LIFE-SPAN DEVELOPMENT

Eleventh Edition

JOHN W. SANTROCK

University of Texas at Dallas

Higher Education

Boston   Burr Ridge, IL   Dubuque, IA   New York   San Francisco   St. Louis
Bangkok   Bogotá   Caracas   Kuala Lumpur   Lisbon   London   Madrid   Mexico City
Milan   Montreal   New Delhi   Santiago   Seoul   Singapore   Sydney   Taipei   Toronto

*With special appreciation to my parents,
Ruth and John Santrock*

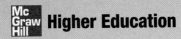

Higher Education

LIFESPAN DEVELOPMENT
Published by McGraw-Hill, an imprint of The McGraw-Hill Companies, Inc., 1221 Avenue of the Americas, New York, NY 10020. Copyright © 2008, 2006, 2004, 2002, 1999, 1997 by the McGraw-Hill Companies, Inc. All rights reserved. No part of this publication may be reproduced or distributed in any form or by any means, or stored in a database or retrieval system, without the prior written consent of The McGraw-Hill Companies, Inc., including, but not limited to, in any network or other electronic storage or transmission, or broadcast for distance learning. Some ancillaries, including electronic and print components, may not be available to customers outside the United States.

This book is printed on acid-free paper.

3 4 5 6 7 8 9 0 DOW/DOW 0 9 8

ISBN: 978-0-07-353191-5
MHID: 0-07-353191-X

Editor in Chief: *Emily Barrosse*
Publisher: *Beth Mejia*
Executive Editor: *Michael J. Sugarman*
Director of Development: *Dawn Groundwater*
Editorial Coordinator: *Kate Russillo*
Development Editor, Supplements: *Meghan Campbell*
Executive Marketing Manager: *Sarah Martin*
Media Producer: *Alexander Rohrs*
Project Manager: *Marilyn Rothenberger*
Manuscript Editor: *Pat Steele*
Art Director: *Jeanne M. Schreiber*
Senior Designer: *Kim Menning*
Senior Production Supervisor: *Tandra Jorgensen*
Illustrators: *John Waller and Judy Waller, Rennie Evans, and Techbooks, York*
Photo Research: *LouAnn Wilson*
Cover photos: *Top to bottom:* © *Digital Vision;* © *Ariel Skelley/CORBIS;* © *Chuck Savage/CORBIS;* © *David Young-Wolff/PhotoEdit*
This book was set in 9.5/12 Meridian by Techbooks, York, and printed on 45# Pub Matte by R.R. Donnelley and Sons.
Photo and text credits can be found following the References on page C-1, a continuation of the copyright page.

Library of Congress Cataloguing-in-Publication Data

Santrock, John W.
    Life-span development / John W. Santrock—11th ed.
        p. cm.
    Includes biographical references and indexes.
    ISBN-13: 978-0-07-353191-5; ISBN-10: 0-07-353191-X
    1. Developmental psychology—Textbooks. I. Title.
BF713.S26 2008
155—dc22   2006566892

BRIEF CONTENTS

iii

CONTENTS

Section 2
BEGINNINGS 70

Section 3
INFANCY 136

Section 4
EARLY CHILDHOOD 236

Section 5

MIDDLE AND LATE CHILDHOOD 312

Chapter 10
PHYSICAL AND COGNITIVE DEVELOPMENT IN MIDDLE AND LATE CHILDHOOD 312

Chapter 11
SOCIOEMOTIONAL DEVELOPMENT IN MIDDLE AND LATE CHILDHOOD 350

Section 6
ADOLESCENCE 386

Section 7
EARLY ADULTHOOD 456

Section 8
MIDDLE ADULTHOOD 526

Section 9
LATE ADULTHOOD 586

Section 10
ENDINGS 676

EXPERT CONSULTANTS

Life-span development has become an enormous, complex field and no single author, or even several authors, can possibly keep up with the rapidly changing content in the many different areas of life-span development. To solve this problem, author John Santrock sought the input of leading experts about content in all age periods of human development. The experts provided detailed evaluations and recommendations for a chapter(s) in their area(s) of expertise. The biographies and photographs of the experts, who literally represent a who's who list in the field of life-span development, follow.

PAUL BALTES

Dr. Baltes is widely recognized as one of the pioneers who created the field of life-span development and continues to be one of the field's leading experts. He is director of the Max Planck Institute for Human Development in Berlin (Germany) and part-time Distinguished Professor of Psychology at the University of Virginia (USA). His research interests include theories and models of adaptive (successful) human development, interdisciplinary perspectives on gerontology, cognitive aging, and the psychology of wisdom. Since 2004, he has directed the newly created Max Planck International Research Network on Aging (MaxnetAging) in which several organizations collaborate. After receiving his doctorate in 1967 from the University of Saarland (Germany), Dr. Baltes spent 12 years as a faculty member and department head with West Virginia University and Penn State University. He was also a three-time fellow at the Center for Advanced Study in the Behavioral Sciences, Stanford University. He has authored or edited 17 books and more than 250 articles and scholarly chapters. Dr. Baltes has been honored for his work with numerous awards including honorary doctorates (Geneva, Jyväsklylä, Stockholm, Humboldt University Berlin), and election to the Academia Europaea, foreign member of the American Academy of Arts and Sciences, and member of the Royal Swedish Academy of Sciences.

TIFFANY FIELD

Dr. Field is one of the world's leading experts on prenatal development, birth, and infancy. She currently is a developmental psychology professor at the University of Miami Medical School where she is also director of the Touch Research Institute, a research group that conducts studies on alternative therapies such as massage therapy, yoga, and tai chi. Dr. Field founded the Touch Research Institute in 1992, which became the first center in the world devoted exclusively to scientific studies of touch and its application to improving human lives. She has been a senior research scientist supported by the National Institutes of Health (NIH) for her research career and has published many books including *Infancy* (Harvard Press) and *Touch* (MIT Press). Her research has been published in more than 400 journal papers. Her research and work at the Touch Research Institute is funded by Johnson & Johnson Pediatric Institutes, Gerber, and Colgate-Palmolive.

JOSEPH CAMPOS

Dr. Campos is one of the world's leading experts on infant emotional development. He currently is a professor in the Department of Psychology at the University of California, Berkeley. Dr. Campos is President of the International Society for Infant Studies, and previously was the first Executive Officer of the International Society for Research on Emotions. He has written *Development in Infancy*, with Michael Lamb, and has co-edited one of the volumes of the *Handbook of Child Psychology*, 1983 edition, as well as the 2003 book, *Emotions Inside Out: 130 Years after Darwin's Expression of the Emotions in Man and Animals*. He holds Distinguished Teaching Awards from the University of Denver and the University of Illinois at Urbana-Champaign, and also is Distinguished Guest Professor at Beijing Normal University.

DAVID MOORE

Dr. Moore is a leading expert in biological foundations of development and infant development. He currently is a professor of psychology at Pitzer College and Claremont Graduate University in Claremont, California. Dr. Moore's research examines perception and cognition in human infants, and has focused recently on the categorization of infant-directed speech. Articles reporting this work have appeared in *Developmental Psychology*, *Developmental Psychobiology*, and *The Journal of Experimental Child Psychology*, among others. His accessible book (2002) about how development contributes to the appearance of our traits is titled *The Dependent Gene: The Fallacy of Nature vs. Nurture*.

L. MONIQUE WARD

Dr. Ward is a leading expert on adolescent development. She obtained her undergraduate degree from Yale University and her Ph.D. from UCLA. Dr. Ward currently is a professor in the Department of Psychology at the University of Michigan. Dr. Ward's research focuses on children's and adolescents' developing conceptions of gender and sexuality, and how these conceptions are linked to their social and sexual decision making. She is especially interested in how children interpret and use the messages they receive about male-female relations from their parents, peers, and the media. One current line of research investigates the role of the media in sexual socialization. A second line examines how adolescents integrate sexual communication from their parents with input from other sources. Dr. Ward's research also explores the intersections between gender ideologies, body image, and sexuality. She currently is a member of the American Psychological Association Task Force on the sexualization of girls.

ROSS PARKE

Dr. Parke is one of the world's leading experts on children's socioemotional development. He is currently Distinguished Professor of Psychology and director of the Center for Family Studies at the University of California, Riverside. Dr. Parke is past President of the Society for Research in Child Development and past President of Division 7, the Developmental Psychology Division, of the American Psychological Association. He is a Fellow of the American Association for the Advancement of Science and has served as editor of both the *Journal of Family Psychology* and *Developmental Psychology*, and as associate editor of *Child Development*. Dr. Parke is the author of *Fatherhood*; co-author of *Throwaway Dads* (with Armin Brott), and co-editor of *Family-Peer Relationships: In Search of the Linkages* (with Gary Ladd), *Children in Time and Place* (with Glen Elder and John Modell), and *Exploring Family Relationships with Other Social Contexts* (with Sheppard Kellam). His research has focused on social relationships, including the effects of punishment, aggression, child abuse, and the father's role. Dr. Parke currently is studying links between family and peer social systems, ethnic variations in families, and the effects of the new reproductive technologies on families.

JEAN BERKO GLEASON

Dr. Gleason is one of the world's leading experts on children's language. She currently is a professor in the Department of Psychology at Boston University and is also a faculty member and former director of BU's Graduate Program in Applied Linguistics. Dr. Gleason has been a visiting scholar at Stanford University, Harvard, and the Linguistics Institute of the Hungarian Academy of Sciences in Budapest. She received her undergraduate and graduate degrees from Harvard/Radcliffe. Dr. Gleason has been president of the International Association for the Study of Child Language and is the author and editor of leading textbooks on language development and psycholinguistics. Since writing her doctoral dissertation on how children learn to make plurals and past tenses in English she has published over one hundred articles on aphasia, language attrition, language development in children, gender differences in parents' speech, and cross-cultural differences. Her work is frequently cited in the professional literature, and has been featured in the popular press and on television.

ELISA VELÁSQUEZ-ANDRADE

Dr. Velásquez-Andrade is a leading expert on diversity. She received an undergraduate and a master's degree in child development at the National University of Mexico. Dr. Velásquez-Andrade obtained her M.A. and Ph.D. in educational psychology at The University of Texas at Austin. She received research training on mother-child attachment relationships at the University of Minnesota and the University of Wisconsin–Madison. She was a research fellow at the University of Texas at Austin and a clinical developmental specialist at the University of Florida. Dr. Velásquez-Andrade taught at the National University of Mexico and the University of New Orleans before joining the Department of Psychology at Sonoma State University. In the past twenty years she has taught undergraduate and graduate courses in child development, developmental psychology, early childhood education, applied research, and cross-cultural and multicultural psychology. Her research interests include understanding the personal and contextual factors associated with the resilience and successful adaptation of immigrant Latino families and their children, as well as the educational success of Latino students. She is a strong advocate for the need to conduct sound research with ethnic minority populations in the United States. Dr. Velásquez-Andrade has been a multicultural consultant to several nonprofit organizations and community programs serving the Latino populations in Northern California, and is a national trainer in the American Psychological Association's ACT (Adults and Children Together) Against Violence Program. Dr. Velásquez-Andrade is a member of the Steering Committee and founding member of the Latino Caucus of the Society for Research in Child Development (SRCD).

JEAN MANDLER

Dr. Mandler is one of the world's leading experts on infant cognitive development. She received her B.A. with Highest Honors from Swarthmore College and her Ph.D. from Harvard University. She is now Distinguished Research Professor of Cognitive Science at the University of California San Diego in La Jolla, California.

Dr. Mandler is also a Fellow of the American Academy of Arts and Sciences. Her wide-ranging research contributions to psychology include studies of animal learning, schema theory, story understanding, and picture recognition. For the past twenty years Dr. Mandler has conducted extensive research on cognitive development in infancy, specializing in how the first concepts are created and used. Her most recent book, *The Foundations of Mind*, was published in 2004.

JOHN SCHULENBERG

Dr. Schulenberg is one of the world's leading experts on adolescence, emerging adulthood, and development in early adulthood. He currently is a Professor of Developmental Psychology at the University of Michigan, and a Research Professor at the University of Michigan's Institute for Social Research and Center for Human Growth and Development. Dr. Schulenberg has published widely on several topics concerning adolescent development and the transition to adulthood, focusing especially on how developmental transitions and tasks relate to health risks and adjustment difficulties. His recent research, published in such journals as *Addiction, Developmental Psychology, Development and Psychopathology, Journal of Studies on Alcohol,* and *Prevention Science,* examines such areas as the prevention of substance use and continuity and discontinuity in adjustment during the transition to adulthood. He is a co–principal investigator on the highly acclaimed National Institute of Drug Abuse–funded national Monitoring the Future study on drug abuse in adolescence. Dr. Schulenberg has served on several policy and review committees for the Society for Research on Adolescence, and on advisory and review committees for the National Institutes of Health and the National Science Foundation. He also is a Fellow of the American Psychological Association.

CAMILLE WORTMAN

Dr. Wortman is one of the world's leading experts on death and grieving. She currently is a Professor of Psychology at the State University of New York at Stony Brook, where for the past decade, she has served as the director of the Social/Health Psychology Graduate Training Program. Prior to coming to Stony Brook, Dr. Wortman was a professor at Northwestern University and the University of Michigan. Her research focuses on bereavement, with a particular emphasis on how people react to the sudden, traumatic death of a loved one.

Dr. Wortman received the Distinguished Scientific Award for an Early Career Contribution in Psychology from the American Psychological Association for this work, which has been funded both by federal agencies (the National Science Foundation, the National Institute of Mental Health, the National Institute on Aging) and private foundations (the MacArthur Foundation, and the Insurance Institute for Highway Safety). Dr. Wortman has authored over 80 articles and book chapters dealing with grief and loss. Following the September 11, 2001, catastrophe, she was invited to develop material on trauma and loss for the American Psychological Association Web site and the Web site for the International Society for Traumatic Stress Studies.

WILLIAM HOYER

Dr. Hoyer is one of the world's leading experts on cognitive development in adult development and aging. He currently is Professor of Psychology and Senior Scientist at the Center for Health and Behavior at Syracuse University. Dr. Hoyer teaches courses in adult development and aging at Syracuse, where he also is an associate of the Gerontology Center, Director of the Graduate Training Program in Experimental Psychology, and Research Professor of Ophthalmology at Upstate Medical University at Syracuse. He received his Ph.D. in experimental psychology from West Virginia University. Dr. Hoyer's research interests center on skill learning, memory, and cognitive expertise from a developmental perspective. He is currently the Principal Investigator on a five-year research grant titled "Aging of Cognitive Mechanisms" from the National Institute on Aging. Dr. Hoyer's publications include seven books and over 100 journal articles, including articles in *Developmental Psychology, Psychology and Aging,* and *Journal of Gerontology: Psychological Sciences.* Dr. Hoyer is a Fellow of the American Psychological Association, the American Psychological Society, and the Gerontological Society of America. He serves or has served on a number of grant review panels and on the editorial boards for a number of journals including *Developmental Psychology, Journal of Gerontology: Psychological Sciences, Aging, Neuropsychology, and Cognition,* and *Psychology and Aging.*

Preparing a new edition of *Life-Span Development* is both a joy and a challenge. I enjoy revising this text because I continue to learn more about the human life span and the journey of life each of us takes. It also is gratifying to revise the text because the feedback from students and instructors has been consistently enthusiastic. The challenge of revising a successful text is always to continue meeting readers' needs and expectations, while keeping the material fresh and up to date. For the eleventh edition of *Life-Span Development*, I have expanded coverage in a number of key areas, incorporated the latest research and applications, and fine-tuned the aspects of the book that make learning easier and more engaging.

RESEARCH

Above all, a text on life-span development must include a solid research foundation. *Life-Span Development* treats research in three ways: (1) it provides students with the most recent research in the field, (2) it covers one in-depth research study per chapter, and (3) it includes expert consultation from premier researchers across the life span.

Recent Research

This edition of *Life-Span Development* presents the latest, most contemporary research on each period of the human life span. The eleventh edition includes more than 2,400 citations from the twenty-first century, with more than 1,700 of these from 2004, 2005, 2006, and 2007. The eleventh edition also includes discussion of material from research reviews in two very recently pubished major handbooks in life-span development: (1) *Handbook of Child Psychology* (2006) and (2) *Handbook of the Psychology of Aging* (2006). As a result, instructors and students can rely on *Life-Span Development* as a scientifically based, up-to-date guide to the latest theories and findings in the field of life-span development.

Here are several examples of new research material on children's development in this edition of *Life-Span Development*:

- Two recent meta-analyses of adopted children's problems and cognitive development (Juffer & van IJzendoorn, 2005; van IJzendoorn, Juffer, & Poelhuis, 2005)
- Recent research on obesity, stress, and pregnancy (Anderson & others, 2005; Kristensen & others, 2005; O'Connor & others, 2005)

- New coverage of recent research on the lower incidence of SIDS in infants who use a pacifier when placed for sleep (Li & others, 2006)
- New section on concept formation in infancy (Mandler, 2004, 2006)
- Recent research conducted by the NICHD Child Care Research Network (2005, 2006)
- Recent research from the Bogalusa Heart Study (Berensen & others, 2005; Lee & others, 2005; Freedman & others, 2005)
- Recent research on exercise and ADHD (Ferrando-Lucas, 2006; Rebollo & Montiel, 2006)
- New section on children's scientific thinking (Bransford & Donovan, 2005; Lehrer & Schauble, 2006)
- New section on metalinguistic awareness (Berko Gleason, 2005; Ely, 2005)
- New section on moral personality (Blasi, 2005; Lapsley & Narvaez, 2006)
- New section on developmental changes in peer relations (Rubin, Bukowski, & Parker, 2006)
- Recent longitudinal research on links between drinking in adolescence and drinking in middle adulthood (Pitkänen, Lyyra, & Pulkkinen, 2005)
- Coverage of longitudinal study on adolescent contraceptive use (Anderson, Santelli, & Moore, 2006)
- Expanded and updated coverage of information processing in adolescence with an emphasis on executive functioning and decision making (Kuhn, 2005; Kuhn & Franklin, 2006)
- Recent research on dating in adolescence and adolescents' adjustment (Furman, Ho, & Lo, 2005; La Greca & Harrison, 2005)
- Recent research on service learning and adolescent development (Reinders & Youniss, 2006)
- Recent research on the role of friendship in suicide attempts (Hacker & others, 2006)
- Discussion of longitudinal study indicating that most bad health habits in adolescence worsen in emerging adulthood (Harris & others, 2006)
- Recent research on post-divorce cohabitation with a spouse and instability of remarriage (Xu, Hudspeth, & Bartkowski, 2006)
- Recent research on the positive effect of marital education on marital relationships (Stanley & others, 2006)
- Recent research on the role of stress in inhibiting neurogenesis (Mirescu & Gould, 2006)

Chapter-by-chapter content changes are described under "What's New in This Edition."

Research in Life-Span Development Interludes

Research in Life-Span Development interludes appear once in each chapter and provide a more in-depth look at research related to a topic in the chapter. I call them interludes rather than boxes because they follow directly in the text after the research has been introduced. In most instances they consist of a description of a research study, including the participants, the methods used to obtain data, and the main results. In most cases they are research studies that have been conducted in the twenty-first century. For example, Chapter 10 includes a new Research in Life-Span Development interlude on Marital Conflict, Individual Hostility, and the Use of Physical Punishment (Kanoy & others, 2003). Chapter 11 includes a new Research in Life-Span Development interlude: Aggressive Victims, Passive Victims, and Bullies (Hanish & Guerera, 2004)

Because students often have more difficulty reading about research studies than other text material, I wrote these with an eye toward student understanding.

Expert Research Consultants

Twelve expert consultants provided author John Santrock with detailed feedback about the content of a chapter or chapters in their area(s) of expertise. The photographs and biographics of the expert consultants appear on pages xiv to xvi. The expert consultants for *Life-Span Development* (Eleventh Edition) were:

Paul Baltes, *Max Planck Institute, Berlin Germany* Life-Span Developmental Theory and Aging Research; Chapters 1, 16, 19, and 20

Elisa Velásquez-Andrade, *Sonoma State University* Culture and Diversity throughout the book

David Moore, *Pitzer College and Claremont Graduate University* Chapter 3: Biological Beginnings

Tiffany Field, *University of Miami* Chapter 4: Prenatal Development and Birth

Jean Mandler, *University of California–San Diego* Chapter 6: Cognitive Development in Infancy

Joseph Campos, *University of California–Berkeley* Chapter 7: Socioemotional Development in Infancy

Jean Berko Gleason, *Boston University* Language Development; Chapters 6, 8, and 10

Ross Parke, *University of California–Riverside* Socioemotional Development in Childhood; Chapters 7, 9, and 11

L. Monique Ward, *University of Michigan* Adolescent Development; Chapters 12 and 13

John Schulenberg, *University of Michigan* Early Adulthood; Chapters 14 and 15

William Hoyer, *Syracuse University* Cognitive Development in Adult Development and Aging; Chapters 14, 16, and 19

Camille Wortman, *State University of New York–Stony Brook* Chapter 21: Death and Grieving

APPLICATIONS

It is important to not only present the scientific foundations of life-span development to students, but also to provide applied examples of concepts and to give students a sense that the field of life-span development has personal meaning for them. To underscore the importance of applications, I have included a new Applications in Life-Span Development interlude in every chapter that focuses on health and well-being, parenting, and education. Among the topics of the 21 Applications interludes are:

- Chapter 1: Family Policy
- Chapter 4: A Healthy Pregnancy
- Chapter 6: How Parents Can Facilitate Infants' and Toddlers' Language Development
- Chapter 8: Tools of the Mind
- Chapter 9: Communicating with Children About Divorce
- Chapter 12: Reducing Adolescent Pregnancy
- Chapter 13: Strategies for Parenting Adolescents
- Chapter 15: Strategies for Reducing Loneliness
- Chapter 17: Strategies for Parents and Their Adult Children
- Chapter 20: Strategies for Effectively Engaging in Optimization with Compensation

In addition to giving special attention throughout the text to health and well-being, parenting, and educational applications, the eleventh edition of *Life-Span Development* also includes a *Careers in Life-Span Development* profile in every chapter. They describe an individual whose career relates to the chapter's content. Most of these inserts have a photograph of the person at work. In addition, a *Careers in Life-Span Development* appendix follows Chapter 1 and describes a number of careers in education/research, clinical/counseling, medical/nursing/physical, and family/relationships categories. Numerous Web links provide students with opportunities to read about these careers in greater depth.

ADULT DEVELOPMENT, AGING, AND DIVERSITY

Two very important aspects of a text on life-span development are strong coverage of adult development and aging, as well as diversity.

Adult Development and Aging

Instructors have repeatedly told me that most life-span texts don't give adequate attention to adult development and aging. In the eleventh edition, I have substantially modified, expanded, and updated the adult development and aging content, continuing a process I began a number of editions ago. Examples of new coverage include:

- Updated coverage of Paul Baltes' views and research on life-span developmental theory and aging, through his role as an expert consultant for the text and his recent publications; new coverage of Baltes' view on the co-construction of life-span development through biological, cultural, and individual factors (Baltes, Lindenberger, & Staudinger, 2006)

- Updated and expanded description of emerging adulthood, including Arnett's (2006) recent elucidation of five key themes
- Significantly updated discussion of attachment in young adults (Fraley, 2004; Wei & others, 2005)
- Substantial updating of marital trends and marital problems (Karney & Bradbury, 2005; Popenoe & Whitehead, 2005)
- New section on marital education and its link with positive relationship outcomes (Stanley & others, 2006)
- New coverage of metabolic syndrome (Deedwania & others, 2005)
- Schaie's recent research on cognitive trajectories of individuals across middle adulthood and how variations in some cognitive areas are more likely to be linked to cognitive impairment in late adulthood than others (Schaie, 2005; Willis & Schaie, 2005)
- New section on metacogniton in middle adulthood (Hertzog & Dixon, 2005; Hertzog & Robinson, 2005)
- Recent research on regrets that older adults have when engaging in a life review (Roese & Summerville, 2005)
- Discussion of longitudinal study from individuals 20 to 94 years of age that focused on links between health and religion (McCullough & Laurenceau, 2005)
- Recent meta-analysis of 87 studies on stability and change in the big five personality factors (Roberts, Walton, & Viechtbauer, 2006)
- Recent research on gender differences in middle adulthood divorce and on the role that divorce plays in intergenerational relations (Amato & Cheadle, 2005; Sakraida, 2005)
- Coverage of recent research on the role of stress in inhibiting neurogenesis (Mirescu & Gould, 2006)
- Discussion of recent research that found increased activity in mitochondria in the cells of older adults following exercise (Menshikova & others, 2006)
- Recent research on the substantial decline in brain volume in late adulthood (Shan & others, 2005)
- Recent research involving the Nun Study (Riley & others, 2005)
- Recent research on centenarians (Selim & others, 2005)
- Recent research on links between exercise and brain/cognitive functioning in older adults (Kiraly & Kiraly, 2005; Kramer, Fabiani, & Colcombe, 2006)
- Recent research on calorie restriction and aging (Sharma & Kaur, 2005; Ward & others, 2005)
- Recent research on mental health, cognitive functioning, and aging (Bierman & others, 2005; van Horren & others, 2005)
- New main section, Cognitive Neuroscience and Aging, with coverage of recent research on links between aging, the brain, and cognitive functioning (Cabeza, Nyberg, & Park, 2005; Kramer, Fabiani, & Colcombe, 2006)

- New main section on language development and aging (Thornton & Light, 2006)
- Expanded and updated coverage of wisdom based on the research of Paul Baltes and his colleagues (Baltes, Lindenberger, & Staudinger, 2006)
- Expanded and updated discussion of Alzheimer disease, including recent research on early cognitive factors that predict Alzheimer disease and drug treatment with Alzheimer patients, as well as links of Alzheimer disease to heredity and exercise (Gatz and others, 2006; Tariot, 2006)
- New section on technology and older adults (Czaja & others, 2006; Scialfa, 2006)
- Coverage of longitudinal study of older adults and the roles that marriage and friendship play in their mortality (Rasulo, Christensen, & Tomassini, 2005)
- Recent research on cohabitation by older adults (Brown, Lee, & Bulanda, 2006)
- Recent meta-analysis of gender and caregivers' stress and health (Pinquart & Sorensen, 2006)
- New section on the recently proposed dual-process model of coping with bereavement (Stroebe, Schut, & Stroebe, 2005)
- New section, Coping and Type of Death (Murphy & others, 2003; Wortman & Boerner, 2007)
- New coverage of the concept of complicated grief (Neimeyer, 2006; Prigerson, 2005)
- Discussion of research on sense making and grief (Currier, Holland, & Neimeyer, 2006)

Diversity

Diversity is another key aspect of life-span development. I made every effort to explore diversity issues in a sensitive manner in each chapter. In addition to weaving diversity into discussions of life-span topics, I've included *Diversity in Life-Span Development* interludes in each chapter. The discussion of diversity also includes new material on these topics:

- Expanded coverage of poverty and children's development (McLoyd, Aikens, & Burton, 2006)
- Expanded and updated discussion of research issues involving ethnic minority children (Parke & Buriel, 2006)
- Latino and Asian American beliefs about pregnancy (American Public Health Association, 2006)
- Coverage of recent research on the Hawaii Health Start program (Duggan & others, 2004)
- New research on children's vocabulary development in low-income families (Pan & others, 2005)
- Discussion of recent research on the WIC program with young children from low-income families (Melgar-Quinonez & Kaiser, 2004)
- New discussion of ethnicity and children's health, including recent research (Andrulis, 2005; Oh, & Hamilton, 2005)
- New coverage of the Hip-Hop to Health Jr program to reduce overweight and obesity in African American and Latino children attending Head Start programs (Fitzgibbon & others, 2005)

- Inclusion of the U.S. Congress' recent consideration to infuse Project Head Start with a stronger academic orientation (Stipek, 2004)
- Description of longitudinal study on the Perry Preschool program participants at age 40 (Schweinhart & others, 2005)
- Inclusion of recent comparisons between early childhood education in the United States and developing countries (Roopnarine & Metindoan, 2006)
- Updated and expanded discussion of bilingual education based on a recent comprehensive research review (Snow & Yang, 2006)
- Expanded coverage of ethnic identity, including recent research (Fuligni, Witkow, & Garcia, 2005; Phinney, 2006)
- New section on immigration and adolescent development (Parke & Buriel, 2006)
- Recent research on African American grandmothers who raise their grandchildren (Minkler & Fuller-Thompson, 2005)
- Coverage of recent research on the role of church attendance in the mortality of older Mexican Americans (Hill & others, 2005, 2006)
- Recent research on gender and stereotyping in older adults (Rupp, Vodanovich, & Crede, 2005)
- New research on social integration in African American older adults (Barnes & others, 2004a)

WRITING, ORGANIZATION, AND THE LEARNING SYSTEM

The new edition of *Life-Span Development* should be even more accessible to students because of the extensive rewriting, organization, and learning system. Every sentence, paragraph, section, and chapter of this book was carefully examined and, when appropriate, revised and rewritten. The result is a much clearer, better-organized presentation of material in this eleventh edition.

I strongly believe that students should not only be challenged to study hard and think more deeply and productively about life-span development, but should also be provided with an effective learning system. Instructors and students have commented about how student-friendly this book has become in recent editions. Now more than ever, students struggle to see the "big picture," especially in courses like life-span development, which include so much material. The learning system centers on learning goals that, together with the main text headings, keep the key ideas in front of the reader from the beginning to the end of the chapter. Each chapter has no more than five main headings and corresponding learning goals, which are presented side-by-side in the chapter-opening spread. At the end of each main section of a chapter, the learning goal is repeated in a feature called "Review and Reflect," which prompts students to review the key topics in the section and poses a question to encourage them to think critically about what they have read. At the end of the chapter, under the heading, "Reach Your Learning Goals," the learning goals guide students through the chapter review.

In addition, maps that link up with the learning goals are presented at the beginning of each major section in the chapter. At the end of each chapter, the section maps are assembled into a complete map of the chapter that provides a visual review guide. The complete learning system, including many additional features not mentioned here, is presented later in a section titled Visual Tour for Students.

WHAT'S NEW IN THIS EDITION?

The eleventh edition focuses on two major goals (1) developing a new feature that enables students to apply life-span concepts outside the classroom, and (2) significant chapter-by-chapter updating, revising, and streamlining.

Applications in Life-Span Development Interludes

As mentioned earlier, the eleventh edition includes a new applications feature called "Applications in Life-Span Development" interludes. These interludes focus on health and well-being, parenting strategies, and education and are designed to help students apply life-span development theories and concepts outside the classroom. For example, Chapter 9 includes an interlude on Communicating with Children About Divorce. Chapter 10 includes an interlude on Strategies for Increasing Children's Creative Thinking, and Chapter 11 includes an interlude on *Increasing Children's Self-Esteem*.

Chapter-By-Chapter Changes

All 21 chapters of *Life-Span Development*, eleventh edition, feature substantial changes. The highlights of these changes follow.

Chapter 1 INTRODUCTION

- Extensive line-by-line rewriting of chapter for improved flow of material and student understanding
- Updating of chapter based on the input of expert consultant Paul Baltes
- New section, The Importance of Studying Life-Span Development, including contemporary research (Benson & others, 2006; Field, Hernandez-Reif, & Freedman, 2004)
- Updated life expectancy figures, United States, 2005: 78 years (Central Intelligence Agency, 2005)
- Important new section in the discussion of the life-span perspective: Development Is a Co-Construction of Biology, Culture, and the Individual (Baltes, Lindenberger, & Staudinger, 2006)
- New Applications in Life-Span Development interlude: Improving Family Policy (Powell, 2006; Ramey, Ramey, & Lanzi, 2006)
- Expanded discussion of poverty and children, including recent statistics on the percentage of U.S. children living in poverty (Federal Register, 2004; McLoyd, Aikens, & Burton, 2006)

Chapter 2 THE SCIENCE OF LIFE-SPAN DEVELOPMENT

- Reduced amount of material on Freud's theory at reviewers' and adopters' requests
- Extensive line-by-line editing and rewriting to improve student understanding
- Revised organization of the section on research methods to include descriptive methods
- New Applications in Life-Span Development interlude: Early Childhood TV Viewing and Adolescent Behavior
- Deletion of final section on Being a Wise Consumer of Information About Life-Span Development to help in reducing chapter length
- Expanded and updated coverage of research issues involving ethnic minority children (Parke & Buriel, 2006)

Chapter 3 BIOLOGICAL BEGINNINGS

- Extensive line-by-line rewriting of chapter and inclusion of a number of new introductions to topics and transitions between topics for improved clarity and understanding
- New Applications in Life-Span Development interlude: Parenting Adopted Children
- Numerous revised and updated descriptions based on evaluations of the chapter's material by leading experts Gilbert Gottlieb and David Moore
- Revised description of the human genome
- Expanded coverage of phenylketonuria and how its link with nutrition reflects the principle of heredity-environment interaction
- New coverage of recent research on IVF babies, indicating risks for singleton IVF babies compared to singleton babies not produced by IVF (Klipstein & others, 2005; Merlob & others, 2005)
- New Research in Life-Span Development interlude: In Vitro Fertilization and Developmental Outcomes in Adolescence
- New description of two recent meta-analyses: One on behavioral problems and mental health referrals in adopted and non-adopted children (Juffer & van IJzendoorn, 2005) and one on the cognitive development of adopted and nonadopted children (van IJzendoorn, Juffer, & Poelhuis, 2005)
- Updated and expanded discussion of the epigenetic view, including criticisms of the heredity-environment correlation view (Gottlieb, Wahlsten, & Lickliter, 2006)

Chapter 4 PRENATAL DEVELOPMENT AND BIRTH

- Extensive rewriting of chapter on a line-by-line basis and rearrangement of some sections (Assessing the Newborn before Low Birth Weight and Preterm Infants, for example) to improve clarity and understanding
- New chapter opening Images of Life-Span Development, Mr. Littles, that describes one couple and the prenatal development and birth of their son
- Coverage of recent study on prescription drug use during pregnancy (Riley & others, 2005)
- Discussion of recent research on caffeine consumption during pregnancy and fetal death (Matijasevich & others, 2006)
- Description of longitudinal study linking maternal cigarette smoking during pregnancy with later cigarette smoking by adolescent offspring (Porath & Fried, 2005)
- Coverage of recent study indicating trends in smoking during pregnancy in the United States (Centers for Disease Control and Prevention, 2004)
- Discussion of recent research on maternal use of cocaine during pregnancy and attention deficits in preschool children (Noland & others, 2005)
- New section on the increase in methamphetamine use during pregnancy (Avria & others, 2006)
- Coverage of recent study on prenatal marijuana exposure and depression in 10-year-old children (Gray & others, 2005)
- New description of maternal diabetes as a risk factor for pregnancy outcomes, including recent research (Rosenberg & others, 2005)
- Discussion of recent study on a link between maternal use of folic acid and iron during early pregnancy and a lower risk of Down syndrome in offspring (Czeizel & Puho, 2005)
- Updated and expanded discussion of overweight, obesity, and pregnancy (Fiala & others, 2006; King, 2006)
- Updated and expanded coverage of the mother's emotional state during prenatal development and birth (Jones & others, 2006; Kapoor & others, 2006)
- Discussion of recent research on pregnancy outcomes in women of very advanced maternal age (Callaway, Lust, & McIntyre, 2005)
- Description of recent research linking heavy paternal smoking to increased risk of early pregnancy loss (Venners & others, 2004)
- New Applications in Life-Span Development interlude, A Healthy Pregnancy, that provides strategies for the expectant mother and her partner (Heaman, 2005; Mogren, 2005)
- New coverage of CenteringPregnancy, a rapidly increasing program for empowering women to take an active role in experiencing a healthy pregnancy (Massey, Rising, & Ickovics, 2006; Moos, 2006)
- Expanded and updated coverage in the Diversity in Life-Span Development interlude on cultural beliefs about pregnancy, with special attention to beliefs in Latino and Asian cultures (American Public Health Association, 2006)
- New section on the increase in various nonmedicated techniques such as waterbirth, massage, acupuncture, hypnosis, and music therapy to reduce pain during childbirth (Geissbuehler, Stein, & Eberhard, 2004; Simpkin & Bolding, 2004; Spencer, 2005)
- Expanded and updated coverage of why cesarean delivery has increased in the United States and recent data on trends in cesarean delivery (Coleman & others, 2005; Martin & others, 2005; Sarsam, Elliott, & Lam, 2005)
- Description of recent study on the reading and mathematics deficits of low birth weight individuals at age 17 (Breslau, Paneth, & Lucia, 2004)

- Discussion of recent study documenting the positive effects of exercise in the postpartum period on maternal well-being (Blum, Beaudoin, & Caton-Lemos, 2005)

Chapter 5   PHYSICAL DEVELOPMENT IN INFANCY

- Updating and revision of shared sleeping controversy (Newton & Vandeven, 2006; Pelayo & others, 2006)
- New description of recent research showing that SIDS is less likely to occur in infants who are given a pacifier when placed for sleep (Hauck, Omojokun, & Siadaty, 2005; Li & others, 2006)
- Revision of material on motor and perceptual development based on input from leading expert Rachael Keen (2005)
- Revised and updated interpretation of variations in motor milestones in infancy, including description of the increasing number of babies who do not crawl (likely linked to parents placing the babies on their backs when sleeping to reduce the risk of SIDS (Adolph & Berger, 2005, 2006)
- Description of recent study involving the Hawaii Healthy Start program and its effect on maternal alcohol use, partner abuse, and child abuse (Duggan & others, 2004)
- Inclusion of recent research review of 61 studies on the link between breast feeding and a lower incidence of obesity in childhood and adulthood (Owen & others, 2005)
- New description of Karen Adolph's research involving little transfer between crawling and walking (Keen, 2005)
- Expanded and updated discussion of reaching and grasping in the first two years of life, as well as coverage of the importance of exercising fine motor skills in infancy (Keen, 2005)
- Expanded and updated description of techniques used to study infant perception, including the orienting response, tracking, and high-amplitude sucking (Keen, 2005; Menn & Stoel-Gammon, 2005)
- New discussion of whether experience is necessary for the vision of infants to develop normally, including recent research (Sugita, 2004)
- New section: Nature, Nurture, and the Development of Infants' Visual Perception (Kellman & Arterberrry, 2006)
- New coverage of developmental changes in stereoacuity during infancy (Biech & others, 2005; Takai & others, 2005)

Chapter 6   COGNITIVE DEVELOPMENT IN INFANCY

- Extensive editing and rewriting of Piagetian material for improved student understanding
- Important new section on concept formation and categorization in infancy (Mandler, 2004, 2006)
- Updated coverage of predicting IQ later in childhood from information processing tasks in infancy (Kaveck, 2004)
- New coverage of Michael Tomasello's (2006) interactionist view of language that stresses the role of intentions
- Substantially updated and revised Research in Life-Span Development interlude, including recent research indicating that the types of maternal speech, vocabulary, and gestures are more important that the sheer amount

of verbal input in predicting children's vocabulary development in low-income families (Pan & others, 2005)
- New Applications in Life-Span Development interlude: How Parents Can Facilitate Infants' and Toddlers' Language Development
- Extensive editing and updating of language material based on input from leading expert John Bonvillian
- Coverage of recent study on the importance of social interaction in advancing the language of infants, including new research (Goldstein, West, & Kay, 2003)

Chapter 7   SOCIOEMOTIONAL DEVELOPMENT IN INFANCY

- Extensive rewriting of chapter for improved student understanding, including addition of numerous concrete examples of concepts and more descriptions of infants' behaviors and emotions
- New Applications in Life-Span Development interlude: Parenting and the Child's Temperament
- Extensively revised discussion of the appearance of early emotions based on expert consultant Joseph Campos' (2005) comments
- New material on strategies for calming crying infants, including the effectiveness of swaddling (Oghi & others, 2004)
- Coverage of recent study on links between maternal separation anxiety and maternal characteristics (Hsu, 2004)
- Inclusion of the contemporary view of the developmentally evolving nature of temperament (Thompson & Goodvin, 2005)
- Description of recent research on goodness of fit in temperament involving a combination of high infant fearlessness and harsh parenting, as well as the type of temperament most likely to reduce the effects of negative environments (Rothbart & Bates, 2006; Shaw & others, 2003)
- Expanded and updated description of self-understanding in infancy (Lewis, 2005; Thompson, 2006)
- Expanded coverage of the nature of attachment and how the infant's and young child's social cognitive advances contribute to attachment (Thompson, 2006)
- Description of the outcomes of early attachment security and later outcomes in childhood and adolescence by Alan Sroufe and his colleagues (2005) and updated conclusions about the importance of early secure attachment *and* later positive social experiences in predicting development (Thompson, 2006)
- Expanded discussion of cultural variations in attachment (Saarni & others, 2006)
- Updated coverage of the NICHD Early Child Care Research Network Study, including recent findings on amount of time spent in child care and child outcomes (Vandell, 2004)
- New coverage of links between long hours spent in center-based care and negative outcomes for children with certain types of temperament (Crockenberg & Leekes, 2005)

- Updated research discussed in the Research in Life-Span Development interlude based on recent findings from the NICHD Child Care Research Network (2005, 2006) study

Chapter 8 PHYSICAL AND COGNITIVE DEVELOPMENT IN EARLY CHILDHOOD

- Coverage of recent fMRI study showing low levels of myelination in young children with development delays in cognitive and motor development (Pujol & others, 2004)
- Expanded emphasis on the importance of the maturation of the prefrontal cortex in cognitive and socioemotional development (Espy & others, 2004; Levesque & others, 2004)
- New coverage of the Hip-Hop to Health Jr program to reduce overweight and obesity in African American and Latino children attending Head Start programs (Fitzgibbon & others, 2005)
- Discussion of recent study on parents' misperceptions of their children's overweight (Eetstein & others, 2006)
- New coverage of cultural variations in promoting right-handedness (Zverev, 2006)
- Expanded and updated coverage of malnutrition in early childhood, including a longitudinal study on malnutrition at age 3 and behavioral problems at ages 8, 11, and 17 (Liu & others, 2004)
- Discussion of recent research studies linking participation in the WIC program with positive nutritional outcomes in young children from low-income families (Melgar-Quinonez & Kaiser, 2004; Siega-Riz & others, 2004)
- New discussion of ethnicity and children's health, including recent research (Andrulis, 2005)
- New Applications in Life-Span Development interlude: Tools of the Mind (Budrova & Leong, 2001, 2007; Hyson, Copple, & Jones, 2006)
- Expanded and updated coverage of young children's control of their attention, including recent research on sustained attention and its link to school readiness (NICHD Child Care Research Network, 2003) and a recent study on how children's early experiences at home can influence their attention and memory later in childhood (NICHD Early Child Care Research Network, 2005)
- Recent recommendations for three changes to improve interviewing techniques with children to reduce their suggestibility (Bruck, Ceci, & Principe, 2006)
- Coverage of recent study showing that older children are more likely to reject the occurrence of false events than younger children (Ghetti & Alexander, 2004)
- Expanded and updated description of the young child's theory of mind (Harris, 2006)
- Expanded and updated discussion of language development in early childhood, including increased emphasis on the regularities in which young children acquire their particular language (Berko Gleason, 2005)
- Inclusion of information about recent consideration by the U.S. Congress to infuse Project Head Start with a stronger academic orientation and some concerns about this (Stipek, 2004)

- Description of recent data on the positive outcomes of the Perry Preschool program at age 40 (Schweinhart & others, 2005)
- Update on the number of states providing education for 3- and 4-year-old children and the percentage of 3- and 4-year-old children who attend center-based programs (NAEYC, 2005)
- Recent information about the surge of interest in Montessori schools in the United States (Whitescarver, 2006)
- Updated and expanded coverage of the Diversity in Life-Span Development interlude to include comparisons of early childhood education between the United States and developing countries (Rooparnine & Metingdogan, 2006)

Chapter 9 SOCIOEMOTIONAL DEVELOPMENT IN EARLY CHILDHOOD

- New chapter opening Images of Life-Span Development: Craig Lesley's Complicated Early Emotional and Social Life (Lesley, 2005)
- New Research in Life-Span Development interlude: Marital Conflict, Individual Hostility, and the Use of Physical Punishment (Kanoy & others, 2003)
- New Applications in Life-Span Development interlude: Communicating with Children About Divorce
- New section, Emotional Regulation and Peer Relations (Eisenberg, Spinrad, & Smith, 2004; Saarni & others, 2006)
- Expanded and updated discussion of developmental changes in peer relations in early childhood based on a recent review (Rubin, Bukowski, & Parker, 2006)
- Description of a recent effective prevention program for child maltreatment (Cicchetti & Cicchetti, Toth, & Rogosch, 2005)
- Discussion of recent research on the importance of secure attachment in divorced children's lives (Brockmeyer, Treboux, & Crowell, 2005)

Chapter 10 PHYSICAL AND COGNITIVE DEVELOPMENT IN MIDDLE AND LATE CHILDHOOD

- New Images of Life-Span Development: The Story of Angie and Her Weight
- Substantial reorganization and rewriting of intelligence coverage for improved understanding
- Coverage of recent study on instruction time in physical education classes and the weight of elementary school girls (Datar & Sturm, 2004)
- New section on Cardiovascular Disease, including a number of recent research studies with an emphasis on the Bogalusa Heart Study (Berensen & others, 2005; Lee & others, 2005; Freedman & others, 2005)
- New survey information about the percentage of U.S. children who have a learning disability or ADHD (Bloom & Dey, 2006)
- New coverage of the very recent interest in the role that exercise might play in ADHD (Ferrando-Lucas, 2006; Rebollo & Montiel, 2006)

- New description of the 2004 reauthorization of IDEA and its link with No Child Left Behind legislation (Halonen & Kauffman, 2006)
- Expanded and updated coverage of James Kauffman and his colleagues' (Kauffman & Hallahan, 2005; Kauffman, McGee, & Brigham, 2004) view that too often children with disabilities are not challenged to be all they can be
- New Applications in Life-Span Development interlude: Strategies for Increasing Children's Creative Thinking
- New section: Children's Scientific Thinking (Lehrer & Schauble, 2006; Bransford & Donovan, 2005)
- New discussion of Pressley and his colleagues' observations of how teachers infrequently use strategy instruction in their classrooms (Pressley & Harris, 2006; Pressley & Hilden, 2006)
- New section: Metalinguistic Awareness (Berko Gleason, 2005; Ely, 2005)
- New coverage of the importance of vocabulary development in reading comprehension (Berninger, 2006; Snow & Yang, 2006)
- Updated and expanded discussion of bilingual education based on a recent comprehensive research review (Snow & Yang, 2006)

Chapter 11 SOCIOEMOTIONAL DEVELOPMENT IN MIDDLE AND LATE CHILDHOOD

- Coverage of recent concern that too many children grow up receiving empty praise, which can harm their school achievement (Graham, 2005; Stipek, 2005)
- New Applications in Life-Span Development interlude: Increasing Children's Self-Esteem
- New section: Self-Efficacy (Bandura, 2004; Schunk, 2004)
- Expanded and updated overview of main changes in emotional development during middle and late childhood (Thompson & Goodvin, 2005)
- Updated and expanded discussion of social conventional reasoning (Smetana, 2006; Turiel, 2006)
- New section on personality that emphasizes moral identity, moral character, and moral exemplars (Lapsley & Narvaez, 2006)
- Updated and expanded discussion of gender differences in emotion and self-regulation (Ruble, Martin, & Berenbaum, 2006)
- Updated national assessment of the gender gap in reading (National Assessment of Educational Progress (2005)
- New section: Developmental Changes in Peer Relations (Rubin, Bukowski, & Parker, 2006)
- Discussion of a recent successful intervention with peer rejected children (DeRosier & Marcus, 2005)
- New Research in Life-Span Development interlude: Aggressive Victims, Passive Victims, and Bullies (Hanish & Guerera, 2004)
- Updated and expanded coverage of coverage of constructivist and direct instruction approaches and the No Child Left Behind legislation (Eby, Herrell, & Jordan, 2006; Lewis, 2005)

- Coverage of Jonathan Kozol's (2005) recent book *The Shame of the Nation* that portrays the continuing educational segregation and inequities of many minority students living in low-income circumstances

Chapter 12 PHYSICAL AND COGNITIVE DEVELOPMENT IN ADOLESCENCE

- Extensive rewriting, editing, and reworking of chapter for improved clarity and student understanding
- Updated and expanded discussion of the brain's development in adolescence (Nelson, Thomas, & de Haan, 2006; Steinberg, 2006)
- Updated and expanded discussion of television and adolescent sexuality (Ward & Friedman, 2006)
- Discussion of recent longitudinal study on adolescent contraceptive use (Anderson, Santelli, & Morrow, 2006)
- Updated description of the reduction in U.S. adolescent pregnancy rates (Child Trends, 2006)
- New Applications in Life-Span Development interlude, Reducing Adolescent Pregnancy, that includes information from a recent review of research on whether schools should have an abstinence-only or contraceptive knowledge approach to sex education (Bennett & Assefi, 2005)
- Updated coverage of adolescent drug use trends (Johnston & others, 2006)
- New coverage of the increased use of prescription painkillers by adolescents (Johnston & others, 2005; Sung & others, 2005)
- Discussion of longitudinal study from 8 to 42 years of age indicating that early onset of drinking is a risk factor for heavy drinking in middle age (Pitkänen, Lyyra, & Pulkkinen, 2005)
- New description of research study on parental behavior and adolescent eating problems (Pakpreo & others, 2004)
- Much expanded, updated, and revised coverage of information processing in adolescence based on Deanna Kuhn's (Kuhn, 2005; Kuhn & Franklin, 2006) review of advances in executive functioning
- Updating of high school dropout rates, including Figure 12.11 (Center for Education Statistics, 2005)
- Updated and expanded discussion of service learning, including recent data on the percentage of schools that require service learning and recent research (Benson & others, 2006; Metz & Youniss, 2005; Reinders & Youniss, 2006)

Chapter 13 SOCIOEMOTIONAL DEVELOPMENT IN ADOLESCENCE

- New chapter opening Images of Life-Span Development: Jewel Cash, Teen Dynamo
- Updated, expanded, and reorganized section on identity
- Expanded coverage of ethnic identity, including recent research (Phinney, 2006; Fuligni, Witkow, & Garcia, 2005)
- New description of the importance of emotion regulation in adolescence and research linking emotional control to higher grades (Gumora & Arsenio, 2002)

- Inclusion of information about early maturing adolescents experiencing more conflict with parents than those who mature on-time or late (Collins & Steinberg, 2006)
- Discussion of recent longitudinal study on a number of dimensions of parenting linked with competent or deviant outcomes in adolescents (Goldstein & others, 2005)
- New Applications in Life-Span Development interlude, Strategies for Parenting Adolescents
- Commentary about developmental changes in reputation-based crowds in adolescence (Collins & Steinberg, 2006)
- New section: Adjustment and Dating in Adolescence, including information about recent research (Furman, Ho, & Low, 2005; La Greca & Harrison, 2005)
- New coverage of gangs in adolescence, including recent research (Dishion, Nelson, & Yasui, 2005; Lauber, Marshall, & Meyers, 2005)
- Updated trends on various aspects of school violence (Brener & others, 2005)
- Description of recent national survey on the percentage of U.S. adolescents who attempted suicide in 2005 (Eaton & others, 2006)
- Coverage of recent study that found a link between not having friends and attempting suicide in adolescence (Hacker & others, 2006)
- New section on immigration in the discussion of ethnicity and culture (Parke & Buriel, 2006)

Chapter 14 PHYSICAL AND COGNITIVE DEVELOPMENT IN EARLY ADULTHOOD

- New chapter opening story, David Eggers, Pursuing a Career in the Face of Stress
- New comparison of the transition to adulthood, with the transition to adolescence in terms of culturally imposed structure and continuity/discontinuity (Schulenberg, Sameroff, & Cicchetti, 2004)
- Updated and expanded discussion of emerging adulthood, including Arnett's (2006) recent description of five main themes of emerging adulthood
- Updated coverage of college freshmen's experiences, including gender differences in feeling overwhelmed with all they had to do (Pryor & others, 2005)
- New discussion of characteristics associated with well-being and success in the transition to adulthood, including recent research (Schulenberg, Bryant, & O'Malley, 2004)
- New description of longitudinal study indicating that most bad health habits in adolescence worsen in emerging adulthood (Harris & others, 2006)
- Coverage of recent analyses indicating that obesity is increasing faster for women than men in many countries around the world (Seidell, 2005)
- Added description of restrained eaters increasing their food intake under stress while unrestrained eaters decrease food intake under stress (Lowe & Kral, 2006)
- Updated discussion of the positive links between exercise and improved mental health (Richardson & others, 2005)
- New Applications in Life-Span Development interlude: Exercise

- Description of two recent longitudinal analyses of the positive effects of Alcoholics Anonymous (Moos & Moos, 2005; Timko, Finney, & Moos, 2005)
- Discussion of recent study of the effectiveness of a combined drug and behavioral Treatment for alcoholism (Anton & others, 2006)
- Updated coverage of HIV and AIDS (UNAIDS, 2005)
- Description of Labouvie-Vief's (2006) recent perspective on cognitive changes in emerging adults
- Updated description of the occupational outlook in the United States (Occupational Outlook Handbook, 2006–2007)

Chapter 15 SOCIOEMOTIONAL DEVELOPMENT IN EARLY ADULTHOOD

- Extensive editing and reorganization of chapter for better student understanding, including new separate sections on adult lifestyles and marriage and the family
- New introductory overview of key aspects of socioemotional development in early adulthood (Thompson & Goodvin, 2005)
- Extensively revised and updated coverage of attachment in early adulthood, including recent research on links between adult attachment styles and many aspects of life (Fraley & others, 2006; Wei & others, 2005)
- Discussion of recent study demonstrating the importance of distinguishing between different domains of similarity in predicting whether a relationship is likely to succeed (Klohnen & Luo, 2005)
- New Applications in Life-Span Development interlude: Strategies for Reducing Loneliness
- Revised organization of marriage and adult lifestyles with these topics now in one main section rather than two, allowing the topics of single adults and cohabiting adults to appropriately precede the discussion of married adults and the topics of divorced adults and remarried adults to follow married adults
- Coverage of recent study on postdivorce cohabitation with a spouse and instability of remarriage (Xu, Hudspeth, & Bartkowski, 2006)
- Significantly updated coverage of marriage trends, including 30-years trends in the percentage of U.S. women and men who say they are "very happy" in their marriage (Popenoe & Whitehead, 2005)
- Discussion of recent study on the types of severe problems in marriages in low-, middle-, and high-income households, including a new research figure (Karney & Bradbury, 2005; Karney, Garvan, & Thomas, 2003)
- New description of factors likely to increase the probability that a marriage will end in a divorce (Popenoe & Whitehead, 2005; Rodriguez, Hall, & Fincham, 2005)
- New section on marital education and its link with positive relationship outcomes (Stanley & others, 2006)
- Coverage of recent studies on divorce and smoking initiation or relapse in women and alcohol consumption in men (Eng & others, 2005; Lee & others, 2005)

- Recent research on remarried adults and symptoms of depression (Barrett & Turner, 2005)
- Updated discussion of gender similarities and differences in communication, including recent meta-analyses (Hyde, 2005; Leaper & Smith, 2004)

Chapter 16   PHYSICAL AND COGNITIVE DEVELOPMENT IN MIDDLE ADULTHOOD

- New description of the "rectangularization" of the age structure across the life span as increasing numbers of people live to be middle-aged and older (Willis & Martin, 2005)
- New coverage of the concept of gains and losses and their balancing in middle adulthood and how this balancing contributes to the uniqueness of the middle adulthood period (Baltes, Lindenberger, & Staudinger, 2006; Willis & Schaie, 2005)
- Expanded discussion of the increasing belief that middle adulthood is lasting longer
- New coverage of the increased interest in describing *late midlife* as the period from 55 to 65 years of age and what characterizes this age period (Deeg, 2005)
- Inclusion from some experts that midlife is influenced more by sociocultural factors than biological factors than the earlier and later periods of the life span (Willis & Martin, 2005)
- Description of longitudinal study examining physical health through the midlife period (Cleary, Zaborski, & Ayanian, 2004)
- Expanded and updated coverage of cardiovascular system changes in middle adulthood, including the most recent thinking on why HDL is a protective factor in reducing cardiovascular disease (Nicholls, Rye, & Barter, 2005)
- New discussion of the increasing problem of metabolic syndrome in middle adulthood (Deedwania & Volkova, 2005; Medina-Gomez & Vidal-Puig, 2005; Otiniano & others, 2005)
- Description of recent study highlighting the factors most likely to be involved when women report elevated menopausal symptoms (Rossi, 2004)
- New discussion of possible cognitive, neuroanatomical, and neurochemical causes of the decline in speed of processing in adulthood (Hartley, 2006)
- New coverage of Schaie's recent analysis of variations in the cognitive trajectories of individuals across middle adulthood and how variations in some cognitive areas are more likely to be linked to cognitive impairment in late adulthood than others (Schaie, 2005; Willis & Schaie, 2005)
- Description of recent meta-analysis indicating that everyday problem solving remains stable across the early and middle adulthood years, then declines in late adulthood (Thornton & Dumke, 2005)
- New section on metacognition in middle adulthood (Hertzog & Dixon, 2005; Hertzog & Robinson, 2005)

- Recent research on leisure and the regrets U.S. adults have about their lives (Roese & Summerville, 2005)
- Discussion of longitudinal study from 20 to 94 years of age focused on links between health and religion (McCullough & Laurenceau, 2005)
- New Applications in Life-Span Development interlude: Religion and Coping, including recent interest in links between religion, meaning-making, coping, and adjustment (Park, 2005)
- New Careers in Life-Span Development Profile: Gabriel Dy Liasco, Pastoral Counselor

Chapter 17   SOCIOEMOTIONAL DEVELOPMENT IN MIDDLE ADULTHOOD

- Coverage of recent data from the MIDUS national survey regarding the percentage of U.S. adults who experience a midlife crisis and why (Wethington, Kessler, & Pixley, 2004)
- Description of recent research on three factors that middle-aged adults perceive they have more control over than younger adults and two factors they have less control over (Lachman & Firth, 2004)
- Discussion of a recent meta-analysis of 87 longitudinal studies spanning the ages of 10 to 100 focused on stability and change in the big five factors of personality (Roberts, Walton, & Viechtbauer, 2006)
- Description of recent study of conscientiousness across the adult years (Roberts, Walton, & Bogg, 2005)
- Updated discussion of conclusions about stability and change in adulthood (Caspi & Roberts, 2006; Caspi & Shiner, 2006; Mroczek, Spiro, & Griffin, 2006)
- Expanded and updated coverage of the "empty nest" and its refilling (Gordon & Shaffer, 2004)
- Description of recent study comparing women who initiated a divorce in midlife and those whose husbands initiated the divorce (Sakraida, 2005)
- New Applications in Life-Span Development interlude: Strategies for Parents and Their Young Adult Children (Furman, 2005; Paul, 2003)
- Discussion of recent research on the role that divorce plays in intergenerational relationships (Amato & Cheadle, 2005)

Chapter 18   PHYSICAL DEVELOPMENT IN LATE ADULTHOOD

- Description of recent research that found increased mitochondria activity in the cells of older adults following exercise (Menshikova & others, 2006)
- Description of recent information that stress inhibits neurogenesis (Mirescu & Gould, 2006)
- Coverage of recent research on the substantial decrease in brain volume in older adults (Shan & others, 2005)
- Updating of the Nun Study, including recent research on the connection between idea density in early adulthood

and brain/cognitive functioning in late adulthood (Riley & others, 2005)

- Updated discussion of centenarians, including recent research (Selim & others, 2005)
- Inclusion of improved brain functioning and cognitive functioning, and reduced oxidative stress based on recent research in the description of positive effects of exercise in older adults (Kiraly & Kiraly, 2005; Kramer, Fabiani, & Colcombe, 2006)
- Description of recent research on exercise and muscle strength in older women (Haykowsky & others, 2005)
- Recent research indicating that caloric restriction may provide neuroprotection for an aging central nervous system in animals (Hiona & Leeuwenburgh, 2005; Sharma & Kaur, 2005)
- Recent research indicating that calorie restrction may increase longevity by slowing the age-related increase in oxidative stress to cells (Ward & others, 2005)
- Description of recent study comparing older adults in a community-based long-term care program with their counterparts in an institutionalized long-term care facility (Marek & others, 2005)
- New Applications in Life-Span Development interlude: Health-Care Providers and Older Adults

Chapter 19 COGNITIVE DEVELOPMENT IN LATE ADULTHOOD

- Coverage of recent study indicating that slower processing of information may be implicated in the link between IQ and mortality (Deary & Der, 2005)
- Discussion of recent research on knowledge and processing speed in older adults and younger adults (Hedden, Lautenschlager, & Park, 2005)
- Discussion of recent study of a link between time of day testing and the explicit and implicit memory of younger and older adults (May, Hasher, & Foong, 2005)
- Description of recent study on training older adults to improve their processing speed (Edwards & others, 2005)
- Description of two recent longitudinal studies on the relation of mental health to cognitive functioning in older adults (Bierman & others, 2005; van Hooren & others, 2005)
- New main section, Cognitive Neuroscience and Aging, with a discussion of the increased research on links between aging, the brain, and cognitive functioning (Cabeza, Nyberg, & Park, 2005; Kramer, Fabiani, & Colcombe, 2006)
- New main section, Language Development, which describes changes in language in older adults (Burke & Shafto, 2004; Obler, 2005; Thornton & Light, 2006)
- Expanded and updated discussion of wisdom based on the research of Paul Baltes and his colleagues (Baltes & Kuntzmann, 2004; Baltes, Lindenberger, & Staudinger, 2006)
- Description of recent study on employers' negative stereotyping of older workers (Gringart, Helmes, & Speelman, 2005)

- Discussion of recent study linking a number of factors to difficulty in adjusting to retirement (van Solinge & Henkens, 2005)
- Coverage of recent study comparing the life satisfaction and health of retired women who were married, remarried, separated, divorced, or never married (Price & Joo, 2005)
- Description of recent study on gender and retirement (Jacobs-Lawson, Hershey, & Seukam, 2005)
- New Applications in Life-Span Development interlude: Meeting the Mental Health Needs of Older Adults
- Expanded and updated coverage of Alzheimer disease, including recent research on links to heredity and exercise (Gatz & others, 2006; Larson & others, 2006)
- New section: Drug Treatment of Alzheimer Disease, including recent research on cholinerase inhibitors and the approval of a new drug that improves cognitive functioning in individuals with moderate to severe Alzheimer disease (Biachanti & others, 2006; Tariot, 2006)
- New coverage of three recent studies on the link between performance on cognitive tasks and the appearance of dementia and Alzheimer disease up to 10 years later (Aggarwal & others, 2005; Jorm & others, 2005; Tierney & others, 2005)
- Recent meta-analysis of gender and caregivers' stress and health (Pinquart & Sorensen, 2006)
- Updated coverage of the mental health needs and treatment of older adults (Knight & others, 2006)
- Description of two recent studies on links between older Mexican Americans' church attendance, cognitive performance, and mortality (Hill & others, 2005)

Chapter 20 SOCIOEMOTIONAL DEVELOPMENT IN LATE ADULTHOOD

- New section, Personality and Aging, that describes links between certain personality traits and mortality (Mroczek, Spiro, & Griffin, 2006)
- New Applications in Life-Span Development interlude: Strategies for Effectively Engaging in Selective Optimization with Compensation (Baltes, Lindenberger, & Staudinger, 2006; Freund & Baltes, 2002)
- Description of recent study that revealed four main themes in reminiscence (Timmer, Westerhof, & Dittmann-Kohli, 2005)
- New discussion of reminiscence therapy with older adults (Woods & others, 2005)
- New section: Self-Control in Late Adulthood
- Coverage of recent study of gender and stereotyping of older adults (Rupp, Vodanovich, & Crede, 2005)
- New section: Technology and Older Adults (Czaja & others, 2006; Scialfa, 2006)
- Coverage of recent study on the stability of self-esteem across the life span (Trzesniewski, Donnellan, & Robins, 2003)
- Discussion of two recent studies on the importance of friendship in older adults (Fiori, Antonucci, & Cortina, 2006; Rasulo, Christensen, & Tomassini, 2005)

- New section: Cohabiting Older Adults, including recent research studies (Brown & others, 2005; King & Scott, 2005; Waite, 2005)
- Coverage of recent study on the influence of attitudes and biomedical factors on sexual desire (DeLamater & Sill, 2005)
- New description of research on social integration in African American older adults (Barnes & others, 2004a)
- Coverage of recent study on perceived discrimination by older adult African Americans and non-Latino Whites (Barnes & others, 2004b)
- Discussion of recent study on links between happiness and self-efficacy and an optimistic outlook in centenarians (Jopp & Rott, 2006)

Chapter 21 DEATH AND GRIEVING

- Description of the highly publicized case of Terri Schiavo to illustrate issues involving passive euthanasia
- Inclusion of recent ideas about what might characterize a "good death" (Carr, 2003; Wortman & Boerner, 2007)
- Coverage of recent research on hospices (Teno & others, 2004; Wortman & Boerner, 2007)
- New section: Coping and Type of Death (Murphy & others, 2003; Wortman & Boerner, 2007)
- New Applications in Life-Span Development interlude: Communicating with a Dying Person
- New section on the recently proposed dual-process model of coping with bereavement (Stroebe, Schut, & Stroebe, 2005)
- New coverage of the increasingly used term of complicated grief (Neimeyer, 2006; Prigerson, 2005)
- Description of recent therapy that was effective in reducing complicated grief (Zuckoff & others, 2006)
- Discussion of research on sense making and grief (Currier, Holland, & Neimeyer, 2006)

ACKNOWLEDGMENTS

I very much appreciate the support and guidance provided to me by many people at McGraw-Hill. Beth Mejia, Publisher, has provided outstanding guidance and support for this text. Mike Sugarman, Executive Editor, has brought a wealth of publishing knowledge and vision to bear on improving my text. Kathy Field, the development editor for this text, provided extensive and remarkable changes that make it more understandable and student-friendly. Dawn Groundwater, Director of Development, has done a superb job of organizing and monitoring the many tasks necessary to move this book through the editorial process. Kate Russillo, Editorial Coordinator, has once again been instrumental in obtaining reviews. Sarah Martin, Marketing Manager, has contributed in numerous positive ways to this book. Kim Menning created a beautiful design for the text. Pat Steele did a superb job as the book's copy editor. Marilyn Rothenberger did a terrific job in coordinating the book's production.

I also want to thank my wife, Mary Jo, our children, Tracy and Jennifer, and our grandchildren, Jordan, Alex, and Luke, for their wonderful contributions to my life and for helping me to better understand the marvels and mysteries of life-span development.

REVIEWERS

I owe a special gratitude to the expert consultants and general reviewers who provided detailed feedback about the book.

Expert Consultants

I have already listed the expert consultants earlier in the preface. Their photographs and biographies appear later on pages xiv and xvi. Life-span development has become an enormous, complex field and no single author can possibly be an expert in all areas of the field. Since the sixth edition, I have sought the input of leading experts in many different areas of life-span development. This tradition continues in the eleventh edition. The experts have provided me with detailed recommendations of new research to include in every period of the life span. The panel of experts is literally a who's who in the field of life-span development.

General Text Reviewers

I gratefully acknowledge the comments and feedback from instructors around the nation who reviewed the tenth edition of *Life-Span Development* and chapters from the eleventh edition.

Jackie Adamson, *South Dakota School of Mines & Technology*
Ryan Allen, *The Citadel*
Renee Babcock, *Central Michigan University*
Gregory Braswell, *Illinois State University*
Dominique Charlottaux, *Broward Community College*
Yiwei Chen, *Bowling Green University*
Arthur Gonchar, *University of LaVerne*
Debra Hollister, *Valencia Community College*
Daysi Mejia, *Florida Gulf Coast University*
Charisse Nixon, *Pennsylvania State University at Erie*
Susan Perez, *University of North Florida*
Cathie Robertson, *Grossmont College*
Karen Salekin, *University of Alabama*
Pamela Schuetze, *Buffalo State College*
Dennis Valone, *Pennsylvania State University at Erie*
Mark Winkel, *University of Texas—Pan American*

Expert Consultants for Previous Editions

Toni C. Antonucci, *University of Michigan–Ann Arbor;* **Paul Baltes,** *Max Planck Institute for Human Development;* **Diana Baumrind,** *University of California–Berkeley;* **Carol Beal,** *University of Massachusetts at Amherst;* **James Birren,** *University of California–Los Angeles;* **Marc H. Bornstein,** *National Institute of Child Health & Development;* **Sue Bredekamp,** *National Association for the Education of Young Children;* **Urie Bronfenbrenner,** *Cornell University;* **Rosalind Charlesworth,** *Weber State*

University; **Florence Denmark,** *Pace University;* **Joseph Durlack,** *Loyola University;* **Glen Elder,** *University of North Carolina–Chapel Hill;* **Tiffany Field,** *University of Miami;* **Alan Fogel,** *University of Utah;* **Jean Berko Gleason,** *Boston University;* **Gilbert Gottlieb,** *University of North Carolina;* **Julia Graber,** *Columbia University;* **Sandra Graham,** *University of California–Los Angeles;* **Jane Halonen,** *Alverno College;* **Yvette R. Harris,** *Miami University–Ohio;* **Algea O. Harrison-Hale,** *Oakland University;* **Craig Hart,** *Brigham Young University;* **Bert Hayslip,** *University of North Texas;* **Ravenna Helson,** *University of California–Berkeley;* **Cigdem Kagitcibasi,** *Koc University (Turkey);* **Robert Kastenbaum,** *Arizona State University;* **Gisela Labouvie-Vief,** *Wayne State University;* **Barry M. Lester,** *Women and Infants' Hospital;* **Jean M. Mandler,** *University of California–San Diego;* **James Marcia,** *Simon Fraser University;* **Scott Miller,** *University of Florida;* **Phyllis Moen,** *Cornell University;* **Ross D. Parke,** *University of California–Riverside;* **James Reid,** *Washington University;* **Carolyn Saarni,** *Sonoma State University;* **Barba Patton,** *University of Houston–Victoria;* **K. Warner Schaie,** *Pennsylvania State University;* **Jan Sinnott,** *Towson State University;* **Margaret Beale Spencer,** *University of Pennsylvania;* **Ross A. Thompson,** *University of Nebraska–Lincoln;* **Marian Underwood,** *University of Texas at Dallas;* **Susan Whitbourne,** *University of Massachusetts–Amherst.*

General Text Reviewers for Previous Editions

Patrick K. Ackles, *Michigan State University;* **Berkeley Adams,** *Jamestown Community College;* **Jackie Adamson,** *South Dakota School of Mines & Technology;* **Pamela Adelmann,** *Saint Paul Technical College;* **Joanne M. Alegre,** *Yavapai College;* **Gary L. Allen,** *University of South Carolina;* **Kristy Allen,** *Ozark Technical College;* **Lilia Allen,** *Charles County Community College;* **Susan E. Allen,** *Baylor University;* **Doreen Arcus,** *University of Massachusetts–Lowell;* **Frank. R. Ashbur,** *Valdosta State College;* **Leslie Ault,** *Hostos Community College–CUNY;* **Renee L. Babcock,** *Central Michigan University;* **Daniel R. Bellack,** *Trident Technical College;* **Helen E. Benedict,** *Baylor University;* **Alice D. Beyrent,** *Hesser College;* **John Biondo,** *Community College of Allegheny County–Boyce Campus;* **James A. Blackburn,** *University of Wisconsin–Madison;* **Stephanie Blecharczyk,** *Keene State College;* **Belinda Blevin-Knabe,** *University of Arkansas–Little Rock;* **Karyn Mitchell Boutlin,** *Massasoit Community College;* **Donald Bowers,** *Community College of Philadelphia;* **Saundra Y. Boyd,** *Houston Community College;* **Michelle Boyer-Pennington,** *Middle Tennessee State University;* **Ann Brandt-Williams,** *Glendale Community College;* **Julia Braungart-Rieke,** *University of Notre Dame;* **Kathy Brown,** *California State University at Fullerton;* **Jack Busky,** *Harrisburg Area Community College;* **Joan B. Cannon,** *University of Lowell;* **Jeri Carter,** *Glendale Community College;* **Vincent Castranovo,** *Community College of Philadelphia;* **Ginny Chappeleau,** *Muskingum Area Technical College;* **Dominique Charlotteaux,** *Broward Community College;* **Yiwei Chen,** *Bowling Green State University;* **Bill Cheney,** *Crichton College;* **M. A. Christenberry,** *Augusta College;* **Saundra Ciccarelli,** *Florida Gulf University;* **Andrea Clements,** *East Tennessee State University;* **Meredith**

Cohen, *University of Pittsburgh;* **Diane Cook,** *Gainesville College;* **Ava Craig,** *Sacramento City College;* **Kathleen Crowley-Long,** *College of Saint Rose;* **Cynthia Crown,** *Xavier University;* **Dana Davidson,** *University of Hawaii at Manoa;* **Diane Davis,** *Bowie State University;* **Tom L. Day,** *Weber State University;* **Doreen DeSantio,** *West Chester University;* **Jill De Villiers,** *Smith College;* **Darryl M. Dietrich,** *College of St. Scholastica;* **Bailey Drechsler,** *Cuesta College;* **Mary B. Eberly,** *Oakland University;* **Margaret Sutton Edmonds,** *University of Massachusetts–Boston;* **Martha M. Ellis,** *Collin County Community College;* **Lena Eriksen,** *Western Washington University;* **Richard Ewy,** *Pennsylvania State University;* **Dan Fawaz,** *Georgia Perimeter College;* **Shirley Feldman,** *Stanford University;* **Roberta Ferra,** *University of Kentucky;* **Linda E. Flickinger,** *St. Claire Community College;* **Lynne Andreozzi Fontaine,** *Community College of Rhode Island;* **Tom Frangicetto,** *Northampton Community College;* **Kathleen Corrigan Fuhs,** *J. Sargeant Reynolds Community College;* **J. Steven Fulks,** *Utah State University;* **Cathy Furlong,** *Tulsa Junior College;* **Duwayne Furman,** *Western Illinois University;* **John Gat,** *Humboldt State University;* **Marvin Gelman,** *Montgomery County College;* **Rebecca J. Glare,** *Weber State College;* **Jean Berko Gleason,** *Boston University;* **David Goldstein,** *Temple University;* **Judy Goodell,** *National University;* **Mary Ann Goodwyn,** *Northeast Louisiana University;* **Caroline Gould,** *Eastern Michigan University;* **Peter C. Gram,** *Pensacola Junior College;* **Dan Grangaard,** *Austin Community College;* **Tom Gray,** *Laredo Community College;* **Michele Gregoire,** *University of Florida at Gainesville;* **Michael Green,** *University of North Carolina;* **Rea Gubler,** *Southern Utah University;* **Gary Gute,** *University of Northern Iowa;* **Laura Hanish,** *Arizona State University;* **Ester Hanson,** *Prince George's Community College;* **Marian S. Harris,** *University of Illinois at Chicago;* **Amanda W. Harrist,** *Oklahoma State University;* **Robert Heavilin,** *Greater Hartford Community College;* **Donna Henderson,** *Wake Forest University;* **Debra Hollister,** *Valencia Community College;* **Heather Holmes-Lonergan,** *Metropolitan State College of Denver;* **Ramona O. Hopkins,** *Brigham Young University;* **Donna Horbury,** *Appalachian State University;* **Susan Horton,** *Mesa Community College;* **Sharon C. Hott,** *Allegany College of Maryland;* **John Hotz,** *Saint Cloud State University;* **Tasha Howe,** *Humboldt State University;* **Kimberley Howe-Norris,** *Cape Fear Community College;* **Stephen Hoyer,** *Pittsburg State University;* **Kathleen Day Hulbert,** *University of Massachusetts–Lowell;* **Derek Isaacowitz,** *Brandeis University;* **Kathryn French Iroz,** *Utah Valley State College;* **Terry Isbell,** *Northwestern State University of Louisiana;* **Erwin Janek,** *Henderson State University;* **James Jasper-Jacobsen,** *Indiana University–Purdue;* **Christina Jose-Kampfner,** *Eastern Michigan University;* **Ursula Joyce,** *St. Thomas Aquinas College;* **Seth Kalichman,** *Loyola University;* **Barbara Kane,** *Indiana State University;* **Kevin Keating,** *Broward Community College;* **James L. Keeney,** *Middle Georgia College;* **Elinor Kinarthy,** *Rio Hondo College;* **Karen Kirkendall,** *Sangamon State University;* **A. Klingner,** *Northwest Community College;* **Steven J. Kohn,** *Nazareth College;* **Amanda Kowal,** *University of Missouri;* **Jane Krump,** *North Dakota State College of Science;* **Nadene L'Amoreaux,** *Indiana University of Pennsylvania;* **Joseph C. LaVoie,** *University of Nebraska at Omaha;* **Kathy Lein,**

Community College of Denver; **Jean Hill Macht,** Montgomery County Community College; **Salvador Macias,** University of South Carolina–Sumter; **Karen Macrae,** University of South Carolina; **Christine Malecki,** Northern Illinois University; **Kathy Manuel,** Bossier Parish Community College; **Myra Marcus,** Florida Gulf Coast University; **Allan Mayotte,** Riverland Community College; **Susan McClure,** Westmoreland Community College; **Dorothy H. McDonald,** Sandhills Community College; **Robert C. McGinnis,** Ancilla College; **Clara McKinney,** Barstow College; **Robert McLaren,** California State University at Fullerton; **Sharon McNeeley,** Northeastern Illinois University; **James Messina,** University of Phoenix; **Heather E. Metcalfe,** University of Windsor; **Karla Miley,** Black Hawk College; **Jessica Miller,** Mesa State College; **Teri M. Miller-Schwartz,** Milwaukee Area Technical College; **David B. Mitchell,** Loyola University; **Joann Montepare,** Emerson College; **Martin D. Murphy,** University of Akron; **Malinda Muzi,** Community College of Philadelphia; **Gordon K. Nelson,** Pennsylvania State University; **Michael Newton,** Sam Houston State University; **Beatrice Norrie,** Mount Royal College; **Jean O'Neil,** Boston College; **Laura Overstreet,** Tarrant County College–Northeast; **Jennifer Parker,** University of South Carolina; **Pete Peterson,** Johnson County Community College; **Richard Pierce,** Pennsylvania State University–Altoona; **David Pipes,** Caldwell Community College; **Leslee Pollina,** Southeast Missouri State University; **Robert Poresky,** Kansas State University; **Christopher Quarto,** Middle Tennessee State University; **Bob Rainey,** Florida Community College; **Nancy Rankin,** University of New England; **H. Ratner,** Wayne State University; **Cynthia Reed,** Tarrant County College–Northeast; **Russell Riley,** Lord Fairfax Community College; **Mark P. Rittman,** Cuyahoga Community College; **Clarence Romeno,** Riverside Community College; **Paul Roodin,** SUNY–Oswego; **Ron Rossac,** University of North Florida; **Julia Rux,** Georgia Perimeter College; **Gayla Sanders,** Community College of Baltimore County–Essex; **Toru Sato,** Shippensburg University; **Nancy Sauerman,** Kirkwood Community College; **Cynthia Scheibe,** Ithaca College; **Robert Schell,** SUNY–Oswego; **Edythe Schwartz,** California State University at Sacramento; **Lisa Scott,** University of Minnesota–Twin Cities; **Owen Sharkey,** University of Prince Edward Island; **Elisabeth Shaw,** Texarkana College; **Susan Nakayama Siaw,** California State Polytechnical University; **Vicki Simmons,** University of Victoria; **Gregory Smith,** University of Maryland; **Jon Snodgrass,** California State University–Los Angeles; **Donald Stanley,** North Dallas Community College; **Jean A. Steitz,** University of Memphis; **Collier Summers,** Florida Community College at Jacksonville; **Barbara Thomas,** National University; **Stacy D. Thompson,** Oklahoma State University; **Debbie Tindell,** Wilkes University; **Stephen Truhon,** Winston-Salem State University; **James Turcott,** Kalamazoo Valley Community College; **Gaby Vandergiessen,** Fairmount State College; **Stephen Werba,** Community College of Baltimore County–Catonsville; **B. D. Whetstone,** Birmingham Southern College; **Nancy C. White,** Reynolds Community College; **Lyn W. Wickelgren,** Metropolitan State College; **Ann M. Williams,** Luzerne County Community College; **Myron D. Williams,** Great Lakes Bible College; **Linda B. Wilson,** Quincy College; **Mary Ann Wisniewski,** Carroll College

SUPPLEMENTS

The eleventh edition of *Life-Span Development* is accompanied by a comprehensive and fully integrated array of supplemental materials, both print and electronic, written specifically for instructors and students of life-span development. In addition, a variety of generic supplements are available to further aid in the teaching and learning of life-span development.

For the Instructor

Once again, based on comprehensive and extensive feedback from instructors, we spent considerable time and effort in expanding and improving the ancillary materials.

Instructor's Manual *Elaine Cassel, Lord Fairfax Community College and Gail Edmunds* This comprehensive manual provides a variety of useful tools for both seasoned instructors and those new to the life-span development course. The Instructor's Manual provides the following tools.

- List of Learning Goals provides detailed components to support each of the chapters' Learning Goals listed in the text.
- Fully integrated chapter outlines to help instructors better use the many resources for the course. Most of the supplementary materials offered in conjunction with *Life-Span Development*, eleventh edition, are represented in this outline and have been correlated to the main concepts in each chapter.
- Lecture suggestions, classroom activities, and research project ideas. As appropriate, these include critical thinking multiple-choice and essay exercises, all of which provide answers where appropriate.
- Classroom activities include logistics for required materials, such as accompanying handouts, varying group sizes, and time needed for completion.
- Personal Application projects guide students in applying life-span development topics to their own lives.
- Media resources for each chapter: Video segments (found on the LifeMap student CD) are listed; as well as Feature Film Suggestions, which provide a synopsis of movies pertaining to chapter topics; as well as updated URLs for useful Internet sites.

Computerized Test Bank on Instructor's Resource CD-ROM *Justina Powers, Cameron University* This comprehensive Test Bank has been extensively revised to include over 2,400 multiple-choice and short answer/brief essay questions for the text's 21 chapters. This Test Bank provides page references that indicate where in the text the answer to each item can be found.

Available on the Instructor's Resource CD-ROM, the Test Bank is compatible with both Windows and Macintosh platforms. The CD-ROM provides an editing feature that enables instructors to integrate their own questions, scramble items, and modify questions.

PowerPoint Slide Presentations *Elaine Cassel, Lord Fairfax Community College* The chapter-by-chapter PowerPoint lectures for this edition integrate the text's learning goals and provide key text material and illustrations. These presentations are designed to be useful in both small- and large-lecture settings, and are easily tailored to suit an individual instructor's lectures.

The McGraw-Hill Developmental Psychology Image Bank This set of 200 full-color images was developed using the best selection of our human development art and tables, and is available online for instructors on the text's Online Learning Center.

Online Learning Center The extensive web site designed especially to accompany Santrock, *Life-Span Development* eleventh edition, offers an array of resources for both instructor and student. For instructors, the web site includes the Instructor's Manual, a full set of PowerPoint Presentations, and hotlinks for the text's topical Web links that appear in the margins and for the Taking It to the Net exercises that appear at the end of each chapter. These resources and more can be found by logging on to the web site at **www.mhhe.com/santrockld11**.

Annual Editions–Developmental Psychology Published by Dushkin/McGraw-Hill, this is a collection of articles on topics related to the latest research and thinking in human development. These editions are updated annually and contain helpful features including a topic guide, an annotated table of contents, unit overviews, and a topical index. An Instructor's Guide containing testing materials is also available.

Sources: Notable Selections in Human Development This volume presents a collection of more than 40 articles, book excerpts, and research studies that have shaped the study of human development and our contemporary understanding of it. The selections are organized topically around major areas of study within human development. Each selection is preceded by a headnote that establishes the relevance of the article or study and provides biographical information about the author.

Taking Sides This debate-style reader is designed to introduce students to controversial viewpoints on the field's most crucial issues. Each issue is carefully framed for the student, and the pro and con essays represent the arguments of leading scholars and commentators in their fields. An Instructor's Guide containing testing material is available.

For the Student

Student Study Guide *Troianne Grayson, Florida Community College* The revised Study Guide provides a complete introduction for students on how best to use each of the various study aids plus invaluable strategies on setting goals, benefiting from class, reading for learning, taking tests, and memory techniques in the section "Being an Excellent Student." Each Study Guide chapter begins with a list of Learning Goals from the text and an outline of the chapter. The self-test sections contain short-answer Checking Your Under-standing questions, multiple-choice and true-false questions, and comprehensive essays with suggested answers. The Study Guide also includes out-of-class research projects, personal application projects, Internet projects, and Web links that complement the revised student research projects and allow for more effective student learning.

LifeMap Interactive CD-ROM for Students The LifeMap CD is especially designed to accompany Santrock, *Life-Span Development,* eleventh edition. Each of the book's 21 chapters features one or more video segments, accompanied by pretest and posttest questions and Web links to further explore issues raised in the video. In addition, each chapter features a multiple-choice quiz with feedback to encourage active learning. The LifeMap CD also features an interactive time line covering the stages of development through the life span.

Online Learning Center (OLC) www.mhhe.com/ santrockld11 This extensive web site designed especially to accompany Santrock, *Life-Span Development,* eleventh edition, offers an array of resources for instructors and students. For students, the web site offers interactive quizzes, matching exercises and English and Spanish glossaries defining the key terms from the text. It also offers Web links for the *Taking It to the Net* exercises that appear at the end of each chapter. Self-assessments related to chapter topics encourage students to examine their personal feelings and experiences in relation to life-span development. The Guide to Life-Span Development can now be found online. These resources and more can be found on the Online Learning Center at **www.mhhe.com/santrockld11**.

Guide to Life-Span Development for Future Nurses

Kathryn Launey, Vance-Granville Community College Revised and improved to facilitate understanding of developmental concepts central to the Life-Span course for future nurses. This new edition contains updated information, exercises, and sample tests designed to help future nurses prepare for licensure exams. This supplement has been put online and can be found on the Online Learning Center at **www.mhhe.com/santrockld11**.

Guide to Life-Span Development for Future Educators This course supplement helps students apply the concepts of human development to careers in education. It contains information, exercises, and sample tests designed to help students prepare for certification and understand human development from a professional perspective.

Resources for Improving Human Development This useful booklet provides descriptions and contact information for organizations and agencies that can provide helpful information, advice, and support related to particular problems or issues in life-span development. Organized in chronological order by periods of the life span, the booklet also describes recommended books and journals.

VISUAL TOUR FOR STUDENTS

This book provides you with important study tools to help you more effectively learn about life-span development. Especially important is the learning goals system that is integrated throughout each chapter. In the visual walkthrough of features, pay special attention to how the learning goals system works.

THE LEARNING GOALS SYSTEM

Using the learning goals system will help you to learn the material more easily. Key aspects of the learning goals system are the learning goals, chapter maps, review and reflect, and reach your learning goals sections, which are all linked together.

At the beginning of each chapter, you will see a page that includes both a chapter outline and three to six learning goals that preview the chapter's main themes and underscore the most important ideas in the chapter. Then, at the beginning of each major section of a chapter, you will see a mini-chapter map that provides you with a visual organization of the key topics you are about to read in the section. At the end of each section is Review and Reflect, in which the learning goal for the section is restated, a series of review questions related to the mini-chapter map are asked, and a question that encourages you to think critically about a topic related to the section appears. At the end of the chapter, you will come to a section titled: Reach Your Learning Goals. This includes an overall chapter map that visually organizes all of the main headings, a restatement of the chapter's learning goals, and a summary of the chapter's content that is directly linked to the chapter outline at the beginning of the chapter. It also includes the questions asked in the Review part of Review and Reflect within the chapter. The summary essentially answers the questions asked in the within-chapter Review sections.

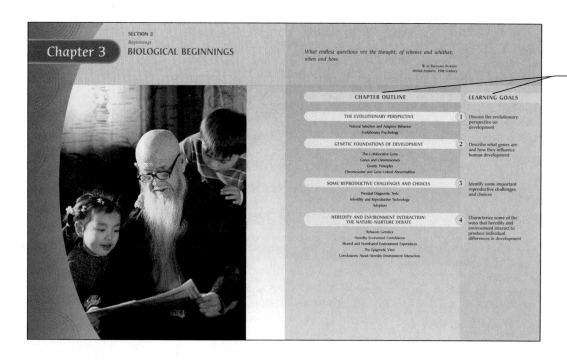

CHAPTER OPENING OUTLINE AND LEARNING GOALS

The outline shows the organization of topics by headings. Primary topic headings are printed in capital letters. The Learning Goals highlight the main ideas in the chapter by section.

MINI-CHAPTER MAP

This visual preview displays the main headings and subheadings for each section of the chapter.

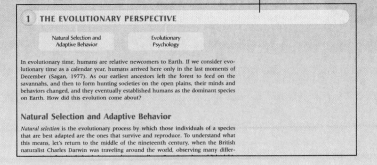

1 THE EVOLUTIONARY PERSPECTIVE

Natural Selection and Adaptive Behavior   Evolutionary Psychology

In evolutionary time, humans are relative newcomers to Earth. If we consider evolutionary time as a calendar year, humans arrived here only in the last moments of December (Sagan, 1977). As our earliest ancestors left the forest to feed on the savannahs, and then to form hunting societies on the open plains, their minds and behaviors changed, and they eventually established humans as the dominant species on Earth. How did this evolution come about?

Natural Selection and Adaptive Behavior

Natural selection is the evolutionary process by which those individuals of a species that are best adapted are the ones that survive and reproduce. To understand what this means, let's return to the middle of the nineteenth century, when the British naturalist Charles Darwin was traveling around the world, observing many differ-

REVIEW AND REFLECT

Review questions enable you to quiz yourself on the key ideas and find out whether you've met the learning goals for one section of a chapter before continuing to the next main topic. The question for reflection helps you to think about what you've just read and apply it. Answering these questions will help you to remember key points and concepts.

Review and Reflect • LEARNING GOAL 3

3 Characterize Some of the Ways that Heredity and Environment Interact to Produce Individual Differences in Development

Review
- What is behavior genetics?
- What are three types of heredity-environment correlations and what is an example of each?
- What is meant by the concepts of shared and nonshared environmental experiences?
- What is the epigenetic view of development?
- What conclusions can be reached about heredity-environment interaction?

Reflect
- A friend tells you that he or she has analyzed his or her genetic background and environmental experiences and reached the conclusion that environment definitely has had little influence on his or her intelligence. What would you say to this person about his or her ability to make this self-diagnosis?

REACH YOUR LEARNING GOALS

This section includes a complete chapter map and a summary restating the Learning Goals and answering the bulleted review questions from the chapter. Use it as a guide to help you organize your study of the chapter—*not* as a substitute for reading the chapter.

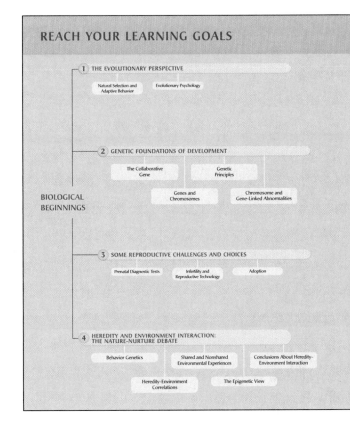

REACH YOUR LEARNING GOALS

1 THE EVOLUTIONARY PERSPECTIVE

Natural Selection and Adaptive Behavior   Evolutionary Psychology

2 GENETIC FOUNDATIONS OF DEVELOPMENT

The Collaborative Gene   Genetic Principles

Genes and Chromosomes   Chromosome and Gene-Linked Abnormalities

BIOLOGICAL BEGINNINGS

3 SOME REPRODUCTIVE CHALLENGES AND CHOICES

Prenatal Diagnostic Tests   Infertility and Reproductive Technology   Adoption

4 HEREDITY AND ENVIRONMENT INTERACTION: THE NATURE-NURTURE DEBATE

Behavior Genetics   Shared and Nonshared Environmental Experiences   Conclusions About Heredity-Environment Interaction

Heredity-Environment Correlations   The Epigenetic View

SUMMARY

1 The Evolutionary Perspective: *Discuss the evolutionary perspective on development*

Natural Selection and Adaptive Behavior
Natural selection is the process by which those individuals of a species that are best adapted survive and reproduce. Darwin proposed that natural selection fuels evolution. In evolutionary theory, adaptive behavior is behavior that promotes the organism's survival in a natural habitat.

Evolutionary Psychology
Evolutionary psychology holds that adaptation, reproduction, and "survival of the fittest" are important in shaping behavior. Ideas proposed by evolutionary developmental psychology include the view that an extended "juvenile" period is needed to develop a large brain and learn the complexity of human social communities. According to Baltes, the benefits resulting from evolutionary selection decrease with age mainly because of a decline in reproductive fitness. At the same time, cultural needs increase. Like other theoretical approaches to development, evolutionary psychology has limitations. Bandura rejects "one-sided evolutionism" and argues for a bidirectional link between biology and environment. Biology allows for a broad range of cultural possibilities.

2 Genetic Foundations of Development: *Describe what genes are and how they influence human development*

The Collaborative Gene
Except in the sperm and egg, the nucleus of each human cell contains 46 chromosomes, which are composed of DNA. Short segments of DNA constitute genes, the units of hereditary information that direct cells to reproduce and manufacture proteins. Genes act collaboratively, not independently.

Genes and Chromosomes
Genes are passed on to new cells when chromosomes are duplicated during the process of mitosis and meiosis, which are two ways in which new cells are formed. When an egg and a sperm unite in the fertilization process, the resulting zygote contains the genes from the chromosomes in the father's sperm and the mother's egg. Despite this transmission of genes from generation to generation, variability is created in several ways, including the exchange of chromosomal segments during meiosis, mutations, and the distinction between a genotype and a phenotype.

Genetic Principles
Genetic principles include those involving dominant-recessive genes, sex-linked genes, genetic imprinting, and polygenic inheritance.

Chromosome and Gene-Linked Abnormalities
Chromosome abnormalities produce Down syndrome, which is caused by the presence of an extra copy of chromosome 21, as well as sex-linked chromosomal abnormalities such as Klinefelter syndrome, fragile X syndrome, Turner syndrome, and XYY syndrome. Gene-linked abnormalities involve harmful genes. Gene-linked disorders include phenylketonuria (PKU) and sickle-cell anemia. Genetic counseling offers couples information about their risk of having a child with inherited abnormalities.

3 Some Reproductive Challenges and Choices: *Identify reproductive challenges and choices*

Prenatal Diagnostic Tests
Amniocentesis, ultrasound sonography, chorionic villi sampling, and maternal blood screening are used to determine whether a fetus is developing normally.

Infertility and Reproductive Technology
Approximately 10 to 15 percent of U.S. couples have infertility problems, some of which can be corrected through surgery or fertility drugs. Additional options include in vitro fertilization and other more recently developed techniques.

Adoption
Although adopted children and adolescents have more problems than their nonadopted counterparts, the vast majority of adopted children adapt effectively. When adoption occurs very early in development, the outcomes for the child are improved. Because of the dramatic changes that occurred in adoption in recent decades, it is difficult to generalize about the average adopted child or average adoptive family.

4 Heredity and Environment Interaction: The Nature-Nurture Debate: *Characterize how heredity and environment interact to produce individual differences in development*

Behavior Genetics
Behavior genetics is the field concerned with the degree and nature of behavior's hereditary basis. Methods used by behavior geneticists include twin studies and adoption studies.

Heredity-Environment Correlations
In Scarr's heredity-environment correlations view, heredity directs the types of environments that children experience. She describes three genotype-environment correlations: passive, evocative, and active (niche-picking). Scarr believes that the relative importance of these three genotype-environment correlations changes as children develop.

FEATURES AND PEDAGOGY

In addition to the learning system, *Life-Span Development*, eleventh edition, offers several special features and pedagogical tools designed to enhance student understanding of the chapter material.

RESEARCH IN LIFE-SPAN DEVELOPMENT INTERLUDE

One Research in Life-Span interlude appears in every in chapter. The research interludes describe a research study or program and are designed to acquaint you with how research in life-span development is conducted.

RESEARCH IN LIFE-SPAN DEVELOPMENT

A National Longitudinal Study of Child Care

In 1991, the National Institute of Child Health and Human Development (NICHD) began a comprehensive, longitudinal study of child-care experiences. Data were collected on a diverse sample of almost 1,400 children and their families at 10 locations across the United States over a period of seven years. Researchers used multiple methods (trained observers, interviews, questionnaires, and testing) and they measured many facets of children's development, including physical health, cognitive development, and socioemotional development. Following are some of the results (NICHD Early Child Care Network, 2001, 2002, 2003, 2004, 2005, 2006).

- *Patterns of Use.* Many families placed their infants in child care very soon after the child's birth, and there was considerable instability in the child care arrangements. By 4 months of age, nearly three-fourths of the infants had entered some form of nonmaternal child care. Almost half of the infants were

APPLICATIONS IN LIFE-SPAN DEVELOPMENT INTERLUDE

Every chapter has one Applications in Life-Span Development interlude, which provides applied information about parenting, education, or health and well-being related to a topic in the chapter

APPLICATIONS IN LIFE-SPAN DEVELOPMENT

Communicating with Children About Divorce

Ellen Galinsky and Judy David (1988) developed a number of guidelines for communicating with children about divorce.

Explain the Separation. As soon as daily activities in the home make it obvious that one parent is leaving, tell the children. If possible, both parents should be present when children are told about the separation to come. The reasons for the separation are very difficult for young children to understand. No matter what parents tell children, children can find reasons to argue against the separation. It is extremely important for parents to tell the children who will take care of them and to describe the specific arrangements for seeing the other parent.

Explain That the Separation Is Not the Child's Fault. Young children often believe their parents' separation or divorce is their own fault. Therefore, it is important to tell children that they are not the cause of the separation. Parents need to repeat this a number of times.

Explain That It May Take Time to Feel Better. Tell young children that it's normal to not feel good about what is happening and that many other children feel this way when their parents become separated. It is also okay for divorced parents to share some of their emotions with children, by saying something like. "I'm having a hard time since the separation just like you, but I know it's going to get better after a while." Such statements are best kept brief and should not criticize the other parent.

Keep the Door Open for Further Discussion. Tell your children to come to you anytime they want to talk about the separation. It is healthy for children to express their pent-up emotions in discussions with their parents and to learn that the parents are willing to listen to their feelings and fears.

Provide as Much Continuity as Possible. The less children's worlds are disrupted by the separation, the easier their transition to a single-parent family will be. This means maintaining the rules already in place as much as possible. Children need

DIVERSITY IN LIFE-SPAN DEVELOPMENT INTERLUDE

One Diversity in Life-Span Development interlude appears in each chapter and provides information about diversity related to a chapter topic.

What chance do you have of living to be 100? Genes play an important role in surviving to an extreme old age (Ford & Tower, 2006; Johnson, 2005; Mackay & others, 2006; Perls, 2006; Perls, Lauerman, & Silver, 1999; Vijg & Suh, 2005; Vogler, 2006). But there are also other factors at work family history, health (weight, diet, smoking, and exercise), education, personality, and lifestyle. To further examine the factors that are involved in living to a very old age, read the following Diversity in Life-Span Development interlude.

DIVERSITY IN LIFE-SPAN DEVELOPMENT

Living Longer in Okinawa

Individuals live longer on the Japanese island of Okinawa in the East China Sea than anywhere else in the world. In Okinawa, there are 34.7 centenarians for every 100,000 inhabitants, the highest ratio in the world. In comparison, the United States has about 10 centenarians for every 100,000 residents. The life expectancy in Okinawa is 81.2 years (86 for women, 78 for men), also highest in the world.

What is responsible for such longevity in Okinawa? Some possible explanations include (Willcox, Willcox, & Suzuki, 2002):

- *Diet.* Okinawans eat very healthy food, heavy on grains, fish, and vegetables, light on meat, eggs, and dairy products. The risk of dying of cancer is far lower among Okinawans than among Japanese and Americans (see figure 18.2). About 100,000 Okinawans moved to Brazil and quickly adopted the eating regimen of their new home, one heavy on red meat. The result: The life expectancy of the Brazilian Okinawans is now 17 years lower than Okinawa's 81 years!
- *Low-stress lifestyle.* The easygoing lifestyle in Okinawa more closely resembles that of a laid-back South Sea island than that of the high-stress world on the Japanese mainland.
- *Caring community.* Okinawans look out for each other and do not isolate or ignore their older adults. If older adults need help, they don't hesitate to ask a neighbor. Such support and caring is likely responsible for Okinawa having the lowest suicide rate among older women in East Asia, an area noted for its high suicide rate among older women.

(continued on next page)

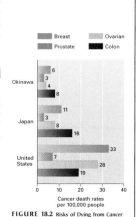

FIGURE 18.2 Risks of Dying from Cancer in Okinawa, Japan, and the United States. The risk of dying from different forms of cancer is lower in Okinawa than in the United States and Japan (Willcox, Willcox, & Suzuki, 2002). Okinawans eat lots of tofu and soy products, which are rich in flavonoids (believed to lower the risk of breast and prostate cancer). They also consume large amounts of fish, especially tuna, mackerel, and salmon, which reduce the risk of breast cancer.

The Hawaii Family Support/Healthy Start Program provides many home-visitor services for overburdened families of newborns and young children. This program has been very successful in reducing abuse and neglect in families. *What are some examples of the home-visitor services in this program?*

CRITICAL THINKING AND CONTENT QUESTIONS IN PHOTOGRAPH CAPTIONS

Most photographs have a caption that ends with a critical thinking or knowledge question in italics to stimulate further thought about a topic.

KEY TERMS AND GLOSSARY

Key terms appear in boldface. Their definitions appear in the margin near where they are introduced.

Intermodal Perception

Imagine yourself playing basketball or tennis. You are experiencing many visual inputs: the ball coming and going, other players moving around, and so on. However, you are experiencing many auditory inputs as well: the sound of the ball bouncing or being hit, the grunts and groans, and so on. There is good correspondence between much of the visual and auditory information: When you see the ball bounce, you hear a bouncing sound; when a player stretches to hit a ball, you hear a groan. When you look at and listen to what is going on, you do not experience just the sounds or just the sights; you put all these things together. You experience a unitary episode. This is **intermodal perception,** which involves integrating information from two or more sensory modalities, such as vision and hearing.

Crude exploratory forms of intermodal perception exist even in newborns (Chen, Striano, & Rakoczy, 2004). For example, newborns turn their eyes and their head toward the sound of a voice or rattle when the sound is maintained for several seconds (Clifton & others, 1981), but the newborn can localize a sound and look at an object only in a crude way (Bechtold, Bushnell, & Salapatek, 1979). These exploratory forms of intermodal perception become sharpened with experience in the first year of life (Hollich, Newman, & Jusczyk, 2005). In one study, infants as young as 3½ months old looked more at their mother when they also heard her voice and longer at their father when they also heard his voice (Spelke & Owsley, 1979); thus even young infants can coordinate visual-auditory information involving people.

intermodal perception The ability to relate and integrate information from two or more sensory modalities, such as vision and hearing.

Key terms also are listed and page-referenced at the end of each chapter.

KEY TERMS

cephalocaudal pattern 139	kwashiorkor 149	gross motor skills 154	visual preference method 161
proximodistal pattern 140	dynamic systems theory 151	fine motor skills 157	habituation 161
lateralization 141	reflexes 153	sensation 159	dishabituation 161
neuron 142	rooting reflex 153	perception 159	size constancy 164
sudden infant death	sucking reflex 153	ecological view 159	shape constancy 164
syndrome (SIDS) 146	Moro reflex 153	affordances 160	intermodal perception 167
marasmus 149	grasping reflex 153		

Key terms are alphabetically listed, defined, and page-referenced in a Glossary at the end of the book.

G·2   Glossary

B

bargaining Kübler-Ross' third stage of dying, in which the dying person develops the hope that death can somehow be postponed.

basal metabolism rate (BMR) The minimum amount of energy a person uses in a resting state. 243

brainstorming A technique in which individuals are encouraged to come up with creative ideas in a group, play off each other's ideas, and say practically whatever comes to mind. 328

Brazelton Neonatal Behavioral Assessment Scale (NBAS) A test given 24 to 36 hours after birth to assess newborns' neurological development, reflexes, and reactions to

chronic disorders Disorders that are characterized by slow onset and long duration. They are rare in early adulthood, they increase during middle adulthood, and they become common in late adulthood.

chronological age The number of years that have elapsed since birth. 20

climacteric The midlife transition in which fertility declines.

QUOTATIONS

These appear occasionally in the margins to stimulate further thought about a topic.

The experiences of the first three years of life are almost entirely lost to us, and when we attempt to enter into a small child's world, we come as foreigners who have forgotten the landscape and no longer speak the native tongue.

—SELMA FRAIBERG
Developmentalist and Child Advocate, 20th Century

as crawling, reaching, and walking, are learned through this process of adaptation: infants modulate their movement patterns to fit a new task by exploring and selecting possible configurations (Adolph & Berger, 2006; Adolph & Joh, 2007; Thelen & Smith, 2006).

To see how dynamic systems theory explains motor behavior, imagine that you offer a new toy to a baby named Gabriel (Thelen & others, 1993). There is no exact program that can tell Gabriel ahead of time how to move his arm and hand and fingers to grasp the toy. Gabriel must adapt to his goal—grasping the toy—and the context. From his sitting position, he must make split-second adjustments to extend his arm, holding his body steady so that his arm and torso don't plow into the toy. Muscles in his arm and shoulder contract and stretch in a host of combinations, exerting a variety of forces. He improvises a way to reach out with one arm and wrap his fingers around the toy.

THE INTERNET

Web icons appear a number of times in each chapter. They signal you to go to the book's Web site where you will find connecting links that provide additional information on the topic discussed in the text. The labels under the Web icon appear as Web links at the Santrock *Life-Span Development,* eleventh edition, Web site, under that chapter for easy access.

The First Year: Milestones and Variations Figure 5.14 summarizes important accomplishments in gross motor skills during the first year, culminating in the ability to walk easily. The timing of these milestones, especially the later ones, may vary by as much as two to four months, and experiences can modify the onset of these accomplishments. For example, since 1992, when pediatricians began recommending that parents keep their infants on their backs at night, fewer babies crawl and the age of onset of crawling is later (Davis & others, 1998). Also, some infants do not follow the standard sequence of motor accomplishments. For example, many American infants never crawl on their belly or on their hands-and-knees. They may discover an idiosyncratic form of locomotion before walking, such as rolling, or they might never locomote until they get upright (Adolph, 2002). In the African Mali tribe, most infants do not crawl (Bril, 1999).

According to Karen Adolph and Sarah Berger (2005), "the old-fashioned view that growth and motor development reflect merely the age-related output of maturation is, at best, incomplete. Rather, infants acquire new skills with the help of their caregivers in a real-world environment of objects, surfaces, and planes" (p. 273).

www.mhhe.com/santrockld11

Developmental Milestones
Karen Adolph's Research

KEY PEOPLE

The most important theorists and researchers in the chapter are listed and page-referenced at the end of each chapter.

KEY PEOPLE

Mark Rosenzweig 143	Arnold Gesell 151	Eleanor and	William James 162
John Watson 147	Esther Thelen 151	James J. Gibson 159	Richard Walk 164
T. Berry Brazelton 149	Karen Adolph 155	Robert Fantz 160	

CAREERS IN LIFE-SPAN DEVELOPMENT APPENDIX

A Careers in Life-Span Development Appendix that describes a number of careers appears following Chapter 1.

APPENDIX

Careers in Life-Span Development

The field of life-span development offers an amazing breadth of careers that can provide extremely satisfying work. College and university professors teach courses in many areas of life-span development. Teachers impart knowledge, understanding, and skills to children and adolescents. Counselors, clinical psychologists, nurses, and physicians help people of different ages to cope more effectively with their lives and improve their well-being.

These and many other careers related to life-span development offer many rewards. By working in the field of life-span development, you can help people to improve their lives, understand yourself and others better, possibly advance the state of knowledge in the field, and have an enjoyable time while you are doing these things. Many careers in life-span development pay reasonably well. For example, psychologists earn well above the median salary in the United States.

If you are considering a career in life-span development, would you prefer to work with infants? children? adolescents? older adults? As you take this course, try to spend some time with people of different ages. Observe their behavior. Talk with them about their lives. Think about whether you would like to work with people of this age in your life's work.

CAREERS IN LIFE-SPAN DEVELOPMENT PROFILES

Throughout the book, Careers in Life-Span Development profiles feature a person working in a life-span field related to the chapter's content.

CAREERS in LIFE-SPAN DEVELOPMENT

Darla Botkin
Marriage and Family Therapist

Darla Botkin is a marriage and family therapist who teaches, conducts research, and engages in marriage and family therapy. She is on the faculty of the University of Kentucky. Darla obtained a bachelor's degree in elementary education with a concentration in special education and then went on to receive a master's degree in early childhood education. She spent the next six years working with children and their families in a variety of settings, including child care, elementary school, and Head Start. These experiences led Darla to recognize the interdependence of the developmental settings that children and their parents experience (such as home, school, and work). She returned to graduate school and obtained a Ph.D. in family studies from the University of Tennessee. She then became a faculty member in the Family Studies program at the University of Kentucky. Completing further coursework and clinical training in marriage and family therapy, she became certified as a marriage and family therapist.

Darla's current interests include working with young children in family therapy, gender and ethnic issues in family therapy, and the role of spirituality in family wellness.

Darla Botkin (left), conducting a family therapy session.

E-LEARNING TOOLS

This feature appears at the end of each chapter and consists of three parts: *Taking It to the Net* Internet problem-solving exercises, *Self-Assessment*, which consists of one or more self-evaluations, and *Health and Well-Being, Parenting, and Education Exercises*, which provide an opportunity to practice decision-making skills related to real-world applications. By going to the On line Learning Center for this book, you can complete these valuable and enjoyable exercises for this book, where you will find many learning activities to improve your knowledge and understanding of the chapter.

E-LEARNING TOOLS

To help you master the material in this chapter, you'll find a number of valuable study tools on the LifeMap CD-ROM that accompanies this book and on the Online Learning Center for *Life-Span Development*, eleventh edition, at **www.mhhe.com/santrockld11**.

Video Clips

In the margins of this book there are icons directing you to the LifeMap CD-ROM that accompanies the book. There you'll find two videos for chapter 5. The first video is called "Nutritional Benefits of Breast Feeding." Is breast feeding better for the infant than bottle feeding? In this segment, a dietician details some of the benefits of breast feeding. The second video is called "Gross Motor Ability at 1 Year." A profile of 1-year-old Cindy illustrates some of the advances in gross motor skills that have occurred during the first year of life.

Self-Assessment

Connect to **www.mhhe.com/santrockld11** to examine your understanding of physical development in infancy by completing the self-assessment, *My Beliefs About Nurturing a Baby's Physical Development*.

Taking It to the Net

Connect to **www.mhhe.com/santrockld11** to research the answers to these questions.

1. Professor Samuels asked his life-span psychology students to write a one-page report explaining how a child's brain develops during infancy and what role parents play in fostering maximal brain development. What comprehensive and current research should this report include?
2. Huy grew up in a traditional Chinese family, where co-sleeping until adolescence was the norm. He sees no problem with allowing his infant daughter to sleep with him and his wife. His wife, Lori, who was born and raised in the United States, is concerned that allowing the baby to sleep in their bed places her at risk for SIDS. Is co-sleeping a significant risk factor for SIDS? What else can Huy and Lori do to reduce the risk?
3. Marianne has landed a part-time job as a nanny for Jack, a 2-month-old boy. What can Marianne expect to see in terms of the child's sensory and motor development as she observes and interacts with Jack over the next six months?

Health and Well-Being, Parenting, and Education Exercises

Build your decision-making skills by trying your hand at the health and well-being, parenting, and education exercises.

Connect to **www.mhhe.com/santrockld11** to research the answers and complete the exercises.

ABOUT THE AUTHOR

JOHN W. SANTROCK

John Santrock received his Ph.D. from the University of Minnesota in 1973. He taught at the University of Charleston and the University of Georgia before joining the School of Behavioral and Brain Sciences at the University of Texas at Dallas, where he currently teaches a number of undergraduate courses and was given the University's Effective Teaching Award in 2006.

John has been a member of the editorial boards of *Child Development* and *Developmental Psychology*. His research on father custody is widely cited and used in expert witness testimony to promote flexibility and alternative considerations in custody disputes. John also has authored these exceptional McGraw-Hill texts: *Psychology* (7th edition), *Children* (9th edition), *Adolescence* (11th edition), *Topical Life-Span Development* (3rd edition), and *Educational Psychology* (3rd edition).

For many years, John was involved in tennis as a player, teaching professional, and coach of professional tennis players. He has been married for more than 35 years to his wife, Mary Jo, who is a realtor. He has two daughters—Tracy, who is studying to become a financial planner at Duke University, and Jennifer, who is a medical sales specialist at Medtronic. He has one granddaughter, Jordan, age 15, and two grandsons, Alex, age 2, and Luke, age 10 months. Tracy recently completed the New York Marathon, and Jennifer was in the top 100 ranked players on the Women's Professional Tennis Tour. In the last decade, John also has spent time painting expressionist art.

John Santrock (*center*) teaching an undergraduate psychology course.

We reach backward to our parents and forward to our children, and through their children to a future we will never see, but about which we need to care.

—CARL JUNG
Swiss Psychiatrist, 20th Century

LEARNING GOALS

1 Discuss the life-span perspective of development

2 Identify the most important developmental processes and periods

3 Describe three key developmental issues

Images of Life-Span Development
How Did Ted Kaczynski Become Ted Kaczynski and Alice Walker Become Alice Walker?

Ted Kaczynski, the convicted Unabomber, traced his difficulties to growing up as a genius in a kid's body and not fitting in when he was a child.

Alice Walker won the Pulitzer Prize for her book *The Color Purple*. Like the characters in her book, Walker overcame pain and anger to triumph and celebrate the human spirit.

Ted Kaczynski sprinted through high school, not bothering with his junior year and making only passing efforts at social contact. Off to Harvard at age 16, Kaczynski was a loner during his college years. One of his roommates at Harvard said that he avoided people by quickly shuffling by them and slamming the door behind him. After obtaining his Ph.D. in mathematics at the University of Michigan, Kaczynski became a professor at the University of California at Berkeley. His colleagues there remember him as hiding from social circumstances—no friends, no allies, no networking.

After several years at Berkeley, Kaczynski resigned and moved to a rural area of Montana where he lived as a hermit in a crude shack for 25 years. Town residents described him as a bearded eccentric. Kaczynski traced his own difficulties to growing up as a genius in a kid's body and sticking out like a sore thumb in his surroundings as a child. In 1996, he was arrested and charged as the notorious Unabomber, America's most wanted killer who sent 16 mail bombs in 17 years that left 23 people wounded or maimed, and 3 people dead. In 1998, he pleaded guilty to the offenses and was sentenced to life in prison.

A decade before Kaczynski mailed his first bomb, Alice Walker, who later won the Pulitzer Prize for her book *The Color Purple,* spent her days battling racism in Mississippi. She had recently won her first writing fellowship, but rather than use the money to follow her dream of moving to Senegal, Africa, she put herself into the heart and heat of the civil rights movement. Walker had grown up knowing the brutal effects of poverty and racism. Born in 1944, she was the eighth child of Georgia sharecroppers who earned $300 a year. When Walker was 8, her brother accidentally shot her in the left eye with a BB gun. By the time her parents got her to the hospital a week later (they had no car), she was blind in that eye and it had developed a disfiguring layer of scar tissue. Despite the counts against her, Walker overcame pain and anger and went on to become not only an award-winning novelist but also an essayist, a poet, a short-story writer, and a social activist.

What leads one individual, so full of promise, to commit brutal acts of violence and another to turn poverty and trauma into a rich literary harvest? If you have ever wondered why people turn out the way they do, you have asked yourself the central question we will explore in this book.

PREVIEW

This chapter previews the themes and issues that we will consider throughout our study of life-span development. First, we will describe the life-span perspective, then we will explore the processes and periods that characterize human development. Finally, we will examine the primary issues that developmentalists debate, issues that will come up repeatedly in this text.

1   THE LIFE-SPAN PERSPECTIVE

| The Importance of Studying Life-Span Development | Characteristics of the Life-Span Perspective |
| A Historical Perspective | Some Contemporary Concerns |

Each of us develops partly like all other individuals, partly like some other individuals, and partly like no other individual. Most of the time, our attention is directed to an individual's uniqueness. But psychologists who study life-span development are drawn to our shared characteristics as well as what makes us unique. As humans, we all have traveled some common paths. Each of us—Leonardo da Vinci, Oprah Winfrey, Ted Kaczynski, Alice Walker, and you—walked at about 1 year, engaged in play as a young child, and searched for an identity as a youth. Each of us, if we live long enough, will experience hearing problems and the death of family members and friends. This is the general course of our **development,** the pattern of movement or change that begins at conception and continues through the human life span.

The Importance of Studying Life-Span Development

Most development involves growth, but it also includes decline. Your ability to speak and write your native language has grown since you were a young child, for example, but your ability to learn to speak a new language has probably declined. In exploring development we will examine the life span from the point of conception until the time when life (at least, life as we know it) ends. You will see yourself as an infant, as a child, and as an adolescent, and be stimulated to think about how those years influenced you. And you will see yourself as a young adult, middle-aged adult, and an adult in old age and be motivated to think how your experiences today will influence your development through the remainder of your adult years.

How might you benefit from examining life-span development? Perhaps you are, or will be, a parent or teacher and you want to learn about children so that you can become a better parent or educator. Perhaps you hope to gain some insight about your own history—as an infant, a child, an adolescent, or a young adult. Perhaps you want to know more about what your life will be like as you grow through the adult years. Or perhaps you think that the study of the human life span might raise some provocative issues. Whatever your reasons for reading this book, you will discover that the study of life-span development is intriguing and filled with information about who we are, how we came to be this way, and where our future will take us.

PEANUTS © United Features Syndicate, Inc.

development The pattern of change that begins at conception and continues through the life span. Most development involves growth, although it also includes decline brought on by aging and dying.

History of Childhood
Children's Issues
Children's Rights
UNICEF

Ah! What would the world be to us
If the children were no more?
We should dread the desert behind us
Worse than the dark before.

—HENRY WADSWORTH LONGFELLOW
American Poet, 19th Century

History of Childhood

An early effort to systematically observe children's behavior was constructed by Arnold Gesell (1928). In his dome, cameras rode on metal tracks at the top of the dome and were moved as needed to record the child's activities. Others could observe from outside the dome without being seen by the child. Today, systematic observation is a cornerstone of learning about how children develop.

original sin The view that children were basically bad and born into the world as evil beings.

tabula rasa The idea, proposed by John Locke, that children are like a "blank tablet."

innate goodness The idea presented by the French philosopher Jean-Jacques Rousseau that children are inherently good.

Researchers who study life-span development aim to describe, explain, and discover ways to optimize development. Consider these research findings:

- Massage therapy facilitates the growth of preterm infants and improves the functioning of their immune system (Field, 2001, 2002, 2003; Field, Hernandez-Reif, & Freedman, 2004; Field & others, 2006).
- When high school students take part in community service projects such as tutoring or helping in a hospital, their grades and self-esteem improve, and they have an increased sense of being able to make a difference for others (Benson & others, 2006; Reinders & Youniss, 2006).
- Friendship is a critical aspect of marital success, even for individuals who rate sexual satisfaction as highly important in a marriage (Gottman & others, 2002).
- When middle-aged and older adults exercise regularly, they lose less brain tissue than sedentary counterparts (Colcombe & others, 2003; Kramer, Fabiani, & Colcombe, 2006).

These are but a few of the thousands of research findings we will examine in this text that can improve your understanding of the human life span.

A Historical Perspective

Today's research on life-span development builds on a long and rich history. Before the latter half of the twentieth century, development was considered to be something that happened only during childhood. A complete view of development, however, requires that we also consider developmental changes in the adult years. In this section, we will look briefly at how the prevailing view of children and adults has changed.

Child Development
Ideas about childhood have varied. Throughout history, philosophers have speculated about the nature of children and how they should be reared (Cairns & Cairns, 2006). In Western civilization, three influential philosophical views are based on the ideas of original sin, tabula rasa, and innate goodness:

- According to the Christian doctrine of **original sin,** children are born into the world corrupted, with an inclination toward evil. The goal of child rearing is to save children from sin.
- Toward the end of the seventeenth century, English philosopher John Locke argued that at birth each child is a **tabula rasa**—a "blank tablet." Locke proposed that people acquire their characteristics through experience and that childhood experiences are important in determining adult characteristics. He advised parents to spend time with their children and help them become contributing members of society.
- In the eighteenth century, Swiss-born, French philosopher Jean-Jacques Rousseau proposed the concept of **innate goodness.** According to Rousseau, children are inherently good and therefore should be permitted to grow naturally with little parental monitoring or constraint.

These conflicting views formed the historical backdrop for the study of childhood and for child-rearing practices. The modern study of children dates only to the late 1800s, when developmentalists stopped relying on a philosophical approach and began to apply the scientific method. That is, they used systematic observation, experimentation, and other methods that we will discuss in Chapter 2 to understand how children develop.

Today, we conceive of childhood as a highly eventful and unique period of life that lays an important foundation for the adult years and is highly differentiated from them. Most approaches to childhood identify distinct periods in which special skills are mastered and new life tasks are confronted. We now value childhood as a special time of growth and change, and we invest great resources in caring for and educating our children, although much yet needs to be accomplished to improve the lives of many children (Cicchetti & Toth, 2006; McLoyd, Aikens, & Burton, 2006; Powell, 2006).

Life-Span Development   Although growth and development are dramatic during the first two decades of life, development is not something that happens only to children and adolescents. The *traditional approach* to studying development emphasizes extensive change from birth to adolescence (especially during infancy), little or no change in adulthood, and decline in old age. But a great deal of change does occur in the five or six decades after adolescence. The *life-span approach* emphasizes developmental change throughout adulthood as well as childhood (Baltes, Lindenberger, & Staudinger, 2006; Birren & Schaie, 2006; Settersen, 2006). Consider this description of adult development:

> The next five or six decades are every bit as important, not only to those adults who are passing through them but to their children, who must live with and understand parents and grandparents. The changes in body, personality, and abilities through these later decades are great. Developmental tasks are imposed by marriage and parenthood, by the waxing and waning of physical prowess and of some intellectual capacities, by the children's flight from the nest, by the achievement of an occupational plateau, and by retirement and the prospect of final extinction. (Sears & Feldman, 1973, pp. v–vi)

Recent changes in human life expectancy contributed to the popularity of the life-span approach to development. The upper boundary of the *human life span* (based on the oldest age documented) is 122 years, as indicated in figure 1.1; this maximum human life span has not changed since the beginning of recorded history. What has changed is *life expectancy*: the average number of years that a person born in a particular year can expect to live. In the twentieth century alone, life expectancy increased by 31 years, thanks to improvements in sanitation, nutrition, and medicine (see figure 1.2). In 2005, the U.S. life expectancy was 78 years of age (U.S. Bureau of the Census, 2006). However, some prognosticators predict that U.S. life expectancy may actually decrease in the future because of the significant increase in obesity (Olshansky & others, 2005).

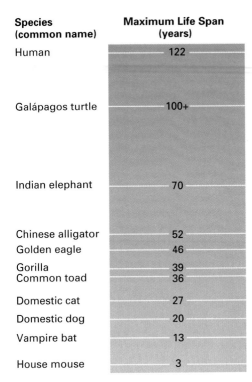

Species (common name)	Maximum Life Span (years)
Human	122
Galápagos turtle	100+
Indian elephant	70
Chinese alligator	52
Golden eagle	46
Gorilla	39
Common toad	36
Domestic cat	27
Domestic dog	20
Vampire bat	13
House mouse	3

FIGURE 1.1 **Maximum Recorded Life Span for Different Species.** Our only competitor for the maximum recorded life span is the Galápagos turtle.

Characteristics of the Life-Span Perspective

The belief that development occurs throughout life is central to the life-span perspective on human development, but this perspective has other characteristics as well. According to life-span development expert Paul Baltes (1987, 2000, 2003; Baltes, Lindenberger, & Staudinger, 2006), the **life-span perspective** views development as lifelong, multidimensional, multidirectional, plastic, multidisciplinary, and contextual, and as a process that involves growth, maintenance, and regulation of loss. It also is important to understand that development is constructed through biological, sociocultural, and individual factors working together. Let's look at each of these characteristics.

Development Is Lifelong   In the life-span perspective, early adulthood is not the endpoint of development; rather, no age period dominates development. Researchers increasingly study the experiences and psychological orientations of adults at different points in their lives. Later in this chapter we will describe the age periods of development and their characteristics.

Development Is Multidimensional   Whatever your age, your body, your mind, your emotions, and your relationships are changing and affecting each other. Consider the development of Ted Kaczynski, the bomber discussed at the opening

www.mhhe.com/santrockld11

Exploring Aging Issues
National Aging Information Center
Global Resources on Aging
Adult Development and Aging
The Gerontological Society of America
Geropsychology Resources

life-span perspective The perspective that development is lifelong, multidimensional, multidirectional, plastic, multidisciplinary, and contextual; involves growth, maintenance, and regulation; and is constructed through biological, sociocultural, and individual factors working together.

Time Period	Average Life Expectancy (years)
2005, USA	78
1954, USA	70
1915, USA	54
1900, USA	47
19th century, England	41
1620, Massachusetts Bay Colony	35
Middle Ages, England	33
Ancient Greece	20
Prehistoric times	18

FIGURE 1.2 Human Life Expectancy at Birth from Prehistoric to Contemporary Times. It took 5,000 years to extend human life expectancy from 18 to 41 years of age.

Paul Baltes, a leading architect of the life-span perspective of development, conversing with one of the long-time research participants (now 96 years of age) in the Berlin Aging Study that he directs. She joined the study in the early 1990s and has participated six times in extensive physical, medical, psychological, and social assessments. In her professional life, she was a practicing medical doctor.

context The setting in which development occurs, which is influenced by historical, economic, social, and cultural factors.

of the chapter. When he was 6 months old, he was hospitalized with a severe allergic reaction, and his parents were rarely allowed to visit the baby. According to his mother, the previously happy baby was never the same. The infant became withdrawn and unresponsive. As Ted grew up, he had periodic "shutdowns" accompanied by rage. In his mother's view, a biological event in infancy warped the development of her son's mind and emotions.

Development consists of biological, cognitive, and socioemotional dimensions. Even within a dimension, there are many components; for example, attention, memory, abstract thinking, speed of processing information, and social intelligence are just a few of the components of the cognitive dimension.

Development Is Multidirectional   Throughout life, some dimensions or components of a dimension expand and others shrink. For example, when one language (such as English) is acquired early in development, the capacity for acquiring second and third languages (such as French and Spanish) decreases later in development, especially after early childhood (Levelt, 1989). During adolescence, as individuals establish romantic relationships, their relationships with friends might decrease. During late adulthood, older adults might become wiser by being able to call on experience to guide their intellectual decision making (Baltes & Kunzmann, 2003; Brugman, 2006), but they perform more poorly on tasks that require speed in processing information (Hartley, 2006; Li & others, 2004; Madden, 2001; Salthouse, 2000).

Development Is Plastic   Even at 10 years old, Ted Kaczynski was extraordinarily shy. Was he destined to remain forever uncomfortable with people? Developmentalists debate how much plasticity people have in various dimensions at different points in their development. *Plasticity* means the capacity for change. For example, can you still improve your intellectual skills when you are in your seventies or eighties? Or might these intellectual skills be fixed by the time you are in your thirties so that further improvement is impossible? In one research study, the reasoning abilities of older adults were improved through retraining (Willis & Schaie, 1994). However, we possibly possess less capacity for change when we become old (Baltes, Reuter-Lorenz, & Rösler, 2006; Baltes & Smith, 2003; Singer, Lindenberger, & Baltes, 2003). The search for plasticity and its constraints is a key element on the contemporary agenda for developmental research (Baltes, Lindenberger, & Staudinger, 2006; Kagan & Herschkowitz, 2005; Prickaerts & others, 2004).

Developmental Science Is Multidisciplinary   Psychologists, sociologists, anthropologists, neuroscientists, and medical researchers all share an interest in unlocking the mysteries of development through the life span. How do your heredity and health limit your intelligence? Do intelligence and social relationships change with age in the same way around the world? How do families and schools influence intellectual development? These are examples of research questions that cut across disciplines.

Development Is Contextual   All development occurs within a **context,** or setting. Contexts include families, schools, peer groups, churches, cities, neighborhoods, university laboratories, countries, and so on. Each of these settings is influenced by historical, economic, social, and cultural factors (Shiraev & Levy, 2007; Yang, 2005).

Contexts, like individuals, change. Thus, individuals are changing beings in a changing world. As a result of these changes, contexts exert three types of influences (Baltes, 2000, 2003): (1) normative age-graded influences, (2) normative history-graded influences, and (3) nonnormative or highly individualized life events. Each of these types can have a biological or environmental impact on development.

Nonnormative life events, such as Hurricane Katrina in August, 2005, are unusual circumstances that have a major impact on a person's life. Here a woman and her children are shown in a Houston shelter for those left homeless by the devastating hurricane.

- **Normative age-graded influences** are similar for individuals in a particular age group. These influences include biological processes such as puberty and menopause. They also include sociocultural, environmental processes such as beginning formal education (usually at about age 6 in most cultures) and retirement (which takes place in the fifties and sixties in most cultures).
- **Normative history-graded influences** are common to people of a particular generation because of historical circumstances. For example, in their youth, American baby boomers shared the experience of the Cuban missile crisis, the assassination of John F. Kennedy, and the Beatles invasion. Other examples of normative history-graded influences include economic, political, and social upheavals such as the Great Depression in the 1930s, World War II in the 1940s, the civil rights and women's rights movements of the 1960s and 1970s, the terrorist attacks of 9/11/2001, as well as the integration of computers and cell phones into everyday life during the 1990s (Modell & Elder, 2002; Schaie, 2007). Long-term changes in the genetic and cultural makeup of a population (due to immigration or changes in fertility rates) are also part of normative historical change.
- **Nonnormative life events** are unusual occurrences that have a major impact on the individual's life. These events do not happen to all people, and when they do occur they can influence people in different ways. Examples include the death of a parent when a child is young, pregnancy in early adolescence, a fire that destroys a home, winning the lottery, or getting an unexpected career opportunity with special privileges. In the life of Alice Walker described at the opening of the chapter, being shot in the eye was a nonnormative life event.

Development Involves Growth, Maintenance, and Regulation of Loss   Baltes and his colleagues assert that the mastery of life often involves conflicts and competition among three goals of human development: growth, maintenance, and regulation of loss (Baltes, 2003; Baltes, Lindenberger, & Staudinger, 2006; Krampe & Baltes, 2003). As individuals age into middle and late adulthood, the maintenance and regulation of loss in their capacities takes center stage away from growth. Thus, a 75-year-old man might aim not to improve his memory or his golf swing but to maintain his independence and to play golf at all. In section 9, "Late Adulthood," we will discuss these ideas about maintenance and regulation of loss in greater depth.

How might growth versus maintenance and regulation be reflected in the development of this grandfather and his two grandchildren?

Development Is a Coconstruction of Biology, Culture, and the Individual   Development is a coconstruction of biological, cultural, and individual factors working together (Baltes, 2003; Baltes, Lindenberger, & Staudinger, 2006; Baltes, Reuter-Lorenz, & Rösler, 2006; Li, 2006). For example, the brain shapes culture, but it is also shaped by culture and the experiences that individuals have or pursue. In terms of individual factors, we can go beyond what our genetic inheritance and environment give us. We can author a unique developmental path by actively choosing from the environment the things that optimize our lives (Rathunde & Csikszentmihalyi, 2006).

Some Contemporary Concerns

Pick up a newspaper or magazine and you might see headlines like these: "Political Leanings May Be Written in the Genes," "Mother Accused of Tossing Children into Bay," "Gender Gap Widens," "FDA Warns About ADHD Drug," "Heart Attack Deaths

normative age-graded influences These are influences that are similar for individuals in a particular age group.

normative history-graded influences Influences that are common to people of a particular generation because of historical circumstances.

nonnormative life events Unusual occurrences that have a major impact on an individual's life.

CAREERS
in LIFE-SPAN DEVELOPMENT

Luis Vargas
Child Clinical Psychologist

Luis Vargas is Director of the Clinical Child Psychology Internship Program and a professor in the Department of Psychiatry at the University of New Mexico Health Sciences Center. He also is Director of Psychology at the University of New Mexico children's Psychiatric Hospital.

Luis obtained an undergraduate degree in psychology from St. Edwards University in Texas, a master's degree in psychology from Trinity University in Texas, and a Ph.D. in clinical psychology from the University of Nebraska–Lincoln.

Luis' main interests are cultural issues and the assessment and treatment of children, adolescents, and families. He is motivated to find better ways to provide culturally responsive mental health services. One of his special interests is the treatment of Latino youth for delinquency and substance abuse.

Luis Vargas (*left*) conducting a child therapy session.

www.mhhe.com/santrockld11

Health Links
Educator's Reference Desk
Diversity
Social Policy
Trends in the Well-Being of
Children and Youth

Children learn to love when they are loved

Higher in African American Patients," "Test May Predict Alzheimer disease." Researchers using the life-span perspective are examining these and many other topics of contemporary concern. The roles that health and well-being, parenting, education, and sociocultural contexts play in life-span development, as well as how social policy is related to these issues, are a particular focus of this textbook.

Health and Well-Being   Does a pregnant woman endanger her fetus if she has a few beers a week? How does a poor diet affect a child's ability to learn? Can exercise help older people maintain their mental abilities? We will discuss many questions like these regarding health and well-being—important goals for just about everyone for most of human history.

Asian physicians in 2600 B.C. and Greek physicians in 500 B.C. did not blame the gods for illness or think that magic would cure it. They recognized that good habits are essential for good health and believed that the physician's role was to be a guide, assisting patients to restore a natural physical and emotional balance. Similarly, health professionals today recognize the power of lifestyles and psychological states in health and well-being (Aldwin, Spiro, & Park, 2006; George, 2006; Hales, 2006; Hahn, Payne, & Lucas, 2007; Hales, 2007; Hahn, Payne, & Lucas, 2007; Wardlaw & Hampl, 2007). In every chapter of this book, issues of health and well-being are integrated into our discussion. They also are highlighted with World Wide Web icons that appear throughout the book.

Clinical psychologists are among the health professionals who help people improve their well-being. You can read about one clinical psychologist who helps adolescents who have become juvenile delinquents or substance abusers in the Careers in Life-Span Development insert. The appendix to the chapter describes the education and training required for this and other careers in life-span development.

Parenting and Education   Can two gay men raise a healthy family? Are children harmed if both parents work outside the home? Do adopted children fare as well as children raised by their biological parents? Are U.S. schools teaching children to be immoral? Are they failing to teach them how to read and write and calculate adequately? We often hear questions like these related to pressures on the contemporary family (Bornstein, 2006; Lamb & Ahnert, 2006; Parke & Buriel, 2006; Powell, 2006) and the failures of U.S. schools (Aldridge & Goldman, 2007; McLaren, 2007; Morrison, 2006; Silberman, 2006). In later chapters, we will analyze child care, the effects of divorce, parenting styles, intergenerational relationships, early childhood education, relationships between childhood poverty and education, bilingual education, new educational efforts to improve lifelong learning, and many other issues related to parenting and education.

Sociocultural Contexts and Diversity   Health, parenting, and education—like development itself—are all shaped by their sociocultural context. To analyze this context, four concepts are especially useful: culture, ethnicity, socioeconomic status, and gender.

Culture encompasses the behavior patterns, beliefs, and all other products of a particular group of people that are passed on from generation to generation. Culture results from the interaction of people over many years. A cultural group can be as large as the United States or as small as an isolated Appalachian town. Whatever its size, the group's culture influences the behavior of its members (Shweder & others, 2006). **Cross-cultural studies** compare aspects of two or more cultures. The comparison provides information about the degree to which development is similar, or universal, across cultures, or is instead culture-specific (Cole, 2006; Greenfield, Shiraev & Levy, 2007; Suzuki, & Rothstein-Fisch, 2006).

Ethnicity (the word *ethnic* comes from the Greek word for "nation") is rooted in cultural heritage, nationality, race, religion, and language. African Americans, Latinos, Asian Americans, Native Americans, Polish Americans, and Italian Americans are a few examples of ethnic groups in the United States. Diversity exists within each ethnic group (Banks, 2006; Koppelman & Goodhart, 2005; Sheets, 2005). Contrary to stereotypes, not all African Americans live in low-income circumstances; not all Latinos are Catholics; not all Asian Americans are high school math whizzes.

Race and ethnicity are sometimes misrepresented. *Race* is a controversial classification of people according to real or imagined biological characteristics such as skin color and blood group (Corsini, 1999). An individual's ethnicity can include his or her race but also many other characteristics. Thus, an individual might be White (a racial category) and a fifth-generation Texan who is a Catholic and speaks English and Spanish fluently.

Socioeconomic status (SES) refers to a person's position within society based on occupational, educational, and economic characteristics. Socioeconomic status implies certain inequalities. Generally, members of a society have (1) occupations that vary in prestige, and some individuals have more access than others to higher-status occupations; (2) different levels of educational attainment, and some individuals have more access than others to better education; (3) different economic resources; and (4) different levels of power to influence a community's institutions. These differences in the ability to control resources and to participate in society's rewards produce unequal opportunities (Conger & Donnellan, 2007; Holden & Hatcher, 2006; Moren-Cross & Lin, 2006; O'Rand, 2006).

Gender is another dimension of the sociocultural context. Whereas sex refers to the biological dimension of being female or male, **gender** involves the psychological and sociocultural dimensions of being female or male. Few aspects of our development are more central to our identity and social relationships than gender (Lippa, 2005; Moen & Spencer, 2006; Poelmans, 2005). How you view yourself,

Two Korean-born children on the day they became United States citizens. Asian American and Latino children are the fastest-growing immigrant groups in the United States. *How diverse are the students in your class on life-span development that you now are taking? How are their experiences in growing up likely similar to or different from yours?*

culture The behavior patterns, beliefs, and all other products of a group that are passed on from generation to generation.

cross-cultural studies Comparison of one culture with one or more other cultures. These provide information about the degree to which development is similar, or universal, across cultures, and the degree to which it is culture-specific.

ethnicity A characteristic based on cultural heritage, nationality characteristics, race, religion, and language.

socioeconomic status (SES) Refers to the grouping of people with similar occupational, educational, and economic characteristics.

gender The psychological and sociocultural dimensions of being female or male.

your relationships with other people, your life and your goals is shaped to a great extent by whether you are male or female and how your culture defines the proper roles of males and females (Hyde, 2007; Smith, 2007).

Each of these dimensions of the sociocultural context—culture, ethnicity, SES, and gender—helps mold how an individual develops through life, as discussions in later chapters will demonstrate. We will explore, for example, questions such as

- Do infants around the world form attachments with their parents in the same way, or do these attachments differ from one culture to another?
- Does poverty influence the likelihood that young children will be aggressive?
- Is there a parenting style that is universally effective, or does the effectiveness of different types of parenting depend on the ethnic group or culture?
- If adolescents from minority groups identify with their ethnic culture, is that likely to help or hinder their social development?
- Do gender differences that appear in heterosexual relationships also occur in same-sex relationships?
- Do men form different types of friendships than women?
- Can your culture help you stay vigorous and live to a ripe old age?
- Why do women live longer than men?

In the United States, the sociocultural context has become increasingly diverse in recent years. Its population includes a greater variety of cultures and ethnic groups than ever before. This changing demographic tapestry promises not only the richness that diversity produces but also difficult challenges in extending the American dream to all individuals (Banks, 2006; Bennett, 2007; Cushner, 2006; Diaz, Pelletier, & Provenzo, 2006; Spring, 2007). We will discuss sociocultural contexts and diversity in each chapter. In addition, a Diversity in Life-Span Development interlude appears in every chapter. The first one, about women's international struggle for equality, appears next.

DIVERSITY IN LIFE-SPAN DEVELOPMENT

Women's Struggle for Equality: An International Journey

The educational and psychological conditions of women around the world are a serious concern (Malley-Morrison, 2004; Sanchez-Carter & Gamble, 2006; UNICEF, 2004). Inadequate educational opportunities, violence, and mental health issues are just some of the problems faced by many women.

A recent analysis found that a higher percentage of girls than boys around the world have never had any education (UNICEF, 2004) (see figure 1.3). The countries with the fewest females being educated are in Africa, where in some areas, girls and women are receiving no education at all. Canada, the United States, and Russia have the highest percentages of educated women. In developing countries, 67 percent of women over the age of 25 (compared with 50 percent of men) have never been to school. At the beginning of the twenty-first century, 80 million more boys than girls were in primary and secondary educational settings around the world (United Nations, 2002).

Women in every country experience violence, often from someone close to them (Malley-Morrison, 2004). Abuse by partners occurs in one of every six households in the United States, with the vast majority of the abuse being directed at women by men (Walker, 2001, 2006). Although most countries around the world now have battered women's shelters, beating women continues to be accepted and expected behavior in some countries (Ashy, 2004).

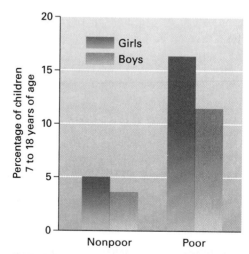

FIGURE 1.3 Percentage of Children 7 to 18 Years of Age Around the World Who Have Never Been to School of Any Kind. When UNICEF (2004) surveyed the education that children around the world are receiving, it found that far more girls than boys receive no formal schooling at all.

Gender also influences mental health. A study of depression in high-income countries found women were twice as likely as men to be diagnosed as depressed (Nolen-Hoeksema, 1990). In the United States, from adolescence through adulthood, females are more likely than males to be depressed (Davison & Neale, 2007; Hammen, 2003). Why? Some experts suggest that more women are diagnosed with depression than actually have depression (Nolen-Hoeksema, 2007). Some argue that inequities such as low pay and unequal employment opportunities have contributed to the greater incidence of depression in females than males (Whiffen, 2001). In the view of some researchers, problems like these are likely to be addressed only when women share equal power with men (Carter, 2004; Parker, 2004).

Social Policy   **Social policy** is a government's course of action designed to promote the welfare of its citizens. Values, economics, and politics all shape a nation's social policy.

Out of concern that policy makers are doing too little to protect the well-being of children and older adults, life-span researchers increasingly are undertaking studies that they hope will lead to effective social policy (Powell, 2006; Renninger & Sigel, 2006; Selman & Dray, 2006).

Social Policy Toward Children   Statistics such as infant mortality rates, mortality among children under 5, and the percentage of children who are malnourished or living in poverty provide benchmarks for evaluating how well children are doing in a particular society. Marian Wright Edelman, a tireless advocate of children's rights, has pointed out that indicators like these place the United States at or near the lowest rank for industrialized nations in the treatment of children (Edelman, 1997).

Children who grow up in poverty represent a special concern (Bernstein, 2004; Evans, 2004; Linver & others, 2004). In 2004, approximately 17 percent of U.S. children lived in poor families and about 4.6 million children lived in families that do not have an employed parent (National Center for Children in Poverty, 2004). As indicated in figure 1.4, one recent study found that a higher percentage of children in poor families than in middle-income families were exposed to family turmoil, separation from a parent, violence, crowding, excessive noise, and poor housing (Evans & English, 2002).

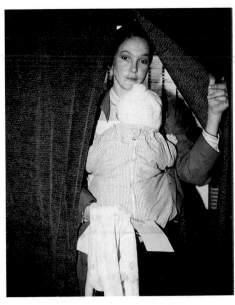

Around the world women too often are treated as burdens rather than assets in the political process. *What can be done to strengthen women's roles in the political process?*

Marian Wright Edelman, president of the Children's Defense Fund (shown here interacting with young children), has been a tireless advocate of children's rights and has been instrumental in calling attention to the needs of children. *What are some of these needs?*

social policy A national government's course of action designed to promote the welfare of its citizens.

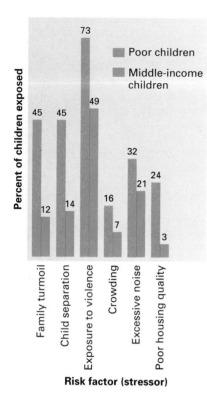

FIGURE 1.4 Exposure to Six Stressors among Poor and Middle-Income Children. One recent study analyzed the exposure to six stressors among poor children and middle-income children (Evans & English, 2002). Poor children were much more likely to face each of these stressors.

These children live in a slum area of a small Vermont town where the unemployment rate is very high because of a decline in industrial jobs. *What should be the government's role in improving the lives of these children?*

How is poverty likely to affect a child's development? One effect was analyzed by Jeanne Brooks-Gunn and her colleagues (2003). In a review of research, they concluded that poverty during the first few years of life is a better predictor of school completion and achievement at age 18 than poverty in the adolescent years. They also found, however, that early intervention for two or three years doesn't permanently reduce disparities in children's achievement. Why? Poor children are likely to continue facing obstacles to success, such as schools that are not conducive to learning, neighborhoods with high levels of violence, and unsafe play areas. Thus, intervention extending into the elementary school years and even the adolescent years may be needed to improve the lives of children living in poverty.

Edelman says that parenting and nurturing the next generation of children is our society's most important function and that we need to take it more seriously than we have in the past. To read about efforts to improve the lives of children through social policies, see the Applications in Life-Span Development interlude that follows.

APPLICATIONS IN LIFE-SPAN DEVELOPMENT

Improving Family Policy

In the United States, the national government, state governments, and city governments all play a role in influencing the well-being of children (Bogenschneider, 2006; Burchinal, 2006; Linver & others, 2004). When families fail or seriously endanger a child's well-being, governments often step in to help (Corbett, 2006; Crouter & Booth, 2004; Ross & Kirby, 2006). At the national and state levels, for decades policy makers have debated whether helping poor parents ends up helping their children as well. Researchers are providing some answers by examining the effects of specific policies (Adams & Snyder, 2006; Ramey, Ramey, & Lanzi, 2006).

For example, the Minnesota Family Investment Program (MFIP) was designed in the 1990s primarily to affect the behavior of adults—specifically, to move adults off the welfare rolls and into paid employment. A key element of the program was it guaranteed that adults who participated in the program would receive more money if they worked than if they did not. When the adults' income rose, how did that affect their children? A study of the effects of MFIP found that increases in the incomes of working poor parents were linked with benefits for their children (Gennetian & Miller, 2002). The children's achievement in school improved, and their behavior problems decreased.

Developmental psychologists and other researchers have examined the effects of many other government policies. They are seeking ways to help families living in poverty improve their well-being, and they have offered many suggestions for improving government policies (Blumenfeld & others, 2005; Coley, Li-Grining, & Chase-Lansdale, 2006; Bogenschneider & others, 2006; Gennetian, Crosby, & Huston, 2006; McLoyd, 2005; Phillips, 2006). One frequent criticism is that the family policies of the United States are overwhelmingly treatment-oriented: only those families and individuals who already have problems are eligible. Few preventive programs are available. For example, families in which the children are on the verge of being placed in foster care are eligible, and often required, to receive counseling; families in which problems are brewing but are not yet full-blown usually cannot qualify for public services.

Social Policy Toward the Aged At the other end of the life span, the well-being of older adults also creates social policy issues (Schultz & Borowski, 2006; Walker, 2006). Special concerns are escalating health-care costs and the access of older adults to adequate health care (Moon, 2006; Stone, 2006). One recent study found that the health-care system fails older adults in many areas (Wenger & others, 2003). For example, older adults received the recommended care for general medical conditions such as heart disease only 52 percent of the time. Appropriate care related to Alzheimer disease and under-nutrition in older adults occurred only 31 percent of the time.

These concerns about the well-being of older adults are heightened by two facts. First, the number of older adults in the United States is growing dramatically, as figure 1.5 shows. Second, many of these older Americans are likely to need society's help. Compared with earlier decades, U.S. adults today are less likely to be married, more likely to be childless, and more likely to be living alone. As the older population continues to increase in the twenty-first century, an increasing number of older adults will be without either a spouse or children—traditionally the main sources of support for older adults (Bennett, 2004; Berado, 2003; Bonanno, Wortman, & Nesse, 2004; Wortman & Boerner, 2007). These individuals will need social relationships, networks, and supports.

FIGURE 1.5 **The Aging of America.** The number of Americans over 65 has grown dramatically since 1900 and is projected to increase further from the present to the year 2040. A significant increase will also occur in the number of individuals in the 85-and-over group. Centenarians—persons 100 years of age or older—are the fastest-growing age group in the United States, and their numbers are expected to swell in the coming decades (Perls, 2005).

The need for social welfare resources far exceeds what policy makers have seen fit to provide. Who should have first claim on government dollars for help—children? Their parents? Older adults? In the last decades of the twentieth century, pensions and government programs such as Social Security and Medicare brought down the percentage of older adults who lived in poverty in the United States. Some argue that the result was *generational inequity,* giving older adults a disproportionately large allocation of resources. Critics of government programs for the elderly ask whether the young have to pay to care for the old, and whether the old should use up resources that might go to disadvantaged children. Life-span expert, Bernice Neugarten (1988) says the resources problem should be viewed not as one of generational inequity, but rather as a major shortcoming of our broader economic and social policies. Also, it is important to keep in mind that children will one day become older adults and will in turn be supported by the efforts of younger people (Williams & Nussbaum, 2001). Furthermore, if there were no Social Security system, many adult children would have to bear the burden of supporting their aging parents and spend less of their resources on educating children.

Maggie Kuhn is founder of the Gray Panthers, an international advocacy group that began in 1970 with five older women committed to improving the social conditions of older adults.

Review and Reflect ● LEARNING GOAL 1

1 Discuss the life-span perspective of development

Review
- What is meant by the concept of development? Why is the study of life-span development important?
- What is the historical background for today's research on life-span development?
- What are eight main characteristics of the life-span perspective? What are three sources of contextual influences?
- What are some contemporary concerns in life-span development?

Reflect
- Imagine what your development would have been like in a culture that offered fewer or distinctly different choices. How might your development have been different if your family had been significantly richer or poorer?

2 DEVELOPMENTAL PROCESSES AND PERIODS

Biological, Cognitive, and Socioemotional Processes

Periods of Development

The Significance of Age

If you wanted to describe how and why Alice Walker or Ted Kaczynski developed during their lifetimes, how would you go about it? A chronicle of the events in any person's life can quickly become a confusing and tedious array of details. Two concepts help provide a framework for describing and understanding an individual's development: developmental processes and periods.

Biological, Cognitive, and Socioemotional Processes

At the beginning of the chapter, we defined *development* as the pattern of change that begins at conception and continues through the life span. The pattern is complex because it is the product of biological, cognitive, and socioemotional processes.

Biological processes produce changes in an individual's physical nature. Genes inherited from parents, the development of the brain, height and weight gains, changes in motor skills, the hormonal changes of puberty, and cardiovascular decline all reflect the role of biological processes in development.

Cognitive processes refer to changes in the individual's thought, intelligence, and language. Watching a colorful mobile swinging above the crib, putting together a two-word sentence, memorizing a poem, imagining what it would be like to be a movie star, and solving a crossword puzzle all involve cognitive processes.

Socioemotional processes involve changes in the individual's relationships with other people, changes in emotions, and changes in personality. An infant's smile in response to her mother's touch, a young boy's aggressive attack on a playmate, a girl's development of assertiveness, an adolescent's joy at the senior prom, and the affection of an elderly couple all reflect the role of the socioemotional processes in development.

Biological, cognitive, and socioemotional processes are inextricably intertwined. Consider a baby smiling in response to its mother's touch. This response depends on biological processes (the physical nature of touch and responsiveness to it), cognitive processes (the ability to understand intentional acts), and socioemotional processes (the act of smiling often reflects a positive emotional feeling and smiling helps to connect us in positive ways with other human beings).

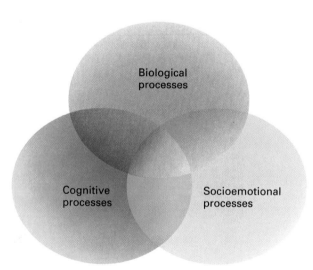

FIGURE 1.6 Processes Involved in Developmental Changes. Biological, cognitive, and socioemotional processes interact as individuals develop.

In many instances biological, cognitive, and socioemotional processes are bidirectional. For example, biological processes can influence cognitive processes and vice versa. In section 9, "Late Adulthood," you will read about how poor health (a biological process) is linked to lower intellectual functioning (a cognitive process). You also will read about how positive thinking about the ability to control one's environment (a cognitive process) can have a powerful effect on an individual's health (a biological process). Thus, although usually we will study the different processes (biological, cognitive, and socioemotional) in separate chapters, keep in mind that we are talking about the development of an integrated individual with a mind and body that are interdependent (see figure 1.6).

Periods of Development

The interplay of biological, cognitive, and socioemotional processes produces the periods of the human life span. A *developmental period* refers to a time frame in a person's life that is characterized by certain features. For the purposes of organization

biological processes Changes in an individual's physical nature.

cognitive processes Changes in an individual's thought, intelligence, and language.

socioemotional processes Changes in an individual's relationships with other people, emotions, and personality.

Periods of Development

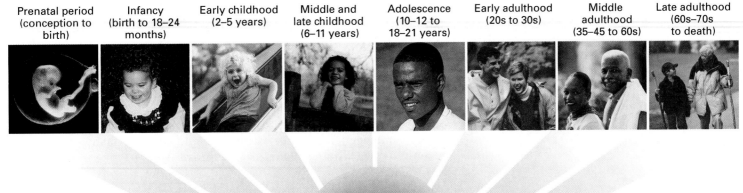

Prenatal period (conception to birth) | Infancy (birth to 18–24 months) | Early childhood (2–5 years) | Middle and late childhood (6–11 years) | Adolescence (10–12 to 18–21 years) | Early adulthood (20s to 30s) | Middle adulthood (35–45 to 60s) | Late adulthood (60s–70s to death)

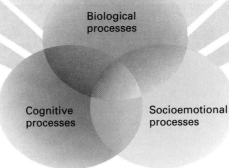

Biological processes

Cognitive processes

Socioemotional processes

Processes of Development

FIGURE 1.7 **Processes and Periods of Development.** The unfolding of life's periods of development is influenced by the interaction of biological, cognitive, and socioemotional processes.

and understanding, we commonly describe development in terms of these periods. The most widely used classification of developmental periods involves the sequence shown in figure 1.7: prenatal period, infancy, early childhood, middle and late childhood, adolescence, early adulthood, middle adulthood, and late adulthood. Approximate age ranges are listed for the periods to provide a general idea of when a period begins and ends.

The *prenatal period* is the time from conception to birth. It involves tremendous growth—from a single cell to an organism complete with brain and behavioral capabilities, produced in approximately a nine-month period.

Infancy is the developmental period from birth to 18 or 24 months. Infancy is a time of extreme dependence on adults. Many psychological activities are just beginning—language, symbolic thought, sensorimotor coordination, and social learning, for example.

Early childhood is the developmental period from the end of infancy to about 5 or 6 years. This period is sometimes called the "preschool years." During this time, young children learn to become more self-sufficient and to care for themselves, develop school readiness skills (following instructions, identifying letters), and spend many hours in play with peers. First grade typically marks the end of early childhood.

Middle and late childhood is the developmental period from about 6 to 11 years of age, approximately corresponding to the elementary school years. This period is sometimes called the "elementary school years." The fundamental skills of reading, writing, and arithmetic are mastered. The child is formally exposed to the larger world and its culture. Achievement becomes a more central theme of the child's world, and self-control increases.

*One's children's children's children.
Look back to us as we look to you; we are
related by our imaginations. If we are able to
touch, it is because we have imagined each
other's existence, our dreams running back
and forth along a cable from age to age.*

—ROGER ROSENBLATT
American Writer, 20th Century

Adolescence is the developmental period of transition from childhood to early adulthood, entered at approximately 10 to 12 years of age and ending at 18 to 22 years of age. Adolescence begins with rapid physical changes—dramatic gains in height and weight, changes in body contour, and the development of sexual characteristics such as enlargement of the breasts, development of pubic and facial hair, and deepening of the voice. At this point in development, the pursuit of independence and an identity are prominent. Thought is more logical, abstract, and idealistic. More time is spent outside the family.

Early adulthood is the developmental period that begins in the late teens or early twenties and lasts through the thirties. It is a time of establishing personal and economic independence, career development, and, for many, selecting a mate, learning to live with someone in an intimate way, starting a family, and rearing children.

Middle adulthood is the developmental period from approximately 40 years of age to about 60. It is a time of expanding personal and social involvement and responsibility; of assisting the next generation in becoming competent, mature individuals; and of reaching and maintaining satisfaction in a career.

Late adulthood is the developmental period that begins in the sixties or seventies and lasts until death. It is a time of adjustment to decreasing strength and health, life review, retirement, and adjustment to new social roles. Late adulthood has the longest span of any period of development, and as noted earlier, the number of people in this age group has been increasing dramatically. As a result, life-span developmentalists have been paying more attention to differences within late adulthood. Increasingly, they distinguish between two age groups in late adulthood: the *young old*, or *old age*, and the *old old*, or *late old age*. Still others distinguish the *oldest old* (85 years and older) from younger older adults.

Paul Baltes and Jacqui Smith (2003) argue that a major change takes place in older adults' lives as they become the oldest old, on average at about 85 years of age. For example, the young old (which was classified as 65 through 84 in this analysis) have substantial potential for physical and cognitive fitness, retain much of their cognitive capacity, and can develop strategies to cope with the gains and losses of aging. In contrast, the oldest old (85 and older) show considerable loss in cognitive skills, experience an increase in chronic stress, and are more frail (Baltes & Smith, 2003).

Thus, Baltes and Smith concluded that considerable plasticity and adaptability characterize adults from their sixties until their mid-eighties but that the oldest old have reached the limits of their functional capacity, which makes interventions to improve their lives difficult. Nonetheless, as we will see in later chapters, considerable variation exists in how much the oldest old retain their capabilities. As you will see next in the Research in Life-Span Development interlude, contexts play an important role in how well older adults perform.

RESEARCH IN LIFE-SPAN DEVELOPMENT

Memory in the A.M. and P.M. and Memory for Something Meaningful

Laura Helmuth (2003) recently described how researchers are finding that certain testing conditions have exaggerated age-related declines in performance in older adults. Optimum testing conditions are not the same for young adults as they are for older adults. Most researchers conduct their studies in the afternoon, a convenient time for researchers and undergraduate participants. Traditional-aged college students in their late teens and early twenties are often more alert and function more optimally in the afternoon, but about 75 percent of older adults are "morning people," performing at their best early in the day (Helmuth, 2003).

Lynn Hasher and her colleagues (2001) tested the memory of college students 18 to 32 years of age and community volunteers 58 to 78 years of age in the late afternoon (about 4 to 5 P.M.) and in the morning (about 8 to 9 A.M.). Regardless of the time of day, the younger college students performed better than the older adults on the memory tests, which involved recognizing sentences from a story and memorizing a list of words. However, when the participants took the memory tests in the morning rather than in the late afternoon, the age difference in performance decreased considerably (see figure 1.8).

The relevance of information also affects memory. Thomas Hess and his colleagues (2003) asked younger adults (18 to 30 years of age) and older adults (62 to 84 years of age) to listen to a drawn-out description that was identified as either someone's experiences on a first job or their experiences while searching for a retirement home. The younger adults remembered the details of both circumstances. However, the older adults showed a keen memory for the retirement-home search but not for the first-job experience.

In short, researchers have found that age differences in memory are robust when researchers ask for information that doesn't matter much, but when older adults are asked about information that is relevant to their lives, differences in the memory of younger and older adults often decline considerably (Hasher, 2003). Thus, the type of information selected by researchers may produce an exaggerated view of declines in memory with age. Determining how age is related to behavior, thought, and feeling can be complicated.

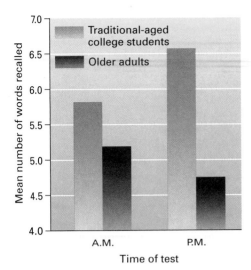

FIGURE 1.8 Memory, Age, and Time of Day Tested (A.M. or P.M.). In a recent study, traditional-aged college students performed better than older adults in both the A.M. and the P.M.. Note, however, that the memory of the older adults was better when they were tested in the morning than in the afternoon, whereas the memory of the traditional-aged college students was not as good in the morning as it was in the afternoon (Hasher & others, 2001).

The Significance of Age

In our description of developmental periods, we linked an approximate age range with each period. But we also have noted that there are variations in the capabilities of individuals of the same age, and we have seen how changes with age can be exaggerated. How important is age when we try to understand an individual?

Age and Happiness Is one age in life better than another? When individuals report how happy they are and how satisfied they are with their lives, no particular age group says they are happier or more satisfied than any other age group (Diener, 2004; Diener, Lucas, & Oishi, 2002). When nearly 170,000 people in 16 countries were surveyed, no differences in their happiness from adolescence into the late adulthood years were found (Inglehart, 1990) (see figure 1.9). About the same percentage of people in each age group—slightly less than 20 percent—reported that they were "very happy."

Why might older people report as much happiness and life satisfaction as younger people? Every period of the life span has its stresses, pluses and minuses, hills and valleys. Although adolescents must cope with developing an identity, feelings of insecurity, mood swings, and peer pressure, the majority of adolescents develop positive perceptions of themselves and their future, feelings of competence about their skills, and positive relationships with friends and family. Although older adults face reduced income and energy, declining physical skills, and concerns about death, they are also less pressured to achieve, have more time for leisurely pursuits, and have many years of experience that may help them adapt to their circumstances with wisdom. Because growing older is a certain outcome of living, it is good to know that we are likely to be just as happy as older adults as when we were younger.

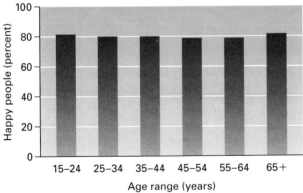

FIGURE 1.9 Age and Happiness. An analysis of surveys of nearly 170,000 people in 16 countries found no age differences in happiness from adolescence into the late adulthood years.

How old would you be if you didn't know how old you were?

—SATCHEL PAIGE
American Baseball Pitcher, 20th Century

(Top) Dawn Russel, competing in the broad jump in a recent Senior Olympics competition in Oregon; (bottom) a sedentary, overweight middle-aged man. *Even if Dawn Russel's chronological age is older, might her biological age be younger than the middle-aged man's?*

chronological age The number of years that have elapsed since birth.

biological age A person's age in terms of biological health.

psychological age An individual's adaptive capacities compared with those of other individuals of the same chronological age.

social age Social roles and expectations related to a person's age.

Conceptions of Age According to some life-span experts, chronological age is not very relevant to understanding a person's psychological development (Botwinick, 1978). **Chronological age** is the number of years that have elapsed since birth. But time is a crude index of experience, and it does not cause anything. Chronological age, moreover, is not the only way of measuring age. Just as there are different domains of development, there are different ways of thinking about age.

Age has been conceptualized not just as chronological age but also as biological age, psychological age, and social age (Hoyer & Roodin, 2003):

- **Biological age** is a person's age in terms of biological health. Determining biological age involves knowing the functional capacities of a person's vital organs. One person's vital capacities may be better or worse than those of others of comparable age. The younger the person's biological age, the longer the person is expected to live, regardless of chronological age.
- **Psychological age** is an individual's adaptive capacities compared with those of other individuals of the same chronological age. Thus, older adults who continue to learn, are flexible, are motivated, control their emotions, and think clearly, are engaging in more adaptive behaviors than their chronological agemates who do not continue to learn, are rigid, are unmotivated, do not control their emotions, and do not think clearly.
- **Social age** refers to social roles and expectations related to a person's age. Consider the role of "mother" and the behaviors that accompany the role (Huyck & Hoyer, 1982). In predicting an adult woman's behavior, it may be more important to know that she is the mother of a 3-year-old child than to know whether she is 20 or 30 years old.

Life-span expert Bernice Neugarten (1988) argues that in U.S. society chronological age is becoming irrelevant. The 28-year-old mayor, the 35-year-old grandmother, the 65-year-old father of a preschooler, the 55-year-old widow who starts a business, and the 70-year-old student illustrate that old assumptions about the proper timing of life events no longer govern our lives. We still have some expectations for when certain life events—such as getting married, having children, and retiring—should occur. However, chronological age has become a less accurate predictor of these life events in our society. Moreover, issues such as how to deal with intimacy and how to cope with success and failure appear and reappear throughout the life span.

From a life-span perspective, an overall age profile of an individual involves not just chronological age but also biological age, psychological age, and social age. For example, a 70-year-old man (chronological age) might be in good physical health (biological age), be experiencing memory problems and not be coping well with the demands placed on him by his wife's recent hospitalization (psychological age), and have a number of friends with whom he regularly golfs (social age).

Review and Reflect ● LEARNING GOAL 2

2 **Identify the most important developmental processes and periods**

Review
- What are three key developmental processes?
- What are eight main developmental periods?
- How is age related to development?

Reflect
- Do you think there is a best age to be? If so, what is it? Why?

3 DEVELOPMENTAL ISSUES

Nature and Nurture

Continuity and Discontinuity

Stability and Change

Evaluating the Developmental Issues

Was Ted Kaczynski born a killer, or did his life turn him into one? Kaczynski himself thought that his childhood was the root of his troubles. He grew up as a genius in a boy's body and never fit in with other children. Did his early experiences determine his later life? Is your own journey through life marked out ahead of time, or can your experiences change your path? Are the experiences you have early in your journey more important than later ones? Is your journey more like taking an elevator up a skyscraper with distinct stops along the way or more like a cruise down a river with smoother ebbs and flows? These questions point to three issues about the nature of development: the roles played by nature and nurture, stability and change, and continuity and discontinuity.

Nature and Nurture

The **nature-nurture issue** involves the extent to which development is influenced by nature and by nurture. *Nature* refers to an organism's biological inheritance, *nurture* to its environmental experiences.

According to those who emphasize the role of nature, just as a sunflower grows in an orderly way—unless flattened by an unfriendly environment—so too the human grows in an orderly way. An evolutionary and genetic blueprint produces commonalities in growth and development (Lewis, 2005, 2007; Promislow, Fedorka, & Burger, 2006). We walk before we talk, speak one word before two words, grow rapidly in infancy and less so in early childhood, experience a rush of sex hormones in puberty, reach the peak of our physical strength in late adolescence and early adulthood, and then physically decline. Proponents of the importance of nature acknowledge that extreme environments—those that are psychologically barren or hostile—can depress development. However, they believe that basic growth tendencies are genetically wired into humans.

By contrast, other psychologists emphasize the importance of nurture, or environmental experiences, in development (Bronfenbrenner & Morris, 2006; Krause, 2006). Experiences run the gamut from the individual's biological environment (nutrition, medical care, drugs, and physical accidents) to the social environment (family, peers, schools, community, media, and culture). Consider the family experiences of adolescents. Researchers have revealed that when parents effectively monitor adolescents' lives, adolescents are less likely to take drugs or engage in delinquency (Collins & Steinberg, 2006). Researchers have also found that when children are rejected by their peers, they often develop behavioral problems (Dodge, Coie, & Lynam, 2006; Ladd, 2006; Rubin, Bukowski, & Parker, 2006).

Stability and Change

Is the shy child who hides behind the sofa when visitors arrive destined to become a wallflower at college dances, or might the child become a sociable, talkative individual? Is the fun-loving, carefree adolescent bound to have difficulty holding down a 9-to-5 job as an adult? These questions reflect the **stability-change issue,** which involves the degree to which early traits and characteristics persist through life or change.

nature-nurture issue Refers to the debate about whether development is primarily influenced by nature or nurture. Nature refers to an organism's biological inheritance, nurture to its environmental experiences. The "nature proponents" claim biological inheritance is the most important influence on development; the "nurture proponents" claim that environmental experiences are the most important.

stability-change issue Involves the degree to which we become older renditions of our early experience (stability) or whether we develop into someone different from who we were at an earlier point in development (change).

What is the nature of the early- and later-experience issue in development?

Many developmentalists who emphasize stability in development argue that stability is the result of heredity and possibly early experiences in life. For example, many argue that if an individual is shy throughout life (as Ted Kaczynski was), this stability is due to heredity and possibly early experiences in which the infant or young child encountered considerable stress when interacting with people.

Developmentalists who emphasize change take the more optimistic view that later experiences can produce change. Recall that in the life-span perspective, plasticity, the potential for change, exists throughout the life span. One reason why adult development was ignored by researchers until fairly recently was the opinion that nothing much changes in adulthood. The major changes were thought to take place in childhood, especially during the first five years of life.

Today, most developmentalists consider that some change is possible throughout the human life span, although they disagree, sometimes vehemently, about just how much change can take place, and how much stability there is. Experts such as Paul Baltes (2003) argue that with increasing age and on average older adults often show less capacity for change in the sense of learning new things than younger adults. However, many older adults continue to be good at practicing what they have learned in earlier times.

The roles of early and later experience are an aspect of the stability-change issue that has long been hotly debated (Caspi & Shiner, 2006; Gottlieb, Wahlsten, & Lickliter, 2006). Some stress that unless infants experience warm, nurturant caregiving in the first year or so of life, their development will never be optimal (Sroufe & others, 2005). Plato was sure that infants who were rocked frequently became better athletes. Nineteenth-century New England ministers told parents in Sunday sermons that the way they handled their infants would determine their children's future character. The emphasis on the importance of early experience rests on the conviction that each life is an unbroken trail on which a psychological quality can be traced back to its origin (Kagan, 1992, 2003).

The later-experience advocates argue that children are malleable throughout development and that later sensitive caregiving is just as important as earlier sensitive caregiving. A number of life-span developmentalists stress that too little attention has been given to later experiences in development (Baltes, Lindenberger, & Staudinger, 2006; Elder & Shanahan, 2006). They argue that early experiences are important contributors to development, but no more important than later experiences. Jerome Kagan (2000, 2003) points out that even children who are shy and timid (qualities of an inhibited temperament, which is linked to heredity) have the capacity to change their behavior. In his research, almost one-third of a group of children who had an inhibited temperament at 2 years of age were not unusually shy or fearful when they were 4 years of age.

People in Western cultures have tended to support the idea that early experiences are more important than later experiences. But the majority of people in the world do not share this belief. For example, people in many Asian countries hold that experiences occurring after about 6 to 7 years of age are more important to development than earlier experiences. This stance stems from the long-standing belief in Eastern cultures that children's reasoning skills begin to develop in important ways in the middle childhood years.

Continuity and Discontinuity

When developmental change occurs, is it gradual or abrupt? Think about your own development for a moment. Did you become the person you are gradually, like the seedling that slowly, cumulatively grows into a giant oak? Or did you experience sudden, distinct changes in your growth, like the caterpillar that changes into a butterfly (see figure 1.10)? For the most part, developmentalists who emphasize nurture usually describe development as a gradual, continuous process. Those who emphasize nature often describe development as a series of distinct stages.

The **continuity-discontinuity issue** focuses on the extent to which development involves gradual, cumulative change (continuity) or distinct stages (discontinuity). In terms of continuity, as the oak grows from seedling to giant oak, it becomes more oak—its development is continuous. Similarly, a child's first word, though seemingly an abrupt, discontinuous event, is actually the result of weeks and months of growth and practice. Puberty might seem abrupt, but it is a gradual process that occurs over several years.

In terms of discontinuity, each person is described as passing through a sequence of stages in which change is qualitatively rather than quantitatively different. As the caterpillar changes to a butterfly, it is not just more caterpillar, it is a different kind of organism—its development is discontinuous. Similarly, at some point a child moves from not being able to think abstractly about the world to being able to. This is a qualitative, discontinuous change in development, not a quantitative, continuous change.

Evaluating the Developmental Issues

Most life-span developmentalists acknowledge that development is not all nature or all nurture, not all stability or all change, and not all continuity or all discontinuity (Gottlieb, Wahlsten, & Lickliter, 2006; Kagan & Fox, 2006; Vogler, 2006). Nature and nurture, stability and change, and continuity and discontinuity characterize development throughout the human life span. With respect to the nature-nurture issue, then, the key to development is the interaction of nature and nurture (Lippa, 2005). For instance, an individual's cognitive development is the result of heredity-environment interaction, not heredity or environment alone. (Much more about heredity-environment interaction appears in chapter 3.)

Although most developmentalists do not take extreme positions on these three important issues, there is spirited debate regarding how strongly development is influenced by each of these factors (Sroufe & others, 2005; Thompson, 2006; Tomasello & Slobin, 2005). Are girls less likely to do well in math because of their "feminine" nature, or because of what they learn as a result of society's masculine bias? How much, if at all, does our memory decline in old age? Can techniques be used to prevent or reduce the decline? Can enriched experiences in adolescence remove "deficits" resulting from childhood experiences of poverty, neglect by parents, and poor schooling? The answers, as we will discuss in coming chapters, depend on the relative importance of nature and nurture, stability and change, and continuity and discontinuity.

Continuity

Discontinuity

FIGURE 1.10 Continuity and Discontinuity in Development. Is our development like that of a seedling gradually growing into a giant oak? Or is it more like that of a caterpillar suddenly becoming a butterfly?

Review and Reflect • LEARNING GOAL 3

3 Describe three key developmental issues

Review
- What is the nature and nurture issue?
- What is the stability and change issue?
- What is the continuity and discontinuity issue?
- What is a good strategy for evaluating the developmental issues?

Reflect
- Can you identify an early experience that you believe contributed in important ways to your development? Can you identify a recent or current (later) experience that you think had (is having) a strong influence on your development?

continuity-discontinuity issue Focuses on the extent to which development involves gradual, cumulative change (continuity) or distinct stages (discontinuity).

REACH YOUR LEARNING GOALS

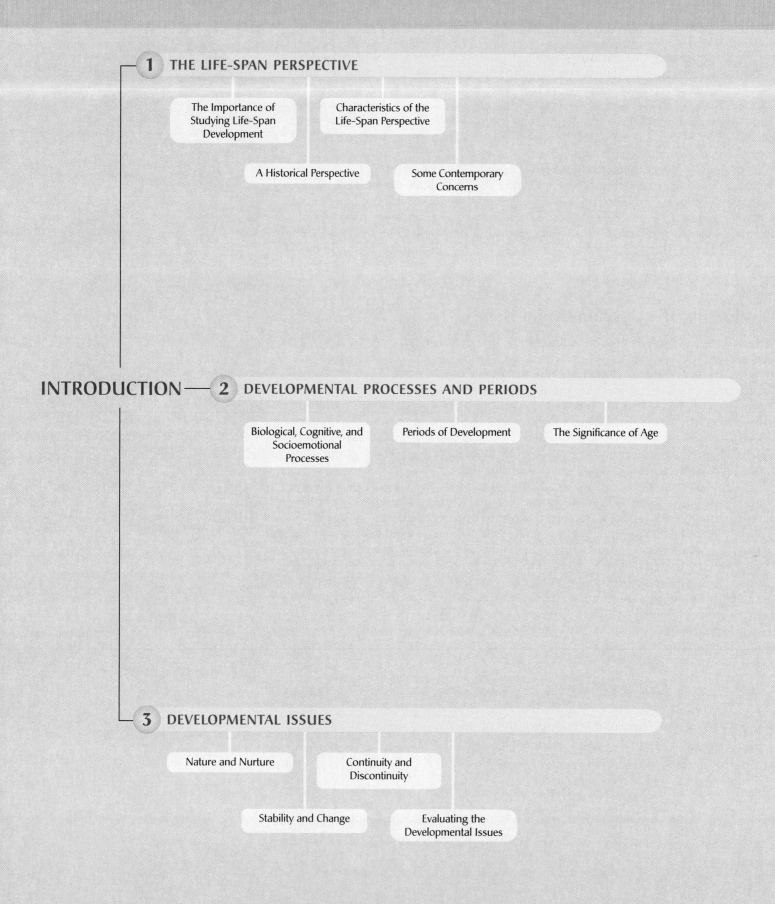

1 THE LIFE-SPAN PERSPECTIVE

The Importance of Studying Life-Span Development

Characteristics of the Life-Span Perspective

A Historical Perspective

Some Contemporary Concerns

INTRODUCTION — **2 DEVELOPMENTAL PROCESSES AND PERIODS**

Biological, Cognitive, and Socioemotional Processes

Periods of Development

The Significance of Age

3 DEVELOPMENTAL ISSUES

Nature and Nurture

Continuity and Discontinuity

Stability and Change

Evaluating the Developmental Issues

SUMMARY

1 The Life-Span Perspective: *Discuss the life-span perspective of development*

The Importance of Studying Life-Span Development

Development is the pattern of change that begins at conception and continues through the human life span. It includes both growth and decline. Studying life-span development helps prepare us to take responsibility for children, gives us insight about our own lives, and gives us knowledge about what our lives will be like as we age.

A Historical Perspective

Prior to the mid-nineteenth century, philosophical views of childhood were prominent, including the notions of original sin, tabula rasa, and innate goodness. The traditional approach to the study of development emphasizes extensive change in childhood but stability in adulthood; the life-span approach emphasizes that change is possible throughout the life span.

Characteristics of the Life-Span Perspective

The life-span perspective includes these basic conceptions: Development is lifelong, multidimensional, multidirectional, and plastic; its study is multidisciplinary; it is embedded in contexts; it involves growth, maintenance, and regulation; and it is a coconstruction of biological, sociocultural, and individual factors. Three important sources of contextual influences are (1) normative age-graded influences, (2) normative history-graded influences, and (3) nonnormative life events.

Some Contemporary Concerns

Health and well-being, parenting, education, sociocultural contexts and diversity, and social policy are all areas of contemporary concern that are closely tied to life-span development. Important dimensions of the sociocultural context include culture, ethnicity, socioecononimc status, and gender.

2 Developmental Processes and Periods: *Identify the most important developmental processes and periods*

Biological, Cognitive, and Socioemotional Processes

Three key developmental processes are biological, cognitive, and socioemotional. Development is influenced by an interplay of these processes.

Periods of Development

The life span is commonly divided into these periods of development: prenatal, infancy, early childhood, middle and late childhood, adolescence, early adulthood, middle adulthood, and late adulthood.

The Significance of Age

According to some experts on life-span development, too much emphasis is placed on chronological age. In studies covering adolescence through old age, people report that they are not happier at one point in development than at others. We often think of age only in terms of chronological age, but a full evaluation of age requires consideration of chronological, biological, psychological, and social age. Neugarten emphasizes that we are moving toward a society in which chronological age is only a weak predictor of development in adulthood.

3 Developmental Issues: *Describe three key developmental issues*

Nature and Nurture

The nature-nurture issue focuses on the extent to which development is mainly influenced by nature (biological inheritance) or nurture (experience).

Stability and Change

The stability-change issue focuses on the degree to which we become older renditions of our early experience or develop into someone different from who we were earlier in development. A special aspect of the stability-change issue is the extent to which development is determined by early versus later experiences.

Continuity and Discontinuity

Developmentalists describe development as continuous (gradual, a cumulative change) or as discontinuous (abrupt, a sequence of stages).

Evaluating the Developmental Issues

Most developmentalists recognize that extreme positions on the nature-nurture, stability-change, and continuity-discontinuity issues are unwise. Despite this consensus, there is still spirited debate on these issues.

KEY TERMS

development 5
original sin 6
tabula rasa 6
innate goodness 6
life-span perspective 7
context 8
normative age-graded
    influences 9

normative history-graded
    influences 9
nonnormative life events 9
culture 11
cross-cultural studies 11
ethnicity 11
socioeconomic status (SES) 11

gender 11
social policy 13
biological processes 16
cognitive processes 16
socioemotional processes 16
chronological age 20
biological age 20

psychological age 20
social age 20
nature-nurture issue 21
stability-change issue 21
continuity-discontinuity
    issue 23

KEY PEOPLE

John Locke 6
Jean-Jacques Rousseau 6

Paul Baltes 7
Marian Wright Edelman 13

Jeanne Brooks-Gunn 14
Bernice Neugarten 20

Jerome Kagan 22

E-LEARNING TOOLS

To help you master the material in this chapter, you'll find a number of valuable study tools on the LifeMap CD-ROM that accompanies this book and on the Online Learning Center for *Life-Span Development*, eleventh edition, at **www.mhhe.com/santrockld11.**

Video Clips

In the margins of this book there are icons directing you to the LifeMap CD-ROM that accompanies the book. In chapter 1 you'll find a video called "Intelligence: The Nature and Nurture of Twins." This segment examines the nature-nurture connection by tracing the development of identical twins Cory and Eric.

Self-Assessment

Connect to **www.mhhe.com/santrockld11** to learn more about your career options by completing the self-assessment, *Evaluating My Interest in a Career in Life-Span Development.*

Taking It to the Net

Connect to **www.mhhe.com/santrockld11** to research the answers to these questions.

1. Janice plans to join a small family practice group on completion of her pediatrics residency. Why should Janice, as a pediatrician, be involved in detecting and helping to prevent violence in the lives of her young patients?
2. Derrick was assigned to write about the challenges of caring for aging adults in the United States in the 21st century. What are some important issues he should address?
3. Carmen is completing her Ph.D. in clinical psychology. She is interested in geropsychology. What are some of the areas in which geropsychologists might conduct research and practice?

Health and Well-Being, Parenting, and Education Exercises

Build your decision-making skills by trying your hand at the health and well-being, parenting, and education exercises. Connect to **www.mhhe.com/santrockld11** to research the answers and complete the exercises.

APPENDIX

Careers in Life-Span Development

The field of life-span development offers an amazing breadth of careers that can provide extremely satisfying work. College and university professors teach courses in many areas of life-span development. Teachers impart knowledge, understanding, and skills to children and adolescents. Counselors, clinical psychologists, nurses, and physicians help people of different ages to cope more effectively with their lives and improve their well-being.

These and many other careers related to life-span development offer many rewards. By working in the field of life-span development, you can help people to improve their lives, understand yourself and others better, possibly advance the state of knowledge in the field, and have an enjoyable time while you are doing these things. Many careers in life-span development pay reasonably well. For example, psychologists earn well above the median salary in the United States.

If you are considering a career in life-span development, would you prefer to work with infants? children? adolescents? older adults? As you take this course, try to spend some time with people of different ages. Observe their behavior. Talk with them about their lives. Think about whether you would like to work with people of this age in your life's work.

In addition, to find out about careers in life-span development you might talk with people who work in various jobs. For example, if you have some interest in becoming a school counselor, call a school, ask to speak with a counselor, and set up an appointment to discuss the counselor's career and work. If you have an interest in becoming a nurse, call the nursing department at a hospital and set up an appointment to speak with the nursing coordinator about a nursing career.

Another way of exploring careers in life-span development is to work in a related job while you are in college. Many colleges and universities offer internships or other work experiences for students who major in specific fields. Course credit or pay is given for some of these jobs. Take advantage of these opportunities. They can help you decide if this is the right career for you, and they can help you get into graduate school, if you decide you want to go.

An advanced degree is not absolutely necessary for some careers in life-span development, but usually you can considerably expand your opportunities (and income) by obtaining a graduate degree. If you think you might want to go to graduate school, talk with one or more professors about your interests, keep a high grade point average, take appropriate courses, and realize that you likely will need to take the Graduate Record Examination at some point.

In the upcoming sections, we will profile a number of careers in four areas: education/research; clinical/counseling; medical/nursing/physical development; and families/relationships. These are not the only career options in life-span development, but the profiles should give you an idea of the range of opportunities available. For each career, we will describe the work and address the amount of education required and the nature of the training. The Web site for this book gives more detailed information about these careers in life-span development.

EDUCATION/RESEARCH

Numerous careers in life-span development involve education or research. The opportunities range from college professor to early childhood educator to school psychologist.

College/University Professor Professors teach courses in life-span development at many types of institutions, including research universities with master's or Ph.D. programs in life-span development, four-year colleges with no graduate programs, and community colleges. The courses in life-span development are offered in many different programs and schools, including psychology, education, nursing, child and family studies, social work, and medicine. In addition to teaching at the undergraduate or graduate level (or both), professors may conduct research, advise students or direct their research, and serve on college or university committees. Research is part of a professor's job description at most universities with master's and Ph.D. programs, but some college professors do not conduct research and focus instead on teaching.

Teaching life-span development at a college or university almost always requires a Ph.D. or master's degree. Obtaining a Ph.D. usually takes four to six years of graduate work; a master's degree requires approximately two years. The training involves taking graduate courses, learning to conduct research, and attending and presenting papers at professional meetings. Many graduate students work as teaching or research assistants for professors in an apprenticeship relationship that helps them to become competent teachers and researchers.

Researcher Some individuals in the field of life-span development work in research positions. They might work for a university, a government agency such as the National Institute of Mental Health, or in private industry. They generate research ideas, plan studies, carry out the research, and usually attempt to publish the research in a scientific journal. A researcher often works in collaboration with other researchers. One researcher might spend much of his or her time in a laboratory; another researcher might work out in the field, such as in schools, hospitals, and so on. Most researchers in life-span development have either a master's or a Ph.D.

Elementary or Secondary School Teacher Elementary and secondary school teachers teach one or more subject areas, preparing the curriculum, giving tests, assigning grades, monitoring students' progress, conducting parent-teacher conferences, and attending workshops. Becoming an elementary or secondary school teacher requires a minimum of an undergraduate degree. The training involves taking a wide range of courses with a major or concentration in education as well as completing supervised practice teaching.

Exceptional Children (Special Education) Teacher Teachers of exceptional children spend concentrated time with children who have a disability such as ADHD, mental retardation, or cerebral palsy or with children who are gifted. Usually some of their work occurs outside of the students' regular classroom and some of it inside the students' regular classroom. The exceptional children teacher works closely with the student's regular classroom teacher and parents to create the best educational program for the student. Teachers of exceptional children often continue their education after obtaining their undergraduate degree and attain a master's degree.

Early Education Educator Early childhood educators work on college faculties and usually teach in community colleges that award an associate degree in early childhood education. They have a minimum of a master's degree in their field. In graduate school, they take courses in early child education and receive supervisory training in child-care or early childhood programs.

Preschool/Kindergarten Teacher   Preschool teachers teach mainly 4-year-old children, and kindergarten teachers primarily teach 5-year-old children. They usually have an undergraduate degree in education, specializing in early childhood education. State certification to become a preschool or kindergarten teacher usually is required.

Family and Consumer Science Educator   Family and consumer science educators may specialize in early childhood education or instruct middle and high school students about such matters as nutrition, interpersonal relationships, human sexuality, parenting, and human development. Hundreds of colleges and universities throughout the United States offer two- and four-year degree programs in family and consumer science. These programs usually require an internship. Additional education courses may be needed to obtain a teaching certificate. Some family and consumer educators go on to graduate school for further training, which provides a background for possible jobs in college teaching or research.

Educational Psychologist   Educational psychologists most often teach in a college or university and conduct research in such areas of educational psychology as learning, motivation, classroom management, and assessment. They help train students for positions in educational psychology, school psychology, and teaching. Most educational psychologists have a doctorate in education, which takes four to six years of graduate work.

School Psychologist   School psychologists focus on improving the psychological and intellectual well-being of elementary, middle/junior, and high school students. They give psychological tests, interview students and their parents, consult with teachers, and may provide counseling to students and their families. They may work in a centralized office in a school district or in one or more schools.

School psychologists usually have a master's or doctoral degree in school psychology. In graduate school, they take courses in counseling, assessment, learning, and other areas of education and psychology.

Gerontologist   Gerontologists usually work in research in some branch of the federal or state government. They specialize in the study of aging with a particular focus on government programs for older adults, social policy, and delivery of services to older adults. In their research, gerontologists define problems to be studied, collect data, interpret the results, and make recommendations for social policy. Most gerontologists have a master's or doctoral degree and have taken a concentration of coursework in adult development and aging.

CLINICAL/COUNSELING

A wide variety of clinical and counseling jobs are linked with life-span development. These range from child clinical psychologist to adolescent drug counselor to geriatric psychiatrist.

Clinical Psychologist   Clinical psychologists seek to help people with psychological problems. They work in a variety of settings, including colleges and universities, clinics, medical schools, and private practice. Some clinical psychologists only conduct psychotherapy; others do psychological assessment and psychotherapy; some also do research. Clinical psychologists may specialize in a particular age group, such as children (child clinical psychologist) or older adults (often referred to as a geropsychologist).

Clinical psychologists have either a Ph.D. (which involves clinical and research training) or a Psy.D. degree (which involves only clinical training). This graduate training usually takes five to seven years and includes courses in clinical psychology and a one-year supervised internship in an accredited setting toward the end of the training. Many geropsychologists pursue a year or two of postdoctoral training. Most states require clinical psychologists to pass a test in order to become licensed in the state and to call themselves clinical psychologists.

Psychiatrist   Psychiatrists obtain a medical degree and then do a residency in psychiatry. Medical school takes approximately four years, and the psychiatry residency another three to four years. Unlike most psychologists (who do not go to medical school), psychiatrists can administer drugs to clients. (Recently, several states gave clinical psychologists the right to prescribe drugs.)

Like clinical psychologists, psychiatrists might specialize in working with children (child psychiatry) or with older adults (geriatric psychiatry). Psychiatrists might work in medical schools in teaching and research roles, in a medical clinic or hospital, or in private practice. In addition to administering drugs to help improve the lives of people with psychological problems, psychiatrists also may conduct psychotherapy.

Counseling Psychologist   Counseling psychologists work in the same settings as clinical psychologists and may do psychotherapy, teach, or conduct research. Many counseling psychologists do not do therapy with individuals who have severe mental disorders, such as schizophrenia.

Counseling psychologists go through much the same training as clinical psychologists, although in a graduate program in counseling rather than clinical psychology. Counseling psychologists have either a master's degree or a doctoral degree. They also must go through a licensing procedure. One type of master's degree in counseling leads to the designation of licensed professional counselor.

School Counselor   School counselors help students to cope with adjustment problems, identify their abilities and interests, develop academic plans, and explore career options. The focus of the job depends on the age of the children. High school counselors advise students about vocational and technical training and admissions requirements for college, as well as about taking entrance exams, applying for financial aid, and choosing a major. Elementary school counselors mainly counsel students about social and personal problems. They may observe children in the classroom and at play as part of their work.

School counselors may work with students individually, in small groups, or even in a classroom. They often consult with parents, teachers, and school administrators when trying to help students. School counselors usually have a master's degree in counseling.

Career Counselor   Career counselors help individuals to identify their best career options and guide them in applying for jobs. They may work in private industry or at a college or university. They usually interview individuals and give them vocational and/or psychological tests to identify appropriate careers that fit their interests and abilities. Sometimes they help individuals to create résumés or conduct mock interviews to help them feel comfortable in a job interview. They might arrange and promote job fairs or other recruiting events to help individuals obtain jobs.

Rehabilitation Counselor   Rehabilitation counselors work with individuals to identify career options, develop adjustment and coping skills to maximize independence, and resolve problems created by a disability. A master's degree in rehabilitation counseling or guidance or counseling psychology is generally considered the minimum education requirement.

Social Worker Many social workers are involved in helping people with social or economic problems. They may investigate, evaluate, and attempt to rectify reported cases of abuse, neglect, endangerment, or domestic disputes. They may intervene in families and provide counseling and referral services to individuals and families. Some social workers specialize in a certain area. For example, a medical social worker might coordinate support services to people with a long-term disability; family-care social workers often work with families with children or an older adult who needs support services. Social workers often work for publicly funded agencies at the city, state, or national level, although increasingly they work in the private sector in areas such as drug rehabilitation and family counseling.

Social workers have a minimum of an undergraduate degree from a school of social work that includes coursework in sociology and psychology. Some social workers also have a master's or doctoral degree. For example, medical social workers have a master's degree in social work (M.S.W.) and complete graduate coursework and supervised clinical experiences in medical settings.

Drug Counselor Drug counselors provide counseling to individuals with drug-abuse problems. Some drug counselors specialize in working with adolescents or older adults. They may work on an individual basis with a substance abuser or conduct group therapy. They may work in private practice, with a state or federal government agency, with a company, or in a hospital.

At a minimum, drug counselors complete an associate's or certificate program. Many have an undergraduate degree in substance-abuse counseling, and some have master's and doctoral degrees. Most states provide a certification procedure for obtaining a license to practice drug counseling.

MEDICAL/NURSING/PHYSICAL DEVELOPMENT

This third main area of careers in life-span development includes a wide range of careers in the medical and nursing areas, as well as jobs pertaining to improving some aspect of a person's physical development.

Obstetrician/Gynecologist An obstetrician/gynecologist prescribes prenatal and postnatal care, performs deliveries in maternity cases, and treats diseases and injuries of the female reproductive system. Becoming an obstetrician/gynecologist requires a medical degree plus three to five years of residency in obstetrics/gynecology. Obstetricians may work in private practice, a medical clinic, a hospital, or a medical school.

Pediatrician A pediatrician monitors infants' and children's health, works to prevent disease or injury, helps children attain optimal health, and treats children with health problems. Pediatricians have earned a medical degree and completed a three- to five-year residency in pediatrics.

Pediatricians may work in private practice, a medical clinic, a hospital, or a medical school. Many pediatricians on the faculty of medical schools also teach and conduct research on children's health and diseases.

Geriatric Physician Geriatric physicians diagnose medical problems of older adults, evaluate treatment options, and make recommendations for nursing care or other arrangements. They have a medical degree and have specialized in geriatric medicine by doing a three- to five-year residency. Like other doctors, geriatric physicians may work in private practice, a medical clinic, a hospital, or a medical school. Those in medical school settings may not only treat older adults but also teach future physicians and conduct research.

Neonatal Nurse Neonatal nurses deliver care to newborn infants. They may work with infants born under normal circumstances or premature and critically ill neonates. A minimum of an undergraduate degree in nursing with a specialization in the newborn is required. This training involves coursework in nursing and the biological sciences, as well as supervised clinical experiences.

Nurse-Midwife A nurse-midwife formulates and provides comprehensive care to expectant mothers as they prepare to give birth, guides them through the birth process, and cares for them after the birth. The nurse-midwife also may provide care to the newborn, counsel parents on the infant's development and parenting, and provide guidance about health practices. Becoming a nurse-midwife generally requires an undergraduate degree from a school of nursing. A nurse-midwife most often works in a hospital setting.

Pediatric Nurse Pediatric nurses monitor infants' and children's health, work to prevent disease or injury, and help children attain optimal health. They may work in hospitals, schools of nursing, or with pediatricians in private practice or at a medical clinic.

Pediatric nurses have a degree in nursing that takes two to five years to complete. They take courses in biological sciences, nursing care, and pediatrics, usually in a school of nursing. They also undergo supervised clinical experiences in medical settings. Some pediatric nurses go on to earn a master's or doctoral degree in pediatric nursing.

Geriatric Nurse Geriatric nurses seek to prevent or intervene in the chronic or acute health problems of older adults. They may work in hospitals, nursing homes, schools of nursing, or with geriatric medical specialists or psychiatrists in a medical clinic or in private practice.

Like pediatric nurses, geriatric nurses take courses in a school of nursing and obtain a degree in nursing, which takes from two to five years. They complete courses in biological sciences, nursing care, and mental health as well as supervised clinical training in geriatric settings. They also may obtain a master's or doctoral degree in their specialty.

Physical Therapist Physical therapists work with individuals who have a physical problem due to disease or injury to help them function as competently as possible. They may consult with other professionals and coordinate services for the individual. Many physical therapists work with people of all ages, although some specialize in working with a specific age group, such as children or older adults.

Physical therapists usually have an undergraduate degree in physical therapy and are licensed by a state. They take courses and experience supervised training in physical therapy.

Occupational Therapist Occupational therapists initiate the evaluation of clients with various impairments and manage their treatment. They help people regain, develop, and build skills that are important for independent functioning, health, well-being, security, and happiness.

An occupational therapist (OTR) may have an associate, bachelor's, master's, and/or doctoral degree with education ranging from two to six years. Training includes occupational therapy courses in a specialized program. National certification is required and licensing/registration is required in some states.

Therapeutic/Recreation Therapist Therapeutic/recreation therapists maintain or improve the quality of life for people with special needs through intervention, leisure education, and recreation. They work in hospitals, rehabilitation centers, local government agencies, at-risk youth programs, as well as other settings. Becoming a therapeutic/recreation therapist requires an undergraduate degree with coursework in leisure studies and a concentration in therapeutic recreation. National certification is usually required. Coursework in anatomy, special education, and psychology is beneficial.

Audiologist Audiologists assess and identify the presence and severity of hearing loss, as well as problems in balance. They may work in a medical clinic, with a physician in private practice, in a hospital, or in a medical school.

An audiologist completes coursework and supervised training to earn a minimum of an undergraduate degree in hearing science. Some audiologists also go on to obtain a master's or doctoral degree.

Speech Therapist Speech therapists identify, assess, and treat speech and language problems. They may work with physicians, psychologists, social workers, and other health-care professionals in a team approach to help individuals with physical or psychological problems that involve speech and language. Some speech therapists specialize in working with individuals of a particular age or people with a particular type of speech disorder.

Speech therapists have a minimum of an undergraduate degree in speech and hearing science or in a type of communications disorder. They may work in private practice, hospitals and medical schools, and government agencies.

Genetic Counselor Genetic counselors identify and counsel families at risk for genetic disorders. They work as members of a health-care team, providing information and support to families who have members who have genetic defects or disorders or are at risk for a variety of inherited conditions. They also serve as educators and resource people for other health-care professionals and the public. Almost one-half work in university medical centers; one-fourth work in private hospital settings.

Genetic counselors have specialized graduate degrees and experience in medical genetics and counseling. Most enter the field after majoring in undergraduate school in such disciplines as biology, genetics, psychology, nursing, public health, or social work.

FAMILIES/RELATIONSHIPS

A number of careers and jobs related to life-span development focus on working with families and relationship problems. These range from home health aide to marriage and family therapist.

Home Health Aide A home health aide provides services to older adults in the older adults' homes, helping them with basic self-care tasks. No higher education is required for this position. There is brief training by an agency.

Child Welfare Worker Child protective services in each state employ child welfare workers. They protect children's rights, evaluate any maltreatment, and may have children removed from their homes if necessary. A child social worker has a minimum of an undergraduate degree in social work.

Child Life Specialist Child life specialists work with children and their families when the child needs to be hospitalized. They monitor the child's activities, seek to reduce the child's stress, and help the child to cope and to enjoy the hospital experience as much as possible. Child life specialists may provide parent education and develop individualized treatment plans based on an assessment of the child's development, temperament, medical plan, and available social supports. Child life specialists have an undergraduate degree. They have taken courses in child development and education and usually completed additional courses in a child life program.

Marriage and Family Therapist Marriage and family therapists work on the principle that many individuals who have psychological problems benefit when psychotherapy is provided in the context of a marital or family relationship. Marriage and family therapists may provide marital therapy, couple therapy to individuals in a relationship who are not married, and family therapy to two or more members of a family.

Marriage and family therapists have a master's or a doctoral degree. They complete a training program in graduate school similar to a clinical psychologist's but with the focus on marital and family relationships. In most states, it is necessary to go through a licensing procedure to practice marital and family therapy.

WEB SITE CONNECTIONS

By going to the Web site for this book, you can obtain more detailed information about the careers described in this appendix. Go to the Web connections in the Career Appendix section, where you will read a description of the Web sites. Then click on the title to go to the Web site described.

There is nothing quite so practical as a good theory.

—KURT LEWIN

American Social Psychologist, 20th Century

CHAPTER OUTLINE

LEARNING GOALS

THEORIES OF DEVELOPMENT

1 Describe theories of life-span development

Psychoanalytic Theories

Cognitive Theories

Behavioral and Social Cognitive Theories

Ethological Theory

Ecological Theory

An Eclectic Theoretical Orientation

RESEARCH IN LIFE-SPAN DEVELOPMENT

2 Explain how research on life-span development is conducted

Methods for Collecting Data

Research Designs

Time Span of Research

FACING UP TO RESEARCH CHALLENGES

3 Discuss research challenges in life-span development

Conducting Ethical Research

Minimizing Bias

Images of Life-Span Development
The Childhoods of Erikson and Piaget

Imagine that you have developed a major theory of development. What would influence you in constructing this theory? A person who develops a theory of development usually has gone through long years of training and has been exposed to many ideas. The person's life experiences may also help explain the theorist's work. Two important developmental theorists, whose views will be described later in the chapter, are Erik Erikson and Jean Piaget. Let's examine a portion of their lives to discover how their experiences might have contributed to the theories they developed.

Erik Homberger Erikson (1902–1994) was born near Frankfurt, Germany, to Danish parents. Before Erik was born, his parents separated, and his mother left Denmark to live in Germany. At age 3, Erik became ill, and his mother took him to see a pediatrician named Homberger. Young Erik's mother fell in love with the pediatrician, married him, and named Erik after his new stepfather.

Erik attended primary school from the age of 6 to 10 and then the gymnasium (high school) from 11 to 18. He studied art and a number of languages. Erik did not like the atmosphere of formal schooling, and this attitude was reflected in his grades. Rather than going to college at age 18, the adolescent Erikson wandered around Europe, keeping a diary about his experiences. After a year of travel through Europe, he returned to Germany and enrolled in an art school, became dissatisfied, and enrolled in another. Later he traveled to Florence, Italy. Psychiatrist Robert Coles described Erikson at this time:

> To the Italians he was the young, tall, thin Nordic expatriate with long blond hair. He wore a corduroy suit and was seen by his family and friends as not odd or "sick" but as a wandering artist who was trying to come to grips with himself, a not unnatural or unusual struggle. (Coles, 1970, p. 15)

Contrast Erikson's experiences with those of Jean Piaget. Piaget (1896–1980) was born in Neuchâtel, Switzerland. Jean's father was an intellectual who taught young Jean to think systematically. Jean's mother was also very bright. His father had an air of detachment from his mother, whom Piaget described as prone to frequent outbursts of neurotic behavior.

In his autobiography, Piaget detailed why he chose to study cognitive development rather than social or abnormal development:

> I started to forego playing for serious work very early. Indeed, I have always detested any departure from reality, an attitude which I relate to . . . my mother's poor health. It was this disturbing factor which at the beginning of my studies in psychology made me keenly interested in psychoanalytic and pathological psychology. Though this interest helped me to achieve independence and widen my cultural background, I have never since felt any desire to involve myself deeper in that particular direction, always much preferring the study of normalcy and of the workings of the intellect to that of the tricks of the unconscious. (Piaget, 1952, p. 238)

These snapshots of Erikson and Piaget illustrate how personal experiences might influence the direction a particular theorist takes. Erikson's wanderings and search for self contributed to his theory of identity development, and Piaget's intellectual experiences with his parents and schooling contributed to his emphasis on cognitive development.

PREVIEW

Theories are part of the science of life-span development. Some individuals have difficulty thinking of life-span development as a science like physics, chemistry, and biology. Can a discipline that studies how parents nurture children, whether watching TV long hours is linked with being overweight, and the factors involved in life satisfaction among older adults be equated with disciplines that study the molecular structure of a compound and how gravity works? The answer is yes. Science is defined not by what it investigates, but by how it investigates.

Whether you're studying photosynthesis, butterflies, Saturn's moons, or human development, it is the way you study that makes the approach scientific or not.

This chapter introduces the theories and methods that are the foundation of the science of life-span development. At the end of the chapter, we will explore some of the ethical challenges and biases that researchers must guard against to protect the integrity of their results and respect the rights of the participants in their studies.

1 THEORIES OF DEVELOPMENT

Psychoanalytic Theories	Behavioral and Social Cognitive Theories	Ecological Theory
Cognitive Theories	Ethological Theory	An Eclectic Theoretical Orientation

All scientific knowledge stems from a rigorous, systematic method of investigation. The *scientific method* is essentially a four-step process:

1. Conceptualize a process or problem to be studied.
2. Collect research information (data).
3. Analyze data.
4. Draw conclusions.

In step 1, when researchers are formulating a problem to study, they often draw on *theories* and develop *hypotheses*. A **theory** is an interrelated, coherent set of ideas that helps to explain and make predictions. For example, a theory on mentoring might attempt to explain and predict why and when sustained support, guidance, and concrete experience make a difference in the lives of children from impoverished backgrounds. **Hypotheses** are specific assumptions and predictions that can be tested to determine their accuracy. For example, a hypothesis might state that individual attention from an adult will improve a child's performance at school.

Numerous theories about life-span development have been proposed, and their diversity makes understanding the field a challenging undertaking (Lerner, 2006; Thomas, 2005). Just when you think one theory has the correct explanation of life-span development, another theory crops up and makes you rethink your earlier conclusion. To keep from getting frustrated, remember that life-span development is complex and multifaceted. As discussed in Chapter 1, it is the product of biological, cognitive, and socioemotional processes. No single theory has been able to account for all aspects of development.

theory An interrelated, coherent set of ideas that helps to explain and make predictions.

hypotheses Specific assumptions and predictions that can be tested to determine their accuracy.

This section outlines key aspects of five theoretical orientations to development: psychoanalytic, cognitive, behavioral and social cognitive, ethological, and ecological. Each contributes an important piece to the life-span development puzzle. Although the theories disagree about certain aspects of development, many of their ideas are complementary rather than contradictory. Together they let us see the total landscape of life-span development in all its richness.

Psychoanalytic Theories

Psychoanalytic theories describe development as primarily unconscious (beyond awareness) and heavily colored by emotion. Psychoanalytic theorists emphasize that behavior is merely a surface characteristic and that a true understanding of development requires analyzing the symbolic meanings of behavior and the deep inner workings of the mind. Psychoanalytic theorists also stress that early experiences with parents extensively shape development. These characteristics are highlighted in the main psychoanalytic theory, that of Sigmund Freud.

Freud's Theory   Freud (1856–1939) was a medical doctor who specialized in neurology. He developed his psychoanalytic theory from work with his patients. After spending most of his years in Vienna, Freud moved to London near the end of his career to flee Nazi anti-Semitism.

Freud (1917) proposed that personality has three structures: the id, the ego, and the superego. The *id* is the Freudian structure of personality that consists of instincts, which are an individual's reservoir of psychic energy. In Freud's view, the id is totally unconscious; it has no contact with reality. As children experience the demands and constraints of reality, a new structure of personality emerges—the *ego*. It deals with the demands of reality and is called the "executive branch" of personality because it uses reasoning to make decisions. The id and the ego have no morality—they do not take into account whether something is right or wrong. The *superego* is the Freudian structure of personality that is the moral branch of personality, the part that considers whether something is right or wrong. Think of the superego as what we often refer to as our "conscience."

In Freud's view, the ego must resolve conflicts between the demands of reality, the wishes of the id, and the constraints of the superego. These conflicts cause anxiety. The anxiety alerts the ego to resolve the conflict by means of *defense mechanisms,* which are the ego's protective methods for reducing anxiety by unconsciously distorting reality.

Repression is the most powerful and pervasive defense mechanism, according to Freud. It pushes unacceptable id impulses (such as intense sexual and aggressive desires) beneath awareness and back into the unconscious mind. Early childhood,

Sigmund Freud, the pioneering architect of psychoanalytic theory. *How did Freud portray the organization of an individual's personality?*

psychoanalytic theories Describe development as primarily unconscious and heavily colored by emotion. Behavior is merely a surface characteristic, and the symbolic workings of the mind have to be analyzed to understand behavior. Early experiences with parents are emphasized.

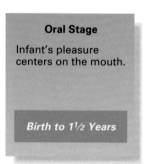

Oral Stage	Anal Stage	Phallic Stage	Latency Stage	Genital Stage
Infant's pleasure centers on the mouth.	Child's pleasure focuses on the anus.	Child's pleasure focuses on the genitals.	Child represses sexual interest and develops social and intellectual skills.	A time of sexual reawakening; source of sexual pleasure becomes someone outside the family.
Birth to 1½ Years	**1½ to 3 Years**	**3 to 6 Years**	**6 Years to Puberty**	**Puberty Onward**

FIGURE 2.1 Freudian Stages. Because Freud emphasized sexual motivation, his stages of development are known as *psychosexual stages*. In his view, if the need for pleasure at any stage is either undergratified or overgratified, an individual may become *fixated*, or locked in, at that stage of development.

in Freud's view, often brings sexually laden experiences that are too threatening and stressful for us to deal with consciously. We reduce the anxiety of this conflict by repressing these experiences.

As Freud listened to, probed, and analyzed his patients, he became convinced that their problems were the result of experiences early in life. He thought that as children grow up, their focus of pleasure and sexual impulses shifts from the mouth to the anus and eventually to the genitals. As a result, we go through five stages of psychosexual development: oral, anal, phallic, latency, and genital (see figure 2.1). Our adult personality, Freud claimed, is determined by the way we resolve conflicts between sources of pleasure at each stage and the demands of reality.

Freud's theory has been significantly revised by a number of psychoanalytic theorists. Many contemporary psychoanalytic theorists reason that Freud overemphasized sexual instincts; they place more emphasis on cultural experiences as determinants of an individual's development. Unconscious thought remains a central theme, but most contemporary psychoanalysts hold that conscious thought plays a greater role than Freud envisioned. Next, we will outline the ideas of an important revisionist of Freud's ideas—Erik Erikson.

Erikson's Psychosocial Theory Erik Erikson recognized Freud's contributions but considered that Freud misjudged some important dimensions of human development. For one thing, Erikson (1950, 1968) said we develop in *psychosocial* stages, rather than in *psychosexual* stages, as Freud maintained. According to Freud, the primary motivation for human behavior is sexual in nature; according to Erikson, it is social and reflects a desire to affiliate with other people. According to Freud, our basic personality is shaped in the first five years of life; according to Erikson, developmental change occurs throughout the life span. Thus, in terms of the early versus later experience issue described in Chapter 1, Freud argued that early experience is far more important than later experiences, whereas Erikson emphasized the importance of both early and later experiences.

In **Erikson's theory,** eight stages of development unfold as we go through life (see figure 2.2). At each stage, a unique developmental task confronts individuals with a crisis that must be resolved. According to Erikson, this crisis is not a catastrophe but a turning point marked by both increased vulnerability and enhanced potential. The more successfully an individual resolves the crises, the healthier development will be (Hopkins, 2000).

Trust versus mistrust is Erikson's first psychosocial stage, which is experienced in the first year of life. Trust in infancy sets the stage for a lifelong expectation that the world will be a good and pleasant place to live.

After gaining trust in their caregivers, infants begin to discover that their behavior is their own. They start to assert their sense of independence, or autonomy. If infants are restrained too much or punished too harshly, they are likely to develop a sense of shame and doubt. This is Erikson's second stage of development, *autonomy versus shame and doubt,* which occurs in late infancy and toddlerhood (1 to 3 years).

Initiative versus guilt, Erikson's third stage of development, occurs during the preschool years. As preschool children encounter a widening social world, they face new challenges that require active, purposeful behavior. Children are asked to assume responsibility for their bodies, their behavior, their toys, and their pets, and they take initiative. Feelings of guilt may arise, though, if the child is irresponsible and is made to feel too anxious.

Industry versus inferiority is Erikson's fourth developmental stage, occurring approximately in the elementary school years. Children's initiative brings them in contact with a wealth of new experiences. As they move into middle and late childhood, they direct their energy toward mastering knowledge and intellectual skills. At no other time is the child more enthusiastic about learning than at the end of early childhood's period of expansive imagination. The danger is that the child can develop a sense of inferiority—feeling incompetent and unproductive.

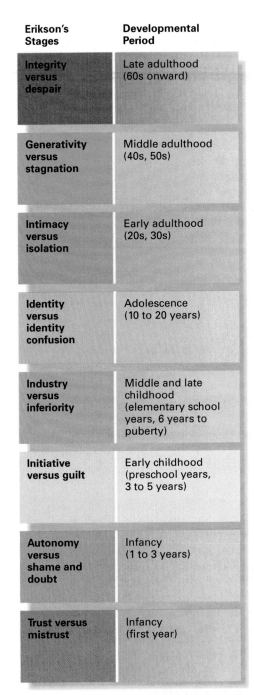

Erikson's Stages	Developmental Period
Integrity versus despair	Late adulthood (60s onward)
Generativity versus stagnation	Middle adulthood (40s, 50s)
Intimacy versus isolation	Early adulthood (20s, 30s)
Identity versus identity confusion	Adolescence (10 to 20 years)
Industry versus inferiority	Middle and late childhood (elementary school years, 6 years to puberty)
Initiative versus guilt	Early childhood (preschool years, 3 to 5 years)
Autonomy versus shame and doubt	Infancy (1 to 3 years)
Trust versus mistrust	Infancy (first year)

FIGURE 2.2 Erikson's Eight Life-Span Stages. Like Freud, Erikson proposed that individuals go through distinct, universal stages of development. Thus, in terms of the continuity-discontinuity issue discussed in Chapter 1, both favor the discontinuity side of the debate. Notice that the timing of Erikson's first four stages is similar to that of Freud's stages. *What are implications of saying that people go through stages of development?*

Erikson's theory Includes eight stages of human development. Each stage consists of a unique developmental task that confronts individuals with a crisis that must be resolved.

Erik Erikson with his wife, Joan, an artist. Erikson generated one of the most important developmental theories of the twentieth century. *Which stage of Erikson's theory are you in? Does Erikson's description of this stage characterize you?*

During the adolescent years individuals are faced with finding out who they are, what they are all about, and where they are going in life. This is Erikson's fifth developmental stage, *identity versus identity confusion*. Adolescents are confronted with many new roles and adult statuses—vocational and romantic, for example. If they explore roles in a healthy manner and arrive at a positive path to follow in life, then they achieve a positive identity. If parents push an identity on adolescents, and if adolescents do not adequately explore many roles and define a positive future path, then identity confusion reigns.

Intimacy versus isolation is Erikson's sixth developmental stage, which individuals experience during the early adulthood years. At this time, individuals face the developmental task of forming intimate relationships. Erikson describes *intimacy* as finding oneself yet losing oneself in another. If the young adult forms healthy friendships and an intimate relationship with another, intimacy will be achieved; if not, isolation will result.

Generativity versus stagnation, Erikson's seventh developmental stage, occurs during middle adulthood. By *generativity* Erikson means primarily a concern for helping the younger generation to develop and lead useful lives. The feeling of having done nothing to help the next generation is stagnation.

Integrity versus despair is Erikson's eighth and final stage of development, which individuals experience in late adulthood. During this stage, a person reflects on the past. Through many different routes, the person may have developed a positive outlook in most or all of the previous stages of development. If so, the person's review of his or her life will reveal a life well spent, and the person will feel a sense of satisfaction—integrity will be achieved. If the person had resolved many of the earlier stages negatively, the retrospective glances likely will yield doubt or gloom—the despair Erikson described.

Each of Erikson's stages has a "positive" pole, such as trust, and a "negative" pole, such as mistrust. In the healthy solution to the crisis of each stage, the positive pole dominates, but Erikson concluded that some exposure or commitment to the negative side is sometimes inevitable. For example, learning to trust is an important outcome of Erikson's first stage, but you cannot trust all people under all circumstances and survive. We will discuss Erikson's theory again in the chapters on socioemotional development.

Evaluating the Psychoanalytic Theories Psychoanalytic theories have contributed to the study of life-span development and have been verified. The contributions include these ideas:

- Early experiences play an important part in development.
- Family relationships are a central aspect of development.
- Personality can be better understood if it is examined developmentally.
- The mind is not all conscious; unconscious aspects of the mind need to be considered.
- In Erikson's theory, changes take place in adulthood as well as in childhood.

These are some criticisms of psychoanalytic theories:

- The main concepts of psychoanalytic theories have been difficult to test scientifically.
- Much of the data used to support psychoanalytic theories come from individuals' reconstruction of the past, often the distant past, and are of unknown accuracy.
- The sexual underpinnings of development are given too much importance (especially in Freud's theory).
- The unconscious mind is given too much credit for influencing development.
- Psychoanalytic theories present an image of humans that is too negative (especially in Freud's theory).
- Psychoanalytic theories are culture-and gender-biased, treating Western culture and males as the measure for evaluating everyone (especially in Freud's theory).

www.mhhe.com/santrockld11

Freud's Theory
Erikson's Theory

Cognitive Theories

Whereas psychoanalytic theories stress the importance of the unconscious, cognitive theories emphasize conscious thoughts. Three important cognitive theories are Piaget's cognitive developmental theory, Vygotsky's sociocultural cognitive theory, and information-processing theory.

Piaget's Cognitive Developmental Theory **Piaget's theory** states that children actively construct their understanding of the world and go through four stages of cognitive development. Two processes underlie this cognitive construction of the world: organization and adaptation. To make sense of our world, we organize our experiences. For example, we separate important ideas from less important ideas, and we connect one idea to another. In addition to organizing our observations and experiences, we *adapt*, adjusting to new environmental demands (Mooney, 2006).

Piaget (1954) also believed that we go through four stages in understanding the world (see figure 2.3). Each stage is age-related and consists of a distinct way of thinking, a *different* way of understanding the world. Thus, according to Piaget, the child's cognition is *qualitatively* different in one stage compared with another (Vidal, 2000). What are Piaget's four stages of cognitive development like?

The *sensorimotor stage,* which lasts from birth to about 2 years of age, is the first Piagetian stage. In this stage, infants construct an understanding of the world by coordinating sensory experiences (such as seeing and hearing) with physical and motor actions—hence the term *sensorimotor.*

The *preoperational stage,* which lasts from approximately 2 to 7 years of age, is Piaget's second stage. In this stage, children begin to go beyond simply connecting sensory information with physical action and represent the world with words, images, and drawings. However, according to Piaget, preschool children still lack the ability to perform what he calls *operations,* which are internalized mental actions that allow children to do mentally what they previously could only do physically. For example, if you imagine putting two sticks together to see whether they would be as long as another stick, without actually moving the sticks, you are performing a concrete operation.

The *concrete operational stage,* which lasts from approximately 7 to 11 years of age, is the third Piagetian stage. In this stage, children can perform operations that involve objects, and they can reason logically as long as reasoning can be applied to specific or concrete examples. For instance, concrete operational thinkers cannot

Jean Piaget, the famous Swiss developmental psychologist, changed the way we think about the development of children's minds. *What are some key ideas in Piaget's theory?*

Piaget's theory States that children actively construct their understanding of the world and go through four stages of cognitive development.

Sensorimotor Stage	Preoperational Stage	Concrete Operational Stage	Formal Operational Stage
The infant constructs an understanding of the world by coordinating sensory experiences with physical actions. An infant progresses from reflexive, instinctual action at birth to the beginning of symbolic thought toward the end of the stage.	The child begins to represent the world with words and images. These words and images reflect increased symbolic thinking and go beyond the connection of sensory information and physical action.	The child can now reason logically about concrete events and classify objects into different sets.	The adolescent reasons in more abstract, idealistic, and logical ways.
Birth to 2 Years of Age	*2 to 7 Years of Age*	*7 to 11 Years of Age*	*11 Years of Age Through Adulthood*

FIGURE 2.3 Piaget's Four Stages of Cognitive Development. According to Piaget, how a child thinks—not how much the child knows—determines the child's stage of cognitive development.

imagine the steps necessary to complete an algebraic equation, which is too abstract for thinking at this stage of development.

The *formal operational stage,* which appears between the ages of 11 and 15 and continues through adulthood, is Piaget's fourth and final stage. In this stage, individuals move beyond concrete experiences and think in abstract and more logical terms. As part of thinking more abstractly, adolescents develop images of ideal circumstances. They might think about what an ideal parent is like and compare their parents to this ideal standard. They begin to entertain possibilities for the future and are fascinated with what they can be. In solving problems, they become more systematic, developing hypotheses about why something is happening the way it is and then testing these hypotheses. We will examine Piaget's cognitive developmental theory further in Chapters 6, 8, 10, 12, and 14.

Vygotsky's Sociocultural Cognitive Theory
Like Piaget, the Russian developmentalist Lev Vygotsky (1896–1934) believed that children actively construct their knowledge. However, Vygotsky (1962) gave social interaction and culture far more important roles in cognitive development than Piaget did. **Vygotsky's theory** is a sociocultural cognitive theory that emphasizes how culture and social interaction guide cognitive development.

Vygotsky portrayed the child's development as inseparable from social and cultural activities (Mooney, 2006; Overton, 2006). He believed that development of memory, attention, and reasoning involves learning to use the inventions of society, such as language, mathematical systems, and memory strategies. Thus in one culture, children might learn to count with the help of a computer; in another, they might learn by using beads. According to Vygotsky, children's social interaction with more-skilled adults and peers is indispensable to their cognitive development (Fidalgo & Pereira, 2005; Kulczewski, 2005). Through this interaction, they learn to use the tools that will help them adapt and be successful in their culture (Hyson, Copple, & Jackson, 2006). For example, if you regularly help a child learn how to read, you not only advance a child's reading skills but also communicate to the child that reading is an important activity in their culture.

Vygotsky's theory has stimulated considerable interest in the view that knowledge is *situated* and *collaborative* (Tudge, 2004). In this view, knowledge is not generated from within the individual but rather is constructed through interaction with other people and objects in the culture, such as books. This suggests that knowledge can best be advanced through interaction with others in cooperative activities.

Vygotsky's theory, like Piaget's, remained virtually unknown to American psychologists until the 1960s, but eventually both became influential among educators as well as psychologists. In Chapter 8 we examine ideas about learning and teaching that are based on Vygotsky's theory.

The Information-Processing Theory
Machines may be the best candidate for the title of "founding father" of information-processing theory. Although many factors stimulated the growth of this theory, none was more important than the computer. Psychologists began to wonder if the logical operations carried out by computers might tell us something about how the human mind works. They drew analogies between a computer's hardware and the brain and between computer software and cognition.

This line of thinking helped to generate **information-processing theory,** which emphasizes that individuals manipulate information, monitor it, and strategize about it. Unlike Piaget's theory but like Vygotsky's theory, information-processing theory does not describe development as stagelike. Instead, according to this theory, individuals develop a gradually increasing capacity for processing information, which allows them to acquire increasingly complex knowledge and skills (Bjorklund, 2005; Munakata, 2006; Reed, 2007).

Robert Siegler (1998, 2003, 2006; Siegler & Alibali, 2005), a leading expert on children's information processing, states that thinking is information processing. In other

www.mhhe.com/santrockld11

Piaget's Theory
Vygotsky's Theory

Lev Vygotsky was born the same year as Piaget, but he died much earlier, at the age of 37. There is considerable interest today in Vygotsky's sociocultural cognitive theory of child development. *What are some key characteristics of Vygotsky's theory?*

Vygotsky's theory A sociocultural cognitive theory that emphasizes how culture and social interaction guide cognitive development.

information-processing theory Emphasizes that individuals manipulate information, monitor it, and strategize about it. Central to this theory are the processes of memory and thinking.

words, when individuals perceive, encode, represent, store, and retrieve information, they are thinking. Siegler emphasizes that an important aspect of development is learning good strategies for processing information. For example, becoming a better reader might involve learning to monitor the key themes of the material being read.

Evaluating the Cognitive Theories   Cognitive theories have contributed to the study of life-span development and have been criticized. These are some contributions:

- The cognitive theories present a positive view of development, emphasizing conscious thinking.
- The cognitive theories (especially Piaget's and Vygotsky's) emphasize the individual's active construction of understanding.
- Piaget's and Vygotsky's theories underscore the importance of examining developmental changes in children's thinking.
- The information-processing theory offers detailed descriptions of cognitive processes.

These are some criticisms of cognitive theories:

- Piaget's stages are not as uniform as he theorized. Piaget also underestimated the cognitive skills of infants and overestimated the cognitive skills of adolescents.
- The cognitive theories do not give adequate attention to individual variations in cognitive development.
- Information-processing theory does not provide an adequate description of developmental changes in cognition.
- Psychoanalytic theorists argue that the cognitive theories do not give enough credit to unconscious thought.

Behavioral and Social Cognitive Theories

At about the same time as Freud was interpreting patients' unconscious minds through their early childhood experiences, Ivan Pavlov and John B. Watson were conducting detailed observations of behavior in controlled laboratory settings. Their work provided the foundations of *behaviorism,* which essentially holds that we can study scientifically only what can be directly observed and measured. Out of the behavioral tradition grew the belief that development is observable behavior that can be learned through experience with the environment (Bugental & Grusec, 2006). In terms of the continuity-discontinuity issue discussed in Chapter 1, the behavioral and social cognitive theories emphasize continuity in development and argue that development does not occur in stagelike fashion. The three versions of the behavioral approach that we will explore are Pavlov's classical conditioning, Skinner's operant conditioning, and Bandura's social cognitive theory.

Pavlov's Classical Conditioning   In the early 1900s, the Russian physiologist Ivan Pavlov (1927) knew that dogs innately salivate when they taste food. He became curious when he observed that dogs also salivate to various sights and sounds before eating their food. For example, when an individual paired the ringing of a bell with the food, the bell ringing subsequently elicited salivation from the dogs when it was presented by itself. With this experiment, Pavlov discovered the principle of *classical conditioning,* in which a neutral stimulus (in our example, ringing a bell) acquires the ability to produce a response originally produced by another stimulus (in our example, food).

In the early twentieth century, John Watson demonstrated that classical conditioning occurs in human beings. In an experiment that would be considered unethical today, he showed an infant named Albert a white rat to see if he was afraid of it. He was not. As Albert played with the rat, a loud noise was sounded behind his head. As you might imagine, the noise caused little Albert to cry. After several pairings of the loud noise and the white rat, Albert began to cry at the sight of the rat even when

B. F. Skinner was a tinkerer who liked to make new gadgets. The younger of his two daughters, Deborah, was raised in Skinner's enclosed Air-Crib, which he invented because he wanted to control her environment completely. The Air-Crib was sound-proofed and temperature controlled. Debbie, shown here as a child with her parents, is currently a successful artist, is married, and lives in London. *What do you think about Skinner's Air-Crib?*

www.mhhe.com/santrockld11

Albert Bandura

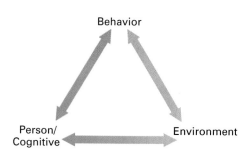

Behavior

Person/
Cognitive   Environment

FIGURE 2.4 Bandura's Social Cognitive Model. The arrows illustrate how relations between behavior, person/cognitive, and environment are reciprocal rather than one way. *Person/cognitive* refers to cognitive processes (for example, thinking and planning) and personal characteristics (for example, believing that you can control your experiences).

social cognitive theory The view of psychologists who emphasize behavior, environment, and cognition as the key factors in development.

the noise was not sounded (Watson & Rayner, 1920). Albert had been classically conditioned to fear the rat. Similarly, many of our fears may result from classical conditioning: fear of the dentist may be learned from a painful experience, fear of driving from being in an automobile accident, fear of heights from falling off a highchair when we were infants, and fear of dogs from being bitten.

Skinner's Operant Conditioning Classical conditioning may explain how we develop many involuntary responses such as fears, but B. F. Skinner argued that a second type of conditioning accounts for the development of other types of behavior. According to Skinner (1938), through *operant conditioning* the consequences of a behavior produce changes in the probability of the behavior's occurrence. A behavior followed by a rewarding stimulus is more likely to recur, whereas a behavior followed by a punishing stimulus is less likely to recur. For example, when a person smiles at a child after the child has done something, the child is more likely to engage in the activity than if the person gives the child a nasty look.

According to Skinner, such rewards and punishments shape development. For example, Skinner's approach argues that shy people learned to be shy as a result of experiences they had while growing up. It follows that modifications in an environment can help a shy person become more socially oriented. Also, for Skinner the key aspect of development is behavior, not thoughts and feelings. He emphasized that development consists of the pattern of behavioral changes that are brought about by rewards and punishments.

Bandura's Social Cognitive Theory Some psychologists agree with the behaviorists' notion that development is learned and is influenced strongly by environmental interactions. Unlike Skinner, they argue that cognition is also important in understanding development (Watson & Tharp, 2007). **Social cognitive theory** holds that behavior, environment, and cognition are the key factors in development.

American psychologist Albert Bandura (1925–) is the leading architect of social cognitive theory. Bandura (1986, 2001, 2004, 2006) emphasizes that cognitive processes have important links with the environment and behavior. His early research program focused heavily on *observational learning* (also called *imitation* or *modeling*), which is learning that occurs through observing what others do. For example, a young boy might observe his father yelling in anger and treating other people with hostility; with his peers, the young boy later acts very aggressively, showing the same characteristics as his father's behavior. A girl might adopt the dominant and sarcastic style of her teacher, saying to her younger brother, "You are so slow. How can you do this work so slowly?" Social cognitive theorists stress that people acquire a wide range of behaviors, thoughts, and feelings through observing others' behavior and that these observations form an important part of life-span development.

What is *cognitive* about observational learning in Bandura's view? He proposes that people cognitively represent the behavior of others and then sometimes adopt this behavior themselves.

Bandura's (2001, 2004, 2006) most recent model of learning and development includes three elements: behavior, the person/cognitive, and the environment. An individual's confidence that he or she can control his or her success is an example of a person factor; strategies to do so are an example of a cognitive factor. As shown in figure 2.4, behavior, person/cognitive, and environmental factors operate interactively. Behavior can influence person factors and vice versa. Cognitive activities can influence the environment, the environment can change the person's cognition, and so on.

Let's consider how Bandura's model might work in the case of a college student's achievement behavior. As the student diligently studies and gets good grades, her behavior produces positive thoughts about her abilities. As part of her effort to make good grades, she plans and develops a number of strategies to make her studying more efficient. In these ways, her behavior has influenced her thought and her thought has influenced her behavior. At the beginning of the term, her college made a special effort to involve students in a study skills program. She decided to join. Her success, along with that of other students who attended the program, has led the college to expand the program next semester. In these ways, environment influenced behavior, and behavior changed the environment. The college administrators' expectations that the study skills program would work made it possible in the first place. The program's success has spurred expectations that this type of program could work in other colleges. In these ways, cognition changed the environment, and the environment changed cognition.

Evaluating the Behavioral and Social Cognitive Theories

Behavioral and social cognitive theories have contributed to the study of life-span development and have been criticized. Contributions include:

- Their emphasis on the importance of scientific research
- Their focus on environmental determinants of behavior
- The identification and explanation of observational learning (by Bandura)
- The inclusion of person/cognitive factors (in social cognitive theory)

Criticisms of the behavioral and social cognitive theories include the objections that they give:

- Too little emphasis on cognition (in Pavlov's and Skinner's theories)
- Too much emphasis on environmental determinants
- Inadequate attention to developmental changes
- Inadequate consideration of human spontaneity and creativity

Behavioral and social cognitive theories emphasize the importance of environmental experiences in human development. Next we turn our attention to a theory that underscores the importance of the biological foundations of development—ethological theory.

Ethological Theory

American developmental psychologists began to pay attention to the biological bases of development thanks to the work of European zoologists who pioneered the field of ethology. **Ethology** stresses that behavior is strongly influenced by biology, is tied to evolution, and is characterized by critical or sensitive periods. These are specific time frames during which, according to ethologists, the presence or absence of certain experiences has a long-lasting influence on individuals.

European zoologist Konrad Lorenz (1903–1989) helped bring ethology to prominence. In his best-known experiment Lorenz (1965) studied the behavior of greylag geese, which will follow their mothers as soon as they hatch.

In a remarkable set of experiments, Lorenz separated the eggs laid by one goose into two groups. One group he returned to the goose to be hatched by her. The other group was hatched in an incubator. The goslings in the first group performed as predicted. They followed their mother as soon as they hatched. However, those in the second group, which saw Lorenz when they first hatched, followed him everywhere, as though he were their mother. Lorenz marked the goslings and then placed both groups under a box. Mother goose and "mother" Lorenz stood aside as the box lifted. Each group of goslings went directly to its "mother." Lorenz called this process *imprinting*, the rapid, innate learning within a limited critical period of time that involves attachment to the first moving object seen.

Albert Bandura has been one of the leading architects of social cognitive theory. *How does Bandura's theory differ from Skinner's?*

ethology Stresses that behavior is strongly influenced by biology, is tied to evolution, and is characterized by critical or sensitive periods.

Konrad Lorenz, a pioneering student of animal behavior, is followed through the water by three imprinted greylag geese. Describe Lorenz's experiment with the geese. *Do you think his experiment would have the same results with human babies? Explain.*

Ethological research and theory at first had little or nothing to say about the nature of social relationships across the human life span, and the theory stimulated few studies with humans. Ethologists' view that normal development requires that certain behaviors emerge during a *critical period,* a fixed time period very early in development, seemed to be overdrawn.

However, John Bowlby (1969, 1989) illustrated an important application of ethological theory to human development. Bowlby argued that attachment to a caregiver over the first year of life has important consequences throughout the life span. In his view, if this attachment is positive and secure, the individual will likely develop positively in childhood and adulthood. If the attachment is negative and insecure, life-span development will likely not be optimal. Thus, in this view the first year of life is a *sensitive period* for the development of social relationships. In chapter 7, "Socioemotional Development in Infancy," we will explore the concept of infant attachment in much greater detail.

Ethological theory has contributed to the study of life-span development and has been criticized. Contributions include:

- Increased focus on the biological and evolutionary basis of development
- Use of careful observations in naturalistic settings
- Emphasis on sensitive periods of development

These are some criticisms of ethological theory:

- Concepts of critical and sensitive periods perhaps too rigid
- Too strong an emphasis on biological foundations
- Inadequate attention to cognition
- Better at generating research with animals than with humans

Another theory that emphasizes the biological aspects of human development—evolutionary psychology—will be presented in chapter 3, "Biological Beginnings," along with views on the role of heredity in development. Also, we will examine a number of biological theories of aging in chapter 18, "Physical Development in Late Adulthood."

Ecological Theory

While ethological theory stresses biological factors, ecological theory emphasizes environmental factors. One ecological theory that has important implications for understanding life-span development was created by Urie Bronfenbrenner (1917–2005).

Bronfenbrenner's **ecological theory** (1986, 2000, 2004; Bronfenbrenner & Morris, 1998, 2006) holds that development reflects the influence of several environmental systems. The theory identifies five environmental systems (see figure 2.5):

Exploring Ethology
Bronfenbrenner's Theory

ecological theory Bronfenbrenner's environmental systems theory holds that development reflects the influence of several environmental systems.

- *Microsystem:* The setting in which the individual lives. These contexts include the person's family, peers, school, and neighborhood. It is in the microsystem that the most direct interactions with social agents take place—with parents, peers, and teachers, for example. The individual is not a passive recipient of experiences in these settings, but someone who helps to construct the settings.

- *Mesosystem:* Relations between microsystems or connections between contexts. Examples are the relation of family experiences to school experiences, school experiences to church experiences, and family experiences to peer experiences. Children whose parents have rejected them may have difficulty developing positive relations with teachers.

- *Exosystem:* Links between a social setting in which the individual does not have an active role and the individual's immediate context. For example, a husband's or child's experience at home may be influenced by a mother's experiences at work. The mother might receive a promotion that requires more travel, which might increase conflict with the husband and change patterns of interaction with the child.

- *Macrosystem:* The culture in which individuals live. Remember from chapter 1 that culture refers to the behavior patterns, beliefs, and all other products of a group of people that are passed on from generation to generation. Remember also that cross-cultural studies—the comparison of one culture with one or more other cultures—provide information about the generality of development.

- *Chronosystem:* The patterning of environmental events and transitions over the life course, as well as sociohistorical circumstances. For example, divorce is one transition. Researchers have found that the negative effects of divorce on children often peak in the first year after the divorce (Hetherington, 1993). By two years after the divorce, family interaction is less chaotic and more stable. As an example of sociohistorical circumstances, consider how the opportunities for women to pursue a career have increased during the last thirty years.

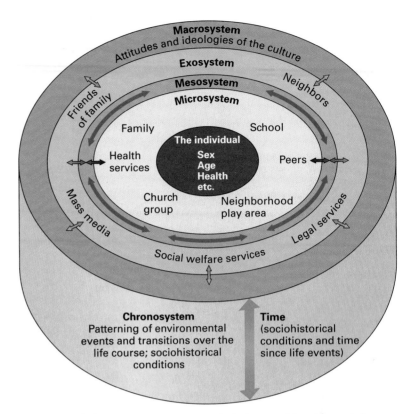

FIGURE 2.5 Bronfenbrenner's Ecological Theory of Development. Bronfenbrenner's ecological theory consists of five environmental systems: microsystem, mesosystem, exosystem, macrosystem, and chronosystem.

Bronfenbrenner (2000, 2004; Bronfenbrenner & Morris, 1998, 2006) has recently added biological influences to his theory and now describes it as a *bioecological* theory. Nonetheless, ecological, environmental contexts still predominate in Bronfenbrenner's theory (Ceci, 2000).

Ecological theory has contributed to the study of life-span development and has been criticized. The contributions include:

- A systematic examination of macro and micro dimensions of environmental systems
- Attention to connections between environmental settings (mesosystem)
- Consideration of sociohistorical influences on development (chronosystem)

These are some criticisms of ecological theory:

- Too little attention to biological foundations of development, even with the added discussion of biological influences
- Inadequate attention to cognitive processes

Urie Bronfenbrenner developed ecological theory, a perspective that is receiving increased attention today. His theory emphasizes the importance of both micro and macro dimensions of the environment in which the child lives.

As an application of Bronfenbrenner's theory, let's take a closer look at the macrosystem, which involves cultural comparisons. The Diversity in Life-Span Development interlude examines cross-cultural variations in child rearing.

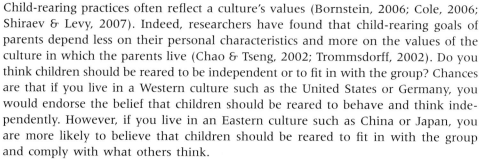

DIVERSITY IN LIFE-SPAN DEVELOPMENT

Culture and Child Rearing

What are some examples of how cultural values shape child-rearing practices?

Child-rearing practices often reflect a culture's values (Bornstein, 2006; Cole, 2006; Shiraev & Levy, 2007). Indeed, researchers have found that child-rearing goals of parents depend less on their personal characteristics and more on the values of the culture in which the parents live (Chao & Tseng, 2002; Trommsdorff, 2002). Do you think children should be reared to be independent or to fit in with the group? Chances are that if you live in a Western culture such as the United States or Germany, you would endorse the belief that children should be reared to behave and think independently. However, if you live in an Eastern culture such as China or Japan, you are more likely to believe that children should be reared to fit in with the group and comply with what others think.

Chinese and Japanese children are reared to show a concern for social harmony (Keller, 2002). They (as well as children in African and Latino communal cultures) grow up with a stronger sense of "family self" than children in the United States and most other Western cultures, believing that what they do reflects not just on one's self but on one's family. Do something wrong or deviant and you shame your family; do something right and you bring honor to your family in these communal cultures. Researchers have found that U.S. adolescents are much less likely to say their parents are disappointed in them than are adolescents in Japan (Atkinson, 1988).

Keep in mind, though, that cultures as large and complex as the United States include people with diverse views on child rearing. This is especially true today as a result of the dramatic increase in immigrants from Asian and Latino countries. Many Asians and Latinos who have immigrated to the United States have brought child-rearing views with them from their native country, views that in many cases conflict with the emphasis on independence in the American culture (Fuligni & Witkow, 2004; Parke & Buriel, 2006).

Such differences in cultural values can pose difficulty when children and adolescents from communal cultures want as much independence as their American peers and friends while their parents and grandparents want to preserve their native culture's traditions. For example, immigrant adolescents may want to date earlier and have more independence in their romantic relationships than their parents believe is appropriate. One recent study of Latina youth in a Midwestern town in the United States found that parents placed strict boundaries on their youths' romantic involvement (Raffaelli & Ontai, 2001). The girls reported that their early dating experiences usually occurred without parental knowledge or permission and over half of the girls engaged in "sneak dating."

An Eclectic Theoretical Orientation

The theories that we have discussed were developed at different points in the twentieth century, as figure 2.6 shows. No single theory described in this chapter can explain entirely the rich complexity of life-span development, but each has contributed to our understanding of development. Psychoanalytic theory best explains the unconscious mind. Erikson's theory best describes the changes that occur in adult development. Piaget's, Vygotsky's, and the information-processing views provide the most complete description of cognitive development. The behavioral and

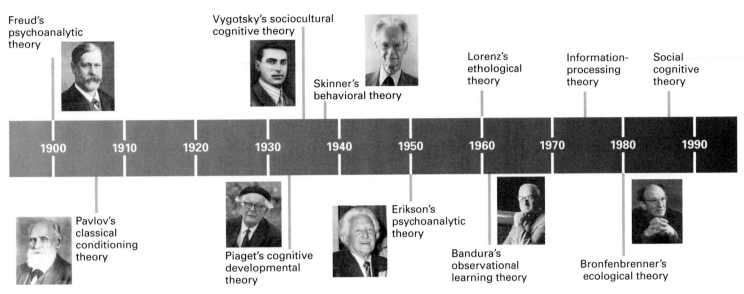

FIGURE 2.6 Time Line for Major Developmental Theories

social cognitive and ecological theories have been the most adept at examining the environmental determinants of development. The ethological theories have highlighted biology's role and the importance of sensitive periods in development.

In short, although theories are helpful guides, relying on a single theory to explain development is probably a mistake. This book instead takes an **eclectic theoretical orientation,** which does not follow any one theoretical approach but rather selects from each theory whatever is considered its best features. In this way, you can view the study of development as it actually exists—with different theorists making different assumptions, stressing different empirical problems, and using different strategies to discover information. Figure 2.7 compares the main theoretical perspectives in terms of how they view important developmental issues in life-span development.

eclectic theoretical orientation An orientation that does not follow any one theoretical approach, but rather selects from each theory whatever is considered its best features.

THEORY	ISSUES	
	Continuity/discontinuity, early versus later experiences	**Biological and environmental factors**
Psychoanalytic	Discontinuity between stages—continuity between early experiences and later development; early experiences very important; later changes in development emphasized in Erikson's theory	Freud's biological determination interacting with early family experiences; Erikson's more balanced biological-cultural interaction perspective
Cognitive	Discontinuity between stages in Piaget's theory; continuity between early experiences and later development in Piaget's and Vygotsky's theories; no stages in Vygotsky's theory or information-processing theory	Piaget's emphasis on interaction and adaptation; environment provides the setting for cognitive structures to develop; information-processing view has not addressed this issue extensively but mainly emphasizes biological-environmental interaction
Behavioral and social cognitive	Continuity (no stages); experience at all points of development important	Environment viewed as the cause of behavior in both views
Ethological	Discontinuity but no stages; critical or sensitive periods emphasized; early experiences very important	Strong biological view
Ecological	Little attention to continuity/discontinuity; change emphasized more than stability	Strong environmental view

FIGURE 2.7 A Comparison of Theories and Issues in Life-Span Development

> *Review and Reflect* • **LEARNING GOAL 1**
>
> **1** **Describe theories of life-span development**
>
> **Review**
> - Define theory and hypotheses. What are two main psychoanalytic theories? What are some contributions and criticisms of the psychoanalytic theories?
> - What are three main cognitive theories? What are some contributions and criticisms of the cognitive theories?
> - What are three main behavioral and social cognitive theories? What are some contributions and criticisms of the behavioral and social cognitive theories?
> - What is the nature of ethological theory? What are some contributions and criticisms of the theory?
> - What characterizes ecological theory? What are some contributions and criticisms of the theory?
> - What is an eclectic theoretical orientation?
>
> **Reflect**
> - Which of the life-span theories do you think best explains your own development? Why?

2 RESEARCH IN LIFE-SPAN DEVELOPMENT

| Methods for Collecting Data | Research Designs | Time Span of Research |

If they follow an eclectic orientation, how do scholars and researchers determine that one feature of a theory is somehow better than another? The scientific method discussed at the beginning of this chapter provides the guide. Through scientific research, the features of theories can be tested and refined.

Generally, research in life-span development is designed to test hypotheses, which in some cases are derived from the theories just described. Through research, theories are modified to reflect new data, and occasionally new theories arise. How are data about life-span development collected? What types of research designs are used to study life-span development? If researchers want to study people of different ages, what research designs can they use?

Methods for Collecting Data

Whether we are interested in studying attachment in infants, the cognitive skills of children, or marital relations in older adults, we can choose from several ways of collecting data. Here we outline the measures most often used, including their advantages and disadvantages, beginning with observation.

*S*cience refines everyday thinking.

—ALBERT EINSTEIN
German-born American Physicist, 20th Century

Observation   Scientific observation requires an important set of skills (Graziano & Raulin, 2007; McMillan & Schumacher, 2006). Unless we are trained observers and practice our skills regularly, we might not know what to look for, we might not remember what we saw, we might not realize that what we are looking for is changing from one moment to the next, and we might not communicate our observations effectively.

For observations to be effective, they have to be systematic (Christiansen, 2007; Elmes, Kantowitz, & Roediger, 2005). We have to have some idea of what we are

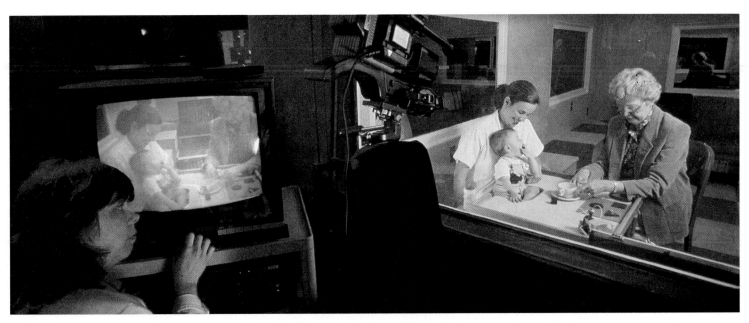

In this research study, mother-child interaction is being videotaped. Later, researchers will code the interaction using precise categories.

looking for. We have to know whom we are observing, when and where we will observe, how the observations will be made, and how they will be recorded.

Where should we make our observations? We have two choices: the laboratory and the everyday world.

When we observe scientifically, we often need to control certain factors that determine behavior but are not the focus of our inquiry (Best & Kahn, 2006; Lammers & Badia, 2005). For this reason, some research in life-span development is conducted in a **laboratory,** a controlled setting with many of the complex factors of the "real world" removed. For example, suppose you want to observe how children react when they see other people act aggressively. If you observe children in their homes or schools, you have no control over how much aggression the children observe, what kind of aggression they see, which people they see acting aggressively, or how other people treat the children. In contrast, if you observe the children in a laboratory, you can control these and other factors and therefore have more confidence about how to interpret your observations.

Laboratory research does have some drawbacks, however, including the following:

- It is almost impossible to conduct research without the participants' knowing they are being studied.
- The laboratory setting is unnatural and therefore can cause the participants to behave unnaturally.
- People who are willing to come to a university laboratory may not fairly represent groups from diverse cultural backgrounds.
- People who are unfamiliar with university settings, and with the idea of "helping science," may be intimidated by the laboratory setting.
- Some aspects of life-span development are difficult if not impossible to examine in the laboratory. Laboratory studies of certain types of stress may even be unethical.

Naturalistic observation provides insights that we sometimes cannot achieve in the laboratory (Billman, 2003). **Naturalistic observation** means observing behavior in real-world settings, making no effort to manipulate or control the situation. Life-span researchers conduct naturalistic observations at sporting events, child-care centers, work settings, malls, and other places people live in and frequent.

laboratory A controlled setting in which many of the complex factors of the "real world" are removed.

naturalistic observation Observing behavior in real-world settings.

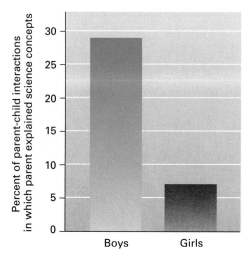

FIGURE 2.8 **Parents' Explanations of Science to Sons and Daughters at a Science Museum.** In a naturalistic observation study at a children's science museum, parents were three times more likely to explain science to boys than to girls (Crowley & others, 2001). The gender difference occurred regardless of whether the father, the mother, or both parents were with the child, although the gender difference was greatest for fathers' science explanations to sons and daughters.

Naturalistic observation was used in one study that focused on conversations in a children's science museum (Crowley & others, 2001). Parents were three times as likely to engage boys as girls in explanatory talk while visiting exhibits at the science museum, suggesting a gender bias that encourages boys more than girls to be interested in science (see figure 2.8). In another study, Mexican American parents who had completed high school used more explanations with their children when visiting a science museum than Mexican American parents who had not completed high school (Tenenbaum & others, 2002).

Survey and Interview   Sometimes the best and quickest way to get information about people is to ask them for it. One technique is to *interview* them directly. A related method is the *survey* (sometimes referred to as a questionnaire), which is especially useful when information from many people is needed. A standard set of questions is used to obtain people's self-reported attitudes or beliefs about a particular topic. In a good survey, the questions are clear and unbiased, allowing respondents to answer unambiguously.

Surveys and interviews can be used to study a wide range of topics from religious beliefs to sexual habits to attitudes about gun control to beliefs about how to improve schools. Surveys and interviews today are conducted in person, over the telephone, and over the Internet.

Some survey and interview questions are unstructured and open-ended, such as "Could you elaborate on your optimistic tendencies?" or "How fulfilling would you say your marriage is?" Such questions allow for unique responses from each person surveyed. Other survey and interview questions are more structured and specific. For example, one national poll on beliefs about what needs to be done to improve U.S. schools asked: "Of the following four possibilities, which one do you think offers the most promise for improving public schools in the community: a qualified, competent teacher in every classroom; free choice for parents among a number of private, church-related, and public schools; rigorous academic standards; the elimination of social promotion; or don't know?" (Rose & Gallup, 2000). More than half of the respondents said that the most important way to improve schools is to have a qualified, competent teacher in every classroom.

One problem with surveys and interviews is the tendency of participants to answer questions in a way that they think is socially acceptable or desirable rather than telling what they truly think or feel (Best & Kahn, 2006; Nardi, 2006). For example, on a survey or in an interview some individuals might say that they do not take drugs even though they do.

Standardized Test   A **standardized test** has uniform procedures for administration and scoring. Many standardized tests allow a person's performance to be compared with the performance of other individuals (Gronlund, 2006; Osterland, 2006); thus they provide information about individual differences among people. One example is the Stanford-Binet intelligence test, which is described in chapter 10, "Physical and Cognitive Development in Middle and Late Childhood." Your score on the Stanford-Binet test tells you how your performance compares with that of thousands of other people who have taken the test.

Standardized tests also have weaknesses (Aiken & Groth-Marnat, 2006; Gregory, 2007). First, they do not always predict behavior in nontest situations. Second, standardized tests are based on the belief that a person's behavior is consistent and stable, yet personality and intelligence—two primary targets of standardized testing—can vary with the situation. For example, a person may perform poorly on a standardized intelligence test in an office setting but score much higher at home, where he or she is less anxious. This criticism is especially relevant for members of minority groups, some of whom have been inaccurately classified as mentally retarded on the basis of their scores on intelligence tests (Valencia & Suzuki, 2001). A third weakness of standardized tests is that many psychological tests developed in Western cultures

standardized test A test with uniform procedures for administration and scoring. Many standardized tests allow a person's performance to be compared with the performance of other individuals.

might not be appropriate in other cultures (Greenfield, Suzuki, & Rothstein-Fisch, 2006; Matsumoto, 2004). The experiences of people in differing cultures may lead them to interpret and respond to questions differently.

Case Study   A **case study** is an in-depth look at a single individual. Case studies are performed mainly by mental health professionals when, for either practical or ethical reasons, the unique aspects of an individual's life cannot be duplicated and tested in other individuals (Dattilio, 2001). A case study provides information about one person's fears, hopes, fantasies, traumatic experiences, upbringing, family relationships, health, or anything that helps the psychologist understand the person's mind and behavior. In later chapters we discuss vivid case studies, such as studies of Michael Rehbein, who had much of the left side of his brain removed at 7 years of age to end severe epileptic seizures, and a modern-day "wild child" named Genie, who lived in near isolation during her childhood.

An illustrative case study is Erik Erikson's (1969) analysis of Mahatma Gandhi, who pioneered the use of nonviolent methods in his fight for India's independence. Erikson studied Gandhi's life in great depth to gain insights into how his positive spiritual identity developed, especially during his youth. In putting the pieces of Gandhi's identity development together, Erikson described how culture, history, family, and various other factors might affect the way other people develop an identity.

Case histories provide dramatic, in-depth portrayals of people's lives, but remember that we must be cautious when generalizing from this information. The subject of a case study is unique, with a genetic makeup and personal history that no one else shares. In addition, case studies involve judgments of unknown reliability. Psychologists who conduct case studies rarely check to see if other psychologists agree with their observations.

Life-History Record   A **life-history record** documents a lifetime chronology of events and activities. It often includes records on education, work, family, and residence. In compiling life-history records, researchers may use a wide array of materials, including public records, historical documents, observations, written and oral reports from the subject, and interviews (Clausen, 1993). During interviews researchers might compile life calendars, which record the age (year and month) at which transitions occur in a variety of domains. Using multiple types of materials to compile the life history allows researchers to contrast information from varied sources and sometimes to resolve discrepancies, resulting in a more accurate life-history record (Elder & Shanahan, 2006).

Physiological Measures   Researchers are increasingly using physiological measures when they study development at different points in the life span. For example, as puberty unfolds, the blood levels of certain hormones increase. To determine the nature of these hormonal changes, researchers take blood samples from willing adolescents (Susman & Rogol, 2004).

Another physiological measure that is increasingly being used is neuroimaging, especially *functional magnetic resonance imaging (fMRI),* in which electromagnetic waves are used to construct images of a person's brain tissue and biochemical activity (Fox & Schott, 2004; Kramer, Fabiani, & Colcombe, 2006; Nelson, Thomas, & de Haan, 2006). We will have much more to say about neuroimaging and other physiological measures at various points in this book.

Research Designs

Suppose you want to find out whether the children of permissive parents are more likely than other children to be rude and unruly. Life-history records are not likely to be very helpful. The data-collection method that researchers choose often depends

Mahatma Gandhi was the spiritual leader of India in the middle of the twentieth century. Erik Erikson conducted an extensive case study of Gandhi's life to determine what contributed to his identity development. *What are some limitations of the case study approach?*

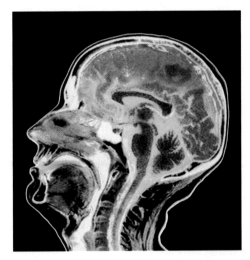

This fMRI scan of a 51-year-old male shows atrophy in the cerebral cortex of the brain, which occurs in various disorders including stroke and Alzheimer disease. The area of the upper cerebral cortex (where higher level brain functioning such as thinking and planning occur) is colored dark red. Neuroimaging techniques such as the fMRI are helping researchers to learn more about how the brain functions as people develop and age, as well as what happens to the brain when aging diseases such as stroke and Alzheimer disease are present.

case study An in-depth look at a single individual.

life-history record A record of information about a lifetime chronology of events and activities that often involve a combination of data records on education, work, family, and residence.

on the goal of their research (McBurney & White, 2007; Mitchell & Jolley, 2007). The goal may be simply to describe a phenomenon, or it may be to describe relationships between phenomena, or to determine the causes or effects of a phenomenon.

Perhaps you decide that you need to observe both permissive and strict parents with their children and compare them. How would you do that? In addition to a method for collecting data, you would need a research design. There are three main types of research design: descriptive, correlational, and experimental.

Descriptive Research

All of the data-collection methods that we have discussed can be used in **descriptive research,** which aims to observe and record behavior. For example, a researcher might observe the extent to which people are altruistic or aggressive toward each other. By itself, descriptive research cannot prove what causes some phenomenon, but it can reveal important information about people's behavior.

Correlational Research

In contrast to descriptive research, correlational research goes beyond describing phenomena to provide information that will help us to predict how people will behave. In **correlational research,** the goal is to describe the strength of the relationship between two or more events or characteristics. The more strongly the two events are correlated (or related or associated), the more effectively we can predict one event from the other.

For example, to study whether children of permissive parents have less self-control than other children, you would need to carefully record observations of parents' permissiveness and their children's self-control. The data could then be analyzed statistically to yield a numerical measure, called a **correlation coefficient,** a number based on a statistical analysis that is used to describe the degree of association between two variables. The correlation coefficient ranges from +1.00 to −1.00. A negative number means an inverse relation. For example, researchers often find a negative correlation between permissive parenting and children's self-control. By contrast, they often find a positive correlation between parental monitoring of children and children's self-control.

The higher the correlation coefficient (whether positive or negative), the stronger the association between the two variables. A correlation of 0 means that there is no association between the variables. A correlation of −.40 is stronger than a correlation of +.20 because we disregard whether the correlation is positive or negative in determining the strength of the correlation.

A caution is in order, however. Correlation does not equal causation (Sprinthall, 2007). The correlational finding just mentioned does not mean that permissive parenting necessarily causes low self-control in children. It could mean that, but it also could mean that a child's lack of self-control caused the parents to simply throw up their arms in despair and give up trying to control the child. It also could mean that other factors, such as heredity or poverty, caused the correlation between permissive parenting and low self-control in children. Figure 2.9 illustrates these possible interpretations of correlational data.

Throughout this book you will read about numerous correlational research studies. Keep in mind how easy it is to assume causality when two events or characteristics merely are correlated.

Experimental Research

To study causality, researchers turn to *experimental research.* An **experiment** is a carefully regulated procedure in which one or more factors believed to influence the behavior being studied are manipulated while all other factors are held constant. If the behavior under study changes when a factor is manipulated, we say that the manipulated factor has caused the behavior to change. In other words, the experiment has demonstrated cause and effect. The cause is the factor that was manipulated. The effect is the behavior that changed because of the manipulation. Nonexperimental research methods (descriptive and

descriptive research Has the purpose of observing and recording behavior.

correlational research The goal is to describe the strength of the relationship between two or more events or characteristics.

correlation coefficient A number based on statistical analysis that is used to describe the degree of association between two variables.

experiment A carefully regulated procedure in which one or more of the factors believed to influence the behavior being studied are manipulated while all other factors are held constant.

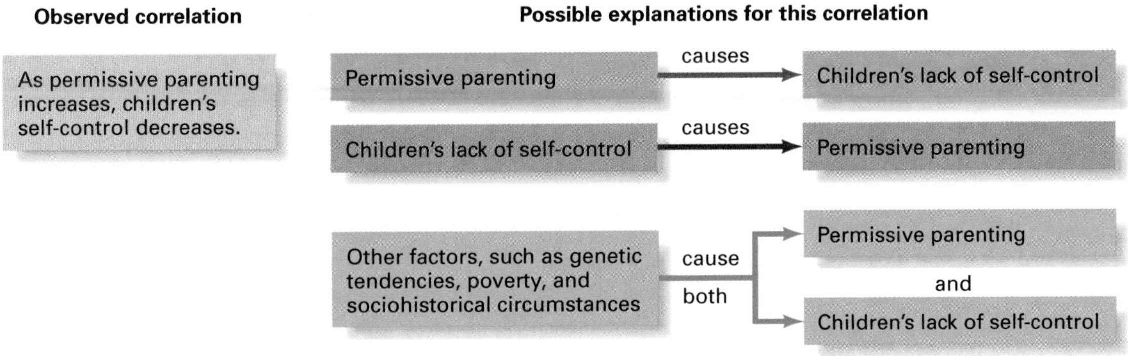

Observed correlation   **Possible explanations for this correlation**

As permissive parenting increases, children's self-control decreases.

Permissive parenting —causes→ Children's lack of self-control

Children's lack of self-control —causes→ Permissive parenting

Other factors, such as genetic tendencies, poverty, and sociohistorical circumstances —cause both→ Permissive parenting   and   Children's lack of self-control

FIGURE 2.9 Possible Explanations for Correlational Data. An observed correlation between two events cannot be used to conclude that one event caused the other. Some possibilities are that the second event caused the first event or that a third, unknown event caused the correlation between the first two events.

correlational research) cannot establish cause and effect because they do not involve manipulating factors in a controlled way (Jackson, 2006; Mitchell & Jolley, 2007).

Independent and Dependent Variables   Experiments include two types of changeable factors, or variables: independent and dependent. An independent variable is a manipulated, influential, experimental factor. It is a potential cause. The label independent is used because this variable can be manipulated independently of other factors to determine its effect. One experiment may include several independent variables.

A dependent variable is a factor that can change in an experiment, in response to changes in the independent variable. As researchers manipulate the independent variable, they measure the dependent variable for any resulting effect.

For example, suppose that you conducted a study to determine whether aerobic exercise by pregnant women changes the breathing and sleeping patterns of newborn babies. You might require one group of pregnant women to engage in a certain amount of exercise each week; the amount of exercise is thus the independent variable. When the infants are born, you would observe and measure their breathing and sleeping patterns. These patterns are the dependent variable, the factor that changes as the result of your manipulation.

Experimental and Control Groups   Experiments can involve one or more experimental groups and one or more control groups. An experimental group is a group whose experience is manipulated. A control group is a comparison group that is as much like the experimental group as possible and that is treated in every way like the experimental group except for the manipulated factor (independent variable). The control group serves as a baseline against which the effects of the manipulated condition can be compared.

Random assignment is an important principle for deciding whether each participant will be placed in the experimental group or in the control group. Random assignment means that researchers assign participants to experimental and control groups by chance. It reduces the likelihood that the experiment's results will be due to any preexisting differences between groups (Myers & Hansen, 2006). In the example of the effects of aerobic exercise by pregnant women on the breathing and sleeping patterns of their newborns, you would randomly assign half of the pregnant women to engage in aerobic exercise over a period of weeks (the experimental group) and the other half to not exercise over the same number of weeks (the control group). Figure 2.10 illustrates the principles of experimental research.

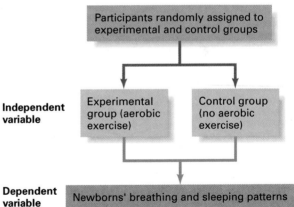

Participants randomly assigned to experimental and control groups

Independent variable   Experimental group (aerobic exercise)   Control group (no aerobic exercise)

Dependent variable   Newborns' breathing and sleeping patterns

FIGURE 2.10 Principles of Experimental Research. Imagine that you decide to conduct an experimental study of the effects of aerobic exercise by pregnant women on their newborns' breathing and sleeping patterns. You would randomly assign pregnant women to experimental and control groups. The experimental-group women would engage in aerobic exercise over a specified number of sessions and weeks. The control group would not. Then, when the infants are born, you would assess their breathing and sleeping patterns. If the breathing and sleeping patterns of newborns whose mothers were in the experimental group are more positive than those of the control group, you would conclude that aerobic exercise caused the positive effects.

Time Span of Research

Researchers in life-span development have a special concern with studies that focus on the relation of age to some other variable. We have several options: Researchers can study different individuals of different ages and compare them; they can study the same individuals as they age over time; or they can use some combination of these two approaches.

Cross-Sectional Approach   The **cross-sectional approach** is a research strategy in which individuals of different ages are compared at one time. A typical cross-sectional study might include a group of 5-year-olds, 8-year-olds, and 11-year-olds. Another might include a group of 15-year-olds, 25-year-olds, and 45-year-olds. The groups can be compared with respect to a variety of dependent variables: IQ, memory, peer relations, attachment to parents, hormonal changes, and so on. All of this can be accomplished in a short time. In some studies data are collected in a single day. Even in large-scale cross-sectional studies with hundreds of subjects, data collection does not usually take longer than several months to complete.

The main advantage of the cross-sectional study is that the researcher does not have to wait for the individuals to grow up or become older. Despite its efficiency, the cross-sectional approach has its drawbacks. It gives no information about how individuals change or about the stability of their characteristics. It can obscure the increases and decreases of development—the hills and valleys of growth and development. For example, a cross-sectional study of life satisfaction might reveal average increases and decreases, but it would not show how the life satisfaction of individual adults waxed and waned over the years. It also would not tell us whether adults who had positive or negative perceptions of life satisfaction as young adults maintained their relative degree of life satisfaction as middle-aged or older adults.

Longitudinal Approach   The **longitudinal approach** is a research strategy in which the same individuals are studied over a period of time, usually several years or more. For example, in a longitudinal study of life satisfaction, the same adults might be assessed periodically over a 70-year time span—at the ages of 20, 35, 45, 65, and 90, for example. The Applications in Life-Span Development interlude that follows describes a longitudinal study on whether certain television viewing experiences (during early childhood) are linked with competencies later, during adolescence.

APPLICATIONS IN LIFE-SPAN DEVELOPMENT

Early Childhood TV Viewing and Adolescent Behavior

Many researchers have examined how watching television influences children (Comstock & Scharrer, 2006). One study examined the long-term relation between the television viewing of 570 U.S. young children and their behavior as adolescents (Anderson & others, 2001). Information about TV viewing when the children were 5 years old was obtained through viewing diaries. If the child was in the room while the TV was turned on, parents were asked to indicate in the diary what channel and program the TV was tuned to. Information about the children when they were adolescents was obtained by interviewing them by phone about their academic achievement, book reading, creativity, and aggression. In addition, high school transcripts were obtained for most participants.

What did the researchers find? The more often children viewed educational programs like *Sesame Street* and *Mr. Rogers' Neighborhood* when they were 5 years old, the higher their grades and creativity, the more they emphasized achievement, the more books they read, and the lower their aggression when they were in high

cross-sectional approach   A research strategy in which individuals of different ages are compared at one time.

longitudinal approach   A research strategy in which the same individuals are studied over a period of time, usually several years or more.

school. The findings were stronger for boys than girls. Figure 2.11 shows the relationship between boys' viewings of educational television during early childhood and their grade point average in high school. The high school girls who had viewed violent programs more often in preschool had lower grades than those who had watched these types of programs less frequently in preschool.

The results of this study support the view that early experiences can have important implications for later development. They also document that watching educational television during childhood is linked with positive outcomes and that exposure to violent television during childhood is associated with negative outcomes.

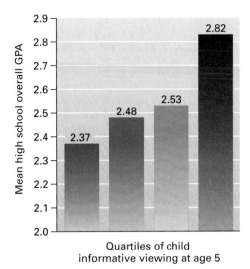

FIGURE 2.11 Educational TV Viewing and High School Grade Point Average for Boys

Longitudinal studies provide a wealth of information about such important issues as stability and change in development and the importance of early experience for later development, but they do have drawbacks (Hartmann & Pelzel, 2005; Hofer & Sliwinski, 2006; Raudenbush, 2001). They are expensive and time consuming. The longer the study lasts, the more participants drop out—they move, get sick, lose interest, and so forth. The participants who remain may be dissimilar to those who drop out, biasing the outcome of the study. Those individuals who remain in a longitudinal study over a number of years may be more compulsive and conformity-oriented, for example, or they might have more stable lives.

Sequential Approach Sometimes developmentalists combine the cross-sectional and longitudinal approaches to learn about life-span development (Schaie, 1993). The **sequential approach** is the combined cross-sectional, longitudinal design. In most instances, this approach starts with a cross-sectional study that includes individuals of different ages. A number of months after the initial assessment, the same individuals are tested again—this is the longitudinal aspect of the design. At this later time, a new group of participants is assessed at each age level. The new groups at each level are added at the later time to control for changes that might have taken place in the original group—some might have dropped out of the study, or retesting might have improved their performance, for example.

The sequential approach is complex, expensive, and time consuming, but it does provide information that is impossible to obtain from cross-sectional or longitudinal approaches alone. The sequential approach has been especially helpful in examining cohort effects in life-span development, which we will discuss next.

Cohort Effects A *cohort* is a group of people who are born at a similar point in history and share similar experiences as a result, such as living through the Great Depression of the 1930s or growing up in the same city around the same time. These shared experiences may produce a range of differences among cohorts. For example, people who were teenagers during the Great Depression are likely to differ from people who were teenagers during the booming 1990s in their educational opportunities; in how they were raised; and in their attitudes toward sex, religious values, and economic status. In life-span development research, **cohort effects** are due to a person's time of birth, era, or generation but not to actual age.

Cohort effects are important because they can powerfully affect the dependent measures in a study ostensibly concerned with age (Hofer & Sliwinski, 2006; Schaie, 2007). Researchers have shown it is especially important to be aware of cohort effects in the assessment of adult intelligence (Schaie, 1996, 2007). Individuals born at different points in time—such as 1920, 1940, and 1960—have had varying opportunities for education. Individuals born in earlier years had less access to education, and this fact may have a significant effect on how this cohort performs on intelligence tests.

Cross-sectional studies can show how different cohorts respond but they can confuse age changes and cohort effects. Longitudinal studies are effective in studying age

sequential approach A combined cross-sectional, longitudinal design.

cohort effects Effects due to a person's time of birth, era, or generation but not to actual age.

Cohort effects are due to a person's time of birth or generation but not actually to age. Think for a moment about growing up in (a) the Roaring Twenties, (b) the Great Depression, (c) the 1940s and World War II, (d) the 1950s, (e) the late 1960s, and (f) today. *How might your development be different depending on which of these time frames has dominated your life? your parents' lives? your grandparents' lives?*

changes but only within one cohort. With sequential studies, both age changes in one cohort can be examined and compared with age changes in another cohort.

So far we have discussed many aspects of scientific research in life-span development. In the Research in Life-Span Development interlude, you can read about the research journals in which such research is published.

RESEARCH IN LIFE-SPAN DEVELOPMENT

Research Journals

Regardless of whether you pursue a career in life-span development, psychology, or some related scientific field, you can benefit by learning about the journal process. As a student you might be required to look up original research in journals. As a parent, teacher, or nurse you might want to consult journals to obtain information that will help you understand and work more effectively with people. As an inquiring person, you might look up information in journals after you have heard or read something that piqued your curiosity.

A journal publishes scholarly and academic information, usually in a specific domain—such as physics, math, sociology, or, our current interest, life-span development. Scholars in these fields publish most of their research in journals, which are the source of core information in virtually every academic discipline.

An increasing number of journals publish information about life-span development. Among the leading journals in life-span development are *Developmental Psychology, Child Development, Pediatrics, Pediatric Nursing, The Journals of Gerontology, Infant Behavior and Development, Journal of Research on Adolescence, Journal of Adult Development, Journal of Gerontological Nursing, Psychology and Aging, Human Development,* and many others. Also, a number of journals that do not focus solely on development include articles on various aspects of human development. These journals include *Journal of Educational Psychology, Sex Roles, Journal of Cross-Cultural Research, Journal of Marriage and the Family,* and *Journal of Consulting and Clinical Psychology.*

Every journal has a board of experts who evaluate articles submitted for publication. Each submitted paper is accepted or rejected on the basis of such factors as its contribution to the field, methodological excellence, and clarity of writing. Some of the most prestigious journals reject as many as 80 to 90 percent of the articles submitted.

Journal articles are usually written for other professionals in the specialized field of the journal's focus; therefore, they often contain technical language and terms specific to the discipline that are difficult for nonprofessionals to understand. Articles are often organized as follows: abstract, introduction, method, results, discussion, and references.

The *abstract* is a brief summary that appears at the beginning of the article. The abstract lets readers quickly determine whether the article is relevant to their interests. The *introduction* introduces the problem or issue that is being studied. It includes a concise review of research relevant to the topic, theoretical ties, and one or more hypotheses to be tested. The *method* section consists of a clear description of the subjects evaluated in the study, the measures used, and the procedures that were followed. The method section should be sufficiently clear and detailed so that by reading it another researcher could repeat or replicate the study. The *results* section reports the analysis of the data collected. In most cases, the results section includes statistical analyses that are difficult for nonprofessionals to understand. The *discussion* section describes the author's conclusions, inferences, and interpretation of what was found. Statements are usually made about whether the hypotheses presented in the introduction were supported, limitations of the study, and suggestions for future research. The last part of the journal article, called *references,* includes bibliographic information for each source cited in the article. The references section is often a good source for finding other articles relevant to the topic that interests you.

www.mhhe.com/santrockld11

**Child Development
Developmental Psychology
The Journals of Gerontology**

Where do you find journals such as those we have described? Your college or university library likely has some of them, and some public libraries also carry journals. Online resources such as PsycINFO, which can facilitate the search for journal articles, are available to students on many campuses.

Review and Reflect • LEARNING GOAL 2

2 Explain how research on life-span development is conducted

Review
- What methods are used to collect data on life-span development?
- What are three main types of research designs?
- What are some ways that researchers study the time span of people's lives?

Reflect
- You have learned that correlation does not equal causation. Develop an example of two variables (two sets of observations) that are correlated but that you believe almost certainly have no causal relationship.

3 FACING UP TO RESEARCH CHALLENGES

Conducting Ethical Research   Minimizing Bias

The scientific foundation of research in life-span development helps to minimize the effect of research bias and maximize the objectivity of the results. Still, subtle challenges remain for each researcher to resolve. One is to ensure that research is conducted in an ethical way; another is to recognize, and try to overcome, deeply buried personal biases.

Conducting Ethical Research

The explosion in technology has forced society to grapple with looming ethical questions that were unimaginable only a few decades ago. The same line of research that enables previously sterile couples to have children might someday let prospective parents "call up and order" the characteristics they prefer in their children or tip the balance of males and females in the world. Should embryos left over from procedures for increasing fertility be saved or discarded? Should people with heritable fatal diseases (such as Huntington disease) be discouraged from having children?

Researchers also face ethical questions both new and old. They have a responsibility to anticipate the personal problems their research might cause and to at least inform the participants of the possible fallout. Safeguarding the rights of research participants is a challenge because the potential harm is not always obvious (McBurney & White, 2007). At first glance, you might not imagine that a questionnaire on dating relationships would have any substantial impact or that an experiment involving treatment of memory loss in older adults would be anything but beneficial. But the failure to consider participants' well-being can have life-altering consequences for them. For example, one investigation of young dating couples asked them to complete a questionnaire (Rubin & Mitchell, 1976). That questionnaire stimulated some participants to think about potentially troublesome issues. In at least one case, discussing those issues led to the end of the relationship.

Ethics in research may affect you personally if you ever serve as a participant in a study. In that event, you need to know your rights as a participant and the responsibilities of researchers to assure that these rights are safeguarded.

If you ever become a researcher in life-span development yourself, you will need an even deeper understanding of ethics. Even if you only carry out experimental projects in psychology courses, you must consider the rights of the participants in those projects. A student might think, "I volunteer in a home for the mentally retarded several hours per week. I can use the residents of the home in my study to see if a particular treatment helps improve their memory for everyday tasks." But without proper permissions, the most well-meaning, kind, and considerate studies still violate the rights of the participants.

Today, proposed research at colleges and universities must pass the scrutiny of a research ethics committee before the research can be initiated. In addition, the American Psychological Association (APA) has developed ethics guidelines for its members. The code of ethics instructs psychologists to protect their participants from mental and physical harm. The participants' best interests need to be kept foremost in the researcher's mind (Graziano & Raulin, 2007; Rosnow & Rosenthal, 2005). APA's guidelines address four important issues:

- *Informed Consent* All participants must know what their participation will involve and what risks might develop. For example, participants in a study on dating should be told beforehand that a questionnaire might stimulate thoughts about issues in their relationship that they have not considered.

www.mhhe.com/santrockld11

Psychologists' Ethical Principles

Participants also should be informed that in some instances a discussion of the issues might improve their relationship, but in others might worsen the relationship and even end it. Even after informed consent is given, participants must retain the right to withdraw from the study at any time and for any reason.

- *Confidentiality* Researchers are responsible for keeping all of the data they gather on individuals completely confidential and, when possible, completely anonymous.

- *Debriefing* After the study has been completed, participants should be informed of its purpose and the methods that were used. In most cases, the experimenter also can inform participants in a general manner beforehand about the purpose of the research without leading participants to behave in a way they think that the experimenter is expecting. When preliminary information about the study is likely to affect the results, participants can at least be debriefed after the study has been completed.

- *Deception* This is an ethical issue that researchers debate extensively (Leary, 2004). In some circumstances, telling the participants beforehand what the research study is about substantially alters the participants' behavior and invalidates the researcher's data. In all cases of deception, however, the psychologist must ensure that the deception will not harm the participants and that the participants will be told the complete nature of the study (debriefed) as soon as possible after the study is completed.

Minimizing Bias

Studies of life-span development are most useful when they are conducted without bias or prejudice toward any particular group of people. Of special concern is bias based on gender and bias based on culture or ethnicity.

Gender Bias For most of its existence, our society has had a strong gender bias, a preconceived notion about the abilities of women and men that prevented individuals from pursuing their own interests and achieving their potential (Helgeson, 2005; Smith, 2007). Gender bias also has had a less obvious effect within the field of life-span development (Etaugh & Bridges, 2006; Worell & Goodheart, 2006). For example, it is not unusual for conclusions to be drawn about females' attitudes and behaviors from research conducted with males as the only participants (Hyde, 2007; Matlin, 2004).

Furthermore, when researchers find gender differences, their reports sometimes magnify those differences (Denmark and her colleagues, 1988). For example, a researcher might report that 74 percent of the men in a study had high achievement expectations versus only 67 percent of the women and go on to talk about the differences in some detail. In reality, this might be a rather small difference. It also might disappear if the study were repeated or the study might have methodological problems that don't allow such strong interpretations.

Pam Reid is a leading researcher who studies gender and ethnic bias in development. To read about Reid's interests, see the Careers in Life-Span Development profile.

Cultural and Ethnic Bias The realization that research on life-span development needs to include more people from diverse ethnic groups has also been building (Graham, 1992, 2006). Historically, people from ethnic minority groups (African American, Latino, Asian American, and Native American) were excluded from most research in the United States and simply thought of as variations from the norm or average. If minority individuals were included in samples and their scores didn't fit the norm, they were viewed as confounds or "noise" in data and discounted. Given the fact that individuals from diverse ethnic groups were excluded

CAREERS
in LIFE-SPAN DEVELOPMENT

Pam Reid
Educational and Developmental Psychologist

When she was a child, Pam Reid liked to play with chemistry sets. Pam majored in chemistry during college and wanted to become a doctor. However, when some of her friends signed up for a psychology class as an elective, she decided to take the course. She was intrigued by learning about how people think, behave, and develop—so much so that she changed her major to psychology. Pam went on to obtain her Ph.D. in psychology (American Psychological Association, 2003, p. 16).

For a number of years, Pam was a professor of education and psychology at the University of Michigan, where she also was a research scientist at the Institute for Research on Women and Gender. Her main focus has been on how children and adolescents develop social skills, with a special interest in the development of African American girls (Reid & Zalk, 2001). In 2004, Pam became provost and executive vice-president at Roosevelt University in Chicago.

Pam Reid (*back row, center*), with graduate students she mentored at the University of Michigan.

from research on life-span development for so long, we might reasonably conclude that people's real lives are perhaps more varied than research data have indicated in the past (Ponterotto & others, 2001).

Researchers also have tended to overgeneralize about ethnic groups (Banks, 2006; Diaz, Pelletier, and Provenzo, 2006; Mays & others, 2007; Spencer, 2006). **Ethnic gloss** is using an ethnic label such as African American or Latino in a superficial way that portrays an ethnic group as being more homogeneous than it really is (Trimble, 1988). For example, a researcher might describe a research sample like this: "The participants were 60 Latinos." A more complete description of the Latino group might be something like this: "The 60 Latino participants were Mexican Americans from low-income neighborhoods in the southwestern area of Los Angeles. Thirty-six were from homes in which Spanish is the dominant language spoken, 24 from homes in which English is the main language spoken. Thirty were born in the United States, 30 in Mexico. Twenty-eight described themselves as Mexican American, 14 as Mexican, 9 as American, 6 as Chicano, and 3 as Latino." Ethnic gloss can cause researchers to obtain samples of ethnic groups that are not representative of the group's diversity, which can lead to overgeneralization and stereotyping.

Ross Parke and Raymond Buriel (2006) recently described how research on ethnic minority children and their families has not been given adequate attention, especially in light of their significant rate of growth. Until recently, ethnic minority families were combined in the category "minority," which masks important differences among ethnic groups as well as diversity within an ethnic group. When research has been conducted on ethnic groups, most often they are compared to non-White Latinos to identify group differences. An assumption in two-group studies is that ethnic minority children have not advanced far enough to be the same as non-White Latino children and that this developmental lag contributes to ethnic

ethnic gloss Using an ethnic label such as African American or Latino in a superficial way that portrays an ethnic group as being more homogeneous than it really is.

Look at these two photographs, one of all White males, the other of a diverse group of females and males from different ethnic groups, including some White individuals. Consider a topic in psychology, such as parenting, love, or cultural values. *If you were conducting research on this topic, might the results of the study be different depending on whether the participants in your study were the individuals in the photograph on the left or those on the right?*

minority children's problems. Recently, some researchers have replaced two-group studies with more in-depth examination of variations within a single ethnic group. For example, a researcher might study how parents in an ethnic group adapt to the challenges they face as a minority in U.S. society and how these experiences contribute to the goals they have for their children.

The continued growth of minority families in the United States in approaching decades will mainly be due to the immigration of Latino and Asian families. Researchers need "to take into account their acculturation level and generational status of parents and children," and how they influence family processes and child outcomes (Parke & Buriel, 2006, p. 487). More attention also needs to be given to *biculturalism* because the complexity of diversity means that some children of color identify with two or more ethnic groups. Language development research needs to focus more on second-language acquisition (usually English) and bilingualism and how they are linked to school achievement.

Review and Reflect ● LEARNING GOAL 3

3 Discuss research challenges in life-span development

Review
- What are researchers' ethical responsibilities to the people they study?
- How can gender, cultural, and ethnic bias affect the outcome of a research study?

Reflect
- Imagine that you are conducting a research study on the sexual attitudes and behaviors of adolescents. What ethical safeguards should you use in conducting the study?

REACH YOUR LEARNING GOALS

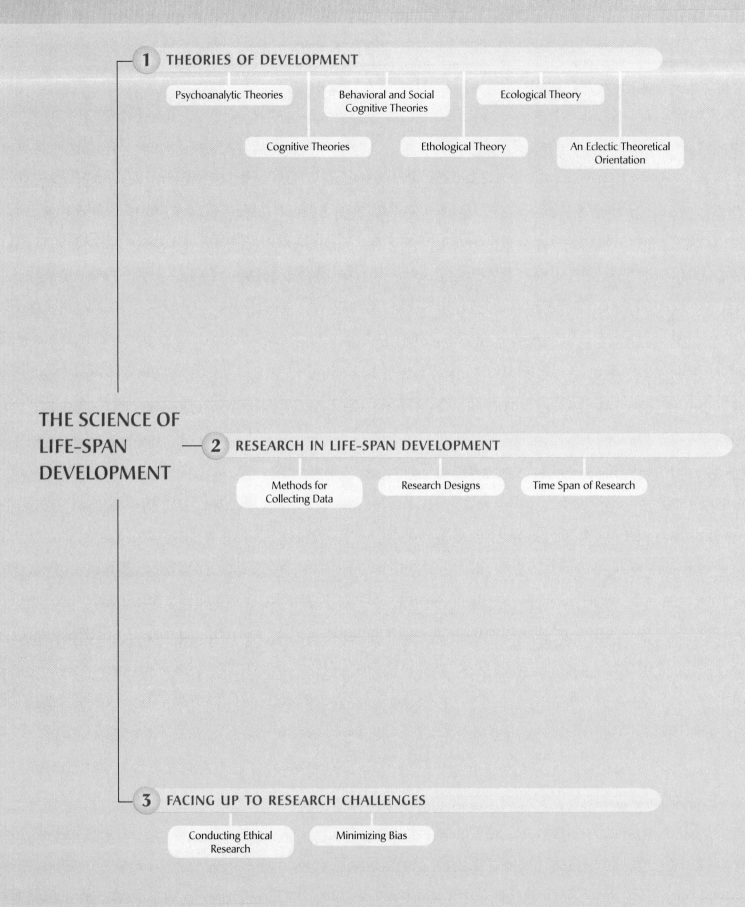

THE SCIENCE OF LIFE-SPAN DEVELOPMENT

1 THEORIES OF DEVELOPMENT

Psychoanalytic Theories

Behavioral and Social Cognitive Theories

Ecological Theory

Cognitive Theories

Ethological Theory

An Eclectic Theoretical Orientation

2 RESEARCH IN LIFE-SPAN DEVELOPMENT

Methods for Collecting Data

Research Designs

Time Span of Research

3 FACING UP TO RESEARCH CHALLENGES

Conducting Ethical Research

Minimizing Bias

SUMMARY

1 Theories of Development: *Describe theories of life-span development*

Psychoanalytic Theories

The scientific method involves four main steps: (1) conceptualize a problem, (2) collect data, (3) analyze data, and (4) draw conclusions. A theory is an interrelated, coherent set of ideas that helps to explain and to make predictions. Theory is often involved in conceptualizing a problem. Hypotheses are specific assumptions and predictions, often derived from theory, that can be tested to determine their accuracy. Psychoanalytic theories describe development as primarily unconscious and as heavily colored by emotion. Psychoanalytic theorists believe that behavior is merely a surface characteristic and that early experiences with parents shape development. The two main psychoanalytic theories in developmental psychology are Freud's and Erikson's. Freud said that personality is made up of three structures—id, ego, and superego. The conflicting demands of these structures produce anxiety. Freud also proposed that individuals go through five psychosexual stages—oral, anal, phallic, latency, and genital. Erikson's theory emphasizes these eight psychosocial stages of development: trust versus mistrust, autonomy versus shame and doubt, initiative versus guilt, industry versus inferiority, identity versus identity confusion, intimacy versus isolation, generativity versus stagnation, and integrity versus despair. Contributions of psychoanalytic theories include an emphasis on early experiences and family relationships. Criticisms include the main concepts being difficult to test scientifically and too much emphasis on sexuality.

Cognitive Theories

The three main cognitive theories are Piaget's cognitive developmental theory, Vygotsky's sociocultural theory, and information-processing theory. Cognitive theories emphasize conscious thoughts. Piaget proposed a cognitive developmental theory in which children use the processes of organization and adaptation (assimilation and accommodation) to understand their world. In Piaget's theory, children go through four cognitive stages: sensorimotor, preoperational, concrete operational, and formal operational. Vygotsky's sociocultural cognitive theory emphasizes how culture and social interaction guide cognitive development. The information-processing theory emphasizes that individuals manipulate information, monitor it, and strategize about it. Contributions of cognitive theories include a positive view of development and an emphasis on the active construction of understanding. Criticisms include skepticism about the accuracy of Piaget's stages and too little attention to individual variations.

Behavioral and Social Cognitive Theories

Three versions of the behavioral approach are Pavlov's classical conditioning, Skinner's operant conditioning, and Bandura's social cognitive theory. In Pavlov's classical conditioning, a neutral stimulus acquires the ability to produce a response originally produced by another stimulus. In Skinner's operant conditioning, the consequences of a behavior produce changes in the probability of the behavior's recurrence. In Bandura's social cognitive theory, observational learning is a key aspect of life-span development. Bandura emphasizes reciprocal interactions among person/cognitive factors, behavior, and environment. Contributions of the behavioral and social cognitive theories include an emphasis on scientific research and environmental determinants of behavior. Criticisms include too little emphasis on cognition in Pavlov's and Skinner's views and giving inadequate attention to developmental changes.

Ethological Theory

Ethology stresses that behavior is strongly influenced by biology, is tied to evolution, and is characterized by critical or sensitive periods. Contributions of ethological theory include a focus on the biological and evolutionary basis of development, and the use of careful observations in naturalistic settings. Criticisms include a belief that the critical and sensitive period concepts might be too rigid and too much emphasis on biological foundations.

Ecological Theory

Ecological theory is Bronfenbrenner's environmental systems view of development. It consists of five environmental systems: microsystem, mesosystem, exosystem, macrosystem, and chronosystem. Contributions of the theory include a systematic examination of macro and micro dimensions of environmental systems, and attention to connections between environmental systems. Criticisms include giving inadequate attention to biological factors, as well as too little emphasis on cognitive factors.

An Eclectic Theoretical Orientation

An eclectic theoretical orientation does not follow any one theoretical approach, but rather selects from each theory whatever factor is considered the best within that theory.

2 Research in Life-Span Development: *Explain how research on life-span development is conducted*

Methods for Collecting Data

Methods for collecting data about life-span development include observation (in a laboratory or a naturalistic setting), survey (questionnaire) or interview, standardized test, case study, life-history record, and physiological measures.

Research Designs

Three main research designs are descriptive, correlational, and experimental. Descriptive research aims to observe and record behavior. In correlational research, the goal is to describe the strength of the relationship between two or more events or characteristics. Experimental research involves conducting an experiment, which can determine cause and effect. An independent variable is the manipulated, influential, experimental factor. A dependent variable is a factor that can change in an experiment, in response to changes in the independent variable. Experiments can involve one or more experimental groups and control groups. In random assignment, researchers assign participants to experimental and control groups by chance.

Time Span of Research

When researchers decide about the time span of their research, they can conduct cross-sectional, longitudinal, or sequential studies. Life-span researchers are especially concerned about cohort effects.

3 Facing Up to Research Challenges: *Discuss research challenges in life-span development*

Conducting Ethical Research

Researchers' ethical responsibilities include seeking participants' informed consent, ensuring their confidentiality, debriefing them about the purpose and potential personal consequences of participating, and avoiding unnecessary deception of participants.

Minimizing Bias

Researchers need to guard against gender, cultural, and ethnic bias in research. Every effort should be made to make research equitable for both females and males. Individuals from varied ethnic backgrounds need to be included as participants in life-span research, and overgeneralization about diverse members within a group must be avoided.

KEY TERMS

theory 39
hypotheses 39
psychoanalytic theories 40
Erikson's theory 41
Piaget's theory 43
Vygotsky's theory 44

information-processing
   theory 44
social cognitive theory 46
ethology 47
ecological theory 48
eclectic theoretical
   orientation 51

laboratory 53
naturalistic observation 53
standardized test 54
case study 55
life-history record 55
descriptive research 56
correlational research 56

correlation coefficient 56
experiment 56
cross-sectional approach 58
longitudinal approach 58
sequential approach 59
cohort effects 59
ethnic gloss 64

KEY PEOPLE

Sigmund Freud 40
Erik Erikson 41
Jean Piaget 43

Lev Vygotsky 44
Robert Siegler 44
Ivan Pavlov 45

B. F. Skinner 46
Albert Bandura 46
Konrad Lorenz 47

John Bowlby 48
Urie Bronfenbrenner 48
Ross Parke and Raymond
   Buriel 64

E-LEARNING TOOLS

To help you master the material in this chapter, you'll find a number of valuable study tools on the LifeMap CD-ROM that accompanies this book and on the Online Learning Center for *Life-Span Development*, eleventh edition, at **www.mhhe.com/santrockld11**.

Video Clips

In the margins of this book there are icons directing you to the LifeMap CD-ROM that accompanies the book. There you'll find a video for chapter 2 called "Self-Report Bias in Surveys." Anyone who conducts a survey must deal with at least two forms of bias: the researcher's own bias in the phrasing of questions, and the reliability of the answers provided for those questions. As this segment demonstrates, forms of bias may involve differences of gender, culture, and ethnicity.

Self-Assessment

Connect to **www.mhhe.com/santrockld11** to reflect on how you've become the person you are today by completing the self-assessment, *Models and Mentors in My Life*.

Taking It to the Net

Connect to **www.mhhe.com/santrockld11** to research the answers to these questions.

1. Like many students of lifespan psychology, Ymelda has a hard time with Freud's theory, insisting that it is "all about sex." Is that the extent of Freud's theoretical perspective?
2. Juan's lifespan psychology teacher asked the class to read about Albert Bandura's famous "Bobo" doll experiment and determine if there were any gender differences in the responses of boys and girls who (1) saw aggressive behavior rewarded and (2) who saw aggressive behavior punished. What should Juan's conclusions be?
3. A requirement for Wanda's methods course is to design and carry out an original research project. Among the many decisions she must make is what type of data she will collect. She decides to research how people adapt to college life. Her instructor asks if she will use an interview or a survey. What are the distinctions between surveys and interviews, and what are the benefits and difficulties of each?

Health and Well-Being, Parenting, and Education Exercises

Build your decision-making skills by trying your hand at the health and well-being, parenting, and education exercises. Connect to **www.mhhe.com/santrockld11** to research the answers and complete the exercises.

*What endless questions vex the thought, of whence and whither,
when and how.*

—Sir Richard Burton
British Explorer, 19th Century

CHAPTER OUTLINE

LEARNING GOALS

THE EVOLUTIONARY PERSPECTIVE

Natural Selection and Adaptive Behavior

Evolutionary Psychology

1 Discuss the evolutionary
perspective on
development

GENETIC FOUNDATIONS OF DEVELOPMENT

The Collaborative Gene

Genes and Chromosomes

Genetic Principles

Chromosome and Gene-Linked Abnormalities

2 Describe what genes are
and how they influence
human development

SOME REPRODUCTIVE CHALLENGES AND CHOICES

Prenatal Diagnostic Tests

Infertility and Reproductive Technology

Adoption

3 Identify some important
reproductive challenges
and choices

HEREDITY AND ENVIRONMENT INTERACTION:
THE NATURE-NURTURE DEBATE

Behavior Genetics

Heredity-Enviroment Correlations

Shared and Nonshared Environment Experiences

The Epigenetic View

Conclusions About Heredity-Environment Interaction

4 Characterize some of the
ways that heredity and
environment interact to
produce individual
differences in development

Images of Life-Span Development
The Jim and Jim Twins

Jim Lewis (*left*) and Jim Springer (*right*).

Jim Springer and Jim Lewis are identical twins. They were separated at 4 weeks of age and did not see each other again until they were 39 years old. Both worked as part-time deputy sheriffs, vacationed in Florida, drive Chevrolets, had dogs named Toy, and married and divorced women named Betty. One twin named his son James Allan, and the other named his son James Alan. Both liked math but not spelling, enjoyed carpentry and mechanical drawing, chewed their fingernails down to the nubs, had almost identical drinking and smoking habits, had hemorrhoids, put on 10 pounds at about the same point in development, first suffered headaches at the age of 18, and had similar sleep patterns.

Jim and Jim do have some differences. One wears his hair over his forehead, the other slicks it back and has sideburns. One expresses himself best orally; the other is more proficient in writing. But, for the most part, their profiles are remarkably similar.

Jim and Jim were part of the Minnesota Study of Twins Reared Apart, directed by Thomas Bouchard and his colleagues. The study brings identical twins (identical genetically because they come from the same fertilized egg) and fraternal twins (who come from different fertilized eggs) from all over the world to Minneapolis to investigate their lives. There the twins complete personality and intelligence tests, and they provide detailed medical histories, including information about diet and smoking, exercise habits, chest X-rays, heart stress tests, and EEGs. The twins are asked more than 15,000 questions about their family and childhood, personal interests, vocational orientation, values, and aesthetic judgments (Bouchard & others, 1990).

Another pair of identical twins in the Minnesota study, Daphne and Barbara, are called the "giggle sisters" because, after being reunited, they were always making each other laugh. A thorough search of their adoptive families' histories revealed no gigglers. The giggle sisters ignored stress, avoided conflict and controversy whenever possible, and showed no interest in politics.

Two other identical twin sisters were separated at 6 weeks and reunited in their fifties. Both described hauntingly similar nightmares in which they had doorknobs and fishhooks in their mouths as they smothered to death. The nightmares began during early adolescence and stopped within the past 10 to 12 years. Both women were bed wetters until about 12 or 13 years of age, and their educational and marital histories are remarkably similar.

When genetically identical twins who were separated as infants show such striking similarities in their tastes and habits and choices, can we conclude that their genes must have caused the development of those tastes and habits and choices? Other possible causes need to be considered. The twins shared not only the same genes but also some experiences. Some of the separated twins lived together for several months prior to their adoption; some of the twins had been reunited prior to testing (in some cases, many years earlier); adoption agencies often place twins in similar homes; and even strangers who spend several hours together and start comparing their lives are likely to come up with some coincidental similarities (Adler, 1991). The Minnesota study of identical twins points to both the importance of the genetic basis of human development and the need for further research on genetic and environmental factors (Bouchard, 1995).

PREVIEW

The examples of Jim and Jim, the giggle sisters, and the identical twins who had the same nightmares stimulate us to think about our genetic heritage and the biological foundations of our existence. Organisms are not like billiard balls, moved by simple, external forces to predictable positions on life's pool table.

Environmental experiences and biological foundations work together to make us who we are. Our coverage of life's biological beginnings focuses on evolution, genetic foundations, challenges and choices regarding reproduction, and the interaction of heredity and environment.

1   THE EVOLUTIONARY PERSPECTIVE

> Natural Selection and Adaptive Behavior

> Evolutionary Psychology

In evolutionary time, humans are relative newcomers to Earth. If we consider evolutionary time as a calendar year, humans arrived here only in the last moments of December (Sagan, 1977). As our earliest ancestors left the forest to feed on the savannahs, and then to form hunting societies on the open plains, their minds and behaviors changed, and they eventually established humans as the dominant species on Earth. How did this evolution come about?

Natural Selection and Adaptive Behavior

Natural selection is the evolutionary process by which those individuals of a species that are best adapted are the ones that survive and reproduce. To understand what this means, let's return to the middle of the nineteenth century, when the British naturalist Charles Darwin was traveling around the world, observing many different species of animals in their natural surroundings. Darwin, who published his observations and thoughts in *On the Origin of Species* (1859), noted that most organisms reproduce at rates that would cause enormous increases in the population of most species and yet populations remain nearly constant. He reasoned that an intense, constant struggle for food, water, and resources must occur among the many young born each generation, because many of the young do not survive. Those that do survive and reproduce pass on their characteristics to the next generation. Darwin argued that these survivors are better *adapted* to their world than are the nonsurvivors (Johnson, 2006; Rose & Mueller, 2006). The best-adapted individuals survive to leave the most offspring. Over the course of many generations, organisms with the characteristics needed for survival make up an increased percentage of the population. Over many, many generations, this could produce a gradual modification of the whole population. If environmental conditions change, however, other characteristics might become favored by natural selection, moving the species in a different direction (Freeman & Herron, 2007; McKee, Poirier, & McGraw, 2005).

All organisms must adapt to particular places, climates, food sources, and ways of life. An eagle's claws are a physical adaptation that facilitates predation. *Adaptive behavior* is behavior that promotes an organism's survival in the natural habitat (Cosmides & others, 2003). For example, attachment between a caregiver and a baby ensures the infant's closeness to a caregiver for feeding and protection from danger, thus increasing the infant's chances of survival. Or consider pregnancy sickness, which

How does the attachment of this Vietnamese baby to its mother reflect the evolutionary process of adaptive behavior?

is a tendency for women to avoid certain foods and become nauseous during pregnancy (Schmitt & Pilcher, 2004). Women with pregnancy sickness tend to avoid foods that are higher in toxins, such as coffee, that may harm the fetus. Thus, pregnancy sickness may be an evolution-based adaptation that enhances the offspring's ability to survive.

Evolutionary Psychology

Although Darwin introduced the theory of evolution by natural selection in 1859, his ideas only recently have become a popular framework for explaining behavior. Psychology's newest approach, **evolutionary psychology,** emphasizes the importance of adaptation, reproduction, and "survival of the fittest" in shaping behavior. "Fit" in this sense refers to the ability to bear offspring that survive long enough to bear offspring of their own. In this view, natural selection favors behaviors that increase reproductive success, the ability to pass your genes to the next generation (Bjorklund, 2006; Geary, 2006).

David Buss (1995, 2000, 2004) has been especially influential in stimulating new interest in how evolution can explain human behavior. He believes that just as evolution shapes our physical features, such as body shape and height, it also pervasively influences how we make decisions, how aggressive we are, our fears, and our mating patterns. For example, assume that our ancestors were hunters and gatherers on the plains and that men did most of the hunting and women stayed close to home gathering seeds and plants for food. If you have to travel some distance from your home in an effort to find and slay a fleeing animal, you need not only certain physical traits but also the ability for certain types of spatial thinking. Men born with these traits would be more likely than men without them to survive, to bring home lots of food, and to be considered attractive mates—and thus to reproduce and pass on these characteristics to their children. In other words, these traits would provide a reproductive advantage for males, and, over many generations, men with good spatial thinking skills might become more numerous in the population. Critics point out that this scenario might or might not have actually happened.

evolutionary psychology Emphasizes the importance of adaptation, reproduction, and "survival of the fittest" in shaping behavior.

Evolutionary Developmental Psychology Recently, interest has grown in using the concepts of evolutionary psychology to understand human development (Geary, 2006). Here are a few ideas proposed by evolutionary developmental psychologists (Bjorklund & Pellegrini, 2002, pp. 336–340):

- *An extended juvenile period evolved because humans require time to develop a large brain and learn the complexity of human social communities.* Humans take longer to become reproductively mature than any other mammal (see figure 3.1). During this juvenile period they develop a large brain and the experiences required for mastering the complexities of human society.

- *"Many aspects of childhood function as preprations for adulthood and were selected over the course of evolution"* (p. 337). Play is one possible example. Beginning in the preschool years, boys in all cultures engage in more rough-and-tumble play than girls. Perhaps rough-and-tumble play prepares boys for fighting and hunting as adults. In contrast to boys, girls engage in play that involves more imitation of parents, such as caring for dolls, and less physical dominance. This, according to evolutionary psychologists, is an evolved tendency that prepares females for becoming the primary caregivers for their offspring.

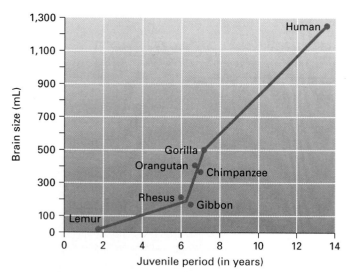

FIGURE 3.1 The Brain Sizes of Various Primates and Humans in Relation to the Length of the Juvenile Period. Compared with other primates, humans have both a larger brain and a longer juvenile period. *What conclusions can you draw from the relationship indicated by this graph?*

- *Some characteristics of childhood were selected because they are adaptive at specific points in development, not because they prepare children for adulthood.* For example, some aspects of play may function, not to prepare us for adulthood, but to help children adapt to their immediate circumstances, perhaps to learn about their current environment.

- *Many evolved psychological mechanisms are domain-specific.* That is, the mechanisms apply only to a specific aspect of a person's makeup (Atkinson & Wheeler, 2004; Rubenstein, 2004). According to evolutionary psychology, information processing is one example. In this view, the mind is not a general-purpose device that can be applied equally to a vast array of problems. Instead, as our ancestors dealt with certain recurring problems, specialized modules evolved that process information related to those problems, such as a module for physical knowledge, a module for mathematical knowledge, and a module for language. Also in this view, "infants enter the world 'prepared' to process and learn some information more readily than others, and these preparations serve as the foundation for social and cognitive development" (p. 338). For example, much as goslings in Lorenz' experiment (described in chapter 2) were "prepared" to follow their mother, human infants are biologically prepared to learn the sounds that are part of human language.

- *Evolved mechanisms are not always adaptive in contemporary society.* Some behaviors that were adaptive for our prehistoric ancestors may not serve us well today. For example, the food-scarce environment of our ancestors likely led to humans' propensity to gorge when food is available and to crave high-caloric foods, a trait that might lead to an epidemic of obesity when food is plentiful.

Evolution
Evolutionary Psychology
Handbook of Evolutionary Psychology
Evolutionary Psychology Resources

Evolution and Life-Span Development   In evolutionary theory, what matters is that individuals live long enough to reproduce and pass on their characteristics (Johnson, 2006; Mader, 2006, 2007; Promislow, Fedorka, & Burger, 2006). So why do humans live so long after reproduction? Perhaps evolution favored longevity because having older people around improves the survival rates of babies. For example, perhaps having grandparents alive to care for the young while parents were out hunting and gathering food created an evolutionary advantage.

According to life-span developmentalist Paul Baltes (2000, 2003; Baltes, Lindenberger, & Staudinger, 2006; Baltes & Smith, 2003), the benefits conferred by evolutionary selection decrease with age. Natural selection has not weeded out many harmful conditions and nonadaptive characteristics that appear among older adults. Why? Natural selection operates primarily on characteristics that are tied to reproductive fitness, which extends through the earlier part of adulthood. Thus, says Baltes, selection primarily operates during the first half of life.

As an example, consider Alzheimer disease, an irreversible brain disorder characterized by gradual deterioration. This disease typically does not appear until age 70 or later. If it were a disease that struck 20-year-olds, perhaps natural selection would have eliminated it eons ago.

Thus, unaided by evolutionary pressures against nonadaptive conditions, we suffer the aches, pains, and infirmities of aging. As the benefits of evolutionary selection decrease with age, argues Baltes, the need for culture increases (see figure 3.2). That is, as older adults weaken biologically, they need culture-based resources such as cognitive skills, literacy, medical technology, and social support. For example, older adults may need help and training from other people to maintain their cognitive skills (Hoyer & Roodin, 2003).

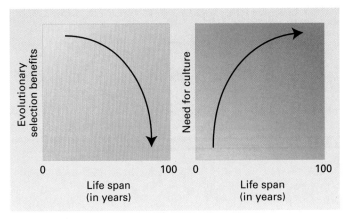

FIGURE 3.2 Baltes' View of Evolution and Culture Across the Life Span. Benefits derived from evolutionary selection decrease as we age, whereas the need for culture increases with age.

Children in all cultures are interested in the tools that adults in their cultures use. For example, this 11-month-old boy from the Efe culture in the Democratic Republic of the Congo in Africa is trying to cut a papaya with an *apopau* (a smaller version of a machete). *Might the infant's behavior be evolutionary-based or be due to both biological and environmental conditions?*

Evaluating Evolutionary Psychology Although the popular press gives a lot of attention to the ideas of evolutionary psychology, it remains just one theoretical approach. Like the theories described in chapter 2, it has limitations, weaknesses, and critics (Buller, 2005). Albert Bandura (1998), whose social cognitive theory was described in chapter 2, acknowledges the important influence of evolution on human adaptation. However, he rejects what he calls "one-sided evolutionism," which sees social behavior as the product of evolved biology. An alternative is a *bidirectional view,* in which environmental and biological conditions influence each other. In this view, evolutionary pressures created changes in biological structures that allowed the use of tools, which enabled our ancestors to manipulate the environment, constructing new environmental conditions. In turn, environmental innovations produced new selection pressures that led to the evolution of specialized biological systems for consciousness, thought, and language.

In other words, evolution gave us bodily structures and biological potentialities; it does not dictate behavior. People have used their biological capacities to produce diverse cultures—aggressive and pacific, egalitarian and autocratic. As American scientist Steven Jay Gould (1981) concluded, in most domains of human functioning, biology allows a broad range of cultural possibilities.

Review and Reflect • LEARNING GOAL 1

1 **Discuss the Evolutionary Perspective on Development**

Review
- Define natural selection and adaptive behavior?
- What is evolutionary psychology? What are some basic ideas about human development proposed by evolutionary psychologists? How might evolutionary influences have different effects at different points in the life span? How can evolutionary psychology be evaluated?

Reflect
- Which is more persuasive to you: the views of evolutionary psychologists or their critics? Why?

---

2 GENETIC FOUNDATIONS OF DEVELOPMENT

The Collaborative Gene	Genetic Principles
Genes and Chromosomes	Chromosome and Gene-Linked Abnormalities

How are characteristics that suit a species for survival transmitted from one generation to the next? Darwin did not know because genes and the principles of genetics had not yet been discovered. Each of us carries a "genetic code" that we inherited from our parents. Because a fertilized egg carries this human code, a fertilized human egg cannot grow into an egret, eagle, or elephant.

The Collaborative Gene

Each of us began life as a single cell weighing about one twenty-millionth of an ounce! This tiny piece of matter housed our entire genetic code—instructions that orchestrated growth from that single cell to a person made of trillions of cells, each containing a replica of the original code. That code is carried by our genes. What are genes and what do they do? For the answer, we need to look into our cells.

The nucleus of each human cell contains **chromosomes,** which are threadlike structures made up of deoxyribonucleic acid, or DNA. **DNA** is a complex molecule that has a double helix shape, like a spiral staircase, and contains genetic information. **Genes,** the units of hereditary information, are short segments of DNA, as you can see in figure 3.3. They direct cells to reproduce themselves and to assemble proteins. Proteins, in turn, are the building blocks of cells as well as the regulators that direct the body's processes (Hartwell, 2008; Johnson, 2006).

Each gene has its own location, its own designated place on a particular chromosome. Today, there is a great deal of enthusiasm about efforts to discover the specific locations of genes that are linked to certain functions (Enger, 2007; Lewin, 2006; Lewis, 2007; Nester & others, 2007; Plomin, 2004). An important step in this direction was accomplished when the Human Genome Project and the Celera Corporation completed a preliminary map of the human *genome*—the complete set of developmental instructions for creating proteins that initiate the making of a human organism (U.S. Department of Energy, 2001).

One of the big surprises of the Human Genome Project was a report indicating that humans have only about 30,000 genes (U.S. Department of Energy, 2001). More recently, the number of human genes has been revised further downward to 20,000 to 25,000 (International Human Genome Sequencing Consortium, 2004). Scientists had thought that humans had as many as 100,000 or more genes. They had also believed that each gene programmed just one protein. In fact, humans appear to have far more proteins than they have genes, so there cannot be a one-to-one correspondence between genes and proteins (Commoner, 2002; Moore, 2001). Each gene is not translated, in automaton-like fashion, into one and only one protein. A gene does not act independently, as developmental psychologist David Moore (2001) emphasized by titling his recent book *The Dependent Gene.*

Rather than being an independent source of developmental information, DNA collaborates with other sources of information to specify our characteristics. The collaboration operates at many points. For example, the cellular machinery mixes, matches, and links small pieces of DNA to reproduce the genes and that machinery is influenced by what is going on around it.

Whether a gene is turned "on," working to assemble proteins, is also a matter of collaboration. The activity of genes (*genetic expression*) is affected by their environment (Gottlieb, 2003, 2004; Gottlieb, Wahlsten, & Lickliter, 2006). For example, hormones that circulate in the blood make their way into the cell where they can turn genes "on" and "off." The flow of hormones can be affected by environmental conditions, such as light, day length, nutrition, and behavior. Numerous studies have shown that external events outside of the original cell and the person, as well as events inside the cell, can excite or inhibit gene expression (Gottlieb, Wahlsten, & Lickliter, 2006; Mauro & others, 1994; Rusak & others, 1990).

In short, a single gene is rarely the source of a protein's genetic information, much less of an inherited trait (Gottlieb, 2003, 2004; Gottlieb, Wahlsten, & Lickliter, 2006; Moore, 2001). Rather than being a group of independent genes, the human genome consists of many genes that collaborate both with each other and with non-genetic factors inside and outside the body.

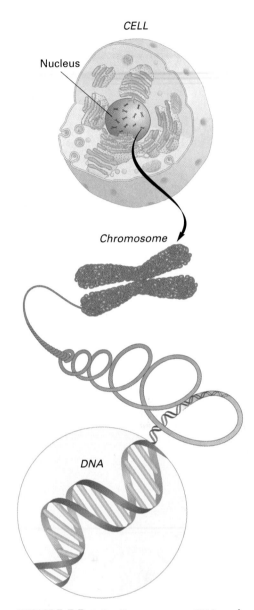

FIGURE 3.3 Cells, Chromosomes, DNA, and Genes. (*Top*) The body contains trillions of cells. Each cell contains a central structure, the nucleus. (*Middle*) Chromosomes are threadlike structures located in the nucleus of the cell. Chromosomes are composed of DNA. (*Bottom*) DNA has the structure of a spiraled double chain. A gene is a segment of DNA.

chromosomes Threadlike structures that come in 23 pairs, one member of each pair coming from each parent. Chromosomes contain the genetic substance DNA.

DNA A complex molecule that contains genetic information.

genes Units of hereditary information composed of DNA. Genes direct cells to reproduce themselves and manufacture the proteins that maintain life.

A positive result from the Human Genome Project. Shortly after Andrew Gobea was born, his cells were genetically altered to prevent his immune system from failing.

mitosis Cellular reproduction in which the cell's nucleus duplicates itself with two new cells being formed, each containing the same DNA as the parent cell, arranged in the same 23 pairs of chromosomes.

meiosis A specialized form of cell division that occurs to form eggs and sperm (or gametes).

fertilization A stage in reproduction whereby an egg and a sperm fuse to create a single cell, called a zygote.

zygote A single cell formed through fertilization.

www.mhhe.com/santrockld11

Landmarks in the History of Genetics

Heredity Resources

Genetics Journals and News

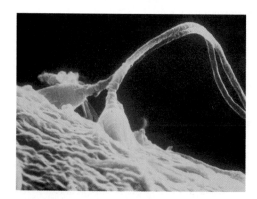

FIGURE 3.4 Union of Sperm and Egg

Calvin and Hobbes   by Bill Watterson

Genes and Chromosomes

Genes are not only collaborative; they are enduring. How do the genes manage to get passed from generation to generation and end up in all of the trillion cells in the body? Three processes explain the heart of the story: mitosis, meiosis, and fertilization.

Mitosis, Meiosis, and Fertilization   All cells in your body, except the sperm and egg, have 46 chromosomes arranged in 23 pairs. These cells reproduce by a process called **mitosis.** During mitosis, the cell's nucleus—including the chromosomes—duplicates itself and the cell divides. Two new cells are formed, each containing the same DNA as the original cell, arranged in the same 23 pairs of chromosomes.

However, a different type of cell division—**meiosis**—forms eggs and sperm (or *gametes*). During meiosis, a cell of the testes (in men) or ovaries (in women) duplicates its chromosomes but then divides *twice,* thus forming four cells, each of which has only half of the genetic material of the parent cell. By the end of meiosis, each egg or sperm has 23 *unpaired* chromosomes.

During **fertilization,** an egg and a sperm fuse to create a single cell, called a **zygote** (see figure 3.4). In the zygote, the 23 unpaired chromosomes from the egg and the 23 unpaired chromosomes from the sperm combine to form one set of 23 paired chromosomes—one chromosome of each pair from the mother's egg and the other from the father's sperm. In this manner, each parent contributes half of the offspring's genetic material.

Figure 3.5 shows 23 paired chromosomes of a male and a female. The members of each pair of chromosomes are both similar and different: Each chromosome in the pair contains varying forms of the same genes, at the same location on the chromosome. A gene for hair color, for example, is located on both members of one pair of chromosomes, in the same location on each. However, one of those chromosomes might carry the gene for blond hair; the other chromosome in the pair might carry the gene for brown hair.

Do you notice any obvious differences between the chromosomes of the male and the chromosomes of the female in figure 3.5? The difference lies in the 23rd pair. Ordinarily, in females this pair consists of two chromosomes called *X chromosomes*; in males the 23rd pair consists of an X and a *Y chromosome*. The presence of a Y chromosome is what makes an individual male.

Sources of Variability   Combining the genes of two parents in offspring increases genetic variability in the population, which is valuable for a species because it provides more characteristics for natural selection to operate on (Dowan, 2007;

Krogh, 2007; Mader, 2006; Lewis, 2007). In fact, the human genetic process creates several important sources of variability.

First, the chromosomes in the zygote are not exact copies of those in mothers' ovaries and the fathers' testes. During the formation of the sperm and egg in meiosis, the members of each pair of chromosomes are separated, but which chromosome in the pair goes to the gamete is a matter of chance. In addition, before the pairs separate, pieces of the two chromosomes in each pair are exchanged, creating a new combination of genes on each chromosome. Thus, when chromosomes from the mother's egg and the father's sperm are brought together in the zygote, the result is a truly unique combination of genes (Belk & Borden, 2007; Starr, 2006).

If each zygote is unique, how do identical twins like those discussed in the opening of the chapter exist? *Identical twins* (also called monozygotic twins) develop from a single zygote that splits into two genetically identical replicas, each of which becomes a person. *Fraternal twins* (called dizygotic twins) develop from separate eggs and separate sperm, making them genetically no more similar than ordinary siblings.

A second source of variability comes from DNA. Chance, a mistake by cellular machinery, or damage from an environmental agent such as radiation may produce a *mutated gene,* which is a permanently altered segment of DNA (Cummings, 2006).

Even when their genes are identical, however, people vary. The difference between genotypes and phenotypes helps us to understand this source of variability. All of a person's genetic material makes up his or her **genotype.** However, not all of the genetic material is apparent in our observed and measurable characteristics. A **phenotype** consists of observable characteristics. Phenotypes include physical characteristics (such as height, weight, and hair color) and psychological characteristics (such as personality and intelligence).

For each genotype, a range of phenotypes can be expressed, providing another source of variability (Gottlieb, Wahlsten, & Lickliter, 2006; Loos & Rankinen, 2005; Wong, Gottesman, & Petronis, 2005). An individual can inherit the genetic potential to grow very large, for example, but good nutrition, among other things, will be essential to achieving that potential. The giggle sisters introduced in the chapter opening might have inherited the same genetic potential to be very tall, but if Daphne had grown up malnourished, she might have ended up noticeably shorter than Barbara. This principle is so widely applicable it has a name: Heredity-environment interaction, or gene-environment interaction (Gottlieb, 2005).

Genetic Principles

What determines how a genotype is expressed to create a particular phenotype? Much is unknown about the answer to this question (Dowan, 2007; Klug, Cummings, & Spencer, 2006; Lewis, 2005, 2007). However, a number of genetic principles have been discovered, among them those of dominant-recessive genes, sex-linked genes, genetic imprinting, and polygenically determined characteristics.

Dominant-Recessive Genes Principle
In some cases, one gene of a pair always exerts its effects; it is *dominant,* overriding the potential influence of the other gene, called the *recessive* gene. This is the *dominant-recessive genes principle.* A recessive gene exerts its influence only if the two genes of a pair are both recessive. If you inherit a recessive gene for a trait from each of your parents, you will show the trait. If you inherit a recessive gene from only one parent, you may never know you carry the gene. Brown hair, farsightedness, and dimples rule over blond hair, nearsightedness, and freckles in the world of dominant-recessive genes.

Can two brown-haired parents have a blond-haired child? Yes, they can. Suppose that each parent has a dominant gene for brown hair and a recessive gene for blond hair. Since dominant genes override recessive genes, the parents have brown

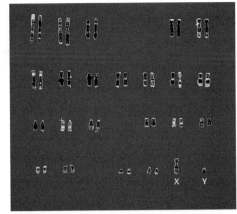

(a)

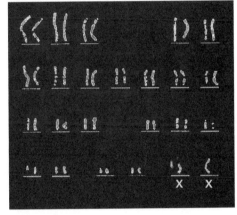

(b)

FIGURE 3.5 The Genetic Difference Between Males and Females. Set (*a*) shows the chromosome structure of a male, and set (*b*) shows the chromosome structure of a female. The last pair of 23 pairs of chromosomes is in the bottom right box of each set. Notice that the Y chromosome of the male is smaller than the X chromosome of the female. To obtain this kind of chromosomal picture, a cell is removed from a person's body, usually from the inside of the mouth. The chromosomes are stained by chemical treatment, magnified extensively, and then photographed.

genotype A person's genetic heritage; the actual genetic material.

phenotype The way an individual's genotype is expressed in observed and measurable characteristics.

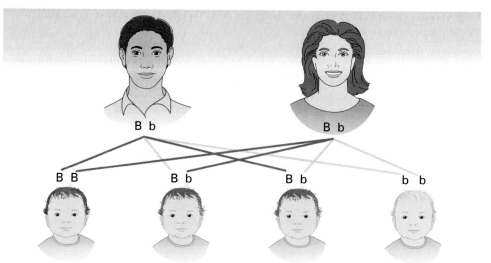

B = Gene for brown hair   b = Gene for blond hair

FIGURE 3.6 How Brown-Haired Parents Can Have a Blond-Haired Child. Although both parents have brown hair, each parent can have a recessive gene for blond hair. In this example, both parents have brown hair, but each parent carries the dominant gene for brown hair (*B*) and the recessive gene for blond hair. Therefore, the odds of their child having blond hair are one in four—the probability the child will receive a recessive gene (*b*) from each parent.

hair, but both are carriers of blondness and pass on their recessive genes for blond hair. With no dominant gene to override them, the recessive genes can make the child's hair blond (see figure 3.6).

Sex-Linked Genes Most mutated genes are recessive. When a mutated gene is carried on the X chromosome, the result is called *X-linked inheritance* (Turner, 2006). It may have very different implications for males than females. Remember that males have only one X chromosome. Thus, if there is an altered, disease-creating gene on the X chromosome, males have no "backup" copy to counter the harmful gene and therefore may carry an X-linked disease. However, females have a second X chromosome, which is likely to be unchanged. As a result, they are not likely to have the X-linked disease. Thus, most individuals who have X-linked diseases are males. Females who have one changed copy of the X gene are known as "carriers," and they usually do not show any signs of the X-linked disease. Hemophilia and fragile X syndrome, which we will discuss later in the chapter, are examples of X-linked inheritance (Gonzalez-del Angel & others, 2000).

Genetic Imprinting *Genetic imprinting* occurs when genes have differing effects depending on whether they are inherited from the mother or the father (Abu-Amero & others, 2006; Federman, 2006). A chemical process "silences" one member of the gene pair. For example, as a result of imprinting, only the maternally derived copy of a gene might be active, while the paternally derived copy of the same gene is silenced—or vice versa. Only a small percentage of human genes appear to undergo imprinting, but it is a normal and important aspect of development. When imprinting goes awry, development is disturbed as in the case of Beckwith-Wiedemann syndrome, a growth disorder, and Wilms tumor, a type of cancer.

Polygenic Inheritance Genetic transmission is usually more complex than the simple example we have examined thus far (Lewis, 2007; Starr, 2006). Few characteristics reflect the influence of only a single gene or pair of genes. Most are determined by the interaction of many different genes; they are said to be *polygenically determined*. Even a simple characteristic such as height, for example, reflects the interaction of many genes, as well as the influence of the environment.

Name	Description	Treatment	Incidence
Down syndrome	An extra chromosome causes mild to severe retardation and physical abnormalities.	Surgery, early intervention, infant stimulation, and special learning programs	1 in 1,900 births at age 20 1 in 300 births at age 35 1 in 30 births at age 45
Klinefelter syndrome (XXY)	An extra X chromosome causes physical abnormalities.	Hormone therapy can be effective	1 in 600 male births
Fragile X syndrome	An abnormality in the X chromosome can cause mental retardation, learning disabilities, or short attention span.	Special education, speech and language therapy	More common in males than in females
Turner syndrome (XO)	A missing X chromosome in females can cause mental retardation and sexual underdevelopment.	Hormone therapy in childhood and puberty	1 in 2,500 female births
XYY syndrome	An extra Y chromosome can cause above-average height.	No special treatment required	1 in 1,000 male births

FIGURE 3.7 **Some Chromosome Abnormalities.** The treatments for these abnormalities do not necessarily erase the problem but may improve the individual's adaptive behavior and quality of life.

Chromosome and Gene-Linked Abnormalities

Sometimes, abnormalities characterize the genetic process (Hartwell, 2008; Lewis, 2007). Some of these abnormalities involve whole chromosomes that do not separate properly during meiosis. Other abnormalities are produced by harmful genes.

Chromosome Abnormalities Sometimes, when a gamete is formed, the sperm and ovum does not have its normal set of 23 chromosomes. The most notable examples involve Down syndrome and abnormalities of the sex chromosomes (see figure 3.7).

Down Syndrome An individual with **Down syndrome** has a round face, a flattened skull, an extra fold of skin over the eyelids, a protruding tongue, short limbs, and retardation of motor and mental abilities (Hodapp & Dykens, 2006). The syndrome is caused by the presence of an extra copy of chromosome 21. It is not known why the extra chromosome is present, but the health of the male sperm or female ovum may be involved (Susanne & others, 2006; Zitanova & others, 2006).

Down syndrome appears approximately once in every 700 live births. Women between the ages of 16 and 34 are less likely to give birth to a child with Down syndrome than are younger or older women. African American children are rarely born with Down syndrome.

Sex-Linked Chromosome Abnormalities Recall that a newborn normally has either an X and a Y chromosome, or two X chromosomes. Human embryos must possess at least one X chromosome to be viable. The most common sex-linked chromosome abnormalities involve the presence of an extra chromosome (either an X or Y) or the absence of one X chromosome in females.

Klinefelter syndrome is a genetic disorder in which males have an extra X chromosome, making them XXY instead of XY (Handelsman & Liu, 2006; Itti & others, 2006). Males with this disorder have undeveloped testes, and they usually have enlarged breasts and become tall. Klinefelter syndrome occurs approximately once in every 600 live male births (Aguirre & others, 2006).

Fragile X syndrome is a genetic disorder that results from an abnormality in the X chromosome, which becomes constricted and often breaks (Irwin & others, 2005). Mental deficiency often is an outcome, but it may take the form of mental retardation, a learning disability, or a short attention span (Lewis, 2007). This disorder occurs

These athletes, many of whom have Down syndrome, are participating in a Special Olympics competition. Notice the distinctive facial features of the individuals with Down syndrome, such as a round face and a flattened skull. *What causes Down syndrome?*

Down syndrome A chromosomally transmitted form of mental retardation, caused by the presence of an extra copy of chromosome 21.

Klinefelter syndrome A chromosomal disorder in which males have an extra X chromosome, making them XXY instead of XY.

fragile X syndrome A genetic disorder involving an abnormality in the X chromosome, which becomes constricted and often breaks.

**Genetic Disorders
Prenatal Testing and Down Syndrome**

During a physical examination for a college football tryout, Jerry Hubbard, 32, learned that he carried the gene for sickle-cell anemia. Daughter Sara is healthy but daughter Avery (in the print dress) has sickle-cell anemia. *If you were a genetic counselor would you recommend that this family have more children? Explain.*

Turner syndrome A chromosome disorder in females in which either an X chromosome is missing, making the person XO instead of XX, or the second X chromosome is partially deleted.

XYY syndrome A chromosomal disorder in which males have an extra Y chromosome.

phenylketonuria (PKU) A genetic disorder in which an individual cannot properly metabolize an amino acid. PKU is now easily detected but, if left untreated, results in mental retardation and hyperactivity.

sickle-cell anemia A genetic disorder that affects the red blood cells and occurs most often in people of African descent.

more frequently in males than in females, possibly because the second X chromosome in females negates the effects of the other abnormal X chromosome (Fanos, Spangner, & Musci, 2006).

Turner syndrome is a chromosome disorder in females in which either an X chromosome is missing, making the person XO instead of XX, or part of one X chromosome is deleted (Kanaka-Gantenbein, 2006; Pasquino & others, 2005). Females with Turner syndrome are short in stature and have a webbed neck (Carel, 2005). They might be infertile and have difficulty in mathematics, but their verbal ability is often quite good. Turner syndrome occurs in approximately 1 of every 2,500 live female births.

The **XYY syndrome** is a chromosomal disorder in which the male has an extra Y chromosome (Briken & others, 2006; Monastirli & others, 2005). Early interest in this syndrome focused on the belief that the extra Y chromosome found in some males contributed to aggression and violence. However, researchers subsequently found that XYY males are no more likely to commit crimes than are XY males (Witkin & others, 1976).

Gene-Linked Abnormalities Abnormalities can be produced not only by an uneven number of chromosomes, but also by harmful genes (Cummings, 2006; Lewis, 2007). More than 7,000 such genetic disorders have been identified, although most of them are rare.

Phenylketonuria (PKU) is a genetic disorder in which the individual cannot properly metabolize phenylalanine, an amino acid (Brosco, Mattingly, & Sanders, 2006; Gassio & others, 2005). It results from a recessive gene and occurs about once in every 10,000 to 20,000 live births. Today, phenylketonuria is easily detected, and it is treated by a diet that prevents an excess accumulation of phenylalanine. If phenylketonuria is left untreated, however, excess phenylalanine builds up in the child, producing mental retardation and hyperactivity. Phenylketonuria accounts for approximately 1 percent of institutionalized individuals who are mentally retarded, and it occurs primarily in Whites.

The story of phenylketonuria has important implications for the nature-nurture issue. Although phenylketonuria is a genetic disorder (nature), how or whether a gene's influence in phenylketonuria is played out depend on environmental influences since the disorder can be treated (nurture) (Hvas, Nexo, & Nielsen, 2006; Zaffanello, Maffeis, & Zamboni, 2005). That is, the presence of a genetic defect *does not* inevitably lead to the development of the disorder *if* the individual develops in the right environment (one free of phenylalanine). This is one example of the important principle of heredity-environment interaction (Gottlieb, 2005). Under one environmental condition (phenylalanine in the diet), mental retardation results, but when other nutrients replace phenylalanine, intelligence develops in the normal range. The same genotype has different outcomes depending on the environment (in this case, the nutritional environment).

Sickle-cell anemia, which occurs most often in people of African descent, is a genetic disorder that impairs the body's red blood cells. Red blood cells carry oxygen to the body's cells and are usually shaped like a disk. In sickle-cell anemia, a recessive gene causes the red blood cell to become a hook-shaped "sickle" that cannot carry oxygen properly and dies quickly (Smith & others, 2006). As a result, the body's cells do not receive adequate oxygen, causing anemia and early death (Benz, 2004). About 1 in 400 African American babies is affected by sickle-cell anemia. One in 10 African Americans is a carrier, as is 1 in 20 Latin Americans.

Other diseases that result from genetic abnormalities include cystic fibrosis, diabetes, hemophilia, Huntington disease, spina bifida, and Tay-Sachs disease. Figure 3.8 provides further information about these diseases. Someday, scientists may identify why these and other genetic abnormalities occur and discover how to cure them. The Human Genome Project has already linked specific DNA variations with increased risk of a number of diseases and conditions, including Huntington disease (in which the central nervous system deteriorates), some forms of cancer, asthma, diabetes, hypertension, and Alzheimer disease.

Name	Description	Treatment	Incidence
Cystic fibrosis	Glandular dysfunction that interferes with mucus production; breathing and digestion are hampered, resulting in a shortened life span.	Physical and oxygen therapy, synthetic enzymes, and antibiotics; most individuals live to middle age.	1 in 2,000 births
Diabetes	Body does not produce enough insulin, which causes abnormal metabolism of sugar.	Early onset can be fatal unless treated with insulin.	1 in 2,500 births
Hemophilia	Delayed blood clotting causes internal and external bleeding.	Blood transfusions/injections can reduce or prevent damage due to internal bleeding.	1 in 10,000 males
Huntington disease	Central nervous system deteriorates, producing problems in muscle coordination and mental deterioration.	Does not usually appear until age 35 or older; death likely 10 to 20 years after symptoms appear.	1 in 20,000 births
Phenylketonuria (PKU)	Metabolic disorder that, left untreated, causes mental retardation.	Special diet can result in average intelligence and normal life span.	1 in 10,000 to 1 in 20,000 births
Sickle-cell anemia	Blood disorder that limits the body's oxygen supply; it can cause joint swelling, as well as heart and kidney failure.	Penicillin, medication for pain, antibiotics, and blood transfusions.	1 in 400 African American children (lower among other groups)
Spina bifida	Neural tube disorder that causes brain and spine abnormalities.	Corrective surgery at birth, orthopedic devices, and physical/medical therapy.	2 in 1,000 births
Tay-Sachs disease	Deceleration of mental and physical development caused by an accumulation of lipids in the nervous system.	Medication and special diet are used, but death is likely by 5 years of age.	One in 30 American Jews is a carrier.

FIGURE 3.8 Some Gene-Linked Abnormalities

Dealing with Genetic Abnormalities   Every individual carries DNA variations that might predispose the person to serious physical disease or mental disorder. But not all individuals who carry a genetic disorder display the disorder. Other genes or developmental events sometimes compensate for genetic abnormalities (Gottlieb, 2004; Gottlieb, Wahlsten, & Lickliter, 2006). For example, recall the earlier example of phenylketonuria: Even though individuals might carry the genetic disorder of phenylketonuria, it is not expressed when phenylalanine is replaced by other nutrients in their diet.

Thus, genes are not destiny, but genes that are missing, nonfunctional, or mutated can be associated with disorders. Identifying such genetic flaws could enable doctors to predict an individual's risks, recommend healthy practices, and prescribe the safest and most effective drugs. A decade or two from now, parents of a newborn baby may be able to leave the hospital with a full genome analysis of their offspring that reveals disease risks.

However, this knowledge might bring important costs as well as benefits. Who would have access to a person's genetic profile? An individual's ability to land and hold jobs or obtain insurance might be threatened if it is known that a person is considered at risk for some disease. For example, should an airline pilot or a neurosurgeon who is predisposed to develop a disorder that makes one's hands shake be required to leave that job early?

Genetic counselors, usually physicians or biologists who are well versed in the field of medical genetics, understand the kinds of problems just described, the odds of encountering them, and helpful strategies for offsetting some of their effects (Berkowitz, Roberts, & Minkoff, 2005; Finn & Smoller, 2006; Mayeux, 2005; Watson & others, 2005). To read about the career and work of a genetic counselor, see the Careers in Life-Span Development Profile.

CAREERS in LIFE-SPAN DEVELOPMENT

Holly Ishmael
Genetic Counselor

Holly Ishmael is a genetic counselor at Children's Mercy Hospital in Kansas City. She obtained an undergraduate degree in psychology and then a master's degree in genetic counseling from Sarah Lawrence College.

Genetic counselors, like Holly, work as members of a health-care team, providing information and support to families with birth defects or genetic disorders. They identify families at risk by analyzing inheritance patterns and explore options with the family. Some genetic counselors, like Holly, become specialists in prenatal and pediatric genetics; others might specialize in cancer genetics or psychiatric genetic disorders.

Holly says, "Genetic counseling is a perfect combination for people who want to do something science-oriented, but need human contact and don't want to spend all of their time in a lab or have their nose in a book" (Rizzo, 1999, p. 3).

Genetic counselors have specialized graduate degrees in the areas of medical genetics and counseling. They enter graduate school with undergraduate backgrounds from a variety of disciplines, including biology, genetics, psychology, public health, and social work. There are approximately thirty graduate genetic counseling programs in the United States. If you are interested in this profession, you can obtain further information from the National Society of Genetic Counselors at www.nsgc.org.

Holly Ishmael (*left*) in a genetic counseling session.

Review and Reflect • LEARNING GOAL 2

2 Describe What Genes Are and How They Influence Human Development

Review
• What are genes?
• How are genes passed on?
• What basic principles describe how genes interact?
• What are some chromosome and gene-linked abnormalities?

Reflect
• What are some possible ethical issues regarding genetics and development that might arise in the future?

---

3 SOME REPRODUCTIVE CHALLENGES AND CHOICES

| Prenatal Diagnostic Tests | Infertility and Reproductive Technology | Adoption |

The facts and principles we have discussed regarding meiosis, genetics, and genetic abnormalities are a small part of the recent explosion of knowledge about human biology. This knowledge not only helps us understand human development but also opens up many new choices to prospective parents, choices that can also raise ethical questions.

Prenatal Diagnostic Tests

One choice open to prospective mothers is the extent to which they should undergo prenatal testing. A number of tests can indicate whether a fetus is developing normally, including ultrasound sonography, chorionic villi sampling, amniocentesis, and maternal blood screening (Allen, Wilson, & Cheung, 2006).

An ultrasound test is often conducted 7 weeks into a pregnancy and at various times later in pregnancy. *Ultrasound sonography* is a prenatal medical procedure in which high-frequency sound waves are directed into the pregnant woman's abdomen. The echo from the sounds is transformed into a visual representation of the fetus's inner structures. This technique can detect many structural abnormalities in the fetus, including microencephaly, a form of mental retardation involving an abnormally small brain; it can also determine the number of fetuses and give clues to the baby's sex (Letterie, 2005; McHugh, Kiely, & Spitz, 2006).

At some point between the 10th and 12th weeks of pregnancy, chorionic villi sampling may be used to detect genetic defects and chromosome abnormalities (Csaba, Bush, & Saphier, 2006; Evans & Wapner, 2005). *Chorionic villi sampling* is a prenatal medical procedure in which a small sample of the placenta (the vascular organ that links the fetus to the mother's uterus) is removed. Diagnosis takes about 10 days.

Between the 15th and 18th weeks of pregnancy, amniocentesis may be performed. *Amniocentesis* is a prenatal medical procedure in which a sample of amniotic fluid is withdrawn by syringe and tested for chromosome or metabolic disorders (Ramsey & others, 2004). The amniotic fluid is found within the amnion, a thin sac in which the embryo is suspended. Ultrasound sonography is often used during amniocentesis so that the syringe can be placed precisely. The later amniocentesis is performed, the better its diagnostic potential. The earlier it is performed, the more useful it is in deciding how to handle a pregnancy (Pinette & others, 2004). It may take two weeks for enough cells to grow and amniocentesis test results to be obtained.

Both amniocentesis and chorionic villi sampling provide valuable information about the presence of birth defects, but they also raise difficult issues for parents about whether an abortion should be obtained if birth defects are present (Li & others, 2006; Papp & Papp, 2003). Chorionic villi sampling allows a decision to made sooner, near the end of the first 12 weeks of pregnancy, when abortion is safer and less traumatic than later, but chorionic villi sampling carries greater risks than amniocentesis. Amniocentesis brings a small risk of miscarriage: about 1 woman in every 200 to 300 miscarries after amniocentesis. Chorionic villi sampling brings a slightly higher risk of miscarriage than amniocentesis and is linked with a slight risk of limb deformities.

During the 16th to 18th weeks of pregnancy, maternal blood screening may be performed. *Maternal blood screening* identifies pregnancies that have an elevated risk for birth defects such as spina bifida (a typically fatal defect in the spinal cord) and Down syndrome (Echevarria & Avellon, 2006; Nicolaides, 2005). The current blood test is called the *triple screen* because it measures three substances in the mother's blood. After an abnormal triple screen result, the next step is usually an ultrasound examination. If an ultrasound does not explain the abnormal triple screen results, amniocentesis is typically used.

Infertility and Reproductive Technology

Recent advances in biological knowledge have also opened up many choices for infertile people. Approximately 10 to 15 percent of couples in the United States experience infertility, which is defined as the inability to conceive a child after 12 months of regular intercourse without contraception. The cause of infertility can rest with the

A 6-month-old infant poses with the ultrasound sonography record taken four months into the baby's prenatal development. *What is ultrasound sonography?*

woman or the man (Amin & others, 2006). The woman may not be ovulating (releasing eggs to be fertilized), she may be producing abnormal ova, her fallopian tubes by which ova normally reach the womb may be blocked, or she may have a disease that prevents implantation of the embryo into the uterus. The man may produce too few sperm, the sperm may lack motility (the ability to move adequately), or he may have a blocked passageway (Heshmat & Lo, 2006; Kumar & others, 2006).

In the United States, more than 2 million couples seek help for infertility every year. In some cases of infertility, surgery may correct the cause; in others, hormone-based drugs may improve the probability of having a child. Of the 2 million couples who seek help for infertility every year, about 40,000 try high-tech assisted reproduction. The three most common techniques are:

- *In vitro fertilization (IVF)*. Eggs and sperm are combined in a laboratory dish. If any eggs are successfully fertilized, one or more of the resulting fertilized eggs are transferred into the woman's uterus.
- *Gamete intrafallopian transfer (GIFT)*. A doctor inserts eggs and sperm directly into a woman's fallopian tube.
- *Zygote intrafallopian transfer (ZIFT)*. This is a two-step procedure. First, eggs are fertilized in the laboratory; then, any resulting fertilized eggs are transferred to a fallopian tube.

A national study in the United States in 2000 by the Centers for Disease Control and Prevention found that IVF is by far the most frequently used technique used (98 percent of all cases in the study) and had the highest success rate (slightly more than 30 percent).

The creation of families by means of the new reproductive technologies raises important questions about the physical and psychological consequences for children (Ito & others, 2006; McDonald & others, 2005; Merlob & others, 2005; Rao & Tan, 2005). One result of fertility treatments is an increase in multiple births (El-Toukhy, Khalaf, & Braude, 2006; Evans & Britt, 2005). Twenty-five to 30 percent of pregnancies achieved by fertility treatments—including in vitro fertilization—now result in multiple births. Any multiple birth increases the likelihood that the babies will have life-threatening and costly problems, such as extremely low birth weight. However, a recent review of 169 studies on IVF babies found that IVF twins do not show greater risks for premature birth, death within a week of birth, or low birth weight than twins not conceived through IVF (Hampton, 2004). The review also revealed no serious physical malformation rates among IVF babies. However, IVF singleton babies were approximately twice as likely to be born prematurely and to die within a week of birth, and almost three times as likely to be low in birth weight compared to singletons not conceived through IVF.

Not nearly as many studies have examined the psychological outcomes of IVF as the physical outcomes. To read about a recent study that addresses these consequences, see the Research in Life-Span Development interlude that follows.

RESEARCH IN LIFE-SPAN DEVELOPMENT

In Vitro Fertilization and Developmental Outcomes in Adolescence

A longitudinal study examined 34 in vitro fertilization families, 49 adoptive families, and 38 families with a naturally conceived child (Golombok, MacCallum, & Goodman, 2001). Each type of family included a similar portion of boys and girls. Also, the age of the young adolescents did not differ according to family type (mean age of 11 years, 11 months).

Children's socioemotional development was assessed by (1) interviewing the mother and obtaining detailed descriptions of any problems the child might have, (2) administering a Strengths and Difficulties questionnaire to the child's mother and teacher, and (3) administering the Social Adjustment Inventory for Children and Adolescents, which examines functioning in school, peer relationships, and self-esteem.

No significant differences between the children from the in vitro fertilization, adoptive, and naturally conceiving families were found. The results from the Social Adjustment Inventory for Children and Adolescents are shown in figure 3.9. Another study also revealed no psychological differences between IVF babies and those not conceived by IVF, but more research is needed to reach firm conclusions in this area (Hahn & Dipietro, 2001).

FIGURE 3.9 Socioemotional Functioning of Children Conceived Through In Vitro Fertilization or Naturally Conceived. This graph shows the results of a study that compared the socioemotional functioning of young adolescents who had either been conceived through in vitro fertilization (IVF) or naturally conceived (Golombok, MacCallum, & Goodman, 2001). For each type of family, the study included a similar portion of boys and girls and children of similar age (mean age of 11 years, 11 months). Although the means for the naturally conceived group were slightly higher, this is likely due to chance: there were no significant differences between the groups.

Adoption

Although surgery and fertility drugs can sometimes solve the infertility problem, another choice is to adopt a child (Grotevant, 2006; Grotevant & others, 2006; Maynard, 2005; Miller, 2005). Adoption is the social and legal process by which a parent-child relationship is established between persons unrelated at birth. As we see next in the Diversity in Life-Span Development interlude, an increase in diversity has characterized the adoption of children in the United States in recent years.

DIVERSITY IN LIFE-SPAN DEVELOPMENT

The Increased Diversity of Adopted Children and Adoptive Parents

Several changes occurred during the last several decades of the twentieth century in the characteristics both of adopted children and of adoptive parents (Brodzinsky & Pinderhughes, 2002, pp. 280–282). Until the 1960s, most U.S. adopted children were healthy, European American infants, who were adopted within a few days or weeks after birth. However, in recent decades, an increasing number of unmarried U.S. mothers decided to keep their babies, and the number of unwanted births decreased as contraception became readily available and abortion was legalized. As a result, the number of healthy European American infants available for adoption dropped dramatically. Increasingly, U.S. couples adopted children who were not European Americans, children from other countries, and children in foster care whose characteristics—such as age, minority status, exposure to neglect or abuse, or physical or mental health problems—"were once thought to be barriers to adoption" (p. 281).

Changes also have characterized adoptive parents. Until the last several decades of the twentieth century, most adoptive parents had a middle- or upper-socioeconomic status and were "married, infertile, European American couples, usually in their 30s and 40s, and free of any disability. Adoption agencies *screened out* couples who did not have these characteristics" (p. 281). Today, however, many adoption agencies *screen in* as many applicants as possible and have no income requirements for adoptive parents. Many agencies now permit single adults, older adults, and gay and lesbian adults to adopt children (Rampage & others, 2003; Ryan, Pearlmutter, & Groza, 2004).

What changes in adopted children and adoptive parents have taken place in the last several decades?

(continued on next page)

Do these changes matter? They open opportunities for many children and many couples, but possible effects of changes in the characteristics of parents on the outcomes for children are still unknown. For example, in one study, adopted adolescents were more likely to have problems if the adopted parents had low levels of education (Miller & others, 2000). In another study, international adoptees showed fewer behavior problems and were less likely to be using mental health services than domestic adoptees (Juffer & van IJzendoorn, 2005). More research is needed before definitive conclusions can be reached about the changing demographic characteristics of adoption.

The changes in adoption practice over the last several decades make it difficult to generalize about the average adopted child or average adopted parent. As we see next, though, some researchers have provided useful comparisons between adopted children and nonadopted children and their families.

How do adopted children fare after they are adopted? Children who are adopted very early in their lives are more likely to have positive outcomes than children adopted later in life. In one study, the later adoption occurred, the more problems the adoptees had. Infant adoptees had the fewest adjustment difficulties; those adopted after they were 10 years of age had the most problems (Sharma, McGue, & Benson, 1996).

In general, adopted children and adolescents are more likely to experience psychological and school-related problems than nonadopted children (Brodzinsky & others, 1984; Brodzinksy, Lang, & Smith, 1995; Brodzinsky & Pinderhughes, 2002). For example, a recent meta-analysis (a statistical procedure that combines the results of a number of studies) revealed that adoptees were far more likely to be using mental health services than their nonadopted counterparts (Juffer & van IJzendoorn, 2005). Adopted children also showed more behavior problems than nonadoptees, but this difference was small.

Research that contrasts adopted and nonadopted adolescents has also found positive characteristics among the adopted adolescents. For example, in one study, although adopted adolescents were more likely than nonadopted adolescents to use illicit drugs and to engage in delinquent behavior, the adopted adolescents were also less likely to be withdrawn and engaged in more prosocial behavior, such as being altruistic, caring, and supportive of others (Sharma, McGue, & Benson, 1998).

Do adopted children show differences in cognitive development as well? A recent meta-analysis of 62 studies involving almost 18,000 adopted children showed that the cognitive development of adopted children differed from that of both (1) children who remained in institutional care or in the birth family and (2) their current nonadopted siblings or peers in their current environment (van IJzendoorn, Juffer, & Poelhuis, 2005). In this meta-analysis, the adopted children scored higher on IQ tests and performed better in school than the children who stayed behind in institutions or their birth families. The IQ of adopted children did not differ from that of nonadopted peers or siblings in their current environment, but their school performance and language abilities were at lower levels, and they were more likely to have learning difficulties. Overall, the meta-analysis documented the positive influence of adoption on children's cognitive development and the normal intellectual ability of adopted children, but a lower level of performance in school.

In short, the vast majority of adopted children (including those adopted at older ages, transracially, and across national borders) adjust effectively, and their parents report considerable satisfaction with their decision to adopt (Brodzinsky & Pinderhughes, 2002). Furthermore, adopted children fare much better than children in long-term foster care or in an institutional environment (Brodzinsky & Pinderhughes, 2002). To read more about adoption, see the Applications in Life-Span Development interlude in which we discuss effective parenting strategies with adopted children.

APPLICATIONS IN LIFE-SPAN DEVELOPMENT

Parenting Adopted Children

Many of the keys to effectively parenting adopted children are no different than those for effectively parenting biological children: Be supportive and caring, be involved and monitor the child's behavior and whereabouts, be a good communicator, and help the child learn to develop self-control. However, parents of adopted children face some unique circumstances. These need to recognize the differences involved in adoptive family life, communicate about these differences, show respect for the birth family, and support the child's search for self and identity.

David Brodzinsky and Ellen Pinderhughes (2002, pp. 288–292) recently discussed how to handle some of the challenges that parents face when their adopted children are at different points in development:

- *Infancy.* Researchers have found few differences in the attachment that adopted and nonadopted infants form with their parents, but attachment can be compromised "when parents have difficulty in claiming the child as their own either because of unresolved fertility issues, lack of support from family and friends, and/or when their expectations about the child have not been met" (p. 288). Competent adoption agencies or counselors can help prospective adoptive parents develop realistic expectations.
- *Early Childhood.* Because many children begin to ask where they came from when they are about 4 to 6 years old, this is a natural time to begin to talk in simple ways to children about their adoption status (Warshak, 2004). Some parents (although not as many as in the past) decide not to tell their children about the adoption. This secrecy may create psychological risks for the child if he or she later finds out about the adoption.
- *Middle and Late Childhood.* During the elementary school years, children begin to express "much more curiosity about their origins: *Where did I come from? What did my birthmother and birthfather look like? Why didn't they keep me? Where are they now? Can I meet them?*" (p. 290). As they grow older, children may become more ambivalent about being adopted and question their adoptive parents' explanations. It is important for adoptive parents to recognize that this ambivalence is normal. Also, problems may come from the desire of adoptive parents to make life too perfect for the adoptive child and to present a perfect image of themselves to the child. The result too often is that adopted children feel that they cannot release any angry feelings and openly discuss problems (Warshak, 2004).
- *Adolescence.* Adolescents are likely to develop more abstract and logical thinking, to focus their attention on their bodies, and to search for an identity. These characteristics provide the foundation for adopted adolescents to reflect on their adoption status in more complex ways, to become "preoccupied with the lack of physical resemblance between themselves and others in the family" (p. 291), and to explore how the fact that they were adopted fits into their identity. Adoptive parents "need to be aware of these many complexities and provide teenagers with the support they need to cope with these adoption-related tasks" (p. 292).

Review and Reflect • **LEARNING GOAL 3**

③ Identify Some Important Reproductive Challenges and Choices

Review
- What are some common prenatal diagnostic tests?
- What are some techniques that help infertile people to have children?
- How does adoption affect children's development?

Reflect
- We discussed a number of studies indicating that adoption is linked with negative outcomes for children. Does that mean that all adopted children have more negative outcomes than all nonadopted children? Explain.

4 HEREDITY AND ENVIRONMENT INTERACTION: THE NATURE-NURTURE DEBATE

Behavior Genetics

Shared and Nonshared Environmental Experiences

Conclusions About Heredity-Environment Interaction

Heredity-Environment Correlations

The Epigenetic View

In each section of this chapter so far we have examined parts of the nature-nurture debate. We have seen how the environment exerts selective pressures on the characteristics of species over generations, examined how genes are passed from parents to children, and discussed how reproductive technologies and adoption influence the course of children's lives. But in all of these situations, heredity and environment interact to produce development. After all, Jim and Jim (and each of the other pairs of identical twins discussed in the opening of the chapter) have the same genotype, but they are not the same person; each is unique. What made them different? Whether we are studying how genes produce proteins, their influence on how tall a person is, or how PKU might affect an individual, we end up discussing heredity-environment interactions.

Is it possible to untangle the influence of heredity from that of environment and discover the role of each in producing individual differences in development? When heredity and environment interact, how does heredity influence the environment, and vice versa?

Behavior Genetics
Twin Research

Behavior Genetics

Behavior genetics is the field that seeks to discover the influence of heredity and environment on individual differences in human traits and development (Bishop & others, 2006; Deater-Deckard & others, 2005; Knafo, Iervolino, & Plomin, 2005; Vogler, 2006). Note that behavior genetics does not determine the extent to which genetics or the environment affects an individual's traits. Instead, what behavior geneticists try to do is to figure out what is responsible for the differences among people—that is, to what extent do people differ because of differences in genes, environment, or a combination of these? To study the influence of heredity on behavior, behavior geneticists often use either twins or adoption situations.

behavior genetics The field that seeks to discover the influence of heredity and environment on individual differences in human traits and development.

Heredity-Environment Correlation	Description	Examples
Passive	Children inherit genetic tendencies from their parents, and parents also provide an environment that matches their own genetic tendencies.	Musically inclined parents usually have musically inclined children and they are likely to provide an environment rich in music for their children.
Evocative	The child's genetic tendencies elicit stimulation from the environment that supports a particular trait. Thus genes evoke environmental support.	A happy, outgoing child elicits smiles and friendly responses from others.
Active (niche-picking)	Children actively seek out "niches" in their environment that reflect their own interests and talents and are thus in accord with their genotype.	Libraries, sports fields, and a store with musical instruments are examples of environmental niches children might seek out if they have intellectual interests in books, talent in sports, or musical talents, respectively.

FIGURE 3.10 Exploring Heredity-Environment Correlations

In the most common **twin study,** the behavioral similarity of identical twins (who are genetically identical) is compared with the behavioral similarity of fraternal twins. Recall that although fraternal twins share the same womb, they are no more genetically alike than brothers or sisters who did not. Thus, by comparing groups of identical and fraternal twins, behavior geneticists capitalize on the basic knowledge that identical twins are more similar genetically than are fraternal twins (Bulik & others, 2006; Mackintosh & others, 2006). For example, a recent study found that conduct problems were more prevalent in identical twins than fraternal twins; the researchers concluded that the study demonstrated an important role for heredity in conduct problems (Scourfield & others, 2004).

However, several issues complicate interpretation of twin studies (Vogler, 2006). For example, perhaps the environments of identical twins are more similar than the environments of fraternal twins. Adults might stress the similarities of identical twins more than those of fraternal twins, and identical twins might perceive themselves as a "set" and play together more than fraternal twins do. If so, the influence of the environment on the observed similarities between identical and fraternal twins might be very significant.

In an **adoption study,** investigators seek to discover whether the behavior and psychological characteristics of adopted children are more like those of their adoptive parents, who have provided a home environment, or more like those of their biological parents, who have contributed their heredity (Haugaard & Hazen, 2004). Another form of the adoption study compares adoptive and biological siblings.

Twin studies compare identical twins with fraternal twins. Identical twins develop from a single fertilized egg that splits into two genetically identical organisms. Fraternal twins develop from separate eggs, making them genetically no more similar than nontwin siblings. *What is the nature of the twin study method?*

Heredity-Environment Correlations

The difficulties that researchers encounter when they interpret the results of twin studies and adoption studies reflect the complexities of heredity-environment interaction. Some of these interactions are *heredity-environment correlations,* which means that individuals' genes may influence the types of environments to which they are exposed. In a sense, individuals "inherit" environments that may be related or linked to genetic "propensities" (Plomin & others, 2003). Behavior geneticist Sandra Scarr (1993) described three ways that heredity and environment are correlated (see figure 3.10):

- **Passive genotype-environment correlations** occur because biological parents, who are genetically related to the child, provide a rearing environment for the child. For example, the parents might have a genetic predisposition to

twin study A study in which the behavioral similarity of identical twins is compared with the behavioral similarity of fraternal twins.

adoption study A study in which investigators seek to discover whether the behavior and psychological characteristics of adopted children are more like their adoptive parents, who provided a home environment, or more like their biological parents, who contributed their heredity. Another form of the adoption study is to compare adoptive and biological siblings.

passive genotype-environment correlations Correlations that exist when the natural parents, who are genetically related to the child, provide a rearing environment for the child.

be intelligent and read skillfully. Because they read well and enjoy reading, they provide their children with books to read. The likely outcome is that their children, given their own inherited predispositions from their parents and their book-filled environment, will become skilled readers.

- **Evocative genotype-environment correlations** occur because a child's characteristics elicit certain types of environments. For example, active, smiling children receive more social stimulation than passive, quiet children do. Cooperative, attentive children evoke more pleasant and instructional responses from the adults around them than uncooperative, distractible children do.

- **Active (niche-picking) genotype-environment correlations** occur when children seek out environments that they find compatible and stimulating. *Niche-picking* refers to finding a setting that is suited to one's abilities. Children select from their surrounding environment some aspect that they respond to, learn about, or ignore. Their active selections of environments are related to their particular genotype. For example, outgoing children tend to seek out social contexts in which to interact with people, whereas shy children don't. Children who are musically inclined are likely to select musical environments in which they can successfully perform their skills. How these "tendencies" come about will be discussed shortly under the topic of the epigenetic view.

Scarr believes that the relative importance of the three genotype-environment correlations changes as children develop from infancy through adolescence. In infancy, much of the environment that children experience is provided by adults. Thus, passive genotype-environment correlations are more common in the lives of infants and young children than they are for older children and adolescents who can extend their experiences beyond the family's influence and create their environments to a greater degree.

Notice that this analysis gives the preeminent role in development to heredity: the analysis describes how heredity may influence the types of environments that children experience. Critics argue that the concept of heredity-environment correlation gives heredity too much of a one-sided influence in determining development because it does not consider the role of prior environmental influences in shaping the correlation itself (Gottlieb, 2003, 2004; Gottlieb, Wahlsten, & Lickliter, 2006). Before considering this criticism and a different view of the heredity-environment linkage, let's take a closer look at how behavior geneticists analyze the environments involved in heredity.

Shared and Nonshared Environmental Experiences

Behavior geneticists have argued that to understand the environment's role in differences between people, we should distinguish between shared and nonshared environments. That is, we should consider experiences that children share in common with other children living in the same home, and experiences that are not shared (Feinberg & Hetherington, 2001; Gatz & others, 2006; Gelhorn & others, 2006; Tholin & others, 2005).

Shared environmental experiences are siblings' common experiences, such as their parents' personalities or intellectual orientation, the family's socioeconomic status, and the neighborhood in which they live. By contrast, **nonshared environmental experiences** are a child's unique experiences, both within the family and outside the family, that are not shared with a sibling. Even experiences occurring within the family can be part of the "nonshared environment." For example, parents often interact differently with each sibling, and siblings interact differently with parents (Hetherington, Reiss, & Plomin, 1994). Siblings often have different peer groups, different friends, and different teachers at school.

evocative genotype-environment correlations Correlations that exist when the child's genotype elicits certain types of physical and social environments.

active (niche-picking) genotype-environment correlations Correlations that exist when children seek out environments they find compatible and stimulating.

shared environmental experiences Siblings' common environmental experiences, such as their parents' personalities and intellectual orientation, the family's socioeconomic status, and the neighborhood in which they live.

nonshared environmental experiences The child's own unique experiences, both within the family and outside the family, that are not shared by another sibling. Thus, experiences occurring within the family can be part of the "nonshared environment."

Behavior geneticist Robert Plomin (1993) has found that shared environment accounts for little of the variation in children's personality or interests. In other words, even though two children live under the same roof with the same parents, their personalities are often very different. Further, Plomin argues that heredity influences the nonshared environments of siblings through the heredity-environment correlations we described earlier (Plomin & others, 2003). For example, a child who has inherited a genetic tendency to be athletic is likely to spend more time in environments related to sports, while a child who has inherited a tendency to be musically inclined is more likely to spend time in environments related to music.

What are the implications of Plomin's interpretation of the role of shared and nonshared environments in development? In the *Nurture Assumption,* Judith Harris (1998) argued that what parents do does not make a difference in their children's and adolescents' behavior. Yell at them. Hug them. Read to them. Ignore them. Harris says it won't influence how they turn out. She argues that genes and peers are far more important than parents in children's and adolescents' development.

Genes and peers do matter, but Harris' descriptions of peer influences do not take into account the complexity of peer contexts and developmental trajectories (Hartup, 1999). In addition, Harris is wrong in saying that parents don't matter. For example, in the early child years parents play an important role in selecting children's peers and indirectly influencing children's development (Baumrind, 1999). A huge parenting literature with many research studies documents the importance of parents in children's development (Collins & others, 2000, 2001; Maccoby, 2002). We will discuss parents' important roles throughout this book.

The Epigenetic View

Does the concept of heredity-environment correlation downplay the importance of environment in our development? The concept emphasizes how heredity directs the kind of environmental experiences individuals have. However, earlier in the chapter we discussed how genes are collaborative, not determining an individual's traits in an independent manner, but rather in an interactive manner with the environment. In line with the concept of a collaborative gene, Gilbert Gottlieb (1998, 2003, 2004; Gottlieb, Wahlsten, & Lickliter, 2006) emphasizes the **epigenetic view,** which states that development is the result of an ongoing, bidirectional interchange between heredity and the environment. Figure 3.11 compares the heredity-environment correlation and epigenetic views of development.

Let's look at an example that reflects the epigenetic view. A baby inherits genes from both parents at conception. During prenatal development, toxins, nutrition, and stress can influence some genes to stop functioning while others become stronger or weaker. During infancy, environmental experiences such as toxins, nutrition, stress, learning, and encouragement continue to modify genetic activity and the activity of the nervous system that directly underlies behavior (Gottlieb, 2005). Heredity and environment operate together—or collaborate—to produce a person's intelligence, temperament, height, weight, ability to pitch a baseball, ability to read, and so on (Gottlieb, Wahlsten, & Lickliter, 1998, 2006; Moore, 2001).

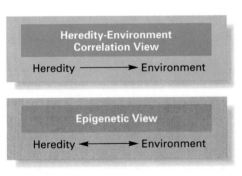

FIGURE 3.11 Comparison of the Heredity-Environment Correlation and Epigenetic Views

Conclusions About Heredity-Environment Interaction

If an attractive, popular, intelligent girl is elected president of her senior class in high school, is her success due to heredity or to environment? Of course, the answer is both.

epigenetic view Emphasizes that development is the result of an ongoing, bidirectional interchange between heredity and environment.

The interaction of heredity and environment is so extensive that to ask which is more important, nature or nurture, is like asking which is more important to a rectangle, height or width.

—WILLIAM GREENOUGH
*Contemporary Developmental Psychologist,
University of Illinois at Urbana*

The relative contributions of heredity and environment are not additive. That is, we can't say that such-and-such a percentage of nature and such-and-such a percentage of experience make us who we are. Nor is it accurate to say that full genetic expression happens once, around conception or birth, after which we carry our genetic legacy into the world to see how far it takes us. Genes produce proteins throughout the life span, in many different environments. Or they don't produce these proteins, depending in part on how harsh or nourishing those environments are.

The emerging view is that complex behaviors have some *genetic loading* that gives people a propensity for a particular developmental trajectory (Plomin & others, 2003; Walker, Petrill, & Plomin, 2005). However, the actual development requires more: an environment. And that environment is complex, just like the mixture of genes we inherit (Bronfenbrenner & Morris, 2006; Parke & Buriel, 2006; Scheidt & Windley, 2006; Spencer, 2006). Environmental influences range from the things we lump together under "nurture" (such as parenting, family dynamics, schooling, and neighborhood quality) to biological encounters (such as viruses, birth complications, and even biological events in cells) (Greenough, 1997, 1999; Greenough & others, 2001).

Imagine for a moment that there is a cluster of genes somehow associated with youth violence. (This example is hypothetical because we don't know of any such combination.) The adolescent who carries this genetic mixture might experience a world of loving parents, regular nutritious meals, lots of books, and a series of masterful teachers. Or the adolescent's world might include parental neglect, a neighborhood in which gunshots and crime are everyday occurrences, and inadequate schooling. In which of these environments are the adolescent's genes likely to manufacture the biological underpinnings of criminality?

Review and Reflect • LEARNING GOAL 3

3 **Characterize Some of the Ways that Heredity and Environment Interact to Produce Individual Differences in Development**

Review

- What is behavior genetics?
- What are three types of heredity-environment correlations and what is an example of each?
- What is meant by the concepts of shared and nonshared environmental experiences?
- What is the epigenetic view of development?
- What conclusions can be reached about heredity-environment interaction?

Reflect

- A friend tells you that he or she has analyzed his or her genetic background and environmental experiences and reached the conclusion that environment definitely has had little influence on his or her intelligence. What would you say to this person about his or her ability to make this self-diagnosis?

REACH YOUR LEARNING GOALS

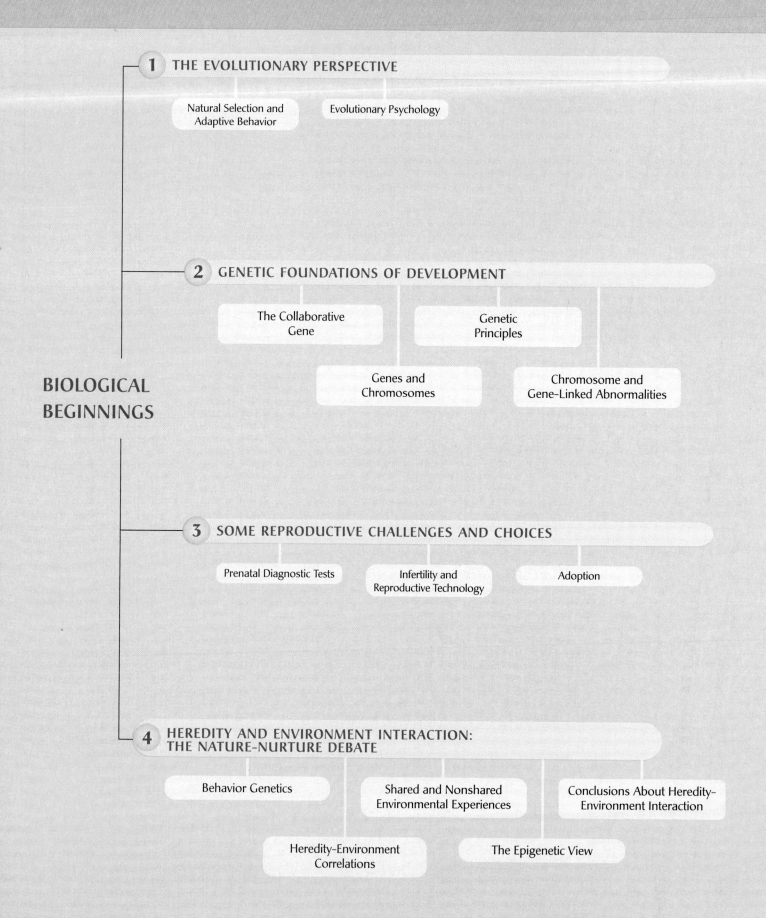

BIOLOGICAL BEGINNINGS

1 THE EVOLUTIONARY PERSPECTIVE

Natural Selection and Adaptive Behavior

Evolutionary Psychology

2 GENETIC FOUNDATIONS OF DEVELOPMENT

The Collaborative Gene

Genetic Principles

Genes and Chromosomes

Chromosome and Gene-Linked Abnormalities

3 SOME REPRODUCTIVE CHALLENGES AND CHOICES

Prenatal Diagnostic Tests

Infertility and Reproductive Technology

Adoption

4 HEREDITY AND ENVIRONMENT INTERACTION: THE NATURE-NURTURE DEBATE

Behavior Genetics

Shared and Nonshared Environmental Experiences

Conclusions About Heredity-Environment Interaction

Heredity-Environment Correlations

The Epigenetic View

SUMMARY

1 The Evolutionary Perspective: *Discuss the evolutionary perspective on development*

Natural Selection and Adaptive Behavior
Natural selection is the process by which those individuals of a species that are best adapted survive and reproduce. Darwin proposed that natural selection fuels evolution. In evolutionary theory, adaptive behavior is behavior that promotes the organism's survival in a natural habitat.

Evolutionary Psychology
Evolutionary psychology holds that adaptation, reproduction, and "survival of the fittest" are important in shaping behavior. Ideas proposed by evolutionary developmental psychology include the view that an extended "juvenile" period is needed to develop a large brain and learn the complexity of human social communities. According to Baltes, the benefits resulting from evolutionary selection decrease with age mainly because of a decline in reproductive fitness. At the same time, cultural needs increase. Like other theoretical approaches to development, evolutionary psychology has limitations. Bandura rejects "one-sided evolutionism" and argues for a bidirectional link between biology and environment. Biology allows for a broad range of cultural possibilities.

2 Genetic Foundations of Development: *Describe what genes are and how they influence human development*

The Collaborative Gene
Except in the sperm and egg, the nucleus of each human cell contains 46 chromosomes, which are composed of DNA. Short segments of DNA constitute genes, the units of hereditary information that direct cells to reproduce and manufacture proteins. Genes act collaboratively, not independently.

Genes and Chromosomes
Genes are passed on to new cells when chromosomes are duplicated during the process of mitosis and meiosis, which are two ways in which new cells are formed. When an egg and a sperm unite in the fertilization process, the resulting zygote contains the genes from the chromosomes in the father's sperm and the mother's egg. Despite this transmission of genes from generation to generation, variability is created in several ways, including the exchange of chromosomal segments during meiosis, mutations, and the distinction between a genotype and a phenotype.

Genetic Principles
Genetic principles include those involving dominant-recessive genes, sex-linked genes, genetic imprinting, and polygenic inheritance.

Chromosome and Gene-Linked Abnormalities
Chromosome abnormalities produce Down syndrome, which is caused by the presence of an extra copy of chromosome 21, as well as sex-linked chromosomal abnormalities such as Klinefelter syndrome, fragile X syndrome, Turner syndrome, and XYY syndrome. Gene-linked abnormalities involve harmful genes. Gene-linked disorders include phenylketonuria (PKU) and sickle-cell anemia. Genetic counseling offers couples information about their risk of having a child with inherited abnormalities.

3 Some Reproductive Challenges and Choices: *Identify reproductive challenges and choices*

Prenatal Diagnostic Tests
Amniocentesis, ultrasound sonography, chorionic villi sampling, and maternal blood screening are used to determine whether a fetus is developing normally.

Infertility and Reproductive Technology
Approximately 10 to 15 percent of U.S. couples have infertility problems, some of which can be corrected through surgery or fertility drugs. Additional options include in vitro fertilization and other more recently developed techniques.

Adoption
Although adopted children and adolescents have more problems than their nonadopted counterparts, the vast majority of adopted children adapt effectively. When adoption occurs very early in development, the outcomes for the child are improved. Because of the dramatic changes that occurred in adoption in recent decades, it is difficult to generalize about the average adopted child or average adoptive family.

4 Heredity and Environment Interaction: The Nature-Nurture Debate: *Characterize how heredity and environment interact to produce individual differences in development*

Behavior Genetics
Behavior genetics is the field concerned with the degree and nature of behavior's hereditary basis. Methods used by behavior geneticists include twin studies and adoption studies.

Heredity-Environment Correlations
In Scarr's heredity-environment correlations view, heredity directs the types of environments that children experience. She describes three genotype-environment correlations: passive, evocative, and active (niche-picking). Scarr believes that the relative importance of these three genotype-environment correlations changes as children develop.

Shared and Nonshared Environmental Influences

Shared environmental experiences refer to siblings' common experiences, such as their parents' personalities and intellectual orientation, the family's socioeconomic status, and the neighborhood in which they live. Nonshared environmental experiences involve the child's unique experiences, both within a family and outside a family, that are not shared with a sibling. Many behavior geneticists argue that differences in the development of siblings are due to nonshared environmental experiences (and heredity) rather than shared environmental experiences.

The Epigenetic View

The epigenetic view emphasizes that development is the result of an ongoing, bidirectional interchange between heredity and environment.

Conclusions About Heredity-Environment Interaction

Complex behaviors have some genetic loading that gives people a propensity for a particular developmental trajectory. However, actual development also requires an environment, and that environment is complex. The interaction of heredity and environment is extensive. Much remains to be discovered about the specific ways that heredity and environment interact to influence development.

KEY TERMS

evolutionary psychology 74
chromosomes 77
DNA 77
genes 77
mitosis 78
meiosis 78
fertilization 78
zygote 78
genotype 79

phenotype 79
Down syndrome 81
Klinefelter syndrome 81
fragile X syndrome 81
Turner syndrome 82
XYY syndrome 82
phenylketonuria (PKU) 82
sickle-cell anemia 82

behavior genetics 90
twin study 91
adoption study 91
passive genotype-environment correlations 91
evocative genotype-environment correlations 92

active (niche-picking) genotype-environment correlations 92
shared environmental experiences 92
nonshared environmental experiences 92
epigenetic view 93

KEY PEOPLE

Thomas Bouchard 72
Charles Darwin 73
David Buss 74

Paul Baltes 75
Albert Bandura 76
Steven Jay Gould 76

David Moore 77
Sandra Scarr 91
Robert Plomin 93

Judith Harris 93
Gilbert Gottlieb 93

E-LEARNING TOOLS

To help you master the material in this chapter, you'll find a number of valuable study tools on the Student CD-ROM that accompanies this book. In addition, visit the Online Learning Center for *Life-Span Development*, eleventh edition, where you'll find these valuable resources and exercises for chapter 3, "Biological Beginnings."

Self-Assessment

Learn more about how genetic screening is done by reviewing the sample assessment, Prenatal Genetic Screening Questionnaire. Then try your hand at developing a family health tree by completing the self-assessment, *My Family Health Tree*.

Taking It to the Net

1. Ahmahl, a biochemistry major, is writing a psychology paper on the potential dilemmas that society and scientists may face as a result of the decoding of the human genome. What are some of the main issues or concerns that Ahmahl should address in his class paper?
2. Brandon and Katie are thrilled to learn that they are expecting their first child. They are curious about the genetic makeup of their unborn child and want to know (a) what disorders might be identified through prenatal genetic testing, and (b) which tests, if any, Katie should undergo to help determine this information?
3. Greg and Courtney have three boys. They would love to have a girl. Courtney read that there is a clinic in Virginia where you can pick the sex of your child. How successful are such efforts? Would you want to have this choice available to you?

Video Clips

View video clips of key researchers, including David Buss as he discusses the importance of evolutionary psychology.

Health and Well-Being, Parenting, and Education Exercises

Build your decision-making skills by trying your hand at the health and well-being, parenting and education exercises.

Connect to **www.mhhe.com/santrockld11** to research the answers and complete these exercises.

Chapter 4

PRENATAL DEVELOPMENT AND BIRTH

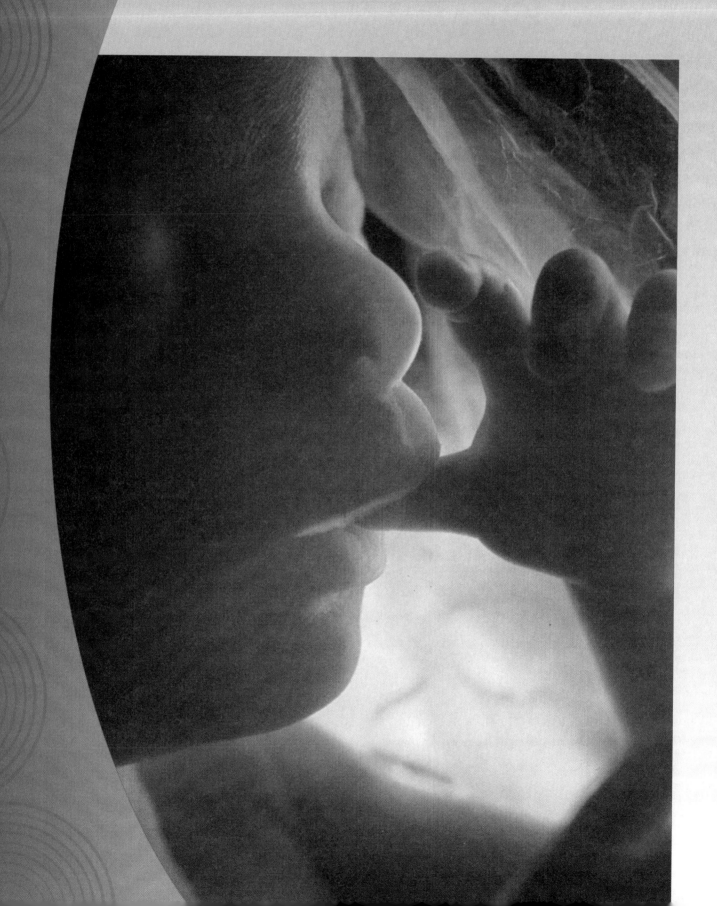

There was a star danced, and under that I was born.

—WILLIAM SHAKESPEARE
English Playwright, 17th Century

CHAPTER OUTLINE

LEARNING GOALS

PRENATAL DEVELOPMENT

The Course of Prenatal Development
Hazards to Prenatal Development
Prenatal Care

1 Describe prenatal development

BIRTH

The Birth Process
Assessing the Newborn
Low Birth Weight and Preterm Infants

2 Discuss the birth process

THE POSTPARTUM PERIOD

Physical Adjustments
Emotional and Psychological Adjustments
Bonding

3 Explain the changes that take place in the postpartum period

Images of Life-Span Development
Mr. Littles

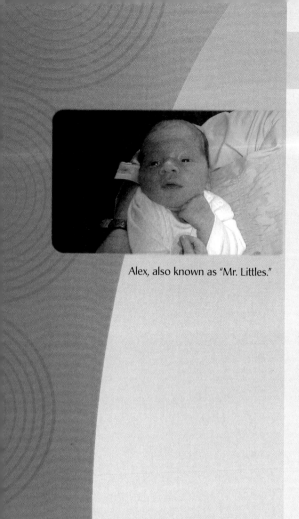

Alex, also known as "Mr. Littles."

Diana and Roger married when he was 38 and she was 34. Both worked full time and were excited when Diana became pregnant. Two months into her pregnancy Diana began to have some unusual pains and bleeding and lost the baby. Diana thought deeply about why she was unable to carry the baby to full term. It was about the time she became pregnant that the federal government began to warn that eating certain types of fish with a high mercury content during pregnancy on a regular basis can cause a miscarriage. Now she eliminated these fish from her diet.

Six months later, Diana became pregnant again. She and Roger read about pregnancy and signed up for birth preparation classes. Each Friday night for eight weeks they practiced simulated contractions. They talked about what kind of parents they wanted to be and discussed what changes in their lives the baby would make. When they found out that their offspring was going to be a boy, they gave him a name: Mr. Littles.

This time, Diana's pregnancy went well, and Alex, also known as Mr. Littles, was born. During the birth, however, Diana's heart rate dropped precipitously and she was given a stimulant to raise it. Apparently the stimulant also increased Alex's heart rate and breathing to a dangerous point and he had to be placed in a newborn intensive care unit (NICU).

Several times a day, Diana and Roger visited Alex in the NICU. They saw that the staff spent large amounts of time filling out charts on computers and little time handling and touching the babies. Several babies in the NICU who had a very low birth weight had been in intensive care for weeks, and these babies were not doing well. Fortunately, Alex was in better health. After several days in the NICU, his parents were permitted to take home a very healthy Alex.

PREVIEW

This chapter chronicles the truly remarkable developments from conception through birth. Imagine . . . at one time you were an organism floating in a sea of fluid in your mother's womb. Let's now explore what your development was like from the time you were conceived through the time you were born.

1 PRENATAL DEVELOPMENT

| The Course of Prenatal Development | Hazards to Prenatal Development | Prenatal Care |

Imagine how Alex ("Mr. Littles") came to be. Out of thousands of eggs and millions of sperm, one egg and one sperm united to produce him. Had the union of sperm and egg come a day or even an hour earlier or later, he might have been very different—maybe even of the opposite sex. Conception occurs when a single sperm cell from the male unites with an ovum (egg) in the female's fallopian tube in a process called fertilization. Over the next few months the genetic code discussed in chapter 3 directs a series of changes in the fertilized egg, but many events and hazards will influence how that egg develops and becomes tiny Alex.

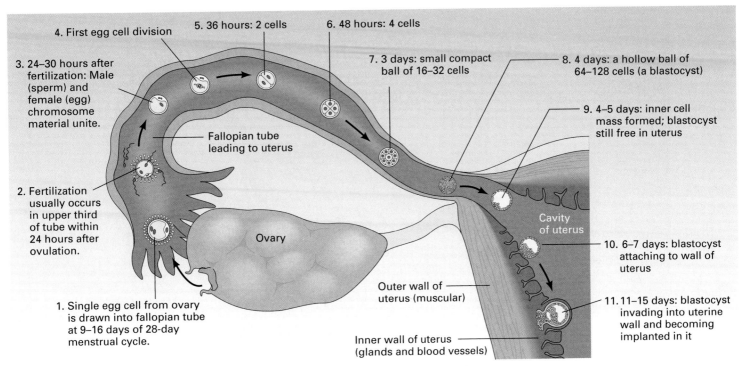

4. First egg cell division

5. 36 hours: 2 cells

6. 48 hours: 4 cells

3. 24–30 hours after fertilization: Male (sperm) and female (egg) chromosome material unite.

7. 3 days: small compact ball of 16–32 cells

8. 4 days: a hollow ball of 64–128 cells (a blastocyst)

9. 4–5 days: inner cell mass formed; blastocyst still free in uterus

Fallopian tube leading to uterus

2. Fertilization usually occurs in upper third of tube within 24 hours after ovulation.

Ovary

Cavity of uterus

10. 6–7 days: blastocyst attaching to wall of uterus

1. Single egg cell from ovary is drawn into fallopian tube at 9–16 days of 28-day menstrual cycle.

Outer wall of uterus (muscular)

Inner wall of uterus (glands and blood vessels)

11. 11–15 days: blastocyst invading into uterine wall and becoming implanted in it

FIGURE 4.1 Significant Developments in the Germinal Period. Just one week after conception, cells of the blastocyst have already begun specializing. The germination period ends when the blastocyst attaches to the uterine wall. *Which of the steps shown in the drawing occur in the laboratory when IVF (described in chapter 3) is used?*

The Course of Prenatal Development

Prenatal development lasts approximately 266 days, beginning with fertilization and ending with birth. It can be divided into three periods: germinal, embryonic, and fetal.

The Germinal Period

The **germinal period** is the period of prenatal development that takes place in the first two weeks after conception. It includes the creation of the fertilized egg, called a zygote, cell division, and the attachment of the zygote to the uterine wall.

Rapid cell division by the zygote begins the germinal period (recall from chapter 3 that this cell divison occurs through a process called *mitosis*). By approximately one week after conception, the differentiation of these cells—their specialization for different tasks—has already begun. At this stage the group of cells, now called the **blastocyst,** consists of an inner mass of cells that will eventually develop into the embryo and the **trophoblast,** an outer layer of cells that later provides nutrition and support for the embryo. *Implantation,* the attachment of the zygote to the uterine wall, takes place about 10 to 14 days after conception. Figure 4.1 illustrates some of the most significant developments during the germinal period.

The Embryonic Period

The **embryonic period** is the period of prenatal development that occurs from two to eight weeks after conception. During the embryonic period, the rate of cell differentiation intensifies, support systems for cells form, and organs appear.

This period begins as the blastocyst attaches to the uterine wall. The mass of cells is now called an *embryo,* and three layers of cells form. The embryo's *endoderm* is the inner layer of cells, which will develop into the digestive and respiratory systems. The *ectoderm* is the outermost layer, which will become the nervous system,

www.mhhe.com/santrockld11

The Visible Embryo
The Trimesters

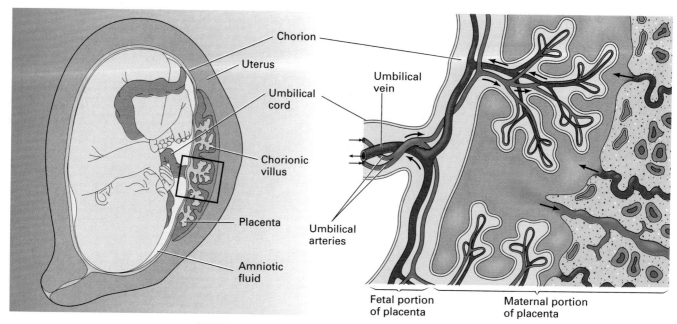

FIGURE 4.2 The Placenta and the Umbilical Cord. The area bound by the square in the left half of the illustration is enlarged in the right half. Arrows indicate the direction of blood flow. Maternal blood flows through the uterine arteries to the spaces housing the placenta, and it returns through the uterine veins to the maternal circulation. Fetal blood flows through the umbilical arteries into the capillaries of the placenta and returns through the umbilical vein to the fetal circulation. The exchange of materials takes place across the layer separating the maternal and fetal blood supplies, so the bloods never come into contact. *What is known about how the placental barrier works and its importance?*

sensory receptors (ears, nose, and eyes, for example), and skin parts (hair and nails, for example). The *mesoderm* is the middle layer, which will become the circulatory system, bones, muscles, excretory system, and reproductive system. Every body part eventually develops from these three layers. The endoderm primarily produces internal body parts, the mesoderm primarily produces parts that surround the internal areas, and the ectoderm primarily produces surface parts.

As the embryo's three layers form, life-support systems for the embryo develop rapidly. These life-support systems include the amnion, the umbilical cord (both of which develop from the fertilized egg, not the mother's body), and the placenta. The **amnion** is like a bag or an envelope that contains a clear fluid in which the developing embryo floats. The amniotic fluid provides an environment that is temperature and humidity controlled, as well as shockproof. The **umbilical cord** contains two arteries and one vein, and connects the baby to the placenta. The **placenta** consists of a disk-shaped group of tissues in which small blood vessels from the mother and the offspring intertwine but do not join.

Figure 4.2 illustrates the placenta, the umbilical cord, and the blood flow in the expectant mother and developing organism. Very small molecules—oxygen, water, salt, food from the mother's blood, as well as carbon dioxide and digestive wastes from the offspring's blood—pass back and forth between the mother and embryo or fetus. Large molecules cannot pass through the placental wall; these include red blood cells and harmful substances, such as most bacteria, maternal wastes, and hormones. The mechanisms that govern the transfer of substances across the placental barrier are complex and are still not entirely understood (Giequel & Le Boue, 2006; Xu & others, 2006).

By the time most women know they are pregnant, the major organs have begun to form in the fetus. **Organogenesis** is the name given to the process of organ formation during the first two months of prenatal development. While they are being formed, the organs are especially vulnerable to environmental changes. In the third

amnion The life-support system that is a bag or envelope that contains a clear fluid in which the developing embryo floats.

umbilical cord A life-support system containing two arteries and one vein that connects the baby to the placenta.

placenta A life-support system that consists of a disk-shaped group of tissues in which small blood vessels from the mother and offspring intertwine.

organogenesis Organ formation that takes place during the first two months of prenatal development.

week after conception, the neural tube that eventually becomes the spinal cord forms. At about 21 days, eyes begin to appear, and at 24 days the cells for the heart begin to differentiate. During the fourth week, the urogenital system becomes apparent, and arm and leg buds emerge. Four chambers of the heart take shape, and blood vessels appear. From the fifth to the eighth week, arms and legs differentiate further; at this time, the face starts to form but still is not very recognizable. The intestinal tract develops and the facial structures fuse. At eight weeks, the developing organism weighs about 1/30 ounce and is just over 1 inch long.

The Fetal Period

The Fetal Period   The **fetal period** is the prenatal period of development that begins two months after conception and lasts for seven months, on the average. Growth and development continue their dramatic course during this time.

Three months after conception, the fetus is about 3 inches long and weighs about 3 ounces. It has become active, moving its arms and legs, opening and closing its mouth, and moving its head. The face, forehead, eyelids, nose, and chin are distinguishable, as are the upper arms, lower arms, hands, and lower limbs. The genitals can be identified as male or female. By the end of the fourth month, the fetus has grown to 6 inches in length and weighs 4 to 7 ounces. At this time, a growth spurt occurs in the body's lower parts. For the first time the mother can feel arm and leg movements.

By the end of the fifth month, the fetus is about 12 inches long and weighs close to a pound. Structures of the skin have formed—toenails and fingernails, for example. The fetus is more active, showing a preference for a particular position in the womb. By the end of the sixth month, the fetus is about 14 inches long and has gained another half pound to a pound. The eyes and eyelids are completely formed, and a fine layer of hair covers the head. A grasping reflex is present and irregular breathing movements occur.

At about seven months, the fetus for the first time has a chance of surviving outside of the womb—that is, it is *viable*. But even when infants are born in the seventh month, they usually need help breathing. By the end of the seventh month, the fetus is about 16 inches long and now weighs about 3 pounds.

During the last two months of prenatal development fatty tissues develop, and the functioning of various organ systems—heart and kidneys, for example—steps up. During the eighth and ninth months, the fetus grows longer and gains substantial weight—about another 4 pounds. At birth, the average American baby weighs 7½ pounds and is about 20 inches long.

Figure 4.3 gives an overview of the main events during prenatal development. Notice that instead of describing development in terms of germinal, embryonic, and fetal periods, figure 4.3 divides prenatal development into equal periods of three months, called *trimesters*. Remember that the three trimesters are not the same as the three prenatal periods we have discussed. The germinal and embryonic periods occur in the first trimester. The fetal period begins toward the end of the first trimester and continues through the second and third trimesters. Viability (the chances of surviving outside the womb) occurs at the beginning of the third trimester.

Hazards to Prenatal Development

For Alex, the baby discussed at the opening of this chapter, the course of prenatal development went smoothly. His mother's womb protected him as he developed. Despite this protection, the environment can affect the embryo or fetus in many well-documented ways.

General Principles   A **teratogen** is any agent that can potentially cause a birth defect or negatively alter cognitive and behavioral outcomes. (The word comes from the Greek word *tera* meaning "monster".) The field of study that investigates

> *The history of man for nine months preceding his birth would, probably, be far more interesting, and contain events of greater moment than all three score and ten years that follow it.*
>
> —Samuel Taylor Coleridge
> *English Poet, Essayist, 19th Century*

fetal period The prenatal period of development that begins two months after conception and lasts for seven months, on the average.

teratogen Any agent that can potentially cause a birth defect or negatively alter cognitive and behavioral outcomes.

First trimester (first 3 months)

Prenatal growth	Conception to 4 weeks	8 weeks	12 weeks	
	• Is less than ¹/₁₀ inch long • Beginning development of spinal cord, nervous system, gastrointestinal system, heart, and lungs • Amniotic sac envelopes the preliminary tissues of entire body • Is called a "zygote"	• Is just over 1 inch long • Face is forming with rudimentary eyes, ears, mouth, and tooth buds • Arms and legs are moving • Brain is forming • Fetal heartbeat is detectable with ultrasound • Is called an "embryo"	• Is about 3 inches long and weighs about 1 ounce • Can move arms, legs, fingers, and toes • Fingerprints are present • Can smile, frown, suck, and swallow • Sex is distinguishable • Can urinate • Is called a "fetus"	

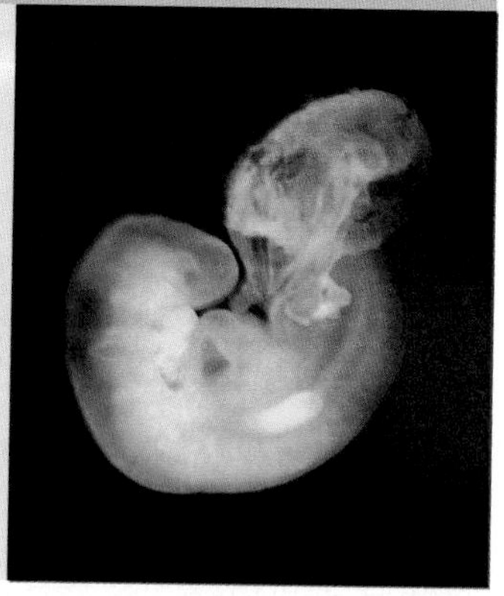

Second trimester (middle 3 months)

Prenatal growth	16 weeks	20 weeks	24 weeks	
	• Is about 6 inches long and weighs about 4 to 7 ounces • Heartbeat is strong • Skin is thin, transparent • Downy hair (lanugo) covers body • Fingernails and toenails are forming • Has coordinated movements; is able to roll over in amniotic fluid	• Is about 12 inches long and weighs close to 1 pound • Heartbeat is audible with ordinary stethoscope • Sucks thumb • Hiccups • Hair, eyelashes, eyebrows are present	• Is about 14 inches long and weighs 1 to 1½ pounds • Skin is wrinkled and covered with protective coating (vernix caseosa) • Eyes are open • Waste matter is collected in bowel • Has strong grip	

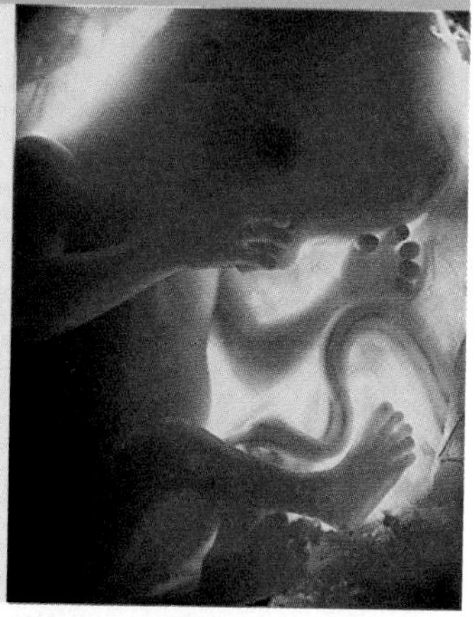

Third trimester (last 3 months)

Prenatal growth	28 weeks	32 weeks	36 to 38 weeks	
	• Is about 16 inches long and weighs about 3 pounds • Is adding body fat • Is very active • Rudimentary breathing movements are present	• Is 16½ to 18 inches long and weighs 4 to 5 pounds • Has periods of sleep and wakefulness • Responds to sounds • May assume the birth position • Bones of head are soft and flexible • Iron is being stored in liver	• Is 19 to 20 inches long and weighs 6 to 7½ pounds • Skin is less wrinkled • Vernix caseosa is thick • Lanugo is mostly gone • Is less active • Is gaining immunities from mother	

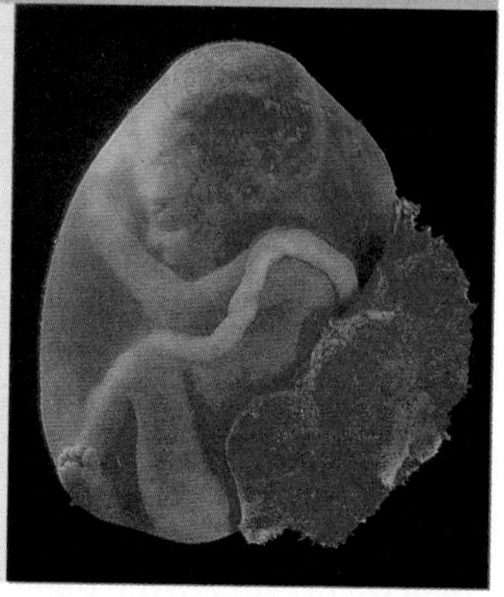

FIGURE 4.3 The Three Trimesters of Prenatal Development. Both the germinal and embryonic periods occur during the first trimester. The end of the first trimester as well as the second and third trimesters are part of the fetal period.

the causes of birth defects is called *teratology*. Teratogens include drugs, incompatible blood types, environmental pollutants, infectious diseases, nutritional deficiencies, maternal stress, advanced maternal and paternal age, and environmental pollutants. In fact, thousands of babies are born deformed or mentally retarded every year as a result of events that occurred in the mother's life as early as one or two months *before* conception. As we further discuss teratogens, you will see that factors related to the father also can influence prenatal development.

So many teratogens exist that practically every fetus is exposed to at least some teratogens. For this reason, it is difficult to determine which teratogen causes which problem. In addition, it may take a long time for the effects of a teratogen to show up. Only about half of all potential effects appear at birth.

The dose, genetic susceptibility, and the time of exposure to a particular teratogen influence both the severity of the damage to an embryo or fetus and the type of defect:

- *Dose* The dose effect is rather obvious—the greater the dose of an agent, such as a drug, the greater the effect.
- *Genetic Susceptibility* The type or severity of abnormalities caused by a teratogen is linked to the genotype of the pregnant woman and the genotype of the embryo or fetus (Lidral & Murray, 2005). For example, how a mother metabolizes a particular drug can influence the degree to which the drug effects are transmitted to the embryo or fetus. Differences in placental membranes and placental transport also affect exposure. The extent to which an embryo or fetus is vulnerable to a teratogen may also depend on its genotype (Graham & Shaw, 2005).
- *Time of Exposure* Teratogens do more damage when they occur at some points in development than at others (Rifas-Shiman & others, 2006). Damage during the germinal period may even prevent implantation. In general, the embryonic period is more vulnerable than the fetal period.

Health and Prenatal Development
Exploring Teratology
High-Risk Situations

Figure 4.4 summarizes additional information about the effects of time of exposure to a teratogen. The probability of a structural defect is greatest early in the embryonic period, when organs are being formed. Each body structure has its own critical period of formation. Recall from chapter 2 that a *critical period* is a fixed time period very early in development during which certain experiences or events can have a long-lasting effect on development. The critical period for the nervous system (week 3) is earlier than for arms and legs (weeks 4 and 5).

After organogenesis is complete, teratogens are less likely to cause anatomical defects. Instead, exposure during the fetal period is more likely instead to stunt growth or to create problems in the way organs function. To examine some key teratogens and their effects, let's begin with drugs.

Prescription and Nonprescription Drugs Many U.S. women are given prescriptions for drugs while they are pregnant—especially antibiotics, analgesics, and asthma medications (Riley & others, 2005). Prescription as well as nonprescription drugs, however, may have effects on the embryo or fetus that the women never imagined.

The damage that drugs can do was tragically highlighted in 1961, when many pregnant women took a popular tranquilizer, thalidomide, to alleviate their morning sickness. In adults, the effects of thalidomide are mild; in embryos, however, they are devastating. Not all infants were affected in the same way. If the mother took thalidomide on day 26 (probably before she knew she was pregnant), an arm might not grow. If she took the drug two days later, the arm might not grow past the elbow. The thalidomide tragedy shocked the medical community and parents and taught a valuable lesson: Taking the wrong drug at the wrong time is enough to physically handicap the offspring for life.

Prescription drugs that can function as teratogens include antibiotics, such as streptomycin and tetracycline; some antidepressants; certain hormones, such as progestin and synthetic estrogen; and Accutane (which often is prescribed for acne) (Ashkenazi & Silberstein, 2006; Jordan, 2005; Scheinfeld & Bangalore, 2006). Nonprescription drugs that can be harmful include diet pills and aspirin (Norgard & others, 2005).

Psychoactive Drugs *Psychoactive drugs* are drugs that act on the nervous system to alter states of consciousness, modify perceptions, and change moods. Examples

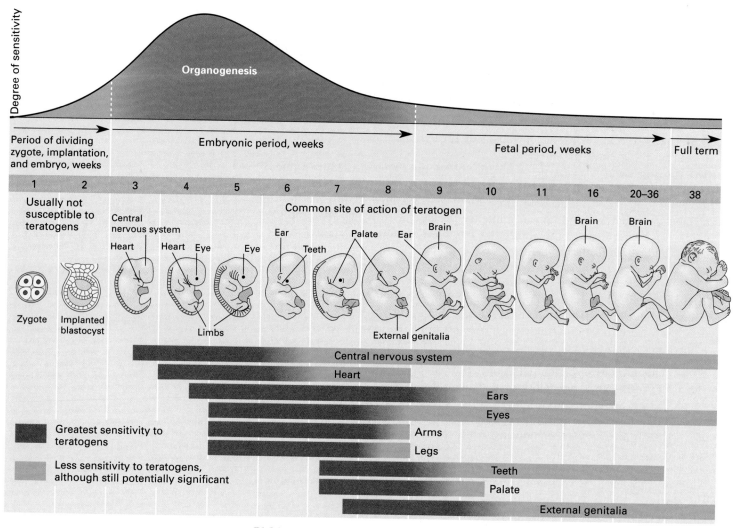

FIGURE 4.4 **Teratogens and the Timing of Their Effects on Prenatal Development**. The danger of structural defects caused by teratogens is greatest early in embryonic development. The period of organogenesis (red color) lasts for about six weeks. Later assaults by teratogens (blue-green color) mainly occur in the fetal period and instead of causing structural damage are more likely to stunt growth or cause problems of organ function.

include caffeine, alcohol, and nicotine, as well as illegal drugs such as cocaine, marijuana, and heroin (Alvik & others, 2006; Noland & others, 2005).

Caffeine   People often consume caffeine by drinking coffee, tea, or colas, or by eating chocolate. A review of studies on caffeine consumption during pregnancy concluded that a small increase in the risks for spontaneous abortion and low birth weight occurs for pregnant women consuming more than 150 milligrams of caffeine (approximately two cups of brewed coffee or two to three 12-ounce cans of cola) per day (Fernandez & others, 1998). (Low birth weight is linked to a variety of health and developmental problems, which we will discuss later in the chapter.) A recent study revealed that pregnant women who consumed 300 or more milligrams of caffeine a day had an increased risk of fetal death (Matijasevich & others, 2006). Taking into account such results, the Food and Drug Administration recommends that pregnant women either not consume caffeine or consume it only sparingly.

Alcohol   Heavy drinking by pregnant women can be devastating to offspring (Caley, Kramer, & Robinson, 2005; Welch-Carre, 2005). **Fetal alcohol syndrome (FAS)**

fetal alcohol syndrome (FAS) A cluster of abnormalities that appears in the offspring of mothers who drink alcohol heavily during pregnancy.

is a cluster of abnormalities that appears in the offspring of mothers who drink alcohol heavily during pregnancy. The abnormalities include facial deformities and defective limbs, face, and heart. Figure 4.5 shows a child with fetal alcohol syndrome. Most of these children are below average in intelligence, and some are mentally retarded (Abel, 2006; Toga, Thompson, & Sowell, 2006; West & Blake, 2005). Although many mothers of FAS infants are heavy drinkers, many mothers who are heavy drinkers do not have children with FAS or have one child with FAS and other children who do not have it.

Drinking alcohol during pregnancy, however, can have serious effects on offspring even when they are not afflicted with FAS. One recent study found that prenatal exposure to binge drinking was linked to a greater likelihood of having IQ scores in the mentally retarded range and a higher incidence of acting-out behavior at 7 years of age (Bailey & others, 2004). Serious malformations such as those produced by FAS are not found in infants born to mothers who are moderate drinkers, but even moderate drinking can have an effect on the offspring (Burden & others, 2005). In one study, children whose mothers drank moderately (one to two drinks a day) during pregnancy were less attentive and alert, even at 4 years of age (Streissguth & others, 1984). Also, a recent study found that pregnant women who had three or more drinks a day faced an increased risk of preterm birth (Parazzini & others, 2003). In a longitudinal study the more alcohol mothers drank in the first trimester of pregnancy, the more 14-year-olds fell behind on growth markers such as weight, height, and head size (Day & others, 2002).

What are some guidelines for alcohol use during pregnancy? Even drinking just one or two servings of beer or wine or one serving of hard liquor a few days a week can have negative effects on the fetus, although it is generally agreed that this level of alcohol use will not cause fetal alcohol syndrome. The U.S. Surgeon General recommends that *no* alcohol be consumed during pregnancy. Recent research suggests that it may not be wise to consume alcohol at the time of conception. One study revealed that "both male and female alcohol intakes during the week of conception increased the risk of early pregnancy loss" (Henriksen & others, 2004, p. 661).

Nicotine   Cigarette smoking by pregnant women can also adversely influence prenatal development, birth, and postnatal development (Huizink & Mulder, 2006; Pringle & others, 2005). Preterm births and low birth weights, fetal and neonatal deaths, respiratory problems, and sudden infant death syndrome (SIDS, also known as crib death) are all more common among the offspring of mothers who smoked during pregnancy (Adgent, 2006; Moore & Davies, 2005).

Prenatal exposure to heavy smoking has been linked in one study to nicotine withdrawal symptoms in newborns (Godding & others, 2004). Other studies have linked prenatal exposure to cigarette smoking during pregnancy to increased incidence of attention deficit hyperactivity disorder at 5 to 16 years of age (Thapar & others, 2003), and to an increased risk of cigarette smoking during adolescence (Porath & Fried, 2005).

A recent analysis indicated a decline in smoking during pregnancy from 1990 to 2002, although smoking by pregnant adolescents still remained high (Centers for Disease Control and Prevention, 2004). Intervention programs designed to help pregnant women stop smoking can reduce some of smoking's negative effects, especially by raising birth weights (Klesges & others, 2001).

Cocaine   Does cocaine use during pregnancy harm the developing embryo and fetus? The most consistent finding is that cocaine exposure during prenatal development is associated with reduced birth weight, length, and head circumference (Minnes & others, 2005; Smith & others, 2001). In other studies, prenatal cocaine exposure has been linked to impaired motor development at 2 years of age (Arendt & others, 1999); to lower arousal, less effective self-regulation, higher excitability,

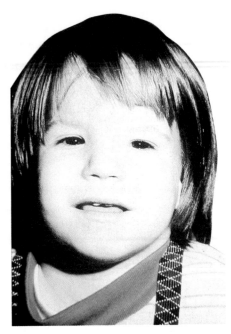

FIGURE 4.5 Fetal Alcohol Syndrome. This child's wide-set eyes, flat bones, and thin upper lip are symptoms of fetal alcohol syndrome. *How much alcohol should women feel safe drinking while they are pregnant?*

www.mhhe.com/santrockld11

Fetal Alcohol Syndrome
Smoking and Pregnancy

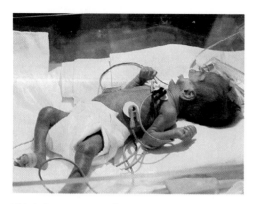

This baby was exposed to cocaine prenatally. *What are some of the possible effects on development of being exposed to cocaine prenatally?*

and lower quality of reflexes at 1 month of age (Lester & others, 2002); and to impaired language development and information processing (Beeghly & others, 2006; Harvey, 2004; Morrow & others, 2003), including attention deficits in preschool children (Noland & others, 2005).

These findings should be interpreted cautiously (Accornero & others, 2006; Vidaeff & Mastrobattista, 2003). Why? Because other factors in the lives of pregnant women who use cocaine (such as poverty, malnutrition, and other substance abuse) often cannot be ruled out as possible contributors to the problems found in their children (Hurt & others, 2005). For example, cocaine users are more likely than nonusers to smoke cigarettes, use marijuana, drink alcohol, and take amphetamines.

Despite these cautions, the weight of research evidence indicates that children born to mothers who use cocaine are likely to have neurological and cognitive deficits (Mayes, 2003; Noland & others, 2005). Cocaine use by pregnant women is not recommended.

Methamphetamine Methamphetamine, like cocaine, is a stimulant, speeding up an individual's nervous system. Babies born to mothers who use methamphetamine, or "meth," during pregnancy are at risk for a number of problems, including high infant mortality, low birth weight, and developmental and behavioral problems (Chang & others, 2004). Meth use during pregnancy is increasing and some experts conclude that meth use during pregnancy has become a greater problem in the United States than cocaine use (Elliott, 2004). A recent survey found that 5 percent of U.S. women used methamphetamine during their pregnancy (Arria & others, 2006).

Marijuana There has not been extensive research on how marijuana use by pregnant women affects their offspring. A recent review of the research concluded that marijuana use by pregnant women is related to negative outcomes in memory and information processing in their offspring (Kalant, 2004). For example, in a longitudinal study, prenatal marijuana exposure was related to learning and memory difficulties at age 11 (Richardson & others, 2002). Another study revealed that prenatal marijuana exposure was linked with depressive symptoms at 10 years of age (Gray & others, 2005). However, because of the small numbers of studies, it is difficult to reach conclusions about the effects of marijuana use by mothers during pregnancy. Nonetheless, marijuana use is not recommended for pregnant women (Huizink & Mulder, 2006).

Heroin It is well documented that infants whose mothers are addicted to heroin show several behavioral difficulties (Thaithumyanon & others, 2005; Yang & others, 2006). The difficulties include withdrawal symptoms, such as tremors, irritability, abnormal crying, disturbed sleep, and impaired motor control. Many still show behavioral problems at their first birthday, and attention deficits may appear later in development. The most common treatment for heroin addiction, methadone, is associated with very severe withdrawal symptoms in newborns.

Incompatible Blood Types Incompatibility between the mother's and father's blood types poses another risk to prenatal development. Blood types are created by differences in the surface structure of red blood cells. One type of difference in the surface of red blood cells creates the familiar blood groups—A, B, O, and AB. A second difference creates what is called Rh-positive and Rh-negative blood. If a surface marker, called the *Rh factor*, is present in an individual's red blood cells, the person is said to be Rh-positive; if the Rh marker is not present, the person is said to be Rh-negative. If a pregnant woman is Rh-negative and her partner is Rh-positive, the fetus may be Rh-positive. If the fetus' blood is Rh-positive and the mother's is Rh-negative, the mother's immune system may produce antibodies that will attack the fetus. This can result in any number of problems, including miscarriage or stillbirth, anemia, jaundice, heart defects, brain damage, or death soon after birth (Moise, 2005).

Generally, the first Rh-positive baby of an Rh-negative mother is not at risk, but with each subsequent pregnancy the risk increases. A vaccine (RhoGAM) may be given to the mother within three days of the child's birth to prevent her body from making antibodies that will attack future Rh-positive fetuses. Also, babies affected by Rh incompatibility can be given blood transfusions before or right after birth (Mannessier & others, 2000).

Maternal Diseases   Maternal diseases and infections can produce defects in offspring by crossing the placental barrier, or they can cause damage during birth (Avgil & Ornoy, 2006; Kirkham, Harris, & Grzybowski, 2005; Tappia & Gabriel, 2006). Rubella (German measles) is one disease that can cause prenatal defects. The greatest damage occurs if a mother contracts rubella in the third or fourth week of pregnancy, although infection during the second month is also damaging (Kobayashi & others, 2005). A rubella outbreak in 1964–1965 resulted in 30,000 prenatal and neonatal (newborn) deaths, and more than 20,000 affected infants were born with malformations, including mental retardation, blindness, deafness, and heart problems. Elaborate preventive efforts ensure that rubella will never again have such disastrous effects. A vaccine that prevents German measles is now routinely administered to children, and women who plan to have children should have a blood test before they become pregnant to determine if they are immune to the disease (Bar-Oz & others, 2004).

Syphilis (a sexually transmitted disease) is more damaging later in prenatal development—four months or more after conception. Rather than affecting organogenesis, as rubella does, syphilis damages organs after they have formed. Damage includes eye lesions, which can cause blindness, and skin lesions. When syphilis is present at birth, problems can develop in the central nervous system and gastrointestinal tract (Mullick, Beksinksa, & Msomi, 2005). Most states require that pregnant women be given a blood test to detect the presence of syphilis.

Another infection that has received widespread attention recently is genital herpes. Newborns contract this virus when they are delivered through the birth canal of a mother with genital herpes (Avgil & Ornoy, 2006; Rupp, Rosenthal, & Stanberry, 2005; Thung & Grobman, 2005). About one-third of babies delivered through an infected birth canal die; another one-fourth become brain damaged. If an active case of genital herpes is detected in a pregnant woman close to her delivery date, a cesarean section can be performed (in which the infant is delivered through an incision in the mother's abdomen) to keep the virus from infecting the newborn.

AIDS is a sexually transmitted disease that is caused by the human immunodeficiency virus (HIV), which destroys the body's immune system. A mother can infect her offspring with the HIV virus in three ways: (1) during gestation across the placenta, (2) during delivery through contact with maternal blood or fluids, and (3) postpartum (after birth) through breast feeding. The transmission of HIV through breast feeding is especially a problem in many developing countries (UNICEF, 2004). Babies born to HIV-infected mothers can be (1) infected and symptomatic (show AIDS symptoms), (2) infected but asymptomatic (not show AIDS symptoms), or (3) not infected at all. An infant who is infected and asymptomatic may still develop HIV symptoms up until 15 months of age.

In the early 1990s, before preventive treatments were available, 1,000 to 2,000 infants were born with HIV each year in the United States. Since then, transmission of the HIV virus from mothers to the fetuses has been reduced dramatically (Kriebs, 2006). Only about one-third as many cases of newborns with the HIV virus appear today as in the early 1990s. This decline is due to the increase in counseling and voluntary testing of pregnant women for HIV and to the use of zidovudine (AZT) by infected women during pregnancy, and for the infant after birth (Rathbun, Lockhart, & Stephens, 2006; Thorne & Newell, 2005). In many poor countries, however, treatment with AZT is limited, and HIV infection of infants remains a major problem (Iyasu & others, 2005; Kirungi & others, 2006).

The more widespread disease of diabetes, characterized by high levels of sugar in the blood, also affects offspring (Casson, 2006). A recent study revealed that both chronic (long-standing) and gestational (onset or first recognition during pregnancy) diabetes were significant risks for cesarean delivery and preterm birth (Rosenberg & others, 2005).

Maternal Diet and Nutrition A developing embryo or fetus depends completely on its mother for nutrition, which comes from the mother's blood. The nutritional status of the embryo or fetus is determined by the mother's total caloric intake, and her intake of proteins, vitamins, and minerals. Children born to malnourished mothers are more likely than other children to be malformed.

Because the fetus depends entirely on its mother for nutrition, it is important for the pregnant woman to have good nutritional habits. In Kenya, this government clinic provides pregnant women with information about how their diet can influence the health of their fetus and offspring. *What might the information about diet be like?*

Being overweight before and during pregnancy can also put the embryo or fetus at risk, and an increasing number of pregnant women in the United States are overweight (Dietl, 2005; Fiala, Egan, & Lashgari, 2006; King, 2006). Three studies found that obese women had a significant risk of fetal death (Cnattingius & others, 1998; Kumari, 2001; Nohr & others, 2005). Other recent studies indicated that prepregnancy maternal obesity doubled the risk of stillbirth and neonatal death, and was linked with defects in the central nervous system of offspring (Anderson & others, 2005; Kristensen & others, 2005).

One aspect of maternal nutrition that is important for normal prenatal development is folic acid, a B-complex vitamin (Bailey & Berry, 2005; Tamura & Picciano, 2006). A lack of folic acid is linked with neural tube defects in offspring, such as spina bifida, a typically fatal defect in the spinal cord (Christian & others, 2006; Felkner & others, 2005). One recent study also found that maternal use of folic acid and iron during the first month of pregnancy was associated with a lower risk of Down syndrome in offspring, although more studies are needed to confirm this connection (Czeizel & Puho, 2005). The U.S. Public Health Service recommends that pregnant women consume a minimum of 400 micrograms of folic acid per day (about twice the amount the average woman gets in one day). Orange juice and spinach are examples of foods rich in folic acid.

Eating fish is often recommended as part of a healthy diet, but pollution has made many fish a risky choice for pregnant women. Some fish contain high levels of mercury, which is released into the air both naturally and by industrial pollution (Fitzgerald & others, 2004). When mercury falls into the water it can become toxic and accumulate in large fish, such as shark, swordfish, king mackerel, and some species of large tuna. Mercury is easily transferred across the placenta, and the embryo's developing brain and nervous system are highly sensitive to the metal (Gliori & others, 2006; Sato, Li, & Shaha, 2006). The U.S. Food and Drug Administration (2004) recently provided the following recommendations for women of childbearing age and young children: Don't eat shark, swordfish, king mackerel, or tilefish; eat up to 12 ounces (2 average meals) a week of fish and shellfish that are lower in mercury, such as shrimp, canned light tuna, salmon, pollock, and catfish.

PCB-polluted fish also pose a risk to prenatal development (Fitzgerald & others, 2004). PCBs (polychlorinated biphenyls) are chemicals that were used in manufacturing until they were banned in the 1970s in the United States, but they are still present in landfills, sediments, and wildlife. One study kept track of the extent to which pregnant women ate PCB-polluted fish from Lake Michigan was examined, and subsequently observed their children as newborns, young children, and at 11 years of age (Jacobson & others, 1984; Jacobson & Jacobson, 2002, 2003). The women who had eaten more PCB-polluted fish were more likely to have smaller, preterm infants who were more likely to react slowly to stimuli. As preschool children, their exposure to PCBs was linked with less effective short-term memory, and at age 11 with lower verbal intelligence and reading comprehension.

Emotional States and Stress Tales abound about how a pregnant woman's emotional state affects the fetus. For centuries it was thought that frightening experiences—such as a severe thunderstorm or a family member's death—leave birthmarks on the child or affect the child in more serious ways. In fact, a mother's stress can be transmitted to the fetus, and we now have a better grasp of how this takes place, although the mechanisms that link fetal health and the mother's emotional states are still far from certain (King & Laplante, 2005; Knackstedt, Hamelmann, & Arck, 2005).

When a pregnant woman experiences intense fears, anxieties, and other emotions, physiological changes occur that may affect her fetus. For example, producing adrenaline in response to fear restricts blood flow to the uterine area and can deprive the fetus of adequate oxygen. Also, maternal stress may increase the level of corticotrophin-releasing hormone (CRH) early in pregnancy (Kapoor & others, 2006; Sljivic & others, 2006). CRH, in turn, has been linked to premature delivery. Women under stress are about four times more likely than their low-stress counterparts to deliver babies prematurely (Dunkel-Schetter & others, 2001). A mother's stress may also influence the fetus indirectly by increasing the likelihood that the mother will engage in unhealthy behaviors, such as taking drugs and engaging in poor prenatal care.

High maternal anxiety and stress during pregnancy might have long-term consequences for the offspring (Jones & others, 2006). One recent study found that infants of mothers who had a low level of CRH during pregnancy showed less fear and distress at 2 months of age than their infant counterparts whose mothers had a high level of CRH during pregnancy (Davis & others, 2005). Also, in a longitudinal study, high maternal anxiety during pregnancy was linked to higher levels of cortisol (a hormone secreted by the adrenal glands in response to stress) in offspring at 10 years of age (O'Connor & others, 2005). In another longitudinal study, preschool children whose mothers had higher concentrations of cortisol during pregnancy had higher concentrations of cortisol themselves than preschool children whose mothers had lower concentrations of cortisol during pregnancy (Gutteling, de Weerth, & Buitelaar, 2005).

The mother's emotional state during pregnancy can influence the birth process, too. An emotionally distraught mother might have irregular contractions and a more difficult labor, which can cause irregularities in the supply of oxygen to the fetus or other problems after birth. Babies born after extended labor also may adjust more slowly to their world and be more irritable.

Positive emotional states also appear to make a difference to the fetus. Pregnant women who are optimistic thinkers have less adverse outcomes than pregnant women who are pessimistic thinkers (Loebel & Yalli, 1999). Optimists are more likely to believe that they have control over the outcomes of their pregnancies.

Maternal Age When possible harmful effects on the fetus and infant are considered, two maternal ages are of special interest: adolescence and 35 and older (Aliyu & others, 2004). One recent study revealed that the rate of stillbirth was elevated for adolescent girls and women 35 years and older (Bateman & Simpson, 2006). The mortality rate of infants born to adolescent mothers is double that of infants born to mothers in their twenties. Although this high rate probably reflects the immaturity of the mother's reproductive system, poor nutrition, lack of prenatal care, and low socioeconomic status may also play a role (Lenders, McElrath, & Scholl, 2000). Prenatal care decreases the probability that a child born to an adolescent girl will have physical problems. However, adolescents are the least likely of women in all age groups to obtain prenatal assistance from clinics, pediatricians, and health services.

Maternal age is also linked to the risk that a child will have Down syndrome (Resta, 2005; Soergel & others, 2006). As discussed in chapter 3, an individual with *Down syndrome* has distinctive facial characteristics, short limbs, and retardation of motor and mental abilities. A baby with Down syndrome rarely is born to a mother 16 to 34

What are some of the risks for infants born to adolescent mothers?

years of age. However, when the mother reaches 40 years of age, the probability is slightly over 1 in 100 that a baby born to her will have Down syndrome, and by age 50 it is almost 1 in 10.

When mothers are 35 years and older, risks also increase for low birth weight, for preterm delivery, and for fetal death. One recent study found that low birth weight delivery increased 11 percent and preterm delivery increased 14 percent in women 35 years and older (Tough & others, 2002). In another study, fetal death was low for women 30 to 34 years of age but increased progressively for women 35 to 39 and 40 to 44 years of age in one recent study (Canterino & others, 2004).

We still have much to learn about the role of the mother's age in pregnancy and childbirth. As women remain active, exercise regularly, and are careful about their nutrition, their reproductive systems may remain healthier at older ages than was thought possible in the past. For example, in a recent study, two-thirds of the pregnancies of women 45 years and older in Australia were free of complications (Callaway, Lust, & McIntyre, 2005).

Paternal Factors So far, we have discussed how characteristics of the mother—such as drug use, disease, nutrition and diet, emotional states, and age—can influence prenatal development and the development of the child. Might there also be some paternal risk factors? Indeed, there are several. Men's exposure to lead, radiation, certain pesticides, and petrochemicals may cause abnormalities in sperm that lead to miscarriage or diseases, such as childhood cancer (Lindbohm, 1991; Trasler, 2000; Trasler & Doerksen, 2000). When fathers have a diet low in vitamin C, their offspring have a higher risk of birth defects and cancer (Fraga & others, 1991). Also, it has been speculated that, when fathers take cocaine, it may attach itself to sperm and cause birth defects, but the evidence for this effect is not yet strong. In one study, long-term use of cocaine by men was related to low sperm count, low motility, and a higher number of abnormally formed sperm (Bracken & others, 1990). Cocaine-related infertility appears to be reversible if users stop taking the drug for at least one year.

The father's smoking during the mother's pregnancy also can cause problems for the offspring. In one investigation, the newborns of fathers who smoked around their wives during the pregnancy were 4 ounces lighter at birth for each pack of cigarettes smoked per day than were the newborns whose fathers did not smoke during their wives' pregnancy (Rubin & others, 1986). In another study, in China, the longer the fathers smoked, the stronger the risk that their children would develop cancer (Ji & others, 1997). In yet another study, heavy paternal smoking was associated with the risk of early pregnancy loss (Venners & others, 2005).

The father's age also makes a difference (Klonoff-Cohen & Natarajan, 2004; Slama & others, 2005; Tang & others, 2006). About 5 percent of children with Down syndrome have older fathers. The offspring of older fathers also face increased risk for other birth defects, including dwarfism and Marfan syndrome, which involves head and limb deformities.

There are also risks to offspring when both the mother and father are older (Dunson, Baird, & Colombo, 2004). In one study, the risk of an adverse pregnancy outcome, such as miscarriage, rose considerably when the woman was 35 years or older and the man was 40 years of age or older (de la Rochebrochard & Thonneau, 2002).

Environmental Hazards Many aspects of our modern industrial world can endanger the embryo or fetus. Earlier, we mentioned that an embryo or fetus may be harmed if the mother's diet includes polluted fish or if the father's exposure to certain chemicals caused abnormalities in his sperm. Some specific hazards to the embryo or fetus that are worth a closer look include radiation, toxic wastes, and other chemical pollutants (Bellinger, 2005; Urbano & Tait, 2004).

Radiation can cause a gene mutation (an abrupt, permanent change in DNA). Chromosomal abnormalities are elevated among the offspring of fathers exposed to high levels of radiation in their occupations (Schrag & Dixon, 1985). X-ray radiation

An explosion at the Chernobyl nuclear power plant in the Ukraine produced radioactive contamination that spread to surrounding areas. Thousands of infants were born with health problems and deformities as a result of the nuclear contamination, including this boy whose arm did not form. *Other than radioactive contamination, what are some other types of environmental hazards to prenatal development?*

also can affect the developing embryo or fetus, especially in the first several weeks after conception, when women do not yet know they are pregnant (Urbano & Tait, 2004). Possible effects include microencephaly (an abnormally small brain), mental retardation, and leukemia. Women and their physicians should weigh the risk of an X-ray when an actual or potential pregnancy is involved (Brent, 2004; Hurwitz & others, 2006; Smits & others, 2006). However, a routine diagnostic X-ray of a body area other than the abdomen, with the women's abdomen protected by a lead apron, is generally considered safe.

Environmental pollutants and toxic wastes are also sources of danger to unborn children. Among the dangerous pollutants are carbon monoxide, mercury, and lead, as well as certain fertilizers and pesticides. Exposure to lead can come from lead-based paint that flakes off the walls of a home or from leaded gasoline emitted by cars on a nearby busy highway. Early exposure to lead can affect children's mental development (Yang & others, 2003). For example, in one study, 2-year-olds who prenatally had high levels of lead in their umbilical-cord blood performed poorly on a test of mental development (Bellinger & others, 1987).

Despite these many potential hazards during prenatal development, it is important to keep in mind that most of the time prenatal development does not go awry and development proceeds along the positive path that we described at the beginning of the chapter (Lester, 2000). In the Applications in Life-Span Development interlude that follows, we outline some of the steps that prospective parents can take to increase the chances for healthy prenatal development.

APPLICATIONS IN LIFE-SPAN DEVELOPMENT

A Healthy Pregnancy

Diana and Roger, the couple described in the opening of this chapter, took several steps to ensure a healthy pregnancy and positive outcome for their offspring. Diane read the popular book, *What to Expect When You are Expecting* (Eisenberg, Murkoff, & Hathaway, 2002) and Roger read *The Expectant Father* (Brott, 2001) to improve their understanding of pregnancy and the prenatal development of "Mr. Littles." Referring to these books as the pregnancy progressed helped them to get a better grasp of the month-to-month changes that characterize a pregnancy and whether they were engaging in healthy practices.

Reading *The Expectant Father* made Roger realize how important the partner's support is to the expectant mother's positive emotional state (Heaman, 2005). One recent study found that a partner's support was related to lower levels of anxiety and depression in expectant mothers (Glazier & others, 2004). Another study revealed that partner support was linked to a lower-level emotional stress in economically disadvantaged pregnant adolescents (Milan & others, 2004).

A helpful initial strategy for women is to begin preparing for pregnancy before becoming pregnant (Anderson & others, 2006; Hofmanova, 2006; Johnson & others, 2006). Women should consult with their physician about discontinuing any medications that might harm the offspring, including acne medications and tranquilizers. If they smoke or drink alcohol, they need to break these habits before becoming pregnant. It also is wise to reduce caffeine intake and begin taking a multiple vitamin with iron, making sure it has at least .4 mg of folic acid. Avoiding fish with high levels of mercury is another good strategy.

In addition to eating healthily, moderate regular exercise is linked with fewer discomforts in pregnancy and an improved sense of well-being (Morris & Johnson, 2005; Poudevigne & O'Connor, 2005, 2006). For example, one recent study revealed that regular exercise during the second half of pregnancy reduced the low back pain

(continued on next page)

Lines of communication should be open between the expectant mother and her partner during pregnancy. *What are some examples of good partner communication during pregnancy?*

of expectant mothers (Garshasbi & Faghihzadeh, 2005). However, it is important for expectant mothers not to "overdo it" and exercise too strenuously, which can increase the probability of bleeding or preterm labor. Walking, swimming, and stretching are among recommended exercises for expectant mothers.

Another important aspect of having a healthy pregnancy is to talk with a physician about the prenatal tests that can be used to assess the health of the developing fetus and which one(s) might be appropriate, a topic that we discussed in chapter 3. Another important step in a healthy pregnancy is to obtain early prenatal care, which we will discuss next.

Prenatal Care

Information about teratogens and other prenatal hazards is one of the many benefits that expectant mothers gain from prenatal care. Although prenatal care varies enormously, it usually involves a defined schedule of visits for medical care, which typically include screening for manageable conditions and treatable diseases that can affect the baby or the mother (Kuppermann & others, 2006). In addition to medical care, prenatal programs often include comprehensive educational, social, and nutritional services (Massey, Rising, & Ickovics, 2006; Moos, 2006).

The education provided in prenatal care varies during the course of pregnancy. Those in the early stages of pregnancy as well as couples who are anticipating a pregnancy may participate in early prenatal classes. In addition to providing information on dangers to the fetus, early prenatal classes often discuss the development of the embryo and the fetus; sexuality during pregnancy; choices about the birth setting and care providers; nutrition, rest, and exercise; common discomforts of pregnancy and relief measures; psychological changes in the expectant mother and her partner; and factors that increase the risk of preterm labor and possible symptoms of preterm labor. Early classes also may include information about the advantages and disadvantages of breast feeding and bottle feeding (50 to 80 percent of expectant mothers decide how they will feed their infant prior to the sixth month of pregnancy). During the second or third trimester of pregnancy, prenatal classes focus on preparing for the birth, infant care and feeding, choices about birth, and postpartum self-care.

A CenteringPregnancy program. This rapidly increasing program alters routine prenatal care by bringing women out of exam rooms and into relationship-oriented groups.

An innovative program that is rapidly expanding in the United States is CenteringPregnancy (Massey, Rising, & Ickovics, 2006; Moos, 2006). This program is relationship-centered and provides complete prenatal care in a group setting. CenteringPregnancy replaces traditional 15-minute physician visits with 90-minute peer group support settings and self-examination, led by a physician or a certified nurse midwife. Groups of up to 10 women (and often their partners) meet regularly beginning at 12- to 16-weeks of pregnancy. The sessions emphasize empowering women to play an active role in experiencing a healthy pregnancy.

Does prenatal care matter? Information about pregnancy, labor, delivery, and caring for the newborn can be especially valuable for first-time mothers (Chang & others, 2003). Prenatal care is also very important for women in poverty because it links them with other social services. The legacy of prenatal care continues after the birth because women who experience this type of care are more likely to get preventive care for their infants (Bates & others, 1994).

Research contrasting the experiences of mothers who had prenatal care and those who did not supports the significance of prenatal care. One recent study found that U.S. women who had no prenatal care were far more likely than their counterparts who received prenatal care to have infants who had low birth weight, increased mortality, and a number of other physical problems (Herbst & others, 2003). In other recent studies, low birth weight and preterm deliveries were common among U.S. mothers who received no prenatal care and the absence of prenatal care increased the risk for preterm birth almost threefold in both non-Latino White and

African American women (Stringer & others, 2005; Vintzileos & others, 2002). Another recent study revealed that the later prenatal care begins, the greater the risk of congenital malformations (Carmichael, Shaw, & Nelson, 2002).

Inadequate prenatal care may help explain a disturbing fact: Rates of infant mortality and low birth weight indicate that many other nations have healthier babies than the United States (Grant, 1996; Smulian & others, 2002). In many countries that have a lower percentage of low birth weight infants than the United States, mothers receive either free or very low-cost prenatal and postnatal care, and can receive paid maternity leave from work that ranges from 9 to 40 weeks. In Norway and the Netherlands, prenatal care is coordinated with a general practitioner, an obstetrician, and a midwife.

Why do some U.S. women receive inadequate prenatal care? Sometimes the reasons are tied to the health-care system, to provider practices, and to their own individual and social characteristics (Conway & Kutinova, 2006). Women who do not want to be pregnant, who have negative attitudes about being pregnant, or who unintentionally become pregnant are more likely to delay prenatal care or to miss appointments. As we noted earlier, adolescent girls are less likely than adult women to obtain prenatal care. Within the United States, there are differences among ethnic groups both in the health of babies and in prenatal care (Madan & others, 2006). In the 1980s, more than one-fifth of all non-Latino White mothers and one-third of all African American mothers did not receive prenatal care in the first trimester of their pregnancy, and 5 percent of White mothers and 10 percent of African American mothers received no prenatal care at all (Wegman, 1986).

The situation has been improving. From 1990 to 2004, the use of timely prenatal care increased for women from a variety of ethnic backgrounds in the United States, although non-Latino White women were still more likely to obtain prenatal care than African American and Latino women (see figure 4.6). The United States needs more comprehensive medical and educational services to improve the quality of prenatal care and to reduce the number of low birth weight and preterm infants (Daniels, Noe, & Mayberry, 2006; Thornton & others, 2006).

Cultures around the world have differing views of pregnancy than the United States. In the Diversity in Life-Span Development interlude that follows, we will explore these beliefs.

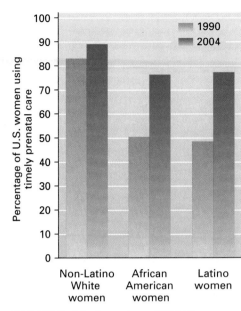

FIGURE 4.6 **Percentage of U.S. Women Using Timely Prenatal Care: 1990 to 2004.** From 1990 to 2004, the use of timely prenatal care increased by 7 percent (to 89.1) for non-Latino White women, by 25 percent (to 76.5) for African American women, and by 28 percent (to 77.4) for Latino women in the United States.

www.mhhe.com/santrockld11

Reproductive Health Links
Exploring Pregnancy
Childbirth Classes
Prenatal Care
Health-Care Providers

DIVERSITY IN LIFE-SPAN DEVELOPMENT

Cultural Beliefs About Pregnancy

All cultures have beliefs and rituals that surround life's major events, including pregnancy. Some cultures treat pregnancy simply as a natural occurrence; others see it as a medical condition (Mathole & others, 2004; Paredes & others, 2005; Walsh, 2006). For Diana and Roger, the couple described at the opening of this chapter, it seemed normal to obtain medical care and turn for help during pregnancy to doctors and other health professionals. But obtaining medical care during pregnancy may not seem important to a woman whose culture defines pregnancy as a natural condition.

How expectant mothers behave during pregnancy may depend in part on the prevalence of traditional home-care remedies and folk beliefs, the importance of indigenous healers, and the influence of health-care professionals in their culture (Walsh, 2006). In various cultures, pregnant women may turn to herbalists, faith healers, root doctors, or spiritualists for help (Mbonye, Neema, & Magnussen, 2006).

(continued on next page)

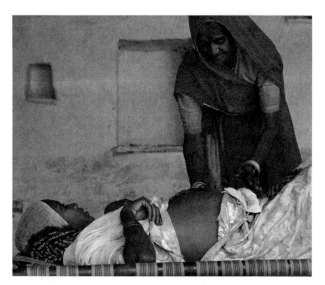

In India, a midwife checks on the size, position, and heartbeat of a fetus. Midwives deliver babies in many cultures around the world. *What are some cultural variations in prenatal care?*

Following are some maternal health beliefs and behaviors that are common to Latino and Asian cultures (American Public Health Association, 2006):

- *Latino.* Latinas are less likely to use family-planning services than non-Latino Whites and African Americans (Hamilton & Ventura, 2006). Further, a common folk belief by Latinos is that using certain contraceptives such as birth control pills will lessen menstrual flow, causing retention of impurities and ultimately health problems. Also, many Mexican American women seek advise about their pregnancy from their mothers and older women in the community. They may call on an indigenous healer known as a *curandero.* Recent immigrant Latinas and undocumented workers tend to initiate prenatal care after the first trimester, while their counterparts who have been residing in the United States for longer periods of time are more likely to begin prenatal care earlier (Taylor, Ko, & Pan, 1999).

- *Asian.* Common among Chinese expectant mothers is the practice of listening to classical music during pregnancy because they believe it will help the offspring develop patience, wisdom, and artistic sensitivity. Many Chinese also think that a child's moral disposition is at least partially developed in the womb. As a consequence, expectant Chinese mothers may avoid contact with people they perceive to be dishonest, engage in charitable deeds, and try to avoid having negative thoughts or feelings. In some Asian countries, such as the Philippines, many expectant mothers will not take any medication during pregnancy. Also, some immigrant Asian women return to their parents' home in their native country to deliver their baby, especially if it is their firstborn child.

When health-care professionals work with expectant mothers, cultural assessment should be an important component of their care (Jansen, 2006; Laditka & others, 2005; Wood & Atkins, 2006). In other words, they should identify beliefs, values, and behaviors related to childbearing. In particular, ethnic background, degree of affiliation with the ethnic group, patterns of decision making, religious preference, language, communication style, and etiquette may all affect a woman's attitudes about the care needed during pregnancy (Atiyeh & El-Mohandes, 2005; Willis & others, 2004). Health-care workers should assess whether a woman's beliefs or practices pose a threat to her or the fetus. If they do, health-care professionals should consider a culturally sensitive way to handle the problem.

Review and Reflect • LEARNING GOAL 1

1 Describe Prenatal Development

Review
- What is the course of prenatal development?
- What are some of the main hazards to prenatal development?
- What do prenatal care programs provide?

Reflect
- What can be done to convince women who are pregnant not to smoke or drink? Consider the role of health-care providers, the role of insurance companies, and specific programs targeted at women who are pregnant.

As we saw in the opening story, sometimes unexpected changes occur during birth, as when Diana's heart rate dropped and Alex's heart and breathing rates became precariously high. Let's further explore the birth process, examining variations in how it occurs and in its outcomes.

The Birth Process

Nature writes the basic script for how birth occurs, but parents make important choices about conditions surrounding birth. We look first at the sequence of physical steps when a child is born.

Stages of Birth   Childbirth—or labor—occurs in three stages. In the first stage, uterine contractions are 15 to 20 minutes apart at the beginning and last up to a minute. These contractions cause the woman's cervix (the opening into the birth canal) to stretch and open. As the first stage progresses, the contractions come closer together, appearing every two to five minutes. Their intensity increases too. By the end of the first birth stage, contractions dilate the cervix to an opening of about 4 inches, so that the baby can move from the uterus to the birth canal. For a woman having her first child, the first stage lasts an average of 12 to 24 hours; it is the longest of the three stages. For later births, the first stage lasts an average of 8 hours.

What is the first stage like for the mother-to-be? Here is a description of one woman's experience:

> It is day 266 of his mother Cindy's pregnancy. She is in the frozen-food isle of a convenience store and feels a sharp pain, starting in the small of her back and reaching around her middle, which causes her to gasp. For weeks, painless Braxton-Hicks spasms (named for the gynecologist who discovered them) have been flexing her uterine muscles. But these practice contractions were not nearly as intense and painful as the one she just experienced. After six hours of irregular spasms, her uterus settles into a more predictable rhythm.
>
> At 3 A.M., Cindy and her husband, Tom, are wide awake. They time Cindy's contractions with a stopwatch. The contractions are now only six minutes apart. It's time to call the hospital. A short time later, Tom and Cindy arrive at the hospital's labor-delivery suite. . . . When the cervix is dilated to more than 4 centimeters, or almost half open, Cindy receives her first medication. As Demorol begins to drip in her veins, the pain of her contractions is less intense . . . (Warrick, 1992, p. E1).

The second birth stage begins when the baby's head starts to move through the cervix and the birth canal. It terminates when the baby completely emerges from the mother's body. For a first birth, this stage lasts approximately $1\frac{1}{2}$ hours, and for later births the second stage averages 45 minutes in length. With each contraction, the mother bears down hard to push the baby out of her body. By the time the baby's head is out of the mother's body, the contractions come almost every minute and last for about a minute.

Afterbirth is the third stage, at which time the placenta, umbilical cord, and other membranes are detached and expelled from the mother's body. This final stage is the shortest of the three birth stages, lasting only minutes.

Childbirth Setting and Attendants   In the United States, 99 percent of births take place in hospitals (Ventura & others, 1997). Some women with good medical histories and low risk for problems may choose a delivery at home or in a

We must respect this instant of birth, this fragile moment. The baby is between two worlds, on a threshold, hesitating . . .

—FREDERICK LEBOYER
French Obstetrician, 20th Century

A woman in the African !Kung culture giving birth in a sitting position. Notice the help and support being given by another woman. *What are some cultural variations in childbirth?*

freestanding birth center, which is usually staffed by nurse-midwives. Births at home are far more common in many other countries; for example, in Holland, 35 percent of the babies are born at home. Some critics worry that the U.S. tendency to view birth through a medical lens may lead to unnecessary medical procedures (Hausman, 2005; Kennedy & Shannon, 2004).

Who helps a mother during birth varies across cultures. In U.S. hospitals it has become the norm for fathers or birth coaches to be with the mother throughout labor and delivery. In the East African Nigoni culture, men are completely excluded from the childbirth process. When a woman is ready to give birth, female relatives move into the woman's hut and the husband leaves, taking his belongings (clothes, tools, weapons, and so on) with him. He is not permitted to return until after the baby is born. In some cultures, childbirth is an open, community affair. For example, in the Pukapukan culture in the Pacific Islands, women give birth in a shelter that is open for villagers to observe.

Midwifery is the norm throughout most of the world. In Holland, more than 40 percent of babies are delivered by midwives rather than doctors (Treffers & others, 1990). But more than 90 percent of U.S. births are attended by physicians and only 6 percent of women who deliver a baby in the United States are attended by a midwife (Tritten, 2004). In the United States, most midwives are nurses who have been specially trained in delivering babies (Kerr, 2005; Marsh-Prelesnik, 2006). Compared to physicians, certified nurse-midwives generally spend more time with patients during prenatal visits, place more emphasis on patient counseling and education, provide more emotional support, and are more likely to be with the patient one-on-one during the entire labor and delivery process, which may explain the more positive outcomes for babies delivered by certified nurse-midwives (Davis, 2005).

In many countries, a doula attends a childbearing woman. *Doula* is a Greek word that means "a woman who helps." A **doula** is a caregiver who provides continuous physical, emotional, and educational support for the mother before, during, and after childbirth. Doulas remain with the mother throughout labor, assessing and responding to her needs. Researchers have found positive effects when a doula is present at the birth of a child. In one study, the mothers who received doula support reported less labor pain than the mothers who did not receive doula support (Klaus, Kennell, & Klaus, 1993).

In the United States, most doulas work as independent providers hired by the expectant mother. Doulas typically function as part of a "birthing team," serving as an adjunct to the midwife or the hospital's obstetric staff (Dundek, 2006; Lantz & others, 2005). Managed care organizations are increasingly offering doula support as a part of regular obstetric care.

Methods of Childbirth   U.S. hospitals often allow the mother and her obstetrician a range of options regarding their method of delivery. Key choices involve the use of medication and when to resort to a cesarean delivery.

Medication   Three basic kinds of drugs that are used for labor are analgesia, anesthesia, and oxytocics.

Analgesia is used to relieve pain. Analgesics include tranquilizers, barbiturates, and narcotics (such as Demerol).

Anesthesia is used in late first-stage labor and during expulsion of the baby to block sensation in an area of the body or to block consciousness. There is a trend toward not using general anesthesia, which blocks consciousness, in normal births because a general anethesia can be transmitted through the placenta to the fetus (Lieberman & others, 2005). An *epidural block* is regional anesthesia that numbs the woman's body from the waist down. Even this drug, thought to be relatively safe, has come under recent criticism because it is associated with fever, extended labor, and increased risk for cesarean delivery (Glantz, 2005).

doula A caregiver who provides continuous physical, emotional, and educational support for the mother before, during, and after childbirth.

Oxytocics are synthetic hormones that are used to stimulate contractions (Kotaska, Klein, & Liston, 2006). Pitocin is the most commonly used oxytocic (Akerlund, 2006).

Predicting how a drug will affect an individual woman and her fetus is difficult (Briggs & Wan, 2006). A particular drug might have only a minimal effect on one fetus yet have a much stronger effect on another. The drug's dosage also is a factor. Stronger doses of tranquilizers and narcotics given to decrease the mother's pain have a potentially more negative effect on the fetus than mild doses. It is important for the mother to assess her level of pain and have a voice in the decision of whether she should receive medication (Young, 2001).

Natural and Prepared Childbirth   For a brief time not long ago, the idea of avoiding all medication during childbirth gained favor in the United States. Instead, many women chose to reduce the pain of childbirth through techniques known as natural childbirth and prepared childbirth became popular. Today, at least some medication is used in the typical childbirth, but elements of natural childbirth and prepared childbirth remain popular.

Natural childbirth is the method that aims to reduce the mother's pain by decreasing her fear through education about childbirth and by teaching her to use breathing methods and relaxation techniques during delivery (Day-Stirk, 2005; Sandiford, 2006). This approach was developed in 1914 by English obstetrician Grantley Dick-Read. Dick-Read believed that the doctor's relationship with the mother plays an important role in reducing her perception of pain and that the doctor should be present, providing reassurance, during her active labor prior to delivery.

French obstetrician Ferdinand Lamaze developed a method similar to natural childbirth that is known as **prepared childbirth** or the Lamaze method. It includes a special breathing technique to control pushing in the final stages of labor, as well as more detailed education about anatomy and physiology than Dick-Read's approach provides. The Lamaze method has become very popular in the United States. The pregnant woman's partner usually serves as a coach, who attends childbirth classes with her and helps her with her breathing and relaxation during delivery.

Many other prepared childbirth techniques have been developed. They usually include elements of Dick-Read's natural childbirth or Lamaze's method, plus one or more other components. For instance, the Bradley method emphasizes the father's role as a labor coach (Signore, 2004). Virtually all of the prepared childbirth methods emphasize education, relaxation and breathing exercises, and support.

In sum, proponents of current prepared childbirth methods believe that when information and support are provided, women *know* how to give birth. To read about one nurse whose research focuses on fatigue during childbearing and breathing exercises during labor, see the Careers in Life-Span Development profile.

Other Nonmedicated Techniques to Reduce Pain   The effort to reduce stress and control pain during labor has recently led to an increase in the use of some older and some newer nonmedicated techniques (Albers & others, 2005; Simkin & Bolding, 2004). These include waterbirth, massage, acupuncture, hypnosis, and music therapy.

Waterbirth involves giving birth in a tub of warm water. Some women go through labor in the water and get out for delivery, others remain in the water for delivery. The rationale for waterbirth is that the baby has been in an amniotic sac for many months and that delivery in a similar environment is likely to be less stressful for the baby and the mother. Mothers get into the warm water when contractions become closer together and more intense. Getting into the water too soon can cause labor to slow or stop. Researchers have recently found positive results for the use of waterbirth (Enning, 2004; Simkin & Bolding, 2004; Thoni & Moroder, 2004; Woodward & Kelly, 2004). In a recent comparison of almost 6,000 landbirths and more than 3,500 waterbirths, waterbirths resulted in a lower incidence of episiotomies (an incision made to widen the vagina for delivery), fewer perineal lacerations (the perineum is

Partners or friends take childbirth classes with prospective mothers as part of prepared or natural childbirth. This is a Lamaze training session. *What are key elements of the Lamaze method?*

natural childbirth Developed in 1914 by Dick-Read, this method attempts to reduce the mother's pain by decreasing her fear through education about childbirth and relaxation techniques during delivery.

prepared childbirth Developed by French obstetrician Ferdinand Lamaze, this childbirth strategy is similar to natural childbirth but includes a special breathing technique to control pushing in the final stages of labor and a more detailed anatomy and physiology course.

CAREERS
in LIFE-SPAN DEVELOPMENT

Linda Pugh
Perinatal Nurse

Perinatal nurses work with childbearing women to support health and growth during the childbearing experience. Linda Pugh, Ph.D., R.N.C., is a perinatal nurse on the faculty at The Johns Hopkins University School of Nursing. She is certified as an inpatient obstetric nurse and specializes in the care of women during labor and delivery. She teaches undergraduate and graduate students, educates professional nurses, and conducts research. In addition, Linda consults with hospitals and organizations about women's health issues and topics we discuss in this chapter. Her research interests include nursing interventions with low-income breast feeding women, discovering ways to prevent and ameliorate fatigue during childbearing, and using breathing exercises during labor.

Linda Pugh (*right*) a perinatal nurse, with a mother and her newborn.

www.mhhe.com/santrockld11

Childbirth Strategies
Childbirth Setting and Attendants
Midwifery
Doula
Fathers and Childbirth
Siblings and Childbirth

a muscle between the vagina and the rectum), fewer vaginal tears, and a lower rate of newborn complications (Geissbuehler, Stein, & Eberhard, 2004). Waterbirth has been practiced more often in European countries such as Switzerland and Sweden in recent decades than in the United States but is increasingly being included in U.S. birth plans.

Massage is increasingly used as a procedure prior to and during delivery (Spencer, 2005). Several research studies have found that massage can reduce pain and anxiety during labor (Chang, Wang, & Chen, 2002; Wang & others, 2005). Massage is a promising procedure for use during childbirth but more research is needed to document its effectiveness (Simkin & Bolding, 2004).

Acupuncture, the insertion of very fine needles into specific locations in the body, has been used as a standard procedure to reduce the pain of childbirth in China for centuries, although it only recently has begun to be used in the United States for this purpose. A recent research review indicated that only a limited number of studies had been conducted on the use of acupuncture in childbirth but that it appears to be safe and may have positive effects (Smith & Crowler, 2004). One recent study found that acupuncture lowered the need for medical inductions and cesarean deliveries (Duke & Don, 2005). Further research is needed to determine the effectiveness of acupuncture as childbirth procedure.

Hypnosis, the induction of a psychological state of altered attention and awareness in which the individual is unusually responsive to suggestions, is also increasingly being used during childbirth (Ketterhagan, VandeVusse, & Berner, 2002; Spencer, 2005). Although several studies have indicated positive effects of hypnosis for reducing pain during childbirth, recent reviews indicate that further research is needed to determine the risks and benefits of this procedure (Cyna, McAuliffe, & Andrew, 2004; Simkin & Bolding, 2004).

Music therapy during childbirth, which involves the use of music to reduce stress and manage pain, is increasingly used (Browning, 2000; Chang & Chen, 2004). Few research studies have been conducted to determine its effectiveness (Simkin & Bolding, 2004).

Cesarean Delivery Normally, as in the birth of Alex ("Mr. Littles") described in the opening of the chapter, the baby's head comes through the vagina first. But if the baby is in a **breech position,** the baby's buttocks are the first part to emerge from the vagina. In 1 of every 25 deliveries, the baby's head is still in the uterus when the rest of the body is out. Breech births can cause respiratory problems. As a result, if the baby is in a breech position, what is called a cesarean section or a cesarean delivery is usually performed. In a *cesarean delivery,* the baby is removed from the mother's uterus through an incision made in her abdomen.

Cesarean deliveries are safer than breech deliveries. Cesarean deliveries also are performed if the baby is lying crosswise in the uterus, if the baby's head is too large to pass through the mother's pelvis, if the baby develops complications, or if the mother is bleeding vaginally. Cesarean deliveries can be life-saving, but they do bring risks. Compared with vaginal deliveries, they involve a higher infection rate, longer hospital stays, and the greater expense and stress that accompany any surgery.

The benefits and risks of cesarean sections continue to be debated (Bailit, Love, & Dawson, 2006; Declercq, Menacker, & Macdorman, 2006; Lee & others, 2005). Some critics believe that too many babies are delivered by cesarean section in the United States. More cesarean sections are performed in the United States than in any other country in the world. The cesarean delivery rate jumped 7.5 percent from 2002 to 2004 in the United States to 29.1 percent of all births, the highest level since these data began to be reported on birth certificates in 1989 (Hoyert & others, 2006). Higher cesarean delivery rates may be due to a better ability to identify infants in distress during birth and the increase in overweight and obese pregnant women (Coleman & others, 2005; Sarsam, Elliott, & Lam, 2005). Also, some doctors may be overly cautious and recommend a cesarean delivery to defend against a potential lawsuit.

The Transition from Fetus to Newborn Much of our discussion of birth so far has focused on the mother. Being born also involves considerable stress for the baby. During each contraction, when the placenta and umbilical cord are compressed as the uterine muscles draw together, the supply of oxygen to the fetus is decreased. If the delivery takes too long, the baby can develop *anoxia,* a condition in which the fetus or newborn has an insufficient supply of oxygen. Anoxia can cause brain damage (Kendall & Peebles, 2005).

The baby has considerable capacity to withstand the stress of birth. Large quantities of adrenaline and noradrenalin, hormones that protect the fetus in the event of oxygen deficiency, are secreted in stressful circumstances. These hormones increase the heart's pumping activity, speed up heart rate, channel blood flow to the brain, and raise the blood-sugar level. Never again in life will such large amounts of these hormones be secreted. This circumstance underscores how stressful it is to be born and also how well prepared and adapted the fetus is for birth (VanBeveren, 2005).

At the time of birth, the baby is covered with what is called *vernix caseosa,* a protective skin grease. This vernix consists of fatty secretions and dead cells, thought to help protect the baby's skin against heat loss before and during birth.

Immediately after birth, the umbilical cord is cut and the baby is on its own. Before birth, oxygen came from the mother via the umbilical cord, but now the baby is self-sufficient and can breathe on its own. Now 25 million little air sacs in the lungs must be filled with air. These first breaths may be the hardest ones an individual takes.

Assessing the Newborn

Almost immediately after birth, after the baby and mother have become acquainted, a newborn is taken to be weighed, cleaned up, and tested for signs of developmental problems that might require urgent attention. The **Apgar Scale** is widely used to assess the health of newborns at 1 and 5 minutes after birth. The Apgar Scale evaluates infants' heart rate, respiratory effort, muscle tone, body color, and reflex irritability. An obstetrician or a nurse does the evaluation and gives the newborn a

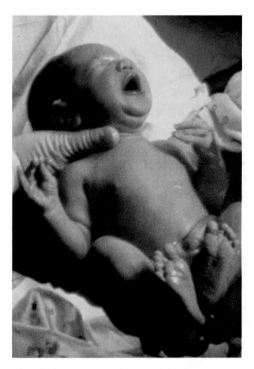

After the long journey of prenatal development, the baby comes to the threshold between two worlds. Birth takes place. *What is the transition to the outside world like for the newborn?*

breech position The baby's position in the uterus that causes the buttocks to be the first part to emerge from the vagina.

Apgar Scale A widely used method to assess the health of newborns at one and five minutes after birth. The Apgar Scale evaluates infants' heart rate, respiratory effort, muscle tone, body color, and reflex irritability.

Score	0	1	2	
Heart rate	Absent	Slow—less than 100 beats per minute	Fast—100–140 beats per minute	
Respiratory effort	No breathing for more than one minute	Irregular and slow	Good breathing with normal crying	
Muscle tone	Limp and flaccid	Weak, inactive, but some flexion of extremities	Strong, active motion	
Body color	Blue and pale	Body pink, but extremities blue	Entire body pink	
Reflex irritability	No response	Grimace	Coughing, sneezing and crying	

FIGURE 4.7 The Apgar Scale. A newborn's score on the Apgar Scale indicates whether the baby has urgent medical problems.

score, or reading, of 0, 1, or 2 on each of these five health signs (see figure 4.7). A total score of 7 to 10 indicates that the newborn's condition is good. A score of 5 indicates there may be developmental difficulties. A score of 3 or below signals an emergency and indicates that the baby might not survive.

The Apgar Scale is especially effective at assessing the newborn's ability to respond to the stress of delivery and the new environment (Al-Suleiman & others, 2006; Fallis & others, 2006). It also identifies high-risk infants who need resuscitation. For a more thorough assessment of the newborn, the Brazelton Neonatal Behavioral Assessment Scale or the Neonatal Intensive Care Unit Network Neurobehavioral Scale may be used.

The **Brazelton Neonatal Behavioral Assessment Scale (NBAS)** is performed within 24 to 36 hours after birth. It is also used as a sensitive index of neurological competence in the weeks or months after birth and as a measure in many studies of infant development (Hart & others, 2006; Nakai & others, 2004; Ohgi, Akiyama, & Fukuda, 2005). The NBAS assesses the newborn's neurological development, reflexes, and reactions to people. The newborn is an active participant, and the score is based on the newborn's best performance. Sixteen reflexes, such as blinking and rooting, are assessed, along with reactions to stimuli, such as the infant's reaction to a rattle. (We will have more to say about reflexes in chapter 6, when we discuss motor development in infancy.)

The examiner rates the newborn on each of 27 items. For example, item 15 is "cuddliness." The examiner uses nine categories to assessing cuddliness and scores the infant on a continuum that ranges from being very resistant to being held to being extremely cuddly and clinging. The 27 items of the NBAS are organized into four categories—physiological, motoric, state, and interaction. Based on these categories, the baby is also classified in global terms, such as "worrisome," "normal," or "superior," based on these categories (Nugent & Brazelton, 2000).

A very low NBAS score can indicate brain damage, or stress to the brain that may heal in time. If an infant merely seems sluggish, parents are encouraged to give the infant attention and become more sensitive to the infant's needs. Parents are shown how the newborn can respond to people and how to stimulate such responses. These communications with parents can improve their interaction skills with both high-risk infants and healthy, responsive infants (Girling, 2006).

An "offspring" of the NBAS, the **Neonatal Intensive Care Unit Network Neurobehavioral Scale (NNNS)** provides a more comprehensive analysis of the newborn's behavior, neurological and stress responses, and regulatory capacities (Brazelton, 2004; Lester, Tronick, & Brazelton, 2004). Whereas the NBAS was

Brazelton Neonatal Behavioral Assessment Scale (NBAS) A test given 24 to 36 hours after birth to assess newborns' neurological development, reflexes, and reactions to people.

Neonatal Intensive Care Unit Neurobehavioral Scale (NNNS) An "offspring" of the NBAS, the NNNS provides a more comprehensive analysis of the newborn's behavior, neurological and stress responses, and regulatory capacities.

developed to assess normal, healthy, term infants, Brazelton, along with Barry Lester and Edward Tronick, developed the NNNS to assess the at-risk infant. It is especially useful for evaluating preterm infants (although it may not be appropriate for those less than 30 weeks' gestational age) and substance-exposed infants (Miller-Loncar & others, 2005). For example, the NNNS includes items to assess the infant's capacity for regulating arousal, "responsiveness to stimulation, self-soothing, and tolerance of handling," and a scale to provide information about "manifestations of drug dependence or environment-related stress" (Boukydis & others, 2004, p. 680). According to Brazelton (2004), although created to evaluate at-risk infants, the NNNS is also appropriate for assessing normal, healthy, full-term infants.

Low Birth Weight and Preterm Infants

Three related conditions pose threats to many newborns: low birth weight, being preterm, and being small-for-date. **Low birth weight infants** weigh less than $5\frac{1}{2}$ pounds at birth. *Very low birth weight* newborns weigh under 3 pounds and *extremely low birth weight* newborns under 2 pounds. **Preterm infants** are those born three weeks or more before the pregnancy has reached its full term—in other words, 35 or fewer weeks after conception. **Small for date infants** (also called *small for gestational age infants*) are those whose birth weight is below normal when the length of the pregnancy is considered. They weigh less than 90 percent of all babies of the same gestational age. Small for date infants may be preterm or full term. One recent study found that small for date infants had more than a fourfold risk of death (Regev & others, 2004).

A "kilogram kid," weighing less than 2.3 pounds at birth. *What are some long-term* potential consequences *for weighing so little at birth?*

The preterm birth rate in the United States increased 18 percent from 1990 to 2004 (Hoyert & others, 2006). One of every eight U.S. births is now preterm. The increase in preterm birth is likely due to such factors as the increasing number of births to women 35 years and older, increasing rates of multiple births, increased management of maternal and fetal conditions (for example, inducing labor preterm if medical technology indicates it will increase the likelihood of survival), increased substance abuse (tobacco, alcohol), and increased stress (Petrini, 2004). African American infants are twice as likely as non-Latino White infants to be born preterm (Dubay & others, 2001). In one recent study, weekly injections of the hormone progesterone, which is naturally produced by the ovaries, lowered the rate of preterm births by one-third (Meis & Peaceman, 2003). Researchers are recommending that further research be conducted to determine the safest and most effective way to administer the drug.

Incidences and Causes of Low Birth Weight   Most, but not all, preterm babies are also low birth weight babies. The incidence of low birth weight varies considerably from country to country. In some developing countries, such as Bangladesh, where poverty is rampant and the health and nutrition of mothers are poor, the percentage of low birth weight babies reaches as high as 50 percent. In the United States, there has been an increase in low birth weight infants in the last two decades, and the U.S. low birth weight rate of 8.1 percent in 2004 is considerably higher than that of many other developed countries (Cuevas & others, 2005; Hoyert & others, 2006). For example, only 4 percent of the infants born in Sweden, Finland, the Netherlands, and Norway are low birth weight, and only 5 percent of those born in New Zealand, Australia, France, and Japan are low birth weight.

The causes of low birth weight also vary. In the developing world, low birth weight stems mainly from the mother's poor health and nutrition (Lasker & others, 2005). Diseases such as diarrhea and malaria, which are common in developing countries, can impair fetal growth if the mother becomes infected while she is pregnant. In developed countries, cigarette smoking during pregnancy is the leading cause of low birth weight (Ashdown-Lambert, 2005; Delpisheh & others, 2006; Hankins & Longo, 2006). In both developed and developing countries, adolescents

low birth weight infants An infant that weighs less than $5\frac{1}{2}$ pounds at birth.

preterm infants Those born three weeks or more before the pregnancy has reached its full term.

small for date infants Also called small for gestational age infants, these infants' birth weights are below normal when the length of pregnancy is considered. Small for date infants may be preterm or full term.

who give birth when their bodies have not fully matured are at risk for having low birth weight babies. In the United States, the increase in the number of low birth weight infants is thought to be due to such factors as the use of drugs, poor nutrition, multiple births, and reproductive technologies (Bacak & others, 2005; Hoyert & others, 2006).

Consequences of Low Birth Weight   Although most low birth weight infants are normal and healthy, as a group they have more health and developmental problems than normal birth weight infants (Hintz & others, 2005; Moss, 2006; Mufti, Setna, & Nazir, 2006). The number and severity of these problems increase as birth weight decreases (Kilbride, Thorstad, & Daily, 2004). Survival rates for infants who are born very early and very small have risen, but with this improved survival rate have come increases in rates of severe brain damage (Yu, 2000). The lower the birth weight, the greater the likelihood of brain injury (Watenberg & others, 2002). Approximately 7 percent of moderately low birth weight infants (3 pounds 5 ounces to 5 pounds 8 ounces) have brain injuries. This figure increases to 20 percent for the smallest newborns (1 pound 2 ounces to 3 pounds 5 ounces). Low birth weight infants are also more likely than normal birth weight infants to have lung or liver diseases.

At school age, children who were born low in birth weight are more likely than their normal birth weight counterparts to have a learning disability, attention deficit hyperactivity disorder, or breathing problems such as asthma (Hintz & others, 2005; Wocadlo & Rieger, 2006). A recent study revealed that 17-year-olds who were born with low birth weight were 50 percent more likely than normal birth weight individuals to have reading and mathematics deficits (Breslau, Paneth, & Lucia, 2004). Approximately 50 percent of all low birth weight children are enrolled in special education programs.

Note that not all of these adverse consequences can be attributed solely to being born low in birth weight. Some of the less severe but more common developmental and physical delays occur because many low birth weight children come from disadvantaged environments (Malamitsi-Puchner & Boutsikou, 2006).

Some effects of being born low in birth weight can be reversed. Intensive enrichment programs that provide medical and educational services for both the parents and children can improve short-term outcomes for low birth weight children. Federal laws mandate that services for school-age children be expanded to include family-based care for infants. At present, these services are aimed at children born with severe disabilities. The availability of services for moderately low birth weight children who do not have severe physical problems varies, but most states do not provide these services.

Kangaroo Care and Massage Therapy   One recent survey found that 82 percent of neonatal intensive-care units in the United States use kangaroo care (Engler & others, 2002). **Kangaroo care** is a way of holding a preterm infant so that there is skin-to-skin contact (Ludington-Hoe & Golant, 1993; Ludington-Hoe & others, 2006). The baby, wearing only a diaper, is held upright against the parent's bare chest, much as a baby kangaroo is carried by its mother. Kangaroo care is typically practiced for two to three hours per day, skin-to-skin over an extended time in early infancy (Feldman & others, 2003).

Why use kangaroo care with preterm infants? Preterm infants often have difficulty coordinating their breathing and heart rate, and the close physical contact with the parent provided by kangaroo care can help to stabilize the preterm infant's heartbeat, temperature, and breathing (Dodd, 2005; Ferber & Makhoul, 2004; Kennell, 2006). Further, preterm infants who experience kangaroo care have longer periods of sleep, gain more weight, decrease their crying, have longer periods of alertness, and earlier hospital discharge (Ludington-Hoe & others, 2004, 2006; Worku & Kassir, 2005). One recent study compared 26 low birth weight infants who received kangaroo care

New mother learning how to practice kangaroo care. *What is kangaroo care?*

kangaroo care A way of holding a preterm infant so that there is skin-to-skin contact.

with 27 low birth weight infants who received standard medical/nursing care (Ohgi & others, 2002). At both 6 and 12 months of age, the kangaroo care infants were more alert and responsive, less irritable and fussy, and had a more positive mood. Another recent study found that preterm infants who received kangaroo care had better control of their arousal, more effectively attended to stimuli, and engaged in more sustained exploration during a toy session than a control group of preterm infants who did not receive kangaroo care (Feldman & others, 2002). Increasingly, kangaroo care is being recommended for full-term infants as well (Johnson, 2005).

Many preterm infants experience less touch than full-term infants because they are isolated in temperature-controlled incubators (Beachy, 2003). The research of Tiffany Field has led to a surge of interest in the role that massage might play in improving the developmental outcomes for preterm infants. To read about her research, see the following Research in Life-Span Development interlude.

RESEARCH IN LIFE-SPAN DEVELOPMENT

Tiffany Field's Research on Massage Therapy

Throughout history and in many cultures, caregivers have massaged infants. In Africa and Asia, infants are routinely massaged by parents or other family members for several months after birth. In the United States, interest in using touch and massage to improve the growth, health, and well-being of infants has been stimulated by the research of Tiffany Field (1998, 2001, 2003; Field, Hernandez-Reif, & Freedman, 2004; Field & others, 2006), director of the Touch Research Institute at the University of Miami School of Medicine.

In Field's first study in this area, massage therapy consisting of firm stroking with the palms of the hands was given three times per day for 15-minute periods to preterm infants (Field & others, 1986). The massage therapy led to 47 percent greater weight gain than standard medical treatment (see figure 4.8). The massaged infants also were more active and alert than preterm infants who were not massaged, and they performed better on developmental tests.

In later studies, Field demonstrated the benefits of massage therapy for infants who faced a variety of problems. For example, preterm infants exposed to cocaine in utero who received massage therapy gained weight and improved their scores on developmental tests (Field, 1992). In another investigation, newborns born to HIV-positive mothers were randomly assigned to a massage therapy group or to a control group that did not receive the therapy (Scafidi & Field, 1996). The massaged infants showed superior performance on a wide range of assessments, including daily weight gain. Another study investigated 1- to 3-month-old infants born to depressed adolescent mothers (Field & others, 1996). The infants of depressed mothers who received massage therapy had lower stress—as well as improved emotionality, sociability, and soothability—compared with the non-massaged infants of depressed mothers.

In a recent study, Field and her colleagues (2004) taught mothers how to massage their full-term infants. Once a day before bedtime the mothers massaged the babies using either light or moderate pressure. Infants who were massaged with moderate pressure "gained more weight, were greater length, performed better on the orientation scale of the Brazelton, had lower Brazelton excitability and depression scores, and exhibited less agitation during sleep" (p. 435).

(continued on next page)

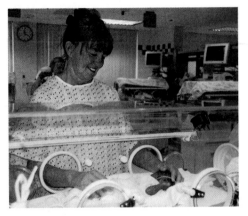

Shown here is Tiffany Field massaging a newborn infant. *What types of infants has massage therapy been shown to help?*

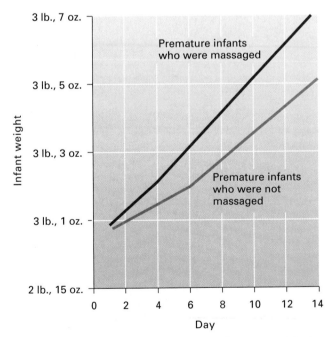

FIGURE 4.8 Weight Gain Comparison of Premature Infants Who Were Massaged or Not Massaged. In Tiffany Field's study (Field & others, 1986), premature infants who were massaged showed a greater mean daily weight gain than premature infants who were not massaged. *Besides the results of this study, what else would you want to know before concluding that massage therapy helps premature infants?*

In a recent review of the use of massage therapy with preterm infants, Field and her colleagues (2004) concluded that the most consistent findings involve two positive results: (1) increased weight gain and (2) discharge from the hospital from three to six days earlier.

Infants are not the only ones who may benefit from massage therapy. In other studies, Field and her colleagues have demonstrated the benefits of massage therapy with women in reducing labor pain (Field, Hernandez-Reif, Taylor, & others, 1997), with children who have arthritis (Field, Hernandez-Reif, Seligman, & others, 1997), with children who have asthma (Field, Henteleff, & others, 1998), with autistic children's attentiveness (Field, Lasko, & others, 1997), and with adolescents who have attention deficit hyperactivity disorder (Field, Quintino, & others, 1998).

Review and Reflect • LEARNING GOAL 2

2 Discuss the Birth Process

Review
- What are the three main stages of birth? What are some different birth strategies? What is the transition from fetus to newborn like for the infant?
- What are three measures of neonatal health and responsiveness?
- What are the outcomes for children if they are born preterm or with a low birth weight?

Reflect
- If you are a female, which birth strategy do you prefer? Why? If you are a male, how involved would you want to be in helping your partner through pregnancy and the birth of your baby?

---

3 THE POSTPARTUM PERIOD

| Physical Adjustments | Emotional and Psychological Adjustments | Bonding |

What would life be like for Diana, Roger, and Alex, the new family described in the opening of the chapter? Diana planned to stay home for Alex's first three months of life before going back to work. Even so, the weeks after childbirth are likely to present many challenges to these new parents and their offspring. This is the **postpartum period,** the period after childbirth or delivery that lasts for about six weeks or until the mother's body has completed its adjustment and has returned to a nearly prepregnant state. It is a time when the woman adjusts, both physically and psychologically, to the process of childbearing.

The postpartum period involves a great deal of adjustment and adaptation. The baby has to be cared for. The mother has to recover from childbirth, to learn how to take care of the baby, and to learn to feel good about herself as a mother. The father needs to learn how to take care of his recovering wife, to learn how to take care of the baby, and to learn to feel good about himself as a father. Many health professionals believe that the best way to meet these challenges is with a family-centered approach that uses the family's resources to support an early and smooth adjustment to the newborn by all family members. The adjustments needed are physical, emotional, and psychological.

postpartum period The period after childbirth when the mother adjusts, both physically and psychologically, to the process of childbirth. This period lasts for about six weeks or until her body has completed its adjustment and returned to a near prepregnant state.

Physical Adjustments

A woman's body makes numerous physical adjustments in the first days and weeks after childbirth. She may have a great deal of energy or feel exhausted and let down. Most new mothers feel tired and need rest. Though these changes are normal, the fatigue can undermine the new mother's sense of well-being and confidence in her ability to cope with a new baby and a new family life.

The physical adjustments during the postpartum period are influenced by what preceded it. During pregnancy, the woman's body gradually adjusted to physical changes, but now it is forced to respond quickly. The method of delivery and circumstances surrounding the delivery affect the speed with which the mother's body readjusts.

After delivery, a mother's body undergoes sudden and dramatic changes in hormone production. When the placenta is delivered, estrogen and progesterone levels drop steeply and remain low until the ovaries start producing hormones again. The woman will probably begin menstruating again in four to eight weeks if she is not breast feeding. If she is breast feeding, she might not menstruate for several months to a year or more, though ovulation can occur during this time. The first several menstrual periods following delivery might be heavier than usual, but periods soon return to normal.

Involution is the process by which the uterus returns to its prepregnant size five or six weeks after birth. Immediately following birth, the uterus weighs 2 to 3 pounds. By the end of five or six weeks, the uterus weighs 2 to $3\frac{1}{2}$ ounces. Nursing the baby helps contract the uterus at a rapid rate.

Some women and men want to resume sexual intercourse as soon as possible after the birth. Others feel constrained or afraid. A sore perineum (the area between the anus and vagina), a demanding baby, lack of help, and extreme fatigue affect a woman's ability to relax and to enjoy making love. Physicians often recommend that women refrain from having sexual intercourse for approximately six weeks following the birth of the baby.

If the woman regularly engaged in conditioning exercises during pregnancy, exercise will help her recover her former body contour and strength. With a caregiver's approval, the new mother can begin some exercises as soon as one hour after delivery. A recent study found that women who maintained or increased their exercise from prepregnancy to postpartum had better maternal well-being than women who engaged in no exercise or decreased their exercise from prepregnancy to postpartum (Blum, Beaudoin, & Caton-Lemos, 2005).

Relaxation techniques are also helpful during the postpartum period. Five minutes of slow breathing on a stressful day in the postpartum period can relax and refresh the new mother, as well as the new baby.

Emotional and Psychological Adjustments

Emotional fluctuations are common for mothers in the postpartum period. These emotional fluctuations may be due to any of a number of factors: hormonal changes, fatigue, inexperience or lack of confidence with newborn babies, or the extensive time and demands involved in caring for a newborn. For some women, emotional fluctuations decrease within several weeks after the delivery, but other women experience more long-lasting emotional swings.

"Baby Blues" and Postpartum Depression
As shown in figure 4.9, about 70 percent of new mothers in the United States have what are called "baby blues." About two to three days after birth, they begin to feel depressed, anxious, and upset. These feelings may come and go for several months after the birth, often peaking about three to five days after birth. Even without treatment, these feelings usually go away after one or two weeks.

Postpartum Adjustment
Postpartum Resources

Postpartum blues
Symptoms appear 2 to 3 days after delivery and usually subside within 1 to 2 weeks.

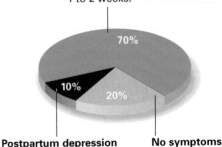

Postpartum depression
Symptoms linger for weeks or months and interfere with daily functioning.

No symptoms

FIGURE 4.9 Postpartum Blues and Postpartum Depression Among U.S. Women. Some health professionals refer to the postpartum period as the "fourth trimester." Though the time span of the postpartum period does not necessarily cover three months, the term "fourth trimester" suggests continuity and the importance of the first several months after birth for the mother.

For other women, emotional fluctuations persist and can produce feelings of anxiety, depression, and difficulty in coping with stress (Beck, 2006; Hall, 2005). Mothers who have such feelings, even when they are getting adequate rest, may benefit from professional help in dealing with their problems. Here are some of the signs that can indicate a need for professional counseling about postpartum adaptation: excessive worrying, depression, extreme changes in appetite, crying spells, and inability to sleep.

Postpartum depression involves a major depressive episode that typically occurs about four weeks after delivery. In other words, women with postpartum depression have such strong feelings of sadness, anxiety, or despair that for at least a two-week period they have trouble coping with their daily tasks. Without treatment, postpartum depression may become worse and last for many months (Driscoll, 2006; Hanley, 2006; Horowitz & Goodman, 2005). About 10 percent of new mothers experience postpartum depression. Between 25 to 50 percent of these depressed new mothers have episodes that last six months or longer (Beck, 2002). If untreated, approximately 25 percent of these women are still depressed a year later.

The hormonal changes occurring after childbirth are believed to play a role in postpartum depression, but the precise role of hormones has not been identified (Flores & Hendrick, 2002; McCoy, Beal, & Watson, 2003). Estrogen helps some women with postpartum depression, but estrogen also has some possible problematic side effects (Gentile, 2005; Spinelli, 2005). Several antidepressant drugs are effective in treating postpartum depression and appear to be safe for breast feeding women (Horowitz & Cousins, 2006). Psychotherapy, especially cognitive therapy, also is an effective treatment of postpartum depression for many women (Beck, 2002, 2006; Lasiuk & Ferguson, 2005).

Can a mother's postpartum depression affect her child? According to one recent study, it can (Righetti-Veltema & others, 2002). A sample of 570 women and their infants were assessed three months after delivery. Ten percent of the mothers were classified as experiencing postpartum depression on the basis of their responses to the Edinburgh Postnatal Depression Scale (Cox, Holden, & Sagovsky, 1987). Compared with nondepressed mothers, the depressed mothers had less vocal and visual communication with their infant, touched the infant less, and smiled less at the infant. The negative effects on the infant involved eating or sleeping problems.

A Father's Adjustment   Fathers also undergo considerable adjustment in the postpartum period, even when they work away from home all day (Cox, 2006; Pinheiro & others, 2006). Many fathers feel that the baby comes first and gets all of the mother's attention; some feel that they have been replaced by the baby.

To help the father adjust, parents should set aside some special time to be together with each other. The father's postpartum reaction also likely will be improved if he has taken childbirth classes with the mother and is an active participant in caring for the baby.

For the father as well as the mother, it is important to put time and thought into being a competent parent of a young infant (Cowan & Cowan, 2000; Hipwell & others, 2005; McVeigh, Baafi, & Williamson, 2002). Both need to become aware of the infant's needs—physical, psychological, and emotional. Both the mother and the father need to develop a sensitive, comfortable relationship with the baby.

Bonding

A special component of the parent-infant relationship is **bonding,** the formation of a connection, especially a physical bond between parents and the newborn in the period shortly after birth. Sometimes hospitals seem determined to deter bonding.

The postpartum period is a time of considerable adjustment and adaptation for both the mother and the father. Fathers can provide an important support system for mothers, especially in helping mothers care for young infants. *What kinds of tasks might the father of a newborn do to support the mother?*

postpartum depression Characteristic of women who have such strong feelings of sadness, anxiety, or despair that for at least a two-week period they have trouble coping with daily tasks in the postpartum period.

bonding The formation of a close connection, especially a physical bond between parents and their newborn in the period shortly after birth.

Drugs given to the mother to make her delivery less painful can make the mother drowsy, interfering with her ability to respond to and stimulate the newborn. Mothers and newborns are often separated shortly after delivery, and preterm infants are isolated from their mothers even more than full-term mothers.

Do these practices do any harm? Some physicians believe that during the period shortly after birth, the parents and newborn need to form an emotional attachment as a foundation for optimal development in years to come (Kennell, 2006; Kennell & McGrath, 1999). Is there evidence that close contact between mothers and infants in the first several days after birth is critical for optimal development later in life? Although some research supports this bonding hypothesis (Klaus & Kennell, 1976), a body of research challenges the significance of the first few days of life as a critical period (Bakeman & Brown, 1980; Rode & others, 1981). Indeed, the extreme form of the bonding hypothesis—that the newborn must have close contact with the mother in the first few days of life to develop optimally—simply is not true.

Nonetheless, the weakness of the bonding hypothesis should not be used as an excuse to keep motivated mothers from interacting with their newborns. Such contact brings pleasure to many mothers. In some mother-infant pairs—including preterm infants, adolescent mothers, and mothers from disadvantaged circumstances—early close contact may establish a climate for improved interaction after the mother and infant leave the hospital.

Many hospitals now offer a *rooming-in* arrangement, in which the baby remains in the mother's room most of the time during its hospital stay. However, if parents choose not to use this rooming-in arrangement, the weight of the research suggests that this decision will not harm the infant emotionally (Lamb, 1994).

Review and Reflect • LEARNING GOAL 3

3 Explain the changes that take place in the postpartum period

Review
- What does the postpartum period involve? What physical adjustments does the woman's body make in this period?
- What emotional and psychological adjustments characterize the postpartum period?
- Is bonding critical for optimal development?

Reflect
- If you are a female, what can you do to adjust effectively in the postpartum period? If you are a male, what can you do to help in the postpartum period?

REACH YOUR LEARNING GOALS

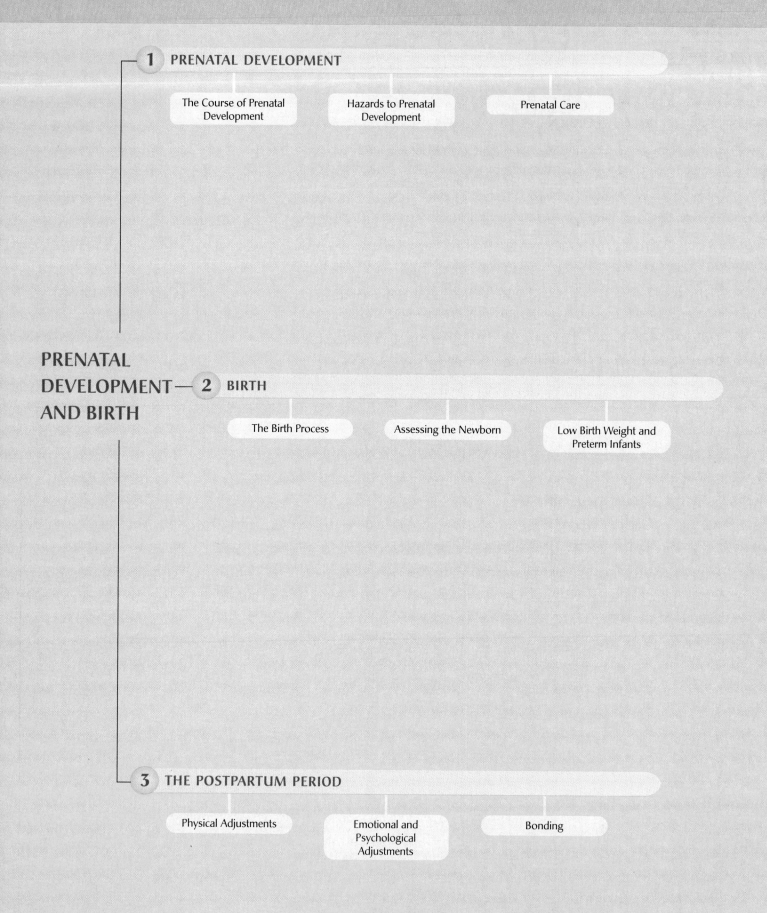

PRENATAL DEVELOPMENT AND BIRTH

1 PRENATAL DEVELOPMENT

The Course of Prenatal Development

Hazards to Prenatal Development

Prenatal Care

2 BIRTH

The Birth Process

Assessing the Newborn

Low Birth Weight and Preterm Infants

3 THE POSTPARTUM PERIOD

Physical Adjustments

Emotional and Psychological Adjustments

Bonding

SUMMARY

1 Prenatal Development: *Describe prenatal development*

The Course of Prenatal Development

Prenatal development is divided into three periods: germinal (conception until 10 to 14 days later), which ends when the zygote (a fertilized egg) attaches to the uterine wall; embryonic (two to eight weeks after conception), during which the embryo differentiates into three layers, life-support systems develop, and organ systems form (organogenesis); and fetal (two months after conception until about nine months, or when the infant is born), a time when organ systems have matured to the point at which life can be sustained outside of the womb.

Hazards to Prenatal Development

A teratogen is any agent that can potentially cause a birth defect or negatively alter cognitive and behavioral outcomes. The dose, time of exposure, and genetic susceptibility influence the severity of the damage to an unborn child and the type of defect that occurs. Prescription drugs that can be harmful include antibiotics, some depressants, and certain hormones; nonprescription drugs that can be harmful include diet pills and aspirin. The psychoactive drugs caffeine, alcohol, nicotine, cocaine, methamphetamine, marijuana, and heroin are potentially harmful to offspring. For example, fetal alcohol syndrome (FAS) is a cluster of abnormalities that appear in offspring of mothers who drink heavily during pregnancy. Even when pregnant women drink moderately (one to two drinks a day), negative effects on their offspring have been found. Cigarette smoking by pregnant women also has serious adverse effects on prenatal and child development (such as low birth weight). Incompatibility of the mother's and the father's blood types can also be harmful to the fetus. Problems may also result if a pregnant woman has rubella (German measles), syphilis, genital herpes, AIDS, or diabetes. A developing fetus depends entirely on its mother for nutrition, and it may be harmed if the mother is malnourished, overweight, has a diet deficient in folic acid, or consumes significant amounts of fish polluted by mercury or PCBs. High anxiety and stress in the mother are linked with less than optimal prenatal and birth outcomes. Maternal age can negatively affect the offspring's development if the mother is an adolescent or 35 and older. Paternal factors that can adversely affect prenatal development include exposure to lead, radiation, certain pesticides, and petrochemicals. Potential environmental hazards include radiation, environmental pollutants, and toxic wastes.

Prenatal Care

Prenatal care varies extensively but usually involves medical care services with a defined schedule of visits and often includes educational, social, and nutritional services. Much needs to be done to improve prenatal care in the United States, especially for low-income families.

2 Birth: *Discuss the birth process*

The Birth Process

Childbirth occurs in three stages. The first stage, which lasts about 12 to 24 hours for a woman having her first child, is the longest stage. The cervix dilates to about 4 inches at the end of the first stage. The second stage begins when the baby's head moves through the cervix and ends with the baby's complete emergence. The third stage is afterbirth. Childbirth strategies involve the childbirth setting and attendants. In many countries, a doula attends a childbearing woman. Methods of delivery include medicated, natural and prepared, and cesarean. An increasing number of nonmedicated techniques, such as waterbirth, are being used to reduce childbirth pain. Being born involves considerable stress for the baby, but the baby is well prepared and adapted to handle the stress. Anoxia—insufficient oxygen supply to the fetus/newborn—is a potential hazard.

Assessing the Newborn

For many years, the Apgar Scale has been used to assess the newborn's health. The Brazelton Neonatal Behavioral Assessment Scale examines the newborn's neurological development, reflexes, and reactions to people. Recently, the Neonatal Intensive Care Unit Network Neurobehavioral Scale (NNNS) was created to assess the at-risk infant.

Low Birth Weight and Preterm Infants

Low birth weight infants weigh less than $5\frac{1}{2}$ pounds and they may be preterm (born three weeks or more before the pregnancy has reached full term) or small for date (also called small for gestational age, which refers to infants whose birth weight is below norm when the length of pregnancy is considered). Small for date infants may be preterm or full term. Although most low birth weight infants are normal and healthy, as a group they have more health and developmental problems than normal birth weight infants. Kangaroo care and massage therapy have been shown to have benefits for preterm infants.

3 The Postpartum Period: *Explain the changes that take place in the postpartum period*

Physical Adjustments

The postpartum period is the period after childbirth that lasts for about six weeks or until the mother's body has completed its adjustment. Physical adjustments in the period include fatigue, involution (the process by which the uterus returns to its prepregnant size five or six weeks after birth), and hormonal changes. Decisions about when to resume sexual intercourse vary. Exercise helps the mother recover body contour and strength.

Emotional and Psychological Adjustments

Emotional fluctuations on the part of the mother are common in this period, and they can vary a great deal from one mother to the next. Postpartum depression characterizes women who have such strong feelings of sadness, anxiety, or despair that they have trouble coping with daily tasks in the postpartum period. Postpartum depression occurs in about 10 percent of new mothers. The father also goes through a postpartum adjustment.

Bonding

Bonding is the formation of a close connection, especially a physical bond between parents and the newborn shortly after birth. Early bonding has not been found to be critical in the development of a competent infant.

KEY TERMS

germinal period 103
blastocyst 103
trophoblast 103
embryonic period 103
umbilical cord 104
placenta 104
amnion 104
organogenesis 104

fetal period 105
teratogen 105
fetal alcohol syndrome (FAS) 108
doula 120
natural childbirth 121
prepared childbirth 121
breech position 123

Apgar Scale 123
Brazelton Neonatal Behavioral Assessment Scale (NBAS) 124
Neonatal Intensive Care Unit Network Neurobehavioral Scale (NNNS) 124

low birth weight infants 125
preterm infants 125
small for date infants 125
kangaroo care 126
postpartum period 128
postpartum depression 130
bonding 130

KEY PEOPLE

Grantley Dick-Read 121   Ferdinand Lamaze 121   T. Berry Brazelton 125   Tiffany Field 127

E-LEARNING TOOLS

To help you master the material in this chapter, you'll find a number of valuable study tools on the Student CD-ROM that accompanies this book. In addition, visit the Online Learning Center for *Life-Span Development*, eleventh edition, where you'll find these valuable resources for chapter 4, "Prenatal Development and Birth."

Video Clips

In the margins of this book there are icons directing you to the LifeMap CD-ROM that accompanies the book. There you'll find a video for chapter 4 called "Transitions to Parenting— Heterosexual Married Couples." In an interview conducted only weeks before the birth of their first child, a couple anticipates some of the transitional issues that all parents must deal with in the weeks immediately following the birth of the child.

Self-Assessment

Connect to **www.mhhe.com/santrockld11** to learn more about how alcohol can affect an unborn baby by completing the self-assessment, *Pregnancy Screening for Alcohol Use*.

Taking It to the Net

1. Denise's sister, Doreen, is pregnant for the first time. Doreen is not particularly known for her healthy lifestyle. What particular things can Denise encourage Doreen to do in order to give birth to a healthy baby?
2. Sienne told her fiancé, Jackson, that he had better stop smoking before they begin trying to conceive a child. Why is Sienne concerned about Jackson's smoking and its effect on their children before they have even started planning their family?
3. Hannah, who gave birth to a healthy baby boy—her first child—two weeks ago, appears to her husband Sean to be sad and lethargic, and is having trouble sleeping. How can Sean determine if Hannah is just going through a natural period of postbaby "blues" or if she might be suffering from postpartum depression?

Health and Well-Being, Parenting, and Education Exercises

Build your decision-making skills by trying your hand at the health and well-being, parenting and education exercises.

Connect to **www.mhhe.com/santrockld11** to research the answers and complete these exercises.

A baby is the most complicated object made by unskilled labor.

—ANONYMOUS

CHAPTER OUTLINE	LEARNING GOALS

PHYSICAL GROWTH AND DEVELOPMENT IN INFANCY

1 Discuss physical growth and development in infancy

Patterns of Growth

Height and Weight

The Brain

Sleep

Nutrition

MOTOR DEVELOPMENT

2 Describe infants' motor development

The Dynamic Systems View

Reflexes

Gross Motor Skills

Fine Motor Skills

SENSORY AND PERCEPTUAL DEVELOPMENT

3 Explain sensory and perceptual development in infancy

What Are Sensation and Perception?

The Ecological View

Visual Perception

Other Senses

Intermodal Perception

Perceptual-Motor Coupling

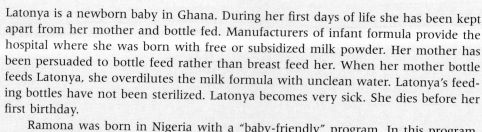

Images of Life-Span Development
Breast and Bottle Feeding in Africa

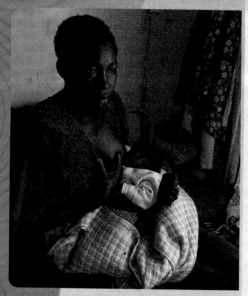

(*Top*) An HIV-infected mother breast feeding her baby in Nairobi, Africa; (*Bottom*) A Rhwandan mother bottle feeding her baby. *What are some concerns about breast versus bottle feeding in impoverished African countries?*

Latonya is a newborn baby in Ghana. During her first days of life she has been kept apart from her mother and bottle fed. Manufacturers of infant formula provide the hospital where she was born with free or subsidized milk powder. Her mother has been persuaded to bottle feed rather than breast feed her. When her mother bottle feeds Latonya, she overdilutes the milk formula with unclean water. Latonya's feeding bottles have not been sterilized. Latonya becomes very sick. She dies before her first birthday.

Ramona was born in Nigeria with a "baby-friendly" program. In this program, babies are not separated from their mothers when they are born, and the mothers are encouraged to breast feed them. The mothers are told of the perils that bottle feeding can bring because of unsafe water and unsterilized bottles. They also are informed about the advantages of breast milk, which include its nutritious and hygienic qualities, its ability to immunize babies against common illnesses, and its role in reducing the mother's risk of breast and ovarian cancer. Ramona's mother is breast feeding her. At 1 year of age, Ramona is very healthy.

For many years, maternity units in hospitals favored bottle feeding and did not give mothers adequate information about the benefits of breast feeding. In recent years, the World Health Organization and UNICEF have tried to reverse the trend toward bottle feeding of infants in many impoverished countries. They instituted the "baby-friendly" program in many countries (Grant, 1993). They also persuaded the International Association of Infant Formula Manufacturers to stop marketing their baby formulas to hospitals in countries where the governments support the baby-friendly initiatives (Grant, 1993). For the hospitals themselves, costs actually were reduced as infant formula, feeding bottles, and separate nurseries became unnecessary. For example, baby-friendly Jose Fabella Memorial Hospital in the Philippines reported saving 8 percent of its annual budget. Still, there are many places in the world where the baby-friendly initiatives have not been implemented (UNICEF, 2004).

The advantages of breast feeding in impoverished countries are substantial. However, these advantages must be balanced against the risk of passing HIV to the baby through breast milk if the mothers have the virus; the majority of mothers don't know that they are infected (Doherty & others, 2006; Piwoz & Ross, 2005; Vogler, 2006). In some areas of Africa, more than 30 percent of mothers have the HIV virus.

PREVIEW

It is very important for infants to get a healthy start. When they do, their first two years of life are likely to be a time of amazing development. In this chapter we focus on the biological domain and the infant's physical development, exploring physical growth, motor development, and sensory and perceptual development.

1 PHYSICAL GROWTH AND DEVELOPMENT IN INFANCY

Patterns of Growth

The Brain

Nutrition

Height and Weight

Sleep

Infants' physical development in the first two years of life is extensive. At birth, newborns have a gigantic head (relative to the rest of the body), which flops around uncontrollably, and some basic reflexes. In the span of 12 months, infants become capable of sitting anywhere, standing, stooping, climbing, and usually walking. During the second year, growth decelerates, but rapid increases in such activities as running and climbing take place. Let's now examine in greater detail the sequence of physical development in infancy.

Patterns of Growth

An extraordinary proportion of the total body is occupied by the head during prenatal development and early infancy (see figure 5.1). The **cephalocaudal pattern** is the sequence in which the earliest growth always occurs at the top—the head—with physical growth and differentiation of features gradually working their way down from top to bottom (for example, shoulders, middle trunk, and so on). This same pattern occurs in the head area, because the top parts of the head—the eyes and brain—grow faster than the lower parts, such as the jaw.

Sensory and motor development generally proceed according to the cephalocaudal principle. For example, infants see objects before they can control their torso, and they can use their hands long before they can crawl or walk. However, development does not follow a rigid blueprint. One recent study found that infants reached for toys with their feet prior to reaching with their hands (Galloway & Thelen, 2004). On average, infants first touched the toy with their feet when they were 12 weeks old and with their hands when they were 16 weeks old.

cephalocaudal pattern The sequence in which the earliest growth always occurs at the top—the head—with physical growth in size, weight, and feature differentiation gradually working from top to bottom.

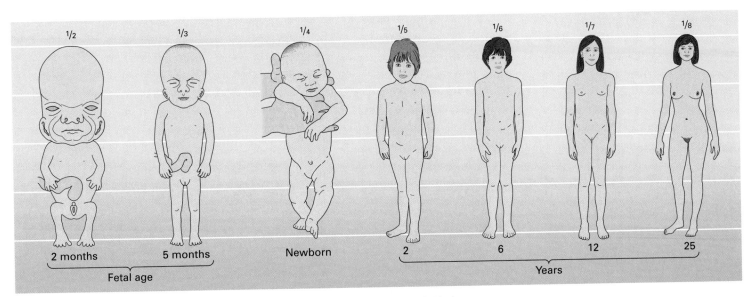

FIGURE 5.1 Changes in Proportions of the Human Body During Growth. As individuals develop from infancy through adulthood, one of the most noticeable physical changes is that the head becomes smaller in relation to the rest of the body. The fractions listed refer to head size as a proportion of total body length at different ages.

Growth also follows the **proximodistal pattern,** the sequence in which growth starts at the center of the body and moves toward the extremities. For example, infants control the muscles of their trunk and arms before they control their hands and fingers, and they use their whole hands before they can control several fingers.

Height and Weight

The average North American newborn is 20 inches long and weighs $7\frac{1}{2}$ pounds. Ninety-five percent of full-term newborns are 18 to 22 inches long and weigh between $5\frac{1}{2}$ and 10 pounds.

In the first several days of life, most newborns lose 5 to 7 percent of their body weight before they adjust to feeding by sucking, swallowing, and digesting. Then they grow rapidly, gaining an average of 5 to 6 ounces per week during the first month. They have doubled their birth weight by the age of 4 months and have nearly tripled it by their first birthday. Infants grow about 1 inch per month during the first year, reaching approximately $1\frac{1}{2}$ times their birth length by their first birthday.

Growth slows considerably in the second year of life. By 2 years of age, infants weigh approximately 26 to 32 pounds, having gained a quarter to half a pound per month during the second year; now they have reached about one-fifth of their adult weight. At 2 years of age, the average infant is 32 to 35 inches in height, which is nearly half of their adult height.

The Brain

By the time the infant is born, what that began as a single cell now has a brain that contains tens of billions of nerve cells, or neurons. Extensive brain development continues after birth, through infancy and later (Nelson, Thomas, & de Haan, 2006). Because the brain is still developing so rapidly in infancy, the infant's head should

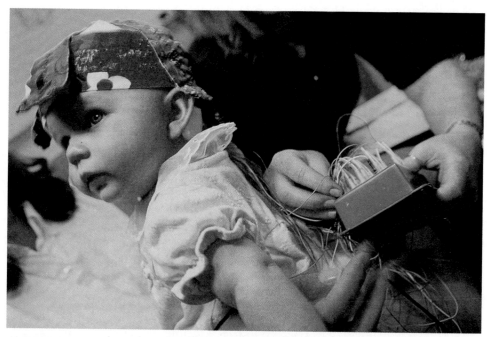

FIGURE 5.2 Measuring the Activity of an Infant's Brain. By attaching up to 128 electrodes to a baby's scalp to measure the brain's activity, Charles Nelson (2003, 2005; Nelson, Thomas, & de Haan, 2006) has found that even newborns produce distinctive brain waves that reveal they can distinguish their mother's voices from another woman's, even while they are asleep. *Why is it so difficult to measure infants' brain activity?*

proximodistal pattern The sequence in which growth starts at the center of the body and moves toward the extremities.

be protected from falls or other injuries and the baby should never be shaken. *Shaken baby syndrome,* which includes brain swelling and hemorrhaging, affects hundreds of babies in the United States each year (Harding, Risdon, & Krous, 2004; Minns & Busuttil, 2004; Newton & Vandeven, 2005).

Studying the brain's development in infancy is challenging. Even the latest brain-imaging technologies (described in chapter 2) cannot make out fine details in adult brains and cannot be used with babies (Nelson, Thomas, & de Haan, 2006). Positron-emission tomography (PET) scans pose a radiation risk to babies, and infants wriggle too much to capture accurate images using magnetic resonance imaging (MRI) (Marcus, Mulrine, & Wong, 1999). As figure 5.2 illustrates, one way researchers have studied the infant's brain is by attaching electrodes to the scalp to monitor the brain's electrical activity (Nelson, 2003, 2005; Nelson, Thomas, & de Haan, 2006).

Using the electroencephalogram (EEG), which measures the brain's electrical activity, researchers have found that a spurt in EEG activity occurs at about $1\frac{1}{2}$ to 2 years of age (Fischer & Rose, 1995). Other spurts seem to take place at about 9, 12, 15, and 18 to 20 years of age. Researchers believe that these spurts of brain activity may coincide with important changes in cognitive development. For example, the increase in EEG brain activity at $1\frac{1}{2}$ to 2 years of age is likely associated with an increase in the infant's capacity for conceptualization and language.

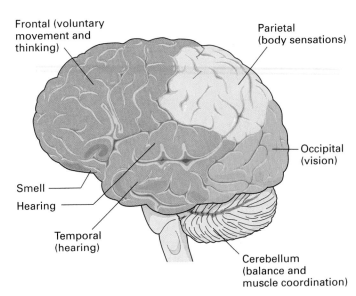

FIGURE 5.3 **The Brain's Four Lobes.** Shown here are the locations of the brain's four lobes: frontal, occipital, temporal, and parietal.

The Brain's Development

At birth, the newborn's brain is about 25 percent of its adult weight. By the second birthday, the brain is about 75 percent of its adult weight. However, the brain's areas do not mature uniformly.

Mapping the Brain Scientists analyze and categorize areas of the brain in numerous ways (Toga, Thompson, & Sowell, 2006). We are most concerned with the portion farthest from the spinal cord known as the *forebrain,* which includes the cerebral cortex and several structures beneath it. The *cerebral cortex* covers the forebrain like a wrinkled cap. It has two halves, or hemispheres (see figure 5.3). Based on ridges and valleys in the cortex, scientists distinguish four main areas, called lobes, in each hemisphere: the *frontal lobes,* the *occipital lobes,* the *temporal lobes,* and the *parietal lobes* (see figure 5.3).

Very often, though, researchers describe areas of the cortex based not on the physical ridges and valleys but on function. For example, *primary motor cortex* refers to areas of the frontal lobe that control the body's muscles. *Primary sensory cortex* is an adjacent region in the parietal lobe that receives information about touch, pressure, and pain. *Visual cortex* is an area in the occipital lobe that processes visual information, and *auditory cortex* is a part of the temporal lobe that processes information about sounds. *Prefrontal cortex* is a part of the frontal lobe involved in thinking, planning, and self-regulation.

Although these areas are found in the cerebral cortex of each hemisphere, the two hemispheres are not identical in anatomy or function (see figure 5.4). **Lateralization** is the specialization of function in one hemisphere of the cerebral cortex or the other. Researchers continue to be interested in the degree to which each is involved in various aspects of thinking, feeling, and behavior (Gandour & others, 2003). The most extensive research on the brain's hemispheres has focused on language (Sakai & others, 2005; Wood & others, 2004). Speech and grammar are localized to the left hemisphere in most people, but some aspects of language, such as appropriate language use in different contexts and the use of metaphor and humor, involve the right hemisphere. Thus, language is not controlled exclusively by the brain's left hemisphere (Jabbour & others, 2005; Johnson, 2005;

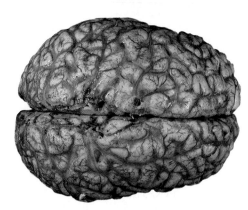

FIGURE 5.4 **The Human Brain's Hemispheres.** The two hemispheres of the human brain are clearly seen in this photograph. It is a myth that the left hemisphere is the exclusive location of language and logical thinking or that the right hemisphere is the exclusive location of emotion and creative thinking.

lateralization Specialization of function in one hemisphere of the cerebral cortex or the other.

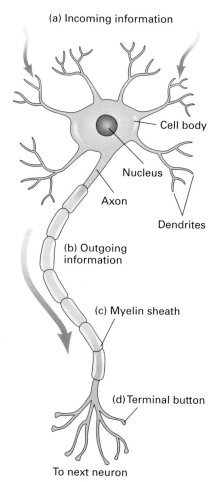

(a) Incoming information

Cell body

Nucleus

Axon

Dendrites

(b) Outgoing information

(c) Myelin sheath

(d) Terminal button

To next neuron

FIGURE 5.5 The Neuron. (a) The dendrites of the cell body receive information from other neurons, muscles, or glands through the axon. (b) Axons transmit information away from the cell body. (c) A myelin sheath covers most axons and speeds information transmission. (d) As the axon ends, it branches out into terminal buttons.

www.mhhe.com/santrockld11

Neural Processes
Charles Nelson's Research

neuron Nerve cell that handles information processing at the cellular level.

Tremblay, Monetta, & Joanette, 2004). Further, most neuroscientists agree that complex functions, such as reading, performing music, and creating art, are the outcome of communication between both sides of the brain.

At birth, the hemispheres of the cerebral cortex already have started to specialize: Newborns show greater electrical brain activity in the left hemisphere than the right hemisphere when they are listening to speech sounds (Hahn, 1987). How are the areas of the brain different in the newborn and the infant than in an adult, and why do the differences matter? Important differences have been documented at both the cellular and the structural level.

Changes in Neurons Within the brain, the type of nerve cells called neurons send electrical and chemical signals, communicating with each other. A **neuron** is a nerve cell that handles information processing (see figure 5.5). Extending from the neuron's cell body are two types of fibers known as axons and dendrites. Generally, the axon carries signals away from the cell body and dendrites carry signals toward it. A *myelin sheath,* which is a layer of fat cells, encases many axons (see figure 5.4). The myelin sheath insulates axons and helps electrical signals travel faster down the axon. At the end of the axon are terminal buttons, which release chemicals called *neurotransmitters* into *synapses,* which are tiny gaps between neurons' fibers. Chemical interactions in synapses connect axons and dendrites, allowing information to pass from neuron to neuron.

Neurons change in two very significant ways during the first years of life. First, *myelination,* the process of encasing axons with fat cells, begins prenatally and continues after birth, even into adolescence. Second, connectivity among neurons increases, creating new neural pathways, as figure 5.6 illustrates. New dendrites grow, connections among dendrites increase, and synaptic connections between axons and dendrites proliferate. Whereas myelination speeds up neural transmissions, the expansion of dendritic connections facilitates the spreading of neural pathways in infant development.

Researchers have discovered an intriguing aspect of synaptic connections. Nearly twice as many of these connections are made as will ever be used (Huttenlocher & Dabholkar, 1997). The connections that are used become strengthened and survive, while the unused ones are replaced by other pathways or disappear (Casey, Durston, & Fossella, 2001). In the language of neuroscience, these connections will be "pruned."

Changes in Regions of the Brain Figure 5.7 vividly illustrates the dramatic growth and later pruning of synapses in the visual, auditory, and prefrontal cortex (Huttenlocher & Dabholkar, 1997). Notice that "blooming and pruning" vary considerably by brain region (Thompson & Nelson, 2001). For example, the peak of synaptic overproduction in the visual cortex occurs at about the fourth postnatal month, followed by a gradual retraction until the middle to end of the preschool years (Huttenlocher & Dabholkar, 1997). In areas of the brain involved in hearing and language, a similar, though somewhat later, course is detected. However, in the *prefrontal cortex,* the area of the brain where higher-level thinking and self-regulation occur, the peak of overproduction takes place at about 1 year of age; it is not until middle to late adolescence that the adult density of synapses is achieved. Both heredity and environment are thought to influence the timing and course of synaptic overproduction and subsequent retraction.

Meanwhile, the pace of myelination also varies in different areas of the brain. Myelination for visual pathways occurs rapidly after birth and is completed in the first six months. Auditory myelination is not completed until 4 or 5 years of age.

In general, some areas of the brain, such as the primary motor areas, develop earlier than others, such as the primary sensory areas. The frontal lobes are immature in the newborn. However, as neurons in the frontal lobes become myelinated and interconnected during the first year of life, infants develop

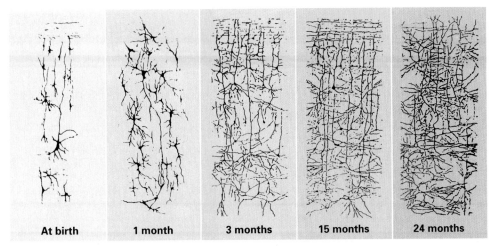

At birth   1 month   3 months   15 months   24 months

FIGURE 5.6 **The Development of Dendritic Spreading.** Note the increase in connectedness between neurons over the course of the first two years of life. Reprinted by permission of the publisher from *The Postnatal Development of the Human Cerebral Cortex, Vols. I–VIII* by Jesse LeRoy Conel, Cambridge, Mass.: Harvard University Press, Copyright © 1939, 1975 by the President and Fellows of Harvard College.

an ability to regulate their physiological states, such as sleep, and gain more control over their reflexes. Cognitive skills that require deliberate thinking do not emerge until later (Bell & Fox, 1992). Indeed, the prefrontal region of the frontal lobe has the most prolonged development of any brain region, with changes detectable at least into the adolescent years (Johnson, 2001, 2005).

Early Experience and the Brain What determines how these changes in the brain occur? Until the middle of the twentieth century, scientists believed that the brain's development was determined almost exclusively by genetic factors. But researcher Mark Rosenzweig (1969) was curious about whether early experiences change the brain's development. He conducted a number of experiments with rats and other animals to investigate this possibility. Animals were randomly assigned to grow up in different environments. Animals in an enriched early environment lived in cages with stimulating features, such as wheels to rotate, steps to climb, levers to press, and toys to manipulate. In contrast, other animals had the early experience of growing up in standard cages or in barren, isolated conditions.

The results were stunning. The brains of the animals growing up in the enriched environment developed better than the brains of the animals reared in standard or isolated conditions. The brains of the "enriched" animals weighed more, had thicker layers, had more neuronal connections, and had higher levels of neurochemical activity. Similar findings occurred when older animals were reared in vastly different environments, although the results were not as strong as for the younger animals. Such results give hope that enriching the lives of infants and young children who live in impoverished environments can produce positive changes in their development.

Depressed brain activity has recently been found in children who grow up in a deprived environment (Cicchetti, 2001). As shown in figure 5.8, a child who grew

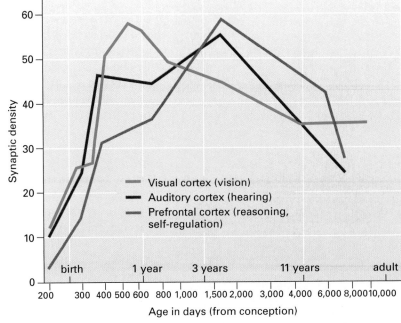

FIGURE 5.7 **Synaptic Density in the Human Brain from Infancy to Adulthood.** The graph shows the dramatic increase and then pruning in synaptic density for three regions of the brain: visual cortex, auditory cortex, and prefrontal cortex. Synaptic density is believed to be an important indication of the extent of connectivity between neurons.

Development of the Brain
Early Development of the Brain
Early Experience and the Brain

FIGURE 5.8 **Early Deprivation and Brain Activity.** These two photographs are PET (positron-emission tomography) scans (which use radioactive tracers to image and analyze blood flow and metabolic activity in the body's organs) of the brains of (a) a normal child and (b) an institutionalized Romanian orphan who experienced substantial deprivation since birth. In PET scans, the highest to lowest brain activity is reflected in the colors of red, yellow, green, blue, and black, respectively. As can be seen, red and yellow show up to a much greater degree in the PET scan of the normal child than the deprived Romanian orphan.

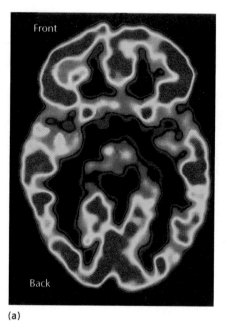

(a)

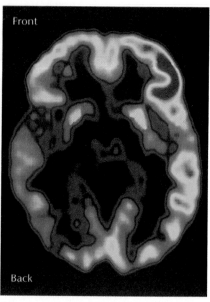

(b)

(a)

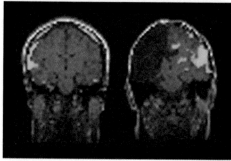

(b)

FIGURE 5.9 **Plasticity in the Brain's Hemispheres.** (a) Michael Rehbein at 14 years of age. (b) Michael's right hemisphere (right) has reorganized to take over the language functions normally carried out by corresponding areas in the left hemisphere of an intact brain (left). However, the right hemisphere is not as efficient as the left, and more areas of the brain are recruited to process speech.

up in the unresponsive and nonstimulating environment of a Romanian orphanage showed considerably depressed brain activity compared with a normal child.

The profusion of connections described earlier provides the growing brain with flexibility and resilience. Consider 16-year-old Michael Rehbein. At age $4\frac{1}{2}$, he began to experience uncontrollable seizures—as many as 400 a day. Doctors said that the only solution was to remove the left hemisphere of his brain where the seizures were occurring. The first major surgery was at age 7 and another at age 10. Recovery was slow but his right hemisphere began to reorganize and take over functions that normally occur in the brain's left hemisphere. One of these functions was speech (see figure 5.9).

Neuroscientists believe that what wires the brain—or rewires it, in the case of Michael Rehbein—is repeated experience (Nash, 1997). Each time a baby tries to touch an attractive object or gazes intently at a face, tiny bursts of electricity shoot through the brain, knitting neurons together into circuits. What results are some of the behavioral milestones that we discuss in this and other chapters. For example, at about 2 months of age, the motor-control centers of the brain develop to the point at which infants can suddenly reach out and grab a nearby object. At about 4 months, the neural connections necessary for depth perception begin to form. And at about 12 months the brain's speech centers are poised to produce one of infancy's magical moments: when the infant utters his or her first word.

In sum, neural connections are formed early in life. The infant's brain literally is waiting for experiences to determine how connections are made (Greenough, 2001; Johnson, 2001, 2005). Before birth, it appears that genes mainly direct how the brain establishes basic wiring patterns. Neurons grow and travel to distant places awaiting further instructions. After birth, environmental experiences guide the brain's development. The inflowing stream of sights, sounds, smells, touches, language, and eye contact help shape the brain's neural connections (Nelson, Thomas, & de Haan, 2006; Neville & Bavelier, 2002).

Sleep

When we were infants, sleep consumed more of our time than it does now. The typical newborn sleeps 16 to 17 hours a day, but newborns vary a lot in how much they sleep. The range is from about 10 hours to about 21 hours.

Infants also vary in their preferred times for sleeping and their patterns of sleep. Although the total amount of time spent sleeping remains somewhat consistent,

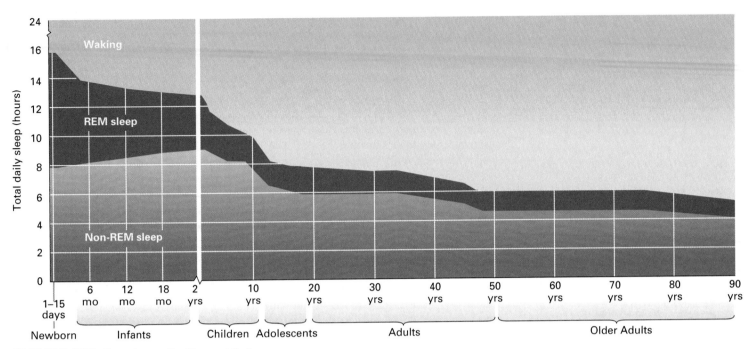

FIGURE 5.10 Sleep Across the Human Life Span

an infant may change from sleeping 7 or 8 hours several times a day to sleeping for only a few hours three or four times a day. By about 1 month of age, many American infants have begun to sleep longer at night. By about 4 months of age, they usually have moved closer to adult-like sleep patterns, spending the most time sleeping at night and the most time awake during the day (Daws, 2000).

Cultural variations influence infant sleeping patterns. For example, in the Kipsigis culture in Kenya, infants sleep with their mothers at night and are permitted to nurse on demand (Super & Harkness, 1997). During the day they are strapped to their mothers' backs, accompanying them on daily rounds of chores and social activities. As a result, the Kipsigis infants do not sleep through the night until much later than American infants do. During the first eight months of postnatal life, Kipsigis infants rarely sleep longer than three hours at a stretch, even at night. This sleep pattern contrasts with that of American infants, many of whom begin to sleep up to eight hours a night by 8 months of age.

REM Sleep Figure 5.10 shows the average number of total hours spent in sleep across the life span, as well as the time spent in *REM (rapid eye-movement) sleep* and non-REM sleep. Most adults spend about one-fifth of their night in REM sleep, and REM sleep usually appears about one hour after non-REM sleep. However, about half of an infant's sleep is REM sleep, and infants often begin their sleep cycle with REM sleep rather than non-REM sleep. A much greater amount of time is taken up by REM sleep in infancy than at any other point in the life span. By the time infants reach 3 months of age, the percentage of time they spend in REM sleep falls to about 40 percent, and REM sleep no longer begins their sleep cycle.

Why do infants spend so much time in REM sleep? Researchers are not certain. The large amount of REM sleep may provide infants with added self-stimulation, since they spend less time awake than do older children. REM sleep also might promote the brain's development in infancy (McNamara & Sullivan, 2000).

Shared Sleeping Sleeping arrangements for newborns vary from culture to culture (Alexander & Radisch, 2005; Berkowitz, 2004; Cortesi & others, 2004). Sharing a bed with a mother is a common practice in many cultures, whereas in others newborns sleep in a crib, either in the same room as the parents or in a separate

*S*leep that knits up the ravelled sleave of care ... Balm of hurt minds, great nature's second course, Chief nourisher in life's feast.

—WILLIAM SHAKESPEARE
English Playwright, 17th Century

room. Whatever the sleeping arrangements, it is recommended that the infant's bedding provide firm support and that cribs should have side rails.

In the United States, sleeping in a crib in a separate room is the most frequent sleeping arrangement for an infant. In one cross-cultural study, American mothers said they have their infants sleep in a separate room to promote the infants' self-reliance and independence (Morelli & others, 1992). By contrast, Mayan mothers in rural Guatemala had infants sleep in their bed until the birth of a new sibling, at which time the infant would sleep with another family member or in a separate bed in the mother's room. The Mayan mothers believed that the co-sleeping arrangement with their infants enhanced the closeness of their relationship with the infants and were shocked when told that American mothers have their babies sleep alone.

Shared sleeping, or co-sleeping, is a controversial issue among experts. According to some child experts, shared sleeping bring several benefits: it promotes breast feeding and a quicker response to the baby's cries, and it allows the mother to detect potentially dangerous breathing pauses in the baby (Nelson & others, 2005). However, shared sleeping remains a controversial issue, with some experts recommending it, others arguing against it (Lehr & others, 2005; Newton & Vandeven, 2006; Pelayo & others, 2006). The American Academy of Pediatrics Task Force on Infant Positioning and SIDS (AAPTFIPS) (2000; Cohen, 2000) recommends against shared sleeping. They argue that in some instances bed sharing might lead to sudden infant death syndrome (SIDS), as could be the case if a sleeping mother rolls over on her baby. Two recent studies found that bed sharing was linked with the incidence of SIDS (Alexander & Radisch, 2005; Unger & others, 2003).

SIDS **Sudden infant death syndrome (SIDS)** is a condition that occurs when infants stop breathing, usually during the night, and die suddenly without an apparent cause. SIDS remains the highest cause of infant death in the United States, with nearly 3,000 infant deaths annually attributed to SIDS. Risk of SIDS is highest at 4 to 6 weeks of age (Matthews, Menacker, & MacDorman, 2003).

Since 1992, the American Academy of Pediatrics (AAP) has recommended that infants be placed to sleep on their backs to reduce the risk of SIDS, and the frequency of prone sleeping among U.S. infants has dropped dramatically (AAPTFIPS, 2000). Researchers have found that SIDS does indeed decrease when infants sleep on their backs rather than their stomachs or sides (Alexander & Radisch, 2005; Alm, Lagercrantz, & Wennergren, 2006). Among the reasons given for prone sleeping being a high risk factor for SIDS are that it impairs the infant's arousal from sleep and restricts the infant's ability to swallow effectively (Ariagno, van Liempt, & Mirmiran, 2006; Spitzer, 2005).

In addition to sleeping in a prone position, researchers have found that the following are risk factors for SIDS (AAPTFIPS, 2000; Kahn & others, 2004):

- Low birth weight infants are 5 to 10 times more likely to die of SIDS than are their normal-weight counterparts (Horne & others, 2002).
- Infants whose siblings have died of SIDS are two to four times as likely to die of it (Getahun & others, 2004).
- Six percent of infants with *sleep apnea,* a temporary cessation of breathing in which the airway is completely blocked, usually for 10 seconds or longer, die of SIDS (McNamara & Sullivan, 2000).
- African American and Eskimo infants are four to six times as likely as all others to die of SIDS (Ige & Shelton, 2004).
- SIDS is more common in lower socioeconomic groups (Mitchell & others, 2000).
- SIDS is more common in infants who are passively exposed to cigarette smoke (Spitzer, 2005; Tong, England, & Glantz, 2005).
- SIDS is more common if infants sleep in soft bedding (McGarvey & others, 2006).

Is this a good sleep position for infants? Why or why not?

www.mhhe.com/santrockld11

SIDS

sudden infant death syndrome (SIDS) A condition that occurs when an infant stops breathing, usually during the night, and suddenly dies without an apparent cause.

- SIDS is less likely to occur in infants who use a pacifier when they go to sleep (Hauck, Omojokun, & Siadaty, 2005; Li & others, 2006; Mitchell, Blair, & L'Hoir, 2006).

Nutrition

From birth to 1 year of age, human infants nearly triple their weight and increase their length by 50 percent. What do they need to sustain this growth?

Decades ago, behaviorist John Watson (1928) argued that infants should be fed on a schedule, and he recommended feeding newborns 4 ounces of formula every six hours. In recent years, *demand feeding*—in which the timing and amount of feeding are determined by the infant—has become more popular. Controversy still characterizes the issue of demand versus scheduled feeding. There is no doubt, however, that the importance of adequate nutrients consumed in a loving and supportive environment during the infant years cannot be overstated (Brom, 2005; Samour, Helm, & Lang, 2000; Sizer & Whitney, 2006). Our coverage of infant nutrition begins with information about their nutritional needs, then turns to the issue of breast versus bottle feeding, and concludes with an overview of malnutrition.

Nutritional Needs   Individual differences among infants in terms of their nutrient reserves, body composition, growth rates, and activity patterns make defining actual nutrient needs difficult. However, because parents need guidelines, nutritionists recommend that infants consume approximately 50 calories per day for each pound they weigh—more than twice an adult's requirement per pound.

Does the same type of nutrition that makes us healthy adults also make young infants healthy? No. Diets designed for adult weight loss and prevention of heart disease may actually retard growth and development in babies. Fat is very important for babies. Nature's food—breast milk—is not low in fat or calories. No child under the age of 2 should be consuming skim milk. For growing infants, high-calorie, high-energy foods are part of a balanced diet.

Some affluent, well-educated parents almost starve their babies by feeding them the low-fat, low-calorie diet they themselves eat. In one investigation, seven babies 7 to 22 months of age were undernourished by their unwitting health-conscious parents (Lifshitz & others, 1987). The well-meaning parents substituted vegetables, skim milk, and other low-fat foods for what they called junk food. But parents who go to the opposite extreme appear to be a more widespread problem. A recent national study of more than 3,000 randomly selected 4- to 24-month-olds documented that many U.S. parents aren't feeding their babies enough fruits and vegetables, but are feeding them too much junk food (Fox & others, 2004). Up to one-third of the babies ate no vegetables and fruit, frequently ate French fries, and almost half of the 7- to 8-month-old babies were fed desserts, sweets, or sweetened drinks. By 15 months, French fries were the most common vegetables the babies ate.

Breast Versus Bottle Feeding   For the first 4 to 6 months of life, human milk or an alternative formula is the baby's source of nutrients and energy. For years, debate has focused on whether breast feeding is better for the infant than bottle feeding. The growing consensus is that breast feeding is better for the baby's health (Gartner & others, 2005; Spatz, 2006; Wardlaw & Hampel, 2007; Wong, 2006). Since the 1970s, breast feeding by U.S. mothers has soared (see figure 5.11). In 2004 more than two-thirds of U.S. mothers breast fed their newborns, and more than a third breast fed their six-month-olds. The American Academy of Pediatrics (AAP) and the

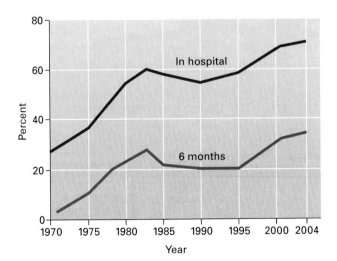

FIGURE 5.11 Trends in Breast Feeding in the United States: 1970–2004

American Dietetic Association strongly endorse breast feeding throughout the infant's first year (AAP Working Group on Breastfeeding, 1997; Gartner & others, 2005; James & Dobson, 2005).

What are some of the benefits of breast feeding? They include these benefits during the first two years of life and later:

- Appropriate weight gain and lowered risk of childhood obesity (Kalies & others, 2005). A recent review of 11 studies found that breast feeding reduces the risk of childhood obesity to a moderate extent (Dewey, 2003). Another recent review of 61 studies concluded that breast feeding protects against obesity in childhood and adulthood (Owen & others, 2005).
- Fewer allergies (Friedman & Zeiger, 2005; Host & Halken, 2005).
- Prevention or reduction of diarrhea, respiratory infections (such as pneumonia and bronchitis), bacterial and urinary tract infections, and otitis media (a middle ear infection) (Chantry, Howard, & Aninger, 2006; Isaacs, 2005; Jackson & Nazar, 2006).
- Denser bones in childhood and adulthood (Gibson & others, 2000).
- Reduced childhood cancer and reduced incidence of breast cancer in mothers and their female offspring (Eisinger & Burke, 2003; Kwan & others 2004).
- Lower incidence of SIDS—in one study, for every month of exclusive breast feeding, the rate of SIDS was cut in half (Fredrickson, 1993).
- More advanced neurological and cognitive development (Eidelman & Feldman, 2004; Gustafsson & others, 2004).
- Better visual acuity (Makrides & others, 1995).

Which women are least likely to breast feed? They include mothers who work full-time outside of the home, mothers under age 25, mothers without a high school education, African American mothers, and mothers in low-income circumstances (Centers for Disease Control and Prevention, 2006; Ryan, 1997; Scott & others, 2006). In one study of low-income mothers in Georgia, interventions (such as counseling focused on the benefits of breast feeding and the free loan of a breast pump) increased the incidence of breast feeding (Ahluwalia & others, 2000). Increasingly, mothers who return to work in the infant's first year of life use a breast pump to extract breast milk that can be stored for later feeding of the infant when the mother is not present.

Although there are clearly advantages to breast feeding, are there circumstances when mothers should not breast feed? Yes, a mother should not breast feed (1) when the mother is infected with AIDS or some other infectious disease that can be transmitted through her milk, (2) if she has active tuberculosis, or (3) if she is taking any drug that may not be safe for the infant (AAPWGB, 1997; Doherty & others, 2006; Merchant & Lala, 2005; Vogler, 2006).

Some women cannot breast feed their infants because of physical difficulties; others feel guilty if they terminate breast feeding early (Walshaw & Owens, 2006). Mothers may also worry that they are depriving their infants of important emotional and psychological benefits if they bottle feed rather than breast feed. Some researchers have found, however, that there are no psychological differences between breast-fed and bottle-fed infants (Ferguson, Harwood, & Shannon, 1987; Young, 1990).

Malnutrition in Infancy Early weaning of infants from breast milk to inadequate sources of nutrients, such as unsuitable and unsanitary cow's milk formula, can cause protein deficiency and malnutrition in infants (Kramer, 2003). Something that looks like milk but is not, usually a form of tapioca or rice, is also often substituted for breast milk. In many of the world's developing countries, mothers used to breast feed their infants for at least two years. To become more modern, they stopped breast feeding much earlier and replaced it with bottle feeding. Comparisons of breast-fed and bottle-fed infants in such countries as Afghanistan, Haiti, Ghana,

Human milk or an alternative formula is a baby's source of nutrients for the first 4 to 6 months. The growing consensus is that breast feeding is better for the baby's health, although controversy still swirls about the issue of breast feeding versus bottle feeding. *Why is breast feeding strongly recommended by pediatricians?*

This Honduran child has kwashiorkor. Notice the tell-tale sign of kwashiorkor—a greatly expanded abdomen. *What are some other characteristics of kwashiorkor?*

and Chile document that the mortality rate of bottle-fed infants is as much as five times that of breast-fed infants (Grant, 1997).

Two life-threatening conditions that can result from malnutrition are marasmus and kwashiorkor. **Marasmus** is caused by a severe protein-calorie deficiency and results in a wasting away of body tissues in the infant's first year. The infant becomes grossly underweight and his or her muscles atrophy. **Kwashiorkor,** caused by severe protein deficiency, usually appears between 1 and 3 years of age. Children with kwashiorkor sometimes appear to be well fed even though they are not because the disease can cause the child's abdomen and feet to swell with water. Kwashiorkor causes a child's vital organs to collect the nutrients that are present and deprive other parts of the body of them. The child's hair also becomes thin, brittle, and colorless, and the child's behavior often becomes listless.

Even if not fatal, severe and lengthy malnutrition is detrimental to physical, cognitive, and social development (Grantham-McGregor, Ani, & Fernald, 2001; Nolan & others, 2002). In one investigation, two groups of extremely malnourished 1-year-old South African infants were studied (Bayley, 1970). The children in one group were given adequate nourishment during the next six years; no intervention took place in the lives of the other group. After the seventh year, the poorly nourished group of children performed much worse on tests of intelligence than did the adequately nourished group.

Another study linked the diets of rural Guatemalan infants with their social development at the time they entered elementary school (Barrett, Radke-Yarrow, & Klein, 1982). Children whose mothers had been given nutritious supplements during pregnancy and who themselves had been given more nutritious, high-calorie foods in their first two years of life were more active, more involved, more helpful with their peers, less anxious, and happier than their counterparts who had not been given nutritional supplements. The results suggest how important it is for parents to be attentive to the nutritional needs of their infants.

In further research on early supplementary feeding and children's cognitive development, Ernesto Pollitt and his colleagues (1993) conducted a longitudinal investigation over two decades in rural Guatemala. They found that early nutritional supplements in the form of protein and increased calories can have positive long-term effects on cognitive development. The researchers also found that the relation of nutrition to cognitive performance is moderated both by the time period during which the supplement is given and by the sociodemographic context. For example, the children in the lowest socioeconomic groups benefited more than did the children in higher socioeconomic groups. Although there still was a positive nutritional influence when supplementation began after 2 years of age, the effect on cognitive development was less powerful.

In sum, adequate early nutrition is an important aspect of healthy development. To be healthy, children need a nurturant, supportive environment (Chopra, 2003). One individual who has stood out as an advocate of caring for children is T. Berry Brazelton, who is featured in the Careers in Life-Span Development profile. And to read about a program that helps infants get a healthy start in the life, see the Applications in Life-Span Development interlude.

marasmus A wasting away of body tissues in the infant's first year, caused by severe protein-calorie deficiency.

kwashiorkor A condition caused by a deficiency in protein in which the child's abdomen and feet become swollen with water; usually appears between 1 to 3 years of age.

CAREERS in LIFE-SPAN DEVELOPMENT

T. Berry Brazelton
Pediatrician

T. Berry Brazelton is America's best-known pediatrician as a result of his numerous books, television appearances, and newspaper and magazine articles about parenting and children's health. He takes a family-centered approach to child development issues and communicates with parents in easy-to-understand ways.

Dr. Brazelton founded the Child Development Unit at Boston Children's Hospital and created the Brazelton Neonatal Behavioral Assessment Scale, a widely used measure of the newborn's health and well-being (which you read about in chapter 4). He also has conducted a number of research studies on infants and children and has been president of the Society for Research in Child Development, a leading research organization.

T. Berry Brazelton, pediatrician, with a young child.

APPLICATIONS IN LIFE-SPAN DEVELOPMENT

A Healthy Start

The Hawaii Family Support/Healthy Start Program began in 1985 (Allen, Brown, & Finlay, 1992). It was designed by the Hawaii Family Stress Center in Honolulu, which already had been making home visits to improve family functioning and reduce child abuse for more than a decade. Participation is voluntary. Families of newborns are screened for family risk factors, including unstable housing, histories of substance abuse, depression, parents' abuse as a child, late or no prenatal care, fewer than 12 years of schooling, poverty, and unemployment. Healthy Start workers screen and interview new mothers in the hospital. They also screen families referred by physicians, nurses, and others. Because the demand for services outstrips available resources, only families with a substantial number of risk factors can participate.

Each new participating family receives a weekly visit from a family support worker. Each of the program's eight home visitors works with approximately 25 families at a time. The worker helps the family cope with any immediate crises, such as unemployment or substance abuse. The family also is linked directly with a pediatrician to ensure that the children receive regular health care. Infants are screened for developmental delays and are immunized on schedule. Pediatricians are notified when a child is enrolled in Healthy Start and when a family at risk stops participating.

The Family Support/Healthy Start Program recently hired a child development specialist to work with families of children with special needs. And, in some instances, the program's male family support worker visits a father to talk about his role in the family. The support workers encourage parents to participate in group activities held each week at the program center located in a neighborhood shopping center.

Over time, parents are encouraged to assume more responsibility for their family's health and well-being. Families can participate in Healthy Start until the child is 5 and enters public school. One recent study found that the Hawaiian Healthy Start program produced a lower incidence of maternal alcohol abuse and partner violence but did not reduce child abuse (Duggan & others, 2004).

The Hawaii Family Support/Healthy Start Program provides many home-visitor services for overburdened families of newborns and young children. This program has been very successful in reducing abuse and neglect in families. *What are some examples of the home-visitor services in this program?*

Review and Reflect • LEARNING GOAL 1

1 **Discuss physical growth and development in infancy**

Review
- What are cephalocaudal and proximodistal patterns?
- What changes in height and weight take place in infancy?
- What are some key features of the brain and its development in infancy?
- What changes occur in sleep during infancy?
- What are infants' nutritional needs?

Reflect
- What three pieces of advice about the infant's physical development would you want to give a friend who has just had a baby? Why those three?

2 MOTOR DEVELOPMENT

The Dynamic Systems View   Gross Motor Skills

Reflexes   Fine Motor Skills

As a newborn, Ramona, whom we met in the chapter opening, could suck, fling her arms, and tightly grip a finger placed in her tiny hand. Within just two years, she would be toddling around on her own, opening doors and jars as she explored her little world. Are her accomplishments inevitable? How do infants develop their motor skills, and which skills do they develop when?

The Dynamic Systems View

Developmentalist Arnold Gesell (1934) thought his painstaking observations had revealed how people develop their motor skills. He had discovered that infants and children develop rolling, sitting, standing, and other motor skills in a fixed order and within specific time frames. These observations, said Gesell, show that motor development comes about through the unfolding of a genetic plan, or *maturation.*

Later studies, however, demonstrated that the sequence of developmental milestones is not as fixed as Gesell indicated and not due as strongly to heredity as Gesell argued (Adolph & Berger, 2005, 2006; Adolph & Joh, 2007). In the 1990s, the study of motor development experienced a renaissance as psychologists developed new insights about *how* motor skills develop (Thelen & Smith, 1998). One increasingly influential theory is dynamic systems theory proposed by · Esther Thelen.

According to **dynamic systems theory,** infants assemble motor skills for perceiving and acting. Notice that perception and action are coupled according to this theory (Thelen, 1995, 2000, 2001; Thelen & Smith, 1998, 2006; Thelen & Whitmeyer, 2005). In order to develop motor skills, infants must perceive something in the environment that motivates them to act and use their perceptions to fine-tune their movements. Motor skills represent solutions to the infant's goals.

How is a motor skill developed according to this theory? When infants are motivated to do something, they might create a new motor behavior. The new behavior is the result of many converging factors: the development of the nervous system, the body's physical properties and its possibilities for movement, the goal the child is motivated to reach, and the environmental support for the skill. For example, babies learn to walk only when maturation of the nervous system allows them to control certain leg muscles, when their legs have grown enough to support their weight, and when they want to move.

Mastering a motor skill requires the infant's active efforts to coordinate several components of the skill (Adolph & Berger, 2006; Adolph & Joh, 2007; Thelen & Smith, 2006). Infants explore and select possible solutions to the demands of a new task; they assemble adaptive patterns by modifying their current movement patterns. The first step occurs when the infant is motivated by a new challenge—such as the desire to cross a room—and gets into the "ball park" of the task demands by taking a couple of stumbling steps. Then, the infant "tunes" these movements to make them smoother and more effective. The tuning is achieved through repeated cycles of action and perception of the consequences of that action. According to the dynamic systems view, even universal milestones, such

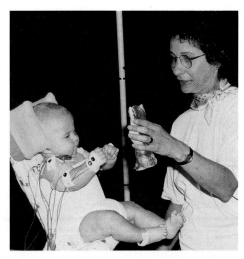

Esther Thelen is shown conducting an experiment to discover how infants learn to control their arms to reach and grasp for objects. A computer device is used to monitor the infant's arm movements and to track muscle patterns. Thelen's research is conducted from a dynamic systems perspective. *What is the nature of this perspective?*

www.mhhe.com/santrockld11

Esther Thelen's Research

dynamic systems theory The perspective on motor development that seeks to explain how motor behaviors are assembled for perceiving and acting.

The experiences of the first three years of life are almost entirely lost to us, and when we attempt to enter into a small child's world, we come as foreigners who have forgotten the landscape and no longer speak the native tongue.

—SELMA FRAIBERG
Developmentalist and Child Advocate, 20th Century

as crawling, reaching, and walking, are learned through this process of adaptation: infants modulate their movement patterns to fit a new task by exploring and selecting possible configurations (Adolph & Berger, 2006; Adolph & Joh, 2007; Thelen & Smith, 2006).

To see how dynamic systems theory explains motor behavior, imagine that you offer a new toy to a baby named Gabriel (Thelen & others, 1993). There is no exact program that can tell Gabriel ahead of time how to move his arm and hand and fingers to grasp the toy. Gabriel must adapt to his goal—grasping the toy—and the context. From his sitting position, he must make split-second adjustments to extend his arm, holding his body steady so that his arm and torso don't plow into the toy. Muscles in his arm and shoulder contract and stretch in a host of combinations, exerting a variety of forces. He improvises a way to reach out with one arm and wrap his fingers around the toy.

Thus, according to dynamic systems theory, motor development is not a passive process in which genes dictate the unfolding of a sequence of skills over time. Rather, the infant actively puts together a skill in order to achieve a goal within the constraints set by the infant's body and environment. Nature and nurture, the infant and the environment, are all working together as part of an ever-changing system (Adolph & Berger, 2006; Adolph & Joh, 2007; Thelen & Smith, 2006).

As we examine the course of motor development, we will describe how dynamic systems theory applies to some specific skills. First, though, let's examine how the story of motor development begins with reflexes.

Reflexes

The newborn is not completely helpless. Among other things, it has some basic reflexes. For example, the newborn automatically holds its breath and contracts

Reflex	Stimulation	Infant's Response	Developmental Pattern
Blinking	Flash of light, puff of air	Closes both eyes	Permanent
Babinski	Sole of foot stroked	Fans out toes, twists foot in	Disappears after 9 months to 1 year
Grasping	Palms touched	Grasps tightly	Weakens after 3 months, disappears after 1 year
Moro (startle)	Sudden stimulation, such as hearing loud noise or being dropped	Startles, arches back, throws head back, flings out arms and legs and then rapidly closes them to center of body	Disappears after 3 to 4 months
Rooting	Cheek stroked or side of mouth touched	Turns head, opens mouth, begins sucking	Disappears after 3 to 4 months
Stepping	Infant held above surface and feet lowered to touch surface	Moves feet as if to walk	Disappears after 3 to 4 months
Sucking	Object touching mouth	Sucks automatically	Disappears after 3 to 4 months
Swimming	Infant put face down in water	Makes coordinated swimming movements	Disappears after 6 to 7 months
Tonic neck	Infant placed on back	Forms fists with both hands and usually turns head to the right (sometimes called the "fencer's pose" because the infant looks like it is assuming a fencer's position)	Disappears after 2 months

FIGURE 5.12 Infant Reflexes. This chart describes some of the infant's reflexes.

its throat to keep water out. **Reflexes** are built-in reactions to stimuli; they govern the newborn's movements, which are automatic and beyond the newborn's control. Reflexes are genetically carried survival mechanisms. They allow infants to respond adaptively to their environment before they have had the opportunity to learn.

The rooting and sucking reflexes are important examples. Both have survival value for newborn mammals, who must find a mother's breast to obtain nourishment. The **rooting reflex** occurs when the infant's cheek is stroked or the side of the mouth is touched. In response, the infant turns its head toward the side that was touched in an apparent effort to find something to suck. The **sucking reflex** occurs when newborns automatically suck an object placed in their mouth. This reflex enables newborns to get nourishment before they have associated a nipple with food.

Another example is the **Moro reflex,** which occurs in response to a sudden, intense noise or movement. When startled, the newborn arches its back, throws back its head, and flings out its arms and legs. Then the newborn rapidly closes its arms and legs. The Moro reflex is believed to be a way of grabbing for support while falling; it would have had survival value for our primate ancestors.

Some reflexes—coughing, sneezing, blinking, shivering, and yawning, for example—persist throughout life. They are as important for the adult as they are for the infant. Other reflexes, though, disappear several months following birth, as the infant's brain matures, and voluntary control over many behaviors develops. The rooting, sucking, and Moro reflexes, for example, all tend to disappear when the infant is 3 to 4 months old.

The movements of some reflexes eventually become incorporated into more complex, voluntary actions. One important example is the **grasping reflex,** which occurs when something touches the infant's palms. The infant responds by grasping tightly. By the end of the third month, the grasping reflex diminishes, and the infant shows a more voluntary grasp. For example, when an infant sees a mobile turning slowly above a crib, it may reach out and try to grasp it. As its motor development becomes smoother, the infant will grasp objects, carefully manipulate them, and explore their qualities. An overview of the reflexes we have discussed, along with others such as stepping and swimming, is given in figure 5.12.

Although reflexes are automatic and inborn, differences in reflexive behavior are soon apparent. For example, the sucking capabilities of newborns vary considerably. Some newborns are efficient at forceful sucking and obtaining milk; others are not as adept and get tired before they are full. Most infants take several weeks to establish a sucking style that is coordinated with the way the mother is holding the infant, the way milk is coming out of the bottle or breast, and the infant's temperament.

Pediatrician T. Berry Brazelton (1956) observed how infants' sucking changed as they grew older. Over 85 percent of the infants engaged in considerable sucking behavior unrelated to feeding. They sucked their finger, their fists, and pacifiers. By the age of 1 year, most had stopped the sucking behavior, but as many as 40 percent of children continue to suck their thumbs after they have started school (Kessen, Haith, & Salapatek, 1970). Most developmentalists do not attach a great deal of significance to this behavior.

Gross Motor Skills

Ask any parents about their baby, and sooner or later you are likely to hear about one or more motor milestone, such as "Cassandra just learned to crawl," "Jesse is finally sitting alone," or "Angela took her first step last week." Parents proudly announce such milestones as their children transform themselves from babies unable to lift their heads to toddlers who grab things off the grocery store shelf, chase a

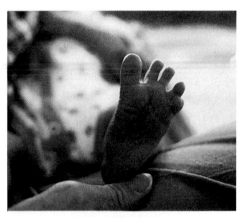
Babinski reflex

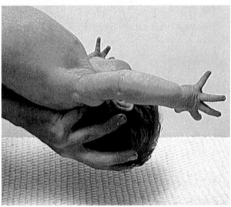
Moro reflex

The Babinski reflex (top) usually disappears around nine months. The Moro reflex (bottom) usually disappears around three months.

Reflexes Built-in reactions to stimuli that govern the newborn's movements, which are automatic and beyond the newborn's control.

rooting reflex A newborn's built-in reaction that occurs when the infant's cheek is stroked or the side of the mouth is touched. In response, the infant turns his or her head toward the side that was touched, in an apparent effort to find something to suck.

sucking reflex A newborn's built-in reaction to automatically suck an object placed in its mouth. The sucking reflex enables the infant to get nourishment before he or she has associated a nipple with food.

Moro reflex A neonatal startle response that occurs in reaction to a sudden, intense noise or movement. When startled, the newborn arches its back, throws its head back, and flings out its arms and legs. Then the newborn rapidly closes its arms and legs to the center of the body.

grasping reflex A neonatal reflex that occurs when something touches the infant's palms. The infant responds by grasping tightly.

What are some developmental changes in posture during infancy?

cat, and participate actively in the family's social life (Thelen, 1995, 2000). These milestones are examples of **gross motor skills,** which are skills that involve large-muscle activities, such as moving one's arms and walking.

The Development of Posture   How do gross motor skills develop? As a foundation, these skills require postural control (Thelen, 1995, 2000; Thelen & Smith, 2006). For example, to track moving objects, you must be able to control your head in order to stabilize your gaze; before you can walk, you must be able to balance on one leg.

Posture is more than just holding still and straight. In Thelen's (1995, 2000; Thelen & Smith, 2006) view, posture is a dynamic process that is linked with sensory information from proprioceptive cues in the skin, joints, and muscles, which tell us where we are in space; from vestibular organs in the inner ear that regulate balance and equilibrium; and from vision and hearing (Spencer & others, 2000).

Newborn infants cannot voluntarily control their posture. Within a few weeks, though, they can hold their heads erect, and soon they can lift their heads while prone. By 2 months of age, babies can sit while supported on a lap or an infant seat, but they cannot sit independently until they are 6 or 7 months of age. Standing also develops gradually during the first year of life. By about 8 months of age, infants usually learn to pull themselves up and hold onto a chair, and they often can stand alone by about 10 to 12 months of age.

Learning to Walk   Locomotion and postural control are closely linked, especially in walking upright (Adolph & Berger, 2005, 2006; Adolph & Joh, 2007). To walk upright, the baby must be able both to balance on one leg as the other is swung forward and to shift the weight from one leg to the other (Thelen, 2000; Thelen & Smith, 2006).

Even young infants can make the alternating leg movements that are needed for walking. The neural pathways that control leg alternation are in place from a very early age, possibly even at birth or before. Infants engage in frequent alternating kicking movements throughout the first six months of life when they are lying on their backs. Also when 1- to 2-month-olds are given support with their feet in contact with a motorized treadmill, they show well-coordinated, alternating steps. Despite these early abilities, most infants do not learn to walk until about the time of their first birthday.

If infants can produce forward stepping movements so early, why does it take them so long to learn to walk? The key skills in learning to walk appear to be stabilizing balance on one leg long enough to swing the other forward and shifting the weight without falling. This is a difficult biomechanical problem to solve, and it takes infants about a year to do it.

Infants also must learn what kinds of places and surfaces are safe for crawling or walking (Adolph & Berger, 2005, 2006; Adolph & Joh, 2002). Karen Adolph (1997) investigated how experienced and inexperienced crawling infants and walking infants go down steep slopes (see figure 5.13). Newly crawling infants, who averaged about $8\frac{1}{2}$ months in age, rather indiscriminately went down the steep slopes, often falling in the process (with their mothers next to the slope to catch them). After weeks of practice, the crawling babies became more adept at judging which slopes were too steep to crawl down and which ones they could navigate safely.

You might expect that babies who learned that a slope was too steep for crawling would know when they began walking whether a slope was safe. But Adolph's research indicated that newly walking infants could not judge the safety of the

gross motor skills Motor skills that involve large-muscle activities, such as walking.

Newly crawling infant

Experienced walker

FIGURE 5.13 The Role of Experience in Crawling and Walking Infants' Judgments of Whether to Go Down a Slope. Karen Adolph (1997) found that locomotor experience rather than age was the primary predictor of adaptive responding on slopes of varying steepness. Newly crawling and walking infants could not judge the safety of the various slopes. With experience, they learned to avoid slopes where they would fall. When expert crawlers began to walk, they again made mistakes and fell, even though they had judged the same slope accurately when crawling. Adolph referred to this as the *specificity of learning* because it does not transfer across crawling and walking.

slopes. Only when infants became experienced walkers were they able to accurately match their skills with the steepness of the slopes. They rarely fell downhill, either refusing to go down the steep slopes or going down backward in a cautious manner. Experienced walkers perceptually assessed the situation—looking, swaying, touching, and thinking before they moved down the slope. With experience, both the crawlers and the walkers learned to avoid the risky slopes where they would fall, integrating perceptual information with the development of a new motor behavior. In this research, we again see the importance of perceptual-motor coupling in the development of motor skills.

What are some practical applications of Adolph's research? Parents should realize how accident-prone children are at this early stage of locomotion (Keen, 2005). They may seem very competent as they motor about, but they don't realize potential dangers they might encounter. It takes many weeks of walking before children learn that drop-offs, steps, and slopes are dangerous. Thus, falls and other accidents are common when infants begin to walk; caregivers should be constantly on guard.

The First Year: Milestones and Variations   Figure 5.14 summarizes important accomplishments in gross motor skills during the first year, culminating in the ability to walk easily. The timing of these milestones, especially the later ones, may vary by as much as two to four months, and experiences can modify the onset of these accomplishments. For example, since 1992, when pediatricians began recommending that parents keep their infants on their backs at night, fewer babies crawl and the age of onset of crawling is later (Davis & others, 1998). Also, some infants do not follow the standard sequence of motor accomplishments. For example, many American infants never crawl on their belly or on their hands-and-knees. They may discover an idiosyncratic form of locomotion before walking, such as rolling, or they might never locomote until they get upright (Adolph, 2002). In the African Mali tribe, most infants do not crawl (Bril, 1999).

According to Karen Adolph and Sarah Berger (2005), "the old-fashioned view that growth and motor development reflect merely the age-related output of maturation is, at best, incomplete. Rather, infants acquire new skills with the help of their caregivers in a real-world environment of objects, surfaces, and planes" (p. 273).

www.mhhe.com/santrockld11

Developmental Milestones
Karen Adolph's Research

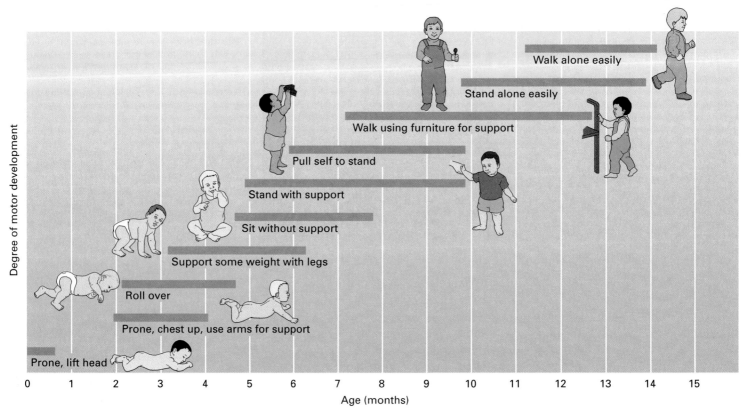

Degree of motor development

Walk alone easily

Stand alone easily

Walk using furniture for support

Pull self to stand

Stand with support

Sit without support

Support some weight with legs

Roll over

Prone, chest up, use arms for support

Prone, lift head

Age (months)

0 1 2 3 4 5 6 7 8 9 10 11 12 13 14 15

FIGURE 5.14 Milestones in Gross Motor Development. The horizontal blue bars indicate the range in which most infants reach various milestones in gross motor development.

Development in the Second Year The motor accomplishments of the first year bring increasing independence, allowing infants to explore their environment more extensively and to initiate interaction with others more readily. In the second year of life, toddlers become more motorically skilled and mobile. They are no longer content in a playpen and want to move all over the place. Child development experts believe that motor activity during the second year is vital to the child's competent development and that few restrictions, except for safety, should be placed on their adventures (Fraiberg, 1959).

By 13 to 18 months, toddlers can pull a toy attached to a string and use their hands and legs to climb up a number of steps. By 18 to 24 months, toddlers can walk quickly or run stiffly for a short distance, balance on their feet in a squat position while playing with objects on the floor, walk backward without losing their balance, stand and kick a ball without falling, stand and throw a ball, and jump in place.

Can parents give their babies a head start on becoming physically fit and physically talented through structured exercise classes? Physical fitness classes for babies range from passive fare—with adults putting infants through the paces—to programs called "aerobic" because they demand crawling, tumbling, and ball skills. Pediatricians point out that when an adult is stretching and moving an infant's limbs, the adult can easily go beyond the infant's physical limits without knowing it. Pediatricians also recommend that exercise for infants should not be of the intense, aerobic variety. Babies cannot adequately stretch their bodies to achieve aerobic benefits.

In short, most infancy experts recommend against structured exercise classes for babies. But there are other ways of guiding infants' motor development. Caregivers in some cultures do handle babies vigorously, and this might advance motor development, as we discuss in the Diversity in Life-Span Development interlude.

A baby is an angel whose wings decrease as his legs increase.

—French Proverb

Cultural Variations in Guiding Infants' Motor Development

Mothers in developing countries tend to stimulate their infants' motor skills more than mothers in more modern countries (Hopkins, 1991). Jamaican mothers regularly massage their infants and stretch their arms and legs (Hopkins, 1991). Mothers in the Gusii culture of Kenya also encourage vigorous movement in their babies (Hopkins & Westra, 1988).

Do these cultural variations make a difference in the infant's motor development? When caregivers provide babies with physical guidance by physically handling them in special ways (such as stroking, massaging, or stretching) or by giving them opportunities for exercise, the infants often reach motor milestones earlier than infants whose caregivers have not provided these activities. For example, Jamaican mothers expect their infants to sit and walk alone two to three months earlier than English mothers do (Hopkins & Westra, 1990).

Nonetheless, even when infants' motor activity is restricted, many infants still reach the milestones of motor development at a normal age. For example, Algonquin infants in Quebec, Canada, spend much of their first year strapped to a cradle board. Despite their inactivity, these infants still sit up, crawl, and walk within an age range similar to that of infants in cultures who have had much greater opportunity for activity.

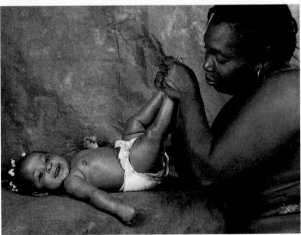

(Top) In the Algonquin culture in Quebec, Canada, babies are strapped to a cradle board for much of their infancy. *(Bottom)* In Jamaica, mothers massage and stretch their infants' arms and legs. *To what extent do cultural variations in the activity infants engage in influence the time at which they reach motor milestones?*

Fine Motor Skills

Whereas gross motor skills involve large muscle activity, **fine motor skills** involve finely tuned movements. Grasping a toy, using a spoon, buttoning a shirt, or anything that requires finger dexterity demonstrates fine motor skills. Infants have hardly any control over fine motor skills at birth, but newborns do have many components of what will become finely coordinated arm, hand, and finger movements (Rosenblith, 1992).

The onset of reaching and grasping marks a significant achievement in infants' ability to interact with their surroundings (McCarty & Ashmead, 1999; Oztop, Bradley, & Arbib, 2004). During the first two years of life, infants refine how they reach and grasp. Initially, infants reach by moving their shoulders and elbows crudely, swinging toward an object. Later, when infants reach for an object they move their wrists, rotate their hands, and coordinate their thumb and forefinger. Infants do not have to see their own hands in order to reach for an object (Clifton & others, 1993). Proprioceptive cues from muscles, tendons, and joints, not sight of the limb, guide reaching by 4-month-old infants.

fine motor skills Motor skills that involve more finely tuned movements, such as finger dexterity.

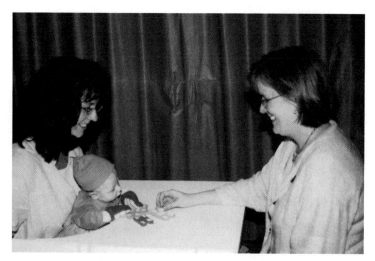

FIGURE 5.15 Infants' Use of "Sticky Mittens" to Explore Objects. Amy Needham and her colleagues (2002) found that "sticky mittens" enhanced young infants' object exploration skills.

Infants refine their ability to grasp objects by developing two types of grasps. Initially, infants grip with the whole hand, which is called the *palmer grasp*. Later, toward the end of the first year, infants grasp small objects with their thumb and forefinger, which is called the *pincer grip*. Their grasping system is very flexible. They vary their grip on an object depending on its size and shape, as well as the size of their own hands relative to the object's size. Infants grip small objects with their thumb and forefinger (and sometimes their middle finger too), whereas they grip large objects with all of the fingers of one hand or both hands.

Perceptual-motor coupling is necessary for the infant to coordinate grasping (Keen, 2005). Which perceptual system the infant is most likely to use in coordinating grasping varies with age. Four-month-old infants rely greatly on touch to determine how they will grip an object; 8-month-olds are more likely to use vision as a guide (Newell & others, 1989). This developmental change is efficient because vision lets infants preshape their hands as they reach for an object.

Experience plays a role in reaching and grasping. In one recent study, 3-month-old infants participated in play sessions wearing "sticky mittens"—"mittens with palms that stuck to the edges of toys and allowed the infants to pick up the toys" (Needham, Barrett, & Peterman, 2002, p. 279) (see figure 5.15). Infants who participated in sessions with the mittens grasped and manipulated objects earlier in their development than a control group of infants who did not receive the "mitten" experience. The experienced infants looked at the objects longer, swatted at them more during visual contact, and were more likely to mouth the objects.

Just as infants need to exercise their gross motor skills, they also need to exercise their fine motor skills (Keen, 2005). Especially when they can manage a pincer grip, infants delight in picking up small objects. Many develop the pincer grip and begin to crawl at about the same time, and infants at this time pick up virtually everything in sight, especially on the floor, and put the objects in their mouth. Thus, parents need to be vigilant in regularly monitoring what objects are within the infant's reach.

Review and Reflect ○ **LEARNING GOAL 2**

2 **Describe infants' motor development**

Review
- What is dynamic systems theory?
- What are some reflexes that infants have?
- How do gross motor skills develop in infancy?
- How do fine motor skills develop in infancy?

Reflect
- Which view of infant motor development do you prefer—the traditional maturational view or the dynamic systems view? Why?

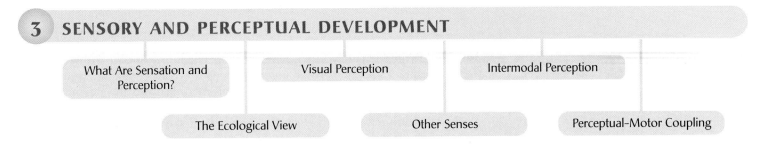

3 SENSORY AND PERCEPTUAL DEVELOPMENT

| What Are Sensation and Perception? | Visual Perception | Intermodal Perception |
| The Ecological View | Other Senses | Perceptual-Motor Coupling |

Right now, I am looking at my computer screen to make sure the words are being printed accurately as I am typing them. My perceptual and motor skills are working together. Recall that even control of posture uses information from the senses. And when people grasp an object, they use perceptual information about the object to adjust their motions.

How do these sensations and perceptions develop? Can a newborn see? If so, what can it perceive? What about the other senses—hearing, smell, taste, and touch? What are they like in the newborn, and how do they develop? Can an infant put together information from two modalities, such as sight and sound? These are among the intriguing questions that we will explore in this section.

What Are Sensation and Perception?

How does a newborn know that her mother's skin is soft rather than rough? How does a 5-year-old know what color his hair is? Infants and children "know" these things as a result of information that comes through the senses. Without vision, hearing, touch, taste, smell, and other senses, we would be isolated from the world; we would live in dark silence, a tasteless, colorless, feelingless void.

Sensation occurs when information interacts with sensory *receptors*—the eyes, ears, tongue, nostrils, and skin. The sensation of hearing occurs when waves of pulsating air are collected by the outer ear and transmitted through the bones of the inner ear to the auditory nerve. The sensation of vision occurs as rays of light contact the eyes, become focused on the retina, and are transmitted by the optic nerve to the visual centers of the brain.

Perception is the interpretation of what is sensed. The air waves that contact the ears might be interpreted as noise or as musical sounds, for example. The physical energy transmitted to the retina of the eye might be interpreted as a particular color, pattern, or shape, depending on how it is perceived.

The Ecological View

For the past several decades, much of the research on perceptual development in infancy has been guided by the ecological view of Eleanor and James J. Gibson (E. Gibson, 1969, 1989, 2001; J. Gibson, 1966, 1979). They argue that we do not have to take bits and pieces of data from sensations and build up representations of the world in our minds. Instead, our perceptual system can select from the rich information that the environment itself provides.

According to the Gibsons' **ecological view,** we directly perceive information that exists in the world around us. Perception brings us into contact with the environment in order to interact with and adapt to it. Perception is designed for action. Perception gives people such information as when to duck, when to turn their bodies through a narrow passageway, and when to put their hands up to catch something.

sensation The product of the interaction between information and the sensory receptors—the eyes, ears, tongue, nostrils, and skin.

perception The interpretation of what is sensed.

ecological view The view that perception functions to bring organisms in contact with the environment and to increase adaptation.

www.mhhe.com/santrockld11

Newborns' Senses
Richard Aslin's Research
Leslie Cohen's Research
Albert Yonas' Research
International Society on Infant Studies

In the Gibsons' view, all objects have **affordances,** which are opportunities for interaction offered by objects that fit within our capabilities to perform activities. A pot may afford you something to cook with, and it may afford a toddler something to bang. Adults immediately know when a chair is appropriate for sitting, when a surface is safe for walking, or when an object is within reach. We directly and accurately perceive these affordances by sensing information from the environment—the light or sound reflecting from the surfaces of the world—and from our own bodies through muscle receptors, joint receptors, and skin receptors, for example.

An important developmental question is, What affordances can infants or children detect and use? In one study, for example, when babies who could walk were faced with a squishy waterbed, they stopped and explored it, then chose to crawl rather than walk across it (Gibson & others, 1987). They combined perception and action to adapt to the demands of the task.

Similarly, as we described earlier in the section on motor development, infants who were just learning to crawl or just learning to walk were less cautious when confronted with a steep slope than experienced crawlers or walkers were (Adolph, 1997; Adolph & Avolio, 2000). The more experienced crawlers and walkers perceived that a slope *affords* the possibility for not only faster locomotion but also for falling. Again, infants coupled perception and action to make a decision about what to do in their environment. Through perceptual development, children become more efficient at discovering and using affordances.

Studying the infant's perception has not been an easy task. The Research in Life-Span Development interlude describes some of the ingenious ways researchers study the infant's perception.

RESEARCH IN LIFE-SPAN DEVELOPMENT

Studying the Infant's Perception

The creature has poor motor coordination and can move itself only with great difficulty. Although it cries when uncomfortable, it uses few other vocalizations. In fact, it sleeps most of the time, about 16 to 17 hours a day. You are curious about this creature and want to know more about what it can do. You think to yourself, "I wonder if it can see. How could I find out?"

You obviously have a communication problem with the creature. You must devise a way that will allow the creature to "tell" you that it can see. While examining the creature one day, you make an interesting discovery. When you move an object horizontally in front of the creature, its eyes follow the object's movement. The creature's head movement suggests that it has at least some vision.

In case you haven't already guessed, the creature you have been reading about is the human infant, and the role you played is that of a researcher interested in devising techniques to learn about the infant's visual perception. After years of work, scientists have developed research methods and tools sophisticated enough to examine the subtle abilities of infants and to interpret their complex actions (Bendersky & Sullivan, 2002; Kellman & Banks, 1998; Menn & Stoel-Gammon, 2005; Slater, 2004).

Visual Preference Method

Robert Fantz (1963) was a pioneer in this effort. Fantz made an important discovery that advanced the ability of researchers to investigate infants' visual perception: infants look at different things for different lengths of time. Fantz placed infants in a "looking chamber," which had two visual displays on the ceiling above the infant's head. An experimenter viewed the infant's eyes by looking through a peephole. If the infant was fixating on one of the displays, the experimenter could

affordances Opportunities for interaction offered by objects that fit within our capabilities to perform functional activities.

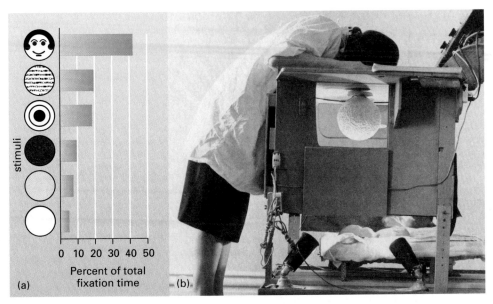

FIGURE 5.16 Fantz' Experiment on Infants' Visual Perception. (*a*) Infants 2 to 3 weeks old preferred to look at some stimuli more than others. In Fantz' experiment, infants preferred to look at patterns rather than at color or brightness. For example, they looked longer at a face, a piece of printed matter, or a bull's-eye than at red, yellow, or white discs. (*b*) Fantz used a "looking chamber" to study infants' perception of stimuli.

see the display's reflection in the infant's eyes. This allowed the experimenter to determine how long the infant looked at each display. Fantz (1963) found that infants only 2 days old look longer at patterned stimuli, such as faces and concentric circles, than at red, white, or yellow disks. Infants 2 to 3 weeks old preferred to look at patterns—a face, a piece of printed matter, or a bull's-eye—rather than at red, yellow, or white disks (see figure 5.16). Fantz' research method—studying whether infants can distinguish one stimulus from another by measuring the length of time they attend to different stimuli—is referred to as the **visual preference method.**

Habituation and Dishabituation

Another way that researchers have studied infant perception is to present a stimulus (such as a sight or a sound) a number of times. If the infant decreases its response to the stimulus after several presentations, it indicates that the infant is no longer interested in the stimulus. If the researcher now presents a new stimulus, the infant's response will recover—indicating the infant could discriminate between the old and new stimulus.

Habituation is the name given to decreased responsiveness to a stimulus after repeated presentations of the stimulus. **Dishabituation** is the recovery of an habituated response after a change in stimulation. Newborn infants can habituate to repeated sights, sounds, smells, or touches (Rovee-Collier, 2002). Among the measures researchers use in habituation studies are sucking behavior (sucking behavior stops when the young infant attends to a novel object), heart and respiration rates, and the length of time the infant looks at an object. Figure 5.17 shows the results of one study of habituation and dishabituation with newborns (Slater, Morison, & Somers, 1988).

Other Methods

To assess an infant's attention to sound, researchers often use a method called *high-amplitude sucking*. In this method, infants are given a nonnutritive nipple to suck and the nipple is connected to "a sound generating system. Each suck causes a noise to

(continued on next page)

visual preference method A method used to determine whether infants can distinguish one stimulus from another by measuring the length of time they attend to different stimuli.

habituation Decreased responsiveness to a stimulus after repeated presentation of the stimulus.

dishabituation Recovery of a habituated response after a change in stimulation.

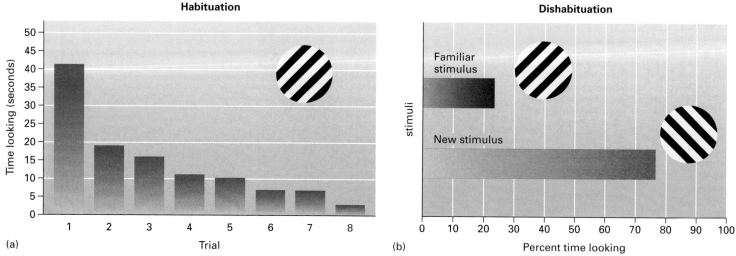

FIGURE 5.17 Habituation and Dishabituation. In the first part of one study, 7-hour-old newborns were shown the stimulus in (a). As indicated, the newborns looked at it an average of 41 seconds when it was first presented to them (Slater, Morison, & Somers, 1988). Over seven more presentations of the stimulus, they looked at it less and less. In the second part of the study, infants were presented with both the familiar stimulus to which they had just become habituated to (a) and a new stimulus (shown in b, which was rotated 90 degrees). The newborns looked at the new stimulus three times as much as the familiar stimulus.

be generated and infant learns quickly that sucking brings about this noise. At first, babies suck frequently, so the noise occurs often. Then, gradually, they lose interest in hearing repetitions of the same noise and begin to suck less frequently. At this point, the experimenter changes the sound that is being generated. If the babies renew vigorous sucking, we infer that they have discriminated the sound change and are sucking more because they want to hear the interesting new sound" (Menn & Stoel-Gammon, 2005, p. 71).

To determine if an infant can see or hear a stimulus, researchers might look for the *orienting response,* which involves turning one's head toward a sight or sound (Keen, 2005). Another technique to determine what an infant can see is to monitor the infant's *tracking,* which consists of eye movements that follow (*track*) a moving object.

Equipment

Technology can facilitate the use of most methods for investigating the infant's perceptual abilities. Videotape equipment allows researchers to investigate elusive behaviors. High-speed computers make it possible to perform complex data analysis in minutes. Other equipment records respiration, heart rate, body movement, visual fixation, and sucking behavior, which provide clues to what the infant is perceiving. For example, some researchers use equipment that detects if a change in infants' respiration follows a change in the pitch of a sound. If so, it suggests that the infants heard the pitch change. Thus, scientists have become ingenious at assessing the development of infants, discovering ways to "interview" them even though they cannot yet talk.

Visual Perception

Psychologist William James (1890/1950) called the newborn's perceptual world a "blooming, buzzing confusion." A century later, we can safely say that he was wrong (Slater, 2004). Even the newborn perceives a world with some order. That world,

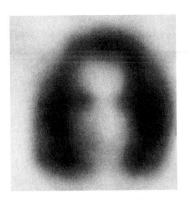   

FIGURE 5.18 Visual Acuity During the First Months of Life. The four photographs represent a computer estimation of what a picture of a face looks like to a 1-month-old, 2-month-old, 3-month-old, and 1-year-old (which approximates that of an adult).

however, is far different than the one perceived by the toddler or the adult. What do newborns see? How does visual perception develop in infancy?

Visual Acuity and Color   Just how well can infants see? At birth, the nerves and muscles and lens of the eye are still developing. As a result, newborns cannot see small things that are far away. The newborn's vision is estimated to be 20/600 on the well-known Snellan chart, with which you are tested when you have your eyes examined (Banks & Salapatek, 1983). In other words, an object 20 feet away is only as clear to the newborn as it would be if it were 600 feet away from an adult with normal vision (20/20). By 6 months of age, though, vision is 20/100 or better, and, by about the first birthday, the infant's vision approximates that of an adult (Banks & Salapatek, 1983). Figure 5.18 shows a computer estimation of what a picture of a face looks like to an infant at different ages from a distance of about 6 inches.

The infant's color vision also improves (Kellman & Arterberry, 2006). By 8 weeks, and possibly even 4 weeks, infants can discriminate some colors (Kelly, Borchert, & Teller, 1997). By 4 months of age, they have color preferences that mirror adults in some cases, preferring saturated colors such as royal blue over pale blue, for example (Bornstein, 1975).

In part, these changes in vision reflect maturation. Experience, however, is also necessary for vision to develop normally. For example, a recent study found that experience is necessary for normal color vision to develop (Sugita, 2004). Early experience is also essential for the normal development of the ability to use the cues to depth and distance that come from binocular vision. *Binocular vision* combines into one image the two different views of the world received by our eyes because they are several inches apart; the difference between the images received by the two eyes provides powerful cues for distance and depth. Newborns do not have binocular vision; it develops at about 3 to 4 months of age (Slater, Field, & Hernandez-Reif, 2002). Researchers have found that deprivation of vision in one eye (called *monocular deprivation*) during infancy produces an irreversible loss of binocular depth perception (Billson, Fitzgerald, & Provis, 1985).

Perceiving Patterns   What does the world look like to infants? Do they recognize patterns? As we discussed in the Research on Life-Span Development interlude, with the help of his "looking chamber, Robert Fantz (1963) revealed that even 2- to 3-week-old infants prefer to look at patterned displays rather than nonpatterned displays. For example, they prefer to look at a normal human face rather than one with scrambled features, and prefer to look at a bull's-eye target or black and white stripes rather than a plain circle. Research on visual preferences

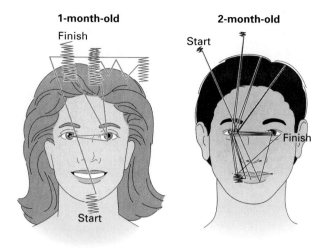

1-month-old   **2-month-old**

FIGURE 5.19 How 1- and 2-Month-Old Infants Scan the Human Face

demonstrates that the newborn's visual world is not the "blooming, buzzing confusion" William James imagined.

Even very young infants soon change the way they gather information from the visual world. By using a special mirror arrangement, researchers projected an image of human faces in front of infants' eyes so that the infants' eye movements could be photographed (Maurer & Salapatek, 1976). As figure 5.19 shows, the 2-month-old scans much more of the face than the 1-month-old, and the 2-month-old spends more time examining the internal details of the face. Thus, the 2-month-old gains more information about the world than the 1-month-old.

Perceptual Constancy Some perceptual accomplishments are especially intriguing because they indicate that the infant's perception goes beyond the information provided by the senses (Bower, 2002; Slater, Field, & Hernandez-Reif, 2002). This is the case in *perceptual constancy*, in which sensory stimulation is changing but perception of the physical world remains constant. If infants did not develop perceptual constancy, each time they saw an object at a different distance or in a different orientation, they would perceive it as a different object. Thus, the development of perceptual constancy allows infants to perceive their world as stable. Two types of perceptual constancy are size constancy and shape constancy.

Size constancy is the recognition that an object remains the same even though the retinal image of the object changes. The farther away from us an object is, the smaller its image is on our eyes. Thus, the size of an object on the retina is not sufficient to tell us its actual size. For example, you perceive a bicycle standing right in front of you as smaller than the car parked across the street, even though the bicycle casts a larger image on your eyes than the car does. When you move away from the bicycle, you do not perceive it to be shrinking even though its image on your retinas shrinks; you perceive its size as constant.

But what about babies? Do they have size constancy? Researchers have found that babies as young as 3 months of age show size constancy (Bower, 1966; Day & McKenzie, 1973). However, at 3 months of age, this ability is not full-blown. It continues to develop until 10 or 11 years of age (Kellman & Banks, 1998).

Shape constancy is the recognition that an object remains the same shape even though its orientation to us changes. Look around the room you are in right now. You likely see objects of varying shapes, such as tables and chairs. If you get up and walk around the room, you will see these objects from different sides and angles. Even though your retinal image of the objects changes as you walk and look, you will still perceive the objects as the same shape.

Do babies have shape constancy? As with size constancy, researchers have found that babies as young as 3 months of age have shape constancy (Bower, 1966; Day & McKenzie, 1973). Three-month-old infants, however, do not have shape constancy for irregularly-shaped objects, such as tilted planes (Cook & Birch, 1984).

Depth Perception Decades ago, the inspiration for what would become a classic experiment came to Eleanor Gibson as she was eating a picnic lunch on the edge of the Grand Canyon. She wondered whether an infant looking over the canyon's rim would perceive the dangerous drop-off and back up. She also was worried that her own two young children would play too close to the canyon's edge and fall off. Might even infants perceive depth?

To investigate this question, Eleanor Gibson and Richard Walk (1960) constructed a miniature cliff with a drop-off covered by glass in their laboratory. They placed infants on the edge of this visual cliff and had their mothers coax them

size constancy The recognition that an object remains the same even though the retinal image of the object changes.

shape constancy The recognition that an object's shape remains the same even though its orientation to us changes.

to crawl onto the glass (see figure 5.20). Most infants would not crawl out on the glass, choosing instead to remain on the shallow side, an indication that they could perceive depth.

The 6- to 12-month-old infants in the visual cliff experiment had extensive visual experience. Do younger infants without this experience still perceive depth? Since younger infants do not crawl, this question is difficult to answer. Two- to 4-month-old infants show differences in heart rate when they are placed directly on the deep side of the visual cliff instead of on the shallow side (Campos, Langer, & Krowitz, 1970). However, these differences might mean that young infants respond to differences in some visual characteristics of the deep and shallow cliffs, with no actual knowledge of depth. Although researchers do not know exactly how early in life infants can perceive depth, we do know, as we noted earlier, that infants develop the ability to use binocular cues to depth by about 3 to 4 months of age.

Researchers also are interested in fine-detail depth perception, which is called *stereoacuity* (Birch & others, 2005). A recent study using random-dot TV patterns showed that stereoacuity did not improve from 6 to 12 months of age but improved rapidly after one year of age (Takai & others, 2005).

FIGURE 5.20 Examining Infants' Depth Perception on the Visual Cliff. Eleanor Gibson and Richard Walk (1960) found that most infants would not crawl out on the glass, which indicated that they had depth perception.

Nature, Nurture, and the Development of Infants' Visual Perception   There has been a long-standing interest in how strongly infants' visual perception is influenced by nature or nurture. A recent analysis concluded that much of vision develops from innate (nature) foundations and that the basic foundation of many visual abilities can be detected at birth while others unfold maturationally (Kellman & Arterberry, 2006). Environmental experiences (nurture) likely refine or calibrate many visual functions, and they may be the driving force behind some functions.

Other Senses

Other sensory systems besides vision also develop during infancy. We will explore development in hearing, touch and pain, smell, and taste.

Hearing   During the last two months of pregnancy, as the fetus nestles in its mother's womb, it can hear sounds such as the mother's voice, music, and so on (Kisilevsky & others, 2004; Saffran, Werker, & Werner, 2006). Two psychologists wanted to find out if a fetus that heard Dr. Seuss' classic story *The Cat in the Hat* while still in the mother's womb would prefer hearing the story after birth (DeCasper & Spence, 1986). During the last months of pregnancy, 16 women read *The Cat in the Hat* to their fetuses. Then shortly after they were born, the mothers read either *The Cat in the Hat* or a story with a different rhyme and pace, *The King, the Mice and the Cheese* (which was not read to them during prenatal development). The infants sucked on a nipple in a different way when the mothers read the two stories, suggesting that the infants recognized the pattern and tone of *The Cat in the Hat* (see figure 5.21). This study illustrates not only that a fetus can hear but also that it has a remarkable ability to learn even before birth.

The fetus can also recognize the mother's voice, as a recent study demonstrated (Kisilevsky & others, 2003). Sixty term fetuses (mean gestational age, 38.4 weeks) were exposed to a tape recording either of their mother or of a female stranger reading a passage. The sounds of the tape were delivered through a loudspeaker held just above the mother's abdomen. Fetal heart rate increased in response to the mother's voice but decreased in response to the stranger's voice.

Newborns will suck more rapidly on a nipple in order to listen to some sounds rather than others. Their sucking behavior indicates that they prefer a recording of

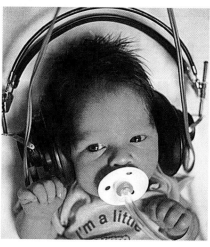

(a)   (b)

FIGURE 5.21 Hearing in the Womb. (*a*) Pregnant mothers read *The Cat in the Hat* to their fetuses during the last few months of pregnancy. (*b*) When they were born, the babies preferred listening to a recording of their mothers reading *The Cat in the Hat*, as evidenced by their sucking on a nipple that produced this recording, rather than another story, *The King, the Mice and the Cheese.*

their mother's voice to the voice of an unfamiliar woman, their mother's native language to a foreign language, and the classical music of Beethoven to the rock music of Aerosmith (Flohr & others, 2001; Spence & DeCasper, 1987). They are especially sensitive to the sounds of human speech.

What kinds of changes in hearing take place during infancy? They involve perception of a sound's loudness, pitch, and localization (Saffran, Werker, & Werner, 2006).

- Immediately after birth, infants cannot hear soft sounds quite as well as adults can; a stimulus must be louder to be heard by a newborn than by an adult (Trehub & others, 1991). For example, an adult can hear a whisper from about 4 to 5 feet away, but a newborn requires that sounds be closer to a normal conversational level to be heard at that distance.
- Infants are also less sensitive to the pitch of a sound than adults are. *Pitch* is the perception of the frequency of a sound. A soprano voice sounds high pitched, a bass voice low pitched. Infants are less sensitive to low-pitched sounds and are more likely to hear high-pitched sounds (Aslin, Jusczyk, & Pisoni, 1998). By 2 years of age, infants have considerably improved their ability to distinguish sounds with different pitches.
- Even newborns can determine the general location from where a sound is coming but by 6 months of age, they are more proficient at *localizing* sounds, detecting their origins. Their ability to localize sounds continues to improve in the second year (Litovsky & Ashmead, 1997; Morrongiello, Fenwick, & Chance, 1990; Saffran, Werker, & Werner, 2006).

Touch and Pain   Do newborns respond to touch? Can they feel pain?

Newborns do respond to touch. A touch to the cheek produces a turning of the head; a touch to the lips produces sucking movements.

Newborns can also feel pain. If and when you have a son and need to consider whether he should be circumcised, the issue of an infant's pain perception probably will become important to you. Circumcision is usually performed on young boys about the third day after birth. Will your young son experience pain if he is circumcised when he is 3 days old? An investigation by Megan Gunnar and her colleagues (1987) found that newborn infant males cried intensely during circumcision. Circumcised infants also display amazing resiliency. Within several minutes after the surgery, they can nurse and interact in a normal manner with their mothers. And, if allowed to, the newly circumcised newborn drifts into a deep sleep, which seems to serve as a coping mechanism.

For many years, doctors performed operations on newborns without anesthesia. This practice was accepted because of the dangers of anesthesia and because of the supposition that newborns do not feel pain. As researchers demonstrated that newborns can feel pain, the practice of operating on newborns without anesthesia is being challenged. Anesthesia now is used in some circumcisions.

The important ability to connect information about vision with information about touch develops during infancy. Coordination of vision and touch has been well-documented in 6-month-olds (Rose, 1990) and in one study was demonstrated in 2- to 3-year-olds (Steri, 1987).

Smell   Newborns can differentiate odors. The expressions on their faces seem to indicate that they like the way vanilla and strawberry smell but do not like the way rotten eggs and fish smell (Steiner, 1979). In one investigation, 6-day-old infants who were breast fed showed a clear preference for smelling their mother's breast pad rather than a clean breast pad (MacFarlane, 1975) (see figure 5.22). However, when they were 2 days old, they did not show this preference, indicating that they require several days of experience to recognize this odor.

Taste   Sensitivity to taste might be present even before birth. When saccharin was added to the amniotic fluid of a near-term fetus, swallowing increased (Windle, 1940). In one study, even at only 2 hours of age, babies made different facial expressions when they tasted sweet, sour, and bitter solutions (Rosenstein & Oster, 1988) (see figure 5.23). At about 4 months of age, infants begin to prefer salty tastes, which as newborns they had found to be aversive (Harris, Thomas, & Booth, 1990).

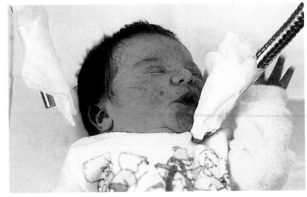

FIGURE 5.22 Newborns' Preference for the Smell of Their Mother's Breast Pad. In the experiment by MacFarlane (1975), 6-day-old infants preferred to smell their mother's breast pad rather than a clean one that had never been used, but 2-day-old infants did not show the preference, indicating that this odor preference requires several days of experience to develop.

Intermodal Perception

Imagine yourself playing basketball or tennis. You are experiencing many visual inputs: the ball coming and going, other players moving around, and so on. However, you are experiencing many auditory inputs as well: the sound of the ball bouncing or being hit, the grunts and groans, and so on. There is good correspondence between much of the visual and auditory information: When you see the ball bounce, you hear a bouncing sound; when a player stretches to hit a ball, you hear a groan. When you look at and listen to what is going on, you do not experience just the sounds or just the sights; you put all these things together. You experience a unitary episode. This is **intermodal perception,** which involves integrating information from two or more sensory modalities, such as vision and hearing.

Crude exploratory forms of intermodal perception exist even in newborns (Chen, Striano, & Rakoczy, 2004). For example, newborns turn their eyes and their head toward the sound of a voice or rattle when the sound is maintained for several seconds (Clifton & others, 1981), but the newborn can localize a sound and look at an object only in a crude way (Bechtold, Bushnell, & Salapatek, 1979). These exploratory forms of intermodal perception become sharpened with experience in the first year of life (Hollich, Newman, & Jusczyk, 2005). In one study, infants as young as $3\frac{1}{2}$ months old looked more at their mother when they also heard her voice and longer at their father when they also heard his voice (Spelke & Owsley, 1979); thus even young infants can coordinate visual-auditory information involving people.

intermodal perception The ability to relate and integrate information from two or more sensory modalities, such as vision and hearing.

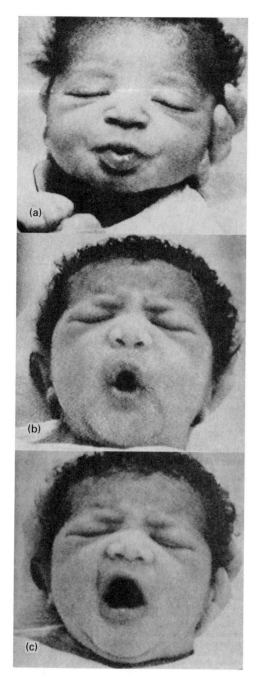

FIGURE 5.23 Newborns' Facial Responses to Basic Tastes. Facial expressions elicited by (a) a sweet solution, (b) a sour solution, and (c) a bitter solution.

Can young infants put vision and sound together as precisely as adults do? In the first six months, infants have difficulty connecting sensory input from different modes, but in the second half of the first year they show an increased ability to make this connection mentally.

Thus, babies are born into the world with some innate abilities to perceive relations among sensory modalities, but their intermodal abilities improve considerably through experience (Banks, 2005). As with all aspects of development, in perceptual development, nature and nurture interact and cooperate (Banks, 2005).

Perceptual-Motor Coupling

As we come to the end of this chapter, we return to the important theme of perceptual-motor coupling. The distinction between perceiving and doing has been a time-honored tradition in psychology. However, a number of experts on perceptual and motor development question whether this distinction makes sense (Bertenthal, 2005; Gibson, 2001; Keen, 2005; Thelen & Whitmeyer, 2005). In particular, Esther Thelen's dynamic systems approach explores how people assemble motor behaviors for perceiving and acting; the ecological approach of Eleanor and James J. Gibson examines how perception guides action. Action can guide perception and perception can guide action. Only by moving your eyes, head, hands, and arms and by moving from one location to another can you fully experience your environment and learn how to adapt to it. Perception and action are coupled.

Babies continually coordinate their movements with perceptual information to learn how to maintain balance, reach for objects in space, and move across various surfaces and terrains (Adolph & Berger, 2006; Adolph & Joh, 2007; Kellman & Arterberry, 2006; Thelen & Smith, 2006; Thelen & Whitmeyer, 2005). They are motivated to move by what they perceive. Suppose infants see an attractive toy across the room. To reach the toy, they must perceive the current state of their bodies and learn how to use their limbs. Although their movements at first are awkward and uncoordinated, babies soon learn to select patterns that are appropriate for reaching their goals.

Equally important is the other part of the perception-action coupling. That is, action educates perception. For example, exploring an object manually helps infants to discriminate its texture, size, and hardness. Locomoting teaches babies about how objects and people look from different perspectives and about whether surfaces will support their weight. Individuals perceive in order to move and move in order to perceive. Perceptual and motor development do not occur in isolation from one another but instead are coupled (Adolph & Berger, 2006; Adolph & Joh, 2007; Bornstein, Arterberry, & Mash, 2005; Thelen & Smith, 2006; Thelen & Whitmeyer, 2005).

Review and Reflect • LEARNING GOAL 3

3 **Explain sensory and perceptual development in infancy**

Review
- What are sensation and perception?
- What is the ecological view of perception?
- How does visual perception develop in infancy?
- How do hearing, touch and pain, smell, and taste develop in infancy?
- What is intermodal perception?
- How is perceptual-motor development coupled?

Reflect
- How much sensory stimulation should caregivers provide for infants? A little? A lot? Could an infant be given too much sensory stimulation? Explain.

REACH YOUR LEARNING GOALS

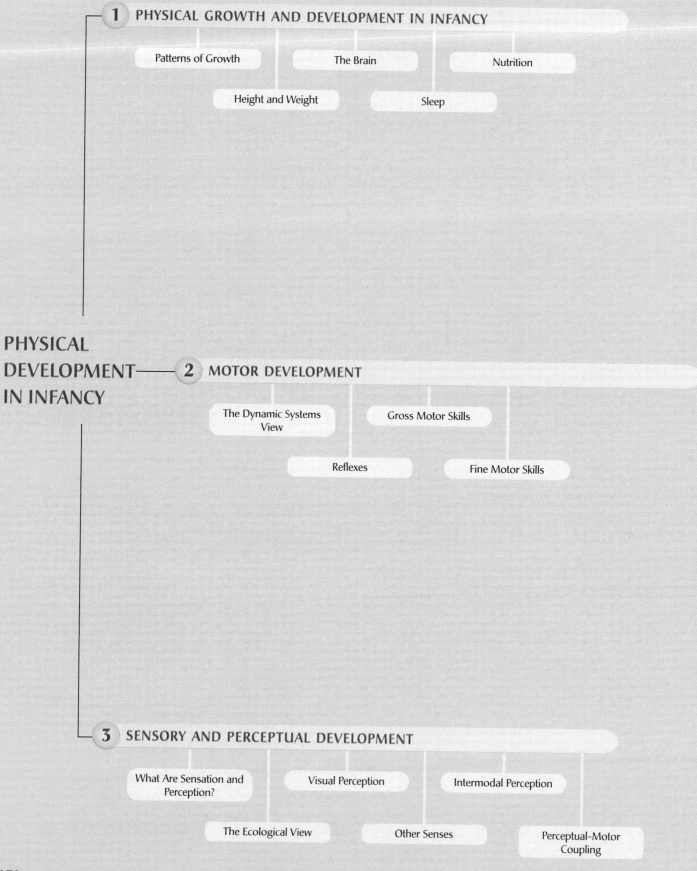

PHYSICAL DEVELOPMENT IN INFANCY

1 PHYSICAL GROWTH AND DEVELOPMENT IN INFANCY

Patterns of Growth

The Brain

Nutrition

Height and Weight

Sleep

2 MOTOR DEVELOPMENT

The Dynamic Systems View

Gross Motor Skills

Reflexes

Fine Motor Skills

3 SENSORY AND PERCEPTUAL DEVELOPMENT

What Are Sensation and Perception?

Visual Perception

Intermodal Perception

The Ecological View

Other Senses

Perceptual-Motor Coupling

SUMMARY

1 Physical Growth and Development in Infancy: *Discuss physical growth and development in infancy*

Patterns of Growth
The cephalocaudal pattern is the sequence in which growth proceeds from top to bottom. The proximodistal pattern is the sequence in which growth starts at the center of the body and moves toward the extremities.

Height and Weight
The average North American newborn is 20 inches long and weighs $7\frac{1}{2}$ pounds. Infants grow about 1 inch per month in the first year and nearly triple their weight by their first birthday. The rate of growth slows in the second year.

The Brain
One of the most dramatic changes in the brain in the first two years of life is dendritic spreading, which increases the connections between neurons. Myelination, which speeds the conduction of nerve impulses, continues through infancy and even into adolescence. The cerebral cortex has two hemispheres (left and right). Lateralization refers to specialization of function in one hemisphere or the other. Research with animals suggests that the environment plays a key role in early brain development. Neural connections are formed early in an infant's life. Before birth, genes mainly direct neurons to different locations. After birth, the inflowing stream of sights, sounds, smells, touches, language, and eye contact help shape the brain's neural connections.

Sleep
Newborns usually sleep 16 to 17 hours a day. By 4 months of age, many American infants approach adult-like sleeping patterns. REM sleep—during which dreaming occurs—is present more in early infancy than in childhood and adulthood. Sleeping arrangements for infants vary across cultures. In America, infants are more likely to sleep alone than in many other cultures. Some experts believe shared sleeping can lead to sudden infant death syndrome (SIDS), a condition that occurs when a sleeping infant suddenly stops breathing and dies without an apparent cause.

Nutrition
Infants need to consume about 50 calories per day for each pound they weigh. The growing consensus is that breast feeding is superior to bottle feeding. Severe infant malnutrition is still prevalent in many parts of the world. A special concern in impoverished countries is early weaning from breast milk.

2 Motor Development: *Describe infants' motor development*

The Dynamic Systems View
Thelen's dynamic systems theory seeks to explain how motor behaviors are assembled for perceiving and acting. Perception and action are coupled. According to this theory, motor skills are the result of many converging factors, such as the development of the nervous system, the body's physical properties and its movement possibilities, the goal the child is motivated to reach, and environmental support for the skill. In the dynamic systems view, motor development is far more complex than the result of a genetic blueprint.

Reflexes
Reflexes—automatic movements—govern the newborn's behavior. They include the sucking, rooting, and Moro reflexes—all of which typically disappear after three to four months, as well as such permanent reflexes as coughing and blinking. For infants, sucking is an especially important reflex because it provides a means of obtaining nutrition.

Gross Motor Skills
Gross motor skills involve large-muscle activities. Key skills developed during infancy include control of posture and walking. Although infants usually learn to walk by their first birthday, the neural pathways that allow walking begin to form earlier. When infants reach milestones in the development of gross motor skills may vary by as much as two to four months, especially for milestones in late infancy.

Fine Motor Skills
Fine motor skills involve finely tuned movements. The onset of reaching and grasping marks a significant accomplishment, and this becomes more refined during the first two years of life.

3 Sensory and Perceptual Development: *Explain sensory and perceptual development in infancy*

What Are Sensation and Perception?
Sensation occurs when information interacts with sensory receptors. Perception is the interpretation of sensation.

The Ecological View
Created by the Gibsons, the ecological view states that we directly perceive information that exists in the world around us. Perception brings people in contact with the environment to interact with and adapt to it. Affordances provide opportunities for interaction offered by objects that fit within our capabilities to perform activities.

Visual Perception

Researchers have developed a number of methods to assess the infant's perception, including the visual preference method (which Fantz used to determine young infants' interest in looking at patterned over non patterned displays), habituation and dishabituation, and tracking. The infant's visual acuity increases dramatically in the first year of life. In color vision, newborns can distinguish green and red. All three color-sensitive receptors function in adult-like ways by 2 months of age. Young infants systematically scan human faces. By 3 months of age, infants show size and shape constancy. In Gibson and Walk's classic study, infants as young as 6 months of age had depth perception. Much of vision develops from biological foundations but environmental experiences can contribute to the development of visual perception.

Other Senses

The fetus can hear several weeks prior to birth. Immediately after birth, newborns can hear, but their sensory threshold is higher than that of adults. Developmental changes in the perception of loudness, pitch, and localization of sound occur during infancy. Newborns can respond to touch and feel pain. Newborns can differentiate odors, and sensitivity to taste may be present before birth.

Intermodal Perception

Crude, exploratory forms of intermodal perception—the ability to relate and integrate information from two or more sensory modalities—are present in newborns and become sharpened over the first year of life.

Perceptual-Motor Coupling

Perception and action are often not isolated but rather are coupled. Individuals perceive in order to move and move in order to perceive.

KEY TERMS

cephalocaudal pattern 139
proximodistal pattern 140
lateralization 141
neuron 142
sudden infant death
    syndrome (SIDS) 146
marasmus 149

kwashiorkor 149
dynamic systems theory 151
reflexes 153
rooting reflex 153
sucking reflex 153
Moro reflex 153
grasping reflex 153

gross motor skills 154
fine motor skills 157
sensation 159
perception 159
ecological view 159
affordances 160

visual preference method 161
habituation 161
dishabituation 161
size constancy 164
shape constancy 164
intermodal perception 167

KEY PEOPLE

Mark Rosenzweig 143
John Watson 147
T. Berry Brazelton 149

Arnold Gesell 151
Esther Thelen 151
Karen Adolph 155

Eleanor and
    James J. Gibson 159
Robert Fantz 160

William James 162
Richard Walk 164

E-LEARNING TOOLS

To help you master the material in this chapter, you'll find a number of valuable study tools on the LifeMap CD-ROM that accompanies this book and on the Online Learning Center for *Life-Span Development*, eleventh edition, at **www.mhhe.com/ santrockld11.**

Video Clips

In the margins of this book there are icons directing you to the LifeMap CD-ROM that accompanies the book. There you'll find two videos for chapter 5. The first video is called "Nutritional Benefits of Breast Feeding." Is breast feeding better for the infant than bottle feeding? In this segment, a dietician details some of the benefits of breast feeding. The second video is called "Gross Motor Ability at 1 Year." A profile of 1-year-old Cindy illustrates some of the advances in gross motor skills that have occurred during the first year of life.

Self-Assessment

Connect to **www.mhhe.com/santrockld11** to examine your understanding of physical development in infancy by completing the self-assessment, *My Beliefs About Nurturing a Baby's Physical Development.*

Taking It to the Net

Connect to **www.mhhe.com/santrockld11** to research the answers to these questions.

1. Professor Samuels asked his life-span psychology students to write a one-page report explaining how a child's brain develops during infancy and what role parents play in fostering maximal brain development. What comprehensive and current research should this report include?
2. Huy grew up in a traditional Chinese family, where co-sleeping until adolescence was the norm. He sees no problem with allowing his infant daughter to sleep with him and his wife. His wife, Lori, who was born and raised in the United States, is concerned that allowing the baby to sleep in their bed places her at risk for SIDS. Is co-sleeping a significant risk factor for SIDS? What else can Huy and Lori do to reduce the risk?
3. Marianne has landed a part-time job as a nanny for Jack, a 2-month-old boy. What can Marianne expect to see in terms of the child's sensory and motor development as she observes and interacts with Jack over the next six months?

Health and Well-Being, Parenting, and Education Exercises

Build your decision-making skills by trying your hand at the health and well-being, parenting, and education exercises.

Connect to **www.mhhe.com/santrockld11** to research the answers and complete the exercises.

I wish I could travel down by the road that crosses the baby's mind where reason makes kites of her laws and flies them. . . .

—RABINDRANATH TAGORE
Bengali Poet, Essayist, 20th Century

CHAPTER OUTLINE

LEARNING GOALS

PIAGET'S THEORY OF INFANT DEVELOPMENT

Cognitive Processes

The Sensorimotor Stage of Development

1 Summarize the cognitive processes in Piaget's theory and the stage of sensorimotor development

LEARNING, REMEMBERING, AND CONCEPTUALIZING

Conditioning

Attention

Imitation

Memory

Concept Formation and Categorization

2 Describe how infants learn, remember, and conceptualize

INDIVIDUAL DIFFERENCES AND ASSESSMENT

Measures of Infant Development

Predicting Intelligence

3 Discuss infant assessment measures and the prediction of intelligence

LANGUAGE DEVELOPMENT

Defining Language

Language's Rule Systems

How Language Develops

Biological and Environmental Influences

An Interactionist View

4 Explain language development in infancy

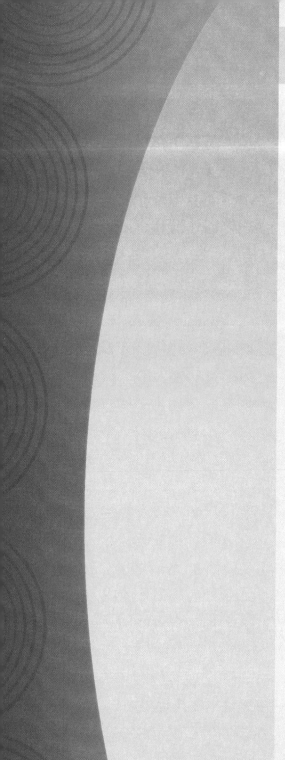

Images of Life-Span Development
Laurent, Lucienne, and Jacqueline

Jean Piaget, the famous Swiss psychologist, was a meticulous observer of his three children—Laurent, Lucienne, and Jacqueline. His books on cognitive development are filled with these observations. Here are a few of Piaget's observations of his children in infancy (Piaget, 1952):

- At 21 days of age, "Laurent found his thumb after three attempts: prolonged sucking begins each time. But, once he has been placed on his back, he does not know how to coordinate the movement of the arms with that of the mouth and his hands draw back even when his lips are seeking them" (p. 27).

- During the third month, thumb sucking becomes less important to Laurent because of new visual and auditory interests. But, when he cries, his thumb goes to the rescue.

- Toward the end of Lucienne's fourth month, while she is lying in her crib, Piaget hangs a doll above her feet. Lucienne thrusts her feet at the doll and makes it move. "Afterward, she looks at her motionless foot for a second, then recommences. There is no visual control of her foot, for the movements are the same when Lucienne only looks at the doll or when I place the doll over her head. On the other hand, the tactile control of the foot is apparent: after the first shakes, Lucienne makes slow foot movements as though to grasp and explore" (p. 159).

- At 11 months, "Jacqueline is seated and shakes a little bell. She then pauses abruptly in order to delicately place the bell in front of her right foot; then she kicks hard. Unable to recapture it, she grasps a ball which she then places at the same spot in order to give it another kick" (p. 225).

- At 1 year, 2 months, "Jacqueline holds in her hands an object which is new to her: a round, flat box which she turns all over, shakes, (and) rubs against the bassinet. . . . She lets it go and tries to pick it up. But she only succeeds in touching it with her index finger, without grasping it. She nevertheless makes an attempt and presses on the edge. The box then tilts up and falls again" (p. 273). Jacqueline shows an interest in this result and studies the fallen box.

- At 1 year, 8 months, "Jacqueline arrives at a closed door with a blade of grass in each hand. She stretches out her right hand toward the [door] knob but sees that she cannot turn it without letting go of the grass. She puts the grass on the floor, opens the door, picks up the grass again, and enters. But when she wants to leave the room, things become complicated. She puts the grass on the floor and grasps the doorknob. But then she perceives that in pulling the door toward her she will simultaneously chase away the grass which she placed between the door and the threshold. She therefore picks it up in order to put it outside the door's zone of movement" (p. 339).

For Piaget, these observations reflect important changes in the infant's cognitive development. Piaget believed that infants go through six substages as they progress in less than two short years from Laurent's thumb sucking to Jacqueline's problem solving.

Piaget's descriptions of infants are just the starting point for our exploration of cognitive development. Excitement and enthusiasm about the study of infant cognition have been fueled by an interest in what newborns and infants know, by continued fascination about innate and learned factors in the infant's cognitive development, and by controversies about whether infants construct their knowledge (Piaget's view) or know their world more directly. In this chapter we will study not only Piaget's theory of infant development but also learning, remembering, and conceptualizing by infants; individual differences; and language development.

1   PIAGET'S THEORY OF INFANT DEVELOPMENT

Cognitive Processes

The Sensorimotor Stage of Development

Poet Nora Perry asks, "Who knows the thoughts of a child?" As much as anyone, Piaget knew. Through careful observations of his own three children—Laurent, Lucienne, and Jacqueline—and observations of and interviews with other children, Piaget changed perceptions of the way children think about the world.

Piaget's theory is a general, unifying story of how biology and experience sculpt cognitive development. Piaget thought that, just as our physical bodies have structures that enable us to adapt to the world, we build mental structures that help us to adapt to the world. *Adaptation* involves adjusting to new environmental demands. Piaget stressed that children actively construct their own cognitive worlds; information is not just poured into their minds from the environment. He sought to discover how children at different points in their development think about the world and how systematic changes in their thinking occur.

Cognitive Processes

What processes do children use as they construct their knowledge of the world? Piaget developed several concepts to answer this question; especially important are schemes, assimilation, accommodation, organization, equilibrium, and equilibration.

Schemes   As the infant or child seeks to construct an understanding of the world, said Piaget (1954), the developing brain creates **schemes.** These are actions or mental representations that organize knowledge. In Piaget's theory, behavioral schemes (physical activities) characterize infancy and mental schemes (cognitive activities) develop in childhood (Lamb, Bornstein, & Teti, 2002). A baby's schemes are structured by simple actions that can be performed on objects such as sucking, looking, and grasping. Older children have schemes that include strategies and plans for solving problems. For example, in the descriptions at the opening of this chapter, Laurent displayed a scheme for sucking; Jacqueline displayed a problem-solving scheme when she was able to open the door without losing her blade of grass. By the time we have reached adulthood, we have constructed an enormous number of diverse schemes, ranging from how to drive a car to balancing a budget to the concept of fairness.

schemes In Piaget's theory, actions or mental representations that organize knowledge.

Assimilation and Accommodation

To explain how children use and adapt their schemes, Piaget offered two concepts: assimilation and accommodation. **Assimilation** occurs when children use their existing schemes to deal with new information or experiences. **Accommodation** occurs when children adjust their schemes to take new information and experiences into account.

Think about a toddler who has learned the word *car* to identify the family's car. The toddler might call all moving vehicles on roads "cars," including motorcycles and trucks; the child has assimilated these objects to his or her existing scheme. But the child soon learns that motorcycles and trucks are not cars and fine-tunes the category to exclude motorcycles and trucks, accommodating the scheme.

Assimilation and accommodation operate even in very young infants. Newborns reflexively suck everything that touches their lips; they assimilate all sorts of objects into their sucking scheme. By sucking different objects, they learn about their taste, texture, shape, and so on. After several months of experience, though, they construct their understanding of the world differently. Some objects, such as fingers and the mother's breast, can be sucked, and others, such as fuzzy blankets, should not be sucked. In other words, they accommodate their sucking scheme.

Organization

To make sense out of their world, said Piaget, children cognitively organize their experiences. **Organization** in Piaget's theory is the grouping of isolated behaviors and thoughts into a higher-order system. Continual refinement of this organization is an inherent part of development. A boy who has only a vague idea about how to use a hammer may also have a vague idea about how to use other tools. After learning how to use each one, he relates these uses, organizing his knowledge.

Equilibration and Stages of Development

Assimilation and accommodation always take the child to a higher ground, according to Piaget. In trying to understand the world, the child inevitably experiences cognitive conflict, or *disequilibrium.* That is, the child is constantly faced with counterexamples to his or her existing schemes and with inconsistencies. For example, if a child believes that pouring water from a short and wide container into a tall and narrow container changes the amount of water, then the child might be puzzled by where the "extra" water came from and whether there is actually more water to drink. The puzzle creates disequilibrium; for Piaget, an internal search for equilibrium creates motivation for change. The child assimilates and accommodates, adjusting old schemes, developing new schemes, and organizing and reorganizing the old and new schemes. Eventually, the organization is fundamentally different from the old organization; it is a new way of thinking.

In short, according to Piaget, children constantly assimilate and accommodate as they seek equilibrium. There is considerable movement between states of cognitive equilibrium and disequilibrium as assimilation and accommodation work in concert to produce cognitive change. **Equilibration** is the name Piaget gave to this mechanism by which children shift from one stage of thought to the next.

The result of these processes, according to Piaget, is that individuals go through four stages of development. A different way of understanding the world makes one stage more advanced than another. Cognition is *qualitatively* different in one stage compared with another. In other words, the way children reason at one stage is different from the way they reason at another stage. Here our focus is on Piaget's stage of infant cognitive development. In later chapters (8, 10, and 12) we will explore the last three Piagetian stages.

The Sensorimotor Stage of Development

The **sensorimotor stage** lasts from birth to about 2 years of age. In this stage, infants construct an understanding of the world by coordinating sensory experiences (such as seeing and hearing) with physical, motoric actions—hence the term "sensorimotor."

---

*W*e are born capable of learning.

—JEAN-JACQUES ROUSSEAU
Swiss-Born French Philosopher, 18th Century

www.mhhe.com/santrockld11

Piaget's Stages

---

assimilation Piagetian concept of the incorporation of new information into existing schemes.

accommodation Piagetian concept of adjusting schemes to fit new information and experiences.

organization Piaget's concept of grouping isolated behaviors into a higher-order, more smoothly functioning cognitive system.

equilibration A mechanism that Piaget proposed to explain how children shift from one stage of thought to the next.

sensorimotor stage The first of Piaget's stages, which lasts from birth to about 2 years of age; infants construct an understanding of the world by coordinating sensory experiences with motoric actions.

Substage	Age	Description	Example
1 Simple reflexes	Birth to 1 month	Coordination of sensation and action through reflexive behaviors.	Rooting, sucking, and grasping reflexes; newborns suck reflexively when their lips are touched.
2 First habits and primary circular reactions	1 to 4 months	Coordination of sensation and two types of schemes: habits (reflex) and primary circular reactions (reproduction of an event that initially occurred by chance). Main focus is still on the infant's body.	Repeating a body sensation first experienced by chance (sucking thumb, for example); then infants might accommodate actions by sucking their thumb differently than they suck on a nipple.
3 Secondary circular reactions	4 to 8 months	Infants become more object-oriented, moving beyond self-preoccupation; repeat actions that bring interesting or pleasurable results.	An infant coos to make a person stay near; as the person starts to leave, the infant coos again.
4 Coordination of secondary circular reactions	8 to 12 months	Coordination of vision and touch—hand-eye coordination; coordination of schemes and intentionality.	Infant manipulates a stick in order to bring an attractive toy within reach.
5 Tertiary circular reactions, novelty, and curiosity	12 to 18 months	Infants become intrigued by the many properties of objects and by the many things they can make happen to objects; they experiment with new behavior.	A block can be made to fall, spin, hit another object, and slide across the ground.
6 Internalization of schemes	18 to 24 months	Infants develop the ability to use primitive symbols and form enduring mental representations.	An infant who has never thrown a temper tantrum before sees a playmate throw a tantrum; the infant retains a memory of the event, then throws one himself the next day.

FIGURE 6.1 Piaget's Six Substages of Sensorimotor Development

At the beginning of this stage, newborns have little more than reflexes with which to work. At the end of the sensorimotor stage, 2-year-olds can produce complex sensorimotor patterns and use primitive symbols. We first will summarize Piaget's descriptions of how infants develop. Later we will consider criticisms of his view.

Substages Piaget divided the sensorimotor stage into six substages: (1) simple reflexes; (2) first habits and primary circular reactions; (3) secondary circular reactions; (4) coordination of secondary circular reactions; (5) tertiary circular reactions, novelty, and curiosity; and (6) internalization of schemes (see figure 6.1).

Simple reflexes, the first sensorimotor substage, corresponds to the first month after birth. In this substage, sensation and action are coordinated primarily through reflexive behaviors, such as rooting and sucking. Soon the infant produces behaviors that resemble reflexes in the absence of the usual stimulus for the reflex. For example, a newborn will suck a nipple or bottle only when it is placed directly in the baby's mouth or touched to the lips. But soon the infant might suck when a bottle or nipple is only nearby. Even in the first month of life, the infant is initiating action and actively structuring experiences.

First habits and primary circular reactions is the second sensorimotor substage, which develops between 1 and 4 months of age. In this substage, the infant coordinates sensation and two types of schemes: habits and primary circular reactions. A *habit* is a scheme based on a reflex that has become completely separated from its eliciting stimulus. For example, infants in substage 1 suck when bottles are put to their lips or when they see a bottle. Infants in substage 2 might suck even when no bottle is present. A *circular reaction* is a repetitive action.

A *primary circular reaction* is a scheme based on the attempt to reproduce an event that initially occurred by chance. For example, suppose an infant accidentally

simple reflexes Piaget's first sensorimotor substage, which corresponds to the first month after birth. In this substage, sensation and action are coordinated primarily through reflexive behaviors.

first habits and primary circular reactions Piaget's second sensorimotor substage, which develops between 1 and 4 months of age. In this substage, the infant coordinates sensation and two types of schemes: habits and primary circular reactions.

secondary circular reactions Piaget's third sensorimotor substage, which develops between 4 and 8 months of age. In this substage, the infant becomes more object-oriented, moving beyond preoccupation with the self.

coordination of secondary circular reactions Piaget's fourth sensorimotor substage, which develops between 8 and 12 months of age. Actions become more outwardly directed, and infants coordinate schemes and act with intentionality.

tertiary circular reactions, novelty, and curiosity Piaget's fifth sensorimotor substage, which develops between 12 and 18 months of age. In this substage, infants become intrigued by the many properties of objects and by the many things that they can make happen to objects.

internalization of schemes Piaget's sixth and final sensorimotor substage, which develops between 18 and 24 months of age. In this substage, the infant develops the ability to use primitive symbols.

sucks his fingers when they are placed near his mouth. Later, he searches for his fingers to suck them again, but the fingers do not cooperate because the infant cannot coordinate visual and manual actions.

Habits and circular reactions are stereotyped: that is, the infant repeats them the same way each time. During this substage, the infant's own body remains the infant's center of attention. There is no outward pull by environmental events.

Secondary circular reactions is the third sensorimotor substage, which develops between 4 and 8 months of age. In this substage, the infant becomes more object-oriented, moving beyond preoccupation with the self. The infant's schemes are not intentional or goal-directed, but they are repeated because of their consequences. By chance, an infant might shake a rattle. The infant repeats this action for the sake of its fascination. This is a *secondary circular reaction:* an action repeated because of its consequences. The infant also imitates some simple actions, such as the baby talk or burbling of adults, and some physical gestures. However, the baby imitates only actions that he or she is already able to produce.

Coordination of secondary circular reactions is Piaget's fourth sensorimotor substage, which develops between 8 and 12 months of age. To progress into this substage the infant must coordinate vision and touch, hand and eye. Actions become more outwardly directed. Significant changes during this substage involve the coordination of schemes and intentionality. Infants readily combine and recombine previously learned schemes in a coordinated way. They might look at an object and grasp it simultaneously, or they might visually inspect a toy, such as a rattle, and finger it simultaneously, exploring it tactilely. Actions are even more outwardly directed than before. Related to this coordination is the second achievement—the presence of intentionality. For example, infants might manipulate a stick in order to bring a desired toy within reach or they might knock over one block to reach and play with another one. Similarly, when 11-month-old Jacqueline, as described in the chapter opening, placed the ball in front of her and kicked it, she was demonstrating intentionality.

Tertiary circular reactions, novelty, and curiosity is Piaget's fifth sensorimotor substage, which develops between 12 and 18 months of age. In this substage, infants become intrigued by the many properties of objects and by the many things that they can make happen to objects. A block can be made to fall, spin, hit another object, and slide across the ground. *Tertiary circular reactions* are schemes in which the infant purposely explores new possibilities with objects, continually doing new things to them and exploring the results. Piaget says that this stage marks the starting point for human curiosity and interest in novelty.

Internalization of schemes is Piaget's sixth and final sensorimotor substage, which develops between 18 and 24 months of age. In this substage, the infant develops the ability to use primitive symbols. For Piaget, a *symbol* is an internalized sensory image or word that represents an event. Primitive symbols permit the infant to think about concrete events without directly acting them out or perceiving them. Moreover, symbols allow the infant to manipulate and transform the represented events in simple ways. In a favorite Piagetian example, Piaget's young daughter saw a matchbox being opened and closed. Later, she mimicked the event by opening and closing her mouth. This was an obvious expression of her image of the event.

This 17-month-old is in Piaget's stage of tertiary circular reactions. *What might the infant do to suggest that she in this stage?*

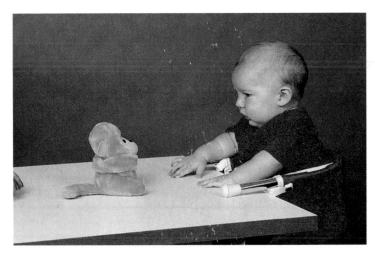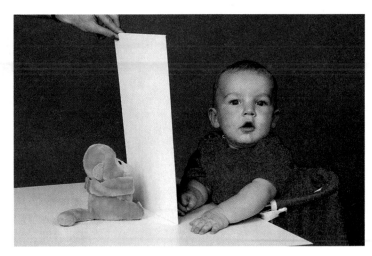

FIGURE 6.2 **Object Permanence.** Piaget argued that object permanence is one of infancy's landmark cognitive accomplishments. For this 5-month-old boy, "out-of-sight" is literally out of mind. The infant looks at the toy monkey (*left*), but, when his view of the toy is blocked (*right*), he does not search for it. Several months later, he will search for the hidden toy monkey, reflecting the presence of object permanence.

Object Permanence Imagine how chaotic and unpredictable your life would be if you could not distinguish between yourself and your world. This is what the life of a newborn must be like, according to Piaget. There is no differentiation between the self and world; objects have no separate, permanent existence.

By the end of the sensorimotor period, objects are both separate from the self and permanent. **Object permanence** is the understanding that objects continue to exist even when they cannot be seen, heard, or touched. Acquiring the sense of object permanence is one of the infant's most important accomplishments, according to Piaget.

How could anyone know whether an infant had a sense of object permanence or not? The principal way that object permanence is studied is by watching an infant's reaction when an interesting object disappears (see figure 6.2). If infants search for the object, it is assumed that they believe it continues to exist.

Object permanence is just one of the basic concepts about the physical world developed by babies. To Piaget, children, even infants, are much like little scientists, examining the world to see how it works. The Research in Life-Span Development interlude describes some of the ways in which adult scientists try to discover what these "baby scientists" are finding out about the world.

RESEARCH IN LIFE-SPAN DEVELOPMENT

Object Permanence and Causality

Two accomplishments of infants that Piaget examined were the development of object permanence and the child's understanding of causality. Let's examine two research studies that address these topics.

In both studies, Renée Baillargeon and her colleagues used a research method that involves *violation of expectations*. In this method, infants see an event happen as it normally would. Then, the event is changed, often in a way that creates a physically impossible event. If infants look longer at the changed event, that indicates they are surprised by it. In other words, the infant's reaction is interpreted to indicate that the infant had certain expectations about the world that were violated.

object permanence The Piagetian term for understanding that objects and events continue to exist, even when they cannot directly be seen, heard, or touched.

(continued on next page)

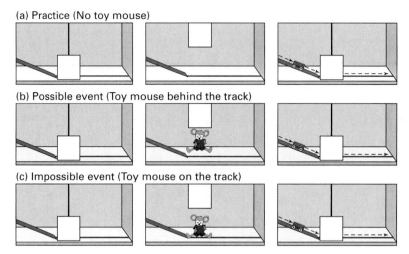

(a) Practice (No toy mouse)

(b) Possible event (Toy mouse behind the track)

(c) Impossible event (Toy mouse on the track)

FIGURE 6.3 Using the Violation of Expectations Method to Study Object Permanence in Infants. If infants looked longer at (c) than at (b), researchers reasoned that the impossible event in (c) violated the infants' expectations and that they remembered that the toy mouse existed.

In one study focused on object permanence, researchers showed infants a toy car that moved down an inclined track, disappeared behind a screen, and then reemerged at the other end, still on the track (Baillargeon & DeVos, 1991) (see figure 6.3) (*a*). After this sequence was repeated several times, something different occurred: A toy mouse was placed *behind* the tracks but was hidden by the screen while the car rolled by (*b*). This was the "possible" event. Then, the researchers created an "impossible event": The toy mouse was placed *on* the tracks but was secretly removed after the screen was lowered so that the car seemed to go through the mouse (*c*). In this study, infants as young as $3\frac{1}{2}$ months of age looked longer at the impossible event than at the possible event, indicating that they were surprised by it. Their surprise suggested that they remembered not only that the toy mouse still existed (object permanence) but its location.

Another study focused on the infant's understanding of causality (Kotovsky & Baillargeon, 1994). In this research, a cylinder rolls down a ramp and hits a toy bug at the bottom of the ramp. By $5\frac{1}{2}$ and $6\frac{1}{2}$ months of age, after infants have seen how far the bug will be pushed by a medium-sized cylinder, their reactions indicate that they understand that the bug will roll farther if it is hit by a large cylinder than if it is hit by a small cylinder. Thus, by the middle of the first year of life these infants understood that the size of a moving object determines how far it will move a stationary object that it collides with.

The research findings discussed in this interlude and other research indicate that infants develop object permanence earlier than Piaget proposed. Indeed, as you will see in the next section, a major theme of infant cognitive development today is that infants are more cognitively competent than Piaget envisioned.

Evaluating Piaget's Sensorimotor Stage Piaget opened up a new way of looking at infants with his view that their main task is to coordinate their sensory impressions with their motor activity. However, the infant's cognitive world is not as neatly packaged as Piaget portrayed it, and some of Piaget's explanations for the cause of change are debated. In the past several decades, sophisticated experimental techniques have been devised to study infants, and there have been a large number of research studies on infant development. Much of the new research suggests that Piaget's view of sensorimotor development needs to be modified (Bremner, 2004; Gouin-Decarie, 1996).

The A-not-B Error One modification concerns Piaget's claim that certain processes are crucial in stage transitions. The data do not always support his explanations. For example, in Piaget's theory, an important feature in the progression into substage 4 is an infant's inclination to search for a hidden object in a familiar location rather than to look for the object in a new location. **AB̄ error** (also called A-not-B error) is the term used to describe infants who make the mistake of selecting the familiar hiding place (A) rather than the new hiding place (B̄), after they have seen it hidden there. For example, if a toy is hidden twice, initially at location A and subsequently at location B̄, 8- to 12-month-old infants search correctly at location A initially. But when the toy is subsequently hidden at location B̄, they make the mistake of continuing to search for it at location A. Older infants are less likely to make the AB̄ error because their concept of object permanence is more complete.

Researchers have found, however, that the AB̄ error does not show up consistently (Corrigan, 1981; Sophian, 1985). The evidence indicates that AB̄ errors are sensitive to the delay between hiding the object at B̄ and the infant's attempt to find it (Diamond, 1985). Thus, the AB̄ error might be due to a failure in memory. Another explanation is that infants tend to repeat a previous motor behavior (Smith, 1999).

Perceptual Development and Expectations A number of theorists, such as Eleanor Gibson (2001) and Elizabeth Spelke (1991; Spelke & Newport, 1998), contend that infants' perceptual abilities are highly developed at a very early age. For example, in chapter 5 we discussed research that demonstrated the presence of intermodal perception—the ability to coordinate information from two or more sensory modalities, such as vision and hearing—by $3\frac{1}{2}$ months of age, much earlier than Piaget would have predicted (Spelke & Owsley, 1979).

Research also suggests that infants develop the ability to understand how the world works at a very early age. For example, by the time they are 3 months of age, infants develop expectations about future events. Marshall Haith and his colleagues (Canfield & Haith, 1991; Haith, Hazen, & Goodman, 1988) presented pictures to infants in either a regular alternating (such as left, right, left, right) or an unpredictable sequence (such as right, right, left, right). When the sequence was predictable, the 3-month-old infants began to anticipate the location of the picture, looking at the side on which it was expected to appear. However, younger infants did not develop expectations about where a picture would be presented.

What kinds of expectations do infants form? Are we born expecting the world to obey basic physical laws, such as gravity, or when do we learn about how the world works? Experiments by Elizabeth Spelke (1991, 2000; Spelke & Hespos, 2001) have addressed these questions. She placed babies before a puppet stage and showed them a series of actions that are unexpected if you know how the physical world works—for example, one ball seemed to roll through a solid barrier, another seemed to leap between two platforms, and a third appeared to hang in midair (Spelke, 1979). Spelke measured and compared the babies' looking times for unexpected and expected actions. She concluded that, by 4 months of age, even though infants do not yet have the ability to talk about objects, move around objects, manipulate objects, or even see objects with high resolution, they expect objects to be solid and continuous. However, at 4 months of age, infants do not expect an object to obey gravitational constraints (Spelke & others, 1992). Similarly, research by Renée Baillargeon and her colleagues (1995, 2004; Aguiar & Baillargeon, 2002) documents that infants as young as 3 to 4 months expect objects to be *substantial* (in the sense that other objects cannot move through them) and *permanent* (in the sense that objects continue to exist when they are hidden).

In sum, researchers believe that infants see objects as bounded, unitary, solid, and separate from their background, possibly at birth or shortly thereafter, but definitely by 3 to 4 months of age, much earlier than Piaget envisioned. Young infants

Cognitive Milestones

AB̄ error Occurs when infants make the mistake of selecting the familiar hiding place (A) rather than the new hiding place (B̄) as they progress into substage 4 in Piaget's sensorimotor stage.

still have much to learn about objects, but the world appears both stable and orderly to them.

By 6 to 8 months, infants have learned to perceive gravity and support—that an object hanging on the end of a table should fall, that ball-bearings will travel farther when rolled down a longer rather than a shorter ramp, and that cup handles will not fall when attached to a cup (Slater, Field, & Hernandez-Reif, 2002). As infants develop, their experiences and actions on objects help them to understand physical laws.

Many researchers conclude that Piaget wasn't specific enough about how infants learn about their world and that infants are more competent than Piaget thought (Bremner, 2004; Cohen & Cashon, 2006; Mandler, 2003, 2004, 2006; Meltzoff, 2004). As they have examined the specific ways that infants learn, the field of infant cognition has become very specialized. There are many researchers working on different questions, with no general theory emerging that can connect all of the different findings (Nelson, 1999). Their theories are local theories, focused on specific research questions, rather than grand theories like Piaget's (Kuhn, 1998). If there is a unifying theme, it is that investigators in infant development seek to understand more precisely how developmental changes in cognition take place and the big issue of nature and nurture.

Review and Reflect • LEARNING GOAL 1

1 **Summarize the cognitive processes in Piaget's theory and the stage of sensorimotor development**

Review
- What cognitive processes are important in Piaget's theory?
- What are some characteristics of Piaget's stage of sensorimotor development? What are some contributions and criticisms of Piaget's sensorimotor stage?

Reflect
- What are some implications of Piaget's theory of infant development for parenting?

---

2 LEARNING, REMEMBERING, AND CONCEPTUALIZING

| Conditioning | Imitation | Concept Formation and Categorization |

| Attention | Memory |

When Piaget hung a doll above 4-month-old Lucienne's feet, as described in the chapter opening, would she remember the doll? If Piaget had rewarded her for moving the doll with her foot, would that have affected Lucienne's behavior? If he had shown her how to shake the doll's hand, could she have imitated him? If he had shown her a different doll, could she have formed the concept of a "doll"?

Questions like these might be examined by researchers taking the behavioral and social cognitive or information processing approaches introduced in chapter 2. In contrast to Piaget's theory, these approaches do not describe infant development in terms of stages. Instead, they document gradual changes in the infant's ability to understand and process information about the world. In this section we explore what researchers using these approaches can tell us about how infants learn, remember, and conceptualize.

Conditioning

In chapter 2, "The Science of Life-Span Development," we described Pavlov's classical conditioning (in which, as a result of pairing, a new stimulus comes to elicit a response previously given to another stimulus) and Skinner's operant conditioning (in which the consequences of a behavior produce changes in the probability of the behavior's occurrence). Infants can learn through both types of conditioning. For example, if an infant's behavior is followed by a rewarding stimulus, the behavior is likely to recur.

Operant conditioning has been especially helpful to researchers in their efforts to determine what infants perceive (Kraebel, Fable, & Gerhardstein, 2004). For example, infants will suck faster on a nipple when the sucking behavior is followed by a visual display, music, or a human voice (Rovee-Collier, 1987; Rovee-Collier & Barr, 2004).

Carolyn Rovee-Collier (1987) has also demonstrated how infants can retain information from the experience of being conditioned. In a characteristic experiment, she places a $2\frac{1}{2}$-month-old baby in a crib under an elaborate mobile (see figure 6.4). She then ties one end of a ribbon to the baby's ankle and the other end to the mobile. Subsequently, she observes that the baby kicks and makes the mobile move. The movement of the mobile is the reinforcing stimulus (which increases the baby's kicking behavior) in this experiment. Weeks later, the baby is returned to the crib, but its foot is not tied to the mobile. The baby kicks, which suggests it has retained the information that if it kicks a leg, the mobile will move.

Attention

Attention, the focusing of mental resources on select information, improves cognitive processing on many tasks. Even newborns can detect a contour and fix their attention on it. Older infants scan patterns more thoroughly. By 4 months, infants can selectively attend to an object.

Closely linked with attention are the processes of habituation and dishabituation that we discussed in chapter 5, "Physical Development in Infancy." If you say the same word or show the same toy to a baby several times in a row, the baby usually pays less attention to it each time. This is *habituation*—decreased responsiveness to a stimulus after repeated presentations of the stimulus. *Dishabituation* is the increase in responsiveness after a change in stimulation. Chapter 5 described some of the measures that researchers use to study whether habituation is occurring, such as sucking behavior (sucking stops when an infant attends to a novel object), heart rates, and the length of time the infant looks at an object.

Infants' attention is strongly governed by novelty and habituation. When an object becomes familiar, attention becomes shorter, making infants more vulnerable to distraction (Oakes, Kannass, & Shaddy, 2002). One recent study found that 10-month-olds were more distractible than 26-month-olds (Ruff & Capozzoli, 2003).

Knowing about habituation and dishabituation can help parents interact effectively with infants. Infants respond to changes in stimulation. Wise parents sense when an infant shows an interest and realize that they may have to repeat something many times for the infant to process information. But if the stimulation is repeated often, the infant stops responding to the parent. In parent-infant interaction, it is important for parents to do novel things and to repeat them often until

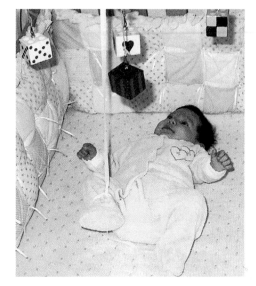

FIGURE 6.4 The Technique Used in Rovee-Collier's Investigation of Infant Memory. In Rovee-Collier's experiment, operant conditioning was used to demonstrate that infants as young as $2\frac{1}{2}$ months of age can retain information from the experience of being conditioned. *What did infants recall in Rovee-Collier's experiment?*

attention The focusing of mental resources.

FIGURE 6.5 Infant Imitation. Infant development researcher Andrew Meltzoff protrudes his tongue in an attempt to get the infant to imitate his behavior. *How do Meltzoff's findings about imitation compare with Piaget's descriptions of infants' abilities?*

the infant stops responding. The parent stops or changes behaviors when the infant redirects his or her attention (Rosenblith, 1992).

Imitation

Can infants imitate someone else's emotional expressions? If an adult smiles, will the baby follow with a smile? If an adult protrudes her lower lip, wrinkles her forehead, and frowns, will the baby show a sad face?

Infant development researcher Andrew Meltzoff (2002, 2004, 2005; Meltzoff & Moore, 1999) has conducted numerous studies of infants' imitative abilities. He sees infants' imitative abilities as biologically based, because infants can imitate a facial expression within the first few days after birth. He also emphasizes that the infant's imitative abilities do not resemble a hardwired response but rather involve flexibility and adaptability. In Meltzoff's observations of infants across the first 72 hours of life, the infants gradually displayed more complete imitation of an adult's facial expression, such as protruding the tongue or opening the mouth wide (see figure 6.5).

Not all experts on infant development accept Meltzoff's conclusions that newborns are capable of imitation. Some say that these babies were engaging in little more than automatic responses to a stimulus.

Meltzoff (2005) also has studied **deferred imitation,** which occurs after a time delay of hours or days. Piaget held that deferred imitation doesn't occur until about 18 months of age. Meltzoff's research suggested that it occurs much earlier. In one study, Meltzoff (1988) demonstrated that 9-month-old infants could imitate actions—such as pushing a recessed button in a box, which produced a beeping sound—that they had seen performed 24 hours earlier.

Memory

Meltzoff's studies of deferred imitation suggest that infants have another important cognitive ability: **memory,** which involves the retention of information over time. Sometimes information is retained only for a few seconds, and at other times it is retained for a lifetime. What can infants remember, when?

Some researchers such as Rovee-Collier have concluded that infants as young as 2 to 6 months of age can remember some experiences through $1\frac{1}{2}$ to 2 years of age (Rovee-Collier & Barr, 2004). However, critics such as Jean Mandler (2000), a leading expert on infant cognition, argue that the infants in Rovee-Collier's experiments are displaying only implicit memory. **Implicit memory** refers to memory without conscious recollection—memories of skills and routine procedures that are performed automatically. In contrast, **explicit memory** refers to the conscious memory of facts and experiences.

When people think about memory, they are usually referring to explicit memory. Most researchers find that babies do not show explicit memory until the second half of the first year (Bauer, 2005, 2006; Bauer & others, 2003; Mandler & McDonough, 1995). Then, explicit memory improves substantially during the second year of life (Bauer, 2004, 2005, 2006; Carver & Bauer, 2001). In one longitudinal study, infants were assessed several times during their second year (Bauer & others, 2000). Older infants showed more accurate memory and required fewer prompts to demonstrate their memory than younger infants.

Let's examine another aspect of memory. Do you remember your third birthday party? Probably not. Most adults can remember little if anything from the first 3 years of their life. This is called *infantile* or *childhood amnesia.* The few reported adult memories of life at age 2 or 3 are at best very sketchy (Neisser, 2004; Newcombe & others, 2000). Elementary school children also do not remember much of their early child years (Lie & Newcombe, 1999).

deferred imitation Imitation that occurs after a delay of hours or days.

memory A central feature of cognitive development, pertaining to all situations in which an individual retains information over time.

implicit memory Memory without conscious recollection; involves skills and routine procedures that are automatically performed.

explicit memory Memory of facts and experiences that individuals consciously know and can state.

What is the cause of infantile amnesia? One reason older children and adults have difficulty recalling events from their infant and early child years is that during these early years the prefrontal lobes of the brain are immature; this area of the brain is believed to play an important role in storing memories for events (Boyer & Diamond, 1992).

In sum, most of young infants' conscious memories appear to be rather fragile and short-lived, although their implicit memory of perceptual-motor actions can be substantial (Mandler, 2000, 2003).

www.mhhe.com/santrockld11

Infant Cognition
Rovee-Collier's Research
Patricia Bauer's Infant Memory Studies

Concept Formation and Categorization

Along with memory, concepts are indispensable to competent cognitive development. To understand what concepts are, we first have to define *categories:* they group objects, events, and characteristics on the basis of common properties. *Concepts* are ideas about what categories represent, or said another way, the sort of thing we think category members are. Concepts and categories help us to simplify and summarize information. Without concepts, you would see each object and event as unique; you would not be able to make any generalizations.

Do infants have concepts? Yes, they do, although we do not know just how early concept formation begins (Mandler, 2004). It is not until about 7 to 9 months of age that infants form *conceptual* categories that are characterized by perceptual variability. For example, in one study of 7- to 11-month-olds, infants classified birds as animals and airplanes as vehicles even though the objects were perceptually similar—airplanes and birds with their wings spread (Mandler & McDonough, 1993).

Further advances in categorization occur in the second year of life. Many infants' "first concepts are broad and global in nature, such as 'animal' or 'indoor thing.' Gradually, over the first two years these broad concepts become more differentiated into concepts such as 'land animal,' then 'dog,' or to 'furniture,' then 'chair'" (Mandler, 2006, p. 1).

In sum, the infant's advances in processing information—through attention, memory, imitation, and concept formation—is much richer, more gradual, and less stage-like, and occurs earlier than was envisioned by earlier theorists, such as Piaget. As leading infant researcher Jean Mandler (2004) concluded, "The human infant shows a remarkable degree of learning power and complexity in what is being learned and in the way it is represented" (p. 304).

Infants are creating concepts and organizing their world into conceptual domains that will form the backbone of their thought throughout life.

—JEAN MANDLER
*Contemporary Psychologist,
University of California-San Diego*

Review and Reflect • LEARNING GOAL 2

2 Describe how infants learn, remember, and conceptualize

Review
- How do infants learn through conditioning?
- What is attention? What characterizes attention in infants?
- How is imitation involved in infant learning?
- To what extent can infants remember?
- When do infants develop concepts and how does concept formation change during infancy?

Reflect
- If a friend told you that she remembers being abused by her parents when she was 2 years old, would you believe her? Explain your answer.

3   INDIVIDUAL DIFFERENCES AND ASSESSMENT

> Measures of Infant
> Development

> Predicting Intelligence

So far, we have discussed how the cognitive development of infants generally progresses. We have emphasized what is typical of the largest number of infants or the average infant, but the results obtained for *most* infants do not apply to *all* infants. It is advantageous to know whether an infant is developing at a slow, normal, or advanced pace during the course of infancy. If an infant advances at an especially slow rate, then some form of enrichment may be necessary. If an infant develops at an advanced pace, parents may be advised to provide toys that stimulate cognitive growth in slightly older infants. How is an infant's cognitive development assessed?

Measures of Infant Development

Individual differences in infant cognitive development have been studied primarily through the use of developmental scales or infant intelligence tests. For example, in chapter 4 we discussed the Brazelton Neonatal Behavioral Assessment Scale (NBAS) and the Neonatal Intensive Care Unit Network Neurobehavioral Scale (NNNS), which are used to evaluate newborns. To read about the work of one infant assessment specialist, see the Careers in Life-Span Development profile.

CAREERS
in LIFE-SPAN DEVELOPMENT

Toosje Thyssen VanBeveren
Infant Assessment Specialist

Toosje Thyssen VanBeveren is a developmental psychologist at the University of Texas Medical Center in Dallas. She has a master's degree in child clinical psychology and a Ph.D. in human development. Currently, Toosje is involved in a 12-week program called New Connections, which is a comprehensive intervention for young children who were affected by substance abuse prenatally and for their caregivers.

In the New Connections program, Toosje assesses infants' developmental status and progress. She might refer the infants to a speech, physical, or occupational therapist and monitor the infants' services and progress. Toosje trains the program staff and encourages them to use the exercises she recommends. She also discusses the child's problems with the primary caregivers, suggests activities, and assists them in enrolling infants in appropriate programs.

During her graduate work at the University of Texas at Dallas, Toosje was author John Santrock's teaching assistant in his undergraduate course on life-span development for four years. As a teaching assistant, she attended classes, graded exams, counseled students, and occasionally gave lectures. Each semester, Toosje returns to give a lecture on prenatal development and infancy. She also teaches part-time in the psychology department at UT-Dallas. In Toosje's words, "My days are busy and full. The work is often challenging. There are some disappointments but mostly the work is enormously gratifying."

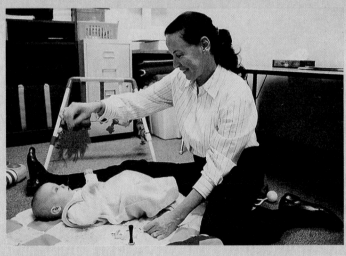

Toosje Thyssen VanBeveren conducting an infant assessment.

The most important early contributor to the testing of infants was Arnold Gesell (1934). He developed a measure that helped sort out potentially normal babies from abnormal ones. This was especially useful to adoption agencies, which had large numbers of babies awaiting placement. Gesell's examination was used widely for many years and still is frequently employed by pediatricians to distinguish normal and abnormal infants. The current version of the Gesell test has four categories of behavior: motor, language, adaptive, and personal-social. The **developmental quotient (DQ)** combines subscores in these categories to provide an overall score.

Bayley Scales of Infant Development (2nd ed.)

The widely used **Bayley Scales of Infant Development** were developed by Nancy Bayley (1969) in order to assess infant behavior and predict later development. The current version, Bayley-II (1993) has three components: a mental scale, a motor scale, and an infant behavior profile.

How should a 6-month-old perform on the Bayley mental scale? The 6-month-old infant should be able to vocalize pleasure and displeasure, persistently search for objects that are just out of immediate reach, and approach a mirror that is placed in front of the infant by the examiner. By 12 months of age, the infant should be able to inhibit behavior when commanded to do so, imitate words the examiner says (such as *Mama*), and respond to simple requests (such as "Take a drink").

The explosion of interest in infant development has produced many new measures, especially tasks that evaluate the ways infants process information (Rose, Feldman, & Wallace, 1992). The Fagan Test of Infant Intelligence is increasingly being used (Fagan, 1992). This test focuses on the infant's ability to process information in such ways as encoding the attributes of objects, detecting similarities and differences between objects, forming mental representations, and retrieving these representations. For example, it uses the amount of time babies look at a new object compared with the amount of time they spend looking at a familiar object to estimate their intelligence. The Fagan test elicits similar performances from infants in different cultures.

Predicting Intelligence

The infant-testing movement grew out of the tradition of IQ testing. However, compared with tests of infants, IQ tests of older children pay more attention to verbal ability. Tests for infants contain far more items related to perceptual-motor development and include measures of social interaction.

Overall scores on such tests as the Gesell and the Bayley scales do not correlate highly with IQ scores obtained later in childhood. In one study conducted by Nancy Bayley, no relation was found between the Bayley scales and intelligence as measured by the Stanford-Binet at the ages of 6 and 7 (Bayley, 1943). This is not surprising because the components tested in infancy are not the same as the components tested by IQ tests.

Unlike the Gesell and Bayley scales, the Fagan test is correlated with measures of intelligence in older children. In fact, evidence is accumulating that measures of habituation and dishabituation predict intelligence in childhood and adolescence (Bornstein & Sigman, 1986; Sigman, Cohen, & Beckwith, 2000). Quicker habituation and greater amounts of looking in dishabituation reflect more efficient information processing. A recent review concluded that when measured between 3 and 12 months, both habituation and dishabituation are related to higher IQ scores on tests given at various times between infancy and adolescence (Kavsek, 2004).

It is important, however, not to go too far and think that connections between cognitive development in early infancy and later cognitive development are so strong that no discontinuity takes place. Some important changes in cognitive development occur after infancy, changes that we will describe in later chapters.

developmental quotient (DQ) An overall score that combines subscores in motor, language, adaptive, and personal-social domains in the Gesell assessment of infants.

Bayley Scales of Infant Development Scales developed by Nancy Bayley that are widely used in the assessment of infant development. The current version has three components: a mental scale, a motor scale, and an infant behavior profile.

4 LANGUAGE DEVELOPMENT

Defining Language   How Language Develops   An Interactionist View

Language's Rule Systems   Biological and Environmental Influences

In 1799, a nude boy was observed running through the woods in France. The boy was captured when he was 11 years old. He was called the Wild Boy of Aveyron and was believed to have lived in the woods alone for six years (Lane, 1976). When found, he made no effort to communicate. He never learned to communicate effectively. Sadly, a modern-day wild child named Genie was discovered in Los Angeles in 1970. Despite intensive intervention, Genie has never acquired more than a primitive form of language. Both cases—the Wild Boy of Aveyron and Genie—raise questions about the biological and environmental determinants of language, topics that we also will examine later in the chapter. First, though, we need to define language.

Defining Language

Language is a form of communication—whether spoken, written, or signed—that is based on a system of symbols. Language consists of the words used by a community and the rules for varying and combining them.

Think how important language is in our everyday lives. We need language to speak with others, listen to others, read, and write. Our language enables us to describe past events in detail and to plan for the future. Language lets us pass down information from one generation to the next and create a rich cultural heritage.

All human languages have some common characteristics. These include infinite generativity and organizational rules. **Infinite generativity** is the ability to produce an endless number of meaningful sentences using a finite set of words and rules. Rules describe the way language works (Berko Gleason, 2004). Let's explore what these rules involve and how they organize language.

Language's Rule Systems

When nineteenth-century American writer Ralph Waldo Emerson said, "The world was built in order and the atoms march in tune," he must have had language in mind. Language is highly ordered and organized (Berko Gleason, 2005). The

language A form of communication, whether spoken, written, or signed, that is based on a system of symbols.

infinite generativity The ability to produce an endless number of meaningful sentences using a finite set of words and rules.

organization involves five systems of rules: phonology, morphology, syntax, semantics, and pragmatics.

Phonology

Every language is made up of basic sounds. **Phonology** is the sound system of the language, including the sounds that are used and how they may be combined (Ballem & Plunkett, 2005; Menn & Stoel-Gammon, 2005). For example, English has the initial consonant cluster *spr* as in *spring*, but no words begin with the cluster *rsp*.

Phonology provides a basis for constructing a large and expandable set of words out of two or three dozen phonemes. A *phoneme* is the basic unit of sound in a language; it is the smallest unit of sound that affects meaning. For example, in English the sound represented by the letter *p*, as in the words *pot* and *spot*, is a phoneme. The /p/ sound is slightly different in the two words, but this variation is not distinguished in English, and therefore the /p/ sound is a single phoneme. In some languages, such as Hindi, the variations of the /p/ sound represent separate phonemes.

Morphology

Morphology refers to the units of meaning involved in word formation. A *morpheme* is a minimal unit of meaning; it is a word or a part of a word that cannot be broken into smaller meaningful parts. Every word in the English language is made up of one or more morphemes. Some words consist of a single morpheme (for example, *help*), whereas others are made up of more than one morpheme (for example, *helper* has two morphemes, *help* + *er*, with the morpheme *-er* meaning "one who," in this case "one who helps"). Thus, not all morphemes are words by themselves; for example, *pre-*, *-tion*, and *-ing* are morphemes.

Just as the rules that govern phonology describe the sound sequences that can occur in a language, the rules of morphology describe the way meaningful units (morphemes) can be combined in words (Ravid, Levi, & Ben-Zvi, 2004; Tager-Flusberg, 2005). Morphemes have many jobs in grammar, such as marking tense (for example, *she walks* versus *she walked*) and number (*she walks* versus *they walk*).

Syntax

Syntax involves the way words are combined to form acceptable phrases and sentences. If someone says to you, "Bob slugged Tom" or "Bob was slugged by Tom," you know who did the slugging and who was slugged in each case because you have a syntactic understanding of these sentence structures. You also understand that the sentence, "You didn't stay, did you?" is a grammatical sentence but that "You didn't stay, didn't you?" is unacceptable and ambiguous.

If you learn another language, English syntax will not get you very far. For example, in English an adjective usually precedes a noun (as in *blue sky*), whereas in Spanish the adjective usually follows the noun (*cielo azul*). Despite the

FRANK & ERNEST: Thaves/Dist. by Newspaper Enterprise Association, Inc.

phonology The sound system of the language, including the sounds that are used and how they may be combined.

morphology Units of meaning involved in word formation.

syntax The ways words are combined to form acceptable phrases and sentences.

differences in their syntactic structures, however, syntactic systems in all the world's languages have some common ground (Chang, Dell, & Bock, 2006; Tager-Flusberg, 2005). For example, no language we know of permits sentences like the following one:

> The mouse the cat the farmer chased killed ate the cheese.

It appears that language users cannot process subjects and objects arranged in too complex a fashion in a sentence.

Semantics   **Semantics** refers to the meaning of words and sentences. Every word has a set of semantic features, which are required attributes related to meaning. *Girl* and *woman*, for example, share many semantic features but they differ semantically in regard to age.

Words have semantic restrictions on how they can be used in sentences (Pan, 2005). The sentence *The bicycle talked the boy into buying a candy bar* is syntactically correct but semantically incorrect. The sentence violates our semantic knowledge that bicycles don't talk.

Pragmatics   A final set of language rules involves **pragmatics,** the appropriate use of language in different contexts. Pragmatics covers a lot of territory. When you take turns speaking in a discussion or use a question to convey a command ("Why is it so noisy in here?" "What is this, Grand Central Station?"), you are demonstrating knowledge of pragmatics. You also apply the pragmatics of English when you use polite language in appropriate situations (for example, when talking to one's teacher) or tell stories that are interesting, jokes that are funny, and lies that convince. In each of these cases, you are demonstrating that you understand the rules of your culture for adjusting language to suit the context (Hoff, 2006).

Pragmatic rules can be complex and differ from one culture to another (Bryant, 2005). Consider the pragmatics of saying "thank you." Even preschoolers' use of the phrase *thank you* varies with sex, socioeconomic status, and the age of the individual they are addressing. If you were to study the Japanese language, you would come face-to-face with countless pragmatic rules about how to say thank you to individuals of various social levels and with various relationships to you.

At this point, we have discussed five important rule systems involved in language. An overview of these rule systems is presented in figure 6.6.

How Language Develops

According to an ancient historian, in the thirteenth century, the Emperor of Germany, Frederick II, had a cruel idea. He wanted to know what language children would speak if no one talked to them. He selected several newborns and threatened their caregivers with death if they ever talked to the infants. Frederick never found out what language the children spoke because they all died. Today, we are still curious about infants' development of language, although our experiments and observations are, to say the least, far more humane than the evil Frederick's.

Whatever language they learn, infants all over the world follow a similar path in language development. What are some key milestones in this development?

semantics The meaning of words and sentences.

pragmatics The appropriate use of language in different contexts.

Babbling and Gestures   Babies actively produce sounds from birth onward. The effect of these early communications is to attract attention (Lock, 2004; Volterra

Rule System	Description	Examples
Phonology	The sound system of a language. A phoneme is the smallest sound unit in a language.	The word *chat* has three phonemes or sounds: /ch/ /ā/ /t/. An example of phonological rule in the English language is while the phoneme /r/ can follow the phonemes /t/ or /d/ in an English consonant cluster (such as *track* or *drab*), the phoneme /l/ cannot follow these letters.
Morphology	The system of meaningful units involved in word formation.	The smallest sound units that have a meaning are called morphemes, or meaning units. The word *girl* is one morpheme, or meaning unit; it cannot be broken down any further and still have meaning. When the suffix *s* is added, the word becomes *girls* and has two morphemes because the *s* changed the meaning of the word, indicating that there is more than one girl.
Syntax	The system that involves the way words are combined to form acceptable phrases and sentences.	Word order is very important in determining meaning in the English language. For example, the sentence "Sebastian pushed the bike" has a different meaning than "The bike pushed Sebastian."
Semantics	The system that involves the meaning of words and sentences.	Knowing the meaning of individual words—that is, vocabulary. For example, semantics includes knowing the meaning of such words as *orange*, *transportation*, and *intelligent*.
Pragmatics	The system of using appropriate conversation and knowledge of how to effectively use language in context.	An example is using polite language in appropriate situations, such as being mannerly when talking with one's teacher. Taking turns in a conversation involves pragmatics.

FIGURE 6.6 The Rule Systems of Language

& others, 2004). Babies' sounds and gestures go through this sequence during the first year:

- *Crying.* Babies cry even at birth. Crying can signal distress, but as we will discuss in chapter 7, there are different types of cries that signal different things.
- *Cooing.* Babies first coo at about 1 to 2 months. These are gurgling sounds that are made in the back of the throat and usually express pleasure during interaction with the caregiver.
- *Babbling.* In the middle of the first year babies babble; that is, they produce strings of consonant-vowel combinations, such as "ba, ba, ba, ba."
- *Gestures.* Infants start using gestures, such as showing and pointing, at about 8 to 12 months of age. They may wave bye-bye, nod to mean "yes," show an empty cup to want more milk, and point to a dog to draw attention to it.

Those deaf infants who are born to deaf parents who use sign language, babble with their hands and fingers at about the same age as hearing children babble vocally (Bloom, 1998). Such similarities in timing and structure between manual and vocal babbling indicate that a unified language capacity underlies signed and spoken language (Petitto, Kovelman, & Harasymowycz, 2003).

Recognizing Language Sounds   Long before they begin to learn words, infants can make fine distinctions among the sounds of the language (Lock, 2004; Menn & Stoel-Gammon, 2005). In Patricia Kuhl's (1993, 2000; Kuhl & others, 2006) research, phonemes from languages all over the world are piped through a speaker for infants to hear (see figure 6.7). A box with a toy bear in it is placed where the infant can see it. A string of identical syllables is played; then the syllables are changed (for example, *ba ba ba ba*, and then *pa pa pa pa*). If the infant turns its

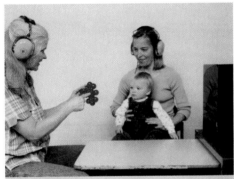

FIGURE 6.7 From Universal Linguist to Language-Specific Listener. In Patricia Kuhl's research laboratory babies listen to tape-recorded voices that repeat syllables. When the sounds of the syllables change, the babies quickly learn to look at the bear. Using this technique, Kuhl has demonstrated that babies are universal linguists until about 6 months of age, but in the next six months become language-specific listeners. *Does Kuhl's research give support to the view that either "nature" or "nurture" is the source of language acquisition?*

Patricia Kuhl's Research
Language Milestones
Babbling
The Naming Explosion

head when the syllables change, the box lights up and the bear dances and drums, rewarding the infant for noticing the change.

Kuhl's research has demonstrated that from birth up to about 6 months of age, infants are "citizens of the world": they recognize when sounds change most of the time no matter what language the syllables come from. But over the next six months, infants get even better at perceiving the changes in sounds from their "own" language, the one their parents speak, and gradually lose the ability to recognize differences that are not important in their own language.

An example involves the English "r" and "l" sounds, which distinguish words such as "rake" and "lake" (Iverson & Kuhl, 1996; Iverson & others, 2003). In the United States, infants from English-speaking homes detect the changes from "ra" to "la" when they are 6 months old and get better at detecting the change by 12 months of age. However, in Japanese there is no such "r" or "l." In Japan, 6-month-old infants perform as well as their American counterparts in recognizing the "r" and "l" distinction, but by 12 months of age they lose this ability.

Infants must fish out individual words from the nonstop stream of sound that makes up ordinary speech (Brownlee, 1998; Jusczyk, 2000). To do so, they must find the boundaries between words, which is very difficult for infants because adults don't pause between words when they speak. Still, infants begin to detect word boundaries by 8 months of age. For example, in one study, 8-month-old infants listened to recorded stories that contained unusual words, such as *hornbill* and *python* (Jusczyk & Hohne, 1997). Two weeks later, the researchers tested the infants with two lists of words, one made up of words in the stories, the other of new, unusual words that did not appear in the stories. The infants listened to the familiar words for a second longer, on average, than to new words.

First Words   Between about 8 to 12 months of age, infants often indicate their first understanding of words. The infant's first spoken word is a milestone eagerly anticipated by every parent. This event usually occurs between 10 to 15 months of age and at an average of about 13 months. However, long before babies say their first words, they have been communicating with their parents, often by gesturing and using their own special sounds. The appearance of first words is a continuation of this communication process (Berko Gleason, 2005).

A child's first words include those that name important people (*dada*), familiar animals (*kitty*), vehicles (*car*), toys (*ball*), food (*milk*), body parts (*eye*), clothes (*hat*), household items (*clock*), and greeting terms (*bye*). These were the first words of babies 50 years ago. They are the first words of babies today. Children often express various intentions with their single words, so that "cookie" might mean, "That's a cookie" or "I want a cookie."

On the average, infants understand about 50 words at about 13 months but they can't say this many words until about 18 months (Menyuk, Liebergott, & Schultz, 1995). Thus, in infancy *receptive vocabulary* (words the child understands) considerably exceeds *spoken vocabulary* (words the child uses).

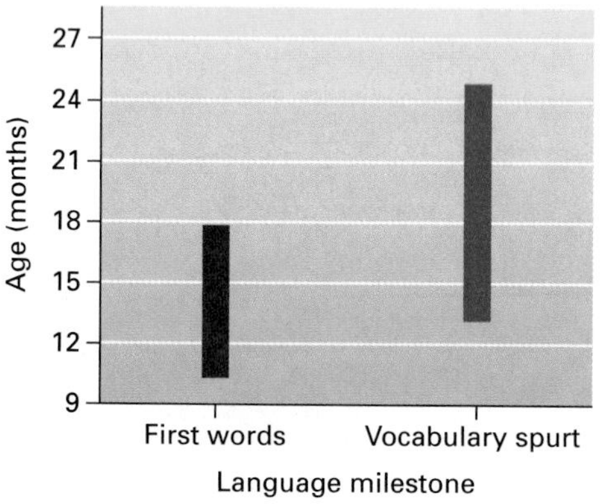

The infant's spoken vocabulary rapidly increases once the first word is spoken (Houston-Price, Plunkett, & Harris, 2005; Waxman & Lidz, 2006). The average 18-month-old can speak about 50 words, but by the age of 2 years can speak about 200 words. This rapid increase in vocabulary that begins at approximately 18 months is called the *vocabulary spurt* (Bloom, Lifter, & Broughton, 1985).

Like the timing of a child's first word, the timing of the vocabulary spurt varies (Bloom, 1998; Dale & Goodman, 2004). Figure 6.8 shows the range for these two language milestones in 14 children. On average, these children said their first word at 13 months and had a vocabulary spurt at 19 months. However, the ages for the first word of individual children varied from 10 to 17 months and for their vocabulary spurt from 13 to 25 months.

Children sometimes overextend or underextend the meanings of the words they use (Woodward & Markman, 1998). *Overextension* is the tendency to apply a

FIGURE 6.8 Variation in Language Milestones. *What are some possible explanations for variations in the timing of these milestones?*

word to objects that are inappropriate for the word's meaning. For example, children at first may say *"dada"* not only for "father" but also for other men, strangers, or boys. With time, overextensions decrease and eventually disappear. *Underextension* is the tendency to apply a word too narrowly; it occurs when children fail to use a word to name a relevant event or object. For example, a child might use the word *boy* to describe a 5-year-old neighbor but not apply the word to a male infant or to a 9-year-old male.

Two-Word Utterances By the time children are 18 to 24 months of age, they usually speak two-word utterances. To convey meaning with just two words, the child relies heavily on gesture, tone, and context. The wealth of meaning children can communicate with a two-word utterance includes the following (Slobin, 1972):

- Identification: "See doggie."
- Location: "Book there."
- Repetition: "More milk."
- Nonexistence: "All gone thing."
- Negation: "Not wolf."
- Possession: "My candy."
- Attribution: "Big car."
- Agent-action: "Mama walk."
- Action-direct object: "Hit you."
- Action-indirect object: "Give Papa."
- Action-instrument: "Cut knife."
- Question: "Where ball?"

These examples are from children whose first language is English, German, Russian, Finnish, Turkish, or Samoan.

Notice that the two-word utterances omit many parts of speech and are remarkably succinct. In fact, in every language, a child's first combinations of words have this economical quality; they are telegraphic. **Telegraphic speech** is the use of short and precise words without grammatical markers such as articles, auxiliary verbs, and other connectives. Telegraphic speech is not limited to two words. "Mommy give ice cream" and "Mommy give Tommy ice cream" also are examples of telegraphic speech.

Biological and Environmental Influences

We have discussed a number of language milestones in infancy; figure 6.9 summarizes the time at which infants typically reach these milestones. But what makes this amazing development possible? Everyone who uses language in some way "knows" its rules and has the ability to create an infinite number of words and sentences. Where does this knowledge come from? Is it the product of biology? Is language learned and influenced by experiences?

Biological Influences The ability to speak and understand language requires a certain vocal apparatus as well as a nervous system with certain capabilities. The nervous system and vocal apparatus of humanity's predecessors changed over hundreds of thousands or millions of years (Fisher & Marcus, 2006). With advances in the nervous system and vocal structures, *Homo sapiens* went beyond the grunting and shrieking of other animals to develop speech. Although estimates vary, many experts believe that humans acquired language about 100,000 years ago, which in evolutionary time, represents a very recent acquisition. It gave humans an enormous edge over other animals and increased the chances of human survival (Lachlan & Feldman, 2003; Pinker, 1994).

Around the world, most young children learn to speak in two-word utterances, at about 18 to 24 months of age. *What are some examples of these two-word utterances?*

Typical Age	Language Milestones
Birth	Crying
1 to 2 months	Cooing begins
6 months	Babbling begins
7 to 11 months	Change from universal linguist to language-specific listener
8 to 12 months	Use gestures, such as showing and pointing Comprehension of words appears
13 months	First word spoken
18 months	Vocabulary spurt starts
18 to 24 months	Uses two-word utterances Rapid expansion of understanding of words

FIGURE 6.9 **Some Language Milestones in Infancy.** Despite great variations in the language input received by infants, around the world they follow a similar path in learning to speak.

telegraphic speech The use of short and precise words without grammatical markers such as articles, auxiliary verbs, and other connectives.

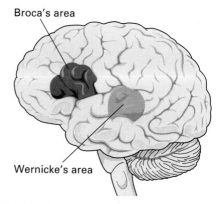

Broca's area

Wernicke's area

FIGURE 6.10 Broca's Area and Wernicke's Area. Broca's area is located in the frontal lobe of the brain's left hemisphere, and it is involved in the control of speech. Wernicke's area is a portion of the left hemisphere's temporal lobe that is involved in understanding language. *How does the role of these areas of the brain relate to lateralization, which was discussed in chapter 5?*

www.mhhe.com/santrockld11

Brain and Language Development

Broca's area An area in the brain's left frontal lobe involved in speech production.

Wernicke's area An area of the brain's left hemisphere that is involved in language comprehension.

aphasia A loss or impairment of language ability caused by brain damage.

language acquisition device (LAD) Chomsky's term that describes a biological endowment that enables the child to detect the features and rules of language, including phonology, syntax, and semantics.

Some language scholars view the remarkable similarities in how children acquire language all over the world as strong evidence that language has a biological basis. There is evidence that particular regions of the brain are predisposed to be used for language (Nakano & Blumstein, 2004; Pizzamiglio & others, 2005). Two regions involved in language were first discovered in studies of brain-damaged individuals: **Broca's area,** an area in the left frontal lobe of the brain involved in producing words, and **Wernicke's area,** a region of the brain's left hemisphere involved in language comprehension (see figure 6.10). Damage to either of these areas produces types of **aphasia,** which is a loss or impairment of language processing. Individuals with damage to Broca's area have difficulty producing words correctly; individuals with damage to Wernicke's area have poor comprehension and often produce fluent but incomprehensible speech.

Linguist Noam Chomsky (1957) proposed that humans are biologically prewired to learn language at a certain time and in a certain way. He said that children are born into the world with a **language acquisition device (LAD),** a biological endowment that enables the child to detect certain features and rules of language, including phonology, syntax, and semantics. Children are prepared by nature with the ability to detect the sounds of language, for example, and follow rules such as how to form plurals and ask questions.

Chomsky's LAD is a theoretical construct, not a physical part of the brain. Is there evidence for the existence of a LAD? Supporters of the LAD concept cite the uniformity of language milestones across languages and cultures, evidence that children create language even in the absence of well-formed input, and biological substrates of language. But as we will see, critics argue that even if infants have something like a LAD, it cannot explain the whole story of language acquisition.

Environmental Influences   Decades ago, behaviorists opposed Chomsky's hypothesis and argued that language represents nothing more than chains of responses acquired through reinforcement (Skinner, 1957). A baby happens to babble "Ma-ma"; Mama rewards the baby with hugs and smiles; the baby says "Mama" more and more. Bit by bit, said the behaviorists, the baby's language is built up. According to behaviorists, language is a complex learned skill, much like playing the piano or dancing.

The behavioral view of language learning has several problems. First, it does not explain how people create novel sentences—sentences that people have never heard or spoken before. Second, children learn the syntax of their native language even if they are not reinforced for doing so. Social psychologist Roger Brown (1973) spent long hours observing parents and their young children. He found that parents did not directly or explicitly reward or correct the syntax of most children's utterances. That is, parents did not say "good," "correct," "right," "wrong," and so on. Also, parents did not offer direct corrections such as, "You should say two shoes, not two shoe." However, as we will see shortly, many parents do expand on their young children's grammatically incorrect utterances and recast many of those that have grammatical errors (Bonvillian, 2005).

The behavioral view is no longer considered a viable explanation of how children acquire language. But a great deal of research describes ways in which children's environmental experiences influence their language skills. Many language experts argue that a child's experiences, the particular language to be learned, and the context in which learning takes place can strongly influence language acquisition (Goorhuis-Brouwer & others, 2004; Marchman, 2003; Snow & Yang, 2006; Tomasello, 2006).

Language is not learned in a social vacuum. Most children are bathed in language from a very early age (Fernald, 2001; Hart & Risley, 1995; Tomasello, 2006).

FIGURE 6.11 Social Interaction and Babbling. One study focused on two groups of mothers and their eighth month-old infants (Goldstein, King, & West, 2003). One group of mothers was instructed to smile and touch their infants immediately after the babies cooed and babbled; the other group was also told to smile and touch their infants but in a random manner, unconnected to sounds the infants made. The infants whose mothers immediately responded in positive ways to their babbling subsequently made more complex, speechlike sounds, such as "da" and "gu." The research setting for this study, which underscores how important caregivers are in the early development of language, is shown above.

The Wild Boy of Aveyron who never learned to communicate effectively had lived in social isolation for years. The support and involvement of caregivers and teachers greatly facilitate a child's language learning (Berko Gleason, 2005; Masur, Flynn, & Eichorst, 2005; Pan & others, 2005; Snow & Yang, 2006). For example, one recent study found that when mothers immediately smiled and touched their 8-month-old infants after they babbled, the infants subsequently made more complex speech-like sounds than when mothers responded to their infants in a random manner (Goldstein, King, & West, 2003) (see figure 6.11).

Michael Tomasello (2002, 2003, 2006) stresses that young children are intensely interested in their social world and that early in their development they can understand the intentions of other people. His *interaction view* of language emphasizes that children learn language in specific contexts. For example, when a toddler and a father are jointly focused on a book, the father might say, "See the birdie." In this case, even a toddler understands that the father intends to name something and knows to look in the direction of the pointing. Through this kind of joint attention, early in their development children are able to use their social skills to acquire language.

In particular, researchers have found that the child's vocabulary development is linked to the family's socioeconomic status and the type of talk that parents direct to their children. To read about these links, see the Diversity in Life-Span Development interlude that follows.

DIVERSITY IN LIFE-SPAN DEVELOPMENT

Language Environment, Poverty, and Language Development

What characteristics of a family make a difference to a child's language development? Socioeconomic status has been linked with how much parents talk to their children and with young children's vocabulary. Betty Hart and Todd Risley (1995) observed the language environments of children whose parents were professionals and children whose parents were on welfare. Compared with the professional parents, the parents on welfare talked much less to their young children, talked less about past events, and provided less elaboration (see figure 6.12). Also, as indicated in figure 6.12, the children of the professional parents had a much larger vocabulary at 36 months of age than the children of the welfare parents.

Other research has linked how much mothers speak to their infants and the infants' vocabularies. For example, in one study by Janellen Huttenlocher and her colleagues (1991), infants whose mothers spoke more often to them had markedly higher vocabularies. By the second birthday, vocabulary differences were substantial.

However, a recent study of 1- to 3-year-old children living in low-income families found that the sheer amount of maternal talk was not the best predictor of a child's vocabulary growth (Pan & others, 2005). Rather, it was maternal language and literacy skills that were positive related to the children's vocabulary development. For example, when mothers used a more diverse vocabulary when talking with their children, their children's vocabulary benefited, but their children's vocabulary was not related to the total amount of their talkativeness with their children. Also, mothers who frequently used pointing gestures had children with a greater vocabulary. Pointing usually occurs in concert with speech and it may enhance the meaning of mothers' verbal input to their children.

These research studies and others (NICHD Early Child Care Research Network, 2005) demonstrate the important effect that early speech input and poverty can have on the development of a child's language skills.

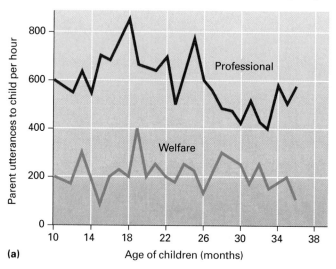

(a)

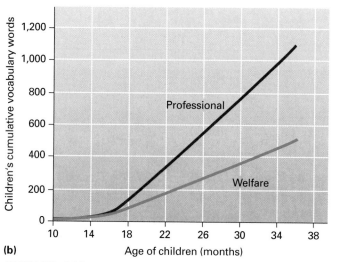

(b)

FIGURE 6.12 Language Input in Professional and Welfare Families and Young Children's Vocabulary Development. (*a*) In this study (Hart & Risley, 1995), parents from professional families talked with their young children more than parents from welfare families. (*b*) All of the children learned to talk, but children from professional families developed vocabularies that were twice as large as those from welfare families. Thus, by the time children go to preschool, they already have experienced considerable differences in language input in their families and developed different levels of vocabulary that are linked to their socioeconomic context. *Does this study indicate that poverty caused deficiencies in vocabulary development?*

child-directed speech Language spoken in a higher pitch than normal with simple words and sentences.

One intriguing component of the young child's linguistic environment is **child-directed speech,** language spoken in a higher pitch than normal with simple words and sentences (Thiessen, Hill, & Saffran, 2005). It is hard to use child-directed speech when not in the presence of a baby. As soon as you start talking to a baby, though, you shift into child-directed speech. Much of this is automatic and something most parents are not aware they are doing. Even 4-year-olds speak in simpler ways to 2-year-olds than to their 4-year-old friends. Child-directed speech has the important function of capturing the infant's attention and maintaining communication.

Adults often use strategies other than child-directed speech to enhance the child's acquisition of language, including recasting, expanding, and labeling:

- *Recasting* is rephrasing something the child has said, perhaps turning it into a question or restating the child's immature utterance in the form of a fully grammatical sentence. For example, if the child says, "The dog was barking," the adult can respond by asking, "When was the dog barking?" Effective recasting lets the child indicate an interest and then elaborates on that interest.

- *Expanding* is restating, in a linguistically sophisticated form, what a child has said. For example, a child says, "Doggie eat," and the parent replies, "Yes, the doggie is eating."
- *Labeling* is identifying the names of objects. Young children are forever being asked to identify the names of objects. Roger Brown (1958) called this "the original word game" and claimed that much of a child's early vocabulary is motivated by this adult pressure to identify the words associated with objects.

Parents use these strategies naturally and in meaningful conversations. Parents do not (and should not) use any deliberate method to teach their children to talk, even for children who are slow in learning language. Children usually benefit when parents guide their children's discovery of language rather than overloading them with language; "following in order to lead" helps a child learn language. If children are not ready to take in some information, they are likely to tell you (perhaps by turning away). Thus, giving the child more information is not always better.

Remember, the encouragement of language development, not drill and practice, is the key. Language development is not a simple matter of imitation and reinforcement. To read further about ways that parents can facilitate children's language development, see the Applications in Life-Span Development interlude.

Communicating with Babies

APPLICATIONS IN LIFE-SPAN DEVELOPMENT

How Parents Can Facilitate Infants' and Toddlers' Language Development

In *Growing Up with Language,* linguist Naomi Baron (1992) provided ideas to help parents facilitate their child's language development. A summary of her ideas follows:

Infants

- *Be an active conversational partner.* Initiate conversation with the infant. If the infant is in a daylong child-care program, ensure that the baby receives adequate language stimulation from adults.
- *Talk as if the infant understands what you are saying.* Parents can generate self-fulfilling prophecies by addressing their young children as if they understand what is being said. The process may take four to five years, but children gradually rise to match the language model presented to them.
- *Use a language style with which you feel comfortable.* Don't worry about how you sound to other adults when you talk with your child. Your affect, not your content, is more important when talking with an infant. Use whatever type of baby talk with which you feel comfortable.

Toddlers

- *Continue to be an active conversational partner.* Engaging toddlers in conversation, even one-sided conversation, is the most important thing a parent can do to nourish a child linguistically.

(continued on next page)

It is a good idea for parents to begin talking to their babies at the start. The best language teaching occurs when the talking is begun before the infant becomes capable of intelligible speech. *What are some other guidelines for parents to follow in helping their infants and toddlers develop their language?*

- *Remember to listen.* Since toddlers' speech is often slow and laborious, parents are often tempted to supply words and thoughts for them. Be patient and let toddlers express themselves, no matter how painstaking the process is or how great a hurry you are in.
- *Use a language style with which you are comfortable, but consider ways of expanding your child's language abilities and horizons.* For example, using long sentences need not be problematic. Use rhymes. Ask questions that encourage answers other than "Yes" and "No." Actively repeat, expand, and recast the child's utterances. Introduce new topics. And use humor in your conversation.
- *Adjust to your child's idiosyncrasies instead of working against them.* Many toddlers have difficulty pronouncing words and making themselves understood. Whenever possible, make toddlers feel that they are being understood.
- *Avoid sexual stereotypes.* Don't let the toddler's sex determine your amount or style of conversation. Many American mothers are more linguistically supportive of girls than of boys, and many fathers talk less with their children than mothers do. Cognitively enriching initiatives from both mothers and fathers benefit both boys and girls.
- *Resist making normative comparisons.* Be aware of the ages at which your child reaches specific milestones (such as the first word, first 50 words), but do not measure this development rigidly against that of other children. Such social comparisons can bring about unnecessary anxiety.

An Interactionist View

If language acquisition depended only on biology, then Genie and the Wild Boy of Aveyron (discussed earlier in the chapter) should have talked without difficulty. A child's experiences influence language acquisition. But we have seen that language does have strong biological foundations. No matter how much you converse with a dog, it won't learn to talk. In contrast, children are biologically prepared to learn language. Children all over the world acquire language milestones at about the same time and in about the same order. An interactionist view emphasizes that both biology and experience contribute to language development (Tomasello & Slobin, 2004).

This interaction of biology and experience can be seen in the variations in the acquisition of language. Children vary in their ability to acquire language, and this variation cannot be readily explained by differences in environmental input alone. For children who are slow in developing language skills, however, opportunities to talk and be talked with are important. Children whose parents provide them with a rich verbal environment show many positive benefits. Parents who pay attention to what their children are trying to say, expand their children's utterances, read to them, and label things in the environment, are providing valuable, if unintentional, benefits (Berko Gleason, 2004).

American psychologist Jerome Bruner (1983, 1996) proposed that the sociocultural context is extremely important in understanding children's language development. His view has some similarities with the ideas of Lev Vygotsky that were briefly described in chapter 2 and will be presented in greater detail in chapter 8. Bruner stresses the role of parents and teachers in constructing what he called a *language acquisition support system (LASS).*

Today, most language researchers believe that children everywhere arrive in the world with special social and linguistic capacities that make language acquisition not just likely, but inevitable. How much of the language is biologically determined and how much depends on interaction with others is a subject of debate among linguists and psychologists. However, all agree that both biological capacity and relevant experience are necessary (Berko Gleason, 2005).

Review and Reflect ● LEARNING GOAL 4

4 **Explain language development in infancy**

Review
- What is language?
- What are language's rule systems?
- How does language develop in infancy?
- What are some biological and environmental influences on language?
- To what extent do biological and environmental influences interact to produce language development?

Reflect
- Would it be a good idea for parents to hold large flash cards of words in front of their infant to help the infant learn language? Why or why not? What do you think Piaget would say about this activity?

REACH YOUR LEARNING GOALS

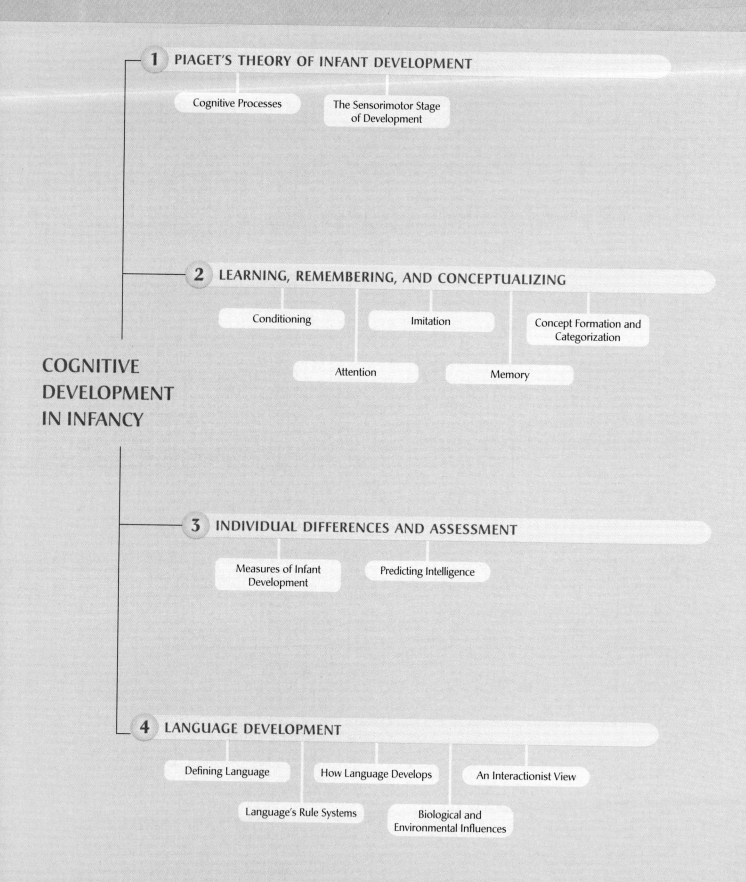

COGNITIVE DEVELOPMENT IN INFANCY

1 PIAGET'S THEORY OF INFANT DEVELOPMENT

Cognitive Processes

The Sensorimotor Stage of Development

2 LEARNING, REMEMBERING, AND CONCEPTUALIZING

Conditioning

Imitation

Concept Formation and Categorization

Attention

Memory

3 INDIVIDUAL DIFFERENCES AND ASSESSMENT

Measures of Infant Development

Predicting Intelligence

4 LANGUAGE DEVELOPMENT

Defining Language

How Language Develops

An Interactionist View

Language's Rule Systems

Biological and Environmental Influences

SUMMARY

1 Piaget's Theory of Cognitive Development: *Summarize the cognitive processes in Piaget's theory and the stage of sensorimotor development*

Cognitive Processes

In Piaget's theory, children construct their own cognitive worlds, building mental structures to adapt to their world. Schemes are actions or mental representations that organize knowledge. Behavioral schemes (physical activities) characterize infancy, whereas mental schemes (cognitive activities) develop in childhood. Assimilation occurs when children incorporate new information into existing schemes; accommodation refers to children's adjustment of their schemes in the face of new information. Through organization, children group isolated behaviors into a higher-order, more smoothly functioning cognitive system. Equilibration is a mechanism Piaget proposed to explain how children shift from one cognitive stage to the next. As children experience cognitive conflict in trying to understand the world, they use assimilation and accommodation to obtain equilibrium. The result is a new stage of thought. According to Piaget, there are four qualitatively different stages of thought.

The Sensorimotor Stage of Development

In sensorimotor thought, the first of Piaget's four stages, the infant organizes and coordinates sensations with physical movements. The stage lasts from birth to about 2 years of age. Sensorimotor thought has six substages: simple reflexes; first habits and primary circular reactions; secondary circular reactions; coordination of secondary circular reactions; tertiary circular reactions, novelty, and curiosity; and internalization of schemes. One key accomplishment of this stage is object permanence, the ability to understand that objects continue to exist even though the infant is no longer observing them. Another aspect involves infants' understanding of cause and effect. Piaget opened up a whole new way of looking at infant development in terms of coordinating sensory input with motoric actions. In the past decades, revisions of Piaget's view have been proposed based on research. For example, researchers have found that a stable and differentiated perceptual world is established earlier than Piaget envisioned, and infants begin to develop concepts as well.

2 Learning, Remembering, and Conceptualizing: *Describe how infants learn, remember, and conceptualize*

Conditioning

Both classical and operant conditioning occur in infants. Operant conditioning techniques have especially been useful to researchers in demonstrating infants' perception and retention of information about perceptual-motor actions.

Attention

Attention is the focusing of mental resources, and in infancy attention is closely linked with habituation. Habituation is the repeated presentation of the same stimulus, causing reduced attention to the stimulus. If a different stimulus is presented and the infant pays increased attention to it, dishabituation is occurring.

Imitation

Meltzoff has shown that newborns can match their behaviors (such as protruding their tongue) to a model. His research also shows that deferred imitation occurs as early as 9 months of age.

Memory

Memory is the retention of information over time. Infants as young as 2 months of age can retain information about perceptual-motor actions. However, many experts argue that what we commonly think of as memory (consciously remembering the past) does not occur until the second half of the first year of life. The phenomenon of not being able to remember events that occurred before the age of 3—known as infantile amnesia—may be due to the immaturity of the prefrontal lobes of the brain at that age.

Concept Formation and Conceptualization

Mandler argues that it is not until about 7 to 9 months of age that infants form conceptual categories. Infants' first concepts are broad. Over the first two years of life, these broad concepts gradually become more differentiated.

3 Individual Differences and Assessment: *Discuss infant assessment measures and the prediction of intelligence*

Measures of Infant Development

Developmental scales for infants grew out of the tradition of IQ testing of older children. These scales are less verbal than IQ tests. Gesell's scale is still widely used by pediatricians to distinguish normal and abnormal infants; it provides a developmental quotient (DQ). The Bayley scales, developed by Nancy Bayley, continue to be widely used today to assess infant development. They consist of a motor scale, a mental scale, and an infant behavior profile. Increasingly used, the Fagan Test of Infant Intelligence assesses how effectively the infant processes information.

Predicting Intelligence

Global scores on the Gesell and Bayley scales are not good predictors of childhood intelligence. However, measures of information processing such as speed of habituation and degree of dishabituation do correlate with intelligence later in childhood. There is both continuity and discontinuity between infant cognitive development and cognitive development later in childhood.

4 Language Development: *Explain language development in infancy*

Defining Language
Language is a form of communication, whether spontaneous, written, or signed, that is based on a system of symbols. Language consists of all the words used by a community and the rules for varying and combining them. It is marked by infinite generativity.

Language's Rule Systems
Phonology is the sound system of the language, including the sounds that are used and how they may be combined. Morphology refers to the units of meaning involved in word formation. Syntax is the way words are combined to form acceptable phrases and sentences. Semantics involves the meaning of words and sentences. Pragmatics is the appropriate use of language in different contexts.

How Language Develops
Among the milestones in infant language development are crying (birth), cooing (1 to 2 months), babbling (6 months), making the transition from universal linguist to language-specific listener (7 to 11 months), using gestures (8 to 12 months), comprehension of words (8 to 12 months), first word spoken (13 months), vocabulary spurt (18 months), rapid expansion of understanding words (18 to 24 months), and two-word utterances (18 to 24 months).

Biological and Environmental Influences
In evolution, language clearly gave humans an enormous advantage over other animals and increased their chance of survival. Broca's area and Wernicke's area are important locations for language processing in the brain's left hemisphere. Chomsky argues that children are born with the ability to detect basic features and rules of language. In other words, they are biologically prepared to learn language with a prewired language acquisition device (LAD). The behavioral view—that children acquire language as a result of reinforcement—has not been supported. Adults help children acquire language through child-directed speech, recasting, expanding, and labeling. Environmental influences are demonstrated by differences in the language development of children as a consequence of being exposed to different language environments in the home. Parents should talk extensively with an infant, especially about what the baby is attending to.

An Interactionist View
Both biology and environment are necessary for competent language development. Bruner's LASS concept emphasizes the importance of both biology and environment in language development. Although biological processes provide the foundation for the acquisition of the basic aspects of language, the contributions of caregivers to children's language competency is extensive.

KEY TERMS

schemes 177
assimilation 178
accommodation 178
organization 178
equilibration 178
sensorimotor stage 178
simple reflexes 179
first habits and primary
    circular reactions 179
secondary circular
    reactions 180

coordination of secondary
    circular reactions 180
tertiary circular reactions,
    novelty, and curiosity 180
internalization of schemes 180
object permanence 181
A$\overline{B}$ error 183
attention 185
deferred imitation 186
memory 186
implicit memory 186

explicit memory 186
developmental
    quotient (DQ) 189
Bayley Scales of Infant
    Development 189
language 190
infinite generativity 190
phonology 191
morphology 191
syntax191

semantics 192
pragmatics 192
telegraphic speech 195
Broca's area 196
Wernicke's area 196
aphasia 196
language acquisition
    device (LAD) 196
child-directed speech 198

KEY PEOPLE

Jean Piaget 177
Renée Baillargeon 181
Eleanor Gibson 183
Elizabeth Spelke 183
Carolyn Rovee-Collier 185

Andrew Meltzoff 186
Jean Mandler 187
Arnold Gesell 189
Nancy Bayley 189
Patricia Kuhl 193

Noam Chomsky 196
Roger Brown 196
Michael Tomasello 197
Betty Hart and Todd Risley 198
Janellen Huttenlocher 198

Naomi Baron 199
Jerome Bruner 200

E-LEARNING TOOLS

To help you master the material in this chapter, you'll find a number of valuable study tools on the LifeMap CD-ROM that accompanies this book and on the Online Learning Center for *Life-Span Development*, eleventh edition, at **www.mhhe.com/santrockld11**.

Video Clips

In the margins of this book there are icons directing you to the LifeMap CD-ROM that accompanies the book. There you'll find two videos for chapter 6. The first video is called "Brain and Infant Cognition." Researchers discuss some of the central issues in the continuing debate over innate versus learned factors in the infant's cognitive development. The second video is called "Language Ability at 2 Years."

A profile of 2-year-old Abby and her communication with her mother offers a snapshot of language development at the two-year mark.

Self-Assessment

Connect to **www.mhhe.com/santrockld11** to examine your understanding of cognitive development in infancy by completing the self-assessment, *My Beliefs About Nurturing a Baby's Mind*.

Taking It to the Net

Connect to **www.mhhe.com/santrockld11** to research the answers to these questions.

1. Toby must make a 15-minute class presentation on an important theorist who has significantly contributed to our understanding of human development. If Toby were to select Piaget, what types of information (written, spoken, visual) should he include in this presentation to his class?
2. Veronica works in an infant child care center that serves mothers who are participating in a welfare-to-work program, advising the mothers about nutrition. What do these mothers need to know about the effect of poor nutrition on their child's cognitive development?
3. Taye is worried that his 1-year-old cousin, Matthew, whom he often baby-sits, is not on track with his language development as compared with his niece Rita. By this age, what are some of the language-related milestones or tasks than an average child usually has achieved?

Health and Well-Being, Parenting, and Education Exercises

Build your decision-making skills by trying your hand at the health and well-being, parenting, and education exercises.

Connect to **www.mhhe.com/santrockld11** to research the answers and complete the exercises.

We never know the love of our parents until we have become parents.

—HENRY WARD BEECHER
American Writer, 19th Century

CHAPTER OUTLINE

EMOTIONAL AND PERSONALITY DEVELOPMENT

Emotional Development

Temperament

Personality Development

ATTACHMENT

What Is Attachment?

Individual Differences in Attachment

Caregiving Styles and Attachment

SOCIAL CONTEXTS

The Family

Child Care

LEARNING GOALS

1 Discuss emotional and personality development in infancy

2 Describe how attachment develops in infancy

3 Explain how social contexts influence the infant's development

Images of Life-Span Development
The Story of Tom's Fathering

Many fathers are spending more time with their infants today than in the past.

Seventeen-month-old Tom is getting excited. His father just asked him if he wants to go outside and play. Tom toddles down the hall as fast as he can to get his shoes, coat, and hat, which he knows he wears when he goes outside. He grabs his hat and says, "Play, play," which at this point in his development is what he labels going outside and exploring the yard and its flowers, bugs, and bees. On the weekend, his parents take him to the zoo, where they point out and name various animals, like lions, tigers, and elephants, as Tom looks wide-eyed at the animals. When they get home, Tom's parents ask him about some of the sounds and movements the zoo animals make. Tom correctly roars at the mention of *lion* and imitates the movements of monkeys.

On weekdays, Tom's father, a writer, cares for him during the day while his mother works full-time away from home. Tom's father is doing a great job of caring for him. Tom's father keeps Tom nearby while he is writing and spends lots of time talking to him and playing with him. From their interactions, it is clear that they genuinely enjoy each other.

Last month, Tom began spending one day a week at a child-care center. His parents carefully selected the center after observing a number of centers and interviewing teachers and center directors. His parents placed him in the center one day a week because they wanted Tom to get some experience with peers and to give his father some time out from caregiving.

Tom's father looks to the future and imagines the Little League games Tom will play in and the many other activities he can enjoy with Tom. Remembering how little time his own father spent with him, he is dedicated to making sure that Tom has an involved, nurturing experience with his father. Of course, not all fathers today are as emotionally involved with their infants as Tom's father is (Connor & White, 2006; Jacobs & Kelley, 2006; Leite & McKenry, 2006).

When Tom's mother comes home in the evening, she spends considerable time with him. Tom shows a positive attachment to both his mother and his father. By cooperating, his parents have successfully juggled their careers and work schedules to provide 1-year-old Tom with excellent child care.

PREVIEW

In chapters 5 and 6, you read about how the infant perceives, learns, and remembers. Infants also are socioemotional beings, capable of displaying emotions and initiating social interaction with people close to *them. The main topics that we will explore in this chapter are emotional and personality development, attachment, and the social contexts of the family and child care.*

1 EMOTIONAL AND PERSONALITY DEVELOPMENT

Emotional Development	Temperament	Personality Development

Anyone who has been around infants for even a brief time detects that they are emotional beings. Not only do infants express emotions, but they also vary in their temperament. Some are shy and others are outgoing. Some are active and others much less so. Let's explore these and other aspects of emotional and personality development in infants.

Emotional Development

Imagine your life without emotion. Emotion is the color and music of life, as well as the tie that binds people together. How do psychologists define and classify emotions, and why are they important to development? How do emotions develop during the first two years of life?

What Are Emotions?   For our purposes, we will define **emotion** as feeling, or affect, that occurs when a person is in a state or an interaction that is important to him or her, especially to his or her well-being (Campos, 2004). Emotion is characterized by behavior that reflects or expresses the pleasantness or unpleasantness of the individual's state or transactions.

When we think about emotions, a few dramatic feelings such as rage or glorious joy spring to mind. Emotions can be specific and take the form of joy, fear, anger, and so on, depending on whether a transaction is a relief, a threat, a frustration, and so on. But emotions can be subtle as well, such as uneasiness in a new situation or the feeling a mother has when she holds her baby. And emotions can vary in how intense they are. For example, an infant may show intense fear or only mild fear in a particular situation.

Psychologists classify the broad range of emotions in many ways, but almost all classifications designate an emotion as either positive or negative. Positive emotions include enthusiasm, joy, and love. Negative emotions include anxiety, anger, guilt, and sadness.

Biological and Environmental Influences   Emotions are influenced both by biological foundations and by a person's experience. In *The Expression of Emotions in Man and Animals*, Charles Darwin (1872/1965) argued that our facial expressions of emotion are innate, not learned; are the same in all cultures around the world; and evolved from the emotions of animals. Today, psychologists still consider that emotions, especially facial expressions of emotions, have a strong biological foundation (Goldsmith, 2002). For example, children who are blind from birth and have never observed the smile or frown on another person's face smile and frown in the same way that children with normal vision do. Also, facial expressions of basic emotions such as happiness, surprise, anger, and fear are the same across cultures.

Biology's importance to emotion is also apparent in the changes in a baby's emotional capacities. Certain regions of the brain that develop early in life (such as the brain stem, hippocampus, and amygdala) play a role in distress, excitement, and rage, and even infants display these emotions (Thompson, Easterbrooks, & Walker, 2003). But, as we discuss later in the chapter, infants only gradually develop the ability to regulate their emotions, and this ability seems tied to the gradual maturation of frontal regions of the cerebral cortex (discussed in chapter 5) that can exert control over other areas of the brain (Porges, Doussard-Roosevelt, & Maiti, 1994).

These biological factors, however, are only part of the story of emotion. Emotions serve important functions in our relationships. As we discuss later in this section, emotions are the first language with which parents and infants communicate (Maccoby, 1992). Emotion-linked interchanges, as when Tom cries and his father sensitively responds, provide the foundation for the infant's developing attachment to the parent.

Social relationships, in turn, provide the setting for the development of a rich variety of emotions. When toddlers hear their parents quarreling, they often react with distress and inhibit their play (Cummings, 1987). Well-functioning families make each other laugh and may develop a light mood to defuse conflicts. Biological evolution has endowed human beings to be *emotional*, but embeddedness in relationships with others provides diversity in emotional experiences (Saarni & others, 2006).

Blossoms are scattered by the wind
And the wind cares nothing, but
The blossoms of the heart
No wind can touch.

—Yoshida Kenko
Buddhist Monk, 14th Century

www.mhhe.com/santrockld11

International Society for Research on Emotions

emotion Feeling, or affect, that occurs when a person is in a state or interaction that is important to them. Emotion is characterized by behavior that reflects (expresses) the pleasantness or unpleasantness of the state a person is in or the transactions being experienced.

FIGURE 7.1 Expression of Different Emotions in Infants

Early Emotions Emotions that infants express in the first six months of life include surprise, interest, joy, anger, sadness, fear, and disgust (see figure 7.1 for infants' facial expressions of some of these early emotions). Researchers debate about how early in the first six months these emotions first appear and their sequence (Campos, 2005; Draghi-Lorenz, Reddy, & Costall, 2001; Lewis, 2002; Saarni & others, 2006). Other emotions that appear in the infant and toddler years include empathy, embarrassment, pride, shame, and guilt, most of these occurring for the first time at some point in the second half of the first year through the second year. These later developing emotions have been called self-conscious emotions or other-conscious emotions, because they involve the emotional reactions of others when they are generated (Lewis, 2002; Saarni & others, 2006).

As an indication of the controversy regarding when certain emotions first are displayed by infants, consider jealousy. Some researchers argue that jealousy does not emerge until approximately 18 months of age (Lewis, 2002), whereas others emphasize that it is displayed much earlier (Campos, 2005; Draghi-Lorenz, Reddy, & Costall, 2001). Recent research studies sway the conclusion about the appearance of emotion to as early as 6 months of age (Hart & Carrington, 2002; Hart & others, 2004). In one study, 6-month-old infants observed their mothers either giving attention to a lifelike baby doll (hugging or gently rocking it, for example) or to a book. When mothers directed their attention to the doll, the infants were more likely to display negative emotions, such as anger and sadness, indicating their jealousy (Hart & Carrington, 2002) (see figure 7.2).

Emotional Expression and Social Relationships Emotional expressions are involved in infants' first relationships. The ability of infants to communicate emotions permits coordinated interactions with their caregivers and the beginning of an emotional bond between them. Not only do parents change their emotional expressions in response to infants' emotional expressions, but infants also modify their emotional expressions in response to their parents' emotional expressions. In other words,

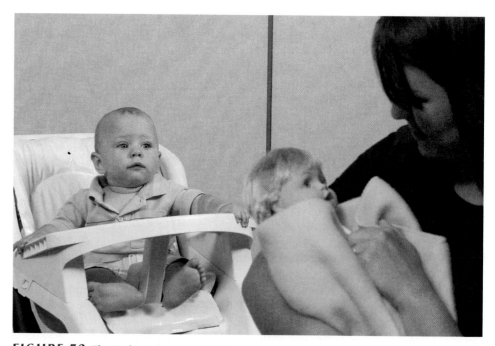

FIGURE 7.2 The Early Appearance of Jealousy

these interactions are mutually regulated. Because of this coordination, the interactions are described as *reciprocal* or *synchronous* when all is going well. Sensitive, responsive parents help their infants grow emotionally, whether the infants respond in distressed or happy ways (Campos, 2001; Thompson, 2006).

Cries and smiles are two emotional expressions that infants display when interacting with parents. These are babies' first forms of emotional communication.

Crying   Crying is the most important mechanism newborns have for communicating with their world. The first cry verifies that the baby's lungs have filled with air. Cries also may provide information about the health of the newborn's central nervous system. Newborns even tend to respond with cries and negative facial expressions when they hear other newborns cry (Dondi, Simion, & Caltran, 1999).

Babies have at least three types of cries:

- **Basic cry:** a rhythmic pattern that usually consists of a cry, followed by a briefer silence, then a shorter whistle that is somewhat higher in pitch than the main cry, then another brief rest before the next cry. Some infancy experts believe that hunger is one of the conditions that incite the basic cry.
- **Anger cry:** A variation of the basic cry in which more excess air is forced through the vocal cords.
- **Pain cry:** A sudden long, initial loud cry followed by breath holding; no preliminary moaning is present. The pain cry is stimulated by a high-intensity stimulus.

What are some different types of cries?

Most adults can determine whether an infant's cries signify anger or pain (Zeskind, Klein, & Marshall, 1992). Parents can distinguish the cries of their own baby better than those of another baby.

Smiling   The power of the infant's smiles was appropriately captured by British theorist John Bowlby (1969): "Can we doubt that the more and better an infant smiles the better he is loved and cared for? It is fortunate for their survival that babies are so designed by nature that they beguile and enslave mothers." Two types of smiling can be distinguished in infants:

- **Reflexive smile:** A smile that does not occur in response to external stimuli and appears during the first month after birth, usually during sleep.
- **Social smile:** A smile that occurs in response to an external stimulus, typically a face in the case of the young infant. Social smiling occurs as early as four months of age in response to a caregiver's voice (Campos, 2005).

Fear   One of a baby's earliest emotions is fear, which typically first appears at about 6 months of age and peaks at about 18 months. However, abused and neglected infants can show fear as early as three months (Campos, 2005). The most frequent expression of an infant's fear involves **stranger anxiety,** in which an infant shows a fear and wariness of strangers.

Stranger anxiety usually emerges gradually. It first appears at about 6 months of age in the form of wary reactions. By age 9 months, the fear of strangers is often more intense, and it continues to escalate through the infant's first birthday (Emde, Gaensbauer, & Harmon, 1976).

Not all infants show distress when they encounter a stranger. Besides individual variations, whether an infant shows stranger anxiety also depends on the social context and the characteristics of the stranger.

Infants show less stranger anxiety when they are in familiar settings. For example, in one study, 10-month-olds showed little stranger anxiety when they met a

basic cry A rhythmic pattern usually consisting of a cry, a briefer silence, a shorter inspiratory whistle that is higher pitched than the main cry, and then a brief rest before the next cry.

anger cry A cry similar to the basic cry, with more excess air forced through the vocal cords.

pain cry A sudden appearance of loud crying without preliminary moaning, followed by breath holding.

reflexive smile A smile that does not occur in response to external stimuli. It happens during the month after birth, usually during sleep.

social smile A smile in response to an external stimulus, which, early in development, typically is a face.

stranger anxiety An infant's fear and wariness of strangers; it tends to appear in the second half of the first year of life.

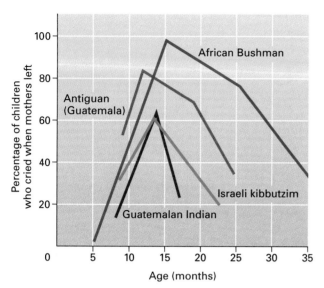

FIGURE 7.3 **Separation Anxiety in Four Cultures.** Note that separation protest peaked at about the same time in all four cultures in this study (13 to 15 months of age) (Kagan, Kearsley, & Zelazo, 1978). However, a higher percentage (100 percent) of infants in an African Bushman culture engaged in separation protest compared to only about 60 percent of infants in Guatemalan Indian and Israeli kibbutzim cultures. *What might explain the fact that separation protest peaks at about the same time in these cultures?*
Reprinted by permission of the publisher from Infancy: Its Place in Human Development by Jerome Kagan, Richard B. Kearsley, and Philip R. Zelazo, p. 107, Cambridge, Mass.: Harvard University Press, Copyright © 1978 by the President and Fellows of Harvard College.

stranger in their own home but much greater fear when they encountered a stranger in a research laboratory (Sroufe, Waters, & Matas, 1974). Also, infants show less stranger anxiety when they are sitting on their mothers' laps than when placed in an infant seat several feet away from their mothers (Bohlin & Hagekull, 1993). Thus, it appears that, when infants feel secure, they are less likely to show stranger anxiety.

Who the stranger is and how the stranger behaves also influence stranger anxiety in infants. Infants are less fearful of child strangers than adult strangers. They also are less fearful of friendly, outgoing, smiling strangers than of passive, unsmiling strangers (Bretherton, Stolberg, & Kreye, 1981).

In addition to stranger anxiety, infants experience fear of being separated from their caregivers. The result is **separation protest**—crying when the caregiver leaves. Separation protest tends to peak at about 15 months among U.S. infants. In fact, one study found that separation protest peaked at about 13 to 15 months in four different cultures (Kagan, Kearsley, & Zelazo, 1978). As indicated in figure 7.3, the percentage of infants who engaged in separation protest varied across cultures, but the infants reached a peak of protest at about the same age—just before the middle of the second year of life.

Social Referencing   Infants not only express emotions like fear but "read" the emotions of other people. **Social referencing** involves "reading" emotional cues in others to help determine how to act in a particular situation. The development of social referencing helps infants to interpret ambiguous situations more accurately, as when they encounter a stranger and need to know whether to fear the person (Mumme, Fernald, & Herrera, 1996; Thompson, 2006). By the end of the first year, a mother's facial expression—either smiling or fearful—influences whether an infant will explore an unfamiliar environment.

Infants become better at social referencing in the second year of life. At this age, they tend to "check" with their mother before they act; they look at her to see if she is happy, angry, or fearful. For example, in one study, 14- to 22-month-old infants were more likely to look at their mother's face as a source of information for how to act in a situation than were 6- to 9-month-old infants (Walden, 1991).

Emotional Regulation and Coping   During the first year of life, the infant gradually develops an ability to inhibit, or minimize, the intensity and duration of emotional reactions (Eisenberg, Spinrad, & Smith, 2004; Zeman, 2006). From early in infancy, babies put their thumbs in their mouths to soothe themselves. But at first, infants mainly depend on caregivers to help them soothe their emotions, as when a caregiver rocks an infant to sleep, sings lullabyes to the infant, gently strokes the infant, and so on.

The caregivers' actions influence the infant's neurobiological regulation of emotions (Saarni & others, 2006; Thompson, 2006; Thompson, Easterbrooks, & Walker, 2003). By soothing the infant, caregivers help infants to modulate their emotion and reduce the level of stress hormones (Gunnar, 2000; Gunnar & Davis, 2003; Gunnar & Quevedo, 2007). Many developmentalists hold it is a good strategy for a caregiver to soothe an infant before the infant gets into an intense, agitated, uncontrolled state (Thompson, 1994).

Later in infancy, when they become aroused, infants sometimes redirect their attention or distract themselves in order to reduce their arousal (Grolnick, Bridges, & Connell, 1996). By 2 years of age, toddlers can use language to define their feeling states and the context that is upsetting them (Kopp & Neufeld, 2002). A toddler

separation protest An infant's distressed reaction when the caregiver leaves.

social referencing "Reading" emotional cues in others to help determine how to act in a particular situation.

might say, "Feel bad. Dog scare." This type of communication may help caregivers to help the child in regulating emotion.

Contexts can influence emotional regulation (Kopp & Neufeld, 2002; Saarni & others, 2006). Infants are often affected by fatigue, hunger, time of day, which people are around them, and where they are. Infants must learn to adapt to different contexts that require emotional regulation. Further, new demands appear as the infant becomes older and parents modify their expectations. For example, a parent may take it in stride if a 6-month-old infant screams in a restaurant but may react very differently if a $1\frac{1}{2}$-year-old starts screaming.

To soothe or not to soothe—should a crying baby be given attention and soothed, or does this spoil the infant? Many years ago, the behaviorist John Watson (1928) argued that parents spend too much time responding to infant crying. As a consequence, he said, parents reward crying and increase its incidence. More recently, behaviorist Jacob Gewirtz (1977) found that a caregiver's quick, soothing response to crying increased crying. In contrast, infancy experts Mary Ainsworth (1979) and John Bowlby (1989) stress that you can't respond too much to infant crying in the first year of life. They believe that a quick, comforting response to the infant's cries is an important ingredient in the development of a strong bond between the infant and caregiver. In one of Ainsworth's studies, infants whose mothers responded quickly when they cried at 3 months of age cried less later in the first year of life (Bell & Ainsworth, 1972).

Controversy still characterizes the question of whether or how parents should respond to an infant's cries (Keefe & others, 2006; Lewis & Ramsay, 1999). However, developmentalists increasingly argue that an infant cannot be spoiled in the first year of life, which suggests that parents should soothe a crying infant. This reaction should help infants develop a sense of trust and secure attachment to the caregiver.

Another technique for calming young infants is *swaddling*, which involves wrapping a young baby in a blanket. Swaddling is popular in many Middle Eastern countries and in the Navajo nation in the United States (Whiting, 1981). However, in the United States swaddling has generally been unpopular because it restricts freedom of movement and is thought to make babies passive (Chisolm, 1989; Saarni & others, 2006). Nonetheless, an increasing number of pediatricians recommend swaddling. Some recent research studies have shown positive outcomes for swaddling. In one recent study, newborns with brain injuries were randomly assigned to a swaddling condition (wrapping the baby in a blanket) or a massage therapy condition (Ohgi & others, 2004). Swaddling reduced the infants' crying more than the massage therapy.

Pediatricians and nurses who recommend swaddling stress that it stops the baby's uncontrolled arm and leg movements that can lead to frenzied crying (Huang & others, 2004; Karp, 2002). They also recommend tucking the baby tightly in the blanket so it does not become loose and become wrapped around the baby's face. An excellent book on how to calm a crying baby, including specific instructions on swaddling, is *The Happiest Baby on the Block* (Karp, 2002).

Temperament

Do you get upset a lot? Does it take much to get you angry, or to make you laugh? Even at birth, babies seem to have different emotional styles. One infant is cheerful and happy much of the time; another baby seems to cry constantly. These tendencies reflect **temperament,** which is an individual's behavioral style and characteristic way of responding.

Describing and Classifying Temperament   How would you describe your temperament or the temperament of a friend? Researchers have described and classified the temperament of individuals in different ways. Here we will examine three of those ways.

temperament An individual's behavioral style and characteristic way of emotionally responding.

"Oh, he's cute, all right, but he's got the temperament of a car alarm." Copyright © The New Yorker Collection 1999 Barbara Smaller from cartoonbank.com. All Rights Reserved.

Infant Temperament

Chess and Thomas' Classification Psychiatrists Alexander Chess and Stella Thomas (Chess & Thomas, 1977; Thomas & Chess, 1991) identified three basic types, or clusters, of temperament:

- **Easy child:** This child is generally in a positive mood, quickly establishes regular routines in infancy, and adapts easily to new experiences.
- **Difficult child:** This child reacts negatively and cries frequently, engages in irregular daily routines, and is slow to accept change.
- **Slow-to-warm-up child:** This child has a low activity level, is somewhat negative, and displays a low intensity of mood.

In their longitudinal investigation, Chess and Thomas found that 40 percent of the children they studied could be classified as easy, 10 percent as difficult, and 15 percent as slow to warm up. Notice that 35 percent did not fit any of the three patterns. Researchers have found that these three basic clusters of temperament are moderately stable across the childhood years.

Kagan's Behavioral Inhibition Another way of classifying temperament focuses on the differences between a shy, subdued, timid child and a sociable, extraverted, bold child. Jerome Kagan (2000, 2002; Kagan & Fox, 2006; Kagan & Snidman, 1991) regards shyness with strangers (peers or adults) as one feature of a broad temperament category called *inhibition to the unfamiliar.* Inhibited children react to many aspects of unfamiliarity with initial avoidance, distress, or subdued affect, beginning about 7 to 9 months of age.

Kagan has found that inhibition shows considerable stability from infancy through early childhood. One recent study classified toddlers into extremely inhibited, extremely uninhibited, and intermediate groups (Pfeifer & others, 2002). Follow-up assessments occurred at 4 and 7 years of age. Continuity was demonstrated for both inhibition and lack of inhibition, although a substantial number of the inhibited children moved into the intermediate groups at 7 years of age.

Rothbart and Bates' Classification New classifications of temperament continue to be forged. Mary Rothbart and John Bates (2006) argue that three broad dimensions best represent what researchers have found to characterize the structure of temperament: extraversion/surgency, negative affectivity, and effortful control (self-regulation):

- *Extraversion/surgency,* which includes "positive anticipation, impulsivity, activity level, and sensation seeking" (Rothbart, 2004, p. 495). Kagan's uninhibited children fit into this category.
- *Negative affectivity,* which includes "fear, frustration, sadness, and discomfort" (Rothbart, 2004, p. 495). These children are easily distressed; they may fret and cry often. Kagan's inhibited children fit this category.
- *Effortful control (self-regulation),* which includes "attentional focusing and shifting, inhibitory control, perceptual sensitivity, and low-intensity pleasure" (Rothbart, 2004, p. 495). Infants who are high on effortful control show an ability to keep their arousal from getting too high and have strategies for soothing themselves. By contrast, children low on effortful control are often unable to control their arousal; they become easily agitated and intensely emotional.

In Rothbart's (2004, p. 497) view, "early theoretical models of temperament stressed the way we are moved by our positive and negative emotions or level of arousal, with our actions driven by these tendencies." The more recent emphasis on effortful control, however, advocates that individuals can engage in a more cognitive, flexible approach to stressful circumstances.

Biological Foundations and Experience How does a child acquire a certain temperament? Kagan (2002, 2003) argues that children inherit a physiology

easy child A child who is generally in a positive mood, who quickly establishes regular routines in infancy, and who adapts easily to new experiences.

difficult child A child who tends to react negatively and cry frequently, who engages in irregular daily routines, and who is slow to accept new experiences.

slow-to-warm-up child A child who has a low activity level, is somewhat negative, and displays a low intensity of mood.

that biases them to have a particular type of temperament. However, through experience they may learn to modify their temperament to some degree. For example, children may inherit a physiology that biases them to be fearful and inhibited, but they learn to reduce their fear and inhibition to some degree.

Biological Influences Physiological characteristics have been linked with different temperaments (Rothbart & Bates, 1998, 2006). In particular, an inhibited temperament is associated with a unique physiological pattern that includes high and stable heart rate, high level of the hormone cortisol, and high activity in the right frontal lobe of the brain (Kagan, 2003; Kagan & Fox, 2006). This pattern may be tied to the excitability of the amygdala, a structure of the brain that plays an important role in fear and inhibition (Kagan, 2003; LeDoux, 1998, 2000). An inhibited temperament or negative affectivity may also be linked to low levels of the neurotransmitter serotonin, which may increase an individual's vulnerability to fear and frustration (Kramer, 1993).

What is heredity's role in the biological foundations of temperament? Twin and adoption studies suggest that heredity has a moderate influence on differences in temperament within a group of people (Plomin & others, 1994). The contemporary view is that temperament is a biologically based but evolving aspect of behavior; it evolves as the child's experiences are incorporated into a network of self-perceptions and behavioral preferences that characterize the child's personality (Thompson & Goodvin, 2005).

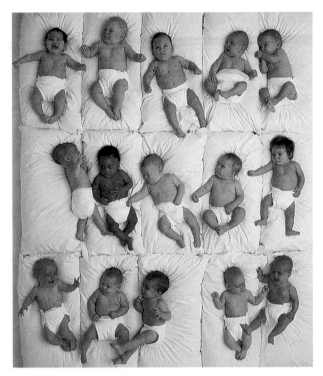

What are some ways that developmentalists have classified infants' temperaments? Which classification makes the most sense to you, based on your observations of infants?

Gender, Culture, and Temperament Gender may be an important factor shaping the context that influences the fate of temperament. Parents might react differently to an infant's temperament depending on whether the baby is a boy or a girl (Kerr, 2001). For example, in one study, mothers were more responsive to the crying of irritable girls than to the crying of irritable boys (Crockenberg, 1986).

Similarly, the reaction to an infant's temperament may depend in part on culture. For example, an active temperament might be valued in some cultures (such as the United States) but not in other cultures (such as China). Indeed, children's temperament can vary across cultures (Putnam, Sanson, & Rothbart, 2002). Behavioral inhibition is more highly valued in China than in North America, and researchers have found that Chinese children are more inhibited than Canadian infants (Chen & others, 1998). The cultural differences in temperament were linked to parent attitude and behaviors. Canadian mothers of inhibited two-year-olds were less accepting of their infants' inhibited temperament while Chinese mothers were more accepting.

In short, many aspects of a child's environment can encourage or discourage the persistence of temperament characteristics (Shiner, 2006). One useful way of thinking about these relationships applies the concept of goodness of fit, which we examine next.

An infant's temperament can vary across cultures. *What do parents need to know about a child's temperament?*

Goodness of Fit and Parenting **Goodness of fit** refers to the match between a child's temperament and the environmental demands the child must cope with (Matheny & Phillips, 2001). Suppose Jason is an active toddler who is made to sit still for long periods of time and Jack is a slow-to-warm-up toddler who is abruptly pushed into new situations on a regular basis. Both Jason and Jack face a lack of fit between their temperament and environmental demands. Lack of fit can produce adjustment problems (Rothbart & Bates, 2006).

Some temperament characteristics pose more parenting challenges than others, at least in modern Western societies (Rothbart & Bates, 2006; Thompson & Goodvin, 2005). When children are prone to distress, as exhibited by frequent crying and

goodness of fit Refers to the match between a child's temperament and the environmental demands with which the child must cope.

irritability, their parents may eventually respond by ignoring the child's distress or trying to force the child to "behave." In one research study, though, extra support and training for mothers of distress-prone infants improved the quality of mother-infant interaction (van den Boom, 1989). The training led the mothers to alter their demands on the child, improving the fit between the child and the environment. Also, in a recent longitudinal study, researchers found that a high level of fearlessness on the part of infants, when combined with harsh parenting, was linked with persistent conduct problems at age eight (Shaw & others, 2003).

Many parents don't become believers in temperament's importance until the birth of their second child. They viewed their first child's behavior as a result of how they treated the child. But then they find that some strategies that worked with their first child are not as effective with the second child. Some problems experienced with the first child (such as those involved in feeding, sleeping, and coping with strangers) do not exist with the second child, but new problems arise. Such experiences strongly suggest that children differ from each other very early in life, and that these differences have important implications for parent-child interaction (Kwak & others, 1999; Rothbart & Putnam, 2002). To read further about some positive strategies for parenting that take into account the child's temperament, see the Applications in Life-Span Development interlude.

APPLICATIONS IN LIFE-SPAN DEVELOPMENT

Parenting and the Child's Temperament

What are the implications of temperamental variations for parenting? Although answers to this question necessarily are speculative, these conclusions regarding the best parenting strategies to use in relation to children's temperament were reached by temperament experts Ann Sanson and Mary Rothbart (1995):

- *Attention to and respect for individuality.* One implication is that it is difficult to generate general prescriptions for "good" parenting. A goal might be accomplished in one way with one child and in another way with another child, depending on the child's temperament. Parents need to be sensitive and flexible to the infant's signals and needs.
- *Structuring the child's environment.* Crowded, noisy environments can pose greater problems for some children (such as a "difficult" child) than others (such as an "easygoing" child). We might also expect that a fearful, withdrawing child would benefit from slower entry into new contexts.
- *The "difficult child" and packaged parenting programs.* Programs for parents often focus on dealing with children who have "difficult" temperaments. In some cases, "difficult child" refers to Thomas and Chess' description of a child who reacts negatively, cries frequently, engages in irregular daily routines, and is slow to accept change. In others, the concept might be used to describe a child who is irritable, displays anger frequently, does not follow directions well, or some other negative characteristic. Acknowledging that some children are harder than others to parent is often helpful, and advice on how to handle particularly difficult characteristics can be useful. However, whether a particular characteristic is difficult depends on its fit with the environment. To label a child "difficult" has the danger of becoming a self-fulfilling prophecy. If a child is identified as "difficult," people may treat the child in a way that actually elicits "difficult" behavior.

Too often, we pigeon-hole children into categories without examining the context (Rothbart & Bates, 2006; Saarni, 2002; Wachs, 2000). Nonetheless, caregivers need to take children's temperament into account. Research does not yet allow for many highly specific recommendations, but, in general, caregivers should (1) be sensitive to the individual characteristics of the child, (2) be flexible in responding to these characteristics, and (3) avoid applying negative labels to the child.

Personality Development

Emotions and temperament form key aspects of *personality*, the enduring personal characteristics of individuals. Let's now examine characteristics that often are thought of as central to personality development during infancy: trust and the development of self and independence.

Trust According to Erik Erikson (1968), the first year of life is characterized by the trust-versus-mistrust stage of development. Following a life of regularity, warmth, and protection in the mother's womb, the infant faces a world that is less secure. Erikson proposed that infants learn trust when they are cared for in a consistent, warm manner. If the infant is not well fed and kept warm on a consistent basis, a sense of mistrust is likely to develop.

Trust versus mistrust is not resolved once and for all in the first year of life. It arises again at each successive stage of development, which can have positive or negative outcomes. For example, children who leave infancy with a sense of trust can still have their sense of mistrust activated at a later stage, perhaps if their parents are separated or divorced under conflicting circumstances.

The Developing Sense of Self Individuals carry with them a sense of who they are and what makes them different from everyone else. They cling to this identity and begin to feel secure in the knowledge that their identity is becoming more stable. Real or imagined, the sense of self is a strong motivating force in life. When does the individual begin to sense a separate existence from others?

Studying the self in infancy is difficult mainly because infants cannot tell us how they experience themselves. Infants cannot verbally express their views of the self. They also cannot understand complex instructions from researchers.

A rudimentary form of self-recognition—being attentive and positive toward one's image in a mirror—appears as early as 3 months of age (Mitchell, 1993; Pipp, Fischer, & Jennings, 1987). However, a central, more complete index of self-recognition—the ability to recognize one's physical features—does not emerge until the second year (Thompson, 2006).

One ingenious strategy to test infants' visual self-recognition is the use of a mirror technique, in which an infant's mother first puts a dot of rouge on the infant's nose. Then an observer watches to see how often the infant touches its nose. Next, the infant is placed in front of a mirror, and observers detect whether nose touching increases. Why does this matter? The idea is that increased nose touching indicates that the infant recognizes the self in the mirror and is trying to touch or rub off the rouge because the rouge violates the infant's view of the self. Increased touching indicates that the infant realizes that it is the self in the mirror but that something is not right since the real self does not have a dot of rouge on it.

Figure 7.4 displays the results of two investigations that used the mirror technique. The researchers found that before they were one year old, infants did not recognize themselves in the mirror (Amsterdam, 1968; Lewis & Brooks-Gunn, 1979). Signs of self-recognition began to appear among some infants when they were 15 to 18 months old. By the time they were two years old, most children recognized themselves in the mirror. In sum, infants begin to develop a self-understanding called self-recognition at approximately 18 months of age (Hart & Karmel, 1996; Lewis & others, 1989).

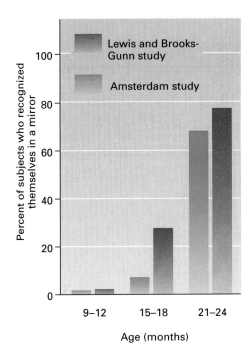

FIGURE 7.4 The Development of Self-Recognition in Infancy. The graph shows the findings of two studies in which infants less than 1 year of age did not recognize themselves in the mirror. A slight increase in the percentage of infant self-recognition occurred around 15 to 18 months of age. By 2 years of age, a majority of children recognized themselves. *Why do researchers study whether infants recognize themselves in a mirror?*

In one recent study, biweekly assessments from 15 to 23 months of age were conducted (Courage, Edison, & Howe, 2004). Self-recognition gradually emerged over this time, first appearing in the form of mirror recognition, followed by use of the personal pronoun and then by recognizing a photo of themselves. These aspects of self-recognition are often referred to as the first indications of toddlers' understanding of the mental state of me, "that they are objects in their own mental representation of the world" (Lewis, 2005, p. 363).

Late in the second year and early in the third year, toddlers show other emerging forms of self-awareness that reflect a sense of me (Thompson, 2006). For example, they refer to themselves such as by saying "me big"; they label their internal experiences such as emotions; they monitor themselves as when a toddler says, "do it myself"; and say that things are theirs (Bates, 1990; Bretherton & others, 1986; Bullock & Lutkenhaus, 1990; Fasig, 2000).

Independence   Not only does the infant develop a sense of self in the second year of life, but independence also becomes a more central theme in the infant's life. The theories of Margaret Mahler and Erik Erikson have important implications for both self-development and independence. Mahler (1979) argues that the child goes through a separation and then an individuation process. *Separation* involves the infant's movement away from the mother. *Individuation* involves the development of self.

Erikson (1968), like Mahler, stressed that independence is an important issue in the second year of life. Erikson describes the second stage of development as the stage of autonomy versus shame and doubt. Autonomy builds as the infant's mental and motor abilities develop. At this point in development, not only can infants walk, but they can also climb, open and close, drop, push and pull, and hold and let go. Infants feel pride in these new accomplishments and want to do everything themselves, whether the activity is flushing a toilet, pulling the wrapping off a package, or deciding what to eat. It is important for parents to recognize the motivation of toddlers to do what they are capable of doing at their own pace. Then they can learn to control their muscles and their impulses themselves. But when caregivers are impatient and do for toddlers what they are capable of doing themselves, shame and doubt develop. Every parent has rushed a child from time to time. It is only when parents consistently overprotect toddlers or criticize accidents (wetting, soiling, spilling, or breaking, for example) that children develop an excessive sense of shame and doubt about their ability to control themselves and their world. As we discuss in later chapters, Erikson believed that the stage of autonomy versus shame and doubt has important implications for the individual's future development.

Erikson believed that autonomy versus shame and doubt is the key developmental theme of the toddler years. *What are some good strategies for parents to use with their toddlers?*

Review and Reflect ● LEARNING GOAL 1

(1) Discuss emotional and personality development in infancy

Review
- What is the nature of an infant's emotions and how do they change?
- What is temperament and how does it develop in infancy?
- What are some important aspects of personality in infancy and how do they develop?

Reflect
- How would you describe your temperament? Does it fit one of Chess and Thomas' three styles—easy, slow to warm up, or difficult? If you have siblings, is your temperament similar or different from theirs?

2   ATTACHMENT

| What Is Attachment? | Individual Differences in Attachment | Caregiving Styles and Attachment |

So far, we have discussed how emotions and emotional competence change as children develop. We have also examined the role of emotional style; in effect, we have seen how emotions set the tone of our experiences in life. But emotions also write the lyrics because they are at the core of our relationships with others. Foremost among these relationships is attachment.

What Is Attachment?

A small curly-haired girl named Danielle, age 11 months, begins to whimper. After a few seconds, she begins to wail. Soon her mother comes into the room, and Danielle's crying ceases. Quickly, Danielle crawls over to where her mother is seated and reaches out to be held. Danielle has just demonstrated attachment to her mother. **Attachment** is a close emotional bond between two people.

There is no shortage of theories about infant attachment. Three theorists discussed in chapter 2—Freud, Erikson, and Bowlby—proposed influential views.

Freud believed that infants become attached to the person or object that provides oral satisfaction. For most infants, this is the mother, since she is most likely to feed the infant. Is feeding as important as Freud thought? A classic study by Harry Harlow (1958) reveals that the answer is no (see figure 7.5).

Harlow removed infant monkeys from their mothers at birth; for 6 months they were reared by surrogate (substitute) "mothers." One surrogate mother was made of wire, the other of cloth. Half of the infant monkeys were fed by the wire mother, half by the cloth mother. Periodically, the amount of time the infant monkeys spent with either the wire or the cloth mother was computed. Regardless of which mother fed them, the infant monkeys spent far more time with the cloth mother. Even if the wire mother, but not the cloth mother provided nourishment, the infant monkeys spent more time with the cloth mother. And when Harlow frightened the monkeys, those "raised" by the cloth mother ran to the mother and clung to it; those raised by the wire mother did not. Whether the mother provided comfort seemed to determine whether the monkeys associated the mother with security. This study clearly demonstrated that feeding is not the crucial element in the attachment process and that contact comfort is important.

Physical comfort also plays a role in Erik Erikson's (1968) view of the infant's development. Recall Erikson's proposal that the first year of life represents the stage of trust versus mistrust. Physical comfort and sensitive care, according to Erikson (1968), are key to establishing a basic trust in infants. The infant's sense of trust, in turn, is the foundation for attachment and sets the stage for a lifelong expectation that the world will be a good and pleasant place to be.

The ethological perspective of British psychiatrist John Bowlby (1969, 1989) also stresses the importance of attachment in the first year of life and the responsiveness of the caregiver. Bowlby believes both infants and their primary caregivers are biologically predisposed to form attachments. He argues that the newborn is biologically equipped to elicit attachment behavior (Weizmann, 2000). The baby cries, clings, coos, and smiles. Later, the infant crawls, walks, and follows the mother. The immediate result is to keep the primary caregiver nearby; the long-term effect is to increase the infant's chances of survival (Thompson, 2006).

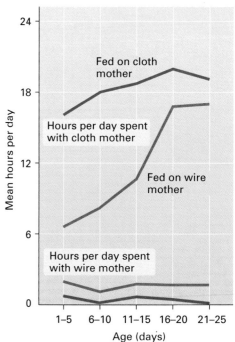

FIGURE 7.5 Contact Time with Wire and Cloth Surrogate Mothers. Regardless of whether the infant monkeys were fed by a wire or a cloth mother, they overwhelmingly preferred to spend contact time with the cloth mother. *How do these results compare with what Freud's theory and Erikson's theory would predict about human infants?*

What is the nature of secure and insecure attachment?

Harry Harlow
Forming a Secure Attachment
Attachment Research

Attachment does not emerge suddenly but rather develops in a series of phases, moving from a baby's general preference for human beings to a partnership with primary caregivers. Following are four such phases based on Bowlby's conceptualization of attachment (Schaffer, 1996):

- *Phase 1: From birth to 2 months.* Infants instinctively direct their attachment to human figures. Strangers, siblings, and parents are equally likely to elicit smiling or crying from the infant.
- *Phase 2: From 2 to 7 months.* Attachment becomes focused on one figure, usually the primary caregiver, as the baby gradually learns to distinguish familiar from unfamiliar people.
- *Phase 3: From 7 to 24 months.* Specific attachments develop. With increased locomotor skills, babies actively seek contact with regular caregivers, such as the mother or father.
- *Phase 4: From 24 months on.* Children become aware of others' feelings, goals, and plans and begin to take these into account in forming their own actions.

In sum, attachment emerges from the social cognitive advances that allow infants to develop expectations for the caregiver's behavior and to determine the affective quality of their relationship (Thompson, 2006). These social cognitive advances include recognizing the caregiver's face, voice, and other features, as well as expecting that the caregiver provides pleasure in social interaction and relief from distress.

Individual Differences in Attachment

Although attachment to a caregiver intensifies midway through the first year, isn't it likely that the quality of babies' attachment experiences varies? Mary Ainsworth (1979) thought so. Ainsworth created the **Strange Situation,** an observational measure of infant attachment in which the infant experiences a series of introductions, separations, and reunions with the caregiver and an adult stranger in a prescribed order. In using the Strange Situation, researchers hope that their observations will provide information about the infant's motivation to be near the caregiver and the degree to which the caregiver's presence provides the infant with security and confidence.

Based on how babies respond in the Strange Situation, they are described as being securely attached or insecurely attached (in one of three ways) to the caregiver:

- **Securely attached babies** use the caregiver as a secure base from which to explore the environment. When in the presence of their caregiver, securely attached infants explore the room and examine toys that have been placed in it. When the caregiver departs, securely attached infants might mildly protest, and when the caregiver returns these infants reestablish positive interaction with her, perhaps by smiling or climbing on her lap. Subsequently, they often resume playing with the toys in the room.
- **Insecure avoidant babies** show insecurity by avoiding the caregiver. In the Strange Situation, these babies engage in little interaction with the caregiver, are not distressed when she leaves the room, usually do not reestablish contact with her on her return, and may even turn their back on her. If contact is established, the infant usually leans away or looks away.
- **Insecure resistant babies** often cling to the caregiver and then resist her by fighting against the closeness, perhaps by kicking or pushing away. In the Strange Situation, these babies often cling anxiously to the caregiver and don't explore the playroom. When the caregiver leaves, they often cry loudly and push away if she tries to comfort them on her return.

attachment A close emotional bond between an infant and a caregiver.

Strange Situation An observational measure of infant attachment that requires the infant to move through a series of introductions, separations, and reunions with the caregiver and an adult stranger in a prescribed order.

securely attached babies Babies that use the caregiver as a secure base from which to explore the environment.

insecure avoidant babies Babies that show insecurity by avoiding the caregiver.

insecure resistant babies Babies that often cling to the caregiver, then resist her by fighting against the closeness, perhaps by kicking or pushing away.

- **Insecure disorganized babies** are disorganized and disoriented. In the Strange Situation, these babies might appear dazed, confused, and fearful. To be classified as disorganized, babies must show strong patterns of avoidance and resistance or display certain specified behaviors, such as extreme fearfulness around the caregiver.

Evaluating the Strange Situation Does the Strange Situation capture important differences among infants? As a measure of attachment, it may be culturally biased. For example, German and Japanese babies often show different patterns of attachment than American infants. As illustrated in figure 7.6, German infants are more likely to show an avoidant attachment pattern and Japanese infants are less likely to display this pattern than American infants (van IJzendoorn & Kroonenberg, 1988). The avoidant pattern in German babies likely occurs because their caregivers encourage them to be independent (Grossmann & others, 1985). Also as shown in figure 7.6, Japanese babies are more likely than American babies to be categorized as resistant. This may have more to do with the Strange Situation as a measure of attachment than with attachment insecurity itself. Japanese mothers rarely let anyone unfamiliar with their babies care for them. Thus, the Strange Situation might create considerably more stress for Japanese infants than for American infants, who are more accustomed to separation from their mothers (Miyake, Chen, & Campos, 1985). Even though there are cultural variations in attachment classification, the most frequent classification in every culture studied so far is secure attachment (Thompson, 2006; van IJzendoorn & Kroonenberg, 1988).

Some critics stress that behavior in the Strange Situation—like other laboratory assessments—might not indicate what infants do in a natural environment. But researchers have found that infants' behaviors in the Strange Situation are closely related to how they behave at home in response to separation and reunion with their mothers (Pederson & Moran, 1996). Thus, many infant researchers believe the Strange Situation continues to show merit as a measure of infant attachment.

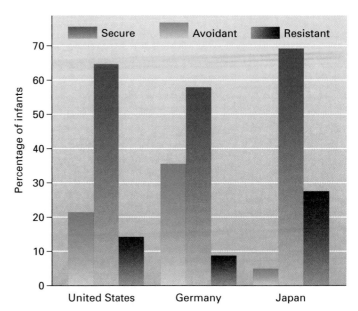

FIGURE 7.6 Cross-Cultural Comparison of Attachment. In one study, infant attachment in three countries—the United States, Germany, and Japan—was measured in the Ainsworth Strange Situation (van IJzendoorn & Kroonenberg, 1988). The dominant attachment pattern in all three countries was secure attachment. However, German infants were more avoidant and Japanese infants were less avoidant and more resistant than U.S. infants. *What are some explanations for differences in how German, Japanese, and American infants respond to the Strange Situation?*

Interpreting Differences in Attachment Do individual differences in attachment matter? Ainsworth believes that secure attachment in the first year of life provides an important foundation for psychological development later in life. The securely attached infant moves freely away from the mother but keeps track of where she is through periodic glances. The securely attached infant responds positively to being picked up by others and, when put back down, freely moves away to play. An insecurely attached infant, by contrast, avoids the mother or is ambivalent toward her, fears strangers, and is upset by minor, everyday separations.

If early attachment to a caregiver is important, it should relate to a child's social behavior later in development. For some children, early attachments seem to foreshadow later functioning (Carlson, Sroufe, & Egeland, 2004; Egeland & Carlson, 2004; Sroufe, Egeland, & Carlson, 1999; Sroufe & others, 2005a, 2005b; Waters, Corcoran, & Anafarta, 2005). In the extensive longitudinal study conducted by Alan Sroufe and his colleagues (2005a, 2005b), early secure attachment (assessed by the Strange Situation at 12 and 18 months) was linked with positive

insecure disorganized babies Babies that show insecurity by being disorganized and disoriented.

emotional health, high self-esteem, self-confidence, and socially competent interaction with peers, teachers, camp counselors, and romantic partners through adolescence. Another recent study found that infants who were securely attached at 15 months of age were more cognitively and socioemotionally competent at 4 years of age than their counterparts who were insecurely attached at 15 months of age (Fish, 2004).

For some children, though, there is little continuity (Thompson & Goodvin, 2005). Not all research reveals the power of infant attachment to predict subsequent development. In one longitudinal study, attachment classification in infancy did not predict attachment classification at 18 years of age (Lewis, 1997). In this study, the best predictor of an insecure attachment classification at 18 was the occurrence of parental divorce in the intervening years. Consistently positive caregiving over a number of years is likely an important factor in connecting early attachment and the child's functioning later in development. Indeed, researchers have found that early secure attachment *and* subsequent experiences, especially maternal care and life stresses, are linked with children's later behavior and adjustment (Belsky & Pasco Fearon, 2002a, 2002b; Thompson, 2006).

Some developmentalists believe that too much emphasis has been placed on the attachment bond in infancy. Jerome Kagan (1987, 2000), for example, believes that infants are highly resilient and adaptive; he argues that they are evolutionarily equipped to stay on a positive developmental course, even in the face of wide variations in parenting. Kagan and others stress that genetic characteristics and temperament play more important roles in a child's social competence than the attachment theorists, such as Bowlby and Ainsworth, are willing to acknowledge (Chaudhuri & Williams, 1999; Young & Shahinfar, 1995). For example, if some infants inherit a low tolerance for stress, this, rather than an insecure attachment bond, may be responsible for an inability to get along with peers.

Another criticism of attachment theory is that it ignores the diversity of socializing agents and contexts that exists in an infant's world. A culture's value system can influence the nature of attachment (Saarni & others, 2006). For example, German and Japanese babies often show different patterns of attachment than American infants. German infants are more likely to show an avoidant attachment pattern and Japanese infants are less likely to show this pattern than U.S. infants (van IJzendoorn & Kroonenberg, 1988). The avoidant pattern in German babies likely occurs because their caregivers encourage them to be more independent. Also, in some cultures, infants show attachments to many people. Among the Hausa (who live in Nigeria), both grandmothers and siblings provide a significant amount of care for infants (Harkness & Super, 1995). Infants in agricultural societies tend to form attachments to older siblings, who are assigned a major responsibility for younger siblings' care. Researchers recognize the importance of competent, nurturant caregivers in an infant's development (Bornstein, 2006; Parke & Buriel, 2006). At issue, though, is whether or not secure attachment, especially to a single caregiver, is critical (Lamb, 2005; Thompson, 2006).

Despite such criticisms, there is ample evidence that security of attachment is important to development (Hofer, 2006; McElwain & Booth-LaForce, 2006; Thompson, 2006). Secure attachment in infancy is important because it reflects a positive parent-infant relationship and provides the foundation that supports healthy socioemotional development in the years that follow.

In the Hausa culture, siblings and grandmothers provide a significant amount of care for infants. *How might these variations in care affect attachment?*

Caregiving Styles and Attachment

Is the style of caregiving linked with the quality of the infant's attachment? Securely attached babies have caregivers who are sensitive to their signals and are consistently available to respond to their infants' needs (Gao, Elliot, & Waters, 1999; Main, 2000). These caregivers often let their babies have an active part in determining the onset and pacing of interaction in the first year of life. One recent study found that maternal sensitivity in parenting was linked with secure attachment in infants in two different cultures: the United States and Colombia (Carbonell & others, 2002).

How do the caregivers of insecurely attached babies interact with them? Caregivers of avoidant babies tend to be unavailable or rejecting (Berlin & Cassidy, 2000). They often don't respond to their babies' signals and have little physical contact with them. When they do interact with their babies, they may behave in an angry and irritable way. Caregivers of resistant babies tend to be inconsistent; sometimes they respond to their babies' needs, and sometimes they don't. In general, they tend not to be very affectionate with their babies and show little sympathy when interacting with them. Caregivers of disorganized babies often neglect or physically abuse them (Cicchetti & Toth, 2006; Lyons-Ruth & others, 2006). In some cases, these caregivers are depressed.

Review and Reflect • LEARNING GOAL 2

2 **Describe how attachment develops in infancy**

Review
- What is attachment?
- What are some individual variations in attachment? What are some criticisms of attachment theory?
- How are caregiving styles related to attachment?

Reflect
- How might the infant's temperament be related to the way in which attachment is classified? Look at the temperament categories we described and reflect on how these might be more likely to show up in infants in some attachment categories than others.

---

3 SOCIAL CONTEXTS

| The Family | Child Care |

Now that we have explored the infant's emotional and personality development and attachment, let's examine the social contexts in which these occur. We will begin by studying a number of aspects of the family and then turn to a social context in which infants increasingly spend time—child care.

The Family

The family can be thought of as a constellation of subsystems—a complex whole made up of interrelated, interracting parts—defined in terms of generation, gender, and role (Minuchin, 2001). Each family member participates in several subsystems. The father and child represent one subsystem, the mother and father another; the mother-father-child represent yet another; and so on.

These subsystems have reciprocal influences on each other, as figure 7.7 highlights (Belsky, 1981). For example, Jay Belsky (1981) suggests that marital relations, parenting, and infant behavior and development can have both direct and indirect

Children socialize parents just as parents socialize children.

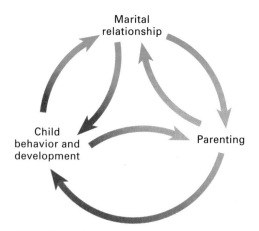

FIGURE 7.7 Interaction Between Children and Their Parents: Direct and Indirect Effects

reciprocal socialization Socialization that is bidirectional; children socialize parents, just as parents socialize children.

effects on each other. An example of a direct effect is the influence of the parents' behavior on the child. An indirect effect is how the relationship between the spouses mediates the way a parent acts toward the child (Hsu, 2004). For example, marital conflict might reduce the efficiency of parenting, in which case marital conflict would indirectly affect the child's behavior. The simple fact that two people are becoming parents may have profound effects on their relationship.

The Transition to Parenthood When people become parents through pregnancy, adoption, or stepparenting, they face disequilibrium and must adapt (Heincke, 2002). Parents want to develop a strong attachment with their infant, but they still want to maintain strong attachments to their spouse and friends, and possibly continue their careers. Parents ask themselves how this new being will change their lives. A baby places new restrictions on partners; no longer will they be able to rush out to a movie on a moment's notice, and money may not be readily available for vacations and other luxuries. Dual-career parents ask, "Will it harm the baby to place her in day care? Will we be able to find responsible baby-sitters?"

In a longitudinal investigation of couples from late pregnancy until $3\frac{1}{2}$ years after the baby was born, couples enjoyed more positive marital relations before the baby was born than after (Cowan & Cowan, 2000). Still, almost one-third showed an increase in marital satisfaction. Some couples said that the baby had both brought them closer together *and* moved them further apart. They commented that being parents enhanced their sense of themselves and gave them a new, more stable identity as a couple. Babies opened men up to a concern with intimate relationships, and the demands of juggling work and family roles stimulated women to manage family tasks more efficiently and pay attention to their own personal growth. A study of young African American and Latino couples from 14 and 24 years of age found that fathers and mothers who had positive relationships with their own parents were more likely to show positive adjustment to parenting than their counterparts who had negative relationships with their parents (Florsheim & others, 2003).

Reciprocal Socialization For many years, socialization between parents and children was viewed as a one-way process: Children were considered to be the products of their parents' socialization techniques. However, parent-child interaction is reciprocal (Parke, 2004; Parke & Buriel, 2006). **Reciprocal socialization** is socialization that is bidirectional. That is, children socialize parents just as parents socialize children. For example, the interaction of mothers and their infants is like a dance or a dialogue in which successive actions of the partners are closely coordinated. This coordinated dance or dialogue can assume the form of mutual synchrony in which each person's behavior depends on the partner's previous behavior (Feldman, 2006; Feldman, Greenbaum, & Yirmiya, 1999). Or it can be reciprocal in the sense that actions of the partners are matched, as when one partner imitates the other or when there is mutual smiling.

When reciprocal socialization has been studied in infancy, mutual gaze, or eye contact, plays an important role in early social interaction. In one investigation, the mother and infant engaged in a variety of behaviors while they looked at each other. By contrast, when they looked away from each other, the rate of such behaviors dropped considerably (Stern & others, 1977). In sum, the behaviors of mothers and infants involve substantial interconnection, mutual regulation, and synchronization (Moreno, Posada, & Goldyn, 2006).

An important form of reciprocal socialization is *scaffolding,* in which parents time interactions in such a way that the infant experiences turn-taking with the parents. Scaffolding involves parental behavior that supports children's efforts, allowing them to be more skillful than they would be if they were to rely only on their own abilities. In using scaffolding, caregivers provide a positive, reciprocal framework in which they and their children interact. For example, in the game peek-a-boo, the mother initially covers the baby. Then she removes the cover and registers "surprise" at the infant's reappearance. As infants become more skilled at peek-a-boo, pat-a-cake, and so on, there are other caregiver games that exemplify scaffolding and turn-taking sequences. In one study, infants who had more extensive scaffolding experiences with their parents (especially in the form of turn-taking) were more likely to engage in turn-taking when they interacted with their peers (Vandell & Wilson, 1988).

Maternal and Paternal Caregiving In stressful circumstances, do infants prefer their mother or father? In one study, 20 12-month-olds were observed interacting with their parents (Lamb, 1977). With both parents present, the infants preferred neither their mother nor their father. The same was true when the infants were alone with the mother or the father. However, the entrance of a stranger, combined with boredom and fatigue, produced a shift in the infants' social behavior toward the mother. In stressful circumstances, then, infants show a stronger attachment to the mother.

Can fathers take care of infants as competently as mothers can? Male primates are notoriously low in their interest in offspring, but when forced to live with infants whose female caregivers are absent, the adult male competently rears the infants. Observations of human fathers and their infants suggest that fathers have the ability to act sensitively and responsively with their infants (Parke, 2000, 2002, 2004; Parke & Buriel, 2006). However, although fathers can be active, nurturant, involved caregivers with their infants, many do not choose to follow this pattern (Chuang, Lamb, & Hwang, 2004; Connor & White, 2006; Hofferth & Casper, 2006; Roopnarine & others, 2005).

The typical father behaves differently toward an infant than the typical mother. Maternal interactions usually center on child-care activities—feeding, changing diapers, bathing. Paternal interactions are more likely to include play. Fathers engage in more rough-and-tumble play. They bounce infants, throw them up in the air, tickle them, and so on (Lamb, 1986, 2000). Mothers do play with infants, but their play is less physical and arousing than that of fathers.

In a recent study, fathers were interviewed about their caregiving responsibilities when their children were 6, 15, 24, and 36 months of age (NICHD Early Child Care Research Network, 2000). A subset was videotaped during father-child play at 6 and 36 months. Several factors predicted the fathers' caregiving activities (such as bathing, feeding, and dressing the child, and taking the child to day care) and their sensitivity during play interactions (such as being responsive to the child's signals and needs, and expressing positive feelings). Fathers were more involved in caregiving when they worked fewer hours and mothers worked more hours, when fathers and mothers were younger, when mothers reported greater marital intimacy, and when the children were boys. Fathers who had less-traditional child-rearing beliefs and reported more marital intimacy were more sensitive during play.

Might the nature of parent-infant interaction be different in families that adopt nontraditional gender roles? This question was investigated by Michael Lamb and his colleagues (1982). They studied Swedish families in which the fathers were the primary caregivers of their firstborn, 8-month-old infants. The mothers were working full-time. In all observations, the mothers were more likely to discipline, hold, soothe, kiss, and talk to the infants than were the fathers. These mothers and fathers dealt with their infants differently, along the lines of American fathers and mothers following traditional gender roles. Having fathers assume the primary caregiving role did not substantially alter the way they interacted with their infants. This may be for biological reasons or because of deeply ingrained socialization patterns in cultures.

How do most fathers and mothers interact differently with infants?

www.mhhe.com/santrockld11

Family Resources
Maternal Resources
The Fatherhood Project

Child Care

Many U.S. children today experience multiple caregivers. Most do not have a parent staying home to care for them; instead, the children have some type of care provided by others—"child care." Many parents worry that child care will reduce their infants' emotional attachment to them, retard the infants' cognitive development, fail to teach them how to control anger, and allow them to be unduly influenced by their peers. How extensive is child care? Are the worries of these parents justified?

Parental Leave Today far more young children are in child care than at any other time in history. About 2 million children in the United States currently receive formal, licensed child care, and uncounted millions of children are cared for by unlicensed baby-sitters. In part, these numbers reflect the fact that U.S. adults cannot receive paid leave from their jobs to care for their young children. However, as described in the Diversity in Life-Span Development interlude, many countries provide extensive parental leave policies.

DIVERSITY IN LIFE-SPAN DEVELOPMENT

Child-Care Policies Around the World

Sheila Kammerman (1989, 2000a, 2000b) has conducted extensive examinations of parental leave policies around the world. Policies vary in eligibility criteria, leave duration, benefit level, and the extent to which parents take advantage of these policies. Europe led the way in creating new standards of parental leave: The European Union (EU) mandated a paid 14-week maternity leave in 1992. Among advanced industrialized countries, the United States grants the shortest period of parental leave and is among the few countries that offers only unpaid leave (Australia and New Zealand are the others).

There are five types of parental leave from employment:

- *Maternity Leave.* In some countries the prebirth leave is compulsory as is a 6- to 10-week leave following birth.

- *Paternity Leave.* This is usually much briefer than maternity leave. It may be especially important when a second child is born and the first child requires care.

- *Parental Leave.* This gender-neutral leave usually follows a maternity leave and allows either women or men to share the leave policy or choose which of them will use it. In 1998, the European Union mandated a three-month parental leave.

- *Child-Rearing Leave.* In some countries, this is a supplement to a maternity leave or a variation on a parental leave. A child-rearing leave is usually longer than a maternity leave and is typically paid at a much lower level.

- *Family Leave.* This covers reasons other than the birth of a new baby and can allow time off from employment to care for an ill child or other family members, time to accompany a child to school for the first time, or time to visit a child's school.

How are child-care policies in many European countries, such as Sweden, different than those in the United States?

Sweden has one of the most extensive leave policies. Paid for by the government at 80 percent of wages, one year of parental leave is allowed (including maternity leave). Maternity leave may begin 60 days prior to the expected birth and ends six weeks after birth. Another six months of parental leave can be used until the child's eighth birthday (Kammerman, 2000a). Virtually all eligible mothers take advantage of the leave policy, and approximately 75 percent of eligible fathers take at least some part of their allowed leave. In addition, employed grandparents now have the right to take time off to care for an ill grandchild.

Variations in Child Care   Because the United States does not have a policy of paid leave for child care, child care in the United States has become a major national concern (Lamb & Ahnert, 2006; Randolph & Kochanoff, 2004; Vandell, 2004). Many factors influence the effects of child care, including the age of the child, the type of child care, and the quality of the program.

When a child's mother works in the first year of life, it can have a negative effect on the child's later development (Belsky & Eggebeen, 1991; Hill & others, 2001). For example, a major longitudinal study found that the 3-year-old children of mothers who went to work before the children were 9 months old had poorer cognitive outcomes than 3-year-old children whose mothers had stayed at home with them in the first nine months of the child's life (Brooks-Gunn, Han, & Waldfogel, 2002). The negative effects of going to work during the child's first nine months were less pronounced when the mothers worked less than 30 hours a week, when the mothers were more responsive and comforting in their caregiving, and when the child care the infants received outside the home was higher in quality.

The type of child care varies extensively (Lamb & Ahnert, 2006; Scarr, 2000). Child care is provided in large centers with elaborate facilities and in private homes. Some child-care centers are commercial operations; others are nonprofit centers run by churches, civic groups, and employers. Some child-care providers are professionals; others are mothers who want to earn extra money.

Use of different types of child care varies by ethnicity (Johnson & others, 2003). For example, Latino families are far less likely than non-Latino White and African American families to have children in child-care centers: 11 percent, 20 percent, and 21 percent, respectively in one recent study (Smith, 2002). Despite indicating a preference for center-based care, African American and Latino families often rely on family-based care, especially by grandmothers. However, there has been a substantial increase in the use of center-based care by African American mothers.

The type of child care makes a difference. Researchers have found that children show more stress when they spend long hours in center-based care than in other types of care (Sagi & others, 2002). Further, children who have a fearful or easily frustrated temperament style are often the most negatively influenced by spending long hours in center-based care (Burrows, Crockenberg, & Leerkes, 2005).

Quality also makes a difference. What constitutes a high-quality child-care program for infants? The demonstration program developed by Jerome Kagan and his colleagues (Kagan, Kearsley, & Zelazo, 1978) at Harvard University is exemplary. The child-care center included a pediatrician, a nonteaching director, and an infant-teacher ratio of 3 to 1. Teachers' aides assisted at the center. The teachers and aides were trained to smile frequently, to talk with the infants, and to provide them with a safe environment, which included many stimulating toys. No adverse effects of child care were observed in this project.

Children are more likely to experience poor-quality child care if they come from families with few resources (psychological, social, and economic) (Lamb, 1994). Many researchers have examined the role of poverty in quality of child

CAREERS in LIFE-SPAN DEVELOPMENT

Rashmi Nakhre
Day-Care Director

Rashmi Nakhre has two master's degrees—one in psychology, the other in child development—and is director of the Hattie Daniels Day Care Center in Wilson, North Carolina. Rashmi received the Distinguished Woman of North Carolina Award for 1999–2000.

Rashmi first worked at the day-care center soon after she arrived in the United States 25 years ago. She says that she took the job initially because she needed the money but "ended up falling in love with my job." Rashmi has turned the Wilson, North Carolina, day-care center into a model for other centers. The center almost closed several years after she began working there because of financial difficulties. Rashmi played a major role in raising funds not only to keep it open but to improve it. The center provides quality day care for the children of many Latino migrant workers.

Rashmi Nakhre, day-care director, working with some of the children at her center.

care (Burchinal, 2006; Cabrera, Hutchens, & Peters, 2006; Giannarelli, Sonenstein, & Stagner, 2006; Phillips, 2006). A recent study found that extensive child care was harmful to low-income children only when the care was of low quality (Votruba-Drzal & others, 2004). Even if the child was in child care more than 45 hours a week, high-quality care was linked with fewer internalizing problems (anxiety, for example) and externalizing problems (aggressive and destructive behaviors, for example).

To read about one individual who provides quality child care to individuals from impoverished backgrounds, see the Careers in Life-Span Development profile. In the Research in Child Development interlude below, you can read about an ongoing national study of child care and its effects.

RESEARCH IN LIFE-SPAN DEVELOPMENT

A National Longitudinal Study of Child Care

In 1991, the National Institute of Child Health and Human Development (NICHD) began a comprehensive, longitudinal study of child-care experiences. Data were collected on a diverse sample of almost 1,400 children and their families at 10 locations across the United States over a period of seven years. Researchers used multiple methods (trained observers, interviews, questionnaires, and testing) and they measured many facets of children's development, including physical health, cognitive development, and socioemotional development. Following are some of the results (NICHD Early Child Care Network, 2001, 2002, 2003, 2004, 2005, 2006).

- *Patterns of Use.* Many families placed their infants in child care very soon after the child's birth, and there was considerable instability in the child care arrangements. By 4 months of age, nearly three-fourths of the infants had entered some form of nonmaternal child care. Almost half of the infants were cared for by a relative when they first entered care; only 12 percent were enrolled in child care centers. Socioeconomic factors were linked to the amount and type of care. For example, mothers with higher incomes and families that were more dependent on the mother's income placed their infants in child care at an earlier age. Mothers who believed that maternal employment has positive effects on children were more likely than other mothers to place their infants in nonmaternal care for more hours. Low-income families were more likely than more affluent families to use child care, but infants from low-income families who were in child care averaged as many hours as other income groups. In the preschool years, mothers who were single, those with more education, and families with higher incomes used more hours of center care than other families. Minority families and mothers with less education used more hours of care by relatives.

- *Quality of Care.* Evaluations of quality of care were based on such characteristics as group size, child–adult ratio, physical environment, caregiver characteristics (such as formal education, specialized training, and child care experience), and caregiver behavior (such as sensitivity to children). An alarming conclusion is that a majority of the child care in the first three years of life was of unacceptable low quality. Positive caregiving by nonparents in child care settings was infrequent—only 12 percent of the children studied experienced positive nonparental child care (such as positive talk, lack of detachment and flat affect, and language stimulation). Further, infants from low-income families experienced lower quality of child care than infants from higher-income families. When quality of caregivers' care was high, children performed better on cognitive and language tasks, were more cooperative with their mothers during play, showed more positive and skilled interaction with peers, and had fewer behavior problems. Caregiver training and good child–staff ratios were linked with higher cognitive and social competence when children were 54 months of age.

    Higher-quality child care was also related to higher-quality mother-child interaction among the families that used nonmaternal care. Further, poor-quality care was related to an increase of insecure attachment to the mother among infants who were 15 months of age, but only when the mother was low in sensitivity and responsiveness. However, child-care quality was not linked to attachment security at 36 months of age.

- *Amount of child care.* The quantity of child care predicted some child outcomes. When children spent extensive amounts of time in child care beginning in infancy, they experienced less sensitive interactions with their mother, showed more behavior problems, and had higher rates of illness (Vandell, 2004). Many of these comparisons involved children in child care for less

What are some important findings from the National Longitudinal Study of Child Care conducted by the National Institute of Child Health and Human Development?

than 30 hours a week versus those in child care for more than 45 hours a week. In general, though, when children spent 30 hours or more per week in child care, their development was less than optimal (Ramey, 2005).

- *Family and Parenting Influences.* The influence of families and parenting was not weakened by extensive child care. Parents played a significant role in helping children to regulate their emotions. Especially important parenting influences were being sensitive to children's needs, being involved with children, and cognitive stimulating them.

What are some strategies parents can follow in regard to child care? Child-care expert Kathleen McCartney (2003, p. 4) offered this advice:

- *Recognize that the quality of your parenting is a key factor in your child's development.*
- *Make decisions that will improve the likelihood you will be good parents.* "For some this will mean working full-time"—for personal fulfillment, income, or both. "For others, this will mean working part-time or not working outside the home."
- *Monitor your child's development.* "Parents should observe for themselves whether their children seem to be having behavior problems." They need to talk with child-care providers and pediatrician about their child's behavior.
- *Take some time to find the best child care.* Observe different child-care facilities and be certain that you like what you see. "Quality child care costs money, and not all parents can afford the child care they want. However, state subsidies, and other programs like Head Start, are available for families in need."

Review and Reflect ● LEARNING GOAL 3

(3) Explain how social contexts influence the infant's development

Review
- What are some important family processes in infant development?
- How does child care influence infant development?

Reflect
- Imagine that a friend of yours is getting ready to put her baby in child care. What advice would you give to her? Do you think she should stay home with the baby? Why or why not? What type of child care would you recommend?

REACH YOUR LEARNING GOALS

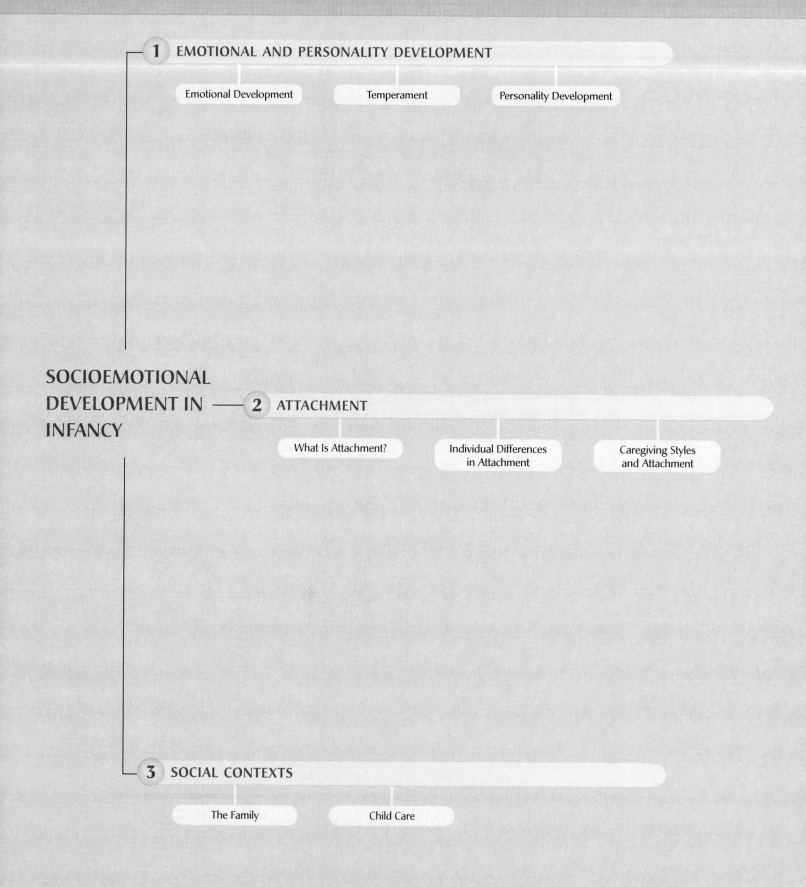

1 EMOTIONAL AND PERSONALITY DEVELOPMENT

Emotional Development

Temperament

Personality Development

SOCIOEMOTIONAL DEVELOPMENT IN INFANCY

2 ATTACHMENT

What Is Attachment?

Individual Differences in Attachment

Caregiving Styles and Attachment

3 SOCIAL CONTEXTS

The Family

Child Care

SUMMARY

1 Emotional and Personality Development: *Discuss emotional and personality development in infancy*

Emotional Development

Emotion is feeling, or affect, that occurs when a person is in a state or an interaction that is important to them. Emotion is characterized by behavior that reflects (expresses) the pleasantness or unpleasantness of the person's state or the transaction being experienced. Psychologists consider that emotions, especially facial expressions of emotions, have a biological foundation. Biological evolution endowed humans to be emotional, but embeddedness in culture and relationships provides diversity in emotional experiences. Emotions play key roles in parent-child relationships. Infants display a number of emotions early in their development, although researchers debate the onset and sequence of these emotions. Crying is the most important mechanism newborns have for communicating with their world. Babies have at least three types of cries—basic, anger, and pain cries. Controversy swirls about whether babies should be soothed when they cry, although increasingly experts recommend immediately responding in a caring way in the first year. Social smiling in response to a caregiver's voice occurs as early as four weeks of age. Two fears that infants develop are stranger anxiety and separation from a caregiver (which is reflected in separation anxiety). Social referencing increases in the second year of life. As infants develop, it is important for them to engage in emotional regulation.

Temperament

Temperament is an individual's behavioral style and characteristic way of emotional responding. Chess and Thomas classified infants as (1) easy, (2) difficult, or (3) slow to warm up. Kagan proposed that inhibition to the unfamiliar is an important temperament category. Rothbart and Bates' view of temperament emphasizes this classification: (1) positive affect and approach, (2) negative affectivity, and (3) effortful control (self-regulation). Physiological characteristics are associated with different temperaments. Children inherit a physiology that biases them to have a particular type of temperament, but through experience they learn to modify their temperament style to some degree. Goodness of fit refers to the match between a child's temperament and the environmental demands the child must cope with. Goodness of fit can be an important aspect of a child's adjustment. Although research evidence is sketchy at this point in time, some general recommendations are that caregivers should (1) be sensitive to the individual characteristics of the child, (2) be flexible in responding to these characteristics, and (3) avoid negative labeling of the child.

Personality Development

Erikson argued that an infant's first year is characterized by the stage of trust versus mistrust. A rudimentary form of self-recognition occurs as early as 3 months of age, but the infant develops a more complete, central form of self-recognition at about 18 months of age. Independence becomes a central theme in the second year of life. Mahler argues that the infant separates herself from her mother and then develops individuation. Erikson stressed that the second year of life is characterized by the stage of autonomy versus shame and doubt.

2 Attachment: *Describe how attachment develops in infancy*

What Is Attachment?

Attachment is a close emotional bond between two people. In infancy, contact comfort and trust are important in the development of attachment. Bowlby's ethological theory stresses that the caregiver and the infant are biologically predisposed to form an attachment. Attachment develops in four phases during infancy.

Individual Differences in Attachment

Securely attached babies use the caregiver, usually the mother, as a secure base from which to explore the environment. Three types of insecure attachment are avoidant, resistant, and disorganized. Ainsworth created the Strange Situation, an observational measure of attachment. Ainsworth believes that secure attachment in the first year of life provides an important foundation for psychological development later in life. The strength of the link between early attachment and later development has varied somewhat across studies. Some critics argue that attachment theorists have not given adequate attention to genetics and temperament. Other critics stress that they have not adequately taken into account the diversity of social agents and contexts. Cultural variations in attachment have been found, but in all cultures studied to date secure attachment is the most common classification.

Caregiving Styles and Attachment

Caregivers of secure babies are sensitive to the babies' signals and are consistently available to meet their needs. Caregivers of avoidant babies tend to be unavailable or rejecting. Caregivers of ambivalent-rejecting babies tend to be inconsistently available to their babies and usually are not very affectionate. Caregivers of disorganized babies often neglect or physically abuse their babies.

3 Social Contexts: *Explain how social contexts influence the infant's development*

The Family

The transition to parenthood requires considerable adaptation and adjustment on the part of parents. Children socialize parents just as parents socialize children. Mutual regulation and scaffolding are important aspects of reciprocal socialization. Belsky's model describes direct and indirect effects. The mother's primary role when interacting with the infant is caregiving; the father's is playful interaction.

Child Care

More U.S. children are in child care now than at any earlier point in history. The quality of child care is uneven, and day care remains a controversial topic. Quality child care can be achieved and seems to have few adverse effects on children. In the NICHD child-care study, infants from low-income families were more likely to receive the lowest quality of care. Also, higher quality of child care was linked with fewer child problems.

KEY TERMS

emotion 209
basic cry 211
anger cry 211
pain cry 211
reflexive smile 211
social smile 211

stranger anxiety 211
separation protest 212
social referencing 212
temperament 213
easy child 214
difficult child 214

slow-to-warm-up child 214
goodness of fit 215
attachment 219
Strange Situation 220
securely attached babies 220

insecure avoidant babies 220
insecure resistant babies 220
insecure disorganized
   babies 221
reciprocal socialization 224

KEY PEOPLE

John Watson 213
Jacob Gewirtz 213
Mary Ainsworth 213
John Bowlby 213
Alexander Chess and Stella
   Thomas 214

Jerome Kagan 214
Mary Rothbart and
   John Bates 214
Erik Erikson 217
Margaret Mahler 218
Harry Harlow 219

Alan Sroufe 221
Jay Belsky 223
Sheila Kammerman 226
Kathleen McCartney 230

E-LEARNING TOOLS

To help you master the material in this chapter, you'll find a number of valuable study tools on the LifeMap CD-ROM that accompanies this book and on the Online Learning Center for *Life-Span Development*, eleventh edition, at **www.mhhe.com/ santrockld11**.

Video Clips

In the margins of this book there are icons directing you to the LifeMap CD-ROM that accompanies the book. There you'll find two videos for chapter 7. The first video is called "Attachment Theory." This segment reviews the three main theories of infant attachment. In an interview, one researcher argues that attachment theory led to a revolution in developmental psychology. The second video is called "Quality Child Care Indicators." More children are placed in child care today than at any other time in history. This segment addresses some of the common anxieties about possible long-term effects of formal child care.

Self-Assessment

Connect to **www.mhhe.com/santrockld11** to examine your understanding of infant emotions and socialization by completing the self-assessment, *My Beliefs About Nurturing a Baby's Socioemotional Development.*

Taking It to the Net

Connect to **www.mhhe.com/santrockld11** to research the answers to these questions.
1. Catherine is conducting a class for new parents at a local clinic. What advice should Catherine give the parents about how parenting practices can affect a child's inborn temperament?
2. Justin read about a new concept known as "attachment parenting." What is it, and how can parents engage in it? Do you think it is a good idea? What specifically can parents do to help ensure that their children develop secure attachment?

Health and Well-Being, Parenting, and Education Exercises

Build your decision-making skills by trying your hand at the health and well-being, parenting, and education exercises.

Connect to **www.mhhe.com/santrockld11** to research the answers and complete the exercises.

The greatest person ever known Is one all poets have outgrown;
The poetry, innate and untold, Of being only four years old.

—CHRISTOPHER MORLEY
American Novelist, 20th Century

CHAPTER OUTLINE

LEARNING GOALS

PHYSICAL CHANGES

1 Identify physical changes in early childhood

Body Growth and Change

Motor Development

Nutrition

Illness and Death

COGNITIVE CHANGES

2 Describe three views of the cognitive changes that occur in early childhood

Piaget's Preoperational Stage

Vygotsky's Theory

Information Processing

LANGUAGE DEVELOPMENT

3 Summarize how language develops in early childhood

Understanding Phonology and Morphology

Changes in Syntax and Semantics

Advances in Pragmatics

Young Children's Literacy

EARLY CHILDHOOD EDUCATION

4 Evaluate different approaches to early childhood education

Variations in Early Childhood Education

Education for Children Who Are Disadvantaged

Controversies in Early Childhood Education

Images of Life-Span Development
Reggio Emilia's Children

A Reggio Emilia classroom in which young children explore topics that interest them.

The Reggio Emilia approach is an educational program for young children that was developed in the northern Italian city of Reggio Emilia. Children of single parents and children with disabilities have priority in admission; other children are admitted according to a scale of needs. Parents pay on a sliding scale based on income.

The children are encouraged to learn by investigating and exploring topics that interest them. A wide range of stimulating media and materials is available for children to use as they learn music, movement, drawing, painting, sculpting, collages, puppets and disguises, and photography, for example.

In this program, children often explore topics in a group, which fosters a sense of community, respect for diversity, and a collaborative approach to problem solving (Hyson, Copple, & Jones, 2006). Two co-teachers are present to serve as guides for children (Edwards, 2002). The Reggio Emilia teachers consider a project as an adventure, which can start from an adult's suggestion, from a child's idea, or from an event, such as a snowfall or something else unexpected. Every project is based on what the children say and do. The teachers allow children enough time to think and craft a project.

At the core of the Reggio Emilia approach is the image of children who are competent and have rights, especially the right to outstanding care and education. Parent participation is considered essential, and cooperation is a major theme in the schools. Many early childhood education experts believe the Reggio Emilia approach provides a supportive, stimulating context in which children are motivated to explore their world in a competent and confident manner (Firlik, 1996; New, 2005; Stegelin, 2003).

PREVIEW

Parents and educators who clearly understand how young children develop can play an active role in creating programs that foster their natural interest in learning, rather than stifling it. In this chapter we will explore the physical, cognitive, and language changes that typically occur as the toddler develops into the preschooler and then examine different approaches to early childhood education.

1 PHYSICAL CHANGES

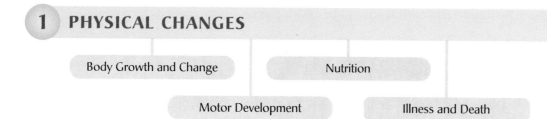

Body Growth and Change

Nutrition

Motor Development

Illness and Death

Remember from chapter 5 that an infant's growth in the first year is rapid and follows cephalocaudal and proximodistal patterns. Around their first birthday, most infants begin to walk. During an infant's second year, the growth rate begins to slow down, but both gross and fine motor skills progress rapidly. The infant develops a sense of mastery through increased proficiency in walking and running. Improvement in fine motor skills—such as being able to turn the pages of a book one at a time—also contributes to the infant's sense of mastery in the second year. The growth rate continues to slow down in early childhood. Otherwise, we would be a species of giants.

Body Growth and Change

Growth in height and weight is the obvious physical change that characterizes early childhood. Unseen changes in the brain and nervous system are no less significant in preparing children for advances in cognition and language.

Height and Weight   The average child grows $2\frac{1}{2}$ inches in height and gains between 5 and 7 pounds a year during early childhood. As the preschool child grows older, the percentage of increase in height and weight decreases with each additional year. Girls are only slightly smaller and lighter than boys during these years, a difference that continues until puberty. During the preschool years, both boys and girls slim down as the trunks of their bodies lengthen. Although their heads are still somewhat large for their bodies, by the end of the preschool years most children have lost their top-heavy look. Body fat also shows a slow, steady decline during the preschool years. The chubby baby often looks much leaner by the end of early childhood. Girls have more fatty tissue than boys; boys have more muscle tissue.

Growth patterns vary individually. Think back to your preschool years. This was probably the first time you noticed that some children were taller than you, some shorter; some were fatter, some thinner; some were stronger, some weaker. Much of the variation was due to heredity, but environmental experiences were also involved. A review of the height and weight of children around the world concluded that the two most important contributors to height differences are ethnic origin and nutrition (Meredith, 1978). The urban, middle-socioeconomic-status, and firstborn children were taller than rural, lower-socioeconomic-status, and later-born children. In the United States, African American children are taller than White children.

Why are some children unusually short? The culprits are

The bodies of 5-year-olds and 2-year-olds are different. Notice that the 5-year-old not only is taller and weighs more, but also has a longer trunk and legs than the 2-year-old. *Can you think of some other physical differences between 2- and 5-year-olds?*

Preschool Growth and Development

- *Congenital factors,* which are genetic or prenatal problems. For example, preschool children whose mothers smoked regularly during pregnancy are half an inch shorter than their counterparts whose mothers did not smoke.
- *A physical problem or an emotional difficulty* that develops in childhood. Children who are chronically sick are shorter than their counterparts who are rarely sick. Children who have been physically abused or neglected may not secrete adequate growth hormone.
- *Growth hormone deficiency,* which is the absence or deficiency of growth hormone produced by the pituitary gland to stimulate the body to grow. Growth hormone deficiency may occur during infancy or later in childhood (Awan, Sattar, & Khattak, 2005; Chernausek, 2004; Mehta & others, 2005).

It is estimated that as many as 10,000 to 15,000 U.S. children have growth hormone deficiency (Stanford University Medical Center, 2006). Without treatment, most children with growth hormone deficiency will not reach a height of 5 feet. Treatment involves regular injections of growth hormone and usually lasts several years (Minczykowski & others, 2005; Rosilio & others, 2005; Sheppard & others, 2006). Some children receive daily injections, others several times a week.

The Brain   One of the most important physical developments during early childhood is the continuing development of the brain and other parts of the nervous system (Nelson, Thomas, & de Haan, 2006). The increasing maturation of the brain, combined with opportunities to experience a widening world, contribute to children's emerging cognitive abilities (Cornish, 2004). In particular, changes in the brain during early childhood enable children to plan their actions, attend to stimuli more effectively, and make considerable strides in language development.

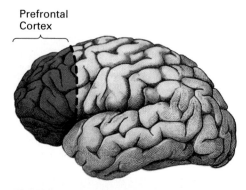

Prefrontal Cortex

FIGURE 8.1 The Prefrontal Cortex. This evolutionarily advanced portion (shaded in purple) of the brain shows extensive development from 3 to 6 years of age and is believed to play important roles in attention and working memory.

Although the brain does not grow as rapidly during early childhood as in infancy, it does undergo dramatic anatomical changes (Thompson & others, 2000). By repeatedly obtaining brain scans of the same children for up to 4 years, researchers have found that children's brains experience rapid, distinct spurts of growth. The overall size of the brain does not increase dramatically from ages 3 to 15; what does dramatically change are local patterns within the brain. The amount of brain material in some areas can nearly double in as little as a year, followed by a drastic loss of tissue as unneeded cells are purged and the brain continues to reorganize itself.

From 3 to 6 years of age the most rapid growth in the brain takes place in part of the frontal lobe involved in planning and organizing new actions and in maintaining attention to tasks (Blumenthal & others, 1999). This part of the frontal lobe is known as the *prefrontal cortex* (see figure 8.1).

The continuation of two changes discussed in chapter 5 contributes to the increase in the brain's size during early childhood. First, the number and size of dendrites increase and second, myelination continues. Recall from chapter 5 that **myelination** is the process in which axons are covered with a layer of fat cells, which increases the speed of information traveling through the nervous system (Meier & others, 2004).

Some developmentalists have linked myelination to the maturation of a number of children's abilities (Nagy, Westerberg, & Klingberg, 2004). For example, myelination in the areas of the brain related to hand-eye coordination is not complete until about 4 years of age. One recent brain imaging study of children with mean age of 4 years found that those who reached motor and cognitive milestones later than average also had significantly reduced levels of myelination (Pujol & others, 2004). Myelination in the areas of the brain related to focusing attention is not complete until the end of middle or late childhood.

Scientists are beginning to chart connections between children's cognitive development and changes in brain structures, *neural circuits* (groups of neurons that communicate with each other), working together to carry out particular functions, and the transmission of information between neurons. For example, the concentration of dopamine in the brain increases considerably from 3 to 6 years of age (Diamond, 2001). Dopamine is a neurotransmitter, or chemical messenger, that is used in a neural circuit that has an important function in attention and working memory (a type of memory that is like a mental workbench, holding information while we perform a cognitive task) (Krimer & Goldman-Rakic, 2001). This neural circuit is located in the prefrontal cortex (Casey, Durston, & Fossella, 2001), the part of the brain that is growing most rapidly between the ages of 3 and 6. The maturation of the prefrontal cortex is important in the development not only of attention but also of memory, math skills, and emotional self-regulation (Espy & others, 2004; Eslinger, Flaherty-Craig, & Benton 2004; Levesque & others, 2004; Tsujimoto & others, 2004). As advances in technology allow scientists to "look inside" the brain and observe its activity, we will likely understand more precisely how the brain functions in cognitive development.

Motor Development

Running as fast as you can, falling down, getting right back up and running just as fast as you can . . . building towers with blocks . . . scribbling, scribbling, and scribbling some more . . . cutting paper with scissors . . . During your preschool years, you probably developed the ability to perform all of these activities.

myelination The process by which the nerve cells are covered and insulated with a layer of fat cells, which increases the speed at which information travels through the nervous system.

Gross Motor Skills The preschool child no longer has to make an effort simply to stay upright and to move around. As children move their legs with more confidence and carry themselves more purposefully, moving around in the environment becomes more automatic (Edwards & Sarwark, 2005; Gallahue & Ozmun, 2006).

At 3 years of age, children enjoy simple movements, such as hopping, jumping, and running back and forth, just for the sheer delight of performing these activities. They take considerable pride in showing how they can run across a room and jump all of 6 inches. The run-and-jump will win no Olympic gold medals, but for the 3-year-old the activity is a source of considerable pride and accomplishment.

At 4 years of age, children are still enjoying the same kind of activities, but they have become more adventurous. They scramble over low jungle gyms as they display their athletic prowess. Although they have been able to climb stairs with one foot on each step for some time, they are just beginning to be able to come down the same way.

At 5 years of age, children are even more adventuresome than when they were 4. It is not unusual for self-assured 5-year-olds to perform hair-raising stunts on practically any climbing object. Five-year-olds run hard and enjoy races with each other and their parents. A summary of development in gross motor skills during early childhood is shown in figure 8.2.

Fine Motor Skills   At 3 years of age, children have the ability to pick up the tiniest objects between their thumb and forefinger for some time, but they are still somewhat clumsy at it. Three-year-olds can build surprisingly high block towers, each block placed with intense concentration but often not in a completely straight line. When 3-year-olds play with a simple jigsaw puzzle, they are rather rough in placing the pieces. Even when they recognize the hole a piece fits into, they are not very precise in positioning the piece. They often try to force the piece in the hole or pat it vigorously.

By 4 years of age, children's fine motor coordination has improved substantially and become much more precise. Sometimes 4-year-old children have trouble building high towers with blocks because, in their desire to place each of the blocks perfectly, they may upset those already stacked. By age 5, children's fine motor coordination has improved further. Hand, arm, and body all move together under better command of the eye. Mere towers no longer interest the 5-year-old, who now wants to build a house or a church, complete with steeple, though adults might still need to be told what each finished project is meant to be. A summary of the development of fine motor skills in early childhood is shown in figure 8.3.

Handedness   As children become able to throw balls and draw pictures, adults are likely to become aware of whether the child is right- or left-handed. For centuries, left-handers have suffered unfair discrimination in a world designed for

How do gross motor skills change in early childhood?

37 to 48 Months	49 to 60 Months	61 to 72 Months
Throws ball underhanded (4 feet)	Bounces and catches ball	Throws ball (44 feet, boys; 25 feet, girls)
Pedals tricycle 10 feet	Runs 10 feet and stops	Carries a 16-pound object
Catches large ball	Pushes/pulls a wagon/doll buggy	Kicks rolling ball
Completes forward somersault (aided)	Kicks 10-inch ball toward target	Skips alternating feet
Jumps to floor from 12 inches	Carries 12-pound object	Roller skates
Hops three hops with both feet	Catches ball	Skips rope
Steps on footprint pattern	Bounces ball under control	Rolls ball to hit object
Catches bounced ball	Hops on one foot four hops	Rides bike with training wheels

FIGURE 8.2 The Development of Gross Motor Skills in Early Childhood. The skills are listed in the approximate order of difficulty within each age period.

37 to 48 Months	49 to 60 Months	61 to 72 Months
Approximates a circle in drawing	Strings and laces shoelace	Folds paper into halves and quarters
Cuts paper	Cuts following a line	Traces around hand
Pastes using pointer finger	Strings 10 beads	Draws rectangle, circle, square, and triangle
Builds three-block bridge	Copies figure X	Cuts interior piece from paper
Builds eight-block tower	Opens and places clothespins (one-handed)	Uses crayons appropriately
Draws 0 and +	Builds a five-block bridge	Makes clay object with two small parts
Dresses and undresses doll	Pours from various containers	Reproduces letters
Pours from pitcher without spilling	Prints first name	Copies two short words

FIGURE 8.3 **The Development of Fine Motor Skills in Early Childhood.** The skills are listed in the approximate order of difficulty within each age period.

right-handers. For many years, teachers forced all children to write with their right hand, even if they had a left-hand tendency. Fortunately, today most teachers let children write with the hand they favor (Wenze & Wenze, 2004). However, in some cultures, such as the Republic of Malawi in Southern Africa, adults still strongly encourage all children to use their right hand rather than their left hand (Zverev, 2006).

Origin and Development of Handedness   What is the origin of hand preference? Genetic inheritance seems to be a strong influence. In one study, the handedness of adopted children was not related to the handedness of their adopted parents, but it was related to the handedness of their biological parents (Carter-Saltzman, 1980).

Right-handedness is dominant in all cultures (it appears in a ratio of about nine right-handers to one left-hander) and it appears before the impact of culture. For example, in one study, ultrasound observations of fetal thumb sucking showed that 9 of 10 fetuses were more likely to be sucking their right hand's thumb (Hepper, Shahidullah, & White, 1990). Newborns also show a preference for one side of their body over the other. In one study, 65 percent of the infants turned their head to the right when they were lying on their back in a crib (Michel, 1981). Fifteen percent preferred to face toward the left and the remaining 20 percent showed no preference. These preferences for the right or the left were linked with handedness later in development.

Handedness, the Brain, and Cognitive Abilities   Approximately 95 percent of right-handed individuals primarily process speech in the brain's left hemisphere (Springer & Deutsch, 1985). However, left-handed individuals show more variation. More than half of left-handers process speech in their left hemisphere, just like right-handers. However, about one-fourth of left-handers process speech equally in both hemispheres (Knecht & others, 2000).

Are there differences in the abilities of left- and right-handers? Regarding language development, the most consistent finding is that left-handers are more likely to have reading problems (Natsopoulos & others, 1998). Left-handers also tend to have unusually good visual-spatial skills and the ability to imagine spatial layouts (Holtzen, 2000). Left-handedness is more common than expected among mathematicians, musicians, architects, and artists (Michelangelo, Leonardo da Vinci, and Picasso were all left-handed) (Schachter & Ransil, 1996). Also, in one study of more than 100,000 students taking the Scholastic Aptitude Test (SAT), 20 percent of the top-scoring group was left-handed, twice the rate of left-handedness found in the general population (10 percent) (Bower, 1985).

Today, most teachers let children write with the hand they favor. *What are the main reasons children become left- or right-handed?*

Nutrition

Eating habits are important aspects of development during early childhood (Gidding & others, 2006; Kwai & others, 2006). What children eat affects their skeletal growth, body shape, and susceptibility to disease.

An average preschool child requires 1,700 calories per day, but energy needs of individual children of the same age, sex, and size vary. Their requirements depend in part on their physical activity, the efficiency with which they use energy, and their **basal metabolism rate (BMR),** which is the minimum amount of energy a person uses in a resting state.

Overeating   Being overweight can be a serious problem in early childhood (Dietz & Robinson, 2005; Mason & others, 2006). The percentage of obese children in the United States has increased dramatically in recent decades, and the percentage is likely to grow unless changes occur in children's lifestyles (Eckstein & others, 2006; Lindsay & others, 2006; Paxson & others, 2006). For example, the popularity of picking up fast-food meals raises the fat levels in children's diets. Many fast-food meals have fat content that is too high for good health (Sizer & Whitney, 2006; Wardlaw, 2006). How much fat should be included in the diet of preschool children? The American Heart Association recommends that the daily limit for calories from fat should be approximately 35 percent.

Childhood obesity contributes to a number of problems. For example, physicians are now seeing Type II (adult-onset) diabetes, a condition directly linked with obesity and a low level of fitness, in children as young as 5 years of age (Berry, Urban, & Grey, 2006; Daniels, 2006). Also, as early as 5 years of age, being overweight is linked with lower self-esteem (Davison & Birth, 2001).

To prevent obesity in children, parents and children should learn to view food as a way to satisfy hunger and nutritional needs, not as proof of love or as a reward for good behavior (Borra & others, 2003; Golan & Crow, 2004). Snack foods should be low in fat, simple sugars, and salt, as well as high in fiber. Routine physical activity should be a daily occurrence (Atlantis, Barnes, & Singh, 2006; Fox, 2004). The child's life should be centered around activities, not meals and television (Robinson, 2006; Salmon, Campbell, & Crawford, 2006).

The Hip-Hop to Health Jr is a family-oriented program for African American and Latino children attending Head Start programs in Chicago that is designed to reduce overweight and obesity (Fitzgibbon & others, 2002, 2005; Stolley & others 2003). The program targets African American and Latino children because they have higher rates of obesity than non-Latino White children. Weight problems are especially acute for African American and Latino young girls with 11 percent of African American and 13 percent of Latino 4- to 5-year-old girls being overweight, compared to only 3 percent of non-Latino White girls (Ogden & others, 1997).

The Hip-Hop to Health Jr program consists of a 45-minute class three times a week for 14 weeks that focuses on hands-on, fun activities that promote healthy eating as well as a 20-minute aerobic activity each class. The parent component of the program consists of a weekly newsletter, homework assignments, and participation in an aerobics class twice a week. In a recent two-year follow-up of the Hip-Hop to Health Jr program, children who were randomly assigned to the program had a smaller increase in body mass index compared to children who did not participate in the program (Fitzgibbon & others, 2005).

Malnutrition   One of the most common nutritional problems in early childhood is iron deficiency anemia, which results in chronic fatigue (Carley, 2003). This problem results from the failure to eat adequate amounts of quality meats and dark green vegetables. Young children from low-income families are most likely to develop iron deficiency anemia (Majumdar & others, 2003).

www.mhhe.com/santrockld11

Exploring Childhood Obesity
Helping an Overweight Child
Preschoolers' Health
Child Health Guide

basal metabolism rate (BMR) The minimum amount of energy a person uses in a resting state.

Poor nutrition affects many young children from low-income families (Drewnowski & Spector, 2004; Gosh & Shah, 2004; Richter, 2003). Many of these children do not get essential amounts of iron, vitamins, or protein. In the United States, the Special Supplemental Nutrition Program for Women, Infants, and Children (WIC), which serves approximately 7,500,000 participants, has positive influences on young children's nutrition and health (Black & others, 2004). For example, one recent study found that participating in the WIC program was linked with a lower risk for being overweight in young Mexican American children (Melgar-Quinonez & Kaiser, 2004). In another study, participation in the WIC program was related to improved nutrition in preschool children, including higher intake of fruit and lower intake of sugar from snacks (Siega-Riz & others, 2004).

Some researchers argue that malnutrition is directly linked to cognitive deficits because of negative effects on brain development (Liu & others, 2003). However, an increasing number of researchers argue that the links between child undernutrition, physical growth, and cognitive development are more complex (Marcon, 2003). The context in which undernutrition occurs must be considered. Children who vary considerably from the norm in physical growth also differ on other biological and socioemotional factors that might influence cognitive development. For example, children who are underfed are also often less supervised, less stimulated, and less educated than children who are well nourished (Wachs, 1995). Poverty interacts with children's nutritional status to affect physical and cognitive development (Marcon, 2003).

Malnutrition may be linked to other aspects of development in addition to cognitive deficits. One longitudinal study found that U.S. children who were malnourished at three years of age showed more aggressive and hyperactive behavior at age eight, more externalizing problems at age eleven, and more excessive motor behavior at age seventeen (Liu & others, 2004).

Illness and Death

Each year, UNICEF (2006) reports the mortality rates for children under 5 in nations around the world. In 2004, 40 nations had a lower under-5 mortality rate than the United States, with Singapore having the lowest rate of all nations. The relatively high under-5 mortality rate of the United States compared with other developed nations is due to such factors as poverty and inadequate health care.

What are the leading causes of death in young children in the United States? What are the greatest risks to their health? How pervasive is death among young children around the world?

The United States   From 1950 to the present, there has been a dramatic decline in deaths of U.S. children under the age of 5 from birth immaturity, birth defects, accidents, cancer, homicide, and heart disease. Vaccines have nearly eradicated disabling bacterial meningitis and have become available to prevent measles, rubella, mumps, and chicken pox. Although the dangers of many contagious diseases for children have greatly diminished, it still is important for parents to keep young children on an immunization schedule to prevent a resurgence of these diseases.

In the United States, motor vehicle accidents are the leading cause of death in young children, followed by cancer and cardiovascular disease (National Vital Statistics Reports, 2004) (see figure 8.4). In addition to motor vehicle accidents, other accidental deaths in children involve drowning, falls, and poisoning (Chen & others, 2005; Coyne-Beasley & others, 2005; Schnake, Peterson, & Corden, 2005).

Children's safety is influenced not only by their own skills and safety behaviors but also by characteristics of their family and home, school and peers, and the community's actions (Langlois, Rutland-Brown, & Thomas, 2005; Sherker & others, 2005; Sutterly & Frost, 2006; Tinsley, 2003). Figure 8.5 describes steps that can be

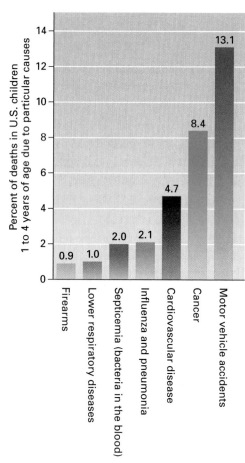

FIGURE 8.4 Main Causes of Death in Children 1 through 4 Years of Age. These figures show the percentage of deaths in U.S. children 1 to 4 years of age due to particular causes in 2002 (National Vital Statistics Reports, 2004).

taken in each of these contexts to enhance children's safety and prevent injury (Sleet & Mercy, 2003).

One characteristic of the home that may threaten children's health is parental smoking. Approximately 22 percent of children and adolescents in the United States are exposed to tobacco smoke in the home. An increasing number of studies conclude that children are at risk for health problems when they live in homes in which a parent smokes (Arshad, 2005; Lloyd & Wise, 2004; Sheehan & Free, 2005). For example, children exposed to tobacco smoke in the home are more likely to develop wheezing symptoms and asthma than children in nonsmoking homes (Arshad, 2005; Murray & others, 2004). They may also have significantly lower levels of vitamin C in their blood than their counterparts in nonsmoking homes. In one recent study, the more parents smoked, the less vitamin C the children and adolescents had in their blood (Strauss, 2001). Children exposed to environmental smoke should be encouraged to eat foods rich in vitamin C or be given this vitamin as a supplement (Preston & others, 2003).

Another concern is the poor health status of many young children from low-income families in the United States (Howell, Pettit, & Kingsley, 2005; Ramey, Ramey, & Lanzi, 2006; Lumeng & others, 2006; Malat, Oh, & Hamilton, 2005). The families of many of these children do not have adequate medical insurance, and thus the children receive less adequate medical care compared with children living in higher socioeconomic conditions (Olson, Tang, & Newacheck, 2005). At the same time, children living in poverty face increased risks to their health, such as malnutrition. Approximately 11 million preschool children in the United States are malnourished, and many have lowered resistance to diseases, including minor ones, such as colds, and major ones, such as influenza.

In addition, children in poverty face a higher risk for lead poisoning than children living in higher-socioeconomic conditions. Lead can get into children's bloodstreams through food or water that is contaminated by lead, from putting lead-contaminated fingers in their mouths, or from inhaling dust from lead-based paint. The negative effects of lead in children's blood are lower intelligence and achievement and attention deficit hyperactivity disorder (Breysse & others, 2004; Canfield & others, 2003). An estimated 3 million children under 6 years of age are thought to be at risk for lead poisoning (Brittle & Zint, 2003; Moya, Bearer, & Etzel, 2004).

Young children's health is also affected by their ethnicity (Andrulis, 2005; Malat, Oh, & Hamilton, 2005; Schneider, Freeman, & McGarvey, 2005). One recent study found that even when socioeconomic status was controlled, Latino, African American, and Asian American children were less likely to have a regular source of health care or to have visited a health professional such as a doctor or dentist in the past year (Shi & Stevens, 2005). Another recent study revealed that children whose parents had limited English proficiency were three times more likely to have fair or poor health status than their counterparts whose parents were proficient in English (Flores, Abreu, & Tomany-Korman, 2005).

The State of Illness and Health of the World's Children   Each year UNICEF produces a report entitled, *The State of the World's Children*. In a recent report, UNICEF (2003) emphasized the importance of information about a nation's under-5 mortality rate. UNICEF concluded that the under-5 mortality rate is the result of a wide range of factors, including the nutritional health and health knowledge of mothers, the level of immunization, dehydration, availability of maternal and child health services, income and food availability in the family, availability of clean water and safe sanitation, and the overall safety of the child's environment.

Many of the deaths of young children around the world could be prevented by a reduction in poverty and improvements in nutrition, sanitation, education, and health services (Bahl & others, 2005; Bhutta & others, 2005; Horton, 2006). High

Individual

- Development of social skills and ability to regulate emotions
- Impulse control (such as not darting out into a street to retrieve a ball)
- Frequent use of personal protection (such as bike helmets and safety seats)

Family/Home

- High awareness and knowledge of child management and parenting skills
- Frequent parent protective behaviors (such as use of child safety seats)
- Presence of home safety equipment (such as smoke alarms and cabinet locks)

School/Peers

- Promotion of home/school partnerships
- Absence of playground hazards
- Injury prevention and safety promotion policies and programs

Community

- Availability of positive activities for children and their parents
- Active surveillance of environmental hazards
- Effective prevention policies in place (such as pool fencing)

FIGURE 8.5 Characteristics That Enhance Young Children's Safety. In each context of a child's life, steps can be taken to create conditions that enhance the child's safety and reduce the likelihood of injury. *How are the contexts listed in the figure related to Bronfenbrenner's theory (described in chapter 2)?*

Many children in impoverished countries die before reaching the age of 5 from dehydration and malnutrition brought about by diarrhea. *What are some of the other main causes of death in young children around the world?*

poverty rates have devastating effects on the health of a country's young children. The poor are the majority in nearly one of every five nations in the world (UNICEF, 2006). They often experience lives of hunger, malnutrition, illness, inadequate access to health care, unsafe water, and a lack of protection from harm (UNICEF, 2006).

In the last decade, there has been a dramatic increase in the number of young children who have died because of HIV/AIDS transmitted to them by their parents (Kalichman & others, 2005). Deaths of young children due to HIV/AIDS especially occur in countries with high rates of poverty and low levels of education. For example, the uneducated are four times more likely to believe that there is no way to avoid AIDS and three times more likely to be unaware that the virus can be transmitted from mother to child (UNICEF, 2006).

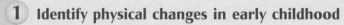

Review and Reflect • LEARNING GOAL 1

1 **Identify physical changes in early childhood**

Review
- How does the body grow and change during early childhood?
- What changes take place in motor development?
- What role does nutrition play in early childhood?
- What are some major causes of illness and death among young children in the United States and around the world?

Reflect
- What were your eating habits as a young child? In what ways are they similar to or different from your current eating habits? Were your early eating habits a forerunner of whether or not you have weight problems today?

2 COGNITIVE CHANGES

Piaget's Preoperational Stage   Vygotsky's Theory   Information Processing

The cognitive world of the preschool child is creative, free, and fanciful. Preschool children's imaginations work overtime, and their mental grasp of the world improves. Our coverage of cognitive development in early childhood focuses on three theories: Piaget's, Vygotsky's, and information processing.

Piaget's Preoperational Stage

Remember from chapter 6 that during Piaget's first stage of development, the sensorimotor stage, the infant progresses in the ability to organize and coordinate sensations and perceptions with physical movements and actions. The **preoperational stage,** which lasts from approximately 2 to 7 years of age, is the second Piagetian stage. In this stage, children begin to represent the world with words, images, and drawings. They form stable concepts and begin to reason. At the same time, the young child's cognitive world is dominated by egocentrism and magical beliefs.

Because Piaget called this stage "preoperational," it might sound like an unimportant waiting period. Not so. However, the label *preoperational* emphasizes that the child does not yet perform **operations,** which are reversible mental actions; they enable children to do mentally what before they could do only physically. Mentally adding and subtracting numbers are examples of operations. *Preoperational thought* is the beginning of the ability to reconstruct in thought what has been established in behavior. It can be divided into two substages: the symbolic function substage and the intuitive thought substage.

The Symbolic Function Substage
The **symbolic function substage** is the first substage of preoperational thought, occurring roughly between the ages of 2 and 4. In this substage, the young child gains the ability to mentally represent an object that is not present. This ability vastly expands the child's mental world (DeLoache, 2001, 2004). Young children use scribble designs to represent people, houses, cars, clouds, and so on; they begin to use language and engage in pretend play. However, although young children make distinct progress during this substage, their thought still has important limitations, two of which are egocentrism and animism.

Egocentrism is the inability to distinguish between one's own perspective and someone else's perspective. The following telephone conversation between 4-year-old Mary, who is at home, and her father, who is at work, typifies Mary's egocentric thought:

Father: Mary, is Mommy there?
Mary: (Silently nods)
Father: Mary, may I speak to Mommy?
Mary: (Nods again silently)

Mary's response is egocentric in that she fails to consider her father's perspective before replying. A nonegocentric thinker would have responded verbally. Piaget and Barbel Inhelder (1969) initially studied young children's egocentrism by devising the three mountains task (see figure 8.6). The child walks around the model of the mountains and becomes familiar with what the mountains look like from different perspectives, and she can see that there are different objects on the mountains. The child is then seated on one side of the table on which the mountains are

preoperational stage Piaget's second stage, lasting from 2 to 7 years of age, during which children begin to represent the world with words, images, and drawings and symbolic thought goes beyond simple connections of sensory information and physical action; stable concepts are formed, mental reasoning emerges, egocentrism is present, and magical beliefs are constructed.

operations In Piaget's theory, internalized sets of actions that enable children to do mentally what they formerly did physically.

symbolic function substage Piaget's first substage of preoperational thought, in which the child gains the ability to mentally represent an object that is not present (between 2 and 4 years of age).

egocentrism The inability to distinguish between one's own perspective and someone else's (salient feature of the first substage of preoperational thought).

View 1

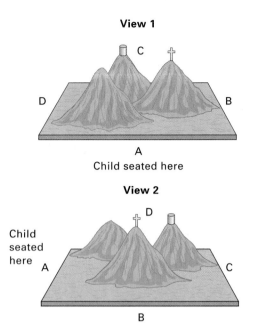

Child seated here

View 2

Child seated here

FIGURE 8.6 The Three Mountains Task. View 1 shows the child's perspective from where he or she is sitting. View 2 is an example of one of the photographs the child would be shown, along with other photographs taken from different perspectives. It shows what the mountains look like to a person sitting at spot B. When asked what a view of the mountains looks like from position B, the preoperational child selects a photograph taken from location A, the child's view at the time. A child who thinks in a preoperational way cannot take the perspective of a person sitting at another spot.

placed. The experimenter moves a doll to different locations around the table, at each location asking the child to select from a series of photos the one photo that most accurately reflects the view that the doll is seeing. Children in the preoperational stage often pick their own view rather than the doll's view. Preschool children frequently show the ability to take another's perspective on some tasks but not others.

Animism, another limitation of preoperational thought, is the belief that inanimate objects have lifelike qualities and are capable of action (Gelman & Opfer, 2004). A young child might show animism by saying, "That tree pushed the leaf off, and it fell down," or "The sidewalk made me mad; it made me fall down." A young child who uses animism fails to distinguish the appropriate occasions for using human and nonhuman perspectives.

Possibly because young children are not very concerned about reality, their drawings are fanciful and inventive. Suns are blue, skies are yellow, and cars float on clouds in their symbolic, imaginative world. One $3\frac{1}{2}$-year-old looked at a scribble he had just drawn and described it as a pelican kissing a seal (see figure 8.7a). The symbolism is simple but strong, like abstractions found in some modern art. Twentieth-century Spanish artist Pablo Picasso commented, "I used to draw like Raphael but it has taken me a lifetime to draw like young children." In the elementary school years, a child's drawings become more realistic, neat, and precise (see figure 8.7b). Suns are yellow, skies are blue, and cars travel on roads (Winner, 1986).

The Intuitive Thought Substage The **intuitive thought substage** is the second substage of preoperational thought, occurring between approximately 4 and 7 years of age. In this substage, children begin to use primitive reasoning and want to know the answers to all sorts of questions. Consider 4-year-old Tommy, who is at the beginning of the intuitive thought substage. Although he is starting to develop his own ideas about the world he lives in, his ideas are still simple, and he is not very good at thinking things out. He has difficulty understanding events that he knows are taking place but which he cannot see. His fantasized thoughts bear little resemblance to reality. He cannot yet answer the question "What if?" in any reliable way. For example, he has only a vague idea of what would happen if a car were to hit him. He also has difficulty negotiating traffic because he cannot do the

www.mhhe.com/santrockld11

Symbolic Thinking

animism The belief that inanimate objects have "lifelike" qualities and are capable of action.

intuitive thought substage Piaget's second substage of preoperational thought, in which children begin to use primitive reasoning and want to know the answers to all sorts of questions (between 4 and 7 years of age).

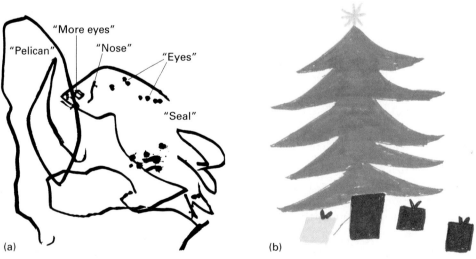

FIGURE 8.7 The Symbolic Drawings of Young Children. (a) A $3\frac{1}{2}$-year-old's symbolic drawing. Halfway into this drawing, the $3\frac{1}{2}$-year-old artist said it was "a pelican kissing a seal." (b) This 11-year-old's drawing is neater and more realistic but also less inventive.

mental calculations necessary to estimate whether an approaching car will hit him when he crosses the road.

By the age of 5 children have just about exhausted the adults around them with "why" questions. The child's questions signal the emergence of interest in reasoning and in figuring out why things are the way they are. Following are some samples of the questions children ask during the questioning period of 4 to 6 years of age (Elkind, 1976):

"What makes you grow up?"

"Why does a woman have to be married to have a baby?"

"Who was the mother when everybody was a baby?"

"Why do leaves fall?"

"Why does the sun shine?"

Piaget called this substage *intuitive* because young children seem so sure about their knowledge and understanding yet are unaware of how they know what they know. That is, they know something but know it without the use of rational thinking.

Centration and the Limits of Preoperational Thought

One limitation of preoperational thought is **centration,** a centering of attention on one characteristic to the exclusion of all others. Centration is most clearly evidenced in young children's lack of **conservation,** the awareness that altering an object's or a substance's appearance does not change its basic properties. For example, to adults, it is obvious that a certain amount of liquid stays the same, regardless of a container's shape. But this is not at all obvious to young children. Instead, they are struck by the height of the liquid in the container; they focus on that characteristic to the exclusion of others.

The situation that Piaget devised to study conservation is his most famous task. In the conservation task, children are presented with two identical beakers, each filled to the same level with liquid (see figure 8.8). They are asked if these beakers have the same amount of liquid, and they usually say yes. Then the liquid from

"I still don't have all the answers, but I'm beginning to ask the right questions."

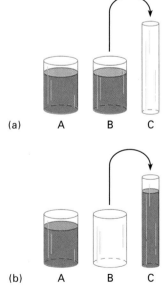

(a) A   B   C

(b) A   B   C

FIGURE 8.8 Piaget's Conservation Task. The beaker test is a well-known Piagetian test to determine whether a child can think operationally—that is, can mentally reverse actions and show conservation of the substance. (*a*) Two identical beakers are presented to the child. Then, the experimenter pours the liquid from B into C, which is taller and thinner than A or B. (*b*) The child is asked if these beakers (A and C) have the same amount of liquid. The preoperational child says "no." When asked to point to the beaker that has more liquid, the preoperational child points to the tall, thin beaker.

centration The focusing of attention on one characteristic to the exclusion of all others.

conservation In Piaget's theory, awareness that altering an object's or a substance's appearance does not change its quantitative properties.

Type of Conservation	Initial Presentation	Manipulation	Preoperational Child's Answer
Number	Two identical rows of objects are shown to the child, who agrees they have the same number.	One row is lengthened and the child is asked whether one row now has more objects.	Yes, the longer row.
Matter	Two identical balls of clay are shown to the child. The child agrees that they are equal.	The experimenter changes the shape of one of the balls and asks the child whether they still contain equal amounts of clay.	No, the longer one has more.
Length	Two sticks are aligned in front of the child. The child agrees that they are the same length.	The experimenter moves one stick to the right, then asks the child if they are equal in length.	No, the one on the top is longer.

FIGURE 8.9 Some Dimensions of Conservation: Number, Matter, and Length. *What characteristics of preoperational thought do children demonstrate when they fail these conservation tasks?*

one beaker is poured into a third beaker, which is taller and thinner than the first two. The children are then asked if the amount of liquid in the tall, thin beaker is equal to that which remains in one of the original beakers. Children who are less than 7 or 8 years old usually say no and justify their answers in terms of the differing height or width of the beakers. Older children usually answer yes and justify their answers appropriately ("If you poured the water back, the amount would still be the same").

In Piaget's theory, failing the conservation-of-liquid task is a sign that children are at the preoperational stage of cognitive development. The failure demonstrates not only centration but also an inability to mentally reverse actions. For example, in the conservation of matter example shown in figure 8.9, preoperational children say that the longer shape has more clay because they assume that "longer is more." Preoperational children cannot mentally reverse the clay-rolling process to see that the amount of clay is the same in both the shorter ball shape and the longer stick shape.

In addition to failing to conserve volume, preoperational children also fail to conserve number, matter, length, and area. However, children often vary in their performance on different conservation tasks. Thus, a child might be able to conserve volume but not number.

Some developmentalists do not believe Piaget was entirely correct in his estimate of when children's conservation skills emerge. For example, Rochel Gelman (1969) showed that when the child's attention to relevant aspects of the conservation task is improved, the child is more likely to conserve. Gelman has also demonstrated that attentional training on one dimension, such as number, improves the preschool child's performance on another dimension, such as mass. Thus, Gelman believes that conservation appears earlier than Piaget thought and that attention is especially important in explaining conservation.

Vygotsky's Theory

social constructivist approach An approach that emphasizes the social contexts of learning and that knowledge is mutually built and constructed. Vygotsky's theory reflects this approach.

Like Piaget, Vygotsky was a constructivist, but Vygotsky's is a **social constructivist approach,** which emphasizes the social contexts of learning and the construction of knowledge through social interaction. In moving from Piaget to Vygotsky, our focus shifts from the individual to collaboration, social interaction, and sociocultural activity (Fidalgo & Pereira, 2005; Harris, 2006; Rogoff, 2003). For Piaget, children construct knowledge by transforming, organizing, and reorganizing previous knowledge. For Vygotsky, children construct knowledge through social interaction (Harris, 2006; Mooney, 2006). In chapter 2, we described some basic ideas about Vygotsky's theory. Here we expand on his theory, exploring his ideas about the zone of proximal development and the young child's use of language.

The Zone of Proximal Development   Vygotsky's belief in the importance of social influences, especially instruction, on children's cognitive development is reflected in his concept of the zone of proximal development. **Zone of proximal development (ZPD)** is Vygotsky's term for the range of tasks that are too difficult for the child to master alone but that can be learned with guidance and assistance of adults or more skilled children. Thus, the lower limit of the ZPD is the level of skill reached by the child working independently. The upper limit is the level of additional responsibility the child can accept with the assistance of an able instructor (see figure 8.10). The ZPD captures the child's cognitive skills that are in the process of maturing and can be accomplished only with the assistance of a more skilled person (Camilleri, 2005; Mooney, 2006). Vygotsky (1962) called these the "buds" or "flowers" of development, to distinguish them from the "fruits" of development, which the child already can accomplish independently.

Let's consider an example that reflects the zone of proximal development (Frede, 1995, p. 125):

> A 5-year-old child is pushing a small shopping cart through the house area of his preschool. His teacher notices that he is putting fruit in the small basket and all other groceries in the larger section of the cart. She has watched him sort objects over the past few weeks and thinks that he may now be able to classify along two dimensions at the same time, with some help from her. She goes to the cash register to pretend to be the cashier and says, "We need to be careful how we divide your groceries into bags. We want to use one bag for things that go in the refrigerator, and other bags for things that will go in the cabinet." Together they devise a system with one bag for each of the following categories: food in cartons that will go into the refrigerator, loose vegetables and fruit for the refrigerator, food cartons that go in the cabinet, and food cans for the cabinet. In this example, the child's unassisted level of classification was fairly gross—fruit versus non-fruit. With the teacher's help, he was able to apply a more sophisticated form of classification.

Scaffolding   Closely linked to the idea of the ZPD is the concept of scaffolding, which was introduced in the context of parent-infant interaction in chapter 7. *Scaffolding* means changing the level of support. Over the course of a teaching session, a more skilled person (a teacher or advanced peer) adjusts the amount of guidance to fit the child's current performance (de Vries, 2005; John-Steiner & Mahn, 2003). When the student is learning a new task, the skilled person may use direct instruction. As the student's competence increases, less guidance is given.

Dialogue is an important tool of scaffolding in the zone of proximal development (Tappan, 1998). Vygotsky viewed children as having rich but unsystematic, disorganized, and spontaneous concepts. In a dialogue, these concepts meet with the skilled helper's more systematic, logical, and rational concepts. As a result, the child's concepts become more systematic, logical, and rational. For example, a dialogue might take place between a teacher and a child when the teacher uses scaffolding to help a child understand a concept like "transportation."

Language and Thought   The use of dialogue as a tool for scaffolding is only one example of the important role of language in a child's development. According to Vygotsky, children use speech not only for social communication,

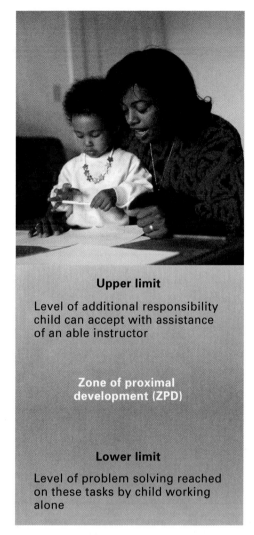

Upper limit

Level of additional responsibility child can accept with assistance of an able instructor

Zone of proximal development (ZPD)

Lower limit

Level of problem solving reached on these tasks by child working alone

FIGURE 8.10 Vygotsky's Zone of Proximal Development. Vygotsky's zone of proximal development has a lower limit and an upper limit. Tasks in the ZPD are too difficult for the child to perform alone. They require assistance from an adult or a more-skilled child. As children experience the verbal instruction or demonstration, they organize the information in their existing mental structures, so they can eventually perform the skill or task alone.

www.mhhe.com/santrockld11

Vygotsky on Language and Thought
Vygotsky: Revolutionary Scientist

zone of proximal development (ZPD) Vygotsky's term for tasks too difficult for children to master alone but that can be mastered with assistance.

but also to help them solve tasks. Vygotsky (1962) further believed that young children use language to plan, guide, and monitor their behavior. This use of language for self-regulation is called *private speech*. For Piaget private speech is egocentric and immature, but for Vygotsky it is an important tool of thought during the early childhood years.

Vygotsky said that language and thought initially develop independently of each other and then merge. He emphasized that all mental functions have external, or social, origins. Children must use language to communicate with others before they can focus inward on their own thoughts. Children also must communicate externally and use language for a long period of time before they can make the transition from external to internal speech. This transition period occurs between 3 and 7 years of age and involves talking to oneself. After a while, the self-talk becomes second nature to children, and they can act without verbalizing. When this occurs, children have internalized their egocentric speech in the form of *inner speech*, which becomes their thoughts.

Vygotsky believed that children who use a lot of private speech are more socially competent than those who don't (Santiago-Delefosse & Delefosse, 2002). He argued that private speech represents an early transition in becoming more socially communicative. For Vygotsky, when young children talk to themselves, they are using language to govern their behavior and guide themselves. For example, a child working on a puzzle might say to herself, "Which pieces should I put together first? I'll try those green ones first. Now I need some blue ones. No, that blue one doesn't fit there. I'll try it over here."

Researchers have found support for Vygotsky's view that private speech plays a positive role in children's development (Winsler, Diaz, & Montero, 1997; Winsler, Carlton, & Barry, 2000). Children use private speech more when tasks are difficult, when they have made errors, and when they are not sure how to proceed (Berk, 1994). Researchers have also found that children who use private speech are more attentive and improve their performance more than children who do not use private speech (Berk & Spuhl, 1995).

Teaching Strategies Vygotsky's theory has been successfully applied to education (Mooney, 2006; Rowe & Wertsch, 2004). Here are some ways Vygotsky's theory can be used by educators:

1. *Assess the child's ZPD*. Like Piaget, Vygotsky did not believe that formal, standardized tests are the best way to assess children's learning. Rather, Vygotsky argued that assessment should focus on determining the child's zone of proximal development. The skilled helper presents the child with tasks of varying difficulty to determine the best level at which to begin instruction.
2. *Use the child's zone of proximal development in teaching*. Teaching should begin toward the zone's upper limit, so that the child can reach the goal with help and move to a higher level of skill and knowledge. Offer just enough assistance. You might ask, "What can I do to help you?" Or simply observe the child's intentions and attempts and provide support when needed. When the child hesitates, offer encouragement. And encourage the child to practice the skill. You may watch and appreciate the child's practice or offer support when the child forgets what to do.
3. *Use more-skilled peers as teachers*. Remember that it is not just adults that are important in helping children learn. Children also benefit from the support and guidance of more-skilled children (John-Steiner & Mahn, 2003).
4. *Monitor and encourage children's use of private speech*. Be aware of the developmental change from externally talking to oneself when solving a problem during the preschool years to privately talking to oneself in the early elementary school years. In the elementary school years, encourage children to internalize and self-regulate their talk to themselves.

5. *Place instruction in a meaningful context.* Educators today are moving away from abstract presentations of material, instead providing students with opportunities to experience learning in real-world settings. For example, instead of just memorizing math formulas, students work on math problems with real-world implications (Santrock, 2006).

The Applications in Life-Span Development interlude further explores the implications of Vygotsky's theory for children's education.

APPLICATIONS IN LIFE-SPAN DEVELOPMENT

Tools of the Mind

Tools of the Mind is an early childhood education curriculum that emphasizes children's development of self-regulation and the cognitive foundations of literacy (Hyson, Copple, & Jones, 2006). The curriculum was created by Elena Bodrova and Deborah Leong (2001) and has been implemented in more than 200 classrooms. Most of the children in the Tools of the Mind programs are at-risk because of their living circumstances, which in many instances involve poverty and other difficult conditions such as being homeless and having parents with drug problems.

Tools of the Mind is grounded in Vygotsky's (1962) theory with special attention given to cultural tools and developing self-regulation, the zone of proximal development, scaffolding, private speech, shared activity, and play as important activity. In a Tools of the Mind classroom, dramatic play has a central role. Teachers guide children in creating themes that are based on the children's interests, such as treasure hunt, store, hospital, and restaurant. Teachers also incorporate field trips, visitor presentations, videos, and books in the development of children's play. They also help children develop a play plan, which increases the maturity of their play. Play plans describe what the children expect to do in the play period, including the imaginary context, roles, and props to be used. The play plans increase the quality of their play and self-regulation.

Scaffolding writing is another important theme in the Tools of the Mind classroom. Teachers guide children in planning their own message by drawing a line to stand for each word the child says. Children then repeat the message, pointing to each line as they say the word. Then, the child writes on the lines, trying to represent each word with some letters or symbols. Figure 8.11 on page 254 shows how the scaffolding writing process improved a 5-year-old child's writing over the course of two months.

Research assessments of children's writing in Tools of the Mind classrooms revealed that they have more advanced writing skills than children in other early childhood programs (Bodrova & Leong, 2001, 2007). For example, they write more complex messages, use more words, spell more accurately, show better letter recognition, and have a better understanding of the concept of a sentence.

Evaluating Vygotsky's Theory How does Vygotsky's theory compare with Piaget's? We already have mentioned several comparisons, such as Vygotsky's emphasis on the importance of inner speech in development and Piaget's view that such speech is immature. Figure 8.12 compares the theories. The implication of Piaget's theory for teaching is that children need support to explore their world and discover knowledge. The main implication of Vygotsky's theory for teaching is that students need many opportunities to learn with a teacher and more-skilled peers. In both Piaget's and Vygotsky's theories, teachers serve as facilitators and guides, rather than as directors and molders.

FIGURE 8.11 Writing Progress of a 5-Year-Old Boy Over Two Months Using the Scaffolding Writing Process in Tools of the Mind. Source: Bodrova, E., & Leong, D. J. (2001, 2007). *Tools of the mind*. Geneva, Switzerland: International Bureau of Education, UNESCO. Available online at http://www.ibe.unesco.org/International/Publications/INNODATAMonograph/inno07.pdf.

Even though their theories were proposed at about the same time, most of the world learned about Vygotsky's theory later than they learned about Piaget's theory, so Vygotsky's theory has not yet been evaluated as thoroughly. Vygotsky's view of the importance of sociocultural influences on children's development fits with the current belief that it is important to evaluate the contextual factors in learning (Hyson, Copple, & Jones, 2006; Kozulin & others, 2003; Rowe & Wertsch, 2004).

Some critics say Vygotsky overemphasized the role of language in thinking. Also, his emphasis on collaboration and guidance has potential pitfalls. Might facilitators be too helpful in some cases, as when a parent becomes too overbearing and controlling? Further, some children might become lazy and expect help when they might have done something on their own.

Information Processing

Piaget's and Vygotsky's theories provided important ideas about how young children think and how their thinking changes. More recently, the information-processing approach has generated research that illuminates how children process information during the preschool years. What are the limitations and advances in the young child's

	Vygotsky	Piaget
Sociocultural Context	Strong emphasis	Little emphasis
Constructivism	Social constructivist	Cognitive constructivist
Stages	No general stages of development proposed	Strong emphasis on stages (sensorimotor, preoperational, concrete operational, and formal operational)
Key Processes	Zone of proximal development, language, dialogue, tools of the culture	Schema, assimilation, accommodation, operations, conservation, classification, hypothetical-deductive reasoning
Role of Language	A major role; language plays a powerful role in shaping thought	Language has a minimal role; cognition primarily directs language
View on Education	Education plays a central role, helping children learn the tools of the culture	Education merely refines the child's cognitive skills that have already emerged
Teaching Implications	Teacher is a facilitator and guide, not a director; establish many opportunities for children to learn with the teacher and more-skilled peers	Also views teacher as a facilitator and guide, not a director; provide support for children to explore their world and discover knowledge

FIGURE 8.12 Comparison of Vygotsky's and Piaget's Theories.

ability to pay attention to the environment, to remember, to develop strategies and solve problems, and to understand their own mental processes and those of others?

Attention   Recall that in chapter 6 we defined *attention* as the focusing of cognitive resources. The child's ability to pay attention improves significantly during the preschool years. Toddlers wander around, shift attention from one activity to another, and seem to spend little time focused on any one object or event. By comparison, the preschool child might be observed watching television for a half hour. One study videotaped young children in their homes (Anderson & others, 1985). In 99 families who were observed for 4,672 hours, visual attention to television dramatically increased during the preschool years.

In at least two ways, however, the preschool child's control of attention is still deficient:

- *Salient versus relevant dimensions.* Preschool children are likely to pay attention to stimuli that stand out, or are *salient,* even when those stimuli are not relevant to solving a problem or performing a task. For example, if a flashy, attractive clown presents the directions for solving a problem, preschool children are likely to pay more attention to the clown than to the directions. After the age of 6 or 7, children attend more efficiently to the dimensions of the task that are relevant, such as the directions for solving a problem. This change reflects a shift to cognitive control of attention, so that children act less impulsively and reflect more.
- *Planfulness.* When experimenters ask children to judge whether two complex pictures are the same, preschool children tend to use a haphazard comparison strategy, not examining all of the details before making a judgment. By comparison, elementary school age children are more likely to systematically compare the details across the pictures, one detail at a time (Vurpillot, 1968) (see figure 8.13).

(a)

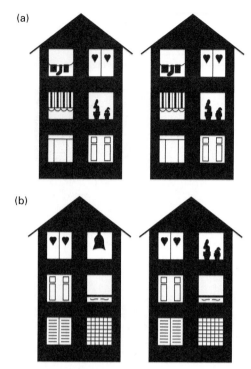

(b)

FIGURE 8.13 The Planfulness of Attention.
In one study, children were given pairs of houses to examine, like the ones shown here (Vurpillot, 1968). For three pairs of houses, what was in the windows was identical (a). For the other three pairs, the windows had different items in them (b). By filming the reflection in the children's eyes, it could be determined what they were looking at, how long they looked, and the sequence of their eye movements. Children under 6 examined only a fragmentary portion of each display and made their judgments on the basis of insufficient information. By contrast, older children scanned the windows in more detailed ways and were more accurate in their judgments of which windows were identical.

short-term memory The memory component in which individuals retain information for up to 30 seconds, assuming there is no rehearsal of the information.

Preschool children's ability to control and sustain their attention is related to both their achievement-related skills and their social skills (NICHD Child Care Research Network, 2005; Ruff & Rothbart, 1996). For example, one recent study of more than 1,000 children found that their ability to sustain their attention at 54 months of age was linked to their school readiness (which included achievement and language skills) (NICHD Early Child Care Research Network, 2005). Also, young children who have difficulty regulating their attention are more likely than other children to experience peer rejection and to engage in aggressive behavior (Eisenberg, Spinrad, & Smith, 2004).

Young children's experiences in their home and child care can influence the development of their attention and memory. One recent study found that stimulating and sensitive care that occurred both early (6 to 36 months of age) and later (54 months and the first grade) in children's home and at child care was linked to better attention and memory, but not planning, in the first grade (NICHD Early Child Care Research Network, 2003).

Memory   *Memory*—the retention of information over time—is a central process in children's cognitive development. In chapter 6, we saw that most of an infant's memories are fragile and, for the most part, short-lived—except for the memory of perceptual-motor actions, which can be substantial (Mandler, 2000, 2004). Thus, we saw that to understand the infant's capacity to remember we need to distinguish *implicit memory* from *explicit memory*. Explicit memory, however, itself comes in many forms. One distinction occurs between relatively permanent or *long-term memory* and short-term memory.

Short-Term Memory   In **short-term memory,** individuals retain information for up to 30 seconds if there is no rehearsal of the information. Using rehearsal (repeating information after it has been presented), we can keep information in short-term memory for a much longer period. One method of assessing short-term memory is the memory-span task. You hear a short list of stimuli—usually digits—presented at a rapid pace (one per second, for example). Then you are asked to repeat the digits.

Research with the memory-span task suggests that short-term memory increases during early childhood. For example, in one investigation, memory span increased from about 2 digits in 2- to 3-year-old children to about 5 digits in 7-year-old children, yet between 7 and 12 years of age memory span increased only by $1\frac{1}{2}$ digits (Dempster, 1981) (see figure 8.14). Keep in mind, though, that memory span varies from one individual to another.

Why does memory span change with age? Rehearsal of information is important; older children rehearse the digits more than younger children. Speed and efficiency of processing information are important, too, especially the speed with which memory items can be identified (Schneider, 2004). For example, in one study, children were tested on their speed at repeating words presented orally (Case, Kurland, & Goldberg, 1982). Speed of repetition was a powerful predictor of memory span. Indeed, when the speed of repetition was controlled, the 6-year-olds' memory spans were equal to those of young adults.

The speed-of-processing explanation highlights a key point in the information-processing perspective: The speed with which a child processes information is an important aspect of the child's cognitive abilities (Halford, 2004; Schneider, 2004). In one recent study, faster processing speed on a memory-span task was linked with higher reading and mathematics achievement (Hitch, Towse, & Hutton, 2001).

How Accurate Are Young Children's Long-Term Memories?   While the toddlers' short-term memory span increases during the early childhood years, their memory also becomes more accurate. Young children can remember a great deal of information if they are given appropriate cues and prompts. Increasingly, young children are even being allowed to testify in court, especially if they are the only witnesses to abuse, a crime, and so forth. However, one recent study found that young children were less likely than older children to reject false suggestions about events (Ghetti & Alexander, 2004). Several factors can influence the accuracy of a young child's memory (Bruck & Ceci, 1999):

- *There are age differences in children's susceptibility to suggestion.* Preschoolers are the most suggestible age group in comparison with older children and adults. For example, preschool children are more susceptible to misleading or incorrect postevent information (Ghetti & Alexander, 2004). Despite these age differences, there is still concern about older children when they are subjected to suggestive interviews (Poole & Lindsay, 1996).
- *There are individual differences in susceptibility.* Some preschoolers are highly resistant to interviewers' suggestions, whereas others immediately succumb to the slightest suggestion (Crossman, Scullin, & Melnyk, 2004; Gilstrap & Ceci, 2005). One recent study found that children with more advanced verbal abilities and self-control were more likely to resist interviewers' suggestive questions (Clarke-Stewart, Malloy, & Allhusen, 2004). A recent research review found that suggestibility is linked to low self-concept, low support from parents, and mothers' insecure attachment in romantic relationships (Bruck & Melnyk, 2004).
- *Interviewing techniques can produce substantial distortions in children's reports about highly salient events.* Children are suggestible not just about peripheral details but also about the central aspects of an event (Bruck, Ceci, & Hembrooke, 1998). Their false claims have been found to persist for at least three months (Ornstein, Gordon, & Larus, 1992). Nonetheless, young children are capable of recalling much that is relevant about an event (Fivush, 1993; Goodman, Batterman-Faunce, & Kenney, 1992). When children do accurately recall an event, the interviewer often has a neutral tone, there is limited use of misleading questions, and there is an absence of any motivation for the child to make a false report (Bruck & Ceci, 1999).

To read further about false memories in children, see the following Research in Life-Span Development interlude.

RESEARCH IN LIFE-SPAN DEVELOPMENT

Suggesting False Events to Children

As described in Bruck and Ceci (1999, pp. 429–430), a study by Deborah Poole and D. Stephen Lindsay revealed how parents can subtly influence their young children's memory for events. Preschool children participated in four activities (such as lifting cans with pulleys) with "Mr. Science" in a university laboratory (Poole & Lindsay, 1995). Four months later, the children's parents were mailed a storybook with a description of their child's visit to see Mr. Science. The storybook described two of the activities in which the child had participated but it also described two in which the child has not participated. Each description also ended with this fabrication of what had happened when it was time to leave the laboratory: "Mr. Science wiped (child's name) hands and face with a wet-wipe. The cloth got close to (child's name) mouth and tasted real yucky."

Parents read the descriptions to their children three times. Later, the children told the experimenter that they had participated in the activities that actually had only been mentioned in the descriptions read by their parents. For example, when asked whether Mr. Science had put anything yucky in their mouths, more than half of the young children say that he had. Subsequently when asked whether Mr. Science put something in their mouth or their mom just read this to them in a story, 71 percent of the young children said that it really happened.

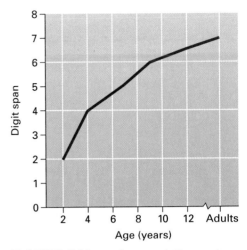

FIGURE 8.14 Developmental Changes in Memory Span. In one study, from 2 years of age to 7 years of age children's memory span increased about 3 digits to 5 digits (Dempster, 1981). By 12 years of age, memory span had increased on average only another $1\frac{1}{2}$ digits, to 7 digits. *What factors might contribute to the increase in memory span during childhood?*

Four-year-old Jennifer Royal was the only eyewitness to one of her playmates' being shot to death. She was allowed to testify in open court and the clarity of her statements helped to convict the gunman. *What are some issues involved in whether young children should be allowed to testify in court?*

This study shows how subtle suggestions can influence children's inaccurate reporting of nonevents. If such inaccurate reports are pursued in follow-up questioning by an interviewer who suspected that something sexual occurred, the result could be a sexual interpretation. This study also revealed the difficulty preschool children have in identifying the source of a suggestion (called *source-monitoring errors*). Children in this study confused their parent reading the suggestion to them with their experience of the suggestion.

In sum, whether a young child's eyewitness testimony is accurate or not may depend on a number of factors such as the type, number, and intensity of the suggestive techniques the child has experienced. It appears that the reliability of young children's reports has as much to do with the skills and motivation of the interviewer as with any natural limitations on young children's memory (Ceci, Fitneva, & Gilstrap, 2003).

According to leading experts who study children's suggestibility, research indicates that these three changes need to be implemented (Bruck, Ceci, & Principe, 2006): (1) Interviewers should be required to electronically preserve their interviews with children, (2) a research-validated interview schedule with children needs to be developed, and (3) programs need to be created to teach interviewers how to use interviewing protocols.

Strategies and Problem Solving   In chapter 2, we mentioned that information-processing theory emphasizes the importance of using good strategies. **Strategies** consist of deliberate mental activities to improve the processing of information (Pressley & Hilden, 2006; Siegler, 2006). For example, rehearsing information and organizing it are two typical strategies that older children and adults use to remember more effectively. For the most part, young children do not use rehearsal and organization to remember (Miller & Seier, 1994).

Even children as young as 2 years of age can learn a strategy. For example, in a study by Zhe Chen and Robert Siegler (2000) 2-year-olds learned to select the best tool to obtain a desired toy. As figure 8.15 illustrates, the experimenters placed young children at a table where an attractive toy was placed too far away for the child to reach it (they were not allowed to crawl on the table). On the table, between the child and the toy, were six potential tools, only one of which was likely to be useful in retrieving the tool. The experimenters either showed the child how to obtain the toy or gave the child a hint. These 2-year-olds learned the strategy.

During early childhood, the relatively stimulus-driven toddler is transformed into a child capable of flexible, goal-directed problem solving (Zelazo & Müller, 2004; Zelazo & others, 2003). For example, 3- to 4-year-olds cannot understand that a single stimulus can be described in incompatible ways from two different perspectives (Perner & others, 2002). Consider a problem in which children must sort stimuli using the rule of *color*. In the course of the color sorting, a child may describe a red rabbit as "a *red one*" to solve the problem. However, in a subsequent task, the child may need to discover a rule that describes the rabbit as just "a *rabbit*" to solve the problem. If 3- to 4-year-olds fail to understand that it is possible to provide multiple descriptions of the same stimulus, they persist in describing the stimulus as "a red rabbit." Researchers have found that at about 4 years of age, children acquire the concept of perspectives, which allows them to appreciate that a single stimulus can be described in two different ways (Frye, 1999).

The Young Child's Theory of Mind   Even young children are curious about the nature of the human mind. They have a **theory of mind,** which refers to awareness of one's own mental processes and the mental processes of others. Studies of theory of mind view the child as "a thinker who is trying to explain, predict,

FIGURE 8.15 The Toy-Retrieval Task in the Study of Young Children's Problem-Solving Strategies. The child needs to choose the toy rake in order to pull in the turtle. In this study (Chen & Siegler, 2000) 2-year-olds were able to learn to select the tool to obtain the toy when the experimenters showed or told them how to do so.

strategies Deliberate mental activities to improve the processing of information.

theory of mind Refers to the awareness of one's own mental processes and the mental processes of others.

and understand people's thoughts, feelings, and utterances" (Harris, 2006). Children's theory of mind changes as they develop through childhood (Flavell, Miller, & Miller, 2002). The main changes occur at 2 to 3 years of age, 4 to 5 years of age, and beyond 5 years.

2 to 3 Years of Age In this time frame, children begin to understand three mental states:

- *Perceptions.* The child realizes that another person sees what is in front of her eyes and not necessarily what is in front of the child's eyes.
- *Emotions.* The child can distinguish between positive (for example, happy) and negative (sad, for example) emotions. A child might say, "Tommy feels bad."
- *Desires.* The child understands that if someone wants something, he or she will try to get it. A child might say, "I want my mommy."

Let's further examine young children's understanding of desires. Children refer to desires earlier and more frequently than they refer to cognitive states such as thinking and knowing (Harris, 2006). Two- to 3-year-olds understand the way that desires are related to actions and to simple emotions (Harris, 2006). For example, they understand that people will search for what they want and that if they obtain it, they are likely to feel happy, but if they don't, they will keep searching for it and are likely to feel sad or angry (Hadwin & Perner, 2001; Wellman & Woolley, 1990).

4 to 5 Years of Age Children come to understand that the mind can represent objects and events accurately or inaccurately. The realization that people can have *false beliefs*—beliefs that are not true—develops in a majority of children by the time they are 5 years old (Wellman, Cross, & Watson, 2001) (see figure 8.16). In one study of false beliefs, young children were shown a Band-Aids box and asked what was inside (Jenkins & Astington, 1996). To the children's surprise, the box actually contained pencils. When asked what a child who had never seen the box would think was inside, 3-year-olds typically responded "pencils." However, the 4- and 5-year-olds, grinning at the anticipation of the false beliefs of other children who had not seen what was inside the box, were more likely to say "Band-Aids."

Children's understanding of thinking has some limitations in early childhood (Harris, 2006; Siegler & Alibali, 2005). They often underestimate when mental activity is likely occurring. For example, they fail to attribute mental activity to someone who is sitting quietly, reading, or talking (Flavell, Green, & Flavell, 1995). Their understanding of their own thinking is also limited. One study revealed that even 5-year-olds have difficulty reporting their thoughts (Flavell, Green, & Flavell, 1995). Children were asked to think quietly about the room in their home where they kept their toothbrushes. Shortly after this, many children denied they had been thinking at all and failed to mention either a toothbrush or a bathroom. In another study, when 5-year-olds were asked to try to have no thoughts at all for about 20 seconds, they reported that they were successful at doing this (Flavell, Green, & Flavell, 2000). By contrast, most of the 8-year-olds said they engaged in mental activity during the 20 seconds and reported specific thoughts.

Beyond Age 5 It is only beyond the preschool years that children have a deepening appreciation of the mind itself rather than just an understanding of mental states (Wellman, 2004). Not until middle and late childhood do children see the mind as an active constructor of knowledge or processing center (Flavell, Green, & Flavell, 1998) and move from understanding that beliefs can be false to realizing that the same event can be open to multiple interpretations (Carpendale & Chandler, 1996).

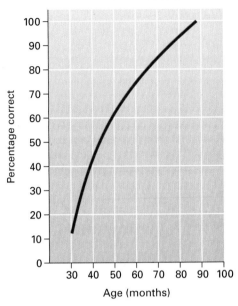

FIGURE 8.16 Developmental Changes in False-Belief Performance. False-belief performance—the child's understanding that a person has a false belief which contradicts reality–dramatically increases from 2½ years of age through the middle of the elementary school years. In a summary of the results of many studies, 2½-year-olds gave incorrect responses about 80 percent of the time (Wellman, Cross, & Watson, 2001). At 3 years, 8 months, they were correct about 50 percent of the time, and after that, gave increasingly correct responses.

Cognitive developmentalist John Flavell (above) has been a pioneer in providing insights into the way children think. Among his many contributions are conducting numerous research studies that have advanced our understanding of developmental changes in theory of mind.

Review and Reflect • LEARNING GOAL 2

> **2** **Describe three views of the cognitive changes that occur in early childhood**
>
> **Review**
> - What characterizes Piaget's stage of preoperational thought?
> - What does Vygotsky's theory suggest about how preschool children construct knowledge?
> - What are some important ways in which information processing changes during early childhood?
>
> **Reflect**
> - Should children be taught concepts such as conservation? Explain.

3 LANGUAGE DEVELOPMENT

Understanding Phonology and Morphology

Advances in Pragmatics

Changes in Syntax and Semantics

Young Children's Literacy

Toddlers move rather quickly from producing two-word utterances to creating three-, four-, and five-word combinations. Between 2 and 3 years of age they begin the transition from saying simple sentences that express a single proposition to saying complex sentences (Bloom, 1998).

Young children's understanding sometimes gets way ahead of their speech. One 3-year-old, laughing with delight as an abrupt summer breeze stirred his hair and tickled his skin, commented, "I got breezed!" Many of the oddities of young children's language sound like mistakes to adult listeners. However, from the children's point of view, they are not mistakes. They represent the way young children perceive and understand their world. As children go through their early childhood years, their grasp of the rule systems that govern language increases.

As young children learn the special features of their own language, there are extensive regularities in how they acquire that particular language (Berko Gleason, 2005). For example, all children learn the prepositions *on* and *in* before other prepositions. Children learning other languages, such as Russian or Chinese, also acquire the particular features of those languages in a consistent order.

Understanding Phonology and Morphology

During the preschool years, most children gradually become more sensitive to the sounds of spoken words and become increasingly capable of producing all the sounds of their language (National Research Council, 1999). They can even produce complex consonant clusters such as *str-* and *-mpt-*. They notice rhymes, enjoy poems, make up silly names for things by substituting one sound for another (such as *bubblegum, bubblebum, bubbleyum*), and clap along with each syllable in a phrase.

By the time children move beyond two-word utterances, they demonstrate a knowledge of morphology rules (Carlisle, 2004). Children begin using the plural and possessive forms of nouns (such as *dogs* and *dog's*). They put appropriate endings on verbs (such as *-s* when the subject is third-person singular and *-ed* for the past tense).

They use prepositions (such as *in* and *on*), articles (such as *a* and *the*), and various forms of the verb *to be* (such as "I *was* going to the store"). Some of the best evidence for changes in children's use of morphological rules occurs in their overgeneralization of the rules, as when a preschool child say "foots" instead of "feet," or "goed" instead of "went."

In a classic experiment that was designed to study children's knowledge of morphological rules, such as how to make a plural, Jean Berko (1958) presented preschool children and first-grade children with cards such as the one shown in figure 8.17. Children were asked to look at the card while the experimenter read aloud the words on the card. Then the children were asked to supply the missing word. This might sound easy, but Berko was interested in the children's ability to apply the appropriate morphological rule, in this case to say "wugs" with the *z* sound that indicates the plural.

Although the children's answers were not perfect, they were much better than chance. What makes Berko's study impressive is that most of the words were made up for the experiment. Thus, the children could not base their responses on remembering past instances of hearing the words. Since they could make the plurals or past tenses of words they had never heard before, this was proof that they knew the morphological rules.

Changes in Syntax and Semantics

Preschool children also learn and apply rules of syntax (Marchman & Thal, 2005). They show a growing mastery of complex rules for how words should be ordered.

Consider *wh-* questions, such as "Where is Daddy going?" or "What is that boy doing?" To ask these questions properly, the child must know two important differences between *wh-* questions and affirmative statements (for instance, "Daddy is going to work" and "That boy is waiting on the school bus"). First, a *wh-* word must be added at the beginning of the sentence. Second, the auxiliary verb must be inverted—that is, exchanged with the subject of the sentence. Young children learn quite early where to put the *wh-* word, but they take much longer to learn the auxiliary-inversion rule. Thus, preschool children might ask, "Where daddy is going?" and "What that boy is doing?"

Gains in semantics also characterize early childhood. Vocabulary development is dramatic. Some experts have concluded that between 18 months and 6 years of age, young children learn about one new word every waking hour (Carey, 1978; Gelman & Kalish, 2006)! By the time they enter first grade, it is estimated that children know about 14,000 words (Clark, 1993).

Advances in Pragmatics

Changes in pragmatics also characterize young children's language development (Bryant, 2005). A 6-year-old is simply a much better conversationalist than a 2-year-old is. What are some of the improvements in pragmatics during the preschool years?

As children get older they become increasingly able to talk about things that are not here (grandma's house, for example) and not now (what happened to them yesterday or might happen tomorrow, for example). A preschool child can tell you what she wants for lunch tomorrow, something that would not have been possible at the two-word stage of language development.

At about 4 years of age, children develop a remarkable sensitivity to the needs of others in conversation. One way in which they show such sensitivity is through their use of the articles *the* and *an* (or *a*). When adults tell a story or describe an event, they generally use *an* (or *a*) when they first refer to an animal or an object, and then use *the* when referring to it later. (For example, "Two boys were walking through the jungle when *a* fierce lion appeared. *The* lion lunged at one boy while the other ran for cover.") Even 3-year-olds follow part of this rule; they consistently

This is a wug.

Now there is another one.
There are two of them.
There are two _____.

FIGURE 8.17 Stimuli in Berko's Study of Young Children's Understanding of Morphological Rules. In Jean Berko's (1958) study, young children were presented cards, such as this one with a "wug" on it. Then the children were asked to supply the missing word; in supplying the missing word, they had to say it correctly too. "Wugs" is the correct response here.

www.mhhe.com/santrockld11

Language Development
Language Growth
Pragmatic Language

How do children's language abilities develop during early childhood?

use the word *the* when referring to previously mentioned things. However, the use of the word *a* when something is initially mentioned develops more slowly. Although 5-year-old children follow this rule on some occasions, they fail to follow it on others.

Around 4 to 5 years of age children learn to change their speech style to suit the situation. For example, even 4-year-old children speak differently to a 2-year-old than to a same-aged peer; they use shorter sentences with the 2-year-old. They also speak differently to an adult than to a same-aged peer, using more polite and formal language with the adult (Shatz & Gelman, 1973).

Young Children's Literacy

The concern about the ability of U.S. children to read and write has led to a careful examination of preschool and kindergarten children's experiences, with the hope that a positive orientation toward reading and writing can be developed early in life (Anderson, Moffatt, & Shapiro, 2006; Antonacci & O'Callaghan, 2006; Hill & Nichols, 2006; Vacca & others, 2006). What should a literacy program for preschool children be like? Instruction should be built on what children already know about oral language, reading, and writing. Further, early precursors of literacy and academic success include language skills, phonological and syntactic knowledge, letter identification, and conceptual knowledge about print and its conventions and functions (Jalongo, 2007; McWhorter, 2006; Rubin, 2006). A longitudinal study found that phonological awareness, letter name and sound knowledge, and naming speed in kindergarten were linked to reading success in the first and second grades (Schattschneider & others, 2004). In another longitudinal study, the number of letters children knew in kindergarten was highly correlated with their reading achievement in high school (Stevenson & Newman, 1986).

All young children should experience feelings of success and pride in their early reading and writing exercises (Graves, Juel, & Graves, 2007; Gunning, 2006; Ruddell, 2006). Parents and teachers need to help them perceive themselves as people who can enjoy exploring oral and written language. Reading should be integrated into the broad communication process, which includes speaking, listening, and writing, as well as other communication systems, such as art, math, and music (Combs, 2006; Christie, Vukelich, & Enz, 2007; May, 2006). Children's early writing attempts should be encouraged without concern for the proper formation of letters or correct conventional spelling. Children should be encouraged to take risks in reading and writing, and errors should be viewed as a natural part of the child's growth (Spandel, 2004; Tompkins, 2006). Parents and teachers should take time to regularly read to children from a wide variety of poetry, fiction, and nonfiction (Temple & others, 2005). They also should present models for young children to emulate by using language appropriately, listening and responding to children's talk, and engaging in their own reading and writing. And children should be encouraged to be active participants in the learning process, rather than passive recipients of knowledge. This can be accomplished by using activities that stimulate experimentation with talking, listening, writing, and reading (Barone, Hardman, & Taylor, 2006).

The devl and the babe goste

† DEVL NAPD iN The BRITE SUNLITE he SED iT IS HOLOWENE I HAV to GET up AND GET. reDE to SCer The littL CHILJRIN WEN ThAEGO to CHRICOR CHRETE FRST He MADE A JACAL ETRN He PUT 2 CEDS iN iT to RELE SCer THEM THN He MADE A COL JRIN to CAST SPELS ON The CHIL JRIN.

Anna Mudd began writing stories when she was 4-years old. Above is her story, "The devl and the babe goste," which she wrote as a 6-year-old. The story includes poetic images, sophisticated syntax, and vocabulary that reflect advances in language development. *What are some guidelines parents and teachers can follow in helping young children develop literacy skills?*

Review and Reflect • LEARNING GOAL 3

③ Summarize how language develops in early childhood

Review
- How do phonology and morphology change during early childhood?
- What characterizes young children's understanding of syntax and semantics in early childhood?
- What advances in pragmatics occur in early childhood?
- How can parents and teachers effectively guide young children's literacy?

Reflect
- How are nature and nurture likely to be involved in the dramatic increase in a young child's spoken vocabulary?

4 EARLY CHILDHOOD EDUCATION

Variations in Early Childhood Education	Educating Children Who Are Disadvantaged	Controversies in Early Childhood Education

To the teachers at a Reggio-Emilia program (described in the chapter opening), preschool children are active learners, exploring the world with their peers, constructing their knowledge of the world in collaboration with their community, aided but not directed by the teachers. In many ways, the Reggio Emilia approach applies ideas consistent with the views of Piaget and Vygotsky discussed in this chapter. Does it matter to the children? How do other early education programs treat children, and how do the children fare? Our exploration of early childhood education focuses on variations in programs, education for children who are disadvantaged, and some controversies in early childhood education.

Variations in Early Childhood Education

Attending preschool is rapidly becoming the norm for U.S. children. In 2002, 43 states funded prekindergarten programs, and 55 percent of U.S. 3- and 4-year-old children attended center-based programs (NAEYC, 2005). Many other 3- and 4-year-old children attend private preschool programs.

There are many variations in the way young children are educated (Henninger, 2005; Hyson, Copple, & Jones, 2006; Morrison, 2006; Roopnarine & Metindogan, 2006). The foundation of early childhood education has been the child-centered kindergarten.

The Child-Centered Kindergarten   In the 1840s, Friedrich Froebel's concern for quality education for young children led to the founding of the kindergarten—literally, "a garden for children." The founder of the kindergarten understood that, like growing plants, children require careful nurturing. Unfortunately, too many of today's kindergartens have forgotten the importance of careful nurturing (Krogh & Slentz, 2001).

Nurturing is still key in the **child-centered kindergarten.** It emphasizes the education of the whole child and concern for his or her physical, cognitive, and socioemotional development (Hendrick & Weissman, 2006). Instruction is organized around the child's needs, interests, and learning styles. Emphasis is on the process of learning, rather than what is learned (Feeney, Christensen, & Moravesik, 2006;

child-centered kindergarten Education that involves the whole child by considering both the child's physical, cognitive, and social development and the child's needs, interests, and learning styles.

Early Childhood Education
NAEYC
High/Scope: Active Learning

White & Coleman, 2000). The child-centered kindergarten honors three principles: Each child follows a unique developmental pattern; young children learn best through firsthand experiences with people and materials; and play is extremely important in the child's total development. *Experimenting, exploring, discovering, trying out, restructuring, speaking,* and *listening* are frequent activities in excellent kindergarten programs. Such programs are closely attuned to the developmental status of 4- and 5-year-old children.

The Montessori Approach Montessori schools are patterned after the educational philosophy of Maria Montessori (1870–1952), an Italian physician-turned-educator, who crafted a revolutionary approach to young children's education at the beginning of the twentieth century (Wentworth, 1999). Her work began in Rome with a group of children who were mentally retarded. She was successful in teaching them to read, write, and pass examinations designed for normal children. Some time later, she turned her attention to poor children from the slums of Rome and had similar success in teaching them. Her approach has since been adopted extensively in private nursery schools in the United States.

The **Montessori approach** is a philosophy of education in which children are given considerable freedom and spontaneity in choosing activities. They are allowed to move from one activity to another as they desire. The teacher acts as a facilitator rather than a director. The teacher shows the child how to perform intellectual activities, demonstrates interesting ways to explore curriculum materials, and offers help when the child requests it. "By encouraging children to make decisions from an early age, Montessori programs seek to develop self-regulated problem solvers who can make choices and manage their time effectively" (Hyson, Copple, & Jones, 2006, p. 14). The number of Montessori schools in the United States has expanded dramatically in recent years, from one school in 1959 to 355 schools in 1970 to approximately 4,000 in 2005 (Whitescarver, 2006).

Some developmentalists favor the Montessori approach, but others believe that it neglects children's social development (Chattin-McNichols, 1992). For example, while Montessori fosters independence and the development of cognitive skills, it deemphasizes verbal interaction between the teacher and child and peer interaction. Montessori's critics also argue that it restricts imaginative play and that its heavy reliance on self-corrective materials may not adequately allow for creativity and for a variety of learning styles (Goffin & Wilson, 2001).

Larry Page and Sergey Brin, founders of the highly successful Internet search engine, Google, recently said that their early years at Montessori schools were a major factor in their success (International Montessori Council, 2006). During an interview with Barbara Walters, they said they learned how to be self-directed and self-starters at Montessori (ABC News, 2005). They commented that Montessori experiences encouraged them to think for themselves and allowed them the freedom to develop their own interests.

Developmentally Appropriate and Inappropriate Education A growing number of educators and psychologists believe that preschool and young elementary school children learn best through active, hands-on teaching methods such as games and dramatic play. They know that children develop at varying rates and that schools need to allow for these individual differences (Miranda, 2004). They also believe that schools should focus on improving children's social development, as well as their cognitive development (Brewer, 2007; Hyson, Copple, & Jones, 2006; Morrison, 2006). Educators refer to this type of schooling as **developmentally appropriate practice,** which is based on knowledge of the typical development of children within an age span (age appropriateness) as well as the uniqueness of the child (individual appropriateness). In contrast, developmentally inappropriate practice for a young child relies on abstract paper-and-pencil activities presented to large groups (McDaniels & others, 2005; Neuman & Roskos, 2005). The Reggio Emilia approach, described in the opening of the chapter, reflects developmentally appropriate practice. Figure 8.18 provides examples of developmentally appropriate and inappropriate practices (Bredekamp & Copple, 1997).

Montessori approach An educational philosophy in which children are given considerable freedom and spontaneity in choosing activities and are allowed to move from one activity to another as they desire.

developmentally appropriate practice Education that focuses on the typical developmental patterns of children (age appropriateness) and the uniqueness of each child (individual appropriateness).

Component	Developmentally Appropriate Practice	Developmentally Inappropriate Practice
Creating a caring community of learners	To promote a positive climate for learning, teachers help children learn how to develop positive relationships with other children and adults.	Little or no effort is made to build a sense of community.
	Teachers foster group cohesiveness and create activities that meet children's individual needs.	The curriculum and environment are essentially the same for each group of children that comes through the program without considering the interests and identities of the children.
	Teachers bring each child's home culture the interests and identities of and language into the shared culture of the school.	Cultural and other individual differences are ignored.
	Teachers recognize the importance of having children work and play collaboratively.	Teachers don't help children develop feelings of caring and empathy for each other.
Teaching to enhance development and learning	Teachers plan and prepare a learning environment that fosters children's initiative, active exploration of material, and sustained engagement with other children, adults, and activities.	The environment is disorderly with little structure.
	In selecting materials, teachers consider children's developmental levels and cultural backgrounds.	The organization of the environment limits children's interaction with other children.
	Teachers maintain a safe, healthy environment and carefully supervise children.	Teachers don't adequately monitor children. Learning materials are mainly drill-and-practice, workbook-type activities rather than interesting and engaging activities.
	Teachers give children opportunities to plan and select many of their program activities from a variety of learning areas and projects.	The program provides few or no opportunities for children to make choices. Children spend too much time sitting and being quiet. Children do a lot of paper-and-pencil seatwork.
	Teachers encourage children's language and communication skills.	Teachers don't provide adequate time for children to develop concepts and skills.
	Teaching strategies involve observing and interacting with children to determine what each child is capable of doing.	Too many activities are uninteresting and unchallenging, or so difficult, that they diminish children's intrinsic motivation to learn.
	Teachers support children's play and child-chosen activities. They also provide many opportunities for children to plan, think about, reflect on, and discuss their own experiences.	Teachers spend too much time providing negative feedback and punishment.
	Activities are interesting and at the right level to challenge children and encourage their intrinsic motivation.	
	Teachers facilitate the development of social skills and self control by providing positive guidance strategies.	
Constructing appropriate curriculum	Curriculum goals assess learning in all developmental areas —physical, social, emotional, language, aesthetic, and intellectual.	Curriculum goals are narrowly focused.
	Curriculum content from various disciplines, such as math, science, or social studies, is integrated through themes, projects, play, and other learning experiences.	The curriculum is too trivial and follows a rigid plan that doesn't take into account children's interests.
	The curriculum plan designed to help children explore key ideas in disciplines appropriate for their age.	In some programs, the curriculum is not adequately planned.
	Culturally diverse and nonsexist materials are provided.	Curriculum expectations are not well matched to children's intellectual capacities and developmental characteristics.
	Teachers use a variety of approaches and daily opportunities to develop children's language and literacy skills through meaningful experiences.	Children's cultural and linguistic backgrounds are ignored.
	Children have daily opportunities for aesthetice expression through art and music, as well as daily opportunities to develop gross- and fine-motor skills.	Reading and writing instruction is too rigid.
		Instruction focuses on isolated skill development through rote memorization.
		Little effort is made to provide children with opportunities to engage in aesthetic activities.
		Little time is spent in gross or fine motor activities.

FIGURE 8.18 Examples of NAEYC Guidelines for Appropriate and Inappropriate Practices for 3- through 5-Year-Olds. Source: Adapted, by permission, from S. Bredekamp and C. Copple, "Developmentally Appropriate Practice for 3- through 5-Year-olds," in Developmentally Appropriate Practice in Early Childhood Programs, Rev. ed., eds. S. Bredekamp and C. Copple (Washington, DC: NAEYC, 1997), 123–38.

One recent study compared 182 children from five developmentally appropriate kindergarten classrooms (with hands-on activities and integrated curriculum tailored to meet age group, cultural, and individual learning styles) and five developmentally inappropriate kindergarten classrooms (which had an academic, direct instruction emphasis with extensive use of workbooks/worksheets, seatwork, and rote drill/practice activities) in a Louisiana school system (Hart & others, 2003). Children from the two types of classrooms did not differ in prekindergarten readiness and the classrooms were balanced in terms of sex and socioeconomic status. Teacher ratings of child behavior and scores on the California Achievement Test were obtained through the third grade. Children taught in developmentally inappropriate classrooms had slower growth in vocabulary, math application, and math computation. In another recent study, the academic achievement of mostly African American and Latino children who were attending Head Start was assessed in terms of whether they were in schools emphasizing developmentally appropriate or inappropriate practices (Huffman & Speer, 2000). The young children in the developmentally appropriate classrooms were more advanced in letter/word identification and showed better performance in applying problems over time.

Education for Young Children Who Are Disadvantaged

For many years, U.S. children from low-income families did not receive any education before they entered the first grade. Often, they began first grade already several steps behind their classmates in their readiness to learn. In the summer of 1965, the federal government began an effort to break the cycle of poverty and poor education for young children in the United States through **Project Head Start.** It is a compensatory program designed to provide children from low-income families the opportunity to acquire the skills and experiences important for success in school.

The goals and methods of Head Start programs vary greatly around the country. The U.S. Congress is considering whether to infuse Head Start programs with a stronger academic focus. Some worry that the emphasis on academic skills will come at the expense of reduced health services and decreased emphasis on socioemotional skills (Stipek, 2004).

Head Start programs are not all created equal. One estimate is that 40 percent of the 1,400 Head Start programs are of questionable quality (Zigler & Styfco, 1994). More attention needs to be given to developing consistently high-quality Head Start programs (Bronfenbrenner, 1995). One individual who is strongly motivated to make Head Start a valuable learning experience for young children from disadvantaged backgrounds is Yolanda Garcia. To read about her work, see the Careers in Life-Span Development insert.

Evaluations support the positive influence of quality early childhood programs on both the cognitive and social worlds of disadvantaged young children (Anderson & others, 2003; Chambers, Chung, & Slavin, 2006; Karoly, Kilburn, & Cannon, 2005; Reynolds, 1999; Ryan, Fauth, & Brooks-Gunn, 2006; Schweinhart & others, 2005; Seifert, 2006). One high-quality early childhood education program (although not a Head Start program) is the Perry Preschool program in Ypsilanti, Michigan, a 2-year preschool program that includes weekly home visits from program personnel. In analyses of the long-term effects of the program, adults who had been in the Perry Preschool program were compared with a control group of adults from the same background who did not receive the enriched early childhood education (Schweinhart & others, 2005; Weikart, 1993). Those who had been in the Perry Preschool program had fewer teen pregnancies and higher high school graduation rates (Weikart, 1993) and at age 40 more were in the workforce, owned their own homes, had a saving account, and had fewer arrests (Schweinhart & others, 2005).

Another longitudinal investigation pooled the data from eleven different early education studies that focused on children ranging in age from 9 to 19 years (Lazar,

**Head Start Resources
Poverty and Learning**

Project Head Start A government-funded program that is designed to provide children from low-income families the opportunity to acquire the skills and experiences important for school success.

Darlington, & others, 1982). The early education models varied substantially, but all were carefully planned and executed by experts in early childhood education. The results indicated that competent preschool education brought low-income children substantial benefits on all four dimensions investigated: school competence (such as special education and grade retention), abilities (as measured by standardized intelligence and achievement tests), attitudes and values, and impact on the family. In sum, ample evidence indicates that well-designed and well-implemented early childhood education programs are successful with low-income children.

Controversies in Early Childhood Education

Currently there is controversy about what the curriculum of U.S. early childhood education should be (Driscoll & Nagel, 2005; Hyson, Copple, & Jones, 2006; Morrison, 2006). On one side are those who advocate a child-centered, constructivist approach much like that emphasized by the NAEYC along the lines of developmentally appropriate practice. On the other side are those who advocate an academic, direct instruction approach.

In reality, many high-quality early childhood education programs include both academic and constructivist approaches. Many education experts like Lilian Katz (1999), though, worry about academic approaches that place too much pressure on young children to achieve and don't provide any opportunities to actively construct knowledge. Competent early childhood programs also should focus on cognitive development *and* socioemotional development, not exclusively on cognitive development (Anderson & others, 2003; Jacobson, 2004; Kagan & Scott-Little, 2004; NAEYC, 2002).

Early childhood education should encourage adequate preparation for learning, varied learning activities, trusting relationships between adults and children, and increased parental involvement (Hildebrand, Phenice, & Hines, 2000). Too many young children go to substandard early childhood programs (Morrison, 2006). According to a report by the Carnegie Corporation (1996), four out of five early childhood programs did not meet quality standards.

Is preschool a good thing for all children? According to developmental psychologist David Elkind (1988), parents who are exceptionally competent and dedicated and who have both the time and the energy can provide the basic ingredients of early childhood education in their home. If parents have the competence and resources to provide young children with a variety of learning experiences and exposure to other children and adults (possibly through neighborhood play groups), along with opportunities for extensive play, then home

CAREERS in LIFE-SPAN DEVELOPMENT

Yolanda Garcia
Director of Children's Services/Head Start

Yolanda Garcia has been the Director of the Children's Services Department for the Santa Clara, California, County Office of Education since 1980. As director, she is responsible for managing child development programs for 2,500 3- to 5-year-old children in 127 classrooms. Her training includes two master's degrees, one in public policy and child welfare from the University of Chicago and another in education administration from San Jose State University.

Yolanda has served on many national advisory committees that have resulted in improvements in the staffing of Head Start programs. Most notably, she served on the Head Start Quality Committee that recommended the development of Early Head Start and revised performance standards for Head Start programs. Yolanda currently is a member of the American Academy of Science Committee on the Integration of Science and Early Childhood Education.

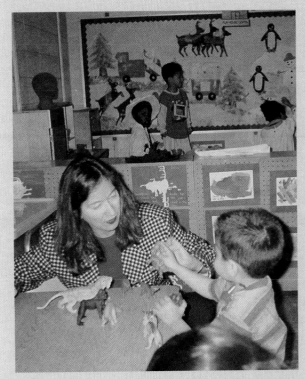

Yolanda Garcia, Director of Children's Services/Head Start, working with some Head Start children in Santa Clara, California.

What is the curriculum controversy in early childhood education?

schooling may sufficiently educate young children. However, if parents do not have the commitment, the time, the energy, and the resources to provide young children with an environment that approximates a good early childhood program, then it *does* matter whether a child attends preschool.

In Japan and many developing countries, the goals of early childhood education are quite different from those of American programs. To read about the differences, see the Diversity in Life-Span Development interlude.

DIVERSITY IN LIFE-SPAN DEVELOPMENT

Early Childhood Education in Japan and Developing Countries

As in America, there is diversity in Japanese early childhood education. Some Japanese kindergartens have specific aims, such as early musical training or the practice of Montessori strategies. In large cities, some kindergartens are attached to universities that have elementary and secondary schools. In most Japanese preschools, however, little emphasis is put on academic instruction.

In one study, 300 Japanese and 210 American preschool teachers, child development specialists, and parents were asked about various aspects of early childhood education (Tobin, Wu, & Davidson, 1989). Only 2 percent of the Japanese respondents listed "to give children a good start academically" as one of their top three reasons for a society to have preschools. In contrast, over half the American respondents chose this as one of their top three choices. Japanese schools do not teach reading, writing, and mathematics but rather skills like persistence, concentration, and the ability to function as a member of a group. The vast majority of young Japanese children are taught to read at home by their parents.

In the comparison of Japanese and American parents, more than 60 percent of the Japanese parents said that the purpose of preschool is to give children experience being a member of the group compared with only 20 percent of the U.S. parents

(Tobin, Wu, & Davidson, 1989) (see figure 8.19). Lessons in living and working together grow naturally out of the Japanese culture. In many Japanese kindergartens, children wear the same uniforms, including caps, which are of different colors to indicate the classrooms to which they belong. They have identical sets of equipment, kept in identical drawers and shelves. This is not intended to turn the young children into robots, as some Americans have observed, but to impress on them that other people, just like themselves, have needs and desires that are equally important (Hendry, 1995).

Japan is a highly advanced industrialized country. What about developing countries—how do they compare to the United States in educating young children? The wide range of programs and emphasis on the education of the whole child—physically, cognitively, and socioemotionally—that characterizes U.S. early childhood does not exist in many developing countries (Rooparnine & Metingdogan, 2006). Economic pressures and parents' belief that education should be academically rigorous have produced teacher-centered rather than child-centered early childhood education programs in most developing countries. Among the countries in which this type of early childhood education has been observed are Jamaica, China, Thailand, Kenya, and Turkey. In these countries, young children are usually given few choices and are educated in highly structured settings. Emphasis is on learning academic skills through rote memory and recitation (Lin, Johnson, & Johnson, 2003). Programs in Mexico, Singapore, Korea, and Hong Kong have been observed to be closer to those in the United States in their emphasis on curriculum flexibility and play-based methods (Cisneros-Cohernour & others, 2000).

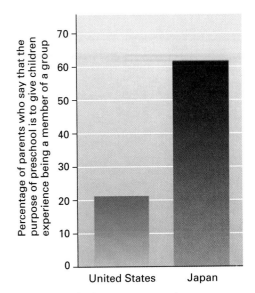

FIGURE 8.19 Comparison of Japanese and U.S. Parents' Views on the Purpose of Preschool

Review and Reflect ● LEARNING GOAL 4

4 **Evaluate different approaches to early childhood education**

Review
- What are some variations in early childhood education?
- What are the main efforts to educate young children who are disadvantaged?
- What are two controversies about early childhood education?

Reflect
- Might preschool be more beneficial to children from middle-income than low-income families? Why?

REACH YOUR LEARNING GOALS

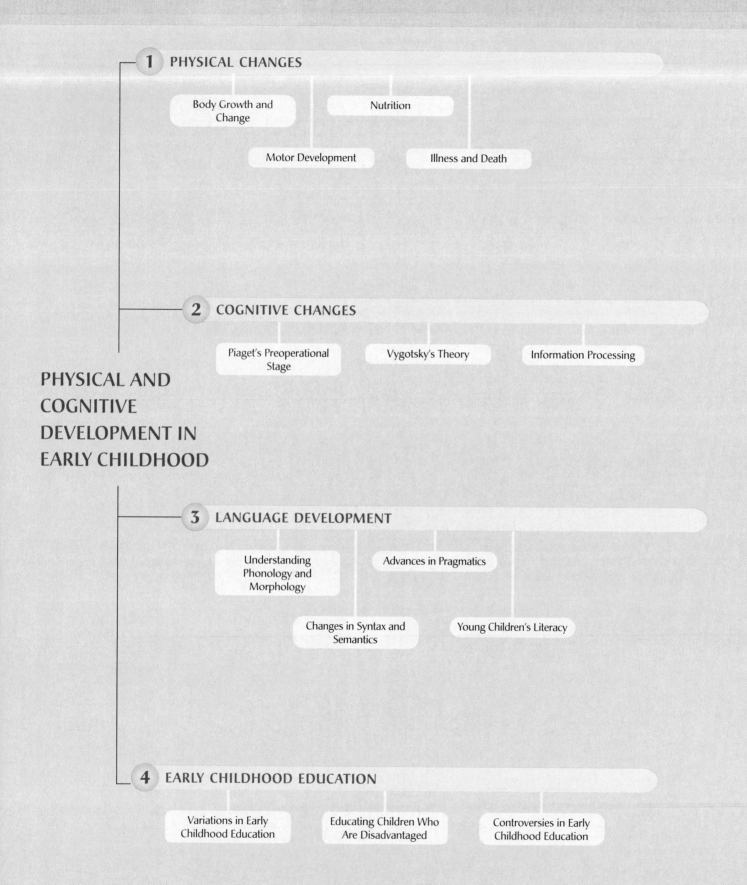

PHYSICAL AND
COGNITIVE
DEVELOPMENT IN
EARLY CHILDHOOD

1 PHYSICAL CHANGES

Body Growth and Change

Nutrition

Motor Development

Illness and Death

2 COGNITIVE CHANGES

Piaget's Preoperational Stage

Vygotsky's Theory

Information Processing

3 LANGUAGE DEVELOPMENT

Understanding Phonology and Morphology

Advances in Pragmatics

Changes in Syntax and Semantics

Young Children's Literacy

4 EARLY CHILDHOOD EDUCATION

Variations in Early Childhood Education

Educating Children Who Are Disadvantaged

Controversies in Early Childhood Education

SUMMARY

1 Physical Changes: *Identify physical changes in early childhood*

Body Growth and Change

The average child grows $2\frac{1}{2}$ inches in height and gains between 5 and 7 pounds a year during early childhood. Growth patterns vary individually, though. Some children are unusually short because of congenital problems, growth hormone deficiency, a physical problem that develops in childhood, or emotional problems. Some of the brain's increase in size in early childhood is due to increases in the number and size of dendrites, some to myelination. From 3 to 6 years of age, the most rapid growth in the brain occurs in the frontal lobes. Brain maturation contributes to improved cognitive abilities.

Motor Development

Gross motor skills increase dramatically during early childhood. Children become increasingly adventuresome as their gross motor skills improve. Fine motor skills also improve substantially during early childhood. Left-handed children are as competent in motor skills and intellect as right-handed children, although left-handers have more reading problems. Both genetic and environmental explanations of handedness have been given.

Nutrition

Energy requirements vary according to basal metabolism, rate of growth, and level of activity. Too many young children in the United States are being raised on diets that are too high in fat. The child's life should be centered on activities, not meals. Other nutritional concerns include malnutrition in early childhood and the inadequate diets of many children living in poverty.

Illness and Death

In recent decades, vaccines have virtually eradicated many diseases that once resulted in the deaths of many young children. The disorders still most likely to be fatal for young children are birth defects, cancer, and heart disease, but accidents are the leading cause of death in young children. A special concern is the poor health status of many young children in low-income families. They often have less resistance to disease, including colds and influenza, than do their higher-socioeconomic-status counterparts. Concerns also have been voiced about the inadequate health care of young children from ethnic minority backgrounds. There has been a dramatic increase in HIV/AIDS in young children in developing countries in the last decade.

2 Cognitive Changes: *Describe three views of the cognitive changes that occur in early childhood*

Piaget's Preoperational Stage

According to Piaget, in the preoperational stage children cannot yet perform operations, which are reversible mental actions, but they begin to present the world with symbols, to form stable concepts, and to reason. During the symbolic function substage, which occurs between 2 and 4 years of age, children begin to create symbols but their thought is limited by egocentrism and animism. During the intuitive thought substage, which stretches from 4 to 7 years of age, children begin to reason and to bombard adults with questions. Thought at this substage is called intuitive because children seem so sure about their knowledge yet are unaware of how they know what they know. Centration and a lack of conservation also characterize the preoperational stage.

Vygotsky's Theory

Vygotsky's theory represents a social constructivist approach to development. According to Vygotsky, children construct knowledge through social interaction, and they use language not only to communicate with others but also to plan, guide, and monitor their own behavior and to help them solve problems. His theory suggests that adults should assess and use the child's zone of proximal development (ZPD), which is the range of tasks that are too difficult for children to master alone but that can be learned with the guidance and assistance of adults or more-skilled children. The theory also suggests that adults and peers should teach through scaffolding, which involves changing the level of support over the course of a teaching session, with the more-skilled person adjusting guidance to fit the student's current performance level.

Information Processing

The child's ability to attend to stimuli dramatically improves during early childhood, but the child attends to the salient rather than the relevant features of a task. Significant improvement in short-term memory occurs during early childhood. With good prompts, young children's long-term memories can be accurate, although young children can be led into developing false memories. Young children usually don't use strategies to remember, but they can learn rather simple problem-solving strategies. Theory of mind is the awareness of one's own mental processes and the mental processes of others. Children begin to understand mental states involving perceptions, desires, and emotions at 2 to 3 years of age and at 4 to 5 years of age realize that people can have false beliefs. It is only beyond the early childhood years that children have a deepening appreciation of the mind itself rather than just understanding mental states.

3 Language Development: *Summarize how language develops in early childhood*

Understanding Phonology and Morphology

Young children increase their grasp of language's rule systems. In terms of phonology, most young children become more sensitive to the sounds of spoken language. Berko's classic experiment demonstrated that young children understand morphological rules.

Changes in Syntax and Semantics
Preschool children learn and apply rules of syntax and how words should be ordered. In terms of semantics, vocabulary development increases dramatically during early childhood.

Advances in Pragmatics
Young children's conversational skills improve, they increase their sensitivity to the needs of others in conversation, and they learn to change their speech style to suit the situation.

Young Children's Literacy
There has been increased interest in young children's literacy. Young children need to develop positive images of reading and writing skills through a supportive environment. Children should be active participants and be immersed in a wide range of interesting and enjoyable listening, talking, writing, and reading experiences.

 4   Early Childhood Education: *Evaluate different approaches to early childhood education*

Variations in Early Childhood Education
The child-centered kindergarten emphasizes the education of the whole child, with particular attention to individual varia-tion, the process of learning, and the importance of play in development. The Montessori approach allows children to choose from a range of activities while teachers serve as facilitators. Developmentally appropriate practice (illustrated by the Reggio Emilia approach) focuses on the typical patterns of children (age-appropriateness) and the uniqueness of each child (individual-appropriateness). Such practice contrasts with developmentally inappropriate practice, which ignores the concrete, hands-on approach to learning.

Educating Children Who Are Disadvantaged
The U.S. government has tried to break the poverty cycle with programs such as Head Start. Model programs have been shown to have positive effects on children who live in poverty.

Controversies in Early Childhood Education
Controversy characterizes early childhood education curricula. On the one side are the child-centered, constructivist advocates; on the other are those who advocate an instructivist, academic approach. Another controversy focuses on whether preschool education matters. Some parents can educate young children as effectively as a school does; however, most parents do not have the skills, time, and commitment to do so.

KEY TERMS

myelination 240
basal metabolism rate
 (BMR) 243
preoperational stage 247
operations 247
symbolic function
 substage 247

egocentrism 247
animism 248
intuitive thought substage 248
centration 249
conservation 249
social constructivist
 approach 250

zone of proximal development
 (ZPD) 251
short-term memory 256
strategies 258
theory of mind 258
child-centered
 kindergarten 263

Montessori approach 264
developmentally appropriate
 practice 264
Project Head Start 266

KEY PEOPLE

Jean Piaget 247
Barbel Inhelder 247

Rochel Gelman 250
Lev Vygotsky 250

Zhe Chen and Robert
 Siegler 258
Jean Berko 261

Maria Montessori 264
Lilian Katz 267
David Elkind 267

E-LEARNING TOOLS

To help you master the material in this chapter, you'll find a number of valuable study tools on the LifeMap CD-ROM that accompanies this book and on the Online Learning Center for *Life-Span Development*, eleventh edition, at **www.mhhe.com/ santrockld11**.

Video Clips

In the margins of this book there are icons directing you to the LifeMap CD-ROM that accompanies the book. There you'll find a video for chapter 8 called "Children and Nutrition." Diet and physical activity, as this segment demonstrates, are important aspects of a healthy lifestyle. These lifestyle choices begin in early childhood.

Self-Assessment

Connect to **www.mhhe.com/santrockld11** to examine your understanding of cognitive development in early childhood by completing the self-assessment, *What I Think Is Important in Early Childhood Education*.

Taking It to the Net

Connect to **www.mhhe.com/santrockld11** to research the answers to these questions.

1. A child's grasp of elementary physics (conservation laws, for example) normally improves during Piaget's preoperational stage. Many adults, however, nevertheless retain a set of incorrect assumptions about motion and matter—what psychologists sometimes refer to as "intuitive physics." Julien is 5 years old. When asked to describe the trajectory a chess piece would follow as it spun off a revolving circular table, Julien answers that it would follow a curved trajectory (an answer inconsistent with Newton's first law of motion). What other misconceptions about the physical world might Julien be likely to retain past the age of 10?

2. Beyonce, who is working in a prosecutor's office for her senior internship, has been asked to write a memo on the suggestibility of child witnesses and how likely a jury is to believe a child's testimony in court cases. How can she find information for the memo that provides research-based facts as well as guidelines for dealing with child witnesses that will be helpful for the prosecutors?

Health and Well-Being, Parenting, and Education Exercises

Build your decision-making skills by trying your hand at the health and well-being, parenting, and education exercises.

Connect to **www.mhhe.com/santrockld11** to research the answers and complete the exercises.

Chapter 9

SOCIOEMOTIONAL DEVELOPMENT IN EARLY CHILDHOOD

Let us play, for it is yet day And we cannot go to sleep; Besides, in the sky the little birds fly And the hills are all covered with sheep.

WILLIAM BLAKE
English Poet, 19th Century

LEARNING GOALS

1 Discuss emotional and personality development in early childhood

2 Explain how families can influence young children's development

3 Describe the roles of peers, play, and television in young children's development

Images of Life-Span Development
Craig Lesley's Complicated Early Emotional and Social Life

In his memoir *Burning Fence: A Western Memoir of Fatherhood,* award-winning novelist Craig Lesley describes one memory from his early childhood:

> Lifting me high above his head, my father placed me in the crotch of the Bing cherry tree growing beside my mother's parents' house in The Dalles. A little frightened at the dizzying height, I pressed my palms into the tree's rough, peeling bark. My father stood close, reassuring. I could see his olive skin, dazzling smile, and sharp-creased army uniform.
>
> "Rudell, don't let him fall." My mother watched, her arms held out halfway, as if to catch me. . . .
>
> The cherries were ripe and robins flittered through the green leaves, pecking at the Bings. Tipping my head back I could see blue sky beyond the extended branches.
>
> "That's enough. Bring him down now." My mother's arms reached out farther.
>
> Laughing, my father grabbed me under the arms, twirled me around, and plunked me into the grass. I wobbled a little. Imprinted on my palms was the pattern of the tree bark, and I brushed off the little bark pieces on my dungarees.
>
> In a moment, my grandmother gave me a small glass of lemonade. . . .
>
> This first childhood memory of my father remains etched in my mind. . . .
>
> When I grew older, I realized that my father had never lifted me into the cherry tree. After Rudell left, I never saw him until I was fifteen. My grandfather had put me in the tree. Still, the memory of my father lifting me into the tree persists. Even today, I remain half-convinced by the details, the press of bark against my palms, the taste of lemonade, the texture of my father's serge uniform. Apparently, my mind has cross-wired the photographs of my handsome father in his army uniform with the logical reality that my grandfather set me in the crotch of the tree.
>
> Why can I remember the event so vividly? I guess because I wanted so much for my father to be there. I have no easy answers. (Lesley, 2005, pp. 8–10)

Like millions of children, Lesley experienced a family torn by divorce; he would also experience abuse by a stepfather. When his father left, Lesley was an infant, but even as a preschooler, he felt his father's absence. Once he planned to win a gift for his father so that his grandmother "could take it to him and then he'd come to see me" (Lesley, 2005, p. 16). In just a few years, the infant had become a child with a complicated emotional and social life.

PREVIEW

In early childhood, children's emotional lives and personalities develop in significant ways and their small worlds widen. In addition to the continuing influence of family relationships, peers take on a more significant role in children's development and play fills the days of many young children's lives.

1 EMOTIONAL AND PERSONALITY DEVELOPMENT

The Self		Moral Development
	Emotional Development	Gender

Numerous changes characterize young children's socioemotional development in early childhood. Their developing minds and social experiences produce remarkable advances in the development of their self, emotional maturity, moral understanding, and gender awareness.

The Self

We learned in chapter 7 that during the second year of life children make considerable progress in self-recognition. In early childhood, their development enables young children to face the issue of initiative versus guilt and to enhance their self-understanding.

Initiative Versus Guilt   According to Erik Erikson (1968), the psychosocial stage that characterizes early childhood is *initiative versus guilt.* By now, children have become convinced that they are persons of their own; during early childhood, they must discover what kind of person they will become. They intensely identify with their parents, who most of the time appear to them to be powerful and beautiful, although often unreasonable, disagreeable, and sometimes even dangerous. During early childhood, children use their perceptual, motor, cognitive, and language skills to make things happen. They have a surplus of energy that permits them to forget failures quickly and to approach new areas that seem desirable—even if they seem dangerous—with undiminished zest and some increased sense of direction. On their own *initiative,* then, children at this stage exuberantly move out into a wider social world.

The great governor of initiative is *conscience.* Children now not only feel afraid of being found out, which causes shame, but they also begin to hear the inner voices of self-observation, self-guidance, and self-punishment (Bybee, 1999). Their initiative and enthusiasm may bring them not only rewards but also guilt, which lowers self-esteem.

Whether children leave this stage with a sense of initiative that outweighs their sense of guilt depends in large part on how parents respond to their children's self-initiated activities. Children who are given the freedom and opportunity to initiate motor play, such as running, bike riding, sledding, skating, tussling, and wrestling, have their sense of initiative supported. Children's initiative is also supported when parents answer their questions and do not deride or inhibit fantasy or play. In contrast, if children are made to feel that their motor activity is bad, that their questions are a nuisance, and that their play is silly and stupid, then they often develop a sense of guilt over self-initiated activities that may persist through life's later stages (Elkind, 1970).

Self-Understanding   In Erikson's portrait of early childhood, the young child clearly has begun to develop **self-understanding,** which is the representation of self, the substance and content of self-conceptions (Harter, 2006). Though not the whole of personal identity, self-understanding provides its rational underpinnings (Damon & Hart, 1992). Mainly through interviews, researchers have probed children's conceptions of many aspects of self-understanding (Harter, 2006).

As we saw in chapter 7, early self-understanding involves self-recognition. For example, we saw that recognizing one's body parts in a mirror takes place by approximately 18 months of age and that a sense of me emerges later in the second year

self-understanding The child's cognitive representation of self, the substance and content of the child's self-conceptions.

and early in the third year. In early childhood, young children think that the self can be described by many material characteristics, such as size, shape, and color. They distinguish themselves from others through many physical and material attributes. Says 4-year-old Sandra, "I'm different from Jennifer because I have brown hair and she has blond hair." Says 4-year-old Ralph, "I am different from Hank because I am taller and I am different from my sister because I have a bicycle." Physical activities are also a central component of the self in early childhood (Keller, Ford, & Meacham, 1978). For example, preschool children often describe themselves in terms of activities such as play. In sum, in early childhood, children often describe themselves in terms of body image, material possessions, and physical activities.

Emotional Development

The young child's growing awareness of self is linked to the ability to feel an expanding range of emotions. Young children, like adults, experience many emotions during the course of a day. At times, they also try to make sense of other people's emotional reactions and to control their own emotions.

A young child expressing the emotion of shame. *Why is shame called a "self-conscious emotion"?*

Self-Conscious Emotions   Recall from chapter 7 that even young infants experience emotions such as joy and fear, but to experience *self-conscious emotions,* children must be able to refer to themselves and be aware of themselves as distinct from others (Lewis, 2002). Pride, shame, embarrassment, and guilt are examples of self-conscious emotions. Self-conscious emotions do not appear to develop until self-awareness appears in the last half of the second year of life.

During the early childhood years, emotions such as pride and guilt become more common. They are especially influenced by parents' responses to children's behavior. For example, a young child may experience shame when a parent says, "You should feel bad about biting your sister."

In one study, girls showed more shame and pride than boys (Stipek, Recchia, & McClintic, 1992). This gender difference is interesting because girls are more at risk for internalizing disorders, such as anxiety and depression, in which feelings of shame and self-criticism often are evident (Cummings, Braungart-Rieker, & Du Rocher-Schudlich, 2003).

Young Children's Emotion Language and Understanding of Emotion   Among the most important changes in emotional development in early childhood are an increased ability to talk about their own and others' emotions and an increased understanding of emotion (Kuebli, 1994). Between 2 and 4 years of age, children considerably increase the number of terms they use to describe emotions (Ridgeway, Waters, & Kuczaj, 1985). They also are learning about the causes and consequences of feelings (Denham, 1998).

When they are 4 to 5 years of age, children show an increased ability to reflect on emotions. They also begin to understand that the same event can elicit different feelings in different people. Moreover, they show a growing awareness that they need to manage their emotions to meet social standards (Bruce, Olen, & Jensen, 1999). Figure 9.1 summarizes the characteristics of young children's talk about emotion and their understanding of it.

Emotion-Coaching and Emotion-Dismissing Parents   Parents can play an important role in helping young children regulate their emotions (Havighurst, Harley, & Prior, 2004; Thompson, 2006; Thompson & Lagattuta, 2005). Depending on how they talk with their children about emotion, parents can be described as taking an *emotion-coaching* or an *emotion-dismissing* approach (Katz, 1999). *Emotion-coaching parents* monitor their children's emotions, view their children's negative emotions as opportunities for teaching, assist them in labeling emotions, and coach them in how to deal effectively with emotions. In contrast, *emotion-dismissing parents*

Approximate Age of Child	Description
2 to 3 years	Increase emotion vocabulary most rapidly
	Correctly label simple emotions in self and others and talk about past, present, and future emotions
	Talk about the causes and consequences of some emotions and identify emotions associated with certain situations
	Use emotion language in pretend play
4 to 5 years	Show increased capacity to reflect verbally on emotions and to consider more complex relations between emotions and situations
	Understand that the same event may call forth different feelings in different people and that feelings sometimes persist long after the events that caused them
	Demonstrate growing awareness about controlling and managing emotions in accord with social standards

FIGURE 9.1 Young Children's Emotion Language and Understanding. Preschoolers become more adept at talking about and understanding their own and others' emotions. *What physical changes (discussed in chapter 8) might be linked with the emotional development of preschoolers?*

view their role as to deny, ignore, or change negative emotions. Researchers have found that when interacting with their children, emotion-coaching parents are less rejecting, use more scaffolding and praise, and are more nurturant than are emotion-dismissing parents (Gottman & DeClaire, 1997). The children of emotion-coaching parents were better at soothing themselves when they got upset, more effective in regulating their negative affect, focused their attention better, and had fewer behavior problems than the children of emotion-dismissing parents.

Regulation of Emotion and Peer Relations Emotions play a strong role in determining whether a child's peer relationships are successful (Eisenberg, Spinrad, & Smith, 2004; Saarni & others, 2006). Moody and emotionally negative children experience greater rejection by their peers, whereas emotionally positive children are more popular (Stocker & Dunn, 1990).

Emotional regulation is an important aspect of getting along with peers (Saarni & others, 2006). In one study conducted in the natural context of young children's everyday peer interactions, self-regulation of emotion enhanced children's social competence (Fabes & others, 1999). Children who made an effort to control their emotional responses were more likely to respond in socially competent ways when peers provoked them—for example, by making a hostile comment or taking something away from them. In sum, the ability to modulate one's emotions is an important skill that benefits children in their relationships with peers (Saarni & others, 2006).

An emotion-coaching parent. *What are some differences in emotion-coaching and emotion-dismissing parents?*

Moral Development

Unlike a crying infant, a screaming 5-year-old is likely to be thought responsible for making a fuss. The parents may worry about whether the 5-year-old is a "bad" child. Although some people think children are innately good (as discussed in chapter 1), many developmentalists believe that just as parents help their children become good readers, musicians, or athletes, parents must nurture goodness and help their children develop morally. **Moral development** involves the development of thoughts, feelings, and behaviors regarding rules and conventions about what people should do in their interactions with other people. Major developmental theories have focused on different aspects of moral development.

moral development Development that involves thoughts, feelings, and actions regarding rules and conventions about what people should do in their interactions with other people.

What is moral is what you feel good after and what is immoral is what you feel bad after.

—ERNEST HEMINGWAY
American Author, 20th Century

Piaget extensively observed and interviewed 4- to 12-year-old children as they played games to learn how they used and thought about the games' rules.

heteronomous morality The first stage of moral development in Piaget's theory, occurring from approximately 4 to 7 years of age. Justice and rules are conceived of as unchangeable properties of the world, removed from the control of people.

autonomous morality The second stage of moral development in Piaget's theory, displayed by older children (about 10 years of age and older). The child becomes aware that rules and laws are created by people and that, in judging an action, one should consider the actor's intentions as well as the consequences.

Moral Feelings   Feelings of anxiety and guilt are central to the account of moral development provided by Freud's psychoanalytic theory (introduced in chapter 2). According to Freud, to reduce anxiety, avoid punishment, and maintain parental affection, children identify with parents, internalizing their standards of right and wrong, and thus form the *superego,* the moral element of personality.

Resolution of the *Oedipal conflict* plays a central role in this development. According to Freud, the young child develops an intense desire to replace the same-sex parent and enjoy the affections of the opposite-sex parent. At about 5 to 6 years of age, children recognize that their same-sex parent might punish them for their incestuous wishes. In fear of losing the parents' love and of being punished for their unacceptable sexual wishes, the child identifies with the same-sex parent, internalizing the parent's standards, and turns inward the hostility that had been aimed at the same-sex parent. This inwardly directed hostility is felt as guilt. In the psychoanalytic account of moral development, the self-punitiveness of guilt is responsible for keeping the child from committing transgressions. That is, children conform to societal standards to avoid guilt.

Freud's ideas about the Oedipal conflict are not backed by research, but guilt certainly can motivate moral behavior. Other emotions, however, also contribute to the child's moral development, including positive feelings. One important example is *empathy,* which is reacting to another person's feelings with an emotional response that is similar to the other's feelings (Eisenberg, 2006; Eisenberg, Fabes, & Spinrad, 2006; Hoffman, 2002; Johansson, 2006).

Infants have the capacity for some purely empathic responses, but empathy often requires the ability to discern another's inner psychological states, or what is called "perspective taking." For effective moral action, children need to learn how to identify a wide range of emotional states in others. They also need to learn to anticipate what kinds of action will improve another person's emotional state (Eisenberg, Fabes, & Spinrad, 2006).

Moral Reasoning   Interest in how children think about moral issues was stimulated by Piaget (1932), who extensively observed and interviewed children from the ages of 4 through 12. Piaget watched children play marbles to learn how they used and thought about the game's rules. He also asked children about ethical issues—theft, lies, punishment, and justice, for example. Piaget concluded that children go through two distinct stages in how they think about morality.

- From 4 to 7 years of age, children display **heteronomous morality,** the first stage of moral development in Piaget's theory. Children think of justice and rules as unchangeable properties of the world, removed from the control of people.
- From 7 to 10 years of age, children are in a transition showing some features of the first stage of moral reasoning and some stages of the second stage, autonomous morality.
- From about 10 years of age and older, children show **autonomous morality.** They become aware that rules and laws are created by people, and in judging an action, they consider the actor's intentions as well as the consequences.

Because young children are heteronomous moralists, they judge the rightness or goodness of behavior by considering its consequences, not the intentions of the actor. For example, to the heteronomous moralist, breaking 12 cups accidentally is worse than breaking one cup intentionally. As children develop into moral autonomists, intentions assume paramount importance.

The heteronomous thinker also believes that rules are unchangeable and are handed down by all-powerful authorities. When Piaget suggested to young children that they use new rules in a game of marbles, they resisted. By contrast, older children—moral autonomists—accept change and recognize that rules are merely convenient conventions, subject to change.

The heteronomous thinker also believes in **immanent justice,** the concept that if a rule is broken, punishment will be meted out immediately. The young child believes that a violation is connected automatically to its punishment. Thus, young children often look around worriedly after doing something wrong, expecting inevitable punishment. Immanent justice also implies that if something unfortunate happens to someone, the person must have transgressed earlier. Older children, who are moral autonomists, recognize that punishment occurs only if someone witnesses the wrongdoing and that, even then, punishment is not inevitable.

How do these changes in moral reasoning occur? Piaget argued that, as children develop, they become more sophisticated in thinking about social matters, especially about the possibilities and conditions of cooperation. Piaget believed that this social understanding comes about through the mutual give-and-take of peer relations. In the peer group, where others have power and status similar to the child's, plans are negotiated and coordinated, and disagreements are reasoned about and eventually settled. Parent-child relations, in which parents have the power and children do not, are less likely to advance moral reasoning, because rules are often handed down in an authoritarian way.

Building on Piaget's ideas, Lawrence Kohlberg developed a theory of moral development that also emphasized moral reasoning and the influence of the give-and-take of peer relations. Like Piaget, Kohlberg concluded from his research that children begin as heteronomous moralists and decide whether an act is right and wrong by whether it is rewarded or punished. Later, in chapter 11, we examine Kohlberg's theory and his stages of moral development, the evidence his theory is based on, and its critics.

How is this child's moral thinking likely to be different about stealing a cookie depending on whether he is in Piaget's heteronomous or autonomous stage?

Moral Behavior   Moral behavior rather than moral reasoning is the focus of the behavioral and social cognitive approach (Bugental & Grusec, 2006; Grusec, 2006). It holds that the processes of reinforcement, punishment, and imitation explain the development of moral behavior. When children are rewarded for behavior that is consistent with laws and social conventions, they are likely to repeat that behavior. When models who behave morally are provided, children are likely to adopt their actions. And, when children are punished for immoral behavior, those behaviors are likely to be reduced or eliminated. However, because punishment may have adverse side effects, as discussed later in this chapter, it needs to be used judiciously and cautiously.

If a 4-year-old boy has been rewarded by his mother for telling the truth when he breaks a glass at home, does that mean that he is likely to tell the truth to his preschool teacher when he knocks over a vase and breaks it? Not necessarily; the situation influences behavior. More than half a century ago, a comprehensive study of thousands of children in many situations—at home, at school, and at church, for example—found that the totally honest child was virtually nonexistent; so was the child who cheated in all situations (Hartshorne & May, 1928–1930). Behavioral and social cognitive researchers emphasize that what children do in one situation is often only weakly related to what they do in other situations. A child might cheat in class but not in a game; a child might steal a piece of candy when alone but not steal it when others are present.

Social cognitive theorists also believe that the ability to resist temptation is closely tied to the development of self-control. To achieve this self-control, children must learn to delay gratification. According to social cognitive theorists, cognitive factors are important in the child's development of self-control (Bandura, 2002).

Gender

When he was 5 years old, Craig Lesley (whose story appeared at the opening of this chapter) spent hours building forts and blazing away with a cap gun in his basement, which his grandfather had turned into a "cowboy room" (Lesley, 2005, p. 20).

immanent justice The concept that, if a rule is broken, punishment will be meted out immediately.

Would a little girl have been as delighted with the chance to play cowboy? Maybe, but even by the time they are 3 years old, most little girls prefer "feminine" toys and most little boys prefer "masculine" toys. In other words, they display *gender-typed preferences.*

Recall that *gender* refers to the social and psychological dimensions of being male or female, and even preschool children display many of these dimensions. By the time he was 2 years old, Craig was probably aware that people can be divided into two categories. If he was like most young children, by the time he was 3 years old he had acquired a **gender identity,** which is the sense of being male or female. He had probably also begun to link dolls with girls and trucks with boys. In other words, even preschoolers begin to learn about **gender roles,** which are sets of expectations that prescribe how females or males should think, act, and feel. During the preschool years, most children increasingly act in ways that match their culture's gender roles.

Biological Influences

How do these and other gender differences come about? Biology clearly plays a role. Among the possible biological influences are chromosomes, hormones, and evolution.

Chromosomes and Hormones   Biologists have learned a great deal about how sex differences develop. Recall that humans normally have 46 chromosomes arranged in pairs (see chapter 3). The 23rd pair consists of a combination of X and Y chromosomes, usually two X chromosomes in a female and an X and a Y in a male. In the first few weeks of gestation, however, female and male embryos look alike.

Males start to differ from females when genes on the Y chromosome in the male embryo trigger the development of testes rather than ovaries; the testes secrete copious amounts of the class of hormones known as androgens, which lead to the development of male sex organs. Low levels of androgens in the female embryo allow the normal development of female sex organs.

Thus, hormones play a critical role in the development of sex differences (Berenbaum & Bailey, 2003; Lippa, 2005). The two main classes of sex hormones are estrogens and androgens, which are secreted by the *gonads* (ovaries in females, testes in males). *Estrogens,* such as estradiol, influence the development of female physical sex characteristics. *Androgens,* such as testosterone, promote the development of male physical sex characteristics.

Biology's role in creating sex differences, however, does not tell the whole story of gender differences. Consider a recent research study of genetic males who were born with ambiguous genitals because of a rare birth defect and who were surgically assigned to be female (Reiner & Gearhart, 2004). In this research, 16 genetically male children 5 to 16 years of age were studied; 14 of them were raised as females. Children and parents were asked detailed questions about the children's play patterns, levels of aggression, career goals, and attitudes about gender roles. The families were followed for 34 to 98 months. In the most recent assessment, 8 of the 14 individuals raised as girls had declared themselves boys, including 4 who had not been told of their surgical transformation. Nature apparently was more important than nurture in the case of these children. However, 5 of the 16 children appeared happy living as girls, implying that in some cases nurture can trump nature. Further, other research and clinical reports indicate many genetic males raised as girls appear to be well adjusted (Gooren, 2002; Slijper & others, 1998).

The Evolutionary Psychology View   How might physical differences between the sexes give rise to psychological differences between males and females? Evolutionary psychology (introduced in chapter 3) offers one answer. According to evolutionary psychology, adaptation during human evolution produced psychological differences between males and females (Buss, 1995, 2000, 2004). Because of their differing roles in reproduction, males and females faced differing pressures when the

Gender Resources

www.mhhe.com/santrockld11

gender identity The sense of being male or female, which most children acquire by the time they are 3 years old.

gender role A set of expectations that prescribes how females or males should think, act, and feel.

human species was evolving. In particular, because having multiple sexual liaisons improves the likelihood that males will pass on their genes, natural selection favored males who adopted short-term mating strategies. These are strategies that allow a male to win the competition with other males for sexual access to females. Therefore, say evolutionary psychologists, males evolved dispositions that favor violence, competition, and risk taking.

In contrast, according to evolutionary psychologists, females' contributions to the gene pool were improved when they secured resources that ensured that their offspring would survive; this outcome was promoted by obtaining long-term mates who could support a family (Jackson, 2004). As a consequence, natural selection favored females who devoted effort to parenting and chose successful, ambitious mates who could provide their offspring with resources and protection.

This evolutionary unfolding, according to some evolutionary psychologists, explains key gender differences in sexual attitudes and sexual behavior. For example, in one study, men said that ideally they would like to have more than 18 sexual partners in their lifetime, whereas women stated that ideally they would like to have only 4 or 5 (Buss & Schmidt, 1993). In another study, 75 percent of the men but none of the women approached by an attractive stranger of the opposite sex consented to a request for sex (Clark & Hatfield, 1989).

Such gender differences, says David Buss (2000, 2004), are exactly the type predicted by evolutionary psychology. Buss argues that men and women differ psychologically in those domains in which they have faced different adaptive problems during evolutionary history. In all other domains, predicts Buss, the sexes will be psychologically similar.

Critics of evolutionary psychology argue that its hypotheses are backed by speculations about prehistory, not evidence, and that in any event people are not locked into behavior that was adaptive in the evolutionary past. Critics also claim that the evolutionary view pays little attention to cultural and individual variations in gender differences.

Social Influences   Many social scientists do not locate the cause of psychological gender differences in biological dispositions. Rather, they argue that these differences are due to social experiences (Denmark, Rabinowitz, & Sechzer, 2005). Explanations for how gender differences come about through experience include both social and cognitive theories.

Social Theories of Gender   Three main social theories of gender have been proposed— social role theory, psychoanalytic theory, and social cognitive theory. Alice Eagly (2000, 2001) proposed **social role theory,** which states that gender differences result from the contrasting roles of women and men. In most cultures around the world, women have less power and status than men have and they control fewer resources (Denmark, Rabinowitz, & Sechzer, 2005; Worell, 2006). Compared with men, women perform more domestic work, spend fewer hours in paid employment, receive lower pay, and are more thinly represented in the highest levels of organizations. In Eagly's view, as women adapted to roles with less power and less status in society, they showed more cooperative, less dominant profiles than men. Thus, the social hierarchy and division of labor are important causes of gender differences in power, assertiveness, and nurture (Betz, 2006; Eagly & Diekman, 2003).

The **psychoanalytic theory of gender** stems from Freud's view that the preschool child develops a sexual attraction to the opposite-sex parent. At 5 or 6 years of age, the child renounces this attraction because of anxious feelings. Subsequently, the child identifies with the same-sex parent, unconsciously adopting the same-sex parent's characteristics. However, developmentalists argue that gender development does not proceed as Freud proposed (Callan, 2001). Children become gender-typed much earlier than 5 or 6 years of age, and they become masculine or feminine even when the same-sex parent is not present in the family.

social role theory A theory that gender differences result from the contrasting roles of men and women.

psychoanalytic theory of gender A theory deriving from Freud's view that the preschool child develops a sexual attraction to the opposite-sex parent, but by approximately 5 or 6 years of age renounces this attraction because of anxious feelings, and subsequently identifies with the same-sex parent, unconsciously adopting the same-sex parent's characteristics.

FIGURE 9.2 A Comparison of the Psychoanalytic and Social Cognitive Views of Gender Development. Parents influence their children's development by action and example.

Theory	Processes	Outcomes
Freud's psychoanalytic theory	Sexual attraction to opposite-sex parent at 3 to 5 years of age; anxiety about sexual attraction and subsequent identification with same-sex parent at 5 to 6 years of age	Gender behavior similar to that of same-sex parent
Social cognitive theory	Rewards and punishments of gender-appropriate and inappropriate behavior by adults and peers; observation and initiation of models' masculine and feminine behavior	Gender behavior

First imagine that this is a photograph of a baby girl. *What expectations would you have for her?* Then imagine that this is a photograph of a baby boy. *What expectations would you have for him?*

www.mhhe.com/santrockld11

Fathers and Sons

social cognitive theory of gender A theory that emphasizes that children's gender development occurs through the observation and imitation of gender behavior and through the rewards and punishments children experience for gender-appropriate and gender-inappropriate behavior.

The social cognitive approach discussed in chapter 2 provides an alternative explanation of how children develop gender-typed behavior (see figure 9.2). According to the **social cognitive theory of gender,** children's gender development occurs through observing and imitating what other people say and do, and through being rewarded and punished for gender-appropriate and gender-inappropriate behavior (Bussey & Bandura, 1999). From birth onward, males and females are treated differently. When infants and toddlers show gender differences, adults tend to reward them. Parents often use rewards and punishments to teach their daughters to be feminine ("Karen, you are being a good girl when you play gently with your doll") and their sons to be masculine ("Keith, a boy as big as you is not supposed to cry"). Parents, however, are only one of many sources through which children learn gender roles (Beal, 1994; Fagot, Rodgers, & Leinbach, 2000). Culture, schools, peers, the media, and other family members also provide gender role models (Smith, 2007). For example, children also learn about gender from observing other adults in the neighborhood and on television (Fagot, Rodgers, & Leinbach, 2000). As children get older, peers become increasingly important. Let's take a closer look at the influence of parents and peers.

Parental Influences Parents, by action and by example, influence their children's gender development (Bronstein, 2006; Lenton & Blair, 2004; Maccoby, 2003). Many parents encourage boys and girls to engage in different types of play and activities (Fagot, 1995). For example, girls are more likely than boys to be given dolls to play, and girls are encouraged to be more nurturant and emotional than boys are. Fathers are more likely to engage in aggressive play with their sons than with their daughters.

Both mothers and fathers are psychologically important to their children's gender development (McHale, Crouter, & Whiteman, 2003). Cultures around the world, however, tend to give them differing roles. Mothers are more consistently given responsibility for nurturance and physical care. Fathers are more likely to engage in playful interaction and to be given responsibility for ensuring that boys and girls conform to existing cultural norms. And, whether or not they have more influence on them, fathers are more involved in socializing their sons than their daughters. Fathers seem to play an especially important part in gender-role development. They are more likely than mothers to act differently toward sons and daughters (Leaper, 2002). Thus, they contribute more to distinctions between the genders (Huston, 1983).

Peer Influences Parents provide the earliest discrimination of gender roles, but before long, peers join the process of responding to and modeling masculine and feminine behavior. In fact, peers become so important to gender development that the playground has been called "gender school" (Luria & Herzog, 1985).

Peers extensively reward and punish gender behavior (Lott & Maluso, 2001). For example, when children play in ways that the culture says are sex-appropriate, their peers tend to reward them. But peers often reject children who act in a manner that is considered more characteristic of the other gender (Matlin, 2004). A little girl who brings a doll to the park may find herself surrounded by new friends; a little boy might be jeered. However, there is greater pressure for boys to conform to a traditional male role than for girls to conform to a traditional female role (Fagot, Rogers, & Leinbach, 2000).

Gender molds important aspects of peer relations. It influences the composition of children's groups, the size of groups, and interactions within a group (Maccoby, 1998, 2002):

- *Gender composition of children's groups.* Around the age of 3, children already show a preference to spend time with same-sex playmates. From 4 to 12 years of age, this preference for playing in same-sex groups increases, and during the elementary school years children spend a large majority of their free time with children of their own sex (see figure 9.3).
- *Group size.* From about 5 years of age onward, boys are more likely to associate together in larger clusters than girls are (Benenson & Heath, 2006). Boys are also more likely to participate in organized group games than girls are. In one study, same-sex groups of six children were permitted to use play materials in any way they wished (Benenson, Apostoleris, & Parnass, 1997). Girls were more likely than boys to play in dyads or triads, while boys were more likely to interact in larger groups and seek to attain a group goal.
- *Interaction in same-sex groups.* Boys are more likely than girls to engage in rough-and-tumble play, competition, conflict, ego displays, risk taking, and seeking dominance. By contrast, girls are more likely to engage in "collaborative discourse," in which they talk and act in a more reciprocal manner.

What effect do the same-sex play groups have on gender differences? In one study, researchers observed preschoolers over six months (Martin & Fabes, 2001). The more time boys spent interacting with other boys, the more their activity level, rough-and-tumble play, and sex-typed choice of toys and games increased, and the less time boys spent near adults. By contrast, the more time preschool girls spent interacting with other girls, the more their activity level and aggression decreased, and the more their girl-type play activities and time spent near adults increased.

Cognitive Influences   Observation, imitation, rewards, and punishment—these are the mechanisms by which gender develops according to social cognitive theory. Interactions between the child and the social environment are the main keys to gender development in this view. Some critics argue that this explanation pays too little attention to the child's own mind and understanding and that it portrays the child as passively acquiring gender roles (Ruble & Martin, 2004). Two cognitive theories—cognitive developmental theory and gender schema theory—stress that individuals actively construct their gender world:

- The **cognitive developmental theory of gender** states that children's gender typing occurs *after* children think of themselves as boys and girls. Once they consistently conceive of themselves as male or female, children prefer activities, objects, and attitudes consistent with this label.
- **Gender schema theory** states that gender typing emerges as children gradually develop gender schemas of what is gender-appropriate and gender-inappropriate in their culture. A *schema* is a cognitive structure, a network of associations that guide an individual's perceptions. A *gender schema* organizes the world in terms of female and male. Children are internally motivated to perceive the world and to act in accordance with their developing schemas.

Initially proposed by Lawrence Kohlberg (1966), the cognitive developmental theory of gender holds that gender development depends on cognition, and it applies the ideas of Piaget's cognitive developmental theory described in chapter 8. As young children develop the conservation and categorization skills described by Piaget, said Kohlberg, they develop a concept of gender. What's more, they come to see that

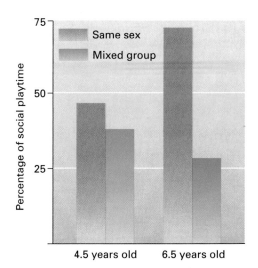

FIGURE 9.3 Developmental Changes in Percentage of Time Spent in Same-Sex and Mixed-Group Settings. Observations of children show that they are more likely to play in same-sex than mixed-sex groups. This tendency increases between 4 and 6 years of age.

cognitive developmental theory of gender
The theory that children's gender typing occurs after they have developed a concept of gender. Once they consistently conceive of themselves as male or female, children often organize their world on the basis of gender.

gender schema theory The theory that an individual's attention and behavior are guided by an internal motivation to conform to gender-based sociocultural standards and stereotypes.

FIGURE 9.4 The Development of Gender Behavior According to the Cognitive Developmental and Gender Schema Theories of Gender Development

Theory	Processes	Emphasis
Cognitive developmental theory	Development of gender constancy, especially around 6 to 7 years of age, when conservation skills develop; after children develop ability to consistently conceive of themselves as male or female, children often organize their world on the basis of gender, such as selecting same-sex models to imitate	Cognitive readiness facilitates gender identity
Gender schema theory	Sociocultural emphasis on gender-based standards and stereotypes; children's attention and behavior are guided by an internal motivation to conform to these gender-based standards and stereotypes, allowing children to interpret the world through a network of gender-organized thoughts	Gender schemas reinforce gender behavior

they will always be male or female. As a result, they begin to select models of their own sex to imitate. The little girl acts as if she is thinking, "I'm a girl, so I want to do girl things. Therefore, the opportunity to do girl things is rewarding."

Notice that in this view gender-typed behavior occurs only after children develop *gender constancy*, which is the understanding that sex remains the same, even though activities, clothing, and hair style might change (Ruble, Martin, & Berenbaum, 2006). However, researchers have found that children do not develop gender constancy until they are about 6 or 7 years old. Before this time, most little girls prefer girlish toys and clothes and games, and most little boys prefer boyish toys and games. Thus, contrary to Kohlberg's description of cognitive developmental theory, gender typing does not appear to depend on gender constancy.

Unlike cognitive developmental theory, gender schema theory does not require children to perceive gender constancy before they begin gender typing (see figure 9.4). Instead, gender schema theory states that gender typing occurs when children are ready to encode and organize information along the lines of what is considered appropriate for females and males in their society (Martin & Dinella, 2001; Martin & Halverson, 1981; Ruble, Martin, & Berenbaum, 2006). Bit by bit, children pick up what is gender-appropriate and gender-inappropriate in their culture, and develop gender schemas that shape how they perceive the world and what they remember. Children are motivated to act in ways that conform with these gender schemas. Thus, gender schemas fuel gender typing (Hyde, 2007).

Review and Reflect • **LEARNING GOAL 1**

1 **Discuss emotional and personality development in early childhood**

Review
- What changes in the self occur during early childhood?
- What changes take place in emotional development in early childhood?
- What are some key aspects of moral development in young children?
- How does gender develop in young children?

Reflect
- Which theory of gender development do you find most persuasive? What might an eclectic theoretical view of gender development be like? (You might want to review the discussion of an eclectic theoretical orientation in chapter 2.)

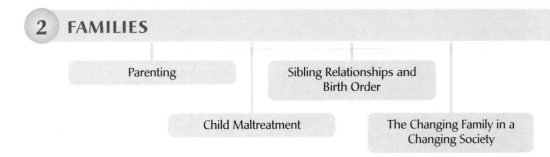

2 **FAMILIES**

Parenting

Sibling Relationships and Birth Order

Child Maltreatment

The Changing Family in a Changing Society

Attachment to a caregiver is a key social relationship during infancy, but we saw in chapter 7 that some experts maintain that secure attachment and the infant years have been overdramatized as determinants of life-span development. Social and emotional development is also shaped by other relationships and by temperament, contexts, and social experiences in the early childhood years and later. Consider Craig Lesley, whose story opened this chapter. As an infant he was securely attached to his mother, but his abandonment by his father also mattered. For years he missed him; he missed his love; he felt "the terrible pull of my father's blood. . . . he drew me like a lodestone" (Lesley, 2005, p. 141). In this section, we will discuss social relationships of early childhood beyond attachment. We will explore the different types of parenting, sibling relationships, and variations in family structures.

Parenting

A few years ago, there was considerable interest in Mozart CDs that were marketed with the promise that playing them would enrich infants' and young children's brains. Some of the parents who bought them probably thought, "I don't have enough time to spend with my children so I'll just play these intellectual CDs and then they won't need me as much." Similarly, one-minute bedtime stories are being marketed for parents to read to their children (Walsh, 2000). There are one-minute bedtime bear books, puppy books, and so on. Parents who buy them know it is good for them to read with their children, but they don't want to spend a lot of time doing it. Behind the popularity of these products is an unfortunate theme that suggests that parenting can be done quickly, with little or no inconvenience (Sroufe, 2000).

What is wrong with these quick-fix approaches to parenting? Good parenting takes time and effort (Bornstein, 2006; Powell, 2005, 2006). You can't do it in a minute here and a minute there. You can't do it with CDs.

Calvin and Hobbes

Parenting

*P*arenting is a very important profession, but no test of fitness for it is ever imposed in the interest of children.

—GEORGE BERNARD SHAW
Irish Playwright, 20th Century

authoritarian parenting A restrictive punitive style in which parents exhort the child to follow their directions and to respect work and effort. The authoritarian parent places firm limits and controls on the child and allows little verbal exchange. Authoritarian parenting is associated with children's social incompetence.

authoritative parenting A parenting style in which parents encourage their children to be independent but still place limits and controls on their actions. Extensive verbal give-and-take is allowed, and parents are warm and nurturant toward the child. Authoritative parenting is associated with children's social competence.

neglectful parenting A style of parenting in which the parent is very uninvolved in the child's life; it is associated with children's social incompetence, especially a lack of self-control.

indulgent parenting A style of parenting in which parents are highly involved with their children but place few demands or controls on them. Indulgent parenting is associated with children's social incompetence, especially a lack of self-control.

Of course, it's not just the quantity of time parents spend with children that is important for children's development—the quality of the parenting is clearly important. To understand variations in parenting, let's consider the styles parents use when they interact with their children, how they discipline their children, and coparenting.

Baumrind's Parenting Styles   Diana Baumrind (1971) believes parents should be neither punitive nor aloof. Rather, they should develop rules for their children and be affectionate with them. She has described four types of parenting styles:

- **Authoritarian parenting** is a restrictive, punitive style in which parents exhort the child to follow their directions and respect their work and effort. The authoritarian parent places firm limits and controls on the child and allows little verbal exchange. For example, an authoritarian parent might say, "You do it my way or else." Authoritarian parents also might spank the child frequently, enforce rules rigidly but not explain them, and show rage toward the child. Children of authoritarian parents are often unhappy, fearful, and anxious about comparing themselves with others, fail to initiate activity, and have weak communication skills.

- **Authoritative parenting** encourages children to be independent but still places limits and controls on their actions. Extensive verbal give-and-take is allowed, and parents are warm and nurturant toward the child. An authoritative parent might put his arm around the child in a comforting way and say, "You know you should not have done that. Let's talk about how you can handle the situation better next time." Authoritative parents show pleasure and support in response to children's constructive behavior. They also expect mature, independent, and age-appropriate behavior by children. Children whose parents are authoritative are often cheerful, self-controlled and self-reliant, and achievement-oriented; they tend to maintain friendly relations with peers, cooperate with adults, and cope well with stress.

- **Neglectful parenting** is a style in which the parent is very uninvolved in the child's life. Children whose parents are neglectful develop the sense that other aspects of the parents' lives are more important than they are. These children tend to be socially incompetent. Many have poor self-control and don't handle independence well. They frequently have low self-esteem, are immature, and may be alienated from the family. In adolescence, they may show patterns of truancy and delinquency.

- **Indulgent parenting** is a style in which parents are highly involved with their children but place few demands or controls on them. Such parents let their children do what they want. The result is that the children never learn to control their own behavior and always expect to get their way. Some parents deliberately rear their children in this way because they believe the combination of warm involvement and few restraints will produce a creative, confident child. However, children whose parents are indulgent rarely learn respect for others and have difficulty controlling their behavior. They might be domineering, egocentric, noncompliant, and have difficulties in peer relations.

These four classifications of parenting involve combinations of acceptance and responsiveness on the one hand and demand and control on the other (Maccoby & Martin, 1983). How these dimensions combine to produce authoritarian, authoritative, neglectful, and indulgent parenting is shown in figure 9.5.

Parenting Styles in Context   Do the benefits of authoritative parenting transcend the boundaries of ethnicity, socioeconomic status, and household composition? Although occasional exceptions have been found, evidence linking authoritative parenting with competence on the part of the child occurs in research across a wide range of ethnic groups, social strata, cultures, and family structures (Steinberg, Blatt-Eisengart, & Cauffman, 2006; Steinberg & Silk, 2002).

Nonetheless, researchers have found that in some ethnic groups, aspects of the authoritarian style may be associated with more positive child outcomes than Baumrind predicts (Parke & Buriel, 2006). Elements of the authoritarian style may take on different meanings and have different effects depending on the context.

For example, Asian American parents often continue aspects of traditional Asian childrearing practices that have sometimes been described as authoritarian. The parents exert considerable control over their children's lives. However, Ruth Chao (2001, 2005; Chao & Tseng, 2002) argues that the style of parenting used by many Asian American parents is distinct from the domineering control of the authoritarian style. Instead, Chao argues that the control reflects concern and involvement in their children's lives and is best conceptualized as a type of training. The high academic achievement of Asian American children may be a consequence of their "training" parents (Stevenson & Zusho, 2002).

An emphasis on requiring respect and obedience is also associated with the authoritarian style, but in Latino child rearing this focus may be positive rather than punitive. Rather than suppressing the child's development, it may encourage the development of a different type of self. Latino child-rearing practices encourage the development of a self and identity that is embedded in the family and requires respect and obedience (Harwood & others, 2002). Furthermore, many Latino families have several generations living together and helping each other (Zinn & Well, 2000). In these circumstances, emphasizing respect and obedience by children may be part of maintaining a harmonious home and may be important in the formation of the child's identity.

Even physical punishment, another characteristic of the authoritarian style, may have varying effects in different contexts. African American parents are more likely than non-Latino White parents to use physical punishment (Deater-Deckard & Dodge, 1997). However, the use of physical punishment has been linked with increased externalized child problems (such as acting out and high levels of aggression) in non-Latino White families but not in African American families. One explanation of this finding points to the need for African American parents to enforce rules in the dangerous environments in which they are more likely to live (Harrison-Hale, McLoyd, & Smedley, 2004). In this context, requiring obedience to parental authority may be an adaptive strategy to keep children from engaging in antisocial behavior that can have serious consequences for the victim or the perpetrator. As we see next, though, overall, the use of physical punishment in disciplining children raises many concerns.

	Accepting, responsive	Rejecting, unresponsive
Demanding, controlling	Authoritative	Authoritarian
Undemanding, uncontrolling	Indulgent	Neglectful

FIGURE 9.5 Classification of Parenting Styles. The four types of parenting styles (authoritative, authoritarian, indulgent, and neglectful) involve the dimensions of acceptance and responsiveness, on the one hand, and demand and control on the other. For example, authoritative parenting involves being both accepting/responsive and demanding/controlling.

Punishment   For centuries, corporal (physical) punishment, such as spanking, has been considered a necessary and even desirable method of disciplining children. Use of corporal punishment is legal in every state in America. A recent national survey of U.S. parents with 3- and 4-year-old children found that 26 percent of parents reported spanking their children frequently and 67 percent of the parents reported yelling at their children frequently (Regaldo & others, 2004). A recent cross-cultural comparison found that individuals in the United States and Canada were among those with the most favorable attitudes toward corporal punishment and were

According to Ruth Chao, what type of parenting style do many Asian American parents use?

the most likely to remember it being used by their parents (Curran & others, 2001) (see figure 9.6).

Despite the widespread use of corporal punishment, there have been surprisingly few research studies on physical punishment, and those that have been conducted are correlational (Baumrind, Larzelere, & Cowan, 2002; Benjet & Kazdin, 2003; Kazdin & Benjet, 2003). Clearly, it would be highly unethical to randomly assign parents to either spank or not spank their children in an experimental study. Recall that cause and effect cannot be determined in a correlational study. In one correlational study, spanking by parents was linked with children's antisocial behavior, including cheating, telling lies, being mean to others, bullying, getting into fights, and being disobedient (Strauss, Sugarman, & Giles-Sims, 1997).

A recent research review concluded that corporal punishment by parents is associated with higher levels of immediate compliance and aggression by the children (Gershoff, 2002). The review also found that corporal punishment is associated with lower levels of moral internalization and mental health (Gershoff, 2002). A longitudinal study found that spanking before age 2 was related to behavioral problems in middle and late childhood (Slade & Wissow, 2004). Some critics, though, argue that the research evidence is not yet sound enough to warrant a blanket injunction against corporal punishment, especially mild corporal punishment (Baumrind, Larzelere, & Cowan, 2002; Kazdin & Benjet, 2003).

What are some reasons for avoiding spanking or similar punishments? The reasons include:

- When adults punish a child by yelling, screaming, or spanking, they are presenting children with out-of-control models for handling stressful situations. Children may imitate this aggressive, out-of-control behavior (Sim & Ong, 2005).
- Punishment can instill fear, rage, or avoidance. For example, spanking the child may cause the child to avoid being around the parent and to fear the parent.
- Punishment tells children what not to do rather than what to do. Children should be given feedback, such as "Why don't you try this?"
- Punishment can be abusive. Parents might unintentionally become so aroused when they are punishing the child that they become abusive (Ateah, 2005; Baumrind, Larzelere, & Cowan, 2002).

Because of reasons such as these, Sweden passed a law in 1979 forbidding parents to physically punish (spank or slap, for example) children. Since the law was enacted, youth rates of delinquency, alcohol abuse, rape, and suicide have dropped in Sweden (Durrant, 2000). These improvements may have occurred for other reasons, such as changing attitudes and opportunities for youth. Nonetheless, the Swedish experience suggests that physical punishment of children may be unnecessary. Many other countries also have passed antispanking laws.

Most child psychologists recommend handling misbehavior by reasoning with the child, especially explaining the consequences of the child's actions for others. *Time out,* in which the child is removed from a setting that offers positive reinforcement, can also be effective. For example, when the child has misbehaved, a parent might take away TV viewing for a specified time.

In chapter 7, we described the family as a system and discussed possible links between marital relationships and parenting practices (Cox & others, 2004). To read about a recent family systems study involving marital conflict and the use of physical punishment, see the Research in Life-Span Development interlude.

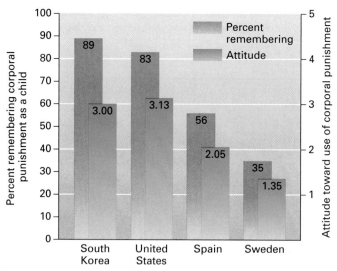

FIGURE 9.6 Corporal Punishment in Different Countries. A 5-point scale was used to assess attitudes toward corporal punishment with scores closer to 1 indicating an attitude against its use and scores closer to 5 suggesting an attitude favoring its use. *Why are studies of corporal punishment correlational studies, and how does that affect their usefulness?*

RESEARCH IN LIFE-SPAN DEVELOPMENT

Marital Conflict, Individual Hostility, and the Use of Physical Punishment

A longitudinal study assessed couples across the transition to parenting to investigate possible links between marital conflict, individual adult hostility, and the use of physical punishment with young children (Kanoy & others, 2003). Before the birth of the first child, the level of marital conflict was observed in a marital problem-solving discussion; answers to questionnaires regarding individual characteristics were also obtained. Thus, these characteristics of the couples were not influenced by characteristics of the child. When the children were 2 and 5 years old, the couples were interviewed about the frequency and intensity of their physical punishment of the children. At both ages, the parents' level of marital conflict was again observed in a marital problem-solving discussion.

The researchers found that both hostility and marital conflict were linked with the use of physical punishment. Individuals with high rates of hostility on the prenatal measures used more frequent and more severe physical punishment with their children. The same was evident for marital conflict—when marital conflict was high, both mothers and fathers were more likely to use physical punishment in disciplining their young children.

If parents who have a greater likelihood of using physical punishment can be identified in prenatal classes, these families could be encouraged to use other forms of discipline before they get into a pattern of physically punishing their children.

How do most child psychologists recommend handling a child's misbehavior?

Coparenting   The relationship between marital conflict and the use of punishment highlights the importance of *coparenting,* which is the support that parents provide one another in jointly raising a child. Poor coordination between parents, undermining of the other parent, lack of cooperation and warmth, and disconnection by one parent are conditions that place children at risk for problems (Doherty & Beaton, 2004; McHale, Kuersten-Hogan, & Rao, 2004; McHale & others, 2002; Van Egeren & Hawkins, 2004). For example, in one study, 4-year-old children from families characterized by low levels of mutuality and support in coparenting were more likely than their classmates to show difficulties in social adjustment on the playground (McHale, Johnson, & Sinclair, 1999). By contrast, parental cooperation and warmth are linked with children's prosocial behavior and competence in peer relations.

Parents who do not spend enough time with their children or who have problems in child rearing can benefit from counseling and therapy. To read about the work of marriage and family counselor Darla Botkin, see the Careers in Life-Span Development insert.

Child Maltreatment

Unfortunately, punishment sometimes leads to the abuse of infants and children. In 2002, approximately 896,000 U.S. children were found to be victims of child abuse (U.S. Department of Health and Human Services, 2003). Eighty-four percent of these children were abused by a parent or parents. Laws in many states now require doctors and teachers to report suspected cases of child abuse, yet many cases go unreported, especially those of battered infants.

Whereas the public and many professionals use the term *child abuse* to refer to both abuse and neglect, developmentalists increasingly use the term *child maltreatment* (Cicchetti & Blender, 2004; Cicchetti & Toth, 2005, 2006). This term does not

CAREERS
in LIFE-SPAN DEVELOPMENT

Darla Botkin
Marriage and Family Therapist

Darla Botkin is a marriage and family therapist who teaches, conducts research, and engages in marriage and family therapy. She is on the faculty of the University of Kentucky. Darla obtained a bachelor's degree in elementary education with a concentration in special education and then went on to receive a master's degree in early childhood education. She spent the next six years working with children and their families in a variety of settings, including child care, elementary school, and Head Start. These experiences led Darla to recognize the interdependence of the developmental settings that children and their parents experience (such as home, school, and work). She returned to graduate school and obtained a Ph.D. in family studies from the University of Tennessee. She then became a faculty member in the Family Studies program at the University of Kentucky. Completing further coursework and clinical training in marriage and family therapy, she became certified as a marriage and family therapist.

Darla's current interests include working with young children in family therapy, gender and ethnic issues in family therapy, and the role of spirituality in family wellness.

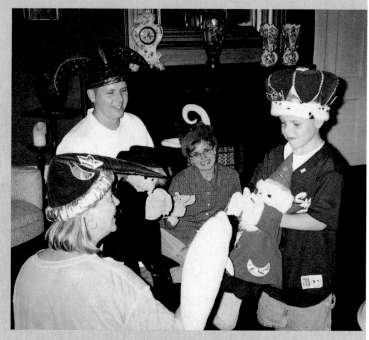

Darla Botkin (*left*), conducting a family therapy session.

Child maltreatment involves grossly inadequate and destructive aspects of parenting.

—DANTE CICCHETTI
Contemporary Developmental Psychologist, University of Minnesota

www.mhhe.com/santrockld11

Child Abuse Prevention Network
International Aspects of Child Abuse
National Clearinghouse on Child Abuse and Neglect

have quite the emotional impact of the term *abuse* and acknowledges that maltreatment includes diverse conditions.

Types of Child Maltreatment The four main types of child maltreatment are physical abuse, child neglect, sexual abuse, and emotional abuse (National Clearinghouse on Child Abuse and Neglect, 2002, 2004):

- *Physical abuse* is characterized by the infliction of physical injury as a result of punching, beating, kicking, biting, burning, shaking, or otherwise harming a child. The parent or other person may not have intended to hurt the child; the injury may have resulted from excessive physical punishment (Hornor, 2005; Maguire & others, 2005).
- *Child neglect* is characterized by failure to provide for the child's basic needs (Sedlak & others, 2006; Trowell, 2006). Neglect can be physical (abandonment, for example), educational (allowing chronic truancy, for example), or emotional (marked inattention to the child's needs, for example).
- *Sexual abuse* includes fondling a child's genitals, intercourse, incest, rape, sodomy, exhibitionism, and commercial exploitation through prostitution or the production of pornographic materials (Edinburgh & others, 2006; London, Bruck, & Ceci, 2005).
- *Emotional abuse (psychological/verbal abuse/mental injury)* includes acts or omissions by parents or other caregivers that have caused, or could cause, serious behavioral, cognitive, or emotional problems (Gelles & Cavanaugh, 2005).

Although any of these forms of child maltreatment may be found separately, they often occur in combination. Emotional abuse is almost always present when other forms are identified.

The Context of Abuse   No single factor causes child maltreatment (Cicchetti & Toth, 2005, 2006). A combination of factors, including the culture, family, and development, likely contribute to child maltreatment (Freisthler, Merritt, & Lascala, 2006).

The extensive violence that takes place in American culture is reflected in the occurrence of violence in the family (Azar, 2002). A regular diet of violence appears on television screens, and parents often resort to power assertion as a disciplinary technique. In China, where physical punishment is rarely used to discipline children, the incidence of child abuse is reported to be very low.

The family itself is obviously a key part of the context of abuse. The interactions of all family members need to be considered, regardless of who performs the violent acts against the child (Kim & Cicchetti, 2004; Margolin, 1994). For example, even though the father may be the one who physically abuses the child, contributions by the mother, the child, and siblings also should be evaluated.

Were parents who abuse children abused by their own parents? About one-third of parents who were abused themselves when they were young abuse their own children (Cicchetti & Toth, 2005, 2006). Thus, some, but not a majority, of parents are locked into an intergenerational transmission of abuse (Dixon, Browne, & Hamilton-Giachritsis, 2005; Leifer & others, 2004). Mothers who break out of the intergenerational transmission of abuse often have at least one warm, caring adult in their background; have a close, positive marital relationship; and have received therapy (Egeland, Jacobvitz, & Sroufe, 1988).

Children at a shelter for domestic violence in Tel Aviv, Israel.

Developmental Consequences of Abuse   Among the developmental consequences of child maltreatment are poor emotion regulation, attachment problems, problems in peer relations, difficulty in adapting to school, and other psychological problems (Cicchetti & Toth, 2005, 2006). Maltreated infants may show excessive negative affect (such as irritability and crying) or they may display blunted positive affect (rarely smiling or laughing). If young children are maltreated, they often show insecure attachment patterns in their social relationships later in development (Cicchetti & Toth, 2005). Maltreated children tend to be overly aggressive with peers or avoid interacting with peers (Bolger & Patterson, 2001). Abused and neglected children are also at risk for academic problems (Cicchetti & Toth, 2005, 2006).

Being physically abused has been linked with children's anxiety, personality problems, depression, suicide attempts, conduct disorder, and delinquency (Cicchetti & Toth, 2005, 2006; Danielson & others, 2005; Kim & Cicchetti, 2006). Later, during the adult years, maltreated children often have difficulty in establishing and maintaining healthy intimate relationships (Colman & Widom, 2004; Minzenberg, Poole, & Vinogradov, 2006). As adults, maltreated children also show increased violence toward other adults, dating partners, and marital partners, as well as increased substance abuse, anxiety, and depression (Sachs-Ericsson & others, 2005; Shea & others, 2005). In sum, maltreated children are at risk for developing a wide range of problems and disorders (Arias, 2004; Haugaard & Hazen, 2004).

An important strategy is to prevent child maltreatment (Cicchetti & Toth, 2006; Lyons, Henly, & Schuerman, 2005). In one recent study of maltreating mothers and their 1-year-olds, two treatments were effective in reducing child maltreatment: (1) home visitation that emphasized

GRANT HILL
Orlando Magic

TAMIA
Recording Artist

We're with the band

We're wearing the blue wristband because it's time to prevent child abuse. To get with the band or learn more, visit www.preventchildabuse.org or call 1-800-688-1275 ext. 2.

Prevent Child Abuse
America

This print ad was created by Prevent Child Abuse America to make people aware of its national blue wristband campaign. The campaign's goal is to educate people about child abuse prevention and encourage them to support the organization. *Source: Prevent Child Abuse America*

improved parenting, coping with stress, and increasing support for the mother, and (2) parent-infant psychotherapy that focused on improving maternal-infant attachment (Cicchetti, Toth, and Rogosch, 2005).

Sibling Relationships and Birth Order

What are sibling relationships like? How extensively does birth order influence behavior?

Sibling Relationships Any of you who have grown up with siblings probably have a rich memory of aggressive, hostile interchanges. But sibling relationships also have many pleasant, caring moments (Volling, 2002; Zukow-Goldring, 2002). Children's sibling relationships include helping, sharing, teaching, fighting, and playing. Children can act as emotional supports, rivals, and communication partners (Carlson, 1995).

Is sibling interaction different from parent-child interaction? There is some evidence that it is. Observations indicate that children interact more positively and in more varied ways with their parents than with their siblings (Baskett & Johnson, 1982). Children also follow their parents' dictates more than those of their siblings, and they behave more negatively and punitively with their siblings than with their parents.

In some instances, siblings may be stronger socializing influences on the child than parents are (Cicirelli, 1994). Someone close in age to the child—such as a sibling—may be able to understand the child's problems and communicate more effectively than parents can. In dealing with peers, coping with difficult teachers, and discussing such taboo subjects as sex, siblings may have more influence than parents.

Is sibling interaction the same around the world? In industrialized societies, such as the United States, parents tend to delegate responsibility for younger siblings to older siblings primarily to give the parents freedom to pursue other activities. However, in nonindustrialized countries, such as Kenya, the older sibling's role as a caregiver to younger siblings has much more importance. In industrialized countries, the older sibling's caregiving role is often discretionary; in nonindustrialized countries, it is more obligatory (Cicirelli, 1994).

Big sisters are the crab grass in the lawn of life.

—Charles Schulz
American Cartoonist, 20th Century

Birth Order Whether a child has older or younger siblings has been linked to development of certain personality characteristics. For example, compared with later-born children, firstborn children are more adult-oriented, helpful, conforming, and self-controlled. Firstborns excel in academic and professional endeavors, and they have more guilt, anxiety, and difficulty in coping with stressful situations, as well as higher admission to child guidance clinics.

What accounts for such differences related to birth order? Proposed explanations usually point to variations in interactions with parents and siblings associated with being in a particular position in the family. This is especially true in the case of the firstborn child (Teti & others, 1993). The oldest child is the only one who does not have to share parental love and affection with other siblings—until another sibling comes along. An infant requires more attention than an older child; this means that the firstborn sibling receives less attention after the newborn arrives. Does this result in conflict between parents and the firstborn? In one research study, mothers became more negative, coercive, and restraining and played less with the firstborn following the birth of a second child (Dunn & Kendrick, 1982).

What is the only child like? The popular conception is that the only child is a "spoiled brat," with such undesirable characteristics as dependency, lack of self-control, and self-centered behavior. But researchers present a more positive portrayal of the only child. Only children often are achievement-oriented and display a desirable personality, especially in comparison with later-borns and children from large families (Falbo & Poston, 1993; Jiao, Ji, & Jing, 1996).

So far, our discussion suggests that birth order might be a strong predictor of behavior. However, an increasing number of family researchers believe that when all of the factors that influence behavior are considered, birth order itself shows limited ability to predict behavior. Think about some of the other important factors in children's lives that influence their behavior beyond birth order. They include heredity, models of competency or incompetency that parents present to children on a daily basis, peer influences, school influences, socioeconomic factors, sociohistorical factors, and cultural variations. When someone says firstborns are always like this but last-borns are always like that, the person is making overly simplistic statements that do not adequately take into account the complexity of influences on a child's development.

The one-child family is becoming much more common in China because of the strong motivation to limit the population growth in the People's Republic of China. The policy is still relatively new, and its effects on children have not been fully examined. *In general, though, what have researchers found the only child to be like?*

The Changing Family in a Changing Society

Beyond variations in the number of siblings, the families that children experience differ in many important ways. The number of children growing up in single-parent families is staggering (Martin, Emery, & Peris, 2004). As shown in figure 9.7, the United States has the highest percentage of single-parent families compared with virtually all other countries. Children may live in families in which both parents work, or have divorced parents, or gay or lesbian parents. Differences in culture and SES also influence their families. How do these variations in families affect children?

Working Parents   More than one of every two U.S. mothers with a child under the age of 5 is in the labor force; more than two of every three with a child from 6 to 17 years of age is. Maternal employment is a part of modern life, but its effects are still debated. According to Lois Hoffman (1989), because household operations have become more efficient and family size has decreased, it is not certain that American children today receive less attention when both parents work outside the home than children in the past whose mothers were not employed. Parents might spend less time than in the past keeping the house clean or pursuing hobbies. Time once split among several children might now be focused on just one or two.

It also cannot be assumed that children would benefit from receiving extra time and attention from stay-at-home parents. Parenting does not always have a positive

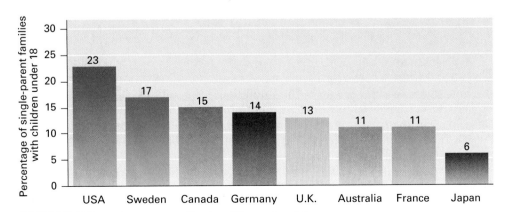

FIGURE 9.7 Single-Parent Families in Different Countries

Family and the Workplace

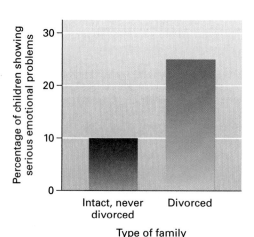

FIGURE 9.8 Divorce and Children's Emotional Problems. In Hetherington's research, 25 percent of children from divorced families showed serious emotional problems compared with only 10 percent of children from intact, never-divorced families. However, keep in mind that a substantial majority (75 percent) of the children from divorced families did not show serious emotional problems.

Divorce Resources
Father Custody

effect on the child. Parents may overinvest in their children, worrying excessively and discouraging the child's independence. The needs of the growing child require parents to give increasing independence to the child, which may be easier for parents whose jobs provide an additional source of identity and self-esteem.

Work can produce positive and negative effects on parenting (Crouter & McHale, 2005). Work-related stress can spill over and harm parenting, but a sense of well-being produced by work can lead to more positive parenting.

When parents work and place their children in child care, how does that affect the children's development? Chapter 7 discussed the research findings. Many studies have found no detrimental effects of maternal employment on children's development (Gottfried, Gottfried, & Bathurst, 2002; Hoffman & Youngblade, 1999). Recall, however, that some research suggests that preschoolers' development may suffer if their mothers worked full-time and they entered child care during their first year (Belsky & Eggebeen, 1991; Brooks-Gunn, Han, & Waldfoge, 2002; Hill & others, 2001, 2005).

Characteristics of preschoolers themselves also influence the effects of child care (Langlois & Liben, 2003). Difficult children and those with poor self-control may be especially at risk in child care (Maccoby & Lewis, 2003). Thus, it may be helpful to teach child care providers how to foster self-regulatory skills in children (Fabes, Hanish, & Martin, 2003) and to invest more effort in building children's attachment to their child-care center or school. For example, one study revealed that when children experienced their group, class, or school as a caring community, they showed increased concern for others, better conflict resolution skills, and a decrease in problem behaviors (Solomon & others, 2000).

Children in Divorced Families   Divorce rates changed rather dramatically in the United States and many countries around the world in the late twentieth century (Amato, 2005). The U.S. divorce rate increased dramatically in the 1960s and 1970s but has declined since the 1980s. However, the divorce rate in the United States is still much higher than in most other countries.

It is estimated that 40 percent of children born to married parents in the United States will experience their parents' divorce (Hetherington & Stanley-Hagan, 2002). Let's examine some important questions about children in divorced families:

Are children better adjusted in intact, never-divorced families than in divorced families? Most researchers agree that children from divorced families show poorer adjustment than their counterparts in nondivorced families (Amato, 2004; Hetherington, 2005; Hetherington & Kelly, 2002; Hetherington & Stanley-Hagan, 2002; Martin, Emery, & Peris, 2004) (see figure 9.8). Those who have experienced multiple divorces are at greater risk. Children in divorced families are more likely than children in nondivorced families to have academic problems, to show externalized problems (such as acting out and delinquency) and internalized problems (such as anxiety and depression), to be less socially responsible, to have less competent intimate relationships, to drop out of school, to become sexually active at an early age, to take drugs, to associate with antisocial peers, to have low self-esteem, and to be less securely attached as young adults (Conger & Chao, 1996). For example, one recent study found that experiencing a divorce in childhood was associated with insecure attachment in early adulthood (Brockmeyer, Treboux, & Crowell, 2005). Nonetheless, keep in mind that a majority of children in divorced families do not have significant adjustment problems. One recent study found that 20 years after their parents had divorced when they were children, approximately 80 percent of adults concluded that their parents' decision to divorce was a wise one (Ahrons, 2004).

Should parents stay together for the sake of the children? Whether parents should stay in an unhappy or conflicted marriage for the sake of their children is one of the most commonly asked questions about divorce (Hetherington, 1999, 2000, 2005). If the stresses and disruptions in family relationships associated with an unhappy, conflictual marriage that erode the well-being of children are reduced by the move to a divorced, single-parent family, divorce can be advantageous. However, if the diminished resources and increased risks associated with divorce also are accompanied by inept parenting and sustained or increased conflict, not only between the divorced couple but also among the parents, children, and siblings, the best choice for the children would be for an unhappy marriage to be retained (Hetherington & Stanley-Hagan, 2002). It is difficult to determine how these "ifs" will play out when parents either remain together in an acrimonious marriage or become divorced. Note that marital conflict may have negative consequences for children in the context of marriage or divorce (Clingempeel & Brand-Clingempeel, 2004; Cummings, Braungart-Rieker, & Du Rocher-Schudlich, 2003).

How much do family processes matter in divorced families? Family processes matter a great deal (Fine & Harvey, 2005; Hetherington & Stanley-Hagan, 2002; Wallerstein & Johnson-Reitz, 2004). When divorced parents' relationship with each other is harmonious and when they use authoritative parenting, the adjustment of children improves (Hetherington, Bridges, & Insabella, 1998). A number of researchers have shown that a disequilibrium, which includes diminished parenting skills, occurs in the year following the divorce but that, by two years after the divorce, restabilization has occurred and parenting skills have improved (Hetherington, 1989).

What factors influence an individual child's vulnerability to suffering negative consequences as a result of living in a divorced family? Among the factors involved in the child's risk and vulnerability are the child's adjustment prior to the divorce, as well as the child's personality and temperament, gender, and custody situation (Hetherington, 2005; Hetherington & Stanley-Hagan, 2002). Children whose parents later divorce show poorer adjustment before the breakup (Amato & Booth, 1996). Children who are socially mature and responsible, who show few behavioral problems, and who have an easy temperament are better able to cope with their parents' divorce. Children with a difficult temperament often have problems in coping with their parents' divorce (Hetherington, 2000).

What concerns are involved in whether parents should stay together for the sake of the children or become divorced?

Earlier studies reported gender differences in response to divorce, with divorce being more negative for girls than boys in mother-custody families. However, more recent studies have shown that gender differences are less pronounced and consistent than was previously believed. Some of the inconsistency may be due to the increase in father custody, joint custody, and increased involvement of noncustodial fathers, especially in their sons' lives (Palmer, 2004). One recent analysis of studies found that children in joint-custody families were better adjusted than children in sole-custody families (Bauserman, 2002). Some studies have shown that boys adjust better in father-custody families, girls in mother-custody families, whereas other studies have not (Maccoby & Mnookin, 1992; Santrock & Warshak, 1979).

What role does socioeconomic status play in the lives of children in divorced families? Custodial mothers experience the loss of about one-fourth to one-half of their predivorce income, in comparison with a loss of only one-tenth by custodial fathers (Emery, 1994). This income loss for divorced mothers is accompanied by increased workloads, high rates of job instability, and residential moves to less desirable neighborhoods with inferior schools.

In sum, many factors are involved in determining how divorce influences a child's development (Hetherington, 2005). In the case of Craig Lesley, whose story opened this chapter, his parents' divorce certainly marked his life, but perhaps not quite in ways we would predict. According to Lesley, his father's "neglect motivated me to raise an alcohol-damaged Indian boy just to show the old man I could succeed as a father where he had fallen down. To be truthful, it was harder than I thought" (Lesley, 2005, p. 7). To read about some strategies for helping children cope with the divorce of their parents, see the Applications in Life-Span Development interlude.

APPLICATIONS IN LIFE-SPAN DEVELOPMENT

Communicating with Children About Divorce

Ellen Galinsky and Judy David (1988) developed a number of guidelines for communicating with children about divorce.

Explain the Separation. As soon as daily activities in the home make it obvious that one parent is leaving, tell the children. If possible, both parents should be present when children are told about the separation to come. The reasons for the separation are very difficult for young children to understand. No matter what parents tell children, children can find reasons to argue against the separation. It is extremely important for parents to tell the children who will take care of them and to describe the specific arrangements for seeing the other parent.

Explain That the Separation Is Not the Child's Fault. Young children often believe their parents' separation or divorce is their own fault. Therefore, it is important to tell children that they are not the cause of the separation. Parents need to repeat this a number of times.

Explain That It May Take Time to Feel Better. Tell young children that it's normal to not feel good about what is happening and that many other children feel this way when their parents become separated. It is also okay for divorced parents to share some of their emotions with children, by saying something like, "I'm having a hard time since the separation just like you, but I know it's going to get better after a while." Such statements are best kept brief and should not criticize the other parent.

Keep the Door Open for Further Discussion. Tell your children to come to you anytime they want to talk about the separation. It is healthy for children to express their pent-up emotions in discussions with their parents and to learn that the parents are willing to listen to their feelings and fears.

Provide as Much Continuity as Possible. The less children's worlds are disrupted by the separation, the easier their transition to a single-parent family will be. This means maintaining the rules already in place as much as possible. Children need parents who care enough to not only give them warmth and nurturance but also set reasonable limits.

Provide Support for Your Children and Yourself. After a divorce or separation, parents are as important to children as before the divorce or separation. Divorced parents need to provide children with as much support as possible. Parents function best when other people are available to give them support as adults and as parents. Divorced parents can find people who provide practical help and with whom they can talk about their problems.

What are the research findings regarding the development and psychological well-being of children raised by gay male and lesbian couples?

Gay Male and Lesbian Parents   Increasingly, gay male and lesbian couples are creating families that include children. Approximately 20 percent of lesbians and 10 percent of gay men are parents (Patterson, 2004). There may be more than 1 million gay and lesbian parents in the United States today.

Like heterosexual couples, gay male and lesbian parents vary greatly. They may be single or they may have same-gender partners. Many lesbian mothers and gay fathers are noncustodial parents because they lost custody of their children to heterosexual spouses after a divorce.

Most children of gay and lesbian parents were born in a heterosexual relationship that ended in a divorce; in most cases, it was probably a relationship in which one or both parents only later identified themselves as gay male or lesbian. In other cases, lesbians and gay men became parents as a result of donor insemination and surrogates, or through adoption.

Parenthood among lesbians and gay men is controversial. Opponents claim that being raised by male or lesbian parents harms the child's development. But researchers have found few differences in children growing up with lesbian mothers or gay fathers and children growing up with heterosexual parents (Patterson, 2002, 2004). For example, children growing up in gay or lesbian families are just as popular with their peers, and there are no differences in the adjustment and mental health of children living in these families when they are compared with children in heterosexual families (Hyde & DeLamater, 2005; Lambert, 2005). Also, the overwhelming majority of children growing up in a gay or lesbian family have a heterosexual orientation (Tasker & Golombok, 1997).

Cultural, Ethnic, and Socioeconomic Variations Parenting can be influenced by culture, ethnicity, and socioeconomic status. In Bronfenbrenner's theory (introduced in chapter 2), these influences are described as part of the macrosystem.

Cross-Cultural Studies Different cultures often give different answers to such basic questions as what the father's role in the family should be, what support systems are available to families, and how children should be disciplined (Harkness & Super, 2002). There are important cross-cultural variations in parenting (Whiting & Edwards, 1988). In some countries, authoritarian parenting is widespread. For example, in the Arab world, many families today are very authoritarian, dominated by the father's rule, and children are taught strict codes of conduct and family loyalty (Booth, 2002). In one recent study, Chinese mothers of preschool children reported that they used more physical coercion, more encouragement of modesty, more shaming and love withdrawal, less warmth, and less democratic participation than U.S. mothers of preschool children (Wu & others, 2006).

What type of parenting is most frequent? In one study of parenting behavior in 186 cultures around the world, the most common pattern was a warm and controlling style, one that was neither permissive nor restrictive (Rohner & Rohner, 1981). The investigators commented that the majority of cultures have discovered, over many centuries, that children's healthy social development is most effectively promoted by love and at least some moderate parental control.

Cultural change is coming to families in many countries around the world (Berry, 2006; Bornstein & Cote, 2006). There are trends toward greater family mobility, migration to urban areas, separation as some family members work in cities or countries far from their homes, smaller families, fewer extended-family households, and increases in maternal employment (Brown & Larson, 2002; Larson, Brown, & Mortimer, 2003). These trends can change the resources that are available to children. For example, when several generations no longer live close by, children may lose support and guidance from grandparents, aunts, and uncles. Also, smaller families may produce more openness and communication between parents and children.

Ethnicity Families within different ethnic groups in the United States differ in their typical size, structure, composition, reliance on kinship networks, and levels of income and education (Harwood & Feng, 2006; Parke & Buriel, 2006). Large and extended families are more common among minority groups than among the White majority. For example, 19 percent of Latino families have three or more children, compared with 14 percent of African American and 10 percent of White families. African American and Latino children interact more with grandparents, aunts, uncles, cousins, and more-distant relatives than do White children.

Single-parent families are more common among African Americans and Latinos than among White Americans (Weinraub, Horvath, & Gringlas, 2002). In comparison with two-parent households, single parents often have more limited resources of time, money, and energy (Gyamfi, Brooks-Gunn, & Jackson, 2001). Ethnic minority parents also are less educated and more likely to live in low-income circumstances

What are some characteristics of families within different ethnic groups?

than their White counterparts. Still, many impoverished ethnic minority families manage to find ways to raise competent children (Coll & Pachter, 2002).

Some aspects of home life can help protect ethnic minority children from injustice. The family can filter out destructive racist messages, and parents can present alternative frames of reference to those presented by the majority. For example, TV shows may tell the 10-year-old boy that he will grow up to be either a star athlete or a bum; his parents can show him that his life holds many possibilities other than these. The extended family also can serve as an important buffer to stress (McAdoo, 2002).

Of course, individual families vary, and how ethnic minority families deal with stress depends on many factors (Fuligni & Yoshikawa, 2004). Whether the parents are native-born or immigrants, how long the family has been in this country, their socioeconomic status, and their national origin all make a difference (Kagiticibasi, 2006). The characteristics of the family's social context also influence its adaptation. What are the attitudes toward the family's ethnic group within its neighborhood or city? Can the family's children attend good schools? Are there community groups that welcome people from the family's ethnic group? Do members of the family's ethnic group form community groups of their own? To read further about ethnic minority parenting, see the Diversity in Life-Span Development interlude.

DIVERSITY IN LIFE-SPAN DEVELOPMENT

Acculturation and Ethnic Minority Parenting

Family Diversity

Ethnic minority children and their parents "are expected to transcend their own cultural background and to incorporate aspects of the dominant culture" into children's development. They undergo varying degrees of *acculturation,* which refers to cultural changes that occur when one culture comes in contact with another. Asian American parents, for example, may feel pressed to modify the traditional training style of parental control discussed earlier as they encounter the more permissive parenting typical of the dominant culture.

The level of family acculturation can affect parenting style by influencing expectations for children's development, parent-child interactions, and the role of the extended family (Ishii-Kuntz, 2004; Martinez & Halgunseth, 2004). For example, in one study, the level of acculturation and maternal education were the strongest predictors of maternal-infant interaction patterns in Latino families (Perez-Febles, 1992).

The family's level of acculturation also influences important decisions about child care and early childhood education. For example, "an African American mother might prefer to leave her children with extended family while she is at work because the kinship network is seen as a natural way to cope with maternal absence. This well-intentioned, culturally appropriate decision might, however, put the child at an educational and social disadvantage relative to other children of similar age who have the benefit of important preschool experiences that may ease the transition into early school years." Less acculturated and more acculturated family members may disagree about the appropriateness of various caregiving practices, possibly creating conflict or confusion.

The opportunities for acculturation that young children experience depend mainly on their parents and extended family. If they send the children to a child-care center, school, church, or other community setting, the children are likely to learn about the values and behaviors of the dominant culture, and they may be expected to adapt to that culture's norms. Thus, Latino children raised in a traditional family in which the family's good is considered more important than the individual's interests may attend a preschool in which children are rewarded for asserting themselves. Chinese American children whose traditional parents value behavioral inhibition (as discussed in chapter 7) may

How is acculturation involved in ethnic minority parenting?

be rewarded outside the home for being active and emotionally expressive. Over time, the differences in the level of acculturation experienced by children and by their parents and extended family may grow. (Source: García Coll & Pachter, 2002, pp. 7–8)

Socioeconomic Status   In America and most Western cultures, differences have been found in child rearing among different socioeconomic-status (SES) groups (Hoff, Laursen, & Tardif, 2002, p. 246):

- "Lower-SES parents (1) are more concerned that their children conform to society's expectations, (2) create a home atmosphere in which it is clear that parents have authority over children," (3) use physical punishment more in disciplining their children, and (4) are more directive and less conversational with their children.
- "Higher-SES parents (1) are more concerned with developing children's initiative" and delay of gratification, (2) "create a home atmosphere in which children are more nearly equal participants and in which rules are discussed as opposed to being laid down" in an authoritarian manner, (3) are less likely to use physical punishment, and (4) "are less directive and more conversational" with their children.

Parents in different socioeconomic groups also tend to think differently about education (Hoff, Laursen, & Tardif, 2002; Magnuson & Duncan, 2002). Middle- and upper-income parents more often think of education as something that should be mutually encouraged by parents and teachers. By contrast, low-income parents are more likely to view education as the teacher's job. Thus, increased school-family linkages especially can benefit students from low-income families.

Review and Reflect • LEARNING GOAL 2

(2) Explain how families can influence young children's development

Review
- What aspects of parenting are linked with young children's development?
- What are the types and consequences of child maltreatment?
- How are sibling relationships and birth order related to young children's development?
- How is children's development affected by having two wage-earning parents, having divorced parents, and being part of a particular cultural, ethnic, and socioeconomic group?

Reflect
- Which style or styles of parenting did your mother and father use in rearing you? What effects do you think their parenting styles have had on your development?

---

(3) PEER RELATIONS, PLAY, AND TELEVISION

Peer Relations	Play	Television

The family is an important social context for children's development. However, children's development also is strongly influenced by what goes on in other social contexts, such as in peer groups and when children are playing or watching television.

What are some characteristics of peer relations in early childhood?

Peer Relations

As children grow older, they spend an increasing amount of time with their *peers*—children of about the same age or maturity level. Even if schools were not age graded and children determined the composition of their groups on their own, they would sort themselves by age (Hartup, 1983).

What are the functions of a child's peer group? One of its most important functions is to provide a source of information and comparison about the world outside the family. Children receive feedback about their abilities from their peer group. Children evaluate what they do in terms of whether it is better than, as good as, or worse than what other children do. It is hard to make these judgments at home because siblings are usually older or younger.

How important are peers for development? Anna Freud (Freud & Dann, 1951) studied six children from different families who banded together after their parents were killed in World War II. The children formed a tightly knit group, dependent on one another and aloof with outsiders. Even though deprived of parental care, they neither became delinquent nor developed serious mental disorders. When peer monkeys who have been reared together are separated, they become depressed and less advanced socially (Suomi, Harlow, & Domek, 1970).

Good peer relations can be necessary for normal social development (Ladd, 2006; Ladd, Herald, & Andrews, 2006). Special concerns focus on children who are withdrawn and aggressive (Bukowski & Adams, 2005; Masten, 2005). Withdrawn children who are rejected by peers or are victimized and feel lonely are at risk for depression. Children who are aggressive with their peers are at risk for developing a number of problems, including delinquency and dropping out of school (Dodge, Coie, & Lynam, 2006; Rubin, Bukowski, & Parker, 2006).

Recall from our discussion of gender that by about the age of 3, children already prefer to spend time with same-sex rather than opposite-sex playmates, and this preference increases in early childhood. During these same years the frequency of peer interaction, both positive and negative, picks up considerably (Hartup, 1983). Although aggressive interaction and rough-and-tumble play increase, the proportion of aggressive exchanges, compared to friendly exchanges, decreases. Many preschool children spend considerable time in peer interaction just conversing with playmates about such matters as "negotiating roles and rules in play, arguing, and agreeing" (Rubin, Bukowski, & Parker, 2006). We will have much more to say about peer relations in chapter 11, "Socioemotional Development in Middle and Late Childhood."

Play

An extensive amount of peer interaction during childhood involves play, but social play is only one type of play (Seifert, 2006). *Play* is a pleasurable activity that is engaged in for its own sake, and its functions and forms vary.

Play's Functions Play is essential to the young child's health. Theorists have focused on different aspects of play and highlighted a long list of functions.

According to Freud and Erikson, play helps the child master anxieties and conflicts. Because tensions are relieved in play, the child can cope with life's problems. Play permits the child to work off excess physical energy and to release pent-up tensions. Therapists use *play therapy* both to allow the child to work off frustrations and to analyze the child's conflicts and ways of coping with them (Drews, Carey, & Schaefer, 2003). Children may feel less threatened and be more likely to express their true feelings in the context of play.

Piaget (1962) maintained that play advances children's cognitive development. At the same time, he said that children's cognitive development *constrains* the way they play. Play permits children to practice their competencies and acquired skills in a relaxed, pleasurable way. Piaget thought that cognitive structures need to be

Mildred Parten classified play into six categories. *Study this photograph. Which of Parten's categories are reflected in the behavior of the children?*

exercised, and play provides the perfect setting for this exercise. For example, children who have just learned to add or multiply begin to play with numbers in different ways as they perfect these operations, laughing as they do so.

Vygotsky (1962) also considered play to be an excellent setting for cognitive development. He was especially interested in the symbolic and make-believe aspects of play, as when a child substitutes a stick for a horse and rides the stick as if it were a horse. For young children, the imaginary situation is real. Parents should encourage such imaginary play, because it advances the child's cognitive development, especially creative thought.

Daniel Berlyne (1960) described play as exciting and pleasurable in itself because it satisfies our exploratory drive. This drive involves curiosity and a desire for information about something new or unusual. Play is a means whereby children can safely explore and seek out new information. Play encourages exploratory behavior by offering children the possibilities of novelty, complexity, uncertainty, surprise, and incongruity.

Play also increases the probability that children will converse and interact with each other. During this interaction, children practice the roles they will assume later in life (Sutton-Smith, 2000). In short, play releases tension, advances cognitive development, increases exploration, provides a safe haven in which children can engage in potentially dangerous behavior, and increases affiliation with peers.

Parten's Classic Study of Play Many years ago, Mildred Parten (1932) developed an elaborate classification of children's play. Based on observations of children in free play at nursery school, Parten proposed the following types of play:

- **Unoccupied play** is not play as it is commonly understood. The child may stand in one spot or perform random movements that do not seem to have a goal. In most nursery schools, unoccupied play is less frequent than other forms of play.
- **Solitary play** happens when the child plays alone and independently of others. The child seems engrossed in the activity and does not care much about anything else that is happening. Two- and 3-year-olds engage more frequently in solitary play than older preschoolers do.
- **Onlooker play** takes place when the child watches other children play. The child may talk with other children and ask questions but does not enter into

unoccupied play Play in which the child is not engaging in play as it is commonly understood and might stand in one spot, or perform random movements that do not seem to have a goal.

solitary play Play in which the child plays alone and independently of others.

onlooker play Play in which the child watches other children play.

*A*nd that park grew up with me; that small world widened as I learned its secrets and boundaries, as I discovered new refuges in its woods and jungles: hidden homes and lairs for the multitudes of imagination, for cowboys and Indians. . . . I used to dawdle on half holidays along the bent and Devonfacing seashore, hoping for gold watches or the skull of a sheep or a message in a bottle to be washed up with the tide.

—DYLAN THOMAS
Welsh Poet, 20th Century

their play behavior. The child's active interest in other children's play distinguishes onlooker play from unoccupied play.

- **Parallel play** occurs when the child plays separately from others but with toys like those the others are using or in a manner that mimics their play. The older children are, the less frequently they engage in this type of play. However, even older preschool children engage in parallel play quite often.
- **Associative play** involves social interaction with little or no organization. In this type of play, children seem to be more interested in each other than in the tasks they are performing. Borrowing or lending toys and following or leading one another in line are examples of associative play.
- **Cooperative play** consists of social interaction in a group with a sense of group identity and organized activity. Children's formal games, competition aimed at winning, and groups formed by a teacher for doing things together are examples of cooperative play. Cooperative play is the prototype for the games of middle childhood. Little cooperative play is seen in the preschool years.

Types of Play Parten's categories represent one way of thinking about the types of play, but it omits some important types. Whereas Parten's categories emphasize the role of play in the child's social world, the contemporary perspective on play emphasizes both the cognitive and the social aspects of play. Among the most widely studied types of children's play today are sensorimotor and practice play, pretense/symbolic play, social play, constructive play, and games (Bergen, 1988).

Sensorimotor and Practice Play **Sensorimotor play** is behavior by infants to derive pleasure from exercising their sensorimotor schemes. The development of sensorimotor play follows Piaget's description of sensorimotor thought, which we discussed in chapter 7. Infants initially engage in exploratory and playful visual and motor transactions in the second quarter of the first year of life. For example, at 9 months of age, infants begin to select novel objects for exploration and play, especially responsive objects, such as toys that make noise or bounce. At 12 months of age, infants enjoy making things work and exploring cause and effect.

Practice play involves the repetition of behavior when new skills are being learned or when physical or mental mastery and coordination of skills are required for games or sports. Sensorimotor play, which often involves practice play, is primarily confined to infancy, while practice play can be engaged in throughout life. During the preschool years, children often engage in practice play. Although practice play declines in the elementary school years, practice play activities such as running, jumping, sliding, twirling, and throwing balls or other objects are frequently observed on the playgrounds at elementary schools.

Pretense/Symbolic Play **Pretense/symbolic play** occurs when the child transforms the physical environment into a symbol. Between 9 and 30 months of age, children increase their use of objects in symbolic play. They learn to transform objects—substituting them for other objects and acting toward them as if they were these other objects (Kavanaugh, 2006). For example, a preschool child treats a table as if it were a car and says, "I'm fixing the car," as he grabs a leg of the table.

Many experts on play consider the preschool years the "golden age" of symbolic/pretense play that is dramatic or sociodramatic in nature (Fein, 1986). This type of make-believe play often appears at about 18 months of age and reaches a peak at 4 to 5 years of age, then gradually declines.

Social Play **Social play** is play that involves interaction with peers, and it is the focus of Parten's classification. Social play increases dramatically during the preschool years.

parallel play Play in which the child plays separately from others, but with toys like those the others are using or in a manner that mimics their play.

associative play Play that involves social interaction with little or no organization.

cooperative play Play that involves social interaction in a group with a sense of group identity and organized activity.

sensorimotor play Behavior engaged in by infants to derive pleasure from exercising their existing sensorimotor schemas.

practice play Play that involves repetition of behavior when new skills are being learned or when physical or mental mastery and coordination of skills are required for games or sports.

pretense/symbolic play Play in which the child transforms the physical environment into a symbol.

social play Play that involves social interactions with peers.

Constructive Play **Constructive play** combines sensorimotor/practice play with symbolic representation. Constructive play occurs when children engage in the self-regulated creation of a product or a solution. Constructive play increases in the preschool years as symbolic play increases and sensorimotor play decreases. In the preschool years, some practice play is replaced by constructive play. For example, instead of moving their fingers around and around in finger paint (practice play), children are more likely to draw the outline of a house or a person in the paint (constructive play). Constructive play is also a frequent form of play in the elementary school years, both in and out of the classroom. Constructive play is one of the few play-like activities allowed in work-centered classrooms. For example, if children create a play about a social studies topic, they are engaging in constructive play.

Games **Games** are activities that are engaged in for pleasure and have rules. Often they involve competition. Preschool children may begin to participate in social games that involve simple rules of reciprocity and turn taking. However, games take on a much stronger role in the lives of elementary school children. In one study, the highest incidence of game playing occurred between 10 and 12 years of age (Eiferman, 1971). After age 12, games decline in popularity (Bergen, 1988).

In sum, play ranges from an infant's simple exercise of a new sensorimotor talent to a preschool child's riding a tricycle to an older child's participation in organized games. It is also important to note that children's play can involve a combination of the play categories we have described. For example, social play can be sensorimotor (rough-and-tumble), symbolic, or constructive.

A preschool "superhero" at play.

Television

Few developments in society in the second half of the twentieth century had a greater impact on children than television (Murray, 2006; Pecora, Murray, & Wartella, 2006; Roberts, Henriksen, & Foehr, 2004; Van Evra, 2004). Although it is only one of the many types of mass media that affect children's behavior, television is the most influential. The persuasive capabilities of television are staggering (Kotler, Wright, & Huston, 2001).

Many children spend more time in front of the television set than they do with their parents. Just how much television do young children watch? In the 1990s, children watched an average of 26 hours of television each week, which is more than any other activity except sleep (National Center for Children Exposed to Violence, 2001). Compared with their counterparts in other developed countries, considerably more children in the United States watch television for long periods (see figure 9.9). The 20,000 hours of television watched by the time the average American adolescent graduates from high school are greater than the number of hours spent in the classroom.

Television can have a negative influence on children by making them passive learners, teaching them stereotypes, providing them with violent models of aggression, and presenting them with unrealistic views of the world. However, television can have a positive influence on children's development by presenting motivating educational programs, increasing their information about the world beyond their immediate environment, and providing models of prosocial behavior (Clifford, Gunter, & McAleer, 1995; Fisch, 2004; Van Evra, 2004).

Effects of Television on Children's Aggression and Prosocial Behavior
The extent to which children are exposed to violence and aggression on television raises special concern (Van Evra, 2004). Saturday morning cartoon shows average more than 25 violent acts per hour. What are the effects of television violence on children's aggression? Does television merely stimulate a child to go out and buy a *Star Wars* ray gun, or can it trigger an attack on a playmate? When children grow up, can television violence increase the likelihood they will violently attack someone?

"Mrs. Horton, could you stop by school today?"
Copyright © Martha Campbell.

constructive play Play that combines sensorimotor and repetitive activity with symbolic representation of ideas. Constructive play occurs when children engage in self-regulated creation or construction of a product or a problem solution.

games Activities engaged in for pleasure that include rules and often competition with one or more individuals.

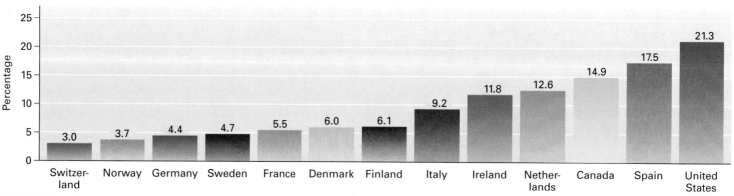

FIGURE 9.9 Percentage of 9-Year-Old Children Who Report Watching More Than Five Hours of Television per Weekday

Children's Television Workshop
Television and Violence

How is television violence linked to children's aggression?

In one experiment, preschool children were randomly assigned to one of two groups: One group watched television shows taken directly from violent Saturday morning cartoons on 11 days; the second group watched television cartoon shows with all of the violence removed (Steur, Applefield, & Smith, 1971). The children were then observed during play at their preschool. The preschool children who had seen the TV cartoon shows with violence kicked, choked, and pushed their playmates more than did the preschool children who watched nonviolent TV cartoon shows. Because the children were randomly assigned to the two conditions (TV cartoons with violence versus nonviolent TV cartoons), we can conclude that exposure to TV violence *caused* the increased aggression in the children in this investigation.

Other research has found links between watching television violence as a child and acting aggressively years later. For example, in one study, exposure to media violence at 6 to 10 years of age was linked with young adult aggressive behavior (Huesmann & others, 2003). In another study, long-term exposure to television violence was significantly related to the likelihood of aggression in 1,565 12- to 17-year-old boys (Belson, 1978). Boys who watched the most aggression on television were the most likely to commit a violent crime, swear, be aggressive in sports, threaten violence toward another boy, write slogans on walls, or break windows. These studies are *correlational,* so we can conclude from them that television violence is *associated with* aggressive behavior.

In addition to television violence, there is increased concern about children who play violent video games, especially those that are highly realistic (Van Mierlo & Van den Buick, 2004; Vastag, 2004). Children can become so deeply immersed in some electronic games that they experience an altered state of consciousness in which rational thought is suspended and arousing aggressive scripts are learned (Roberts, Henrikson, & Foehr, 2004). The direct rewards that players receive ("winning points") for their actions may also enhance the influence of video games.

Correlational studies indicate that children who extensively play violent electronic games are more aggressive than their counterparts who spend less time playing the games or do not play them at all (Cohen, 1995). Experiments have not yet been conducted to demonstrate increased aggression subsequent to playing violent video games, although a recent analysis of research studies concluded that playing violent video games is linked to aggression in both males and females (Anderson & Bushman, 2001).

Television also can teach children that it is better to behave in positive, prosocial ways than in negative, antisocial ways (Dorr, Rabin, & Irlen, 2002; Wilson, 2001), as Aimee Leifer (1973) demonstrated. She selected episodes from the television show *Sesame Street* that reflected positive social interchanges that taught children how to use their social skills. For example, in one interchange, two men were fighting over the amount of space available to them; they gradually began to cooperate and to share the space. Children who watched these episodes copied these behaviors, and in later social situations they applied the prosocial lessons they had learned.

Television, Cognitive Development, and Achievement   In general, television has not been shown to influence children's creativity but is negatively related to their mental ability (Comstock & Scharrer, 2006; Schmidt & Anderson, 2006). As we will discuss in chapter 10, watching television is also linked with reductions in school achievement. However, some types of television—such as educational programming for young children—may enhance achievement. Recall from chapter 2 our description of one longitudinal study in which viewing educational programs such as *Sesame Street* and *Mr. Rogers' Neighborhood* as preschoolers was associated with a host of desirable characteristics in adolescence: getting higher grades, reading more books, placing a higher value on achievement, being more creative, and acting less aggressively (Anderson & others, 2001). These associations were more consistent for boys than girls.

Review and Reflect • LEARNING GOAL 3

3 **Describe the roles of peers, play, and television in young children's development**

Review
- How do peers affect young children's development?
- What are some theories and types of play?
- How does television influence children's development?

Reflect
- What guidelines would you recommend to parents to help them to make television a more positive influence on their children's development? Consider factors such as the child's age, the child's activities other than TV, the parents' patterns of interaction with the children, and types of TV shows.

REACH YOUR LEARNING GOALS

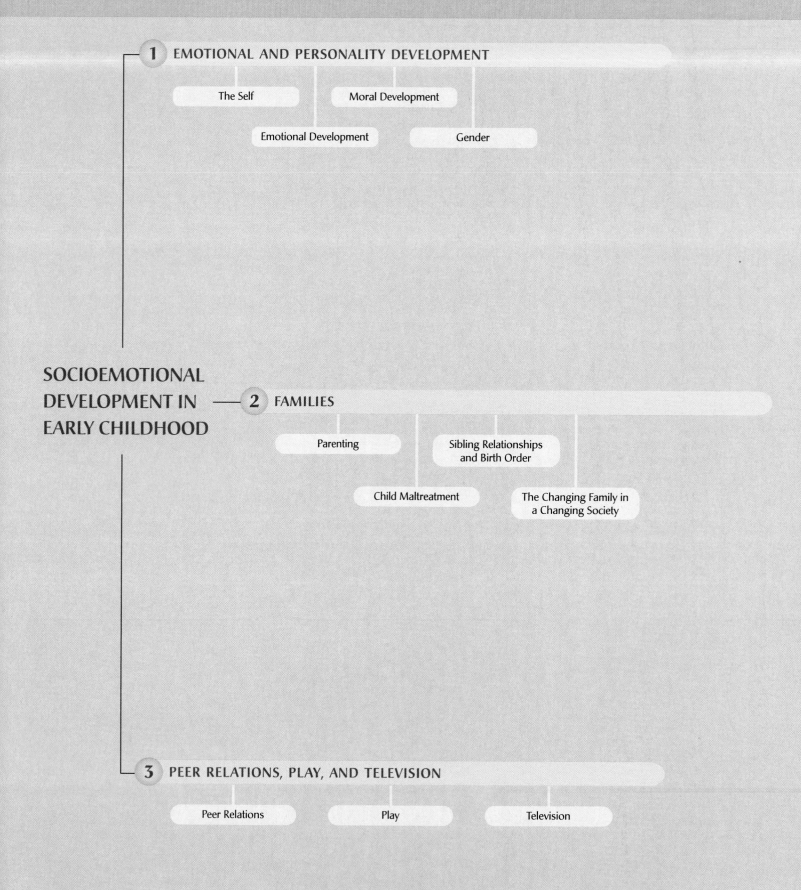

SOCIOEMOTIONAL DEVELOPMENT IN EARLY CHILDHOOD

1 EMOTIONAL AND PERSONALITY DEVELOPMENT

- The Self
- Emotional Development
- Moral Development
- Gender

2 FAMILIES

- Parenting
- Child Maltreatment
- Sibling Relationships and Birth Order
- The Changing Family in a Changing Society

3 PEER RELATIONS, PLAY, AND TELEVISION

- Peer Relations
- Play
- Television

SUMMARY

1 Emotional and Personality Development: *Discuss emotional and personality development in early childhood*

The Self
In Erikson's theory early childhood is a period when development involves resolving the conflict of initiative versus guilt. The toddler's rudimentary self-understanding develops into the preschooler's representation of the self in terms of body image, material possessions, and physical activities.

Emotional Development
Young children's range of emotions expands during early childhood as they increasingly experience self-conscious emotions such as pride, shame, and guilt. Two- and three-year-olds use an increasing number of terms to describe emotion and learn more about the causes and consequences of feelings. At 4 to 5 years of age, children show an increased ability to reflect on emotions and understand that a single event can elicit different emotions in different people. They also show a growing awareness of the need to manage emotions to meet social standards. Emotion-coaching parents have children who engage in more effective self-regulation of their emotions than do emotion-dismissing parents. Emotional regulation plays an important role in successful peer relations.

Moral Development
Moral development involves thoughts, feelings, and actions regarding rules and regulations about what people should do in their interactions with others. Freud's psychoanalytic theory emphasizes the importance of feelings in the development of the superego, the moral branch of personality. In Freud's view, the superego develops through identification with the same-sex parent, and children conform to societal standards to avoid guilt. Positive emotions, such as empathy, also contribute to the child's moral development. Piaget analyzed moral reasoning and concluded that children from 4 to 7 years of age display heteronomous morality, judging behavior by its consequences. According to behavioral and social cognitive theorists, moral behavior develops as a result of reinforcement, punishment, and imitation, and there is considerable situational variability in moral behavior. Self-control is an important aspect of understanding children's moral behavior.

Gender
Gender refers to the social and psychological dimensions of being male or female. Gender identity is acquired by 3 years of age for most children. A gender role is a set of expectations that prescribes how females or males should think, act, and feel. The 23rd pair of chromosomes may have two X chromosomes to produce a female, or one X and one Y chromosome to produce a male. The two main classes of sex hormones are estrogens, which are dominant in females, and androgens, which are dominant in males. Biology is not completely destiny in gender development; children's socialization experiences matter a great deal. Both psychoanalytic theory and social cognitive theory emphasize the adoption of parents' gender characteristics. Peers are especially adept at rewarding gender-appropriate behavior. Both cognitive developmental and gender schema theories emphasize the role of cognition in gender development.

2 Families: *Explain how families can influence young children's development*

Parenting
Authoritarian, authoritative, neglectful, and indulgent are four main parenting styles. Authoritative parenting is the most widely used style around the world and is the style most often associated with children's social competence. However, ethnic variations in parenting styles suggest that in African American and Asian American families, some aspects of control may benefit children. Latino parents often emphasize connectedness with the family and respect and obedience in their child rearing. Physical punishment is widely used by U.S. parents, but there are a number of reasons why it is not a good choice. Coparenting has positive effects on children's development.

Child Maltreatment
Child maltreatment may take the form of physical abuse, child neglect, sexual abuse, and emotional abuse. Child maltreatment places the child at risk for academic, emotional, and social problems. Adults who suffered child maltreatment are also vulnerable to a range of problems.

Sibling Relationships and Birth Order
Siblings interact with each other in positive and negative ways. Birth order is related in certain ways to child characteristics, but by itself it is not a good predictor of behavior.

The Changing Family in a Changing Society
In general, having both parents employed full-time outside the home has not been shown to have negative effects on children. However, in specific circumstances, when a mother works outside the home, such as when the infant is less than 1 year old, negative effects can occur. Divorce can have negative effects on children's adjustment, but so can an acrimonious relationship between parents who stay together for their children's sake. If divorced parents develop a harmonious relationship and practice authoritative parenting, children's adjustment improves. Researchers have found few differences between children growing up in gay or lesbian families and children growing up in heterosexual families. Cultures vary on a number of issues regarding families. African American and Latino children are more likely than White American children to live in single-parent families and larger families and to have

extended family connections. Lower-SES parents create a home atmosphere that involves more authority and physical punishment with children than higher-SES parents. Higher-SES parents are more concerned about developing children's initiative and delay of gratification.

 ### 3 Peer Relations, Play, and Television: *Describe the roles of peers, play, and television in young children's development*

Peer Relations

Peers are powerful socialization agents. Peers provide a source of information and comparison about the world outside the family.

Play

Play's functions include affiliation with peers, tension release, advances in cognitive development, exploration, and provision of a safe haven. Parten developed the categories of unoc-cupied, solitary, onlooker, parallel, associative, and coopera-tive play. The contemporary perspective on play emphasizes both the cognitive and the social aspects of play. Among the most widely studied types of children's play are sensorimotor play, practice play, pretense/symbolic play, social play, con-structive play, and games.

Television

Television can have both negative influences (such as turning children into passive learners and presenting them with aggressive models) and positive influences (such as providing models of prosocial behavior) on children's development. TV violence is not the only cause of children's aggression, but it can induce aggression. Prosocial behavior on TV can teach children positive behavior. Television viewing has not been shown to be linked to children's creativity but is negatively related to their mental ability although some types of educa-tional television may enhance achievement in school.

KEY TERMS

self-understanding 277
moral development 279
heteronomous morality 280
autonomous morality 280
immanent justice 281
gender identity 282
gender role 282
social role theory 283

psychoanalytic theory of gender 283
social cognitive theory of gender 284
cognitive developmental theory of gender 285
gender schema theory 285
authoritarian parenting 288

authoritative parenting 288
neglectful parenting 288
indulgent parenting 288
unoccupied play 303
solitary play 303
onlooker play 303
parallel play 304
associative play 304

cooperative play 304
sensorimotor play 304
practice play 304
pretense/symbolic play 304
social play 304
constructive play 305
games 305

KEY PEOPLE

Erik Erikson 277
Sigmund Freud 280
Jean Piaget 280

Lawrence Kohlberg 285
Diana Baumrind 288
Ruth Chao 289

Lois Hoffman 295
Anna Freud 302
Lev Vygotsky 303

Daniel Berlyne 303
Mildred Parten 303

E-LEARNING TOOLS

To help you master the material in this chapter, you'll find a number of valuable study tools on the LifeMap CD-ROM that accompanies this book and on the Online Learning Center for *Life-Span Development*, eleventh edition, at **www.mhhe.com/ santrockld11**.

Video Clips

In the margins of this book there are icons directing you to the LifeMap CD-ROM that accompanies the book. There you'll find two videos for chapter 9. The first video is called "When a Second Baby Comes Along." Are there patterns among the personality traits of firstborn siblings? A researcher discusses the significance of birth order and offers some practical advice about preparing a child for a new brother or sister. The second video is called "Cultural Variations in Father's Role." A son will typically speak of his father as a role model, but the actual role that fathers play in their sons' and daughters' development continues to be a subject of research. This segment looks at some of that research.

Self-Assessment

Connect to **www.mhhe.com/santrockld11** to examine your beliefs about caring for young children by completing the self-assessment, *My Parenting Style*.

Taking It to the Net

Connect to www.mhhe.com/santrockld11 to research the answers to these questions.

1. Doris and Ken are in the process of getting a divorce. Each wants full custody of the two children, Kevin, age 10, and Chrissie, age 3. Although the divorce process has been very stressful for both of them, Doris and Ken share concerns about the effects their divorce might have on their children. What immediate effects can they expect, especially given the context of the custody battle? How might Kevin's reactions differ from Chrissie's? What might the long-term effects of the divorce be on their children?
2. Karen's mother is concerned about how to best help her daughter, Teresa, whose husband has abandoned her and their 5-year-old son. What are some of the challenges that Teresa may have to face, and how can her mother help her through this difficult time?
3. Jonathan and Diedre want to shield their children from the violence on television, but they are not sure how to go about it—other than by not allowing any television viewing at all. What recommendations does the APA have for parents?

Health and Well-Being, Parenting, and Education Exercises

Build your decision-making skills by trying your hand at the health and well-being, parenting, and education exercises.

Connect to **www.mhhe.com/santrockld11** to research the answers and complete the exercises.

The thirst to know and understand . . . These are the good in life's rich hand.

—SIR WILLIAM WATSON
English Poet, 20th Century

CHAPTER OUTLINE

LEARNING GOALS

PHYSICAL CHANGES AND HEALTH

Body Growth and Change

Motor Development

Exercise and Sports

Health, Illness, and Disease

1 Describe physical changes and health in middle and late childhood

CHILDREN WITH DISABILITIES

Learning Disabilities

Attention Deficit Hyperactivity Disorder (ADHD)

Educational Issues

2 Identify children with different types of disabilities and issues in educating them

COGNITIVE CHANGES

Piaget's Cognitive Developmental Theory

Information Processing

Intelligence

Interpreting Differences in IQ Scores

Extremes of Intelligence

3 Explain cognitive changes in middle and late childhood

LANGUAGE DEVELOPMENT

Vocabulary, Grammar, and Metalinguistic Awareness

Reading

Bilingualism and Second Language Learning

4 Discuss language development in middle and late childhood

The following comments are by Angie, an elementary-school-aged girl:

> When I was eight years old, I weighed 125 pounds. My clothes were the size that large teenage girls wear. I hated my body and my classmates teased me all the time. I was so overweight and out of shape that when I took at P.E. class my face would get red and I had trouble breathing. I was jealous of the kids who played sports and weren't overweight like I was.
>
> I'm nine years old now and I've lost 30 pounds. I'm much happier and proud of myself. How did I lose the weight? My mom said she had finally decided enough was enough. She took me to a pediatrician who specializes in helping children lose weight and keep it off. The pediatrician counseled my mom about my eating and exercise habits, then had us join a group that he had created for overweight children and their parents. My mom and I go to the group once a week and we've now been participating in the program for six months. I no longer eat fast food meals and my mom is cooking more healthy meals. Now that I've lost weight, exercise is not as hard for me and I don't get teased by the kids at school. My mom's pretty happy too because she's lost 15 pounds herself since we've been in the counseling program.

Not all overweight children are as successful as Angie at reducing their weight. Indeed, being overweight or obese in childhood has become a major national concern in the United States. Later in the chapter, we will further explore being overweight and obese in childhood, including obesity's causes and outcomes.

PREVIEW

During the middle and late childhood years children grow taller, heavier, and stronger. They become more adept at using their physical skills, and they develop new cognitive skills. This chapter is about physical and cognitive development in middle and late childhood. To begin, we will explore some changes in physical development.

1 PHYSICAL CHANGES AND HEALTH

- Body Growth and Change
- Motor Development
- Exercise and Sports
- Health, Illness, and Disease

Continued change characterizes children's bodies during middle and late childhood, and their motor skills improve. As children move through the elementary school years, they gain greater control over their bodies and can sit and attend for longer periods of time. Regular exercise is one key to making these years a time of healthy growth and development.

Body Growth and Change

The period of middle and late childhood involves slow, consistent growth. This is a period of calm before the rapid growth spurt of adolescence. During the elementary school years, children grow an average of 2 to 3 inches a year until, at the age of

11, the average girl is 4 feet, $10\frac{1}{4}$ inches tall, and the average boy is 4 feet, 9 inches tall. During the middle and late childhood years, children gain about 5 to 7 pounds a year. The weight increase is due mainly to increases in the size of the skeletal and muscular systems, as well as the size of some body organs.

Proportional changes are among the most pronounced physical changes in middle and late childhood. Head circumference, waist circumference, and leg length decrease in relation to body height (Hockenberry, 2005). A less noticeable physical change is that bones continue to ossify during middle and late childhood but yield to pressure and pull more than mature bones.

Muscle mass and strength gradually increase during these years as "baby fat" decreases. The loose movements and knock-knees of early childhood give way to improved muscle tone. Thanks to both heredity and to exercise, children double their strength capabilities during these years. Because of their greater number of muscle cells, boys are usually stronger than girls.

Motor Development

During middle and late childhood, children's motor skills become much smoother and more coordinated than they were in early childhood. For example, only one child in a thousand can hit a tennis ball over the net at the age of 3, yet by the age of 10 or 11 most children can learn to play the sport. Running, climbing, skipping rope, swimming, bicycle riding, and skating are just a few of the many physical skills elementary school children can master. In gross motor skills involving large activity, boys usually outperform girls.

Increased myelination of the central nervous system is reflected in the improvement of fine motor skills during middle and late childhood. Children can more adroitly use their hands as tools. Six-year-olds can hammer, paste, tie shoes, and fasten clothes. By 7 years of age, children's hands have become steadier. At this age, children prefer a pencil to a crayon for printing, and reversal of letters is less common. Printing becomes smaller. At 8 to 10 years of age, the hands can be used independently with more ease and precision. Fine motor coordination develops to the point at which children can write rather than print words. Cursive letter size becomes smaller and more even. At 10 to 12 years of age, children begin to show manipulative skills similar to the abilities of adults. They can master the complex, intricate, and rapid movements needed to produce fine-quality crafts or to play a difficult piece on a musical instrument. Girls usually outperform boys in their use of fine motor skills.

Exercise and Sports

Elementary school children are far from physical maturity, so they need to be active. They become more fatigued by long periods of sitting than by running, jumping, or bicycling. Physical action, such as batting a ball, skipping rope, or balancing on a beam, is essential for these children to refine their developing skills. It is becoming increasingly clear that exercise plays an important role in children's growth and development (Dencker & others, 2006; Riddell & Iscoe, 2006).

Are U.S. children getting enough exercise? In a 1997 national poll, only 22 percent of children in grades 4 through 12 were physically active for 30 minutes every day of the week (Harris, 1997). Their parents said their children were too busy watching TV, spending time on the computer, or playing video games to exercise much. Boys were more physically active at all ages than girls. In one historical comparison, the percentage of children involved in daily P.E. programs in schools decreased from 80 percent in 1969 to 20 percent in 1999 (Health Management Resources, 2001) (see figure 10.1). Further, a recent study found that 61 percent of 9- to 13-year-old U.S. children do not participate in any organized physical activity

*E*very forward step we take we leave *some phantom of ourselves behind.*

—JOHN LANCASTER SPALDING
American Educator, 19th Century

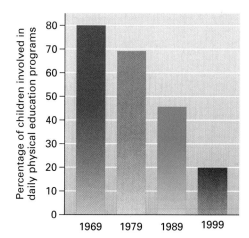

FIGURE 10.1 Percentage of Children Involved in Daily Physical Education Programs in the United States from 1969 to 1999. There has been a dramatic drop in the percentage of children participating in daily physical education programs in the United States, from 80 percent in 1969 to only 20 percent in 1999.

What are some good strategies for increasing children's exercise?

What are some potential positive and negative consequences for children's participation in sports?

during their nonschool hours and that 23 percent do not engage in any free-time physical activity (Centers for Disease Control and Prevention, 2003).

Here are some ways to get children to exercise more:

- Offer more physical activity programs run by volunteers at school facilities.
- Improve physical fitness activities in schools.
- Have children plan community and school activities that really interest them.
- Encourage families to focus more on physical activity and encourage parents to exercise more. Caregivers who model an active lifestyle and provide children with opportunities to be active influence children's activity level (Ruxton, 2004).

Participation in sports can have both positive and negative consequences for children. Participation can provide exercise, opportunities to learn how to compete, self-esteem, and a setting for developing peer relations and friendships. However, sports also can bring pressure to achieve and win, physical injuries, a distraction from academic work, and unrealistic expectations for success as an athlete (Browne & Lamb, 2006).

Few people challenge the value of sports for children when conducted as part of a school's physical education or intramural program. However, some critics question the appropriateness of highly competitive, win-oriented sports teams, especially when they involve championship play and media publicity. Such activities not only put undue stress on children but also may teach them a win-at-all-costs philosophy (Pratt, Patel, & Greydanus, 2003). Overly ambitious parents, coaches, and community boosters can unintentionally create a highly stressful atmosphere in children's sports. When parental, organizational, or community prestige becomes the central focus of the child's participation in sports, the danger of exploitation clearly is present. Programs oriented toward such purposes often require long and arduous training sessions over many months and years, frequently leading to specialization at too early an age. In such circumstances, adults often transmit to the child the distorted view that the sport is the most important aspect of the child's existence.

Health, Illness, and Disease

For the most part, middle and late childhood is a time of excellent health. Disease and death are less prevalent during this period than during others in childhood and in adolescence.

Accidents and Injuries Injuries are the leading cause of death during middle and late childhood, and the most common cause of severe injury and death in this period is motor vehicle accidents, either as a pedestrian or as a passenger (Hockenberry, 2005). The use of safety-belt restraint greatly reduces the severity of motor vehicle injuries (Bolen, Bland, & Sacks, 1999). Other serious injuries involve bicycles, skateboards, roller skates, and other sports equipment.

Most accidents occur in or near the child's home or school. The most effective prevention strategy is to educate the child about the hazards of risk taking and improper use of equipment (Aitken & others, 2004; Philippakis & others, 2004). Wearing appropriate safety helmets, protective eye and mouth shields, and protective padding are recommended for children who engage in active sports (Briem & others, 2004).

Cancer Cancer is the second leading cause of death in U.S. children 5 to 14 years of age. Three percent of all children's deaths in this age period are due to cancer. Currently, 1 in every 330 children in the United States develops cancer before the age of 19. Moreover, the incidence of cancer in children is increasing (Neglia & others, 2001).

Child cancers mainly attack the white blood cells (leukemia), brain, bone, lymph system, muscles, kidneys, and nervous system. All are characterized by an uncontrolled proliferation of abnormal cells (Savell & others, 2004). As indicated in figure 10.2, the most common cancer in children is leukemia, a cancer in which bone marrow manufactures an abundance of abnormal white blood cells, which crowd out normal cells, making the child susceptible to bruising and infection.

Child life specialists are among the health professionals who work to make the lives of children with diseases such as cancer less stressful. To read about the work of child life specialist Sharon McCleod, see the Careers in Life-Span Development profile.

Cardiovascular Disease Cardiovascular disease is uncommon in children. Nonetheless, environmental experiences and behavior in the childhood years can sow the seeds for cardiovascular disease in adulthood. Many elementary-school-aged children already possess one or more of the risk factors for cardiovascular disease, such as hypertension and obesity (Cohen, 2004; Hanevold & others, 2004; Katzmarzyk & others, 2004; Sorof & others, 2004). A recent study of more than 5,000 U.S. children revealed that high blood pressure was most likely to be present in Latino children (25 percent) and least characteristic of Asian American (14 percent) children (Sorof & others, 2004).

Another recent study examined the role of diet and exercise on cardiovascular functioning in 82 overweight 9- to 12-year-old children (Woo & others, 2004). Children were randomly assigned to either a dietary only or a dietary plus supervised exercise program for six weeks and subsequently for one year. After six weeks, both treatments were linked with a decrease in waist-hip ratio, lower cholesterol, and improved functioning of arteries. After one year, the carotid wall of the children was thinner and body fat content was lower in the children in the dietary/exercise group.

More information comes from the Bogalusa Heart Study, also called "Heart Smart," an ongoing evaluation of 8,000 boys and girls in Bogalusa, Louisiana (Berenson, 2005; Berenson & others, 2005; Chen & others, 2005; Freedman & others, 2004, 2005;

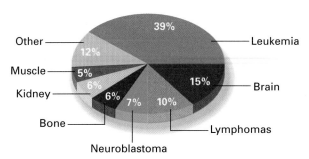

FIGURE 10.2 Types of Cancer in Children. Cancers in children have a different profile from adult cancers, which attack mainly the lungs colon, breast, prostate, and pancreas.

CAREERS
in LIFE-SPAN DEVELOPMENT

Sharon McLeod
Child Life Specialist

Sharon McLeod is a child life specialist who is clinical director of the Child Life and Recreational Therapy Department at the Children's Hospital Medical Center in Cincinnati.

Under Sharon's direction, the goals of the Child Life Department are to promote children's optimal growth and development, reduce the stress of health-care experiences, and provide support to child patients and their families. These goals are accomplished through therapeutic play and developmentally appropriate activities, educating and psychologically preparing children for medical procedures, and serving as a resource for parents and other professionals regarding children's development and health-care issues.

Sharon says that human growth and development provides the foundation for her profession of child life specialist. She also describes her best times as a student when she conducted fieldwork, had an internship, and experienced hands-on theories and concepts she learned in her courses.

Sharon McLeod, child life specialist, working with a child at Children's Hospital Medical Center in Cincinnati.

Child Health
Child Health Guide

Janssen & others, 2006; Katzmarzyk & others, 2004; Li & others, 2004; Nicklas & others, 2003, 2004a, 2004b; Rajeshwari & others, 2005). Following are some results from the Bogalusa Heart Study:

- More than half of the children exceeded the recommended intake of salt, fat, cholesterol, and sugar (Nicklas & others, 1995).
- Consumption of sweetened beverages, sweets (desserts, candy), and total consumption of low-quality food were associated with being overweight in childhood (Nicklas & others, 2003).
- Adiposity (having excess body weight) beginning in childhood was related to cardiovascular problems in adulthood (Li & others, 2004).
- Higher body mass index (BMI) in childhood was linked to the likelihood of developing metabolic syndrome (a cluster of characteristics that include excessive fat around the abdomen, high blood pressure, and diabetes) in adulthood (Freedman & others, 2005)

Obesity Childhood obesity is an increasing problem (Insel & Roth, 2006; Sizer & Whitney, 2006). The prevalence of being overweight among children from 6 to 11 years of age in the United States increased 325 percent from 1974 to 1999 (NHANES, 2001). Males are considered to be obese when their weight is 20 percent or more over their maximum desirable weight for their height, and females are considered obese when their weight is 25 percent over (Medline Plus, 2006). Girls are more likely to be obese than boys. Obesity at 6 years of age results in approximately a 25 percent probability that the child will be obese as an adult; obesity at age 12 results in approximately a 75 percent chance that the adolescent will be obese as an adult.

The increase in obesity is cause for great concern because obesity raises the risk for many medical and psychological problems (Arif & Rohrer, 2006; Johnson & others, 2006). Obese children can develop pulmonary problems and hip problems (Perez-Perdomo & others, 2003). Obese children also are prone to have high blood pressure, elevated blood cholesterol levels, and type 2 diabetes (Bindler & Bruya, 2006; Daniels, 2006). The problems faced by Angie, whose comments opened this chapter, illustrate some of the psychological difficulties encountered by many obese children. Low self-esteem and depression are common outgrowths of obesity. Furthermore, obese children often have problems in peer relations and may be excluded from peer groups (Datar & Sturm, 2004; Janssen & others, 2004). One recent study found that obese children are often teased by their peers, have difficulty playing sports, and have health problems (Schwimmer, Burwinkle, & Varni, 2003).

What are the causes for the increase in obesity? Changes in diet are one suspect. From the late 1970s through the late 1990s, key dietary shifts took place among U.S. children as young as 2 years of age through the adult years: greater away-from-home consumption, large increases in total calories from salty snacks, soft drinks, and pizza; and large decreases in calories from low- and medium-fat milk and medium- and high-fat beef and pork (Nielsen, Siega-Riz, & Popkin, 2002). Children's total caloric intake also increased.

Another recent national assessment found that most children's diets are poor or in need of improvement (Federal Interagency Forum on Child and Family Statistics, 2002). In this assessment, only 27 percent of 2- to 5-year-old children were categorized as having good diets. Their diets worsened as they became older—only 13 percent of 6- to 9-year-old children had healthy diets.

Other characteristics of how today's children live may also be culprits in the rise of obesity (Lindsay & others, 2006; Salmon, Campbell, & Crawford, 2006). One recent study found that time spent watching TV and the number of soft drinks consumed were both related to children's obesity (Giammattei & others, 2003). The context in which children eat may also play a role. In one recent study, children who ate with their families were more likely to eat more vegetables and low-fat foods (such as low-fat milk and salad dressing and lean meats), and drink fewer

What are some concerns about children's cardiovascular health and obesity?

sodas than children who ate alone (Cullen, 2001). In this study, overweight children ate 50 percent of their meals in front of a TV, compared with only 35 percent of normal-weight children.

Inadequate levels of exercise are also linked with being overweight (Riddell & Iscoe, 2006; Williams, 2005). One recent study found that one additional hour of physical education per week in the first grade was linked to girls being less likely to be overweight (Datar & Sturm, 2004). In chapter 14, we will discuss the most effective treatments for obesity, with a special focus on the importance of exercise.

www.mhhe.com/santrockld11

Overweight Children
Heart Smart
Diseases and Illnesses
Medical Links
Cancer in Children

Review and Reflect • LEARNING GOAL 1

1 **Describe physical changes and health in middle and late childhood**

Review
- What are some changes in body growth and proportion in middle and late childhood?
- How do children's motor skills develop in middle and late childhood?
- What roles do exercise and sports play in children's lives?
- What are some characteristics of health, illness, and disease in middle and late childhood?

Reflect
- Should parents be discouraged from coaching their children in sports or watching their children play in sports? Explain.

---

2 CHILDREN WITH DISABILITIES

Learning Disabilities   Attention Deficit Hyperactivity Disorder (ADHD)   Educational Issues

The elementary school years are a time when children with disabilities become more sensitive about their differentness and how it is perceived by others. Approximately 10 percent of children in the United States receive special education or related services. As figure 10.3 shows, among children with disabilities who receive special education services, more than 40 percent have a learning disability (National Center for Education Statistics, 2003). Substantial percentages of children have speech or language impairments, mental retardation, or serious emotional disturbance.

Learning Disabilities

Bobby's second-grade teacher complains that his spelling is awful. Eight-year-old Tim says reading is really hard for him, and a lot of times the words don't make much sense. Alisha has good oral language skills but has considerable difficulty in computing correct answers to arithmetic problems. Each of these students has a learning disability.

After examining the research on learning disabilities, leading expert Linda Siegel (2003) recently concluded that a definition of **learning disabilities** should include these components: (1) a minimum IQ level; (2) a significant difficulty in a school-related area, especially reading and/or mathematics; and (3) exclusion of only severe

learning disability Includes three components: (1) a minimum IQ level; (2) a significant difficulty in a school-related area (especially reading and/or mathematics); and (3) exclusion of only severe emotional disorders, second-language background, sensory disabilities, and/or specific neurological deficits.

Disability	Number of Children	Percentage of All Children with Disabilities
Learning disabilities	2,846,000	44.4
Speech and language impairments	1,084,000	16.9
Mental retardation	592,000	9.2
Emotional disturbance	476,000	7.4

FIGURE 10.3 U.S. Children with a Disability Who Receive Special Education Services. Figures are for the 2001–2002 school year and represent the four categories with the highest number and percentage of children. Both learning disability and attention deficit hyperactivity disorder are combined in the learning disabilities category (National Center for Education Statistics, 2003).

www.mhhe.com/santrockld11

Exploring Disabilities
Learning Disabilities
Learning Disabilities Association

dyslexia A category of learning disabilities involving a severe impairment in the ability to read and spell.

attention deficit hyperactivity disorder (ADHD) A disability in which children consistently show one or more of the following characteristics: (1) inattention, (2) hyperactivity, and (3) impulsivity.

emotional disorders, second-language background, sensory disabilities, and/or specific neurological deficits.

A recent national survey found that 8 percent of U.S. children have a learning disability (Bloom & Dey, 2006). About three times as many boys as girls are classified as having a learning disability (U.S. Department of Education, 1996). Among the explanations for this gender difference are a greater biological vulnerability among boys and *referral bias*. That is, boys are more likely to be referred by teachers for treatment because of their behavior (Liederman, Kantrowitz, & Flannery, 2005).

In the past two decades, the percentage of children classified as having a learning disability has increased substantially—from less than 30 percent of all children receiving special education and related services in 1977 to more than 40 percent today. Some experts say that the dramatic increase reflects poor diagnostic practices. They suggest that teachers sometimes are too quick to label children with the slightest learning problem as having a learning disability, instead of recognizing that the problem may rest in their ineffective teaching. Other experts say the increase in children being labeled with a "learning disability" is justified (Hallahan & Kaufmann, 2005, 2006).

The most common problem that characterizes children with a learning disability involves reading (Spafford & Grosser, 2005). **Dyslexia** is a category that is reserved for individuals who have a severe impairment in their ability to read and spell (Rosen, 2006; Snowling, 2004). Children with learning disabilities often have difficulties in handwriting, spelling, or composition. Their writing may be extremely slow, it may be virtually illegible, and they may make numerous spelling errors because of their inability to match up sounds and letters.

About 5 percent of all school-age children in the United States receive special education or related services because of a learning disability. In the federal classification of children receiving special education and related services, attention deficit hyperactivity disorder (ADHD) is included in the learning disabilities category. Because of the significant interest in ADHD today, we will discuss it by itself next.

Attention Deficit Hyperactivity Disorder (ADHD)

Matthew has attention deficit hyperactivity disorder, and the outward signs are fairly typical. He has trouble attending to the teacher's instructions and is easily distracted. He can't sit still for more than a few minutes at a time, and his handwriting is messy. His mother describes him as very fidgety.

Attention deficit hyperactivity disorder (ADHD) is a disability in which children consistently show one or more of these characteristics over a period of time: (1) inattention, (2) hyperactivity, and (3) impulsivity. Children who are inattentive have difficulty focusing on any one thing and may get bored with a task after only a few minutes. Children who are hyperactive show high levels of physical activity and almost always seem to be in motion. Children who are impulsive have difficulty curbing their reactions and do not do a good job of thinking before they act. Depending on the characteristics that children with ADHD display, they can be diagnosed as (1) ADHD with predominantly inattention, (2) ADHD with predominantly hyperactivity/impulsivity, or (3) ADHD with both inattention and hyperactivity/impulsivity.

The number of children diagnosed and treated for ADHD has increased substantially, by some estimates doubling in the 1990s. A recent national survey found that 7 percent of U.S. children 3 to 17 years of age had ADHD (Bloom & Dey, 2006). The disorder occurs as much as four to nine times more in boys than in girls. There is controversy, however, about the increased diagnosis of ADHD (Terman & others, 1996). Some experts attribute the increase mainly to heightened awareness of the disorder. Others are concerned that many children are being incorrectly diagnosed.

Causes and Course of ADHD   Definitive causes of ADHD have not been found. However, a number of causes have been proposed, such as heredity, low levels of certain neurotransmitters (chemical messengers in the brain), prenatal and postnatal abnormalities, and environmental toxins, such as lead (Voeller, 2004; Waldman & Gizer, 2006; Weyandt, 2006). Thirty to 50 percent of children with ADHD have a sibling or parent who has the disorder (Farane & Doyle, 2001).

Many children with ADHD are difficult to discipline, have a low frustration tolerance, and have problems in peer relations (Farone & Doyle, 2001). Other common characteristics of children with ADHD include general immaturity and clumsiness. Signs of ADHD may be present in the preschool years. Parents and preschool or kindergarten teachers may notice that the child has an extremely high activity level and a limited attention span. They may say the child is "always on the go," "can't sit still even for a second," or "never seems to listen." Despite these signs of ADHD, children are often not diagnosed with the disorder until the elementary school years (Ross & Ross, 2006; Zentall, 2006; Wolraich, 2006).

The increased academic and social demands of formal schooling, as well as stricter standards for behavioral control, often illuminate the problems of the child with ADHD. Elementary school teachers typically report that the child with ADHD has difficulty working independently, completing seatwork, and organizing work. Restlessness and distractibility also are often noted. These problems are more likely to be observed during repetitive or taxing tasks, or tasks the child perceives to be boring (such as completing worksheets or doing homework) (Hoza & others, 2001).

It used to be thought that ADHD decreased in adolescence, but now it is thought that this often is not the case. Estimates suggest that ADHD decreases in only about one-third of adolescents. Increasingly, it is being recognized that these problems may continue into adulthood (Faraone, Biederman, & Mick, 2006).

Many children with ADHD show impulsive behavior, such as this child who is jumping out of his seat and throwing a paper airplane at other children. *How would you handle this situation if you were a teacher and this were to happen in your classroom?*

www.mhhe.com/santrockld11

ADHD

Treatment of ADHD   About 85 to 90 percent of children with ADHD are taking stimulant medication such as Ritalin or Adderall (which has fewer side effects than Ritalin) to enable them to control their behavior (Denney, 2001). Ritalin and Adderall are stimulants, and for most individuals, they speed up the nervous system and behavior. However, in many children with ADHD, the drug speeds up underactive areas of the prefrontal cortex that control attention, impulsivity, and planning, enhancing the children's ability to focus. This enhanced ability to focus their attention results in what *appears* to be a "slowing down" of behavior in these children (Reeves & Schweitzer, 2004).

Stimulant medication has been found to be effective in improving the attention of many children with ADHD, but it usually does not improve their attention to the same level as that of children who do not have ADHD (Barbaresi & others, 2006; Tucha & others, 2006). Further, in 2006, the U.S. government issued a warning about the cardiovascular risks of stimulant medications used to treat ADHD.

Researchers have found that a combination of medication (such as Ritalin) and behavior management improves the behavior of children with ADHD better than medication alone or behavior management alone (Chronis & others, 2004; Swanson & others, 2001). Critics argue that many physicians are too quick to prescribe stimulants for children with milder forms of ADHD (Marcovitch, 2004).

Recent studies also are focusing on the possibility that exercise might reduce ADHD (Tantillo & others, 2002). For example, researchers have found that exercise increases the levels of two neurotransmitters—dopamine and norepinephrine—that improve concentration (Ferrando-Lucas, 2006; Rebollo & Montiel, 2006). Some mental health professionals are recommending that children and youth with ADHD exercise several times a day (Ratey, 2006). They also speculate that the increase in rates of ADHD have coincided with the decrease in exercise that children are getting.

IDEA mandates free, appropriate education for all children. *What services does IDEA mandate for children with disabilities?*

www.mhhe.com/santrockld11

Education of Children
Who Are Exceptional
Inclusion

Educational Issues

Until the 1970s most public schools either refused enrollment to children with disabilities or inadequately served them. In 1975, *Public Law 94-142*, the Education for All Handicapped Children Act, required that all students with disabilities be given a free, appropriate public education. In 1990, Public Law 94-142 was recast as the *Individuals with Disabilities Education Act* (IDEA). IDEA was amended in 1997 and then reauthorized in 2004 and renamed the Individuals with Disabilities Education Improvement Act.

IDEA spells out broad mandates for services to all children with disabilities (Hallahan & Kauffman, 2006; Hardman, Drew, & Egan, 2006; Smith, 2007; Turnbull, Turnbull, & Hopkins, 2007). These include evaluation and eligibility determination, appropriate education and an individualized education plan (IEP), and education in the least restrictive environment (LRE).

An **individualized education plan (IEP)** is a written statement that spells out a program that is specifically tailored for the student with a disability (Friend, 2005, 1006; Werts, Culatta, & Tompkins, 2007). In general, the IEP should be (1) related to the child's learning capacity, (2) specifically constructed to meet the child's individual needs and not merely a copy of what is offered to other children, and (3) designed to provide educational benefits.

The **least restrictive environment (LRE)** is a setting that is as similar as possible to the one in which children who do not have a disability are educated. This provision of the IDEA has given a legal basis to efforts to educate children with a disability in the regular classroom (Friend, 2005, 2006; Mastropieri, & Scruggs, 2007). The term **inclusion** describes educating a child with special education needs full-time in the regular classroom (Haager & Klingner, 2005; Vaughn, Bos, & Schumm, 2007).

A major aspect of the 2004 reauthorization of IDEA involved aligning it with the government's No Child Left Behind (NCLB) legislation, which mandates general assessments of educational progress that include students with disabilities. This alignment includes requiring most students with disabilities "to take standard tests of academic achievement and to achieve at a level equal to that of students without disabilities. Whether this expectation is reasonable is an open question" (Hallahan & Kauffman, 2006, pp. 28–29).

Many legal changes regarding children with disabilities have been extremely positive (Turnbull, Turnbull, & Tompkins, 2007). Compared with several decades ago, far more children today are receiving competent, specialized services. For many children, inclusion in the regular classroom, with modifications or supplemental services, is appropriate (Hardman, Drew, & Egan, 2006; Smith, 2007). However, some leading experts on special education argue that in some cases the effort to educate children with disabilities in the regular classroom has become too extreme. For example, James Kauffman and his colleagues (Kauffman & Hallahan, 2005; Kaufman, McGee, and Brigham, 2004) state that inclusion too often has meant making accommodations in the regular classroom that do not always benefit children with disabilities. They advocate a more individualized approach that does not always involve full inclusion but allows options such as special education outside the regular classroom. Kauffman and his colleagues (2004, p. 620) acknowledge that children with disabilities "*do* need the services of specially trained professionals" and "*do* sometimes need altered curricula or adaptations to make their learning possible." However, "we sell students with disabilities short when we pretend that they are not different from typical students. We make the same error when we pretend that they must *not* be expected to put forth extra effort if they are to learn to do some things—or learn to do something in a different way." Like general education, special education should challenge students with disabilities "to become all they can be."

Review and Reflect • LEARNING GOAL 2

2 **Identify children with different types of disabilities and issues in educating them**

Review
- Who are children with disabilities? What characterizes children with learning disabilities?
- How would you describe children with attention deficit hyperactivity disorder?
- What are some issues in educating children with disabilities?

Reflect
- Think back on your own schooling and how children with learning disabilities or ADHD either were or were not diagnosed. Were you aware of such individuals in your classes? Were they helped by specialists? You may know one or more individuals with a learning disability or ADHD. Ask them about their educational experiences and whether they think schools could have done a better job of helping them.

3 **COGNITIVE CHANGES**

Piaget's Cognitive Developmental Theory

Intelligence

Extremes of Intelligence

Information Processing

Interpreting Differences in IQ Scores

Do children enter a new stage of cognitive development in middle and late childhood? How do children process information in this age period? What is the nature of children's intelligence? Let's explore these questions.

Piaget's Cognitive Developmental Theory

According to Piaget (1952), the preschool child's thought is preoperational. Preschool children can form stable concepts, and they have begun to reason, but their thinking is flawed by egocentrism and magical belief systems. As we discussed in chapter 8, however, Piaget may have underestimated the cognitive skills of preschool children. Some researchers argue that under the right conditions, young children may display abilities that are characteristic of Piaget's next stage of cognitive development, the stage of concrete operational thought (Gelman, 1969). Here we will cover the characteristics of concrete operational thought, an evaluation of Piaget's portrait of this stage, and applications of Piaget's ideas to education.

The Concrete Operational Stage   Piaget proposed that the *concrete operational stage* lasts from approximately 7 to 11 years of age. In this stage, children can perform concrete operations, and they can reason logically as long as reasoning can be applied to specific or concrete examples. Remember that *operations* are mental actions that are reversible, and *concrete operations* are operations that are applied to real, concrete objects.

The conservation tasks described in chapter 8 indicate whether children are capable of concrete operations. For example, recall that in one task involving conservation

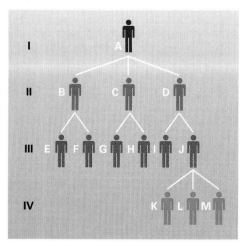

FIGURE 10.4 Classification: An Important Ability in Concrete Operational Thought. A family tree of four generations (*I to IV*): The preoperational child has trouble classifying the members of the four generations; the concrete operational child can classify the members vertically, horizontally, and obliquely (up and down and across). For example, the concrete operational child understands that a family member can be a son, a brother, and a father, all at the same time.

We owe to Piaget the present field of cognitive development with its image of the developing child, who through its own active and creative commerce with its environment, builds an orderly succession of cognitive structures enroute to intellectual maturity.

—JOHN FLAVELL
Contemporary Developmental Psychologist, Stanford University

seriation The concrete operation that involves ordering stimuli along a quantitative dimension (such as length).

transitivity The ability to logically combine relations to understand certain conclusions.

of matter, the child is presented with two identical balls of clay. The experimenter rolls one ball into a long, thin shape; the other remains in its original ball shape. The child is then asked if there is more clay in the ball or in the long, thin piece of clay. By the time children reach the age of 7 or 8, most answer that the amount of clay is the same. To answer this problem correctly, children have to imagine the clay rolling back into a ball. This type of imagination involves a reversible mental action applied to a real, concrete object. Concrete operations allow the child to consider several characteristics rather than focus on a single property of an object. In the clay example, the preoperational child is likely to focus on height *or* width. The concrete operational child coordinates information about both dimensions.

What other abilities are characteristic of children who have reached the concrete operational stage? One important skill is the ability to classify or divide things into different sets or subsets and to consider their interrelationships. Consider the family tree of four generations that is shown in figure 10.4 (Furth & Wachs, 1975). This family tree suggests that the grandfather (A) has three children (B, C, and D), each of whom has two children (E through J), and that one of these children (J) has three children (K, L, and M). A child who comprehends the classification system can move up and down a level, across a level, and up and down and across within the system. The concrete operational child understands that person J can at the same time be father, brother, and grandson, for example.

Children who have reached the concrete operational stage are also capable of **seriation,** which is the ability to order stimuli along a quantitative dimension (such as length). To see if students can serialize, a teacher might haphazardly place eight sticks of different lengths on a table. The teacher then asks the students to order the sticks by length. Many young children end up with two or three small groups of "big" sticks or "little" sticks, rather than a correct ordering of all eight sticks. Another mistaken strategy they use is to evenly line up the tops of the sticks but ignore the bottoms. The concrete operational thinker simultaneously understands that each stick must be longer than the one that precedes it and shorter than the one that follows it.

Another aspect of reasoning about the relations between classes is **transitivity,** which is the ability to logically combine relations to understand certain conclusions. In this case, consider three sticks (A, B, and C) of differing lengths. A is the longest, B is intermediate in length, and C is the shortest. Does the child understand that, if A is longer than B and B is longer than C, then A is longer than C? In Piaget's theory, concrete operational thinkers do; preoperational thinkers do not.

Evaluating Piaget's Concrete Operational Stage Has Piaget's portrait of the concrete operational child stood the test of research? According to Piaget, various aspects of a stage should emerge at the same time. In fact, however, some concrete operational abilities do not appear in synchrony. For example, children do not learn to conserve at the same time they learn to cross-classify.

Furthermore, education and culture exert stronger influences on children's development than Piaget believed (Cole, 2005, 2006; Greenfield, Suzuki, & Rothstein-Fisch, 2006). Some preoperational children can be trained to reason at a concrete operational stage. And the age at which children acquire conservation skills is related to how much practice their culture provides in these skills. Among Wolof children in the West African nation of Senegal, for example, only 50 percent of the 10- to 13-year-olds understood the principle of conservation (Greenfield, 1966). Comparable studies among cultures in central Australia, New Guinea (an island north of Australia), the Amazon jungle region of Brazil, and rural Sardinia (an island off the coast of Italy) yielded similar results (Dasen, 1977).

Thus, although Piaget was a giant in the field of developmental psychology, his conclusions about the concrete operational stage have been challenged. In chapter 12, after examining the final stage in his theory of cognitive development, we will evaluate Piaget's contributions and the criticisms of his theory.

Neo-Piagetians argue that Piaget got some things right, but that his theory needs considerable revision. They give more emphasis to how children use attention, memory, and strategies to process information (Case, 1987, 1999; Case & Mueller, 2001). They especially believe that a more accurate portrayal of children's thinking requires attention to children's strategies, the speed at which children process information, the particular task involved, and the division of problems into smaller, more precise steps (Demetriou, 2001). These are issues addressed by the information processing approach, and we discuss some of them later in this chapter.

Another alternative comes from Vygotsky. As we discussed in chapter 8, Vygotsky, like Piaget, held that children construct their knowledge of the world. But Vygotsky did not propose stages of cognitive development, and he emphasized the importance of social interaction, the social contexts of learning, and the young child's use of language to plan, guide, and monitor behavior.

An outstanding teacher and education in the logic of science and mathematics are important cultural experiences that promote the development of operational thought. *Might Piaget have underestimated the roles of culture and schooling in children's cognitive development?*

Applications to Education   Piaget was not an educator but he provided a sound conceptual framework for viewing learning and education. Following are some ideas in Piaget's theory that can be applied to teaching children (Elkind, 1976; Heuwinkel, 1996).

1. *Take a constructivist approach.* Piaget emphasized that children learn best when they are active and seek solutions for themselves. Piaget opposed teaching methods that treat children as passive receptacles. The educational implication of Piaget's view is that, in all subjects, students learn best by making discoveries, reflecting on them, and discussing them, rather than blindly imitating the teacher or doing things by rote.

2. *Facilitate, rather than direct, learning.* Effective teachers design situations that allow students to learn by doing. These situations promote students' thinking and discovery. Teachers listen, watch, and question students, to help them gain better understanding. Don't just examine what students think and the product of their learning. Rather, carefully observe them and find out how they think. Ask relevant questions to stimulate their thinking, and ask them to explain their answers.

3. *Consider the child's knowledge and level of thinking.* Students do not come to class with empty minds. They have many ideas about the physical and natural world. They have concepts of space, time, quantity, and causality. These ideas differ from the ideas of adults. Teachers need to interpret what a student is saying and respond in a way that is not too far from the student's level. Also, Piaget suggested that it is important to examine children's mistakes in thinking, not just what they get correct, to help guide them to a higher level of understanding.

4. *Use ongoing assessment.* Individually constructed meanings cannot be measured by standardized tests. Math and language portfolios (which contain work in progress as well as finished products), individual conferences in which students discuss their thinking strategies, and students' written and verbal explanations of their reasoning can be used to evaluate progress.

5. *Promote the student's intellectual health.* When Piaget came to lecture in the United States, he was asked, "What can I do to get my child to a higher cognitive stage sooner?" He was asked this question so often here compared with other countries that he called it "the American question." For Piaget, children's learning should occur naturally. Children should not be pushed and pressured into achieving too much too early in their development, before they are ready.

6. *Turn the classroom into a setting of exploration and discovery.* What do actual classrooms look like when the teachers adopt Piaget's views? Several first- and second-grade math classrooms provide some examples (Kamii, 1985, 1989). The teachers emphasize students' own exploration and discovery. The classrooms

neo-Piagetians Developmentalists who have elaborated on Piaget's theory, giving more emphasis to information processing, strategies, and precise cognitive steps.

What are some educational strategies that can be derived from Piaget's theory?

Piaget and Education

are less structured than what we think of as a typical classroom. Workbooks and predetermined assignments are not used. Rather, the teachers observe the students' interests and natural participation in activities to determine the course of learning. For example, a math lesson might be constructed around counting the day's lunch money or dividing supplies among students. Often, games are used to stimulate mathematical thinking. For example, a version of dominoes teaches children about even-numbered combinations; a variation on tic-tac-toe replaces *X*s and *O*s with numbers. Teachers encourage peer interaction during the lessons and games because students' different viewpoints can contribute to advances in thinking.

Educators have also applied Vygotsky's ideas. His theory suggests that teachers should encourage elementary school children to internalize and regulate their talk to themselves. They should provide students with opportunities to experience learning in real-world settings—for example, instead of memorizing math formulas, students should work on math problems with real-world implications (Santrock, 2006). In chapter 8 we described other ways in which teachers have applied Vygotsky's ideas.

What does a Vygotskian classroom look like? The Kamehameha Elementary Education Program (KEEP) is based on Vygotsky's theory (Tharp, 1994). Many of the learning activities take place in small groups. The key element in this program is use of the zone of proximal development (the range of tasks that are too difficult for the child to master alone but that can be learned with guidance and assistance from others). Children might read a story and then interpret its meaning. Scaffolding is used to improve children's literary skills. The instructor asks questions, responds to students' queries, and builds on the ideas that students generate. Thousands of children from low-income families have attended KEEP public schools—in Hawaii, on an Arizona Navajo Indian reservation, and in Los Angeles. Compared with a control group of non-KEEP children, the KEEP children participated more actively in classroom discussion, were more attentive in class, and had higher reading achievement (Tharp & Gallimore, 1988).

Information Processing

If instead of analyzing the type of thinking that children display we examine how they handle information during middle and late childhood, what do we find? During these years most children dramatically improve their ability to sustain and control attention. As we discussed in chapter 8, they pay more attention to task-relevant stimuli than to salient stimuli. Other changes in information processing during middle and late childhood involve memory, thinking, and metacognition.

Memory   In chapter 8, we concluded that short-term memory increases considerably during early childhood but after the age of 7 does not show as much increase. **Long-term memory,** a relatively permanent and unlimited type of memory, increases with age during middle and late childhood. In part, improvements in memory reflect children's increased knowledge and their increased use of strategies (National Research Council, 1999; Schraw, 2006).

Knowledge and Expertise   Much of the research on the role of knowledge in memory has compared experts and novices (Siegler & Alibali, 2005). *Experts* have acquired extensive knowledge about a particular content area; this knowledge influences what they notice and how they organize, represent, and interpret information. This in turn affects their ability to remember, reason, and solve problems. When individuals have expertise about a particular subject, their memory also tends to be good regarding material related to that subject.

For example, one study found that 10- and 11-year-olds who were experienced chess players ("experts") were able to remember more information about chess

long-term memory A relatively permanent type of memory that holds huge amounts of information for a long period of time.

pieces than college students who were not chess players ("novices") (Chi, 1978) (see figure 10.5). In contrast, when the college students were presented with other stimuli, they were able to remember them better than the children were. Thus, the children's expertise in chess gave them superior memories, but only in chess.

There are developmental changes in expertise. Older children usually have more expertise about a subject than younger children do, which can contribute to their better memory for the subject.

Strategies   If we know anything at all about long-term memory, it is that long-term memory depends on the learning activities individuals engage in when learning and remembering information (Alexander, 2006; Pressley & Hilden, 2006; Siegler, 2006). Recall from chapter 8 that *strategies* consist of deliberate mental activities to improve the processing of information (Pressley & Hilden, 2006; Siegler, 2006). They do not occur automatically but require effort and work. Strategies, which are also called *control processes,* are under the learner's conscious control and can be used to improve memory (Siegler, 2006; Siegler & Alibali, 2005). Two important strategies are creating mental images and elaborating on information.

Mental imagery can help even young school children to remember pictures (Schneider & Pressley, 1997). However, for remembering verbal information, mental imagery works better for older children than for younger children (Schneider, 2004; Schneider & Pressley, 1997). In one study, 20 sentences were presented to first- through sixth-grade children to remember—such as "The angry bird shouted at the white dog" and "The policeman painted the circus tent on a windy day" (Pressley & others, 1987). Children were randomly assigned either to an imagery condition in which they were told to make a picture in their head for each sentence or a control condition in which they were told just to try hard. The instructions to form images helped older elementary school children (grades 4 through 6) but did not help the younger elementary school children (grades 1 through 3).

Elaboration is an important strategy that involves engaging in more extensive processing of information. When individuals engage in elaboration, their memory benefits (Terry, 2006). Thinking of examples and referencing one's self are good ways to elaborate information. Thinking about personal associations with information makes the information more meaningful and helps children to remember it.

The use of elaboration changes developmentally (Schneider, 2004; Schneider & Pressley, 1997). Adolescents are more likely to use elaboration spontaneously than children. Elementary school children can be taught to use elaboration strategies on a learning task, but they will be less likely than adolescents to use the strategies on other learning tasks in the future. Nonetheless, verbal elaboration can be an effective strategy for processing information even for young elementary school children.

Fuzzy Trace Theory   Might something other than knowledge and strategies be responsible for the improvement in memory during the elementary school years? Charles Brainerd and Valerie Reyna (1993; Reyna, 2004; Reyna & Brainerd, 1995) argue that fuzzy traces account for much of this improvement. Their **fuzzy trace theory** states that memory is best understood by considering two types of memory representations: (1) verbatim memory trace and (2) gist. The *verbatim memory trace* consists of the precise details of the information, whereas *gist* refers to the central idea of the information. When gist is used, fuzzy traces are built up. Although individuals of all ages extract gist, young children tend to store and retrieve verbatim traces. At some point during the early elementary school years, children begin to use gist more and, according to the theory, this contributes to the improved memory and reasoning of older children because fuzzy traces are more enduring and less likely to be forgotten than verbatim traces.

Thinking   Three important aspects of thinking are being able to think critically, creatively, and scientifically.

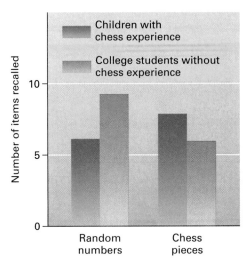

FIGURE 10.5 The Role of Expertise in Memory. Notice that when 10 to 11-year-old children and college students were asked to remember a string of random numbers that had been presented to them, the college students fared better. However, the 10 to 11-year-olds who had experience playing chess ("experts") had better memory for the location of chess pieces on a chess board than college students with no chess experience ("novices") (Chi, 1978).

elaboration An important strategy that involves engaging in more extensive processing of information.

fuzzy trace theory States that memory is best understood by considering two types of memory representations: (1) verbatim memory trace and (2) gist. In this theory, older children's better memory is attributed to the fuzzy traces created by extracting the gist of information.

Critical Thinking **Critical thinking** involves thinking reflectively and productively, as well as evaluating the evidence. In this book, the second part of the Review and Reflect sections of each chapter challenges you to think critically about a topic or an issue related to the discussion.

Jacqueline and Martin Brooks (2001) lament that few schools really teach students to think critically and develop a deep understanding of concepts. Deep understanding occurs when students are stimulated to rethink previously held ideas. In Brooks and Brooks' view, schools spend too much time getting students to give a single correct answer in an imitative way, rather than encouraging them to expand their thinking by coming up with new ideas and rethinking earlier conclusions. They observe that too often teachers ask students to recite, define, describe, state, and list, rather than to analyze, infer, connect, synthesize, criticize, create, evaluate, think, and rethink. Many successful students complete their assignments, do well on tests and get good grades, yet they don't ever learn to think critically and deeply. They think superficially, staying on the surface of problems rather than stretching their minds and becoming deeply engaged in meaningful thinking.

Creative Thinking Cognitively competent children not only think critically, but also creatively (Sternberg, Grigorenko, & Singer, 2004). **Creative thinking** is the ability to think in novel and unusual ways and to come up with unique solutions to problems. Thus, intelligence and creativity are not the same thing. This difference was recognized by J. P. Guilford (1967), who distinguished between **convergent thinking,** which produces one correct answer and characterizes the kind of thinking that is required on conventional tests of intelligence, and **divergent thinking,** which produces many different answers to the same question and characterizes creativity. For example, a typical item on a conventional intelligence test is "How many quarters will you get in return for 60 dimes?" In contrast, the following question has many possible answers: "What image comes to mind when you hear the phrase 'sitting alone in a dark room' or 'some unique uses for a paper clip'?"

It is important to recognize that children will show more creativity in some domains than others (Kaufman & Steinberg, 2006; Runco, 2004, 2006). A child who shows creative thinking skills in mathematics may not exhibit these skills in art, for example.

An important goal is to help children become more creative. The following Applications in Life-Span Development interlude examines some recommendations for ways to accomplish this goal.

What do you mean, "What is it?" It's the spontaneous, unfettered expression of a young mind not yet bound by the restraints of narrative or pictorial representation.
Science Cartoons Plus. Used with permission.

critical thinking Thinking reflectively and productively, as well as evaluating the evidence.

creative thinking The ability to think in novel and unusual ways and to come up with unique solutions to problems.

convergent thinking Thinking that produces one correct answer and is characteristic of the kind of thinking tested by standardized intelligence tests.

divergent thinking Thinking that produces many answers to the same question and is characteristic of creativity.

brainstorming A technique in which individuals are encouraged to come up with creative ideas in a group, play off each other's ideas, and say practically whatever comes to mind.

APPLICATIONS IN LIFE-SPAN DEVELOPMENT

Strategies for Increasing Children's Creative Thinking

Some strategies for increasing children's creative thinking include:

• *Have children engage in brainstorming and come up with as many ideas as possible.* **Brainstorming** is a technique in which children are encouraged to come up with creative ideas in a group, play off each other's ideas, and say practically whatever comes to mind. However, a recent review of research on brainstorming concluded that for many individuals, working alone can generate more ideas and better ideas than working in groups (Rickards & deCock, 2003). One reason for this is that in groups, some individuals loaf while others do most of the creative thinking. Nonetheless, there may be benefits to brainstorming, such as team building.

Whether in a group or individually, a good creativity strategy is to come up with as many new ideas as possible. The more ideas children produce, the better their chance of creating something unique. Famous twentieth-century Spanish artist Pablo Picasso produced more than 20,000 works of art; not all of them were masterpieces. Creative children are not afraid of failing or getting something wrong. They may go down 20 dead-end streets before they come up with an innovative idea. They recognize that it's okay to win some and lose some. They are willing to take risks, just as Picasso was.

What are some good strategies for guiding children in thinking more creatively?

- *Provide children with environments that stimulate creativity.* Some settings nourish creativity; others depress it (Sternberg, Grigorenko, & Singer, 2004). People who encourage children's creativity often rely on children's natural curiosity. They provide exercises and activities that stimulate children to find insightful solutions to problems, rather than asking a lot of questions that require rote answers. Adults also encourage creativity by taking children to locations where creativity is valued. Science, discovery, and children's museums may offer rich opportunities to stimulate children's creativity (Gardner, 1993).

- *Don't overcontrol.* Teresa Amabile (1993) says that telling children exactly how to do things leaves them feeling that any originality is a mistake and any exploration is a waste of time. Adults are less likely to destroy children's natural curiosity if they allow children to select their own interests and support their inclinations rather than dictating activities for the children. Amabile also believes that, when adults constantly hover over children, the children feel they are being watched while they are working. When children are under constant surveillance, their creative risk taking and adventurous spirit wane. Another strategy that can harm creativity is to have grandiose expectations for a child's performance and expect the child to do something perfectly, according to Amabile.

- *Encourage internal motivation.* The excessive use of prizes, such as gold stars, money, or toys, can stifle creativity by undermining the intrinsic pleasure children derive from creative activities. Creative children's motivation is the satisfaction generated by the work itself. Competition for prizes and formal evaluations often undermine intrinsic motivation and creativity (Amabile & Hennessey, 1992).

- *Introduce children to creative people.* Think about the identity of the most creative people in your community. Teachers can invite these people to their classrooms and ask them to describe what helps them become creative or to demonstrate their creative skills. A writer, poet, musician, scientist, and many others can bring their props and productions to the class, turning it into a theater for stimulating students' creativity.

Scientific Thinking   Children's problem solving is often compared to that of scientists. Both children and scientists ask fundamental questions about the nature of reality. Both also seek answers to problems that often seem utterly trivial or unanswerable to other people (such as why is the sky blue?). And like scientists, children often emphasize causal mechanisms (Frye & others, 1996).

This "child as scientist" metaphor has led researchers to ask whether children generate hypotheses, perform experiments, and reach conclusions concerning the meaning of their data in ways resembling those of scientists (Clinchy, Mansfield, & Schott, 1995). In comparing children and scientists, researchers have found that preadolescents have much greater difficulty in separating their prior theories from the evidence that they have obtained. Often, when they try to learn about new phenomena, children maintain their old theories regardless of the evidence (Kuhn, Schauble, & Garcia-Mila, 1992).

Another difference between scientists and children is that children are influenced more by happenstance events than by the overall pattern of occurrences (Kuhn, 2004; Kuhn, Amsel, & O'Laughlin, 1988). Children also have difficulty designing new experiments that can distinguish conclusively among alternative causes. Instead, they tend to bias the experiments in favor of whichever hypothesis they began with, and sometimes they will see the results as supporting their original hypothesis even when the results directly contradict it (Schauble, 1990). Thus, although there are important similarities between children and scientists, there are also important differences in the degree to which they can separate theory and evidence and in their ability to design conclusive experiments (Lehrer & Schauble, 2006; Lehrer, Schauble, & Petrosino, 2001).

Scientists typically engage in certain kinds of thinking and behavior. For example, they regularly make careful observations; collect, organize, and analyze data; measure, graph, and understand spatial relations; pay attention to and regulate their own thinking; and know when and how to apply their knowledge to solve problems (Chapman, 2000). These skills, which are essential to the practice of science, are not routinely taught in schools, especially elementary schools. As a result, many students are not competent at them. Many scientists and educators believe that schools need to guide students in learning how to use these skills (Bransford & Donovan, 2005; Chiappetta & Koballa, 2006; Lehrer & Schauble, 2006; Lynn & Eylon, 2006; Peters & Stout, 2006).

Metacognition One expert in children's thinking, Deanna Kuhn (1999), suggests that to help students become better thinkers, schools should pay more attention to helping students develop skills that entail knowing about their own (and others') knowing. In other words, schools should do more to develop **metacognition,** which is cognition about cognition, or knowing about knowing (Flavell, 1999, 2004; Flavell, Miller, & Miller, 2002).

The majority of developmental studies classified as "metacognitive" have focused on *metamemory,* or knowledge about memory (DeMarie, Abshier, & Ferron, 2001). This includes general knowledge about memory, such as knowing that recognition tests are easier than recall tests. It also encompasses knowledge about one's own memory, such as a student's ability to monitor whether she has studied enough for a test that is coming up next week.

Young children do have some general knowledge about memory. By 5 or 6 years of age, children usually already know that familiar items are easier to learn than unfamiliar ones, that short lists are easier than long ones, that recognition is easier than recall, and that forgetting is more likely to occur over time (Lyon & Flavell, 1993). However, in other ways young children's metamemory is limited. They don't understand that related items are easier to remember than unrelated ones and that remembering the gist of a story is easier than remembering information verbatim (Kreutzer, Leonard, & Flavell, 1975). By the fifth grade, students understand that gist recall is easier than verbatim recall.

Young children also have only limited knowledge about their own memory. They have an inflated opinion of their memory abilities. For example, in one study a majority of young children predicted that they would be able to recall all 10 items on a list of 10 items. When tested for this, none of the young children managed this feat (Flavell, Friedrichs, & Hoyt, 1970). As they move through the elementary school years, children give more realistic evaluations of their memory skills (Schneider & Pressley, 1997).

In addition to metamemory, metacognition includes knowledge about strategies. In the view of Michael Pressley (2000), the key to education is helping students

Mary Lynn Peacher, a fourth-grade teacher at Jenks East Elementary School, in Oklahoma, demonstrates airfoil "charks" to students. Peacher tells students that they are scientists and asks them to describe what they see as they carry out various exercises.

metacognition Cognition about cognition, or knowing about knowing.

learn a rich repertoire of strategies that result in solutions to problems. Good thinkers routinely use strategies and effective planning to solve problems. Good thinkers also know when and where to use strategies. Understanding when and where to use strategies often results from monitoring the learning situation (McCormick, 2003).

Pressley and his colleagues (Pressley & Harris, 2006; Pressley & Hilden, 2006; Pressley & others, 2001, 2003, 2004) have spent considerable time in recent years observing strategy instruction by teachers and strategy use by students in elementary and secondary school classrooms. They conclude that strategy instruction is far less complete and intense than what students need in order to learn how to use strategies effectively. They argue that education needs to be restructured so that students are provided with more opportunities to become competent strategic learners.

Intelligence

Parents, teachers, and children themselves are likely to think and talk about children's cognitive abilities in terms different than those we have used so far. Rather than considering a child's skills as a critical thinker or scientific thinker, for example, they might ask whether a child is smart or intelligent.

Just what is meant by the concept of "intelligence"? Some experts describe intelligence as problem-solving skills. Others describe it as the ability to adapt to and learn from life's everyday experiences. Combining these ideas, we can arrive at a definition of **intelligence** as problem-solving skills and the ability to learn from and adapt to life's everyday experiences.

Interest in intelligence has often focused on individual differences and assessment. **Individual differences** are the stable, consistent ways in which people are different from each other. We can talk about individual differences in personality or any other domain, but it is in the domain of intelligence that the most attention has been directed at individual differences. For example, an intelligence test purports to inform us about whether a student can reason better than others who have taken the test. Let's go back in history and see what the first intelligence test was like.

The Binet Tests In 1904, the French Ministry of Education asked psychologist Alfred Binet to devise a method of identifying children who were unable to learn in school. School officials wanted to reduce crowding by placing students who did not benefit from regular classroom teaching in special schools. Binet and his student Théophile Simon developed an intelligence test to meet this request. The test is called the 1905 Scale. It consisted of 30 questions on topics ranging from the ability to touch one's ear to the ability to draw designs from memory and define abstract concepts.

Binet developed the concept of **mental age (MA),** an individual's level of mental development relative to others. Not much later, in 1912, William Stern created the concept of **intelligence quotient (IQ),** a person's mental age divided by chronological age (CA), multiplied by 100. That is: $IQ = MA/CA \times 100$. If mental age is the same as chronological age, then the person's IQ is 100. If mental age is above chronological age, then IQ is more than 100. If mental age is below chronological age, then IQ is less than 100.

The Binet test has been revised many times to incorporate advances in the understanding of intelligence and intelligence tests. These revisions are called the *Stanford-Binet tests* (Stanford University is where the revisions have been done). By administering the test to large numbers of people of different ages from different backgrounds, researchers have found that scores on the Stanford-Binet approximate a normal distribution (see figure 10.6). A **normal distribution** is symmetrical, with a majority of the scores falling in the middle of the possible range of scores and few scores appearing toward the extremes of the range.

intelligence Problem-solving skills and the ability to learn from and adapt to the experiences of everyday life.

individual differences The stable, consistent ways in which people are different from each other.

mental age (MA) Binet's measure of an individual's level of mental development, compared with that of others.

intelligence quotient (IQ) A person's mental age divided by chronological age, multiplied by 100.

normal distribution A symmetrical distribution with most scores falling in the middle of the possible range of scores and a few scores appearing toward the extremes of the range.

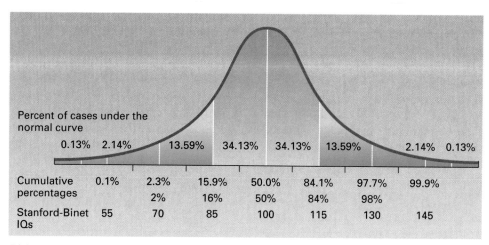

FIGURE 10.6 The Normal Curve and Stanford Binet IQ Scores. The distribution of IQ scores approximates a normal curve. Most of the population falls in the middle range of scores. Notice that extremely high and extremely low scores are very rare. Slightly more than two-thirds of the scores fall between 85 and 115. Only about 1 in 50 individuals has an IQ of more than 130, and only about 1 in 50 individuals has an IQ of less than 70.

The current Stanford-Binet is administered individually to people from the age of 2 through the adult years. It includes a variety of items, some of which require verbal responses, others nonverbal responses. For example, items that reflect a 6-year-old's performance on the test include the verbal ability to define at least six words, such as *orange* and *envelope,* as well as the nonverbal ability to trace a path through a maze. Items that reflect an average adult's intelligence include defining words such as *disproportionate* and *regard,* explaining a proverb, and comparing idleness and laziness.

An individual's responses to the Stanford-Binet can be analyzed in terms of four content areas: verbal reasoning, quantitative reasoning, abstract/visual reasoning, and short-term memory. A general composite score is still obtained to reflect overall intelligence. The Stanford-Binet continues to be one of the most widely used tests to assess a student's intelligence (Naglieri, 2000).

The Wechsler Scales   Another set of widely used tests is called the *Wechsler scales,* developed by David Wechsler. They include the Wechsler Preschool and Primary Scale of Intelligence—III (WPPSI–III) to test children 4 to 6½ years of age; the Wechsler Intelligence Scale for Children—IV Integrated (WISC-IV Integrated) for children and adolescents 6 to 16 years of age; and the Wechsler Adult Intelligence Scale (WAIS-III).

Not only do the Wechsler scales provide an overall IQ, but they also yield verbal and performance IQs. Verbal IQ is based on six verbal subscales, performance IQ on five performance subscales. This allows the examiner to quickly see patterns of strengths and weaknesses in different areas of the student's intelligence. Three of the Wechsler subscales are shown in figure 10.7.

Types of Intelligence   Is it more appropriate to think of a child's intelligence as a general ability or as a number of specific abilities? Charles Spearman (1927) said that people have both a general intelligence, which he called *g,* and specific types of intelligence, which he called *s.* As early as the 1930s, L. L. Thurstone (1938) said people have seven of these specific abilities, which he called primary abilities: verbal comprehension, number ability, word fluency, spatial visualization, associative memory, reasoning, and perceptual speed. More recently, Robert Sternberg and Howard Gardner have proposed influential theories that describe specific types of intelligence.

Verbal Subscales

Similarities

A child must think logically and abstractly to answer a number of questions about how things might be similar.

Example: "In what way are a lion and a tiger alike?"

Comprehension

This subscale is designed to measure an individual's judgment and common sense.

Example: "What is the advantage of keeping money in a bank?"

Nonverbal Subscales

Block Design

A child must assemble a set of multicolored blocks to match designs that the examiner shows. Visual-motor coordination, perceptual organization, and the ability to visualize spatially are assessed.

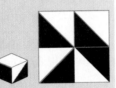

Example: "Use the four blocks on the left to make the pattern on the right."

FIGURE 10.7 Sample Subscales of the Wechsler Intelligence Scale for Children (WISC–IV Integrated). The Wechsler includes 11 subscales, 6 verbal and 5 nonverbal. Three of the subscales are shown here. Simulated items similar to those found in the *Wechsler Intelligence Scale for Children–Fourth Edition*. Copyright © 2003 by Harcourt Assessment, Inc. Reproduced by permission. All rights reserved.

Sternberg's Triarchic Theory Robert J. Sternberg (1986, 2003, 2004) developed the **triarchic theory of intelligence,** which states that intelligence comes in three forms:

- *Analytical intelligence.* This refers to the ability to analyze, judge, evaluate, compare, and contrast.
- *Creative intelligence.* This consists of the ability to create, design, invent, originate, and imagine.
- *Practical intelligence.* This involves the ability to use, apply, implement, and put ideas into practice.

Sternberg (2002) says that children with different triarchic patterns "look different" in school. Students with high analytic ability tend to be favored in conventional schooling. They often do well under direct instruction, in which the teacher lectures and gives students objective tests. They often are considered to be "smart" students who get good grades, show up in high-level tracks, do well on traditional tests of intelligence and the SAT, and later get admitted to competitive colleges.

In contrast, children who are high in creative intelligence often are not on the top rung of their class. Many teachers have expectations about how assignments should be done, and creatively intelligent students may not conform to those expectations. Instead of giving conformist answers, they give unique answers, for which they might get reprimanded or marked down. No teacher wants to discourage creativity, but Sternberg believes that too often a teacher's desire to improve students' knowledge depresses creative thinking.

Like children high in creative intelligence, children who are practically intelligent often do not relate well to the demands of school. However, many of these children do well outside of the classroom's walls. They may have excellent social skills and good common sense. As adults, some become successful managers, entrepreneurs, or politicians, yet they have undistinguished school records.

Gardner's Eight Frames of Mind Howard Gardner (1983, 1993, 2002) suggests there are eight types of intelligence, or "frames of mind." These are described here, with

"You're wise, but you lack tree smarts."
© The New Yorker Collection, 1988, by Donald Reilly from cartoonbank.com. All Rights Reserved.

www.mhhe.com/santrockld11

Sternberg's Theory

triarchic theory of intelligence Sternberg's theory that intelligence consists of analytical intelligence, creative intelligence, and practical intelligence.

Multiple Intelligence Links
Multiple Intelligences and Education

Children in the Key School form "pods," in which they pursue activities of special interest to them. Every day, each child can choose from activities that draw on Gardner's eight frames of mind. The school has pods that range from gardening to architecture to gliding to dancing. *What are some of the main ideas of Gardner's theory and its application to education?*

examples of the types of vocations in which they are reflected as strengths (Campbell, Campbell, & Dickinson, 2004):

- *Verbal:* The ability to think in words and use language to express meaning. Occupations: Authors, journalists, speakers.
- *Mathematical:* The ability to carry out mathematical operations. Occupations: Scientists, engineers, accountants.
- *Spatial:* The ability to think three-dimensionally. Occupations: Architects, artists, sailors.
- *Bodily-Kinesthetic:* The ability to manipulate objects and be physically adept. Occupations: Surgeons, craftspeople, dancers, athletes.
- *Musical:* A sensitivity to pitch, melody, rhythm, and tone. Occupations: Composers, musicians, and sensitive listeners.
- *Interpersonal:* The ability to understand and effectively interact with others. Occupations: Successful teachers, mental health professionals.
- *Intrapersonal:* The ability to understand oneself. Occupations: Theologians, psychologists.
- *Naturalist:* The ability to observe patterns in nature and understand natural and human-made systems. Occupations: Farmers, botanists, ecologists, landscapers.

According to Gardner, everyone has all of these intelligences but to varying degrees. As a result, we prefer to learn and process information in different ways. People learn best when they can apply their strong intelligences to the task.

Evaluating the Multiple-Intelligence Approaches Sternberg's and Gardner's approaches have much to offer. They have stimulated teachers to think more broadly about what makes up children's competencies. And they have motivated educators to develop programs that instruct students in multiple domains. These approaches also have contributed to interest in assessing intelligence and classroom learning in innovative ways, such as by evaluating student portfolios (Birney & others, 2005; Kornhaber, Fierros, & Veenema, 2005; Moran & Gardner, 2006; Weber, 2005).

Still, doubts about multiple-intelligences approaches persist. If musical skill reflects a distinct type of intelligence, some critics ask, why not label the skills of outstanding chess players, prizefighters, writers, politicians, physicians, lawyers, ministers, and poets as types of intelligence? Some critics say that a research base to support the three intelligences of Sternberg or the eight intelligences of Gardner has not yet emerged. A number of psychologists think that the multiple-intelligence views have taken the concept of specific intelligences too far (Johnson & others, 2004). For example, one expert on intelligence, Nathan Brody (2000, 2006), argues that people who excel at one type of intellectual task are likely to excel in others. Thus, individuals who do well at memorizing lists of digits are also likely to be good at solving verbal problems and spatial layout problems. The argument between those who support Spearman's concept of g (general intelligence) and those who advocate the multiple-intelligences view is ongoing.

Culture and Intelligence Differences in conceptions of intelligence occur not only among psychologists but also among cultures. What is viewed as intelligent in one culture may not be thought of as intelligent in another (Benson, 2003; Cole, 2005, 2006; Serpell, 2000). For example, people in Western cultures tend to view intelligence in terms of reasoning and thinking skills, whereas people in Eastern cultures see intelligence as a way for members of a community to successfully engage in social roles (Nisbett, 2003). One study found that Taiwanese Chinese conceptions of intelligence emphasize understanding and relating to others, including when to show and when not to show one's intelligence (Yang & Sternberg, 1997).

Robert Serpell (1974, 2000) has studied concepts of intelligence in rural African communities since the 1970s. He has found that people in rural African communities, especially those in which Western schooling is not common, tend to blur the distinction between being intelligent and being socially competent. In rural Zambia, for example, the concept of intelligence involves being both clever and responsible. Elena Grigorenko and her colleagues (2001) have also studied the concept of intelligence among rural Africans. They found that people in the Luo culture of rural Kenya view intelligence as consisting of four domains: (1) academic intelligence; (2) social qualities such as respect, responsibility, and consideration; (3) practical thinking; and (4) comprehension. In another study in the same culture, children who scored highly on a test of knowledge about medicinal herbs—a measure of practical intelligence—tended to score poorly on tests of academic intelligence (Sternberg & others, 2001). These results indicated that practical and academic intelligence can develop independently and may even conflict with each other. They also suggest that the values of a culture may influence the direction in which a child develops.

Interpreting Differences in IQ Scores

The IQ scores that result from tests such as the Stanford-Binet and Wechsler scales provide information about children's mental abilities. However, interpreting what performance on an intelligence test means is debated. One issue focuses on what determines individual and group differences in these scores.

The Influence of Genetics Arthur Jensen (1969) argued that intelligence is primarily inherited and that environment plays only a minimal role in intelligence. Jensen reviewed the research on intelligence, much of which involved comparisons of identical and fraternal twins, and which also used IQ as the indicator of intelligence. Identical twins have exactly the same genetic makeup; if intelligence is genetically determined, Jensen reasoned, identical twins' IQs should be more similar than the intelligence of fraternal twins.

The studies on intelligence in identical twins that Jensen examined showed an average correlation of .82, a very high positive association. Investigations of fraternal twins, however, produced an average correlation of .50, a moderately high positive correlation. A difference of .32 is substantial. However, a more recent research review that included many studies conducted since Jensen's original review found that the difference in the average correlation of intelligence between identical and fraternal twins was .15, substantially less than what Jensen found (Grigorenko, 2000) (see figure 10.8).

Jensen also compared the correlation of IQ scores for identical twins reared together with those reared apart. The correlation for those reared together was .89, and for those reared apart was .78, a difference of .11. Jensen argued that if environmental factors were more important than genetic factors, the difference should have been greater.

Adoption studies have been inconclusive about the relative importance of genetics in intelligence. In most *adoption studies,* researchers determine whether the behavior of adopted children is more like that of their biological parents or their adopted parents. In one study, the educational levels attained by biological parents were better predictors of children's IQ scores than were the IQs of the children's adoptive parents (Scarr & Weinberg, 1983). Because of the stronger genetic link between the adopted children and their biological parents, the implication is that heredity is more important than environment. Environmental effects also have been found in studies of adoption. For example, moving children into an adoptive family with a better environment than the child had in the past increased the children's IQs by an average of 12 points (Locurto, 1990).

How strong is the effect of genetics on intelligence? The concept of heritability attempts to tease apart the effects of heredity and environment in a population. **Heritability** is the fraction of the variance in a population that is attributed to genetics. The heritability index is computed using correlational techniques. Thus, the

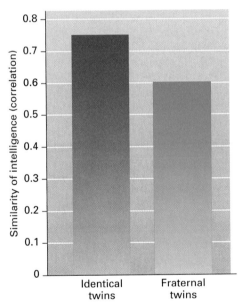

FIGURE 10.8 Correlation Between Intelligence Test Scores and Twin Status. The graph represents a summary of research findings that have compared the intelligence test scores of identical and fraternal twins. An approximate .15 difference has been found with a higher correlation for identical twins (.75) and a lower correlation for fraternal twins (.60).

heritability The fraction of variance in a population that is attributed to genetics and is computed using correlational techniques.

highest degree of heritability is 1.00 and correlations of .70 and above suggest a strong genetic influence. A committee of respected researchers convened by the American Psychological Association concluded that by late adolescence, the heritability of intelligence is about .75, which reflects a strong genetic influence (Neisser & others, 1996).

An important point to keep in mind about heritability is that it refers to a specific group (population), *not* to individuals (Okagaki, 2000). Researchers use the concept of heritability to try to describe why people differ. Heritability says nothing about why a single individual, like yourself, has a certain intelligence; nor does it say anything about differences *between* groups.

Most research on heredity and environment does not include environments that differ radically. Thus, it is not surprising that many genetic studies show environment to be a fairly weak influence on intelligence (Fraser, 1995).

The heritability index has several flaws. It is only as good as the data entered into its analysis and the interpretations made from it (Sternberg, Grigorenko, & Kidd, 2005). The data are virtually all from traditional IQ tests, which some experts think are not always the best indicator of intelligence (Gardner, 2002; Sternberg, 2002). Also, the heritability index assumes that we can treat genetic and environmental influences as factors that can be separated, with each part contributing a distinct amount of influence. As we discussed in chapter 3, genes and the environment always work together. Genes always exist in an environment and the environment shapes their activity.

Today, most researchers agree that genetics does not determine intelligence to the extent Jensen claimed (Gottlieb, Wahlsten, & Lickliter, 2006; Ramey, Ramey, & Lanzi, 2006; Sternberg, Grigorenko, & Kidd, 2006). For most people, this means that modifications in environment can change their IQ scores considerably. Although genetic endowment may always influence a person's intellectual ability, the environmental influences and opportunities we provide children and adults do make a difference (Ramey, Ramey, & Lanzi, 2006; Sternberg, 2006).

Environmental Influences In chapter 5 we described one study that demonstrated the influence of parents on cognitive abilities. Researchers went into homes and observed how extensively parents from welfare and middle-income professional families talked and communicated with their young children (Hart & Risley, 1995). They found that the middle-income professional parents were much more likely to communicate with their young children than the welfare parents were. How much the parents communicated with their children in the first three years of their lives was correlated with the children's Stanford-Binet IQ scores at age 3. The more parents communicated with their children, the higher the children's IQs were.

Schooling also influences intelligence (Ceci & Gilstrap, 2000; Christian, Bachman, & Morrison, 2001). The biggest effects have been found when large groups of children have been deprived of formal education for an extended period, resulting in lower intelligence. One study examined the IQ scores of children in South Africa whose schooling was delayed for four years because teachers were not available (Ramphal, 1962). Compared with children in nearby villages who had teachers, the children whose entry into school was delayed experienced a 5-point drop in IQ for every year of delay.

Another possible effect of education can be seen in rapidly increasing IQ test scores around the world (Flynn, 1999, 2006). IQ scores have been increasing so fast that a high percentage of people regarded as having average intelligence at the turn of the century would be considered below average in intelligence today (Howard, 2001) (see figure 10.9). If a representative sample of people today took the Stanford-Binet test used in 1932, about one-fourth would be defined as having very superior intelligence, a label usually accorded to fewer than 3 percent of the population (Horton, 2001). Because the increase has taken place in a relatively short time, it can't be due to heredity, but rather may be due to increasing levels

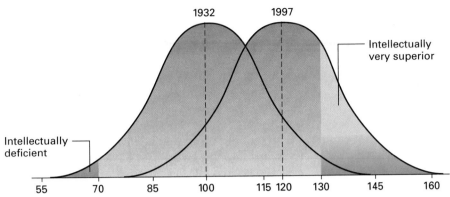

FIGURE 10.9 **The Increase in IQ Scores from 1932 to 1997.** As measured by the Stanford-Binet intelligence test, American children seem to be getting smarter. Scores of a group tested in 1932 fell along a bell-shaped curve with half below 100 and half above. Studies show that if children took that same test today, half would score above 120 on the 1932 scale. Very few of them would score in the "intellectually deficient" end, on the left side, and about one-fourth would rank in the "very superior" range.

of education attained by a much greater percentage of the world's population or to other environmental factors such as the explosion of information to which people are exposed. The worldwide increase in intelligence test scores that has occurred over a short time frame has been called the *Flynn effect*, after the researcher who discovered it—James Flynn.

Keep in mind that environmental influences are complex (Neisser & others, 1996; Sternberg, 2006; Sternberg, Grigorenko, & Kidd, 2006). Growing up with all the "advantages," for example, does not guarantee success. Children from wealthy families may have easy access to excellent schools, books, travel, and tutoring, but they may take such opportunities for granted and fail to develop the motivation to learn and to achieve. In the same way, "poor" or "disadvantaged" does not automatically equal "doomed."

Researchers increasingly are interested in manipulating the early environment of children who are at risk for impoverished intelligence (Blair & Ramey, 1996; Campbell, 2006; Ramey, Ramey, & Lanzi, 2006). The emphasis is on prevention rather than remediation. Many low-income parents have difficulty providing an intellectually stimulating environment for their children. Programs that educate parents to be more sensitive caregivers and better teachers, as well as support services such as quality child-care programs, can make a difference in a child's intellectual development.

A recent review of the research on early interventions concluded that (1) high-quality center-based interventions are associated with increases in children's intelligence and school achievement; (2) the interventions are most successful with poor children and children whose parents have little education; (3) the positive benefits continue through adolescence, but are not as strong as in early childhood or the beginning of elementary school; and (4) the programs that are continued into middle and late childhood have the best long-term results (Brooks-Gunn, 2003). To read further about environmental influences on intelligence, see the Research in Life-Span Development interlude.

RESEARCH IN LIFE-SPAN DEVELOPMENT

The Abecedarian Project

Each morning a young mother waited with her child for the bus that would take the child to school. The child was only 2 months old, and "school" was an experimental program at the University of North Carolina at Chapel Hill. There the child experienced a number of interventions designed to improve her intellectual development—everything from bright objects dangled in front of her eyes while she was a baby to language instruction and counting activities when she was a toddler (Wickelgren, 1999). The child's mother had an IQ of 40 and could not read signs or determine how much change she should receive from a cashier. Her grandmother had a similarly low IQ.

Today, at age 20, the child's IQ measures 80 points higher than her mother's did when the child was 2 months old. Not everyone agrees that IQ can be affected this extensively, but environment can make a substantial difference in a child's intelligence. As behavior geneticist Robert Plomin (1999) says, even something that is highly heritable (like intelligence) may be malleable through interventions.

The child we just described was part of the Abecedarian Intervention program at the University of North Carolina at Chapel Hill conducted by Craig Ramey and his associates (Ramey & Campbell, 1984; Ramey & Ramey, 1998; Ramey, Ramey, & Lanzi, 2001, 2006). They randomly assigned 111 young children from low-income, poorly educated families to either an intervention group, which received full-time, year-round child care along with medical and social work services, or a control group, which received medical and social benefits but no child care. The child-care program included gamelike learning activities aimed at improving language, motor, social, and cognitive skills.

The success of the program in improving IQ was evident by the time the children were 3 years old. At that age, the experimental group showed normal IQs averaging 101, a 17-point advantage over the control group. Recent follow-up results suggest that the effects are long-lasting. More than a decade later at age 15, children from the intervention group still maintained an IQ advantage of 5 points over the control-group children (97.7 to 92.6) (Campbell & others, 2001; Ramey, Ramey, & Lanzi, 2001, 2006). They also did better on standardized tests of reading and math, and were less likely to be held back a year in school. Also, the greatest IQ gains were made by the children whose mothers had especially low IQs—below 70. At age 15, these children showed a 10-point IQ advantage over a group of children whose mothers' IQs were below 70 but did not experience the child-care intervention.

Group Differences   In the United States, children from African American and Latino families score below children from White families on standardized intelligence tests. On the average, African American schoolchildren score 10 to 15 points lower on standardized intelligence tests than White American schoolchildren do (Brody, 2000; Lynn, 1996). These are *average scores,* however. About 15 to 25 percent of African American schoolchildren score higher than half of White schoolchildren do, and many White schoolchildren score lower than most African American schoolchildren. The reason is that the distribution of scores for African American and White schoolchildren overlap.

As African Americans have gained social, economic, and educational opportunities, the gap between African Americans and Whites on standardized intelligence tests has begun to narrow (Ogbu & Stern, 2001; Onwuegbuzie & Daley, 2001). This gap especially narrows in college, where African American and White students often experience more similar environments than in the elementary and high school years (Myerson & others, 1998). Also, when children from disadvantaged African American families are adopted into more-advantaged middle-socioeconomic-status families, their scores on intelligence tests more closely resemble national averages for middle-socioeconomic-status children than for lower-socioeconomic-status children (Scarr & Weinberg, 1983).

One potential influence on intelligence test performance is **stereotype threat,** the anxiety that one's behavior might confirm a negative stereotype about one's

stereotype threat The anxiety that one's behavior might confirm a negative stereotype about one's group.

group (Steele & Aronson, 2004). For example, when African Americans take an intelligence test, they may experience anxiety about confirming the old stereotype that African Americans are "intellectually inferior." In one study, the verbal part of the GRE was given individually to African American and White students at Stanford University (Steele & Aronson, 1995). Half the students of each ethnic group were told that the researchers were interested in assessing their intellectual ability. The other half were told that the researchers were trying to develop a test and that it might not be reliable and valid (therefore, it would not mean anything in relation to their intellectual ability). The White students did equally well on the test in both conditions. However, the African American students did more poorly when they thought the test was assessing their intellectual ability; when they thought the test was just in the development stage and might not be reliable or valid, they performed as well as the White students.

Other studies have confirmed the existence of stereotype threat (Cohen & Sherman, 2005; Helms, 2005). African American students do more poorly on standardized tests if they believe they are being evaluated. If they believe the test doesn't count, they perform as well as White students (Aronson, 2002; Aronson & others, 1999; Aronson, Fried, & Good, 2002). However, some critics believe the extent to which stereotype threat explains the testing gap has been exaggerated (Ackerman & Lohman, 2006; Sackett, Hardison, & Cullen, 2004).

Biased tests may also contribute to group differences in average IQ scores. Many of the early tests of intelligence favored urban children over rural children, children from middle-SES families over children from low-income families, and White children over minority children (Miller-Jones, 1989). The standards for the early tests were almost exclusively based on White middle-SES children. And some of the items were culturally biased. For example, one item on an early test asked what you should do if you find a 3-year-old in the street. The correct answer was "Call the police." However, children from impoverished inner-city families might not choose this answer if they have had bad experiences with the police. Children living in rural areas might not have police nearby. The contemporary versions of intelligence tests attempt to reduce such cultural bias.

Even if the content of test items is appropriate, however, another problem can characterize intelligence tests. Since many items are verbal, minority groups may encounter problems in understanding the language of the items.

Creating Culture-Fair Tests **Culture-fair tests** are tests of intelligence that are intended to be free of cultural bias. Two types of culture-fair tests have been devised. The first includes items that are familiar to children from all socioeconomic and ethnic backgrounds, or items that at least are familiar to the children taking the test. For example, a child might be asked how a bird and a dog are different, on the assumption that all children have been exposed to birds and dogs. The second type of culture-fair test has no verbal questions. Figure 10.10 shows a sample question from the Raven's Progressive Matrices Test. Even though tests such as the Raven's Progressive Matrices are designed to be culture-fair, people with more education still score higher than those with less education do.

Why is it so hard to create culture-fair tests? Most tests tend to reflect what the dominant culture thinks is important (Greenfield, Suzuki, & Rothstein-Fisch, 2006; Greenfield & others, 2006). If tests have time limits, that will bias the test against groups not concerned with time. If languages differ, the same words might have different meanings for different language groups. Even pictures can produce bias because some cultures have less experience with drawings and photographs (Anastasi & Urbina, 1996). Within the same culture, different groups could have different attitudes, values, and motivation, and this could affect their performance on intelligence tests. Items that ask why buildings should be made of brick are biased against children who have little or no experience with brick houses. Questions about railroads, furnaces, seasons of the year, distances between cities, and so on can be biased

How might stereotype threat affect African American children's scores on tests?

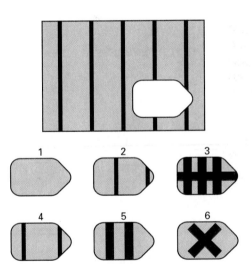

FIGURE 10.10 **Sample Item from the Raven's Progressive Matrices Test.** Individuals are presented with a matrix arrangement of symbols, such as the one at the top of this figure, and must then complete the matrix by selecting the appropriate missing symbol from a group of symbols, such as the ones at the bottom. Simulated item similar to those found in the *Raven's Progressive Matrices.* Copyright © 1998 by Harcourt Assessment, Inc. Reproduced with permission. All rights reserved.

culture-fair tests Tests of intelligence that are designed to be free of cultural bias.

against groups who have less experience than others with these contexts. Recall, too, that cultures define what is intelligent differently.

These attempts to produce culture-fair tests remind us that conventional intelligence tests probably are culturally biased, yet the effort to create a truly culture-fair test has not yielded a successful alternative.

Using Intelligence Tests Psychological tests are tools. Like all tools, their effectiveness depends on the knowledge, skill, and integrity of the user. A hammer can be used to build a beautiful kitchen cabinet, or it can be used as a weapon of assault. Like a hammer, psychological tests can be used for positive purposes, or they can be badly abused. Here are some cautions about IQ that can help you avoid the pitfalls of using information about a child's intelligence in negative ways:

- *Avoid stereotyping and expectations.* A special concern is that the scores on an IQ test easily can lead to stereotypes and expectations about students. Sweeping generalizations are too often made on the basis of an IQ score. An IQ test should always be considered a measure of current performance. It is not a measure of fixed potential. Maturational changes and enriched environmental experiences can advance a student's intelligence.
- *Know that IQ is not a sole indicator of competence.* Another concern about IQ tests occurs when they are used as the main or sole assessment of competence. A high IQ is not the ultimate human value. As we have seen in this chapter, it is important to consider not only students' intellectual competence in such areas as verbal skills but also their creative and practical skills.
- *Use caution in interpreting an overall IQ score.* In evaluating a child's intelligence, it is wiser to think of intelligence as consisting of a number of domains. Keep in mind the different types of intelligence described by Sternberg and Gardner. Remember that, by considering the different domains of intelligence, you can find that every child has at least one or more strengths.

Extremes of Intelligence

Intelligence tests have been used to discover indications of mental retardation or intellectual giftedness, the extremes of intelligence. At times, intelligence tests have been misused for this purpose. Keeping in mind the theme that an intelligence test should not be used as the sole indicator of mental retardation or giftedness, we will explore the nature of these intellectual extremes.

Mental Retardation **Mental retardation** is a condition of limited mental ability in which an individual has a low IQ, usually below 70 on a traditional intelligence test, and has difficulty adapting to everyday life. About 5 million Americans fit this definition of mental retardation.

There are several classifications of mental retardation (Hodapp & Dykens, 2006). About 89 percent of the mentally retarded fall into the mild category, with IQs of 55 to 70. About 6 percent are classified as moderately retarded, with IQs of 40 to 54; these people can attain a second-grade level of skills and may be able to support themselves as adults through some types of labor. About 3.5 percent of the mentally retarded are in the severe category, with IQs of 25 to 39; these individuals learn to talk and engage in very simple tasks but require extensive supervision. Less than 1 percent have IQs below 25; they fall into the profoundly mentally retarded classification and need constant supervision (Drew & Hardman, 2000).

Mental retardation can have an organic cause, or it can be social and cultural in origin:

- **Organic retardation** is mental retardation that is caused by a genetic disorder or by brain damage; the word *organic* refers to the tissues or organs of the body, so there is some physical damage in organic retardation. Most people

A child with Down syndrome. *What causes a child to develop Down syndrome? In which major classification of mental retardation does the condition fall?*

mental retardation A condition of limited mental ability in which an individual has a low IQ, usually below 70 on a traditional test of intelligence, and has difficulty adapting to everyday life.

organic retardation Mental retardation that involves some physical damage and is caused by a genetic disorder or brain damage.

who suffer from organic retardation have IQs that range between 0 and 50. However, children with Down syndrome have an average IQ of approximately 50. As discussed in chapters 3 and 4, Down syndrome occurs when an individual has an extra copy of chromosome 21.

- **Cultural-familial retardation** is a mental deficit in which no evidence of organic brain damage can be found; individuals' IQs range from 50 to 70. Psychologists suspect that such mental deficits result from the normal variation that distributes people along the range of intelligence scores combined with growing up in a below-average intellectual environment.

Giftedness   There have always been people whose abilities and accomplishments outshine others'—the whiz kid in class, the star athlete, the natural musician. People who are **gifted** have above-average intelligence (an IQ of 130 or higher) and/or superior talent for something. When it comes to programs for the gifted, most school systems select children who have intellectual superiority and academic aptitude. Children who are talented in the visual and performing arts (arts, drama, dance), athletics, or other special aptitudes tend to be overlooked (Hargrove, 2005; Smith, 2005; Tassell-Baska & Stambaugh, 2006; Winner, 2000, 2006).

What are the characteristics of children who are gifted? There has been speculation that giftedness is linked with having a mental disorder. However, no relation between giftedness and mental disorder has been found. Similarly, the idea that gifted children are maladjusted is a myth, as Lewis Terman (1925) found when he conducted an extensive study of 1,500 children whose Stanford-Binet IQs averaged 150. The children in Terman's study were socially well adjusted, and many went on to become successful doctors, lawyers, professors, and scientists. Recent studies support the conclusion that gifted people tend to be more mature than others, have fewer emotional problems than others, and grow up in a positive family climate (Davidson, 2000; Feldman, 2001).

Ellen Winner (1996) described three criteria that characterize gifted children, whether in art, music, or academic domains:

1. *Precocity.* Gifted children are precocious. They begin to master an area earlier than their peers. Learning in their domain is more effortless for them than for ordinary children. In most instances, these gifted children are precocious because they have an inborn high ability in a particular domain or domains.
2. *Marching to their own drummer.* Gifted children learn in a qualitatively different way than ordinary children. One way that they march to a different drummer is that they need minimal help, or scaffolding, from adults to learn. In many instances, they resist any kind of explicit instruction. They also often make discoveries on their own and solve problems in unique ways.
3. *A passion to master.* Gifted children are driven to understand the domain in which they have high ability. They display an intense, obsessive interest and an ability to focus. They are not children who need to be pushed by their parents. They motivate themselves, says Winner.

Is giftedness a product of heredity or environment? Likely both. Individuals who are gifted recall that they had signs of high ability in a particular area at a very young age, prior to or at the beginning of formal training (Howe & others, 1995). This suggests the importance of innate ability in giftedness. However, researchers also have found that individuals with world-class status in the arts, mathematics, science, and sports all report strong family support and years of training and practice (Bloom, 1985). Deliberate practice is an important characteristic of individuals who become experts in a particular domain. For example, in one study, the best musicians engaged in twice as much deliberate practice over their lives as the least successful ones did (Ericsson, Krampe, & Tesch-Römer, 1993).

At 2 years of age, art prodigy Alexandra Nechita colored in coloring books for hours and also took up pen and ink. She had no interest in dolls or friends. By age 5 she was using watercolors. Once she started school, she would start painting as soon as she got home. At the age of 8, in 1994, she saw the first public exhibit of her work. In succeeding years, working quickly and impulsively on canvases as large as 5 feet by 9 feet, she has completed hundreds of paintings, some of which sell for close to $100,000 apiece. As a teenager, she continues to paint—relentlessly and passionately. It is, she says, what she loves to do. *What are some characteristics of children who are gifted?*

www.mhhe.com/santrockld11

Children Who Are Gifted

cultural-familial retardation Retardation that is characterized by no evidence of organic brain damage, but the individual's IQ is between 50 and 70.

gifted Having above-average intelligence (an IQ of 130 or higher) and/or superior talent for something.

> ### *Review and Reflect* • LEARNING GOAL 3
>
> **(3) Explain cognitive changes in middle and late childhood**
>
> **Review**
> - What characterizes Piaget's stage of concrete operational thought? What are some contributions and criticisms of Piaget?
> - How do children process information in the middle and late childhood years?
> - What is intelligence, and how is it assessed?
> - What determines individual and group differences in IQ scores?
> - What are the key characteristics of mental retardation and giftedness?
>
> **Reflect**
> - A CD-ROM, *Children's IQ and Achievement Test*, now lets parents test their child's IQ and how well the child is performing in relation to their grade in school. What might be some problems with parents giving their children an IQ test?

4 LANGUAGE DEVELOPMENT

Vocabulary, Grammar, and Metalinguistic Awareness	Reading	Bilingualism and Second Language Learning

Children gain new skills as they enter school that make it possible to learn to read and write: These include increasingly using language to talk about things that are not physically present, learning what a word is, and learning how to recognize and talk about sounds (Berko Gleason, 2003). They have to learn the *alphabetic principle,* that the letters of the alphabet represent sounds of the language. As children develop during middle and late childhood, changes in their vocabulary and grammar also take place (Hoff, 2003).

Vocabulary, Grammar, and Metalinguistic Awareness

During middle and late childhood, changes occur in the way children's mental vocabulary is organized. When asked to say the first word that comes to mind when they hear a word, young children typically provide a word that often follows the word in a sentence. For example, when asked to respond to "dog" the young child may say "barks," or to the word "eat" say "lunch." At about 7 years of age, children begin to respond with a word that is the same part of speech as the stimulus word. For example, a child may now respond to the word "dog" with "cat" or "horse." To "eat," they now might say "drink." This is evidence that children now have begun to categorize their vocabulary by parts of speech (Berko Gleason, 2003).

The process of categorizing becomes easier as children increase their vocabulary. Children's vocabulary increases from an average of about 14,000 words at 6 years of age to an average of about 40,000 words by 11 years of age.

Children make similar advances in grammar. During the elementary school years, children's improvement in logical reasoning and analytical skills helps them understand such constructions as the appropriate use of comparatives (*shorter, deeper*) and subjectives ("If you were president . . ."). During the elementary school years, children become increasingly able to understand and use complex grammar, such as the following sentence: *The boy who kissed his mother wore a hat.* They also learn to use language in a more connected way, producing connected discourse. They become able to relate sentences to one another to produce descriptions, definitions, and narratives that make sense. Children must be able to do these things orally before they can be expected to deal with them in written assignments.

These advances in vocabulary and grammar during the elementary school years are accompanied by the development of **metalinguistic awareness,** which is knowledge about language, such as knowing what a preposition is or the ability to discuss the sounds of a language. Metalinguistic awareness allows children "to think about their language, understand what words are, and even define them" (Berko Gleason, 2005, p. 4). It improves considerably during the elementary school years. Defining words becomes a regular part of classroom discourse, and children increase their knowledge of syntax as they study and talk about the components of sentences such as subjects and verbs (Ely, 2005).

Children also make progress in understanding how to use language in culturally appropriate ways—pragmatics. By the time they enter adolescence, most children know the rules for the use of language in everyday contexts, that is, what is appropriate to say and what is inappropriate to say.

Reading

Before learning to read, children learn to use language to talk about things that are not present; they learn what a word is; and they learn how to recognize sounds and talk about them (Berko Gleason, 2003). If they develop a large vocabulary, their path to reading is eased. Children who begin elementary school with a small vocabulary are at risk when it comes to learning to read (Berko Gleason, 2003).

Vocabulary development plays an important role in reading comprehension (Berninger, 2006; Paris & Paris, 2006; Snow & Yang, 2006). For example, a recent study revealed that a good vocabulary was linked with reading comprehension in second-grade students (Berninger & Abbott, 2005). Having a good vocabulary helps readers access word meaning effortlessly.

How should children be taught to read? Currently, debate focuses on the whole-language approach versus the basic-skills-and-phonics approach (May, 2006; Ruddell, 2006; Vacca & others, 2006).

The **whole-language approach** stresses that reading instruction should parallel children's natural language learning. In some whole-language classes beginning readers are taught to recognize whole words or even entire sentences, and to use the context of what they are reading to guess at the meaning of words. Reading materials should be whole and meaningful—that is, children should be given material in its complete form, such as stories and poems, so that they learn to understand language's communicative function. Reading should be connected with listening and writing skills. Although there are variations in whole-language programs, most share the premise that reading should be integrated with other skills and subjects, such as science and social studies, and that it should focus on real-world material. Thus, a class might read newspapers, magazines, or books, and then write about and discuss them.

In contrast, the **basic-skills-and-phonics approach** emphasizes that reading instruction should teach phonics and its basic rules for translating written symbols into sounds. Early reading instruction should involve simplified materials. Only after children have learned correspondence rules that relate spoken phonemes to the alphabet letters that are used to represent them should they be given complex reading materials, such as books and poems.

Which approach is better? Children can benefit from both approaches (Vacca & others, 2006). Researchers have found strong evidence that the basic-skills-and-phonics approach should be used in teaching children to read but that students also benefit from the whole-language approach (Fox & Hull, 2002; Heilman, Blair, & Rupley, 2002; Silva & Martins, 2003). Training for phonological awareness is best when it is integrated with reading and writing, is simple, and is conducted in small groups rather than with a whole class (Stahl, 2002).

Whichever approach is used, reading, like other important skills, takes time and effort. In a national assessment, children in the fourth grade had higher scores on a national reading test when they read 11 or more pages daily for school and

What are the main approaches to teaching children how to read?

www.mhhe.com/santrockld11

Reading Research

metalinguistic awareness Refers to knowledge about language, such as knowing what a preposition is or the ability to discuss the sounds of a language.

whole-language approach An approach to reading instruction based on the idea that instruction should parallel children's natural language learning. Reading materials should be whole and meaningful.

basic-skills-and-phonics approach The idea that reading instruction should teach both phonics and the basic rules for translating written symbols into sounds.

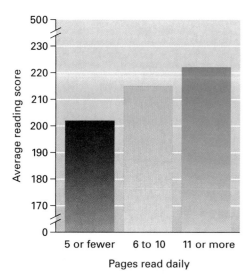

FIGURE 10.11 The Relation of Reading Achievement to Number of Pages Read Daily. In the recent analysis of reading in the fourth grade in the National Assessment of Educational Progress (2000), reading more pages daily in school and as part of homework assignments was related to higher scores on a reading test in which scores ranged from 0 to 500.

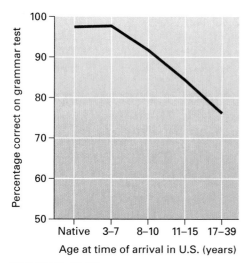

FIGURE 10.12 Grammar Proficiency and Age at Arrival in the United States. In one study, 10 years after arriving in the United States, individuals from China and Korea took a grammar test (Johnson & Newport, 1991). People who arrived before the age of 8 had a better grasp of grammar than those who arrived later.

homework (National Assessment of Educational Progress, 2000) (see figure 10.11). Teachers who required students to read a great deal on a daily basis had students who were more proficient at reading than teachers who required little reading by their students.

Bilingualism and Second Language Learning

Learning a second language is more readily accomplished by children than adolescents or adults. Adults make faster initial progress, but their eventual success in the second language is not as great as children's. For example, in one study, Chinese and Korean adults who immigrated to the United States at different ages were given a test of grammatical knowledge (Johnston & Newport, 1991). Those who began learning English when they were 3 to 7 years old scored as well as native speakers on the test, but those who arrived in the United States and started learning English in later childhood or adolescence had lower test scores (see figure 10.12). Children's ability to pronounce words with the correct accent in a second language also decreases with age, with an especially sharp drop occurring after the age of about 10 to 12 (Asher & Garcia, 1969). In sum, researchers have found that early exposure to a second language is optimal and ensures the least amount of damage to the home language and to the new language (Lesaux & Siegel, 2003; Lessow-Hurley, 2005; Petitto, Kovelman, & Harasymowycz, 2003).

Students in the United States are far behind their counterparts in many developed countries in learning a second language. For example, in Russia, schools have 10 grades, called *forms*, which roughly correspond to the 12 grades in American schools. Children begin school at age 7 in Russia and begin learning English in the third form. Because of this emphasis on teaching English, most Russian citizens under the age of 40 today are able to speak at least some English. The United States is the only technologically advanced Western nation that does not require foreign language study in high school, even for students in rigorous academic programs.

U.S. students may be missing more than the chance to acquire a skill by not learning to speak a second language (Soltero, 2004). *Bilingualism*—the ability to speak two languages—has a positive effect on children's cognitive development (Gibbons & Ng, 2004). Children who are fluent in two languages perform better than their single-language counterparts on tests of control of attention, concept formation, analytical reasoning, cognitive flexibility, and cognitive complexity (Bialystok, 1999, 2001). They also are more conscious of the structure of spoken and written language and better at noticing errors of grammar and meaning, skills that benefit their reading ability (Bialystok, 1993, 1997).

In the United States, many immigrant children go from being monolingual in their home language to bilingual in that language and in English, only to end up monolingual speakers of English. This is called *subtractive bilingualism* and it can have negative effects on children, who often become ashamed of their home language.

A current controversy related to bilingualism involves bilingual education (Padilla, 2006). To read about this controversy, see the Diversity in Life-Span Development interlude.

DIVERSITY IN LIFE-SPAN DEVELOPMENT

Bilingual Education

A current controversy related to bilingualism involves the millions of U.S. children who come from homes in which English is not the primary language (Adamson, 2004). What is the best way to teach these children?

For the last two decades, the preferred strategy has been *bilingual education*, which teaches academic subjects to immigrant children in their native language while slowly teaching English (Diaz-Rico & Weed, 2006; Gottlieb, 2006; Ovando, Combs, & Collier, 2006). Advocates of bilingual education programs argue that if children who do not know English are taught only in English, they will fall behind in academic subjects. How, they ask, can 7-year-olds learn arithmetic or history taught only in English when they do not speak the language?

Some critics of bilingual programs argue that too often it is thought that immigrant children need only one year of bilingual education. However, in general it takes immigrant children approximately three to five years to develop speaking proficiency and seven years to develop reading proficiency in English (Hakuta, Butler, & Witt, 2000). Also, immigrant children of course vary in their ability to learn English (Diaz-Rico & Weed, 2006; Rueda & Yaden, 2006; Wiese & Garcia, 2006). Children who come from lower socioeconomic backgrounds have more difficulty than those from higher socioeconomic backgrounds (Hakuta, 2001). Thus, especially for immigrant children from low-socioeconomic backgrounds, more years of bilingual education may be needed than they currently are receiving.

Critics who oppose bilingual education argue that as a result of these programs, the children of immigrants are not learning English, which puts them at a permanent disadvantage in U.S. society. California, Arizona, and Massachusetts have significantly reduced the number of bilingual education programs. Some states continue to endorse bilingual education, but the emphasis that test scores be reported separately for English Language Learners (students whose main language is not English) in the No Child Left Behind state assessments has shifted attention to literacy in English (Rivera & Collum, 2006; Snow & Yang, 2006).

What have researchers found regarding outcomes of bilingual education programs? Drawing conclusions about the effectiveness of bilingual education programs is difficult because of variations across programs in the number of years they are in effect, type of instruction, qualities of schooling other than bilingual education, teachers, children, and other factors. Further, no effectively conducted experiments that compare bilingual education with English-only education in the United States have been conducted (Snow & Yang, 2006). Some experts have concluded that the quality of instruction is more important in determining outcomes than the language in which it is delivered (Lesaux & Siegel, 2003).

Research supports bilingual education in that (1) children have difficulty learning a subject when it is taught in a language they do not understand, and (2) when both languages are integrated in the classroom, children learn the second language more readily and participate more actively (Gonzales, Yawkey, & Minaya-Rowe, 2006; Hakuta, 2000, 2001, 2005; Soltero, 2004). However, many of the research results report only modest rather than strong support for bilingual education and some supporters of bilingual education now acknowledge that English-only instruction can produce positive outcomes for English Language Learners (Lesaux & Siegel, 2003).

A first- and second-grade bilingual English–Cantonese teacher instructing students in Chinese in Oakland, California. *What have researchers found about the effectiveness of bilingual education?*

Review and Reflect • LEARNING GOAL 4

4 Discuss language development in middle and late childhood

Review
- What are some changes in vocabulary and grammar in the middle and late childhood years?
- What controversy characterizes how to teach children to read?
- What is bilingual education? What issues are involved in bilingual education?

Reflect
- What are some of the key considerations in using a balanced approach to teaching reading?

REACH YOUR LEARNING GOALS

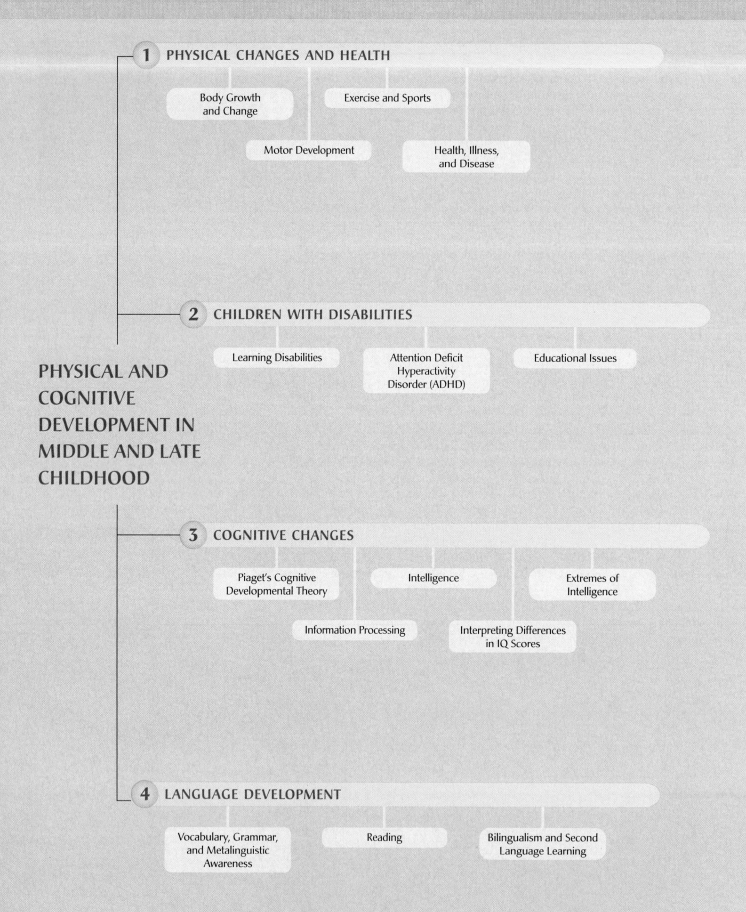

PHYSICAL AND COGNITIVE DEVELOPMENT IN MIDDLE AND LATE CHILDHOOD

1 PHYSICAL CHANGES AND HEALTH

- Body Growth and Change
- Motor Development
- Exercise and Sports
- Health, Illness, and Disease

2 CHILDREN WITH DISABILITIES

- Learning Disabilities
- Attention Deficit Hyperactivity Disorder (ADHD)
- Educational Issues

3 COGNITIVE CHANGES

- Piaget's Cognitive Developmental Theory
- Information Processing
- Intelligence
- Interpreting Differences in IQ Scores
- Extremes of Intelligence

4 LANGUAGE DEVELOPMENT

- Vocabulary, Grammar, and Metalinguistic Awareness
- Reading
- Bilingualism and Second Language Learning

SUMMARY

 Physical Changes and Health: *Describe physical changes and health in middle and late childhood*

Body Growth and Change
The period of middle and late childhood involves slow, consistent growth. During this period, children grow an average of 2 to 3 inches a year. Muscle mass and strength gradually increase. Among the most pronounced changes in body growth and proportion are decreases in head circumference, waist circumference, and leg length in relation to body height.

Motor Development
During the middle and late childhood years, motor development becomes much smoother and more coordinated. Children gain greater control over their bodies and can sit and attend for longer periods of time. However, their lives should be activity-oriented and very active. Increased myelination of the central nervous system is reflected in improved motor skills. Improved fine motor skills appear in the form of handwriting development. Boys are usually better at gross motor skills, girls at fine motor skills.

Exercise and Sports
Most American children do not get nearly enough exercise. Children's participation in sports can have consequences that are either positive (exercise and self-esteem) or negative (pressure to win and physical injuries).

Health, Illness, and Disease
For the most part, middle and late childhood is a time of excellent health. The most common cause of severe injury and death in childhood is motor vehicle accidents, with most occurring at or near the child's home or school. Cancer is the second leading cause of death in children (after accidents). Leukemia is the most common childhood cancer. Cardiovascular disease is uncommon in children but the precursors to adult cardiovascular disease are often already apparent in children. Obesity in children poses serious health risks. The increase in the prevalence of obesity among children is linked to poor diet, inadequate exercise, and poor eating habits.

 Children with Disabilities: *Identify children with different types of disabilities and issues in educating them*

Learning Disabilities
An estimated 10 percent of U.S. children receive special education or related services. Slightly more than 40 percent of students with disabilities are classified as having a learning disability. In the federal government classification, this category includes attention deficit hyperactivity disorder, or ADHD. Children with learning disabilities (1) exceed a minimum IQ level; (2) have a significant difficulty in a school-related area; and

(3) do not have severe emotional disorders, second-language background, sensory disabilities, or specific neurological deficits. Dyslexia is a category of learning disabilities that involves a severe impairment in the ability to read and spell.

Attention Deficit Hyperactivity Disorder (ADHD)
Attention deficit hyperactivity disorder (ADHD) is a disability in which individuals consistently show problems in one or more of these areas: (1) inattention, (2) hyperactivity, and (3) impulsivity. ADHD has been increasingly diagnosed.

Educational Issues
In 1975, Public Law 94-142, the Education for All Handicapped Children Act, required that all children with disabilities be given a free, appropriate public education. This law was renamed the Individuals with Disabilities Education Act (IDEA) in 1990 and updated in 2004. IDEA includes requirements that children with disabilities receive an individual education plan (IEP), which is a written plan that spells out a program tailored to the child, and that they be educated in the least restrictive environment (LRE), which is a setting that is as similar as possible to the one in which children without disabilities are educated. The term *inclusion* means educating children with disabilities full-time in the regular classroom.

 Cognitive Changes: *Explain cognitive changes in middle and late childhood*

Piaget's Cognitive Developmental Theory
Piaget said that the stage of concrete operational thought characterizes children from about 7 to 11 years of age. During this stage children are capable of concrete operations, conservation, classification, seriation, and transitivity. Piaget's ideas have been applied extensively to education. Critics argue that some abilities emerge earlier than Piaget thought, that elements of a stage do not appear at the same time, and that education and culture have more influence on development than Piaget predicted. Neo-Piagetians place more emphasis on how children process information, strategies, speed of information processing, and the division of cognitive problems into more precise steps.

Information Processing
Long-term memory increases in middle and late childhood. Knowledge and expertise influence memory. Strategies, such as imagery and elaboration, can be used by children to improve their memory. Fuzzy trace theory has been proposed to explain developmental changes in memory. Critical thinking involves thinking reflectively and productively, as well as evaluating the evidence. A special concern is the lack of emphasis on critical thinking in many schools. Creative thinking is the ability to think in novel and unusual ways and to come up with unique solutions to problems. Guilford distinguished between convergent and divergent thinking. A number of strategies can be used to encourage children's creative

thinking, including brainstorming. Children think like scientists in some ways, but in others they don't. Metacognition is knowing about knowing. Most metacognitive studies have focused on metamemory. Pressley views the key to education as helping students learn a rich repertoire of strategies.

Intelligence

Intelligence consists of problem-solving skills and the ability to adapt to and learn from life's everyday experiences. Interest in intelligence often focuses on individual differences and assessment. Widely used intelligence tests today include the Stanford-Binet tests and Wechsler scales. Results on these tests may be reported in terms of an overall IQ or in terms of performance on specific areas of the tests. Spearman proposed that people have a general intelligence (*g*) and specific types of intelligence (*s*). Sternberg proposed that intelligence comes in three main forms: analytical, creative, and practical. Gardner proposes that there are eight types of intelligence: verbal, math, spatial, bodily-kinesthetic, musical skills, interpersonal skills, intrapersonal skills, and naturalist skills. The multiple-intelligence approaches have expanded our conception of intelligence, but critics argue that the research base for these approaches is not well established. Cultures, however, vary in the way they define intelligence.

Interpreting Differences in IQ Scores

IQ scores are influenced by both genetics and characteristics of the environment. Studies of heritability indicate that genetics has a strong influence on the variance in IQ scores within a population, but environmental changes can alter the IQ scores of most people considerably. Parents, home environments, schools, and intervention programs can influence these scores. Intelligence test scores have risen considerably around the world in recent decades—called the Flynn effect—and this supports the role of environment in intelligence. Group differences in IQ scores may reflect many influences, including stereotype threat and cultural bias. Tests may be biased against certain groups because they are not familiar with a standard form of English, with the content tested, or with the testing situation. Tests are likely to reflect the values and experience of the dominant culture.

Extremes of Intelligence

Mental retardation involves low IQ and problems in adapting to everyday life. One classification of mental retardation distinguishes organic and cultural-familial retardation. A child who is gifted has above-average intelligence and/or superior talent for something. Terman contributed to our understanding that gifted children are not more maladjusted than nongifted children. Three characteristics of gifted children are precocity, individuality, and a passion to master a domain.

④ Language Development: *Discuss language development in middle and late childhood*

Vocabulary, Grammar, and Metalinguistic Awareness

Children become more analytical and logical in their approach to words and grammar. In terms of grammar, children now better understand comparatives and subjectives. They become increasingly able to use complex grammar and produce narratives that make sense. Improvements in metalinguistic awareness—knowledge about language—are evident during the elementary school years as children increasingly define words, increase their knowledge of syntax, and understand better how to use language in culturally appropriate ways.

Reading

A current debate in reading focuses on the basic-skills-and-phonics approach versus the whole-language approach. The basic-skills-and-phonics approach advocates phonetics instruction and giving children simplified materials. The whole-language approach stresses that reading instruction should parallel children's natural language learning and giving children whole-language materials, such as books and poems.

Bilingualism and Second Language Learning

Bilingual education aims to teach academic subjects to immigrant children in their native languages (most often in Spanish) while gradually adding English instruction. Researchers have found that bilingualism does not interfere with performance in either language. Success in learning a second language is greater in childhood than in adolescence.

KEY TERMS

KEY PEOPLE

E-LEARNING TOOLS

To help you master the material in this chapter, you'll find a number of valuable study tools on the LifeMap CD-ROM that accompanies this book and on the Online Learning Center for *Life-Span Development*, eleventh edition, at **www.mhhe.com/ santrockld11**.

Video Clips

In the margins of this book there are icons directing you to the LifeMap CD-ROM that accompanies the book. There you'll find a video for chapter 10 called "Interactivity: Sensorimotor Neural Circuits." One of the more noticeable developments of the middle and late childhood years is a refinement of motor skills. This segment looks at how different children achieve this new level of physical coordination.

Self-Assessment

Connect to **www.mhhe.com/santrockld11** to learn more about various kinds of intelligence by completing the self-assessments, *Evaluating Myself on Gardner's Eight Types of Intelligence* and *How Emotionally Intelligent Am I?*

Taking It to the Net

Connect to **www.mhhe.com/santrockld11** to research the answers to these questions.
1. Clarence wants to teach his fifth-grade students good dietary, nutritional, and exercise habits. What lessons can they be taught now that will benefit them later in life?
2. Noah's parents are upset to hear that their fourth-grader may have dyslexia. Noah's father is concerned that people will think Noah is stupid. What should Noah's teacher tell these parents about the nature and causes of dyslexia?

Health and Well-Being, Parenting, and Education Exercises

Build your decision-making skills by trying your hand at the health and well-being, parenting, and education exercises. Connect to **www.mhhe.com/santrockld11** to research the answers and complete the exercises.

Children are busy becoming something they have not quite grasped yet, something which keeps changing.

—ALASTAIR REID
American Poet, 20th Century

CHAPTER OUTLINE

LEARNING GOALS

EMOTIONAL AND PERSONALITY DEVELOPMENT

1 Discuss emotional and personality development in middle and late childhood

The Self

Emotional Development

Moral Development

Gender

FAMILIES

2 Describe parent-child issues and societal changes in families

Parent-Child Issues

Stepfamilies

Latchkey Children

PEERS

3 Identify changes in peer relationships in middle and late childhood

Developmental Changes

Peer Status

Social Cognition

Bullying

Friends

SCHOOLS

4 Characterize contemporary approaches to student learning and sociocultural aspects of schooling and achievement

Contemporary Approaches to Student Learning

Socioeconomic Status and Ethnicity

Cross-Cultural Comparisons of Achievement

Images of Life-Span Development
The South Bronx to Pax, a Make-Believe Planet

At P.S. 30 in the South Bronx, Mr. Bedrock teaches fifth grade. One student in his class, Serafina, recently lost her mother to AIDS. When author Jonathan Kozol visited the class, he was told that two other children had taken the role of "allies in the child's struggle for emotional survival" (Kozol, 2005, p. 291).

Textbooks are in short supply for the class, and the social studies text is so out of date it claims that Ronald Reagan is the country's president. But Mr. Bedrock told Kozol that it's a "wonderful" class this year. About their teacher, 56-year-old Mr. Bedrock, one student said, "He's getting old, . . . but we love him anyway" (p. 292). Kozol found the students orderly, interested, and engaged. He describes one day when Mr. Bedrock is asking the students "about reading charts and graphs."

> "Okay, Ashley! Get it right!"
> Before she can answer, he walks over to her desk. "If you mess it up, I'll have to punish Alejandro."
> "Hey!" says Alejandro.
> "That's not fair," says Serafina. "If someone messes up, you have to punish *her*, not someone else."
> "Unfair to Alejandro!" several children say.
> "Poor me!" says Alejandro. (p. 294)

By late childhood, most children, like these students at P.S. 30, have developed friendships, learned to interact with adults other than their parents, and developed ideas about fairness and other moral concepts.

Can children understand such concepts as discrimination, economic inequality, affirmative action, and comparable worth? Probably not, if we use those terms, but might we be able to construct circumstances involving those concepts that they are able to understand? Phyllis Katz (1987) asked elementary-school-age children to pretend that they had taken a long ride on a spaceship to a make-believe planet called Pax. She asked for their opinions about various situations in which they found themselves. The situations involved conflict, socioeconomic inequality, and civil-political rights. For example, regarding conflict she asked them what a teacher should do when two students were tied for a prize or when they have been fighting. The economic equality dilemmas included a proposed field trip that not all students could afford, a comparable-worth situation in which janitors were paid more than teachers, and an employment situation that discriminated against those with dots on their noses instead of stripes. The civil rights items dealt with minority rights and freedom of the press.

The elementary school children did indeed recognize injustice and often came up with interesting solutions to problems. For example, all but two children believed that teachers should earn as much as janitors—the holdouts said teachers should make less because they stay in one room or because cleaning toilets is more disgusting and therefore deserves higher wages. Children were especially responsive to the economic inequality items. All but one thought that not giving a job to a qualified applicant who had different physical characteristics (a dotted rather than a striped nose) was unfair. The majority recommended an affirmative action solution—giving the job to the one from the discriminated-against minority. None of the children verbalized the concept of freedom of the press or seemed to understand that a newspaper has the right to criticize a mayor in print without being punished. War was mentioned as the biggest problem on Earth, although children were not certain whether it was presently occurring. Other problems mentioned were crime, hatred, school, smog, and meanness. Overall, the types of rules the children believed a society should abide by were quite sensible—almost all included the need for equitable sharing of resources and work and prohibitions against aggression.

PREVIEW

The years of middle and late childhood bring many changes to children's social and emotional lives. Transformations in their relationships with parents and peers occur, and schooling takes on a more academic flavor. The development of their self-conceptions, moral reasoning, and moral behavior is also significant.

1 EMOTIONAL AND PERSONALITY DEVELOPMENT

The Self	Moral Development

Emotional Development	Gender

The young students in Katz's study could come up with imaginative solutions to the problems on Pax in part because of their cognitive development, as discussed in previous chapters, but their responses also reflect their socioemotional development. Here we will focus on the development of the self, emotional development, moral development, and gender during middle and late childhood.

The Self

What is the nature of the child's self-understanding and self-esteem during the elementary school years? What role does self-efficacy play in children's achievement?

The Development of Self-Understanding In middle and late childhood, children recognize differences between inner and outer states, and they become more likely to include subjective inner states in their definition of self. In one investigation, second-grade children were much more likely than younger children to name psychological characteristics (such as preferences or personality traits) in their self-definition and less likely to name physical characteristics (such as eye color or possessions) (Aboud & Skerry, 1983). For example, 8-year-old Todd includes in his self-description, "I am smart and I am popular." Ten-year-old Tina says about herself, "I am pretty good about not worrying most of the time. I used to lose my temper but I'm better about that now. I also feel proud when I do well in school."

In addition, during the elementary school years, children become more likely to recognize social aspects of the self. They include references to social groups in their self-descriptions, such as referring to themselves as Girl Scouts, as Catholics, or as someone who has two close friends (Livesley & Bromley, 1973).

Children's self-understanding in the elementary school years also includes increasing reference to social comparison. At this point in development, children are more likely to distinguish themselves from others in comparative rather than in absolute terms. That is, elementary-school-age children are no longer as likely to think about what they do or do not do, but are more likely to think about what they can do in comparison with others.

Consider a series of studies in which Diane Ruble (1983) investigated children's use of social comparison in their self-evaluations. Children were given a difficult task and then offered feedback on their performance, as well as information about the performances of other children their age. The children were then asked for self-evaluations. Children younger than 7 made virtually no reference to the information about other children's performances. However, many children older than 7 included socially comparative information in their self-descriptions.

In short, in middle and late childhood, self-understanding increasingly shifts from defining oneself through external characteristics to defining oneself through internal characteristics. Also, elementary-school-age children are more likely to define themselves in terms of social characteristics and social comparison. Increasingly, children establish their differences as an individual apart from others.

Self-Esteem and Self-Concept   High self-esteem and a positive self-concept are important characteristics of children's well-being (Donnellan, Trzesniewski, & Robins, 2006; Dusek & McIntyre, 2003; Harter, 1999, 2006). Investigators sometimes use the terms *self-esteem* and *self-concept* interchangeably or do not precisely define them, but there is a meaningful difference between them. **Self-esteem** refers to global evaluations of the self; it is also called *self-worth* or *self-image*. For example, a child may perceive that she is not merely a person but a *good* person. **Self-concept** refers to domain-specific evaluations of the self. Children can make self-evaluations in many domains of their lives—academic, athletic, appearance, and so on. In sum, *self-esteem* refers to global self-evaluations, *self-concept* to domain-specific evaluations.

Self-esteem reflects perceptions that do not always match reality (Baumeister & others, 2003). A child's self-esteem might reflect a belief about whether he or she is intelligent and attractive, for example, but that belief is not necessarily accurate. Thus, high self-esteem may refer to accurate, justified perceptions of one's worth as a person and one's successes and accomplishments, but it can also refer to an arrogant, grandiose, unwarranted sense of superiority over others. In the same manner, low self-esteem may reflect either an accurate perception of one's shortcomings or a distorted, even pathological insecurity and inferiority.

Variations in self-esteem have been linked with many aspects of children's development. However, much of the research is *correlational* rather than *experimental*. Recall from chapter 2 that correlation does not equal causation. Thus, if a correlational study finds an association between children's low self-esteem and low academic achievement, low academic achievement could cause the low self-esteem as much as low self-esteem causes low academic achievement (Bowles, 1999).

In fact, there are only moderate correlations between school performance and self-esteem, and these correlations do not suggest that high self-esteem produces better school performance (Baumeister & others, 2003). Efforts to increase students' self-esteem have not always led to improved school performance (Davies & Brember, 1999).

Children with high self-esteem have greater initiative but this can produce positive or negative outcomes (Baumeister & others, 2003). High-self-esteem children are prone to both prosocial and antisocial actions.

In fact, a current concern is that too many of today's children grow up receiving praise for mediocre or even poor performance and as a consequence have inflated self-esteem (Graham, 2005; Stipek, 2005). They may have difficulty handling competition and criticism. This theme is vividly captured by the title of a book, *Dumbing Down Our Kids: Why America's Children Feel Good about Themselves but Can't Read, Write, or Add* (Sykes, 1995).

What are some good strategies for effectively increasing children's self-esteem? See the Applications in Life-Span Development interlude for some answers to this question.

What are some issues involved in understanding children's self-esteem in school?

self-esteem The global evaluative dimension of the self. Self-esteem is also referred to as self-worth or self-image.

self-concept Domain-specific evaluations of the self.

APPLICATIONS IN LIFE-SPAN DEVELOPMENT

Increasing Children's Self-Esteem

Four ways children's self-esteem can be improved include identifying the causes of low self-esteem, providing emotional support and social approval, helping children achieve, and helping children cope (Bednar, Wells, & Peterson, 1995; Harter, 1999, 2006).

- *Identify the causes of low self-esteem.* Intervention should target the causes of low self-esteem. Children have the highest self-esteem when they perform competently in domains that are important to them. Therefore, children should be encouraged to identify and value areas of competence. These areas might include academic skills, athletic skills, physical attractiveness, and social acceptance.
- *Provide emotional support and social approval.* Some children with low self-esteem come from conflicted families or conditions in which they experienced abuse or neglect—situations in which support was not available. In some cases, alternative sources of support can be arranged either informally through the encouragement of a teacher, a coach, or another significant adult, or more formally, through programs such as Big Brothers and Big Sisters.
- *Help children achieve.* Achievement also can improve children's self-esteem. For example, the straightforward teaching of real skills to children often results in increased achievement and, thus, in enhanced self-esteem. Children develop higher self-esteem because they know the important tasks that will achieve their goals, and they have performed them or similar behaviors in the past.
- *Help children cope.* Self-esteem is often increased when children face a problem and try to cope with it, rather than avoid it. If coping rather than avoidance prevails, children often face problems realistically, honestly, and nondefensively. This produces favorable self-evaluative thoughts, which lead to the self-generated approval that raises self-esteem.

How can parents help children develop higher self-esteem?

Self-Efficacy Another aspect of the self that plays an important role in children's achievement and adjustment is **self-efficacy,** the belief that one can master a situation and produce favorable outcomes. Albert Bandura (1997, 2001, 2004), whose social cognitive theory we described in chapter 1, holds that self-efficacy is a critical factor in whether or not students achieve. Self-efficacy is the belief that "I can"; helplessness is the belief that "I cannot" (Bandura, 2004; Stipek, 2002; Maddux, 2002). Students with high self-efficacy endorse such statements as "I know that I will be able to learn the material in this class" and "I expect to be able to do well at this activity."

Dale Schunk (1991, 2001, 2004) has applied the concept of self-efficacy to many aspects of students' achievement. In his view, self-efficacy influences a student's choice of activities. Students with low self-efficacy for learning may avoid many learning tasks, especially those that are challenging. By contrast, high-self-efficacy counterparts eagerly work at learning tasks (Schunk & Zimmerman, 2003, 2006 Zimmerman & Schunk, 2004). Students with high self-efficacy are more likely to expend effort and persist longer at a learning task than students with low self-efficacy.

Industry Versus Inferiority In chapter 2, we described Erik Erikson's (1968) eight stages of human development. His fourth stage, industry versus inferiority, appears during middle and late childhood. The term *industry* expresses a dominant theme of this period: Children become interested in how things are made and how they work. It is the Robinson Crusoe age, in that the enthusiasm and minute

self-efficacy The belief that one can master a situation and produce favorable outcomes.

detail Crusoe uses to describe his activities appeal to the child's budding sense of industry. When children are encouraged in their efforts to make, build, and work—whether building a model airplane, constructing a tree house, fixing a bicycle, solving an addition problem, or cooking—their sense of industry increases. However, parents who see their children's efforts at making things as "mischief" or "making a mess" encourage children's development of a sense of inferiority.

Children's social worlds beyond their families also contribute to a sense of industry. School becomes especially important in this regard. Consider children who are slightly below average in intelligence. They are too bright to be in special classes but not bright enough to be in gifted classes. They fail frequently in their academic efforts, developing a sense of inferiority. By contrast, consider children whose sense of industry is derogated at home. A series of sensitive and committed teachers may revitalize their sense of industry (Elkind, 1970).

Emotional Development

In chapter 9, we saw that preschoolers become more adept at talking about their own and others' emotions. They also show a growing awareness of the need to control and manage their emotions to meet social standards. In middle and late childhood, children further develop their understanding and self-regulation of emotion (Rubin, 2000; Saarni, 1999, 2006; Saarni & others, 2006).

Developmental Changes Important developmental changes in emotions during the middle and late childhood years include the following (Kuebli, 1994; Thompson & Goodvin, 2005; Wintre & Vallance, 1994):

- *Improved emotional understanding* (Thompson & Goodvin, 2005). For example, children in elementary school develop an increased ability to understand such complex emotions as pride and shame (Kuebli, 1994). These emotions become less tied to the reactions of other people; they become more self-generated and integrated with a sense of personal responsibility.
- *Increased understanding that more than one emotion can be experienced in a particular situation.*
- *An increased tendency to take into fuller account the events leading to emotional reactions.*
- *Marked improvements in the ability to suppress or conceal negative emotional reactions.* Elementary-school children often intentionally hide their emotions (Thompson & Goodvin, 2005).
- *The use of self-initiated strategies for redirecting feelings.* In the elementary-school years, children become more reflective and develop better strategies to cope with emotional matters. They can more effectively manage their emotions with cognitive strategies, such as engaging in distracting thoughts (Thompson & Goodvin, 2005).
- A capacity for genuine empathy (Thompson & Goodvin, 2005).

Emotional Intelligence One way of viewing these developments in children's ability to understand and regulate emotions is to say that they are developing social aspects of intelligence. In terms of the theories discussed in chapter 10, they are developing what is called "practical intelligence" in Sternberg's theory and "intrapersonal" and "interpersonal" intelligence in Gardner's theory. Another approach, first proposed in 1990, identifies **emotional intelligence** as a form of social intelligence that involves the ability to monitor one's own and others' feelings and emotions, to discriminate among them, and to use this information to guide one's thinking and action (Salovey & Mayer, 1990).

Interest in emotional intelligence grew with the publication of Daniel Goleman's book *Emotional Intelligence* (1995). Goleman maintains that to predict an individual's

emotional intelligence A form of social intelligence that involves the ability to monitor one's own and others' feelings and emotions, to discriminate among them, and to use this information to guide one's thinking and action.

competence, performance on standardized intelligence tests matters less than emotional intelligence. In Goleman's view, emotional intelligence involves four main areas:

- *Developing emotional self-awareness* (such as the ability to separate feelings from actions)
- *Managing emotions* (such as being able to control anger)
- *Reading emotions* (such as taking the perspective of others)
- *Handling relationships* (such as the ability to solve relationship problems)

Some schools have programs that are designed to help children with their emotional lives. For example, one private school near San Francisco, the Nueva School, offers a class in what is called "self science," and the list of the class's contents echoes Goleman's definition of the components of emotional intelligence. The subject of self science is feelings—the child's own and those involved in relationships. Teachers speak to issues such as hurt over being left out, envy, and disagreements.

Coping with Stress An important aspect of children's lives is learning how to cope with stress. As children get older, they are able to more accurately appraise a stressful situation and determine how much control they have over it. Older children generate more coping alternatives to stressful conditions and use more cognitive coping strategies (Compas & others, 2001; Saarni, 1999; Saarni & others, 2006). For example, older children are better than younger children at intentionally shifting their thoughts to something that is less stressful. Older children are also better at reframing, or changing one's perception of a stressful situation. For example, younger children may be very disappointed that their teacher did not say hello to them when they arrived at school. Older children may reframe this type of situation and think, "She may have been busy with other things and just forgot to say hello."

By 10 years of age, most children are able to use these cognitive strategies to cope with stress (Saarni, 1999). However, in families that have not been supportive and are characterized by turmoil or trauma, children may be so overwhelmed by stress that they do not use such strategies.

The terrorist attacks on the World Trade Center in New York City and the Pentagon in Washington, D.C., on September 11, 2001, and hurricanes Katrina and Rita in August and September 2005, raised special concerns about how to help children cope with such stressful events. Children who have a number of coping techniques have the best chance of adapting and functioning competently in the face of traumatic events. Here are some recommendations for helping children cope with the stress of these types of events (Gurwitch & others, 2001, pp. 4–11):

- *Reassure children of their safety and security.* This may need to be done numerous times.
- *Allow children to retell events and be patient in listening to them.*
- *Encourage children to talk about any disturbing or confusing feelings.* Tell them that these are normal feelings after a stressful event.
- *Help children make sense of what happened.* Children may misunderstand what took place. For example, young children "may blame themselves, believe things happened that did not happen, believe that terrorists are in the school, etc. Gently help children develop a realistic understanding of the event" (p. 10).
- *Protect children from reexposure to frightening situations and reminders of the trauma.* This includes limiting conversations about the event in front of the children.

What are some effective strategies to help children cope with traumatic events, such as the terrorist attacks on the United States on 9/11/2001 and hurricane Katrina in September, 2005?

Traumatic events may cause individuals to think about the moral aspects of life. Hopelessness and despair may short-circuit moral development when a child is confronted by the violence of war zones and impoverished inner cities (Garbarino & others, 1992; Nadar, 2001). Let's further explore children's moral development.

Lawrence Kohlberg, the architect of a provocative cognitive developmental theory of moral development. *What is the nature of his theory?*

Kohlberg's Theory

preconventional reasoning The lowest level in Kohlberg's theory of moral development. The individual's moral reasoning is controlled primarily by external rewards and punishment.

heteronomous morality (Kohlberg's theory) Kohlberg's first stage in preconventional reasoning, in which moral thinking is tied to punishment.

individualism, instrumental purpose, and exchange The second Kohlberg stage of moral development. At this stage, individuals pursue their own interests but also let others do the same.

conventional reasoning The second, or intermediate, level in Kohlberg's theory of moral development. At this level, individuals abide by certain standards of others, such as parents or the laws of society.

mutual interpersonal expectations, relationships, and interpersonal conformity Kohlberg's third stage of moral development. At this stage, individuals value trust, caring, and loyalty to others as a basis of moral judgments.

Moral Development

Remember from chapter 9 our description of Piaget's view of moral development. Piaget proposed that younger children are characterized by heteronomous morality but that, by 10 years of age, they have moved into a higher stage called autonomous morality. According to Piaget, older children consider the intentions of the individual, believe that rules are subject to change, and are aware that punishment does not always follow wrongdoing.

A second major perspective on moral development was proposed by Lawrence Kohlberg (1958, 1986). Piaget's cognitive stages of development serve as the underpinnings for Kohlberg's theory, but Kohlberg suggested that there are six stages of moral development. These stages, he argued, are universal. Development from one stage to another, said Kohlberg, is fostered by opportunities to take the perspective of others and to experience conflict between one's current stage of moral thinking and the reasoning of someone at a higher stage.

Kohlberg arrived at his view after 20 years of using a unique interview with children. In the interview, children are presented with a series of stories in which characters face moral dilemmas. The following is the most popular Kohlberg dilemma:

> In Europe a woman was near death from a special kind of cancer. There was one drug that the doctors thought might save her. It was a form of radium that a druggist in the same town had recently discovered. The drug was expensive to make, but the druggist was charging ten times what the drug cost him to make. He paid $200 for the radium and charged $2,000 for a small dose of the drug. The sick woman's husband, Heinz, went to everyone he knew to borrow the money, but he could only get together $1,000 which is half of what it cost. He told the druggist that his wife was dying and asked him to sell it cheaper or let him pay later. But the druggist said, "No, I discovered the drug, and I am going to make money from it." So Heinz got desperate and broke into the man's store to steal the drug for his wife. (Kohlberg, 1969, p. 379)

This story is one of 11 that Kohlberg devised to investigate the nature of moral thought. After reading the story, the interviewee answers a series of questions about the moral dilemma. Should Heinz have stolen the drug? Was stealing it right or wrong? Why? Is it a husband's duty to steal the drug for his wife if he can get it no other way? Would a good husband steal? Did the druggist have the right to charge that much when there was no law setting a limit on the price? Why or why not?

The Kohlberg Stages Based on the answers interviewees gave for this and other moral dilemmas, Kohlberg described three levels of moral thinking, each of which is characterized by two stages (see figure 11.1).

Preconventional reasoning is the lowest level of moral reasoning, said Kohlberg. At this level, good and bad are interpreted in terms of external rewards and punishments.

- *Stage 1.* **Heteronomous morality** is the first stage in preconventional reasoning. At this stage, moral thinking is tied to punishment. For example, children think that they must obey because they fear punishment for disobedience.
- *Stage 2.* **Individualism, instrumental purpose, and exchange** is the second stage of preconventional reasoning. At this stage, individuals reason that pursuing their own interests is the right thing to do but they let others do the same. Thus, they think that what is right involves an equal exchange. They reason that if they are nice to others, others will be nice to them in return.

Conventional reasoning is the second, or intermediate, level in Kohlberg's theory of moral development. At this level, individuals apply certain standards, but they are the standards set by others, such as parents or the government.

- *Stage 3.* **Mutual interpersonal expectations, relationships, and interpersonal conformity** is Kohlberg's third stage of moral development. At this

LEVEL 1 Preconventional Level No Internalization	LEVEL 2 Conventional Level Intermediate Internalization	LEVEL 3 Postconventional Level Full Internalization
Stage 1 Heteronomous Morality *Children obey because adults tell them to obey. People base their moral decisions on fear of punishment.*	**Stage 3** Mutual Interpersonal Expectations, Relationships, and Interpersonal Conformity *Individuals value trust, caring, and loyalty to others as a basis for moral judgments.*	**Stage 5** Social Contract or Utility and Individual Rights *Individuals reason that values, rights, and principles undergird or transcend the law.*
Stage 2 Individualism, Purpose, and Exchange *Individuals pursue their own interests but let others do the same. What is right involves equal exchange.*	**Stage 4** Social System Morality *Moral judgments are based on understanding of the social order, law, justice, and duty.*	**Stage 6** Universal Ethical Principles *The person has developed moral judgments that are based on universal human rights. When faced with a dilemma between law and conscience, a personal, individualized conscience is followed.*

FIGURE 11.1 Kohlberg's Three Levels and Six Stages of Moral Development. Kohlberg argued that people everywhere develop their moral reasoning by passing through these age-based *stages*. *Where does Kohlberg's theory stand on the nature-nurture and continuity-discontinuity issues discussed in chapter 1?*

stage, individuals value trust, caring, and loyalty to others as a basis of moral judgments. Children and adolescents often adopt their parents' moral standards at this stage, seeking to be thought of by their parents as a "good girl" or a "good boy."

- *Stage 4.* **Social systems morality** is the fourth stage in Kohlberg's theory of moral development. At this stage, moral judgments are based on understanding the social order, law, justice, and duty. For example, adolescents may reason that in order for a community to work effectively, it needs to be protected by laws that are adhered to by its members.

Postconventional reasoning is the highest level in Kohlberg's theory of moral development. At this level, the individual recognizes alternative moral courses, explores the options, and then decides on a personal moral code.

- *Stage 5.* **Social contract or utility and individual rights** is the fifth Kohlberg stage. At this stage, individuals reason that values, rights, and principles undergird or transcend the law. A person evaluates the validity of actual laws, and social systems can be examined in terms of the degree to which they preserve and protect fundamental human rights and values.
- *Stage 6.* **Universal ethical principles** is the sixth and highest stage in Kohlberg's theory of moral development. At this stage, the person has developed a moral standard based on universal human rights. When faced with a conflict between law and conscience, the person reasons that conscience should be followed, even though the decision might bring risk.

Kohlberg believed that these levels and stages occur in a sequence and are age related: Before age 9, most children use level 1, preconventional reasoning based on external rewards and punishments, when they consider moral choices. By early adolescence, their moral reasoning is increasingly based on the application of standards set by others. Most adolescents reason at stage 3, with some signs of stages 2 and 4. By early adulthood, a small number of individuals reason in postconventional ways.

social systems morality The fourth stage in Kohlberg's theory of moral development. Moral judgments are based on understanding the social order, law, justice, and duty.

postconventional reasoning The highest level in Kohlberg's theory of moral development. At this level, the individual recognizes alternative moral courses, explores the options, and then decides on a personal moral code.

social contract or utility and individual rights The fifth Kohlberg stage. At this stage, individuals reason that values, rights, and principles undergird or transcend the law.

universal ethical principles The sixth and highest stage in Kohlberg's theory of moral development. Individuals develop a moral standard based on universal human

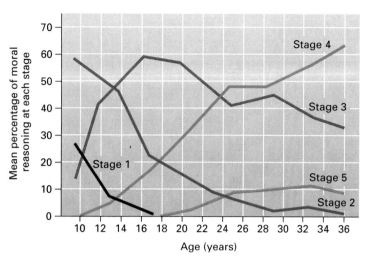

FIGURE 11.2 Age and the Percentage of Individuals at Each Kohlberg Stage. In one longitudinal study of males from 10 to 36 years of age, at age 10 most moral reasoning was at stage 2 (Colby & others, 1983). At 16 to 18 years of age, stage 3 became the most frequent type of moral reasoning, and it was not until the mid-twenties that stage 4 became the most frequent. Stage 5 did not appear until 20 to 22 years of age and it never characterized more than 10 percent of the individuals. In this study, the moral stages appeared somewhat later than Kohlberg envisioned and stage 6 was absent. *Do you think it matters that all of the participants in this study were males? Why or why not?*

What evidence supports this description of development? A 20-year longitudinal investigation found that use of stages 1 and 2 decreased with age (Colby & others, 1983) (see figure 11.2). Stage 4, which did not appear at all in the moral reasoning of 10-year-olds, was reflected in the moral thinking of 62 percent of the 36-year-olds. Stage 5 did not appear until age 20 to 22 and never characterized more than 10 percent of the individuals.

Thus, the moral stages appeared somewhat later than Kohlberg initially envisioned, and reasoning at the higher stages, especially stage 6, was rare. Although stage 6 has been removed from the Kohlberg moral judgment scoring manual, it still is considered to be theoretically important in the Kohlberg scheme of moral development.

Influences on the Kohlberg Stages What factors influence movement through Kohlberg' stages? Although moral reasoning at each stage presupposes a certain level of cognitive development, Kohlberg argued that advances in children's cognitive development did not ensure development of moral reasoning. Instead, moral reasoning also reflects children's experiences in dealing with moral questions and moral conflict.

Several investigators have tried to advance individuals' levels of moral development by having a model present arguments that reflect moral thinking one stage above the individuals' established levels. This approach applies the concepts of equilibrium and conflict that Piaget used to explain cognitive development. By presenting arguments slightly beyond the children's level of moral reasoning, the researchers created a disequilibrium that motivated the children to restructure their moral thought. The upshot of studies using this approach is that virtually any plus-stage discussion, for any length of time, seems to promote more advanced moral reasoning (Walker, 1982).

Kohlberg believed that peer interaction is a critical part of the social stimulation that challenges children to change their moral reasoning. Whereas adults characteristically impose rules and regulations on children, the give-and-take among peers gives children an opportunity to take the perspective of another person and to generate rules democratically. Kohlberg stressed that in principle, encounters with any peers can produce perspective-taking opportunities that may advance a child's moral reasoning.

Kohlberg's Critics Kohlberg's theory provoked debate, research, and criticism (Gibbs, 2003; Lapsley, 2006; Lapsley & Narvaez, 2004, 2006; Rest & others, 1999; Smetana, 2006; Turiel, 2006; Walker, 2004, 2006). Key criticisms involve the link between moral thought and moral behavior, the roles of culture and the family in moral development, and the significance of concern for others.

Moral Thought and Moral Behavior Kohlberg's theory has been criticized for placing too much emphasis on moral thought and not enough emphasis on moral behavior (Walker, 2004). Moral reasons can sometimes be a shelter for immoral behavior. Corrupt CEOs and politicians endorse the loftiest of moral virtues in public before their own behavior is exposed. Whatever the latest public scandal, you will probably find that the culprits displayed virtuous thoughts but engaged in immoral behavior. No one wants a nation of cheaters and thieves who can reason at the postconventional level. The cheaters and thieves may know what is right yet still do what is wrong. Heinous actions can be cloaked in a mantle of moral virtue.

The mantle of virtue is not necessarily a ruse; it is often taken on sincerely. Social cognitive theorist Albert Bandura (1999, 2002) argues that people usually do not engage in harmful conduct until they have justified the morality of their actions to themselves. Immoral conduct is made personally and socially acceptable by portraying it as serving socially worthy or moral purposes or even as doing God's will. Bandura provides the examples of Islamic extremists who mount jihad (holy war) against what they see as a tyrannical, decadent people seeking to enslave the Islamic world and antiabortion activists who bomb abortion clinics or murder doctors in order to discourage abortions.

Culture and Moral Reasoning Kohlberg emphasized that his stages of moral reasoning are universal, but some critics claim his theory is culturally biased (Banks, 1993; Miller, 2006; Shweder & others, 2006; Wainryb, 2006). Both Kohlberg and his critics may be partially correct.

One review of 45 studies in 27 cultures around the world, mostly non-European, provided support for the universality of Kohlberg's first four stages (Snarey, 1987). Individuals in diverse cultures developed through these four stages in sequence as Kohlberg predicted. Stages 5 and 6, however, were not found in all cultures. Furthermore, this review found that Kohlberg's scoring system does not recognize the higher-level moral reasoning of certain cultures and thus that moral reasoning is more culture-specific than Kohlberg envisioned (Snarey, 1987).

In particular, researchers had heard moral judgments based on the principles of communal equity and collective happiness in Israel, the unity and sacredness of all life forms in India, and collective moral responsibility in New Guinea (Snarey, 1987). These examples of moral reasoning would not be scored at the highest level in Kohlberg's system because they are not based on principles of justice. Similar results occurred in a study that assessed the moral development of 20 adolescent male Buddhist monks in Nepal (Huebner & Garrod, 1993). Justice, a basic theme in Kohlberg's theory, was not of paramount importance in the monks' moral views, and their concerns about the prevention of suffering and the role of compassion are not captured by Kohlberg's theory.

In sum, although Kohlberg's approach does capture much of the moral reasoning voiced in various cultures around the world, his approach misses or miscontrues some important moral concepts in particular cultures (Fang & others, 2003; Gibbs, 2003; Lapsley & Narvaez, 2004; Miller, 2006; Shweder & others, 2006; Wainryb, 2006).

Families and Moral Development Kohlberg argued that family processes are essentially unimportant in children's moral development. As noted earlier, he argued that parent-child relationships usually provide children with little opportunity for give-and-take or perspective taking. Rather, Kohlberg said that such opportunities are more likely to be provided by children's peer relations (Brabeck, 2000).

Did Kohlberg underestimate the contribution of family relationships to moral development? A number of developmentalists emphasize that *inductive discipline,* which uses reasoning and focuses children's attention on the consequences of their actions for others, positively influences moral development (Hoffman, 1970). They also stress that parents' moral values influence children's developing moral thoughts (Gibbs, 1993). Nonetheless, most developmentalists agree with Kohlberg, and Piaget, that peers play an important role in the development of moral reasoning.

Gender and the Care Perspective Perhaps the most publicized criticism of Kohlberg's theory has come from Carol Gilligan (1982, 1992, 1996), who argues that Kohlberg's theory reflects a gender bias. According to Gilligan, Kohlberg's theory is based on a male norm that puts abstract principles above relationships and concern for others and sees the individual as standing alone and independently making moral decisions. It puts justice at the heart of morality. In contrast to Kohlberg's

This 14-year-old boy in Nepal is thought to be the sixth holiest Buddhist in the world. *How might the moral reasoning of this boy be different than Kohlberg's theory predicts?*

Carol Gilligan is shown with some of the students she has interviewed about the importance of relationships in a female's development. *What is Gilligan's view of moral development?*

Gilligan's Care Perspective

justice perspective A moral perspective that focuses on the rights of the individual; individuals independently make moral decisions.

care perspective The moral perspective of Carol Gilligan, which views people in terms of their connectedness with others and emphasizes interpersonal communication, relationships with others, and concern for others.

social conventional reasoning Thoughts about social consensus and convention, in contrast to moral reasoning, which stresses ethical issues.

---

justice perspective, Gilligan argues for a **care perspective,** which is a moral perspective that views people in terms of their connectedness with others and emphasizes interpersonal communication, relationships with others, and concern for others. According to Gilligan, Kohlberg greatly underplayed the care perspective, perhaps because he was a male, because most of his research was with males rather than females, and because he used male responses as a model for his theory.

In extensive interviews with girls from 6 to 18 years of age, Gilligan and her colleagues found that girls consistently interpret moral dilemmas in terms of human relationships and base these interpretations on listening and watching other people (Gilligan, 1992, 1996; Gilligan & others, 2003). However, a meta-analysis (a statistical analysis that combines the results of many different studies) cast doubt on Gilligan's claim of substantial gender differences in moral judgment (Jaffee & Hyde, 2000). Overall, this analysis found only a small gender difference in care-based reasoning, and the difference was greater in adolescence than childhood. When differences in moral reasoning occurred, they were better explained by the nature of the dilemma than by gender. For example, both males and females tended to use care reasoning to deal with interpersonal dilemmas and justice reasoning to handle societal dilemmas.

Along with this lack of support for gender differences in moral reasoning, however, other research does find differences in how boys and girls tend to interpret situations (Eisenberg & Morris, 2004). In support of this idea, one recent study found that females rated prosocial dilemmas (those emphasizing altruism and helping) as more significant than males did (Wark & Krebs, in press). Another recent study revealed that young adolescent girls used more care-based reasoning about dating dilemmas than boys (Weisz & Black, 2002).

Social Conventional Reasoning   Some theorists and researchers argue that Kohlberg did not adequately distinguish between moral reasoning and social conventional reasoning (Smetana, 2006; Smetana & Turiel, 2003; Turiel, 1998, 2003, 2006; Lapsley, 2006; Lapsley & Narvaez, 2006). **Social conventional reasoning** focuses on conventional rules that have been established by social consensus in order to control behavior and maintain the social system. The rules themselves are arbitrary, such as using a fork at meals and raising your hand in class before speaking.

In contrast, moral reasoning focuses on ethical issues and rules of morality. Unlike conventional rules, moral rules are not arbitrary. They are obligatory, widely accepted, and somewhat impersonal (Turiel, 2006). Rules pertaining to lying, cheating, stealing, and physically harming another person are moral rules because violation of these rules affronts ethical standards that exist apart from social consensus and convention. Moral judgments involve concepts of justice, whereas social conventional judgments are concepts of social organization.

Prosocial Behavior   Whereas Kohlberg's and Gilligan's theories have focused primarily on the development of moral reasoning, the study of prosocial moral behavior has placed more emphasis on the behavioral aspects of moral development (Grusec, Davidov, & Lundell, 2002). Children engage in both immoral antisocial acts such as lying and cheating and prosocial moral behavior such as showing empathy or acting altruistically (Carlo, 2006; Eisenberg, Spinrad, & Sadovsky, 2006; Hoffman, 2002). Even during the preschool years children may care for others or comfort others in distress, but prosocial behavior occurs more often in adolescence than in childhood (Eisenberg & Fabes, 1998; Eisenberg & Morris, 2004).

William Damon (1988) described how sharing develops. During their first years, when children share, it is usually not for reasons of empathy but for the fun of the social play ritual or out of imitation. Then, at about 4 years of age, a combination of empathic awareness and adult encouragement produces a sense of obligation on the part of the child to share with others. Most 4-year-olds are not selfless saints, however. Children believe they have an obligation to share but do not necessarily think they should be as generous to others as they are to themselves.

Children's sharing comes to reflect a more complex sense of what is just and right during middle and late childhood. By the start of the elementary school years, children begin to express objective ideas about fairness (Eisenberg, Fabes, & Spinrad, 2006). It is common to hear 6-year-old children use the word *fair* as synonymous with *equal* or *same*. By the mid to late elementary school years, children believe that equity instead sometimes means that people with special merit or special needs deserve special treatment.

Missing from the factors that guide children's sharing is one that many adults might expect to be the most influential: the motivation to obey adult authority figures. Surprisingly, a number of studies have shown that adult authority has only a small influence on children's sharing (Eisenberg, 1982). Parental advice and prodding certainly foster standards of sharing, but the give-and-take of peer requests and arguments provides the most immediate stimulation of sharing.

Moral Personality   Beyond the development of moral reasoning and specific moral feelings and prosocial behaviors, do children also develop a pattern of moral characteristics that is distinctively their own? In other words, do children develop a *moral personality*, and if so, what are its components? Researchers have focused attention on three possible components: (1) moral identity, (2) moral character, and (3) moral exemplars:

How does children's sharing change from the preschool to the elementary school years?

- *Moral identity.* Individuals have a moral identity when moral notions and moral commitments are central to their lives (Blasi, 2005). They construct the self with reference to moral categories. Violating their moral commitment would place the integrity of their self at risk (Lapsley & Narvaez, 2006).
- *Moral character.* A person with moral character has the willpower, desires, and integrity to stand up to pressure, overcome distractions and disappointments, and behave morally. A person of good moral character displays moral virtues such as "honesty, truthfulness, and trustworthiness, as well as those of care, compassion, thoughtfulness, and considerateness. Other salient traits revolve around virtues of dependability, loyalty, and conscientiousness" (Walker, 2002, p. 74).
- *Moral exemplars.* Moral exemplars are people who have lived exemplary moral lives. Their moral personality, identity, character, and set of virtues reflect moral excellence and commitment.

In sum, moral development is a multifaceted, complex concept. Included in this complexity are their thoughts, feelings, behaviors, and personality.

Gender

Gilligan's claim that Kohlberg's theory of moral development reflects gender bias reminds us of the pervasive influence of gender on development. Long before elementary school, boys and girls show preferences for different toys and activities. As we discussed in chapter 9, preschool children display a gender identity and gender-typed behavior that reflects biological, cognitive, and social influences. Here we will examine gender stereotypes, gender similarities and differences, and gender-role classification.

Gender Stereotypes   According to the old ditty, boys are made of "frogs and snails" and girls are made of "sugar and spice and all that's nice." In the past, a well-adjusted boy was supposed to be independent, aggressive, and powerful. A well-adjusted girl was supposed to be dependent, nurturant, and uninterested in power. The masculine characteristics were considered to be healthy and good by society; the feminine characteristics were considered undesirable. These notions reflect **gender stereotypes,** which are broad categories that reflect general impressions and beliefs about females and males.

gender stereotypes Broad categories that reflect our impressions and beliefs about females and males.

What are little boys made of? Frogs and snails And puppy-dogs' tails. What are little girls made of? Sugar and spice And all that's nice.

—J. O. HALLIWELL
English Author, 19th Century

Researchers have found that gender stereotyping is extensive (Lenton & Blair, 2004; Ruble, Martin, & Berenbaum, 2006; Smith, 2007). In one far-ranging study of college students in 30 countries, males were widely believed to be dominant, independent, aggressive, achievement-oriented, and enduring, while females were widely believed to be nurturant, affiliative, less esteemed, and more helpful in times of distress (Williams & Best, 1982).

In a subsequent study, women and men who lived in more highly developed countries perceived themselves as more similar than women and men who lived in less developed countries (Williams & Best, 1989). In the more highly developed countries, the women were more likely to attend college and be gainfully employed. Thus, as sexual equality increases, male and female stereotypes, as well as actual behavioral differences, may diminish. In this study, the women were more likely to perceive similarity between the sexes than the men were (Williams & Best, 1989). And the sexes were perceived more similarly in the Christian than in the Muslim societies. Other research continues to find that gender stereotyping is pervasive (Arima, 2003; Best, 2001; Bigler, Averhart, & Liben, 2003).

Gender Similarities and Differences

What is the reality behind gender stereotypes? Let's examine some of the similarities and differences between the sexes, keeping in mind that (1) the differences are averages—not all females versus all males; (2) even when differences are reported, there is considerable overlap between the sexes; and (3) the differences may be due primarily to biological factors, sociocultural factors, or both. First, we will examine physical similarities and differences, and then we will turn to cognitive and socioemotional similarities and differences.

Physical Development   Women have about twice the body fat of men, most concentrated around breasts and hips. In males, fat is more likely to go to the abdomen. On the average, males grow to be 10 percent taller than females. Other physical differences are less obvious. From conception on, females have a longer life expectancy than males, and females are less likely than males to develop physical or mental disorders. Males have twice the risk of coronary disease as females.

Differences in hormones contribute to many of these physical differences between the sexes. Recall that androgens such as testosterone are male sex hormones and estrogens are female sex hormones, although both males and females produce androgens and estrogens. Male hormones promote the growth of long bones; female hormones stop such growth at puberty. Estrogen strengthens the immune system, making females more resistant to infection, for example. Female hormones also signal the liver to produce more "good" cholesterol, which makes females' blood vessels more elastic than males'. In contrast, testosterone triggers the production of low-density lipoprotein, which clogs blood vessels. Higher levels of stress hormones cause faster clotting in males, but also higher blood pressure than in females.

Does gender matter when it comes to brain structure and function? Human brains are much alike, whether the brain belongs to a male or a female (Halpern, 2001). However, researchers have found some differences in the brains of males and females (Goldstein & others, 2001; Kimura, 2000). Among the differences that have been discovered are:

- Female brains are smaller than male brains, but female brains have more folds; the larger folds (called convolutions) allow more surface brain tissue within the skulls of females than males (Luders & others, 2004).
- One part of the hypothalamus responsible for sexual behavior is larger in men than women (Swaab & others, 2001).
- Portions of the corpus callosum—the band of tissues through which the brain's two hemispheres communicate—is larger in females than males (LeVay, 1981).

- An area of the parietal lobe that functions in visuospatial skills is larger in males than females (Frederikse & others, 2000).
- The areas of the brain involved in emotional expression show more metabolic activity in females than males (Gur & others, 1995).

Cognitive Development   In a classic review of gender differences, Eleanor Maccoby and Carol Jacklin (1974) concluded that males have better math and visuospatial skills (the kinds of skills an architect needs to design a building's angles and dimensions), whereas females have better verbal abilities. Subsequently, Maccoby (1987) revised her conclusion about several gender dimensions. She said that the accumulation of research evidence now suggests that verbal differences between females and males have virtually disappeared but that the math and visuospatial differences still exist. For example, despite equal participation in the National Geography Bee, in most years all 10 finalists are boys (Liben, 1995).

Some experts in gender, such as Janet Shibley Hyde (2005, 2007; Hyde & Mezulis, 2001), suggest that the cognitive differences between females and males have been exaggerated. For example, there is considerable overlap in the distributions of female and male scores on math and visuospatial tasks (Halpern, 2006).

In a national study, boys did slightly better than girls did at math and science (National Assessment of Educational Progress, 2005). Overall, though, girls were far superior students, and they were significantly better than boys in reading (see figure 11.3). In another recent national study, females had better writing skills than males in grades 4, 8, and 12, with the gap widening as students progressed through school (Coley, 2001).

Socioemotional Development   Three areas of socioemotional development in which gender similarities and differences have been studied extensively are aggression, emotion, and prosocial behavior.

One of the most consistent gender differences is that boys are more physically aggressive than girls are. The difference occurs in all cultures and appears very early in children's development (Ostrov, Keating, & Ostrov, 2004; White, 2001). The physical aggression difference is especially pronounced when children are provoked. Both biological and environmental factors have been proposed to account for gender differences in aggression. Biological factors include heredity and hormones. Environmental factors include cultural expectations, adult and peer models, and social agents that reward aggression in boys and punish aggression in girls.

Although boys are consistently more physically aggressive than girls, might girls show as much or more verbal aggression, such as yelling, than boys? When verbal aggression is examined, gender differences often disappear; sometimes, though, verbal aggression is more pronounced in girls (Eagly & Steffen, 1986). Girls are much more likely than boys to engage in what is called *relational aggression*, which involves behaviors such as trying to make others dislike a certain child by spreading malicious rumors about the child or ignoring another child when angry at him or her (Crick, 2005; Crick & others, 2004; Underwood, 2003, 2004).

Are there gender differences in emotion? Beginning in the elementary school years, boys are more likely to hide their negative emotions, such as sadness, and girls are less likely to express disappointment that might hurt others' feelings (Eisenberg, Martin, & Fabes, 1996). Beginning in early adolescence, girls say they experience more sadness, shame, and guilt, and report more intense emotions, while boys are more likely to deny that they experience these emotions (Ruble, Martin, & Berenbaum, 2006). Males usually show less self-regulation of emotion than females, and this low self-control can translate into behavioral problems (Eisenberg & others, 2002). In one study, children's low self-regulation was linked with greater

"So according to the stereotype, you can put two and two together, but I can read the handwriting on the wall."

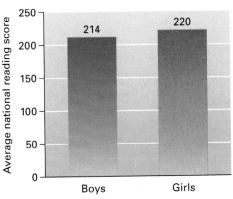

FIGURE 11.3 National Reading Scores for Fourth-Grade Boys and Girls. In the National Assessment of Educational Progress, data collected in 2005 indicated that girls did better in reading in the fourth grade (National Assessment of Educational Progress, 2005). For the eighth-grade students in this national assessment, the gender gap had widened (266 girls, 255 boys). The national assessment was scored on a scale from 0 to 500.

aggression, the teasing of others, overreaction to frustration, low cooperation, and inability to delay gratification (Block & Block, 1980).

Are there gender differences in prosocial behavior? Females view themselves as more prosocial and empathic (Eisenberg & Morris, 2004). Across childhood and adolescence, females engage in more prosocial behavior, (Eisenberg & Fabes, 1998; Eisenberg, Fabes, & Spinrad, 2006). The biggest gender difference occurs for kind and considerate behavior, with a smaller difference in sharing.

Earlier in the chapter, we discussed Carol Gilligan's theory that many females are more sensitive about relationships and have better relationship skills than males do. In chapter 15, "Socioemotional Development in Early Adulthood," we will further explore this area of gender.

Androgyny

Gender-Role Classification Not very long ago, it was accepted that boys should grow up to be masculine and girls to be feminine. In the 1970s, however, as both females and males became dissatisfied with the burdens imposed by their stereotypic roles, alternatives to femininity and masculinity were proposed. Instead of describing masculinity and femininity as a continuum in which more of one means less of the other, it was proposed that individuals could have both masculine and feminine traits.

This thinking led to the development of the concept of **androgyny,** the presence of positive masculine and feminine characteristics in the same person (Bem, 1977; Spence & Helmreich, 1978). The androgynous boy might be assertive (masculine) and nurturant (feminine). The androgynous girl might be powerful (masculine) and sensitive to others' feelings (feminine). Recent studies confirmed that societal changes are leading females to be more assertive (Spence & Buckner, 2000) and that sons were more androgynous than their fathers (Guastello & Guastello, 2003).

Gender experts, such as Sandra Bem, argue that androgynous individuals are more flexible, competent, and mentally healthy than their masculine or feminine counterparts. To some degree, though, which gender-role classification is best depends on the context involved. For example, in close relationships, feminine and androgynous orientations might be more desirable. One recent study found that girls and individuals high in femininity showed a stronger interest in caring than did boys and individuals high in masculinity (Karniol, Grosz, & Schorr, 2003). However, masculine and androgynous orientations might be more desirable in traditional academic and work settings because of the achievement demands in these contexts.

Despite talk about the "sensitive male," William Pollack (1999) argues that little has been done to change traditional ways of raising boys. He says that the "boy code" tells boys that they should show little if any emotion and should act tough. Boys learn the boy code in many contexts—sandboxes, playgrounds, schoolrooms, camps, hangouts. The result, according to Pollack, is a "national crisis of boyhood." Pollack and others suggest that boys would benefit from being socialized to express their anxieties and concerns and to better regulate their aggression.

Gender in Context Both the concept of androgeny and gender stereotypes talk about people in terms of personality traits such as "aggressive" or "caring." However, which traits people display may vary with the situation (Galambos, 2004). Thus, the nature and extent of gender differences may depend on the context.

Consider helping behavior. The stereotype is that females are better than males at helping. But it depends on the situation. Females are more likely than males to volunteer their time to help children with personal problems and to engage in caregiving behavior. However, in situations in which males feel a sense of competence and that involve danger, males are more likely than females to help (Eagly & Crowley, 1986). For example, a male is more likely than a female to stop and help a person stranded by the roadside with a flat tire. Indeed, one recent study documented that males are more likely to help when the context is masculine in nature (MacGeorge, 2003).

androgyny The presence of positive masculine and feminine characteristics in the same individual.

"She is emotional; he is not"—that is the master emotional stereotype. However, like differences in helping behavior, emotional differences in males and females depend on the particular emotion involved and the context in which it is displayed (Shields, 1991). Males are more likely to show anger toward strangers, especially male strangers, when they feel they have been challenged. Males also are more likely to turn their anger into aggressive action. Emotional differences between females and males often show up in contexts that highlight social roles and relationships. For example, females are more likely to discuss emotions in terms of relationships, and they are more likely to express fear and sadness.

The importance of considering gender in context is nowhere more apparent than when examining what is culturally prescribed behavior for females and males in different countries around the world (Denmark, Rabinowitz, & Sechzer, 2005; Gibbons, 2000). Although there has been greater acceptance of androgyny and similarities in male and female behavior in the United States, in many countries gender roles have remained gender-specific. For example, in many Middle Eastern countries, the division of labor between males and females is dramatic. Males are socialized and schooled to work in the public sphere, females in the private world of home and child rearing. For example, in Iran, the dominant view is that the man's duty is to provide for his family and the woman's is to care for her family and household. China also has been a male-dominant culture. Although women have made some strides in China, the male role is still dominant. Most males in China do not accept androgynous behavior and gender equity.

In China, females and males are usually socialized to behave, feel, and think differently. The old patriarchal traditions of male supremacy have not been completely uprooted. Chinese women still make considerably less money than Chinese men do, and, in rural China (such as here in the Lixian Village of Sichuan) male supremacy still governs many women's lives.

Review and Reflect • LEARNING GOAL 1

1 Discuss emotional and personality development in middle and late childhood

Review
- What changes take place in the self during the middle and late childhood years?
- How does emotion change during middle and late childhood?
- What is Kohlberg's theory of moral development and how has it been criticized? How do prosocial behavior and altruism develop during the middle and late childhood years?
- What are gender stereotypes, and what are some important gender differences?

Reflect
- A young man who had been sentenced to serve 10 years for selling a small amount of marijuana walked away from a prison camp six months after he was sent there. He is now in his fifties and has been a model citizen. Should he be sent back to prison? Why or why not? At which Kohlberg stage should your response be placed?

2 FAMILIES

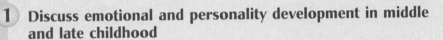

Parent-Child Issues   Stepfamilies   Latchkey Children

As children move into the middle and late childhood years, parents spend considerably less time with them. In one study, parents spent less than half as much time with their children aged 5 to 12 in caregiving, instruction, reading, talking, and playing as when the children were younger (Hill & Stafford, 1980). This drop in parent-child interaction may be even more extensive in families with little parental

What are some changes in the focus of parent-child relationships in middle and late childhood?

School-Family Linkages

education. Although parents spend less time with their children in middle and late childhood than in early childhood, parents continue to be extremely important in their children's lives. How do parent-child interactions typically change in middle and late childhood? How are elementary school children affected by living with stepparents or by being left on their own after school?

Parent–Child Issues

Parent-child interactions during early childhood focus on matters such as modesty, bedtime regularities, control of temper, fighting with siblings and peers, eating behavior and manners, autonomy in dressing, and attention seeking. Although some of these issues—fighting and reaction to discipline, for example—are carried forward into the elementary school years, many new issues appear by the age of 7 (Maccoby, 1984). These include whether children should be made to perform chores and, if so, whether they should be paid for them; how to help children learn to entertain themselves, rather than relying on parents for everything; and how to monitor children's lives outside the family in school and peer settings.

Compared with parents of preschool children, parents of elementary school children use less physical discipline. They are more likely to use deprivation of privileges, appeals to the child's self-esteem, comments designed to increase the child's sense of guilt, and statements that the child is responsible for his or her actions.

Discipline during middle and late childhood is often easier for parents than it was during early childhood; it may also be easier than during adolescence. In middle and late childhood, children's cognitive development has matured to the point that parents can reason with children about resisting deviation and controlling their behavior. By adolescence, children's reasoning has become more sophisticated, and they may push more strongly for independence, which contributes to parenting difficulties.

During middle and late childhood, some control is transferred from parent to child. The process is gradual, and it produces *coregulation* rather than control by either the child or the parent alone. Parents continue to exercise general supervision and control, while children are allowed to engage in moment-to-moment self-regulation. The major shift to autonomy does not occur until about the age of 12 or later. School-related matters are especially important for families during middle and late childhood (Collins, Madsen, & Susman-Stillman, 2002). School-related difficulties are the number one reason that children in this age group are referred for clinical help. Children must learn to relate to adults outside the family on a regular basis—adults who interact with the child much differently than parents. During middle and late childhood, interactions with adults outside the family involve more formal control and achievement orientation.

Stepfamilies

Not only has divorce become commonplace in the United States, so has getting remarried (Dunn & others, 2001; Marsiglio, 2004). It takes time for parents to marry, have children, get divorced, and then remarry. Consequently, there are far more elementary and secondary school children than infant or preschool children living in stepfamilies.

The number of remarriages involving children has grown steadily in recent years. Also, divorces occur at a 10 percent higher rate in remarriages than in first marriages (Cherlin & Furstenberg, 1994). About half of all children whose parents divorce will have a stepparent within four years of the separation.

Remarried parents face some unique tasks. The couple must define and strengthen their marriage and at the same time renegotiate the biological parent-child relationships and establish stepparent-stepchild and stepsibling relationships (Coleman, Ganong, & Fine, 2004). The complex histories and multiple relationships make adjustment difficult in a stepfamily (Hetherington & Stanley-Hagan, 2002). Only one-third of stepfamily couples stay remarried.

In some cases, the stepfamily may have been preceded by the death of a spouse. However, by far the largest number of stepfamilies are preceded by divorce rather than death (Pasley & Moorefield, 2004). Three common types of stepfamily structure are (1) stepfather, (2) stepmother, and (3) blended or complex. In stepfather families, the mother typically had custody of the children and remarried, introducing a stepfather into her children's lives. In stepmother families, the father usually had custody and remarried, introducing a stepmother into his children's lives. In a blended or complex stepfamily, both parents bring children from previous marriages to live in the newly formed stepfamily.

Children often have better relationships with their custodial parents (mothers in stepfather families, fathers in stepmother families) than with stepparents (Santrock, Sitterle, & Warshak, 1988). Also, children in simple families (stepmother, stepfather) often show better adjustment than their counterparts in complex (blended) families (Anderson & others, 1999; Hetherington & Kelly, 2002).

As in divorced families, children in stepfamilies show more adjustment problems than children in nondivorced families (Hetherington, Bridges, & Insabella, 1998; Hetherington & Kelly, 2002). The adjustment problems are similar to those found among children of divorced parents—academic problems and lower self-esteem, for example (Anderson & others, 1999). However, it is important to recognize that a majority of children in stepfamilies do not have problems. In one recent analysis, 25 percent of children from stepfamilies showed adjustment problems compared to 10 percent in intact, never-divorced families (Hetherington & Kelly, 2002; Hetherington & Stanley-Hagan, 2002).

Adolescence is an especially difficult time for the formation of a stepfamily (Anderson & others, 1999). This may occur because becoming part of a stepfamily exacerbates normal adolescent concerns about identity, sexuality, and autonomy.

How does living in a stepfamily influence a child's development?

Stepfamilies
Stepfamily Resources
Stepfamily Support

Latchkey Children

We concluded in chapter 9 that when both parents work outside the home it does not necessarily have negative outcomes for their children. However, the subset of children sometimes called "latchkey children" deserves further scrutiny. These children are given the key to their home, take the key to school, and then use it to let themselves into the home while their parents are still at work. Latchkey children are largely unsupervised for two to four hours a day during each school week. During the summer months, they might be unsupervised for entire days, five days a week.

How do latchkey children handle the lack of limits and structure during the latchkey hours? In one study, researchers interviewed more than 1,500 latchkey children (Long & Long, 1983). They concluded that a slight majority of these children had had negative latchkey experiences. Some latchkey children may grow up too fast, hurried by the responsibilities placed on them. Without limits and parental supervision, latchkey children find their way into trouble more easily, possibly stealing, vandalizing, or abusing a sibling. Ninety percent of the juvenile delinquents in Montgomery County, Maryland, are latchkey children. Joan Lipsitz (1983), in testifying before the Select Committee on Children, Youth, and Families, called the lack of adult supervision of children in the after-school hours a major problem. Lipsitz called it the "three-to-six o'clock problem" because it was during this time that the Center for Early Adolescence in North Carolina, when Lipsitz was director, experienced a peak of referrals for clinical help.

Although latchkey children may be vulnerable to problems, the experiences of latchkey children vary enormously, as do the experiences of all children with working parents (Belle, 1999; Morris & Kalil, 2006). Parents need to give special attention to the ways in which their latchkey children's lives can be effectively monitored (Huston & Ripke, 2006). Variations in latchkey experiences suggest that parental monitoring and authoritative parenting help the child cope more effectively with latchkey experiences, especially in resisting peer pressure (Galambos & Maggs, 1989; Steinberg, 1986).

For parents who work, are there good alternatives to allowing their school-children to be home by themselves after school? One recent study of 819 10- to 14-year-olds found that out-of-home care, whether supervised or unsupervised, was

What are some strategies parents can adopt that benefit latchkey children?

linked to delinquency, drug and alcohol use, and school problems (Coley, Morri, & Hernandez, 2004). Other research, however, found more positive outcomes for children in some after-school programs. In one study, attending a formal after-school program that included academic, recreational, and remedial activities was associated with better academic achievement and social adjustment, in comparison with other types of after-school care such as informal adult supervision or with self-care (Posner & Vandell, 1994).

Participation in five types of out-of-school care (before- and after-school programs, extracurricular activities, father care, and nonadult care—usually an older sibling) was examined in one recent study to determine their possible link with children's academic achievement toward the end of the first grade (NICHD Early Child Care Research Network, 2004). "Children who consistently participated in extracurricular activities during kindergarten and first grade obtained higher standardized math test scores than children who did not consistently participate in these activities. Participation in other types of out-of-school care was not related to child functioning in the first grade" (p. 280). These results, however, might reflect a difference among the parents of children in different programs. Parents who enroll their children in extracurricular activities may be more achievement-oriented and have higher achievement expectations for their children than parents who don't place their children in these activities.

A recent study found that low-income parents were especially dissatisfied with the quality of options available in after-school programs (The Wallace Foundation, 2004). Practitioners and policymakers recommend that after-school programs have warm and supportive staff, a flexible and relaxed schedule, multiple activities, and opportunities for positive interactions with staff and peers (Pierce, Hamm, & Vandell, 1997).

Review and Reflect • LEARNING GOAL 2

2 **Describe parent-child issues and societal changes in families**

Review
- What are some important parent-child issues in middle and late childhood?
- How does being in a stepfamily influence children's development?
- How are children likely to be affected by being left on their own after school?

Reflect
- What was your relationship with your parents like when you were in elementary school? How do you think it influenced your development?

3 PEERS

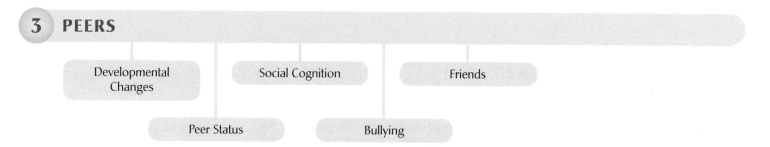

Developmental Changes

Social Cognition

Friends

Peer Status

Bullying

During middle and late childhood the amount of time children spend in peer interaction increases. Children play games with peers, function in groups, and cultivate friendships. First, we will discuss how relations with peers change during middle and late childhood. We then examine variations in how children relate to their peers, such as the characteristics of popular children and of children who are bullied, before turning to the important role that friends play in children's lives.

Developmental Changes

As children enter the elementary school years, reciprocity becomes especially important in peer interchanges. Researchers estimate that the percentage of time spent in social interaction with peers increases from approximately 10 percent at 2 years of age to more than 30 percent in middle and late childhood (Rubin, Bukowski, & Parker, 2006). In one early study, a typical day in elementary school included approximately 300 episodes with peers (Barker & Wright, 1951). As children move through middle and late childhood, the size of their peer group increases, and peer interaction is less closely supervised by adults (Rubin, Bukowski, & Parker, 2006). Until about 12 years of age, children's preference for same-sex groups increases.

What are some statuses that children have with their peers?

Peer Status

Which children are likely to be popular with their peers and which ones are disliked? Developmentalists address this and similar questions by examining *sociometric status*, a term that describes the extent to which children are liked or disliked by their peer group (Cillessen & Mayeux, 2004; Ladd 2006). Sociometric status is typically assessed by asking children to rate how much they like or dislike each of their classmates. Or it may be assessed by asking children to nominate the children they like the most and those they like the least.

Developmentalists have distinguished five peer statuses (Wentzel & Asher, 1995):

- **Popular children** are frequently nominated as a best friend and are rarely disliked by their peers.
- **Average children** receive an average number of both positive and negative nominations from their peers.
- **Neglected children** are infrequently nominated as a best friend but are not disliked by their peers.
- **Rejected children** are infrequently nominated as someone's best friend and are actively disliked by their peers.
- **Controversial children** are frequently nominated both as someone's best friend and as being disliked.

Popular children have a number of social skills that contribute to their being well liked. They give out reinforcements, listen carefully, maintain open lines of communication with peers, are happy, control their negative emotions, act like themselves, show enthusiasm and concern for others, and are self-confident without being conceited (Hartup, 1983; Rubin, Bukowski, & Parker, 1998).

Neglected children engage in low rates of interaction with their peers and are often described as shy by peers. The goal of many training programs for neglected children is to help them attract attention from their peers in positive ways and to hold that attention by asking questions, by listening in a warm and friendly way, and by saying things about themselves that relate to the peers' interests. They also are taught to enter groups more effectively.

Rejected children often have more serious adjustment problems than those who are neglected (Coie, 2004; Ladd, 2006; Parker & Asher, 1987; Sandstrom & Zakriski, 2004). One recent study found that in kindergarten, children who were rejected by their peers were less likely to engage in classroom participation, more likely to express a desire to avoid school, and more likely to report being lonely than children who were accepted by their peers (Buhs & Ladd, 2001). The combination of being rejected by peers and being aggressive forecasts problems. One study evaluated 112 fifth-grade boys over a period of 7 years until the end of high school

popular children Children who are frequently nominated as a best friend and are rarely disliked by their peers.

average children Children who receive an average number of both positive and negative nominations from peers.

neglected children Children who are infrequently nominated as a best friend but are not disliked by their peers.

rejected children Children who are infrequently nominated as a best friend and are actively disliked by their peers.

controversial children Children who are frequently nominated both as someone's best friend and as being disliked.

(Kupersmidt & Coie, 1990). The best predictor of whether rejected children would engage in delinquent behavior or drop out of school later during adolescence was aggression toward peers in elementary school. Another recent study found that when third-grade boys were highly aggressive and rejected by their peers, they showed markedly higher levels of delinquency as adolescents and young adults than other boys (Miller-Johnson, Coie, & Malone, 2003).

John Coie (2004, pp. 252–253) provided three reasons why aggressive peer-rejected boys have problems in social relationships:

- "First, the rejected, aggressive boys are more impulsive and have problems sustaining attention. As a result, they are more likely to be disruptive of ongoing activities in the classroom and in focused group play.
- Second, rejected, aggressive boys are more emotionally reactive. They are aroused to anger more easily and probably have more difficulty calming down once aroused. Because of this they are more prone to become angry at peers and attack them verbally and physically . . .
- Third, rejected children have fewer social skills in making friends and maintaining positive relationships with peers."

Not all rejected children are aggressive (Ladd, 2006; Rubin, Bukowski, & Parker, 2006; Hymel, McDougall, & Renshaw, 2004). Although aggression and its related characteristics of impulsiveness and disruptiveness underlie rejection about half the time, approximately 10 to 20 percent of rejected children are shy.

How can rejected children be trained to interact more effectively with their peers? Rejected children may be taught to more accurately assess whether the intentions of their peers are negative (Bierman, 2004). They may be asked to engage in role playing or to discuss hypothetical situations involving negative encounters with peers, such as when a peer cuts into a line ahead of them. In some programs, children are shown videotapes of appropriate peer interaction and asked to draw lessons from what they have seen (Ladd, Buhs, & Troop, 2004).

One recent social-skills intervention program was successful in increasing social acceptance and self-esteem and decreasing depression and anxiety in peer-rejected children (DeRosier & Marcus, 2005). Students participated in the program once a week (50 to 60 minutes) for eight weeks. The program included instruction in how to manage emotions, how to improve prosocial skills, how to become better communicators, and how to compromise and negotiate.

Social Cognition

A boy accidentally trips and knocks another boy's soft drink out of his hand. That boy misinterprets the encounter as hostile, which leads him to retaliate aggressively against the boy who tripped. Through repeated encounters of this kind, the aggressive boy's classmates come to perceive him as habitually acting in inappropriate ways.

This encounter demonstrates the importance of *social cognition*—thoughts about social matters, such as the aggressive boy's interpretation of an encounter as hostile and his classmates' perception of his behavior as inappropriate (Lewis & Carpendale, 2004). Children's social cognition about their peers becomes increasingly important for understanding peer relationships in middle and late childhood. Of special interest are the ways in which children process information about peer relations and their social knowledge (Dodge, 2000; Dodge, Coie, & Lynam, 2006; Gifford-Smith & Rabiner, 2004).

Kenneth Dodge (1983) argues that children go through five steps in processing information about their social world. They decode social cues, interpret, search for a response, select an optimal response, and enact. Dodge has found that aggressive boys are more likely to perceive another child's actions as hostile when the child's intention is ambiguous. And, when aggressive boys search for cues to determine a peer's intention, they respond more rapidly, less efficiently, and less reflectively than do nonaggressive children. These are among the social cognitive factors believed to be involved in children's conflicts.

Social knowledge also is involved in children's ability to get along with peers. They need to know what goals to pursue in poorly defined or ambiguous situations, how to initiate and maintain a social bond, and what scripts to follow to get other children to be their friends. For example, as part of the script for getting friends, it helps to know that saying nice things, regardless of what the peer does or says, will make the peer like the child more.

Bullying

Significant numbers of students are victimized by bullies (DeRosier & Marcus, 2005; Espelage & Swearer, 2004; Evertson & Weinstein, 2006; Roberts, 2005; Snell & Hirschstein, 2005). In one national survey of more than 15,000 sixth- through tenth-grade students, nearly one of every three students said that they had experienced occasional or frequent involvement as a victim or perpetrator in bullying (Nansel & others, 2001). In this study, bullying was defined as verbal or physical behavior intended to disturb someone less powerful. As shown in figure 11.4, being belittled about looks or speech was the most frequent type of bullying.

Who is likely to be bullied? In the study just described, boys and younger middle school students were most likely to be affected (Nansel & others, 2001). Children who said they were bullied reported more loneliness and difficulty in making friends, while those who did the bullying were more likely to have low grades and to smoke and drink alcohol. Researchers have found that anxious, socially withdrawn, and aggressive children are often the victims of bullying (Hanish & Guerra, 2004). Anxious and socially withdrawn children may be victimized because they are nonthreatening and unlikely to retaliate if bullied while aggressive children may be the targets of bullying because their behavior is irritating to bullies (Rubin, Bukowski, & Parker, 2006).

What are the outcomes of bullying? A recent study of 9- to 12-year-old children in the Netherlands found that the victims of bullies had a much higher incidence of headaches, sleeping problems, abdominal pain, tiredness, and depression than children not involved in bullying behavior (Fekkes, Pijpers, & Verloove-Vanhorick, 2004). A study of U.S. sixth-grade students examined three groups: bullies, victims, and those who were both bullies and victims (Juvonen, Graham, & Schuster, 2003). Bully-victims were the most troubled group, displaying the highest level of conduct, school, and relationship problems. Despite increased conduct problems, bullies enjoyed the highest standing of the three groups among their classmates. To read further about bullying, see the Research in Life-Span Development interlude.

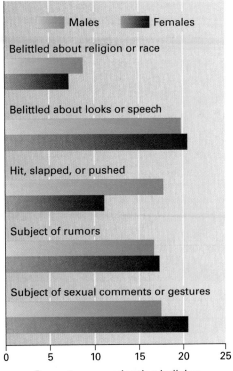

FIGURE 11.4 Bullying Behaviors Among U.S. Youth. This graph shows the type of bullying most often experienced by U.S. youth. The percentages reflect the extent to which bullied students said that they had experienced a particular type of bullying. In terms of gender, note that when they were bullied, boys were more likely to be hit, slapped, or pushed than girls were.

Reducing Bullying

RESEARCH IN LIFE-SPAN DEVELOPMENT

Aggressive Victims, Passive Victims, and Bullies

One recent study examined the extent to which aggressive victims (who provoke their peers and respond to threats or attacks with reactive aggression), passive victims (who submit to aggressors' demands), and bullies (who act aggressively toward their peers but are rarely attacked in return) showed different developmental pathways (Hanish & Guerra, 2004). The children were assessed initially in the fourth grade and then again in the sixth grade.

Peer sociometric ratings were used to identify children as aggressive victims, passive victims, bullies, uninvolved, and average. Each child received a booklet containing randomized lists (separated by gender) of the names of all children in the

What are some characteristics of bullying? What are some strategies to reduce bullying?

class. The children were asked to mark all peers' names that were applicable to certain questions. The questions included items that assessed aggression and victimization, such as "Who starts a fight over nothing?" and "Who are the children who are getting picked on?"

The results indicated that "aggressive victims became less prevalent and passive victims and bullies became more prevalent with age. Although it was common for aggressive victims and bullies to move from one group to the other across time, there was little overlap with the passive victim group" (p. 17).

To reduce bullying, teachers and schools can (Cohn & Canter, 2003; Hyman & others, 2006; Limber, 1997, 2004; Milsom & Gallo, 2006):

- Get older peers to serve as monitors for bullying and intervene when they see it taking place.
- Develop school-wide rules and sanctions against bullying and post them throughout the school.
- Form friendship groups for children and youth who are regularly bullied by peers.
- Be aware that bullying often occurs outside the classroom, so school personnel may not actually see it taking place. Also, many victims of bullying don't report the bullying to adults. Unsupervised areas such as the playground, bus, and school corridors are common places where students are bullied. If bullying is observed in a classroom or in other locations, a decision needs to be made about whether it is serious enough to report to school authorities or parents.
- Incorporate the message of the antibullying program into places of worship, school, and other community activities where children and youth are involved.
- Encourage parents to reinforce their children's positive behaviors and model appropriate interpersonal interactions.
- Identify bullies and victims early and use social skills training to improve their behavior. Teaching empathy, especially perspective taking, promoting self-control, and training social skills have been found to reduce the negative behavior of bullies (Macklem, 2003). Researchers have also found that when victims of bullying develop assertiveness skills, bullying is reduced (Kaiser & Raminsky, 2003; Macklem, 2003). They also have documented that improving students' social skills, including friendship skills and how to approach people, can reduce a victim's chances of being bullied (Rigby, 2002).

Friends

"My best friend is nice. She is honest and I can trust her. I can tell her my innermost secrets and know that nobody else will find out about them. I have other friends, but she is my best friend. We consider each other's feelings and don't want to hurt each other. We help each other out when we have problems. We make up funny names for people and laugh ourselves silly. We make lists of which boys we think are the ugliest, which are the biggest jerks, and so on. Some of these things we share with other friends, some we don't." This is a description of a friendship by a 10-year-old girl. It demonstrates that children are interested in specific peers—not just any peers. They want to share concerns, interests, information, and secrets with them.

Like adult friendships, children's friendships are typically characterized by similarity. Throughout childhood, friends are more similar than dissimilar in terms of age, sex, race, and many other factors. Friends often have similar attitudes toward school, similar educational aspirations, and closely aligned achievement orientations.

Why are children's friendships important? Willard Hartup (1996, 2000; Hartup & Abecassis, 2004) has studied peer relations and friendship for more than three decades. He recently concluded that friends can be cognitive and emotional resources from childhood through old age. Friends can foster self-esteem and a sense of well-being.

More specifically, children's friendships can serve six functions (Gottman & Parker, 1987):

- *Companionship.* Friendship provides children with a familiar partner and play-mate, someone who is willing to spend time with them and join in collaborative activities.
- *Stimulation.* Friendship provides children with interesting information, excitement, and amusement.
- *Physical support.* Friendship provides time, resources, and assistance.
- *Ego support.* Friendship provides the expectation of support, encouragement, and feedback, which helps children maintain an impression of themselves as competent, attractive, and worthwhile individuals.
- *Social comparison.* Friendship provides information about where the child stands vis-à-vis others and whether the child is doing okay.
- *Affection and intimacy.* Friendship provides children with a warm, close, trusting relationship with another individual. **Intimacy in friendships** is characterized by self-disclosure and the sharing of private thoughts. Research reveals that intimate friendships may not appear until early adolescence (Berndt & Perry, 1990).

What are some functions of friendship?

Although having friends can be a developmental advantage, not all friendships are alike (Bagwell, 2004). People differ in the company they keep—that is, who their friends are. Developmental advantages occur when children have friends who are socially skilled and supportive. However, it is not developmentally advantageous to have coercive and conflict-ridden friendships (Berndt, 2002; Rubin, Bukowski, & Parker, 2006).

The importance of friendship was recently underscored in a two-year longitudinal study (Wentzel, Barry, & Caldwell, 2004). Sixth-grade students who did not have a friend engaged in less prosocial behavior (cooperation, sharing, helping others), had lower grades, and were more emotionally distressed (depression, low well-being) than their counterparts who had one or more friends. Two years later, in the eighth grade, the students who did not have a friend in the sixth grade were still more emotionally distressed.

Review and Reflect • LEARNING GOAL 3

3 **Identify changes in peer relationships in middle and late childhood**

Review
- What developmental changes characterize peer relations in middle and late childhood?
- How does children's peer status influence their development?
- How is social cognition involved in children's peer relations?
- What is the nature of bullying?
- What are children's friendships like?

Reflect
- If you were a school principal, what would you do to reduce bullying in your school?

intimacy in friendships Self-disclosure and the sharing of private thoughts.

4 SCHOOLS

Contemporary Approaches to Student Learning	Socioeconomic Status and Ethnicity	Cross-Cultural Comparisons of Achievement

For most children, entering the first grade signals a change from being a "home-child" to being a "schoolchild." They take up a new role (being a student) and experience new obligations. They develop new relationships and develop new standards by which to judge themselves. School provides children with a rich source of new ideas to shape their sense of self. The children will spend many years in schools as members of small societies in which there are tasks to be accomplished, people to be socialized and socialized by, and rules that define and limit behavior, feelings, and attitudes. By the time students graduate from high school, they have spent 12,000 hours in the classroom. In short, it is justifiable to be concerned about the impact of schools on children.

www.mhhe.com/santrockld11

Pathways to School Improvement

Contemporary Approaches to Student Learning

Controversy swirls about the best way to teach children and how to hold schools and teachers accountable for whether children are learning.

Constructivist and Direct Instruction Approaches The **constructivist approach** is a learner-centered approach that emphasizes the importance of individuals actively constructing their knowledge and understanding with guidance from the teacher. In the constructivist view, teachers should not attempt to simply pour information into children's minds. Rather, children should be encouraged to explore their world, discover knowledge, reflect, and think critically with careful monitoring and meaningful guidance from the teacher (Eby, Herrell, & Jordan, 2006; Eggen & Kauchak, 2006; Morrison, 2006). The constructivist belief is that for too long in American education children have been required to sit still, be passive learners, and rotely memorize irrelevant as well as relevant information (Henson, 2004; Silberman, 2006).

Today, constructivism may include an emphasis on collaboration—children working with each other in their efforts to know and understand (Pontecorvo, 2004). A teacher with a constructivist instructional philosophy would not have children memorize information rotely but would give them opportunities to meaningfully construct the knowledge and understand the material while guiding their learning (Ornstein, Lasley, & Mindes, 2005).

Is this classroom more likely constructivist or direct instruction? Explain.

Consider an elementary school classroom that is investigating a school bus (Katz & Chard, 1989). The children write to the district's school superintendent and ask if they can have a bus parked at their school for a few days. They study the bus, discover the functions of its parts, and discuss traffic rules. Then, in the classroom, they build their own bus out of cardboard. The children are having fun, but they also are practicing writing, problem solving, and even some arithmetic. When the class has their parents' night, all that the parents want to see is the bus because their children have been talking about it at home for weeks. Many education experts believe that this is the kind of education all children deserve. That is, they believe that children should be active, constructivist learners and taught through concrete, hands-on experience.

By contrast, the **direct instruction approach** is a structured, teacher-centered approach that is characterized by teacher direction and control, high teacher expectations for students' progress, maximum time spent by students on academic tasks,

constructivist approach A learner-centered approach that emphasizes the importance of individuals actively constructing their knowledge and understanding with guidance from the teacher.

direct instruction approach A structured, teacher-centered approach that is characterized by teacher direction and control, mastery of academic skills, high expectations for students' progress, maximum time spent on learning tasks, and efforts to keep negative affect to a minimum.

and efforts by the teacher to keep negative affect to a minimum. An important goal in the direct instruction approach is maximizing student learning time.

Advocates of the constructivist approach argue that the direct instruction approach turns children into passive learners and does not adequately challenge them to think in critical and creative ways (Duffy & Kirkley, 2004). The direct instruction enthusiasts say that the constructivist approaches do not give enough attention to the content of a discipline, such as history or science. They also believe that the constructivist approaches are too relativistic and vague.

Some experts in educational psychology believe that many effective teachers use both a constructivist *and* a direct instruction approach rather than either exclusively (Darling-Hammond & Bransford, 2005; Schwartz & others, 1999). Further, some circumstances may call more for a constructivist approach, others for a direct instruction approach. For example, experts increasingly recommend an explicit, intellectually engaging direct instruction approach when teaching students with a reading or a writing disability (Berninger, 2006).

Accountability Since the 1990s, the U.S. public and governments at every level have demanded increased accountability from schools. One result was the spread of state-mandated tests to measure just what students had or had not learned (Hambleton, 2002; Houston, 2005; Lewis, 2005). Many states identified objectives for students in their state and created tests to measure whether students were meeting those objectives. This approach became national policy in 2002 when the No Child Left Behind (NCLB) legislation was signed into law.

Advocates argue that statewide standardized testing will have a number of positive effects. These include improved student performance; more time teaching the subjects that are tested; high expectations for all students; identification of poorly performing schools, teachers, and administrators; and improved confidence in schools as test scores rise.

Most educators support high expectations and high standards for students (Revelle, 2004). At issue, however, is whether the tests and procedures mandated by NCLB are the best ones for achieving high standards (Kubrick & McLaughlin, 2005).

What are some issues involved in the No Child Left Behind legislation?

Critics argue that the NCLB legislation will do more harm than good (Ambrosio, 2004; Fair Test, 2004; Goldberg, 2005; Lewis, 2005). One criticism stresses that using a single test as the sole indicator of students' progress and competence presents a very narrow view of students' skills. This criticism is similar to the one leveled at IQ tests, which we described in chapter 10. To assess student progress and achievement, many psychologists and educators emphasize that a number of measures should be used, including tests, quizzes, projects, portfolios, classroom observations, and so on. Also, the tests used as part of NCLB don't measure creativity, motivation, persistence, flexible thinking, and social skills (Droege, 2004). Critics point out that teachers end up spending far too much class time "teaching to the test" by drilling students and having them memorize isolated facts at the expense of teaching that focuses on thinking skills, which students need for success in life. Despite such criticisms, most U.S. schools are making accommodations to meet the requirements of NCLB.

Socioeconomic Status and Ethnicity

Children from low-income, ethnic minority backgrounds have more difficulties in school than do their middle-socioeconomic-status, White counterparts. Why? Critics argue that schools have not done a good job of educating low-income, ethnic minority students to overcome the barriers to their achievement (Cooter, 2004; Scott-Jones, 1995). Let's further explore the roles of socioeconomic status and ethnicity in schools.

The Education of Students from Low-Income Backgrounds

Many children in poverty face problems that present barriers to their learning (Diaz, Pelletier, & Provenzo, 2006; Ryan, Fauth, & Brooks-Gunn, 2006). They might have parents who don't set high educational standards for them, who are incapable of reading to them, and who don't have enough money to pay for educational materials and experiences, such as books and trips to zoos and museums. They might be malnourished and live in areas where crime and violence are a way of life.

Compared with schools in higher-income areas, schools in low-income areas are more likely to have more students with low achievement test scores, low graduation rates, and small percentages of students going to college; they are more likely to have young teachers with less experience; and they are more likely to encourage rote learning (McLoyd, Aikens, & Burton, 2006; Spring, 2007). Too few schools in low-income neighborhoods provide students with environments that are conducive to learning (Tozer, Senese, & Violas, 2005). Many of the schools' buildings and classrooms are old and crumbling.

Ethnicity in Schools   More than one third of all African American and almost one third of all Latino students attend schools in the 47 largest city school districts in the United States, compared with only 5 percent of all White and 22 percent of all Asian American students. Many of these inner-city schools are still segregated, are grossly underfunded, and do not provide adequate opportunities for children to learn effectively. Thus, the effects of SES and the effects of ethnicity are often intertwined.

In a recent book, *The Shame of the Nation,* Jonathan Kozol (2005) described his visits to 60 U.S. schools in low-income areas of cities in 11 states. He saw many schools in which the minority population was 80 to 90 percent, concluding that school segregation is still present for many poor minority students. Kozol saw many of the inequities just summarized—unkempt classrooms, hallways, and restrooms; inadequate textbooks and supplies; and lack of resources. He also saw teachers mainly instructing students to rotely memorize material, especially as preparation for mandated tests, rather than engage in higher-level thinking. Kozol also frequently observed teachers using threatening disciplinary tactics to control the classroom.

Even outside of inner-city schools, school segregation remains a factor in U.S. education. Almost one third of all African American and Latino students attend schools in which 90 percent or more of the students are from minority groups (Banks, 2003, 2006).

The school experiences of students from different ethnic groups vary considerably (Bennett, 2007; Cushner, 2006; Spring, 2006, 2007; Pang, 2005; Spencer, 2006). African American and Latino students are much less likely than non-Latino White or Asian American students to be enrolled in academic, college preparatory programs and are much more likely to be enrolled in remedial and special education programs. Asian American students are far more likely than other ethnic minority groups to take advanced math and science courses in high school. African American students are twice as likely as Latinos, Native Americans, or Whites to be suspended from school.

Some experts say that a form of institutional racism permeates many American schools by which teachers accept a low level of performance from children of color (Ogbu & Stern, 2001). American anthropologist John Ogbu (1989) proposed that ethnic minority students are placed in a position of subordination and exploitation in the American educational system. He believes that students of color, especially African Americans and Latinos, have inferior educational opportunities, are exposed to teachers and school administrators who have low academic expectations for them, and encounter negative stereotypes (Ogbu & Stern, 2001). In one study of middle schools in predominantly Latino areas of Miami, Latino and White teachers rated

www.mhhe.com/santrockld11

Interview with Jonathan Kozol
Diversity and Education
Multicultural Education

African American students as having more behavioral problems than African American teachers rated the same students as having (Zimmerman & others, 1995).

Following are some strategies for improving relationships among ethnically diverse students (Santrock, 2006).

- *Turn the class into a jigsaw classroom.* When Eliot Aronson was a professor at the University of Texas at Austin, the school system contacted him for ideas on how to reduce the increasing racial tension in classrooms. Aronson (1986) developed the concept of "jigsaw classroom," in which students from different cultural backgrounds are placed in a cooperative group in which they have to construct different parts of a project to reach a common goal. Aronson used the term *jigsaw* because he saw the technique as much like a group of students cooperating to put different pieces together to complete a jigsaw puzzle. How might this work? Team sports, drama productions, and music performances are examples of contexts in which students cooperatively participate to reach a common goal.

- *Use technology to foster cooperation with students from around the world.*

- *Encourage students to have positive personal contact with diverse other students.* Contact alone does not do the job of improving relationships with diverse others. For example, busing ethnic minority students to predominantly White schools, or vice versa, has not reduced prejudice or improved interethnic relations (Minuchin & Shapiro, 1983). What matters is what happens after children get to school. Especially beneficial in improving interethnic relations is sharing one's worries, successes, failures, coping strategies, interests, and other personal information with people of other ethnicities. When this happens, people tend to look at others as individuals rather than as members of a homogeneous group.

- *Encourage students to engage in perspective taking.* Exercises and activities that help students see others' perspectives can improve interethnic relations. This helps students "step into the shoes" of peers who are culturally different and feel what it is like to be treated in fair or unfair ways.

- *Help students think critically and be emotionally intelligent about cultural issues.* Students who learn to think critically and deeply about interethnic relations are likely to decrease their prejudice. Becoming more emotionally intelligent includes understanding the causes of one's feelings, managing anger, listening to what others are saying, and being motivated to share and cooperate.

- *Reduce bias.* Teachers can reduce bias by displaying images of children from diverse ethnic and cultural groups, selecting play materials and classroom activities that encourage cultural understanding, helping students resist stereotyping, and working with parents.

- *View the school and community as a team.* James Comer (1988, 2004) believes that a community, team approach is the best way to educate children. Three important aspects of the Comer Project for Change are (1) a governance and management team that develops a comprehensive school plan, assessment strategy, and staff development plan; (2) a mental health or school support team; and (3) a parents' program. Comer believes that the entire school community should have a cooperative rather than an adversarial attitude. The Comer program is currently operating in more than 600 schools in 26 states. To read further about James Comer's work, see the Careers in Life-Span Development profile.

- *Be a competent cultural mediator.* Teachers can play a powerful role as a cultural mediator by being sensitive to racist content in materials and classroom interactions, learning more about different ethnic groups, being sensitive to children's ethnic attitudes, viewing students of color positively, and thinking of positive ways to get parents of color more involved as partners with teachers in educating children (Jones & Fuller, 2003).

CAREERS
in LIFE-SPAN DEVELOPMENT

James Comer
Child Psychiatrist

James Comer grew up in a low-income neighborhood in East Chicago, Indiana, and credits his parents with leaving no doubt about the importance of education. He obtained a BA degree from Indiana University. He went on to obtain a medical degree from Howard University College of Medicine, a Master of Public Health degree from the University of Michigan School of Public Health, and psychiatry training at the Yale University School of Medicine's Child Study Center. He currently is the Maurice Falk professor of Child Psychiatry at the Yale University Child Study Center and an associate dean at the Yale University Medical School. During his years at Yale, James has concentrated his career on promoting a focus on child development as a way of improving schools. His efforts in support of healthy development of young people are known internationally.

James, perhaps, is best known for the founding of the School Development Program in 1968, which promotes the collaboration of parents, educators, and community to improve social, emotional, and academic outcomes for children.

James Comer (*left*) is shown with some of the inner-city African American children who attend a school that became a better learning environment because of Comer's intervention.

Cross-Cultural Comparisons of Achievement

American children are more achievement-oriented than their counterparts in many countries. However, in the last several decades, the poor performance of American children in math and science has become well publicized. For example, in one cross-national comparison of the math and science achievement of 9- to 13-year-old students, the United States finished 13th (out of 15) in science and 15th (out of 16) in math achievement (Educational Testing Service, 1992). In this study, Korean and Taiwanese students placed first and second, respectively. Critics of cross-national comparisons argue that, in many comparisons, virtually all U.S. children are being compared with a "select" group of children from other countries; therefore, they conclude, it is no wonder that American students don't fare so well. That criticism holds for some international comparisons. However, when the top 25 percent of students in different countries were compared, U.S. students moved up some, but not a lot (Mullis, 1999). In the Diversity in Life-Span Development interlude, you can read about Harold Stevenson's efforts to find out why American students fare so poorly in mathematics.

DIVERSITY IN LIFE-SPAN DEVELOPMENT

Cross-Cultural Comparisons in Learning Math and Math Instruction

The University of Michigan's Harold Stevenson has been conducting research on children's learning for five decades. His current research explores reasons for the poor performance of American students. Stevenson and his colleagues (Stevenson,

1995, 2000; Stevenson & Hofer, 1999; Stevenson & others, 1990; Stevenson & Zusko, 2002) have completed five cross-cultural comparisons of students in the United States, China, Taiwan, and Japan. In these studies, Asian students consistently outperform American students in mathematics. And, the longer the students are in school, the wider the gap becomes between Asian and American students—the lowest difference is in the first grade, the highest in the eleventh grade (the highest grade studied).

To learn more about the reasons for these large cross-cultural differences, Stevenson and his colleagues spent thousands of hours observing in classrooms, as well as interviewing and surveying teachers, students, and parents. They found that the Asian teachers spent more of their time teaching math than did the American teachers. For example, more than one fourth of total classroom time in the first grade was spent on math instruction in Japan, compared with only one tenth of the time in the U.S. first-grade classrooms. Also, the Asian students were in school an average of 240 days a year, compared with 178 days in the United States.

In addition, differences were found between the Asian and American parents. The American parents had much lower expectations for their children's education and achievement than did the Asian parents. Also, the American parents were more likely to believe that their children's math achievement was due to innate ability; the Asian parents were more likely to say that their children's math achievement was the consequence of effort and training (see figure 11.5). The Asian students were more likely to do math homework than were the American students, and the Asian parents were far more likely to help their children with their math homework than were the American parents (Chen & Stevenson, 1989).

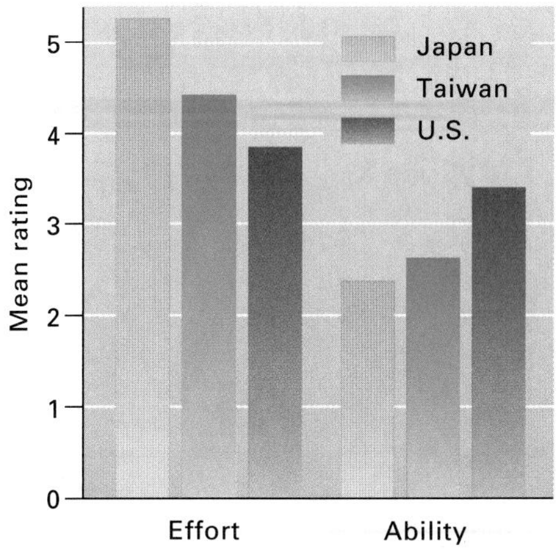

FIGURE 11.5 Mothers' Beliefs About the Factors Responsible for Children's Math Achievement in Three Countries. In one study, mothers in Japan and Taiwan were more likely to believe that their children's math achievement was due to effort rather than innate ability, while U.S. mothers were more likely to believe their children's math achievement was due to innate ability (Stevenson, Lee, & Stigler, 1986). If parents believe that their children's math achievement is due to innate ability and their children are not doing well in math, the implication is that they are less likely to think their children will benefit from putting forth more effort.

Review and Reflect • LEARNING GOAL 4

4 **Characterize contemporary approaches to student learning and sociocultural aspects of schooling and achievement**

Review
- What are two major contemporary issues in educating children?
- How do socioeconomic status and ethnicity influence schooling?
- What are some cross-cultural comparisons of achievement?

Reflect
- Should the United States be worried about the low performance of its students in mathematics and science in comparison to Asian students? Why or why not? Are Americans' expectations for students too low? Explain.

REACH YOUR LEARNING GOALS

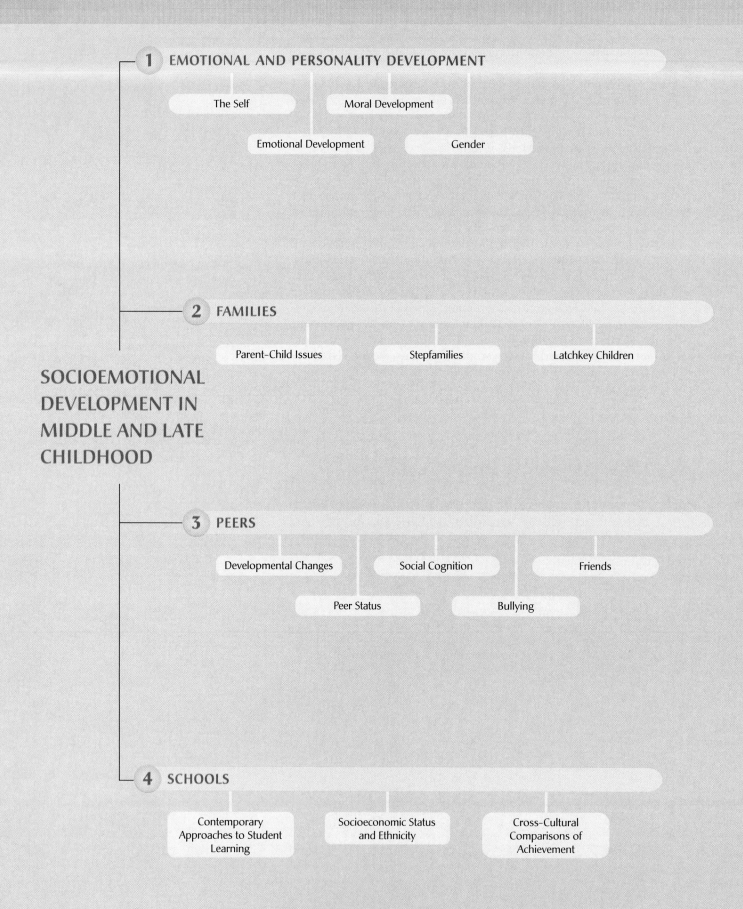

SOCIOEMOTIONAL DEVELOPMENT IN MIDDLE AND LATE CHILDHOOD

1 EMOTIONAL AND PERSONALITY DEVELOPMENT

The Self

Moral Development

Emotional Development

Gender

2 FAMILIES

Parent-Child Issues

Stepfamilies

Latchkey Children

3 PEERS

Developmental Changes

Social Cognition

Friends

Peer Status

Bullying

4 SCHOOLS

Contemporary Approaches to Student Learning

Socioeconomic Status and Ethnicity

Cross-Cultural Comparisons of Achievement

SUMMARY

1 Emotional and Personality Development: *Discuss emotional and personality development in middle and late childhood*

The Self

The internal self, the social self, and the socially comparative self become more prominent in middle and late childhood. Self-concept refers to domain-specific evaluations of the self. Self-esteem refers to global evaluations of the self and is also referred to as self-worth or self-image. Self-esteem is only moderately related to school performance but is more strongly linked to initiative. Four ways to increase self-esteem are to (1) identify the causes of low self-esteem, (2) provide emotional support and social approval, (3) help children achieve, and (4) help children cope. Self-efficacy is the belief that one can master a situation and produce positive outcomes. Bandura considers that self-efficacy is a critical factor in whether students will achieve. Schunk argues that self-efficacy influences a student's choice of tasks, with low-efficacy students avoiding many learning tasks. Erikson's fourth stage of development, industry versus inferiority, characterizes the middle and late childhood years.

Emotional Development

Developmental changes in emotion include increased understanding of complex emotions such as pride and shame, detecting that more than one emotion can be experienced in a particular situation, taking into account the circumstances that led up to an emotional reaction, improvements in the ability to suppress and conceal negative emotions, and using self-initiated strategies to redirect feelings. Emotional intelligence is a form of social intelligence that involves the ability to monitor one's own and others' feelings and emotions, to discriminate among them, and to use this information to guide one's own thinking and action. Goleman maintains that emotional intelligence involves four main areas: emotional self-awareness, managing emotions, reading emotions, and handling relationships. As children get older, they use a greater variety of coping strategies and more cognitive strategies.

Moral Development

Kohlberg argued that moral development consists of three levels—preconventional, conventional, and postconventional—and six stages (two at each level). Kohlberg believed that these stages were age-related. Influences on movement through the stages include cognitive development, imitation and cognitive conflict, peer relations, and perspective taking. Criticisms of Kohlberg's theory have been made, especially by Gilligan, who advocates a stronger care perspective. Other criticisms focus on the inadequacy of moral reasoning to predict moral behavior, culture and family influences, and the distinction between moral reasoning and social conventional reasoning. Prosocial behavior involves positive moral behaviors such as sharing. Most sharing in the first three years is not done for empathy, but at about 4 years of age empathy contributes to sharing. By the start of the elementary school years, children express objective ideas about fairness. Recently, there has been a surge of interest in moral personality.

Gender

Gender stereotypes are widespread around the world. A number of physical differences exist between males and females. Some experts argue that cognitive differences between males and females have been exaggerated. In terms of socioemotional differences, males are more physically aggressive than females, whereas females regulate their emotions better and engage in more prosocial behavior than males. Gender-role classification focuses on how masculine, feminine, or androgynous individuals are. Androgyny means having both positive feminine and masculine characteristics. It is important to think about gender in terms of context.

2 Families: *Describe parent-child issues and societal changes in families*

Parent-Child Issues

Parents spend less time with children during middle and late childhood than in early childhood. New parent-child issues emerge and discipline changes. Control is more coregulatory.

Stepfamilies

As in divorced families, children living in stepparent families have more adjustment problems than their counterparts in nondivorced families. However, a majority of children in stepfamilies do not have adjustment problems.

Latchkey Children

Children who are not monitored by adults in the after-school hours may find their way into trouble more easily than other children, although contextual variations characterize latchkey children's experiences.

3 Peers: Identify changes in peer relationships in middle and late childhood

Developmental Changes

Among the developmental changes in peer relations in middle and late childhood are increased preference for same-sex groups, an increase in time spent in peer interaction and the size of the peer group, and less supervision of the peer group by adults.

Peer Status

Popular children are frequently nominated as a best friend and are rarely disliked by their peers. Average children receive an average number of both positive and negative nominations from their peers. Neglected children are infrequently nominated as a best friend but are not disliked by their peers. Rejected children are infrequently nominated as a best friend and are actively disliked by their peers. Controversial children are frequently nominated both as a best friend and as being disliked by peers. Rejected children are especially at risk for a number of problems.

Social Cognition

Social information-processing skills and social knowledge are two important dimensions of social cognition in peer relations.

Bullying

Significant numbers of children are bullied, and this can result in short-term and long-term negative effects for both the victims and bullies.

Friends

Like adult friends, children who are friends tend to be similar to each other. Children's friendships serve six functions: companionship, stimulation, physical support, ego support, social comparison, and intimacy/affection.

4 Schools: *Characterize contemporary approaches to student learning and sociocultural aspects of schooling and achievement*

Contemporary Approaches to Student Learning

Contemporary approaches to student learning include constructivist (a learner-centered approach) and direct instruction (a teacher-centered approach). In the United States standardized testing of elementary schools students has been mandated by both many state governments and by the No Child Left Behind federal legislation.

Socioeconomic Status and Ethnicity

Children in poverty face many barriers to learning at school as well as at home. The effects of SES and ethnicity on schools are intertwined as many U.S. schools are segregated. Low expectations for ethnic minority children represent one of the barriers to their learning.

Cross-Cultural Comparisons of Achievement

American children are more achievement-oriented than children in many countries, but perform more poorly in math and science than many children in Asian countries, such as China, Taiwan, and Japan.

KEY TERMS

self-esteem 354
self-concept 354
self-efficacy 355
emotional intelligence 356
preconventional
    reasoning 358
heteronomous morality 358
individualism, instrumental
    purpose, and exchange 358
conventional reasoning 358

mutual interpersonal
    expectations, relationships,
    and interpersonal
    conformity 358
social systems morality 359
postconventional
    reasoning 359
social contract or utility and
    individual rights 359

universal ethical
    principles 359
justice perspective 362
care perspective 362
social conventional
    reasoning 362
gender stereotypes 363
androgyny 366
popular children 371

average children 371
neglected children 371
rejected children 371
controversial children 371
intimacy in friendships 375
constructivist approach 376
direct instruction
    approach 376

KEY PEOPLE

Albert Bandura 355
Dale Schunk 355
Erik Erikson 355
Daniel Goleman 356
Lawrence Kohlberg 358

Carol Gilligan 361
William Damon 362
Eleanor Maccoby 365
Carol Jacklin 365
Janet Shibley Hyde 365

Sandra Bem 366
William Pollack 366
Joan Lipsitz 369
John Coie 372
Kenneth Dodge 372

Willard Hartup 375
Jonathan Kozol 378
John Ogbu 378
Eliot Aronson 379
Harold Stevenson 380

E-LEARNING TOOLS

To help you master the material in this chapter, you'll find a number of valuable study tools on the LifeMap CD-ROM that accompanies this book and on the Online Learning Center for *Life-Span Development*, eleventh edition, at **www.mhhe.com/santrockld11.**

Video Clips

In the margins of this book there are icons directing you to the LifeMap CD-ROM that accompanies the book. There you'll find two videos for chapter 11. The first video is called "Characteristics of Children Who Bully." How are bullies made? What causal factors distinguish those who are likely to bully from those likely to be bullied? This segment explores the power dynamics of childhood bullying. The second video is called "Schools and Public Policy." The transition to middle school can be a major paradigm shift for the student. In this segment, Dr. Jacquelynne Eccles describes how her study of the social parameters of middle school has led to changes in public policy.

Self-Assessment

Connect to **www.mhhe.com/santrockld11** to reflect on your childhood by completing the self-assessment, *My Socioemotional Development as a Child.*

Taking It to the Net

Connect to **www.mhhe.com/santrockld11** to research the answers to these questions.

1. Ling, a third-grade teacher, overheard a talk-show discussion on emotional intelligence. She has seen several books on the subject in the local library but was unaware of its impact on learning. What is emotional intelligence and how can Ling and her students' parents facilitate this type of development in children?
2. Frank is researching the latest information on bullying after his younger brother told him of his recent experiences with bullies at his junior high school. What information is available on the prevalence of bullying, the make-up of the children who bully, and the reason for the increase in this type of behavior?

Health and Well-Being, Parenting, and Education Exercises

Build your decision-making skills by trying your hand at the health and well-being, parenting, and education exercises.

Connect to **www.mhhe.com/santrockld11** to research the answers and complete the exercises.

In youth, we clothe ourselves with rainbows, and go brave as the zodiac.

—RALPH WALDO EMERSON
American Poet, 19th Century

CHAPTER OUTLINE	LEARNING GOALS
THE NATURE OF ADOLESCENCE	**1** Discuss the nature of adolescence
PHYSICAL CHANGES Puberty The Brain Adolescent Sexuality	**2** Describe the changes involved in puberty as well as changes in the brain and sexuality during adolescence
ISSUES IN ADOLESCENT HEALTH Adolescent Health Substance Use and Abuse Eating Disorders	**3** Identify adolescent problems related to health, substance use and abuse, and eating disorders
ADOLESCENT COGNITION Piaget's Theory Adolescent Egocentrism Information Processing	**4** Explain cognitive changes in adolescence
SCHOOLS The Transition to Middle or Junior High School Effective Schools for Young Adolescents High School Service Learning	**5** Summarize some key aspects of how schools influence adolescent development

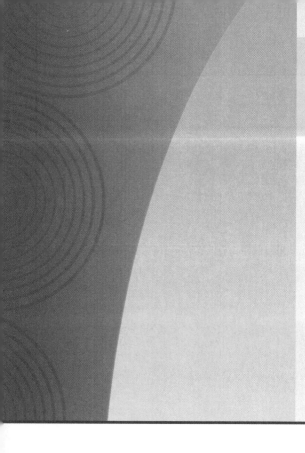

Images of Life-Span Development
The Best of Times and the Worst of Times for Today's Adolescents

It is both the best of times and the worst of times for adolescents. Their world possesses powers and perspectives inconceivable 50 years ago: computers, longer life expectancies, the entire planet accessible through television, satellites, air travel. But so much knowledge and choice can be chaotic and dangerous. . . . The hazards of the adult world, its sometimes fatal temptations, descend upon children so early that the ideal of childhood is demolished. . . . Strange fragments of violence come flashing out of the television set and lodge in minds too young to understand them. The messages are powerful and contradictory. Rock videos suggest orgiastic sex. Public health officials counsel "safe sex." Television pours into the imaginations of children a bizarre version of reality. (Morrow, 1988, pp. 32–33)

Adolescence is not a time of rebellion, crisis, pathology, and deviance. A far more accurate vision of adolescence is of a time of evaluation, decision making, commitment, and carving out a place in the world. Most of the problems of today's youth are not with the youth themselves. What adolescents need is access to a range of legitimate opportunities and to long-term support from adults who care deeply about them (Hamburg & Hamburg, 2004).

PREVIEW

Adolescence is a transitional period in the human life span, linking childhood and adulthood. We begin the chapter by examining some general characteristics of adolescence followed by coverage of major physical changes and health issues of adolescence. Then we describe the significant cognitive changes that characterize adolescence and various aspects of schools for adolescents.

1 THE NATURE OF ADOLESCENCE

As in development during childhood, genetic, biological, environmental, and social factors interact in adolescent development. During their previous 10 to 13 years of development, adolescents experienced thousands of hours of interactions with parents, peers, and teachers, but now they face dramatic biological changes, new experiences, and new developmental tasks. Relationships with parents take a different form, moments with peers become more intimate, and dating occurs for the first time, as do sexual exploration and possibly intercourse. The adolescent's thoughts are more abstract and idealistic. Biological changes trigger a heightened interest in body image. Adolescence has both continuity and discontinuity with childhood.

There is a long history of worrying about how adolescents will turn out. In 1904, G. Stanley Hall proposed the "storm-and-stress" view that adolescence is a turbulent time charged with conflict and mood swings. However, when Daniel Offer and his colleagues (1988) studied the self-images of adolescents in the United States, Australia, Bangladesh, Hungary, Israel, Italy, Japan, Taiwan, Turkey, and West Germany, at least 73 percent of the adolescents displayed a healthy self-image. Although there were differences among them, the adolescents were happy most of the time, they enjoyed

Growing up has never been easy. However, adolescence is not best viewed as a time of rebellion, crisis, pathology, and deviance. A far more accurate vision of adolescence describes it as a time of evaluation, of decision making, of commitment, and of carving out a place in the world. Most of the problems of today's youth are not with the youth themselves. What adolescents need is access to a range of legitimate opportunities and to long-term support from adults who deeply care about them. *What might be some examples of such support and caring?*

life, they perceived themselves as able to exercise self-control, they valued work and school, they expressed confidence about their sexual selves, they expressed positive feelings toward their families, and they felt they had the capability to cope with life's stresses: not exactly a storm-and-stress portrayal of adolescence.

Public attitudes about adolescence emerge from a combination of personal experience and media portrayals, neither of which produce an objective picture of how normal adolescents develop (Feldman & Elliott, 1990). Some of the readiness to assume the worst about adolescents likely involves the short memories of adults. Many adults measure their current perceptions of adolescents by their memories of their own adolescence. Adults may portray today's adolescents as more troubled, less respectful, more self-centered, more assertive, and more adventurous than they were.

However, in matters of taste and manners, the young people of every generation have seemed radical, unnerving, and different from adults—different in how they look, in how they behave, in the music they enjoy, in their hairstyles, and in the clothing they choose. It is an enormous error, though, to confuse adolescents' enthusiasm for trying on new identities and enjoying moderate amounts of outrageous behavior with hostility toward parental and societal standards. Acting out and boundary testing are time-honored ways in which adolescents move toward accepting, rather than rejecting, parental values.

Most adolescents negotiate the lengthy path to adult maturity successfully, but too large a group does not (Nichols & Good, 2004). Ethnic, cultural, gender, socioeconomic, age, and lifestyle differences influence the actual life trajectory of every adolescent. Different portrayals of adolescence emerge, depending on the particular group of adolescents being described (Benson & others, 2006; Schulenberg, 2006; Wigfield & others, 2006). Today's adolescents are exposed to a complex menu of lifestyle options through the media, and many face the temptations of drug use and sexual activity at increasingly young ages (Larson & Wilson, 2004). Too many adolescents are not provided with adequate opportunities and support to become competent adults (Benson & others, 2006; Youngblade & Theokas, 2006).

www.mhhe.com/santrockld11

Practical Resources and Research
Adolescent Issues
Profile of America's Youth
Trends in the Well-Being
of America's Youth

1 **Discuss the nature of adolescence**

Review
- What characterizes adolescent development?

Reflect
- How much have adolescents changed or stayed the same over the last 30 to 40 years?

---

2 PHYSICAL CHANGES

Puberty	The Brain	Adolescent Sexuality

One father remarked that the problem with his teenage son was not that he grew, but that he did not know when to stop growing. As we will see, there is considerable variation in the timing of the adolescent growth spurt. In addition to pubertal changes, other physical changes we will explore involve sexuality and the brain.

Puberty

Puberty is not the same as adolescence. For most of us, puberty ends long before adolescence does, although puberty is the most important marker of the beginning of adolescence. **Puberty** is a period of rapid physical maturation involving hormonal and bodily changes that occur primarily during early adolescence. Puberty is not a single, sudden event (Dorn & others, 2006; Ojeda & others, 2006). We know whether a young boy or girl is going through puberty, but pinpointing puberty's beginning and end is difficult. Among the most noticeable changes are signs of sexual maturation and increases in height and weight.

Sexual Maturation, Height, and Weight   Think back to the onset of your puberty. Of the striking changes that were taking place in your body, what was the first change that occurred? Researchers have found that male pubertal characteristics develop in this order: increase in penis and testicle size, appearance of straight pubic

ZITS By Jerry Scott and Jim Borgman

© ZITS Partnership. Reprinted with permission of King Features Syndicate.

puberty A period of rapid physical and sexual maturation that occurs mainly during early adolescence.

hair, minor voice change, first ejaculation (which usually occurs through masturbation or a wet dream), appearance of kinky pubic hair, onset of maximum growth, growth of hair in armpits, more detectable voice changes, and growth of facial hair.

What is the order of appearance of physical changes in females? First, either the breasts enlarge or pubic hair appears. Later, hair appears in the armpits. As these changes occur, the female grows in height, and her hips become wider than her shoulders. **Menarche**—a girl's first menstruation—comes rather late in the pubertal cycle. Initially, her menstrual cycles may be highly irregular. For the first several years, she may not ovulate every menstrual cycle; some girls do not ovulate at all until a year or two after menstruation begins. No voice changes comparable to those in pubertal males occur in pubertal females. By the end of puberty, the female's breasts have become more fully rounded.

Marked weight gains coincide with the onset of puberty. During early adolescence, girls tend to outweigh boys, but by about age 14 boys begin to surpass girls. Similarly, at the beginning of the adolescent period, girls tend to be as tall as or taller than boys of their age, but by the end of the middle school years most boys have caught up or, in many cases, surpassed girls in height.

As indicated in figure 12.1, the growth spurt occurs approximately two years earlier for girls than for boys (Abbassi, 1998). The mean age at the beginning of the growth spurt in girls is 9 years of age; for boys, it is 11 years of age. The peak rate of pubertal change occurs at $11\frac{1}{2}$ years for girls and $13\frac{1}{2}$ years for boys. During their growth spurt, girls increase in height about $3\frac{1}{2}$ inches per year, boys about 4 inches. Boys and girls who are shorter or taller than their peers before adolescence are likely to remain so during adolescence; however, as much as 30 percent of an individual's height in late adolescence is unexplained by his or her height in the elementary school years.

Hormonal Changes

Behind the first whisker in boys and the widening of hips in girls is a flood of **hormones**, powerful chemical substances secreted by the endocrine glands and carried through the body by the bloodstream. The endocrine system's role in puberty involves the interaction of the hypothalamus, the pituitary gland, and the gonads. The **hypothalamus** is a structure in the higher portion of the brain that monitors eating, drinking, and sex. The **pituitary gland** is an important endocrine gland that controls growth and regulates other glands. The **gonads** are the sex glands—the testes in males, the ovaries in females.

How does the hormonal system work? The pituitary sends a signal via *gonadotropins* (hormones that stimulate the testes or ovaries) to the appropriate gland to manufacture the hormone. Then the pituitary gland, through interaction with the hypothalamus, detects when the optimal level of hormones is reached and responds and maintains it with additional gonadotropin secretion.

Not only does the pituitary gland release gonadotropins that stimulate the testes and ovaries, but through interaction with the hypothalamus the pituitary gland also secretes hormones that either directly lead to growth and skeletal maturation or that produce growth effects through interaction with the thyroid gland, located in the neck region (Clarkson & Herbison, 2006).

The concentrations of certain hormones increase dramatically during adolescence (Hughes & Kumanan, 2006; Susman, 2006; Whitlock & others, 2006). *Testosterone* is a hormone associated in boys with the development of genitals, an increase in height, and a change in voice. *Estradiol* is a hormone associated in girls with breast, uterine, and skeletal development. In one study, testosterone levels increased eighteenfold in boys but only twofold in girls during puberty; estradiol increased eightfold in girls but only twofold in boys (Nottelmann & others, 1987) (see figure 12.2). Note that both testosterone and estradiol are present in the hormonal makeup of both boys and girls but that testosterone dominates in male pubertal development, estradiol in female pubertal development.

The same influx of hormones that puts hair on a male's chest and imparts curvature to a female's breast may contribute to psychological development in adolescence

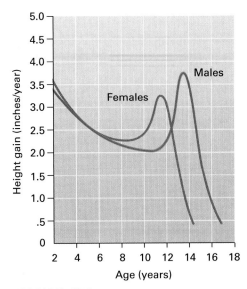

FIGURE 12.1 Pubertal Growth Spurt. On the average, the peak of the growth spurt during puberty occurs 2 years earlier for girls ($11\frac{1}{2}$) than for boys ($13\frac{1}{2}$). *How are hormones related to the growth spurt and to the difference between the average height of adolescent boys and girls?*

Biological Changes

menarche A girl's first menstruation.

hormones Powerful chemical substances secreted by the endocrine glands and carried through the body by the bloodstream.

hypothalamus A structure in the higher portion of the brain that monitors eating, drinking, and sex.

pituitary gland An important endocrine gland that controls growth and regulates other glands.

gonads The sex glands—the testes in males and the ovaries in females.

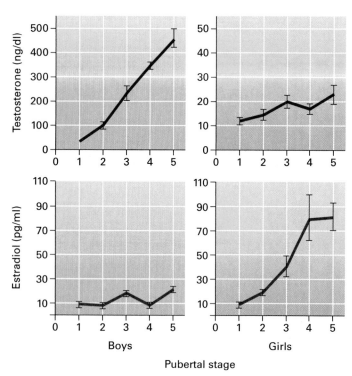

FIGURE 12.2 Hormone Levels by Sex and Pubertal Stage for Testosterone and Estradiol. The five stages range from the early beginning of puberty (stage 1) to the most advanced stage of puberty (stage 5). Notice the significant increase in testosterone in boys and the significant increase in estradiol in girls.

What are some of the differences in the ways girls and boys experience pubertal growth?

(Rapkin & others, 2006). In one study of 108 normal boys and girls ranging in age from 9 to 14, a higher concentration of testosterone was present in boys who rated themselves as more socially competent (Nottelmann & others, 1987). In another study of 60 normal boys and girls in the same age range, girls with higher estradiol levels expressed more anger and aggression (Inoff-Germain & others, 1988). However, hormonal effects by themselves do not account for adolescent development (Graber & Brooks-Gunn, 2002; Rowe & others, 2004). For example, in one study, social factors accounted for two to four times as much variance as did hormonal factors in young adolescent girls' depression and anger (Brooks-Gunn & Warren, 1989). Behavior and moods also can affect hormones (Paikoff, Buchanan, & Brooks-Gunn, 1991). Stress, eating patterns, exercise, sexual activity, tension, and depression can activate or suppress various aspects of the hormonal system. In sum, the hormone-behavior link is complex (Susman, 2006).

Timing and Variations in Puberty Imagine a toddler displaying all the features of puberty—a 3-year-old girl with fully developed breasts or a boy just slightly older with a deep voice. That is what we would see by the year 2250 if the age at which puberty arrives were to keep getting younger at its present pace. In Norway today, menarche occurs at just over 13 years of age, compared with 17 years of age in the 1840s. In the United States—where children mature up to a year earlier than children in European countries—the average age of menarche declined significantly since the mid-nineteenth century (Hermann-Giddens, 2006) (see figure 12.3). Fortunately, however, we are unlikely to see pubescent toddlers, since what has happened in the past century is likely the result of improved nutrition and health (Delemarre-van de Waal, 2005). The available information suggests that menarche began to occur earlier at about the time of the Industrial Revolution, a period associated with increased standards of living and advances in medical science (Petersen, 1979).

Why do the changes of puberty occur when they do, and how can variations in their timing be explained? The basic genetic program for puberty is wired into the species (Sharp & others, 2004; Waylen & Wolke, 2004), but nutrition, health, and other environmental factors also affect puberty's timing and makeup (Graham, 2005; Himes, 2006).

One key factor that triggers puberty is body mass (Cervero & others, 2006). Menarche occurs at a relatively consistent weight in girls. A body weight approximating 106 ± 3 pounds can trigger menarche and the end of the pubertal growth spurt. For menarche to begin and continue, fat must make up 17 percent of the girl's body weight. As a result, teenage anorexics whose weight drops dramatically and some female athletes in sports such as gymnastics do not menstruate (Beals & Hill, 2006).

For most boys, the pubertal sequence may begin as early as 10 years of age or as late as 13½. It may end as early as 13 years or as late as 17 years for most boys. The normal range is wide enough that, given two boys of the same chronological age, one might complete the pubertal sequence before the other one has begun it. Menarche is considered within a normal range if it appears between the ages of 9 and 15.

Body Image One psychological aspect of physical change in puberty is certain: Adolescents are preoccupied with their bodies and develop individual images of what their bodies are like. Perhaps you looked in the mirror daily and sometimes even hourly to see if you could detect anything different about your changing body. Preoccupation with body image is strong throughout adolescence, but it is especially acute during puberty, a time when adolescents are more dissatisfied with their bodies than in late adolescence (Graber & Brooks-Gunn, 2001).

There are gender differences in adolescents' perceptions of their bodies. In general, compared with boys, girls are less happy with their bodies and have more negative body images throughout puberty (Bearman & others, 2006; Dyl & others, 2006). As pubertal change proceeds, girls often become more dissatisfied with their bodies, probably because their body fat increases, whereas boys become more satisfied as they move through puberty, probably because their muscle mass increases (Gross, 1984).

Early and Late Maturation   Some of you entered puberty early, others late, and yet others on time. Adolescents who mature earlier or later than their peers perceive themselves differently. In the Berkeley Longitudinal Study some years ago, early-maturing boys perceived themselves more positively and had more successful peer relations than did their late-maturing counterparts (Jones, 1965). When the late-maturing boys were in their thirties, however, they had developed a stronger sense of identity than the early-maturing boys had (Peskin, 1967). Possibly this occurred because the late-maturing boys had more time to explore life's options or because the early-maturing boys continued to focus on their advantageous physical status instead of on career development and achievement. More recent research confirms, though, that at least during adolescence it is advantageous to be an early-maturing rather than a late-maturing boy (Simmons & Blyth, 1987).

For girls, early and late maturation have been linked with body image. In the sixth grade, early-maturing girls show greater satisfaction with their figures than do late-maturing girls, but by the tenth grade late-maturing girls are more satisfied (Simmons & Blyth, 1987) (see figure 12.4). One possible reason for this is that in late adolescence early-maturing girls are shorter and stockier, whereas late-maturing girls are taller and thinner. Thus, late-maturing girls in late adolescence have bodies that more closely approximate the current American ideal of feminine beauty—tall and thin.

An increasing number of researchers have found that early maturation increases girls' vulnerability to a number of problems (DeRose & Brooks-Gunn, 2006; Graber & others, 2004; Graber, Brooks-Gunn, & Warren, 2006). Early-maturing girls are more likely to smoke, drink, be depressed, have an eating disorder, request earlier independence from their parents, and have older friends; and their bodies are likely to elicit responses from males that lead to earlier dating and earlier sexual experiences (Wiesner & Ittel, 2002). One recent study of 1,225 urban middle school girls found that those who entered puberty early experimented with alcohol and marijuana at much higher rates than their ethnic minority peers who developed later (Graber, 2003). In another study, early-maturing girls had lower educational and occupational attainment in adulthood (Stattin & Magnusson, 1990). Apparently as a result of their early physical development and hanging out with older peers, early-maturing girls are easily lured into problem behaviors, not recognizing the possible long-term effects of these on their development (Petersen, 1993; Sarigiani & Petersen, 2000).

Some researchers now question whether the effects of puberty are as strong as once believed (Petersen, 1993). Puberty affects some adolescents more strongly than others and some behaviors more strongly than others. Body image, dating interest, and sexual behavior are affected by pubertal change. In terms of overall development and adjustment in the human life span, however, variations such as early and late maturation have less dramatic effects than once thought. In thinking about puberty's effects, keep in mind that an adolescent's world involves cognitive and socioemotional changes, as well as physical changes. As with all periods of development, these processes work in concert to produce who we are in adolescence.

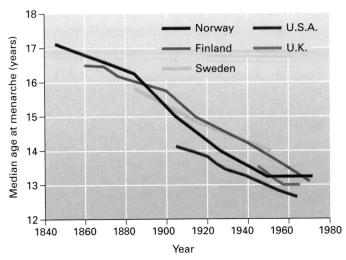

FIGURE 12.3 Median Ages at Menarche in Selected Northern European Countries and the United States from 1845 to 1969. Notice the steep decline in the age at which girls experienced menarche in four northern European countries and the United States from 1845 to 1969. Recently the age at which girls experience menarche has been leveling off.

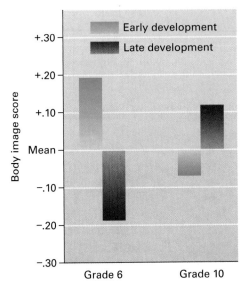

FIGURE 12.4 Early- and Late-Maturing Adolescent Girls' Perceptions of Body Image in Early and Late Adolescence. The sixth-grade girls in this study had positive body images scores if they were early-maturers but negative body image scores if they were late-maturers (Simmons & Blyth, 1987). Positive body image scores indicated satisfaction with their figures. By the tenth-grade, however, it was the late-maturers who had positive body image scores.

The Brain

Along with the rest of the body, the brain is changing during adolescence, but what we know about brain development in adolescence is in its infancy. As advances in technology take place, significant strides will also likely be made in charting developmental changes in the adolescent brain (Giedd & others, 2006; Kuhn & Franklin, 2006; Nelson, Thomas, & de Haan, 2006; Steinberg, 2006). What do we know now?

In chapter 8, "Physical and Cognitive Development in Early Childhood," we described how the pruning of synapses continues through late adolescence. Spurts in the brain's electrical activity seem to occur at about 9, 12, 15, and 18 to 20 years of age. These spurts may signal changes in cognitive development. During puberty, neural activity using the neurotransmitter dopamine increases while activity using the neurotransmitter serotonin decreases (Walker, 2002). What does this mean? Scientists do not know, but some have speculated that the increased risk for some mental disorders, such as schizophrenia, during adolescence and early adulthood may be due to this elevation of dopamine activity.

In one study, researchers used magnetic resonance imaging (MRI) to discover if brain activity during the processing of emotional information differed in adolescents (10 to 18 years of age) and adults (20 to 40 years of age) (Baird & others, 1999). In this study, participants were asked to view pictures of faces displaying fearful expressions while they underwent an MRI. When adolescents (especially younger ones) processed the emotional information, brain activity was more pronounced in the amygdala than in the frontal lobe (see figure 12.5). The reverse occurred in the adults. The amygdala is involved in processing information about emotion, while the frontal lobes are involved in higher-level reasoning and thinking. The researchers interpreted their findings to mean that adolescents tend to respond with "gut" reactions to emotional stimuli while adults are more likely to respond in rational, reasoned ways. The researchers also concluded that these changes are linked to growth in the frontal lobe of the brain from adolescence to adulthood. However, more research is needed to clarify these findings (Dahl, 2001; DeBellis & others, 2001; Spear, 2000, 2004; Steinberg, 2004, 2005, 2006).

Leading researcher Charles Nelson (2003) argues that while adolescents are capable of very strong emotions, their prefrontal cortex hasn't developed enough to allow them to control these passions. It is as if their brains don't have the brakes to slow down their emotions. Or consider this interpretation of the development of emotion and cognition in adolescents: "early activation of strong 'turbo-charged' feelings with a relatively unskilled set of 'driving skills' or cognitive abilities to modulate strong emotions and motivations" (Dahl, 2004, p. 18).

Other researchers have found that the amygdala and hippocampus increase in volume during adolescence (Giedd & others, 1999; Sowell & Jernigan, 1998). Both structures are involved in emotion and are part of the group of structures sometimes called the *limbic system*. Changes in the limbic system during puberty may lead adolescents to seek novelty and to need higher levels of stimulation in order to experience pleasure (Spear, 2000, 2004). However, because of the relatively slow development of the prefrontal cortex, which is still maturing during adolescence, adolescents may lack the cognitive skills to effectively control their pleasure seeking (Blakemore & Choudhury, 2006; Toga, Thompson, & Sowell, 2006). This developmental disjunction between the limbic system and prefrontal cortex may account for an increase in risk taking and other problems in adolescence.

Adolescent Sexuality

Adolescence is a time of sexual exploration and experimentation, of sexual fantasies and realities, of incorporating sexuality into one's identity. Adolescents have an almost insatiable curiosity about sexuality. They think about whether they are

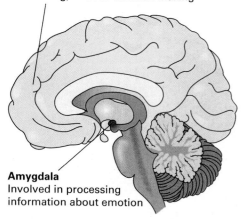

Prefrontal cortex
Involved in higher-order cognitive functioning, such as decision making

Amygdala
Involved in processing information about emotion

FIGURE 12.5 Developmental Changes in the Adolescent's Brain. The amygdala, which is responsible for processing information about emotion, matures earlier than the prefrontal cortex, which is responsible for making decisions and other higher-order cognitive functions. *What are some possible implications of this difference in the maturation rate of different brain regions for adolescents' behavior?*

sexually attractive, how to do sex, and what the future holds for their sexual lives. The majority of adolescents eventually manage to develop a mature sexual identity, but most experience times of vulnerability and confusion (Brown & Brown, 2006).

Adolescence is a bridge between the asexual child and the sexual adult (Feldman, 1999). Every society gives some attention to adolescent sexuality. In some societies, adults clamp down and protect adolescent females from males by chaperoning them. Other societies promote very early marriage. Yet others allow some sexual experimentation.

In the United States children and adolescents learn a great deal about sex from television (Collins, 2005; Collins & others, 2004; Ward & Caruthers, 2001; Ward & Friedman, 2006; Ward, Hansbrough, & Walker, 2005). The messages come from TV commercials, which use sex to sell just about everything, as well as from the content of TV shows. A recent study of 1,762 12- to 17-year-olds found that those who watched more sexually explicit TV shows were more likely than their counterparts who watched these shows less to initiate sexual intercourse in the next 12 months (Collins & others, 2004). Adolescents in the highest 10 percent of viewing sexually explicit TV shows were twice as likely to engage in sexual intercourse as those in the lowest 10 percent. The results held regardless of whether the exposure to explicit sex involved actual sexual behavior or just talk about sex. Sexual messages also come from videos, the lyrics of popular music, and Web sites (Roberts, Henriksen, & Foehr, 2004). A recent research review found that frequent watching of soap operas and music videos was linked with greater acceptance of casual attitudes about sex and higher expectations of engaging in sexual activity (Ward, 2003).

Sex is virtually everywhere in the American culture and is used to sell just about everything. *What evidence is cited in the text to indicate that messages from the media influence adolescents' attitudes or behavior?*

Developing a Sexual Identity   Mastering emerging sexual feelings and forming a sense of sexual identity is a multifaceted and lengthy process. It involves learning to manage sexual feelings (such as sexual arousal and attraction), developing new forms of intimacy, and learning the skills to regulate sexual behavior to avoid undesirable consequences (Crockett, Raffaelli, & Moilanen, 2003). The sexual identity must also be related to other developing identities, which are discussed in chapter 13.

An adolescent's sexual identity involves activities, interests, styles of behavior, and an indication of sexual orientation (whether an individual has same-sex or other-sex attractions) (Buzwell & Rosenthal, 1996). For example, some adolescents have a high anxiety level about sex, others a low level. Some adolescents are strongly aroused sexually, others less so. Some adolescents are very active sexually, others not at all. Some adolescents are sexually inactive in response to their strong religious upbringing; others go to church regularly, yet their religious training does not inhibit their sexual activity (Thornon & Camburn, 1989).

It is commonly believed that most gay and lesbian individuals quietly struggle with same-sex attractions in childhood, do not engage in heterosexual dating, and gradually recognize that they are gay or lesbian in mid to late adolescence (Diamond, 2003). Many youth do follow this developmental pathway but others do not. For example, many youth have no recollection of same-sex attractions and experience a more abrupt sense of their same-sex attraction in late adolescence (Savin-Williams, 2001, 2005). Researchers also have found that the majority of adolescents with same-sex attractions also experience some degree of other-sex attractions (Garofalo & others, 1999). Even though some adolescents who are attracted to same-sex individuals fall in love with these individuals, others claim that their same-sex attractions are purely physical (Savin-Williams, 2001, 2005, 2006; Savin-Williams & Diamond, 2004).

In sum, gay and lesbian youth have diverse patterns of initial attraction, often have bisexual attractions, and may have physical or emotional attraction to same-sex individuals but do not always fall in love with them (Diamond, 2003; Savin-Williams

What is the progression of sexual behaviors in adolescence?

& Cohen, 2006; Savin-Williams & Diamond, 2004). In chapter 14, "Physical and Cognitive Development in Early Adulthood," we will further explore homosexuality as well as heterosexuality.

The Progression of Adolescent Sexual Behaviors Adolescents engage in a rather consistent progression of sexual behaviors (DeLamater & MacCorquodale, 1979). One study in which 452 individuals 18 to 25 years of age were asked about their sexual experiences found the following: kissing preceded petting, which preceded sexual intercourse and oral sex (Feldman, Turner, & Araujo, 1999). Male adolescents reported engaging in these sexual behaviors approximately one year earlier than female adolescents.

The timing of sexual initiation varies by country as well as by gender and other socioeconomic characteristics. In one study, among females, the proportion having first intercourse by age 17 ranged from 72 percent in Mali to 47 percent in the United States and 45 percent in Tanzania (Singh & others, 2000). The percentage of males who had their first intercourse by age 17 ranged from 76 percent in Jamaica to 64 percent in the United States and 63 percent in Brazil. Within the United States, male, African American, and inner-city adolescents report being the most sexually active (Feldman, Turner, & Araujo, 1999). Asian American adolescents have the most restrictive sexual timetable.

Here is information from a national survey of U.S. adolescents that further reveals the timing of their sexual activities (Alan Guttmacher Institute, 1998):

- Most young adolescents have not had sexual intercourse: 8 in 10 girls and 7 in 10 boys are virgins at age 15.
- The probability that adolescents will have sexual intercourse increases steadily with age, but 1 in 5 individuals have not yet had sexual intercourse by age 19.
- Most teenagers first have sexual intercourse in the mid- to late-adolescent years, about eight years before they marry.
- The first voluntary sexual partner for most adolescent girls is younger, the same age, or no more than two years older.

Psychologists are exploring ways to encourage adolescents to make less risky sexual decisions. Here an adolescent participates in an interactive video session developed by Julie Downs and her colleagues at the Department of Social and Decision Making Sciences at Carnegie Mellon University. The videos help adolescents evaluate their responses and decisions in high-risk sexual contexts.

In sum, by the end of adolescence the majority of U.S. adolescents have had sexual intercourse.

Many adolescents are not emotionally prepared to handle sexual experiences, especially in early adolescence. In one study, the earlier boys and girls engaged in sexual intercourse, the more they were likely to show adjustment problems (Bingham & Crockett, 1996). Early sexual activity also is linked with other risky behaviors such as excessive drinking, drug use, delinquency, and school-related problems (Dryfoos, 1990). Adolescents who engage in sex before age 16 and experience a number of partners over time are the least effective users of contraception and are at risk for early, unintended pregnancy and for sexually transmitted infections (Cavanaugh, 2004).

Contraceptive Use Sexual activity is a normal activity necessary for procreation, but if appropriate safeguards are not taken it brings the risk of unintended, unwanted pregnancy and sexually transmitted infections (Carroll, 2007; Davies & others, 2006). Both of these risks can be reduced significantly by using certain forms of contraception and barriers (such as condoms) (Breheny & Stephens, 2004). The good news is that adolescents are increasing their use of contraceptives (Schaalma & others, 2004). A recent study examined trends in U.S. ninth- to twelfth-graders' contraceptive use from 1991 to 2003 (Anderson, Santelli, & Morrow, 2006). Approximately one-third of the adolescents reported being sexually active in the previous three months. The use of a condom by males increased from 46 percent in 1991 to 63 percent in 2003. The percentage of adolescents who used either withdrawal or no method steadily declined from 33 percent in 1991 to 19 percent in 2003.

Although adolescent contraceptive use is increasing, many sexually active adolescents still do not use contraceptives, or they use them inconsistently (Brindis, 2006; Davies & others, 2006; Feldman, 2006; Hock & Williams, 2007). Sexually active younger adolescents are less likely than older adolescents to take contraceptive precautions. Younger adolescents are more likely to use a condom or withdrawal, whereas older adolescents are more likely to use the pill or a diaphragm. In one study, adolescent females reported changing their behavior in the direction of safer sex practices more than did adolescent males (Rimberg & Lewis, 1994).

Sexually Transmitted Infections Some forms of contraception, such as birth control pills or implants, do not protect against sexually transmitted infections, or STIs. **Sexually transmitted infections (STIs)** are contracted primarily through sexual contact, including oral-genital and anal-genital contact. Every year more than 3 million American adolescents (about one-fourth of those who are sexually experienced) acquire an STI (Centers for Disease Control and Prevention, 2006). In a single act of unprotected sex with an infected partner, a teenage girl has a 1 percent risk of getting HIV, a 30 percent risk of acquiring genital herpes, and a 50 percent chance of contracting gonorrhea (Glei, 1999). Yet another very widespread STI is chlamydia. In chapter 14, we will describe these and other sexually transmitted infections.

Adolescent Pregnancy In cross-cultural comparisons, the United States continues to have one of the highest adolescent pregnancy and childbearing rates in the industrialized world, despite a considerable decline in the 1990s (Centers for Disease Control and Prevention, 2002) (see figure 12.6). The U.S. adolescent pregnancy rate is eight times as high as in the Netherlands. Although U.S. adolescents are no more sexually active than their counterparts in the Netherlands, their adolescent pregnancy rate is dramatically higher.

There are encouraging trends, though, in U.S. adolescent pregnancy rates. In 2004, births to adolescent girls fell to a record low (Child Trends, 2006). The rate of births to adolescent girls has dropped 25 percent since 1991. Reasons for the decline include increased contraceptive use, fear of sexually transmitted infections such as AIDS, and the economic prosperity of the 1990s, which may have motivated adolescents to delay starting a family so that they could take jobs. The greatest drop in U.S. adolescent pregnancy rates in the 1990s came among 15- to 17-year-old girls. There is a special concern about the continued high rate of adolescent pregnancy in Latinas (Nadeem, Whaley, & Anthony, 2006; Talashek, Alba, & Patel, 2006).

Adolescent pregnancy creates health risks for both the baby and the mother. Infants born to adolescent mothers are more likely to have low birth weights—a prominent factor in infant mortality—as well as neurological problems and childhood illness (Malamitsi-Puchner & Boutsikou, 2006). Adolescent mothers often drop out of school. Although many adolescent mothers resume their education later in

www.mhhe.com/santrockld11

The Alan Guttmacher Institute
CDC National Prevention Network
American Social Health Association
HIV/AIDS and Adolescents
Adolescent Pregnancy

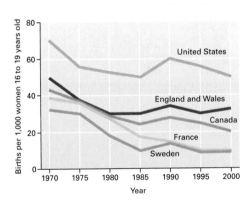

FIGURE 12.6 Cross-Cultural Comparisons of Adolescent Pregnancy Rates. Pregnancy rates among U.S. adolescents are among the highest in the industrialized world (Centers for Disease Control and Prevention, 2002).

sexually transmitted infections (STIs) Infections that are contracted primarily through sexual contact, which is not limited to sexual intercourse. Oral-genital and anal-genital contact also can transmit STIs.

CAREERS in LIFE-SPAN DEVELOPMENT

Lynn Blankenship, Family and Consumer Science Educator

Lynn Blankenship is a family and consumer science educator. She has an undergraduate degree in this area from the University of Arizona. She has taught for more than 20 years, the last 14 at Tucson High Magnet School.

Lynn was awarded the Tucson Federation of Teachers Educator of the Year Award for 1999–2000 and the Arizona Teacher of the Year in 1999.

Lynn especially enjoys teaching life skills to adolescents. One of her favorite activities is having students care for an automated baby that imitates the needs of real babies. She says that this program has a profound impact on students because the baby must be cared for around the clock for the duration of the assignment. Lynn also coordinates real-world work experiences and training for students in several child-care facilities in the Tucson area.

Lynn Blankenship (*center*) teaching life skills to students.

life, they generally do not catch up economically with women who postpone childbearing until their twenties. One longitudinal study found that the children of women who had their first birth during their teens had lower achievement test scores and more behavioral problems than did children whose mothers had their first birth as adults (Hofferth & Reid, 2002).

However, often it is not pregnancy alone that leads to negative consequences for an adolescent mother and her offspring (Hillis & others, 2004; Leadbetter & Way, 2001; Oxford & others, 2006). Adolescent mothers are more likely to come from low-income backgrounds (Mehra & Agrawal, 2004). Many adolescent mothers also were not good students before they became pregnant. One recent study found that adolescent childbearers were more likely to have a history of conduct problems, less educational attainment, and lower childhood socioeconomic status than later child-bearers (Jaffee, 2002). However, in this study, early childbearing exacerbated the difficulties associated with these risks.

Of course, some adolescent mothers do well in school and have positive outcomes (Barnet & others, 2004; Whitman & others, 2001). Serious, extensive efforts are needed to help pregnant adolescents and young mothers enhance their educational and occupational opportunities. Adolescent mothers also need help in obtaining competent child care and in planning for the future.

All adolescents can benefit from age-appropriate family-life education (Weyman, 2003). Family and consumer science educators teach life skills, such as effective decision making, to adolescents. To read about the work of one family and consumer science educator, see the Careers in Life-Span Development profile. And to learn more about ways to reduce adolescent pregnancy, see the Applications in Life-Span Development interlude.

APPLICATIONS IN LIFE-SPAN DEVELOPMENT

Reducing Adolescent Pregnancy

One strategy for reducing adolescent pregnancy, called the Teen Outreach Program (TOP), focuses on engaging adolescents in volunteer community service and stimulates discussions that help adolescents appreciate the lessons they learn through volunteerism. In one study, 695 adolescents in grades 9 to 12 were randomly assigned to either a Teen Outreach group or a control group (Allen & others, 1997). They were assessed at both program entry and at program exit nine months later. The rate of pregnancy was substantially lower for the Teen Outreach adolescents. These adolescents also had a lower rate of school failure and academic suspension.

Girls, Inc., has four programs that are intended to increase adolescent girls' motivation to avoid pregnancy until they are mature enough to make responsible decisions about motherhood (Roth & others, 1998). Growing Together, a series of five

2-hour workshops for mothers and adolescents, and Will Power/Won't Power, a series of six 2-hour sessions that focus on assertiveness training, are for 12- to 14-year-old girls. For older adolescent girls, Taking Care of Business provides nine sessions that emphasize career planning as well as information about sexuality, reproduction, and contraception. Health Bridge coordinates health and education services—girls can participate in this program as one of their club activities. Girls who participated in these programs were less likely to get pregnant than girls who did not participate (Girls, Inc., 1991).

Currently, a major controversy in sex education is whether schools should have an abstinence-only program or a program that emphasizes contraceptive knowledge (Cabezon & others, 2005; Santelli & others, 2006). A recent review of research found that some abstinence-only programs and some contraceptive-knowledge programs were effective in changing adolescents' sexual behavior (Bennett & Assefi, 2005). However, the positive outcomes were modest and most lasted only for a short time. Contrary to critics of contraceptive-knowledge programs, the research review found that they do not increase adolescent sexual activity. An important point to note about comparing sex education programs is that the variation in samples, interventions, and outcome measures make conclusions about which programs are most effective difficult.

These are not adolescent mothers, but rather adolescents who are participating in the Teen Outreach Program (TOP), which engages adolescents in volunteer community service. These adolescent girls are serving as volunteers in a child care center for crack babies. Researchers have found that such volunteer experiences can reduce the rate of adolescent pregnancy.

Review and Reflect • LEARNING GOAL 2

2 **Describe the changes involved in puberty as well as changes in the brain and sexuality during adolescence**

Review
- What are some key aspects of puberty?
- What changes typically occur in the brain during adolescence?
- What are some important aspects of sexuality in adolescence?

Reflect
- Did you experience puberty early or late? How did this timing affect your development?

3 ISSUES IN ADOLESCENT HEALTH

| Adolescent Health | Substance Use and Abuse | Eating Disorders |

Many health experts argue that whether adolescents are healthy depends primarily on their own behavior. To improve adolescent health, adults should aim to (1) increase adolescents' health-enhancing behaviors, such as eating nutritiously, exercising, wearing seat belts, and getting adequate sleep, and (2) reduce adolescents' health-compromising behaviors, such as drug abuse, violence, unprotected sexual intercourse, and dangerous driving.

Adolescent Health

Adolescence is a critical juncture in the adoption of behaviors relevant to health (Blum & Nelson-Mmari, 2004; Levine & Smolak, 2006). Many factors linked to poor health in adulthood begin during adolescence. Healthy behavior such as eating foods low in fat and cholesterol and engaging in regular exercise not only has immediate benefits but contributes to the delay or prevention of major causes of premature disability and mortality in adulthood—heart disease, stroke, diabetes, and cancer (Ramey, Ramey, & Lanzi, 2006; Richter, 2006; Turbin & others, 2006).

Nutrition and Exercise   Since the 1960s, the percentage of adolescents who are overweight has increased (see figure 12.7). As discussed in chapter 10, poor diet and inadequate exercise probably contribute to the problem.

A recent study of more than 3,000 U.S. adolescents found that 34 percent were in the lowest fitness category (Carnethon, Gulati, & Greenland, 2005). In a comparison of adolescents in 28 countries, U.S. adolescents exercised less and ate more junk food than adolescents in most other countries (World Health Organization, 2000). U.S. adolescents were more likely to eat fried food and less likely to eat fruits and vegetables than adolescents in most other countries studied. U.S. adolescents' eating choices were similar to those of adolescents in England. Just two-thirds of U.S. adolescents exercised at least twice a week, compared with 80 percent or more of adolescents in Ireland, Austria, Germany, and the Slovak Republic.

Individuals tend to become less active as they reach and progress through adolescence (Dwyer & others, 2006; Merrick & others, 2005), but ethnic differences are noteworthy (Sánchez-Johnsen & others, 2004; Viner & others, 2006). One study examined the activity habits of more than 1,000 African American and more than 1,000 non-Latino White girls annually from 9 to 10 years of age to 18 to 19 years of age (Kimm & others, 2002). At 9 to 10 years of age, most girls reported they were engaging in some physical activity outside of school. However, by 16 to 17 years of age, 56 percent of African American girls and 31 percent of non-Latino White girls were not engaging in any regular physical activity in their spare time. By 18 to 19 years of age, the figures were 70 percent and 29 percent, respectively. In sum, physical activity declines substantially in girls during adolescence and more in African American than non-Latino White girls (Kimm & Obarzanek, 2002; Shaibi & others, 2006).

Sleep Patterns   Like nutrition and exercise, sleep has a huge influence on well-being. One recent study of 2,259 U.S. 11- to 14-year-olds found that not getting enough sleep was associated with lower self-esteem and higher levels of depression (Fredriksen & others, 2004). Thanks in part to the belief that many adolescents are not getting enough sleep, interest in adolescent sleep patterns has surged

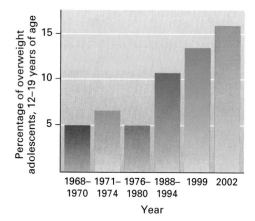

FIGURE 12.7 The Increase in Being Overweight in Adolescence from 1968 to 2002 in the United States. In this study, being overweight was determined by body mass index (BMI), which is computed by a formula that takes into account height and weight (National Center for Health Statistics, 2005). There was a substantial increase in the percentage of adolescents who were overweight from 1968 to 2002.

Adolescent Health

(Carskadon, 2004, 2005, 2006; Chen, Wang, & Jeng, 2006; Dahl, 2006; Hansen & others, 2005; Ireland & Culpin, 2006; Yang & others, 2005).

Mary Carskadon and her colleagues (Carskadon, 2002, 2004, 2005, 2006; Acebo & Carskadon, 2002; Carskadon, Acebo, & Jenni, 2004) found that when given the opportunity, adolescents will sleep an average of nine hours and 25 minutes a night. Most get considerably less than nine hours of sleep, especially during the week. This shortfall creates a sleep deficit, which adolescents often attempt to make up on the weekend.

Carskadon and her colleagues also found that older adolescents tend to be sleepier during the day than younger adolescents. Their research suggests that adolescents' biological clocks undergo a shift as they get older, delaying their period of wakefulness by about one hour. A delay in the nightly release of the sleep-inducing hormone melatonin, which is produced in the brain's pineal gland, seems to underlie this shift. Melatonin is secreted at about 9:30 P.M. in younger adolescents and approximately an hour later in older adolescents.

Their sleep patterns influence the hours during which adolescents learn most effectively in school (Carstensen, Mindell, & Drake, 2006; National Sleep Foundation, 2006). Carskadon has suggested that early school starting times may cause grogginess, inattention in class, and poor performance on tests. Based on her research, school officials in Edina, Minnesota, decided to start classes at 8:30 A.M. rather than 7:25 A.M. Since then, there have been fewer referrals for discipline problems and the number of students who report being ill or depressed has decreased. The school system reports that test scores have improved for high school students, but not for middle school students. This finding supports Carskadon's suspicion that early start times are likely to be more stressful for older than for younger adolescents.

How might changing sleep patterns in adolescents affect their school performance?

Leading Causes of Death in Adolescence   The three leading causes of death in adolescence are accidents, homicide, and suicide. More than half of all deaths in adolescents ages 10 to 19 are due to accidents, and most of those, especially among older adolescents, involve motor vehicles. Risky driving habits, such as speeding, tailgating, and driving under the influence of alcohol or other drugs, may be more important causes of these accidents than is lack of driving experience. In about 50 percent of the motor vehicle fatalities involving an adolescent, the driver has a blood alcohol level of 0.10 percent, twice the level needed to be "under the influence" in some states. A high rate of intoxication is also often present in adolescents who die as pedestrians or while using recreational vehicles.

Homicide is the second leading cause of death in adolescence (National Center for Health Statistics, 2004), especially among African American male adolescents. Since the 1950s, the adolescent suicide rate has tripled. Suicide accounts for 6 percent of the deaths in the 10-to-14 age group and 12 percent of deaths in the 15-to-19 age group. We will discuss suicide further in chapter 13.

Risk-Taking Behavior   One type of health-compromising behavior that increases in adolescence is risk taking (Baskin-Summers & Summers, 2006; Youngblade & others, 2006). Beginning in early adolescence, individuals *seek* experiences that create high-intensity feelings. Of course, there is a wide range of individual differences (Dahl, 2004, p. 6), but generally adolescents *like* intensity, excitement, and arousal. They are drawn to music videos that shock and bombard the senses. Teenagers flock to horror and slasher movies. They dominate queues waiting to ride the high-adrenaline rides at amusement parks. Adolescence is a time when sex, drugs, *very* loud music, and other high-stimulation experiences take on great appeal. It is a developmental period when an appetite for adventure, a predilection for risks, and a desire for novelty and thrills seem to reach naturally high levels.

Two important factors in sexual risk taking are *self-regulation*—the ability to regulate one's emotions and behavior—and parent-adolescent relationships. One longitudinal study found that a lower level of self-regulation at 12 to 13 years of

What are some characteristics of adolescents' risk-taking behavior?

age was linked with a higher level of sexual risk taking four years later (Rafaelli & Crockett, 2003). Other researchers have also found a relation between low self-regulation and high sexual risk taking (Kahn & others, 2002). In another recent study, sexual risk taking in adolescence was linked with low parental monitoring and poor parent-adolescent communication (Huebner & Howell, 2003). A research review found these aspects of parenting were linked with reduced risk of adolescent pregnancy: parent/adolescent closeness or connectedness, parental supervision or regulation of adolescents' activities, and parental values against intercourse or unprotected intercourse in adolescence (Miller, Benson, and Galbraith, 2001)

What can be done to help adolescents satisfy their motivation for risk taking without compromising their health? As Laurence Steinberg (2004, p. 58) argues, one strategy is to limit "opportunities for immature judgment to have harmful consequences. Thus, strategies such as raising the price of cigarettes, more vigilantly enforcing laws governing the sale of alcohol, expanding access to mental health and contraceptive services, and raising the driving age would likely be more effective in limiting adolescent smoking, substance abuse, suicide, pregnancy, and automobile fatalities than strategies aimed at making adolescents wiser, less impulsive, and less short-sighted."

It also is important for parents, teachers, mentors, and other responsible adults to effectively monitor adolescents' behavior (Dahl, 2004). In many cases, adults decrease their monitoring of adolescents too early, leaving them to cope with tempting situations alone or with friends and peers (Masten, 2004). When adolescents are in tempting and dangerous situations with minimal adult supervision, their inclination to engage in risk-taking behavior combined with their lack of self-regulatory skills can make them vulnerable to a host of negative outcomes.

Substance Use and Abuse

Each year since 1975, Lloyd Johnston and his colleagues at the Institute of Social Research at the University of Michigan have monitored the drug use of America's high school seniors in a wide range of public and private high schools. Since 1991, they also have surveyed drug use by eighth- and tenth-graders. In 2005, the University of Michigan study, called the Monitoring the Future Study, surveyed approximately 50,000 students in nearly 400 secondary schools.

According to this study, as figure 12.8 illustrates, the proportions of tenth- and twelfth-grade students who use any illicit drug declined in the late 1990s and first

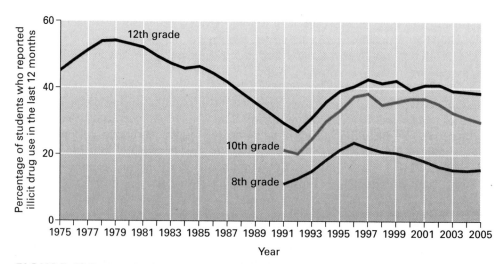

FIGURE 12.8 Trends in Drug Use by U.S. Eighth-, Tenth-, and Twelfth-Grade Students. This graph shows the percentage of U.S. eighth-, tenth-, and twelfth-grade students who reported having taken an illicit drug in the last 12 months from 1991 to 2005 for eighth- and tenth-graders, and from 1975 to 2005 for twelfth-graders (Johnston & others, 2006).

years of the twenty-first century (Johnston & others, 2006). The United States has the highest rate of adolescent drug use of any industrialized nation. Also, the University of Michigan survey likely underestimates the percentage of adolescents who take drugs because it does not include high school dropouts, who have a higher rate of drug use than do students who are still in school.

Alcohol How extensive is alcohol use by U.S. adolescents? Sizable declines have occurred in recent years (Johnston & others, 2006). The percentage of U.S. eighth-graders saying that they had any alcohol to drink in the past 30 days fell from a 1996 high of 26 percent to 17 percent in 2005. The 30-day prevalence fell among tenth-graders from 39 percent in 2001 to 33 percent in 2005 and among high school seniors from 72 percent in 1980 to 47 percent in 2005. Binge drinking (defined in the University of Michigan surveys as having five or more drinks in a row in the last two weeks) by high school seniors declined from 41 percent in 1980 to 30 percent in 2005. Binge drinking by eighth- and tenth-graders also has dropped in recent years. A consistent sex difference occurs in binge drinking, with males engaging in this more than females.

Although alcohol use by secondary school students has declined in recent years, college students show little drop in alcohol use and an increase in heavy drinking. Heavy drinking at parties among college males is common and is becoming more common (Wechsler & others, 2002).

Cigarette Smoking Cigarette smoking (in which the active drug is nicotine) is one of the most serious yet preventable health problems. One study found that smoking in the adolescent years causes permanent genetic changes in the lungs and forever increases the risk of lung cancer, even if the smoker quits (Weincke & others, 1999). The damage was much less likely among smokers in the study who started in their twenties. The early age of onset of smoking was more important in predicting genetic damage than how heavily the individuals smoked.

Smoking is likely to begin in grades 7 through 9, although sizable portions of youth are still establishing regular smoking habits during high school and college. Since 1975, cigarettes have been the substance most frequently used on a daily basis by high school seniors. Risk factors for becoming a regular smoker in adolescence include having a friend who smoked, a weak academic orientation, and low parental support (Tucker, Ellickson, & Klein, 2003).

Cigarette smoking among adolescents peaked in 1996 and 1997 and has gradually declined since then (Johnston & others, 2006). Following peak use in 1996, smoking rates for U.S. eighth-graders have fallen by 50 percent. In 2005, the percentages of adolescents who said they smoked cigarettes in the last 30 days were 23 percent (twelfth grade), 15 percent (tenth grade), and 9 percent (eighth grade).

There are a number of explanations for the decline in cigarette use by U.S. youth. These include increasing prices, less tobacco advertising reaching adolescents, more antismoking advertisements, and an increase in negative publicity about the tobacco industry (Myers & MacPherson, 2004). Since the mid-1990s an increasing percentage of adolescents have reported that they perceive cigarette smoking as dangerous, that they disapprove of it, that they are less accepting of being around smokers, and that they prefer to date nonsmokers (Johnston, O'Malley, & Bachman, 2004).

www.mhhe.com/santrockld11

National Clearinghouse for
Alcohol and Drug Information
Monitoring the Future

Painkillers An alarming recent trend is use of prescription painkillers by adolescents. A 2004 survey revealed that 18 percent of U.S. adolescents had used Vicodin at some point in their lifetime, while 10 percent had used Oxycontin (Partnership for a Drug-Free America, 2005). These drugs fall into the general class of drugs called narcotics and they are highly addictive. In this recent national survey, 9 percent of adolescents said they had abused cough medications to intentionally get high. The

University of Michigan began including Oxycontin in its survey of twelfth-graders in 2002. From 2002 to 2005 adolescents' reports of using it at any time in the previous year increased from 4 percent to 5.5 percent (Johnston & others, 2006). Adolescents cite the medicine cabinets of their parents or of friends' parents as the main source for their prescription painkillers.

A recent analysis of data from the National Survey on Drug Use and Health revealed that abuse of prescription painkillers by U.S. adolescents may have become an epidemic (Sung & others, 2005). In this survey, adolescents especially at risk for abusing prescription painkillers were likely to already be using illicit drugs, came from low-socioeconomic-status families, had favorable attitudes toward illicit drugs, had detached parents, or had friends who used drugs.

What roles do parents play in adolescents' drug use?

The Roles of Development, Parents, and Peers   Most adolescents use drugs at some point in their development, whether limited to alcohol, caffeine, and cigarettes or extended to marijuana, cocaine, and hard drugs. Using drugs as a way of coping with stress, however, can interfere with the development of competent coping skills and responsible decision making. If they use drugs to cope with stress, many young adolescents enter adult roles of marriage and work prematurely, without adequate socioemotional growth, and risk failure in these roles. Researchers have found that drug use in childhood or early adolescence has more detrimental long-term effects on the development of responsible, competent behavior than when drug use occurs in late adolescence (Newcomb & Bentler, 1988). A longitudinal study of individuals from 8 to 42 years of age found that early onset of drinking was linked to increased risk of heavy drinking in middle age (Pitkanen, Lyyra, & Pulkkinen, 2005).

One longitudinal study linked early substance abuse with several characteristics of early childhood (Kaplow & others, 2002). Risk factors at kindergarten age for substance use at 10 to 12 years of age included being male, having a parent who abused substances, having a low level of verbal reasoning by parents, and having low social problem-solving skills.

Parents, peers, and social support can play important roles in preventing adolescent drug abuse (Eitle, 2005; Fromme, 2006; Nash, McQueen, & Bray, 2005; Nation & Heflinger, 2006; Riggs, Elfenbaum, & Pentz, 2006). Positive relationships with parents and others can reduce adolescents' drug use (Little & others, 2004; Wood & others, 2004). In one recent study, parental control and monitoring were linked with a lower incidence of problem behavior by adolescents, including substance abuse (Fletcher, Steinberg, & Williams-Wheeler, 2004). In another study low parental involvement, peer pressure, and associating with problem-behaving friends were linked with higher use of drugs by adolescents (Simons-Morton & others, 2001). Also, a recent national survey revealed that parents who were more involved in setting limits, such as where adolescents went after school and what they were exposed to on TV and the Internet, were more likely to have adolescents who did not use drugs (National Center on Addiction and Substance Abuse, 2001). To read about a program created to reduce adolescent drinking and smoking, see the Research in Life-Span Development interlude.

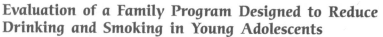

RESEARCH IN LIFE-SPAN DEVELOPMENT

Evaluation of a Family Program Designed to Reduce Drinking and Smoking in Young Adolescents

Few experimental studies have been conducted to determine if family programs can reduce drinking and smoking in young adolescents. In one recent experimental study, 1,326 families with 12- to 14-year-old adolescents living throughout the

United States were interviewed (Bauman & others, 2002). After the baseline interviews, participants were randomly assigned either to go through the Family Matters program (experimental group) or to not experience the program (control group) (Bauman & others, 2002).

The families assigned to the Family Matters program received four mailings of booklets. Each mailing was followed by a telephone call from a health educator to "encourage participation by all family members, answer any questions, and record information" (Bauman & others, 2002, pp. 36–37). The first booklet focused on the negative consequences of adolescent substance abuse to the family. The second emphasized "supervision, support, communication skills, attachment, time spent together, educational achievement, conflict reduction, and how well adolescence is understood." The third booklet asked parents to "list things that they do that might inadvertently encourage their child's use of tobacco or alcohol, identify rules that might influence the child's use, and consider ways to monitor use. Then adult family members and the child meet to agree upon rules and sanctions related to adolescent use." Booklet four deals with what "the child can do to resist peer and media pressures for use."

Two follow-up interviews with the parents and adolescents were conducted three months and one year after the experimental group completed the program. Adolescents in the Family Matters program reported lower alcohol and cigarette use both at three months and again one year after the program had been completed. Figure 12.9 shows the results for alcohol.

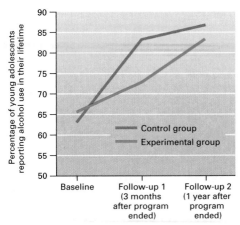

FIGURE 12.9 Young Adolescents' Reports of Alcohol Use in the Family Matters Program. Note that at baseline (before the program started) the young adolescents in the Family Matters program (experimental group) and their counterparts who did not go through the program (control group) reported approximately the same lifetime use of alcohol (slightly higher use by the experimental group). However, three months after the program ended, the experimental group reported lower alcohol use, and this reduction was still present one year after the program ended, although at a reduced level.

Eating Disorders

Eating disorders have become increasingly common among adolescents (Casazza & Ciccazzo, 2006; Fiore & others, 2006; Lowrey & others, 2005). Here are some research findings involving adolescent eating disorders:

- *Body Image.* Girls who felt negatively about their bodies in early adolescence were more likely to develop eating disorders, two years later, than their counterparts who did not feel negatively about their bodies (Attie & Brooks-Gunn, 1989).
- *Parenting.* Adolescents who reported observing more healthy eating patterns and exercise by their parents had more healthy eating patterns and exercised more themselves (Pakpreo & others, 2004). Negative parent-adolescent relationships were linked with increased dieting by girls over a one-year period (Archibald, Graber, & Brooks-Gunn, 1999).
- *Sexual Activity.* Girls who were both sexually active with their boyfriends and in pubertal transition were the most likely to be dieting or engaging in disordered eating patterns (Cauffman, 1994).
- *Role Models.* Girls who were highly motivated to look like same-sex figures in the media were more likely than their peers to become very concerned about their weight (Field & others, 2001). Watching commercials with idealized thin female images increased adolescent girls' dissatisfaction with their bodies (Hargreaves & Tiggemann, 2004).
- *Television.* Adolescent girls who watched four hours of television or more per day were more likely to be overweight than those who watched less than four hours a day (Dowda & others, 2001).

Let's now examine two eating disorders that may appear in adolescence: anorexia nervosa and bulimia nervosa.

Anorexia Nervosa Although most U.S. girls have been on a diet at some point, slightly less than 1 percent ever develop anorexia nervosa (Walters &

Anorexia nervosa has become an increasing problem for adolescent girls and young adult women. *What are some possible causes of anorexia nervosa?*

Kendler, 1994). **Anorexia nervosa** is an eating disorder that involves the relentless pursuit of thinness through starvation. It is a serious disorder that can lead to death (Agras & others, 2004; Jacoangeli & others, 2006). Three main characteristics of anorexia nervosa are:

- Weighing less than 85 percent of what is considered normal for a person's age and height.
- Having an intense fear of gaining weight. The fear does not decrease with weight loss.
- Having a distorted image of their body shape (Striegel-Moore & others, 2004; Wiseman, Sunday, & Becker, 2005). Even when they are extremely thin, they see themselves as too fat. They never think they are thin enough, especially in the abdomen, buttocks, and thighs. They usually weigh themselves frequently, often take their body measurements, and gaze critically at themselves in mirrors (Seidenfeld, Sosin, & Rickert, 2004).

Anorexia nervosa typically begins in the early to middle teenage years, often following an episode of dieting and some type of life stress (Lee & others, 2005). It is about 10 times more likely to occur in females than males. When anorexia nervosa does occur in males, the symptoms and other characteristics (such as a distorted body image and family conflict) are usually similar to those reported by females who have the disorder (Araceli & others, 2005).

Most anorexics are White adolescent or young adult females from well-educated, middle- and upper-income families and are competitive and high-achieving (Schmidt, 2003). They set high standards, become stressed about not being able to reach the standards, and are intensely concerned about how others perceive them (Striegel-Moore, Silberstein, & Rodin, 1993). Unable to meet these high expectations, they turn to something they can control: their weight.

The fashion image in U.S. culture that emphasizes "thin is beautiful" contributes to the incidence of anorexia nervosa (Hsu, 2004; Polivy & others, 2003). This image is reflected in the saying, "You never can be too rich or too thin." The media portrays thin as beautiful in their choice of fashion models, which many adolescent girls want to emulate (Strasburger, 2006; Wiseman, Sunday, & Becker, 2005).

Bulimia Nervosa Whereas anorexics control their eating by restricting it, most bulimics cannot (Mitchell & Mazzeo, 2004). **Bulimia nervosa** is an eating disorder in which the individual consistently follows a binge-and-purge pattern. The bulimic goes on an eating binge and then purges by self-inducing vomiting or using a laxative. Although many people binge and purge occasionally and some experiment with it, a person is considered to have a serious bulimic disorder only if the episodes occur at least twice a week for three months.

As with anorexics, most bulimics are preoccupied with food, have a strong fear of becoming overweight, and are depressed or anxious (Garcia-Alba, 2004; Ramacciotti & others, 2005; Speranza & others, 2005). Unlike anorexics, people who binge-and-purge typically fall within a normal weight range, which makes bulimia more difficult to detect.

Approximately 1 to 2 percent of U.S. women are estimated to develop bulimia nervosa (Gotesdam & Agras, 1995), and about 90 percent of bulimics are women. Bulimia nervosa typically begins in late adolescence or early adulthood. Many women who develop bulimia nervosa were somewhat overweight before the onset of the disorder, and the binge eating often began during an episode of dieting. One recent study of adolescent girls found that increased dieting, pressure to be thin, exaggerated emphasis on appearance, body dissatisfaction, depression symptoms, low self-esteem, and low social support predicted binge eating two years later (Stice, Presnell, & Spangler, 2002). As with anorexia nervosa, about 70 percent of individuals who develop bulimia nervosa eventually recover from the disorder (Agras & others, 2004; Keel & others, 1999).

anorexia nervosa An eating disorder that involves the relentless pursuit of thinness through starvation.

bulimia nervosa An eating disorder in which the individual consistently follows a binge-and-purge pattern.

Review and Reflect ● LEARNING GOAL 3

3 **Identify adolescent problems related to health, substance use and abuse, and eating disorders**

Review
- What are key concerns about the health of adolescents?
- What are some characteristics of adolescents' substance use and abuse?
- What are the characteristics of the major eating disorders?

Reflect
- What do you think should be done to reduce the use of drugs by adolescents?

4 ADOLESCENT COGNITION

| Piaget's Theory | Adolescent Egocentrism | Information Processing |

Adolescents' developing power of thought opens up new cognitive and social horizons. Let's examine what their developing power of thought is like, beginning with Piaget's theory (1952).

Piaget's Theory

As we discussed in chapter 10, Piaget proposed that at about 7 years of age children enter the *concrete operational stage* of cognitive development. They can reason logically about concrete events and objects, and they make gains in the ability to classify objects and to reason about the relationships between classes of objects. The concrete operational stage lasts until the child is about 11 years old, according to Piaget, when the fourth and final stage of cognitive development begins, the formal operational stage.

The Formal Operational Stage What are the characteristics of the formal operational stage? Formal operational thought is more abstract than concrete operational thought. Adolescents are no longer limited to actual, concrete experiences as anchors for thought. They can conjure up make-believe situations, events that are purely hypothetical possibilities or abstract propositions, and can try to reason logically about them.

The abstract quality of thinking during the formal operational stage is evident in the adolescent's verbal problem-solving ability. Whereas the concrete operational thinker needs to see the concrete elements A, B, and C to be able to make the logical inference that, if A = B and B = C, then A = C, the formal operational thinker can solve this problem merely through verbal presentation.

Another indication of the abstract quality of adolescents' thought is their increased tendency to think about thought itself. One adolescent commented, "I began thinking about why I was thinking what I was. Then I began thinking about why I was thinking about what I was thinking about what I was." If this sounds abstract, it is, and it characterizes the adolescent's enhanced focus on thought and its abstract qualities.

Might adolescents' ability to reason hypothetically and to evaluate what is ideal versus what is real lead them to engage in demonstrations, such as this protest related to better ethnic relations? What other causes might be attractive to adolescents' newfound cognitive abilities of hypothetical-deductive reasoning and idealistic thinking?

Accompanying the abstract nature of formal operational thought is thought full of idealism and possibilities, especially during the beginning of the formal operational stage, when assimilation dominates. Adolescents engage in extended speculation about ideal characteristics—qualities they desire in themselves and in others. Such thoughts often lead adolescents to compare themselves with others in regard to such ideal standards. And their thoughts are often fantasy flights into future possibilities. It is not unusual for the adolescent to become impatient with these new-found ideal standards and to become perplexed over which of many ideal standards to adopt.

At the same time that adolescents think more abstractly and idealistically, they also think more logically. Children are likely to solve problems through trial-and-error; adolescents begin to think more as a scientist thinks, devising plans to solve problems and systematically testing solutions. This type of problem solving requires **hypothetical-deductive reasoning,** which involves creating a hypothesis and deducing its implications, which provides ways to test the hypothesis. Thus, formal operational thinkers develop hypotheses about ways to solve problems and then systematically deduce the best path to follow to solve the problem.

One example of hypothetical-deductive reasoning involves a modification of the familiar game Twenty Questions. Individuals are shown a set of 42 color pictures, displayed in a rectangular array (six rows of seven pictures each) and are asked to determine which picture the experimenter has in mind (that is, which is "correct"). The individuals are allowed to ask only questions to which the experimenter can answer yes or no. The object of the game is to select the correct picture by asking as few questions as possible. Adolescents who are deductive hypothesis testers formulate a plan and test a series of hypotheses, which considerably narrows the field of choices. The most effective plan is a "halving" strategy (Q: Is the picture in the right half of the array? A: No. Q: Okay. Is it in the top half? And so on.). A correct halving strategy guarantees the answer in seven questions or less. By contrast, concrete operational thinkers may persist with questions that continue to test some of the same possibilities that previous questions could have eliminated. For example, they may ask whether the correct picture is in row 1 and are told that it is not. Later, they may ask whether the picture is *X,* which is in row 1.

Thus, formal operational thinkers test their hypotheses with judiciously chosen questions and tests. By contrast, concrete operational thinkers often fail to understand the relation between a hypothesis and a well-chosen test of it, stubbornly clinging to ideas that already have been discounted.

Evaluating Piaget's Theory

Some of Piaget's ideas on the formal operational stage have been challenged (Keating, 2004; Kuhn & Franklin, 2006). There is much more individual variation than Piaget envisioned. Only about one in three young adolescents is a formal operational thinker. Many American adults never become formal operational thinkers, and neither do many adults in other cultures.

Furthermore, education in the logic of science and mathematics promotes the development of formal operational thinking. This point recalls a criticism of Piaget's theory that we discussed in chapter 10: Culture and education exert stronger influences on cognitive development than Piaget believed (Cole, 2005, 2006; Greenfield, Suzuki, & Rothstein-Fisch, 2006).

Piaget's theory of cognitive development has been challenged on other points as well (Bauer, 2006; Cohen & Cashon, 2006; Mandler, 2004). As we noted in chapter 10, Piaget conceived of stages as unitary structures of thought, with various aspects of a stage emerging at the same time. However, most contemporary developmentalists agree that cognitive development is not as stage-like as Piaget thought (Bjorklund, 2005; Kellman & Arterberry, 2006). Furthermore, children can be trained to reason at a higher cognitive stage, and some cognitive abilities emerge earlier than Piaget thought (Bjorklund, 2005; Mandler, 2004). For example, even 2-year-olds are non-egocentric in some contexts. When they realize that another person will not see an

The thoughts of youth are long, long thoughts.

—Henry Wadsworth Longfellow
American Poet, 19th Century

hypothetical-deductive reasoning Piaget's formal operational concept that adolescents have the cognitive ability to develop hypotheses, or best guesses, about ways to solve problems, such as an algebraic equation.

object, they investigate whether the person is blindfolded or looking in a different direction. Some understanding of the conservation of number has been demonstrated as early as age 3, although Piaget did not think it emerged until 7. Other cognitive abilities can emerge later than Piaget thought (Keating, 2004; Kuhn & Franklin, 2006). As we noted, many adolescents still think in concrete operational ways or are just beginning to master formal operations. Even many adults are not formal operational thinkers.

Despite these challenges to Piaget's ideas, we owe him a tremendous debt. Piaget was the founder of the present field of cognitive development, and he developed a long list of masterful concepts of enduring power and fascination: assimilation, accommodation, object permanence, egocentrism, conservation, and others. Psychologists also owe him the current vision of children as active, constructive thinkers. And they have a debt to him for creating a theory that generated a huge volume of research on children's cognitive development.

Piaget also was a genius when it came to observing children. His careful observations demonstrated inventive ways to discover how children act on and adapt to their world. He also showed us how children need to make their experiences fit their schemes yet simultaneously adapt their schemes to experience. Piaget also revealed how cognitive change is likely to occur if the context is structured to allow gradual movement to the next higher level. Concepts do not emerge suddenly, full-blown, but instead develop through a series of partial accomplishments that lead to increasingly comprehensive understanding (Haith & Benson, 1998).

Adolescent Egocentrism

"Oh, my gosh! I can't believe it. Help! I can't stand it!" Tracy desperately yells. "What is wrong? What is the matter?" her mother asks. Tracy responds, "Everyone in here is looking at me." The mother queries, "Why?" Tracy says, "Look, this one hair just won't stay in place," as she rushes to the restroom of the restaurant. Five minutes later, she returns to the table in the restaurant after she has depleted an entire can of hairspray.

Tracy's reaction illustrates the egocentrism that is another characteristic of adolescent cognition. **Adolescent egocentrism** is the heightened self-consciousness of adolescents. David Elkind (1976) believes that adolescent egocentrism has two key components—the imaginary audience and personal fable. The **imaginary audience** is adolescents' belief that others are as interested in them as they themselves are, as well as attention-getting behavior—attempts to be noticed, visible, and "on stage." An adolescent might think that others are as aware of a small spot on his trousers as he is, possibly knowing that he has masturbated. Another adolescent, an eighth-grade girl, walks into her classroom and thinks that all eyes are riveted on her complexion. Adolescents sense that they are "on stage" in early adolescence, believing they are the main actors and all others are the audience.

According to Elkind, the **personal fable** is the part of adolescent egocentrism involving a sense of uniqueness and invincibility. For example, during a conversation between two 14-year-old girls, one named Margaret says, "Are you kidding, I won't get pregnant." And 13-year-old Adam describes himself, "No one understands me, particularly my parents. They have no idea of what I am feeling." Adolescents' sense of personal uniqueness makes them feel that no one can understand how they really feel. As part of their effort to retain a sense of personal uniqueness, adolescents might craft a story about the self that is filled with fantasy, immersing themselves in a world that is far removed from reality. Personal fables frequently show up in adolescent diaries.

Adolescents also often show a sense of invincibility, believing that they themselves will never suffer the terrible experiences (such as deadly car wrecks) that happen to other people. This sense of invincibility likely is involved in the reckless behavior of some adolescents, such as drag racing, drug use, suicide, and having sexual intercourse without using contraceptives or barriers against STIs.

Many adolescent girls spend long hours in front of the mirror, depleting cans of hairspray, tubes of lipstick, and jars of cosmetics. *How might this behavior be related to changes in adolescent cognitive and physical development?*

adolescent egocentrism The heightened self-consciousness of adolescents.

imaginary audience Involves adolescents' belief that others are as interested in them as they themselves are; attention-getting behavior motivated by a desire to be noticed, visible, and "on stage."

personal fable The part of adolescent egocentrism that involves an adolescent's sense of uniqueness and invincibility.

Information Processing

According to Deanna Kuhn (2005; Kuhn & Franklin, 2006), the most important cognitive change in adolescence is improvement in *executive functioning*, which involves higher-order cognitive activities such as monitoring and managing cognitive resources, reasoning, making decisions, and thinking critically. Improvements in executive functioning permit more effective learning and an improved ability to determine how attention will be allocated, to make decisions, and to engage in critical thinking.

Although driver-training courses can improve adolescents' cognitive and motor skills related to driving, these courses have not been effective in reducing adolescents' high rate of traffic accidents. *Why might this be so?*

Decision Making Adolescence is a time of increased decision making—which friends to choose, which person to date, whether to have sex, buy a car, go to college, and so on (Byrnes, 2003, 2005; Wigfield, Byrnes, & Eccles, 2006). How competent are adolescents at making decisions? In some reviews, older adolescents are described as more competent than younger adolescents, who in turn are more competent than children (Keating, 1990). Compared with children, young adolescents are more likely to generate different options, examine a situation from a variety of perspectives, anticipate the consequences of decisions, and consider the credibility of sources.

However, older adolescents' decision-making skills are far from perfect, as are adults' (Jacobs & Klaczynski, 2002; Keating, 2004; Klaczynski, 1997, 2005). Indeed, some researchers have found that adolescents and adults do not differ in their decision-making skills (Quadrel, Fischoff, & Davis, 1993). Furthermore, some personality traits may influence decision making. Adolescents who are impulsive and seek sensation are often not very effective decision makers, for example (Byrnes, 1998, 2005).

Being able to make competent decisions does not guarantee that one will make them in everyday life, where breadth of experience often comes into play (Jacobs & Potenza, 1990; Keating, 1990). For example, driver-training courses improve adolescents' cognitive and motor skills to levels equal to, or sometimes superior to, those of adults. However, driver training has not been effective in reducing adolescents' high rate of traffic accidents (Potvin, Champagne, & Laberge-Nadeau, 1988).

Most people make better decisions when they are calm rather than emotionally aroused. That may especially be true for adolescents, who have a tendency to be emotionally intense. The same adolescent who makes a wise decision when calm may make an unwise decision when emotionally aroused (Dahl, 2004). In the heat of the moment, emotions may overwhelm decision-making ability.

Adolescents need more opportunities to practice and discuss realistic decision making (Jones, Rasmussen, & Moffitt, 1997). Many real-world decisions on matters such as sex, drugs, and daredevil driving occur in an atmosphere of stress that includes time constraints and emotional involvement. One strategy for improving adolescent decision making is to provide more opportunities for them to engage in role playing and group problem solving.

Critical Thinking Adolescence is an important transitional period in the development of critical thinking (Keating, 1990). In one study of fifth-, eighth-, and eleventh-graders, critical thinking increased with age but still occurred in only 43 percent of even the eleventh-graders, and many adolescents showed self-serving biases in their reasoning (Klaczynski & Narasimham, 1998).

If fundamental skills (such as literacy and math skills) are not developed during childhood, critical-thinking skills are unlikely to mature in adolescence. For the subset of adolescents who lack such fundamental skills, potential gains in adolescent thinking are not likely. For other adolescents, however, cognitive changes that allow improved critical thinking in adolescence include the following:

- Increased speed, automaticity, and capacity of information processing, which free cognitive resources for other purposes
- More breadth of content knowledge in a variety of domains
- Increased ability to construct new combinations of knowledge

- A greater range and more spontaneous use of strategies or procedures for applying or obtaining knowledge, such as planning, considering alternatives, and cognitive monitoring

---

Review and Reflect ● LEARNING GOAL 4

4 Explain cognitive changes in adolescence

Review
- What is Piaget's theory of adolescent cognitive development?
- What is adolescent egocentrism?
- What are some important aspects of information processing in adolescence?

Reflect
- Using Piaget's theory of cognitive development as a guide, suppose an 8-year-old and a 16-year-old are watching a political convention on television. How might their perceptions of the proceedings differ? What Piagetian concepts would these perceptions reflect?

---

5 SCHOOLS

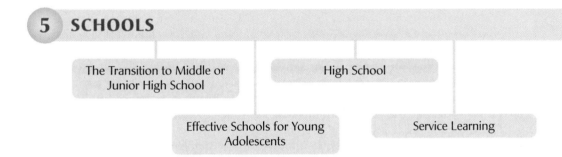

What is the transition from elementary to middle or junior high school like? What are the characteristics of effective schools for adolescents?

The Transition to Middle or Junior High School

The emergence of junior high schools in the 1920s and 1930s was justified on the basis of the changes that characterize early adolescence, as well as the need for more schools for the growing student population. Old high schools became junior high schools, and new regional high schools were built. Gradually, the ninth grade was restored to the high school, as many school systems developed middle schools that include the seventh and eighth grades, or sixth, seventh, and eighth grades. The creation of middle schools was influenced by the earlier onset of puberty in recent decades.

The first year of middle or junior high school can be difficult for many students (Hawkins & Berndt, 1985). For example, in one study of the transition from sixth grade in an elementary school to the seventh grade in a junior high school, adolescents' perceptions of the quality of their school life plunged in the seventh grade (Hirsch & Rapkin, 1987). In the seventh grade, the students were less satisfied with school, were less committed to school, and liked their teachers less. The drop in school satisfaction occurred regardless of how academically successful the students were.

The transition to middle school or junior high school can be stressful (Eccles, 2003; Wigfield, Byrnes, & Eccles, 2006; Wigfield & others, 2006). Why? The transition takes place at a time when many changes—in the individual, in the family,

The transition from elementary to middle or junior high school occurs at the same time as a number of other developmental changes. *What are some of these other developmental changes?*

Schools for Adolescents
National Center for Education Statistics
United States Department of Education
Middle Schools

and in school—are occurring simultaneously. These changes include puberty and related concerns about body image; the emergence of at least some aspects of formal operational thought, including accompanying changes in social cognition; increased responsibility and decreased dependency on parents; change to a larger, more impersonal school structure; change from one teacher to many teachers and from a small, homogeneous set of peers to a larger, more heterogeneous set of peers; and an increased focus on achievement and performance and their assessment. Also, when students make the transition to middle or junior high school, they experience the **top-dog phenomenon,** moving from being the oldest, biggest, and most powerful students in the elementary school to being the youngest, smallest, and least powerful students in the middle or junior high school.

There can also be positive aspects to the transition to middle or junior high school. Students are more likely to feel grown up, have more subjects from which to select, have more opportunities to spend time with peers and locate compatible friends, and enjoy increased independence from direct parental monitoring. They also may be more challenged intellectually by academic work.

Effective Schools for Young Adolescents

Educators and psychologists worry that junior high and middle schools have become watered-down versions of high schools, mimicking their curricular and extracurricular schedules. Critics argue that these schools should offer activities that reflect a wide range of individual differences in biological and psychological development among young adolescents. In 1989 the Carnegie Corporation issued an extremely negative evaluation of our nation's middle schools. It concluded that most young adolescents attended massive, impersonal schools; learned from irrelevant curricula; trusted few adults in school; and lacked access to health care and counseling. It recommended that the nation should develop smaller "communities" or "houses" to lessen the impersonal nature of large middle schools; have lower student-to-counselor ratios (10 to 1 instead of several-hundred-to-1); involve parents and community leaders in schools; develop new curricula; have teachers team teach in more flexibly designed curriculum blocks that integrate several disciplines; boost students' health and fitness with more in-school programs; and help students who need public health care to get it. In sum, middle schools throughout the nation need a major redesign if they are to be effective in educating adolescents (Eccles & Roeser, 2005).

High School

Just as there are concerns about U.S. middle school education, so are there concerns about U.S. high school education. Critics stress that many high schools foster passivity and that schools should create a variety of pathways for students to achieve an identity. Many students graduate from high school with inadequate reading, writing, and mathematical skills, including many who go on to college and have to enroll in remediation classes there. Other students drop out of high school and do not have skills that will allow them to obtain decent jobs much less to be informed citizens.

High School Dropouts   In the last half of the twentieth century and the first several years of the twenty-first century, U.S. high school dropout rates declined (National Center for Education Statistics, 2005). For example, in the 1940s, more than half of U.S. 15- to 24-year-olds had dropped out of school; in 2003, this figure had decreased to only 9.9 percent. Figure 12.10 shows the trends in high school dropout rates. Notice that the dropout rate of Latino adolescents remains high, although it is decreasing in the twenty-first century. The highest dropout rate in the United States, though, likely occurs for Native American youth—less than 50 percent finish their high school education.

top-dog phenomenon The circumstance of moving from the top position in elementary school to the lowest position in middle or junior high school.

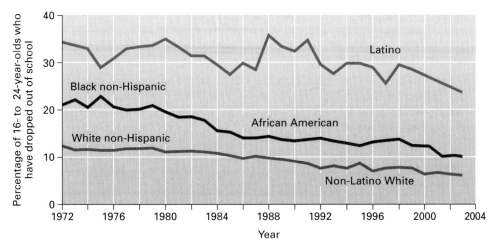

FIGURE 12.10 Trends in High School Dropout Rates. From 1972 through 2003, the school dropout rate for Latinos remained very high (23.5 percent of 16- to 24-year-olds in 2003). The African American dropout rate was still higher (10.9 percent) than the White non-Latino rate (6.3 percent) in 2000. The overall dropout rate declined considerably from the 1940s through the 1960s but has declined only slightly since 1972. (Source: National Center for Education Statistics, 2005).

Students drop out of schools for many reasons (Christensen & Thurlow, 2004; Gewertz, 2006). In one study, almost 50 percent of the dropouts cited school-related reasons for leaving school, such as not liking school or being expelled or suspended (Rumberger, 1995). Twenty percent of the dropouts (but 40 percent of the Latino students) cited economic reasons for leaving school. One-third of the female students dropped out for personal reasons, such as pregnancy or marriage.

According to a recent review, the most effective programs to discourage dropping out of high school provide early reading programs, tutoring, counseling, and mentoring (Lehr & others, 2003). They also emphasize the creation of caring environments and relationships, use block scheduling, and offer community-service opportunities.

Toward Effective High Schools   Many high school graduates not only are poorly prepared for college, they also are poorly prepared for the demands of the modern workplace. Many major companies expect new employees to be able to read at relatively high levels, do at least elementary algebra, use personal computers for straightforward tasks such as word processing, solve semistructured problems in which hypotheses must be formed and tested, communicate effectively (orally and in writing), and work effectively in groups with persons of various backgrounds (Murnane & Levy, 1996).

An increasing number of educators believe that the nation's high schools need a new mission for the twenty-first century that addresses the problems listed here (National Commission on the High School Senior Year, 2001):

- More support is needed to enable all students to graduate from high school with the knowledge and skills needed to succeed in post–secondary education and careers. Many parents and students, especially those in low-income and minority communities, are unaware of the knowledge and level of skills required to succeed in post–secondary education.
- High schools need to have higher expectations for student achievement. The senior year of high school has become too much of a party time; some students who have been accepted to college routinely ignore the academic demands of their senior year. Low academic expectations harm students from all backgrounds.
- U.S. high school students spend too much time working in low-level service jobs. Researchers have found that when tenth-graders work more than 14 hours a week, their grades drop, and when eleventh-graders work 20 or

www.mhhe.com/santrockld11

Reducing the Dropout Rate
High School Education

more hours a week, their grades drop (Greenberger & Steinberg, 1986). At the same time, shorter, higher-quality work experiences, including community service and internships, benefit high school students.

- There has been too little coordination and communication across the different levels of K–12, as well as between K–12 schools and institutions of higher education.
- At the middle and secondary school levels, every student needs strong, positive connections with adults, preferably many of them, as they explore options for school, post–secondary education, and work.

Are American secondary schools different from those in other countries? To explore this question, see the Diversity in Life-Span Development interlude.

DIVERSITY IN LIFE-SPAN DEVELOPMENT

Cross-Cultural Comparisons of Secondary Schools

Secondary schools in different countries share a number of features, but differ on others. Let's explore the similarities and differences in secondary schools in five countries: Australia, Brazil, Germany, Japan, and the United States.

Most countries mandate that children begin school at 6 to 7 years of age and stay in school until they are 14 to 17 years of age. Brazil requires students to go to school only until they are 14 years old, whereas Russia mandates that students stay in school until they are 17. Germany, Japan, Australia, and the United States require school attendance until at least 15 to 16 years of age, with some states, such as California, recently raising the mandatory age to 18.

Most secondary schools around the world are divided into two or more levels, such as middle school (or junior high school) and high school. However, Germany's schools are divided according to three educational ability tracks: (1) The main school provides a basic level of education, (2) the middle school gives students a more advanced education, and (3) the academic school prepares students for entrance to a university. German schools, like most European schools, offer a classical education, which includes courses in Latin and Greek. Japanese secondary schools have an entrance exam, but secondary schools in the other four countries do not. Only Australia and Germany have comprehensive exit exams.

The United States is the only country in the world in which sports are an integral part of the public school system. Only a few private schools in other countries have their own sports teams, sports facilities, and highly organized sports events.

In Brazil, students are required to take Portuguese (the native language) and four foreign languages (Latin, French, English, and Spanish). Brazil requires these languages because of the country's international character and emphasis on trade and commerce. Seventh-grade students in Australia take courses in sheep husbandry and weaving, two areas of economic and cultural interest in the country. In Japan, students take a number of Western courses in addition to their basic Japanese courses; these courses include Western literature and languages (in addition to Japanese literature and language), Western physical education (in addition to Japanese martial arts classes), and Western sculpture and handicrafts (in addition to Japanese calligraphy). The Japanese school year is also much longer than that of other countries (225 days versus 180 days in the United States, for example).

The juku, or "cramming school," is available to Japanese children and adolescents in the summertime and after school. It provides coaching to help them improve their grades and their entrance exam scores for high schools and universities. The Japanese practice of requiring an entrance exam for high school is a rarity among the nations of the world.

Service Learning

Service learning is a form of education that promotes social responsibility and service to the community. In service learning, students engage in activities such as tutoring, helping older adults, working in a hospital, assisting at a child-care center, or cleaning up a vacant lot to make a play area. Thus, service learning takes education out into the community (Benson & others, 2006; Flanagan, 2004; Hart, Atkins, & Donnelly, 2006; Metz & Youniss, 2005; Reinders & Youniss, 2006).

What are some of the positive effects of service training?

One goal of service learning is to help students to become less self-centered and more strongly motivated to help others (Pritchard & Whitehead, 2004). One eleventh-grade student worked as a reading tutor for students from low-income homes with reading skills well below their grade levels. She commented that until she did the tutoring she didn't realize how many students had not experienced the same opportunities that she had had. An especially rewarding moment occurred when one young girl told her, "I want to learn to read like you do so I can go to college when I grow up." A key feature of service learning is that it benefits both the student volunteers and the recipients of their help (Hamilton & Hamilton, 2004).

Students who engage in service learning tend to share certain characteristics, such as being extraverted, having a high level of self-understanding, and showing a commitment to others (Eisenberg & Morris, 2004). Also, females are more likely to volunteer to engage in community service than males (Eisenberg & Morris, 2004).

Researchers have found that service learning benefits students in a number of ways:

- Their grades improve, they become more motivated, and set more goals (Johnson & others, 1998; Search Institute, 1995).
- Their self-esteem improves (Hamburg, 1997; Johnson & others, 1998).
- They have an improved sense of being able to make a difference for others (Search Institute, 1995).
- They become less alienated (Calabrese & Schumer, 1986).
- They increasingly reflect on society's political organization and moral order (Yates, 1995).

www.mhhe.com/santrockld11

Service Learning

Recent figures indicate that 26 percent of U.S. public high schools require students to participate in service learning (Metz & Youniss, 2005). One recent study found that participating in the required 40 hours of community service improved the civic attitudes and behaviors of the twelfth-grade students who had never participated in a service learning program (Metz & Youniss, 2005). The benefits of service learning, both for the volunteer and for the recipient, suggest that more students should be required to participate in service learning programs (Arenas & others, 2006; Benson & others, 2006).

Review and Reflect • LEARNING GOAL 5

5 **Summarize some key aspects of how schools influence adolescent development**

Review
- What is the transition to middle or junior high school like?
- What are some characteristics of effective schools for young adolescents?
- What are some important things to know about high school dropouts and improving high schools?
- What is service learning and how does it affect adolescent development?

Reflect
- What was your middle or junior high school like? How did it measure up to the Carnegie Foundation's recommendations?

service learning A form of education that promotes social responsibility and service to the community.

REACH YOUR LEARNING GOALS

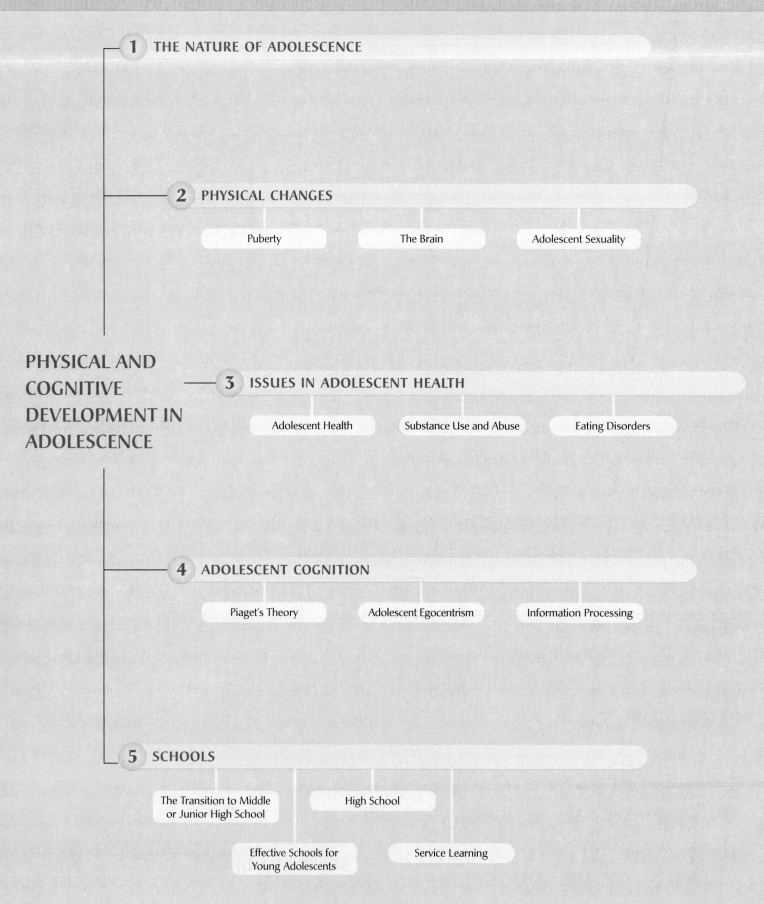

PHYSICAL AND
COGNITIVE
DEVELOPMENT IN
ADOLESCENCE

1 THE NATURE OF ADOLESCENCE

2 PHYSICAL CHANGES

Puberty

The Brain

Adolescent Sexuality

3 ISSUES IN ADOLESCENT HEALTH

Adolescent Health

Substance Use and Abuse

Eating Disorders

4 ADOLESCENT COGNITION

Piaget's Theory

Adolescent Egocentrism

Information Processing

5 SCHOOLS

The Transition to Middle
or Junior High School

High School

Effective Schools for
Young Adolescents

Service Learning

SUMMARY

1. The Nature of Adolescence: *Discuss the nature of adolescence*

Many stereotypes of adolescents are too negative. Most adolescents today successfully negotiate the path from childhood to adulthood. However, too many of today's adolescents are not provided with adequate opportunities and support to become competent adults. It is important to view adolescents as a heterogeneous group because different portraits of adolescents emerge depending on the particular set of adolescents being described.

2. Physical Changes: *Describe the changes involved in puberty as well as changes in the brain and sexuality during adolescence*

Puberty

Puberty is a period of rapid physical maturation involving hormonal and bodily changes that occur primarily during early adolescence. Puberty's determinants include nutrition, health, heredity, and body mass. The endocrine system's influence on puberty involves an interaction of the hypothalamus, the pituitary gland, and the gonads (sex glands). Testosterone plays a key role in the pubertal development of males, whereas estradiol serves this function in females. The initial onset of the pubertal growth spurt occurs on the average at 9 years for girls and 11 for boys, reaching a peak change for girls at $11\frac{1}{2}$ and for boys at $13\frac{1}{2}$. Sexual maturation is a predominant feature of pubertal change. Individual variation in pubertal changes is substantial. Adolescents show considerable interest in their body image, with girls having more negative body images than boys do. For boys, early maturation brings benefits, at least during early adolescence. Early-maturing girls are vulnerable to a number of risks.

The Brain

Spurts in the brain's electrical activity seem to occur at about 9, 12, 15, and 18 to 20 years of age. The amygdala, which handles the processing of information about emotion, develops earlier than the prefrontal cortex, which is involved in higher-level cognitive processing. This means that the brain region responsible for putting the brakes on risky, impulsive behavior is still under construction in adolescence.

Adolescent Sexuality

Adolescence is a time of sexual exploration and sexual experimentation. Mastering emerging sexual feelings and forming a sense of sexual identity are two challenges of the period. National U.S. data indicate that by age 19, four of five individuals have had sexual intercourse. Contraceptive use by adolescents is increasing. About one in four sexually experienced adolescents acquire a sexually transmitted infection (STI). America's adolescent pregnancy rate is high but has been decreasing in recent years.

3. Issues in Adolescent Health: *Identify adolescent problems related to health, substance use and abuse, and eating disorders*

Adolescent Health

Adolescence is a critical juncture in health because many of the factors related to poor health habits and early death in the adult years begin during adolescence. Poor nutrition, lack of exercise, and inadequate sleep are concerns. Risk-taking behavior increases during adolescence. Strategies for controlling the consequences of risk taking include limiting the opportunities for bad judgment to have harmful consequences and monitoring adolescents' behavior. The three leading causes of death in adolescence are accidents, homicide, and suicide.

Substance Use and Abuse

Despite recent declines in use, the United States has the highest rate of adolescent drug use of any industrialized nation. Alcohol abuse is a major adolescent problem, although its rate has been dropping in recent years, as has cigarette smoking. A recent concern is the increased use of prescription painkillers by adolescents. Drug use in childhood or early adolescence has more negative outcomes than drug use that begins in late adolescence. Parents and peers play important roles in whether adolescents take drugs.

Eating Disorders

Eating disorders have increased in adolescence, with a substantial increase in the percentage of adolescents who are overweight. Two eating disorders that may emerge in adolescence are anorexia nervosa and bulimia nervosa.

4. Adolescent Cognition: *Explain cognitive changes in adolescence*

Piaget's Theory

During the formal operational stage, Piaget's fourth stage of cognitive development, thought is more abstract, idealistic, and logical than during the concrete operational stage. Adolescents become capable of hypothetical-deductive reasoning. However, many adolescents are not formal operational thinkers but are consolidating their concrete operational thought.

Adolescent Egocentrism

Elkind describes adolescent egocentrism as the heightened self-consciousness of adolescents that consists of two parts: imaginary audience and personal fable.

Information Processing

Changes in information processing in adolescence are mainly reflected in improved executive functioning, which includes advances in decision making and critical thinking. Older adolescents make better decisions than younger adolescents, who in turn are better at this than children are. Being able to make competent decisions, however, does not mean they actually will be made in everyday life, where breadth of experience comes into play. Increased speed of processing, automaticity, and capacity, as well as more content knowledge and a greater range and spontaneous use of strategies, allow for improved critical thinking in adolescence.

5 Schools: *Summarize some key aspects of how schools influence adolescent development*

The Transition to Middle or Junior High School

The transition to middle or junior high school coincides with many social, familial, and individual changes in the adolescent's life, and this transition is often stressful. One source of stress is the move from the top-dog to the lowest position in school.

Effective Schools for Young Adolescents

In 1989, the Carnegie Foundation recommended a major redesign of U.S. middle schools that included an increase in smaller "communities," lower student-to-counselor ratios, and an increase in parental and community involvement.

High School

The overall high school dropout rate declined considerably in the last half of the twentieth century, but the dropout rates of Latino and Native American youth remain very high. A number of strategies have been proposed for improving U.S. high schools, including better support and higher expectations.

Service Learning

Service learning involves educational experiences that promote social responsibility and service to the community. Researchers have found that service learning benefits students in a number of ways.

KEY TERMS

puberty 390
menarche 391
hormones 391
hypothalamus 391
pituitary gland 391

gonads 391
sexually transmitted
   infections (STIs) 397
anorexia nervosa 406

bulimia nervosa 406
hypothetical-deductive
   reasoning 408
adolescent egocentrism 409

imaginary audience 409
personal fable 409
top-dog phenomenon 412
service learning 415

KEY PEOPLE

Mary Carskadon 401
Lloyd Johnston 402

Jean Piaget 407
David Elkind 409

Deanna Kuhn 410

E-LEARNING TOOLS

To help you master the material in this chapter, you'll find a number of valuable study tools on the LifeMap CD-ROM that accompanies this book and on the Online Learning Center for *Life-Span Development*, eleventh edition, at **www.mhhe.com/ santrockld11**.

Video Clips

In the margins of this book there are icons directing you to the LifeMap CD-ROM that accompanies the book. There you'll find two videos for chapter 12. The first video is called "Sex Among Teens at Age 15." These informal interviews with 15-year-olds offer a snapshot of contemporary adolescent attitudes toward sex. The second video is called "Eating Disorders." Obesity, anorexia nervosa, and bulimia are described in this segment, which also addresses the question of why these problems have become so common among adolescents.

Self-Assessment

Connect to **www.mhhe.com/santrockld11** to reflect on your early teenage years by completing the self-assessment, *My Romantic and Sexual Involvement in Adolescence.*

Taking It to the Net

Connect to **www.mhhe.com/santrockld11** to research the answers to these questions.

1. Al is the student member of his high school's substance abuse awareness educational forum. He has been asked to address the incoming freshmen on the latest statistics about teen use of tobacco, marijuana, cocaine, heroin, alcohol, and methamphetamine. What are these statistics?

2. Mrs. Karpacz, an elementary school principal, wants to help prepare her fourth-grade students for transition to middle school. What can parents, teachers, and students do to prepare for a smooth transition and cause the least amount of upheaval?

Health and Well-Being, Parenting, and Education Exercises

Build your decision-making skills by trying your hand at the health and well-being, parenting, and education exercises. Connect to **www.mhhe.com/santrockld11** to research the answers and complete the exercises.

Chapter 13

SOCIOEMOTIONAL DEVELOPMENT IN ADOLESCENCE

In case you're worried about what's going to become of the younger generation, it's going to grow up and start worrying about the younger generation.

—ROGER ALLEN
Contemporary American Writer

CHAPTER OUTLINE		LEARNING GOALS
THE SELF AND EMOTIONAL DEVELOPMENT	**1**	**Discuss changes in the self and emotional development during adolescence**
Self-Esteem		
Identity		
Emotional Development		
FAMILIES	**2**	**Describe changes that take place in adolescents' relationships with their parents**
Autonomy and Attachment		
Parent-Adolescent Conflict		
PEERS	**3**	**Characterize the changes that occur in peer relations during adolescence**
Friendships		
Peer Groups		
Dating and Romantic Relationships		
CULTURE AND ADOLESCENT DEVELOPMENT	**4**	**Explain how culture influences adolescent development**
Cross-Cultural Comparisons		
Ethnicity		
ADOLESCENT PROBLEMS	**5**	**Identify adolescent problems in socioemotional development and strategies for helping adolescents with problems**
Juvenile Delinquency		
Depression and Suicide		
The Interrelation of Problems and Successful Prevention/Intervention Programs		

Images of Life-Span Development
Jewel Cash, Teen Dynamo

Jewel Cash, seated next to her mother, participating in a crime watch meeting at a community center.

The mayor of the city says that she is "everywhere." She recently persuaded the city's school committee to consider ending the practice of locking tardy students out of their classrooms. She also swayed a neighborhood group to support her proposal for a winter jobs program. According to one city councilman, "People are just impressed with the power of her arguments and the sophistication of the argument" (Silva, 2005, pp. B1, B4). She is Jewel E. Cash, and she is just 16 years old.

A junior at Boston Latin Academy, Jewel was raised in one of Boston's housing projects by her mother, a single parent. Today she is a member of the Boston Student Advisory Council, mentors children, volunteers at a woman's shelter, manages and dances in two troupes, and is a member of a neighborhood watch group—among other activities. Jewel is far from typical, but her activities illustrate that cognitive and socioemotional development allows even adolescents to be capable, effective individuals.

PREVIEW

Significant changes characterize socioemotional development in adolescence. These changes include increased efforts to understand one's self, searching for identity, and emotional fluctuations. Changes also occur in the social contexts of adolescents' lives, with transformations occurring in relationships with families and peers in cultural contexts. Adolescents also may develop socioemotional problems, such as delinquency and depression.

1 THE SELF AND EMOTIONAL DEVELOPMENT

| Self-Esteem | Identity | Emotional Development |

Jewel Cash told an interviewer from the *Boston Globe*, "I see a problem and I say, 'How can I make a difference?' . . . I can't take on the world, even though I can try. . . . I'm moving forward but I want to make sure I'm bringing people with me" (Silva, 2005, pp. B1, B4). Jewel's confidence, sense of self, and emotional maturity sound at least as impressive as her activities. This section examines how adolescents develop characteristics like these. How much did you understand yourself during adolescence, and how did you acquire the stamp of your identity? This section examines self-esteem, identity, and emotional development during adolescence.

Self-Esteem

Recall from chapter 11 that *self-esteem* is the overall way we evaluate ourselves and that self-esteem is also referred to as self-image or self-worth. Controversy characterizes the extent to which self-esteem changes during adolescence and whether there are gender differences in adolescents' self-esteem (Harter, 2006). In one recent study, both boys and girls had particularly high self-esteem in childhood, but their self-esteem dropped considerably during adolescence (Robins & others, 2002). The self-esteem of girls declined more than the self-esteem of boys during adolescence in this study. Another recent study also found that the self-esteem of girls declined during early adolescence, but it found that the self-esteem of boys increased in early adolescence (Baldwin & Hoffman, 2002). In this study, high adolescent self-esteem was related to positive family relationships.

Some critics argue that developmental changes and gender differences in self-esteem during adolescence have been exaggerated (Harter, 2002). For example, in one analysis of research studies on self-esteem in adolescence, it was concluded that girls have only slightly more negative self-esteem than do boys (Kling & others, 1999). Despite the differing results and interpretations, the self-esteem of girls is likely to decline at least somewhat during early adolescence.

Why would the self-esteem of girls decline during early adolescence? One explanation points to girls' negative body images during pubertal change. Another explanation involves the greater interest young adolescent girls take in social relationships and society's failure to reward that interest. To read further about self-esteem in adolescence, see the Research in Life-Span Development interlude.

RESEARCH IN LIFE-SPAN DEVELOPMENT

Adolescents' Self-Images

One recent study examined the self-images of 675 adolescents (289 males and 386 females) from 13 to 19 years of age in Naples, Italy (Bacchini & Magliulo, 2003). Self-image was assessed using the Offer Self-Image Questionnaire (Offer & others, 1989), which consists of 130 items grouped into 11 scales that define five different aspects of self-image:

- The *psychological self* (made up of scales that assess impulse control, emotional tone, and body image)
- The *social self* (consists of scales that evaluate social relationships, morals, and vocational and educational aspirations)
- The *coping self* (composed of scales to measure mastery of the world, psychological problems, and adjustment)
- The *familial self* (made up of only one scale that evaluates how adolescents feel about their parents)
- The *sexual self* (composed of only one scale that examines adolescents' feelings and attitudes about sexual matters)

The adolescents had positive self-images, with their scores being above a neutral score (3.5) on all 11 scales. For example, the adolescents' average body self-image score was 4.2. The aspect of their lives in which adolescents had the most positive self-image involved their educational and vocational aspirations (average score of 4.8). The lowest self-image score was for impulse control (average score of 3.9). These results support the view that adolescents have a more positive perception of themselves than is commonly believed.

Gender differences were found on a number of the self-image scales, with boys consistently having more positive self-images than did girls. Keep in mind, though, that as we indicated earlier, even though girls reported lower self-images than boys, their self-images still were mainly in the positive range.

Identity

Who am I? What am I all about? What am I going to do with my life? What is different about me? How can I make it on my own? These questions reflect the search for an identity. By far the most comprehensive and provocative theory of identity development is Erik Erikson's. In this section we examine his views on identity. We also discuss contemporary research on how identity develops and how social contexts influence that development.

What Is Identity? Identity is a self-portrait composed of many pieces, including these:

What are some important dimensions of identity?

- The career and work path the person wants to follow (vocational/career identity)
- Whether the person is conservative, liberal, or middle-of-the-road (political identity)
- The person's spiritual beliefs (religious identity)
- Whether the person is single, married, divorced, and so on (relationship identity)
- The extent to which the person is motivated to achieve and is intellectual (achievement, intellectual identity)
- Whether the person is heterosexual, homosexual, or bisexual (sexual identity)
- Which part of the world or country a person is from and how intensely the person identifies with his or her cultural heritage (cultural/ethnic identity)
- The kind of things a person likes to do, which can include sports, music, hobbies, and so on (interest)
- The individual's personality characteristics (such as being introverted or extraverted, anxious or calm, friendly or hostile, and so on) (personality)
- The individual's body image (physical identity)

At the bare minimum, identity involves commitment to a vocational direction, an ideological stance, and a sexual orientation. We put these pieces together to form a sense of ourselves continuing through time within a social world.

Synthesizing the identity components can be a long and drawn-out process, with many negations and affirmations of various roles and faces. Identity development gets done in bits and pieces. Decisions are not made once and for all, but have to be made again and again. Identity development does not happen neatly, and it does not happen cataclysmically (Kroger, 2003, 2006).

As long as one keeps searching, the answers come.

—JOAN BAEZ
American Folk Singer, 20th Century

www.mhhe.com/santrockld11

Identity Development
Identity Development in Literature

Erikson's View Questions about identity surface as common, virtually universal, concerns during adolescence. Some decisions made during adolescence might seem trivial: whom to date, whether or not to break up, which major to study, whether to study or play, whether or not to be politically active, and so on. Over the years of adolescence, however, such decisions begin to form the core of what the individual is all about as a human being—what is called his or her identity.

It was Erik Erikson (1950, 1968) who first understood how central questions about identity are to understanding adolescent development. That identity is now believed to be a key aspect of adolescent development is a result of Erikson's masterful thinking and analysis. His ideas reveal rich insights into adolescents' thoughts and feelings, and reading one or more of this books is worthwhile. A good starting point is *Identity: Youth and Crisis* (1968). Other works that portray identity development are *Young Man Luther* (1962) and *Gandhi's Truth* (1969).

Erikson's theory was introduced in chapter 2. Recall that his fifth developmental stage, which individuals experience during adolescence, is **identity versus identity confusion.** During this time, said Erikson, adolescents are faced with deciding who they are, what they are all about, and where they are going in life.

identity versus identity confusion Erikson's fifth developmental stage, which occurs during adolescence. At this time, individuals are faced with deciding on who they are, what they are all about, and where they are going in life.

These questions about identity occur throughout life, but they become especially important for adolescents. Erikson believes that adolescents face an overwhelming number of choices. As they gradually come to realize that they will be responsible for themselves and their own lives, adolescents search for what those lives are going to be.

The search for an identity during adolescence is aided by a **psychosocial moratorium,** which is Erikson's term for the gap between childhood security and adult autonomy. During this period, society leaves adolescents relatively free of responsibilities and free to try out different identities. Adolescents in effect search their culture's identity files, experimenting with different roles and personalities. They may want to pursue one career one month (lawyer, for example) and another career the next month (doctor, actor, teacher, social worker, or astronaut, for example). They may dress neatly one day, sloppily the next. This experimentation is a deliberate effort on the part of adolescents to find out where they fit in the world. Most adolescents eventually discard undesirable roles.

Youth who successfully cope with conflicting identities emerge with a new sense of self that is both refreshing and acceptable. Adolescents who do not successfully resolve this identity crisis suffer what Erikson calls identity confusion. The confusion takes one of two courses: Individuals withdraw, isolating themselves from peers and family, or they immerse themselves in the world of peers and lose their identity in the crowd.

"Who are you?" said the Caterpillar. Alice replied, rather shyly, "I—I hardly know, Sir, just at present—at least I know who I was when I got up this morning, but I must have changed several times since then."

—LEWIS CARROLL
English Writer, 19th Century

Developmental Changes   Although questions about identity may be especially important during adolescence, identity formation neither begins nor ends during these years. It begins with the appearance of attachment, the development of the sense of self, and the emergence of independence in infancy; the process reaches its final phase with a life review and integration in old age. What is important about identity development in adolescence, especially late adolescence, is that for the first time, physical development, cognitive development, and socioemotional development advance to the point at which the individual can sort through and synthesize childhood identities and identifications to construct a viable path toward adult maturity.

How do individual adolescents go about the process of forming an identity? Eriksonian researcher James Marcia (1980, 1994) believes that Erikson's theory of identity development contains four *statuses* of identity, or ways of resolving the identity crisis: identity diffusion, identity foreclosure, identity moratorium, and identity achievement. What determines an individual's identity status? Marcia classifies individuals based on the existence or extent of their crisis or commitment (see figure 13.1). **Crisis** is defined as a period of identity development during which the individual is exploring alternatives. Most researchers use the term *exploration* rather than crisis. **Commitment** is personal investment in identity.

The four statuses of identity are:

- **Identity diffusion,** the status of individuals who have not yet experienced a crisis or made any commitments. Not only are they undecided about occupational and ideological choices, they are also likely to show little interest in such matters.

psychosocial moratorium Erikson's term for the gap between childhood security and adult autonomy that adolescents experience as part of their identity exploration.

crisis Marcia's term for a period of identity development during which the adolescent is choosing among meaningful alternatives.

commitment Marcia's term for the part of identity development in which adolescents show a personal investment in what they are going to do.

identity diffusion Marcia's term for adolescents who have not yet experienced a crisis (explored meaningful alternatives) or made any commitments.

Position on Occupation and Ideology	Identity Status			
	Identity diffusion	Identity foreclosure	Identity moratorium	Identity achievement
Crisis	Absent	Absent	Present	Present
Commitment	Absent	Present	Absent	Present

FIGURE 13.1 Marcia's Four Statuses of Identity. According to Marcia, an individual's status in developing an identity can be described as identity diffusion, identity foreclosure, identity moratorium, or identity achievement. The status depends on the presence or absence of (1) a crisis or exploration of alternatives and (2) a commitment to an identity. *What is the identity status of most young adolescents?*

Once formed, an identity furnishes individuals with a historical sense of who they have been, a meaningful sense of who they are now, and a sense of who they might become in the future.

—JAMES MARCIA
*Contemporary Psychologist,
Simon Fraser University*

- **Identity foreclosure** is the status of individuals who have made a commitment but not experienced a crisis. This occurs most often when parents hand down commitments to their adolescents, usually in an authoritarian way, before adolescents have had a chance to explore different approaches, ideologies, and vocations on their own.
- **Identity moratorium** is the status of individuals who are in the midst of a crisis but whose commitments are either absent or are only vaguely defined.
- **Identity achievement** is the status of individuals who have undergone a crisis and made a commitment.

Let's explore some examples of Marcia's identity statuses. Thirteen-year-old Sarah has neither begun to explore her identity in any meaningful way nor made an identity commitment; she is identity diffused. Eighteen-year-old Tim's parents want him to be a medical doctor so he is planning on majoring in premedicine in college and has not explored other options; he is identity foreclosed. Nineteen-year-old Sasha is not quite sure what life paths she wants to follow, but she recently went to the counseling center at her college to find out about different careers; she is in identity moratorium status. Twenty-one-year-old Marcelo extensively explored several career options in college, eventually getting his degree in science education, and is looking forward to his first year of teaching high school students; he is identity achieved. These examples focused on the career dimension of identity, but remember that identity has a number of dimensions.

In Marcia's terms, young adolescents are primarily in the identity statuses of diffusion, foreclosure, or moratorium. In order to move to the status of identity achievement, young adolescents need three things (Marcia, 1987, 1996): They must be confident that they have parental support, must have an established sense of industry, and must be able to adopt a self-reflective stance toward the future.

Beyond Erikson Some researchers believe the most important identity changes take place during *emerging adulthood,* the period from about 18 to 25 years of age. For example, Alan Waterman (1985, 1989, 1992) has found that from the years preceding high school through the last few years of college, the number of individuals who are identity achieved increases while the number who are identity diffused decreases. Many young adolescents are identity diffused. College upperclassmen are more likely than high school students or college freshmen to be identity achieved.

The timing of changes in identity status may depend on the particular area of life involved (Kroger, 2006). For example, for religious beliefs and political ideology, many college students have identity-foreclosure and identity-moratorium status. Many college students are still wrestling with ideological commitments (Arehart & Smith, 1990; Harter, 1990).

In any event, resolution of the identity issue during adolescence does not mean that identity will be stable through the remainder of life. Many individuals who develop positive identities follow what are called "MAMA" cycles; that is, their identity status changes from *m*oratorium to *a*chievement to *m*oratorium to *a*chievement (Archer, 1989). These cycles may be repeated throughout life (Francis, Fraser, & Marcia, 1989). Marcia (2002) believes that the first identity is just that—it is not, and should not be expected to be, the final product.

In short, questions about identity come up throughout life. An individual who develops a healthy identity is flexible and adaptive, open to changes in society, in relationships, and in careers (Adams, Gulotta, & Montemayor, 1992). This openness assures numerous reorganizations of identity throughout the individual's life.

Family Influences Parents are important figures in the adolescent's development of identity. For example, one recent study found that poor communication between mothers and adolescents, as well as persistent conflicts with friends, was linked to less positive identity development (Reis & Youniss, 2004). Do parenting styles influence

identity foreclosure Marcia's term for adolescents who have made a commitment but have not experienced a crisis.

identity moratorium Marcia's term for adolescents who are in the midst of a crisis, but their commitments are either absent or vaguely defined.

identity achievement Marcia's term for adolescents who have undergone a crisis and have made a commitment.

identity development? Parents who encourage adolescents to participate in family decision making—*democratic* parents—foster identity achievement. In contrast, parents who control the adolescent's behavior without giving the adolescent an opportunity to express opinions—*autocratic* parents—encourage identity foreclosure. *Permissive* parents, who provide little guidance to adolescents and allow them to make their own decisions, promote identity diffusion (Enright & others, 1980).

The search for balance between the need for autonomy and the need for connectedness becomes especially important to identity during adolescence. Developmentalist Catherine Cooper and her colleagues (Carlson, Cooper, & Hsu, 1990; Cooper & Grotevant, 1989; Grotevant & Cooper, 1985, 1998) found that the presence of a family atmosphere that promotes both individuality and connectedness are important in the adolescent's identity development:

- **Individuality** consists of two dimensions: self-assertion (the ability to have and communicate a point of view) and separateness (the use of communication patterns to express how one is different from others).
- **Connectedness** also consists of two dimensions: mutuality, which involves sensitivity to and respect for others' views, and permeability, which involves openness to others' views.

In general, Cooper's research indicates that identity formation is enhanced by family relationships that are both individuated, which encourages adolescents to develop their own point of view, and connected, which provides a secure base from which adolescents can explore their widening social worlds. When connectedness is strong and individuation weak, adolescents often have an identity foreclosure status. When connectedness is weak, adolescents often reveal identity confusion (Archer & Waterman, 1994).

Ethnic Identity   Throughout the world, ethnic minority groups have struggled to maintain their ethnic identities while blending in with the dominant culture (Erikson, 1968). **Ethnic identity** is an enduring aspect of the self that includes a sense of membership in an ethnic group, along with the attitudes and feelings related to that membership (Phinney, 1996). Erikson thought that this struggle for a separate ethnic identity within the larger culture has been the driving force in the founding of churches, empires, and revolutions throughout history.

Many aspects of sociocultural contexts may influence ethnic identity (Berry & others, 2006; French & others, 2006; Phinney & others, 2006). Ethnic identity tends to be stronger among members of minority groups than among members of mainstream groups. For example, in one study, the exploration of ethnic identity was higher among ethnic minority college students than among White non-Latino college students (Phinney & Alipuria, 1990). Time is another aspect of the context that influences ethnic identity (Berry & others, 2006). The indicators of identity often differ for each succeeding generation of immigrants (Phinney, 2003, 2006). First-generation immigrants are likely to be secure in their identities and unlikely to change much; they may or may not develop a new identity. The degree to which they begin to feel "American" appears to be related to whether or not they learn English, develop social networks beyond their ethnic group, and become culturally competent in their new country. Second-generation immigrants are more likely to think of themselves as "American," possibly because citizenship is granted at birth. For second-generation immigrants, ethnic identity is likely to be linked to retention of their ethnic language and social networks. In the third and later generations, the issues become more complex. Broad social factors may affect the extent to which members of this generation retain their ethnic identities. For example, media images may either discourage or encourage members of an ethnic group from identifying with their group or retaining parts of its culture. Discrimination may force people to see themselves as cut off from the majority group and encourage them to seek the support of their own ethnic culture.

Michelle Chin, age 16: "Parents do not understand that teenagers need to find out who they are, which means a lot of experimenting, a lot of mood swings, a lot of emotions and awkwardness. Like any teenager, I am facing an identity crisis. I am still trying to figure out whether I am a Chinese American or an American with Asian eyes."

*M*any *ethnic minority youth must bridge "multiple worlds" in constructing their identities.*

—CATHERINE COOPER
Contemporary Psychologist,
University of California at Santa Cruz

www.mhhe.com/santrockld11

Cultural Identity in Canada
Exploring Ethnic Identities
An Adolescent Talks
About Ethnic Identity
Ethnic Identity Research

individuality Individuality consists of two dimensions: self-assertion (the ability to have and communicate a point of view) and separateness (the use of communication patterns to express how one is different from others).

connectedness Connectedness consists of two dimensions: mutuality (sensitivity to and respect for others' views) and permeability (openness to others' views).

ethnic identity An enduring, basic aspect of the self that includes a sense of membership in an ethnic group and the attitudes and feelings related to that membership.

Researcher Margaret Beale Spencer, shown here talking with adolescents, believes that adolescence is often a critical juncture in the identity development of ethnic minority individuals. Most ethnic minority individuals consciously confront their ethnicity for the first time in adolescence.

The immediate contexts in which ethnic minority youth live also influence their identity development (Spencer, 2006). In the United States, many ethnic minority youth live in pockets of poverty; are exposed to drugs, gangs, and crime; and interact with youth and adults who have dropped out of school or are unemployed. Support for developing a positive identity is scarce. In such settings, programs for youth can make an important contribution to identity development.

Researchers are increasingly finding that a positive ethnic identity is linked to positive outcomes for ethnic minority adolescents (Rieckmann, Wadsworth, & Deyhle, 2004; Umana-Taylor, 2004; Yasui, Dorham, & Dishion, 2004). Consider these three recent studies:

- Ethnic identity was related to higher school engagement and lower aggression (Van Buren & Graham, 2003)
- A stronger ethnic identity was associated with higher self-esteem in African American, Latino, and Asian American youth (Bracey, Bamaca, & Umana-Taylor, 2004).
- The strength of ninth-grade students' ethnic identification was a better predictor of their academic success than the specific ethnic labels they used to describe themselves (Fuligni, Witkow, & Garcia, 2005). In this study, the ethnic groups most likely to incorporate more of their family's national origin and cultural background into their ethnic identification were Mexican and Chinese immigrants.

Emotional Development

Adolescence has long been described as a time of emotional turmoil (Hall, 1904). In its extreme form, this view is too stereotypical because adolescents are not constantly in a state of "storm and stress." Nonetheless, early adolescence is a time when emotional highs and lows increase (Rosenblum & Lewis, 2003; Scaramella & Conger, 2004). Young adolescents can be on top of the world one moment and down in the dumps the next. In many instances, the intensity of their emotions seems out of proportion to the events that elicit them (Steinberg & Levine, 1997). Young adolescents might sulk a lot, not knowing how to adequately express their feelings. With little or no provocation, they might blow up at their parents or siblings, which could involve using the defense mechanism of displacing their feelings onto another person.

Reed Larson and Maryse Richards (1994) found that adolescents reported more extreme emotions and more fleeting emotions than their parents did. For example, adolescents were five times more likely to report being "very happy" and three times more likely to report being "very sad" than their parents (see figure 13.2). These findings lend support to the perception of adolescents as moody and changeable (Rosenblum & Lewis, 2003).

Researchers have also found that from the fifth through the ninth grades, both boys and girls experience a 50 percent decrease in being "very happy" (Larson & Lampman-Petraitis, 1989). In this same study, adolescents were more likely than preadolescents to report mildly negative mood states.

It is important for adults to recognize that moodiness is a *normal* aspect of early adolescence, and most adolescents make it through these moody times to become competent adults. Nonetheless, for some adolescents, such emotions can reflect serious problems. For example, rates of depressed moods become more elevated for girls during adolescence (Nolen-Hoeksema, 2007). We will have more to say about depression later in the chapter.

What causes the emotional swings of early adolescence? As we saw in chapter 12, "Physical and Cognitive Development in Adolescence," significant hormonal changes characterize puberty. Emotional fluctuations in early adolescence may be related to the variability of hormones during this time period. Moods become less

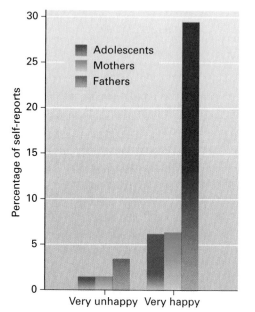

FIGURE 13.2 Self-Reported Extremes of Emotion by Adolescents, Mothers, and Fathers Using the Experience Sampling Method. In the study by Reed Larson and Maryse Richards (1994), adolescents and their mothers and fathers were beeped at random times by researchers using the experience sampling method. The researchers found that adolescents were more likely to report more emotional extremes than their parents.

extreme as adolescents move into adulthood, and this decrease in emotional fluctuation may be due to adaptation to hormone levels over time (Rosenbaum & Lewis, 2003).

Researchers have discovered that pubertal change is associated with an increase in negative emotions (Adam, 2006; Archibald, Graber, & Brooks-Gunn, 2003; Brooks-Gunn, Graber, & Paikoff, 1994; Dorn, Williamson, & Ryan, 2002). However, most researchers conclude that hormonal influences are small and that when they occur they usually are associated with other factors, such as stress, eating patterns, sexual activity, and social relationships (Rosenbaum & Lewis, 2003; Susman, Dorn, & Schiefelbein, 2003; Susman & Rogol, 2004).

Indeed, environmental experiences may contribute more to the emotions of adolescence than hormonal changes. Recall from chapter 12 that in one study, social factors accounted for two to four times as much variance as hormonal factors in young adolescent girls' depression and anger (Brooks-Gunn & Warren, 1989). In sum, both hormonal changes and environmental experiences are involved in the changing emotional landscape of adolescence.

Being able to control one's emotions is an important aspect of adolescent development. For example, one study revealed the importance of emotion regulation and mood in academic success (Gumora & Arsenio, 2002). Even when their level of cognitive ability was controlled, young adolescents who said they experienced more negative emotion regarding academic routines had lower grade point averages.

Review and Reflect ● LEARNING GOAL 1

(1) Discuss changes in the self and emotional development during adolescence

Review
- What are some changes in self-esteem that take place in adolescence?
- How does identity develop in adolescence?
- What factors affect emotional development in adolescence?

Reflect
- Where are you in your identity development? Get out a sheet of paper and list each of the pieces of identity (vocational, political, religious, relationship achievement/intellectual, sexual, gender, cultural/ethnic, interest, personality, and physical) in a column on the left side of the paper. Then write the four identity statuses (diffused, foreclosed, moratorium, and achieved) across the top of the page. Next to each dimension of identity, place a check mark in the appropriate space that reflects your identity status for the particular aspect of identity. If you checked diffused or foreclosed for any of the dimensions, think about what you need to do to move on to a moratorium status in those areas.

---

2 FAMILIES

Autonomy and Attachment   Parent–Adolescent Conflict

In chapter 11, we discussed how, during middle and late childhood, parents spend less time with their children than in early childhood. We saw that discipline during these years involves an increased use of reasoning and deprivation of

When I was a boy of 14, my father was so ignorant I could hardly stand to have the man around. But when I got to be 21, I was astonished at how much he had learnt in 7 years.

—MARK TWAIN
American Writer and Humorist, 19th Century

What are strategies parents can use to guide adolescents in effectively handling their increased motivation for autonomy?

privileges, and that there is a gradual transfer of control from parents to children, producing coregulation. Adolescence typically alters the relationship between parents and their children. Among the most important aspects of family relationships in adolescence are those that involve autonomy, attachment, and parent-adolescent conflict.

Autonomy and Attachment

Jewel, whom we met in the chapter opening, has an unusual relationship with her mother. When Jewel was a child, her mother would take her to community events around the city. Now the two still often attend events together, and Jewel jokes that her mother is her press secretary (Silva, 2005).

If Jewel and her mother instead matched stereotypes, Jewel would probably be doing all that she could to escape her mother's company. Jewel's actual behavior illustrates the dangers of overgeneralization, but it is, after all, the typical adolescent that we're most interested in. With most adolescents, parents are likely to find themselves engaged in a delicate balancing act, weighing competing needs for autonomy and control, for independence and connection.

The Push for Autonomy   The typical adolescent's push for autonomy and responsibility puzzles and angers many parents. Parents see their teenager slipping from their grasp. They may have an urge to take stronger control as the adolescent seeks autonomy and responsibility. Heated emotional exchanges may ensue, with either side calling names, making threats, and doing whatever seems necessary to gain control. Parents may seem frustrated because they *expect* their teenager to heed their advice, to want to spend time with the family, and to grow up to do what is right. Most parents anticipate that their teenager will have some difficulty adjusting to the changes that adolescence brings, but few parents imagine and predict just how strong an adolescent's desires will be to spend time with peers or how much adolescents will want to show that it is they—not their parents—who are responsible for their successes and failures.

The ability to attain autonomy and gain control over one's behavior in adolescence is acquired through appropriate adult reactions to the adolescent's desire for control (Collins & Steinberg, 2006; Laursen & Collins, 2004). At the onset of adolescence, the average individual does not have the knowledge to make appropriate or mature decisions in all areas of life. As the adolescent pushes for autonomy, the wise adult relinquishes control in those areas in which the adolescent can make reasonable decisions but continues to guide the adolescent to make reasonable decisions in areas in which the adolescent's knowledge is more limited. Gradually, adolescents acquire the ability to make mature decisions on their own.

Gender differences characterize autonomy-granting in adolescence. Boys are given more independence than girls. In one recent study, this was especially true in U.S. families with a traditional gender-role orientation (Bumpus, Crouter, & McHale, 2001).

The Role of Attachment   Recall from chapter 7 that one of the most widely discussed aspects of socioemotional development in infancy is secure attachment to caregivers. In the past decade, researchers have explored whether secure attachment also might be an important concept in adolescents' relationships with their parents (Allen & others, 2003; Collins & Steinberg, 2006; Egeland & Carlson, 2004). For example, Joseph Allen and his colleagues (Allen, Hauser, & Borman-Spurrell, 1996; Allen, Kuperminc, & Moore, 2005; Allen & others, 1998, 2002) found that securely attached adolescents were less likely than those who were insecurely attached to engage in problem behaviors, such as juvenile delinquency and drug abuse.

Other research has examined possible links between secure attachment to parents and good relations with peers. Researchers have found that securely attached adolescents had better peer relations than their insecurely attached counterparts

(Kobak, 1999; Laible, Carlo, & Raffaelli, 2000). However, the correlations between adolescent-parent attachments and adolescent outcomes are moderate, indicating that the success or failure of parent-adolescent attachments does not necessarily guarantee success or failure in peer relationships (Buhrmester, 2003).

Clearly, secure attachment with parents can be an asset for the adolescent, fostering the trust to engage in close relationships with others and laying the foundation for skills in close relationships. But a significant minority of adolescents from strong, supportive families nonetheless struggle in peer relations for a variety of reasons, such as being physically unattractive, maturing late, and experiencing cultural and SES discrepancies. On the other hand, some adolescents from troubled families find a positive, fresh start with peer relations that can compensate for their problematic family backgrounds.

Balancing Freedom and Control We have seen that parents play very important roles in adolescent development (Collins & Laursen, 2004). Although adolescents are moving toward independence, they still need to stay connected with families (Bradshaw & Garbarino, 2004; Harold, Colarossi, & Mercier, 2007; Laursen & Collins, 2004). The following studies document the important roles that parents play in adolescents' development:

- In the National Longitudinal Study on Adolescent Health (Council of Economic Advisors, 2000) of more than 12,000 adolescents, those who did not eat dinner with a parent five or more days a week had dramatically higher rates of smoking, drinking, marijuana use, getting into fights, and initiation of sexual activity.
- In another study, parents who played an active role in monitoring and guiding their adolescents' development were more likely to have adolescents with positive peer relations and lower drug use than parents who had a less active role (Mounts, 2002).

A recent longitudinal study provides further evidence of links between adolescents' relationship with their parents and their behavior (Goldstein, Davis-Kean, & Eccles, 2005). Young adolescents' perceptions of autonomy and warmth in relationships with parents in the seventh grade were linked with the adolescents' participation in risky peer contexts (such as going along with a peer to engage in deviant behavior) in the eighth grade, which in turn was related to the adolescents' engagement in deviant behavior (such as delinquency or drug use) in the eleventh grade. In terms of autonomy, young adolescents who perceived that they had a high degree of freedom over their daily activities (such as how late they could stay out and whether they could date) participated in extensive unsupervised interactions with peers, which in turn was related to deviant behaviors in the eleventh grade. Also, young adolescents who perceived their parents as too intrusive tended to frequently interact with peers who engaged in deviant behavior, which in turn was linked with deviant behavior in the eleventh grade. Thus, it is important for parents to maintain a delicate balance between not permitting too much freedom with peers and being too intrusive in their young adolescents' lives. Another important result in this study was that young adolescents who indicated they had less positive relationships with their parents tended to have an extreme peer orientation, which in turn was linked to engaging in deviant behavior in the eleventh grade.

Parent-Adolescent Conflict

While attachment to parents remains strong for many adolescents, the connectedness is not always smooth (Harold, Colarossi, & Mercier, 2007). Early adolescence is a time when conflict with parents escalates beyond childhood levels. This increase may be due to a number of factors: the biological changes of puberty, cognitive changes involving increased idealism and logical reasoning, social changes focused

It is not enough for parents to understand children. They must accord children the privilege of understanding them.

—MILTON SAPIRSTEIN
American Psychiatrist, 20th Century

www.mhhe.com/santrockld11

Parenting Today's Adolescents
Parent-Adolescent Conflict
Reengaging Families with Adolescents

on independence and identity, maturational changes in parents, and expectations that are violated by parents and adolescents. Regarding puberty, researchers have found that early-maturing adolescents experience more conflict with their parents than those who mature on time or late (Collins & Steinberg, 2006). Regarding increased idealism, many adolescents compare their parents to an ideal standard and then criticize their flaws.

Many parents see their adolescent changing from a compliant child to someone who is noncompliant, oppositional, and resistant to parental standards. When this happens, parents tend to clamp down and put more pressure on the adolescent to conform to parental standards. Parents often expect their adolescents to become mature adults overnight, instead of understanding that the journey takes 10 to 15 years. Parents who recognize that this transition takes time handle their youth more competently and calmly than those who demand immediate conformity to adult standards. The opposite tactic—letting adolescents do as they please without supervision—is also unwise.

Although parent-adolescent conflict increases in early adolescence, it does not reach the tumultuous proportions G. Stanley Hall envisioned at the beginning of the twentieth century (Collins & Laursen, 2004; Collins & Steinberg, 2006; Smetana, Campione-Barr, & Metzger, 2006). Rather, much of the conflict involves the everyday events of family life, such as keeping a bedroom clean, dressing neatly, getting home by a certain time, and not talking forever on the phone. The conflicts rarely involve major dilemmas, such as drugs and delinquency.

It is not unusual to hear parents of young adolescents ask, "Is it ever going to get better?" Things usually do get better as adolescents move from early to late adolescence. Conflict with parents often escalates during early adolescence, remains somewhat stable during the high school years, and then lessens as the adolescent reaches 17 to 20 years of age. Parent-adolescent relationships become more positive if adolescents go away to college than if they attend college while living at home (Sullivan & Sullivan, 1980).

The everyday conflicts that characterize parent-adolescent relationships may actually serve a positive developmental function. These minor disputes and negotiations facilitate the adolescent's transition from being dependent on parents to becoming an autonomous individual. For example, in one study, adolescents who expressed disagreement with their parents explored identity development more actively than did adolescents who did not express disagreement with their parents (Cooper & others, 1982). Recognizing that conflict and negotiation can serve a positive developmental function can tone down parental hostility. Understanding parent-adolescent conflict, though, is not simple (Conger & Ge, 1999).

In sum, the old model of parent-adolescent relationships suggested that as adolescents mature they detach themselves from parents and move into a world of autonomy apart from parents. The old model also suggested that parent-adolescent conflict is intense and stressful throughout adolescence. The new model emphasizes that parents serve as important attachment figures and support systems as adolescents explore a wider, more complex social world. The new model also emphasizes that, in most families, parent-adolescent conflict is moderate rather than severe and that the everyday negotiations and minor disputes are normal and can serve the positive developmental function of helping the adolescent make the transition from childhood dependency to adult independence (see figure 13.3).

Still, a high degree of conflict characterizes some parent-adolescent relationships. One estimate of the proportion of parents and adolescents who engage in prolonged, intense, repeated, unhealthy conflict is about one in five families (Montemayor, 1982). While this figure represents a minority of adolescents, it indicates that 4 to 5 million American families encounter serious, highly stressful parent-adolescent conflict. And this prolonged, intense conflict is associated with a number of adolescent problems—movement out of the home, juvenile delinquency, school dropout, pregnancy and early marriage, membership in religious cults, and drug

Old Model		New Model

Old Model

Autonomy, detachment from parents; parent and peer worlds are isolated

Intense, stressful conflict throughout adolescence; parent-adolescent relationships are filled with storm and stress on virtually a daily basis

New Model

Attachment and autonomy; parents are important support systems and attachment figures; adolescent-parent and adolescent-peer worlds have some important connections

Moderate parent-adolescent conflict is common and can serve a positive developmental function; conflict greater in early adolescence

FIGURE 13.3 Old and New Models of Parent-Adolescent Relationships

abuse (Brook & others, 1990). To read about some strategies for parenting adolescents, see the Applications in Life-Span Development interlude.

APPLICATIONS IN LIFE-SPAN DEVELOPMENT

Strategies for Parenting Adolescents

Competent adolescent development is most likely when adolescents have parents who (Santrock, 2007; Small, 1990)

1. *Show them warmth and respect, and avoid the tendency to be too controlling or too permissive.*
2. *Demonstrate sustained interest in their lives.* Parents need to spend time with their adolescents and monitor their lives.
3. *Understand and adapt to their cognitive and socioemotional development.*
4. *Communicate expectations for high standards of conduct and achievement.*
5. *Display constructive ways of dealing with problems and conflict.* Moderate conflict is a normal part of the adolescent's desire for independence and search for an identity.
6. *Understand that adolescents don't become adults overnight.* Adolescence is a long journey.

Review and Reflect • LEARNING GOAL 2

2 **Describe changes that take place in adolescents' relationships with their parents**

Review
- How do needs for autonomy and for attachment affect development in adolescence?
- What is the nature of parent-adolescent conflict?

Reflect
- How much autonomy did your parents give you in adolescence? Too much? Too little? How intense was your conflict with your parents during adolescence? What were the conflicts mainly about? Would you behave differently toward your own adolescents than your parents did with you? If so, how?

3   PEERS

| Friendships | Peer Groups | Dating and Romantic Relationships |

What changes take place in friendship during the adolescent years?

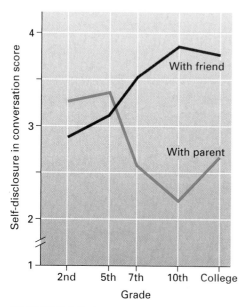

FIGURE 13.4 Self-Disclosing Conversations. In this study children and youth completed a 5-point rating scale, with a higher score representing greater self-disclosure (Buhrmester, 1998). The data shown here represent the means for each age group. Self-disclosing conversations with friends increased dramatically in adolescence while declining in an equally dramatic fashion with parents. However, self-disclosing conversations with parents began to pick up somewhat during the college years.

During middle and late childhood children spend more time with their peers than they did in early childhood, as we discussed in chapter 11, and friendships become more important to them. They can take the perspective of their peers and friends more readily than they could in the past, and their social knowledge of how to make and keep friends increases. Being overlooked or, worse yet, being rejected can have damaging effects that sometimes are carried forward to adolescence (Ladd, 2006; Rubin, Bukowski, & Parker, 2006).

Peers play powerful roles in the lives of adolescents. When you think back to your adolescent years, many of your most enjoyable moments probably were spent with peers—on the telephone, in school activities, in the neighborhood, at dances, or just hanging out. Peer relations undergo important changes in adolescence, including changes in friendships and in peer groups and the beginning of romantic relationships. In childhood, the focus of peer relations is on being liked by classmates and being included in games or lunchroom conversations. Being overlooked or, worse yet, being rejected can have damaging effects on children's development that sometimes are carried forward to adolescence (Ladd, 2006; Rubin, Bukowski, & Parker, 2006).

Friendships

For most children, being popular with their peers is a strong motivator. The focus of their peer relations is on being liked by classmates and being included in games or lunchroom conversations. Beginning in early adolescence, however, teenagers typically prefer to have a smaller number of friendships that are more intense and intimate than those of young children.

Harry Stack Sullivan (1953) was the most influential theorist to discuss the importance of adolescent friendships. In contrast to other psychoanalytic theorists who focused almost exclusively on parent-child relationships, Sullivan argued that friends are also important in shaping the development of children and adolescents. Everyone, said Sullivan, has basic social needs, such as the need for tenderness (secure attachment), playful companionship, social acceptance, intimacy, and sexual relations. Whether or not these needs are fulfilled largely determines our emotional well-being. For example, if the need for playful companionship goes unmet, then we become bored and depressed; if the need for social acceptance is not met, we suffer a lowered sense of self-worth.

During adolescence, said Sullivan, friends become increasingly important in meeting social needs. In particular, Sullivan argued that the need for intimacy intensifies during early adolescence, motivating teenagers to seek out close friends. If adolescents fail to forge such close friendships, they experience loneliness and a reduced sense of self-worth.

Many of Sullivan's ideas have withstood the test of time (Buhrmester, 2005). For example, adolescents report disclosing intimate and personal information to their friends more often than do younger children (Buhrmester, 1998) (see figure 13.4). Adolescents also say they depend more on friends than on parents to satisfy their needs for companionship, reassurance of worth, and intimacy. The ups and downs of experiences with friends shape adolescents' well-being (Berndt, 2002).

Although most adolescents develop friendships with individuals who are close to their own age, some adolescents become best friends with younger or older individuals. Do older friends encourage adolescents to engage in delinquent behavior or early sexual behavior? Adolescents who interact with older youths do engage in these behaviors more frequently, but it is not known whether the older youth guide younger adolescents toward deviant behavior or whether the younger adolescents were already prone to deviant behavior before they developed the friendship with the older youth (Billy, Rodgers, & Udry, 1984).

Peer Groups

Unlike children, whose groups are usually informal collections of friends or neighborhood acquaintances, adolescents are often members of formal and heterogeneous groups, including adolescents beyond their friends and neighborhood acquaintances. For example, try to recall the student council, honor society, or football team at your junior high school. These organizations probably included many people you had not met before and may have included adolescents from various ethnic groups.

Do these and other peer groups matter? Yes, they do. Researchers have found that the standards of peer groups and the influence of crowds and cliques become increasingly important during adolescence.

Peer Pressure   Young adolescents conform more to peer standards than do children. Around the eighth and ninth grades, conformity to peers—especially to their antisocial standards—peaks (Leventhal, 1994). At this point, adolescents are most likely to go along with a peer to steal hubcaps off a car, draw graffiti on a wall, or steal cosmetics from a store counter. U.S. adolescents are more likely to put pressure on their peers to resist parental influence than Japanese adolescents are (Rothbaum & others, 2000).

Cliques and Crowds   Cliques and crowds assume more important roles in the lives of adolescents than children (Brown, 2003, 2004). **Cliques** are small groups that range from 2 to about 12 individuals and average about 5 to 6 individuals. The clique members are usually of the same sex and about the same age.

Cliques can form because adolescents engage in similar activities, such as being in a club or on a sports team. Some cliques also form because of friendship. Several adolescents may form a clique because they have spent time with each other and enjoy each other's company. Not necessarily friends, they often develop a friendship if they stay in the clique.

What do adolescents do in cliques? They share ideas and hang out together. Often they develop an in-group identity in which they believe that their clique is better than other cliques.

Crowds are larger than cliques and less personal. Adolescents are usually members of a crowd based on reputation, and they may or may not spend much time together. Many crowds are defined by the activities adolescents engage in (such as "jocks" who are good at sports or "druggies" who take drugs) (Brown, 2004). Reputation-based crowds often appear for the first time in early adolescence and usually become less prominent in late adolescence (Collins & Steinberg, 2006).

In one study, crowd membership was associated with adolescent self-esteem (Brown & Lohr, 1987). The crowds included jocks (athletically oriented), populars (well-known students who led social activities), normals (middle-of-the-road students who made up the masses), druggies or toughs (known for illicit drug use or other delinquent activities), and nobodies (low in social skills or intellectual abilities). The self-esteem of the jocks and the populars was highest, whereas that of the nobodies was lowest. One group of adolescents not in a crowd had self-esteem equivalent to that of the jocks and the populars; this group was the independents, who indicated that crowd membership was not important to them. Keep in mind that these data are correlational; self-esteem could increase an adolescent's probability of becoming a crowd member, just as crowd membership could increase the adolescent's self-esteem.

www.mhhe.com/santrockld11

**Adolescent Peer Relationships
Youth Connections**

Most adolescents conform to the mainstream standards of their peers. However, the rebellious or anticonformist adolescent reacts counter to the mainstream peer group's expectations, deliberately moving away from the actions or beliefs this group advocates.

clique A small group that ranges from 2 to about 12 individuals, averaging about 5 to 6 individuals, and can form because adolescents engage in similar activities.

crowd A larger group structure than a clique, a crowd is usually formed based on reputation and members may or may not spend much time together.

What are dating relationships like in adolescence?

Dating and Romantic Relationships

Adolescents spend considerable time either dating or thinking about dating. Dating can be a form of recreation, a source of status, a setting for learning about close relationships, as well as a way of finding a mate.

Developmental Changes in Dating   Can you remember confiding to a friend in middle school or junior high that you "liked" someone? Or what it was like when you first had an exclusive relationship with someone, "going out" with that person and only that person? One recent study found that 40 percent of the sixth-graders studied had announced that "I like" someone (Buhrmester, 2001) (see figure 13.5). But it wasn't until the tenth grade that half of the adolescents had had a romantic relationship that lasted two months or longer. By the twelfth grade, a quarter of the adolescents still had not had a romantic relationship that lasted two months or longer. Another study found that 35 percent of 15- to 16-year-olds and almost 60 percent of 17- and 18-year-olds had had dating relationships that endured for 11 months or longer (Carver, Joyner, & Udry, 2003).

In their early exploration of romantic relationships, today's adolescents often find comfort in numbers and begin hanging out together in mixed-sex groups. Sometimes they just hang out at someone's house or get organized enough to get someone to drive them to a mall or a movie (Peterson, 1997). Or they may try *cyberdating*—"dating" over the Internet—as another alternative to traditional dating (Thomas, 1998). Cyberdating is especially popular among middle-school students. Of course, cyberdating is hazardous since one does not know who is really at the other end of the computer link. By the time they reach high school and are able to drive, most adolescents are more interested in real-life dating.

The functions of dating and romantic relationships also tend to change over the course of adolescence. Young adolescents are likely to see romantic relationships, not as a way of fulfilling attachment or sexual needs, but as a context for exploring how attractive they are, how they should romantically interact with someone, and how all of this looks to the peer group (Brown, 1999). In one study of heterosexual adolescents, young adolescents frequently mentioned companionship, intimacy, and support as positive aspects of romantic relationships, but not love and security (Feiring, 1996). Also, the young adolescents described physical attraction more in terms of cute, pretty, or handsome than in sexual terms (such as being a good kisser). (Possibly the failure to discuss sexual interests was due to

FIGURE 13.5 Age of Onset of Romantic Activity. In this study, announcing that "I like someone" occurred earliest, followed by going out with the same person three or more times, having an exclusive relationship for over two months, and finally planning an engagement or marriage (which characterized only a very small percentage of participants by the twelfth grade) (Buhrmester, 2001).

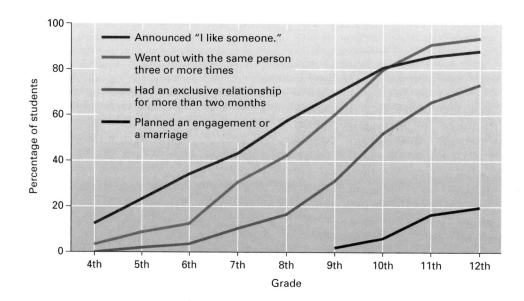

the adolescents' discomfort in talking about such personal feelings with an unfamiliar adult.) Attachment and sexual needs become central to these relationships only after adolescents learn how to interact with romantic partners (Bouchey & Furman, 2003; Furman & Shaeffer, 2003; Furman & Simon, 2006).

Dating in Gay and Lesbian Youth Recently, researchers have begun to study romantic relationships in gay, lesbian, and bisexual youth (Diamond & Savin-Williams, 2003; Savin-Williams & Diamond, 2004; Savin-Williams, 2005, 2006). Many sexual minority youth date other-sex peers, which can help them to clarify their sexual orientation or disguise it from others (Savin-Williams & Cohen, 2006; Savin-Williams & Diamond, 2004). Most gay and lesbian youth have had some same-sex sexual experience, often with peers who are "experimenting" and then go on to a primarily heterosexual orientation. However, relatively few have same-sex romantic relationships because of limited opportunities and social disapproval of same-sex relationships (Savin-Williams, 2005). In one study gay and lesbian youth rated the breakup of a current romance as their second most stressful problem, second only to disclosure of their sexual orientation to their parents (D'Augelli, 1991).

Gender Differences How adolescents behave on a date depends on their **dating scripts,** which are cognitive models that guide dating interactions. In one study of heterosexual adolescents, first dates were highly scripted along gender lines that gave males more power than females (Rose & Frieze, 1993). The male's script involved initiating the date (asking for and planning it), controlling the public domain (driving and opening doors), and initiating sexual interactions (making physical contact, making out, and kissing). The female's script focused on the private domain (concern about appearance, enjoying the date), participating in the structure of the date established by the male (being picked up, having doors opened), and responding to sexual overtures. Gender differences also occur in the motivations that adolescents bring to dating. In one study of heterosexual adolescents, 15-year-old girls were more likely to describe romance in terms of interpersonal qualities, the boys in terms of physical attraction (Feiring, 1996).

Sociocultural Contexts and Dating The sociocultural context exerts a powerful influence on adolescents' dating patterns. This influence may be seen in differences in dating patterns among ethnic groups within the United States. For example, one recent study found that Asian American adolescents were less likely to be involved in a romantic relationship in the past 18 months than African American or Latino adolescents (Carver, Joyner, & Udry, 2003).

Values, religious beliefs, and traditions often dictate the age at which dating begins, how much freedom in dating is allowed, whether dates must be chaperoned by adults or parents, and the roles of males and females in dating. For example, Latino and Asian American cultures have more conservative standards regarding adolescent dating than does the Anglo-American culture. Dating may become a source of conflict within a family if the parents have immigrated from cultures in which dating begins at a late age, little freedom in dating is allowed, dates are chaperoned, and adolescent girl dating is especially restricted. When immigrant adolescents choose to adopt the ways of the dominant U.S. culture (such as unchaperoned dating), they often clash with parents and extended-family members who have more traditional values.

In recent studies, Latina young adults in the midwestern United States reflected on their experiences in dating during adolescence (Raffaelli & Ontai, 2001, 2004). They said that their parents placed strict boundaries on their romantic involvement. As a result, the young women said that their adolescent dating experiences were filled with tension and conflict. Over half of the Latinas engaged in "sneak dating" without their parents' knowledge.

What are some ethnic variations in dating during adolescence?

dating scripts The cognitive models that individuals use to guide and evaluate dating interactions.

Dating and Romantic Relationships
Teen Chat

Dating and Adjustment Researchers have linked dating and romantic relationships with various measures of how well adjusted adolescents are (Barber, 2006; Fisher, 2006). Not surprisingly, one study of tenth-grade adolescents found that those who dated were more likely than those who did not date to be accepted by their peers and to be perceived as more physically attractive (Furman, Ho, & Low, 2005). Another recent study of 14- to 19-year-olds found that adolescents who were not involved in a romantic relationship had more social anxiety than their counterparts who were dating or romantically involved (La Greca & Harrison, 2005). But tenth-grade adolescents who dated also had more externalized problems such as delinquency and engaged in substance use (as well as genital sexual behavior) more than their counterparts who did not date (Furman, How, & Low, 2005).

Dating and romantic relationships at an unusually early age have been linked with several problems (Smetana, Campione-Barr, & Metzger, 2006). Early dating and "going with" someone is associated with adolescent pregnancy and problems at home and school (Florsheim, Moore, & Edgington, 2003). In one study (Buhrmester, 2001), girls' early romantic involvement was linked with lower grades, less active participation in class discussion, and school-related problems.

Review and Reflect ● LEARNING GOAL 3

3 Characterize the changes that occur in peer relations during adolescence

Review
• What changes take place in friendship during adolescence?
• What are adolescents' peer groups like?
• What is the nature of adolescent dating and romantic relationships?

Reflect
• What were your peer relationships like during adolescence? What peer groups were you involved in? How did they influence your development? What were your dating and romantic relationships like in adolescence? If you could change anything about the way you experienced peer relations in adolescence, what would it be?

---

4 CULTURE AND ADOLESCENT DEVELOPMENT

Cross-Cultural Comparisons   Ethnicity

We live in an increasingly diverse world, one in which there is increasing contact between adolescents from different cultures and ethnic groups. In this section, we will explore how adolescents vary cross-culturally and how ethnicity affects U.S. adolescents and their development.

Cross-Cultural Comparisons

What are the world's youth like? What traditions remain for adolescents around the globe? What circumstances are changing adolescents' lives?

Some experts argue that adolescence too often is thought of in a "Eurocentric" way (Nsamenang, 2002). Others note that advances in transportation and telecommunication are spawning a global youth culture in which adolescents everywhere wear the same type of clothing and have similar hairstyles, listen to the same music, and use similar slang expressions (Schegel, 2000). But cultural differences among adolescents have by no means disappeared (Larson & Wilson, 2004).

Traditions and Changes in Adolescence Around the Globe Consider some of the variations of adolescence around the world (Brown & Larson, 2002):

- Two-thirds of Asian Indian adolescents accept their parents' choice of a marital partner for them (Verma & Saraswathi, 2002).
- In the Philippines, many female adolescents sacrifice their own futures by migrating to the city to earn money that they can send home to their families.
- In the Middle East, many adolescents are not allowed to interact with the other sex, even in school (Booth, 2002).
- Street youth in Kenya and other parts of the world learn to survive under highly stressful circumstances (Nsamenang, 2002). In some cases abandoned by their parents, they may engage in delinquency or prostitution to provide for their economic needs.
- Whereas individuals in the United States are marrying later than in past generations, youth in Russia are marrying earlier to legitimize sexual activity (Stetsenko, 2002).

Thus, depending on the culture being observed, adolescence may involve many different experiences (Larson & Wilson, 2004).

Some cultures have retained their traditions regarding adolescence, but rapid global change is altering the experience of adolescence in many places, presenting new opportunities and challenges to young people's health and well-being. Around the world, adolescents' experiences may differ (Brown & Larson, 2002; Larson & Wilson, 2004).

Health Adolescent health and well-being have improved in some respects but not in others. Overall, fewer adolescents around the world die from infectious diseases and malnutrition now than in the past (Call & others, 2002; World Health Organization, 2002). However, a number of adolescent health-compromising behaviors (especially illicit drug use and unprotected sex) are increasing in frequency (Blum & Nelson-Mmari, 2004). Extensive increases in the rates of HIV in adolescents have occurred in many sub-Saharan countries (World Health Organization, 2002).

Gender Around the world, the experiences of male and female adolescents continue to be quite different (Brown & Larson, 2002; Larson & Wilson, 2004). Except in a few areas, such as Japan, the Philippines, and Western countries, males have far greater access to educational opportunities than females. In many countries, adolescent females have less freedom to pursue a variety of careers and engage in various leisure acts than males. Gender differences in sexual expression are widespread, especially in India, Southeast Asia, Latin America, and Arab countries, where there are far more restrictions on the sexual activity of adolescent females than on males. These gender differences do appear to be narrowing over time, however. In some countries, educational and career opportunities for women are expanding and in some parts of the world control over adolescent girls' romantic and sexual relationships is weakening.

Family In some countries, adolescents grow up in closely knit families with extensive extended kin networks "that provide a web of connections and reinforce a traditional way of life" (Brown & Larson, 2002, p. 6). For example, in Arab countries, "adolescents are taught strict codes of conduct and loyalty" (p. 6). However, in Western countries such as the United States, parenting is less authoritarian than in the

Asian Indian adolescents in a marriage ceremony

Muslim school in Middle East with boys only

Street youth in Rio de Janeiro

past, and much larger numbers of adolescents are growing up in divorced families and stepfamilies.

In many countries around the world current trends "include greater family mobility, migration to urban areas, family members working in distant cities or countries, smaller families, fewer extended-family households, and increases in mothers' employment" (Brown & Larson, 2002, p. 7). Unfortunately, many of these changes may reduce the ability of families to provide time and resources for adolescents.

The typical relationship between parents and adolescents varies among cultures. For example, in some cultures there is less parent-adolescent conflict than in others. American psychologist Reed Larson (1999) spent six months in India studying middle-socioeconomic-status adolescents and their families. He observed that in India there seems to be little parent-adolescent conflict and that many families likely would be described as "authoritarian" in Baumrind's categorization (discussed in chapter 9). Researchers also have found considerably less conflict between parents and adolescents in Japan than in the United States (Rothbaum & others, 2000).

The extent to which adolescents push for autonomy also varies. Larson observed that in India many adolescents do not go through a process of breaking away from their parents and that parents choose their youths' marital partners. In one study, U.S. adolescents sought autonomy earlier than Japanese adolescents (Rothbaum & others, 2000). In the transition to adulthood, Japanese youth are less likely to live outside the home than Americans (Hendry, 1999).

School In general, the number of adolescents in school in developing countries is increasing. However, schools in many parts of the world—especially Africa, South Asia, and Latin America—still do not provide education to all adolescents. Indeed, there has been a decline in recent years in the percentage of Latin American adolescents who have access to secondary and higher education (Welti, 2002). Furthermore, many schools do not provide students with the skills they need to be successful in adult work.

Peers Some cultures give peers a stronger role in adolescence than others (Brown, 2004; Brown & Larson, 2002). In most Western nations, peers figure prominently in adolescents' lives, in some cases taking on roles that are otherwise assumed by parents. Among street youth in South America, the peer network serves as a surrogate family that supports survival in dangerous and stressful settings. In other regions of the world, such as in Arab countries, peers have a very restrictive role, especially for girls (Booth, 2002).

In sum, adolescents' lives are characterized by a combination of change and tradition. Researchers have found both similarities and differences in the experiences of adolescents in different countries (Larson & Wilson, 2004). To read about how adolescents around the world spend their time, see the Diversity in Life-Span Development interlude.

DIVERSITY IN LIFE-SPAN DEVELOPMENT

How Adolescents Around the World Spend Their Time

Reed Larson and Suman Verma (Larson, 2001; Larson & Varma, 1999) have examined how adolescents spend their time in work, play, and developmental activities such as school. U.S. adolescents spend about 60 percent as much time on schoolwork as East Asian adolescents do, which is mainly due to U.S. adolescents doing less homework.

What U.S. adolescents have in greater quantities than adolescents in other industrialized countries is discretionary time (Larson & Wilson, 2004). About 40 to 50 percent of U.S. adolescents' waking hours (not counting summer vacations) is spent in discretionary activities compared with 25 to 35 percent in East Asia and 35 to 45 percent in Europe. Whether this additional discretionary time is a liability or an asset for U.S. adolescents, of course, depends on how they use it.

According to Larson (2001), for optimal development, U.S. adolescents may have too much unstructured time because when adolescents are allowed to choose what they do with their time, they typically engage in unchallenging activities such as hanging out and watching TV. Although relaxation and social interaction are important aspects of adolescence, it seems unlikely that spending large numbers of hours per week in unchallenging activities fosters development. Structured voluntary activities may provide more promise for adolescent development than unstructured time, especially if adults give responsibility to adolescents, challenge them, and provide competent guidance in these activities (Larson, 2001).

Rites of Passage   Another variation in the experiences of adolescents in different cultures is whether the adolescents go through a rite of passage. Some societies have elaborate ceremonies that signal the adolescent's move to maturity and achievement of adult status (Kottak, 2004). A **rite of passage** is a ceremony or ritual that marks an individual's transition from one status to another. Most rites of passage focus on the transition to adult status. In many primitive cultures, rites of passage are the avenue through which adolescents gain access to sacred adult practices, to knowledge, and to sexuality. These rites often involve dramatic practices intended to facilitate the adolescent's separation from the immediate family, especially the mother. The transformation is usually characterized by some form of ritual death and rebirth, or by means of contact with the spiritual world. Bonds are forged between the adolescent and the adult instructors through shared rituals, hazards, and secrets to allow the adolescent to enter the adult world. This kind of ritual provides a forceful and discontinuous entry into the adult world at a time when the adolescent is perceived to be ready for the change.

Africa has been the location of many rites of passage for adolescents, especially sub-Saharan Africa. Under the influence of Western culture, many of the rites are disappearing today, although some vestiges remain. In locations where formal education is not readily available, rites of passage are still prevalent.

Do we have such rites of passage for American adolescents? We certainly do not have universal formal ceremonies that mark the passage from adolescence to adulthood. Certain religious and social groups do have initiation ceremonies that indicate that an advance in maturity has been reached—the Jewish bar mitzvah, the Catholic confirmation, and social debuts, for example.

School graduation ceremonies come the closest to being culture-wide rites of passage in the United States. The high school graduation ceremony has become nearly universal for middle-class adolescents and increasing numbers of adolescents from low-income backgrounds. Nonetheless, high school graduation does not result in universal changes; many high school graduates continue to live with their parents, continue to be economically dependent on them, and continue to be undecided about career and lifestyle matters.

Another rite of passage for increasing numbers of American adolescents is sexual intercourse (Halonen & Santrock, 1999). By 19 years of age, four out of five American adolescents have had sexual intercourse.

These Congolese Kota boys painted their faces as part of a rite of passage to adulthood. *What rites of passage do American adolescents have?*

rite of passage A ceremony or ritual that marks an individual's transition from one status to another. Most rites of passage focus on the transition to adult status.

Ethnicity

It is important for adolescents to learn to take the perspective of individuals from ethnic and cultural groups that are different from theirs and think, "If I were in

Jason Leonard, age 15: "I want America to know that most of us black teens are not troubled people from broken homes and headed to jail. . . . In my relationships with my parents, we show respect for each other and we have values in our house. We have traditions we celebrate together, including Christmas and Kwanzaa."

their shoes, what kind of experiences might I have had?" "How would I feel if I were a member of their ethnic or cultural group?" "How would I think and behave if I had grown up in their world?" Such perspective taking often increases an adolescent's empathy and understanding of individuals from ethnic and cultural groups different from their own (Gudykunst, 2004; Pang, 2005).

Earlier in this chapter, we explored the identity development of ethnic minority adolescents. Here we will further examine immigration and the relationship between ethnicity and socioeconomic status.

Immigration Relatively high rates of immigration are contributing to the growth of ethnic minorities in the United States (Cushner, 2006; McLoyd, 2005; Phinney, 2003). Immigrants often experience stressors uncommon to or less prominent among longtime residents, such as language barriers, dislocations and separations from support networks, changes in SES status, and the dual struggle to preserve identity and to acculturate (Chun & Akutsu, 2003).

The adjustment of immigrants to their new country may be complicated by the fact that both native-born Americans and immigrants may be torn between two values related to ethnic issues: assimilation and pluralism (Sue, 1990).

- **Assimilation** is the absorption of ethnic minority groups into the dominant group, which often means the loss of some or virtually all of the behavior and values of the ethnic group. Individuals who endorse assimilation usually advocate that ethnic minority groups become more American.
- **Pluralism** is the coexistence of distinct ethnic and cultural groups in the same society, each of which maintains its cultural differences.

Many of the families that have immigrated in recent decades to the United States, such as Mexican Americans and Asian Americans, come from collectivist cultures in which family obligation and duty to one's family is strong (Fuligni & Hardway, 2004). For adolescents this family obligation may take the form of assisting parents in their occupations and contributing to the family's welfare (Parke & Buriel, 2006). This often means helping out in jobs in construction, gardening, cleaning, or restaurants. In some cases, the large number of hours immigrant youth work in such jobs can be detrimental to their academic achievement.

Ethnicity and Socioeconomic Status Much of the research on ethnic minority adolescents has failed to tease apart the influences of ethnicity and socioeconomic status. Ethnicity and socioeconomic status can interact in ways that exaggerate the influence of ethnicity because ethnic minority individuals are overrepresented in the lower socioeconomic levels of American society. Consequently, researchers too often have given ethnic explanations for aspects of adolescent development that were largely due instead to socioeconomic status. For example, decades of research on group differences in self-esteem failed to consider the socioeconomic status of African American and White children and adolescents. When African American adolescents from low-income backgrounds are compared with White adolescents from middle-income backgrounds, the differences often are large but not informative because of the confounding of ethnicity and socioeconomic status (Scott-Jones, 1995).

Although some ethnic minority youth have middle-income backgrounds, economic advantage does not entirely enable them to escape the burdens of ethnic minority status (Diaz, Pelletier, & Provenzo, 2006; Spencer, 2006). Middle-income ethnic minority youth still encounter much of the prejudice, discrimination, and bias associated with being a member of an ethnic minority group. Often characterized as a "model minority" because of their strong achievement orientation and family cohesiveness, Japanese Americans still experience stress associated with ethnic minority status (Sue, 1990).

assimilation The absorption of ethnic minority groups into the dominant group, which often involves the loss of some or virtually all of the behavior and values of the ethnic minority group.

pluralism The coexistence of distinct ethnic and cultural groups in the same society. Individuals with a pluralistic stance usually advocate that cultural differences be maintained and appreciated.

Not all ethnic minority families are poor. However, poverty contributes to the stressful life experiences of many ethnic minority adolescents (Fox & others, 2004; Leventhal & Brooks-Gunn, 2004; Schellenbach, Leadbetter, & Moore, 2004). Thus, many ethnic minority adolescents experience a double disadvantage: (1) prejudice, discrimination, and bias because of their ethnic minority status; and (2) the stressful effects of poverty.

Changing Contexts

Review and Reflect • LEARNING GOAL 4

4 **Explain how culture influences adolescent development**

Review
- What are some comparisons of adolescents in different cultures? How do adolescents around the world spend their time? What are rites of passage?
- How does ethnicity influence adolescent development?

Reflect
- What is your ethnicity? Have you ever been stereotyped because of your ethnicity? How different is your identity from the mainstream culture?

---

5 ADOLESCENT PROBLEMS

Juvenile Delinquency

Depression and Suicide

The Interrelation of Problems and Successful Prevention/Intervention Programs

In chapter 12, we described these adolescent problems: substance abuse, sexually transmitted infections, and eating disorders. Here, we will examine the problems of juvenile delinquency, depression, and suicide.

Juvenile Delinquency

The label **juvenile delinquent** is applied to an adolescent who breaks the law or engages in behavior that is considered illegal. Like other categories of disorders, juvenile delinquency is a broad concept; legal infractions range from littering to murder. Because the adolescent technically becomes a juvenile delinquent only after being judged guilty of a crime by a court of law, official records do not accurately reflect the number of illegal acts juvenile delinquents commit. Estimates of the number of juvenile delinquents in the United States are sketchy, but FBI statistics indicate that at least 2 percent of all youth are involved in juvenile court cases.

U.S. government statistics reveal that 8 of 10 cases of juvenile delinquency involve males (Snyder & Sickmund, 1999). In the last two decades, however, there has been a greater increase in female delinquency than in male delinquency (Snyder & Sickmund, 1999). For both male and female delinquents, rates for property offenses are higher than for other rates of offenses (such as offenses

juvenile delinquent An adolescent who breaks the law or engages in behavior that is considered illegal.

against persons, drug offenses, and public order offenses). Arrests of adolescent males for delinquency still are much higher than for adolescent females.

Delinquency rates among minority groups and lower-socioeconomic-status youth are especially high in proportion to the overall population of these groups. However, such groups have less influence over the judicial decision-making process in the United States and, therefore, may be judged delinquent more readily than their White, middle-socioeconomic-status counterparts.

In the Pittsburgh Youth Study, a longitudinal study focused on more than 1,500 inner-city boys, three developmental pathways to delinquency were (Loeber & Farrington, 2001; Loeber & others, 1998; Stoutheimer-Loeber & others, 2002):

- *Authority conflict.* Youth on this pathway showed stubbornness prior to age 12, then moved on to defiance and avoidance of authority.
- *Covert.* This pathway included minor covert acts, such as lying, followed by property damage and moderately serious delinquency, then serious delinquency.
- *Overt.* This pathway included minor aggression followed by fighting and violence.

One issue in juvenile justice is whether an adolescent who commits a crime should be tried as an adult (Steinberg & Cauffman, 2001). In a recent study, trying adolescent offenders as adults increased rather than reduced their crime rate (Myers, 1999). The study evaluated more than 500 violent youth in Pennsylvania, which has adopted a "get tough" policy. Although these 500 offenders had been given harsher punishment than a comparison group retained in juvenile court, they were more likely to be rearrested—and rearrested more quickly—for new offenses once they were returned to the community. This suggests that the price of short-term public safety attained by prosecuting juveniles as adults might increase the number of criminal offenses over the long run.

Causes of Delinquency What causes delinquency? Many causes have been proposed, including heredity, identity problems, community influences, and family experiences. Erik Erikson (1968), for example, believes that adolescents whose development has restricted them from acceptable social roles or made them feel that they cannot measure up to the demands placed on them may choose a negative identity. Adolescents with a negative identity may find support for their delinquent image among peers, reinforcing the negative identity. For Erikson, delinquency is an attempt to establish an identity, although a negative one.

Although delinquency is less exclusively a phenomenon of lower-socioeconomic status than it was in the past, some characteristics of lower-class culture might promote delinquency. The norms of many lower-SES peer groups and gangs are antisocial, or counterproductive, to the goals and norms of society at large. Getting into and staying out of trouble are prominent features of life for some adolescents in low-income neighborhoods (Flannery & others, 2003). Adolescents from low-income backgrounds may sense that they can gain attention and status by performing antisocial actions. Being "tough" and "masculine" are high-status traits for lower-SES boys, and these traits are often measured by the adolescent's success in performing and getting away with delinquent acts. Furthermore, adolescents in communities with high crime rates observe many models who engage in criminal activities. These communities may be characterized by poverty, unemployment, and feelings of alienation toward the middle class. Quality schooling, educational funding, and organized neighborhood activities may be lacking in these communities (Sabol, Coulton, & Korbin, 2004).

Certain characteristics of family support systems are also associated with delinquency (Dodge, Coie, & Lynam, 2006; Farrington, 2004). Parents of delinquents are less skilled in discouraging antisocial behavior and in encouraging skilled behavior than are parents of nondelinquents. Parental monitoring of adolescents

**Office of Juvenile Justice and
Delinquency Prevention
Justice Information Center
Preventing Crime**

Common parenting weaknesses in the families of antisocial boys include a lack of supervision, poor disciplining skills, limited problem-solving abilities, and a tendency to be uncommunicative with sons.

—GERALD PATTERSON
*Contemporary American Psychologist,
University of Oregon*

is especially important in determining whether an adolescent becomes a delinquent (Coley, Morris, & Hernandez, 2004; Patterson, DeBaryshe, & Ramsey, 1989). Family discord and inconsistent and inappropriate discipline also are associated with delinquency (Bor, McGee, & Fagan, 2004). An increasing number of studies have also found that siblings can have a strong influence on delinquency (Bank, Burraston, & Snyder, 2004; Conger & Reuter, 1996). In one recent study, high levels of hostile sibling relationships and older sibling delinquency were linked with younger sibling delinquency in both brother and sister pairs (Slomkowski & others, 2001). Having delinquent peers greatly increases the risk of becoming delinquent (Dodge, Coie, & Lynam, 2006; Laird & others, 2005; Lauber, Marshall, & Meyers, 2005).

Youth Violence   Youth violence is a special concern in the United States today (Barton, 2005; Taylor & others, 2005). Estimates indicate that there are more than 750,000 gang members in more than 24,000 gangs in the United States with the average age of gang members being 17 to 18 years (Egley, 2002). Gangs often engage in violent and criminal activities and use these activities as an indication of gang identity and loyalty (Lauber, Marshall, & Meyers, 2005).

Among the risk factors that increase the likelihood an adolescent will become a gang member are disorganized neighborhoods characterized by economic hardship, having other family members in a gang, drug use, lack of family support, and peer pressure (Lauber, Marshall, & Meyers, 2005). Also, a recent study found that peer rejection, doing poorly in school, and engaging in antisocial behavior were linked with whether middle school students were members of a gang (Dishion, Nelson, & Yasui, 2005).

School violence is also a concern (Cheurprakobkit & Bartsch, 2005; Molina, Dulmus, & Sowers, 2005; Robinson & Clay, 2005). A national survey revealed that in 2003, 13 percent of U.S. high school students reported that they had been in a physical fight on school property and six percent said they carry a weapon on school property (Brener & others, 2005). The good news is that there has been a decline in violence-related behaviors in schools. In the national survey just mentioned, from 1991 to 2003, physical fighting declined from 16 percent to 13 percent of students and weapon carrying declined from 12 percent to 6 percent. However, being injured in a fist fight remained stable and not going to school because of safety concerns increased from 4.4 percent of students in 1993 to 5.5 percent of students in 2003.

Since the late 1990s, a series of school shootings gained national attention. In April 1999, in Littleton, Colorado, two Columbine High School students, Eric Harris and Dylan Klebold, shot and killed 12 students and a teacher, wounded 23 others, and then killed themselves. In May 1998, slightly built Kip Kinkel strode into a cafeteria at Thurston High School in Springfield, Oregon, and opened fire on his fellow students, murdering two and injuring many others. Later that day, police went to his home and found his parents lying dead on the floor, also victims of Kip's violence. In 2001, 15-year-old Charles "Andy" Williams fired shots at Santana High School in Southern California, killing two classmates and injuring 13 others. According to students at the school, Andy was a victim of bullying and had joked the previous weekend of his violent plans, but no one took him seriously after he later said he was just kidding.

Is there any way psychologists can predict whether a youth will turn violent? It's a complex task, but researchers have pieced together some clues (Cowley, 1998). Violent youth are overwhelmingly male, and many are driven by feelings of powerlessness. Violence seems to infuse these youth with a sense of power. In one study based on data collected in the National Longitudinal Study of Adolescent Health, secure attachment to parents, living in an intact family, and attending church services with parents were linked with lower incidences of violent behavior in seventh-through twelfth-graders (Franke, 2000).

A current concern is gang violence. *What are some reasons that adolescents join a gang?*

"Andy" Williams, escorted by police after being arrested for killing two classmates and injuring 13 others at Santana High School. *What factors might contribute to youth murders?*

Small-town shooting sprees attract attention, but youth violence is far greater in poverty-infested areas of inner cities. Urban poverty fosters powerlessness and rage, and many inner-city neighborhoods provide almost daily opportunities to observe violence. Many urban youth who live in poverty also lack adequate parent involvement and supervision (Tolan, 2001).

James Garbarino (1999, 2001) says there is a lot of ignoring that goes on in these kinds of situations. Parents often do not want to acknowledge what might be a very upsetting reality. Harris and Klebold were members of the "Trenchcoat Mafia" clique of Columbine outcasts. The two even had made a video for a school media class the previous fall that depicted them walking down the halls at the school shooting other students. Allegations were made that a year earlier the sheriff's department had been given information that Harris had bragged openly on the Internet that he and Klebold had built four bombs. Kip Kinkel had an obsession with guns and explosives, a history of abusing animals, and a nasty temper when crossed. When police examined his room, they found two pipe bombs, three larger bombs, and bomb-making recipes Kip had downloaded from the Internet. Clearly, some signs were present in these students' lives to suggest that they had some serious problems, but it is still very difficult to predict whether youths like these will act on their anger and sense of powerlessness to commit murder.

Garbarino (1999, 2001) has interviewed a number of youth killers. He concludes that nobody really knows precisely why a tiny minority of youth kill but that it might be a lack of a spiritual center. In the youth killers he interviewed, Garbarino often found a spiritual or emotional emptiness in which the youth sought meaning in the dark side of life.

Some interventions can reduce or prevent youth violence (Barton, 2004; Carnegie Council on Adolescent Development, 1995). Prevention efforts should include developmentally appropriate schools, supportive families, and youth and community organizations. At a more specific level, one promising strategy for preventing youth violence is the teaching of conflict management as part of health education in elementary and middle schools. To build resources for such programs, the Carnegie Foundation is supporting a national network of violence prevention practitioners based at the U.S. Department of Education, linked with a national research center on youth violence at the University of Colorado.

These are some of the Oregon Social Learning Center's recommendations for reducing youth violence (Walker, 1998, p. 1C):

- *Recommit to raising children safely and effectively.* This includes engaging in "parenting practices that produce healthy, well-adjusted children. Such practices involve consistent, fair discipline that is never harsh or severely punitive, careful monitoring and supervision, positive family management techniques, involvement in the child's daily life, daily debriefings about the child's experiences, and teaching problem-solving strategies."
- *Make prevention a reality.* Too often lip service is given to prevention strategies without investing in them at the necessary levels to make them effective.
- "*Give greater support to our schools, which are struggling to educate an increasingly diverse and at-risk student population.*"
- "*Forge effective partnerships among families, schools, social service systems, public safety, churches, and other agencies to create the socializing experiences that will give all of our youth a chance to develop along positive lines.*"

One individual whose goal is to reduce violence in adolescence and help at-risk adolescents cope more effectively with their lives is Rodney Hammond. To read about his work, see the Careers in Life-Span Development profile.

Depression and Suicide

What is the nature of depression in adolescence? What causes an adolescent to commit suicide?

CAREERS
in LIFE-SPAN DEVELOPMENT

Rodney Hammond
Health Psychologist

Rodney Hammond described his college experiences:

> When I started as an undergraduate at the University of Illinois, Champaign-Urbana, I hadn't decided on my major. But to help finance my education, I took a part-time job in a child development research program sponsored by the psychology department. There, I observed inner-city children in settings designed to enhance their learning. I saw firsthand the contribution psychology can make, and I knew I wanted to be a psychologist. (American Psychological Association, 2003, p. 26)

Rodney Hammond went on to obtain a doctorate in school and community psychology with a focus on children's development. For a number of years, he trained clinical psychologists at Wright State University in Ohio and directed a program to reduce violence in ethnic minority youth. There, he and his associates taught at-risk youth how to use social skills to effectively manage conflict and to recognize situations that could lead to violence. Today, Rodney is Director of Violence Prevention at the Centers for Disease Control and Prevention in Atlanta. Rodney says that if you are interested in people and problem solving, psychology is a wonderful way to put these together.

(Source: American Psychological Association, 2003, pp. 26–27)

Rodney Hammond, counseling an adolescent girl about the risks of adolescence and how to effectively cope with them.

Depression Depression is more likely to occur in adolescence than in childhood and more likely to occur in adulthood than adolescence. Further, adolescent girls consistently have higher rates of depression than adolescent boys (Graber, 2004; Logsdon, 2004; Nolen-Hoeksema, 2007). Among the reasons for this gender difference are that

- Females tend to ruminate in their depressed mood and amplify it.
- Females' self-images, especially their body images, are more negative than males'.
- Females face more discrimination than males do.
- Puberty occurs earlier for girls than for boys, and as a result girls experience a piling up of changes and life experiences in the middle school years, which can increase depression.

Certain family factors place adolescents at risk for developing depression (Eley & others, 2004; Graber, 2004; Seroczynski, Jacquez, & Cole, 2003). These include having a depressed parent, emotionally unavailable parents, parents who have high marital conflict, and parents with financial problems.

Poor peer relationships also are associated with adolescent depression (Bearman & Moody, 2004; Kistner, 2006). Not having a close relationship with a best friend, having less contact with friends, and experiencing peer rejection all increase depressive tendencies in adolescents. Problems in adolescent romantic relationships can also trigger depression, especially for girls (Davila & Steinberg, 2006).

The experience of difficult changes or challenges also is associated with depressive symptoms in adolescence (Compas & Grant, 1993), and parental divorce increases depressive symptoms in adolescents. Also, when adolescents go through puberty at the same time as they move from elementary school to middle or junior

Adolescent Depression
Suicide

What are some characteristics of adolescents who become depressed? What are some factors that are linked with suicide attempts by adolescents?

high school, they report being depressed more than do adolescents who go through puberty after the school transition.

Suicide Suicidal behavior is rare in childhood but escalates in early adolescence (Judge & Billick, 2004). Suicide is the third leading cause of death today among adolescents 13 through 19 years of age in the United States (National Center for Health Statistics, 2004). After increasing to high levels in the 1990s, suicide rates in adolescents have declined in recent years (Gould & others, 2003). In 2001, 1 in 10,000 U.S. 15- to 24-year-olds committed suicide (National Vital Statistics Reports, 2003). In 2005, a national survey found that 8.4 percent of U.S. adolescents had attempted suicide (Eaton & others, 2006).

Far more adolescents contemplate suicide or attempt suicide unsuccessfully (Holmes & Holmes, 2005; Judge & Billick, 2004). In a national study, one-fifth of U.S. high school students said that they had seriously considered or attempted suicide in the last 12 months (National Center for Health Statistics, 2000). Less than 3 percent reported a suicide attempt that resulted in an injury, poisoning, or drug overdose that had been treated by a doctor. Females were more likely to attempt suicide than males but males were more likely to commit suicide. Males use more lethal means, such as a gun, in their suicide attempts, while adolescent females are more likely to cut their wrists or take an overdose of sleeping pills, which is less likely to result in death. A recent study of adolescents indicated that suicide ideation peaked at age 15 (Rueter & Kwon, 2005).

A recent concern related to adolescent suicide is a possible link between the use of antidepressants and suicidal thoughts (Kaizar & others, 2006). The Federal Drug Administration (2004) issued a report based on its review of a number of research studies; the report concluded that 2 to 3 percent of adolescents taking antidepressants experience an increase in suicidal thoughts. It is estimated that antidepressants are prescribed for approximately 1 million U.S. children and adolescents. However, a recent study found no link between adolescents' antidepressant use and suicidal behavior (Valuck & others, 2004).

One issue focuses on whether lesbian and gay male adolescents are especially vulnerable to suicide (Savin-Williams, 2005). In one study of 12,000 adolescents, approximately 15 percent of lesbian and gay male youth said that they had attempted suicide compared with 7 percent of heterosexual youth (Russell & Joyner, 2001). However, Richard Savin-Williams (2001) found that lesbian and gay male adolescents were only slightly more likely than heterosexual adolescents to attempt suicide. He argues that most studies have exaggerated the suicide rates for lesbian and gay male adolescents because they only survey the most disturbed youth who are attending support groups or hanging out at shelters for lesbian and gay male youth.

Both early and later experiences may be involved in suicide attempts. The adolescent might have a long-standing history of family instability and unhappiness. Lack of affection and emotional support, high control, and pressure for achievement by parents during childhood are likely to show up as factors in suicide attempts. One recent review of research found a link that adolescents who had been physically or sexually abused were more likely to have suicidal thoughts than adolescents who had not experienced such abuse (Evans, Hawton, & Rodham, 2005). A recent study also found that not having friends was linked to suicide attempts by both ninth- and eleventh-graders (Hacker & others, 2006). Recent and current stressful circumstances, such as getting poor grades in school and experiencing the breakup of a romantic relationship, may trigger suicide attempts (Antai-Otong, 2003).

Just as genetic factors are associated with depression, they also are associated with suicide. The closer a person's genetic relationship to someone who has committed suicide, the more likely that person is to also commit suicide (Baud, 2005; Marusic, 2005).

What is the psychological profile of the suicidal adolescent? Suicidal adolescents often have depressive symptoms (Sinclair & others, 2005). Although not all depressed adolescents are suicidal, depression is the most frequently cited factor associated with adolescent suicide (Pelkonen & Marttunen, 2003). A recent study also found that the psychological factors of being overly self-critical and having a sense of hopelessness were also related to suicide ideation and behavior (Cox, Enns, & Clara, 2004). Low self-esteem and a dissatisfied body image also are associated with adolescent suicide (Harter & Whitesell, 2001; Rodriguez-Cano, Beato-Fernandez, & Liario, 2006).

The Interrelation of Problems and Successful Prevention/Intervention Programs

We have described some of the major adolescent problems in this chapter and in chapter 12: substance abuse; juvenile delinquency; school-related problems, such as dropping out of school; adolescent pregnancy and sexually transmitted infections; depression; and suicide.

The most at-risk adolescents have more than one problem. Researchers are increasingly finding that problem behaviors in adolescence are interrelated (Camenga, Klein, & Ray, 2006; Tubman & Windle, 1995). For example, heavy substance abuse is related to early sexual activity, lower grades, dropping out of school, and delinquency. Early initiation of sexual activity is associated with the use of cigarettes and alcohol, the use of marijuana and other illicit drugs, lower grades, dropping out of school, and delinquency. Delinquency is related to early sexual activity, early pregnancy, substance abuse, and dropping out of school. As many as 10 percent of all adolescents in the United States have serious multiple-problem behaviors (for example, adolescents who have dropped out of school, are behind in their grade level, are users of heavy drugs, regularly use cigarettes and marijuana, and are sexually active but do not use contraception). Another 15 percent of adolescents participate in many of these behaviors but with slightly lower frequency and less deleterious consequences. These high-risk youth often engage in two- or three-problem behaviors (Dryfoos, 1990).

In a review of the programs that have been successful in preventing or reducing adolescent problems, adolescence researcher Joy Dryfoos (1990) described the common components of successful programs:

1. *Intensive individualized attention.* In successful programs, high-risk children are attached to a responsible adult, who gives the child attention and deals with the child's specific needs. This theme occurs in a number of programs. In a successful substance-abuse program, a student assistance counselor is available full-time for individual counseling and referral for treatment.
2. *Community-wide multiagency collaborative approaches.* The basic philosophy of community-wide programs is that a number of different programs and services have to be in place. In one successful substance-abuse program, a community-wide health promotion campaign has been implemented that uses local media and community education, in concert with a substance-abuse curriculum in the schools.
3. *Early identification and intervention.* Reaching children and their families before children develop problems, or at the beginning of their problems, is a successful strategy (Pianta, 2005). One preschool program serves as an excellent model for the prevention of delinquency, pregnancy, substance abuse, and dropping out of school. Operated by the High/Scope Foundation in Ypsilanti, Michigan, the Perry Preschool has had a long-term positive impact on its students. This enrichment program, directed by David Weikart, serves disadvantaged African American children. They attend a high-quality two-year preschool program and receive weekly home visits from program personnel.

Based on official police records, by age 19, individuals who had attended the Perry Preschool program were less likely to have been arrested and reported fewer adult offenses than a control group did. The Perry Preschool students also were less likely to drop out of school, and teachers rated their social behavior as more competent than that of a control group who had not received the enriched preschool experience.

One current program that seeks to prevent adolescent problems is called Fast Track (Dodge, 2001; Conduct Problems Prevention Research Group, 2002, 2004). High-risk children who show conduct problems at home and at kindergarten were identified. Then, during the elementary school years, the at-risk children and their families are given support and training in parenting, problem-solving and coping skills, peer relations, classroom atmosphere and curriculum, academic achievement, and home-school relations. Ten project interventionists work with the children, their families, and schools to increase the protective factors and decrease the risk factors in these areas. Thus far, results show that the intervention effectively improved parenting practices and children's problem-solving and coping skills, peer relations, reading achievement, and problem behavior at home and school during the elementary school years compared with a control group of high-risk children who did not experience the intervention.

Review and Reflect ● LEARNING GOAL 5

5 **Identify adolescent problems in socioemotional development and strategies for helping adolescents with problems**

Review
- What is juvenile delinquency? What causes it? What is the nature of youth violence?
- What is the nature of depression and suicide in adolescence?
- How are adolescent problems interrelated? What are some components of successful prevention/intervention programs for adolescents?

Reflect
- Are the consequences of risk taking in adolescence today more serious than in the past? If so, why?

REACH YOUR LEARNING GOALS

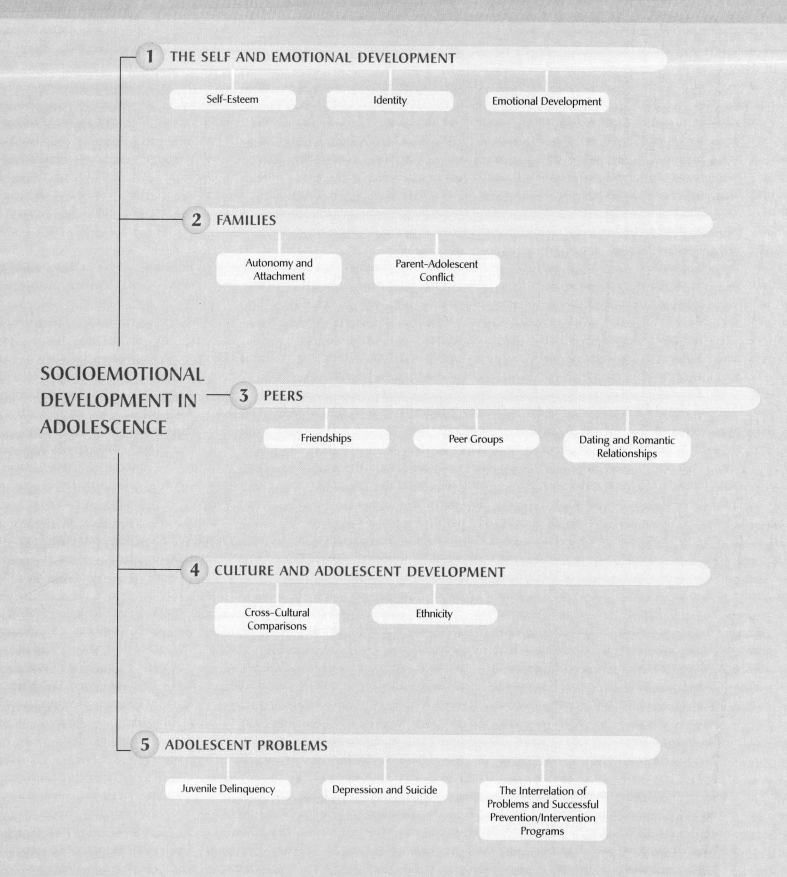

SOCIOEMOTIONAL DEVELOPMENT IN ADOLESCENCE

1 THE SELF AND EMOTIONAL DEVELOPMENT

- Self-Esteem
- Identity
- Emotional Development

2 FAMILIES

- Autonomy and Attachment
- Parent-Adolescent Conflict

3 PEERS

- Friendships
- Peer Groups
- Dating and Romantic Relationships

4 CULTURE AND ADOLESCENT DEVELOPMENT

- Cross-Cultural Comparisons
- Ethnicity

5 ADOLESCENT PROBLEMS

- Juvenile Delinquency
- Depression and Suicide
- The Interrelation of Problems and Successful Prevention/Intervention Programs

SUMMARY

1 The Self and Emotional Development: *Discuss changes in the self and emotional development during adolescence*

Self-Esteem

Some researchers have found that self-esteem declines in early adolescence for both boys and girls, but the drop for girls is greater. Other researchers caution that these declines are often exaggerated and actually are small.

Identity

Identity development is complex and is done in bits and pieces. Erikson argues that identity versus identity confusion is the fifth stage of the human life span, which individuals experience during adolescence. A psychosocial moratorium during adolescence allows the personality and role experimentation that are important aspects of identity development. Identity development begins during infancy and continues through old age. James Marcia proposed four identity statuses—identity diffusion, foreclosure, moratorium, and achievement—that are based on crisis (exploration) and commitment. Some experts argue the main changes in identity occur in emerging adulthood rather than adolescence. Individuals often follow moratorium-achievement-moratorium-achievement (MAMA) cycles in their lives. Parents are important figures in adolescents' identity development. Democratic parenting facilitates identity development; autocratic and permissive parenting do not. Identity development is also facilitated by family relations that promote both individuality and connectedness. Throughout the world ethnic minority groups have struggled to maintain their identities while blending into the majority culture.

Emotional Development

Adolescents report more extreme and fleeting emotions than their parents, and as individuals go through early adolescence they are less likely to report being very happy. However, it is important to view moodiness as a normal aspect of early adolescence. Although pubertal change is associated with an increase in negative emotions, hormonal influences are often small and environmental experiences may contribute more to the emotions of adolescence than hormonal changes.

2 Families: *Describe changes that take place in adolescents' relationships with their parents*

Autonomy and Attachment

Many parents have a difficult time handling the adolescent's push for autonomy, even though the push is one of the hallmarks of adolescence. Adolescents do not simply move into a world isolated from parents; attachment to parents increases the probability that an adolescent will be socially competent.

Parent-Adolescent Conflict

Parent-adolescent conflict increases in adolescence. The conflict is usually moderate rather than severe, and the increased conflict may serve the positive developmental function of promoting autonomy and identity. A subset of adolescents experience high parent-adolescent conflict, which is linked with negative outcomes.

3 Peers: *Characterize the changes that occur in peer relations during adolescence*

Friendships

Harry Stack Sullivan was the most influential theorist to discuss the importance of adolescent friendships. He argued that there is a dramatic increase in the psychological importance and intimacy of close friends in early adolescence.

Peer Groups

Children's groups are less formal and less heterogeneous than adolescent groups. The pressure to conform to peers is strong during adolescence, especially during the eighth and ninth grades. Cliques and crowds assume more importance in the lives of adolescents than in the lives of children. Membership in certain crowds—especially jocks and populars—is associated with increased self-esteem. Independents also show high self-esteem.

Dating and Romantic Relationships

Dating can have many functions. Younger adolescents often begin to hang out together in mixed-sex groups. Many gay and lesbian youth date other-sex peers, which can help them to clarify their sexual orientation or disguise it from others. Male and female adolescents engage in different dating scripts. Culture can exert a powerful influence on adolescent dating. Dating shows mixed connections with adjustment during adolescence. Early dating is linked with developmental problems.

4 Culture and Adolescent Development: *Explain how culture influences adolescent development*

Cross-Cultural Comparisons

There are both similarities and differences in adolescents across different countries. With technological advances, a youth culture with similar characteristics may be emerging. However, there still are many variations in adolescents across cultures. In some countries, traditions are being continued in the socialization of adolescents, whereas in others, substantial changes in the experiences of adolescents are taking place. Adolescents often fill their time with different activities, depending on the culture in which they live. Ceremonies mark an individual's transition from one status to another, especially into adulthood. In primitive cultures, rites of passage are often well defined. In contemporary America, rites of passage to adulthood are ill-defined.

Ethnicity

Many of the families that have immigrated in recent decades to the United States come from collectivist cultures in which there is a strong sense of family obligation. Much of the research on ethnic minority adolescents has not teased apart the influences of ethnicity and socioeconomic status. Because of this failure, too often researchers have given ethnic explanations for characteristics that were largely due to socioeconomic factors. While not all ethnic minority families are poor, poverty contributes to the stress of many ethnic minority adolescents.

5 Adolescent Problems: *Identify adolescent problems in socioemotional development and strategies for helping adolescents with problems*

Juvenile Delinquency

A juvenile delinquent is an adolescent who breaks the law or engages in conduct that is considered illegal. Heredity, identity problems, community influences, and family experiences have been proposed as causes of juvenile delinquency. An increasing concern is the high rate of violence among youth, especially in gangs and at school.

Depression and Suicide

Adolescents have a higher rate of depression than children. Female adolescents are more likely to have mood and depressive disorders than male adolescents are. Adolescent suicide is the third leading cause of death in U.S. adolescents. Both proximal (recent) and distal (earlier) factors are likely involved in suicide's causes.

The Interrelation of Problems and Successful Prevention/Intervention Programs

Researchers are increasingly finding that problem behaviors in adolescence are interrelated. Dryfoos found a number of common components in successful programs designed to prevent or reduce adolescent problems: They provide individual attention to high-risk adolescents, they develop community-wide intervention, and they include early identification and intervention.

KEY TERMS

identity versus identity confusion 424	identity diffusion 425	connectedness 427	rite of passage 441
psychosocial moratorium 425	identity foreclosure 426	ethnic identity 427	assimilation 442
crisis 425	identity moratorium 426	clique 435	pluralism 442
commitment 425	identity achievement 426	crowd 435	juvenile delinquent 443
	individuality 427	dating scripts 437	

KEY PEOPLE

Erik Erikson 424	Catherine Cooper 427	G. Stanley Hall 432	Richard Savin-Williams 448
James Marcia 425	Reed Larson and Maryse Richards 428	Harry Stack Sullivan 434	Joy Dryfoos 449
Alan Waterman 426		James Garbarino 446	

E-LEARNING TOOLS

To help you master the material in this chapter, you'll find a number of valuable study tools on the LifeMap CD-ROM that accompanies this book and on the Online Learning Center for *Life-Span Development*, eleventh edition, at **www.mhhe.com/santrockld11**.

Video Clips

In the margins of this book there are icons directing you to the LifeMap CD-ROM that accompanies the book. There you'll find two videos for chapter 13. The first is called "Adolescent Self-Esteem." In this segment, Dr. Susan Harter examines the connection between self-concept and self-esteem and the way adolescents form attitudes about themselves. The second video is called "Girls and Body Image." Interviews with 14-year-old girls, about their emerging image of themselves as female, test the validity of the so-called "gender intensification hypothesis."

Self-Assessment

Connect to **www.mhhe.com/santrockld11** to reflect on your feelings and your early teenage years by completing the self-assessments, *My Self-Esteem, How Much Did My Parents Monitor My Behavior in Adolescence?* and *Am I Depressed?*

Taking It to the Net

Connect to **www.mhhe.com/santrockld11** to research the answers to these questions.

1. Shelley's mother is Euro-American and her father is Japanese. Many people who do not know her have a hard time identifying her ethnic background, and she is continually asked, "What are you?" There are several other minority students at her school, although few of them openly identify themselves as biracial or multiracial. Shelley is now in the process of figuring out who she is. What are some of the challenges biracial or multiracial adolescents face? How might their identity development progress?

2. Fourteen-year-old Denise, an only child, and her mother, Doris, always had a great relationship—until recently. Now it seems that they are constantly arguing. Doris is trying to understand what is going on with her daughter. How can she tell if Denise's behavior is normal for a 14-year-old?

3. The local school board wants to try to prevent violent and tragic incidents like those in Littleton, Colorado, and Springfield, Oregon. It has asked its principals and teachers to study an APA publication that identifies warning signs of violence and suggests interventions. What will they learn from it, and how can they try to prevent similar situations in their school district?

Health and Well-Being, Parenting, and Education Exercises

Build your decision-making skills by trying your hand at the health and well-being, parenting, and education exercises. Connect to **www.mhhe.com/santrockld11** to research the answers and complete the exercises.

Whatever you can do, or dream you can, begin it. Boldness has genius, power, and magic.

—JOHANN WOLFGANG VON GOETHE
German Playwright and Novelist, 19th Century

LEARNING GOALS

1 Describe the transition from adolescence to adulthood

2 Identify the changes in physical development in young adults

3 Discuss sexuality in young adults

4 Characterize cognitive changes in early adulthood

5 Explain the key dimensions of careers and work in early adulthood

Images of Life-Span Development
David Eggers, Pursuing a Career in the Face of Stress

David Eggers, talented and insightful author

He was a senior in college when both of his parents died of cancer within five weeks of each other. What would he do? He and his 8-year-old brother left Chicago to live in California, where his older sister was entering law school. David would take care of his younger brother, but he needed a job. That first summer, he took a class in furniture-painting; then he worked for a geological surveying company, re-creating maps on a computer. Soon, though, he did something very different: with friends from high school, David Eggers started *Might,* a satirical magazine for twenty-somethings. It was an edgy, highly acclaimed publication, but not a money-maker. After a few years, Eggers had to shut down the magazine, and he abandoned California for New York.

This does not sound like a promising start for a career. But within a decade after his parents' death, Eggers had not only raised his young brother but had also founded a quarterly journal and Web site, *McSweeney's,* and had written a best-seller, *A Heartbreaking Work of Staggering Genius,* which received the National Book Critics Circle Award and was nominated for a Pulitzer Prize. It is a slightly fictionalized account of Eggers' life as he helped care for his dying mother, raised his brother, and searched for his own place in the world. Despite the pain of his loss and the responsibility for his brother, Eggers quickly built a record of achievement as a young adult.

PREVIEW

In this chapter, we will explore many aspects of physical and cognitive development in early adulthood. These include some of the areas that were so important in David Eggers' life, such as maximizing his creative talents and pursuing a career. We also will explore changes in physical development, sexuality,

and cognitive development, However, we will begin where we left off in section 6, "Adolescence," and address the transition from adolescence to adulthood, a time during which David Eggers displayed resilience in face of intense stress.

1 THE TRANSITION FROM ADOLESCENCE TO ADULTHOOD

Becoming an Adult	The Transition from High School to College

As singer Bob Dylan asks, "How many roads must a man walk down before you call him a man?" When does an adolescent become an adult? In chapter 12, we saw that it is not easy to tell when a girl or a boy enters adolescence. The task of determining when an individual becomes an adult is more difficult.

Becoming an Adult

An important transition occurs from adolescence to adulthood (Arnett, 2004, 2006; Arnett & Tanner, 2006; Nelson & Barry, 2005; Lefkowitz, 2005; Schulenberg & Zarrett, 2006). It has been said that adolescence begins in biology and ends in culture. That is, the transition from childhood to adolescence begins with the onset of pubertal maturation, whereas the transition from adolescence to adulthood is determined by cultural standards and experiences.

Indeed, there is less culturally imposed structure on individuals as they make the transition to adulthood than when they make the transition to adolescence (Labouvie-Vief, 2006; Schulenberg, Sameroff, & Cicchetti, 2004). This lack of structure can be positive for some individuals, negative for others. The relative lack of structure allows for more self-direction and flexibility in the selection of activities and pursuits, but it can result in avoidance of life tasks and considerable floundering.

An increasing number of experts argue that the transition from adolescence to adulthood is a critical juncture in life-span development (Arnett, 2004, 2006; Arnett & Tanner, 2006; Masten, Obradovic, & Burt, 2006; Tanner, 2006). As recently described by John Schulenberg and his colleagues (2004), many individuals who were well adjusted in childhood and adolescence continue to be so in the transition to adulthood, and many individuals who were poorly adjusted continue to be in the transition to adulthood as well. However, some individuals who were troubled as adolescents get their lives together in the transition to adulthood, while others who were doing well as adolescents have difficulty coping with the transition to adulthood. Thus, the transition to adulthood is marked by continuity for many individuals, but discontinuity for others. An important theme of this transition is "taking hold of some kind of life" in a responsible, competent manner (Schulenberg, Bryant, & O'Malley, 2004).

Around the world, youth are increasingly expected to delay their entry into adulthood, in large part because contemporary society requires adults who are more educated and skilled than previous generations (Mortimer & Larson, 2002). Thus, the transition between adolescence and adulthood can be a long one. **Emerging adulthood** is the term now given to the transition from adolescence to adulthood (Arnett, 2000; 2004; 2006). The age range for emerging adulthood is approximately 18 to 25 years of age. Experimentation and exploration characterize the emerging adult. At this point in their development, many individuals are still exploring which career path they want to follow, what they want their identity to be, and which lifestyle they want to adopt (for example, single, cohabiting, or married).

Jeffrey Arnett (2006) recently described five features of emerging adulthood:

- *Identity exploration, especially in love and work.* As we saw in chapter 13, emerging adulthood is the time during which key changes in identity take place for many individuals (Cote, 2006).
- *Instability.* Residential changes peak during early adulthood, a time during which there also is often instability in love, work, and education.
- *Self-focused.* According to Arnett (2006, p. 10), emerging adults "are self-focused in the sense that they have little in the way of social obligations, little in the way of duties and commitments to others, which leaves them with a great deal of autonomy in running their own lives."
- *Feeling in-between.* Many emerging adults don't consider themselves adolescents or full-fledged adults.
- *The age of possibilities, a time when individuals have an opportunity to transform their lives.* Arnett (2006) describes two ways in which emerging adulthood is the age of possibilities: (1) Many emerging adults are optimistic about their future and (2) for emerging adults who have experienced difficult times while growing up, emerging adulthood presents an opportunity to direct their lives in a more positive direction (Schulenberg & Zarrett, 2006).

Is there a specific age at which individuals become adults? One study examined emerging adults' perception of whether they were adults (Arnett, 2000). The majority of the 18- to 25-year-olds responded neither "yes" nor "no," but "in some respects yes, in some respects no" (see figure 14.1). In this study, not until the late twenties and early thirties did a clear majority of respondents agree that they had reached adulthood. Thus, these emerging adults saw themselves as neither adolescents nor

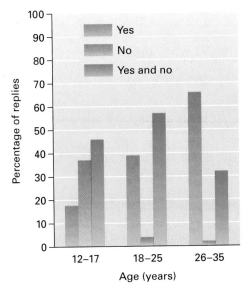

FIGURE 14.1 Self-Perceptions of Adult Status. In one study, individuals were asked, "Do you feel that you have reached adult status?" and were given a choice of answering "yes," "no," or "in some respects yes, in some respects no" (Arnett, 2000). As indicated in the graph, the majority of the emerging adults (18 to 25) responded "in some respects yes, in some respects no."

emerging adulthood The transition from adolescence to adulthood (approximately 18 to 25 years of age) that involves experimentation and exploration.

full-fledged adults, reflecting the characteristic of emerging adulthood we described earlier—feeling in-between.

In another study, however, 21-year-olds said that they had reached adult status when they were 18 to 19 years old (Scheer, 1996). In this study, both social status factors (financial status and graduation/education) and cognitive factors (being responsible and making independent decisions) were cited as markers for reaching adulthood. Clearly, reaching adulthood involves more than just attaining a specific chronological age.

In the United States, the most widely recognized marker of entry into adulthood is holding a more or less permanent, full-time job, which usually happens when an individual finishes school—high school for some, college for others, graduate or professional school for still others. However, other criteria are far from clear. Economic independence is one marker of adult status but achieving it is often a long process. College graduates are increasingly returning to live with their parents as they attempt to establish themselves economically. A recent longitudinal study found that at age 25 only slightly more than half of the participants were fully financially independent of their family of origin (Cohen & others, 2003). The most dramatic findings in this study, though, involved the extensive variability in the individual trajectories of adult roles across 10 years from 17 to 27 years of age; many of the participants moved back and forth between increasing and decreasing dependency.

Taking responsibility for oneself is likely an important marker of adult status for many individuals. One recent study found that increased responsibility was a marker for adult status (Shulman & Ben-Artzi, 2003). And in another study, more than 70 percent of college students said that being an adult means accepting responsibility for the consequences of one's actions, deciding on one's own beliefs and values, and establishing a relationship with parents as an equal adult (Arnett, 1995).

What we have said about the determinants of adult status mainly characterize individuals in industrialized societies, especially Americans. Are the criteria for adulthood the same in developing countries as they are in the United States? In developing countries, marriage is more often a significant marker for entry into adulthood, and this usually occurs much earlier than the adulthood markers in the United States (Arnett, 2000, 2004). Further, a recent study found that a majority of Chinese college students in their early twenties said that they had reached adult status (Nelson, Badger, & Wu, 2004).

At some point in the late teens through the early twenties, then, individuals reach adulthood. In becoming an adult, they accept responsibility for themselves, become capable of making independent decisions, and gain financial independence from their parents (Arnett, 2000, 2004).

The new freedoms and responsibilities of emerging adulthood represent major changes in individuals' lives. Keep in mind, though, that considerable continuity still glues adolescence and adulthood together. For example, one recent longitudinal study found that religious views and behaviors of emerging adults were especially stable and that their attitudes toward drugs were stable to a lesser degree as well (Bachman & others, 2002).

What determines an individual's well-being in the transition to adulthood? In a review of research, three types of assets were especially important to well-being during this transition: intellectual (academic success, planfulness, and good decision-making skills); psychological (mental health, mastery motivation, confidence in one's competence, identity, values, and community contributions); and social (connectedness to others through friendship and positive peer relations) (Eccles & Goodman, 2002). In one study of individuals from 18 to 26 years of age, succeeding rather than stalling in developmental tasks such as work, romantic involvement, and citizenship was linked to a positive trajectory of well-being (Schulenberg, Bryant, & O'Malley, 2004).

The Transition from High School to College

Just as the transition from elementary school to middle or junior high school involves change and possible stress, so does the transition from high school to college. The two transitions have many parallels. Going from being a senior in high school to being a freshman in college replays the top-dog phenomenon of transferring from the oldest and most powerful group of students to the youngest and least powerful group of students that occurred earlier as adolescence began. For many students, the transition from high school to college involves movement to a larger, more impersonal school structure; interaction with peers from more diverse geographical and sometimes more diverse ethnic backgrounds; and increased focus on achievement and its assessment. And like the transition from elementary to middle or junior high school, the transition from high school to college can involve positive features. Students are more likely to feel grown up, have more subjects from which to select, have more time to spend with peers, have more opportunities to explore different lifestyles and values, enjoy greater independence from parental monitoring, and be challenged intellectually by academic work (Santrock & Halonen, 2006).

Stress   Today's college students experience more stress and are more depressed than in the past, according to a national study of more than 300,000 freshmen at more than 500 colleges and universities (Pryor & others, 2005). In 2005, 27 percent (up from 16 percent in 1985) said they frequently "felt overwhelmed with what I have to do." College females were more than twice as likely as their male counterparts (36 to 16 percent respectively) to say that they felt overwhelmed with all they had to do. And college freshmen in 2005 indicated that they felt more depressed than their counterparts from the 1980s had indicated. The pressures to succeed in college, get a great job, and make lots of money were pervasive concerns of these students.

In one study, the academic circumstances creating the most stress for students were tests and finals, grades and competition, professors and class environment, too many demands, papers and essay exams, career and future success, and studying (Murphy, 1996). The personal circumstances that caused the most stress for students were intimate relationships, finances, parental conflicts and expectations, and roommate conflicts.

Let's examine some ways to cope with stress, beginning with the negative ways:

- Repress it so you don't have to think about it.
- Take it out on other people when you feel angry or depressed.
- Keep your feelings to yourself.
- Tell yourself the problem will go away.
- Refuse to believe what is happening.
- Try to reduce the tension by drinking and eating more.

Fortunately, you can cope with stress in these positive ways:

- See stress as a challenge to be overcome rather than an overwhelming threat (Steptoe & Ayers, 2005).
- Have good coping resources, such as friends, family, and a mentor (Olpin & Hesson, 2007). One study found that first-year students showed better adaptation to college when they had less family conflict (Feenstra & others, 2001).
- Develop an optimistic outlook and think positively. Thinking optimistically gives you the sense that you are controlling your environment rather than letting it control you. One recent study found that greater optimism, assessed at the beginning of the first semester of college, was linked with less stress and depression over the course of the semester (Brissette, Scheier, & Carver, 2002).

The transition from high school to college often involves positive as well as negative features. In college, students are likely to feel grown up, be able to spend more time with peers, have more opportunities to explore different lifestyles and values, and enjoy greater freedom from parental monitoring. However, college involves a larger, more impersonal school structure and an increased focus on achievement and its assessment. *What was your transition to college like?*

CAREERS
in LIFE-SPAN DEVELOPMENT

Grace Leaf
College/Career Counselor

Grace Leaf is a counselor at Spokane Community College in Washington. She has a master's degree in educational leadership and is working toward a doctoral degree in educational leadership at Gonzaga University in Washington. Her job involves teaching orientation for international students, conducting individual and group advising, and doing individual and group career planning. Grace tries to connect students with goals and values and help them design an educational program that fits their needs and visions.

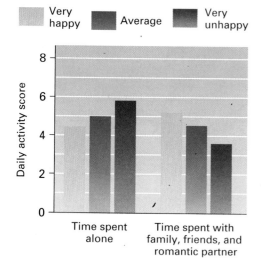

Grace Leaf, counseling college students at Spokane Community College about careers.

FIGURE 14.2 Daily Activity Self-Ratings and College Student's Happiness. In this study of undergraduates the daily activity scores reflect mean times with 1 representing no time and 8 reflecting 8 hours per day (Diener & Seligman, 2002). Students were classified as very happy, average, or very unhappy based on their self-ratings.

- Learn how to relax.
- Seek counseling. Most college campuses have a counseling center with access to mental health professionals who can help you to learn effective ways to cope with stress.

Happiness What makes college students happy? One recent study of 222 undergraduates compared the upper 10 percent of college students who were very happy with average and very unhappy college students (Diener & Seligman, 2002). The very happy college students were highly social, more extraverted, and had stronger romantic and social relationships than the less happy college students, who spent more time alone (see figure 14.2).

Education The United States is becoming a more educated country. In 2001, 29 percent of 25- to 29-year-olds had at least a bachelor's degree, compared with only 17 percent in 1971 (U.S. Department of Education, 2003). Total college enrollment is expected to increase in the next decade as increasing numbers of high school graduates pursue higher education. In the last several decades, there has been a dramatic increase in the number of individuals who attend community colleges rather than four-year colleges, and the community college movement continues to expand.

Returning students make up an increasing percentage of the college population in the United States. Returning students either did not go to college right out of high school or went to college, dropped out, and now have returned. More than one of every five full-time college students today is a returning student, and about two-thirds of part-time college students are returning students (Pryor & others, 2005). Many returning students have to balance their course work with commitments to a partner, children, job, and community responsibilities. Despite the many challenges that returning students face, they bring many strengths to campus, such as life experiences that can be applied to a wide range of issues and topics.

College counselors can provide good information about coping with stress and academic matters. To read about the work of college counselor Grace Leaf, see the Careers in Life-Span Development profile.

Review and Reflect • LEARNING GOAL 1

1 Describe the transition from adolescence to adulthood

Review
- What is the nature of emerging adulthood? What are the criteria for becoming an adult?
- What is the transition from high school to college like?

Reflect
- What do you think is the most important criterion for becoming an adult? Does it make sense to describe becoming an adult in terms of "emerging adulthood" over a period of years or is there a specific age at which someone becomes an adult? Explain.

2 PHYSICAL DEVELOPMENT

The Peak and Slowdown in
Physical Performance

Regular Exercise

Eating and Weight

Substance Abuse

For most individuals, physical status not only reaches its peak in early adulthood, it also begins to decline during this period. Interest in health has increased among young adults, with special concerns about diet, weight, exercise, and addiction.

The Peak and Slowdown in Physical Performance

Most of us reach our peak physical performance before the age of 30, often between the ages of 19 and 26. This peak of physical performance occurs not only for the average young adult, but for outstanding athletes as well. Even though athletes as a group keep getting better than their predecessors—running faster, jumping higher, and lifting more weight—the age at which they reach their peak performance has remained virtually the same (Schulz & Curnow, 1988).

Most swimmers and gymnasts reach their peak performance in their late teens. Golfers and marathon runners tend to peak in their late twenties. In other areas of athletics, peak performance is often in the early to mid-twenties.

Not only do we reach our peak physical performance during early adulthood, but during this time we are also the healthiest. Few young adults have chronic health problems, and they have fewer colds and respiratory problems than when they were children. Most college students know what it takes to prevent illness and promote health. In one study, college students' ranking of health-protective activities—nutrition, sleep, exercise, watching one's weight, and so on—virtually matched that of licensed nurses (Turk, Rudy, & Salovey, 1984).

Although most college students know what it takes to prevent illness and promote health, they don't fare very well when it comes to applying this information to themselves. In one study, college students reported that they probably would never have a heart attack or drinking problem, but that other college students would (Weinstein, 1984). The college students also said no relation exists between their risk of heart attack and how much they exercise, smoke, or eat meat or high-cholesterol food such as eggs, even though they correctly recognized that factors such as family history influence risk. Many college students, it seems, have unrealistic, overly optimistic beliefs about their future health risks.

In early adulthood, few individuals stop to think about how their personal lifestyles will affect their health later in their adult lives. As young adults, many of us develop a pattern of not eating breakfast, not eating regular meals, and relying on snacks as our main food source during the day, eating excessively to the point where we exceed the normal weight for our age, smoking moderately or excessively, drinking moderately or excessively, failing to exercise, and getting by with only a few hours of sleep at night. These poor personal lifestyles were associated with poor health in one investigation of 7,000 individuals from the ages of 20 to 70 (Belloc & Breslow, 1972). In the Berkeley Longitudinal Study—in which individuals were evaluated over a period of 40 years—physical health at age 30 predicted life satisfaction at age 70, more so for men than women (Mussen, Honzik, & Eichorn, 1982).

A longitudinal study revealed that most bad health habits engaged in during adolescence (assessed at 12 through 18 years of age) increased in emerging adulthood (assessed at 19 through 25 years of age (Harris & others, 2006). Inactivity,

Why might it be easy to develop bad health habits in early adulthood?

diet, obesity, substance use, reproductive health care, and health care access worsened in emerging adulthood. For example, when they were 12 to 18 years of age, only 5 percent reported no weekly exercise but when they became 19 to 26 years of age, 46 percent said they did not exercise during a week.

There are some hidden dangers in the peaks of performance and health in early adulthood. Young adults can draw on physical resources for a great deal of pleasure, often bouncing back easily from physical stress and abuse. However, this can lead them to push their bodies too far. The negative effects of abusing one's body may not show up in the first part of early adulthood, but they probably will surface later in early adulthood or in middle adulthood (Csikszentmihalyi & Rathunde, 1998).

Not only do we reach our peak in physical performance during early adulthood, but it is during this age period that we also begin to decline in physical performance. Muscle tone and strength usually begin to show signs of decline around the age of 30. Sagging chins and protruding abdomens also may begin to appear for the first time. The lessening of physical abilities is a common complaint among the just-turned thirties. Says one 30-year-old, "I played tennis last night. My knees are sore and my lower back aches. Last month, it was my elbow that hurt. Several years ago it wasn't that way. I could play all day and not be sore the next morning." Sensory systems show little change in early adulthood, but the lens of the eye loses some of its elasticity and becomes less able to change shape and focus on near objects. Hearing peaks in adolescence, remains constant in the first part of early adulthood, and then begins to decline in the last part of early adulthood. And in the mid to late twenties, the body's fatty tissue increases.

The health profile of our nation's young adults can be improved by reducing the incidence of certain health-impairing lifestyles, such as overeating, and by engaging in health-improving lifestyles that include good eating habits, exercising regularly, and not abusing drugs (Hahn, Payne, & Lucas, 2007; Hales, 2007; Teague, Mackenzie, & Rosenthal, 2007).

After thirty, a body has a mind of its own.

—Bette Midler
American Actress, 20th Century

Eating and Weight

In chapters 8 and 10, we explored obesity in childhood and examined the eating disorders of anorexia nervosa and bulimia nervosa in adolescence (chapter 12). Now, we will turn our attention to obesity in the adult years and the extensive preoccupation that many adults have with dieting.

Obesity Obesity is a serious and pervasive health problem for many individuals (Centers for Disease Control and Prevention, 2005; Corbin & others, 2006; Wardlaw & Hampl, 2007). More than 60 percent of U.S. adults are either overweight or obese (National Center for Health Statistics, 2006). Obesity is linked to increased risk of hypertension, diabetes, and cardiovascular disease (Behn & Ur, 2006; Insel & Roth, 2006; Wardlaw & Smith, 2007). For individuals who are 30 percent overweight, the probability of dying in middle adulthood increases by about 40 percent. *Body mass index*, a measure of weight in relation to height, is often used to determine whether an individual is underweight, a healthy weight, overweight, or obese (see figure 14.3).

What factors are involved in obesity? The possible culprits are heredity, leptin, set point and metabolism, environmental factors, ethnicity, and gender.

Heredity Until recently, the genetic component of obesity had been underestimated by scientists (Lyon & Hirschhorn, 2005; Sadof Farooqi, 2005). Some individuals do inherit a tendency to be overweight. Researchers have documented that animals can be inbred to have a propensity for obesity (Liu & others, 2005). Further, identical human twins have similar weights, even when they are reared apart (Collaku &

others, 2004). Estimates of the variance in body mass that can be explained by heredity range from 25 to 70 percent.

Leptin Leptin (from the Greek word *leptos,* which means "thin") is a protein that is involved in satiety (the condition of being full to satisfaction) and released by fat cells, resulting in decreased food intake and increased energy expenditure. Leptin acts as an antiobesity hormone (Popovic & Duntas, 2005; Zhang & others, 2005).

Initial research focused on a strain of mice called the *ob mouse.* A particular gene called *ob* normally produces leptin, but because of a genetic mutation, the fat cells of *ob* mice cannot produce leptin. The *ob* mice also have a low metabolism, overeat, and get extremely fat. But when *ob* mice are given daily injections of leptin, their metabolic rate increases, they become more active, and they eat less. Consequently, their weight falls to normal. Figure 14.4 shows an untreated *ob* mouse and an *ob* mouse that has received injections of leptin.

In humans, leptin concentrations have been linked with weight, percentage of body fat, weight loss in a single diet episode, and cumulative percentage of weight loss (Haynes, 2005; Kelesidis & Mantzoros, 2006; Monti & others, 2006). Today, scientists are interested in the possibility that leptin might help obese individuals lose weight.

Set Point The amount of stored fat in your body is an important factor in your *set point,* the weight maintained when no effort is made to gain or lose weight. Fat is stored in what are called adipose cells. When these cells are filled, you do not get hungry. When people gain weight—because of genetic predisposition, childhood eating patterns, or adult overeating—the number of their fat cells increases, and they might not be able to get rid of them. A normal-weight individual has 30 to 40 billion fat cells. An obese individual has 80 to 120 billion fat cells. Some scientists have proposed that these fat cells can shrink but might not go away.

Environmental Factors Environmental factors play an important role in obesity (Boyle & Long, 2007; Hales, 2007). The human genome has not changed markedly in the last century, yet obesity has noticeably increased (Roche, Phillips, & Gibney, 2005). The obesity rate has doubled in the United States since 1900. This dramatic increase in obesity likely is due to greater availability of food (especially food high in fat), energy-saving devices, and declining physical activity. One recent study found that in 2000, U.S. women ate 335 calories more a day and men 168 more a day than they did in the early 1970s (National Center for Health Statistics, 2004).

Sociocultural factors are involved in obesity, which is six times more prevalent among women with low incomes than among women with high incomes. Americans also are more obese than Europeans and people in many other areas of the world (Williams, 2005).

Ethnicity and Gender Obesity rates vary across ethnic groups (Howarth & others, 2006; Shai & others, 2006; Tremblay & others, 2005). One study found that African American and Latino women in their twenties and thirties become obese faster than their White counterparts, and Latino men become obese faster than White and African American men (McTigue, Garrett, & Popkin, 2002). Two possibilities might explain these findings (Brownell, 2002). There may be some biological

Weight (pounds)

Height	120	130	140	150	160	170	180	190	200	210	220	230	240	250
4'6"	29	31	34	36	39	41	43	46	48	51	53	56	58	60
4'8"	27	29	31	34	36	38	40	43	45	47	49	52	54	56
4'10"	25	27	29	31	34	36	38	40	42	44	46	48	50	52
5'0"	23	25	27	29	31	33	35	37	39	41	43	45	47	49
5'2"	22	24	26	27	29	31	33	35	37	38	40	42	44	46
5'4"	21	22	24	26	28	29	31	33	34	36	38	40	41	43
5'6"	19	21	23	24	26	27	29	31	32	34	36	37	39	40
5'8"	18	20	21	23	24	26	27	29	30	32	34	35	37	38
5'10"	17	19	20	22	23	24	26	27	29	30	32	33	35	36
6'0"	16	18	19	20	22	23	24	26	27	28	30	31	33	34
6'2"	15	17	18	19	21	22	23	24	26	27	28	30	31	32
6'4"	15	16	17	18	20	21	22	23	24	26	27	28	29	30
6'6"	14	15	16	17	19	20	21	22	23	24	25	27	28	29
6'8"	13	14	15	17	18	19	20	21	22	23	24	25	26	28

■ Underweight　■ Healthy weight　■ Overweight　■ Obese

FIGURE 14.3 Determining Your Body Mass Index. Body mass index is a measure of weight in relation to height. Anyone with a BMI of 25 or more is considered overweight. People who have a body mass index of 30 or more (a BMI of 30 is roughly 30 pounds over a healthy weight) are considered obese. BMI has some limitations: It can overestimate body fat in people who are very muscular, and it can underestimate body fat in people who have lost muscle mass, such as the elderly.

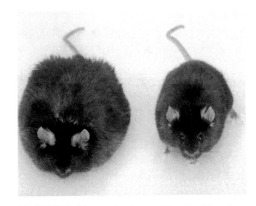

FIGURE 14.4 Obesity and Leptin. The *ob* mouse on the left is untreated; the one on the right has been given injections of leptin.

vulnerability that makes some ethnic-gender groups more susceptible to obesity. Also, some individuals may be at risk for obesity because of their environment, as when their exposure to junk food and fast food is high and their opportunities to be active are minimal.

Recent analyses indicate that in many countries around the world, especially developing countries, obesity rates are increasing faster for women than men (Seidell, 2005). Obesity is especially common in women living in low-income circumstances.

Dieting Ironically, while obesity is on the rise, dieting has become an obsession with many Americans. It has also become the subject of controversy (Cunningham & Hyson, 2006; Last & Wilson, 2006). On one side are the societal norms that promote a very lean, athletic body. This ideal is supported by $50 billion a year in sales of diet books, programs, videos, foods, and pills. On the other side are health professionals and a growing minority of the press. Although they recognize the alarmingly high rate of obesity, they are frustrated by high relapse rates among dieters and the obsession with excessive thinness that can lead to chronic dieting and serious health risks (Brownell, 2000).

Many people live their lives as one big long diet, interrupted by occasional hot fudge sundaes or chocolate chip cookies. They are **restrained eaters,** individuals who chronically restrict their food intake to control their weight. Restrained eaters are often on diets, are very conscious of what they eat, and tend to feel guilty after splurging on sweets (de Lauzon-Guillain & others, 2006; Johnson & Wardle, 2005; Roefs & others, 2005). An interesting characteristic of restrained eaters is that when they stop dieting, they tend to binge eat—that is, eat large quantities of food in a short time (Lowe & Timko, 2004). Also, when under stress, restrained eaters tend to increase their food intake, while unrestrained eaters decrease their food intake (Lowe & Kral, 2005, 2006).

Overweight Americans regularly embark on a diet and some are successful in keeping weight off short-term. However, they find it far more difficult to shed pounds for a year or longer. When overweight people diet and maintain their weight loss, they do become less depressed and reduce their risk for a number of health-impairing disorders (Christensen, 1996).

One recent study compared the effectiveness of four weight-loss programs (Dansinger & others, 2005). One hundred sixty overweight adults 22 to 72 years of age who had high cholesterol, high blood pressure, or high blood sugar were randomly assigned to participate in one of four weight-loss programs for one year: Atkins (low carbohydrate), Zone (macronutrient balance), Weight Watchers (low calorie), or Ornish (low fat). Results of the study included:

- After one year, approximately 25 percent of the participants in each group had lost 10 to 20 pounds. For each group, at least one person had lost 30 to 60 pounds after one year.
- Individuals who lost the most weight had the best improvements in cholesterol—those on the Ornish diet lowered their low-density lipoprotein, or LDL (bad), cholesterol the most, whereas those on the other three diets raised their high-density lipoprotein, or HDL (good), cholesterol the most.
- Only about 25 percent of the participants stuck to their diets on a regular basis for the full year of the study.

In sum, none of the four diets was more effective than the others, and the average weight loss after being on the diets for one year was only modest. This study examined only eating behavior. If exercise patterns had also been examined, the combination of dieting and exercise may have led to greater weight loss.

Indeed, the most effective weight-loss programs include exercise (Eckel, 2005). Exercise not only burns off calories, but continues to elevate the person's metabolic rate for several hours after the exercise. Also, exercise lowers a person's *set point* for

www.mhhe.com/santrockld11

Why People Are Getting Fatter
Obesity

How effective are diet programs?

restrained eaters Individuals who chronically restrict their food intake to control their weight. Restrained eaters are often on diets, are very conscious of what they eat, and tend to feel guilty after splurging on sweets.

weight, which makes it easier to maintain a lower weight (Bennett & Gurin, 1982). In sum, as with children and adolescents, a combination of moderate calorie reduction and regular exercise is the best recipe for losing weight, especially over the long term (Boyle & Long, 2007; Greenwald, 2006; Kruger, Blanck, & Gillespie, 2006).

Regular Exercise

In 1961, President John F. Kennedy offered this message: "We are under-exercised as a nation. We look instead of play. We ride instead of walk. Our existence deprives us of the minimum of physical activity essential for healthy living." Without question, people are jogging, cycling, and aerobically exercising more today than in 1961, but far too many of us are still couch potatoes, spending most of our leisure time in front of the TV or a computer screen.

One of the main reasons that health experts want people to exercise is that it helps to prevent heart disease, diabetes, and other diseases (Corbin & others, 2006; Hales, 2007; Kukkonen-Harjula & others, 2005; Randall & others, 2005). Although exercise designed to strengthen muscles and bones or to improve flexibility is important to fitness, many health experts have stressed aerobic exercise. **Aerobic exercise** is sustained exercise—jogging, swimming, or cycling, for example—that stimulates heart and lung activity.

People in some occupations get more vigorous exercise than those in others (Bertrais & others, 2005; Howley, 2001; Wandel & Roos, 2005). For example, longshoremen, who are on their feet all day and lift, push, and carry heavy cargo, have about half the risk of fatal heart attacks as coworkers like crane drivers and clerks, who have physically less demanding jobs. Elaborate studies of 17,000 male alumni of Harvard University found that those who exercised strenuously on a regular basis had a lower risk of heart disease and were more likely to still be alive in their middle adulthood years than their more sedentary counterparts (Lee, Hsieh, & Paffenbarger, 1995; Paffenbarger & others, 1986).

Some experts conclude that, regardless of other risk factors (smoking, high blood pressure, overweight, heredity), if you exercise enough to burn more than 2,000 calories a week, you can cut your risk of heart attack by an impressive two-thirds (Sherwood, Light, & Blumenthal, 1989). Burning up 2,000 calories a week through exercise requires considerable effort, far more than most individuals are willing to expend. To burn 300 calories a day, through exercise, you would have to do one of the following: swim or run for about 25 minutes, walk for 45 minutes at about 4 miles an hour, or participate in aerobic dancing for 30 minutes.

As a more realistic goal, health experts recommend that adults engage in 30 minutes or more of moderate-intensity physical activity on most, preferably all, days of the week. Most recommend that you should try to raise your heart rate to at least 60 percent of your maximum heart rate. However, only about one-fifth of adults are active at these recommended levels of physical activity. Examples of the physical activities that qualify as moderate or vigorous are listed in figure 14.5.

Researchers have found that exercise benefits not only physical health, but mental health as well (Annesi, 2005; Peluso & Andrade, 2005). In particular, exercise improves self-concept and reduces anxiety and depression (Kirby, 2005; Wise & others, 2006). Meta-analyses have shown that exercise can be as effective in reducing depression as psychotherapy (Richardson & others, 2005). One recent study of more than 600 adults found that exercise was associated with positive mental health and obesity with poor mental health (Rohrer, Pierce, & Blackburn, 2005).

Research on the benefits of exercise suggests that both moderate and intense activities produce important physical and psychological gains (Gostic, 2005). Some people enjoy rigorous, intense exercise. Others enjoy more moderate exercise routines. The enjoyment and pleasure we derive from exercise added to its aerobic benefits make exercise one of life's most important activities (Brownson, Boehmer, & Luke, 2005;

What are some strategies for incorporating exercise into your life?

www.mhhe.com/santrockld11

**Aerobic Institute
Women and Exercise**

aerobic exercise Sustained exercise (such as jogging, swimming, or cycling) that stimulates heart and lung activity.

Moderate
Walking, briskly (3 to 4 mph)
Cycling, for pleasure or transportation (≤10 mph)
Swimming, moderate effort
Conditioning exercise, general calisthenics
Racket sports, table tennis
Golf, pulling cart or carrying clubs
Canoeing, leisurely (2.0 to 3.9 mph)
Home care, general cleaning
Mowing lawn, with power mower
Home repair, painting

Vigorous
Walking, briskly uphill or with a load
Cycling, fast or racing (>10 mph)
Swimming, fast-treading crawl
Conditioning exercise, stair ergometer or ski machine
Racket sports, singles tennis or racketball
Golf, practice at driving range
Canoeing, rapidly (≥ 4 mph)
Moving furniture
Mowing lawn, with hand mower
Home repair, fix-up projects

FIGURE 14.5 Moderate and Vigorous Physical Activities

Corbin & others, 2006; Hahn, Payne, & Lucas, 2007). To read about ways to incorporate regular exercise into your life, see the Applications in Life-Span Development interlude.

APPLICATIONS IN LIFE-SPAN DEVELOPMENT

Exercise

Here are some helpful strategies for building exercise into your life:

- *Reduce TV time.* Heavy TV viewing by college students is linked to poor health (Astin, 1983). Replace some of your TV time with exercise.
- *Chart your progress.* Systematically recording your exercise workouts will help you to chart your progress. This strategy is especially helpful over the long term.
- *Get rid of excuses.* People make up all kinds of excuses for not exercising. A typical excuse is, "I don't have enough time." You likely do have enough time.
- *Imagine the alternative.* Ask yourself whether you are too busy to take care of your own health. What will your life be like if you lose your health?
- *Learn more about exercise.* The more you know about exercise, the more you are likely to start an exercise program and continue it.

Substance Abuse

In chapter 12, "Physical and Cognitive Development in Adolescence," we explored substance abuse in adolescence. Fortunately, by the time individuals reach their mid-twenties, many have reduced their use of alcohol and drugs. That is the conclusion reached by Jerald Bachman and his colleagues (1996, 2002) in a longitudinal analysis of more than 38,000 individuals who were evaluated from the time they were high school seniors through their twenties. Here are some of the main findings in the study:

- College students drink more than youth who end their education after high school.
- Those who don't go to college smoke more.
- Singles use marijuana more than married individuals.
- Drinking is heaviest among singles and divorced individuals. Becoming engaged, married, or even remarried quickly brings down alcohol use. Thus, living arrangements and marital status are key factors in alcohol and drug use rates during the twenties.
- Individuals who consider religion to be very important in their lives and who frequently attend religious services are less likely to take drugs than their less religious counterparts.

Let's take a closer look at use of alcohol and nicotine by college students and young adults and at the nature of addiction.

Alcohol   Around the world, there are differences in alcohol use. Europeans, especially the French, drink alcohol at high rates. Estimates are that about 30 percent of French adults have impaired health related to alcohol consumption. Alcohol use is also high in Russia but its use in China is low. Alcohol use also varies significantly with religion and gender (Bjarnason & others, 2003; Weijers & others, 2003). Some religions, such as Islam, forbid the use of alcohol, but Catholics, Reform Jews, and liberal Protestants all consume alcohol at a fairly high level. Males drink alcohol more than females. Our focus here, though, is not on use of alcohol in general but on two problems associated with drinking: binge drinking and alcoholism.

Binge Drinking Figure 14.6 shows the findings on binge drinking from the longitudinal study by Jerald Bachman and his colleagues (Bachman & others, 1996, 2002). Heavy, binge drinking often increases in college, and it can take its toll on students (Broadwater & others, 2005; Murphy & others, 2005; Wechsler & Murphy, 2006; White, Kraus, & Swartzwelder, 2006). Chronic binge drinking is more common among college men than women and in students living away from home, especially in fraternity houses (Schulenberg & others, 2000).

In a national survey of drinking patterns on 140 campuses, almost half of the binge drinkers reported problems that included (Wechsler & others, 1994):

- missing classes,
- physical injuries,
- troubles with police, and
- having unprotected sex.

What kinds of problems are associated with binge drinking in college?

For example, binge-drinking college students were 11 times more likely to fall behind in school, 10 times more likely to drive after drinking, and twice as likely to have unprotected sex than college students who did not binge drink. Also, one recent study found that after an evening of binge drinking, memory retrieval was significantly impaired during the alcohol hangover the next morning (Verster & others, 2003).

More than 40,000 full-time U.S. college students were asked about their drinking habits in 1993, 1997, 1999, and 2001 (Wechsler & others, 2002). Binge-drinking rates (men who drank five or more drinks in a row and women who drank four or more drinks at least once in the two weeks prior to the questionnaire) remained remarkably consistent—at about 44 percent—over the eight years. Further, almost 75 percent of underage students living in fraternities or sororities were binge drinkers, and 70 percent of traditional-age college students who lived away from home were binge drinkers. The lowest rate of binge drinking—25 percent—occurred for students living at home with their parents.

A special concern is the increase in binge drinking by females during emerging adulthood. One study found a 125 percent increase in binge drinking at all-women colleges from 1993 through 2001 (Wechsler & others, 2002).

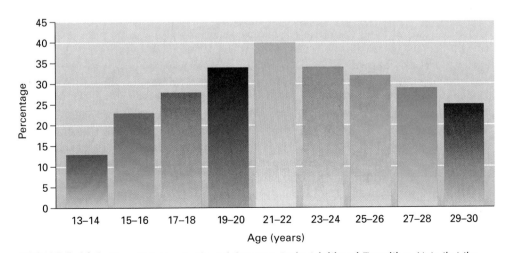

FIGURE 14.6 Binge Drinking in the Adolescence–Early Adulthood Transition. Note that the percentage of individuals engaging in binge drinking peaked at 21 or 22 years of age and then began to gradually decline through the remainder of the twenties. Binge drinking was defined as having five or more alcoholic drinks in a row in the past two weeks.

Alcoholism   *Alcoholism* is a disorder that involves long-term, repeated, uncontrolled, compulsive, and excessive use of alcoholic beverages and that impairs the drinker's health and social relationships. One in nine individuals who drink continues the path to alcoholism. Those who do are disproportionately related to alcoholics (Jang, 2005). Family studies consistently find a high frequency of alcoholism in the first-degree relatives of alcoholics (Conway, Swendsen, & Merikangas, 2003; Pastor & Evans, 2003). Indeed, researchers have found that heredity likely plays a role in alcoholism, although the precise hereditary mechanism has not been found (Crews & others, 2005; Diao & Lin, 2006; Dick & Bierut, 2006; Quickfall & el-Guebaly, 2006). An estimated 50 to 60 percent of individuals who become alcoholics are believed to have a genetic predisposition for it.

Although studies reveal a genetic influence on alcoholism, they also show that environmental factors play a role (Matthews & others, 2005; McCrady & others, 2006). For example, family studies indicate that many alcoholics do not have close relatives who are alcoholics (Martin & Sher, 1994). The large cultural variations in alcohol use mentioned earlier also underscore the environment's role in alcoholism.

About one-third of alcoholics recover whether or not they are in a treatment program. This figure was found in a long-term study of 700 individuals over 50 years and has consistently been found by other researchers as well (Vaillant, 1992). There is a "one-third rule" for alcoholism: by age 65, one-third are dead or in terrible shape, one-third are abstinent or drinking socially, and one-third are still trying to beat their addiction. A positive outcome and recovery from alcoholism are predicted by certain factors: (1) a strong negative experience related to drinking, such as a serious medical emergency or condition; (2) finding a substitute dependency to compete with alcohol abuse, such as meditation, exercise, or overeating (which of course has its own negative health consequences); (3) having new social supports (such as a concerned, helpful employer or a new marriage); and (4) joining an inspirational group, such as a religious organization or Alcoholics Anonymous (Vaillant, 1992).

Cigarette Smoking   Converging evidence from a number of studies underscores the dangers of smoking or being around those who do (Moons & others, 2006; Naess & others, 2004; Tewolde, Ferguson, & Benson, 2006). For example, smoking is linked to 30 percent of cancer deaths, 21 percent of heart disease deaths, and 82 percent of chronic pulmonary disease deaths. Secondhand smoke is implicated in as many as 9,000 lung cancer deaths a year. Children of smokers are at special risk for respiratory and middle-ear diseases (Wallace-Bell, 2003).

Fewer people smoke today than in the past, and almost half of all living adults who ever smoked have quit. The prevalence of smoking in men has dropped from over 50 percent in 1965 to about 28 percent today (National Center for Health Statistics, 2004). However, more than 50 million Americans still smoke cigarettes today. And cigar smoking and tobacco chewing, with risks similar to those of cigarette smoking, have increased.

Most adult smokers would like to quit, but their addiction to nicotine often makes quitting a challenge (Rose, 2006; Thompson & others, 2003). Nicotine, the active drug in cigarettes, is a stimulant that increases the smoker's energy and alertness, a pleasurable and reinforcing experience. Nicotine also stimulates neurotransmitters that have a calming or pain-reducing effect.

How can smokers quit? Four main methods are used to help smokers quit:

- *Using a substitute source of nicotine.* Nicotine gum, the nicotine patch, the nicotine inhaler, and nicotine spray work on the principle of supplying small amounts of nicotine to diminish the intensity of withdrawal. Recent research shows that the percentage of individuals who are still not smoking after five months ranges from 18 percent for the nicotine patch to 30 percent for the nicotine spray (Centers for Disease Control and Prevention, 2001).

"there's no shooting—we just make you keep smoking."

- *Taking an antidepressant.* Bupropion, an antidepressant sold as Zyban, helps smokers control their cravings while they ease off nicotine. Recent research indicates that smokers using Zyban to quit have had a 30 percent average success rate for five months after they started taking the drug (Centers for Disease Control and Prevention, 2001).
- *Controlling stimuli associated with smoking.* This behavior modification technique sensitizes the smoker to social cues associated with smoking. For example, the smoker might associate a morning cup of coffee or a social drink with smoking. Stimulus control strategies help the smoker to avoid these cues or learn to substitute other behaviors for smoking.
- *Going "cold turkey."* Some people succeed by simply stopping smoking without making any major changes in their lifestyle. They decide they are going to quit and they do. Lighter smokers usually have more success with this approach than heavier smokers.

Studies indicate that when people do stop smoking their risk of cancer is reduced (Centers for Disease Control and Prevention, 2001; Hughes, 2003). Five years after people stop smoking their health risk is noticeably lower than people who continue to smoke (U.S. Surgeon General's Report, 1990).

Addiction **Addiction** is a pattern of behavior characterized by an overwhelming involvement with using a drug and securing its supply. This can occur despite adverse consequences associated with the use of the drug. There is a strong tendency to relapse after quitting or withdrawal. Withdrawal symptoms consist of significant changes in physical functioning and behavior. Depending on the drug, these symptoms might include insomnia, tremors, nausea, vomiting, cramps, elevation of heart rate and blood pressure, convulsions, anxiety, and depression when a physically dependent person stops taking the drug. Experts on drug abuse use the term *addiction* to describe either a physical or psychological dependence on the drug or both (Fields, 2007; Kinney, 2006; Ksir, Hart, & Ray, 2006).

Controversy continues about whether addictions are diseases (Fields, 2007; Heather, 2004; Kinney, 2006). The **disease model of addiction** describes addictions as biologically based, lifelong diseases that involve a loss of control over behavior and require medical and/or spiritual treatment for recovery. In the disease model, addiction is either inherited or developed early in life. Current or recent problems or relationships are not believed to be causes of the disease. Once involved in the disease, you can never completely rid yourself of it, according to this model. The disease model has been strongly promoted and supported by the medical profession and Alcoholics Anonymous (AA) (Humphreys, 2000). Recent research studies have found that AA is often successful in reducing substance abuse (Humphreys, 2003; McKellar, Stewart, & Humphreys, 2003; Timko, Finney, & Moos, 2005). For example, a recent longitudinal study of individuals who sought professional help or help through AA found that individuals who entered AA in the first year after seeking help for their alcohol problem reduced their drinking the most over a period of 16 years (Moos & Moos, 2005). Another recent study revealed that women benefited from AA more than men (Timko, Finney, & Moos, 2005). Reasons given for the success of AA include the spiritual aspects of the treatment and the social network and support provided by the AA group (Babor & Del Boca, 2003; Vaillant, 2005).

In contrast to the disease model of addiction, which focuses on biological mechanisms, some psychologists believe that understanding addiction requires that it be placed in context as part of people's lives, their personalities, their relationships, their environments, and their perspectives. In this **life-process model of addiction,** addiction is not a disease but rather a habitual response and a source of gratification or security that can be understood best in the context of social relationships and experiences.

www.mhhe.com/santrockld11

**Clearinghouse for Drug Information
Alcoholism
Smoking/Tobacco Control
Smoking Cessation**

What are two models of addiction?

addiction A pattern of behavior characterized by an overwhelming involvement with using a drug and securing its supply.

disease model of addiction The view that addictions are biologically based, lifelong diseases that involve a loss of control over behavior and require medical and/or spiritual treatment for recovery.

life-process model of addiction The view that addiction is not a disease but rather a habitual response and a source of gratification and security that can be understood only in the context of social relationships and experiences.

Each of these views of addiction—the disease model and the nondisease, life-process model—has its supporters. A recent study found that a combination of biological and environmental factors was effective in decreasing alcohol consumption by alcoholics (Anton & others, 2006). The drug naltrexone (a medication designed to treat alcohol dependence) and a behavioral intervention combined were more effective than either treatment alone in reducing alcohol consumption by alcoholics.

Review and Reflect • LEARNING GOAL 2

2 Identify the changes in physical development in young adults

Review
- How does physical performance peak and then slow down in early adulthood?
- What are some important things to know about eating and weight?
- What are the benefits of exercise?
- How extensive is substance abuse in young adults? What effects does it have on their lives?

Reflect
- To discourage smoking, many governments now levy heavy taxes on cigarettes because of their negative health effects. Would you recommend that the U.S. government levy similar heavy taxes on fatty foods because of their negative health effects? Explain.

---

3 SEXUALITY

| Sexual Orientation and Behavior | Sexually Transmitted Infections | Forcible Sexual Behavior and Sexual Harassment |

We do not need sex for everyday survival the way we need food and water, but we do need it for the survival of the species. In chapter 12 we looked briefly at how adolescents develop a sexual identity and become sexually active. What happens to their sexuality in adulthood? Let's examine the sexual activity of Americans and their sexual orientation, as well as some of the problems that can be associated with sexual activity.

Sexual Orientation and Behavior

Obtaining accurate information about such a private activity as sexual behavior is not easy. The best information we currently have comes from what is often referred to as the 1994 Sex in America survey. In this well-designed, comprehensive study of Americans' sexual patterns, Robert Michael and his colleagues (1994) interviewed more than 3,000 people from 18 to 59 years of age who were randomly selected, a sharp contrast from earlier samples that were based on unrepresentative groups of volunteers.

Heterosexual Attitudes and Behavior   Here are some of the key findings from the 1994 *Sex in America* survey:

- Americans tend to fall into three categories: One-third have sex twice a week or more, one-third a few times a month, and one-third a few times a year or not at all.

- Married (and cohabiting) couples have sex more often than noncohabiting couples (see figure 14.7).
- Most Americans do not engage in kinky sexual acts. When asked about their favorite sexual acts, the vast majority (96 percent) said that vaginal sex was "very" or "somewhat" appealing. Oral sex was in third place, after an activity that many have not labeled a sexual act—watching a partner undress.
- Adultery is clearly the exception rather than the rule. Nearly 75 percent of the married men and 85 percent of the married women indicated that they have never been unfaithful.
- Men think about sex far more than women do—54 percent of the men said they think about it every day or several times a day, whereas 67 percent of the women said they think about it only a few times a week or a few times a month.

In sum, one of the most powerful messages in the 1994 survey was that Americans' sexual lives are more conservative than previously believed. Although 17 percent of the men and 3 percent of the women said they have had sex with at least 21 partners, the overall impression from the survey was that sexual behavior is ruled by marriage and monogamy for most Americans.

Sources of Sexual Orientation

In the Sex in America survey, 2.7 percent of the men and 1.3 percent of the women reported that they had had same-sex relations in the past year (Michael & others, 1994). Why are some individuals lesbian, gay, or bisexual (LGB) and others heterosexual? Speculation about this question has been extensive (Hock & Williams, 2007; Kelly, 2006; King, 2005).

Until the end of the nineteenth century, it was generally believed that people were either heterosexual or homosexual. Today, it is more accepted to view sexual orientation, not as an either/or proposition, but as a continuum from exclusive male-female relations to exclusive same-sex relations (King, 2005). Some individuals are also *bisexual*, being sexually attracted to people of both sexes.

All people, regardless of their sexual orientation, have similar physiological responses during sexual arousal and seem to be aroused by the same types of tactile stimulation. Investigators typically find no differences between LGBs and heterosexuals in a wide range of attitudes, behaviors, and adjustments (Hyde & DeLamater, 2006). One recent review did find a higher prevalence of mental disorders in lesbians, gay men, and bisexuals than in heterosexuals and concluded that the difference was due to the stress associated with minority status involving stigma, prejudice, and discrimination (Meyer, 2003). Homosexuality once was classified as a mental disorder, but both the American Psychiatric Association and the American Psychological Association discontinued this classification as a mental disorder in the 1970s.

Recently, researchers have explored the possible biological basis of same-sex relations (James, 2005; Quinsey, 2003). The results of hormone studies have been inconsistent. If gay males are given male sex hormones (androgens), their sexual orientation doesn't change. Their sexual desire merely increases. A very early prenatal critical period might influence sexual orientation (James, 2005; Meek, Schulz, & Keith, 2005; Swaab & others, 2002). In the second to fifth months after conception, exposure of the fetus to hormone levels characteristic of females might cause the individual (male or female) to become attracted to males (Ellis & Ames, 1987). If this critical-period hypothesis turns out to be correct, it would explain why clinicians have found that sexual orientation is difficult, if not impossible, to modify.

With regard to anatomical structures, neuroscientist Simon LeVay (1991) found that an area of the hypothalamus that governs sexual behavior is twice as large (about the size of a grain of sand) in heterosexual males as in gay males. This area was found to be about the same size in gay males and heterosexual females. Critics of this research point out that many of the gay males in the study had AIDS and suggest that their brains could have been altered by the disease.

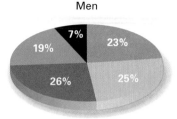

Noncohabiting

Men

Women

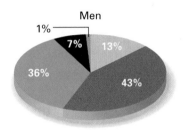

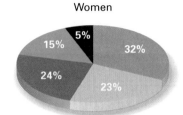

Cohabiting (married)

Men

Women

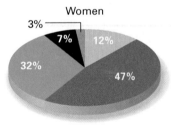

- Never
- A few times a year
- A few times a month
- 2–3 times a week
- 4 or more times a week

FIGURE 14.7 The Sex in America Survey. The percentages show noncohabiting and cohabiting (married) males' and female's responses to the question "How often have you had sex in the past year?" in a 1994 survey (Michael & others, 1994). *What was one feature of the Sex in America survey that made it superior to most surveys of sexual behavior?*

What likely determines an individual's sexual preference?

An individual's sexual orientation—same-sex, heterosexual, or bisexual—is most likely determined by a combination of genetic, hormonal, cognitive, and environmental factors (Baldwin & Baldwin, 1998). Most experts on same-sex relations believe that no one factor alone causes sexual orientation and that the relative weight of each factor can vary from one individual to the next.

In effect, no one knows exactly why some individuals are lesbian, gay, or bisexual (Gooren, 2006). Nevertheless, scientists have a clearer picture of what does not cause individuals to be lesbian or gay. For example, as we saw in chapter 9, "Socioemotional Development in Early Childhood," children raised by gay or lesbian parents or couples are no more likely to be LGB than are children raised by heterosexual parents (Patterson, 2002). There also is no evidence that being a gay male is caused by a dominant mother or a weak father, or that being a lesbian is caused by girls choosing male role models. Researchers have found that having an older brother increases the odds of being a gay male but the route by which this occurs has not been determined (Mustanski, Chivers, & Bailey, 2003).

Attitudes and Behavior of Lesbians and Gay Males   Many gender differences that appear in heterosexual relationships occur in same-sex relationships (Savin-Williams & Diamond, 2004). For example, like heterosexual women, lesbians have fewer sexual partners than gay men and lesbians have less permissive attitudes about casual sex outside a primary relationship than gay men (Peplau, 2002, 2003; Peplau, Fingerhut, & Beals, 2004).

How can lesbians and gay males adapt to a world in which they are a minority? According to psychologist Laura Brown (1989), lesbians and gay males experience life as a minority in a dominant, majority culture. For lesbians and gay men, developing a *bicultural identity* creates new ways of defining themselves. Brown believes that lesbians and gay males adapt best when they don't define themselves in polarities, such as trying to live in an encapsulated lesbian or gay male world completely divorced from the majority culture or completely accepting the dictates and bias of the majority culture. Balancing the demands of the two cultures—the minority lesbian/gay male culture and the majority heterosexual culture—can often lead to more effective coping for lesbians and gay males, says Brown.

Sexually Transmitted Infections

Sexually transmitted infections (STIs) are diseases that are primarily contracted through sex—intercourse as well as oral-genital and anal-genital sex. STIs affect about one of every six U.S. adults (National Center for Health Statistics, 2004). Among the most prevalent STIs are bacterial infections (such as gonorrhea, syphilis, and chlamydia), and STIs caused by viruses—genital herpes, genital warts, and AIDS. Figure 14.8 describes these sexually transmitted infections.

No single STI has had a greater impact on sexual behavior, or created more public fear in the last several decades than AIDS (Carroll, 2007; Kelly, 2006). **Acquired immune deficiency syndrome (AIDS)** is a sexually transmitted infection that is caused by the human immunodeficiency virus (HIV), which destroys the body's immune system. Following exposure to HIV, an individual's body is vulnerable to germs that a normal immune system could destroy.

Through 2004, 944,000 cases of AIDS had been reported in the United States, with about 80 percent of these being males and almost half intravenous (IV) drug users (Centers for Disease Control and Prevention, 2006; Rhodes, 2005). Because of education and the development of more effective drug treatments, deaths due to AIDS have begun to decline in the United States (Centers for Disease Control and Prevention, 2006).

Globally, the total number of individuals with the HIV virus reached 40 million in 2005 (UNAIDS, 2006). The greatest concern about AIDS is in sub-Saharan Africa,

STI	Description/cause	Incidence	Treatment
Gonorrhea	Commonly called the "drip" or "clap." Caused by the bacterium *Neisseria gonorrhoeae*. Spread by contact between infected moist membranes (genital, oral-genital, or anal-genital) of two individuals. Characterized by discharge from penis or vagina and painful urination. Can lead to infertility.	500,000 cases annually in U.S.	Penicillin, other antibiotics
Syphilis	Caused by the bacterium *Treponema pallidum*. Characterized by the appearance of a sore where syphilis entered the body. The sore can be on the external genitals, vagina, or anus. Later, a skin rash breaks out on palms of hands and bottom of feet. If not treated, can eventually lead to paralysis or even death.	100,000 cases annually in U.S.	Penicillin
Chlamydia	A common STI named for the bacterium *Chlamydia trachomatis*, an organism that spreads by sexual contact and infects the genital organs of both sexes. A special concern is that females with chlamydia may become infertile. It is recommended that adolescent and young adult females have an annual screening for this STI.	About 3 million people in U.S. annually.	Antibiotics
Genital herpes	Caused by a family of viruses with different strains. Involves an eruption of sores and blisters. Spread by sexual contact.	One of five U.S. adults	No known cure but antiviral medications can shorten outbreaks
AIDS	Caused by a virus, the human immunodeficiency virus (HIV), which destroys the body's immune system. Semen and blood are the main vehicles of transmission. Common symptoms include fevers, night sweats, weight loss, chronic fatigue, and swollen lymph nodes.	More than 300,000 cumulative cases of HIV virus in U.S. 25–34-year-olds; epidemic incidence in sub-Saharan countries	New treatments have slowed the progression from HIV to AIDS; no cure
Genital warts	Caused by the human papillomavirus, which does not always produce symptoms. Usually appear as small, hard painless bumps in the vaginal area, or around the anus. Very contagious. Certain high-risk types of this virus cause cervical cancer and other genital cancers. May recur despite treatment.	About 5.5 million new cases annually; considered the most common STI in the U.S.	A topical drug, freezing, or surgery

FIGURE 14.8 Sexually Transmitted Infections

where it has reached epidemic proportions (Ford, Odallo, & Chorlton, 2003; UNAIDS, 2006).

Just asking a date about his or her sexual behavior does not guarantee protection from AIDS and other sexually transmitted infections (Caron, 2006; Emmers-Sommer & Allen, 2005). For example, in one investigation, 655 college students were asked to answer questions about lying and sexual behavior (Cochran & Mays, 1990). Of the 422 respondents who said they were sexually active, 34 percent of the men and 10 percent of the women said they had lied so their partner would have sex with them. Much higher percentages—47 percent of the men and 60 percent of the women—said they had been lied to by a potential sexual partner. When asked what aspects of their past they would be most likely to lie about, more than 40 percent of the men and women said they would understate the number of their sexual partners. Twenty percent of the men, but only 4 percent of the women, said they would lie about their results from an AIDS blood test.

What are some good strategies for protecting against AIDS and other sexually transmitted infections? They include:

- *Knowing your and your partner's risk status.* Anyone who has had previous sexual activity with another person might have contracted an STI without being aware of it. Spend time getting to know a prospective partner before you have sex. Use this time to inform the other person of your STI status and inquire about your partner's. Remember that many people lie about their STI status.

www.mhhe.com/santrockld11

Human Sexuality
American Sexual Behavior
Lesbian and Gay Issues
Center for AIDS Prevention Studies
HIV/STD Education
Signs of HIV Infection in Females

sexually transmitted infections (STIs) Diseases that are contracted primarily through sex.

acquired immune deficiency syndrome (AIDS) A sexually transmitted disease caused by the HIV virus, which destroys the body's immune system.

What are some good strategies for protecting against AIDS and other sexually transmitted infections? How effectively have you practiced these strategies?

- *Obtaining medical examinations.* Many experts recommend that couples who want to begin a sexual relationship should have a medical checkup to rule out STIs before they engage in sex. If cost is an issue, contact your campus health service or a public health clinic.
- *Having protected, not unprotected, sex.* When correctly used, latex condoms help to prevent many STIs from being transmitted. Condoms are most effective in preventing gonorrhea, syphilis, chlamydia, and AIDS. They are less effective against the spread of herpes.
- *Not having sex with multiple partners.* One of the best predictors of getting an STI is having sex with multiple partners. Having more than one sex partner elevates the likelihood that you will encounter an infected partner.

Forcible Sexual Behavior and Sexual Harassment

Too often, sex involves the exercise of power. Here we will briefly look at two of the problems that may result: rape and sexual harassment.

Rape **Rape** is forcible sexual intercourse with a person who does not give consent. Legal definitions of rape differ from state to state. For example, in some states, husbands are not prohibited from forcing their wives to have intercourse, although this has been challenged in several states (Kilpatrick, 2004). Because victims may be reluctant to suffer the consequences of reporting rape, the actual incidence is not easily determined (Kelly, 2006; Rickert, Wiemann, & Vaughan, 2005). Rape occurs most often in large cities, where it has been reported that 8 of every 10,000 women 12 years and older are raped each year. Nearly 200,000 rapes are reported each year in the United States.

Although most victims of rape are women, rape of males does occur (McLean, Balding, & White, 2005). Men in prisons are especially vulnerable to rape, usually by heterosexual males who use rape as a means of establishing their dominance and power. Though it might seem impossible for a man to be raped by a woman, a man's erection is not completely under his voluntary control, and some cases of men being raped by women have been reported (Sarrel & Masters, 1982). Male victims account for fewer than 5 percent of all rapes.

Why does rape of women occur so often in the United States? Among the causes given are that males are socialized to be sexually aggressive, to regard women as inferior beings, and to view their own pleasure as the most important objective in sexual relations (Adams-Curtis & Forbes, 2004; Kalmuss, 2004). Researchers have found that male rapists share the following characteristics: aggression enhances their sense of power or masculinity; they are angry at women in general; and they want to hurt and humiliate their victims (Chiroro & others, 2004; Mahlstedt & Welsh, 2005).

Rape is a traumatic experience for the victims and those close to them (Herrera & others, 2006). Victims initially feel shock and numbness and often are acutely disorganized. Some show their distress through words and tears, others internalize their suffering. As victims strive to get their lives back to normal, they may experience depression, fear, anxiety, and increased substance use for months or years (McFarlane & others, 2005; White & Frabutt, 2006). Sexual dysfunctions, such as reduced sexual desire and an inability to reach orgasm, occur in 50 percent of female rape victims (Sprei & Courtois, 1988). Many victims make changes in their lives—such as moving to a new apartment or refusing to go out at night. Recovery depends on the victim's coping abilities, psychological adjustments prior to the assault, and social support. Parents, partner, and others close to the victim can provide important support for recovery, as can mental health professionals (Favero & others, 2004; Hyde & DeLamater, 2006).

rape Forcible sexual intercourse with a person who does not consent to it.

An increasing concern is **date or acquaintance rape,** which is coercive sexual activity directed at someone with whom the victim is at least casually acquainted (Caron, 2006; Sahu, Mohanty, & Dash, 2005; White & Frabutt, 2006). By some estimates, one in three adolescent girls will be involved in a controlling, abusive relationship before she graduates from high school, and two-thirds of college freshman women report having been date-raped or having experienced an attempted date rape at least once (Watts & Zimmerman, 2002). About two-thirds of college men admit that they fondle women against their will, and half admit to forcing sexual activity. To read further about rape on college campuses, see the Research in Life-Span Development interlude.

Sexual Assault

RESEARCH IN LIFE-SPAN DEVELOPMENT

Campus Sexual Assault

A major study that focused on campus sexual assault involved a phone survey of 4,446 women attending two- or four-year colleges (Fisher, Cullen, & Turner, 2001). Sexual victimization was measured in a two-stage process. First, a series of screening questions were asked to determine if the respondent had experienced an act that might possibly be a victimization. Second, if the respondent answered "yes," the respondent was asked detailed questions about the incident, such as the type of unwanted contact and the means of coercion. In addition, respondents were asked about other aspects of their lives, including their lifestyles, routine activities, living arrangements, and prior sexual victimization.

Slightly less than 3 percent said that they either had experienced a rape or an attempted rape during the academic year. About 1 of 10 college women said that they had experienced rape in their lifetime. Unwanted or uninvited sexual contacts were widespread with more than one-third of the college women reporting these incidents. As shown in figure 14.9, in this study, most women (about 9 of 10) knew the person who sexually victimized them. Most of the women attempted to take protective actions against their assailants but were then reluctant to report the victimization to the police for a number of reasons (such as embarrassment, not clearly understanding the legal definition of rape, or not wanting to define someone they knew who victimized them as a rapist). Several factors were associated with sexual victimization: living on campus, being unmarried, getting drunk frequently, and experiencing prior sexual victimization. The majority of rapes occurred in living quarters.

In addition, this research examined a form of sexual victimization that has been studied infrequently: stalking. Thirteen percent of the female students said they had been stalked since the school year began. As with other sexual victimizations, 80 percent knew their stalkers, who most often were boyfriends (42 percent) or classmates (24 percent). Stalking incidents lasted an average of 60 days.

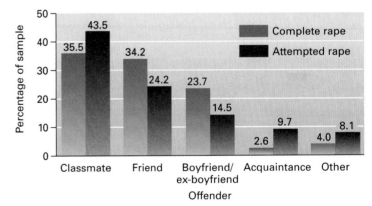

FIGURE 14.9 Relationship Between Victim and Offender in Completed and Attempted Rapes of College Women. In a recent phone survey of college women, slighly less than 3 percent of the women said they had experienced a rape or attempted rape during the academic year (Fisher, Cullen, & Turner, 2001). The percentages shown here indicate the relationship between the victim and the offender. *What were some possible advantages and disadvantages of using a phone survey rather than face-to-face interviews to conduct this study?*

Sexual Harassment   Sexual harassment takes many forms—from inappropriate sexual remarks and physical contact (patting, brushing against one's body) to blatant propositions and sexual assaults (Cortina, 2004; Gregg, 2004). Millions of

date or acquaintance rape Coercive sexual activity directed at someone with whom the perpetrator is at least casually acquainted.

women experience sexual harassment each year in work and educational settings (Lapierre, Spector, & Leck, 2005; Lim & Cortina, 2005; Signal & others, 2005). Sexual harassment of men by women also occurs but to a far lesser extent than sexual harassment of women by men.

Sexual harassment can result in serious psychological consequences for the victim (Cortina & Wasti, 2005; Hoffman, 2004). Sexual harassment is a manifestation of power of one person over another. The elimination of such exploitation requires the development of work and academic environments that provide equal opportunities to develop a career and obtain education in a climate free of sexual harassment (Bildt, 2005; Eyres, 2005; Hyde & DeLamater, 2006).

Review and Reflect • LEARNING GOAL 3

(3) Discuss sexuality in young adults

Review
- What is the nature of heterosexuality and same-sex sexual orientation?
- What are sexually transmitted infections? What are some important things to know about AIDS?
- What are the effects of forcible sexual behavior and sexual harassment?

Reflect
- What can be done to reduce forcible sexual behavior and sexual harassment?

---

4 COGNITIVE DEVELOPMENT

Cognitive Stages | Creativity

The physical changes of young adulthood extend to the brain. Recall from chapter 12 that the prefrontal cortex is still maturing during adolescence. Are there also changes in cognitive performance during these years? To explore the nature of cognition in early adulthood, we will focus on issues related to cognitive stages and creative thinking.

Cognitive Stages

Are young adults more advanced in their thinking than adolescents are? Let's explore what Piaget and others have said about this intriguing question.

Piaget's View Piaget believed that an adolescent and an adult think qualitatively in the same way. That is, Piaget argued that at approximately 11 to 15 years of age, adolescents enter the formal operational stage, which is characterized by more logical, abstract, and idealistic thinking than the concrete operational thinking of 7- to 11-year-olds. Piaget did believe that young adults are more *quantitatively* advanced in their thinking in the sense that they have more knowledge than adolescents. He also believed, as do information-processing psychologists, that adults especially increase their knowledge in a specific area, such as a physicist's understanding of physics or a financial analyst's knowledge about finance. According to Piaget, however, formal operational thought is the final stage in cognitive development, and it characterizes adults as well as adolescents.

Some developmentalists believe it is not until adulthood that many individuals consolidate their formal operational thinking. That is, they may begin to plan and hypothesize about intellectual problems in adolescence, but they become more systematic and sophisticated at this as young adults. Nonetheless, even many adults do not think in formal operational ways at all (Keating, 1990).

Realistic and Pragmatic Thinking According to other developmentalists, Piaget overlooked some important cognitive changes that occur after individuals use formal operational thought. One proposal is that the idealism Piaget described as part of formal operational thinking decreases in early adulthood. This especially occurs as young adults move into the world of work and face the constraints of reality (Labouvie-Vief, 1986).

A related perspective on adult cognitive change was proposed by K. Warner Schaie and Sherry Willis (2000). They concluded that it is unlikely that adults go beyond the powerful methods of scientific thinking characteristic of the formal operational stage. However, Schaie argued that adults do progress beyond adolescents in their *use* of intellect. For example, he said that in early adulthood, individuals often switch from acquiring knowledge to applying knowledge. This especially occurs as individuals pursue long-term career goals and attempt to achieve success in their work.

What are some ways that young adults might think differently than adolescents?

Reflective and Relativistic Thinking William Perry (1970, 1999) also described some changes in cognition that take place in early adulthood. He said that adolescents often view the world in terms of polarities—right/wrong, we/they, good/bad. As youth move into adulthood, they gradually move away from this type of absolute thinking as they become aware of the diverse opinions and multiple perspectives of others. Thus, in Perry's view, the *absolute, dualistic thinking* (either/or) of adolescence gives way to the *reflective, relativistic thinking* of adulthood.

Expanding on Perry's view, Gisela Labouvie-Vief (2006) recently proposed that the increasing complexity of cultures in the past century has generated a greater need for reflective, more complex thinking that takes into account the changing nature of knowledge and challenges. She also emphasizes that key aspects of cognitive development in emerging adulthood include deciding on a particular worldview, recognizing that the worldview is subjective, and understanding that diverse worldviews should be acknowledged. In her perspective, considerable individual variation characterizes the thinking of emerging adults, with the highest level of thinking attained only by some. She argues that the level of education emerging adults achieve especially influences how likely they will maximize their thinking potential.

Is There a Fifth, Postformal Stage? Some theorists have pieced together cognitive changes in young adults and proposed a new stage of cognitive development, **postformal thought,** which is qualitatively different from Piaget's formal operational thought. Postformal thought involves understanding that the correct answer to a problem requires reflective thinking and can vary from one situation to another, and that the search for truth is often an ongoing, neverending process. Postformal thought also includes the belief that solutions to problems need to be realistic and that emotion and subjective factors can influence thinking (Kramer, Kahlbaugh, & Goldston, 1992).

What is postformal thought like in practice? As young adults engage in more reflective judgment when solving problems, they might think deeply about many aspects of politics, their career and work, relationships, and other areas of life (Kitchener, King, & DeLuca, 2006; Labouvie-Vief & Diehl, 1999). They might understand that what might be the best solution to a problem at work (with a co-worker or boss) might not be the best solution at home (with a romantic partner). Many

postformal thought A form of thought that is qualitatively different from Piaget's formal operational thought. It involves understanding that the correct answer to a problem can require reflective thinking, that the correct answer can vary from one situation to another, and that the search for truth is often an ongoing, never-ending process. It also involves the belief that solutions to problems need to be realistic and that emotion and subjective factors can influence thinking.

young adults also become more skeptical about there being a single truth and often are not willing to accept an answer as final. They also often recognize that thinking can't just be abstract but rather has to be realistic and pragmatic. And many young adults understand that emotions can play a role in thinking—for example, that they are likely to think more clearly when they are in a calm and collected state than when they are angry and highly aroused.

How strong is the research evidence for a fifth, postformal, stage of cognitive development? Researchers have found that young adults are more likely to engage in this postformal thinking than adolescents are (Commons & Bresette, 2006; Commons & others, 1989). The fifth stage is controversial, however, and some critics argue that the research evidence has yet to be provided to document it as a qualitatively more advanced stage than formal operational thought.

Creativity

Young adulthood is a time of great creativity for some people. At the age of 30, Thomas Edison invented the phonograph, Hans Christian Andersen wrote his first volume of fairy tales, and Mozart composed *The Marriage of Figaro*. One early study of creativity found that individuals' most creative products were generated in their thirties and that 80 percent of the most important creative contributions were completed by age 50 (Lehman, 1960).

More recently, researchers have found that creativity does peak in adulthood and then decline, but that the peak often occurs in the forties. However, qualifying any conclusion about age and creative accomplishments are (1) the magnitude of the decline in productivity, (2) contrasts across creative domains, and (3) individual differences in lifetime output (Simonton, 1996).

Even though a decline in creative contributions is often found in the fifties and later, the decline is not as great as commonly thought. An impressive array of creative accomplishments occur in late adulthood. Benjamin Franklin invented the bifocal lens when he was 78 years old; Harriet Doerr wrote her first novel—*Stones from Ibarra*, which won the National Book Award in 1984—at the age of 73. And one of the most remarkable examples of creative accomplishment in late adulthood can be found in the life of Henri Chevreul. After a distinguished career as a physicist, Chevreul switched fields in his nineties to become a pioneer in gerontological research. He published his last research paper just a year prior to his death at the age of 103!

Any consideration of decline in creativity with age requires consideration of the domain involved. In such fields as philosophy and history, older adults often show as much creativity as when they were in their thirties and forties. By contrast, in such fields as lyric poetry, abstract math, and theoretical physics, the peak of creativity is often reached in the twenties or thirties.

There also is extensive individual variation in the lifetime output of creative individuals. Typically, the most productive creators in any field are far more prolific than their least productive counterparts. The contrast is so extreme that the top 10 percent of creative producers frequently account for 50 percent of the creative output in a particular domain. For instance, only sixteen composers account for half of the music regularly performed in the classical repertoire.

Can you make yourself more creative? In chapter 10, "Physical and Cognitive Development in Middle and Late Childhood," we presented some strategies for stimulating creative thinking in children, and these strategies can also be used by adults. Other strategies for becoming more creative have been suggested by Mihaly Csikszentmihalyi (pronounced ME-high CHICK-sent-me-high-ee).

Csikszentmihalyi (1995) interviewed 90 leading figures in art, business, government, education, and science to learn how creativity works. He discovered that creative people regularly experience a state he calls *flow*, a heightened state of pleasure experienced when we are engaged in mental and physical challenges that absorb us. Csikszentmihalyi (1997, 2000; Csikszentmihalyi & Nakamura, 2006; Nakamura & Csikszentmihalyi, 2002) believes everyone is capable of achieving flow. Based on his interviews with some of the most creative people in the world, the first step toward a more creative life is cultivating your curiosity and interest. How can you do this?

- *Try to be surprised by something every day.* Maybe it is something you see, hear, or read about. Become absorbed in a lecture or a book. Be open to what the world is telling you. Life is a stream of experiences. Swim widely and deeply in it, and your life will be richer.

- *Try to surprise at least one person every day.* In a lot of things you do, you have to be predictable and patterned. Do something different for a change. Ask a question you normally would not ask. Invite someone to go to a show or a museum you never have visited.

- *Write down each day what surprised you and how you surprised others.* Most creative people keep a diary, notes, or lab records to ensure that their experience is not fleeting or forgotten. Start with a specific task. Each evening record the most surprising event that occurred that day and your most surprising action. After a few days, reread your notes and reflect on your past experiences. After a few weeks, you might see a pattern of interest emerging in your notes, one that might suggest an area you can explore in greater depth.

- *When something sparks your interest, follow it.* Usually when something captures your attention, it is short-lived—an idea, a song, a flower. Too often we are too busy to explore the idea, song, or flower further. Or we think these areas are none of our business because we are not experts about them. Yet the world is our business. We can't know which part of it is best suited to our interests until we make a serious effort to learn as much about as many aspects of it as possible.

- *Wake up in the morning with a specific goal to look forward to.* Creative people wake up eager to start the day. Why? Not necessarily because they are cheerful, enthusiastic types but because they know that there is something meaningful to accomplish each day, and they can't wait to get started.

- *Spend time in settings that stimulate your creativity.* In Csikszentmihalyi's (1995) research, he gave people an electronic pager and beeped them randomly at different times of the day. When he asked them how they felt, they reported the highest levels of creativity when walking, driving, or swimming. I (your author) do my most creative thinking when I'm jogging. These activities are semiautomatic in that they take a certain amount of attention while leaving some time free to make connections among ideas. Another setting in which highly creative people report coming up with novel ideas is the sort of half-asleep, half-awake state we are in when we are deeply relaxed or barely awake.

Mihaly Csikszentmihalyi, in the setting where he gets his most creative ideas. *When and where do you get your most creative thoughts?*

Review and Reflect ● LEARNING GOAL 4

4 **Characterize cognitive changes in early adulthood**

Review
- What changes in cognitive development in young adults have been proposed?
- Does creativity decline in adulthood? How can people lead more creative lives?

Reflect
- What do you think are the most important cognitive changes that take place in young adults?

5 CAREERS AND WORK

Developmental Changes — Values and Careers — The Impact of Work

Personality Types — Monitoring the Occupational Outlook

Earning a living, choosing an occupation, establishing a career, and developing in a career—these are important themes of early adulthood. Even for people as talented as David Eggers, who was described at the opening of this chapter, the path to becoming financially independent and establishing a career can be rocky. What are some of the factors that go into choosing a job or career, and how does work typically affect the lives of young adults?

Developmental Changes

Many children have idealistic fantasies about what they want to be when they grow up. For example, many young children want to be superheroes, sports stars, or movie stars. In the high school years, they often have begun to think about careers on a somewhat less idealistic basis. In their late teens and early twenties, their career decision making has usually turned more serious as they explore different career possibilities and zero in on the career they want to enter. In college, this often means choosing a major or specialization that is designed to lead to work in a particular field. By their early and mid-twenties, many individuals have completed their education or training and started to enter a full-time occupation. From the mid-twenties through the remainder of early adulthood, individuals often seek to establish their emerging career in a particular field. They may work hard to move up the career ladder and improve their financial standing.

"Your son has made a career choice, Mildred. He's going to win the lottery and travel a lot."
© 2004. Reprinted courtesy of Bunny Hoest and Parade Magazine.

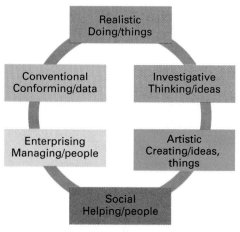

FIGURE 14.10 Holland's Model of Personality Types and Career Choices

Personality Types

Personality type theory is John Holland's view that it is important to match an individual's personality with a particular career. Holland believes that when individuals find careers that fit their personality, they are more likely to enjoy the work and stay in the job longer than if they'd taken a job not suited to their personality. Holland proposed six basic career-related personality types: realistic, investigative, artistic, social, enterprising, and conventional (see figure 14.10):

- *Realistic.* They like the outdoors and working in manual activities. They often are less social than other personality types, have difficulty in demanding situations, and prefer to work alone. This personality type matches up best with such jobs as laborer, farmer, truck driver, construction worker, engineer, and pilot.
- *Investigative.* They are interested in ideas more than people, are rather indifferent to social relationships, are troubled by emotional situations, and are often aloof and intelligent. This personality type matches up well with scientific, intellectually oriented professions.
- *Artistic.* They are creative and enjoy working with ideas and materials that allow them to express themselves in innovative ways. They value nonconformity. Sometimes they have difficulties in social relationships. Not many jobs match up with the artistic personality type. Consequently, some artistic individuals work in jobs that are their second or third choices and express their artistic interests through hobbies and leisure.
- *Social.* They like to work with people and tend to have a helping orientation. They like doing social things considerably more than engaging in intellectual

personality type theory John Holland's view that it is important for individuals to select a career that matches up well with their personality type.

tasks. This personality type matches up with jobs in teaching, social work, and counseling.

- *Enterprising.* They also are more oriented toward people than things or ideas. They may try to dominate others to reach their goals. They are often good at persuading others to do things. The enterprising type matches up with careers in sales, management, and politics.
- *Conventional.* They function best in well-structured situations and are skilled at working with details. They often like to work with numbers and perform clerical tasks rather than working with ideas or people. The conventional type matches up with such jobs as accountant, bank teller, secretary, or file clerk.

If all individuals (and careers) fell conveniently into Holland's personality types, career counselors would have an easy job. However, individuals are typically more varied and complex than Holland's theory suggests. Even Holland (1987) states that individuals rarely are pure types, and most persons are a combination of two or three types. Still, the basic idea of matching personality traits to particular careers is an important contribution to the career development field. Holland's personality types are incorporated into the Strong-Campbell Interest Inventory, a widely used measure in career guidance.

Values and Careers

An important aspect of choosing a career is that it also match up with your values. When people know what they value most—what is important to them in life—they can refine their career choice more effectively. Some values are reflected in Holland's personality types, such as whether a person values working in a career that involves helping others or in a career in which creativity is valued. Among the values that some individuals think are important in choosing a career are working with people they like, working in a career with prestige, making a lot of money, being happy, not having to work long hours, being mentally challenged, having plenty of time for leisure pursuits, working in the right geographical location, and working where physical and mental health are important.

Monitoring the Occupational Outlook

As you explore the type of work you are likely to enjoy and in which you can succeed, it is important to be knowledgeable about different fields and companies. Occupations may have many job openings one year but few in another year as economic conditions change. Thus, it is critical to keep up with the occupational outlook in various fields. An excellent source for doing this is the U.S. government's *Occupational Outlook Handbook*, which is revised every two years.

According to the 2006–2007 handbook, service industries, especially education and health services, and professional and business services, are projected to account for the most new jobs in the next decade. Education and health services, as well as professional and business services, are projected to have significant growth through 2014.

Projected job growth varies widely by education requirements. Jobs that require a college degree are expected to grow the fastest. Most of the highest-paying occupations require a college degree (*Occupational Outlook Handbook*, 2006–2007).

The Impact of Work

Do you work to live or live to work? Most individuals spend about one-third of their lives at work. In one survey, 35 percent of Americans worked 40 hours a week, but 18 percent worked 51 hours or more per week (Center for Survey Research at the University of Connecticut, 2000). Only 10 percent worked less than 30 hours a week.

www.mhhe.com/santrockld11

Holland's Personality Types
Steps to Successful Career Planning
Journal of Vocational Behavior
Career Development Quarterly
Journal of Counseling Psychology

"Uh-huh. Uh-huh. And for precisely how long were you a hunter-gatherer at I.B.M.?"
© The New Yorker Collection, 1989 Jack Ziegler from cartoonbank.com. All Rights Reserved.

www.mhhe.com/santrockld11

Occupational Outlook
Career and Job-Hunting Resources
What Color Is Your Parachute?
Job Interviewing
Work and Family Issues

What are some characteristics of work settings linked with employees' stress?

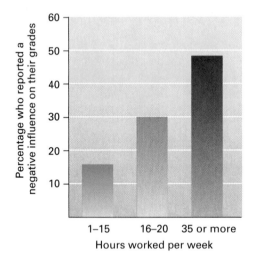

FIGURE 14.11 **The Relation of Hours Worked Per Week in College to Grades.** Among students working to pay for school expenses, 16 percent of those working 1 to 15 hours per week reported that working negatively influenced their grades (National Center for Education Statistics, 2002). Thirty percent of college students who worked 16 to 20 hours a week said the same, as did 48 percent who worked 35 hours or more per week.

Work defines people in fundamental ways (Blustein, 2006; Hoare, 2006; Osipow, 2000). It is an important influence on their financial standing, housing, the way they spend their time, where they live, their friendships, and their health (Warr, 2004). Some people define their identity through their work. Work also creates a structure and rhythm to life that is often missed when individuals do not work for an extended period (Stankunas & others, 2006). When unable to work, many individuals experience emotional distress and low self-esteem.

Of course, work also creates stress (Jedryka-Goral & others, 2006; Lyonette & Yardley, 2006). Four characteristics of work settings are linked with employee stress and health problems (Moos, 1986): (1) high job demands such as having a heavy workload and time pressure, (2) inadequate opportunities to participate in decision making, (3) a high level of supervisor control, and (4) a lack of clarity about the criteria for competent performance.

Work During College   Eighty percent of U.S. undergraduate students worked during the 1999–2000 academic year (National Center for Education Statistics, 2002). Forty-eight percent of undergraduates identified themselves mainly as students working to meet school expenses and 32 percent as employees who decided to enroll in school. Undergraduate students who identified themselves as working to meet expenses worked an average of 26 hours per week; those who considered themselves to be employees worked an average of 40 hours per week.

Working can pay or help offset some costs of schooling, but working also can restrict students' opportunities to learn. For those who identified themselves primarily as students, one recent national study found that as the number of hours worked per week increased, their grades suffered (National Center for Education Statistics, 2002) (see figure 14.11). Other research has found that as the number of hours college students work increases, the more likely they are to drop out of college (National Center for Education Statistics, 2002). Thus, college students need to carefully examine whether the number of hours they work is having a negative impact on their college success.

Of course, jobs also can contribute to your education. More than 1,000 colleges in the United States offer *cooperative (co-op) programs*, which are paid apprenticeships in a field that you are interested in pursuing. (You may not be permitted to participate in a co-op program until your junior year.) Other useful opportunities for working while going to college include internships and part-time or summer jobs relevant to your field of study. In a national survey of employers, almost 60 percent said their entry-level college hires had co-op or internship experience (Collins, 1996). Participating in these work experiences can be a key factor in whether you land the job you want when you graduate.

Unemployment   Unemployment produces stress regardless of whether the job loss is temporary, cyclical, or permanent (Christiansen & others, 2006; Cook & others, 2005; Mantler & others, 2005). Researchers have found that unemployment is related to physical problems (such as heart attack and stroke), mental problems (such as depression and anxiety), marital difficulties, and homicide (Gallo & others, 2006; Hill & Angel, 2005). A recent 15-year longitudinal study of more than 24,000 adults found that life satisfaction dropped considerably following unemployment and increased after becoming re-employed but did not completely return to the life satisfaction level previous to being unemployed (Lucas & others, 2004).

Stress comes not only from a loss of income and the resulting financial hardships but also from decreased self-esteem (Voydanoff, 1990). Individuals who cope best with unemployment have financial resources to rely on, often savings or the earnings of other family members. The support of understanding, adaptable family members also helps individuals cope with unemployment. Job counseling and self-help groups can provide practical advice on job searching, résumés, and interviewing skills, and also give emotional support.

Dual-Career Couples Dual-career couples may have particular problems finding a balance between work and the rest of life (Crossfield, Kinman, & Jones, 2005; Pitt-Catsouphes, Kossek, & Sweet, 2006; Rubin, 2006). If both partners are working, who cleans up the house or calls the repairman or takes care of the other endless details involved in maintaining a home? If the couple has children, who is responsible for being sure that the children get to school or to piano practice, who writes the notes to approve field trips or meets the teacher or makes the dental appointments?

Although single-earner married families still make up a sizeable minority of families, the two-earner couple has increased considerably in the last three decades (Barnett, 2001) (see figure 14.12). As more U.S. women worked outside the home, the division of responsibility for work and family changed. Recent research suggests that (Barnett, 2001; Barnett & others, 2001):

- *U.S. husbands are taking increased responsibility for maintaining the home.* Men in dual-career families do about 45 percent of the housework.
- *U.S. women are taking increased responsibility for breadwinning.* In about one-third of two-earner couples, wives earn as much as or more than their husbands.
- *U.S. men are showing greater interest in their families and parenting.* Young adult men are reporting that family is at least as important to them as work. Among men with egalitarian attitudes toward gender roles, fatherhood is linked with a decrease of 9 hours per week at work; among men with more traditional views about gender roles, fatherhood is associated with an increase of almost 11 hours per week.

In the Diversity in Life-Span Development interlude, we further explore gender and work by examining gender in the workplace. Ethnic diversity in the workplace also is discussed in the interlude.

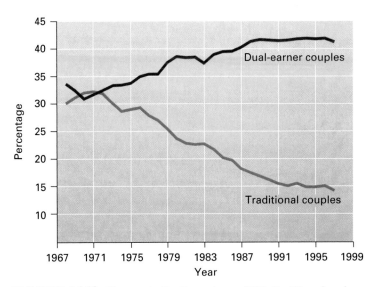

FIGURE 14.12 Changes in the Percentage of U.S. Traditional and Dual-Career Couples. Notice the dramatic increase in dual-earner couples in the last three decades. Traditional couples are those in which the husband is the sole breadwinner.

DIVERSITY IN LIFE-SPAN DEVELOPMENT

Diversity in the Workplace

The workplace is becoming increasingly diverse (Blustein, 2006; Roberson & Stevens, 2006; *Occupational Outlook Handbook,* 2006–2007). Whereas at one time few women were employed outside the home, in developed countries women have increasingly entered the labor force (Helgeson, 2005; Lakes & Carter, 2004). In 2004 in the United States men made up 53.6 percent of the labor force, women 46.4 percent (*Occupational Outlook Handbook,* 2006–2007). Only in Scandinavian countries such as Sweden did women participate in the labor force at the same rate as American women. In the United States, more than one-fourth of all lawyers, physicians, computer scientists, and chemists today are females.

Ethnic diversity also is increasing in the workplace in every developed country except France. In the United States, between 1980 and 2004, the percentage of Latinos and Asian Americans more than doubled, a trend that is expected to continue (*Occupational Outlook Handbook,* 2006–2007; U.S. Bureau of Labor Statistics,

How has the diversity of the workplace changed in recent years?

(continued on next page)

2005). Latinos are projected to constitute a larger percentage of the labor force than African Americans by 2014, growing from 12 percent to 15 percent (*Occupational Outlook Handbook,* 2006–2007). Asian Americans will continue to be the fastest growing of the labor force groups. The increasing diversity in the workplace requires a sensitivity to cultural differences, and the cultural values that workers bring to a job need to be recognized and appreciated (Powell, 2004).

Despite the increasing diversity in the workplace, women and ethnic minorities experience difficulty in breaking through the *glass ceiling*. This invisible barrier to career advancement prevents women and ethnic minorities from holding managerial or executive jobs regardless of their accomplishments and merits (Dipboye & Colella, 2005). Females' share of executive management positions dropped from 32 percent in 1990 to 19 percent in 2000 (U.S. Bureau of Labor Statistics, 2005). However, over the same period, the percentage of ethnic minorities in management jobs increased from 13 percent in 1990 to 17 percent in 2000.

> ### *Review and Reflect* • LEARNING GOAL 5
>
> **5** **Explain the key dimensions of careers and work in early adulthood**
>
> *Review*
> - What are some developmental changes in careers and work?
> - How might personality types be linked to career choice?
> - Why is it important to examine your values when thinking about a career?
> - Which areas are likely to offer the greatest increase in jobs through 2014?
> - What are some important things to know about work?
>
> *Reflect*
> - What careers do you want to pursue? How much education will they take? What are some changes in men's roles in home and family matters in the last 40 years?

REACH YOUR LEARNING GOALS

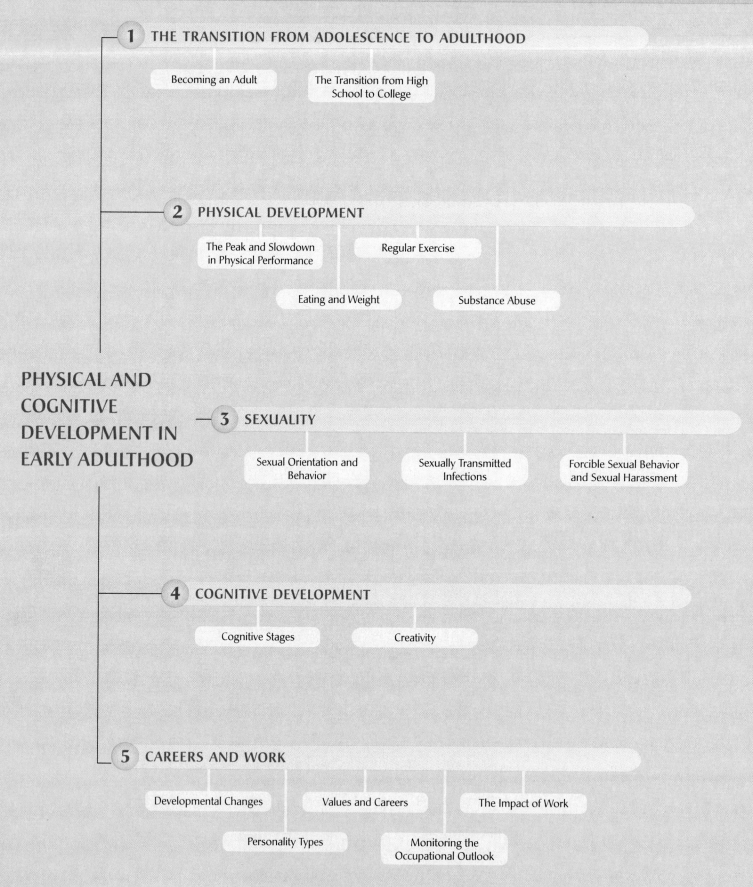

PHYSICAL AND COGNITIVE DEVELOPMENT IN EARLY ADULTHOOD

1 THE TRANSITION FROM ADOLESCENCE TO ADULTHOOD

- Becoming an Adult
- The Transition from High School to College

2 PHYSICAL DEVELOPMENT

- The Peak and Slowdown in Physical Performance
- Regular Exercise
- Eating and Weight
- Substance Abuse

3 SEXUALITY

- Sexual Orientation and Behavior
- Sexually Transmitted Infections
- Forcible Sexual Behavior and Sexual Harassment

4 COGNITIVE DEVELOPMENT

- Cognitive Stages
- Creativity

5 CAREERS AND WORK

- Developmental Changes
- Values and Careers
- The Impact of Work
- Personality Types
- Monitoring the Occupational Outlook

SUMMARY

1 The Transition from Adolescence to Adulthood: *Describe the transition from adolescence to adulthood*

Becoming an Adult
Emerging adulthood is the term now given to the transition from adolescence to adulthood. Its age range is about 18 to 25 years of age, and it is characterized by experimentation and exploration. There is both continuity and change in the transition from adolescence to adulthood. Two criteria for adult status are economic independence and independent decision making.

The Transition from High School to College
The transition from high school to college can involve both positive and negative features. U.S. college students today report experiencing more stress than did college students of the 1980s. An increasing number of college students are returning students.

2 Physical Development: *Identify the changes in physical development in young adults*

The Peak and Slowdown in Physical Performance
Peak physical performance is often reached between 19 and 26 years of age. There is a hidden hazard in this time period—bad health habits are often formed then. Toward the latter part of early adulthood, a detectable slowdown in physical performance is apparent for most individuals.

Eating and Weight
Obesity is a serious problem. Heredity and set point are biological factors involved in obesity. Environmental factors and culture influence obesity. Ethnicity-gender factors are linked to obesity. Many people live their lives as one big long diet—they are referred to as restrained eaters. The most effective weight loss programs involve moderate calorie reduction and regular exercise.

Regular Exercise
Both moderate and intense exercise produce important physical and psychological gains, such as lowered risk of heart disease and lowered anxiety.

Substance Abuse
By the mid-twenties a reduction in drug use often takes place. Although some reduction in alcohol use has occurred among college freshmen, binge drinking is still a major concern. Alcoholism is a disorder that involves long-term, repeated, uncontrolled, compulsive, and excessive use of alcoholic beverages and that impairs the drinker's health and social relationships. A number of strategies, such as nicotine substitutes, have shown some success in getting smokers to quit, but quitting is difficult because of the addictive properties of nicotine. Two views of addiction are the disease model and the life-process model, each of which has supporters.

3 Sexuality: *Discuss sexuality in young adults*

Sexual Orientation and Behavior
In the 1994 Sex in America survey, Americans' sexual lives were portrayed as more conservative than in earlier surveys. It generally is accepted to view sexual orientation along a continuum from exclusively heterosexual to exclusively homosexual. An individual's sexual preference likely is the result of a combination of genetic, hormonal, cognitive, and environmental factors.

Sexually Transmitted Infections
Also called STIs, sexually transmitted infections are contracted primarily through sexual contact. Gonorrhea, syphilis, chlamydia, and genital herpes are among the most common STIs. The STI that has received the most attention in the last several decades is AIDS (acquired immune deficiency syndrome), which is caused by HIV, a virus that destroys the body's immune system. Some good strategies for protecting against AIDS and other STIs are to (1) know your and your partner's risk status; (2) obtain medical examinations; (3) have protected, not unprotected, sex; and (4) not have sex with multiple partners.

Forcible Sexual Behavior and Sexual Harassment
Rape is forcible sexual intercourse with a person who does not give consent. Rape usually produces traumatic reactions in its victims. Date or acquaintance rape involves coercive sexual activity directed at someone with whom the victim is at least casually acquainted. Sexual harassment occurs when one person uses his or her power over another individual in a sexual manner and can result in serious psychological consequences for the victim.

4 Cognitive Development: *Characterize cognitive changes in early adulthood*

Cognitive Stages
Formal operational thought, entered at age 11 to 15, is Piaget's final cognitive stage. According to Piaget, although adults are quantitatively more knowledgeable than adolescents, adults do not enter a new, qualitatively different stage. Some experts argue that the idealism of Piaget's formal operational stage declines in young adults, replaced by more realistic, pragmatic thinking. Perry said that adolescents often engage in dualistic, absolute thinking, whereas young adults are more likely to engage in reflective, relativistic thinking. Some propose that differences like these constitute a qualitatively different, fifth cognitive stage, postformal thought. It involves understanding that the correct answer might require reflective thinking and might vary from one situation to

another, that the search for truth is often never-ending, that solutions to problems need to be realistic, and that emotion and subjective factors can be involved in thinking.

Creativity

Creativity peaks in adulthood, often in the forties, and then declines. However, (1) the magnitude of the decline is often slight; (2) the creativity-age link varies by domain; and (3) there is extensive individual variation in lifetime creative output. Based on interviews with leading experts in different domains, Csikszentmihalyi proposed that the first step toward living a creative life is to cultivate your curiosity and interest.

 5 **Careers and Work:** *Explain the key dimensions of careers and work in early adulthood*

Developmental Changes

Many young children have idealistic fantasies about a career. In the late teens and early twenties, their career thinking has usually turned more serious. By their early to mid-twenties, many individuals have completed their education or training and started in a career. In the remainder of early adulthood, they seek to establish their emerging career and start moving up the career ladder.

Personality Types

John Holland proposed that it is important for individuals to choose a career that is compatible with their personality type. He proposed six personality types: realistic, conventional, artistic, enterprising, investigative, and social.

Values and Careers

It is important to match up a career to your values. There are many different values, ranging from the importance of money to working in a preferred geographical location.

Monitoring the Occupational Outlook

Service industries, especially education and health services, and professional and business services, will account for the most new jobs in America in the next decade. Employment in the computer industry is especially projected to grow rapidly. Jobs that require a college education will be the fastest growing and highest paying.

The Impact of Work

Work defines people in fundamental ways and is a key aspect of their identity. Most individuals spend about one-third of their adult life at work. People often become stressed if they are unable to work but work also can produce stress, as when there is a heavy workload and time pressure. Eighty percent of U.S. college students work while going to college. Working during college can have negative outcomes, especially when students work long hours, or positive outcomes, especially when students participate in co-op programs, internships, or part-time or summer work relevant to their field of study. Unemployment produces stress regardless of whether the job loss is temporary, cyclical, or permanent. Unemployment is related to physical problems, mental problems, and other difficulties. The increasing number of women who work in careers outside the home has led to new work-related issues. There has been a considerable increase in the time men spend in household work and child care.

KEY TERMS

emerging adulthood 459
restrained eaters 466
aerobic exercise 467
addiction 471

disease model of
  addiction 471
life-process model of
  addiction 471

sexually transmitted
  infections (STIs) 475
acquired immune deficiency
  syndrome (AIDS) 475

rape 476
date or acquaintance rape 477
postformal thought 479
personality type theory 482

KEY PEOPLE

Jeffrey Arnett 459
Robert Michael 472
Simon LeVay 473
Laura Brown 474

Jean Piaget 477
K. Warner Schaie and Sherry
  Willis 479
William Perry 479

Gisela Labouvie-Vief 479
Mihaly Csikszentmihalyi 480
John Holland 482

E-LEARNING TOOLS

To help you master the material in this chapter, you'll find a number of valuable study tools on the LifeMap CD-ROM that accompanies this book and on the Online Learning Center for *Life-Span Development*, eleventh edition, at **www.mhhe.com/ santrockld11**.

Video Clips

In the margins of this book there are icons directing you to the LifeMap CD-ROM that accompanies the book. There you'll find a video for chapter 14 called "On Being a Working Mom." The working parents profiled in this segment offer two perspectives on the problem of maintaining the proper balance between work and the rest of life.

Self-Assessment

Connect to **www.mhhe.com/santrockld11** to examine some topics that are important to young adults by completing the self-assessments, *How Much Do I Know About STDs?*, *Matching My Personality Type to Careers*, and *My Career Goals*.

Taking It to the Net

Connect to **www.mhhe.com/santrockld11** to research the answers to these questions.

1. Irina has always considered herself overweight but not obese. She is 5'4" and weighs 160 pounds. Calculate her body mass index (BMI), and use the guidelines to determine whether or not she is overweight or obese. What is your BMI?
2. Nanette is working part-time in her college human resources office. She has been asked to start gathering information for a sexual harassment information booklet. What are the essential characteristics of sexual harassment, and how should Nanette communicate how the signs are identified?

Health and Well-Being, Parenting, and Education Exercises

Build your decision-making skills by trying your hand at the health and well-being, parenting, and education exercises. Connect to **www.mhhe.com/santrockld11** to research the answers and complete the exercises.

Love is a canvas furnished by nature and embroidered by imagination.

—VOLTAIRE
French Essayist, 18th Century

CHAPTER OUTLINE

LEARNING GOALS

STABILITY AND CHANGE FROM CHILDHOOD TO ADULTHOOD

1 Describe stability and change in temperament and attachment from childhood to adulthood

Temperament

Attachment

ATTRACTION, LOVE, AND CLOSE RELATIONSHIPS

2 Identify some key aspects of attraction, love, and close relationships

Attraction

The Faces of Love

Falling Out of Love

Loneliness

ADULT LIFESTYLES

3 Characterize adult lifestyles

Single Adults

Cohabiting Adults

Married Adults

Divorced Adults

Remarried Adults

Gay and Lesbian Adults

MARRIAGE AND THE FAMILY

4 Discuss the family life cycle, parenting, making marriage work, and divorce

The Family Life Cycle

Becoming a Parent

Making Marriage Work

Dealing with Divorce

GENDER, RELATIONSHIPS, AND SELF-DEVELOPMENT

5 Summarize the role of gender in relationships

Gender and Communication

Women's Development

Men's Development

Images of Life-Span Development
Gwenna and Greg: Her Pursuit and His Lack of Commitment

Commitment is an important issue in a romantic relationship for most individuals. Consider Gwenna, who decides that it is time to have a talk with Greg about his commitment to their relationship (Lerner, 1989, pp. 44–45):

> She shared her perspective on both the strengths and weaknesses of their relationship and what her hopes were for the future. She asked Greg to do the same. Unlike earlier conversations, this one was conducted without her pursuing him, pressuring him, or diagnosing his problems with women. At the same time, she asked Greg some clear questions, which exposed his vagueness.
>
> "How will you know when you are ready to make a commitment? What specifically would you need to change or be different than it is today?"
>
> "I don't know," was Greg's response. When questioned further, the best he could come up with was that he'd just feel it.
>
> "How much more time do you need to make a decision one way or another?"
>
> "I'm not sure," Greg replied. "Maybe a couple of years, but I really can't answer a question like that. I can't predict my feelings."
>
> And so it went.
>
> Gwenna really loved this man, but two years (and maybe longer) was longer than she could comfortably wait. So, after much thought, she told Greg that she would wait till fall (about ten months), but that she would move on if he couldn't commit himself to marriage by then. She was open about her wish to marry and have a family with him, but she was equally clear that her first priority was a mutually committed relationship. If Greg was not at that point by fall, then she would end the relationship—painful though it would be.
>
> During the waiting period, Gwenna was able to not pursue him and not get distant or otherwise reactive to his expressions of ambivalence and doubt. In this way she gave Greg emotional space to struggle with his dilemma and the relationship had its best chance of succeeding. Her bottom-line position ("a decision by fall") was not a threat or an attempt to rope Greg in, but rather, a clear statement of what was acceptable to her.
>
> When fall arrived, Greg told Gwenna he needed another six months to make up his mind. Gwenna deliberated a while and decided she could live with that. But when the six months were up, Greg was uncertain and asked for more time. It was then that Gwenna took the painful but ultimately empowering step of ending their relationship.

PREVIEW

Love is of central importance in each of our lives, as it is in Gwenna and Greg's lives. Shortly, we will discuss the many faces of love, as well as marriage and the family, the diversity of adult lifestyles, and the role of gender in relationships. To begin, though, we will return to an issue we initially raised in chapter 1: stability and change.

1 STABILITY AND CHANGE FROM CHILDHOOD TO ADULTHOOD

Temperament

Attachment

For adults, socioemotional development revolves around "the adaptive integration of emotional experience into satisfying daily life and successful relationships with others" (Thompson & Goodvin, 2005, p. 402). Young adults like Gwenna and Greg must make "choices of occupation, partners, and other activities" that will create lifestyles that are "emotionally satisfying, predictable, and manageable." They do not come to these tasks as blank slates, but do their decisions and actions simply reflect the persons they had already become when they were 5 years old or 10 years old or 20 years old?

We no longer believe in the infant determinism of Freud's psychosexual theory, which argued that our socioemotional lives as adults are virtually cast in stone by the time we are 5 years of age. But the first 20 years of life are not meaningless in predicting an adult's socioemotional life (Caspi & Shiner, 2006). And there is every reason to believe that experiences in the early adult years are important in determining what the individual is like later in adulthood. A common finding is that the smaller the time intervals over which we measure socioemotional characteristics, the more similar an individual will look from one measurement to the next. Thus, if we measure an individual's self-concept at the age of 20 and then again at the age of 30, we will probably find more stability than if we measured the individual's self-concept at the age of 10 and then again at the age of 30.

In trying to understand the young adult's socioemotional development, it would be misleading to look at an adult's life only in the present tense, ignoring the unfolding of social relationships and emotions. So, too, it would be a mistake to search only through a 30-year-old's first 5 to 10 years of life in trying to understand why he or she is having difficulty in a close relationship. The truth about adult socioemotional development lies somewhere between the infant determinism of Freud and a contextual approach that ignores the antecedents of the adult years altogether. Let's look at what is known about stability and change in two key aspects of socioemotional development: temperament and attachment.

Temperament

How stable is temperament? Recall that *temperament* is an individual's behavioral style and characteristic emotional responses. In early adulthood most individuals show fewer emotional mood swings than they did in adolescence, and they become more responsible and engage in less risk-taking behavior (Caspi, 1998). Along with these signs of a general change in temperament, researchers also find links between some dimensions of childhood temperament and adult personality. For example, in one longitudinal study, children who were highly active at age 4 were likely to be very outgoing at age 23 (Franz, 1996).

Are other aspects of temperament in childhood linked with adjustment in adulthood? In chapter 7 we saw that researchers have proposed various ways of describing and classifying types and dimensions of personality. Research has linked several of these types and dimensions during childhood with characteristics of adult personality. For example:

To what extent is temperament in childhood linked to temperament in adulthood?

- *Easy and difficult temperaments (two categories in Chess and Thomas' classification of types of temperament).* Here is what we know based on the few longitudinal studies that have been conducted on this topic (Caspi, 1998). In one longitudinal study, children who had an easy temperament at 3 to 5 years of age were likely to be well adjusted as young adults (Chess & Thomas, 1987). In contrast, many children who had a difficult temperament at 3 to 5 years of age were not well adjusted as young adults. Also, other researchers have found that boys with a difficult temperament in childhood are less likely as adults to continue their formal education, whereas girls with a difficult temperament in childhood are more likely to experience marital conflict as adults (Wachs, 2000).
- *Inhibition, a characteristic studied extensively by Jerome Kagan* (2000, 2002, 2003). Individuals who had an inhibited temperament in childhood are less likely than other adults to be assertive or experience social support, and more likely to delay entering a stable job track (Wachs, 2000).

- *Ability to control one's emotions (a dimension in Mary Rothbart and John Bates' analysis of temperament)*. In one longitudinal study, when 3-year-old children showed good control of their emotions and were resilient in the face of stress, they were likely to continue to handle emotions effectively as adults (Block, 1993). By contrast, when 3-year-olds had low emotional control and were not very resilient, they were likely to show problems in these areas as young adults.

In sum, these studies reveal some continuity between certain aspects of temperament in childhood and adjustment in early adulthood. However, keep in mind that these connections between childhood temperament and adult adjustment are based on only a small number of studies, and more research is needed to verify these linkages. Indeed, Theodore Wachs (1994, 2000) proposed ways that linkages between temperament in childhood and personality in adulthood might vary depending on the intervening contexts in individuals' experience. For example, figure 15.1 describes contexts in which an infant who displayed an inhibited temperament might develop a relatively sociable adult personality. As discussed in chapter 7, many aspects of the environment—including gender, culture, parenting, and goodness of fit generally—may influence the persistence of aspects of a child's temperament through life.

Attachment

Like temperament, attachment appears during infancy and plays an important part in socioemotional development. We discussed its role in infancy, childhood, and adolescence (see chapters 7, 9, and 13). How do these earlier patterns of attachment and adults' attachment styles influence the lives of adults?

Although relationships with romantic partners differ from those with parents, romantic partners fulfill some of the same needs for adults as parents do for their children. Recall from chapter 7 that *securely attached* infants are defined as those who use the caregiver as a secure base from which to explore the environment. Similarly,

Initial Temperament Trait: Inhibition

	Child A	Child B
	Intervening Context	
Caregivers	Caregivers (parents) who are sensitive and accepting, and let child set his or her own pace.	Caregivers who use inappropriate "low-level control" and attempt to force the child into new situations.
Physical Environment	Presence of "stimulus shelters" or "defensible spaces" that the children can retreat to when there is too much stimulation.	Child continually encounters noisy, chaotic environments that allow no escape from stimulation.
Peers	Peer groups with other inhibited children with common interests, so the child feels accepted.	Peer groups consist of athletic extroverts, so the child feels rejected.
Schools	School is "undermanned," so inhibited children are more likely to be tolerated and feel they can make a contribution.	School is "overmanned," so inhibited children are less likely to be tolerated and more likely to feel undervalued.
	Personality Outcomes	
	As an adult, individual is closer to extraversion (outgoing, sociable) and is emotionally stable.	As an adult, individual is closer to introversion and has more emotional problems.

FIGURE 15.1 Temperament in Childhood, Personality in Adulthood, and Intervening Contexts. Varying experiences with caregivers, the physical environment, peers, and schools can modify links between temperament in childhood and personality in adulthood. The example given here is for inhibition.

adults may count on their romantic partners to be a secure base to which they can return and obtain comfort and security in stressful times (Powers & others, 2006).

Do adult attachment patterns with partners reflect childhood attachment patterns with parents? In a retrospective study, Cindy Hazen and Phillip Shaver (1987) revealed that young adults who were securely attached in their romantic relationships were more likely to describe their early relationship with their parents as securely attached. In a longitudinal study, infants who were securely attached at 1 year of age were securely attached 20 years later in their adult romantic relationships (Steele & others, 1998). However, in another longitudinal study, links between early attachment styles and later attachment styles were lessened by stressful and disruptive experiences, such as the death of a parent or instability of caregiving (Lewis, Feiring, & Rosenthal, 2000).

How do we know whether adults are "securely attached"? Researchers have used varying methods to describe and classify adult attachment. Increasingly, they are conceptualizing and measuring adult attachment in terms of two dimensions (Brennan, Clark, & Shaver, 1998):

Adult Attachment

- **Attachment-related anxiety:** Involves the extent to which individuals feel secure or insecure about whether a partner will be available, responsive, and attentive.
- **Attachment-related avoidance:** Involves the degree to which individuals feel secure or insecure in relying on others, opening up to them, and being intimate with them.

Thus, saying that adults are "securely attached" indicates that they score low on measures of attachment-related anxiety and attachment-related avoidance.

Researchers also are studying links between adults' current attachment styles and many aspects of adults' lives (Carvallo & Gabriel, 2006; Fraley & others, 2006; Sumer & Cozzarelli, 2004; Wei & others, 2005). Securely attached adults are more satisfied with their close relationships than insecurely attached adults, and the relationships of securely attached are more likely to be characterized by trust, commitment, and longevity (Feeney, Noller, Callan, 1994). Securely attached adults also are more likely than insecurely attached adults to provide support when they are distressed and more likely to give support when their partner is distressed (Simpson, Rholes, & Nelligan, 1992). One recent study found that adults with avoidant and anxious attachment styles were more likely to be depressed than securely attached adults (Hankin, Kassel, & Abela, 2005). Another study revealed that women with anxious or avoidant attachment styles and men with an avoidant attachment style were more likely to have unwanted but consensual sexual experiences than securely attached adults (Gentzler & Kerns, 2004).

In sum, we have examined two aspects of attachment, which researchers are continuing to study: (1) the extent to which attachment to a caregiver in infancy is linked to attachment styles in adulthood, and (2) links between adults' current attachment patterns and their other social relationships and well-being.

What are some key dimensions of attachment in adulthood and how are they related to relationship patterns and well-being?

Review and Reflect ● LEARNING GOAL 1

1 **Describe stability and change in temperament and attachment from childhood to adulthood**

Review
- How stable is temperament from childhood to adulthood?
- How much does attachment change from childhood to adulthood?

Reflect
- What was your temperament like as a child? What is it like now?

attachment-related anxiety Involves the extent to which individuals feel secure or insecure about whether a partner will be available, responsive, and attentive.

attachment-related avoidance Involves the degree to which individuals feel secure or insecure in relying on others, opening up to them, and being intimate with them.

2 ATTRACTION, LOVE, AND CLOSE RELATIONSHIPS

| Attraction | | Falling Out of Love |
| The Faces of Love | | Loneliness |

What makes two people care about each other? What is love? Should we be cautious in our pursuit of love and follow the Czech proverb, "Do not choose your wife at a dance, but in the fields among the harvesters." Why do relationships dissolve? Many of us know all too well that an individual we thought was a marvelous human being may not turn out to be so marvelous after all. But often it is said that it is better to have loved and lost than never to have loved at all. Loneliness is a dark cloud over many individuals' lives. These are the themes of our exploration of close relationships: how they get started in the first place, the faces of love, falling out of love, and loneliness.

Attraction

What attracts people like Gwenna and Greg to each other and motivates them to spend more time with each other? How important are physical attraction and personality traits in determining the relationships we form?

Familiarity and Similarity Familiarity may breed contempt, as the old saying goes, but social psychologists have found that familiarity is a necessary condition for a close relationship to develop. For the most part, friends and lovers are people who have been around each other for a long time; they may have grown up together, gone to high school or college together, worked together, or gone to the same social events (Brehm, 2002).

Another old saying, "Birds of a feather flock together," also helps to explain attraction. Overall, our friends and lovers are much more like us than unlike us (Berscheid, 2000). Friends and lovers tend to have similar attitudes, values, lifestyles, and physical attractiveness. For some characteristics, though, opposites may attract. An introvert may wish to be with an extravert, or someone with little money may wish to associate with someone who is wealthy, for example.

A recent study focused on almost 300 couples who had been married for less than a year and had dated each other for about three years prior to their marriage (Luo & Klohnen, 2005). The couples had very similar attitudes and values, but many

DILBERT © Scott Adams/Dist. by United Feature Syndicate, Inc.

had dissimilar personality attributes. (For example, they differed in whether they were extraverted or introverted and whether they displayed positive or negative emotionality and conscientiousness.) Those who did have similar personality attributes reported higher marital satisfaction than their counterparts with dissimilar personality attributes. Similarity in personality predicted marital satisfaction, but similarity in attitudes and values did not. The researchers concluded that individuals usually don't have much difficulty determining another person's attitudes and values but that figuring out the individual's personality attributes often takes much longer and may play an important role later in relationships.

Why are people attracted to others who have similar attitudes, values, and lifestyles? **Consensual validation** is one reason. Our own attitudes and values are supported when someone else's attitudes and values are similar to ours—their attitudes and values validate ours. Another reason that similarity matters is that people tend to shy away from the unknown. We often prefer to be around people whose attitudes and values we can predict. And similarity implies that we will enjoy doing things with another person who likes the same things and has similar attitudes.

Physical Attractiveness You may be thinking at this point that something is missing from our discussion of attraction. As important as familiarity and similarity may be, they do not explain the spark that often ignites a romantic relationship: physical attractiveness. How important is physical attractiveness in relationships?

Many advertising agencies would have us believe that physical attractiveness is the most important factor in establishing and maintaining a relationship. Psychologists do not consider the link between physical beauty and attraction to be so clear-cut. For example, they have determined that heterosexual men and women differ on the importance of good looks when they seek an intimate partner. Women tend to rate as most important such traits as considerateness, honesty, dependability, kindness, and understanding; men prefer good looks, cooking skills, and frugality (Buss & Barnes, 1986).

Complicating research about the role of physical attraction is changing standards of what is deemed attractive. The criteria for beauty can differ, not just across cultures, but over time within cultures as well (Lamb & others, 1993). In the 1950s, the ideal of female beauty in the United States was typified by the well-rounded figure of Marilyn Monroe. Today, Monroe's 135-pound, 5-foot, 5-inch physique might be regarded as a bit overweight. The current ideal physique for both men and women is neither pleasingly plump nor extremely slender.

The force of similarity also operates at a physical level. We usually seek out someone at our own level of attractiveness in physical characteristics as well as social attributes. Research validates the **matching hypothesis**—which states that, although we may prefer a more attractive person in the abstract, in the real world, we end up choosing someone who is close to our own level of attractiveness (Kalick & Hamilton, 1986).

Much of the research on physical attraction has focused on initial or short-term encounters; researchers have not often evaluated attraction over the course of months and years.

The Faces of Love

Once attraction initiates a relationship, other opportunities exist to deepen the relationship to love. Love refers to a vast and complex territory of human behavior, spanning a range of relationships that includes friendship, romantic love, affectionate love, and even, according to some experts, altruism (Berscheid, 1988). In most of these types of love, one recurring theme is intimacy.

Intimacy Self-disclosure and the sharing of private thoughts are hallmarks of intimacy. As we discussed in chapter 13, adolescents have an increased need for intimacy. At the same time, they are engaged in the essential tasks of developing an

consensual validation An explanation of why individuals are attracted to people who are similar to them. Our own attitudes and behavior are supported and validated when someone else's attitudes and behavior are similar to our own.

matching hypothesis States that although we prefer a more attractive person in the abstract, in the real world we end up choosing someone who is close to our own level.

*W*e are what we love.

—ERIK ERIKSON
Danish-Born American Psychoanalyst and Author,
20th Century

Intimate Relationships
Ellen Berscheid's Research
Friendship

friendship A form of close relationship that involves enjoyment, acceptance, trust, respect, mutual assistance, confiding, understanding, and spontaneity.

identity and establishing their independence from their parents. Juggling the competing demands of intimacy, identity, and independence also becomes a central task of adulthood.

Erikson's Stage: Intimacy Versus Isolation Recall from our discussion in chapter 13 that Erik Erikson (1968) believes that identity versus identity confusion—pursuing who we are, what we are all about, and where we are going in life—is the most important issue to be negotiated in adolescence. In early adulthood, according to Erikson, after individuals are well on their way to establishing stable and successful identities, they enter the sixth developmental stage, which is intimacy versus isolation. Erikson describes intimacy as finding oneself while losing oneself in another person, and it requires a commitment to another person. If a person fails to develop an intimate relationship in early adulthood, according to Erikson, isolation results.

An inability to develop meaningful relationships with others can harm an individual's personality. It may lead individuals to repudiate, ignore, or attack those who frustrate them. Such circumstances account for the shallow, almost pathetic attempts of youth to merge themselves with a leader. Many youth want to be apprentices or disciples of leaders and adults who will shelter them from the harm of the "out-group" world. If this fails, and Erikson believes that it must, sooner or later the individuals recoil into a self-search to discover where they went wrong. This introspection sometimes leads to painful depression and isolation. It also may contribute to a mistrust of others.

Intimacy and Independence Development in early adulthood often involves balancing intimacy and commitment on the one hand, and independence and freedom on the other. At the same time as individuals are trying to establish an identity, they face the difficulty of having to cope with increasing their independence from their parents, developing an intimate relationship with another individual, and increasing their friendship commitments. They also face the task of being able to think for themselves and do things without always relying on what others say or do.

The extent to which young adults develop autonomy has important implications for them. Young adults who have not sufficiently moved away from parental ties may have difficulty in both interpersonal relationships and a career. Consider a daughter who is overprotected by her mother and continues to depend on her mother for financial support in early adulthood. The daughter may have difficulty developing mature intimate relationships and a career. When a promotion comes up that involves more responsibility and possibly more stress, she may turn it down. When things do not go well in her relationship with a young man, she may go crying to her mother.

The balance between intimacy and commitment, on the one hand, and independence and freedom, on the other, is delicate. Some individuals are able to experience a healthy independence and freedom along with an intimate relationship. Keep in mind that intimacy and commitment, and independence and freedom, are not just concerns of early adulthood. They are important themes of development that are worked and reworked throughout the adult years.

Friendship Increasingly researchers are finding that friendship plays an important role in development throughout the human life span (Dow & Wood, 2006; Monsour, 2006; Pruchno & Rosenbaum, 2003). In the words of American historian Henry Adams, "One friend in life is much, two are many, and three hardly possible." **Friendship** is a form of close relationship that involves enjoyment (we like to spend time with our friends), acceptance (we accept our friends without trying to change them), trust (we assume our friends will act in our best interest), respect (we think our friends make good judgments), mutual assistance (we help and support our friends and they us), confiding (we share experiences and confidential matters with a friend), understanding (we feel that a friend knows us well and understands what we like), and spontaneity (we feel free to be ourselves around a friend). In an inquiry of more than 40,000 individuals, many of these characteristics were given when people were asked what a best friend should be like (Parlee, 1979).

As we saw in chapter 11, friendship can serve many functions—such as companionship, intimacy/affection, support, and a source of self-esteem. In some cases, friends can provide a better buffer from stress and be a better source of emotional support than family members. This might be because friends choose each other, whereas family ties are obligatory. Individuals often select a friend in terms of such criteria as loyalty, trustworthiness, and support. Thus, it is not surprising that in times of stress individuals turn to their friends for emotional support (Fehr, 2000).

As with children, adult friends usually come from the same age group. For many individuals, friendships formed in the twenties often continue through the twenties and into the thirties, although some new friends may be made in the thirties and some lost because of moving or other circumstances.

Gender Differences in Friendships   As in the childhood years, there are gender differences in adult friendship (Winstead & Griffin, 2001). Compared with men, women have more close friends and their friendships involve more self-disclosure and exchange of mutual support (Wood, 2001). Women are more likely to listen at length to what a friend has to say and be sympathetic, and women have been labeled as "talking companions" because talk is so central to their relationship (Gouldner & Strong, 1987). Women's friendships tend to be characterized not only by depth but also by breadth: Women share many aspects of their experiences, thoughts, and feelings (Wood, 2001).

When female friends get together, they like to talk, but male friends are more likely to engage in activities, especially outdoors. Thus, the adult male pattern of friendship often involves keeping one's distance while sharing useful information. Men are less likely than women to talk about their weaknesses with their friends, and men want practical solutions to their problems rather than sympathy (Tannen, 1990). Also, adult male friendships are more competitive than those of women (Wood, 2001). For example, male friends disagree with each other more.

Friendships Between Women and Men   What about female-male friendship? Cross-gender friendships are more common among adults than among elementary school children, but not as common as same-gender friendships in adulthood (Fehr, 2000). Cross-gender friendships can provide both opportunities and problems. The opportunities involve learning more about common feelings and interests and shared characteristics, as well as acquiring knowledge and understanding of beliefs and activities that historically have been typical of one gender.

Problems can arise in cross-gender friendships because of different expectations. For example, a woman might expect sympathy from a male friend but might receive a proposed solution rather than a shoulder to cry on (Tannen, 1990). Another problem that can plague an adult cross-gender friendship is unclear sexual boundaries, which can produce tension and confusion (Swain, 1992).

Friends and Lovers   We may like or love our friends, or both. Zick Rubin (1970) argues that liking involves our sense that someone else is similar to us and includes a positive evaluation of the individual. Loving, he believes, involves being close to someone; it includes dependency, a more selfless orientation toward the individual, and qualities of absorption and exclusiveness.

Friends and lovers are similar in some ways. In one study, friends and romantic partners shared the characteristics of acceptance, trust, respect, confiding, understanding, spontaneity, mutual assistance, and happiness (Davis, 1985). However, relationships with spouses or lovers were more likely than friendships to also involve fascination and exclusiveness.

How is adult friendship different among female friends, male friends, and cross-sex friends?

Romantic Love Some friendships evolve into **romantic love,** which is also called passionate love, or eros. Poets, playwrights, and musicians through the ages have lauded the fiery passion of romantic love—and lamented the searing pain when it fails. Think for a moment about songs and books that hit the top of the charts. Chances are they are about love.

Romantic love has strong components of sexuality and infatuation, and it often predominates in the early part of a love relationship (Aron & others, 2005; Brown, 2005; Gonzaga & others, 2006; Hendrick & Hendrick, 2004). Well-known love researcher Ellen Berscheid (1988) says that it is romantic love that we are talking about when we say that we are "in love" with someone. It is romantic love she believes we need to understand if we are to learn what love is all about. Berscheid believes that sexual desire is the most important ingredient of romantic love.

A complex intermingling of different emotions goes into romantic love—including fear, anger, sexual desire, joy, and jealousy, for example (Harris, 2002). Obviously, some of these emotions are a source of anguish (Daley & Hammen, 2002). One study found that romantic lovers were more likely than friends to be the cause of depression (Berscheid & Fei, 1977).

In our culture, romantic love is the main reason to get married. In 1967, a famous study showed that most men maintained that they would not get married if they were not "in love." Women either were undecided or said that they would get married even if they did not love their prospective husband (Kephart, 1967). In the 1980s, however, both women and men tended to agree that they would not get married unless they were "in love." And more than half of the men and women said that not being "in love" is sufficient reason to dissolve a marriage (Berscheid, Snyder, & Omoto, 1989).

Romantic love is especially important among college students. One study of unattached college men and women found that more than half identified a romantic partner, rather than a parent, sibling, or friend, as their closest relationship (Berscheid, Snyder, & Omoto, 1989).

Affectionate Love Love is more than just passion. **Affectionate love,** also called *companionate love,* is the type of love that occurs when someone desires to have the other person near and has a deep, caring affection for the person.

There is a growing belief that the early stages of love have more romantic ingredients but that as love matures, passion tends to give way to affection (Berscheid & Reis, 1998; Harvey & Weber, 2002). Phillip Shaver (1986) proposed a developmental model of love in which the initial phase of romantic love is fueled by a mixture of sexual attraction and gratification, a reduced sense of loneliness, uncertainty about the security of developing another attachment, and excitement from exploring the novelty of another human being. With time, he says, sexual attraction wanes, attachment anxieties either lessen or produce conflict and withdrawal, novelty is replaced with familiarity, and lovers either find themselves securely attached in a deeply caring relationship or distressed—feeling bored, disappointed, lonely, or hostile, for example. In the latter case, one or both partners may eventually end the relationship, as Gwenna did with Greg in the chapter-opening story, and then move on to another relationship.

Consummate Love So far we have discussed two forms of love: romantic (or passionate) and affectionate (or companionate). According to Robert J. Sternberg (1988), these are not the only forms of love. Sternberg proposed a triarchic theory of love in which love can be thought of as a triangle with three main dimensions—passion, intimacy, and commitment. Passion, as described earlier, is physical and sexual attraction to another. Intimacy is emotional feelings of warmth, closeness, and sharing in a relationship. Commitment is the cognitive appraisal of the relationship and the intent to maintain the relationship even in the face of problems

romantic love Also called passionate love, or eros, romantic love has strong sexual and infatuation components and often predominates in the early period of a love relationship.

affectionate love In this type of love, also called companionate love, an individual desires to have the other person near and has a deep, caring affection for the other person.

(Rusbult & others, 2001). Passion and intimacy were present in Gwenna and Greg's relationship, but commitment was absent on Greg's part.

In Sternberg's theory, the strongest, fullest form of love is *consummate love*, which involves all three dimensions (see figure 15.2). If passion is the only ingredient in a relationship (with intimacy and commitment low or absent), we are merely *infatuated*. An affair or a fling in which there is little intimacy and even less commitment is an example. A relationship marked by intimacy and commitment but low or lacking in passion is called *affectionate love*, a pattern often found among couples who have been married for many years. If passion and commitment are present but intimacy is not, Sternberg calls the relationship *fatuous love*, as when one person worships another from a distance. But if couples share all three dimensions—passion, intimacy, and commitment—they experience consummate love.

Falling Out of Love

The collapse of a close relationship may feel tragic. In the long run, however, as was the case for Gwenna, our happiness and personal development may benefit from getting over being in love and ending a close relationship.

In particular, falling out of love may be wise if you are obsessed with a person who repeatedly betrays your trust; if you are involved with someone who is draining you emotionally or financially; or if you are desperately in love with someone who does not return your feelings, which was occurring in Gwenna's relationship with Greg.

Being in love when love is not returned can lead to depression, obsessive thoughts, sexual dysfunction, inability to work effectively, difficulty in making new friends, and self-condemnation (Sbarra & Ferrer, 2006). Thinking clearly in such relationships is often difficult, because our thoughts are so colored by arousing emotions.

Some people get taken advantage of in relationships. For example, without either person realizing it, a relationship can evolve in a way that creates dominant and submissive roles. Detecting this pattern is an important step toward learning either to reconstruct the relationship or to end it if the problems cannot be worked out. To read further about breakups of romantic relationships, see the Research in Life-Span Development interlude.

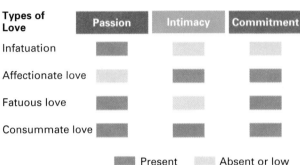

Types of Love	Passion	Intimacy	Commitment
Infatuation	Present	Absent or low	Absent or low
Affectionate love	Absent or low	Present	Present
Fatuous love	Present	Absent or low	Present
Consummate love	Present	Present	Present

FIGURE 15.2 Sternberg's Triangle of Love. Sternberg identified three types of love: passion, intimacy, and commitment. Various combinations of these result in infatuation, affectionate love, fatuous love, and consummate love.

What are some negative aspects of being in love when love is not returned?

RESEARCH IN LIFE-SPAN DEVELOPMENT

Personal Growth Following a Romantic Relationship Breakup

Studies of romantic breakups have mainly focused on their negative aspects (Frazier & Cooke, 1993; Kato, 2005; Kurdek, 1997). Few studies have examined the possibility that a romantic breakup might lead to positive changes.

One recent study assessed the personal growth that can follow the breakup of a romantic relationship (Tashiro & Frazier, 2003). The participants were 92 undergraduate students who had experienced a relationship breakup in the past nine months. They were asked to describe "what positive changes, if any, have happened as a result of your breakup that might serve to improve your future romantic relationships" (p. 118).

Self-reported positive growth was common following a romantic breakup. Changes were categorized in terms of person, relational, and environmental changes.

(continued on next page)

Change category	Exemplars of frequently mentioned responses
Person positives	1. "I am more self-confident." 2. "Through breaking up I found I could handle more on my own." 3. "I didn't always have to be the strong one, it's okay to cry or be upset without having to take care of him."
Relational positives	1. "Better communication." 2. "I learned many relationship skills that I can apply in the future (for example, the importance of saying you're sorry)." 3. "I know not to jump into a relationship too quickly."
Environmental positives	1. "I rely on my friends more. I forgot how important friends are when I was with him." 2. "Concentrate on school more: I can put so much more time and effort toward school." 3. "I believe friends' and family's opinions count—will seek them out in future relationships."

FIGURE 15.3 Examples of Positive Changes in the Aftermath of a Romantic Breakup

The most commonly reported types of growth were person changes, which included feeling stronger and more self-confident, more independent, and better off emotionally. Relational positive changes included gaining relational wisdom, and environmental positive changes included having better friendships because of the breakup. Figure 15.3 provides examples of these positive changes. Women reported more positive growth than did men.

Loneliness

In some cases, loneliness can set in when individuals leave a close relationship, and individuals who don't have friends are vulnerable to loneliness. Each of us has times in our lives when we feel lonely, but for some people loneliness is a chronic condition. More than just an unwelcome social situation, chronic loneliness is linked with impaired physical and mental health (Cacioppo & Hawkley, 2003; Hawkley & others, 2006; Karnick, 2005; Pressman & others, 2005). Chronic loneliness even can lead to an early death (Cuijpers, 2001).

Our society's emphasis on self-fulfillment and achievement, the importance we attach to commitment in relationships, and a decline in stable close relationships are among the reasons loneliness is common today (de Jong-Gierveld, 1987). Researchers have found that married individuals are less lonely than their nonmarried counterparts (never married, divorced, or widowed) in studies conducted in more than 20 countries (Perlman & Peplau, 1998).

It is important to distinguish loneliness from the desire for solitude. Some individuals, especially those with intense careers that involve extensive interactions with people, value solitary time. How do you determine if you are lonely? Scales of loneliness ask you to respond to items like "I don't feel in tune with the people around me" and "I can't find companionship when I want it." If you consistently respond that you never or rarely feel in tune with people around you and rarely or never can find companionship when you want it, you are likely to fall into the category of people who are described as moderately or intensely lonely (Russell, 1996).

Loneliness is often interwoven with the passage through life transitions, such as a move to a different part of the country, a divorce, or the death of a close friend or family member (Beal, 2006; Valeri, 2003). Another situation that often creates loneliness is the first year of college, especially if students leave the familiar world of their hometown and family to enter college. As one student commented:

> My first year here at the university has been pretty lonely. I wasn't lonely at all in high school. I lived in a fairly small town—I knew everybody and everyone knew me. I was a member of several clubs and played on the basketball team. It's not that way at the university. It is a big place and I've felt like a stranger on so many occasions. I'm starting to get used to my life here and the last few months I've been making myself meet people and get to know them, but it has not been easy.

As this comment illustrates, freshmen rarely bring their popularity and social standing from high school into the college environment. There may be a dozen high school basketball stars, National Merit scholars, and former student council presidents in a single dormitory wing. Especially if students attend college away from home, they face the task of forming completely new social relationships.

One study found that two weeks after the school year began, 75 percent of 354 college freshmen felt lonely at least part of the time (Cutrona, 1982). More than 40 percent said their loneliness was moderate to severe. Students who were the most optimistic and had the highest self-esteem were more likely to overcome their loneliness by the end of their freshman year. Loneliness is not reserved for college freshmen, though. Upperclassmen are often lonely as well.

In one recent study of more than 2,600 undergraduates, lonely individuals were less likely to actively cope with stress than individuals who were able to make friends (Cacioppo & others, 2000). Also in this study, lonely college students had higher levels of stress-related hormones and poorer sleep patterns than students who had positive relationships with others.

To read about some strategies for reducing loneliness, see the Applications in Life-Span Development interlude.

Why might loneliness increase in the college transition for some individuals?

Loneliness
Shyness

APPLICATIONS IN LIFE-SPAN DEVELOPMENT

Strategies for Reducing Loneliness

If you are lonely, how can you become better connected with others? Here are some strategies:

- Participate in activities that you can do with others. Join organizations or volunteer your time for a cause you believe in. You likely will get to know others whose views are similar to yours. Going to just one social gathering can help you develop social contacts. When you go, introduce yourself to others and start a conversation. Another strategy is to sit next to new people in your classes or find someone to study with.
- Engage in positive behaviors when you meet new people. You will improve your chances of developing enduring relationships if, when you meet new people, you are nice, considerate, honest, trustworthy, and cooperative. Have a positive attitude, be supportive of the other person, and make positive comments about him or her.
- See a counselor or read a book on loneliness. If you can't get rid of your loneliness on your own, you might want to contact the counseling services at your college. The counselor can talk with you about strategies for reducing your loneliness. You also might want to read a good book on loneliness such as *Intimate Connections* by David Burns (1985).

Review and Reflect • LEARNING GOAL 2

2 **Identify some key aspects of attraction, love, and close relationships**

Review
- What attracts someone to another person?
- What are some different types of love?
- What characterizes falling out of love?
- What is the nature of loneliness and how does it affect people?

Reflect
- If you were to give someone advice about love, what would it be?

3 ADULT LIFESTYLES

Single Adults   Married Adults   Remarried Adults

Cohabiting Adults   Divorced Adults   Gay and Lesbian Adults

Should I get married? If I wait any longer, will it be too late? Will I get left out? Should I stay single or is it too lonely a life? Do I want to have children? How will it affect my marriage? These are questions that many young adults pose to themselves as they consider their lifestyle options.

One of the most striking social changes in recent decades is the decreased stigma attached to people who do not maintain what were long considered conventional families. Adults today choose many lifestyles and form many types of families. They live alone, cohabit, marry, divorce, remarry, or live with someone of the same sex. Let's explore each of these lifestyles and how they affect adults.

Single Adults

There is no rehearsal. One day you don't live alone, the next day you do. College ends. Your wife walks out. Your husband dies. Suddenly, you live in this increasingly modern condition, living alone. Maybe you like it, maybe you don't. Maybe you thrive on the solitude, maybe you ache as if in exile. Either way, chances are you are only half prepared, if at all, to be sole proprietor of your bed, your toaster, and your time. Most of us were raised in the din and clutter of family life, jockeying for a place in the bathroom in the morning, fighting over the last piece of cake, and obliged to compromise on the simplest of choices—the volume of the stereo or the channel on the TV, for example. Few of us grew up thinking that home would be a way station in our life course.

There has been a dramatic rise in the percentage of single adults. In 2000, 25 percent of American adults lived alone (National Center for Health Statistics, 2002). This is more than three times the percentage in 1970 (8 percent).

Even when singles enjoy their lifestyles and are highly competent individuals, they often are stereotyped (DePaulo & Morris, 2005). Stereotypes associated with being single range from the "swinging single" to the "desperately lonely, suicidal" single. Of course, most single adults are somewhere between these extremes. Common problems of single adults may include forming intimate relationships with other adults, confronting loneliness, and finding a niche in a society that is marriage-oriented.

Advantages of being single include having time to make decisions about one's life course, time to develop personal resources to meet goals, freedom to make autonomous decisions and pursue one's own schedule and interests, opportunities to explore new places and try out new things, and privacy. One woman who never married commented, "I enjoy knowing that I can satisfy my own whims without someone else's interferences. If I want to wash my hair at two o'clock in the morning, no one complains. I can eat when I'm hungry and watch my favorite television shows without contradictions from anyone. I enjoy these freedoms."

Once adults reach the age of 30, there can be increasing pressure to settle down and get married. This is when many single adults make a conscious decision to marry or to remain single. As one 30-year-old male recently commented, "It's real. You are supposed to get married by 30—that is a standard. It is part of getting on with your life that you are supposed to do. You have career and who-am-I concerns in your twenties. In your thirties, you have to get on with it, keep on track, make headway, financially and family-wise." But, to another 30-year-old, getting married is less important than buying a house and some property. A training manager for a computer company, Jane says, "I'm competent in making relationships and being committed, so I don't feel a big rush to get married. When it happens, it happens."

Approximately 8 percent of all individuals in the United States who reach the age of 65 have never been married. Contrary to the popular stereotype, older adults who have never been married seem to have the least difficulty coping with loneliness in old age. Many of them discovered long ago how to live autonomously and how to become self-reliant.

Cohabiting Adults

Cohabitation refers to living together in a sexual relationship without being married. Cohabitation has undergone considerable changes in recent years (Popenoe & Whitehead, 2005, 2006; Seltzer, 2004; Smock, Manning, & Porter, 2005) (see figure 15.4). The percentage of U.S. couples who cohabit before marriage has increased from approximately 11 percent in 1970 to almost 60 percent at the beginning of the twenty-first century (Bumpass & Lu, 2000). Cohabiting rates are even higher in some countries—in Sweden, cohabitation before marriage is virtually universal (Hoem, 1995).

A number of couples view their cohabitation not as a precursor to marriage but as an ongoing lifestyle. These couples do not want the official aspects of marriage. In the United States, cohabiting arrangements tend to be short-lived, with one-third lasting less than a year (Hyde & DeLamater, 2006). Less than 1 out of 10 lasts 5 years. Of course, it is easier to dissolve a cohabitation relationship than to divorce.

Do cohabiting relationships differ from marriage in other ways? Relationships between cohabiting men and women tend to be more equal than those between husbands and wives (Wineberg, 1994).

Although cohabitation offers some advantages, it also can produce some problems (Seltzer, 2004; Whitehead & Popenoe, 2005). Disapproval by parents and other family members can place emotional strain on the cohabiting couple. Some cohabiting couples have difficulty owning property jointly. Legal rights on the dissolution of the relationship are less certain than in a divorce.

Does cohabiting help or harm the chances that a couple will have a stable and happy marriage? Some researchers have found no differences in marital quality between individuals who earlier cohabited and those who did not (Newcomb & Bentler, 1980; Watson & DeMeo, 1987). Other researchers have found lower rates of marital satisfaction in couples who lived together before getting married (Booth & Johnson, 1988; Whitehead & Popenoe, 2003). For example, in one study of 13,000 individuals, married couples who cohabited prior to their marriage reported lower levels of happiness with and commitment to their marital relationship than their counterparts who had not previously cohabited (Nock, 1995). In another

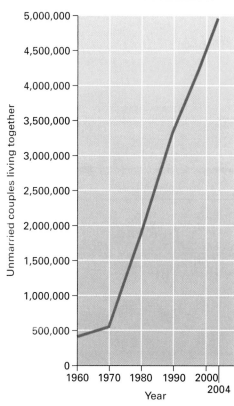

FIGURE 15.4 The Increase in Cohabitation in the United States. Since 1970, there has been a dramatic increase in the number of unmarried adults living together in the United States.

What are some potential advantages and disadvantages of cohabitation?

study, couples who had cohabited before marriage were more likely to divorce than couples who had not cohabited (DeMaris & Rao, 1992). And in one recent study, after 10 years of marriage, 40 percent of couples who lived together before marriage had divorced, whereas 31 percent of those who had not cohabited first had divorced (Centers for Disease Control and Prevention, 2002). A longitudinal study found that the timing of cohabitation is a key factor in marital outcomes (Kline & others, 2004). Couples who cohabitated before they became engaged were at greater risk for poor marital outcomes than those who cohabited only after becoming engaged. Further, a recent study revealed that postdivorce cohabitation with a future spouse was linked with a higher level of instability in a remarriage (Xu, Hudspeth, & Bartkowski, 2006).

In sum, researchers have found either that cohabitation leads to no differences or that cohabitation is not good for a marriage. What might explain the finding that cohabiting is linked with divorce more than not cohabiting? The most frequently given explanation is that the less traditional lifestyle of cohabitation may attract less conventional individuals who are not great believers in marriage in the first place (Manning & Smock, 2002; Whitehead & Popenoe, 2003). An alternative explanation is that the experience of cohabiting changes people's attitudes and habits in ways that increase their likelihood of divorce (Solot & Miller, 2002).

Married Adults

Until about 1930, stable marriage was widely accepted as the endpoint of adult development. In the last 60 years, however, personal fulfillment both inside and outside marriage has emerged as a goal that competes with marital stability. The changing norm of male-female equality in marriage has produced marital relationships that are more fragile and intense than they were earlier in the twentieth century (Bradbury, Fincham, & Beach, 2000).

Marital Trends   In recent years marriage rates in the United States have declined. More adults are remaining single longer today, and the average duration of a marriage in the United States is currently just over nine years. In 2005, the U.S. average age for a first marriage climbed to just over 27 years for men and 26 years for women, higher than at any point in history (U.S. Bureau of the Census, 2005). In addition, the increase in cohabitation and a slight decline in the percentage of divorced individuals who remarry contribute to the decline in marriage rates in the United States (Popenoe & Whitehead, 2005, 2006).

Despite the decline in marriage rates, more than 90 percent of U.S. women still marry at some point in their lives, although projections indicate that in the future this rate will drop into the 80 to 90 percent range (Popenoe & Whitehead, 2005). For example, one projection is that for U.S. individuals born in 1995, 88 percent of the females and 82 percent of the males will likely marry (Schoen & Standish, 2001). If women and men are going to marry, virtually all do so by the time they are 45 years of age (Popenoe & Whitehead, 2005).

How happy are people who do marry? As indicated in figure 15.5, the percentage of married individuals in the United States who said their marriages were "very happy" declined from the 1970s through the early 1990s, but recently has begun to increase (Popenoe & Whitehead, 2005). Notice in figure 15.5 that men consistently report being happier in their marriage than women.

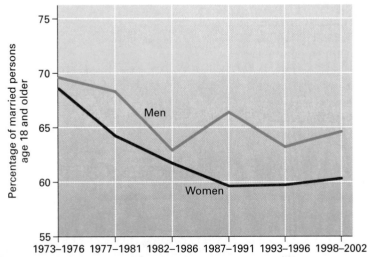

FIGURE 15.5 Percentage of Married Persons Age 18 and Older with "Very Happy" Marriages. Source: Popenoe, D., & Whitehead, B. (2005). *The State of Our Unions*: 2005.

Social Contexts Contexts within a culture and across cultures are powerful influences on marriage (Karney & Bradbury, 2005). One recent U.S. study found that although communication was rated as a relatively severe problem regardless of household income, it was rated most severe in high-income households (Karney, Garvan, & Thomas, 2003) (see figure 15.6). By contrast, drugs and infidelity were rated as more severe problems in low-income households.

Many aspects of marriage vary across cultures. For example, as part of China's efforts to control population growth, a 1981 law sets the minimum age for marriage at 22 years for males, 20 for females. More information about marriage in different cultures appears in the Diversity in Life-Span Development interlude.

DIVERSITY IN LIFE-SPAN DEVELOPMENT

Marriage Around the World

The traits that people look for in a marriage partner vary around the world (Hamon & Ingoldsby, 2003). In one large-scale study of 9,474 adults from 37 cultures on six continents and five islands, people varied most regarding how much they valued chastity—desiring a marital partner with no previous experience in sexual intercourse (Buss & others, 1990). Chastity was the most important characteristic in selecting a marital partner in China, India, Indonesia, Iran, Taiwan, and the Palestinian Arab culture. Adults from Ireland and Japan placed moderate importance on chastity. In contrast, adults in Sweden, Finland, Norway, the Netherlands, and Germany generally said that chastity was not important in selecting a marital partner.

Domesticity is also valued in some cultures and not in others. In this study, adults from the Zulu culture in South Africa, Estonia, and Colombia placed a high value on housekeeping skills in their marital preference. By contrast, adults in the United States, Canada, and all Western European countries except Spain said that housekeeping skill was not an important trait in their partner.

Religion plays an important role in marital preferences in many cultures. For example, Islam stresses the honor of the male and the purity of the female. It also emphasizes the woman's role in childbearing, child rearing, educating children, and instilling the Islamic faith in their children.

International comparisons of marriage also reveal that individuals in Scandinavian countries marry later than Americans, whereas their counterparts in Eastern Europe marry earlier (Bianchi & Spani, 1986). In Denmark, for example, almost 80 percent of the women and 90 percent of the men aged 20 to 24 have never been married.

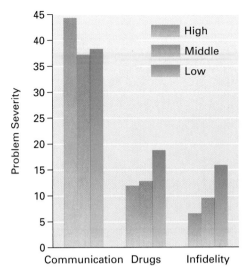

FIGURE 15.6 Severity of Specific Relationship Problems in Low-, Middle-, and High-Income Households. *Why do you think communication was rated the most severe in high income households?*

(a) (b) (c)

(a) In Scandinavian countries, cohabitation is popular; only a small percentage of 20- to 24-year-olds are married. *(b)* Islam stresses male honor and female purity. *(c)* Japanese young adults live at home longer with their parents before marrying than young adults in most countries.

(continued on next page)

In Hungary, less than 40 percent of the women and 70 percent of the men the same age have never been married. In Scandinavian countries, cohabitation is popular among young adults; however, most Scandinavians eventually marry (Popenoe & Whitehead, 2005). In Sweden, on average women delay marriage until they are 31, men until they are 33. Some countries, such as Hungary, encourage early marriage and childbearing to offset declines in the population. Like Scandinavian countries, Japan has a high proportion of unmarried young people. However, rather than cohabiting as the Scandinavians do, unmarried Japanese young adults live at home longer with their parents before marrying.

Premarital Education Premarital education occurs in a group and focuses on relationship advice. Might premarital education improve the quality of a marriage and possibly reduce the chances that the marriage will end in a divorce? Researchers have found that it can (Carroll & Doherty, 2003; Halford & others, 2006). For example, a recent survey of more than 3,000 adults revealed that premarital education was linked to a higher level of marital satisfaction and commitment to a spouse, a lower level of destructive marital conflict, and a 31 percent lower likelihood of divorce (Stanley & others, 2006). The premarital education programs in the study ranged from several hours to 20 hours with a median of 8 hours. It is recommended that premarital education begin approximately six months to a year before the wedding.

The Benefits of a Good Marriage Are there any benefits to having a good marriage? There are. Individuals who are happily married live longer, healthier lives than either divorced individuals or those who are unhappily married (Cotten, 1999). One recent study of 493 women 42 to 50 years of age found that women in happy marriages had lower levels of biological and cardiovascular risk factors—such as high blood pressure, elevated cholesterol levels, and greater body mass index—and lower levels of depression, anxiety, and anger than women in unhappy marriages (Gallo & others, 2003). Another recent study revealed that negative spousal behaviors were linked to a middle-aged adult's health problems (Bookwala, 2005).

What are the reasons for these benefits of a happy marriage? People in happy marriages likely feel less physically and emotionally stressed, which puts less wear and tear on a person's body. Such wear and tear can lead to numerous physical ailments, such as high blood pressure and heart disease, as well as psychological problems such as anxiety, depression, and substance abuse.

There is increasing evidence that stressful events of many types reduce the immune system's capabilities, rendering the person vulnerable to disease and infection. One study compared unhappily and happily married individuals and found that unhappily married individuals had immune systems that were not functioning as effectively as those of happily married individuals (Kiecolt-Glaser & Glaser, 1988). An unhappy marriage increases an individual's risk of getting sick by approximately one-third and can even shorten a person's life by an average of four years (Gove, Style, & Hughes, 1990).

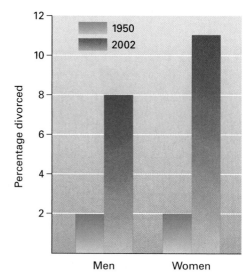

FIGURE 15.7 Percentage of Divorced U.S. Men and Women: 1950 and 2002. *Why do you think more women are divorced than men?*

Divorced Adults

Divorce has become epidemic in our culture (Fine & Harvey, 2006). The number of divorced adults rose from 2 percent of the adult population in 1950 to 3 percent in 1970 to 10 percent in 2002. Figure 15.7 shows the percentage of divorced men and women in the United States in 1950 and 2002 (U.S. Bureau of the Census, 2003).

The divorce rate was increasing annually by 10 percent, but has been declining since the 1980s (Amato & Irving, 2006).

Although divorce has increased for all socioeconomic groups, those in disadvantaged groups have a higher incidence of divorce. Youthful marriage, low educational level, low income, not having a religious affiliation, having parents who are divorced, and having a baby before marriage are associated with increases in divorce (Popenoe & Whitehead, 2005; Rodrigues, Hall, & Fincham, 2006).

If a divorce is going to occur, it usually takes place early in a marriage; most occur in the fifth to tenth year of marriage (National Center for Health Statistics, 2000) (see figure 15.8). This timing may reflect an effort by partners in troubled marriages to stay in the marriage and try to work things out. If after several years these efforts don't improve the relationship, they may then seek a divorce.

Even those adults who initiated their divorce experience challenges after a marriage dissolves (Amato, 2000; Amato & Irving, 2006; Hetherington, 2000; Martin, Emery, & Paris, 2004; Wallerstein & Lewis, 2005). Both divorced women and divorced men complain of loneliness, diminished self-esteem, anxiety about the unknowns in their lives, and difficulty in forming satisfactory new intimate relationships.

The stress of separation and divorce places both men and women at risk for psychological and physical difficulties (Braver, Goodman, & Shapiro, 2006; Fine, Ganong, & Demo, 2005; Hetherington & Stanley-Hagan, 2002; Lee & others, 2005; Lorenz & others, 2006; Waite, 2005). Separated and divorced women and men have higher rates of psychiatric disorders, admission to psychiatric hospitals, clinical depression, alcoholism, and psychosomatic problems, such as sleep disorders, than do married adults. One recent analysis of more than 8,000 51- to 61-year-olds revealed that divorce was associated with an increase in chronic health problems (Waite, 2005). Another recent study found that among nonsmokers and past smokers, women who divorced had more than a twofold increased risk of relapsing or starting smoking (Lee & others, 2005). Yet another recent study indicated that following divorce, men are more likely to increase their alcohol consumption (Eng & others, 2005).

The challenges of divorce differ somewhat for custodial and noncustodial parents and for men and women (Sayer, 2006). Custodial parents have concerns about child rearing and overload in their lives. Noncustodial parents register complaints about alienation from or lack of time with their children. Men show only modest declines in income following a divorce, but women face a significant decline. As we discussed in chapter 9, for divorced women, the financial decline means living in a less desirable neighborhood with fewer resources, less effective schools, and more deviant peer groups for their children. However, the economic decline for women following a divorce has diminished as fewer women follow the conventional role of stay-at-home homemaker and more have experience in the workforce before divorce.

Despite all of these stresses and challenges, people do cope with divorce. Later in this chapter, we consider the varied paths people take after a divorce and some suggested strategies for coping.

Remarried Adults

On average, divorced adults remarry within four years after their divorce, with men remarrying sooner than women. Stepfamilies come in many sizes and forms. The custodial and noncustodial parents and stepparent all might have been married and divorced, in some cases more than once. These parents might have residential children from prior marriages and a large network of grandparents and other relatives.

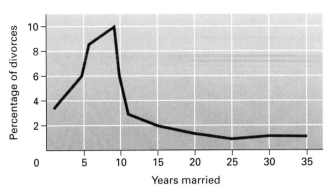

FIGURE 15.8 **The Divorce Rate in Relation to Number of Years Married.** Shown here is the percentage of divorces as a function of how long couples have been married. Notice that most divorces occur in the early years of marriage, peaking in the fifth to tenth years of marriage.

www.mhhe.com/santrockld11

Psychological Aspects of Divorce
Divorced and Remarried Parents
Remarried Adults' Resources
Stepfamily Interventions

Researchers have found that remarried adults are more likely to have higher levels of depressive symptoms than adults in intact, never-divorced families (Barrett & Turner, 2005).

Why do remarried adults find it so difficult to stay remarried? For one thing, many remarry not for love but for financial reasons, for help in rearing children, and to reduce loneliness. They also might carry into the stepfamily negative patterns that produced failure in an earlier marriage. Remarried couples also experience more stress in rearing children than parents in never-divorced families (Ganong, Coleman, & Hans, 2005).

Gay and Lesbian Adults

The legal and social context of marriage creates barriers to breaking up that do not usually exist for same-sex partners. But in other ways researchers have found that gay and lesbian relationships are similar—in their satisfactions, loves, joys, and conflicts—to heterosexual relationships (Hyde & DeLamater, 2006; Julien & others, 2003; Oswald & Clausell, 2005; Peplau & Beals, 2004; Peplau & Fingerhut, 2007). For example, like heterosexual couples, gay and lesbian couples need to find the balance of romantic love, affection, autonomy, and equality that is acceptable to both partners (Kurdek, 2003, 2006). In one study, gay and lesbian couples listed their areas of conflict in order of frequency: finances, driving style, affection and sex, being overly critical, and household tasks (Kurdek, 1995). The components of this list are likely to be familiar to heterosexual couples. As discussed in chapter 9, an increasing number of gay and lesbian couples are creating families that include children (see figure 15.9).

Lesbian couples especially place a high priority on equality in their relationships (Kurdek, 1995). Indeed, some researchers have found that gay and lesbian couples are more flexible in their gender roles than heterosexual individuals are (Marecek, Finn, & Cardell, 1988).

There are a number of misconceptions about homosexual couples (Kurdek, 2004, 2006; Peplau & Fingerhut, 2007). Contrary to stereotypes, one partner is masculine and the other feminine in only a small percentage of homosexual couples. Only a small segment of the gay male population have a large number of sexual partners, and this is uncommon among lesbians. Furthermore, researchers have found that homosexuals prefer long-term, committed relationships (Peplau & Beals, 2002). About half of committed gay male couples do have an open relationship that allows the possibility of sex (but not affectionate love) outside of the relationship. Lesbian couples usually do not have this open relationship.

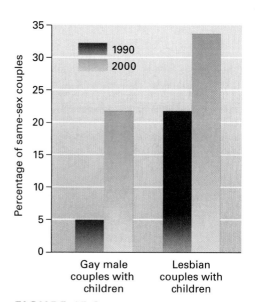

FIGURE 15.9 Percentage of Gay Male and Lesbian Couples with Children: 1990 and 2000. *Why do you think more lesbian couples have children than gay male couples?*

Gay and Lesbian Relationships

www.mhhe.com/santrockld11

Review and Reflect • LEARNING GOAL 3

3 Characterize adult lifestyles

Review
- What are characteristics of the lives of single adults?
- What are key features of the lives of cohabiting adults?
- What are current marital trends?
- How does divorce affect adults?
- What are the lives of remarried parents like?
- How are gay and lesbian couples like or unlike heterosexual couples?

Reflect
- Which type of lifestyle are you living today? What do you think are the advantages and disadvantages of this lifestyle for you? If you could have a different lifestyle, which one would it be? Why?

4 MARRIAGE AND THE FAMILY

The Family Life Cycle

Making Marriage Work

Becoming a Parent

Dealing with Divorce

Whatever lifestyles young adults choose, they will bring certain challenges. Let's examine some of the specific challenges posed by marriage and family life and some strategies for dealing with them.

The Family Life Cycle

No family is static. Families can be thought of as going through a life cycle. For married couples with children who do not experience a divorce or the death of a spouse, the stages of the family life cycle are (Carter & McGoldrick, 1989) (see figure 15.10):

- **Leaving home and becoming a single adult** is the first stage in the family life cycle, and it involves **launching,** the process in which youth move into adulthood and exit their family of origin. In a successful launching, the young adult separates from the family of origin without cutting off ties completely or fleeing to some substitute emotional refuge. Complete cutoffs from parents rarely solve emotional problems. Launching is a time to formulate life goals, to develop an identity, and to become more independent before joining with another person to form a new family. This is a time for young people to sort out emotionally what they will take along from the family of origin, what they will leave behind, and what persons they want to become.

  Young adults no longer feel compelled to comply with parental expectations and wishes. They shift to dealing with their parents adult-to-adult, which requires a mutually respectful relationship in which young adults appreciate and accept their parents as they are.
- The **new couple** is the second stage in the family life cycle. Marriage is usually described as the union of two individuals from separate families, but in reality it is the union of two entire family systems and the development of a new, third system. This stage also involves a realignment as the families of origin and friends include the spouse. Changes in gender roles, marriage of partners from divergent cultural backgrounds, and physical distances between family members increase the burden on couples to define their relationships for themselves. Some experts on marriage and the family reason that marriage represents such a different phenomenon for women and men that we need to speak of "her" marriage and "his" marriage. In American society, women have anticipated marriage with greater enthusiasm and more positive expectations than men have.
- **Becoming parents and a family with children** is the third stage in the family life cycle. When they enter this stage, adults move up a generation and become caregivers to the younger generation. Moving through this lengthy stage successfully requires a commitment of time as a parent, an understanding of the parenting role, and a willingness to adapt to developmental changes in children. Couples in this stage may face struggles with each other about their responsibilities, as well as a refusal or inability to function as competent parents.

Family Life-Cycle Stages	Emotional Process of Transition: Key Principles
1. Leaving home: single young adults	Accepting emotional and financial responsibility for self
2. The joining of families through marriage: the new couple	Commitment to new system
3. Becoming parents and families with children	Accepting new members into the system
4. The family with adolescents	Increasing flexibility of family boundaries to include children's independence and grandparents' frailties
5. The family at midlife	Accepting a multitude of exits and entries into the family system
6. The family in later life	Accepting the shifting of generational roles

FIGURE 15.10 The Family Life Cycle

leaving home and becoming a single adult The first stage in the family life cycle. It involves launching.

launching The process in which youth move into adulthood and exit their family of origin.

new couple Forming the new couple is the second stage in the family life cycle. Two individuals from separate families of origin unite to form a new family system.

becoming parents and a family with children The third stage in the family life cycle. Adults who enter this stage move up a generation and become caregivers to the younger generation.

- The **family with adolescents** represents the fourth stage of the family life cycle. Adolescence is a period in which individuals push for autonomy and seek to develop their own identity. This is a lengthy process, transpiring over at least 10 to 15 years. Compliant children may become noncompliant adolescents. In response, parents may either clamp down, pressuring the adolescent to conform to parental values, or become more permissive, giving the adolescent extensive freedom. Neither is a wise strategy. A flexible, adaptive approach is best.
- The **family at midlife** is the fifth stage in the family life cycle. It is a time of launching children, linking generations, and adapting to midlife changes. Until about a generation ago, most families were involved in raising their children for much of their adult lives until old age. Because of the lower birth rate and longer life of most adults, parents now launch their children about 20 years before retirement, which frees many midlife parents to pursue other activities.
- The **family in later life** is the sixth and final stage in the family life cycle. Retirement alters a couple's lifestyle, requiring adaptation. Grandparenting also characterizes many families in this stage.

Some critics argue that talking about stages of the family life cycle is misleading. Clearly defined stages often do not develop, and the stages do not always occur in a sequential fashion (Azar, 2003; Elder, 1998). Further, critics state that it is the variability associated with the stages that should be emphasized. For example, some people have children early during adolescence or in their forties; some have children outside of marriage. Entry into these stages is increasingly independent from age. Further, many individuals have multiple families (such as children from a first marriage and children from a remarriage). Still, this description of the family life cycle does provide an overview of the varying tasks and challenges that parents face over time.

Becoming a Parent

For many adults, parental roles are well planned, coordinated with other roles in life, and developed with the individual's economic situation in mind. For others, the discovery that they are about to become parents is a startling surprise. In either event, the prospective parents may have mixed emotions and romantic illusions about having a child.

Parenting Myths and Reality   The needs and expectations of parents have stimulated many myths about parenting:

- The birth of a child will save a failing marriage.
- As a possession or extension of the parent, the child will think, feel, and behave like the parents did in their childhood.
- Children will take care of parents in their old age.
- Having a child gives the parents a "second chance" to achieve what they should have achieved.
- Mothers are naturally better parents than fathers.
- Parenting is an instinct and requires no training.

Parenting requires a number of interpersonal skills and imposes emotional demands, yet there is little in the way of formal education for this task. Most parents learn parenting practices from their own parents—some they accept, some they discard. Husbands and wives may bring different viewpoints of parenting practices to the marriage (Huston & Holmes, 2004). Unfortunately, when methods of parents are passed on from one generation to the next, both desirable and undesirable practices are perpetuated.

What are some parenting myths?

family with adolescents The fourth stage of the family life cycle, in which adolescent children push for autonomy and seek to develop their own identities.

family at midlife The fifth stage in the family life cycle, a time of launching children, linking generations, and adapting to midlife developmental changes.

family in later life The sixth and final stage in the family life cycle, involving retirement and, in many families, grandparenting.

Parent educators seek to help individuals to become better parents. To read about the work of one parent educator, see the Careers in Life-Span Development profile.

Trends in Childbearing As birth control has become common practice, many individuals consciously choose when they will have children and how many children they will rear. The number of one-child families is increasing, for example, and U.S. women overall are having fewer children. These childbearing trends are having several results: (1) By giving birth to fewer children and reducing the demands of child care, women free up a significant portion of their life spans for other endeavors; (2) as working women increase in number, they invest less actual time in the child's development; (3) men are apt to invest a greater amount of time in fathering; and (4) parental care in the home is often supplemented by institutional care (child care, for example).

As more women show an increased interest in developing a career, they are not only marrying later, but also having children later (Azar, 2003; Popenoe & Whitehead, 2006). What are some of the advantages of having children early or late? Some of the advantages of having children early (in the twenties) are that the parents are likely to have more physical energy (for example, they can cope better with such matters as getting up in the middle of the night with infants and waiting up until adolescents come home at night); the mother is likely to have fewer medical problems with pregnancy and childbirth; and the parents may be less likely to build up expectations for their children, as do many couples who have waited many years to have children. There are also advantages to having children later (in the thirties): The parents will have had more time to consider their goals in life, such as what they want from their family and career roles; the parents will be more mature and will be able to benefit from their life experiences to engage in more competent parenting; and the parents will be better established in their careers and have more income for child-rearing expenses.

CAREERS in LIFE-SPAN DEVELOPMENT

Janis Keyser
Parent Educator

Janis Keyser is a parent educator and teaches in the Department of Early Childhood Education at Cabrillo College in California. In addition to teaching college classes and conducting parenting workshops, she also has co-authored a book with Laura Davis (1997), *Becoming the Parent You Want to Be: A Source-Book of Strategies for the First Five Years.*

Janis also writes as an expert on the iVillage website (www.parentsplace.com). And she also co-authors a nationally syndicated parenting column, "Growing Up, Growing Together." She is the mother of three, stepmother of five, grandmother of twelve, and great-grandmother of six.

Janis Keyser *(right),* conducting a parenting workshop.

In earlier times, motherhood was considered a full-time occupation and the natural occupation for women. Nurturing children and having a career were thought to be incompatible. We have come to recognize that the balance between caring and achieving, nurturing and working—although difficult to manage—can be accomplished. But as more and more U.S. women moved into the workplace and delayed childbirth in recent years, popular magazine and books began warning women that they would regret this delay and risked ending up childless.

A recent book, *Creating a Life: Professional Women and the Quest for Children* (Hewlett, 2002), described the results of interviews with 1,186 high-achieving career women (income in the top 10 percent of their age group) from 28 to 55 years of age. Among the findings were that 33 percent were childless at age 40, and 49 percent of the "ultraachievers" (earning more than $100,000 a year) were childless. Furthermore, 25 percent of the childless high achievers from 41 to 55 years of age said that they would still like to have a child, and 31 percent of "ultraachievers" would still like to have one. But no high achiever from 41 to 55 years of age had a first child after age 39 and no "ultraachiever" had one after age 36.

We never know the love of our parents until we have become parents.

—Henry Ward Beecher
American Clergyman, 19th Century

Many of the study's childless women in their forties and fifties recommended that younger women spend more time envisioning what their life will be like when they become middle-aged and whether they want their life to include a child. They argue that many high-achieving women will ultimately be happier if they have a child in their twenties or thirties. Critics argue that the optimal age for motherhood depends on the individual and that many women become mothers after they are 35 years of age.

Making Marriage Work

John Gottman (1994; Gottman & Notarius, 2000; Gottman & Silver, 2000; Gottman & others, 1998) has been studying married couples' lives since the early 1970s. He uses many methods to analyze what makes marriages work. Gottman interviews couples about the history of their marriage, their philosophy about marriage, and how they view their parents' marriages. He videotapes them talking to each other about how their day went and evaluates what they say about the good and bad times of their marriages. Gottman also uses physiological measures to measure their heart rate, blood flow, blood pressure, and immune functioning moment by moment. He also checks back in with the couples every year to see how their marriage is faring. Gottman's research represents the most extensive assessment of marital relationships available. Currently he and his colleagues are following 700 couples in seven studies.

In his research, Gottman has found that seven main principles determine whether a marriage will work or not:

- *Establishing love maps.* Individuals in successful marriages have personal insights and detailed maps of each other's life and world. They aren't psychological strangers. In good marriages, partners are willing to share their feelings with each other. They use these "love maps" to express not only their understanding of each other but also their fondness and admiration.
- *Nurturing fondness and admiration.* In successful marriages, partners sing each other's praises. More than 90 percent of the time, when couples put a positive spin on their marriage's history, the marriage is likely to have a positive future.
- *Turning toward each other instead of away.* In good marriages, spouses are adept at turning toward each other regularly. They see each other as friends. This friendship doesn't keep arguments from occurring, but it can prevent differences from overwhelming the relationship. In these good marriages, spouses respect each other and appreciate each other's point of view despite disagreements.
- *Letting your partner influence you.* Bad marriages often involve one spouse who is unwilling to share power with the other. Although power-mongering is more common in husbands, some wives also show this trait. A willingness to share power and to respect the other person's view is a prerequisite to compromising.
- *Solving solvable conflicts.* Two types of problems occur in marriage: (1) perpetual and (2) solvable. Perpetual problems include differences about whether to have children and how often to have sex. Solvable problems include not helping each other reduce daily stresses and not being verbally affectionate. Unfortunately, more than two-thirds of marital problems fall into the perpetual category—those that won't go away. Fortunately, marital therapists have found that couples often don't have to solve their perpetual problems for the marriage to work.

Work, stress, in-laws, money, sex, housework, a new baby: these are among the typical areas of marital conflict, even in happy marriages. When there is conflict in these areas, it usually means that a husband and wife have different ideas about the tasks involved, their importance, or how they should be accomplished. If the conflict is perpetual, no amount of problem-solving expertise will fix it. The tension will decrease only when both partners feel comfortable living with the ongoing difference. However, when the issue is solvable, the challenge is to find the right strategy for dealing with it.

What makes marriages work? What are the benefits of having a good marriage?

In his research, Gottman has found that to resolve conflicts, couples should start out with a soft rather than a harsh approach, try to make and receive "repair attempts," regulate their emotions, compromise, and be tolerant of each other's faults. Conflict resolution is not about one person making changes, it is about negotiating and accommodating each other (Driver & others, 2003).

- *Overcoming gridlock*. One partner wants the other to attend church, the other is an atheist. One partner is a homebody, the other wants to go out and socialize a lot. Such problems often produce gridlock. Gottman believes the key to ending gridlock is not to solve the problem, but to move from gridlock to dialogue and be patient.
- *Creating shared meaning*. The more partners can speak candidly and respectfully with each other, the more likely it is that they will create shared meaning in their marriage. This also includes sharing goals with one's spouse and working together to achieve each other's goals.

For remarried couples, strategies for coping with the stress of living in a stepfamily include these (Visher & Visher, 1989):

- *Have realistic expectations*. Allow time for loving relationships to develop, and look at the complexity of the stepfamily as a challenge to overcome.
- *Develop new positive relationships within the family*. Create new traditions and ways of dealing with difficult circumstances. Allocation of time is especially important because so many people are involved. The remarried couple needs to allot time alone for each other.

Dealing with Divorce

If a marriage doesn't work, what happens after divorce? Psychologically, one of the most common characteristics of divorced adults is difficulty in trusting someone else in a romantic relationship. Following a divorce, though, people's lives can take diverse turns (Tashiro, Frazier, & Berman, 2005). In E. Mavis Hetherington's research, men and women took six common pathways in exiting divorce (Hetherington & Kelly, 2002, pp. 98–108):

- *The enhancers*. Accounting for 20 percent of the divorced group, most were females who "grew more competent, well-adjusted, and self-fulfilled" following their divorce" (p. 98). They were competent in multiple areas of life, showed a remarkable ability to bounce back from stressful circumstances, and created something meaningful out of problems.
- *The good-enoughs*. The largest group of divorced individuals, they were described as average people coping with divorce. They showed some strengths and some weaknesses, some successes and some failures. When they experienced a problem, they tried to solve it. Many of them attended night classes, found new friends, developed active social lives, and were motivated to get higher-paying jobs. However, they were not as good at planning and were less persistent than the enhancers. Good-enough women usually married men who educationally and economically were similar to their first husbands, often going into a new marriage that was not much of an improvement over the first one.
- *The seekers*. These individuals were motivated to find new mates as soon as possible. "At one year post-divorce, 40 percent of the men and 38 percent of women had been classified as seekers. But as people found new partners or remarried, or became more secure or satisfied in their single life, this category shrank and came to be predominated by men" (p. 102).
- *The libertines*. They often spent more time in singles' bars and had more casual sex than their counterparts in the other divorce categories. However, by the end of the first year postdivorce, they often grew disillusioned with their sensation-seeking lifestyle and wanted a stable relationship.

www.mhhe.com/santrockld11

Marriage Support
Journal of Family Psychology

*U*nlike most approaches to helping couples, mine is based on knowing what makes marriages succeed rather than fail.

—JOHN GOTTMAN
Contemporary Psychologist,
University of Washington

What are some pathways adults follow after they divorce?

• *The competent loners.* These individuals, which made up only about 10 percent of the divorced group, were "well-adjusted, self-sufficient, and socially skilled." They had a successful career, an active social life, and a wide range of interests. However, "unlike enhancers, competent loners had little interest in sharing their lives with anyone else" (p. 105).
• *The defeated.* Some of these individuals had problems before their divorce, and these problems increased after the breakup when "the added stress of a failed marriage was more than they could handle. Others had difficulty coping because divorce cost them a spouse who had supported them, or in the case of a drinking problem, restricted them" (p. 106).

Hetherington recommends these strategies for divorced adults (Hetherington & Kelly, 2002):

• Think of divorce as a chance to grow personally and to develop more positive relationships.
• Make decisions carefully. The consequences of your decision making regarding work, lovers, and children may last a lifetime.
• Focus more on the future than the past. Think about what is most important for you going forward in your life, set some challenging goals, and plan how to reach them.
• Use your strengths and resources to cope with difficulties.
• Don't expect to be successful and happy in everything you do. "The road to a more satisfying life is bumpy and will have many detours" (p. 109).
• Remember that "you are never trapped by one pathway. Most of those who were categorized as defeated immediately after divorce gradually moved on to a better life, but moving onward usually requires some effort" (p. 109).

Review and Reflect • LEARNING GOAL 4

 Discuss the family life cycle, parenting, making marriage work, and divorce

Review
• What are the six stages of the family life cycle?
• What are some current trends in childbearing?
• What makes a marriage work?
• What paths do people take after a divorce?

Reflect
• What do you predict will be some major changes in families by the end of the twenty-first century?

---

5 GENDER, RELATIONSHIPS, AND SELF-DEVELOPMENT

| Gender and Communication | Women's Development | Men's Development |

If the story of Gwenna and Greg in the chapter opening sounded familiar, that may be because both acted in some ways that match stereotypes about gender differences. Gwenna was eager to discuss the relationship and to make a commitment; Greg preferred to avoid both. To explore the role of gender differences in adult relationships, we will focus on some issues involving communication and self-development.

Gender and Communication

Stereotypes about differences in men's and women's attitudes toward communication and about differences in how they communicate with each other have spawned countless cartoons and jokes. Are the supposed differences real?

When Deborah Tannen (1990) analyzed the talk of women and men, she found that many wives complain about their husbands that "He doesn't listen to me anymore" and "He doesn't talk to me anymore." Lack of communication, though high on women's lists of reasons for divorce, is mentioned much less often by men.

Communication problems between men and women may come in part from differences in their preferred ways of communicating. Tannen distinguishes rapport talk from report talk. **Rapport talk** is the language of conversation; it is a way of establishing connections and negotiating relationships. **Report talk** is talk that is designed to give information, which includes public speaking. According to Tannen, women enjoy rapport talk more than report talk, and men's lack of interest in rapport talk bothers many women. In contrast, men prefer to engage in report talk. Men hold center stage through such verbal performances as telling stories and jokes. They learn to use talk as a way of getting and keeping attention.

How extensive are the gender differences in communication? Research has yielded somewhat mixed results. Recent studies do reveal some gender differences (Anderson, 2006). One study of a sampling of students' e-mails found that people could guess the writer's gender two-thirds of the time (Thompson & Murachver, 2001). Another study revealed that women make 63 percent of phone calls and when talking to another woman stay on the phone longer (7.2 minutes) than men do when talking with other men (4.6 minutes) (Smoreda & Licoppe, 2000). However, recent meta-analyses suggest that overall gender differences in communication are small in children and adults (Hyde, 2005; Leaper & Smith, 2004).

Women's Development

Tannen's analysis of women's preference for rapport talk suggests that women place a high value on relationships and focus on nurturing their connections with others. This view echoes some ideas of Jean Baker Miller (1986), who has been an important voice in stimulating the examination of psychological issues from a female perspective. Miller argues that when researchers examine what women have been doing in life, a large part of it is active participation in the development of others. In Miller's view, women often try to interact with others in ways that will foster the other person's development along many dimensions—emotionally, intellectually, and socially.

Most experts conclude it is important for women to not only maintain their competency in relationships but to be self-motivated too (Bannon, 2005; Denmark, Rabinowitz, & Sechzer, 2005; Donelson, 1998). As Harriet Lerner (1989) concludes in her book *The Dance of Intimacy*, it is important for women to bring to their relationships nothing less than a strong, assertive, independent, and authentic self. She emphasizes that competent relationships are those in which the separate "I-ness" of both persons can be appreciated and enhanced while still staying emotionally connected to each other.

In sum, Miller, Tannen, and other gender experts such as Carol Gilligan, whose ideas you read about in chapter 11, believe that women are more relationship-oriented than men—and that this relationship orientation should be prized as a skill in our culture more than it currently is. Critics of this view of gender differences in

"You have no idea how nice it is to have someone to talk to."
Copyright © 1964 Don Orehek.

*U*nderstanding the other's ways of talking is a giant leap across the communication gap between women and men, and a giant step toward opening lines of communication.

—DEBORAH TANNEN
Contemporary Sociologist, Georgetown University

www.mhhe.com/santrockld11

Gender and Communication
Women's Issues
Gender and Society

rapport talk The language of conversation; a way to establish connections and negotiate relationships; preferred by women.

report talk Language designed to give information, including public speaking; preferred by men.

How might men be able to reconstruct their masculinity in positive ways?

The Men's Bibliography
Psychological Study of Men and Masculinity
Male Issues

relationships contend that it is too stereotypical (Dindia, 2006; Hyde, 2004, 2005, 2007; Matlin, 2004). They argue that there is greater individual variation in the relationship styles of men and women than this view acknowledges (Edwards & Hamilton, 2004; MacGeorge, 2004).

Men's Development

The male of the species—what is he really like? What are his concerns? According to Joseph Pleck's (1995) *role-strain view,* male roles are contradictory and inconsistent. Men not only experience stress when they violate men's roles, they also are harmed when they do act in accord with men's roles. Here are some of the areas where men's roles can cause considerable strain (Levant, 2002; Levant & Brooks, 1997):

- *Health.* Men live 8 to 10 years less than women do. They have higher rates of stress-related disorders, alcoholism, car accidents, and suicide. Men are more likely than women to be the victims of homicide. In sum, the male role is hazardous to men's health.
- *Male-female relationships.* Too often, the male role involves expectations that men should be dominant, powerful, and aggressive and should control women. "Real men," according to many traditional definitions of masculinity, look at women in terms of their bodies, not their minds and feelings, have little interest in rapport talk and relationships, and do not consider women equal to men in work or many other aspects of life. Thus, the traditional view of the male role encourages men to disparage women, be violent toward women, and refuse to have equal relationships with women.
- *Male-male relationships.* Too many men have had too little interaction with their fathers, especially fathers who are positive role models. Nurturing and being sensitive to others have been considered aspects of the female role, not the male role. And the male role emphasizes competition rather than cooperation. All of these aspects of the male role have left men with inadequate positive, emotional connections with other males.

To reconstruct their masculinity in more positive ways, Ron Levant (2002) suggests that every man should (1) reexamine his beliefs about manhood, (2) separate out the valuable aspects of the male role, and (3) get rid of those parts of the masculine role that are destructive. All of this involves becoming more "emotionally intelligent"—that is, becoming more emotionally self-aware, managing emotions more effectively, reading emotions better (one's own emotions and others'), and being motivated to improve close relationships.

Review and Reflect • LEARNING GOAL 5

(5) **Summarize the role of gender in relationships**

Review
- Are there differences in how men and women communicate?
- What are some important aspects of the woman's role in relationships?
- What are some important aspects of the man's role in relationships?

Reflect
- If you are female, what would you change about the way men function in relationships? If you are male, what would you change about the way women function in relationships?

REACH YOUR LEARNING GOALS

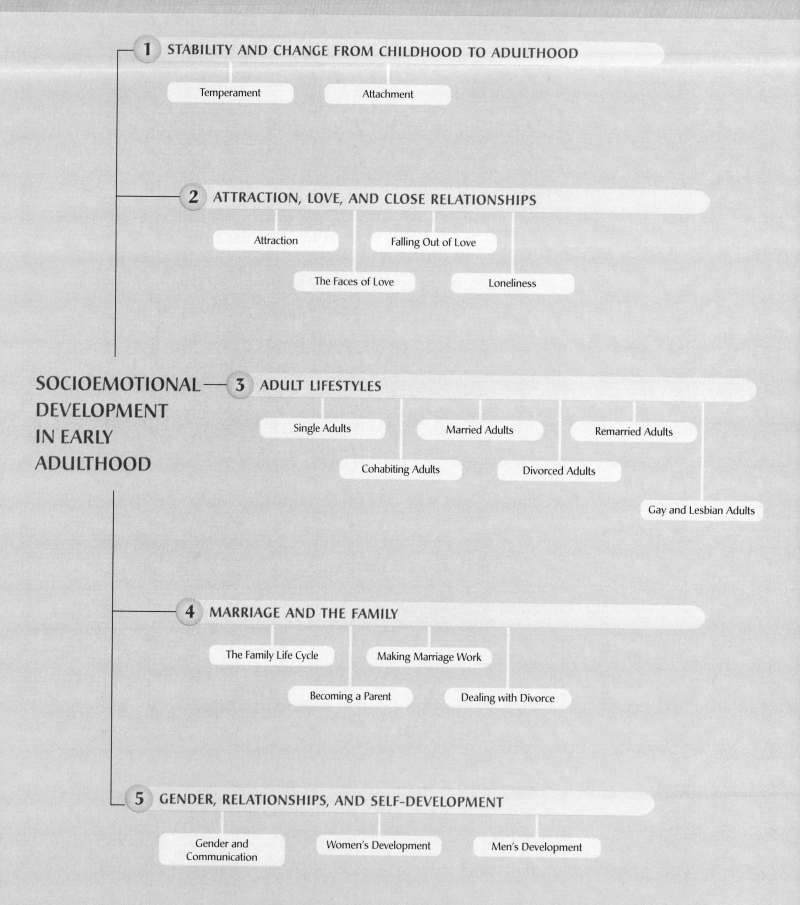

1 STABILITY AND CHANGE FROM CHILDHOOD TO ADULTHOOD

- Temperament
- Attachment

2 ATTRACTION, LOVE, AND CLOSE RELATIONSHIPS

- Attraction
- The Faces of Love
- Falling Out of Love
- Loneliness

SOCIOEMOTIONAL DEVELOPMENT IN EARLY ADULTHOOD

3 ADULT LIFESTYLES

- Single Adults
- Cohabiting Adults
- Married Adults
- Divorced Adults
- Remarried Adults
- Gay and Lesbian Adults

4 MARRIAGE AND THE FAMILY

- The Family Life Cycle
- Becoming a Parent
- Making Marriage Work
- Dealing with Divorce

5 GENDER, RELATIONSHIPS, AND SELF-DEVELOPMENT

- Gender and Communication
- Women's Development
- Men's Development

SUMMARY

1 Stability and Change from Childhood to Adulthood: *Describe stability and change in temperament and attachment from childhood to adulthood*

Temperament

The first 20 years are important in predicting an adult's personality, but so, too, are continuing experiences in the adult years. Activity level in early childhood is linked with being an outgoing young adult. Young adults show fewer mood swings, are more responsible, and engage in less risk taking than adolescents. In some cases, certain dimensions of temperament in childhood are linked with adjustment problems in early adulthood.

Attachment

Two main dimensions characterize adult attachment: attachment-related anxiety and attachment-related avoidance. Attachment styles in early adulthood are linked with a number of relationship patterns and developmental outcomes. For example, securely attached adults often show more positive relationship patterns than insecurely attached adults. Also, adults with avoidant and anxious attachment styles tend to be more depressed than securely attached adults.

2 Attraction, Love, and Close Relationships: *Identify some key aspects of attraction, love, and close relationships*

Attraction

Familiarity precedes a close relationship. We like to associate with people who are similar to us. The principles of consensual validation and matching can explain this. Similarity in personality attributes may be especially important in a relationship's success. Physical attraction is usually most important in the early part of relationships, and criteria for physical attractiveness vary across cultures and historical time.

The Faces of Love

Erikson theorized that intimacy versus isolation is the key developmental issue in early adulthood. There is a delicate balance between intimacy and commitment, on the one hand, and independence and freedom on the other. Friendship plays an important role in adult development, especially in terms of emotional support. Female, male, and female-male friendships often have different characteristics. For example, self-disclosure is more common in female friendships. Romantic love, also called passionate love, is involved when we say we are "in love." It includes passion, sexuality, and a mixture of emotions, not all of which are positive. Affectionate love, also called companionate love, usually becomes more important as relationships mature. Shaver proposed a developmental model of love and Sternberg a triarchic model of love (passion, intimacy, and commitment).

Falling Out of Love

The collapse of a close relationship can be traumatic, but for some individuals it results in happiness and personal development. For most individuals, falling out of love is painful and emotionally intense.

Loneliness

Chronic loneliness is linked with impaired physical and mental health. Loneliness often emerges when people make life transitions, so it is not surprising that loneliness is common among college freshmen.

3 Adult Lifestyles: *Characterize adult lifestyles*

Single Adults

Being single has become an increasingly prominent lifestyle. Autonomy is one of its advantages. Intimacy, loneliness, and finding a positive identity in a marriage-oriented society are challenges faced by single adults.

Cohabiting Adults

Cohabitation is an increasingly popular lifestyle. Cohabitation does not lead to greater marital happiness but rather to no differences or differences suggesting that cohabitation is not good for a marriage.

Married Adults

The age at which individuals marry in the U.S. is increasing. Despite a decline in marriage rates, a large percentage of Americans still marry. Gottman's research has found a number of factors that characterize what makes marriages work. The sociocultural context plays an important role in marriage. Premarital education is associated with positive relationship outcomes. The benefits of marriage include better physical and mental health and a longer life.

Divorced Adults

The U.S. divorce rate increased dramatically in the twentieth century but began to decline in the 1980s. Divorce is complex and emotional.

Remarried Adults

Stepfamilies are complex and adjustment is difficult. Only about one-third of remarried adults stay remarried.

Gay and Lesbian Adults

One of the most striking findings about gay and lesbian couples is how similar they are to heterosexual couples.

Marriage and the Family: *Discuss the family life cycle, parenting, making marriage work, and divorce*

The Family Life Cycle
There are six stages in the family life cycle: leaving home and becoming a single adult; the new couple; becoming parents and a family with children; the family with adolescents; the midlife family; and the family in later life.

Becoming a Parent
Families are becoming smaller, and many women are delaying childbirth until they have become well established in a career. There are some advantages to having children earlier in adulthood, and some advantages to having them later.

Making Marriage Work
Gottman's research indicates that in marriages that work couples establish love maps, nurture fondness and admiration, turn toward each other, accept the influence of the partner, solve solvable conflicts, overcome gridlock, and create shared meaning.

Dealing with Divorce
Hetherington identified six pathways taken by people after divorce. About 20 percent became better adjusted and more competent after the divorce.

5 **Gender, Relationships, and Self-Development:** *Summarize the role of gender in relationships*

Gender and Communication
Tannen distinguishes between rapport talk, which many women prefer, and report talk, which many men prefer. A recent meta-analysis found small gender differences in communication.

Women's Development
Some gender experts contend that women are more relationship-oriented than men and that their interactions focus on fostering the development of other people. Critics argue that there is more individual variation in women's and men's relationship styles than this view acknowledges. Many experts conclude that it is important for females to retain their competence and interest in relationships, but also to direct more effort into self-development.

Men's Development
The traditional male role involves considerable strain, which takes a toll on men's health. The role also discourages interest in relationships, equal relationships with women, and positive emotional connections with other men.

KEY TERMS

attachment-related anxiety 497
attachment-related
  avoidance 497
consensual validation 499
matching hypothesis 499

friendship 500
romantic love 502
affectionate love 502
leaving home and becoming a
  single adult 513

launching 513
new couple 513
becoming parents and a
  family with children 513
family with adolescents 514

family at midlife 514
family in later life 514
rapport talk 519
report talk 519

KEY PEOPLE

Theodore Wachs 496
Cindy Hazan and Phillip
  Shaver 497

Erik Erikson 500
Zick Rubin 501
Ellen Berscheid 502

Robert J. Sternberg 502
John Gottman 516
Deborah Tannen 519

Jean Baker Miller 519
Harriet Lerner 519
Joseph Pleck 520

E-LEARNING TOOLS

To help you master the material in this chapter, you'll find a number of valuable study tools on the LifeMap CD-ROM that accompanies this book and on the Online Learning Center for *Life-Span Development*, eleventh edition, at **www.mhhe.com/santrockld11**.

Video Clips

In the margins of this book there are icons directing you to the LifeMap CD-ROM that accompanies the book. There you'll find two videos for chapter 15. The first is called "Falling in Love." Are there patterns in the process of falling in love that apply generally? When does romantic love lead to companionate love? One couple offer themselves as a case study. The second video is called "Choosing Not to Cohabitate." This segment explores some of the motives for cohabitation (i.e., living together out of wedlock), as well as some of the advantages and disadvantages of this life choice.

Self-Assessment

Connect to **www.mhhe.com/santrockld11** to learn more about falling in love and finding a mate by completing the self-assessments, What Is My Love Like?, The Characteristics I Desire in a Potential Mate, and My Attitudes Towards Women.

Taking It to the Net

Connect to **www.mhhe.com/santrockld11** to research the answers to these questions.

1. Yolanda, who is divorced with two young children, is contemplating a marriage proposal from her boyfriend Dana, divorced with one young child. She is concerned about the potential issues that may arise from this union. What should Yolanda consider before making a decision?

2. Kelly, 29 years old, is surprised to hear about two close friends from college who are getting divorced after only a few years of marriage. One of these friends, April, tells her that "starter marriages" are happening more and more frequently. Is April correct about a growing trend of divorces before the age of 30? If so, what are some of the factors causing this trend?

Health and Well-Being, Parenting, and Education Exercises

Build your decision-making skills by trying your hand at the health and well-being, parenting, and education exercises. Connect to **www.mhhe.com/santrockld11** to research the answers and complete the exercises.

When more time stretches before one, some assessments, however reluctantly and incompletely, begin to be made.

—JAMES BALDWIN
American Novelist, 20th Century

CHAPTER OUTLINE		LEARNING GOALS
THE NATURE OF MIDDLE ADULTHOOD	**1**	Explain how midlife is changing and define middle adulthood
Changing Midlife		
Defining Middle Adulthood		
PHYSICAL DEVELOPMENT	**2**	Discuss physical changes in middle adulthood
Physical Changes		
Health and Disease		
Mortality Rates		
Sexuality		
COGNITIVE DEVELOPMENT	**3**	Identify cognitive changes in middle adulthood
Intelligence		
Information Processing		
CAREERS, WORK, AND LEISURE	**4**	Characterize career development, work, and leisure in middle adulthood
Work in Midlife		
Career Challenges and Changes		
Leisure		
RELIGION AND MEANING IN LIFE	**5**	Explain the roles of religion and meaning in life during middle adulthood
Religion and Adult Lives		
Religion and Health		
Meaning in Life		

Images of Life-Span Development
Time Perspectives

Our perception of time depends on where we are in the life span. We are more concerned about time at some points in life than others (Schroots, 1996). Jim Croce's song "Time in a Bottle" reflects a time perspective that develops in the adult years:

> If I could save Time in a bottle
>
> The first thing that I'd like to do
>
> Is to save every day
>
> Til Eternity passes away
>
> Just to spend them with you . . .
>
> But there never seems to be enough time
>
> To do the things you want to do
>
> Once you find them
>
> I've looked around enough to know
>
> That you're the one I want to go
>
> Through time with
>
> —Jim Croce, "Time in a Bottle"

Jim Croce's song connects time with love and the hope of going through time with someone we love. Love and intimacy are important themes of adult development. So is time. Middle-aged adults begin to look back to where they have been, reflecting on what they have done with the time they have had. They look toward the future more in terms of how much time remains to accomplish what they hope to do with their lives.

PREVIEW

When young adults look forward in time to what their lives might be like as middle-aged adults, too often they anticipate that things will go downhill. However, like all periods of the human life span, for most individuals there usually are positive and negative features of middle age. In this first chapter on middle adulthood, we will discuss physical changes; cognitive changes; changes in careers, work, and leisure; as well as the importance of religion and meaning in life during middle adulthood. To begin, though, we will explore how middle age is changing.

1 THE NATURE OF MIDDLE ADULTHOOD

Changing Midlife

Defining Middle Adulthood

Is midlife experienced the same way today as it was 100 years ago? How can middle adulthood be defined and what are some of its main characteristics?

Changing Midlife

Each year, for $12.50, about 2.5 to 3 million Americans who have turned 50 become members of the American Association for Retired Persons, now called simply, AARP. There is something incongruous about so many 50-year-olds joining a retirement group when hardly any of them are retired. Indeed, many of today's 50-year-olds are in better shape, more alert, and more productive than their 40-year-old counterparts from a generation or two earlier. As more people lead healthier lifestyles and medical discoveries help to stave off the aging process, the boundaries of middle age are being pushed upward. It looks like middle age is starting later and lasting longer for increasing numbers of active, healthy, and productive people. One study found that almost half of the individuals 65 to 69 years of age considered themselves middle-aged (National Council on Aging, 2000) and another study found a similar pattern: Half of the 60- to 75-year-olds viewed themselves as in middle age (Lachman, Maier, & Budner, 2000). Also, some individuals consider the upper boundary of midlife as the age at which they make the transition from work to retirement.

When Carl Jung studied midlife transitions early in the twentieth century, he referred to midlife as the afternoon of life (Jung, 1933). Midlife serves as an important preparation for late adulthood, "the evening of life" (Lachman, 2004, p. 306). But "midlife" came much earlier in Jung's time. In 1900 the average life expectancy was only 47 years of age; only 3 percent of the population lived past 65. Today, the average life expectancy is 78 and 12 percent of the U.S. population is older than 65. As a much greater percentage of the population lives to an older age, the midpoint of life and what constitutes middle age or middle adulthood are getting harder to pin down (Staudinger & Bluck, 2001). Statistically, the middle of life today is about 38 years of age—hardly any 38-year-olds, though, wish to be called "middle-aged"! What we think of as middle age comes later—anywhere from 40 to about 60 or 65 years of age. And as more people live longer, the 60 to 65 years upper boundary will likely be nudged upward.

Compared to previous decades and centuries, an increasing percentage of the population is made up of middle-aged and older adults. In the past, the age structure of the population could be represented by a pyramid, with the largest percentage of the population in the childhood years. Today, the percentages of people at different ages in the life span are more similar, creating what is called the "rectangularization" of the age distribution (a vertical rectangle) (Willis & Martin, 2005).

How is midlife changing?

Although middle adulthood has been a relatively neglected period of the human life span (except for pop psychology portrayals of the midlife crisis), life-span developmentalists are beginning to give more attention to this age period (Brim, Ryff, & Kessler, 2004; Lachman, 2001, 2004; Willis & Martin, 2005; Willis & Reid, 1999). One reason for the increased attention is that the largest cohort in U.S. history is currently moving through the middle-age years. From 1990 to 2015, the middle-aged U.S. population is projected to increase from 47 million to 80 million, a 72 percent increase. Because of the size of the baby-boom cohort (recall from chapter 2 that a *cohort* is a group of people born in a particular year or time period), the median age of the U.S. population will increase from 33 years in 1990 to 42 years in 2050. The baby boomers, born from 1946 to 1964, are of interest to developmentalists not only because of their increased numbers but also because they are the best-educated and most affluent cohort in history to pass through middle age (Martin & Willis, 2005).

Middle age is a mix of new opportunities and expanding resources accompanied by declines in physical abilities.

—LOIS VERBRUGGE
University of Michigan

Network on Successful Midlife Development
Exploring Middle Age

Defining Middle Adulthood

Though the age boundaries are not set in stone, we will consider **middle adulthood** as the developmental period that begins at approximately 40 years of age and extends to about 60 to 65 years of age. For many people, middle adulthood is a time of declining physical skills and expanding responsibility; a period in which people become more conscious of the young-old polarity and the shrinking amount of time left in life; a point when individuals seek to transmit something meaningful to the next generation; and a time when people reach and maintain satisfaction in their careers. In sum, middle adulthood involves "balancing work and relationship responsibilities in the midst of the physical and psychological changes associated with aging" (Lachman, 2004, p. 305).

In midlife, as in other age periods, individuals make choices, selecting what to do, how to invest time and resources, and evaluating what aspects of their lives they need to change. In midlife, "a serious accident, loss, or illness" may be a "wake-up call" and produce "a major restructuring of time and a reassessment" of life's priorities (Lachman, 2004, p. 310).

The concept of gains (growth) and losses (decline) is an important one in life-span development. An increasing number of experts conclude that middle adulthood is the age period in which gains and losses as well as biological and sociocultural factors balance each other (Baltes, Lindenberger, & Staudinger, 2006; Willis & Schaie, 2005). Although biological functioning declines in middle adulthood, sociocultural supports such as education, career, and relationships may peak in middle adulthood (Willis & Schaie, 2005). Thus, middle adulthood may be a unique developmental period in which growth and loss balance each other for many individuals.

Remember from our discussion in chapter 1 that we have not only a chronological age, but also biological, psychological, and social ages. Some experts conclude that compared with earlier and later periods, middle age is influenced more by sociocultural factors (Dittmann-Kohli, 2005; Willis & Martin, 2005; Willis & Schaie, 2005).

As we mentioned earlier, for many increasingly healthy adults, middle age is lasting longer. Indeed, an increasing number of experts on middle adulthood describe the age period of 55 to 65 as *late midlife* (Deeg, 2005). Compared to earlier midlife, late midlife is more likely to be characterized by "the death of a parent, the last child leaving the parental home, becoming a grandparent, the preparation for retirement, and in most cases actual retirement. Many people in this age range experience their first confrontation with health problems. Overall, then, although gains and losses may balance each other in early midlife, losses may begin to dominate gains for many individuals in late midlife (Baltes, Lindenberger, & Staudinger, 2006).

Keep in mind, though, that midlife is characterized by individual variations (Brim, Ryff, Kessler, 2004; Perrig-Chiello & Perren, 2005). As life-span expert Gilbert Brim (1992) commented, middle adulthood is full of changes, twists, and turns; the path is not fixed. People move in and out of states of success and failure.

middle adulthood The developmental period beginning at approximately 40 years of age and extending to about 60 to 65 years of age.

Review and Reflect • LEARNING GOAL 1

1 **Explain how midlife is changing and define middle adulthood**

Review
- How is middle age today different than in past generations?
- How is middle adulthood defined and what are some of its characteristics?

Reflect
- How do you think you will experience (are experiencing or have experienced) middle age differently from your parents or grandparents?

2   PHYSICAL DEVELOPMENT

Physical Changes   Mortality Rates

Health and Disease   Sexuality

When I was a college student and my father was 45 years old, I thought he was really old. I could not conceive of myself ever being that old! But it happened, and now I have a few gray hairs. I'm wearing reading glasses while I'm typing this sentence. I can't run as fast as I could, although I still run 15 to 20 miles every week to keep my body from falling apart. What physical changes accompany this change to middle adulthood?

Physical Changes

Unlike the rather dramatic physical changes that occur in early adolescence and the sometimes abrupt decline in old age, midlife physical changes are usually gradual (Ebersole, Hess, & Luggen, 2004; Merrill & Verbrugge, 1999). A recent study found that self-ratings of physical health became more negative as individuals aged through the midlife period (Cleary, Zaborski, & Ayanian, 2004). In a national survey of baby boomers at midlife (American Association of Retired Persons, 2002), baby boomers said that their health was worse off than they had expected but that they had a good deal of control over their health outcomes.

Although everyone experiences some physical change due to aging in the middle adulthood years, the rates of this aging vary considerably from one individual to another. Genetic makeup and lifestyle factors play important roles in whether chronic disease will appear and when. Middle age is a window through which we can glimpse later life while there is still time to engage in prevention and to influence some of the course of aging (Lachman, 2004). Let's now explore some of the physical changes of middle age.

Visible Signs   One of the most visible signs of physical changes in middle adulthood is physical appearance. The first outwardly noticeable signs of aging usually are apparent by the forties or fifties. The skin begins to wrinkle and sag because of a loss of fat and collagen in underlying tissues. Small, localized areas of pigmentation in the skin produce aging spots, especially in areas that are exposed to sunlight, such as the hands and face (McCullough & Kelly, 2006). Hair becomes thinner and grayer due to a lower replacement rate and a decline in melanin production. Fingernails and toenails develop ridges and become thicker and more brittle.

Since a youthful appearance is stressed in our culture, many individuals whose hair is graying, whose skin is wrinkling, whose bodies are sagging, and whose teeth are yellowing strive to make themselves look younger. Undergoing cosmetic surgery, dyeing hair, purchasing wigs, enrolling in weight reduction programs, participating in exercise regimens, and taking heavy doses of vitamins are common in middle age. Baby boomers have shown a strong interest in plastic surgery and Botox, which may reflect their desire to take control of the aging process (Lachman & Firth, 2004).

In our culture, some aspects of aging in middle adulthood are taken as signs of attractiveness in men. Facial wrinkles and gray hair symbolize strength and maturity in men but may be perceived as unattractive in women. One study found that middle-aged women focus more attention on facial attractiveness than do older or younger women (Nowak, 1977). In this same study, middle-aged women were more likely than middle-aged men to perceive the signs of aging as having a negative effect on their physical appearance.

Famous actor Sean Connery as a young adult in his twenties (*top*) and as a middle-aged adult in his fifties (*bottom*). *What are some of the most outwardly noticeable signs of aging in the middle adulthood years?*

Middle age is when your age starts to show around your middle.

—Bob Hope
American Comedian, 20th Century

Women's Health in Middle Age
Midlife Baby-Boomer
Characteristics

Height and Weight Individuals lose height in middle age, and many gain weight. On average, from 30 to 50 years of age, men lose about $\frac{1}{2}$ inch in height, then may lose another $\frac{3}{4}$ inch from 50 to 70 years of age (Hoyer & Roodin, 2003). The height loss for women can be as much as 2 inches from 25 to 75 years of age. Note that there are large variations in the extent to which individuals become shorter with aging. The decrease in height is due to bone loss in the vertebrae. On average, body fat accounts for about 10 percent of body weight in adolescence; it makes up 20 percent or more in middle age.

Being overweight is a critical health problem in middle adulthood (Aldwin, Spiro, & Park, 2006). For individuals who are 30 percent or more overweight, the probability of dying in middle adulthood increases by about 40 percent. Obesity increases the probability that an individual will suffer a number of other ailments, among them hypertension and digestive disorders (Lebrun & others, 2006; McDermott & others, 2006).

In a large-scale study of middle-aged individuals, 7 of 10 said that they are overweight (Brim, 1999). Nearly half of the individuals over the age of 45 said they are less fit than they were five years ago.

Strength, Joints, and Bones As we saw in chapter 14, maximum physical strength often is attained in the twenties. The term *sarcopenia* is given to age-related loss of muscle mass and strength (Fujita & Volpi, 2006; McCarter, 2006; Schaap & others, 2006). The rate of muscle loss with age occurs at a rate of approximately 1 to 2 percent per year past the age of 50 (Marcell, 2003). A loss of strength especially occurs in the back and legs. Exercise can reduce the decline involved in sarcopenia (Taafe, 2006).

Peak functioning of the body's joints also usually occurs in the twenties. The cushions for the movement of bones (such as tendons and ligaments) become less efficient in the middle-adult years, a time when many individuals experience joint stiffness and more difficulty in movement.

Maximum bone density occurs by the mid to late thirties, from which point there is a progressive loss of bone. The rate of this bone loss begins slowly but accelerates in the fifties (Whitbourne, 2001). Women experience about twice the rate of bone loss as men. By the end of midlife, bones break more easily and heal more slowly (Wehren & others, 2005).

Vision and Hearing *Accommodation* of the eye—the ability to focus and maintain an image on the retina—experiences its sharpest decline between 40 and 59 years of age. In particular, middle-aged individuals begin to have difficulty viewing close objects, which means that many individuals have to wear glasses with bifocal lenses (Fozard & Gordon-Salant, 2001).

The eye's blood supply also diminishes, although usually not until the fifties or sixties. The reduced blood supply may decrease the visual field's size and account for an increase in the eye's blind spot. Also, there is some evidence that the retina becomes less sensitive to low levels of illumination.

Hearing also can start to decline by the age of 40. Sensitivity to high pitches usually declines first. The ability to hear low-pitched sounds does not seem to decline much in middle adulthood, though. Men usually lose their sensitivity to high-pitched sounds sooner than women do. However, this sex difference might be due to men's greater exposure to noise in occupations such as mining, automobile work, and so on (Kline & Scialfa, 1996).

Researchers are identifying new possibilities for improving the vision and hearing of people as they age (Fozard & Gordon-Salant, 2001; Schieber, 2006). One way this is being carried out is through better control of glare or background noise. Further, recent advances in hearing aids dramatically improve hearing for many individuals (Birren, 2002).

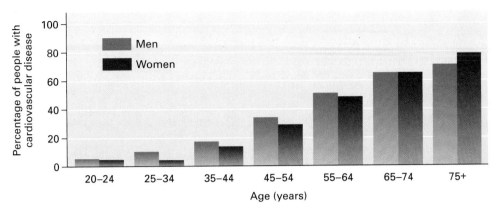

FIGURE 16.1 The Relation of Age and Gender to Cardiovascular Disease. Notice the sharp increase in cardiovascular disease in middle age.

Cardiovascular System   Midlife is the time when high blood pressure and high cholesterol "often take adults by surprise" (Lachman, 2004, p. 307). Indeed, the cardiovascular system changes in middle adulthood and, as indicated in figure 16.1, cardiovascular disease increases considerably in middle age (Safar & Smulyan, 2004). Fatty deposits and scar tissue slowly accumulate in the linings of blood vessels, gradually reducing blood flow to various organs, including the heart and brain (Masoro, 2006). Fatty deposits can begin in adolescence. Thus, eating food high in fat content and being overweight in adolescence may have consequences in later life (Harrell, Jessup, & Greene, 2006; Harmsen & others, 2006).

The level of cholesterol in the blood increases through the adult years and in midlife begins to accumulate on the artery walls, increasing the risk of cardiovascular disease (Masoro, 2006). The type of cholesterol in the blood, however, influences its effect. Cholesterol comes in two forms: LDL (low-density lipoprotein) and HDL (high-density lipoprotein). LDL is often referred to as "bad" cholesterol because when the level of LDL is too high, it sticks to the lining of blood vessels, which can lead to atherosclerosis (hardening of the arteries). HDL is often referred to as "good" cholesterol because when it is high and LDL is low, the risk of cardiovascular disease is lessened (Kim, Han, & Park, 2006). Scientists are not sure why HDL is protective but theorize that it may scour the walls of blood vessels and help to remove LDL from them (Nicholls, Rye, & Barter, 2005; Shao & others, 2006).

Blood pressure (hypertension), too, usually rises in the forties and fifties (Grossman & Messerli, 2006; Uchino & others, 2005). At menopause, a woman's blood pressure rises sharply and usually remains above that of a man through life's later years (Narkiewicz & others, 2005).

An increasing problem in middle and late adulthood is *metabolic disorder*, a condition characterized by hypertension, obesity, and insulin resistance (Grundy, 2006; Patel & others; Reaven, 2006). Metabolic disorder often leads to the development of diabetes and cardiovascular disease (Lin & others, 2006). In a recent longitudinal study, metabolic disorder was a significant predictor of experiencing a heart attack or death over the course of seven years in elderly Mexican Americans (Otiniano & others, 2005).

Exercise, weight control, and a diet rich in fruits, vegetables, and whole grains can often help to stave off many cardiovascular problems in middle age (Chiuve & others, 2006; Stanner, 2006). For example, cholesterol levels are influenced by heredity, but LDL can be reduced and HDL increased by eating food that is low in saturated fat and cholesterol and by exercising regularly (Kelly & Kelly, 2005). Weight loss and exercise are strongly recommended in the treatment of metabolic disorder (Deedwania & Volkova, 2005). To read further about the link between exercise and cardiovascular disease, see the Research in Life-Span Development interlude.

Fitness in Young Adults and Heart Health in Middle Age

A recent longitudinal study was the first large-scale observational study to examine the role of fitness on healthy young adults' development of risk factors for heart disease (Carnethon & others, 2003). Previous studies had focused on the relation between fitness and death from heart disease and stroke.

The study involved 4,487 men and women in four cities (Birmingham, Alabama; Chicago, Illinois; Minneapolis, Minnesota; and Oakland, California). Initial assessments were made when the participants were 18 to 30 years of age with follow-up assessments conducted 2, 5, 7, 10, and 15 years later. Cardiorespiratory fitness was measured with an exercise treadmill test, which consisted of up to nine 2-minute stages of progressive difficulty.

Poor cardiorespiratory fitness in young men and women, determined by the duration of their treadmill exercise test, was associated with the risk of developing hypertension, diabetes, and metabolic syndrome (a constellation of factors closely related to metabolic disorder that includes excess abdominal fat, elevated blood pressure and triglycerides, and low levels of HDL, the "good" cholesterol) in middle age. Improved fitness over seven years was related to a reduced risk of developing diabetes and metabolic syndrome.

FIGURE 16.2 The Relation of Lung Capacity to Age and Cigarette Smoking. Lung capacity shows little change through middle age for individuals who have not smoked. However, smoking is linked with reduced lung capacity in middle-aged and older adults. When individuals stop smoking, their lung capacity becomes greater than those who continue to smoke, but not as great as the lung capacity of individuals who have never smoked.

Lungs There is little change in lung capacity through most of middle adulthood. However, at about the age of 55, the proteins in lung tissue become less elastic. This change, combined with a gradual stiffening of the chest wall, decreases the lungs' capacity to shuttle oxygen from the air people breathe to the blood in their veins. As shown in figure 16.2, the lung capacity of individuals who are smokers drops precipitously in middle age, but if the individuals quit smoking their lung capacity improves, although not to the level of individuals who have never smoked (Williams, 1995).

Sleep Some aspects of sleep become more problematic in middle age (Ingelsson & others, 2006; Vitiello, Larsen, & Moe, 2004). The total number of hours slept usually remains the same as in early adulthood, but beginning in the forties, wakeful periods are more frequent and there is less of the deepest type of sleep (stage 4). The amount of time spent lying awake in bed at night begins to increase in middle age, and this can produce a feeling of being less rested in the morning (Abbot, 2003). Sleep problems in middle-aged adults are more common in individuals who use a higher number of prescription and nonprescription drugs, are obese, have cardiovascular disease, or are depressed (Drapeau & others, 2006; Eqan, 2006; Foley & others, 2004; Hoffman, 2003).

Health and Disease

In middle adulthood, the frequency of accidents declines and individuals are less susceptible to colds and allergies than in childhood, adolescence, or early adulthood. Indeed, many individuals live through middle adulthood without having a disease or persistent health problem. However, disease and persistent health problems become more common in middle adulthood for other individuals (Spiro, 2001).

Only 7 percent of individuals in their early forties report having a disability but that number more than doubles by the early fifties (16 percent), and by the early sixties, 30 percent report having a disability (Bumpass & Aquilino, 1995; Lachman, 2004). When individuals were asked to rate their health in early, middle, and late adulthood, they indicated that their health was not as good as in early adulthood but better than in late adulthood (National Center for Health Statistics, 1999). Men rated their health as somewhat better than women in midlife but in late adulthood the gender differences virtually disappeared.

Chronic disorders are characterized by a slow onset and a long duration. Chronic disorders are rare in early adulthood, increase in middle adulthood, and become common in late adulthood. Overall, arthritis is the leading chronic disorder in middle age, followed by hypertension, but the frequency of chronic disorders in middle age varies by gender. Men have a higher incidence of fatal chronic conditions (such as coronary heart disease, cancer, and stroke); women have a higher incidence of nonfatal ones (such as arthritis, varicose veins, and bursitis).

Stress and Disease Stress is increasingly being found to be a factor in disease. For example, people who have had major life changes such as loss of a spouse or a job have an increased incidence of cardiovascular disease and early death. The cumulative effect of stress often takes a toll on the health of individuals by the time they reach middle age (Aldwin, Spiro, & Park, 2006). Stress is linked to disease through both the immune system and cardiovascular disease (Graham, Christian, & Kiecolt-Glaser, 2006).

The Immune System and Stress The immune system keeps us healthy by recognizing foreign materials such as bacteria, viruses, and tumors and then destroying them. Its machinery consists of billions of white blood cells located in the circulatory system. The number of white blood cells and their effectiveness in killing foreign viruses or bacteria are related to stress levels. When a person is under stress, viruses and bacteria are more likely to multiply and cause disease. Immune system functioning decreases with normal aging (Pawelec & others, 2006; Weng, 2006).

Stress and the Cardiovascular System Sometimes the link between stress and cardiovascular disease is indirect. For example, people who live in a chronically stressed condition are more likely to take up smoking, start overeating, and avoid exercising. All of these stress-related behaviors are linked with the development of cardiovascular disease (Schneiderman & others, 2001). In addition, however, researchers have found that stress and negative emotions can affect the development and course of cardiovascular disease by altering underlying physiological processes (Aldwin, Spiro, & Park, 2006; Das & O'Keefe, 2006).

You may have heard someone say something like "It's no wonder she died of a heart attack with all of the stress he put her through." But is it true that emotional stress can cause a person to have a heart attack? A clear link has not been found, but there is evidence that chronic emotional stress is associated with high blood pressure, heart disease, and early death (Kiecolt-Glaser & others, 2002). Apparently, the surge in adrenaline caused by severe emotional stress causes the blood to clot more rapidly, and blood clotting is a major factor in heart attacks (Fogoros, 2001).

Culture and Health Culture plays an important role in coronary disease. Cross-cultural psychologists believe that studies of immigrants shed light on the role culture plays in health. When people migrate to another culture, their health practices are likely to change while their genetic predispositions to certain disorders remain constant (Ilola, 1990; Jorgensen, Borch-Johnsen, & Bjerregaard, 2006).

Consider the Ni-Hon-San Study (Nippon–Honolulu–San Francisco), an ongoing study of approximately 12,000 Japanese men in Hiroshima and Nagasaki (Japan), Honolulu, and San Francisco. In the study, the Japanese men living in Japan have had the lowest rate of coronary heart disease, those living in Honolulu have had an intermediate rate, and those living in San Francisco have had the highest rate. The Japanese men's cholesterol level, glucose level, and weight all increased as they migrated. Why? As the Japanese men migrated farther away from Japan, they

chronic disorders Disorders that are characterized by slow onset and long duration. They are rare in early adulthood, they increase during middle adulthood, and they become common in late adulthood.

In the Ni-Hon-San study, what health variations were found for Japanese men living in Japan (top), Honolulu (middle), and San Francisco (bottom)?

acculturated, and their health practices, such as diet, changed. The Japanese men in California, for example, ate 40 percent more fat than the men in Japan.

Conversely, Japanese men in California have much lower rates of cerebrovascular disease (stroke) than Japanese men living in Japan. Businessmen in Japan tend to consume vast quantities of alcohol and to chain-smoke, both of which are high-risk factors for stroke. Stroke was the leading cause of death in Japan until it was surpassed by cancer in 1981. However, death rates from stroke for Japanese American men are at the same level as those of White American men. Researchers suspect that this level is related to a change in behavior. That is, Japanese American men consume less alcohol and smoke less than their counterparts in Japan. To read more about cultural factors in health, see the Diversity in Life-Span Development interlude.

DIVERSITY IN LIFE-SPAN DEVELOPMENT

Health Promotion in African Americans, Latinos, Asian Americans, and Native Americans

There are differences within ethnic groups as well as among them. This is just as true of health within ethnic groups as it is of, say, family structure. Asian Americans, for example, are strikingly varied in their national backgrounds, lifestyles, and health. They range from highly acculturated Japanese Americans, who may be well educated and have excellent access to health care, to the many Indochinese refugees who have few economic resources and may be in poor health. The living conditions and lifestyles of individuals within an ethnic group are influenced by their socioeconomic status, immigrant status, social and language skills, occupational opportunities, and such social resources as the availability of meaningful support networks—all of which play a role in health (Mainous & others, 2006; Punzalan & others, 2006; Shaya & Saunders, 2006; Whitfield, 2006).

Despite these variations within ethnic groups, it is useful to know about differences between ethnic groups. African Americans, for example, have an above-average rate of high blood pressure, and there is increasing evidence that diabetes occurs at an above-average rate among Latinos, making this disease a major health problem (Hertz, Unger, & Ferrario, 2006).

Prejudice and racial segregation are the historical underpinnings for the chronic stress of discrimination and poverty that adversely affects the health of many African Americans (Shavers & Shavers, 2006; Trivedi & Ayanian, 2006). Support systems, such as an extended family network, may be especially important resources to improve the health of African Americans and help them cope with stress.

Prejudice and discrimination may also be significant stressors affecting the heath of immigrants from Puerto Rico, Mexico, and elsewhere in Latin America. Immigrants may also face cultural barriers to adequate health care including a lack of financial resources and poor language skills, which often prevent effective doctor-patient communications. In addition, immigrants often are unfamiliar with how the medical system operates, confused about the need to see numerous people, and uncertain about why they have to wait so long for service (Snowden & Cheung, 1990).

Health-care professionals can increase their effectiveness with ethnic minority patients by improving their knowledge of patients' attitudes, beliefs, and folk practices regarding health and disease. Such information should be integrated into Western treatment rather than ignored at the risk of alienating patients.

Personality, Social Relationships, and Health The importance of socioemotional and personality factors in middle adulthood can be seen in the influence of emotional stability, personality, and social relationships on the health of middle-aged adults. For example, as individuals in the Berkeley Longitudinal Study aged from 34 to 50, those who were the most healthy were also the most calm, the most self-controlled, and the most responsible (Livson & Peskin, 1981). Let's explore how two personality profiles and social relationships are linked to health.

Type A/Type B Behavioral Patterns   In the middle of the twentieth century, a secretary for two California cardiologists, Meyer Friedman and Ray Rosenman, observed that the chairs in their waiting rooms were tattered and worn, but only on the front edges. The cardiologists had noticed the impatience of their cardiac patients, who often arrived exactly on time for an appointment and were in a great hurry to leave. Subsequently they conducted a study of 3,000 healthy men between the ages of 35 and 59 over a period of eight years (Friedman & Rosenman, 1974). During the eight years, one group of men had twice as many heart attacks or other forms of heart disease as anyone else. And autopsies of the men who died revealed that this same group had coronary arteries that were more obstructed than those of other men. Friedman and Rosenman described the group that had a high incidence of coronary disease as being characterized by **Type A behavior pattern,** a cluster of characteristics that includes being excessively competitive, hard-driven, impatient, and hostile. Rosenman and Friedman labeled the behavior of the other group, who were relaxed and easygoing, **Type B behavior pattern.**

Type Z behavior
© 1987 The New Yorker Collection, Donald Reilly from cartoonbank.com. All Rights Reserved.

Further research found that the link between Type A behavior and coronary disease is not as strong as Friedman and Rosenman believed (Suls & Swain, 1998; Williams, 1995, 2001). When researchers have examined specific components of Type A behavior, the component most consistently associated with coronary problems is hostility (Aldwin, Spiro, & Park, 2006; Das & O'Keefe, 2006; Williams, 2001). People who are hostile outwardly or turn anger inward are more likely to develop heart disease than their less angry counterparts (Allan & Scheidt, 1996). Such people have been called "hot reactors" because of their intense physiological reactions to stress. Their hearts race, their breathing quickens, and their muscles tense up. Redford Williams (1995), a leading behavioral medicine researcher, holds that such people can develop the ability to control their anger and develop more trust in others, which he thinks can reduce their risk for heart disease.

The role of personality factors, including hostility, in health were examined in one longitudinal study of more than 1,500 men from 28 to 80 years of age with an average age of 47 at the initial assessment (Aldwin & others, 2001). Men who had high, increasing symptoms of poor health were characterized by hostility and anxiety, were overweight, and smoked. Those with few symptoms of poor health were emotionally stable, educated, thin nonsmokers.

www.mhhe.com/santrockld11

Behavioral Medicine
Controlling Anger and Developing Life Skills

Hardiness   Evidence of a link between other personality characteristics and health comes from the Chicago Stress Project, in which male business managers 32 to 65 years of age were studied over a five-year period. During the five years, most of the managers experienced stressful events, such as divorce, job transfers, the death of a close friend, inferior performance evaluations at work, and working at a job with an unpleasant boss. In one study, managers who developed an illness (ranging from the flu to a heart attack) were compared with those who did not (Kobasa, Maddi, & Kahn, 1982). The latter group was more likely to have a hardy personality. **Hardiness** is a personality style characterized by a sense of commitment (rather than alienation), control (rather than powerlessness), and a perception of problems as challenges (rather than threats).

A related study investigated whether hardiness along with exercise and social support buffered stress and reduced illness in executives' lives (Kobasa & others, 1986). When all three factors were present in an executive's life, the level of illness dropped dramatically (see figure 16.3). This suggests the power of multiple buffers of stress, rather than a single buffer, in maintaining health (Harris, 2004; Maddi & others, 2006; Ouellette & DiPlacido, 2001).

Type A behavior pattern A cluster of characteristics—being excessively competitive, hard-driven, impatient, and hostile—thought to be related to the incidence of heart disease.

Type B behavior pattern Being primarily calm and easygoing.

hardiness A personality style characterized by a sense of commitment (rather than alienation), control (rather than powerlessness), and a perception of problems as challenges (rather than threats).

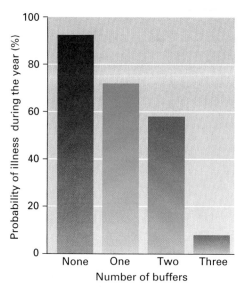

FIGURE 16.3 Illness in High-Stress Business Executives. In one study of high-stress business executives (all of whom were selected for this analysis because they were above the stress mean for the entire one year of the study), three buffers (hardiness, exercise, and social support) were examined (Kobasa & others, 1986). Having one buffer reduced the probability of illness, two buffers reduced the illness risk further, but high-stress business executives with all three buffers had by far the lowest probability of illness.

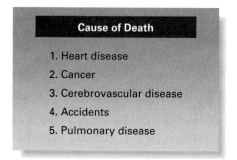

Cause of Death

1. Heart disease
2. Cancer
3. Cerebrovascular disease
4. Accidents
5. Pulmonary disease

FIGURE 16.4 Leading Causes of Death in Middle Adulthood

climacteric The midlife transition in which fertility declines.

menopause The complete cessation of a woman's menstruation, which usually occurs in the late forties or early fifties.

Health and Social Relationships In chapter 15, "Socioemotional Development in Early Adulthood," we saw that being in a happy marriage is linked with getting sick less, having less physical and emotional stress, and living longer than those in unhappy marriages. These results hold for middle-aged as well as young adults.

Researchers also have revealed links between health in middle age and earlier relationships (Ryff & Singer, 2000). In one recent longitudinal study, individuals who were on a positive pathway in their relationships from childhood to middle age had significantly fewer biological problems (cardiovascular disease, physical decline) than their counterparts whose relationships were on a negative pathway (Ryff & others, 2001). In another longitudinal study, adults who experienced more warmth and closeness with their parents during childhood had fewer diagnosed diseases (coronary artery disease, hypertension, ulcer, alcoholism) than those who did not experience warmth and closeness with their parents in childhood (Russek & Schwartz, 1997). These studies reflect continuity in development over many years. Thus, health in middle age is related both to the current quality of social relationships and to the pathways of those relationships earlier in development.

Mortality Rates

Infectious disease was the main cause of death until the middle of the twentieth century. As infectious disease rates declined and more individuals lived through middle age, chronic disorders increased. Chronic diseases are now the main causes of death for individuals in middle adulthood (Merrill & Verbrugge, 1999).

In middle age, many deaths are caused by a single, readily identifiable condition, whereas in old age, death is more likely to result from the combined effects of several chronic conditions (Gessert, Elliott, & Haller, 2003). Figure 16.4 shows the leading causes of death in middle age. Heart disease is the leading cause, followed by cancer and cerebrovascular disease (National Center for Health Statistics, 2004). In the first half of middle age, cancer claims more lives than heart disease; this is reversed in the second half. Men have higher mortality rates than women for all of the leading causes of death.

Sexuality

What kinds of changes characterize the sexuality of women and men as they go through middle age? **Climacteric** is a term that is used to describe the midlife transition in which fertility declines. Let's explore the substantial differences in the climacteric of women and men.

Menopause Most of us know something about menopause. But is what we know accurate? What is menopause, when does it occur, and what are its side effects?

Menopause is the time in middle age, usually in the late forties or early fifties, when a woman's menstrual periods completely cease. The average age at which women have their last period is 51 (Wise, 2006). However, there is large variation in the age at which menopause occurs—from 39 to 59 years of age. *Perimenopause* is the transitional period from normal menstrual periods to no menstrual periods at all, which often takes up to 10 years (Maitland & others, 2006). Perimenopause is most common in the forties but can occur in the thirties (McVeigh, 2005). One recent study of 30- to 50-year-old women found that depressed feelings, headaches, moodiness, and palpitations were the symptoms that women in perimenopause most frequently discussed with health-care providers (Lyndaker & Hulton, 2004).

Not only the timing but also the side effects of menopause vary greatly (Rossi, 2004; Shakhatreh & Mas'ad, 2006; Wilbur & others, 2005). In menopause, production of estrogen by the ovaries declines dramatically, and this decline produces uncomfortable symptoms in some women—"hot flashes," nausea, fatigue, and rapid heartbeat, for example (Fitzpatrick, 2004; Joffe, Soares, & Cohen, 2003). Cross-cultural studies reveal wide variations in the menopause experience (Avis, 1999). For example, hot flashes are uncommon in Mayan women (Beyene, 1986). Asian women report fewer hot flashes than women in Western societies (Payer, 1991). It is difficult to determine the extent to which these cross-cultural variations are due to genetic, dietary, reproductive, or cultural factors.

In the United States, research based on small samples of women who go to physicians or therapists because they are having problems associated with menopause sometimes creates the impression that menopause is necessarily a traumatic event. In fact, in a large-scale study of Americans in midlife, just over 50 percent of middle-aged women reported having no hot flashes at all (Brim, 1999). Almost two-thirds of postmenopausal women said they were relieved that their periods had stopped. Only 1 percent said they felt "only regret" that they no longer had their period. Some menopausal women report depression and irritability, but in some instances these feelings are related to other circumstances such as becoming divorced, losing a job, caring for a sick parent, and so on (Gannon, 1998). A recent study found that elevated side effects of menopause are most likely to occur when women have a history of menstrual pain and of stress at home or at work (Rossi, 2004).

Although menopause overall is not the negative experience for most women it was once thought to be, the loss of fertility is an important marker for women—it means that they have to make final decisions about having children (Huffman & others, 2005; Wise, 2006). Women in their thirties who have never had children sometimes speak about being "up against the biological clock" because they cannot postpone choices about having children much longer.

Until recently, hormone replacement therapy was often prescribed as treatment for unpleasant side-effects of menopause. *Hormone replacement therapy (HRT)* augments the declining levels of reproductive hormone production by the ovaries (Ekstrom, 2005; Quilliam, 2004). HRT can consist of various forms of estrogen, and usually a progestin. A study of HRT's effects was halted as evidence emerged that participants who were receiving HRT faced an increased risk of stroke (National Institutes of Health, 2004). Estrogen alone increased the risk of stroke by about the same amount as estrogen combined with progestin. Preliminary data also indicated a trend toward increased risk of dementia (deterioration of mental functioning) among those receiving HRT. On the positive side, the study found that estrogen lowered the risk of hip fractures and did not increase the risk of heart attacks or breast cancer.

The National Institutes of Health recommend that women with a uterus who are currently taking hormones should consult with their doctor to determine whether they should continue the treatment. If they are taking HRT for short-term relief of symptoms, the benefits may outweigh the risks (Schindler, 2006). However, the recent evidence of risks associated with HRT suggests that long-term hormone therapy should be seriously reevaluated (Turgeon & others, 2004; Warren & Valente, 2004; Crosignani, 2006; Wathen, 2006).

Hormonal Changes in Middle-Aged Men   Do men go through anything like the menopause that women experience? That is, is there a male menopause? During middle adulthood, most men do not lose their capacity to father children, although there usually is a modest decline in their sexual hormone level and activity. Men experience hormonal changes in their fifties and sixties, but nothing like the dramatic drop in estrogen that women experience (Leonard, 2004; Sommer, 2001). Testosterone production begins to decline about 1 percent a year during middle adulthood, and sperm count usually shows a slow decline, but men do not lose their fertility in middle age (Mooradian & Korenman, 2006). What has been referred to as "male menopause," then, probably has less to do with hormonal change than with the psychological adjustment men must make when they are faced with declining physical energy and with family and work pressures. Testosterone therapy has not been found to relieve such symptoms, suggesting that they may not be induced by hormonal change (Harman, 2006).

Researchers have found that almost 50 percent of Canadian and American women have occasional hot flashes, but only 1 in 7 Japanese women do (Lock, 1998). *What factors might account for these variations?*

www.mhhe.com/santrockld11

Menopause: Information and Resources
National Institute of Aging: Menopause
Medline: Menopause

Medline: Middle-Age Sexuality
Midlife Male Hormone Changes

The gradual decline in men's testosterone levels in middle age can reduce their sexual drive (Beutel, Weidner, & Brahler, 2006). Their erections are less full and less frequent, and require more stimulation to achieve them. Researchers once attributed these changes to psychological factors, but increasingly they find that as many as 75 percent of the erectile dysfunctions in middle-aged men stem from physiological problems. Smoking, diabetes, hypertension, and elevated cholesterol levels are at fault in many erectile problems in middle-aged men (Shiri & others, 2003).

Treatment for men with erectile dysfunction has focused recently on the drug Viagra (Padma-Nathan, 2006) and on similar drugs that appeared after Viagra became popular, such as Levitra and Cialis (Wright, 2006). Viagra works by allowing increased blood flow into the penis, which produces an erection. Its success rate is in the range of 60 to 80 percent (Carson, 2003). The possible side effects of Viagra are headaches in 1 of 10 men, blackouts (Viagra can trigger a sudden drop in blood pressure), and seeing blue (because the eyes contain an enzyme similar to the one on which Viagra works in the penis, about 3 percent of users develop temporary vision problems ranging from blurred vision to a blue or green halo effect). Viagra should not be taken by men using nitroglycerin for the treatment of cardiovascular disease because the combination can significantly lower blood pressure and lead to fainting or even death in some men (Cheitlin, 2003). Also, scientists do not know the long-term effects of taking the drug, although in short-term trials it appears to be a relatively safe drug (Burnett, 2004). Early studies indicate that Levitra and Cialis are as successful as Viagra in treating erectile dysfunction and have similar side effects (Morgentaler & others, 2006; Rajfer & others, 2006).

Sexual Attitudes and Behavior   Although the ability of men and women to function sexually shows little biological decline in middle adulthood, sexual activity usually occurs on a less frequent basis than in early adulthood (Burgess, 2004). Career interests, family matters, energy level, and routine may contribute to this decline (Avis & others, 2005).

Figure 16.5 shows the age trends in frequency of sex from the Sex in America survey (described in chapter 14). The frequency of having sex was greatest for individuals aged 25 to 29 years old (47 percent had sex twice a week or more) and dropped off for individuals in their fifties (23 percent of 50- to 59-year-old males said they had sex twice a week or more, while only 14 percent of the females in this age group reported this frequency) (Michael & others, 1994). Note, though, that the Sex in America survey may underestimate the frequency of sexual activity of

		Percentage engaging in sex			
Age groups	*Not at all*	*A few times per year*	*A few times per month*	*2–3 times a week*	*4 or more times a week*
Men					
18–24	15	21	24	28	12
25–29	7	15	31	36	11
30–39	8	15	37	23	6
40–49	9	18	40	27	6
50–59	11	22	43	20	3
Women					
18–24	11	16	2	9	12
25–29	5	10	38	37	10
30–39	9	16	6	33	6
40–49	15	16	44	20	5
50–59	30	22	35	12	2

FIGURE 16.5 The Sex in America Survey: Frequency of Sex at Different Points in Adult Development. *Why do you think the frequency of sex declines as men and women get older?*

middle-aged adults because the data were collected prior to the widespread use of erectile dysfunction drugs such as Viagra.

Living with a spouse or partner makes all the difference in whether people engage in sexual activity, especially for women over 40 years of age. In one study conducted by the MacArthur Foundation, 95 percent of women in their forties with partners said that they have been sexually active in the last six months, compared with only 53 percent of those without partners (Brim, 1999). By their fifties, 88 percent of women living with a partner have been sexually active in the last six months, but only 37 percent of those who are neither married nor living with someone say they have had sex in the last six months.

Review and Reflect ● LEARNING GOAL 2

2 **Discuss physical changes in middle adulthood**

Review
- What are some key physical changes in middle adulthood?
- How would you characterize health and disease in middle adulthood?
- What are the main causes of death in middle age?
- What are the sexual lives of middle-aged adults like?

Reflect
- Were you surprised by any of the characteristics of the sexual lives of middle-aged adults? If so, which ones?

---

3 COGNITIVE DEVELOPMENT

| Intelligence | | Information Processing |

We have seen that middle-aged adults may not see as well, run as fast, or be as healthy as they were in their twenties and thirties. But what about their cognitive skills? Do they decline as we enter and move through middle adulthood? To answer this question we will explore the possibility of cognitive changes in intelligence and information processing.

Intelligence

Our exploration of possible changes in intelligence in middle adulthood focuses on the concepts of fluid and crystallized intelligence, the Seattle Longitudinal Study, and cohort effects.

Fluid and Crystallized Intelligence John Horn believes that some abilities begin to decline in middle age while others increase (Horn & Donaldson, 1980). Horn argues that **crystallized intelligence,** an individual's accumulated information and verbal skills, continues to increase in middle adulthood, while **fluid intelligence,** one's ability to reason abstractly, begins to decline in the middle adulthood years (see figure 16.6).

Horn's data were collected in a cross-sectional manner. Remember from chapter 2, "The Science of Life-Span Development," that a cross-sectional study assesses individuals of different ages at the same point in time. For example, a cross-sectional study might assess the intelligence of different groups of 40-, 50-, and 60-year-olds

crystallized intelligence Accumulated information and verbal skills, which increase with age, according to Horn.

fluid intelligence The ability to reason abstractly, which steadily declines from middle adulthood on, according to Horn.

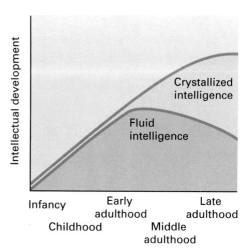

FIGURE 16.6 Fluid and Crystallized Intellectual Development Across the Life Span. According to Horn, crystallized intelligence (based on cumulative learning experiences) increases throughout the life span, but fluid intelligence (the ability to perceive and manipulate information) steadily declines from middle adulthood.

in a single evaluation, such as in 1980. The 40-year-olds in the study would have been born in 1940 and the 60-year-olds in 1920—different eras that offered different economic and educational opportunities. The 60-year-olds likely had fewer educational opportunities as they grew up. Thus, if we find differences between 40- and 60-year-olds on intelligence tests when they are assessed cross-sectionally, these differences might be due to cohort effects related to educational differences rather than to age.

By contrast, remember from chapter 2 that in a longitudinal study, the same individuals are studied over a period of time. Thus, a longitudinal study of intelligence in middle adulthood might consist of giving the same intelligence test to the same individuals when they are 40, 50, and 60 years of age. As we see next, whether data on intelligence are collected cross-sectionally or longitudinally can make a difference in what is found about changes in crystallized and fluid intelligence and about intellectual decline.

The Seattle Longitudinal Study   K. Warner Schaie and Sherry Willis (1996, 2007; Willis & Schaie, 1999, 2005) is conducting an extensive study of intellectual abilities in the adulthood years. Five hundred individuals initially were tested in 1956. New waves of participants are added periodically. The main focus in the Seattle Longitudinal Study has been on individual change and stability in intelligence.

The main mental abilities tested are:

- *Vocabulary* (ability to understand ideas expressed in words)
- *Verbal memory* (ability to encode and recall meaningful language units, such as a list of words)
- *Number* (ability to perform simple mathematical computations such as addition, subtraction, and multiplication)
- *Spatial orientation* (ability to visualize and mentally rotate stimuli in two- and three-dimensional space)
- *Inductive reasoning* (ability to recognize and understand patterns and relationships in a problem and use this understanding to solve other instances of the problem)
- *Perceptual speed* (ability to quickly and accurately make simple discriminations in visual stimuli)

As shown in figure 16.7, the highest level of functioning for four of the six intellectual abilities occurred in the middle adulthood years (Willis & Schaie,

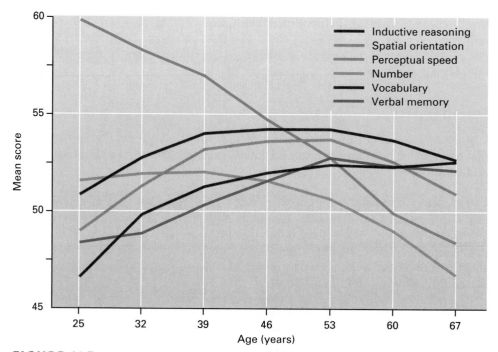

FIGURE 16.7 Longitudinal Changes in Six Intellectual Abilities from Age 25 to Age 67

1999). For both women and men, peak performance on vocabulary, verbal memory, inductive reasoning, and spatial orientation was attained in middle age. For only two of the six abilities—numerical ability and perceptual speed—were there declines in middle age. Perceptual speed showed the earliest decline, actually beginning in early adulthood. Interestingly, in terms of John Horn's ideas that were discussed earlier, for the participants in the Seattle Longitudinal Study, middle age was a time of peak performance for some aspects of both crystallized intelligence (vocabulary) and fluid intelligence (spatial orientation and inductive reasoning).

When Schaie (1994) assessed intellectual abilities both cross-sectionally and longitudinally, he found decline more likely in the cross-sectional than in the longitudinal assessments. For example, as shown in figure 16.8, when assessed cross-sectionally, inductive reasoning showed a consistent decline in the middle adulthood years. In contrast, when assessed longitudinally, inductive reasoning increased until toward the end of middle adulthood, when it began to show a slight decline. In Schaie's view, it is in middle adulthood, not early adulthood, that people reach a peak in their cognitive functioning for many intellectual skills.

The results from and Willis' study that have been described so far focus on *average* cognitive stability or change for all participants across the middle adulthood years. Schaie and Willis (Schaie, 2005; Willis & Schaie, 2005) recently examined individual differences for the participants in the Seattle study and found substantial individual variations. They classified participants as "decliners," "stable," and "gainers" for three categories—number ability, delayed recall (a verbal memory task), and word fluency—from 46 to 60 years of age. The largest percentage of decline (31 percent) or gain (16 percent) occurred for delayed recall; the largest percentage with stable scores (79 percent) occurred for numerical ability. Word fluency declined for 20 percent of the individuals from 46 to 60 years of age.

Might the individual variations in cognitive trajectories in midlife be linked to cognitive impairment in late adulthood? In Willis and Schaie's analysis, cognitively normal and impaired older adults did not differ on measures of vocabulary, spatial orientation, and numerical ability in middle adulthood. However, declines in memory (immediate recall and delayed recall), word fluency, and perceptual speed in middle adulthood were linked to neuropsychologists' ratings of the individuals' cognitive impairment in late adulthood.

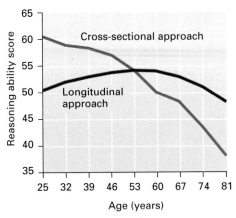

FIGURE 16.8 Cross-Sectional and Longitudinal Comparisons of Intellectual Change in Middle Adulthood. *Why do you think reasoning ability peaks during middle adulthood.*

K. Warner Schaie

Information Processing

As we saw in our discussion of theories of development (chapter 2) and of cognitive development from infancy through adolescence (chapters 6, 8, 10, and 12), the information-processing approach provides another way of examining cognitive abilities. Among the information-processing changes that take place in middle adulthood are those involved in speed of processing information, memory, expertise, practical problem-solving skills, and metacognition.

Speed of Information Processing As we saw in Schaie's (1994, 1996) Seattle Longitudinal Study, perceptual speed begins declining in early adulthood and continues to decline in middle adulthood. A common way to assess speed of information is through a reaction-time task, in which individuals simply press a button as soon as they see a light appear (Hartley, 2006). Middle-aged adults are slower to push the button when the light appears than young adults are. However, keep in mind that the decline is not dramatic—under 1 second in most investigations. Also, for unknown reasons, the decline in reaction time is stronger for women than for men (Salthouse, 1994).

A current interest focuses on possible causes for the decline in speed of processing information in adults (Hartley, 2006; Salthouse, 2005). The causes may occur at different levels of analysis, such as cognitive ("maintaining goals, switching between tasks, or preserving internal representations despite distraction"), neuroanatomical ("changes in specific brain regions, such as the prefrontal cortex"), and neurochemical ("changes in neurotransmitter systems") such as dopamine (Hartley, 2006, p. 201).

Memory In Schaie's (1994, 1996) Seattle Longitudinal Study, verbal memory peaked in the fifties. However, in some other studies, verbal memory has shown a decline in middle age, especially when assessed in cross-sectional studies. For example, in several studies, when asked to remember lists of words, numbers, or meaningful prose, younger adults outperformed middle-aged adults (Salthouse & Skovronek, 1992). Although there still is some controversy about whether memory declines in the middle adulthood years, most experts conclude that it does decline (Hoyer & Verhaeghen, 2006; Salthouse, 2000). However, some experts argue that studies that have concluded there is a decline in memory during middle age often have compared young adults in their twenties with older middle-aged adults in their late fifties and even have included some individuals in their sixties (Schaie, 2000). In this view, memory decline either is nonexistent or minimal in the early part of middle age but does occur in the latter part of middle age or late adulthood (Backman, Small, & Wahlin, 2001).

Aging and cognition expert Denise Park (2001) argues that starting in late middle age, more time is needed to learn new information. The slowdown in learning new information has been linked to changes in **working memory,** the mental "workbench" where individuals manipulate and assemble information when making decisions, solving problems, and comprehending written and spoken language (Baddeley, 2000). In this view, in late middle age, working memory capacity—the amount of information that can be immediately retrieved and used—becomes more limited (Leonards, Ibanez, & Giannakopoulos, 2002). Think of this situation as an overcrowded desk with many items in disarray. As a result of the overcrowding and disarray, long-term memory becomes less reliable, more time is needed to enter new information into long-term storage, and more time is required to retrieve the information. Thus, Park believes that much of the blame for declining memory in late middle age is a result of information overload that builds up as we go through the adult years.

Memory decline is more likely to occur when individuals don't use effective memory strategies, such as organization and imagery (Hess, Osowski, & Leclerc, 2005; Hoyer & Verhaeghen, 2006). By organizing lists of phone numbers into different categories or imagining the phone numbers as representing different objects around the house, many people can improve their memory in middle adulthood.

Expertise Because it takes so long to attain, expertise often shows up more in the middle adulthood than in the early adulthood years (Hess, Osowski, & Leclerc, 2005; Kim & Hasher, 2005). Recall from chapter 10 that *expertise* involves having extensive, highly organized knowledge and understanding of a particular domain. Developing expertise and becoming an "expert" in a field usually is the result of many years of experience, learning, and effort.

Strategies that distinguish experts from novices include these:

- Experts are more likely to rely on their accumulated experience to solve problems.
- Experts often process information automatically and analyze it more efficiently when solving a problem in their domain than novices do.
- Experts have better strategies and shortcuts to solving problems in their domain than novices do.
- Experts are more creative and flexible in solving problems in their domain than novices are (Csikszentmihalyi, 1997).

Stephen J. Hawking is a world-renowned expert in physics. Hawking authored the best-selling book, *A Brief History of Time*. Hawking has a neurological disorder that prevents him from walking or talking. He communicates with the aid of a voice-equipped computer. *What distinguishes experts from novices?*

working memory Closely related to short-term memory but places more emphasis on mental work. Working memory is like a "workbench" where individuals can manipulate and assemble information when making decisions, solving problems, and comprehending written and spoken language.

Practical Problem Solving Everyday problem solving is another important aspect of cognition (Parish-Stephens & Marson, 2006). Nancy Denney (1986, 1990) observed circumstances such as how young and middle-aged adults handled a landlord who would not fix their stove and what they did if a bank failed to deposit a check. She found that the ability to solve such practical problems improved through the forties and fifties as individuals accumulated practical experience. However, since Denney's research other studies on everyday problem-solving and decision-making effectiveness across the adult years have been conducted (Marsiske & Margrett, 2006). A recent meta-analysis of these studies indicated that everyday problem-solving and decision-making effectiveness remained stable in early and middle adulthood, then declined in late adulthood (Thornton & Dumke, 2005). However, in late adulthood, older adults' everyday problem-solving and decision-making effectiveness benefited when individuals were highly educated and the content of the problems involved interpersonal matters.

Metacognition Recall from chapter 10, that *metacognition* involves cognition about cognition, or knowing about knowing. In middle age, it is likely that many adults have accumulated a great deal of metacognitive knowledge, such as knowing which strategies are more important to use than others. They may draw on this metacognitive knowledge to help them combat a decline in memory skills. For example, they may understand that they need to have good organizational skills and reminders to maintain their memory skills. They may also know that they need to monitor their progress in solving a problem and re-evaluate whether they are using the best strategy at particular points in the problem-solving activity.

Given the high level of cognitive skills shown in many areas by middle-aged adults and their extensive experience and accumulation of knowledge, metacognitive knowledge and monitoring may peak in middle adulthood (Hertzog & Dixon, 2005). However, very few research studies have examined metacognition in middle adulthood (Hertzog & Dixon, 2005; Hertzog & Robinson, 2005).

Review and Reflect • LEARNING GOAL 3

3 **Identify cognitive changes in middle adulthood**

Review
- How does intelligence develop in middle adulthood?
- What changes take place in processing information during middle age?

Reflect
- What do you think are the most important cohort effects that can influence the development of intelligence in middle age? How are these likely to change in the future?

---

4 **CAREERS, WORK, AND LEISURE**

| Work in Midlife | Career Challenges and Changes | Leisure |

What are some issues that workers face in midlife? What role does leisure play in the lives of middle-aged adults?

Work in Midlife

The role of work, whether one works in a full-time career, a part-time job, as a volunteer, or a homemaker, is central during the middle years. Middle-aged adults may reach their peak in position and earnings. They may also be saddled with multiple financial burdens from rent or mortgage, child care, medical bills, home repairs, college tuition, loans to family members, or bills from nursing homes.

The progression of career trajectories in middle age is diverse. Some individuals have stable careers, with little mobility, while others move in and out of the labor force, experiencing layoffs and unemployment. Middle-aged adults may experience age discrimination in some job situations, and finding a job in midlife may be difficult because pay demands of older workers are higher than those of younger workers, or technological advances may render the midlife worker's skills outdated or obsolete. (Lachman, 2004, p. 323)

In the United States, approximately 80 percent of individuals 40 to 59 years of age are employed. In the 51-to-59 age group, slightly less than 25 percent do not work. More than half of this age group say that a health condition or an impairment limits the type of paid work that they do (Sterns & Huyck, 2001). Further, U.S. labor force participation is projected to grow to 37 percent for the 55-and-older age group, a 6.5 percent increase over the participation rate for 1996 with the 55-to-64 age group to add 7.3 million workers (Schwerha & McMullin, 2002). The majority of these increases are expected to be in the service industry.

An important issue in midlife is whether individuals will continue to do the type of work that they want to do. Mental and physical capabilities will not be a major impediment for many middle-aged adults if they want to continue working.

For many people, midlife is a time of evaluation, assessment, and reflection in terms of the work they do and want to do in the future (Moen & Spencer, 2006). Among the work issues that some people face in midlife are recognizing limitations in career progress, deciding whether to change jobs or careers, deciding whether to rebalance family and work, and planning for retirement (Sterns & Huyck, 2001).

Career Challenges and Changes

The current middle-aged worker faces several important challenges in the twenty-first century (Avolio & Sosik, 1999). These include the globalization of work, rapid developments in information technologies, downsizing of organizations, early retirement, and concerns about pensions and health care.

Globalization has replaced what was once a primarily White male workforce with employees of different ethnic and national backgrounds. The proliferation of computer technology compels middle-aged adults to become increasingly computer literate to maintain their work competence (Czaja, 2001). To improve profits, many companies are restructuring, downsizing, and outsourcing jobs. One of the outcomes of this is to offer incentives to middle-aged employees to retire early—in their fifties, or in some cases even forties, rather than their sixties.

Reprinted with special permission of King Features North American Syndicate.

The decline in defined-benefit pensions and increased uncertainty about the fate of health insurance are decreasing the sense of personal control for middle-aged workers. As a consequence, many are delaying retirement plans.

Some midlife career changes are self-motivated, others are the consequence of losing one's job (Moen, 1998; Moen & Spencer, 2006; Moen & Wethington, 1999). Some individuals in middle age decide that they don't want to do the same work they have been doing for the rest of their lives (Hoyer & Roodin, 2003). One aspect of middle adulthood involves adjusting idealistic hopes to realistic possibilities in light of how much time individuals have before they retire and how fast they are reaching their occupational goals (Levinson, 1978). If individuals perceive that they are behind schedule, if their goals are unrealistic, they don't like the work they are doing, or their job has become too stressful, they could become motivated to change jobs.

Leisure

As adults, not only must we learn how to work well, but we also need to learn how to relax and enjoy leisure (Ahmed & others, 2005; Stebbins, 2005; Strain & others, 2002). **Leisure** refers to the pleasant times after work when individuals are free to pursue activities and interests of their own choosing—hobbies, sports, or reading, for example. A recent analysis of research on what U.S. adults regret the most, not engaging in more leisure was one of the top six regrets (Roese & Summerville, 2005).

Leisure can be an especially important aspect of middle adulthood (Mannell, 2000; Parkes, 2006). By middle adulthood, more money is available to many individuals, and there may be more free time and paid vacations. In short, midlife changes may produce expanded opportunities for leisure. For many individuals, middle adulthood is the first time in their lives when they have the opportunity to diversify their interests.

In one study, 12,338 men 35 to 57 years of age were assessed each year for five years regarding whether they took vacations or not (Gump & Matthews, 2000). Then, the researchers examined the medical and death records over nine years for men who lived for at least a year after the last vacation survey. Compared with those who never took vacations, men who went on annual vacations were 21 percent less likely to die over the nine years and 32 percent less likely to die of coronary heart disease. The qualities that lead men to pass on a vacation tend to promote heart disease, such as not trusting anyone to fill in while you are gone or fearing that you will get behind in your work and someone will replace you. These are behaviors that sometimes have been described as part of the Type A behavioral pattern.

Adults at midlife need to begin preparing psychologically for retirement. Constructive and fulfilling leisure activities in middle adulthood are an important part of this preparation (Kelly, 1996). If an adult develops leisure activities that can be continued into retirement, the transition from work to retirement can be less stressful.

Sigmund Freud once commented that the two things adults need to do well to adapt to society's demands are to work and to love. To his list we add "to play." In our fast-paced society, it is all too easy to get caught up in the frenzied, hectic pace of our achievement-oriented work world and ignore leisure and play. *Imagine your life as a middle-aged adult. What would be the ideal mix of work and leisure? What leisure activities do you want to enjoy as a middle-aged adult?*

Review and Reflect • LEARNING GOAL 4

4 **Characterize career development, work, and leisure in middle adulthood**

Review
- What are some issues that workers face in midlife?
- What career challenges and changes might people experience in middle adulthood?
- What characterizes leisure in middle age?

Reflect
- What do you want your work life and leisure to be like in middle age? If you are middle aged, what is your work life and leisure like? If you are an older adult, what were they like in middle age?

leisure The pleasant times after work when individuals are free to pursue activities and interests of their own choosing.

5 RELIGION AND MEANING IN LIFE

Religion and Adult Lives   Religion and Health   Meaning in Life

What role does religion play in our development as adults? Is meaning of life an important theme for many middle-aged adults?

Religion and Adult Lives

Religion is an important aspect of people's lives around the world—98 percent of respondents in India, 88 percent in Italy, 72 percent in France, and 63 percent in Scandinavia say that they believe in God (Gallup, 1987). In the MacArthur Study of Midlife Development, more than 70 percent of U.S. middle-aged adults said they are religious and consider spirituality a major part of their lives (Brim, 1999). However, that does not mean they are committed to a single religion or house of worship. About half said they attend religious services less than once a month or never. In another study, about three-fourths of Americans said that they pray (*Religion in America*, 1993).

In thinking about religion and adult development, it is important to consider the role of individual differences (McCullough & others, 2005). Religion is a powerful influence in some adults' lives, whereas it plays little or no role in others' lives (Myers, 2000). Further, the influence of religion in people's lives may change as they develop. In John Clausen's (1993) longitudinal investigation, some individuals who had been strongly religious in their early adult years became less so in middle age; others became more religious in middle age. In a recent longitudinal study of individuals from their early thirties through their late sixties/early seventies, a significant increase in spirituality occurred between late middle (mid-fifties/early sixties) and late adulthood (Wink & Dillon, 2002) (see figure 16.9).

Females have consistently shown a stronger interest in religion than males have (Bijur & others, 1993). Compared with men, they participate more in both organized and personal forms of religion, are more likely to believe in a higher power or presence, and are more likely to feel that religion is an important dimension of their lives. In the recent longitudinal study just described, the spirituality of women increased more than men in the second half of life (Wink & Dillon, 2002).

At the same time that many Americans show a strong interest in religion and believe in God, they also reveal a declining faith in mainstream religious institutions, in religious leaders, and in the spiritual and moral stature of the nation (*Religion in America*, 1993; Sollod, 2000). A series of recent studies have found that Americans are becoming less committed to particular religious denominations (such as Baptist or Catholic). They are more tolerant of other faiths and more focused on their own spiritual journeys (Paloutzian, 2000). This change may be partly generational, a consequence of postwar baby boomers' emphasis on experimentation and independent thinking that is reflected in a fluid religious orientation.

Religion and Health

What might be some of the effects of religion on physical health? Some cults and religious sects encourage behaviors that are damaging to health such as ignoring sound medical advice. For individuals in the religious mainstream, however, there is generally either no link between religion and physical health or a positive effect (Koenig, 2004; Krause, 2004, 2006; McCullough & Laureneeau, 2005; Yates, 2004). A longitudinal study of individuals from 20 to 94 years of age found that women who were highly religious in their twenties had higher self-rated health throughout their lives than did less religious women (McCullough & Laurenceau, 2005). No association between religiousness and health were found for men. Researchers have found that religious commitment helps to moderate blood pressure and hypertension

FIGURE 16.9 Level of Spirituality in Four Adult Age Periods. In a longitudinal study, the spirituality of individuals in four different adult age periods—early (30s), middle (40s), late middle (mid-50s/early 60s), and late (late 60s/early 70s) adulthood—was assessed (Wink & Dillon, 2002). Based on responses to open-ended questions in interviews, the spirituality of the individuals was coded on a 5-point scale with 5 being the highest level of spirituality and 1 the lowest.

www.mhhe.com/santrockld11

Exploring the Psychology of Religion
Psychology of Religion Journals
Mental Health, Religion, and Culture

(Levin & Vanderpool, 1989). Also, a number of studies have confirmed a positive association between religious participation and longevity (Hummer & others, 2004; Thoresen & Harris, 2002).

Why might religion promote physical health? There are several possible answers (Hill & Butter, 1995):

- *Lifestyle issues.* For example, religious individuals have lower drug use than their nonreligious counterparts (Gartner, Larson, & Allen, 1991).
- *Social networks.* The degree to which individuals are connected to others affects their health. Well-connected individuals have fewer health problems (Hill & Pargament, 2003). Religious groups, meetings, and activities provide social connectedness for individuals.
- *Coping with stress.* Religion offers a source of comfort and support when individuals are confronted with stressful events. Although research has not clearly demonstrated prayer's positive effect on physical health, some investigators argue that prayer might be associated with such positive health-related changes as a decrease in the perception of pain and reduced muscle tension (McCullough, 1995). In the Applications in Life-Span Development interlude that follows, we further explore links between religion and coping.

What roles do religion and spirituality play in the lives of middle-aged adults?

APPLICATIONS IN LIFE-SPAN DEVELOPMENT

Religion and Coping

What is the relation between religion and the ability to cope with stress? Some psychologists have categorized prayer and religious commitment as defensive coping strategies, arguing that they are less effective in helping individuals cope than are life-skill, problem-solving strategies. However, recently researchers have found that some styles of religious coping are associated with high levels of personal initiative and competence, and that even when defensive religious strategies are initially adopted, they sometimes set the stage for the later appearance of more-active religious coping (Ano & Vasconcelles, 2005; Dunn & Horgas, 2004; Krause, 2006; Paloutzian & Park, 2005). In a study of 850 medically ill patients admitted to an acute-care hospital, religious coping was related to low depression (Koenig & others, 1992). In one study, depression decreased during times of high stress when there was an increase in collaborative coping (in which people see themselves as active partners with God in solving problems) (Brickel & others, 1998).

Religious coping behaviors appear to function quite well during times of high stress (Koenig, 1998, 2001). In one study, individuals were divided into those who were experiencing high stress and those with low stress (Manton, 1989). In the high-stress group, spiritual support was significantly related to low depression and high self-esteem. No such links were found in the low-stress group.

A recent interest in linking religion and coping focuses on **meaning-making coping,** which involves drawing on beliefs, values, and goals to change the meaning of a stressful situation, especially in times of chronic stress as when a loved one dies (Park, 2005; Park & Folkman, 1997). In Crystal Park's (2005) view, individuals who are religious experience more disruption of their beliefs, values, and goals immediately after the death of a loved one than individuals who are not religious. Eventually, though, individuals who are religious often show better adjustment to the loss. Initially, religion is linked with more depressed feelings about a loved one's death. Over time, however, as religious individuals search for a type of meaning in their loss, the depressed feelings lessen. Thus, religion can serve as a meaning system through which bereaved individuals are able to reframe their loss and even find avenues of personal growth.

How is religion linked to the ability to cope with stress?

meaning-making coping Involves drawing on beliefs, values, and goals to change the meaning of a stressful situation, especially in times of chronic stress as when a loved one dies.

(continued on next page)

In sum, various dimensions of religiousness can help some individuals cope more effectively with their lives (Krause, 2003, 2006; Paloutzian & Park, 2005; Thoresen & Harris, 2002; Thrasher, Campbell, & Oates, 2004). Religious beliefs can shape a person's psychological perception of pain or disability. Religious cognitions can play an important role in maintaining hope and stimulating motivation toward recovery. Because of its effectiveness in reducing distress, religious coping can help prevent denial of the problem and thus facilitate early recognition and more appropriate health-seeking behavior. Religion also can forestall the development of anxiety and depression disorders by promoting communal or social interaction. Houses of religious worship are a readily available, acceptable, and inexpensive source of support for many individuals, especially the elderly. The socialization provided by religious organizations can help prevent isolation and loneliness (Koenig & Larson, 1998).

Religious counselors often advise people about mental health and coping. To read about the work of one religious counselor, see the Careers in Life-Span Development interlude.

Are people who have a meaningful faith happier than those who do not? Reviews of the happiness literature suggest that happy people do tend to have a meaningful religious faith; religiously active individuals report greater happiness than do those who are religiously inactive (Diener, Lucas, & Oishi, 2002). Remember, though, that knowing that two factors correlate does not mean that one causes the other (just as in the case of religion and mental disorder co-occurring in a few individuals). We don't know whether faith enhances happiness, whether happiness induces faith, or whether some other factor is creating the connection.

Meaning in Life

Austrian psychiatrist Viktor Frankl's mother, father, brother, and wife died in the concentration camps and gas chambers in Auschwitz, Poland. Frankl survived the concentration camp and went on to write about meaning in life. In his book, *Man's Search for Meaning,* Frankl (1984) emphasized each person's uniqueness and the finiteness of life. He believed that examining the finiteness of our existence and the certainty of death adds meaning to life. If life were not finite, said Frankl, we could spend our life doing just about whatever we please because time would continue forever.

Frankl said that the three most distinct human qualities are spirituality, freedom, and responsibility. Spirituality, in his view, does not have a religious underpinning. Rather, it refers to a human being's uniqueness—to spirit, philosophy, and mind. Frankl proposed that people need to ask themselves such questions as why they exist, what they want from life, and what the meaning of their life is.

It is in middle adulthood that individuals begin to be faced with death more often, especially the deaths of parents and other older relatives. Also faced with less time in their life, many individuals in middle age begin to ask and evaluate the questions that Frankl proposed. And as we indicated in the discussion of religion and coping, meaning-making coping is especially helpful in times of chronic stress and loss.

CAREERS in LIFE-SPAN DEVELOPMENT

Gabriel Dy-Liasco
Pastoral Counselor

Gabriel Dy-Lisasco is a pastoral counselor at the Pastoral Counseling and Consultation Centers of Greater Washington, D.C. He obtained his Ph.D. in pastoral counseling from Loyola College in Maryland and also has experience as a psychotherapist in such mental health settings as a substance abuse program, military family center, psychiatric clinic, and community mental health center. As a pastoral counselor, he works with adolescents and adults in the aspects of their life that they show the most concern about—psychological, spiritual, or the interface of both. Having lived in Peru, Japan, and the Philippines, he brings considerable multicultural experience to the counseling setting. Dr. Dy-Liasco also is a professor in the Graduate School of Psychology and Counseling at Regent University in the Washington, D.C., area.

Roy Baumeister and Kathleen Vohs (2002, pp. 610–611) argue that the quest for a meaningful life can be understood in terms of four main needs for meaning that guide how people try to make sense of their lives:

- *Need for purpose.* "Present events draw meaning from their connection with future events." Purposes can be divided into (1) goals and (2) fulfillments. Life can be oriented toward a future anticipated state, such as living happily ever after or being in love.
- *Need for values.* This "can lend a sense of goodness or positive characterization of life and justify certain courses of action. Values enable people to decide whether certain acts are right or wrong." Frankl's (1984) view of meaning in life emphasized value as the main form of meaning that people need.
- *Need for a sense of efficacy.* This involves the "belief that one can make a difference. A life that had purposes and values but no efficacy would be tragic. The person might know what is desirable but could not do anything with that knowledge." With a sense of efficacy, people believe that they can control their environment, which has positive physical and mental health benefits (Bandura, 2001).
- *Need for self-worth.* Most individuals want to be "good, worthy persons. Self-worth can be pursued individually, such as" finding out that one is very good at doing something, or collectively, as when people find self-esteem from belonging to a group or category of people.

What characterizes the search for meaning in life?

Review and Reflect ● LEARNING GOAL 5

5 **Explain the roles of religion and meaning in life during middle adulthood**

Review
- What are some characteristics of religion in middle-aged individuals?
- How is religion linked to physical and mental health?
- What role does meaning in life play in middle adulthood?

Reflect
- What are the most important aspects of meaning in life? Might the components of meaning in life vary depending on how old someone is? Explain.

REACH YOUR LEARNING GOALS

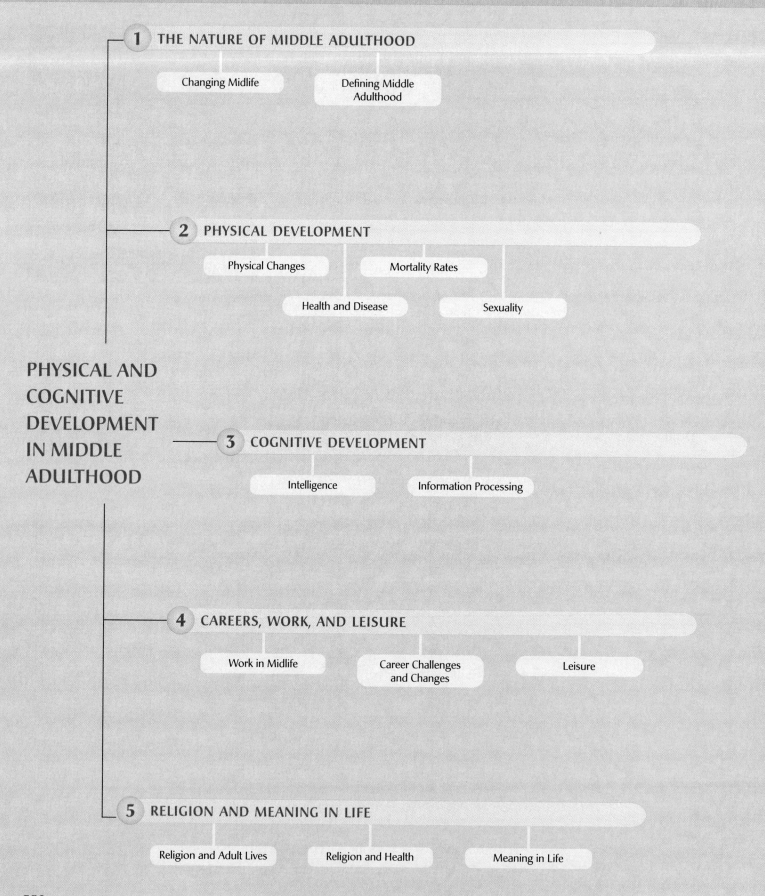

PHYSICAL AND COGNITIVE DEVELOPMENT IN MIDDLE ADULTHOOD

1 THE NATURE OF MIDDLE ADULTHOOD

Changing Midlife

Defining Middle Adulthood

2 PHYSICAL DEVELOPMENT

Physical Changes

Health and Disease

Mortality Rates

Sexuality

3 COGNITIVE DEVELOPMENT

Intelligence

Information Processing

4 CAREERS, WORK, AND LEISURE

Work in Midlife

Career Challenges and Changes

Leisure

5 RELIGION AND MEANING IN LIFE

Religion and Adult Lives

Religion and Health

Meaning in Life

SUMMARY

1 The Nature of Middle Adulthood: *Explain how midlife is changing and define middle adulthood*

Changing Midlife

As more people live to an older age, what we think of as middle age seems to be occurring later. A major reason developmentalists are beginning to study middle age is because of the dramatic increase in the number of individuals entering this period of the life span.

Defining Middle Adulthood

Middle age involves extensive individual variation. With this variation in mind, we will consider middle adulthood to be entered at about 40 and exited at approximately 60 to 65 years of age. Middle adulthood is the age period in which gains and losses as well as biological and sociocultural factors balance each other. Some experts conclude that sociocultural influence development in midlife more than biological factors.

2 Physical Development: *Discuss physical changes in middle adulthood*

Physical Changes

The physical changes of midlife are usually gradual. Genetic and lifestyle factors play important roles in whether chronic diseases will appear and when. Among the physical changes of middle adulthood are outwardly noticeable changes in physical appearance (wrinkles, aging spots); height (decrease) and weight (increase); strength, joints, and bones; vision and hearing; cardiovascular system; lungs; and sleep. In middle age, the frequency of accidents declines and individuals are less susceptible to colds and allergies.

Health and Disease

Chronic disorders rarely appear in early adulthood, increase in middle adulthood, and become more common in late adulthood. Arthritis is the leading chronic disorder in middle age, followed by hypertension. Men have more fatal chronic disorders, women more nonfatal ones in middle age. Immune system functioning declines with aging. Emotional stress likely is an important factor contributing to cardiovascular disease. People who live in a chronically stressed condition are likelier to smoke, overeat, and not exercise. All of these stress-related behaviors are linked with cardiovascular disease. Culture plays an important role in coronary disease. The Type A behavior pattern has been proposed as having a link with heart disease, but hostility is the component of the pattern that is most consistently associated with heart disease. Hardiness is a buffer of stress and is related to reduced illness. Health in middle age is linked to the current quality of social relationships and to developmental pathways of relationships.

Mortality Rates

In middle age, the leading causes of death, in order, are heart disease, cancer, and cerebrovascular disease.

Sexuality

Climacteric is the midlife transition in which fertility declines. The vast majority of women do not have serious physical or psychological problems related to menopause, which usually arrives in the late forties and early fifties, but menopause is an important marker because it signals the end of childbearing capability. Hormone replacement therapy (HRT) augments the declining levels of reproductive hormone production by the ovaries. HRT consists of various forms of estrogen, and usually progestin. Recent evidence of risks associated with HRT suggests that its long-term use should be seriously evaluated. Men do not experience an inability to father children in middle age, although their testosterone levels decline. A male menopause, like the dramatic decline in estrogen in women, does not occur. Sexual behavior occurs less frequently in middle adulthood than in early adulthood. Nonetheless, a majority of middle-aged adults show a moderate or strong interest in sex.

3 Cognitive Development: *Identify cognitive changes in middle adulthood*

Intelligence

Horn argued that crystallized intelligence (accumulated information and verbal skills) continues to increase in middle adulthood, whereas fluid intelligence (ability to reason abstractly) declines. Schaie and Willis found that longitudinal assessments of intellectual abilities are less likely than cross-sectional assessments to find declines in middle adulthood and are even more likely to find improvements. The highest level of four intellectual abilities (vocabulary, verbal memory, inductive reasoning, and spatial orientation) occurred in middle age. Recent analysis shows considerable individual variation in intellectual abilities across middle adulthood and indicates that variations in some abilities are more predictive of cognitive impairment in late adulthood than others.

Information Processing

Speed of information processing, often assessed through reaction time, declines in middle adulthood. Although Schaie found that verbal memory increased in middle age, some researchers have found that memory declines in middle age. Working memory declines in late middle age. Memory is more likely to decline in middle age when individuals don't use effective strategies. Expertise involves having an extensive, highly organized knowledge and an understanding of a domain. Expertise often increases in the middle adulthood years. Practical problem solving remains stable in the early and middle adulthood years but declines in late adulthood.

Metacognition likely peaks in middle adulthood although there have been few research studies of metacognition in the middle adulthood years.

 4   Careers, Work, and Leisure: *Characterize career development, work, and leisure in middle adulthood*

Work in Midlife

For many people midlife is a time of reflection, assessment, and evaluation of their current work and what they plan to do in the future. One important issue is whether individuals will continue to do the type of work they want to do.

Career Challenges and Changes

The current middle-aged worker faces such challenges as the globalization of work, rapid developments in information technologies, downsizing of organizations, early retirement, and concerns about pensions and health care. Midlife job or career changes can be self-motivated or forced on individuals.

Leisure

We not only need to learn to work well, but we also need to learn to enjoy leisure. Midlife may be an especially important time for leisure because of the physical changes that occur and because of preparation for an active retirement.

5   Religion and Meaning in Life: *Explain the roles of religion and meaning in life during middle adulthood*

Religion and Adult Lives

Religion is an important dimension of many Americans' lives, as well as the lives of people around the world. Females show a stronger interest in religion than males do. It is important to consider individual differences in religious interest.

Religion and Health

In some cases, religion can be negatively linked to physical health, as when cults or religious sects discourage individuals from obtaining medical care. In mainstream religions, religion usually shows either a positive association or no association with physical health. Religion can play an important role in coping for some individuals. Happy people tend to have a meaningful religious faith, but it is important to remember that the link is correlational, not causal.

Meaning in Life

Frankl believes that examining the finiteness of our existence leads to exploration of meaning in life. Faced with the death of older relatives and less time to live themselves, many middle-aged individuals increasingly examine life's meaning. Baumeister and Vohs argue that a quest for a meaningful life involves four main needs: purpose, values, efficacy, and self-worth.

KEY TERMS

middle adulthood 530	Type B behavior pattern 537	menopause 538	working memory 544
chronic disorders 535	hardiness 537	crystallized intelligence 541	leisure 547
Type A behavior pattern 537	climacteric 538	fluid intelligence 541	meaning-making coping 549

KEY PEOPLE

Gilbert Brim 530	John Horn 541	Nancy Denney 545	Victor Frankl 550
Meyer Friedman and Ray Rosenman 537	K. Warner Schaie 542	John Clausen 548	Roy Baumeister and Kathleen Vohs 551
	Denise Park 544	Crystal Park 549	

E-LEARNING TOOLS

To help you master the material in this chapter, you'll find a number of valuable study tools on the LifeMap CD-ROM that accompanies this book and on the Online Learning Center for *Life-Span Development*, eleventh edition, at **www.mhhe.com/santrockld11**.

Video Clips

In the margins of this book there are icons directing you to the LifeMap CD-ROM that accompanies the book. There you'll find a video for chapter 16 called "Interview with Stay-Home Dad." An increasing number of fathers in developed countries have the choice of staying home to raise their children. In this segment, a father reflects on the choice he made to stay home.

Self-Assessment

Connect to **www.mhhe.com/santrockld11** to reflect on philosophical issues by completing the self-assessments, *My Spiritual Well-Being* and *What Is My Purpose in Life?*

Taking It to the Net

Connect to **www.mhhe.com/santrockld11** to research the answers to this question:

> In the past year, 58-year-old Alan has experienced some lapses in memory. He sometimes forgets where he put his car keys; it may take him a few minutes to recall the name of someone he met on the golf course last week; and it takes him longer to balance his checkbook than it used to. Is Alan showing signs of dementia or normal age-related forgetfulness? What strategies can Alan use to maintain or even improve his memory?

Health and Well-Being, Parenting, and Education Exercises

Build your decision-making skills by trying your hand at the health and well-being, parenting, and education exercises. Connect to **www.mhhe.com/santrockld11** to research the answers and complete the exercises.

The generations of living things pass in a short time, and like runners, hand on the torch of life.

—LUCRETIUS
Roman Poet, 1st Century B.C.

CHAPTER OUTLINE

LEARNING GOALS

PERSONALITY THEORIES AND DEVELOPMENT

Stages of Adulthood

The Life-Events Approach

Stress in Midlife

Contexts of Midlife Development

1 Describe personality theories and development in middle adulthood

STABILITY AND CHANGE

Longitudinal Studies

Conclusions

2 Discuss stability and change in development during middle adulthood, including longitudinal studies

CLOSE RELATIONSHIPS

Love and Marriage at Midlife

The Empty Nest and Its Refilling

Sibling Relationships and Friendships

Grandparenting

Intergenerational Relationships

3 Identify some important aspects of close relationships in middle adulthood

Images of Life-Span Development
Middle-Age Variations

Forty-five-year-old Sarah feels tired, depressed, and angry when she looks back on the way her life has gone. She became pregnant when she was 17 and married Ben, the baby's father. They stayed together for three years after their son was born, and then Ben left her for another woman. Sarah went to work as a salesclerk to make ends meet. Eight years later, she married Alan, who had two children of his own from a previous marriage. Sarah stopped working for several years to care for the children. Then, like Ben, Alan started going out on her. She found out about it from a friend. Nevertheless, Sarah stayed with Alan for another year. Finally he was gone so much that she could not take it anymore and decided to divorce him. Sarah went back to work again as a salesclerk; she has been in the same position for 16 years now. During those 16 years, she has dated a number of men, but the relationships never seemed to work out. Her son never finished high school and has drug problems. Her father just died last year, and Sarah is trying to help her mother financially, although she can barely pay her own bills. Sarah looks in the mirror and does not like what she sees. She sees her past as a shambles, and the future does not look rosy, either.

Forty-five-year-old Wanda feels energetic, happy, and satisfied. As a young woman, she graduated from college and worked for three years as a high school math teacher. She married Andy, who had just finished law school. One year later, they had their first child, Josh. Wanda stayed home with Josh for two years, and then returned to her job as a math teacher. Even during her pregnancy, Wanda stayed active and exercised regularly, playing tennis almost every day. After her pregnancy, she kept up her exercise habits. Wanda and Andy had another child, Wendy. Now, as they move into their middle-age years, their children are both off to college, and Wanda and Andy are enjoying spending more time with each other. Last weekend they visited Josh at his college, and the weekend before they visited Wendy at her college. Wanda continued working as a high school math teacher until six years ago. She had developed computer skills as part of her job and taken some computer courses at a nearby college, doubling up during the summer months. She resigned her math teaching job and took a job with a computer company, where she has already worked her way into management. Wanda looks in the mirror and likes what she sees. She sees her past as enjoyable, although not without hills and valleys, and she looks to the future with zest and enthusiasm.

PREVIEW

As with Sarah and Wanda, there are individual variations in the way people experience middle age. To begin the chapter we will examine personality theories and development in middle age, including ideas about individual variation. Then we will turn our attention to how much individuals change or stay the same as they go through the adult years and finally explore a number of aspects of close relationships during the middle adulthood years.

1 PERSONALITY THEORIES AND DEVELOPMENT

- Stages of Adulthood
- Stress in Midlife
- The Life-Events Approach
- Contexts of Midlife Development

What is the best way to conceptualize middle age? Is it a stage or a crisis? How extensively is middle age influenced by life events? Do middle-aged adults experience stress differently than young and older adults? Is personality linked with contexts such as the point in history in which individuals go through midlife, their culture, and their gender?

Stages of Adulthood

Adult stage theories have been plentiful, and they have contributed to the view that midlife brings a crisis in development. Two prominent theories that define stages of adult development are Erik Erikson's life-span view and Daniel Levinson's seasons of a man's life.

Erikson's Stage of Generativity Versus Stagnation Erikson (1968) proposed that middle-aged adults face a significant issue—generativity versus stagnation, which is the name Erikson gave to the seventh stage in his life-span theory. *Generativity* encompasses adults' desire to leave legacies of themselves to the next generation (Petersen, 2002). Through these legacies adults achieve a kind of immortality. By contrast, *stagnation* (sometimes called "self-absorption") develops when individuals sense that they have done nothing for the next generation.

Middle-aged adults can develop generativity in a number of ways (Kotre, 1984). Through biological generativity, adults have offspring. Through parental generativity, adults nurture and guide children. Through work generativity, adults develop skills that are passed down to others. And through cultural generativity, adults create, renovate, or conserve some aspect of culture that ultimately survives.

Through generativity, adults promote and guide the next generation by parenting, teaching, leading, and doing things that benefit the community (Pratt & others, 2001). One of the participants in a study of aging said: "From twenty to thirty I learned how to get along with my wife. From thirty to forty I learned how to be a success at my job, and at forty to fifty I worried less about myself and more about the children" (Vaillant, 2002, p. 114). Generative adults commit themselves to the continuation and improvement of society as a whole through their connection to the next generation. Generative adults develop a positive legacy of the self and then offer it as a gift to the next generation.

Does research support Erikson's theory that generativity is an important dimension of middle age? Yes, it does. For example, in one study, Carol Ryff (1984) examined the views of women and men at different ages and found that middle-aged adults especially were concerned about generativity. In another study, generative women with careers found gratification through work; generative women who had not worked in a career experienced gratification through parenting (Peterson & Stewart, 1996). In a longitudinal study of Smith College women, generativity increased from the thirties through the fifties (Cole & Stewart, 1996; Roberts & Helson, 1997; Stewart, Ostrove, & Helson, 2001; Zucker, Ostrove, & Stewart, 2002) (see figure 17.1).

One modification of Erikson's theory proposes that Erikson's three adult stages—involving intimacy (early adulthood), generativity (middle adulthood), and integrity

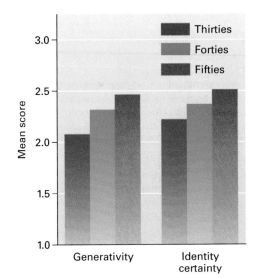

FIGURE 17.1 Changes in Generativity and Identity Certainty from the Thirties Through the Fifties. Both generativity and identity certainty increased in Smith College women as they aged from their thirties through their fifties (Stewart, Ostrove, & Helson, 2001). The women rated themselves on a 3-point scale indicating the extent to which they thought the statements about generativity and identity certainty were descriptive of their lives. *Do the findings in the study of Smith College women contradict Erikson's views of identity development?*

Generativity

Feeling needed by people

Effort to ensure that young people get their chance to develop

Influence in my community or area of interest

A new level of productivity or effectiveness

Appreciation and awareness of older people

Having a wider perspective

Interest in things beyond my family

Identity certainty

A sense of being my own person

Excitement, turmoil, confusion about my impulses and potential (reversed)

Coming near the end of one road and not yet finding another (reversed)

Feeling my life is moving well

Searching for a sense of who I am (reversed)

Wishing I had a wider scope to my life (reversed)

Anxiety that I won't live up to opportunities (reversed)

Feeling secure and committed

FIGURE 17.2 Items Used to Assess Generativity and Identity Certainty. These items were used to assess generativity and identity certainty in the longitudinal study of Smith College women (Stewart, Ostrove, & Helson, 2001). In the assessment of identity certainty, five of the items involved reversed scoring. For example, if an individual scored high on the item "Searching for a sense of who I am," it was an indication of identity uncertainty rather than identity certainty.

www.mhhe.com/santrockld11

**Midlife Crisis
The MacArthur Foundation
Study of Midlife Development**

(late adulthood)—are best viewed as developmental phases within identity. In this view, identity remains the central core of the self's development across all of the adult years (Whitbourne & Connolly, 1999).

Whether or not identity holds this central place in adult development, research does support its continuing importance during middle adulthood. For example, in one study, having a positive identity was linked with generativity in middle age (Vandewater, Ostrove, & Stewart, 1997). In the longitudinal study of Smith College women, identity certainty increased from the thirties through the fifties. Figure 17.2 describes the items that were used to assess generativity and identity certainty in the Smith College study.

Levinson's Seasons of a Man's Life   In *The Seasons of a Man's Life* (1978), clinical psychologist Daniel Levinson reported the results of extensive interviews with forty middle-aged men. The interviews were conducted with hourly workers, business executives, academic biologists, and novelists. Levinson bolstered his conclusions with information from the biographies of famous men and the development of memorable characters in literature. Although Levinson's major interest focused on midlife change, he described a number of stages and transitions during the period from 17 to 65 years of age, as shown in figure 17.3. Levinson emphasizes that developmental tasks must be mastered at each stage.

At the end of one's teens, according to Levinson, a transition from dependence to independence should occur. This transition is marked by the formation of a dream—an image of the kind of life the youth wants to have, especially in terms of a career and marriage. Levinson sees the twenties as a *novice phase* of adult development. It is a time of reasonably free experimentation and of testing the dream in the real world. In early adulthood, the two major tasks to be mastered are exploring the possibilities for adult living and developing a stable life structure.

From about the ages of 28 to 33, the man goes through a transition period in which he must face the more serious question of determining his goals. During the thirties, he usually focuses on family and career development. In the later years of this period, he enters a phase of *Becoming One's Own Man* (or BOOM, as Levinson calls it). By age 40, he has reached a stable location in his career, has outgrown his earlier, more tenuous attempts at learning to become an adult, and now must look forward to the kind of life he will lead as a middle-aged adult.

According to Levinson, the transition to middle adulthood lasts about five years (ages 40 to 45) and requires the adult male to come to grips with four major conflicts that have existed in his life since adolescence: (1) being young versus being old, (2) being destructive versus being constructive, (3) being masculine versus being feminine, and (4) being attached to others versus being separated from them. Seventy to 80 percent of the men Levinson interviewed found the midlife transition tumultuous and psychologically painful, as many aspects of their lives came into question. According to Levinson, the success of the midlife transition rests on how effectively the individual reduces the polarities and accepts each of them as an integral part of his being.

Because Levinson interviewed middle-aged males, we can consider the data about middle adulthood more valid than the data about early adulthood. When individuals are asked to remember information about earlier parts of their lives, they may distort and forget things. The original Levinson data included no females, although Levinson (1996) reported that his stages, transitions, and the crisis of middle age hold for females as well as males. Levinson's work included no statistical analysis. However, the quality and quantity of the Levinson biographies make them outstanding examples of the clinical tradition.

How Pervasive Are Midlife Crises?   Levinson (1978) views midlife as a crisis, believing that the middle-aged adult is suspended between the past and the future, trying to cope with this gap that threatens life's continuity. George Vaillant

(1977) has a different view. Vaillant's study—called the "Grant Study"—involved Harvard University men in their early thirties and in their late forties who initially had been interviewed as undergraduates. He concludes that just as adolescence is a time for detecting parental flaws and discovering the truth about childhood, the forties are a decade of reassessing and recording the truth about the adolescent and adulthood years. However, whereas Levinson sees midlife as a crisis, Vaillant believes that only a minority of adults experience a midlife crisis:

> Just as pop psychologists have reveled in the not-so-common high drama of adolescent turmoil, also the popular press, sensing good copy, had made all too much of the mid-life crisis. The term mid-life crisis brings to mind some variation of the renegade minister who leaves behind four children and the congregation that loved him in order to drive off in a magenta Porsche with a 25-year-old striptease artiste. As with adolescent turmoil, mid-life crises are much rarer in community samples. (pp. 222–223)

The following research studies all document that midlife is not characterized by pervasive crises:

- A recent study found that 26 percent of middle-aged U.S. adults said they had experienced a midlife crisis but most attributed the crisis to negative life events rather than aging (Wethington, Kessler, & Pixley, 2004). In this study that assessed 3,032 Americans from 25 to 72 years of age, the individuals from 40 to 60 years of age were less nervous and worried than those under 40 (Brim, 1999). The middle-aged adults reported a growing sense of control in their work and more financial security. The middle-aged adults also indicated a greater sense of environmental mastery—the ability to handle daily responsibilities—and autonomy than their younger counterparts.
- A longitudinal study of 2,247 individuals found few midlife crises (McCrae & Costa, 1990; Siegler & Costa, 1999). In this study, the emotional instability of individuals did not significantly increase through their middle-aged years (see figure 17.4).
- A study found that adults experienced a peak of personal control and power in middle age (Clark-Plaskie & Lachman, 1999).
- A study of individuals described as young (average age 19), middle-aged (average age 46), and older (average age 73) adults found that their ability to manage their environmental surroundings (environmental mastery) and self-determination (autonomy) increased in middle age (Keyes & Ryff, 1999). Their investment in living (purpose in life) and desire for continued self-realization (personal growth) dropped slightly from early to middle adulthood but still remained high before declining in late adulthood.

Adult development experts are virtually unanimous in their belief that midlife crises have been exaggerated (Brim, Ryff, & Kessler, 2004; Etaugh & Bridges, 2001; Lachman, 2004; Reid & Willis, 1999; Wethington, Kessler, & Pixley, 2004). In sum:

- The stage theories place too much emphasis on crises in development, especially midlife crises.
- There often is considerable individual variation in the way people experience the stages, a topic that we will turn to next.

Late adult transition: Age 60 to 65

Era of late adulthood: 60 to ?

Middle adult transition: Age 40 to 45

Culminating life structure for middle adulthood: 55 to 60

Age 50 transition: 50 to 55

Entry life structure for middle adulthood: 45 to 50

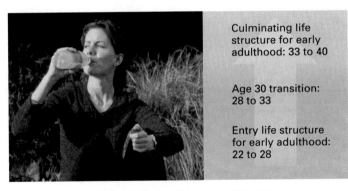

Early adult transition: Age 17 to 22

Culminating life structure for early adulthood: 33 to 40

Age 30 transition: 28 to 33

Entry life structure for early adulthood: 22 to 28

FIGURE 17.3 Levinson's Periods of Adult Development. According to Levinson, adulthood for men has three main stages, which are surrounded by transition periods. Specific tasks and challenges are associated with each stage.

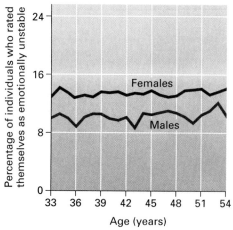

FIGURE 17.4 Emotional Instability and Age. In one longitudinal study, the emotional instability of individuals was assessed from age 33 to age 54 (Costa & McCrae, 1999; McCrae & Costa, 1990). No significant increase in emotional instability occurred during the middle-aged years.

Individual Variations Stage theories focus on the universals of adult personality development as they try to pin down stages that all individuals go through in their adult lives. These theories do not adequately address individual variations in adult development. One extensive study of a random sample of 500 men at midlife, for example, found extensive individual variation among men (Farrell & Rosenberg, 1981). In the individual variations view, middle-aged adults interpret, shape, alter, and give meaning to their lives (Arpanantikui, 2004).

Some individuals may experience a midlife crisis in some contexts of their lives but not others (Lachman, 2004). For example, turmoil and stress may characterize a person's life at work even while things are going smoothly at home.

Researchers have found that in one-third of the cases in which individuals have reported having a midlife crisis, the "crisis is triggered by life events such as a job loss, financial problems, or illness" (Lachman, 2004, p. 315). Let's now explore the role of life events in midlife development.

The Life-Events Approach

Age-related stages represent one major way to examine adult personality development. A second major way to conceptualize adult personality development is to focus on life events (Lorenz & others, 2006; Schwarzer & Schultz, 2003). In the early version of the life-events approach, life events were viewed as taxing circumstances for individuals, forcing them to change their personality (Holmes & Rahe, 1967). Such events as the death of a spouse, divorce, marriage, and so on were believed to involve varying degrees of stress, and therefore likely to influence the individual's development.

Today's life-events approach is more sophisticated (Cui & Vaillant, 1996; Hultsch & Plemons, 1979; McLeod, 1996). The **contemporary life-events approach** emphasizes that how life events influence the individual's development depends not only on the life event itself but also on mediating factors (physical health, family supports, for example), the individual's adaptation to the life event (appraisal of the threat, coping strategies, for example), the life-stage context, and the sociohistorical context (see figure 17.5). For example, if individuals are in poor health and have little family support, life events are likely to be more stressful. And a divorce may be more stressful after many years of marriage when adults are in their fifties than when they have only been married several years and are in their twenties (Chiriboga, 1982); the life-stage context of an event makes a difference. So does the sociohistorical context. For example, adults may be able to cope more effectively with divorce today than in the 1950s because divorce has become more commonplace and accepted in today's society. Whatever the context or mediating variables, however, one individual may perceive a life event as highly stressful while another individual may perceive the same event as a challenge.

Though the life-events approach is a valuable addition to understanding adult development, like other approaches to adult development, it has its drawbacks (Dohrenwend & Dohrenwend, 1978). One of the most significant drawbacks is that the life-events approach places too much emphasis on change. It does not adequately recognize the stability that, at least to some degree, characterizes adult development.

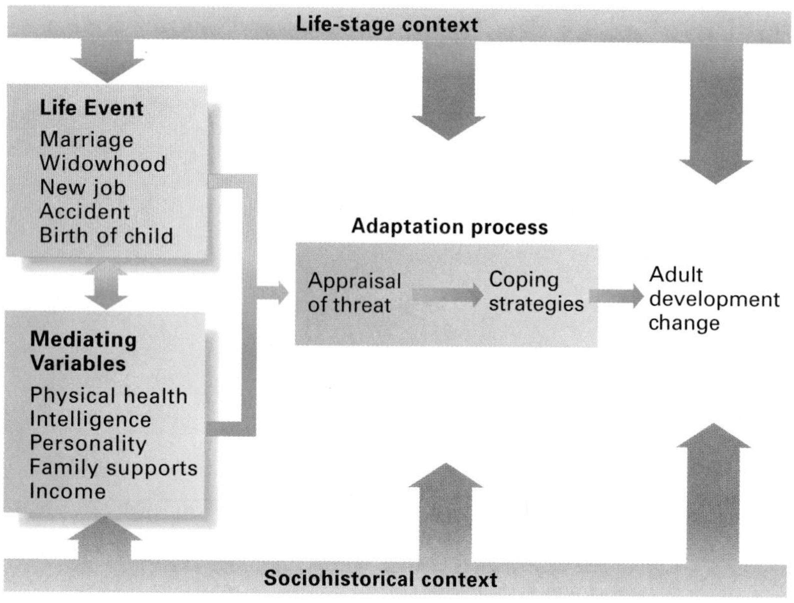

FIGURE 17.5 A Contemporary Life-Events Framework for Interpreting Adult Developmental Change. According to the contemporary life-events approach, the influence of a life event depends on the event itself, on mediating variables, on the life-stage and sociohistorical context, and on the individual's appraisal of the event and coping strategies.

contemporary life-events approach Emphasizes that how a life event influences the individual's development depends not only on the life event, but also on mediating factors, the individual's adaptation to the life event, the life-stage context, and the sociohistorical context.

Daily Hassles	Percentage of Times Checked		Daily Uplifts
Concerns about weight	52.4	76.3	Relating well with your spouse or lover
Health of family member	48.1	74.4	Relating well with friends
Rising prices of common goods	43.7	73.3	Completing a task
Home maintenance	42.8	72.7	Feeling healthy
Too many things to do	38.6	69.7	Getting enough sleep
Misplacing or losing things	38.1	68.4	Eating out
Yardwork or outside home maintenance	38.1	68.1	Meeting your responsibilities
Property, investment, or taxes	37.6	67.7	Visiting, phoning, or writing someone
Crime	37.1	66.7	Spending time with family
Physical appearance	35.9	65.5	Home (inside) pleasing to you

FIGURE 17.6 The Ten Most Frequent Daily Hassles and Uplifts of Middle-Aged Adults over a Nine-Month Period. *How do these hassles and uplifts compare with your own?*

Another drawback of the life-events approach is that it may not be life's major events that are the primary sources of stress, but our daily experiences (Baker, 2006; Jacobs & others, 2006; Mak & others, 2005). Enduring a boring but tense job or marriage and living in poverty do not show up on scales of major life events. Yet the everyday pounding we take from these living conditions can add up to a highly stressful life and eventually illness. In one study of 210 Florida police officers, the day-to-day friction associated with an inefficient justice system and distorted press accounts of police work were more stressful than responding to a felony in progress or making an arrest (Spielberger & Grier, 1983). Some psychologists believe we can gain greater insight into the source of life's stresses by focusing less on major events and more on daily hassles and daily uplifts (Lazarus & Folkman, 1984).

Many researchers have worked to identify the most significant daily hassles and daily uplifts. For example, one study found that the most frequent daily hassles of college students were wasting time, concerns about meeting high standards, and being lonely (Kanner & others, 1981). Among the most frequent uplifts of the college students were entertainment, getting along well with friends, and completing a task. In this same study, the most frequent daily hassles of middle-aged adults were concerns about weight and the health of a family member, while their most frequent daily uplifts involved relating well with a spouse or lover, or a friend (see figure 17.6). And the middle-aged adults were more likely than the college students to report that their daily hassles involved economic concerns (rising prices and taxes, for example). Critics of the daily hassles approach argue that some of the same problems involved with life-events scales occur when daily hassles are assessed (Dohrenwend & Shrout, 1985). For example, knowing about an adult's daily hassles tells us nothing about physical changes, about how the individual copes with hassles, or about how the individual perceives hassles.

Stress in Midlife

As we have seen, there is conclusive evidence that midlife is not a time when a majority of adults experience a tumultuous crisis, and when they do experience a midlife crisis it is often linked to stressful life events. Do middle-aged adults experience stress differently than young adults and older adults? A recent review by Margie Lachman (2004, p. 320) addressed this question, the highlights of which follow. One recent study using daily diaries over a one-week period found that both young and middle-aged adults had more stressful days "and more days with multiple stresses than older adults" (Almeida & Horn, 2004). This finding supports previous research that revealed stress is highest in young and middle-aged adults, then declines in older adults (Chiriboga, 1997). In the recent study, although young adults experienced daily stressors more frequently than middle-aged adults, middle-aged adults experienced more "overload" stressors that involved juggling too many activities at once (Almeida & Horn, 2004). Compared with older adults, however, both young and middle-aged adults experienced more overload stressors, especially involving children and financial risk (Almeida & Horn, 2004). Other researchers have found that middle-aged adults experience fewer stressors that they cannot control than young or older adults (Clark-Plaskie & Lachman, 1999). However, some aspects of personal control increase with age while others decrease. For example, middle-aged adults feel they have a greater sense of control over their finances, work, and marriage than younger adults but less control over their children and sex life (Lachman & Firth, 2004; Lachman & Weaver, 1998).

According to the study using adults' daily diaries, the most frequent daily stressor among middle-aged adults is interpersonal tension (Almeida & Horn, 2004). Gender and educational status, however, influence the stress experienced. Midlife women shouldered more "crossover" stressors—simultaneous demands from multiple contexts such as work and family—than their midlife male counterparts, and as a result they reported more distress. Further, midlife adults with lower-educational status reported the same number of stressors as midlife adults with higher educational status, but the individuals with lower-educational status were more likely to rate the stressors as more severe.

Contexts of Midlife Development

Both Sarah and Wanda, whose stories appeared at the opening to this chapter, are working mothers. In almost every other way, however, their lives could scarcely be more different. Why? Part of the answer might lie in the different contexts of their lives. The contemporary life-events approach (like Bronfenbrenner's theory, discussed in chapter 2) highlights the importance of the complex setting of our lives—of everything from our income and family supports to our sociohistorical circumstances. Let's examine how three aspects of the contexts of life influence development during middle adulthood: historical contexts (cohort effects), gender, and culture.

Historical Contexts (Cohort Effects)   Some developmentalists believe that changing historical times and different social expectations influence how different cohorts—groups of individuals born in the same year or time period—move through the life span (Schaie, 2007). Bernice Neugarten (1964) has been emphasizing the power of age-group or cohort since the 1960s. Our values, attitudes, expectations, and behaviors are influenced by the period in which we live. For example, individuals born during the difficult times of the Great Depression may have a different outlook on life than those born during the optimistic 1950s, says Neugarten.

Neugarten (1986) believes that the social environment of a particular age group can alter its **social clock**—the timetable according to which individuals are expected to accomplish life's tasks, such as getting married, having children, or establishing themselves in a career. Social clocks provide guides for our lives; individuals whose lives are not synchronized with these social clocks find life to be more stressful than those who are on schedule, says Neugarten. For example, the fact that Sarah's pregnancy occurred when she was a teenager probably increased the stressfulness of that pregnancy. Neugarten argues that today there is much less agreement than in the past on the right age or sequence for the occurrence of major life events such as having children or retiring. Indeed, one study found that, between the late 1950s and the late 1970s, there was a dramatic decline in adults' beliefs that there is a "right age" for major life events and achievements (Passuth, Maines, & Neugarten, 1984) (see figure 17.7).

social clock The timetable according to which individuals are expected to accomplish life's tasks, such as getting married, having children, or establishing themselves in a career.

Activity/event	Appropriate age range	Percent who agree (late '50s study)		Percent who agree (late '70s study)	
		Men	**Women**	**Men**	**Women**
Best age for a man to marry	20–25	80	90	42	42
Best age for a woman to marry	19–24	85	90	44	36
When most people should become grandparents	45–50	84	79	64	57
Best age for most people to finish school and go to work	20–22	86	82	36	38
When most men should be settled on a career	24–26	74	64	24	26
When most men hold their top jobs	45–50	71	58	38	31
When most people should be ready to retire	60–65	83	86	66	41
When a man has the most responsibilities	35–50	79	75	49	50
When a man accomplishes most	40–50	82	71	46	41
The prime of life for a man	35–50	86	80	59	66
When a woman has the most responsibilities	25–40	93	91	59	53
When a woman accomplishes most	30–45	94	92	57	48

FIGURE 17.7 Individuals' Conceptions of the Right Age for Major Life Events and Achievements: Late 1950s and Late 1970s

Trying to tease out universal truths and patterns about adult development from one birth cohort is complicated because the findings may not apply to another birth cohort. Most of the individuals studied by Levinson and Vaillant, for example, were born before and during the Great Depression. What was true for these individuals may not be true for today's 50-year-olds, born in the optimistic aftermath of World War II, or for the post–baby-boom generation as they approach the midlife transition. The midlife men in Levinson's and Vaillant's studies might have been burned out at a premature age rather than being representatives of a normal developmental pattern (Rossi, 1989).

Gender Contexts   Critics say that the stage theories of adult development have a male bias (Deutsch, 1991). For example, the central focus of stage theories is on career choice and work achievement, which historically have dominated men's life choices and life chances more than women's. The stage theories do not adequately address women's concerns about relationships, interdependence, and caring (Gilligan, 1982). The adult stage theories have also placed little importance on childbearing and child rearing. Women's family roles are complex and often have a higher salience in their lives than in men's lives. The role demands that women experience in balancing career and family are usually not experienced as intensely by men. And the type of stressors experienced by middle-aged women and men may differ. One recent study revealed that middle-aged women had more interpersonal stressors, whereas their male counterparts had more self-focused stressors (Almeida & Horn, 2004).

Many women who are now at midlife and beyond experienced a role shift in their late twenties, thirties, or beyond (Fodor & Franks, 1990). As they were engaging in traditional roles, the women's movement began and changed the lives of a substantial number of traditionally raised women and their families. Changes are still

Critics say the stage theories of adult development have a male bias by emphasizing career choice and achievement, and that they do not adequately address women's concerns about relationships, interdependence, and caring. The stage theories assume a normative sequence of development, but as women's roles have become more varied and complex, determining what is normative is difficult. *What kinds of changes have taken place in middle-aged women's lives in recent years?*

occurring for many midlife women. Basic changes in social attitudes regarding labor force participation, families, and gender roles have begun to broaden the opportunities available for women in middle adulthood as well as other life-span periods (Moen & Wethington, 1999). The effects of these changes are the most far-reaching for the baby-boom cohort now moving through midlife. The employment patterns across the life span for women now in their middle adult years more closely resemble those of men than they did in the past (Contemporary Research Press, 1993).

Should midlife and the years beyond be feared by women as bringing the loss of youth and opportunity, a time of decline? Or is it a new prime of life, a time for renewal, for shedding preoccupations with a youthful appearance and body, and for seeking new challenges, valuing maturity, and enjoying change?

In one study, the early fifties were indeed a new prime of life for many women (Mitchell & Helson, 1990). In the sample of 700 women aged 26 to 80, women in their early fifties most often described their lives as "first-rate." Conditions that distinguished the lives of women in their early fifties from those of women in other age periods included more "empty nests," better health, higher income, and more concern for parents. Women in their early fifties showed confidence, involvement, security, and breadth of personality.

In sum, the view that midlife is a negative age period for women is stereotypical, as so many perceptions of age periods are (Aldwin & Levenson, 2001; Huyck, 1999). Midlife is a diversified, heterogeneous period for women, just as it is for men.

Cultural Contexts In many cultures, especially nonindustrialized cultures, the concept of middle age is not very clear, or in some cases is absent. It is common in nonindustrialized societies to describe individuals as young or old, but not as middle-aged (Grambs, 1989). Some cultures have no words for "adolescent," "young adult," or "middle-aged adult."

Consider the Gusii culture, located south of the equator in the African country of Kenya. The Gusii divide the life course differently for females and males (LeVine, 1979):

Females	**Males**
1. Infant	1. Infant
2. Uncircumcised girl	2. Uncircumcised boy
3. Circumcised girl	3. Circumcised boy warrior
4. Married woman	4. Male elder
5. Female elder	

Thus, movement from one status to the next is due primarily to life events, not age, in the Gusii culture.

Although the Gusii do not have a clearly labeled midlife transition, some of the Gusii adults do reassess their lives around the age of 40. At this time, these Gusii adults examine their current status and the limited time they have remaining in their lives. Their physical strength is decreasing, and they know they cannot farm their land forever, so they seek spiritual powers by becoming ritual practitioners or healers. As in the American culture, however, a midlife crisis in the Gusii culture is the exception rather than the rule.

What is middle age like for women in other cultures? It depends on the modernity of the culture and the culture's view of gender roles (Dittmann-Kohli, 2005). Some anthropologists believe that when women become middle-aged in nonindustrialized societies they may experience certain advantages (Brown, 1985). First, they are often freed from cumbersome restrictions that were placed on them when they were younger. For example, in middle age they enjoy greater geographical mobility. Child care has ceased or can be delegated, and domestic chores are reduced. They may venture forth from the village for commercial opportunities, visits to relatives living at a distance, and religious events. Second, with middle age a woman

Gusii dancers perform on habitat day in Nairobi, Kenya. Movement from one status to another in the Gusii culture is due primarily to life events, not age. The Gusii do not have a clearly labeled midlife transition.

has the right to exercise authority over specified younger kin. Middle-aged women can extract labor from younger family members. The work of middle-aged women tends to be administrative, delegating tasks and making assignments to younger women. Middle-aged women also make important decisions for certain members of the younger generation: what a grandchild is to be named, who is ready to be initiated, and who is eligible to marry whom. A third major change brought on by middle age in nonindustrialized societies is eligibility for special statuses and the possibility that these provide recognition beyond the household. These statuses include the vocations of midwife, curer, holy woman, and matchmaker.

Even among industrialized cultures, the cultural context of middle age development may differ in significant ways. Consider the social clock. In one study, Australian adults were asked the same questions about the best age for experiencing various life circumstances as Neugarten had asked American adults (Peterson, 1996). Compared with the Americans, the Australian adults advocated later ages for marriage and grandparenthood, a younger age for leaving school, and a broader age range for retiring.

Review and Reflect • LEARNING GOAL 1

1 **Describe personality theories and development in middle adulthood**

Review
- What are some theories of adult stages of development?
- What is the life-events approach?
- How do middle-aged adults experience stress differently than young and older adults?
- How do contexts influence midlife development?

Reflect
- Which approach makes more sense to you—adult stage or life events? Or do you think both approaches should be considered in understanding an adult's development? Explain your answer.

2 STABILITY AND CHANGE

| Longitudinal Studies | Conclusions |

Sarah's adult life, described in the chapter opening, has followed a painful path. Were her sorrows inevitable as a result of how she learned to cope with problems earlier in life? Now middle-aged, is it possible for her to change her coping strategies or how she relates to other people? Recall from chapter 1 that questions like these about stability and change are an important issue in life-span development.

Longitudinal Studies

We will examine five longitudinal studies to help us understand the extent to which there is stability or change in adult development: Neugarten's Kansas City Study, Costa and McCrae's Baltimore Study, the Berkeley Longitudinal Studies, Helson's Mills College Study, and Vaillant's studies.

Openness	**C**onscientiousness	**E**xtraversion	**A**greeableness	**N**euroticism (emotional stability)
• Imaginative or practical	• Organized or disorganized	• Sociable or retiring	• Softhearted or ruthless	• Calm or anxious
• Interested in variety or routine	• Careful or careless	• Fun-loving or somber	• Trusting or suspicious	• Secure or insecure
• Independent or conforming	• Disciplined or impulsive	• Affectionate or reserved	• Helpful or uncooperative	• Self-satisfied or self-pitying

FIGURE 17.8 The Big Five Factors of Personality. Each of the broad supertraits that encompasses more narrow traits and characteristics. Use the acronym OCEAN to remember the big five personality factors (openness, conscientiousness, extraversion, agreeableness, neuroticism).

Neugarten's Kansas City Study   One of the earliest longitudinal studies of adult personality development was conducted by Bernice Neugarten (1964). Known as the "Kansas City Study," it studied individuals 40 to 80 years of age over a 10-year period. The adults were given personality tests, they filled out questionnaires, and they were interviewed.

Neugarten concluded that both stability and change characterized the adults as they aged. The characteristics that showed the most stability were styles of coping (such as avoiding problems or tackling them head-on), being satisfied with life, and being goal directed. In terms of change, as individuals aged from 40 to 60 they became more passive and were more likely to be threatened by the environment. For Sarah, these results suggest that change would likely be very difficult.

Costa and McCrae's Baltimore Study   Another major study of adult personality development continues to be conducted by Paul Costa and Robert McCrae (1995, 1998; McCrae & Costa, 2003, 2006). They focus on what are called the **big five factors of personality,** which are openness to experience, conscientiousness, extraversion, agreeableness, and neuroticism (emotional stability); they are described in figure 17.8. (Notice that if you create an acronym from these factor names, you will get the word *OCEAN.*) A number of research studies point toward these factors as important dimensions of personality (Costa & McCrae, 1995, 1998; McCrae & Costa, 2003, 2006).

Using their five-factor personality test, Costa and McCrae (1995, 2000) studied approximately a thousand college-educated men and women ages 20 to 96, assessing the same individuals over many years. Data collection began in the 1950s to the mid-1960s and is ongoing. Costa and McCrae concluded that considerable stability occurs in the five personality factors—emotional stability, extraversion, openness, agreeableness, and conscientiousness. However, in one recent study, conscientiousness peaked in midlife (Lachman & Bertrand, 2001), and another recent study found some indication that conscientiousness might continue to develop in late adulthood (Roberts, Walton, & Bogg, 2005).

In one study, McCrae and his colleagues (1999) found consistent age trends in personality in a number of cultures. In Germany, Croatia, Italy, Portugal, and Korea, older adults scored lower on extraversion and openness to experience than did younger adults. In these countries, the older adults scored higher in agreeableness and conscientiousness than younger adults. Similar patterns of age changes also were found in a study of Chinese and American adults (Yang, McCrae, & Costa, 1998). Few cultural variations were found in these studies.

A recent meta-analysis of personality stability and change organized according to the Big-Five framework included 87 longitudinal studies spanning 10 to 101 years of age (Roberts, Walton, & Viechtbauer, 2006):

www.mhhe.com/santrockld11

The Big Five
Paul Costa's Research

big five factors of personality Openness to experience, conscientiousness, extraversion, agreeableness, and neuroticism (emotional stability).

- Results for extraversion were complex until it was subdivided into social dominance (assertiveness, dominance) and social vitality (talkativeness, sociability). Social dominance increased from adolescence through middle adulthood while social vitality increased in adolescence and then decreased in early and late adulthood.
- Agreeableness and conscientiousness increased in early and middle adulthood.
- Neuroticism decreased in early adulthood.
- Openness-to-experience increased in adolescence and early adulthood and then decreased in late adulthood.

In general, personality traits changed most during early adulthood.

Berkeley Longitudinal Studies   In the Berkeley Longitudinal Studies more than 500 children and their parents were initially studied in the late 1920s and early 1930s. The book *Present and Past in Middle Life* (Eichorn & others, 1981) profiles these individuals as they became middle-aged. The results from early adolescence through a portion of midlife did not support either extreme in the debate over whether personality is characterized by stability or change. Some characteristics were more stable than others, however. The most stable characteristics were the degree to which individuals were intellectually oriented, self-confident, and open to new experiences. The characteristics that changed the most included the extent to which the individuals were nurturant or hostile and whether or not they had good self-control.

John Clausen (1993), one of the researchers in the Berkeley Longitudinal Studies, stresses that too much attention has been given to discontinuities for all members of the human species, as exemplified in the adult stage theories. Rather, he considers that some people experience recurrent crises and change a great deal over the life course, whereas others have more stable, continuous lives and change far less.

Helson's Mills College Study   Another longitudinal investigation of adult personality development was conducted by Ravenna Helson and her colleagues (Helson, 1997; Helson, Mitchell, & Moane, 1984; Helson & Wink, 1992; Stewart, Osgrove, & Helson, 2001). They initially studied 132 women who were seniors at Mills College in California in the late 1950s and then studied them again when they were in their thirties, forties, and fifties. Helson and her colleagues distinguished three main groups among the Mills women: family-oriented, career-oriented (whether or not they also wanted families), and those who followed neither path (women without children who pursued only low-level work).

Despite their different college profiles and their diverging life paths, the women in all three groups experienced some similar psychological changes over their adult years. Between the ages of 27 and the early forties, there was a shift toward less traditionally feminine attitudes, including greater dominance, greater interest in events outside the family, and more emotional stability. This may have been due to societal changes from the 1950s to the 1980s rather than to age changes. The women in the third group (women without children who pursued low-level work) changed less than those committed to career or family.

During their early forties, many of the women shared the concerns that stage theorists such as Levinson found in men: concern for young and old, introspectiveness, interest in roots, and awareness of limitations and death. However, the researchers in the Mills College Study concluded that rather than being in a midlife crisis, the women were experiencing *midlife consciousness*. The researchers also indicated that commitment to the tasks of early adulthood—whether to a career or family (or both)—helped women learn to control their impulses, develop interpersonal skills, become independent, and work hard to achieve goals. Women who did not commit themselves to one of these lifestyle patterns faced fewer challenges and did not develop as fully as the other women (Rosenfeld & Stark, 1987).

In the Mills College Study, some women moved toward becoming "pillars of society" in their early forties to early fifties. Menopause, caring for aging parents, and an empty nest were not associated with an increase in responsibility and self-control (Helson & Wink, 1992). The identity certainty and awareness of aging of the Mills College women increased from their thirties through their fifties (Stewart, Osgrove, & Helson, 2001).

George Vaillant's Studies Longitudinal studies by George Vaillant help us examine a somewhat different question than the studies described so far: Does personality at middle age predict what a person's life will be like in late adulthood? Vaillant (2002) has conducted three longitudinal studies of adult development and aging: (1) a sample of 268 socially advantaged Harvard graduates born about 1920 (called the Grant Study); (2) a sample of 456 socially disadvantaged inner-city men born about 1930; and (3) a sample of 90 middle-SES, intellectually gifted women born about 1910. These individuals have been assessed numerous times (in most cases, every two years), beginning in the 1920s to 1940s and continuing today for those still living. The main assessments involve extensive interviews with the participants, their parents, and teachers.

Vaillant categorized 75- to 80-year-olds as "happy-well," "sad-sick," and "dead." He used data collected from these individuals when they were 50 years of age to predict which categories they were likely to end up in at 75 to 80 years of age. Alcohol abuse and smoking at age 50 were the best predictors of which individuals would be dead at 75 to 80 years of age. Other factors at age 50 were linked with being in the "happy-well" category at 75 to 80 years of age:

- Getting regular exercise
- Avoiding being overweight
- Being well-educated
- Having a stable marriage
- Being future-oriented
- Being thankful and forgiving
- Empathizing with others
- Being active with other people
- Having good coping skills

Wealth and income at age 50 were not linked with being in the "happy-well" category at 75 to 80 years of age. Generativity in middle age (defined as "taking care of the next generation") was more strongly related than intimacy to whether individuals would have an enduring and happy marriage at 75 to 80 years of age (Vaillant, 2002).

The results for one of Vaillant's studies, the Grant Study of Harvard men, are shown in figure 17.9. Note that when individuals at 50 years of age were not heavy smokers, did not abuse alcohol, had a stable marriage, exercised, maintained a normal weight, and had good coping skills, they were more likely to be alive and happy at 75 to 80 years of age.

Conclusions

What can be concluded about stability and change in personality development during the adult years? Avshalom Caspi and Brent Roberts (2001) recently concluded that the evidence does not support the view that personality traits become completely fixed at a certain age in adulthood. However, they argue that change is typically limited, and in some cases the changes in personality are small. They also say that age is positively related

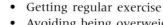

FIGURE 17.9 Links Between Characteristics at Age 50 and Health and Happiness at Age 75 to 80. In a longitudinal study, the characteristics shown above at age 50 were related to whether individuals were happy-well, sad-sick, or dead at age 75 to 80 (Vaillant, 2002).

to stability and that stability peaks in the fifties and sixties. That is, people show greater stability in their personality when they reach midlife than when they were younger adults. These findings support what is called a *cumulative personality model* of personality development, which states that with time and age people become more adept at interacting with their environment in ways that promote the stability of personality.

This does not mean that change is absent throughout midlife. Ample evidence shows that social contexts, new experiences, and sociohistorical changes can affect personality development (Mroczek, Spiro, & Griffin, 2006). However, Caspi and Roberts (2001) concluded that as people get older, stability increasingly outweighs change.

Other researchers argue that stability in personality begins to set in at about 30 years of age (Costa & McCrae, 2000; McCrae, 2001). However, some researchers conclude that personality change can be extensive in the adult years (Lewis, 2001). And some people likely change more than others (Mroczek, Spiro, & Griffin, 2006; Mroczek & others, 2006). In sum, there still is disagreement on how much stability and change characterize personality development in adulthood (Bertrand & Lachman, 2003; Caspi & Shiner, 2006; Mroczek, Spiro, & Griffin, 2006; Roberts, 2006).

At age 55, actor Jack Nicholson said "I feel exactly the same as I've always felt: a slightly reined-in voracious beast." Nicholson felt his personality had not changed much. Some others might think they have changed more. *How much does personality change and how does it stay the same through adulthood?*

Review and Reflect ● LEARNING GOAL 2

2 **Discuss stability and change in development during middle adulthood, including longitudinal studies**

Review
- Identify five longitudinal studies and explain their results.
- What conclusions can be reached about stability and change in development during middle adulthood?

Reflect
- Why is it important to conduct longitudinal studies when investigating stability and change in development?

3 CLOSE RELATIONSHIPS

Love and Marriage at Midlife · Sibling Relationships and Friendships · Intergenerational Relationships

The Empty Nest and Its Refilling · Grandparenting

There is a consensus among middle-aged Americans that a major component of well-being involves positive relationships with others, especially parents, spouse, and offspring (Lachman, 2004; Markus & others, 2004). To begin our examination of midlife relationships, let's explore love and marriage in middle-aged adults.

Love and Marriage at Midlife

Remember from chapter 15 that two major forms of love are romantic love and affectionate love. The fires of romantic love are strong in early adulthood. Affectionate, or companionate, love increases during middle adulthood. That is, physical

What characterizes marriage in middle adulthood?

attraction, romance, and passion are more important in new relationships, especially in early adulthood. Security, loyalty, and mutual emotional interest become more important as relationships mature, especially in middle adulthood.

Even some marriages that were difficult and rocky during early adulthood turn out to be better adjusted during middle adulthood. Although the partners may have lived through a great deal of turmoil, they eventually discover a deep and solid foundation on which to anchor their relationship. In middle adulthood, the partners may have fewer financial worries, less housework and chores, and more time with each other. Middle-aged partners are more likely to view their marriage as positive if they engage in mutual activities.

Most individuals in midlife who are married voice considerable satisfaction with being married. In a large-scale study of individuals in middle adulthood, 72 percent of those who were married said their marriage was either "excellent" or "very good" (Brim, 1999). Possibly by middle age, many of the worst marriages already have dissolved.

Are there any differences in the factors that predict whether couples will divorce in midlife compared with when they were younger adults? In chapter 15, "Socioemotional Development in Early Adulthood," we described John Gottman's extensive research on the factors that make a successful marriage. In a 14-year longitudinal study, Gottman and Robert Levenson (2000) found that couples who divorce in midlife tended to be cool, distant, and suppress their emotions. The midlife divorcing couples were alienated and avoidant. They were the kind of people you see in a restaurant who aren't talking with each other. It is a distant relationship with little or no laughter, love, or interest in each other. One of the divorcing midlife parents often feels as if his or her life is "empty." The researchers found that when divorce occurs among younger adults (often in the first seven years of a marriage), it is characterized by heated emotions that tend to burn out the marriage early. The young divorcing couples frequently were volatile and expressive, full of disappointment that they let each other know about.

Divorce in middle adulthood may be more positive in some ways, more negative in others, than divorce in early adulthood. On the one hand, for mature individuals, the perils of divorce can be fewer and less intense than for younger individuals. They have more resources, and they can use this time as an opportunity to simplify their lives by disposing of possessions, such as a large home, which they no longer need. Their children are adults and may be able to cope with their parents' divorce more effectively. The partners may have gained a better understanding of themselves and may be searching for changes that could include the end to a poor marriage.

On the other hand, the emotional and time commitment to marriage that has existed for so many years may not be lightly given up. Many midlife individuals perceive a divorce as failing in the best years of their lives. The divorcer might see the situation as an escape from an untenable relationship, but the divorced partner usually sees it as betrayal, the ending of a relationship that had been built up over many years and that involved a great deal of commitment and trust.

A recent survey by AARP (2004) of 1,148 40- to 79-year-olds who were divorced at least once in their forties, fifties, or sixties found that staying married because of their children was by far the main reason many people took so long to become divorced. Despite the worry and stress involved in going through a divorce, three in four of the divorcees said they had made the right decision to dissolve their marriage and reported a positive outlook on life. Sixty-six percent of the divorced women said they initiated the divorce compared with only 41 percent of the divorced men. The divorced women were much more afraid of having financial problems (44 percent) than the divorced men (11 percent). Following are the main reasons the middle-aged and older adults cited for their divorce:

Main Causes for Women	**Main Causes for Men**
1. Verbal, physical, or emotional abuse (23 percent)	1. No obvious problems, just fell out of love (17 percent)
2. Alcohol or drug abuse (18 percent)	2. Cheating (14 percent)
3. Cheating (17 percent)	3. Different values, lifestyles (14 percent)

A recent study found that women who initiated a divorce in midlife were characterized more by self-focused growth and optimism than women whose husbands initiated the divorce (Sakraida, 2005).

The Empty Nest and Its Refilling

An important event in a family is the launching of a child into adult life. Parents face new adjustments as a result of the child's absence. Students usually think that their parents suffer from their absence. In fact, parents who live vicariously through their children might experience the **empty nest syndrome,** which includes a decline in marital satisfaction after children leave the home. For most parents, however, marital satisfaction does not decline after children have left home. Rather, for most parents marital satisfaction increases during the years after child rearing (Fingerman, 2003, 2006; Fingerman & Lang, 2004). With their children gone, marital partners have time to pursue career interests and more time for each other (Ward & Spitze, 2004).

In today's uncertain economic climate, the refilling of the empty nest is becoming a common occurrence as adult children return to live at home after several years of college, after graduating from college, or to save money after taking a full-time job (Furman, 2005; Perlman & Shaffer, 2004; Noriko, 2005; Owen, 2005). Young adults also may move back in with their parents after an unsuccessful career or a divorce. And some individuals don't leave home at all until their middle to late twenties because they cannot financially support themselves. Numerous labels have been applied to these young adults who return to their parents' homes to live, including "boomerang kids," and "B2B" (or Back-to-Bedroom) (Furman, 2005).

The middle generation has always provided support for the younger generation, even after the nest is bare. Through loans and monetary gifts for education, and through emotional support, the middle generation has helped the younger generation. Adult children appreciate the financial and emotional support their parents provide them at a time when they often feel considerable stress about their career, work, and lifestyle. And parents feel good that they can provide this support.

However, as with most family living arrangements, there are both pluses and minuses when adult children return to live at home. One of the most common complaints voiced by both adult children and their parents is a loss of privacy. The adult

Doonesbury   BY GARRY TRUDEAU

empty nest syndrome A decrease in marital satisfaction after children leave home, because parents derive considerable satisfaction from their children.

children complain that their parents restrict their independence, cramp their sex lives, reduce their rock music listening, and treat them as children rather than adults. Parents often complain that their quiet home has become noisy, that they stay up late worrying when their adult children will come home, that meals are difficult to plan because of conflicting schedules, that their relationship as a married couple has been invaded, and that they have to shoulder too much responsibility for their adult children. In sum, when adult children return home to live, a disequilibrium in family life is created, which requires considerable adaptation on the part of parents and their adult children. To read about strategies that young adults and their parents can use to get along better, see the Applications in Life-Span Development interlude.

APPLICATIONS IN LIFE-SPAN DEVELOPMENT

Strategies for Parents and Their Young Adult Children

When adult children ask to return home to live, parents and their adult children should agree on the conditions and expectations beforehand. For example, they might discuss and agree on whether young adults will pay rent, wash their own clothes, cook their own meals, do any household chores, pay their phone bills, come and go as they please, be sexually active or drink alcohol at home, and so on. If these conditions aren't negotiated at the beginning, conflict often results because the expectations of parents and young adult children will likely be violated.

Parents need to treat young adult children more like adults than children and let go of much of their parenting role. Parents should not interact with young adult children as if they are dependent children who need to be closely monitored and protected but rather as adults who are capable of responsible, mature behavior. Adult children have the right to choose how much they sleep and eat, how they dress, who they choose as friends and lovers, what career they pursue, and how they spend their money. However, if the young adult children act in ways that interfere with their parents' lifestyles, parents need to say so. The discussion should focus not on the young adult children's choices but on how their activities are unacceptable while living together in the same home.

Some parents don't let go of their young adult children when they should. They engage in "permaparenting," which can impede not only their adult children's movement toward independence and responsibility but also their own postparenting lives. "Helicopter parents" is another label used for parents who hover too closely in their effort to ensure that their children succeed in college and adult life (Paul, 2003). Although well intentioned, this intrusiveness by parents can slow the process by which their children become responsible adults.

When they move back home, young adult children need to think about how they will need to change their behavior to make the living arrangement work. Elina Furman (2005) provides some good recommendations in *Boomerang nation: How to survive with your parents . . . the second time around.* She recommends that when young adult children move back home they expect to make adjustments. And as recommended earlier, she urges young adults to sit down with their parents and negotiate the ground rules for living at home before they actually move back. Furman also recommends that young adults set a deadline for how long they will live at home and then stay focused on their goals (whether to save enough money to pay off their debts, save enough to start a business or buy their own home, finish graduate school, and so on). Too often young adults spend the money they save by moving home on such luxuries as spending binges, nights on the town, expensive clothes, and unnecessary travel, which only delay their ability to move out of their parents' home.

What are some strategies that can help parents and their young adult children get along better?

Sibling Relationships and Friendships

Sibling relationships persist over the entire life span for most adults (Teti, 2001; White, 2001). Eighty-five percent of today's adults have at least one living sibling. Sibling relationships in adulthood may be extremely close, apathetic, or highly rivalrous. The majority of sibling relationships in adulthood have been found to be close (Cicirelli, 1991). Those siblings who are psychologically close to each other in adulthood tended to be that way in childhood. It is rare for sibling closeness to develop for the first time in adulthood (Dunn, 1984).

Friendships continue to be important in middle adulthood just as they were in early adulthood (Antonucci, 1989). It takes time to develop intimate friendships, so friendships that have endured over the adult years are often deeper than those that have just been formed in middle adulthood.

Grandparenting

Many adults become grandparents for the first time during middle age. Researchers have consistently found that grandmothers have more contact with grandchildren than grandfathers (Reitzes & Mutran, 2004; Roberto, Allen, & Blieszner, 2001; Watson, Randolph, & Lyons, 2005). Perhaps women tend to define their role as grandmothers as part of their responsibility for maintaining ties between family members across generations. Men may have fewer expectations about the grandfather role and see it as more voluntary.

How satisfying is it to be a grandparent? What roles do grandparents assume, and what styles do they use with their grandchildren?

Satisfaction with Grandparenting
A majority of grandparents say that grandparenting is easier than parenting. In one study, frequent contact with grandchildren predicted high levels of satisfaction with grandparenting for both grandmothers and grandfathers (Peterson, 1999). Opportunities to observe their grandchildren's development and share in their activities were described as the best features of being a grandparent; lack of frequent contact with grandchildren was pointed to as the worst feature. Only a small minority (8 percent) of Australian grandparents said that they were more dissatisfied than satisfied with their grandparenting role (Peterson, 1999).

What are some grandparents roles and styles?

Grandparent Roles and Styles
What is the meaning of the grandparent role? Three prominent meanings are attached to being a grandparent (Neugarten & Weinstein, 1964). For some older adults, being a grandparent is a source of biological reward and continuity. For others, being a grandparent is a source of emotional self-fulfillment, generating feelings of companionship and satisfaction that may have been missing in earlier adult-child relationships. And for yet others, being a grandparent is a remote role.

The grandparent role may have different functions in different families, in different ethnic groups and cultures, and in different situations (Kivnick & Sinclair, 1996; Lee, Ensminger, & LaVeist, 2005; Watson, Randolph, & Lyons, 2005). For example, in one study of White, African American, and Mexican American grandparents and grandchildren, the Mexican American grandparents saw their grandchildren more frequently, provided more support for the grandchildren and their parents, and had more satisfying relationships with their grandchildren (Bengtson, 1985). And in a study of three generations of families in Chicago, grandmothers had closer relationships with their children and grandchildren and gave more personal advice than grandfathers did (Hagestad, 1985).

The diversity of grandparenting also was apparent in an early investigation of how grandparents interacted with their grandchildren (Neugarten & Weinstein, 1964). Three styles were dominant—formal, fun-seeking, and distant. In the formal

Today's Grandparent
Foundation of Grandparenting
The Grandparent Network
Adult Children and Their Elderly Parents
Grandparent Visitation Rights

style, the grandparent performed what was considered to be a proper and prescribed role. These grandparents showed a strong interest in their grandchildren, but were careful not to give child-rearing advice. In the fun-seeking style, the grandparent was informal and playful. Grandchildren were a source of leisure activity; mutual satisfaction was emphasized. A substantial portion of grandparents were distant figures. In the distant-figure style, the grandparent was benevolent but interaction was infrequent. Grandparents who were over the age of 65 were more likely to display a formal style of interaction; those under 65 were more likely to display a fun-seeking style.

The Changing Profile of Grandparents

An increasing number of U.S. grandchildren live with their grandparents (Gerard, Landry-Meyer, & Roe, 2006; Minkler & Fuller-Thompson, 2005; Ross & Aday, 2006). In 1980, 2.3 million grandchildren lived with their grandparents, but in 2000 that figure had reached 5.6 million (U.S. Bureau of the Census, 2001). Forty-two percent of those grandparents are responsible for their grandchildren. Divorce, adolescent pregnancies, and drug use by parents are the main reasons that grandparents are thrust back into the "parenting" role they thought they had shed. One recent study of grandparents raising their grandchildren found that stress was linked with three conditions: younger grandparents, grandchildren with physical and psychological problems, and low family cohesion (Sands & Goldberg-Glen, 2000).

Less than 20 percent of grandparents whose grandchildren move in with them are 65 years old or older. Almost half of the grandchildren who move in with grandparents are raised by a single grandmother. These families are mainly African American (53 percent). When both grandparents are raising grandchildren, the families are overwhelmingly White.

Grandparents who take in grandchildren are in better health, are better educated, are more likely to be working outside the home, and are younger than grandparents who move in with their children. According to the 2000 U.S. Census report, a majority of the grandparents living with their children contributed to the family income and provided child care while parents worked. Only about 10 percent of the grandparents who move in with their children and grandchildren are in poverty. Almost half of the grandparents who move in with their children are immigrants. Partly because women live longer than men, there are more grandmothers than grandfathers (2.9 million versus 1.7 million) who live with their children. About 70 percent of the grandparents who move in with their children are grandmothers.

As divorce and remarriage have become more common, a special concern of grandparents is visitation privileges with their grandchildren. In the last 10 to 15 years, more states have passed laws giving grandparents the right to petition a court for visitation privileges with their grandchildren, even if a parent objects. Whether such forced visitation rights for grandparents are in the child's best interest is still being debated.

Intergenerational Relationships

Adults in midlife play important roles in the lives of the young and the old (Lachman, 2004). Middle-aged adults share their experience and transmit values to the younger generation (McAdams, 2001). They may be launching children and experiencing the empty nest, adjusting to having grown children return home, or becoming grandparents. They also may be giving or receiving financial assistance, caring for a widowed or sick parent, or adapting to being

What is the nature of intergenerational relationships?

the oldest generation after both parents have died (Acquilino, 2005; Putney & Bengtson, 2001; Silverstein, Gans, & Yang, 2006; Wolff & Casper, 2006).

With each new generation, personality characteristics, attitudes, and values are replicated or changed. As older family members die, their biological, intellectual, emotional, and personal legacies are carried on in the next generation (De Litvan & Manzano, 2005; Soenens & others 2005). Their children become the oldest generation and their grandchildren the second generation. As adult children become middle-aged they often develop more positive perceptions of their parents (Field, 1999). In one recent study, conflicts between mothers and daughters decreased across the life course in both the United States and Japan (Akiyama & Antonucci, 1999).

For the most part, family members maintain considerable contact across generations (Allen, Blieszner, & Roberto, 2000; Bengtson, 2001; Miller-Day, 2004). As we continue to stay connected with our parents and our children as we age, both similarity and dissimilarity across generations are found. For example, similarity between parents and an adult child is most noticeable in religion and politics, least in gender roles, lifestyle, and work orientation.

What are the most common conflicts between parents and their adult children? In one study, they included communication and interaction style (such as "He is always yelling" and "She is too critical"), habits and lifestyle choices (such as sexual activity, living arrangements), child-rearing practices and values (such as decisions about having children, being permissive or controlling), politics, religion, and ideology (such as lack of religious involvement) (Clarke & others, 1999). In this study, there were generational differences in perceptions of the main conflicts between parents and adult children. Parents most often listed habits and lifestyle choices; adult children cited communication and interaction style.

The relationship between parents and their adult children is related to the nature of their earlier relationship, as these studies indicate:

- In a New Zealand study of the child-rearing antecedents of intergenerational relations, supportive family environments and parenting in childhood (assessed when the children were 3 to 15 years of age) were linked with more positive relationships (in terms of contact, closeness, conflict, and reciprocal assistance) between the children and their middle-aged parents when the children were 26 years of age (Belsky & others, 2001).
- In another study, individuals who felt trusted by their parents in adolescence reported greater closeness to their parents in early adulthood (Jacobs & Tanner, 1999). Also in this study, daughters who had experienced long-term lack of trust during adolescence were more alienated from their parents as young adults than sons who had similar experiences.
- In another study, the motivation of adult children to provide social support to their older parents was linked with earlier family experiences (Silverstein & others, 2002). Children who spent more time in shared activities with their parents and were given more financial support by them earlier in their lives provided more support to their parents when they became older.
- In a recent study, divorce in the grandparent generation was linked to less education and marital conflict in the grandchild generation (Amato & Cheadle, 2005). These links were mediated by these characteristics of the middle generation: less education, increased marital conflict, and more tension in early parent-child relationships.

Gender differences also characterize intergenerational relationships (Bengtson, 2001; Etaugh & Bridges, 2001, 2004; Miller-Day, 2004; Nauck & Suckow, 2006). In one study, mothers and their daughters had much closer relationships during their adult years than mothers and sons, fathers and daughters, and fathers and sons (Rossi, 1989). Also in this study, married men were more involved with their wives' kin than with their own. And maternal grandmothers and maternal aunts were cited twice as often as their counterparts on the paternal side of the family as the most important

In case you're worried about what's going to become of the younger generation, it's going to grow up and start worrying about the younger generation.

—Roger Allen
American Writer, 20th Century

The Sandwich Generation

or loved relative. To read further about intergenerational relationships between mothers and daughters, see the Research in Life-Span Development interlude.

RESEARCH IN LIFE-SPAN DEVELOPMENT

"We Had a Nice Little Chat": Mothers' and Daughters' Descriptions of Enjoyable Visits at Different Points in Adult Development

Although researchers have documented that mothers and daughters in adulthood generally have frequent contact and mutually positive feelings, little is known about what mothers and daughters like about their relationship. To examine this topic, Karen Fingerman (2000) studied 48 pairs of older adult mothers (mean age = 76 years) and their middle-aged daughters (mean age = 46 years) and 44 pairs of middle-aged mothers (mean age = 47 years) and their young adult daughters (mean age = 21 years). Interviewers asked participants:

Think about the last time you had a particularly enjoyable visit with your daughter/mother. By visit, I mean a time when you got together, went to the other's house (or your daughter came home from college), or talked on the phone. Tell a little about what went on. Please provide as much information as you can about the visit, what happened, and why it was particularly enjoyable (p. 98).

Transcriptions of the visits were coded and the results for the coded categories were (Fingerman, 2000, pp. 100–102):

- *Investment and connection.* Mothers in both age groups were more invested in their relationship with their daughters than their daughters were with them.
- *Family.* Older mothers and daughters were more likely than younger pairs to describe the larger kin network, such as the daughter's children, siblings, father, husband, or the family in general. By contrast, younger pairs "were more likely to stick to their own relationship and to discuss situations in which the two of them had enjoyed a special event."
- *Nurturance.* "Young adult daughters and older adult mothers were more likely to report pleasure from having the other party help them in some way than were middle-aged women."
- *Interacting.* Younger mothers tended to focus on activities in which they enjoyed their daughters' emergence as a young adult. "Younger daughters derived pleasure from having their mothers around as sounding boards, whereas older daughters" enjoyed the link to the past that their mothers represented.
- *Negative comments.* Mothers and daughters in the older pairs "were more likely to say something negative than were younger mothers and daughters," although these comments were still infrequent.

In sum, mothers' and daughters' perceptions of their visits reflected a combination of individual developmental needs. Although the focus of mothers' and daughters' relationships may change, in general, mothers were more invested in their daughters than the reverse throughout adulthood.

Middle-aged adults have been described as the "sandwich," "squeezed," or "overload" generation because of the responsibilities they have for their adolescent and young adult children on the one hand and their aging parents on the other (Etaugh & Bridges, 2004; Riley & Bowen, 2005). These simultaneous pressures from adolescents or young adult children and aging parents may contribute to stress in middle adulthood. Many middle-aged adults experience considerable stress when their parents become very ill and die. One survey found that when adults enter midlife, 41 percent have both parents alive but that 77 percent leave midlife with no parents alive (Bumpass & Aquilino, 1994).

Recent analyses suggest, however, that fewer middle-aged adults are "sandwiched" between multiple roles as caregiver to a parent and to their own children than often is reported in the media (Hoyer & Roodin, 2003). In one study, a large majority of middle-aged children did not have the responsibility of providing direct care for their parents (Rosenthal, Martin-Matthews, & Matthews, 1996). When this type of responsibility was required, it most often was assumed by daughters in their mid-to-late fifties who did not simultaneously have direct child-care or child-rearing responsibilities. In another study, the point at which some adult children have to take responsibility for caring for their parents usually coincided with the launch of their own adult children who were beginning their own careers and families.

When adults immigrate to another country, intergenerational stress may be increased. To read about the role of immigration and acculturation in intergenerational relationships among Mexican Americans, see the Diversity in Life-Span Development interlude.

DIVERSITY IN LIFE-SPAN DEVELOPMENT

Intergenerational Relationships in Mexican American Families: The Effects of Immigration and Acculturation

In the last several decades, increasing numbers of Mexicans have immigrated to the United States, and their numbers are expected to increase. The pattern of immigration usually involves separation from the extended family (Crowley, Lichter, & Qian, 2006; Parra-Cardona & others, 2006). It may also involve separation of immediate family members, with the husband coming first and then later bringing his wife and children. Those initially isolated, especially the wife, experience considerable stress due to relocation and the absence of family and friends. Within several years, a social network is usually established in the ethnic neighborhood.

As soon as some stability in their lives is achieved, Mexican families may sponsor the immigration of extended family members, such as a maternal or paternal sister or mother who provides child care and enables the mother to go to work. In some cases, the older generation remains behind and joins their grown children in old age. The accessibility of Mexico facilitates visits to and from the native village for vacations or at a time of crisis, such as when an adolescent runs away from home.

Three levels of acculturation often exist within a Mexican American family (Falicov & Karrer, 1980). The mother and the grandparents may be at the beginning level, the father at an intermediate level, and the children at an advanced level. The discrepancies between acculturation levels can give rise to conflicting expectations within the family (Sarkisian, Gerena, & Gerstel, 2006). The immigrant parents' model of child rearing may be out of phase with the dominant culture's model, which may cause reverberations through the family's generations, as we discussed in earlier chapters. For example, the mother and grandparents may be especially resistant to the demands for autonomy and dating made by adolescent daughters, and so may the father (Wilkinson-Lee & others, 2006). And in recent years an increasing number of female youth leave their Mexican American homes to further their education, an event that is often stressful for families with strong ties to Mexican values.

As children leave home, parents begin to face their future as a middle-aged couple. This may be difficult for many Mexican American middle-aged couples because their value orientations have prepared them better for parenting than for relating

(continued on next page)

as a married couple. Family therapists who work with Mexican Americans frequently report that a common pattern is psychological distance between the spouses and a type of emotional separation in midlife. The marital partners continue to live together and carry on their family duties but relate to each other only at a surface level. The younger generation of Mexican Americans may find it difficult to accept their parents' lifestyle, may question their marital arrangement, and may rebel against their value orientations. Despite the intergenerational stress that may be brought about by immigration and acculturation, the majority of Mexican American families maintain considerable contact across generations and continue to have a strong family orientation (Escandon, 2006).

Lilian Troll has conducted research on intergenerational relations and women's development in midlife. To read about her work, see the Careers in Life-Span Development profile.

CAREERS
in LIFE-SPAN DEVELOPMENT

Lillian Troll
Professor of Psychology and Life-Span
Development and Researcher on Families
and Aging Women

Lillian Troll has been a leading figure in the field of adult development and aging. She graduated from the University of Chicago with a joint major in psychology and premedicine. During World War II she dropped out of graduate school to work in Washington, where she helped develop the array of Army screening and achievement tests. After the war she became a suburban housewife and mother, following her husband's career moves from city to city. For a decade, the closest Lillian came to a career in life-span development was founding a nursery school in New Jersey.

Many years later, after her divorce, Lillian returned to the University of Chicago and, in 1967, completed a Ph.D. in life-span development. She then began teaching and conducting research on generations in the family and women's development, first at Wayne State University in Detroit and then, as a 60-year-old grandmother, at Rutgers University Psychology Department. In 1986 she retired and moved to California, where she continued research at the University of California at San Francisco, by collaborating with Colleen Johnson on a longitudinal study of the "oldest old" (people over 85).

Lillian Troll (*left*) with participants in a study of aging women.

Review and Reflect • LEARNING GOAL 3

3 **Identify some important aspects of close relationships in middle adulthood**

Review
- How can love and marriage at midlife be characterized?
- What is the empty nest? How has it been refilling?
- What are sibling relationships and friendships like in middle adulthood?
- What is the nature of grandparenting?
- What are relationships across generations like?

Reflect
- Might there be distinctive phases of middle adulthood? Think about what you have read in this chapter and chapter 16 and describe what these subphases might be. Would they be linked to age? If so, how?

REACH YOUR LEARNING GOALS

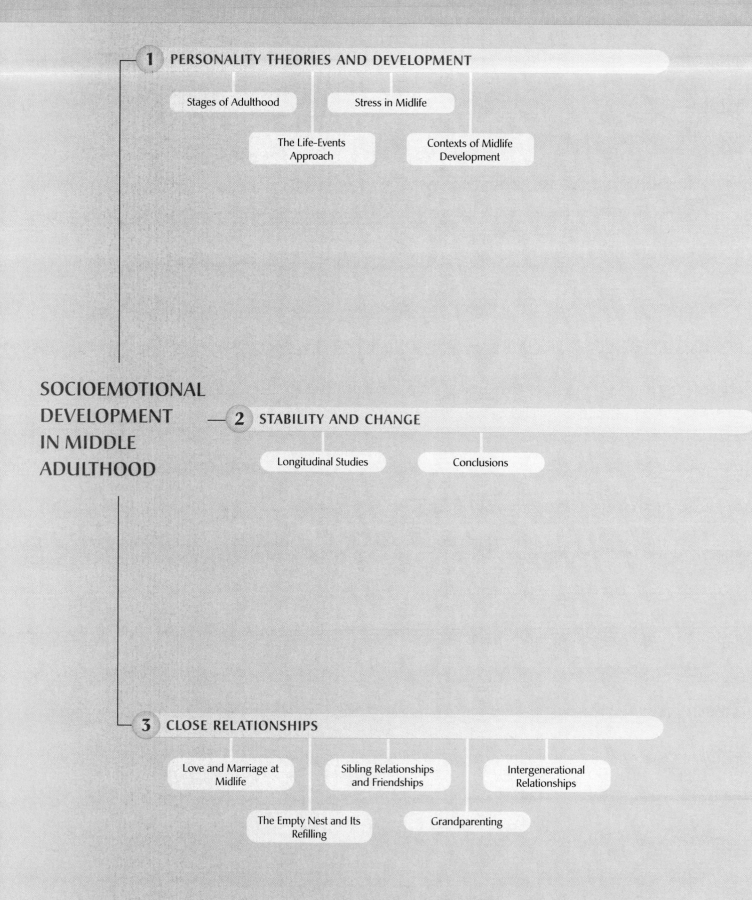

SOCIOEMOTIONAL DEVELOPMENT IN MIDDLE ADULTHOOD

1 PERSONALITY THEORIES AND DEVELOPMENT

- Stages of Adulthood
- The Life-Events Approach
- Stress in Midlife
- Contexts of Midlife Development

2 STABILITY AND CHANGE

- Longitudinal Studies
- Conclusions

3 CLOSE RELATIONSHIPS

- Love and Marriage at Midlife
- The Empty Nest and Its Refilling
- Sibling Relationships and Friendships
- Grandparenting
- Intergenerational Relationships

SUMMARY

1 Personality Theories and Development: *Describe personality theories and development in middle adulthood*

Stages of Adulthood

Erikson says that the seventh stage of the human life span, generativity versus stagnation, occurs in middle adulthood. Four types of generativity are biological, parental, work, and cultural. In Levinson's theory, developmental tasks should be mastered at different points in development and changes in middle age focus on four conflicts: being young versus being old, being destructive versus being constructive, being masculine versus being feminine, and being attached to others versus being separated from them. Levinson proposed that a majority of Americans, especially men, experience a midlife crisis. Research, though, indicates that midlife crises are not pervasive. There is considerable individual variation in development during the middle adulthood years.

The Life-Events Approach

According to the early version of the life-events approach, life events produce taxing circumstances that create stress in people's lives. In the contemporary version of the life-events approach, how life events influence the individual's development depends not only on the life event but also on mediating factors, adaptation to the event, the life-stage context, and the sociohistorical context.

Stress in Midlife

Researchers have found that young and middle-aged adults experience more stressful days, more multiple stressors, and more overload stressors than do older adults. Midlife adults report fewer stressors over which they have no control than young and older adults.

Contexts of Midlife Development

Neugarten believes that the social environment of a particular cohort can alter its social clock—the timetable according to which individuals are expected to accomplish life's tasks. Critics say that the adult stage theories are male biased because they place too much emphasis on achievement and careers and do not adequately address women's concerns about relationships. Midlife is a heterogeneous period for women, as it is for men. For some women, midlife is the prime of their lives. Many cultures do not have a clear concept of middle age. In many nonindustrialized societies, a woman's status improves in middle age.

2 Stability and Change: *Discuss stability and change in development during middle adulthood, including longitudinal studies*

Longitudinal Studies

In Neugarten's Kansas City Study, both stability and change were found. Styles of coping, life satisfaction, and being goal-directed were the most stable. Individuals became more passive and feared the environment more as they aged through middle adulthood. In Costa and McCrae's Baltimore Study, the big five personality factors—emotional stability, extraversion, openness to experience, agreeableness, and conscientiousness—showed considerable stability. However, a recent meta-analysis of the big five personality factors found increases and declines of specific factors across the adult years, with the most change occurring in early adulthood. In the Berkeley Longitudinal Studies, the extremes in the stability-change argument were not supported. The most stable characteristics were intellectual orientation, self-confidence, and openness to new experiences. The characteristics that changed the most were nurturance, hostility, and self-control. In Helson's Mills College Study of women, there was a shift toward less traditional feminine characteristics from age 27 to the early forties, but this might have been due to societal changes. In their early forties, women experienced many of the concerns that Levinson described for men. However, rather than a midlife crisis, this is best called midlife consciousness. George Vaillant's research revealed links between a number of characteristics at age 50 and health and well-being at 75 to 80 years of age.

Conclusions

The issue of whether personality is stable or changes in adulthood continues to be debated. Some researchers believe that stability peaks in the fifties and sixties (Caspi & Roberts, 2001), others that it begins to stabilize at about 30 (Costa & McCrae, 2000), and yet others argue for more change (Lewis, 2001). Some people change more than others.

3 Close Relationships: *Identify some important aspects of close relationships in middle adulthood*

Love and Marriage at Midlife

Affectionate love increases in midlife, especially in marriages that have endured many years. A majority of middle-aged adults who are married say that their marriage is good or excellent. Researchers recently have found that couples who divorce in midlife are more likely to have a cool, distant, emotionally suppressed relationship, whereas divorcing young adults are more likely to have an emotionally volatile and expressive relationship.

The Empty Nest and Its Refilling

Rather than decreasing marital satisfaction as once thought, the empty nest increases it for most parents. An increasing number of young adults are returning home to live with their parents.

Sibling Relationships and Friendships

Sibling relationships continue throughout life. Some are close, others are distant. Friendships continue to be important in middle age.

Grandparenting

Most grandparents are satisfied with their role. There are different grandparent roles and styles. Grandmothers spend more time with grandchildren than grandfathers and the grandmother role involves greater expectations for maintaining ties across generations than the grandfather role. The profile of grandparents is changing, due to such factors as divorce and remarriage. An increasing number of U.S. grandchildren live with their grandparents.

Intergenerational Relationships

Family members usually maintain contact across generations. Mothers and daughters have the closest relationships. The middle-aged generation, which has been called the "sandwich" or "squeezed" generation, plays an important role in linking generations.

KEY TERMS

contemporary life-events
    approach 562
social clock 564

big five factors of
    personality 568
empty nest syndrome 573

KEY PEOPLE

Erik Erikson 559
Carol Ryff 559
George Vaillant 560
Daniel Levinson 560
Bernice Neugarten 564

Paul Costa and Robert
    McCrae 568
John Clausen 569
Ravenna Helson 569

Avshalom Caspi and Brent
    Roberts 570
John Gottman and Robert
    Levenson 572
Karen Fingerman 578

E-LEARNING TOOLS

To help you master the material in this chapter, you'll find a number of valuable study tools on the LifeMap CD-ROM that accompanies this book and on the Online Learning Center for *Life-Span Development*, eleventh edition, at **www.mhhe.com/santrockld11**.

Video Clips

In the margins of this book there are icons directing you to the LifeMap CD-ROM that accompanies the book. There you'll find a video for chapter 17 called "Balancing Work and Family." In this segment, a working mother describes her strategies for dealing with this challenge.

Self-Assessment

Connect to **www.mhhe.com/santrockld11** to learn more about the stress-illness relationship, how extraverted or introverted you are, and how generative you are by completing the self-assessments, *Life Events and My Chance of Significant Illness in the Coming Year, Extraversion*, and *How Generative Am I?*

Taking It to the Net

Connect to **www.mhhe.com/santrockld11** to research the answers to this question:

What did psychologist Daniel Goleman find out about how Erik Erikson and his wife Joan dealt with Erikson's seventh developmental stage, generativity vs. stagnation, in their own lives?

Health and Well-Being, Parenting, and Education Exercises

Build your decision-making skills by trying your hand at the health and well-being, parenting, and education exercises. Connect to **www.mhhe.com/santrockld11** to research the answers and complete the exercises.

Each of us stands alone at the heart of the earth, pierced through by a ray of sunshine: And suddenly it is evening.

—SALVATORE QUASIMODO
Italian Poet, 20th Century

CHAPTER OUTLINE

LEARNING GOALS

LONGEVITY

Life Expectancy and Life Span
Young-Old, the Old-Old, and the Oldest-Old
Biological Theories of Aging

1 Characterize longevity and the biological theories of aging

THE COURSE OF PHYSICAL DEVELOPMENT IN LATE ADULTHOOD

The Aging Brain
The Immune System
Physical Appearance and Movement
Sensory Development
The Circulatory System and Lungs
Sexuality

2 Describe how a person's brain and body change in late adulthood

HEALTH

Health Problems
Substance Abuse
Exercise, Nutrition, and Weight
Health Treatment

3 Identify health problems in older adults and how they can be treated

Images of Life-Span Development
Learning to Age Successfully

Jonathan Swift said, "No wise man ever wished to be younger." Without a doubt, a 70-year-old body does not work as well as it once did. It is also true that an individual's fear of aging is often greater than need be. As more individuals live to a ripe *and* active old age, our image of aging is changing. While on the average a 75-year-old's joints should be stiffening, people can practice not to be average. For example, a 75-year-old man might *choose* to train for and run a marathon; an 80-year-old woman whose capacity for work is undiminished might *choose* to make and sell children's toys.

Consider 85-year-old Sadie Halperin, who has been working out for 11 months at a rehabilitation center for the aged in Boston. She lifts weights and rides a stationary bike. She says that before she started working out, about everything she did—shopping, cooking, walking—was a major struggle. Sadie says she always felt wobbly and held on to a wall when she walked. Now she walks down the center of the hallways and reports that she feels wonderful. Initially she could lift only 15 pounds with both legs; now she lifts 30 pounds. At first she could bench-press only 20 pounds; now she bench-presses 50 pounds. Sadie's exercise routine has increased her muscle strength and helps her to battle osteoporosis by slowing the calcium loss from her bones, which can lead to deadly fractures (Ubell, 1992).

Eighty-five-year-old Sadie Halperin doubled her strength in exercise after just 11 months. Before developing an exercise routine, she felt wobbly and often had to hold on to a wall when she walked. Now she walks down the middle of hallways and says she feels wonderful.

PREVIEW

The story of Sadie Halperin's physical development and well-being raises some truly fascinating questions about life-span development, which we will explore in this chapter. They include: Why do we age, and what, if anything, can we do to slow down the process? How long can we live? What chance do you have of living to be 100? How does the body change in old age? Can certain eating habits and exercise help us live longer?

1 LONGEVITY

Life Expectancy and Life Span	The Young-Old, the Old-Old, and the Oldest-Old	Biological Theories of Aging

In his eighties, Nobel-winning chemist Linus Pauling argued that vitamin C slows the aging process. Aging researcher Roy Walford fasted two days a week because he believed calorie restriction slows the aging process. What do we really know about longevity?

Life Expectancy and Life Span

We are no longer a youthful society. The proportion of individuals at different ages has become increasingly similar. Since the beginning of recorded history, **life span,** the maximum number of years an individual can live, has remained at approximately 120 to 125 years of age. But since 1900 improvements in medicine, nutrition, exercise, and lifestyle have increased our life expectancy an average of 30 additional years.

life span The upper boundary of life, the maximum number of years an individual can live. The maximum life span of human beings is about 120 to 125 years of age.

Recall from chapter 1 that **life expectancy** is the number of years that the average person born in a particular year will probably live. Sixty-five-year-olds in the United States today can expect to live an average of 18 more years (20 for females, 16 for males) (National Center for Health Statistics, 2006). The average life expectancy of individuals born today in the United States is 78 years (Minino, Heron, & Smith, 2006).

Differences in Life Expectancy How does the United States fare in life expectancy, compared with other countries around the world? We do considerably better than some, a little worse than some others. Japan has the highest life expectancy at birth today (81 years) (UNICEF, 2004). Differences in life expectancies across countries are due to such factors as health conditions and medical care throughout the life span.

Life expectancy also differs for various ethnic groups within the United States and for men and women (Land & Yang, 2006). For example, the life expectancy of African Americans (70) in the United States is 7 years lower than the low expectancy for non-Latino Whites (77) (National Center for Health Statistics, 2006). (The gap was 8 years in 1970.) In 2004, the life expectancy for females was 80 years of age, while for males it was 75. Beginning in the mid-thirties, females outnumber males; this gap widens during the remainder of the adult years. By the time adults are 75 years of age, more than 61 percent of the population is female; for those 85 and over, the figure is almost 70 percent female.

Why can women expect to live longer than men? Social factors such as health attitudes, habits, lifestyles, and occupation are probably important (Land & Yang, 2006). For example, men are more likely than women to die from the leading causes of death in the United States, such as cancer of the respiratory system, motor vehicle accidents, cirrhosis of the liver, emphysema, and coronary heart disease (Goldman & others, 2004). These causes of death are associated with lifestyle. For example, the sex difference in deaths due to lung cancer and emphysema occurs because men are heavier smokers than women.

The sex difference in longevity also is influenced by biological factors (Vina & others, 2005). In virtually all species, females outlive males. Women have more resistance to infections and degenerative diseases. For example, the female's estrogen production helps to protect her from arteriosclerosis (hardening of the arteries). And the additional X chromosome that women carry in comparison to men may be associated with the production of more antibodies to fight off disease.

What about yourself? What is the likelihood that you will live to be 100? To evaluate this possibility, see figure 18.1.

Centenarians In 1980, there were only 15,000 centenarians (individuals 100 years and older) in the United States. In 2000, there were 77,000, and it is projected that this number will be 834,000 in 2050. Many people expect that "the older you get, the sicker you get." However, researchers are finding that is not true for some centenarians (Anderson & others, 2005; Motta & others, 2005; Perls, 2006; Terry & others, 2004). One recent study of 400 centenarians found that 32 percent of the males and 15 percent of the females had never been diagnosed with common age-associated diseases such as heart disease, cancer, and stroke (Evert & others, 2003). Another recent study of 93 centenarians revealed that despite some physical limitations, they had a low rate of age-associated diseases and most had good mental health (Selim & others, 2005).

A disproportionate number of centenarians are women who have never been married. In the ongoing New England Centenarian Study, a majority of the centenarians have had difficult lives, such as surviving the Holocaust and living in extreme poverty as an immigrant to the United States (Perls, Lauerman, & Silver, 1999). What has contributed to their survival is their ability to cope successfully

*T*o me old age is always fifteen years older than I am.

–Bernard Baruch
American Statesman, 20th Century

www.mhhe.com/santrockld11

Aging Research Center

life expectancy The number of years that will probably be lived by the average person born in a particular year.

This test gives you a rough guide for predicting your longevity. The basic life expectancy for males is age 74, and for females it is 80. Write down your basic life expectancy. If you are in your fifties or sixties, you should add ten years to the basic figure because you have already proved yourself to be a durable individual. If you are over age 60 and active, you can even add another two years.

Life Expectancy

Decide how each item applies to you and add or subtract the appropriate number of years from your basic life expectancy.

1. Family history

___ Add five years if two or more of your grandparents lived to 80 or beyond.
___ Subtract four years if any parent, grandparent, sister, or brother died of a heart attack or stroke before 50.
___ Subtract two years if anyone died from these diseases before 60.
___ Subtract three years for each case of diabetes, thyroid disorder, breast cancer, cancer of the digestive system, asthma, or chronic bronchitis among parents or grandparents.

2. Marital status

___ If you are married, add four years.
___ If you are over 25 and not married, subtract one year for every unmarried decade.

3. Economic status

___ Add two years if your family income is over $60,000 per year.
___ Subtract three years if you have been poor for the greater part of your life.

4. Physique

___ Subtract one year for every 10 pounds you are overweight.
___ For each inch your girth measurement exceeds your chest measurement deduct two years.
___ Add three years if you are over 40 and not overweight.

5. Exercise

___ Add three years if you exercise regularly and moderately (jogging three times a week).
___ Add five years if you exercise regularly and vigorously (long-distance running three times a week).
___ Subtract three years if your job is sedentary.
___ Add three years if your job is active.

6. Alcohol

___ Add two years if you are a light drinker (one to three drinks a day).
___ Subtract five to ten years if you are a heavy drinker (more than four drinks per day).
___ Subtract one year if you are a teetotaler.

7. Smoking

___ Subtract eight years if you smoke two or more packs of cigarettes per day.
___ Subtract two years if you smoke one to two packs per day.
___ Subtract two years if you smoke less than one pack.
___ Subtract two years if you regularly smoke a pipe or cigars.

8. Disposition

___ Add two years if you are a reasoned, practical person.
___ Subtract two years if you are aggressive, intense, and competitive.
___ Add one to five years if you are basically happy and content with life.
___ Subtract one to five years if you are often unhappy, worried, and often feel guilty.

9. Education

___ Subtract two years if you have less than a high school education.
___ Add one year if you attended four years of school beyond high school.
___ Add three years if you attended five or more years beyond high school.

10. Environment

___ Add four years if you have lived most of your life in a rural environment.
___ Subtract two years if you have lived most of your life in an urban environment.

11. Sleep

___ Subtract five years if you sleep more than nine hours a day.

12. Temperature

___ Add two years if your home's thermostat is set at no more than 68° F.

13. Health care

___ Add three years if you have regular medical checkups and regular dental care.
___ Subtract two years if you are frequently ill.

___ **Your Life Expectancy Total**

FIGURE 18.1 Can You Live to Be 100?

**New England Centenarian Study
Life Expectancy Calculator**

with stress. In one study, 1,200 centenarians were interviewed about many aspects of their lives (Segerberg, 1982). Through their eyes, life looks like this:

- Mary Butler said that finding something to laugh about every day is important. She believes a good laugh is better than a dose of medicine anytime.
- Elza Wynn concluded that he has been able to live so long because he made up his mind to live. He was thinking about dying when he was 77, but decided he would wait a while.
- Anna Marie Robertson ("Grandma") Moses commented that she felt older at 16 than at any time since then. Even when she became very old, she said that she never thought about being old.
- Billy Red Fox believes that being active and not worrying are important keys to living to be 100. At 95, he switched jobs to become a public relations representative. Even at 100, Billy travels 11 months of the year, making public appearances and talking to civic clubs.

Three participants in the New England Centenarian Study: (*Left*) Adelaide Kruger, age 101, watering her flowers; (*middle*) Waldo McBurney, age 104, is an active beekeeper, gardener, and runner who has earned 5 gold medals and set international records in track and field events in his age group. (*right*) Daphne Brann, age 110, voting in an election.

What chance do you have of living to be 100? Genes play an important role in surviving to an extreme old age (Ford & Tower, 2006; Johnson, 2005; Mackay & others, 2006; Perls, 2006; Vijg & Suh, 2005; Vogler, 2006). But there are also other factors at work such as family history, health (weight, diet, smoking, and exercise), education, personality, and lifestyle (Warburton, Nicol, & Bredin, 2006). To further examine the factors that are involved in living to a very old age, read the following Diversity in Life-Span Development interlude.

DIVERSITY IN LIFE-SPAN DEVELOPMENT

Living Longer in Okinawa

Individuals live longer on the Japanese island of Okinawa in the East China Sea than anywhere else in the world. In Okinawa, there are 34.7 centenarians for every 100,000 inhabitants, the highest ratio in the world. In comparison, the United States has about 10 centenarians for every 100,000 residents. The life expectancy in Okinawa is 81.2 years (86 for women, 78 for men), also highest in the world.

What is responsible for such longevity in Okinawa? Some possible explanations include (Willcox, Willcox, & Suzuki, 2002):

- *Diet.* Okinawans eat very healthy food, heavy on grains, fish, and vegetables, light on meat, eggs, and dairy products. The risk of dying of cancer is far lower among Okinawans than among Japanese and Americans (see figure 18.2). About 100,000 Okinawans moved to Brazil and quickly adopted the eating regimen of their new home, one heavy on red meat. The result: The life expectancy of the Brazilian Okinawans is now 17 years lower than Okinawa's 81 years!
- *Low-stress lifestyle.* The easygoing lifestyle in Okinawa more closely resembles that of a laid-back South Sea island than that of the high-stress world on the Japanese mainland.
- *Caring community.* Okinawans look out for each other and do not isolate or ignore their older adults. If older adults need help, they don't hesitate to ask a neighbor. Such support and caring is likely responsible for Okinawa having the lowest suicide rate among older women in East Asia, an area noted for its high suicide rate among older women.

(continued on next page)

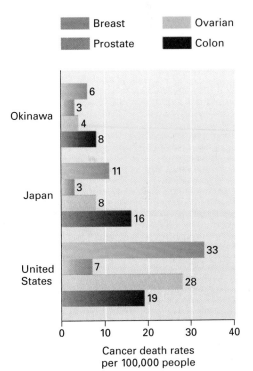
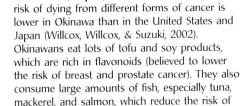

FIGURE 18.2 Risks of Dying from Cancer in Okinawa, Japan, and the United States. The risk of dying from different forms of cancer is lower in Okinawa than in the United States and Japan (Willcox, Willcox, & Suzuki, 2002). Okinawans eat lots of tofu and soy products, which are rich in flavonoids (believed to lower the risk of breast and prostate cancer). They also consume large amounts of fish, especially tuna, mackerel, and salmon, which reduce the risk of breast cancer.

Toshiko Taira, 80, weaves cloth from the fibers of banana trees on a loom in Okinawa. She, like many Okinawans, believes that such sense of purpose helps people to live longer.

- *Activity.* Many older adults in Okinawa are active, engaging in such activities as taking walks and working in their gardens. Many older Okinawans also continue working at their jobs.
- *Spirituality.* Many older adults in Okinawa find a sense of purpose in spiritual matters. Prayer is commonplace and believed to ease the mind of stress and problems.

The Young-Old, the Old-Old, and the Oldest-Old

Do you want to live to be 100, or 90? As we discussed in chapter 1, these ages are part of late adulthood, which begins in the sixties and extends to approximately 120 to 125 years of age. This is the longest span of any period of human development— 50 to 60 years. Some developmentalists distinguish between the *young-old* (65 to 74 years of age) and the *old-old*, or *old age* (75 years and older) (Charness & Bosman, 1992). Yet others distinguish the *oldest-old* (85 years and older) from younger older adults (Baltes & Smith, 2003).

An increased interest in successful aging is producing a portrayal of the oldest-old that is more optimistic than past stereotypes (Freund & Riediger, 2003; Motta & others, 2005). Interventions such as cataract surgery and a variety of rehabilitation strategies are improving the functioning of the oldest-old. In one study, eight weeks of leg-strength training markedly improved the walking ability of nursing home residents who averaged 90 years of age (Fiatarone & others, 1990). And there is cause for optimism in the development of new regimens of prevention and intervention (Abeles & others, 2006; Kaplan, 2006; Kramer, Fabiani, & Colcombe, 2006).

Many experts on aging prefer to talk about such categories as the young-old, old-old, and oldest-old in terms of *function* rather than age. Remember from chapter 1

(a)

(b)

(a) Frenchwoman Jeanne Louise Calment, who recently died at the age of 122. Greater ages have been claimed, but scientists say the maximum human life span is about 120 to 125. (b) Heredity is an important component of how long we will live. For example, in figure 18.1, you were able to add five years to your life expectancy if two or more of your grandparents lived to 80 or beyond. And if you were born a female, you start out with a basic life expectancy that is seven years more than if you were born a male. The three sisters shown here are all in their eighties.

that we described age not only in terms of chronological age, but also in terms of biological age, psychological age, and social age. Thus, in terms of *functional age*—the person's actual ability to function—an 85-year-old might well be more biologically and psychologically fit than a 65-year-old.

Still, there are some significant differences between adults in their sixties or seventies and adults who are 85 and older (Baltes, Lindenberger, & Staudinger, 2006; Baltes & Smith, 2003; Suzman & others, 1992). As we discussed in chapter 1, Paul Baltes (Baltes, 2000; Baltes & Smith, 2003) argues that the oldest-old (85 and over) face a number of problems, including sizable losses in cognitive potential and ability to learn; an increase in chronic stress; a sizable prevalence of physical and mental disabilities; high levels of frailty; increased loneliness; and the difficulty of dying at older ages with dignity. He contrasts the problems of the oldest-old with the increase in successful aging of adults in their sixties and seventies. Compared with the oldest-old, the young-old have a substantial potential for physical and cognitive fitness, higher levels of emotional well-being, and more effective strategies for mastering the gains and losses of old age.

The oldest-old today are mostly female and the majority of these women are widowed and live alone, if not institutionalized. The majority also are hospitalized at some time in the last years of life, and the majority die alone in a hospital or institution (Baltes & Smith, 2003). Their needs, capacities, and resources are often different from those of older adults in their sixties and seventies.

Despite Baltes' negative portrait of the oldest-old, they are a heterogeneous, diversified group (Roberts, Dunkle, & Haug, 1994; Jeste, 2005; Perls, 2006). Many of the oldest-old have outlived their social and financial supports and depend on society for their daily living, but this is not true of all. A significant number have cognitive impairments, but many do not. Almost one-fourth of the oldest-old are institutionalized, and many report some limitation of activity or difficulties in caring for themselves. However, more than three-fourths are not institutionalized. The majority of older adults aged 80 and over continue to live in the community. More than one-third of older adults 80 and over who live in the community report that their health is excellent or good; 40 percent say that they have no activity limitation (Suzman & others, 1992). Less than 50 percent of U.S. 85- to 89-year-olds have a disability (Siegler, Bosworth, & Poon, 2003); a substantial subgroup of the oldest-old are robust and active. The oldest-old who have aged successfully have often been unnoticed and unstudied.

Biological Theories of Aging

Even if we stay remarkably healthy, we begin to age at some point. In fact, lifespan experts argue that biological aging begins at birth (Schaie, 2000). What are the biological explanations of aging? Intriguing explanations of why we age are provided by four biological theories: cellular clock theory, free-radical theory, mitochondrial theory, and hormonal stress theory.

Cellular Clock Theory   **Cellular clock theory** is Leonard Hayflick's (1977) theory that cells can divide a maximum of about 75 to 80 times and that, as we age, our cells become less capable of dividing. Hayflick found that cells extracted from adults in their fifties to seventies divided fewer than 75 to 80 times. Based on the ways cells divide, Hayflick places the upper limit of the human life-span potential at about 120 to 125 years of age.

In the last decade, scientists have tried to fill in a gap in cellular clock theory (Chai & others, 2006; Gatza & others, 2006; Sharpless & DePinho, 2004). Hayflick did not know why cells die. The answer may lie at the tips of chromosomes, at *telomeres*, which are DNA sequences that cap chromosomes (Aviv & others, 2005; Shay & Wright, 2000, 2004, 2005, 2006).

Each time a cell divides, the telomeres become shorter and shorter (see figure 18.3). After about 70 or 80 replications, the telomeres are dramatically reduced and

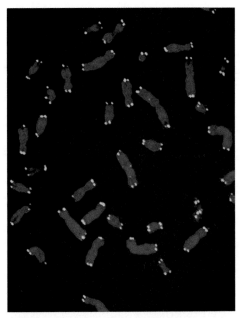

FIGURE 18.3 Telomeres and Aging. The photograph shows actual telomeres lighting up the tips of chromosomes.

cellular clock theory Leonard Hayflick's theory that the maximum number of times that human cells can divide is about 75 to 80. As we age, our cells have less capability to divide.

What Causes Aging?
Telomeres Research
Research on Telomeres and Telomerase
Genetic Studies of Aging

the cell no longer can reproduce. Injecting the enzyme *telomerase* into human cells grown in the laboratory can substantially extend the life of the cells beyond the approximately 70 to 80 normal cell divisions (Shay & Wright, 1999). In one study, age-related telomere erosion was linked with an impaired ability to recover from stress and an increased rate of cancer (Rudolf & others, 1999).

Free-Radical Theory A second microbiological theory of aging is **free-radical theory,** which states that people age because when cells metabolize energy, the by-products include unstable oxygen molecules known as *free radicals*. The free radicals ricochet around the cells, damaging DNA and other cellular structures (Frisard & Ravussin, 2006; Harman, 2006; Mariani & others, 2005; Rodrigo & others, 2005). The damage can lead to a range of disorders, including cancer and arthritis (Katakura, 2006). Overeating is linked with an increase in free radicals, and researchers recently have found that calorie restriction—a diet restricted in calories although adequate in proteins, vitamins, and minerals—reduces the oxidative damage created by free radicals (Sanz & others, 2005).

Mitochondrial Theory There is increasing interest in the role that *mitochondria*—tiny bodies within cells that supply energy for function, growth, and repair—might play in aging (Bulteau, Szweda, & Friguet, 2006; Golden & others, 2006; LaFrance & others, 2005). **Mitochondrial theory** states that aging is due to the decay of mitochondria. It appears that this decay is primarily due to oxidative damage and loss of critical micronutrients supplied by the cell (Capri & others, 2006; Singh, 2006).

How does this damage and loss of nutrients occur? Among the by-products of mitochondrial energy production are the free radicals we just described. According to the mitochondrial theory, the damage caused by free radicals initiates a self-perpetuating cycle in which oxidative damage impairs mitochondrial function, which results in the generation of even greater amounts of free radicals. The result is that over time, the affected mitochondria become so inefficient that they cannot generate enough energy to meet cellular needs (Golden & others, 2006). One recent study found that exercise in older adults increased mitochondrial activity in their cells (Menshikova & others, 2006). The researchers concluded that the increased mitochondrial activity might lead to an increase in mitochondria.

Defects in mitochondria are linked with cardiovascular disease, neurodegenerative diseases such as dementia, and decline in liver functioning (Mariani & others, 2005). However, it is not known whether the defects in mitochondria cause aging or are merely accompaniments of the aging process (DiMauro & others, 2002).

Hormonal Stress Theory The three theories—cellular clock, free radical, and mitochondrial—of aging that we have discussed so far attempt to explain aging at the cellular level. In contrast, **hormonal stress theory** argues that aging in the body's hormonal system can lower resistance to stress and increase the likelihood of disease (Finch & Seeman, 1999; Parsons, 2003).

Normally, when people experience stressors, the body responds by releasing certain hormones. As people age, the hormones stimulated by stress remain at elevated levels longer than when people were younger (Traustadottir, Bosch, & Matt, 2005; Uchino & others, 2005, 2006). These prolonged, elevated levels of stress-related hormones are associated with increased risks for many diseases, including cardiovascular disease, cancer, diabetes, and hypertension (Epel & others, 2006; Magri & others, 2006).

Recently, a variation of hormonal stress theory has emphasized the contribution of a decline in immune system functioning with aging (Graham, Christian, & Kiecolt-Glaser, 2006; Hawkley & Cacioppo, 2004; Pawelec & others, 2006). Aging contributes to immune system deficits that give rise to infectious diseases in older adults. The extended duration of stress and diminished restorative processes in older

free-radical theory A microbiological theory of aging that states that people age because inside their cells normal metabolism produces unstable oxygen molecules known as free radicals. These molecules ricochet around inside cells, damaging DNA and other cellular structures.

mitochondrial theory The theory that aging is caused by the decay of mitochondria, tiny cellular bodies that supply energy for function, growth, and repair.

hormonal stress theory The theory that aging in the body's hormonal system can lower resilience to stress and increase the likelihood of disease.

adults may accelerate the effects of aging on immunity (Fuente, Hernanz, & Vallejo, 2005; Weng, 2006).

Which of these biological theories best explains aging? That question has not yet been answered. It might turn out that all of these biological processes contribute to aging.

Review and Reflect • LEARNING GOAL 1

1 **Characterize longevity and the biological theories of aging**

Review
- What is the difference between life span and life expectancy? What characterizes centenarians? What sex differences exist in longevity?
- How can the differences between the young-old, old-old, and oldest-old be summarized?
- What are the four main biological theories of aging?

Reflect
- If we could increase the maximum human life span, would this be beneficial? If so, to whom?

---

2 THE COURSE OF PHYSICAL DEVELOPMENT IN LATE ADULTHOOD

The Aging Brain	Physical Appearance and Movement	The Circulatory System and Lungs

The Immune System	Sensory Development	Sexuality

Physical decline is inevitable if we manage to live to an old age, but the timing of problems related to aging is not uniform. One analysis involved the MacArthur Research Network on Successful Aging Study, a three-site longitudinal study of successful aging in women and men 70 to 79 years of age. In this study, physical performance (such as walking efficiency, maintaining balance, and repeatedly standing up and sitting down) did decline with age, but there was considerable individual variation (Seeman & others, 1994). Healthy, higher-income participants performed better than older adults in poor health from low-income backgrounds. A majority of the older adults also maintained their physical performance over a three-year period in their seventies, and some even improved their performance during this time.

Recent research on aging underscores that bodily powers decline slowly and that sometimes even lost function can be restored. What are the main physical changes behind the losses of late adulthood?

The Aging Brain

How does the brain change during late adulthood? Does it retain plasticity?

The Shrinking, Slowing Brain On average, the brain loses 5 to 10 percent of its weight between the ages of 20 and 90. Brain volume also decreases (Enzinger & others, 2005). One recent study found that the volume of the brain was 15 percent less in older adults than younger adults (Shan & others, 2005). Scientists are not sure

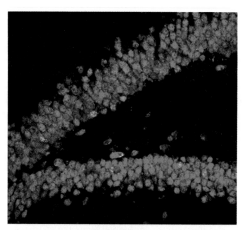

Exercise

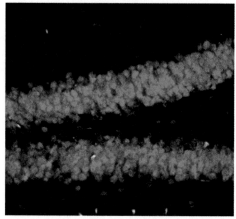

Enriched Environment

FIGURE 18.4 Generating New Nerve Cells in Adult Mice. Researchers have found that exercise (running) and an enriched environment (a larger cage and many toys) can cause brain cells to divide and form new brain cells (Kempermann, van Praag, & Gage, 2000). Cells were labeled with a chemical marker that becomes integrated into the DNA of dividing cells (red). Four weeks later, they were also labeled to mark neurons (nerve cells). As shown here, both the running mice and the mice in an enriched environment had many cells that were still dividing (red) and others that had differentiated into new nerve cells (orange).

why these changes occur but believe they might result from a decrease in dendrites, damage to the myelin sheath that covers axons, or simply the death of brain cells.

Some areas shrink more than others. The prefrontal cortex is one area that shrinks with aging, and recent research has linked this shrinkage with a decrease in working memory and other cognitive activities in older adults (Grady & others, 2006; Nordahl & others, 2006; Rajah & D'Esposito, 2005).

A general slowing of function in the brain and spinal cord begins in middle adulthood and accelerates in late adulthood (Birren, 2002). Both physical coordination and intellectual performance are affected. For example, after age 70, many adults no longer show a knee jerk and by age 90 most reflexes are much slower (Spence, 1989). The slowing of the brain can impair the performance of older adults on intelligence tests, especially timed tests (Birren, Woods, & Williams, 1980).

Aging has also been linked to a reduction in the production of some neurotransmitters, including acetylcholine, dopamine, and gamma-aminobutyric acid (GABA). Some researchers believe that reductions in acetylcholine may be responsible for small declines in memory functioning and even with the severe memory loss associated with Alzheimer disease, which we discuss in chapter 19 (Akaike, 2006; Nordberg, 2006; Wenk, 2006). Normal age-related reductions in dopamine may cause problems in planning and carrying out motor activities (Erixon-Lindroth & others, 2005). Severe reductions in the production of dopamine have been linked with age-related diseases characterized by a loss of motor control, such as Parkinson disease (Chen & others, 2005). GABA helps to control the preciseness of the signal sent from one neuron to another, decreasing "noise," and its production decreases with aging (Betts & others, 2005; Ge & others, 2006; Yu & others, 2006).

The Adapting Brain If the brain were a computer, this description of the aging brain might lead you to think that it could not do much of anything. However, unlike a computer, the brain has remarkable repair capability (Burke & Barnes, 2006). Even in late adulthood, the brain loses only a portion of its ability to function (Anderton, 2002).

As the adult brain ages, it adapts in several ways. First, humans can grow new brain cells throughout their lives (Briones, 2006; Emsley & others, 2005; Ernst & others, 2006; Gould & others, 1999; Kempermann, Wiskott, & Gage, 2004). The extent to which we do so, however, may depend in part on environmental stimulation through such activities as physical activity and learning (Komitova & others, 2005; Kramer, Fabiani, & Colcombe, 2006; Olson & others, 2006; Schaffer & Gage, 2004; van Praag & others, 2005). Figure 18.4 shows the results of one study in which adult mice that ran and adult mice that were placed in an enriched environment generated new brain cells. Researchers also have found that stress inhibits neurogenesis (Mirescu & Gould, 2006).

A second type of adaptation was demonstrated in a study that compared the brains of adults at various ages (Coleman, 1986). From the forties through the seventies, the growth of dendrites increased. However, in people in their nineties, dendritic growth no longer occurred. This dendritic growth might compensate for the possible loss of neurons through the seventies but not in the nineties. Lack of dendritic growth in older adults could be due to a lack of environmental stimulation and activity.

Stanley Rapaport (1994), chief of the neurosciences laboratory at the National Institute on Aging, demonstrated another way in which the aging brain can adapt. He compared the brains of younger and older people engaged in the same tasks. The older brains had rewired themselves to compensate for losses. If one neuron was not up to the job, neighboring neurons helped to pick up the slack. Rapaport concluded that as brains age, they can shift responsibilities for a given task from one region to another.

Changes in lateralization may provide one type of adaptation in aging adults. Recall that lateralization is the specialization of function in one hemisphere of the brain or the other. Using neuroimaging techniques, researchers recently found that brain activity in the prefrontal cortex is lateralized less in older adults than in younger adults when they are engaging in cognitive tasks (Cabeza, 2002; Dixit & others, 2000; Rossi & others, 2005). For example, figure 18.5 shows that when younger adults are given the task of recognizing words they have previously seen, they process the information primarily in the right hemisphere; older adults are more likely to use both hemispheres (Madden & others, 1999).

The decrease in lateralization in older adults might play a compensatory role in the aging brain. That is, using both hemispheres may improve the cognitive functioning of older adults. Support for this view comes from another study in which older adults who used both brain hemispheres were faster at completing a working memory task than their counterparts who primarily used only one hemisphere (Reuter-Lorenz & others, 2000). However, the decrease in lateralization may be a mere by-product of aging; it may reflect an age-related decline in the brain's ability to specialize functions. In this view, during childhood the brain becomes increasingly differentiated in terms of its functions; as adults become older, this process may reverse. Support for the dedifferentiation view is found in the higher intercorrelations of performance on cognitive tasks in older adults than in younger adults (Baltes & Lindenberger, 1997). To read further about aging and the brain, see the Research in Life-Span Development interlude.

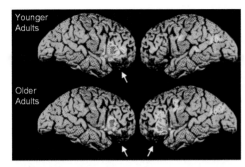

FIGURE 18.5 The Decrease in Brain Lateralization in Older Adults. Younger adults primarily used the right prefrontal region of the brain (*top left photo*) during a recall memory task, while older adults used both the left and right prefrontal regions (*bottom two photos*).

RESEARCH IN LIFE-SPAN DEVELOPMENT

The Nun Study

The Nun Study, directed by David Snowdon, is an intriguing ongoing investigation of aging in 678 nuns, many of whom are from a convent in Mankato, Minnesota (Danner, Snowdon, & Friesen, 2001; Kemper & others, 2001; Riley, Snowdon & Markesbery, 2002; Snowdon, 1995, 1997, 2002, 2003). Each of the 678 nuns agreed to participate in annual assessments of their cognitive and physical functioning. They also agreed to donate their brains for scientific research when they die and they are the largest group of brain donors in the world. Examination of the nuns' donated brains, as well as others, has led neuroscientists to believe that the brain has a remarkable capacity to change and grow, even in old age. The Sisters of Notre Dame in Mankato lead an intellectually challenging life, and brain researchers believe this contributes to their quality of life as older adults and possibly to their longevity.

Findings from the Nun Study so far include:

*   Idea density, a measure of linguistic ability assessed early in the adult years (age 22), was linked with higher brain weight, fewer incidences of mild cognitive impairment, and fewer characteristics of Alzheimer disease in 75- to 95-year-old nuns (Riley & others, 2005).
*   Positive emotions early in adulthood were linked to longevity (Danner, Snowdon, & Friesen, 2001). Handwritten autobiographies from 180 nuns, composed when they were 22 years of age, were scored for emotional content. The nuns whose early writings had higher scores for positive emotional content were more likely to still be alive at 75 to 95 years of age than their counterparts whose early writings were characterized by negative emotional content.
*   Sisters who had taught for most of their lives showed more moderate declines in intellectual skills than those who had spent most of their lives in

Top: Sister Marcella Zachman (*left*) finally stopped teaching at age 97. Now, at 99, she helps ailing nuns exercise their brains by quizzing them on vocabulary or playing a card game called Skip-Bo, at which she deliberately loses. Sister Mary Esther Boor (*right*), also 99 years of age, is a former teacher who stays alert by doing puzzles and volunteering to work the front desk. *Below:* A technician holds the brain of a deceased Mankato nun. The nuns donate their brains for research that explores the effects of stimulation on brain growth.

(continued on next page)

service-based tasks, which supports the notion that stimulating the brain with intellectual activity keeps neurons healthy and alive (Snowdon, 2002).

- Sisters with high levels of folic acid showed little evidence of Alzheimer-like damage to their brain after death (Snowdon & others, 2000). Possibly the substantial folic acid in the blood means less chance of having a stroke and possibly helps to protect the brain from decline.

This and other research provides hope that scientists will discover ways to tap into the brain's capacity to adapt in order to prevent and treat brain diseases (Dobrossy & Dunnett, 2005). For example, scientists might learn more effective ways to help older adults recover from strokes. Even when areas of the brain are permanently damaged by stroke, new message routes can be created to get around the blockage or to resume the function of that area.

The Immune System

Decline in the functioning of the body's immune system with aging is well documented (Pawelec & others, 2006; Weng, 2006). As we indicated earlier in our discussion of hormonal stress theory, the extended duration of stress and diminished restorative processes in older adults may accelerate the effects of aging on immunity (Graham, Christian, & Kiecolt-Glaser, 2006; Hawkley & Cacioppo, 2004). Also, malnutrition involving low levels of protein is linked to a decrease in T cells that destroy infected cells and hence to deterioration in the immune system (Virts, Phillips, & Thoman, 2006). Exercise can improve immune system functioning (Strasser, Skalicky, & Viidik, 2006). Because of the decline in the functioning of their immune systems, vaccination against influenza is especially important in older adults (De la Fuente, Hernanz, & Vallejo, 2006).

Physical Appearance and Movement

In late adulthood, the changes in physical appearance that began occurring during middle age (as discussed in chapter 16) become more pronounced (Gilhar & others, 2004; McCarter, 2006). Wrinkles and age spots are the most noticeable changes.

We also get shorter when we get older. As we saw in chapter 16, both men and women become shorter in late adulthood because of bone loss in their vertebrae (Hoyer & Roodin, 2003).

Our weight usually drops after we reach 60 years of age. This likely occurs because we lose muscle, which also gives our bodies a "sagging" look (Nair, 2005). Figure 18.6 shows the decline in percentage of muscle and bone from age 25 to age 75, and the corresponding increase in the percentage of fat.

Older adults move more slowly than young adults, and this slowing occurs for movements with a wide range of difficulty (see figure 18.7). Even when they perform everyday tasks such as reaching and grasping, moving from one place to another, and continuous movement, older adults tend to move more slowly than when they were young (Lan & others, 2003; Newell, Vaillancourt, & Sosnoff, 2006). Walking rapidly over a distance requires not only muscle strength but also cardiovascular fitness, vision, and postural stability (Morley, 2004).

The good news is that regular walking decreases the onset of physical disability in older adults (Newman & others, 2006; Visser & others, 2005). Also, exercise and appropriate weight lifting can help to reduce the decrease in muscle mass and improve the older person's body appearance (Ferrara & others, 2006). We will have more to say about the benefits of exercise later in this chapter.

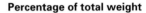

Percentage of total weight

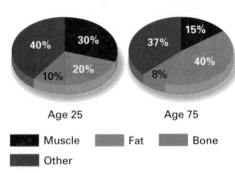

Age 25   Age 75

■ Muscle   ■ Fat   ■ Bone
■ Other

FIGURE 18.6 Changes in Body Composition of Bone, Muscle, and Fat from 25 to 75 Years of Age. Notice the decrease in bone and muscle and the increase in fat from 25 to 75 years of age.

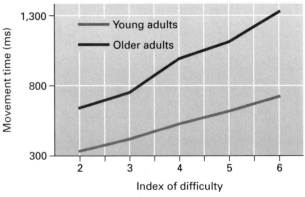

FIGURE 18.7 Movement and Aging. Older adults take longer to move than young adults and this occurs across a range of movement difficulty (Ketcham & Stelmach, 2001).

Sensory Development

Seeing, hearing, and other aspects of sensory functioning are linked with our ability to perform everyday activities. This link was documented in a study of more than 500 adults, 70 to 102 years of age, in which sensory acuity, especially in vision, was related to whether and how well older adults bathed and groomed themselves, completed household chores, engaged in intellectual activities, and watched TV (Marsiske, Klumb, & Baltes, 1997). How do vision, hearing, taste, smell, touch, and pain change in late adulthood?

Vision With aging, visual acuity, color vision, and depth perception decline. Several diseases of the eye also may emerge in aging adults.

Visual Acuity In late adulthood, the decline in vision that began for most adults in early or middle adulthood becomes more pronounced (Crews & Campbell, 2004; Fozard, 2000; Schieber, 2006). Night driving is especially difficult, to some extent because tolerance for glare diminishes. *Dark adaptation* is slower, meaning that older individuals take longer to recover their vision when going from a well-lighted room to semidarkness. The area of the visual field becomes smaller, suggesting that the intensity of a stimulus in the peripheral area of the visual field needs to be increased if the stimulus is to be seen. Events taking place away from the center of the visual field might not be detected (Fozard & Gordon-Salant, 2001).

This visual decline often can be traced to a reduction in the quality or intensity of light reaching the retina. In extreme old age, these changes might be accompanied by degenerative changes in the retina, causing severe difficulty in seeing. Large print books and magnifiers might be needed in such cases.

One recent extensive study of visual changes in adults found that the age of older adults was a significant factor in how extensively their visual functioning differed from that of younger adults (Brabyn & others, 2001). Beyond 75, and more so beyond age 85, older adults showed significantly worse performance on a number of visual tasks when compared with young adults and older adults in their sixties and early seventies. The greatest decline in visual perception beyond 75, and especially beyond 85, involved glare. The older adults, especially those 85 and older, fared much worse in being able to see clearly when glare was present, and they took much longer to recover from glare than younger adults (see figure 18.8). For example, whereas young adults recover vision following glare in less than 10 seconds, 50 percent of 90-year-olds have not recovered vision after 1.5 minutes.

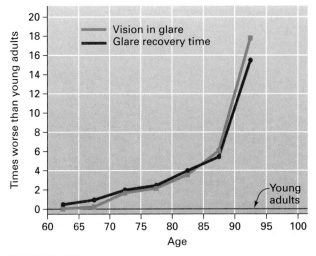

FIGURE 18.8 Rates of Decline in Visual Functioning Related to Glare in Adults of Different Ages. Older adults, especially those 85 and older, fare much worse than younger adults in being able to see clearly when glare is present, and their recovery from glare is much slower. These data were collected from a random sample of community-dwelling older adults living in Marin County, California. For each age, the factor by which the group's median performance was worse than normative values for young adults is shown.

Color Vision Color vision also may decline with age in older adults as a result of the yellowing of the lens of the eye (Suzuki & others, 2006). This decline is most likely to occur in the green-blue-violet part of the color spectrum. As a result, older adults may have trouble accurately matching closely related colors such as navy socks and black socks.

Depth Perception As with many areas of perception, depth perception changes little after infancy until adults become older. Depth perception typically declines in late adulthood, which can make it difficult for the older adult to determine how close or far away or how high or low something is (Brabyn & others, 2001; Norman & others, 2006; Zarof & others, 2003). A decline in depth perception can make steps or street curbs difficult to manage.

A decrease in contrast sensitivity is one factor that diminishes the older adult's ability to perceive depth. Light-dark contrast is produced by the amount of light reflected by surfaces (a light object is brighter than a dark object). The difference in

Aging and Sensory Changes
Aging and Vision Problems

contrast makes objects that contrast with the background easier to see. Compared with younger adults, older adults need sharper contrasts and sharper edges around an object to differentiate it from its background.

Diseases of the Eye Three diseases that can impair the vision of older adults are cataracts, glaucoma, and macular degeneration:

- **Cataracts** involve a thickening of the lens of the eye that causes vision to become cloudy, opaque, and distorted (Fujikado & others, 2004; Knudtson, Klein, & Klein, 2006). By age 70, approximately 30 percent of individuals experience a partial loss of vision due to cataracts. Initially, cataracts can be treated by glasses; if they worsen, a simple surgical procedure can remove them (Muskesh & others, 2006; Stifer & others, 2004).
- **Glaucoma** involves damage to the optic nerve because of the pressure created by a buildup of fluid in the eye (Babalola & others, 2003; Mok, Lee, & So, 2004). Approximately 1 percent of individuals in their seventies and 10 percent of those in their nineties have glaucoma, which can be treated with eyedrops. If left untreated, glaucoma can ultimately destroy a person's vision.
- **Macular degeneration** is a disease that involves deterioration of the *macula* of the retina, which corresponds to the focal center of the visual field. Individuals with macular degeneration may have relatively normal peripheral vision but be unable to see clearly what is right in front of them. It affects 1 in 25 individuals from 66 to 74 years of age and 1 in 6 of those 75 years old and older. If the disease is detected early, it can be treated with laser surgery (Howe, 2003). However, macular degeneration is difficult to treat and thus a leading cause of blindness in older adults (Guymer & Chong, 2006; Schmier, Jones, & Halpern, 2006).

Hearing For hearing as for vision, the age of older adults is important in determining the degree of decline (Stenklev, Vik, & Laukli, 2004) (see figure 18.9). The decline in vision and hearing is much greater in individuals 75 years and older than in individuals 65 to 74 years of age (Charness & Bosman, 1992).

Hearing impairment usually does not become much of an impediment until late adulthood (Crews & Campbell, 2004; Fozard, 2000; Fozard & Gordon-Salant, 2001). Only 19 percent of individuals from 45 to 54 years of age experience some type of hearing problem, but for those 75 to 79, the figure reaches 75 percent (Harris, 1975). It has been estimated that 15 percent of the population over the age of 65 is legally deaf, usually due to degeneration of the *cochlea*, the primary neural receptor for hearing in the inner ear (Olsho, Harkins, & Lenhardt, 1985).

Even in late adulthood, some, but not all, hearing problems can be corrected by hearing aids (Cook & Hawkins, 2006). Wearing two hearing aids that are balanced to correct each ear separately can sometimes help hearing-impaired adults.

cataracts Involve a thickening of the lens of the eye that causes vision to become cloudy, opaque, and distorted.

glaucoma Damage to the optic nerve because of the pressure created by a buildup of fluid in the eye.

macular degeneration A disease that involves deterioration of the macula of the retina, which corresponds to the focal center of the visual field.

Perceptual System	Young-Old (65 to 74 years)	Old-Old (75 years and older)
Vision	There is a loss of acuity even with corrective lenses. Less transmission of light occurs through the retina (half as much as in young adults). Greater susceptibility to glare occurs. Color discrimination ability decreases.	There is a significant loss of visual acuity and color discrimination, and a decrease in the size of the perceived visual field. In late old age, people are at significant risk for visual dysfunction from cataracts and glaucoma.
Hearing	There is a significant loss of hearing at high frequencies and some loss at middle frequencies. These losses can be helped by a hearing aid. There is greater susceptibility to masking of what is heard by noise.	There is a significant loss at high and middle frequencies. A hearing aid is more likely to be needed than in young-old age.

FIGURE 18.9 Vision and Hearing Decline in the Young-Old and the Old-Old

Smell and Taste Most older adults lose some of their sense of smell or taste, or both (Fukunaga, Uematsu, & Sugimoto, 2005; Hawkes, 2006; Wang & others, 2005). These losses often begin around 60 years of age. Smell and taste decline less in healthy older adults than in their less healthy counterparts.

Reductions in the ability to smell and taste can reduce enjoyment of food and life satisfaction (Roberts & Rosenberg, 2006). Also, a decline in the sense of smell can reduce the ability to detect smoke from a fire. If elderly individuals need to be encouraged to eat more, compounds that stimulate the olfactory nerve are sometimes added to food. However, many older adults compensate for their diminished taste and smell by eating sweeter, spicier, and saltier foods (Hoyer & Roodin, 2003), which can lead to eating more low-nutrient, highly seasoned "junk food."

Touch and Pain Changes in touch are also associated with aging (Donat & others, 2005; Gescheider, 1997). One study found that, with aging, individuals could detect touch less in the lower extremities (ankles, knees, and so on) than in the upper extremities (wrists, shoulders, and so on) (Corso, 1977). For most older adults, a decline in touch sensitivity is not problematic (Hoyer & Roodin, 2003).

Older adults are less sensitive to pain and suffer from it less than younger adults (Harkins, Price, & Martinelli, 1986). Although decreased sensitivity to pain can help older adults cope with disease and injury, it can also mask injury and illness that need to be treated.

The Circulatory System and Lungs

Not long ago it was believed that cardiac output—the amount of blood the heart pumps—declines with age even in healthy adults. However, we now know that when heart disease is absent, the amount of blood pumped is the same regardless of an adult's age.

In the past, a 60-year-old with a blood pressure reading of 160/90 would have been told, "For your age, that is normal." Now medication, exercise, and/or a healthier diet might be prescribed to lower blood pressure. Today, most experts on aging even recommend that consistent blood pressures above 120/80 should be treated to reduce the risk of heart attack, stroke, or kidney disease (Franklin, 2006; Safar & Smulyan, 2004). A rise in blood pressure with age can be linked with illness, obesity, anxiety, stiffening of blood vessels, or lack of exercise (Franklin, 2006). The longer any of these factors persist, the worse the individual's blood pressure gets (Hawkins & Dunn, 2006; Wexler & Avkerman, 2006). A recent longitudinal study found that older adults with cardiovascular disease had a lower probability of subsequent successful aging (defined as remaining free of cardiovascular disease, cancer, and obstructive pulmonary disease, and with intact physical and cognitive functioning) than their counterparts without cardiovascular disease (Newman & others, 2003).

Lung capacity drops 40 percent between the ages of 20 and 80, even without disease (Fozard, 1992). Lungs lose elasticity, the chest shrinks, and the diaphragm weakens (Simpson & others, 2005). The good news, though, is that older adults can improve lung functioning with diaphragm-strengthening exercises. Severe impairments in lung functioning and death can result from smoking (Whincup & others, 2006).

Sexuality

In the absence of two circumstances—disease and the belief that old people are or should be asexual—sexuality can be lifelong. Aging, however, does induce some changes in human sexual performance, more so in the male than in the female (Bellastella & others, 2005; Mallis & others, 2006).

What are some characteristics of sexuality in older adults?

Orgasm becomes less frequent in males with age, occurring in every second to third attempt rather than every time. More direct stimulation usually is needed to produce an erection. From 65 to 80 years of age, approximately one out of four men have serious problems getting and/or keeping erections, and after 80 years of age the percentage rises to one out of two men (Butler & Lewis, 2002).

In one study of older adults in their sixties, many were still having sex (Wiley & Bortz, 1996). The women rated kissing as one of the most satisfying sexual activities, while the men rated oral sex as the most satisfying. In another study of more than 1,200 older adults (mean age = 77), almost 30 percent had participated in sexual activity in the past month (Matthias & others, 1997). Two-thirds of the older adults were satisfied with their current level of sexual activity.

Various therapies for older adults who report sexual difficulties have been effective (Burgess, 2004; Carbone & Seftel, 2002). In one study, sex education—which consisted largely of simply giving sexual information—led to increased sexual interest, knowledge, and activity in older adults (White & Catania, 1981). Even when intercourse is impaired by infirmity, other relationship needs persist, among them closeness, sensuality, and being valued as a man or a woman (Hurd, 2006; Johnson, 1996). We discuss these needs in chapter 20.

Review and Reflect • LEARNING GOAL 2

2 **Describe how a person's brain and body change in late adulthood**

Review
- How much plasticity and adaptability does the aging brain have?
- How does the immune system change with aging?
- What changes in physical appearance and movement characterize late adulthood?
- How do vision, hearing, smell and taste, touch, and sensitivity to pain change in older adults?
- How does the circulatory system change in older adults? How do the lungs change in older adults?
- What is the nature of sexuality in late adulthood?

Reflect
- If you could interview the Mankato nuns, what questions would you want to ask them?

---

3 HEALTH

Health Problems

Exercise, Nutrition, and Weight

Substance Abuse

Health Treatment

How healthy are older adults? What types of health problems do they have, and what can be done to maintain or improve their health and ability to function in everyday life?

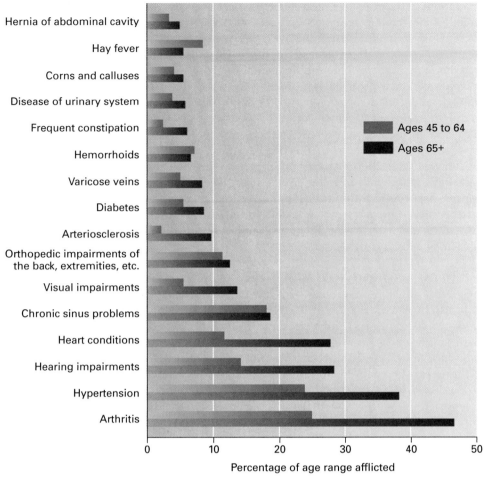

FIGURE 18.10 The Most Prevalent Chronic Conditions in Middle and Late Adulthood

Health Problems

As we age, the probability increases that we will have some disease or illness. The majority of adults still alive at 80 years of age or older are likely to have some type of impairment. Chronic diseases (those with a slow onset and a long duration) are rare in early adulthood, increase in middle adulthood, and become more common in late adulthood.

As shown in figure 18.10, arthritis is the most common chronic disorder in late adulthood, followed by hypertension. Older women have a higher incidence of arthritis and hypertension and are more likely to have visual problems, but are less likely to have hearing problems, than older men are.

Although adults over the age of 65 often have a physical impairment, many of them can still carry on their everyday activities or work. Chronic conditions associated with the greatest limitation on work are heart conditions (52 percent), diabetes (34 percent), asthma (27 percent), and arthritis (27 percent). Conflict in relationships has been linked with greater decline in older adults with diabetes or hypertension (Seeman & Chen, 2002). Low income is also strongly related to health problems in late adulthood (Ferraro, 2006; Holden & Hatcher, 2006). Approximately three times as many poor as non-poor older adults report that their activities are limited by chronic disorders.

Causes of Death in Older Adults   Nearly three-fourths of all older adults die of heart disease, cancer, or cerebrovascular disease (stroke). Chronic lung diseases,

How many of us older persons have really been prepared for the second half of life, for old age, and eternity?

—CARL JUNG
Swiss Psychoanalyst, 20th Century

pneumonia and influenza, and diabetes round out the six leading causes of death among older adults. If cancer, the second leading cause of death in older adults, were completely eliminated, the average life expectancy would rise by only 1 to 2 years. However, if all cardiovascular and kidney diseases were eradicated, the average life expectancy of older adults would increase by approximately 10 years. This increase in longevity is already under way as the number of strokes among older adults has declined considerably in the last several decades. The decline in strokes is due to improved treatment of high blood pressure, a decrease in smoking, better diet, and an increase in exercise.

Ethnicity is linked with the death rates of older adults (National Center for Health Statistics, 2006). Among ethnic groups in the United States, African Americans have high death rates for stroke, heart disease, lung cancer, and female breast cancer. Asian Americans and Latinos have low death rates for these diseases. In the last decade, death rates for most diseases in African Americans, Latinos, and Asian Americans have decreased. However, death rates for most diseases still remain high for African Americans (National Center for Health Statistics, 2006).

Arthritis   **Arthritis** is an inflammation of the joints accompanied by pain, stiffness, and movement problems. Arthritis is especially common in older adults (Blumstein & Gorevic, 2005; Nour & others, 2006). This disorder can affect hips, knees, ankles, fingers, and vertebrae. Individuals with arthritis often experience pain and stiffness, as well as problems in moving about and performing routine daily activities. There is no known cure for arthritis. However, the symptoms of arthritis can be reduced by drugs, such as aspirin, range-of-motion exercises for the afflicted joints, weight reduction, and, in extreme cases, replacement of the crippled joint with a prosthesis (Davenport, 2004; Edwards, 2005; Fontaine & Haaz, 2006).

Osteoporosis   Normal aging brings some loss of bone tissue, but in some instances loss of bone tissue can become severe. **Osteoporosis** involves an extensive loss of bone tissue. Osteoporosis is the main reason many older adults walk with a marked stoop. Women are especially vulnerable to osteoporosis, the leading cause of broken bones in women (Kuehn, 2005; Sambrook & Cooper, 2006). Approximately 80 percent of osteoporosis cases in the United States occur in females, 20 percent in males. Almost two-thirds of all women over the age of 60 are affected by osteoporosis. It is more common in non-Latina White, thin, and small-framed women.

Osteoporosis is related to deficiencies in calcium, vitamin D, estrogen, and lack of exercise (Mauck & Clarke, 2006; Nieves, 2005). To prevent osteoporosis, young and middle-aged women should eat foods rich in calcium (such as dairy products, broccoli, turnip greens, and kale), get more exercise, and avoid smoking (Whitehead & others, 2004). Drugs such as Fosimax can be used to reduce the risk of osteoporosis. Aging women should also get bone density checks (Burke & others, 2003; Dolan & others, 2004).

A program of regular exercise has the potential to reduce osteoporosis (Kuehn, 2005; Lespessailles & Prouteau, 2006; Turner & Robling, 2005). In one study, women aged 50 to 70 lifted weights twice a week, including three sets of eight repetitions on machines to strengthen muscles in the abdomen, back, thighs, and buttocks (Nelson & others, 1994). Their risk of osteoporosis (and resulting broken bones) was sharply reduced, while their balance and muscular strength improved.

Accidents   Accidents are the seventh leading cause of death among older adults. Injuries resulting from a fall at home or during a traffic accident in which an older adult is a driver or an older pedestrian is hit by a vehicle are common (Aschkenasy & Rothenhaus, 2006; Mayhew & others, 2005). Each year, approximately 200,000

www.mhhe.com/santrockld11

Arthritis
Osteoporosis

arthritis Inflammation of the joints that is accompanied by pain, stiffness, and movement problems; especially common in older adults.

osteoporosis A chronic condition that involves an extensive loss of bone tissue and is the main reason many older adults walk with a marked stoop. Women are especially vulnerable to osteoporosis.

adults over the age of 65 (most of them women) fracture a hip in a fall. Half of these older adults die within 12 months, frequently from pneumonia. Because healing and recuperation are slower in older adults, an accident that is only a temporary setback for a younger person may result in long-term hospital or home care for an older adult. In one study, an exercise program reduced the risk of falls in elderly adults (Province & others, 1995). In another study, Tai Chi, a form of balance training, improved the coordination of older adults in challenging conditions (Wong & others, 2001).

Substance Abuse

In many cases, older adults are taking multiple medications, which can increase the risks associated with consuming alcohol or other drugs. For example, when combined with tranquilizers or sedatives, alcohol use can impair breathing, produce excessive sedation, and be fatal.

How extensive is substance abuse in older adults? A recent national survey found that binge drinking (having five or more drinks in one day) declines through the late adulthood years (National Center for Health Statistics, 2002) (see figure 18.11). Indeed, a majority (58 percent) of U.S. adults 65 years and older completely abstain from alcohol, an increase from 38 percent of 45- to 64-year-olds. These declines are usually attributed to an increase in illness and disease (Aldwin, Spiro, & Park, 2006).

Despite these declines in alcohol use, the Substance Abuse and Mental Health Services Administration (2002) has identified substance abuse among older adults as the "invisible epidemic" in the United States. The belief is that substance abuse often goes undetected in older adults, and there is concern about older adults who not only abuse illicit drugs but prescription drugs as well (Scott & Popovich, 2001). Too often, screening questionnaires are not appropriate for older adults, and the consequences of alcohol abuse—such as depression, inadequate nutrition, congestive heart failure, and frequent falls—may erroneously be attributed to other medical or psychological conditions (Hoyer & Roodin, 2003). Because of the dramatic increase in the number of older adults anticipated over the twenty-first century, substance abuse is likely to characterize an increasing number of older adults (Atkinson, Ryan, & Turner, 2001).

Late-onset alcoholism is the label used to describe the onset of alcoholism after the age of 65. Late-onset alcoholism is often related to loneliness, loss of a spouse, or a disabling condition.

Exercise, Nutrition, and Weight

Although adults over the age of 65 often have a physical impairment, many still carry on their everyday activities or work. And according to one survey, disabilities among older adults declined almost 15 percent from 1982 to 1994 (Manton, Corder, & Stallard, 1997). Exercise, fewer smokers, and improvements in medical care account for much of the decline in disability among older adults (Suzman, 1997). The variability in how functioning declines with age and chronic disorders has generated increased attention to how older adults can maintain their functional abilities (Rincon, Muzumdar, & Barzilai, 2006).

Lifestyle, social, and psychological factors all influence the health and functioning of older adults (Abeles & others, 2006; Aldwin, Spiro, & Park, 2006; van Gool & others, 2006). For example, in the McArthur Studies of Successful Aging, emotional support was linked with better functioning in individuals with cardiovascular disease, and self-efficacy was a protective factor for individuals with a history of cancer (Seeman & Chen, 2002). Engaging in physical activity had a protective effect on health in virtually every group of older adults assessed. Let's take a closer

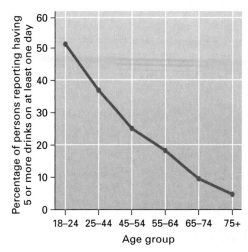

FIGURE 18.11 Age and the Consumption of Five or More Drinks on at Least One Day in the United States. The graph shows the considerable decline in having five or more drinks on at least one day as people get older (National Center for Health Statistics, 2002).

Trends in Health and Aging
Health and Aging:
Cross-Cultural Comparisons

All we know about older adults indicates that they are healthier and happier the more active they are. Several decades ago, it was believed that older adults should be more passive and inactive to be well adjusted and satisfied with life. In today's world, we believe that while older adults may be in the evening of their life span, they are not meant to live out their remaining years passively.

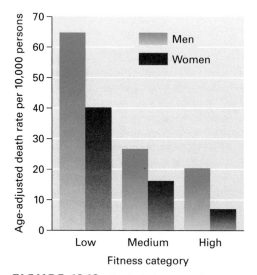

FIGURE 18.12 Physical Fitness and Mortality. In this study of middle-aged and older adults, being moderately fit or highly fit meant that individuals were less likely to die over a period of eight years than their low-fitness (sedentary) counterparts (Blair & others, 1989).

look at how exercise and diet might help prevent health problems in older adults and improve their health.

Exercise   Although we may be in the evening of our lives in late adulthood, we are not meant to live out our remaining years passively. Everything we know about older adults suggests they are healthier and happier the more active they are. Can regular exercise lead to a healthier late adulthood and increase longevity? Let's examine several research studies on exercise and aging.

In one study, the cardiovascular fitness of 101 older men and women (average age = 67 years) was examined (Blumenthal & others, 1989). The older adults were randomly assigned to an aerobic exercise group, a yoga and flexibility control group, and a waiting list control group. The program lasted four months. Prior to and following the four-month program, the older adults underwent comprehensive physiological examinations. In the aerobics group, the older adults participated in three supervised exercise sessions per week for 16 weeks. Each session consisted of a 10-minute warm-up, 30 minutes of continuous exercise on a stationary bicycle, 15 minutes of brisk walking/jogging, and a 5-minute cool-down. In the yoga and flexibility control group, the older adults participated in 60 minutes of supervised yoga exercises at least twice a week for 16 weeks. Over the four-month period, the cardiovascular fitness—such as peak oxygen consumption, cholesterol level, and blood pressure—of the aerobic exercise group significantly improved. In contrast, the cardiovascular fitness of the yoga and waiting list groups did not improve.

In another study, exercise literally meant a difference in life or death for middle-aged and older adults (Blair, 1990). More than 10,000 men and women were divided into categories of low fitness, medium fitness, and high fitness (Blair & others, 1989). Then they were studied over a period of eight years. As shown in figure 18.12, sedentary participants (low fitness) were more than twice as likely to die during the eight-year time span of the study than those who were moderately fit and more than three times as likely to die as those who were highly fit. The positive effects of being physically fit occurred for both men and women in this study.

Gerontologists increasingly recommend strength training in addition to aerobic activity and stretching for older adults (Ferrara & others, 2006; Holviala & others, 2006; Wieser & Haber, 2006). The average person's lean body mass declines with age—about 6.6 pounds of lean muscle are lost each decade during the adult years. The rate of loss accelerates after age 45. Weight lifting can preserve and possibly increase muscle mass in older adults (Seguin & Nelson, 2003). A recent study found that strength training alone or combined aerobic and strength training were more effective than aerobic training alone in improving older adults' muscle strength (Haykowsky & others, 2005). In one study, it also reduced depression in the elderly (Singh, Clements, & Fiatarone, 1997). A recent review of 62 research studies concluded that strength training can improve muscle strength and some aspects of functional limitation, such as gait speed, in older adults (Latham & others, 2004).

Exercise is an excellent way to maintain health. Researchers continue to document its positive effects in older adults (Kramer, Fabiani, & Colcombe, 2006; Okazaki & others, 2005; Rincon, Muzumdar, & Barzilai, 2006; Villareal & others, 2006; Weerdesteyn & others, 2006). Exercise helps people to live independent lives with dignity in late adulthood. At 80, 90, and even 100 years of age, exercise can help prevent older adults from falling down or even being institutionalized. Being physically fit means being able to do the things you want to do, whether you are young or old. More about research on exercise's positive benefits for health is shown in figure 18.13.

Recent reviews of research on exercise and aging reached these conclusions (Singh, 2002, 2004):

- *Exercise can minimize the physiological changes associated with aging and contribute to health and well-being.* Changes that can be modified by exercise include motor coordination, cardiovascular function, metabolism (cholesterol, for example), oxidative stress, brain functioning, attention span, and cognitive fitness (Ferrera, 2004; Kiraly & Kiraly, 2005; Kramer & others, 2005; Singh & others, 2006; Tarpenning & others, 2006).
- *Exercise can optimize body composition as aging occurs.* Exercise can increase muscle mass and bone mass, as well as decrease bone fragility (Issa & Sharma, 2006; Karlsson, 2004).
- *Exercise is related to prevention of common chronic diseases.* Exercise can reduce the risk of cardiovascular disease, Type II diabetes, osteoporosis, stroke, and breast cancer (Ferrara & others, 2006; Petersen & Petersen, 2005).
- *Exercise is associated with improvement in the treatment of many diseases.* When exercise is used as part of the treatment, individuals with these diseases show improvement in symptoms: arthritis, pulmonary disease, congestive heart failure, coronary artery disease, hypertension, Type II diabetes, and obesity (Dishman & others, 2006; Nazarian, 2004; Rosa & others, 2005).
- *Exercise is linked to increased longevity.* Energy expenditure during exercise of at least 1,000 kcal/week reduces mortality by about 30 percent, while 2,000 kcal/week reduces mortality by about 50 percent (Lee & Skerrett, 2001).

Nutrition and Weight Two aspects of undernutrition in older adults especially interest researchers: (1) vitamin and mineral deficiency and (2) the role of calorie restriction in improving health and extending life.

Some older adults engage in dietary restriction that is harmful to their health, especially when they do not get adequate vitamins and minerals (Aldwin, Spiro, & Park, 2006; Kennedy, 2006; Nino & Nino, 2006). One change in eating behavior in older adults is decreased snacking between meals, which may contribute to harmful weight loss, especially in women (Morley, 2003). Among the strategies for increasing weight gain in these women are the use of taste enhancers and of calorie supplements between meals (Morley, 2003; Thomas, 2003).

Seventeenth-century English philosopher and essayist Francis Bacon was the first author to recommend scientific evaluation of diet and longevity. He advocated a frugal diet. Does a restricted intake of food increase longevity or could it possibly even extend the human life span?

Scientists have accumulated considerable evidence that calorie restriction (CR) in laboratory animals (in most cases rats) can increase the animals' life span (Guarente & Picard, 2005; Sinclair & Howitz, 2006; Wolf, 2006). Animals fed diets restricted in calories, although adequate in protein, vitamins, and minerals, live as much as 40 percent longer than animals given unlimited access to food (Jolly, 2005; Piper, Mair, & Partridge, 2005). And chronic problems such as kidney disease appear at a later age (Bodkin, Ortmeyer, & Hansen, 2005; Yu, 2006). CR also delays biochemical alterations such as the age-related rise in cholesterol and triglycerides observed in both humans and animals (Skrha & others, 2005). And recent research indicates that CR may provide neuroprotection for an aging central nervous system (Hiona & Leeuwenburgh, 2005; Sharma & Kaur, 2005) (see figure 18.14).

No one knows for certain how CR works to increase the life span of animals. Some scientists believe it might lower the level of free radicals and reduce oxidative stress in cells (Hunt & others, 2006; Lopez-Lluch & others, 2006). For example, one recent study found that calorie restriction slowed the age-related increase in oxidative stress (Ward & others, 2005). Others believe calorie restriction might trigger a state of emergency called "survival mode" in which the body eliminates all unnecessary functions to focus only on staying alive.

Whether similar very-low-calorie diets can stretch the human life span is not known (Dirks & Leeuwenburgh, 2006; Lane & others, 2004; Shanley &

FIGURE 18.13 The Jogging Hog Experiment. Jogging hogs reveal the dramatic effects of exercise on health. In one investigation, a group of hogs was trained to run approximately 100 miles per week (Bloor & White, 1983). Then, the researchers narrowed the arteries that supplied blood to the hogs' hearts. The hearts of the jogging hogs developed extensive alternate pathways for blood supply, and 42 percent of the threatened heart tissue was salvaged compared with only 17 percent in a control group of nonjogging hogs.

www.mhhe.com/santrockld11

**Exercise and Aging
Roy Walford's Views**

FIGURE 18.14 Calorie Restriction in Monkeys. Shown here are two monkeys at the Wisconsin Primate Research Center. Both are 24 years old. The monkey in the top photograph was raised on a calorie-restricted diet, while the monkey in the bottom photograph was raised on a normal diet. Notice that the monkey on the calorie-restricted diet looks younger; he also has lower glucose and insulin levels. The monkey raised on a normal diet has higher triglycerides and more oxidative damage to his cells.

Kirkwood, 2006). In some instances the animals in these studies ate 40 percent less than normal. In humans, a typical level of calorie restriction involves a 30 percent decrease, which translates into about 1,120 calories a day for the average woman and 1,540 for the average man.

Leaner men do live longer, healthier lives. In one study of 19,297 Harvard alumni, those weighing the least were less likely to die over the past three decades (Lee & others, 1993). The men were divided into five categories according to body mass index (a complex formula that takes into account weight and height; see figure 14.3, page 465). As body mass increased, so did risk of death. The most overweight men had a 67 percent higher risk of dying than the thinnest men. For example, the heaviest men (such as 181 pounds or more for a 5-foot-10-inch man) also had 2½ times the risk of death from cardiovascular disease. Currently, these researchers are studying the relation of body mass index to longevity in women and predict similar results to the study with men.

The Growing Controversy over Vitamins and Aging
For years, most experts on aging and health argued that a balanced diet was all that was needed for successful aging; vitamin supplements were not recommended. However, recent research suggests the possibility that some vitamin supplements—mainly a group called "antioxidants," which includes vitamin C, vitamin E, and beta-carotene—help to slow the aging process and improve the health of older adults.

The theory is that antioxidants counteract the cell damage caused by free radicals, which are produced both by the body's own metabolism and by environmental factors such as smoking, pollution, and bad chemicals in the diet. When free radicals cause damage (oxidation) in one cell, a chain reaction of damage follows. Antioxidants act much like a fire extinguisher, helping to neutralize free-radical activity.

Some research studies find links between the antioxidant vitamins and health (Maxwell & others, 2005). One recent study linked low blood vitamin C concentration in older adults with an earlier incidence of death (Fletcher, Breeze, & Shetty, 2003). Another study found that people who took vitamin E supplements for two years significantly reduced their risk of heart disease—by up to 40 percent (Rimm & others, 1993). However, a recent analysis of 19 studies of vitamin E revealed that middle-aged and older adults who took 200 IU of vitamin E or more a day were more likely to die than their counterparts who did not take vitamin E (Miller & others, 2005). The researchers concluded that most individuals get enough vitamin E in their diet and should not take vitamin E supplements. They argue that vitamin E in low doses may be a powerful antioxidant but in higher doses may increase oxidative damage.

There is no evidence that antioxidants can increase the human life span, but some aging and health experts believe that vitamin C and beta-carotene can reduce a person's risk of becoming frail and sick in the later adult years (Korantzopoulos & others, 2006). However, there are still a lot of blanks and uncertainties in what we know (Stern, 1993). That is, we don't know which vitamins should be taken, how large a dose should be taken, what the restraints are, and so on. Critics also argue that the key experimental studies documenting the effectiveness of the vitamins in slowing the aging process have not been conducted. The studies in this area thus far have been so-called population studies that are correlational rather than experimental in nature. Other factors—such as exercise, better health practices, and good nutritional habits—might be responsible for the positive findings about vitamins and aging rather than vitamins per se. Also, the free-radical theory is a theory and not a fact, and is only one of a number of theories about why we age.

With these uncertainties in mind, some aging experts still recommend vitamin supplements in the following range (Blumberg, 1993): 250 to 1,000 milligrams of vitamin C and 15 to 30 milligrams of beta-carotene.

Possible links between vitamins and cognitive performance in older adults also have been the focus of increased research attention. A recent review of cross-sectional and longitudinal research studies concluded that taking B vitamins, especially folate, B_6, and B_{12}, is positively related to cognitive performance in older adults (Calvaresi & Bryan, 2001). This review also presented some evidence that supplementation with B vitamins can improve cognitive performance in older adults.

Health Treatment

What is the quality of health treatment that older adults in the United States receive? A recent study of older adults with health problems revealed that they receive the recommended medical care they need only half the time (Wenger & others, 2003). The researchers examined the medical records of 372 frail older adults who had been treated by two managed-care organizations over the course of one year. Then they documented the medical care each patient received and judged it using standard indicators of quality. For example, many older adults with an unsteady gait don't get the help they need, such as physical therapy to improve their walking ability. Clearly, the quality of health treatment older adults receive needs to be significantly improved (Gatz, 2006; Rantz & others, 2004).

Geriatric nurses can be especially helpful in treating the health-care problems of older adults. To read about the work of one geriatric nurse, see the Careers in Life-Span Development profile.

About 3 percent of adults 65 years of age and older in the United States reside in a nursing home at any point in time. However, as older adults age, their probability of being in a nursing home or other extended-care facility increases. Twenty-three percent of adults 85 years of age and older live in nursing homes or other extended-care facilities. What is the quality of nursing homes and extended-care facilities for older adults? What is the relationship between older adults and health-care providers?

The quality of nursing homes and other extended-care facilities for older adults varies enormously and is a source of continuing national concern (Briesacher & others, 2005; Castle & Engberg, 2005; Kurrle, 2006; Stevenson, 2006). More than one-third are seriously deficient. They fail federally mandated inspections because they do not meet the minimum standards for physicians, pharmacists, and various rehabilitation specialists (such as occupational and physical therapists). Further concerns focus on the patient's right to privacy, access to medical information, safety, and lifestyle freedom within the individual's range of mental and physical capabilities.

Because of the inadequate quality of many nursing homes and the escalating costs for nursing home care, many specialists in the health problems of the aged believe that home health care, day-care centers, and preventive medicine clinics are good alternatives (Castle, 2001). They are potentially less expensive than hospitals and nursing homes. They also are less likely to engender the feelings of depersonalization and dependency that occur so often in residents of institutions (Greene & others, 1995). One recent study found that older adults in a community-based long-term care

CAREERS in LIFE-SPAN DEVELOPMENT

Sarah Kagan
Geriatric Nurse

Sarah Kagan is a professor of nursing at the University of Pennsylvania School of Nursing. She provides nursing consultation to patients, their families, nurses, and physicians on the complex needs of older adults related to their hospitalization. She also consults on research and the management of patients who have head and neck cancers. Sarah also teaches in the undergraduate nursing program, where she directs the course Nursing Care in the Older Adult. In 2003, she was awarded a MacArthur Fellowship for her work in the field of nursing.

In Sarah's own words:

> I'm lucky to be doing what I love—caring for older adults and families—and learning from them so that I can share this knowledge and develop or investigate better ways of caring. My special interests in the care of older adults who have cancer allow me the intimate privilege of being with patients at the best and worst times of their lives. That intimacy acts as a beacon—it reminds me of the value I and nursing as a profession contribute to society and the rewards offered in return (Kagan, 2004, p. 1).

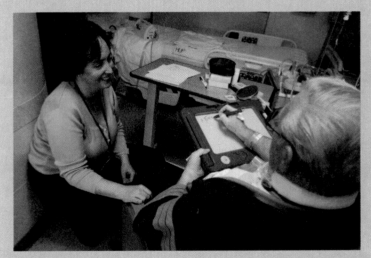

Sarah Kagan with a patient.

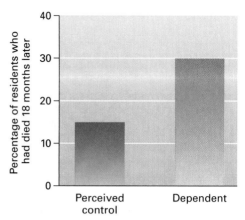

FIGURE 18.15 Perceived Control and Mortality. In the study by Rodin and Langer (1977), nursing home residents who were encouraged to feel more in control of their lives were more likely to be alive 18 months later than those who were treated to feel more dependent on the nursing home staff.

program performed better on cognitive tasks and were less depressed than their counterparts in an institutional-based long-term care facility (Marek & others, 2005).

In a classic study, Judith Rodin and Ellen Langer (1977) found that an important factor related to health, and even survival, in a nursing home is the patient's feelings of control and self-determination. A group of elderly nursing home residents were encouraged to make more day-to-day choices and thus feel they had more responsibility for control over their lives. They began to decide such matters as what they ate, when their visitors could come, what movies they saw, and who could come to their rooms. A similar group in the same nursing home was told by the administrator how caring the nursing home was and how much the staff wanted to help, but these residents were given no opportunity to take more control over their lives. Eighteen months later, the residents given responsibility and control were more alert and active, and said they were happier, than the residents who were only encouraged to feel that the staff would try to satisfy their needs. And the "responsible" or "self-control" group had significantly better improvement in their health than did the "dependent" group. Even more important was the finding that after 18 months only half as many nursing home residents in the "responsibility" group had died as in the "dependent" group (see figure 18.15). Perceived control over one's environment, then, can literally be a matter of life or death.

In another research study, Rodin (1983) measured stress-related hormones in several groups of nursing home residents. Then she taught the residents coping skills to help them deal better with day-to-day problems. They were taught how to say no when they did not want something, without worrying whether they would offend someone. They were given assertiveness training and learned time-management skills. After the training, the nursing home residents had greatly reduced levels of cortisol (a hormone closely related to stress that has been implicated in a number of diseases). The cortisol levels of the assertiveness-training residents remained lower, even after 18 months. Further, these nursing home residents were healthier and had a reduced need for medication, compared with residents who had not been taught the coping skills.

Rodin's research shows that simply giving nursing home residents options for control and teaching them coping skills can change their behavior and improve their health. To read further about health-care providers and older adults, see the Applications in Life-Span Development interlude.

What are some characteristics of health-care providers and their older adult patients?

APPLICATIONS IN LIFE-SPAN DEVELOPMENT

Health-Care Providers and Older Adults

The attitudes of both the health-care provider and the older adult are important aspects of the older adult's health care (Aud & others, 2006; Burbank & others, 2006; Varkey, Chutka, & Lesnick, 2006). Unfortunately, health-care providers too often share society's stereotypes and negative attitudes toward older adults. In a health-care setting, these attitudes can take the form of avoidance, dislike, and begrudged tolerance rather than positive, hopeful treatment. Health-care personnel are more likely to be interested in treating younger persons, who more often have acute problems with a higher prognosis for successful recovery. They often are less motivated to treat older persons, who are more likely to have chronic problems with a lower prognosis for successful recovery.

Not only are physicians less responsive to older patients, but older patients often take a less active role in medical encounters with health-care personnel than do younger patients (Woodward & Wallston, 1987). Older adults should be encouraged to take a more active role in their own health care.

Review and Reflect • LEARNING GOAL 3

3 **Identify health problems in older adults and how they can be treated**

Review

- What are some common health problems in older adults? What are the main causes of death in older adults?
- What characterizes substance abuse in late adulthood?
- How do exercise, nutrition, and weight influence development in late adulthood?
- What are some options and issues in the health treatment of older adults?

Reflect

- What changes in your lifestyle now might help you age more successfully when you become an older adult?

REACH YOUR LEARNING GOALS

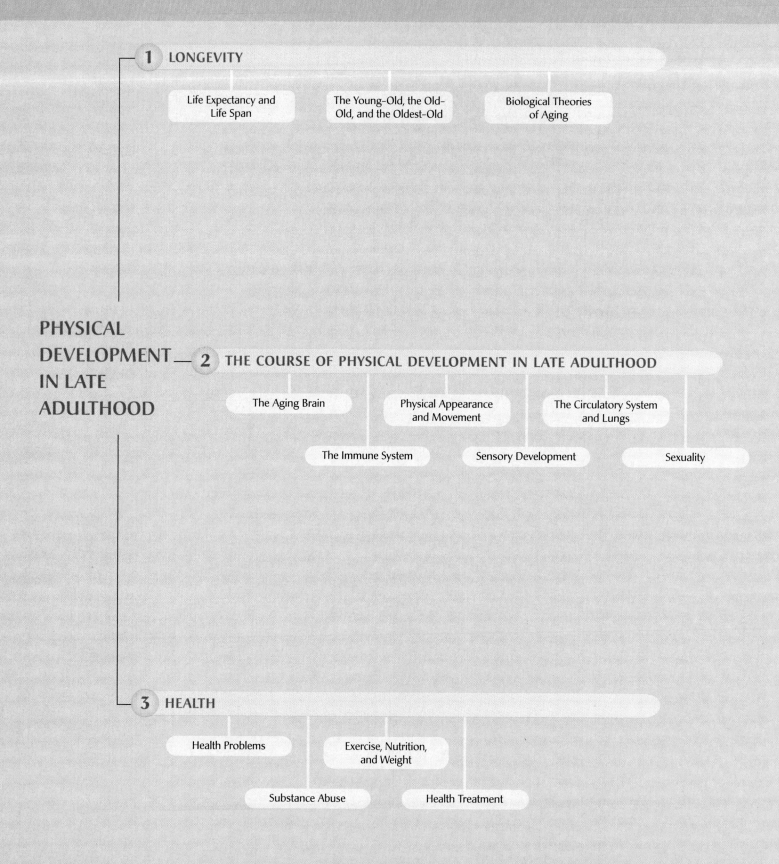

PHYSICAL DEVELOPMENT IN LATE ADULTHOOD

1 LONGEVITY

- Life Expectancy and Life Span
- The Young-Old, the Old-Old, and the Oldest-Old
- Biological Theories of Aging

2 THE COURSE OF PHYSICAL DEVELOPMENT IN LATE ADULTHOOD

- The Aging Brain
- Physical Appearance and Movement
- The Circulatory System and Lungs
- The Immune System
- Sensory Development
- Sexuality

3 HEALTH

- Health Problems
- Exercise, Nutrition, and Weight
- Substance Abuse
- Health Treatment

612

SUMMARY

1 Longevity: *Characterize longevity and the biological theories of aging*

Life Expectancy and Life Span

Life expectancy refers to the number of years that will probably be lived by an average person born in a particular year. Life span is the maximum number of years any member of a species has been known to live. Life expectancy has dramatically increased; life span has not. An increasing number of individuals live to be 100 or older. On the average, females live about six years longer than males do. The sex difference is likely due to biological and social factors.

The Young-Old, the Old-Old, and the Oldest-Old

In terms of chronological age, the young-old have been described as being 65 to 74 years of age, the old-old as 75 years and older, and the oldest-old as 85 years and older. Many experts on aging prefer to describe the young-old, old-old, and oldest-old in terms of functional age rather than chronological age. This view accounts for the fact that some 85-year-olds are more biologically and psychologically fit than some 65-year-olds. However, those 85 and older face significant problems, whereas those in their sixties and seventies are experiencing an increase in successful aging.

Biological Theories of Aging

Four biological theories are cellular clock theory, free-radical theory, mitochondrial theory, and hormonal stress theory. Hayflick proposed the cellular clock theory, which states that cells can divide a maximum of about 75 to 80 times and that as we age, our cells become less capable of dividing. Telomeres are likely involved in explaining why cells lose their capacity to divide. According to free-radical theory, people age because unstable oxygen molecules called free radicals are produced in the cells and damage cellular structures. According to mitochondrial theory, aging is due to the decay of mitochondria, tiny cellular bodies that supply energy for function, growth, and repair. According to hormonal stress theory, aging in the body's hormonal system can lower resilience to stress and increase the likelihood of disease.

2 The Course of Physical Development in Late Adulthood: *Describe how a person's brain and body change in late adulthood*

The Aging Brain

The brain loses weight and volume with age, and there is a general slowing of function in the central nervous system that begins in middle adulthood and increases in late adulthood. However, researchers have recently found that older adults can generate new neurons and, at least through the seventies, new dendrites. The aging brain retains considerable plasticity and adaptiveness. For example, it may compensate for losses in some regions of the brain by shifting responsibilities to other regions. A decrease in lateralization may reflect this kind of compensation, or it may reflect an age-related decline in the specialization of function.

The Immune System

Decline in immune system functioning with aging is well documented. Exercise can improve immune system functioning.

Physical Appearance and Movement

The most obvious signs of aging are wrinkled skin and age spots on the skin. People get shorter as they age, and their weight often decreases after age 60 because of loss of muscle. The movement of older adults slows across a wide range of movement tasks.

Sensory Development

Declines in visual acuity, color vision, and depth perception usually occur with age, especially after age 75. The yellowing of the eye's lens with age reduces color differentiation. The ability to see the periphery of a visual field also declines in older adults. Significant declines in visual functioning related to glare characterize adults 75 years and older and even more so those 85 and older. Three diseases that can impair the vision of older adults are cataracts, glaucoma, and macular degeneration. Hearing decline can begin in middle age but usually does not become much of an impediment until late adulthood. Hearing aids can diminish hearing problems for many older adults. Smell and taste can decline, although the decline is minimal in healthy older adults. Changes in touch sensitivity are associated with aging, although this does not present a problem for most older adults. Sensitivity to pain decreases in late adulthood.

The Circulatory System and Lungs

When heart disease is absent, the amount of blood pumped is the same regardless of an adult's age. High blood pressure is treated with medication, exercise, and/or a healthy diet. Lung capacity does drop with age, but older adults can improve lung functioning with diaphragm-strengthening exercises.

Sexuality

Aging in late adulthood does include some changes in sexual performance, more for males than females. Nonetheless, there are no known age limits to sexual activity.

3 Health: *Identify health problems in older adults and how they can be treated*

Health Problems

As we age, our probability of disease or illness increases. Chronic disorders are rare in early adulthood, increase in middle adulthood, and become more common in late adulthood. The most common chronic disorder in late adulthood is arthritis. Nearly three-fourths of older adults die of heart disease, cancer, or stroke. Osteoporosis is the main reason many older adults walk with a stoop; women are especially vulnerable. Accidents are usually more debilitating to older than to younger adults.

Substance Abuse

Alcohol use and abuse declines in older adults, although this is more difficult to detect in older adults than in younger adults.

Exercise, Nutrition, and Weight

The physical benefits of exercise have clearly been demonstrated in older adults. Aerobic exercise and weight lifting are both recommended if the adults are physically capable of them. There is concern about older adults who do not get adequate vitamins and minerals, especially women. Calorie restriction in animals can increase the animals' life span, but whether this works with humans is not known. In humans, being overweight is associated with an increased mortality rate. Most nutritional experts recommend a well-balanced, low-fat diet for older adults, but do not recommend an extremely low-calorie diet. Controversy surrounds the question of whether vitamin supplements—especially the antioxidants vitamin C, vitamin E, and beta-carotene—can slow the aging process and improve older adults' health. Recent research has found a link between taking B vitamins and positive cognitive performance in older adults.

Health Treatment

Although only 3 percent of adults over 65 reside in nursing homes, 23 percent of adults 85 and over do. The quality of nursing homes varies enormously. Alternatives to nursing homes are being proposed. Simply giving nursing home residents options for control and teaching coping skills can change their behavior and improve their health. The attitudes of both the health-care provider and the older adult patient are important aspects of the older adult's health care. Too often health-care personnel share society's negative view of older adults.

KEY TERMS

life span 588
life expectancy 589
cellular clock theory 593

free-radical theory 594
mitochondrial theory 594
hormonal stress theory 594

cataracts 600
glaucoma 600
macular degeneration 600

arthritis 604
osteoporosis 604

KEY PEOPLE

Leonard Hayflick 593

Stanley Rapaport 596

Ellen Langer 610

Judith Rodin 610

E-LEARNING TOOLS

To help you master the material in this chapter, you'll find a number of valuable study tools on the LifeMap CD-ROM that accompanies this book and on the Online Learning Center for *Life-Span Development,* eleventh edition, at **www.mhhe.com/ santrockld11**.

Video Clips

In the margins of this book there are icons directing you to the LifeMap CD-ROM that accompanies the book. There you'll find a video for chapter 18 called "Human Development: Cognitive Functioning in Centenarians." Do mental faculties invariably diminish as one gets older? Or is the brain, as Dr. Marjorie Silver claims in this segment, a muscle that requires regular exercise?

Self-Assessment

Connect to **www.mhhe.com/santrockld11** to reflect on what aging means to you by completing the self-assessment, *My Beliefs About Aging.*

Taking It to the Net

Connect to **www.mhhe.com/santrockld11** to research the answers to these questions.

1. Do you think you will live to be 100? Investigate your chances of becoming a centenarian by reading the results from an ongoing Harvard University Medical School study.
2. Seventy-year-old Jack knows that regular exercise is important to maintain a healthy heart. But what are the other benefits to staying active, and how much exercising should Jack do?
3. Patty's 85-year-old mother, who lives with her and her family, has begun eating less and less. She tells Patty, "Eating is no fun anymore. I can't taste anything." What can Patty do to make meals more appealing for her mother?

Health and Well-Being, Parenting, and Education Exercises

Build your decision-making skills by trying your hand at the health and well-being, parenting, and education exercises. Connect to **www.mhhe.com/santrockld11** to research the answers and complete the exercises.

Chapter 19 COGNITIVE DEVELOPMENT IN LATE ADULTHOOD

The night hath not yet come: We are not quite cut off from labor by the failing of light; some work remains for us to do and dare.

—HENRY WADSWORTH LONGFELLOW
American Poet, 19th Century

LEARNING GOALS

1 Describe the cognitive functioning of older adults

2 Characterize changes in language in older adults

3 Discuss aging and adaptations to work and retirement

4 Describe mental health problems in older adults

5 Explain the role of religion in the lives of older adults

Images of Life-Span Development
Lily Hearst and Sister Mary, Active Minds

Throughout her life, Lily Hearst has pursued a range of interests including the arts, music, science, and politics. She has a degree in music and reads and speaks three languages. Now, at 101 years old, she lives independently and exercises every day. She reads *The Wall Street Journal* daily, teaches piano, and plays in a classical trio at the North Berkeley Senior Center (in Berkeley, California).

Lily keeps a strict daily routine that begins at seven o'clock, when she gets out of bed, exercises, and fixes her own breakfast. At nine she goes to the pool and swims eight laps. A friend drives her to the senior center where she attends classes, reads, watches movies, and plays piano. Lily keeps track of her life with a date book, writing down engagements and other things she needs to remember. She takes pride in the fact that she is never late for an appointment (Exploratorium, 2004, pp. 1–2).

Another centenarian, Sister Mary, was a participant in the Nun Study, which we described in chapter 18. She died in 1993 at 101 years of age. Even at 100, Sister Mary continued to score high on measures of cognitive skills (Snowdon, 1997). She loved to read, and late in her life was often observed looking through a magnifying glass as she read books, magazines, and newspapers.

PREVIEW

Lily Hearst and Sister Mary led very active cognitive lives as older adults. Just how well older adults can and do function cognitively is an important question *we will explore in this chapter. We also will examine the important topics of language development, work and retirement, mental health, and religion.*

1 COGNITIVE FUNCTIONING IN OLDER ADULTS

- Multidimensionality and Multidirectionality
- Use It or Lose It
- Cognitive Neuroscience and Aging
- Education, Work, and Health
- Training Cognitive Skills

Grandma Moses, known in her time as the "grand old lady of American art," took up painting at the age of 76 and continued to paint past her hundredth birthday.

At the age of 70, John Rock invented the birth control pill. At age 76, Anna Mary Robertson Moses, better known as Grandma Moses, took up painting and became internationally famous, staging fifteen one-woman shows throughout Europe. At age 89, Arthur Rubinstein gave one of his best performances at New York's Carnegie Hall. When Pablo Casals was 95, a reporter asked him, "Mr. Casals, you are the greatest cellist who ever lived. Why do you still practice six hours a day?" Mr. Casals replied, "Because I feel like I am making progress" (Canfield & Hansen, 1995).

Multidimensionality and Multidirectionality

In thinking about the nature of cognitive change in adulthood, it is important to consider that cognition is a multidimensional concept (Craik & Bialystok, 2006; Schaie, 2006; Schaie & Zanjani, 2006). It is also important to consider that although some dimensions of cognition might decline as we age, others might remain stable or even improve (Salthouse & Baltes, 2006).

Cognitive Mechanics and Cognitive Pragmatics

Paul Baltes (2000, 2003; Baltes, Lindenberger, & Staudinger, 2006) clarified the distinction between those aspects of the aging mind that show decline and those that remain stable or even improve. (This distinction is similar to the one between fluid and crystallized intelligence that was described in Chapter 16.)

- **Cognitive mechanics** are the "hardware" of the mind and reflect the neuro-physiological architecture of the brain developed through evolution. Cognitive mechanics consist of these components: speed and accuracy of the processes involved in sensory input, attention, visual and motor memory, discrimination, comparison, and categorization. Because of the strong influence of biology, heredity, and health on cognitive mechanics, their decline with aging is likely. Some researchers conclude that the decline in cognitive mechanics may begin as soon as early midlife (Li & others, 2004).
- **Cognitive pragmatics** are the culture-based "software programs" of the mind. Cognitive pragmatics include reading and writing skills, language comprehension, educational qualifications, professional skills, and also the type of knowledge about the self and life skills that help us to master or cope with life. Because of the strong influence of culture on cognitive pragmatics, their improvement into old age is possible. Thus, although cognitive mechanics may decline in old age, cognitive pragmatics may actually improve, at least until individuals become very old (see figure 19.1).

One recent study focused on older adults (age range: 70 to 100 years of age with a mean age of 85) over a six-year period (Singer & others, 2003). In support of the cognitive mechanics/pragmatics distinction, they found that perceptual speed, memory, and categorization declined with age but that knowledge remained stable up to age 90 before it began to decline.

Now that we have examined the distinction between cognitive mechanics and cognitive pragmatics, let's explore some of the more specific cognitive processes that reflect these two general domains. We begin with these aspects of cognitive mechanics: sensory/motor and speed of processing.

Sensory/Motor and Speed-of-Processing Dimensions

In the Berlin Study of Aging, the key factors that accounted for age differences in intelligence were visual and auditory acuity (Lindenberger & Baltes, 1994). Thus, sensory functioning was a strong late-life predictor of individual differences in intelligence. It is also now well accepted that the speed of processing information declines in late adulthood (Hartley, 2006; Hoyer & Verhaeghen, 2006; Salthouse, 1996, 2000; Salthouse & Miles, 2002) (see figure 19.2).

Although speed of processing information slows down in late adulthood, there is considerable individual variation in this ability (Hartley, 2006). And it is not clear that this slowdown affects our lives in substantial ways. For example, in one experiment, the reaction time and typing skills of typists of varying ages were studied (Salthouse, 1994). The older typists usually had slower reactions, but they actually typed just as fast as the younger typists. Possibly the older typists were faster when they were younger and had slowed down, but the results in another experimental condition suggested that something else was involved. When the number of characters that the typists could look ahead at was limited, the older typists slowed considerably; the younger typists were affected much less by this restriction. Thus, the older typists had learned to look farther ahead, allowing them to type as fast as their younger counterparts.

Accumulated knowledge may compensate to some degree for slower processing speed in older adults. For example, one recent study found that knowledge was

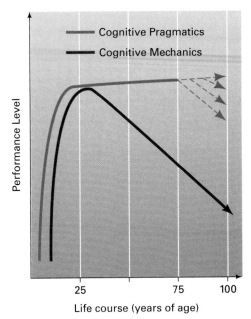

FIGURE 19.1 Theorized Age Changes in Cognitive Mechanics and Cognitive Pragmatics. Baltes argues that cognitive mechanics decline during aging, whereas cognitive pragmatics do not, at least for many people until they become very old. Cognitive mechanics have a biological/genetic foundation; cognitive pragmatics have an experiential/cultural foundation. The broken lines from 75 to 100 years of age indicate possible individual variations in cognitive pragmatics.

cognitive mechanics The "hardware" of the mind, reflecting the neurophysiological architecture of the brain as developed through evolution. Cognitive mechanics involve the speed and accuracy of the processes involving sensory input, attention, visual and motor memory, discrimination, comparison, and categorization.

cognitive pragmatics The culture-based "software programs" of the mind. Cognitive pragmatics include reading and writing skills, language comprehension, educational qualifications, professional skills, and also the type of knowledge about the self and life skills that help us to master or cope with life.

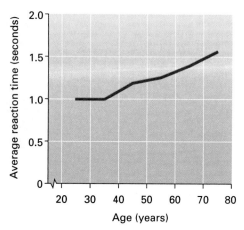

FIGURE 19.2 The Relation of Age to Reaction Time. In one study, the average reaction time began to slow in the forties, and this decline accelerated in the sixties and seventies (Salthouse, 1994). The task used to assess reaction time required individuals to match numbers with symbols on a computer screen.

more important on a memory task for older adults than younger adults and that older adults may rely on age-related increases in knowledge to partially compensate for a decline in processing speed (Hedden, Lautenschlager, & Park, 2005).

The decline in processing speed in older adults is likely due to a decline in functioning of the brain and central nervous system (Fabiani & others, 2006; Groth, Gilmore, & Thomas, 2003). Health and exercise may influence how much decline in processing speed occurs (Gerrotsen & others, 2003). One study found that following six months of aerobic exercise older adults showed improvement on reaction time tasks (Kramer & others, 1999).

The importance of processing speed was underscored in a recent study (Deary & Der, 2005). Researchers have found that lower IQ is linked to earlier death but have not explained why this association exists. In the recent study, 898 56-year-old individuals were monitored with respect to their survival until the age of 70. The link between IQ and mortality was present but after the reaction time of the study's participants was considered, the association of IQ and mortality disappeared. This suggests that slower processing of information might be responsible for the association of lower IQ and mortality.

Attention Three aspects of attention that have been investigated in older adults are selective attention, divided attention, and sustained attention:

- **Selective attention** is focusing on a specific aspect of experience that is relevant while ignoring others that are irrelevant. An example of selective attention is the ability to focus on one voice among many in a crowded room or a noisy restaurant. Another is making a decision about which stimuli to attend to when making a left turn at an intersection. Generally, older adults are less adept at selective attention than younger adults are (Brown, McKenzie, & Doan, 2005; Hoyer & Verhaeghen, 2006; Pesce & others, 2005). However, on simple tasks involving a search for a feature, such as determining whether a target item is present on a computer screen, age differences are minimal when individuals are given sufficient practice.
- **Divided attention** involves concentrating on more than one activity at the same time. When the two competing tasks are reasonably easy, age differences among adults are minimal or nonexistent. However, the more difficult the competing tasks are, the less effectively older adults divide attention than younger adults (Maciokas & Crognale, 2003; Wood, 2002). In one study, the ability to engage in a conversation while simultaneously driving a simulator through highway traffic (in an experimental laboratory) was examined in 17- to 25-year-olds, 26- to 49-year-olds, and 50- to 80-year-olds (McKnight & McKnight, 1993). A nondistraction control condition also was included. Overall, the participants performed more poorly in the divided attention condition than in the nondistraction control condition. Also, the older adults (50 to 80 years old) performed worse in the divided attention condition than the younger two groups but not in the control condition. Thus, placing more demands on the attention of the older adults led them to perform more poorly on the driving task.
- **Sustained attention** is the state of readiness to detect and respond to small changes occurring at random times in the environment. Sometimes sustained attention is referred to as *vigilance*. Researchers have found that older adults perform as well as middle-aged and younger adults on measures of sustained attention (Berardi, Parasuraman, & Haxby, 2001).

Memory Let's examine a research study that addresses how we remember as we age. Non-Latino adults of various ages in the United States were studied to determine how much Spanish they remembered from classes they had taken in high school or college (Bahrick, 1984). The individuals chosen for the study had used

selective attention Focusing on a specific aspect of experience that is relevant while ignoring others that are irrelevant.

divided attention Concentrating on more than one activity at the same time.

sustained attention The state of readiness to detect and respond to small changes occurring at random times in the environment.

Spanish very little since they initially learned it in high school or college. Not surprisingly, the young adults who had taken Spanish within the last three years remembered Spanish best. After that, the deterioration in memory was gradual (see figure 19.3). For example, older adults who had studied Spanish 50 years earlier remembered about 80 percent of what young adults did who had studied it in the last three years! The most important factor in the adults' memory of Spanish was not how long ago they studied it but how well they initially learned it—those who got an A in Spanish 50 years earlier remembered more Spanish than adults who got a C when taking Spanish only one year earlier.

Memory does change during aging, but not all memory changes with age in the same way (Balota, Dolan, & Duchek, 2000; Hoyer & Verhaeghen, 2006). The main dimensions of memory and aging that have been studied include episodic memory, semantic memory, cognitive resources (such as working memory and perceptual speed), memory beliefs, and noncognitive factors such as health, education, and socioeconomic factors (Smith, 1996).

Episodic Memory   **Episodic memory** is the retention of information about the where and when of life's happenings (Tulving, 2000). For example, what was it like when your younger sister or brother was born, what happened to you on your first date, what were you doing when you heard that the Persian Gulf War had begun, and what did you eat for breakfast this morning?

Younger adults have better episodic memory than older adults have (Hoyer & Verhaeghen, 2006; Jacoby & Rhodes, 2006; Persson & others, 2005; Ronnlund & others, 2005). Also, older adults think that they can remember older events better than more recent events, typically reporting that they can remember what happened to them years ago but can't remember what they did yesterday. However, researchers consistently have found that, contrary to such self-reports, in older adults the older the memory, the less accurate it is. This has been documented in studies of memory for high school classmates, foreign language learned in school over the life span, names of grade school teachers, and autobiographical facts kept in diaries (Smith, 1996).

Semantic Memory   **Semantic memory** is a person's knowledge about the world. It includes a person's fields of expertise, such as knowledge of chess for a skilled chess player; general academic knowledge of the sort learned in school, such as knowledge of geometry; and "everyday knowledge" about the meanings of words, famous individuals, important places, and common things, such as what day is Valentine's Day. Semantic memory appears to be independent of an individual's personal identity with the past. For example, you can access a fact—such as "Lima is the capital of Peru"—and not have the foggiest idea of when and where you learned it.

Does semantic memory decline during aging? Older adults do often take longer to retrieve semantic information, but usually they can ultimately retrieve it. For the most part, episodic memory declines more in older adults than semantic memory (Hoyer & Verhaeghen, 2006; Ronnlund & others, 2005).

Cognitive Resources: Working Memory and Perceptual Speed   One view of memory suggests that a limited number of cognitive resources can be devoted to any cognitive task. Two important cognitive resource mechanisms are working memory and perceptual speed. Recall from chapter 16 that *working memory* is closely linked to short-term memory but places more emphasis on memory as a place for mental work. Working memory is like a mental "workbench" that allows individuals to manipulate and assemble information when making decisions, solving problems, and comprehending written and spoken language (Baddeley, 2000). Researchers have found declines in working memory during the late adulthood years (Bopp & Verhaeghen, 2005; Gazzaley & others, 2005; Missonnier & others, 2004).

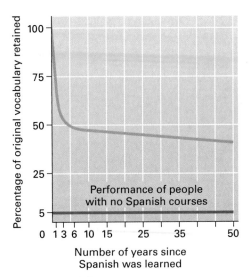

FIGURE 19.3 Memory for Spanish as a Function of Age Since Spanish Was Learned. An initial steep drop over about a three-year period in remembering the vocabulary learned in Spanish classes occurred. However, there was little dropoff in memory for Spanish vocabulary from 3 years after taking Spanish classes to 50 years after taking them. Even 50 years after taking Spanish classes, individuals still remembered almost 50 percent of the vocabulary.

www.mhhe.com/santrockld11

Cognitive Psychology Laboratory
Timothy Salthouse's Research
Fredda Blanchard-Fields' Research

episodic memory The retention of information about the where and when of life's happenings.

semantic memory A person's knowledge about the world—including a person's fields of expertise, general academic knowledge of the sort learned in school, and "everyday knowledge."

Perceptual speed is another cognitive resource that has been studied by researchers on aging. Perceptual speed is the ability to perform simple perceptual-motor tasks such as deciding whether pairs of two-digit or two-letter strings are the same or different or determining the time required to step on the brakes when the car directly ahead stops. Perceptual speed shows considerable decline in late adulthood, and it is strongly linked with decline in working memory (Hartley, 2006; Hoyer & others, 2004). One recent study found that speed of processing training improved the performance of older adults on perceptual speed tasks (Edwards & others, 2005).

Explicit and Implicit Memory   Researchers also have found that aging is linked with changes in explicit memory (Hoyer & Verhaeghen, 2006; Tulving, 2000). **Explicit memory** is memory of facts and experiences that individuals consciously know and can state. Explicit memory also is sometimes called *declarative memory*. Examples of explicit memory include being at a grocery store and remembering what you wanted to buy, being able to name the capital of Illinois, or recounting the events of a movie you have seen. **Implicit memory** is memory without conscious recollection; it involves skills and routine procedures that are automatically performed. Examples of implicit memory include driving a car, swinging a golf club, or typing on a computer keyboard, without having to consciously think about it.

Implicit memory is less likely to be adversely affected by aging than explicit memory (Fleischman & others, 2004; Kessels, Boekhorst, & Postma, 2005; Tulving, 2000). Thus, older adults are more likely to forget what items they wanted to buy at a grocery store (unless they write them down on a list and take it with them) than they are to forget how to drive a car. Their perceptual speed might be slower in driving the car, but they remember how to do it.

In chapter 1, we described research by Lynn Hasher and her colleagues (2001) that indicated that the explicit memory of evening-type younger adults was better when tested in the p.m., while the explicit memory of morning-type older adults was better when it was tested in the a.m. A recent study replicated that finding but also examined a possible link between implicit memory and time of day testing (May, Hasher, & Foong, 2005). For implicit memory, morning-type older adults and evening-type young adults performed better at off-peak times (morning for young adults, evening for older adults).

Source Memory   **Source memory** is the ability to remember where one learned something. Failures of source memory increase with age in the adult years and they can create awkward situations, as when an older adult forgets who told a joke and retells it to the source (Gilbert & others, 2006; Mitchell & others, 2006; Swick, Senkfor, & Van Petten, 2006).

One recent study found that awareness of character can compensate for the age declines in source memory (Rahal, May, & Hasher, 2002). In a typical memory source study, before playing a tape, participants listen to a series of statements spoken by either a male or a female voice. At the end, participants read the statements and say which voice spoke to them. The researchers added this twist to their study. Before playing the tape, some of the older adults were told that one voice belonged to a saintly person who never told a lie and that the other person was a dishonest cad. As in past studies, the older adults had difficulty in remembering which voice spoke which given line. However, those who were told about the trustworthiness of the speakers more accurately judged whether a given statement was likely to be true or false, suggesting that older adults can remember information about a source when it is important to them.

Lynn Hasher (2003, p. 1301), one of the researchers who conducted the memory source study just described, argues that age differences are substantial when individuals are asked "for a piece of information that just doesn't matter much. But if you ask for information that is important, old people do every bit as well as young

explicit memory Memory of facts and experiences that individuals consciously know and can state.

implicit memory Memory without conscious recollection; involves skills and routine procedures that are automatically performed.

source memory The ability to remember where one learned something.

adults . . . young people have mental resources to burn. As people get older, they get more selective in how they use their resources."

Prospective Memory **Prospective memory** involves remembering to do something in the future, such as remembering to take your medicine or remembering to do an errand. Although some researchers have found a decline in prospective memory with age, a number of studies show that whether there is a decline is complex and depends on such factors as the nature of the task and what is being assessed (Einstein & others, 2000; Einstein & McDaniel, 2005; Henry & others, 2004; McDaniel & others, 2003). For example, age-related deficits occur more often in time-based (such as remembering to call someone next Friday) than in event-based (remembering to tell your friend to read a particular book the next time you see her) prospective memory tasks.

Beliefs, Expectations, and Feelings An increasing number of studies are finding that people's beliefs and expectancies about memory play a role in their actual memory (Cavanaugh, 2000; McDougall, 2004). It matters what people tell themselves about their ability to remember. Positive or negative beliefs or expectancies about one's memory skills are related to actual memory performance (Glass & others, 2005; Hess, 2005; Hess, Hinson, & Statham, 2004). Recall from the Research in Life-Span Development interlude in chapter 1 our description of a recent study in which older adults were randomly assigned to read one of two mock newspaper articles at the beginning of a testing situation (Hess & others, 2003). One described the declines in memory that characterize aging; the other emphasized research on the preservation of memory skills in older adults. The older adults who read the pessimistic account of memory and aging remembered 20 to 30 percent fewer words than people who read about the ability to maintain memory in old age.

Attitudes and feelings also matter (Reese & Cherry, 2004). One study found that individuals with low anxiety about their memory skills and high self-efficacy regarding their use of memory in everyday contexts had better memory performance than their high-anxiety/low-self-efficacy counterparts (McDougall & others, 1999).

Noncognitive Factors Health, education, and socioeconomic status can influence an older adult's performance on memory tasks (Peters, 2006; Roman & others, 2004). Although such noncognitive factors as good health are associated with less memory decline in older adults, they do not eliminate memory decline.

One criticism of research on memory and aging is that it has relied primarily on laboratory tests of memory. The argument is that such tasks are contrived and do not represent the everyday cognitive tasks performed by older adults. If researchers used more everyday life memory tasks, would memory decline be found in older adults? A number of researchers have found that using more familiar tasks reduces age decrements in memory but does not eliminate them. Younger adults are better than older adults at remembering faces, routes through town, grocery items, and performed activities. In one study, young adults (20 to 40 years old) remembered news content in print, audio, and TV format better than old adults did (60 to 80 years old) (Frieske & Park, 1999).

Conclusions About Memory and Aging Some, but not all, aspects of memory decline in older adults. The decline occurs primarily in episodic and working memory, not in semantic memory or implicit memory. A decline in perceptual speed is associated with memory decline. Successful aging does not mean eliminating memory decline, but reducing it and adapting to it. As we will see later in this chapter, older adults can use certain strategies to reduce memory decline.

Wisdom
Does wisdom, like good wine, improve with age? What is this thing we call "wisdom"? **Wisdom** is expert knowledge about the practical aspects of life that

prospective memory Involves remembering to do something in the future.

wisdom Expert knowledge about the practical aspects of life that permits excellent judgment about important matters.

Older adults might not be as quick with their thoughts or behavior as younger people, but wisdom may be an entirely different matter. This older woman shares the wisdom of her experience with a classroom of children. *How is wisdom described by life-span developmentalists?*

permits excellent judgment about important matters. This practical knowledge involves exceptional insight into human development and life matters, good judgment, and an understanding of how to cope with difficult life problems. Thus, wisdom, more than standard conceptions of intelligence, focuses on life's pragmatic concerns and human conditions (Baltes & Kunzmann, 2003, 2004; Baltes, Lindenberger, & Staudinger, 2006; Brugman, 2006).

In regard to wisdom, research by Baltes and his colleagues (Baltes, Glück, & Kunzmann, 2002; Baltes & Kunzmann, 2003, 2004; Baltes, Lindenberger, & Staudinger, 2006) has found that:

- High levels of wisdom are rare. Few people, including older adults, attain a high level of wisdom (Baltes & Smith, 1990). That only a small percentage of adults show wisdom supports the contention that it requires experience, practice, or complex skills.
- The time frame of late adolescence and early adulthood is the main age window for wisdom to emerge. No further advances in wisdom have been found for middle-aged and older adults beyond the level they attained as young adults.
- Factors other than age are critical for wisdom to develop to a high level. For example, certain life experiences, such as being trained and working in a field concerned with difficult life problems and having wisdom-enhancing mentors, contribute to higher levels of wisdom. Also, people higher in wisdom have values that are more likely to consider the welfare of others rather than their own happiness.
- Personality-related factors, such as openness to experience, generativity, and creativity, are better predictors of wisdom than cognitive factors such as intelligence.

Education, Work, and Health

Education, work, and health are three important influences on the cognitive functioning of older adults. They are also three of the most important factors involved in understanding why cohort effects need to be taken into account in studying the cognitive functioning of older adults.

Education   Successive generations in America's twentieth century were better educated. Not only were today's older adults more likely to go to college when they were young adults than were their parents or grandparents, but more older adults are returning to college today to further their education than in past generations. Educational experiences are positively correlated with scores on intelligence tests and information-processing tasks, such as memory (Ronnlund & others, 2005; Schaie & Elder, 2006; Springer & others, 2005; Verhaeghen, Marcoen, & Goossens, 1995; Willis & Schaie, 2005).

Older adults might seek more education for a number of reasons. They might want to better understand the nature of their aging. They might want to learn more about the social and technological changes that have produced dramatic changes in their lives. They might want to discover relevant knowledge and to learn relevant skills to cope with societal and job demands in later life. They might recognize that they need further education to remain competitive and stay in the workforce. Earlier, in the twentieth century, most individuals made career choices in adolescence and young adulthood and never wavered from those choices throughout their adult years. Today, that is not always the pattern. Technological changes have meant that some of the occupations of 15 years ago no longer exist. And some of today's occupations could not even be identified 15 years ago. Finally, older adults may seek more education to enhance their self-discovery and the leisure activities that will enable them to make a smoother adjustment to retirement.

It is always in season for the old to learn.

—Aeschylus
Greek Playwright, 5th Century B.C.

Work Successive generations have also had work experiences that include a stronger emphasis on cognitively oriented labor. Our great-grandfathers and grandfathers were more likely to be manual laborers than were our fathers, who are more likely to be involved in cognitively oriented occupations. As the industrial society continues to be replaced by the information society, younger generations will have more experience in jobs that require considerable cognitive investment. The increased emphasis on complex information processing in jobs likely enhances an individual's intellectual abilities (Schaie & Elder, 2006; Schooler, Mulatu, & Oates, 2004).

In one study, substantive complex work was linked with higher intellectual functioning in older adults (Schooler, Mulatu, & Oates, 1999). This research is consistent with findings in a wide range of disciplines, including animal-based neurobiology studies, which strongly suggest that exposure to complex environments increases intellectual functioning throughout the life course (Kempermann, Kuhn, & Gage, 1997).

Health Successive generations have also been healthier in late adulthood as better treatments for a variety of illnesses (such as hypertension) have been developed. Many of these illnesses have a negative impact on intellectual performance (Hultsch, Hammer, & Small, 1993; Schaie & Elder, 2006). Hypertension has been linked to lower cognitive performance in a number of studies, not only in older adults but also in young and middle-aged adults (Elias & others, 2005; Vicario & others, 2005; Willis & Schaie, 2005). In one study, physical health and physical activity were positively related to cognitive performance in older adults (Anstey & Smith, 1999). The older the population, the more persons with health problems. Thus, some of the decline in intellectual performance found for older adults is likely due to health-related factors rather than to age per se (Arvanitakis & others, 2006; Comijs & others, 2002; Lyketsos & others, 2006).

K. Warner Schaie (1994) concluded that although some diseases—such as hypertension and diabetes—are linked to cognitive dropoffs, they do not directly cause mental decline. Rather, the lifestyles of the individuals with the diseases might be the culprits. For example, overeating, inactivity, and stress are related to both physical and mental decline (Christensen & others, 1996).

A number of research studies have found that lifestyle and exercise are linked to improved cognitive functioning (Kramer, Fabiani, & Colcombe, 2006; Kramer & others, 2002; Lautenschlager & Almeida, 2006; Newson & Kemps, 2005). Here are the results of two of these studies:

- Community-dwelling women 65 years of age and older did not have cognitive impairment or physical limitations when they were initially assessed (Yaffe & others, 2001). Six to eight years later, the women with higher physical activity when they were initially assessed were less likely to experience cognitive decline.
- One hundred twenty-four individuals 60 to 75 years of age whose primary activity was sitting around the house were tested for their level of aerobic endurance and their level of cognitive functioning (Kramer & others, 1999). Cognitive functioning was assessed by tasks on working memory, planning, and scheduling. Half the group was randomly assigned to engage in yoga-type stretching activities and the other half was randomly assigned to start walking three times a week. After six months, the walkers averaged a mile in 16 minutes, a minute faster than at the beginning, and the stretchers had become more flexible. When their cognitive functioning was retested after six months, the walkers scored up to 25 percent higher on the cognitive tests than the stretchers did.

How are education, work, and health linked to cognitive functioning in older adults?

Other researchers have found that aerobic exercise is related to improved memory and reasoning (Clarkson-Smith & Hartley, 1989). Walking or any other aerobic exercise appears to get blood and oxygen pumping to the brain, which can help people think more clearly (Studenski & others, 2006).

Two recent studies documented that the mental health of older adults can also influence their memory. A six-year longitudinal study found that higher levels of anxiety and depression assessed at the beginning of the study were linked to poorer memory functioning six years later (van Hooren & others, 2005). Another longitudinal study revealed that higher levels of anxiety and depression were related to poorer cognitive performance in older adults in a number of areas: general cognitive functioning, episodic memory, fluid intelligence, and processing speed (Bierman & others, 2005).

Use It or Lose It

Changes in cognitive activity patterns might result in disuse and consequent atrophy of cognitive skills. This concept is captured in the adage "Use it or lose it." The mental activities that likely benefit the maintenance of cognitive skills in older adults are activities such as reading books, doing crossword puzzles, and going to lectures and concerts. These studies support this idea:

- In an analysis of participants in the Victoria Longitudinal Study, when middle-aged and older adults participated in intellectually engaging activities it served to buffer them against cognitive decline (Hultsch & others, 1999). This also was found in another longitudinal study over a 45-year time frame (Arbuckle & others, 1998).
- In a $4\frac{1}{2}$-year longitudinal study of 801 Catholic priests 65 years and older, those who regularly read books, did crossword puzzles, or otherwise exercised their minds were 47 percent less likely to develop Alzheimer disease than the priests who rarely engaged in these activities (Wilson & others, 2002). Shortly, we will have much more to say about Alzheimer disease.
- In a study of chess players from 20 to 80 years of age, their success in chess tournaments was more closely linked with the amount of time they engaged in deliberate practice than with their age (Charness, Krampe, & Mayr, 1996).

Training Cognitive Skills

If an older adult is losing cognitive skills, can they be retrained? Two key conclusions can be derived from research: (1) Training can improve the cognitive skills of many older adults, but (2) there is some loss in plasticity in late adulthood, especially in the oldest-old, 85 years and older (Baltes, Lindenberger, & Staudinger, 2006; Baltes & Smith, 2003).

Evidence of plasticity and the effectiveness of cognitive training comes from the research of Sherry Willis and K. Warner Schaie (1986), who studied approximately 400 adults, most of whom were older adults. Using individualized training, they improved the spatial orientation and reasoning skills of two-thirds of the adults. Nearly 40 percent of those whose abilities had declined returned to a level they had reached 14 years earlier. Further, the effects of training on reasoning lasted up to seven years after training (Saczynski & Willis, 2001). In another study, instructing older adults to notice distinctions in pictures improved their memory of the pictures (Levy, Jennings, & Langer, 2001) (see figure 19.4).

What activities are part of successful cognitive training? A seven-year longitudinal study by Sherry Willis and Carolyn Nesselroade (1990) used cognitive training to help adults maintain fluid intelligence (the ability to reason abstractly) with advancing age. The older adults were taught strategies for identifying the rule or pattern required to solve problems. After this cognitive training, adults in their seventies and eighties performed at a higher level than they had in their late sixties. The trainer modeled correct strategies for solving problems. Individuals practiced on training items, received feedback about the correct solutions to practice problems, and participated in

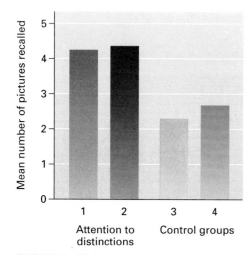

FIGURE 19.4 Improving Attention and Memory in Older Adults. In one study, older adult participants were randomly assigned to one of four attention interventions (Levy, Jennings, & Langer, 2001). In two of the groups, participants studying a set of pictures were told to notice either 3 (group 1) or 5 (group 2) distinctions. In two control groups, participants either were not given any directions related to attention (group 3) or just told to "pay attention." The older adults who viewed the pictures in terms of distinctions remembered more pictures than did the control groups.

group discussion. Other research supports the finding that cognitive training interventions can improve the mental functioning and daily functioning of older adults (Ball & others, 2003; Dunlosky, Kubat-Silman, & Hertzog, 2003).

As we discussed earlier in the chapter, researchers are also finding that improving the physical fitness of older adults can improve their cognitive functioning (Kramer, Fabiani, & Colcombe, 2006; Kramer & Willis, 2002). A recent review of studies revealed that aerobic fitness training improved the planning, scheduling, working memory, resistance to distraction, and processing involving multiple tasks in older adults (Colcombe & Kramer, 2003).

In sum, the cognitive vitality of older adults can be improved through cognitive and fitness training (Colcombe & others, 2004; Kramer, Fabiani, & Colcombe, 2006; Kramer & Willis, 2002; Noice, Noice, & Staines, 2004; Willis & Schaie, 2005). However, benefits have not been observed in all studies (Salthouse, 1991). Further research is needed to determine more precisely which cognitive improvements occur in older adults (Dixon & Cohen, 2003).

To what extent can training improve the cognitive functioning of older adults?

Cognitive Neuroscience and Aging

On several occasions in this chapter and in chapter 18, we have indicated that certain regions of the brain are involved in links between aging and cognitive functioning. In this section, we further explore the substantial increase in interest in the brain's role in aging and cognitive functioning. The field of *cognitive neuroscience* has emerged as the major discipline that studies links between brain and cognitive functioning. This field especially relies on brain imaging techniques, such as fMRI and PET, to reveal the areas of the brain that are activated when individuals are engaging in certain cognitive activities (Chee & others, 2006; Kramer, Fabiani, & Colcombe, 2006; Park & Gutchess, 2006). For example, as an older adult is asked to encode and then retrieve verbal materials or images of scenes, the older adult's brain activity will be monitored by an fMRI brain scan.

Changes in the brain can influence cognitive functioning and changes in cognitive functioning can influence the brain (Cabeza, Nyberg, & Park, 2005). For example, aging of the brain's prefrontal cortex may produce a decline in working memory. And when older adults do not regularly use their working memory (recall the section on "Use it or Lose it"), neural connections in the prefrontal lobe may atrophy. Further, cognitive interventions that activate older adults' working memory may increase these neural connections.

Although in its infancy as a field, the cognitive neuroscience of aging is beginning to uncover some important links between aging, the brain, and cognitive functioning. These include:

- Neural circuits in specific regions of the brain's prefrontal cortex decline and this decline is linked to poorer performance by older adults on complex reasoning tasks, working memory, and episodic memory tasks (Hedden & Gabrielli, 2004; Grady & others, 2006; Nordahl & others, 2006).
- Recall from chapter 18 that older adults are more likely than younger adults to use both hemispheres of the brain to compensate for aging declines in attention, memory, and language (Cabeza, 2002).
- Functioning of the hippocampus declines less than the functioning of the frontal lobes in older adults, but further indication of possible compensation for memory decline in aging was found in a recent study of increased activation of the frontal lobes to possibly compensate for declining activation of the hippocampus (Gutchess & others, 2005).
- Patterns of neural differences with age are larger for retrieval than encoding (Park & Gutchess, 2005).

We are likely to see increased effort to uncover links between aging, the brain, and cognitive functioning in the next several decades.

Review and Reflect • LEARNING GOAL 1

1 **Describe the cognitive functioning of older adults**

Review
- How is cognition multidimensional and multidirectional in older adults? What changes in cognitive processes take place in aging adults?
- How do education, work, and health affect cognition in aging adults?
- What is the concept of "use it or lose it"?
- To what extent can older adults' cognitive skills be trained?
- What characterizes the cognitive neuroscience of aging?

Reflect
- Can you think of older adults who have made significant contributions in late adulthood other than those we mentioned in the chapter? Spend some time reading about these individuals and evaluate how their intellectual interests contributed to their life satisfaction as older adults.

2 LANGUAGE DEVELOPMENT

What are some changes in language development in older adults?

Most research on language development has focused on infancy and childhood. It is generally thought that for most of adulthood individuals maintain their language skills (Thornton & Light, 2006). The vocabulary of individuals often continues to increase throughout most of the adult years, at least until late adulthood (Schaie, 1996; Willis & Schaie, 2005). Many older adults "maintain or improve their knowledge of words and word meanings" (Burke & Shafto, 2004, p. 24).

In late adulthood, however, some decrements in language may appear. For example, if older adults develop hearing problems, they may have difficulty distinguishing speech sounds (Gordon-Salant & others, 2006). Because of a decline in memory skills, older adults may have difficulty in retrieving words from long-term memory (O'Hanlon, Kemper, & Wilcox, 2005; Thornton & Light, 2006). This often involves the *tip-of-the-tongue phenomenon*, in which individuals are confident that they can remember something but just can't quite seem to retrieve it from memory (Heine, Ober, & Shenaut, 1999; Thornton & Light, 2006). To compensate for this decline, older adults may use words that they are very familiar with and shorten the length of their sentences. In conversations, older adults often "produce more ambiguous references and more filled pauses (for example, saying 'um' or 'er') and reformulate their words more than young adults do." These dysfluencies suggest that older adults have difficulty retrieving the appropriate words when speaking (Burke & Shafto, 2004, p. 21). In general, though, most language skills decline little among older adults if they are healthy (Stine, Soederberg, & Morrow, 1996; Thornton & Light, 2006).

Researchers have found conflicting information about changes in *discourse* (extended verbal expression in speech or writing) with aging. "Some (researchers) have reported increased elaborateness, while others have reported less varied and less complex syntax" (Obler, 2005, p. 468).

Nonlanguage factors may be responsible for some of the decline in language skills that do occur in older adults (Obler, 2005). Slower information processing speed and a decline in working memory, especially in being able to keep information in mind while processing, likely contribute to lowered language efficiency in older adults (Stine-Morrow, Miller, & Hertzog, 2006; Waters & Caplan, 2005).

Language does change among individuals with Alzheimer disease, which we will discuss later in the chapter (Forbes-McKay & others, 2005; Nordlund & others, 2005; Thornton & Light, 2006). Word-finding/generating difficulties are one of the earliest symptoms of Alzheimer disease, but most individuals with Alzheimer disease retain much of their ability to produce well-formed sentences until the late stages of the disease. Nonetheless, they do make more grammatical errors than older adults without Alzheimer disease.

Review and Reflect • LEARNING GOAL 2

2 **Characterize changes in language in older adults**

Review
- How can changes in the language development of older adults be described?

Reflect
- Imagine that you are a researcher who is going to study the tip-of-the-tongue phenomena in older adults. What type of task would you use to study this phenomena?

---

3 **WORK AND RETIREMENT**

| Work | Retirement in the United States and Other Countries | Adjustment to Retirement |

What percentage of older adults continue to work? How productive are they? Who adjusts best to retirement? What is the changing pattern of retirement in the United States and around the world? These are some of the questions we now examine.

Work

In the beginning of the twenty-first century, the percentage of men over the age of 65 who continue to work full-time is less than at the beginning of the twentieth century. The decline from 1900 to 2000 has been as much as 70 percent. An important change in older adults' work patterns is the increase in part-time work (Hardy, 2006). The percentage of older adults who work part-time has steadily increased since the 1960s. Aging and work expert James House (1998) believes that many middle-aged workers would like to do less paid work, whereas many older adults would like to do more.

Some individuals maintain their productivity throughout their lives. Some of these older workers work as many or more hours than younger workers. In the National Longitudinal Survey of Older Men, good health, a strong psychological commitment to work, and a distaste for retirement were the most important characteristics related to continued employment into old age (seventies and eighties) (Parnes & Sommers, 1994). The probability of employment also was positively correlated with educational attainment and being married to a working wife.

Especially important to think about is the large cohort of baby boomers—78 million people who will begin to reach traditional retirement age in 2010. Because this cohort is so large, we are likely to see increasing numbers of older adults continue to work (Louria, 2005; Yeats, Folts, & Knapp, 1999; Rogerson & Kim, 2005).

Cognitive ability is one of the best predictors of job performance in older adults. And older workers have lower rates of absenteeism, fewer accidents, and increased job satisfaction, compared with their younger counterparts (Warr, 1994, 2004). This means that the older worker can be of considerable value to a company, above and beyond the older worker's cognitive competence. Changes in federal law now allow individuals over the age of 65 to continue working (Shore & Goldberg, 2005). Also,

Ninety-two-year-old Russell "Bob" Harrell (*right*) puts in 12-hour days at Sieco Consulting Engineers in Columbus, Indiana. A highway and bridge engineer, he designs and plans roads. James Rice (age 48), a vice president of client services at Sieco, says that "Bob" wants to learn something new every day and that he has learned many life lessons from being around him. Harrell says he is not planning on retiring. *What are some variations in work and retirement in older adults?*

AARP
Exploring Retirement
Baby Boomers and Retirement
Health and Retirement

remember from our discussion earlier in the chapter that substantively complex work is linked with a higher level of intellectual functioning (Schooler, Mulatu, & Oates, 1999). This likely is a reciprocal relation—that is, individuals with higher cognitive ability likely continue to work as older adults, and when they work in substantively complex jobs, this likely enhances their intellectual functioning (Schooler, 2001).

An increasing number of middle-aged and older adults are embarking on a second or a third career (Moen & Spencer, 2006; Moen & Wethington, 1999). In some cases, this is an entirely different type of work or a continuation of previous work but at a reduced level. Many older adults also participate in unpaid work—as a volunteer or as an active participant in a voluntary association. These options afford older adults opportunities for productive activity, social interaction, and a positive identity.

Significant numbers of retirees only partially retire, moving to part-time employment by either reducing the number of hours they work on their career jobs or by taking on new (and frequently lower-paying) jobs (Dendinger, Adams, & Jacobson, 2005; Dychtwald, Erickson, & Morison, 2004; Hardy, 2006). Self-employed men are especially likely to continue paid employment, either on the same job or on a new job. Nearly one-third of the men who take on a part-time job do not do so until two years after their retirement (Burkhauser & Quinn, 1989).

In a recent survey, 80 percent of baby boomers said that they expect to work during the retirement years (Roper Starch Worldwide, 2000). The main reason they plan to work when they get older is to engage in part-time work for interest or enjoyment (35 percent), followed by income (23 percent), desire to start a business (17 percent), and the desire to try a different field of work (5 percent). In another recent survey, nearly 70 percent of current employees said that they expect to work for pay once they retire, mainly because they enjoy working and want to stay active and involved (Anthony Greenwald & Associates, 2000).

In summary, age affects many aspects of work (Hardy, 2006; Moen & Spencer, 2006; Rogerson & Kim, 2005). Nonetheless, many studies of work and aging—such as evaluation of hiring and performance—reveal inconsistent results. Important contextual factors, such as age composition of departments or applicant pools, occupations, and jobs, all affect decisions about older workers. It also is important to recognize that ageist stereotypes of workers and of tasks can limit older workers' career opportunities and can encourage early retirement or other forms of downsizing that adversely affect older workers (Hardy, 2006). For example, one recent study found that extensive negative stereotyping of older adults was involved in not hiring them (Gringart, Helmes, & Speelman, 2005). Also, employers' attributes of negative ageist stereotyping often focus on trainability, adaptability, creativity, and interest in new technology (Scialfa & Fernie, 2006).

Retirement in the United States and Other Countries

At what age do most people retire in the United States? Do many people return to the workforce at some point after they have retired? What is retirement like in other countries?

The option to retire is a late-twentieth-century phenomenon in the United States (Atchley & Barusch, 2004). It exists largely thanks to the implementation in 1935 of the Social Security system, which gives benefits to older workers when they retire. On the average, today's workers will spend 10 to 15 percent of their lives in retirement.

Today, many Americans don't retire forever (Moen & Spencer, 2006). Approximately 7 million retired Americans return to work after they have retired (Putnam Investments, 2006). When retired adults return to the labor force, it occurs on average four years after retirement (Hardy, 2006). In many instances, the jobs pay much less than their preretirement jobs (Hardy, 2006). In one study of older adults who returned to work, approximately two-thirds said they were happy they had done so while about one-third indicated they were forced to go back to work to meet financial needs (Putnam Investments, 2006).

In many European countries, officials have experimented with financial inducements designed to reduce unemployment by encouraging the retirement of older workers (Vaupel & Loichinger, 2006). Germany, Sweden, Great Britain, Italy, France, the Czech Republic, Hungary, and Russia are among the nations that are moving toward earlier retirement. In the Netherlands, however, there is currently an effort to recruit retired persons to reenter the workforce because of low unemployment. More information about cultural variations in retirement appears in the following Diversity in Life-Span Development interlude.

DIVERSITY IN LIFE-SPAN DEVELOPMENT

Work and Retirement in Japan, the United States, and Europe

Are a larger percentage of older adults in Japan in the labor force than in the United States and other industrialized countries? What are the attitudes of older Japanese adults toward work and retirement compared with their counterparts in other industrialized countries? To answer these questions, the Japanese Prime Minister's Office conducted national surveys of adults 60 years of age and older in four industrialized nations—Japan, the United States, England, and France. A much larger percentage of the men over 60 in Japan were in the labor force (57 percent) than in the United States (33 percent), England (13 percent), and France (8 percent).

When asked, "What do you think is the best age to retire?" a majority of the older men in England and France said 60 years of age. In sharp contrast, only 14 percent of the older men in Japan and 16 percent of the older men in the United States chose such an early age to retire. Another question the older men in the four countries were asked was, "Where should an older person's income come from?" In Japan and the United States, the proportion of older men who favored saving while working was at least twice that advising reliance on Social Security. In contrast, older adult men in France and England favored reliance on Social Security.

The marked differences in the rate of employment among those over 60 in Japan and the United States, compared with England and France, are mainly due to attitudes and values about work, and about reliance on oneself (and on relatives, in the case of Japan) rather than on the government and its Social Security system (Raymo & others, 2004).

How are work and retirement different in Japan than the United States?

Adjustment to Retirement

Retirement is a process, not an event (Kim & Moen, 2002; Moen & Spencer, 2006). Much of the research on retirement has been cross-sectional rather than longitudinal and has focused on men rather than women. One recent study found that men had higher morale when they had retired within the last two years compared with men who had been retired for longer periods of time (Kim & Moen, 2002). Another recent study revealed that retired married and remarried women reported being more satisfied with their lives and in better health than retired women who were widowed, separated, divorced, or had never been married (Price & Joo, 2005). And a recent study indicated that women spend less time planning for retirement than men do (Jacobs-Lawson, Hershey, & Neukam, 2005).

Older adults who adjust best to retirement are healthy, have adequate income, are active, are better educated, have an extended social network including both friends and family, and usually were satisfied with their lives before they retired (Elovainio & others, 2003; Lee, 2003; Raymo & Sweeney, 2006). Older adults with inadequate income and poor health, and who must adjust to other stress that occurs at the same time as retirement, such as the death of a spouse, have the most difficult time adjusting to retirement (Blekesaune & Solem, 2005; Karpansalo & others, 2005; Kim, 2006). A recent study also found that individuals who had difficulty in adjusting to retirement had a strong attachment to work, including full-time jobs and a long work history, lack of control over the transition to retirement, and low self-efficacy (van Solinge & Henkens, 2005).

Flexibility is also a key factor in whether individuals adjust well to retirement (Taylor, 2006). When people retire, they no longer have the structured environment they had when they were working, so they need to be flexible and discover and pursue their own interests (Eisdorfer, 1996). Cultivating interests and friends unrelated to work improves adaptation to retirement (Zarit & Knight, 1996).

Individuals who view retirement planning only in terms of finances don't adapt as well to retirement as those who have a more balanced retirement plan (Birren, 1996). It is important not only to plan financially for retirement, but to consider other areas of your life as well (Choi, 2001; Cole, 2003). What are you going to do with your leisure time? What are you going to do to stay active? What are you going to do socially? What are you going to do to keep your mind active?

Review and Reflect • LEARNING GOAL 3

3 **Discuss aging and adaptations to work and retirement**

Review
- What characterizes the work of older adults?
- Compare retirement in the United States with other countries.
- How can individuals adjust effectively to retirement?

Reflect
- At what age would you like to retire? Or would you prefer to continue working as an older adult as long as you are healthy? At what age did your father and/or mother retire? How well did they adjust to retirement? Explain.

---

4 MENTAL HEALTH

| Depression | Dementia, Alzheimer Disease, and Other Afflictions | Fear of Victimization, Crime, and Elder Maltreatment |

Although a substantial portion of the population can now look forward to a longer life, that life may unfortunately be hampered by a mental disorder in old age. This prospect is both troubling to the individual and costly to society. Mental disorders make individuals increasingly dependent on the help and care of others. The cost of mental health disorders in older adults is estimated at more than $40 billion per year in the United States. More important than the loss in dollars, though, is the loss of human potential and the suffering. Although mental disorders in older adults are a major concern, older adults do not have a higher incidence of mental disorders than younger adults do (Busse & Blazer, 1996).

Depression

Major depression is a mood disorder in which the individual is deeply unhappy, demoralized, self-derogatory, and bored. The person does not feel well, loses stamina easily, has a poor appetite, and is listless and unmotivated. Major depression has been called the "common cold" of mental disorders. Researchers have found that depressive symptoms vary from less frequent to no more frequent in late adulthood than in middle adulthood (Blazer, 2003; Hybels & Blazer, 2004). One recent study found that the lower frequency of depressive symptoms in older adults compared with middle-aged adults was linked to fewer economic hardships, fewer negative social interchanges, and increased religiosity (Schieman, van Gundy, & Taylor, 2002). Depressive symptoms increase in the oldest-old (85 years and older), and this increase is associated with a higher percentage of women in the group, more physical disability, more cognitive impairment, and lower socioeconomic status (Blazer, 2002; Hybels & Blazer, 2004).

In the child, adolescent, and early adulthood years, females show greater depression than males do (Nolen-Hoeksema & Ahrens, 2002). Does this gender difference hold for middle-aged and older adults? One recent longitudinal study found greater depression in women than men at 50 and 60 years of age, but not at 80 years of age (Barefoot & others, 2001). Men showed increases in depressive symptoms from 60 to 80 but women did not. In this cohort, men may have undergone more profound role shifts after 60 years of age because they were more likely than women to have retired from active involvement in the work world. Thus, the absence of a gender difference in depression in older adults may be cohort-specific and may not hold as women who have entered the workforce in greater numbers are assessed in late adulthood.

Among the most common predictors of depression in older adults are earlier depressive symptoms, poor health, loss events such as the death of a spouse, and low social support (Kraehenbuhl & others, 2004; Loughlin, 2004; Steck & others, 2004). In one longitudinal study, widows showed elevated depressive symptoms up to two years following the death of a spouse (Turvey & others, 1999). In another study, depressive symptoms were higher in U.S. older adults who lived alone, especially immigrants (Wilmoth & Chen, 2003). However, good social support and being socially integrated in the community helped to buffer the effects of declining health on depression in these individuals (Hybels & Blazer, 2004).

One recent study of older adults (average age = 72.5 years) compared those with chronic mild depression and those who were not depressed (McGuire, Kiecolt-Glaser, & Glaser, 2002). The older adults who had chronic mild depression had worse immune system functioning, which resulted in less ability to fight off an infectious agent than their nondepressed counterparts.

Depression is a treatable condition, not only in young adults but in older adults as well (Knight & others, 2006; Pollock, 2005; Steffens & others, 2006). Unfortunately, as many as 80 percent of older adults with depressive symptoms receive no treatment at all. Combinations of medications and psychotherapy produce significant improvement in almost four out of five older adults with depression (Koenig & Blazer, 1996).

Major depression can result not only in sadness, but also in suicidal tendencies (Conner & others, 2006; Preville & others, 2005). Nearly 25 percent of individuals who commit suicide in the United States are 65 years of age or older (Church, Siegel, & Fowler, 1988). The older adult most likely to commit suicide is a male who lives alone, has lost his spouse, and is experiencing failing health (Juurlink & others, 2004; Moscicki & Caine, 2004; Ono, 2004).

What characterizes depression in older adults?

Dementia, Alzheimer Disease, and Other Afflictions

Among the most debilitating of mental disorders in older adults are the dementias (Breitner, 2006; Knight & others, 2006; Reisberg, 2006). In recent years, extensive attention has been focused on the most common dementia, Alzheimer disease. Other afflictions common in older adults are multi-infarct dementia and Parkinson disease.

major depression A mood disorder in which the individual is deeply unhappy, demoralized, self-derogatory, and bored. The person does not feel well, loses stamina easily, has poor appetite, and is listless and unmotivated. Major depression is so widespread that it has been called the "common cold" of mental disorders.

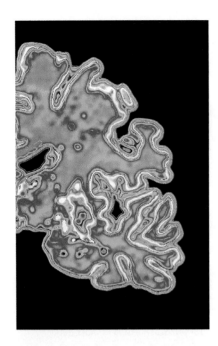

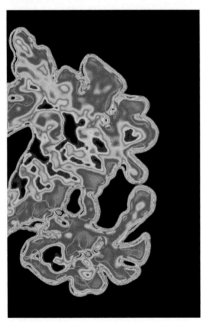

FIGURE 19.5 Two Brains: Normal Aging and Alzheimer Disease. The top computer graphic shows a slice of a normal aging brain, the bottom photograph a slice of a brain ravaged by Alzheimer disease. Notice the deterioration and shrinking in the Alzheimer disease brain.

dementia A global term for any neurological disorder in which the primary symptoms involve a deterioration of mental functioning.

Alzheimer disease A progressive, irreversible brain disorder characterized by a gradual deterioration of memory, reasoning, language, and eventually physical function.

Dementia **Dementia** is a global term for any neurological disorder in which the primary symptoms involve a deterioration of mental functioning. Individuals with dementia often lose the ability to care for themselves and can lose the ability to recognize familiar surroundings and people (including family members) (Boustani & others, 2005; Clarke, 2006; Steeman & others, 2006).

It is estimated that 20 percent of individuals over the age of 80 have dementia. More than 70 types or causes of dementia have been identified (Skoog, Blennow, & Marcusson, 1996).

Alzheimer Disease One form of dementia is **Alzheimer disease**—a progressive, irreversible brain disorder that is characterized by a gradual deterioration of memory, reasoning, language, and eventually, physical function.

In 2005, 4.5 million adults in the United States had Alzheimer disease. It is predicted that Alzheimer disease could triple in the next 50 years, as increasing numbers of people live to older ages. Because of the increasing prevalence of Alzheimer disease, researchers have stepped up their efforts to discover the causes of the disease and find more effective ways to treat it (Harman, 2006).

Because of differences in onset, Alzheimer also is now described as *early-onset* (initially occurring in individuals younger than 65 years of age) or *late-onset* (which has its initial onset in individuals 65 years of age and older). Early-onset Alzheimer disease is rare (about 10 percent of all cases) and generally affects people 30 to 60 years of age.

Alzheimer disease involves a deficiency in the important brain messenger chemical acetylcholine, which plays an important role in memory (Akaike, 2006; Birks, 2006; Lleo, Greenberg, & Growdon, 2006). Also, as Alzheimer disease progresses, the brain shrinks and deteriorates (see figure 19.5). The deterioration of the brain in Alzheimer disease is characterized by the formation of *amyloid plaques* (dense deposits of protein that accumulate in the blood vessels) and *neurofibrillary tangles* (twisted fibers that build up in neurons) (Francis, 2006; Zhuang, Kung, & Kung, 2006). Researchers are especially seeking ways to interrupt the progress of amyloid plaques and neurofibrillary tangles in Alzheimer patients (Devanand & others, 2005; Wenk, 2006).

Although scientists are not certain what causes Alzheimer disease, age is an important risk factor and genes also likely play an important role (Cacabelos, 2005; Gatz & others, 2006; Hansen, 2006; Hough & Ursano, 2006). The number of individuals with Alzheimer disease doubles every five years after the age of 65. A protein called *apolipoprotein E (apoE)*, which is linked to increasing presence of plaques and tangles in the brain, could play a role in as many as one-third of the cases of Alzheimer disease (Aggarwal & others, 2005). A recent study of almost 12,000 pairs of twins in Sweden found that identical twins were both more likely to develop Alzheimer disease than fraternal twins, suggesting a genetic influence on the disease (Gatz & others, 2006).

Although individuals with a family history of Alzheimer disease are at greater risk, the disease is complex and likely caused by a number of factors, including lifestyles. For many years, scientists have known that a healthy diet, exercise, and weight control can lower the risk of cardiovascular disease. Now, they are finding that these healthy lifestyle factors may also lower the risk of Alzheimer disease. Researchers have revealed older adults with Alzheimer disease are more likely to also have cardiovascular disease than individuals who do not have Alzheimer disease (Beeri & others, 2006; Girouard & Iadecola, 2006; Hayden & others, 2006). Autopsies show that brains with the telltale signs of tangles and plaques of Alzheimer patients are three times more common in individuals with cardiovascular disease (Sparks & others, 1990). In the Honolulu-Asia Aging Study, the higher individuals' blood pressure, the more tangles and plaques they had on autopsy (Petrovich & others, 2000). Recently, more cardiac risk factors have been implicated in Alzheimer disease—obesity, smoking, atherosclerosis, and high cholesterol (Hayden & others, 2006; Moreira & others, 2006).

As with many problems associated with aging, exercise may also reduce the risk of Alzheimer disease (Briones, 2006; Nunomura & others, 2006; Stevens & Killeen, 2006). One recent study of more than 2,000 men 71 to 93 years of age revealed that those who walked less than one-fourth of a mile a day were almost twice as likely to develop Alzheimer disease as their male counterparts who walked more than two miles a day (Abbott & others, 2004). Another recent study of older adults found that those who exercised three or more times a week were less likely to develop Alzheimer disease over a six-year period than those who exercised less (Larson & others, 2006).

Former president Ronald Reagan was diagnosed with Alzheimer disease at age 83.

Early Detection and Alzheimer Disease　*Mild cognitive impairment (MCI)* represents a transitional state between the cognitive changes of normal aging and very early Alzheimer disease and other dementias (Petrella & others, 2006). MCI is increasingly recognized as a risk factor for Alzheimer disease (Alexopoulos & others, 2006; Apostolova & others, 2006; Galvin & others, 2005; Hansen, 2006). Three recent longitudinal studies indicate that certain aspects of memory may provide indicators of subsequent dementia and Alzheimer disease:

- Older adults showed deficits in episodic memory three to six years before being diagnosed with dementia, and up to three years before onset of dementia episodic memory worsened and new deficits in verbal fluency, language, and orientation emerged (Jorm & others, 2005).
- Performance on a short verbal recall memory task in individuals with no indication of the presence of Alzheimer disease was linked to whether Alzheimer disease was present in the individuals 10 years later (Tierney & others, 2005).
- Older adults whose episodic memory was impaired in an initial assessment were more than twice as likely to develop Alzheimer disease over a 10-year period as those with impairments in other cognitive domains such as semantic memory, working memory, and visual-spatial ability (Aggarwal & others, 2005).

In sum, deficits in episodic memory appear to be an especially important early indication of risk for subsequent development of Alzheimer disease. Also, special brain scans, such as fMRI (functional magnetic resonance imaging) can detect changes in the brain that are fairly typical of early-Alzheimer disease even before symptoms develop (Bassett & others, 2006; Mimura & Yano, 2006; Mosconi & others, 2005; Staub & others, 2005).

www.mhhe.com/santrockld11

Dementia Web
Exploring Dementia
Dementia Research and Treatment
Dementia Caregivers
Alzheimer Disease
Alzheimer Resources

Drug Treatment of Alzheimer Disease　Several drugs called cholinerase inhibitors have been approved by the U.S. Food and Drug Administration to treat Alzheimer disease. Three of these drugs are now widely used to treat Alzheimer disease: donepezil (Aricept), rivastigmine (Exelon), and galantamine (Razadyne). They are designed to improve memory and other cognitive functions by increasing levels of acetylcholine in the brain (Bianchetti & others, 2006; Souder, 2005). The drugs have been effective in slowing down the progression of Alzheimer symptoms in mild to moderate stages of the disease, but they have not been approved for advanced stages of Alzheimer disease. One recent study revealed that the three cholinerase inhibitors improved cognitive functioning in individuals with Alzheimer disease for as long as four to five years (Bullock & Dengiz, 2005). In 2003, memantine (Namenda) was approved for use in treating moderate to severe Alzheimer disease and it works differently than the cholinerase inhibitors. Memantine is in the class of drugs called NMDA antagonists and it regulates the information-processing activities of the neurotransmitter glutamate. Researchers have found that memantine improves cognitive and behavioral functioning in individuals with moderate to severe Alzheimer disease (Aerosa, Sherriff, & McShane, 2005; Ringman & Cummings, 2006). Researchers are beginning to study how combinations of drugs might further reduce

Alzheimer symptoms. One recent review found that memantine combined with donepezil improved cognitive and behavioral functioning in individuals with moderate or severe Alzheimer disease (Xiong & Doraiswamy, 2005). Keep in mind, though, that the drugs used to treat Alzheimer disease only slow the downward progression of the disease; they do not treat its cause (Pal & Netravathi, 2005; Tariot, 2006).

Caring for Individuals with Alzheimer Disease A special concern is caring for Alzheimer patients (Garity, 2006; Pinquart & Sorensen, 2006). Health-care professionals believe that the family can be an important support system for the Alzheimer patient, but this support can have costs for the family, who can become emotionally and physically drained by the extensive care required for a person with Alzheimer disease (Croog & others, 2006). For example, depression has been reported in 50 percent of family caregivers for Alzheimer patients (Redinbaugh, MacCallum, & Kiecolt-Glaser, 1995). A recent meta-analysis found that female caregivers reported providing more caregiving hours, higher levels of burden and depression, as well as lower levels of well-being and physical health, than male caregivers (Pinquart & Sorensen, 2006).

Respite care (services that provide temporary relief for those who are caring for individuals with disabilities, illnesses, or the elderly) has been developed to help people who have to meet the day-to-day needs of Alzheimer patients. This type of care provides an important break away from the burden of providing chronic care (Robinson, Buckwalter, & Reed, 2005; Zhu & others, 2006). To read further about individuals who care for Alzheimer patients, see the Research in Life-Span Development interlude.

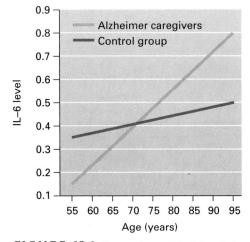

FIGURE 19.6 Comparison of IL-6 Levels in Alzheimer Caregivers and a Control Group of Noncaregivers. Notice that IL-6 (an immune chemical that places individuals at risk for a number of diseases) increased for both the Alzheimer caregivers and the control group of noncaregivers. However, also note that IL-6 increased significantly more in the Alzheimer caregivers. A higher score for IL-6 reflects a higher level of the immune chemical.

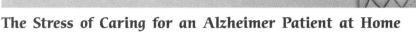

RESEARCH IN LIFE-SPAN DEVELOPMENT

The Stress of Caring for an Alzheimer Patient at Home

Researchers have recently found that the stress of caring for an Alzheimer patient at home can prematurely age the immune system, putting caregivers at risk for developing age-related diseases (Glaser & Kiecolt-Glaser, 2005; Graham, Christian, & Kiecolt-Glaser, 2006; Kiecolt-Glaser & Yehuda, 2005). In one study, 119 older adults who were caring for a spouse with Alzheimer disease or another form of dementia (which can require up to 100 hours a week of time) were compared with 106 older adults who did not have to care for a chronically ill spouse (Kiecolt-Glaser & others, 2003). The age of the older adults upon entry into the study ranged from 55 to 89 with an average of 70.

Periodically during the six-year study, blood samples were taken and the levels of a naturally produced immune chemical called interleukin-6, or IL-6, were measured. IL-6 increases with age and can place people at risk for a number of illnesses, including cardiovascular disease, Type II diabetes, frailty, and certain cancers. The researchers found that the levels of IL-6 increased four times as fast in the Alzheimer caregivers as in the older adults who did not have to care for a critically ill spouse (see figure 19.6). "There were no systematic differences in chronic health problems, medications, or health-relevant behaviors that might have accounted for" (Kiecolt-Glaser & others, 2003, p. 9090) the steeper increase in IL-6 levels for the Alzheimer caregivers.

Each time IL-6 was assessed by drawing blood, the participants also completed a 10-item perceived stress scale to assess the extent they perceived their daily life during the prior week as "unpredictable, uncontrollable, and overloading" (Kiecolt-Glaser & others, 2003, p. 9091). Participants rated each item from 0 (never) to 4 (very often). Alzheimer caregivers reported greater stress than the noncaregiver controls across each of the six annual assessments.

There are many career opportunities for working with individuals who have Alzheimer disease. To read about the work of a director of an Alzheimer association, see the Careers in Life-Span Development profile.

Multi-Infarct Dementia **Multi-infarct dementia** involves a sporadic and progressive loss of intellectual functioning caused by repeated temporary obstruction of blood flow in cerebral arteries (Charlton & others 2006; Morelti & others, 2006). The result is a series of mini-strokes. The term *infarct* refers to the temporary obstruction of blood vessels. It is estimated that 15 to 25 percent of dementias involve the vascular impairment of multi-infarct dementia.

Multi-infarct dementia is more common among men with a history of high blood pressure. The clinical picture of multi-infarct dementia is different than for Alzheimer disease—many patients recover from multi-infarct dementia, whereas

multi-infarct dementia Sporadic and progressive loss of intellectual functioning caused by repeated temporary obstruction of blood flow in cerebral arteries.

CAREERS
in LIFE-SPAN DEVELOPMENT

Jan Weaver
Director of the Alzheimer's
Association of Dallas

Dr. Jan Weaver joined the Alzheimer's Association, Greater Dallas Chapter, as director of services and education in 1999. Prior to that time, she served as associate director of education for the Texas Institute for Research and Education on Aging and director of the National Academy for Teaching and Learning About Aging at the University of North Texas. As a gerontologist, Jan plans and develops services and educational programs that address patterns of human development related to aging. Among the services of the Alzheimer's Association that Jan supervises are a resource center and helpline, a family assistance program, a care program, support groups, referral and information, educational conferences, and community seminars.

Jan recognizes that people of all ages should have an informed and balanced view of older adults that helps them perceive aging as a process of growth and fulfillment rather than a process of decline and dependency. Jan earned her Ph.D. in sociology, with an emphasis in gerontology, from the University of North Texas in 1996.

Jan Weaver giving a lecture on Alzheimer disease.

Muhammad Ali, one of the world's leading sports figures, has Parkinson disease.

Multi-Infarct Dementia
National Parkinson Foundation
World Parkinson Disease Foundation
Resources for Parkinson Disease
Stages in Parkinson Disease

Parkinson disease A chronic, progressive disease characterized by muscle tremors, slowing of movement, and partial facial paralysis.

Alzheimer disease shows a progressive deterioration. The symptoms of multi-infarct dementia include confusion, slurring of speech, writing impairment, and numbness on one side of the face, arm, or leg (Hoyer & Roodin, 2003). However, after each occurrence, there usually is a rather quick recovery, although each succeeding occurrence is usually more damaging. Approximately 35 to 50 percent of individuals who have these transient attacks will have a major stroke within five years unless the underlying problems are treated. Especially recommended for these individuals are exercise, improved diet, and appropriate drugs, which can slow or stop the progression of the underlying vascular disease.

Parkinson Disease   Another type of dementia is **Parkinson disease,** a chronic, progressive disease characterized by muscle tremors, slowing of movement, and partial facial paralysis. Parkinson disease is triggered by degeneration of dopamine-producing neurons in the brain (Bonci & Singh, 2006; Lang & others, 2005). Dopamine is a neurotransmitter that is necessary for normal brain functioning. Why these neurons degenerate is not known. The main treatment for Parkinson disease involves administering drugs that enhance the effect of dopamine (dopamine agonists) in the disease's earlier stages and later administering the drug L-dopa, which is converted by the brain into dopamine (Mir & others, 2005; Schapira, 2005; Swarztrauber, Koudelka, & Brodsky, 2006; Thobis, 2006). However, it is difficult to determine the correct level of dosage of L-dopa and it loses its efficacy over time (Sammi, Nutt, & Ransom, 2004; Stocchi, 2005, 2006).

Fear of Victimization, Crime, and Elder Maltreatment

Some of the physical decline and limitations that characterize development in late adulthood contribute to a sense of vulnerability and fear among older adults (Gray & Acierno, 2002). For some older adults, the fear of crime may become a deterrent to travel, attendance at social events, and the pursuit of an active lifestyle. Almost one-fourth of older adults say they have a basic fear of being the victim of a crime. However, in reality, possibly because of the precautions they take, older adults are less likely than younger adults to be the victim of a crime. However, the crimes committed against older adults are likely to be serious offenses, such as armed robbery (Cohn & Harlow, 1993). Older adults are also victims of nonviolent crimes such as fraud, vandalism, purse snatching, and harassment (Fulmer, Guadagno, & Bolton, 2004). Estimates of the incidence of crimes against older adults may be low because older adults may not report crimes, fearing retribution from criminals or believing the criminal justice system cannot help them.

Elder maltreatment can be perpetrated by anyone, but it is primarily carried out by family members (Brownell & Heiser, 2006; Geroff & Olshaker, 2006). As with child maltreatment, elder maltreatment can involve neglect or physical abuse. Older adults are most often abused by their spouses. A special concern is the burden older women carry in facing possible physical violence. In one study of 614 cases of abuse in Hillsborough County, Florida, 37 percent involved physical assault, most of the abused were women, they were most likely to be living with their spouse, and they were most likely to be over 60 years of age (VandeWeerd & Paveza, 1999). The perpetrators were most likely to be male spouses. Older women also were more likely than elderly men to suffer property damage and robbery, but in these cases the perpetrator was most likely to be a young male (18 to 29 years of age) who was not related to the victim.

Maltreated older adults, as well as older adults who are depressed, have a dementia, or another mental disorder may need mental health treatment. To read about this topic, see the Applications in Life-Span Development interlude.

APPLICATIONS IN LIFE-SPAN DEVELOPMENT

Meeting the Mental Health Needs of Older Adults

Older adults receive disproportionately fewer mental health services (Karlin & Norris, 2005; Knight & others, 2006). One estimate is that only 2.7 percent of all clinical services provided by psychologists go to older adults, although individuals aged 65 and over make up more than 11 percent of the population. Psychotherapy can be expensive. Although reduced fees and sometimes no fee can be arranged in public hospitals for older adults from low-income backgrounds, many older adults who need psychotherapy do not get it (Knight & others, 1996, 2006). It has been said that psychotherapists like to work with young, attractive, verbal, intelligent, and successful clients (called YAVISes) rather than those who are quiet, ugly, old, institutionalized, and different (called QUOIDs). Psychotherapists have been accused of failing to see older adults because they perceive that older adults have a poor prognosis for therapy success, they do not feel they have adequate training to treat older adults, who may have special problems requiring special treatment, and they may have stereotypes that label older adults as low-status and unworthy recipients of treatment (Knight, Nordhus, & Satre, 2003; Virnig & others, 2004).

How can we better meet the mental health needs of older adults? First, psychologists must be encouraged to include more older adults in their client lists, and older adults must be convinced that they can benefit from therapy. Second, we must make mental health care affordable. For example, Medicare continues to fall short of providing many mental health services for older adults, especially those in need of long-term care (Knight & others, 2006).

Margaret Gatz (*right*) has been a crusader for better mental health treatment of older adults. She believes that mental health professionals need to be encouraged to include more older adults in their client lists and that we need to better educate the elderly about how they can benefit from therapy. *What are some common mechanisms of change that can be used to improve the mental health of older adults?*

Review and Reflect • LEARNING GOAL 4

4 **Describe mental health problems in older adults**

Review
- What is the nature of depression in older adults?
- What are dementia, Alzheimer disease, and other afflictions like in older adults?
- How extensive is fear of victimization, crime, and maltreatment in older adults?

Reflect
- Older adults do not have more mental health problems than younger adults do, although many people perceive that older adults have more mental problems. What might account for this misperception?

5 RELIGION

In chapter 16, we described religion and meaning in life with a special focus on middle age, including links between religion and health. Here we will continue our exploration of religion by describing its importance in the lives of many older adults.

In many societies around the world, older adults are the spiritual leaders in their churches and communities. For example, in the Catholic Church, more popes have been elected in their eighties than in any other 10-year period of the human life span.

The religious patterns of older adults have increasingly been studied (Consedine, Magai, & Conway, 2004; Krause, 2004, 2006; Levin, Taylor, & Chatters, 1994; Moberg, 2005). In one analysis, both older African Americans and older Whites attended religious services several times a month, said religion was important in their lives, read religious materials, listened to religious programming, and prayed frequently (Levin, Taylor, & Chatters, 1994). Also, in this analysis, older women had a stronger interest in religion than did older men.

Is religion related to a sense of well-being and life satisfaction in old age? In one recent study it was. Interviews were conducted with 1,500 U.S. White and African American individuals 66 years of age and older (Krause, 2003). Older adults who derived a sense of meaning in life from religion had higher levels of life satisfaction, self-esteem, and optimism. Also, older African American adults were more likely to find meaning in religion than their White counterparts. In another study, religious practices—such as prayer and scripture reading—and religious feelings were associated with a sense of well-being, especially for women and individuals over 75 years of age (Koenig, Smiley, & Gonzales, 1988). In one study of low-income Latinos in San Diego, a strong religious orientation was associated with better health (Cupertino & Haan, 1999). And in two recent studies, across an 8-year period, Mexican Americans aged 65 and older had slower rates of cognitive decline and a 32 percent reduction in risk of mortality compared to their counterparts who never attended church (Hill & others, 2005, 2006).

Religion can provide some important psychological needs in older adults, helping them face impending death, find and maintain a sense of meaningfulness and significance in life, and accept the inevitable losses of old age (Daaleman, Perera, & Studenski, 2004; Fry, 1999; Koenig & Larson, 1998). In one recent study, although church attendance decreased in older adults in their last year of life, their feelings of religiousness and the strength or comfort they received from religion were either stable or increased (Idler, Kasl, & Hays, 2001). Socially, the religious community can provide a number of functions for older adults, such as social activities, social support, and the opportunity to assume teaching and leadership roles. Older adults can become deacons, elders, or religion teachers, assuming leadership roles they might have been unable to take on before they retired (Cox & Hammonds, 1988).

Might praying or meditating actually be associated with longevity? In one recent study, they were (McCullough & others, 2000). Nearly 4,000 women and men 65 years and older, mostly Christians, were asked about their health and whether they prayed or meditated. Those who said they rarely or never prayed had about a 50 percent greater risk of dying during the six-year study compared with those who prayed or meditated at least once a month. In this study, the researchers controlled for many factors known to place people at risk for dying, such as smoking, drinking, and social isolation. It is possible that prayer and meditation lower

During late adulthood, many individuals increasingly engage in prayer. *How might this be linked with longevity?*

www.mhhe.com/santrockld11

Spirituality and Health in Older Adults

the incidence of death in older adults because they reduce stress and dampen the body's production of stress hormones such as adrenaline. A decrease in stress hormones is linked with a number of health benefits, including a stronger immune system (McCullough & others, 2000).

Review and Reflect • LEARNING GOAL 5

5 Explain the role of religion in the lives of older adults

Review
- What are some characteristics of religion in older adults?

Reflect
- Do you think you will become more or less religious as an older adult? Explain.

REACH YOUR LEARNING GOALS

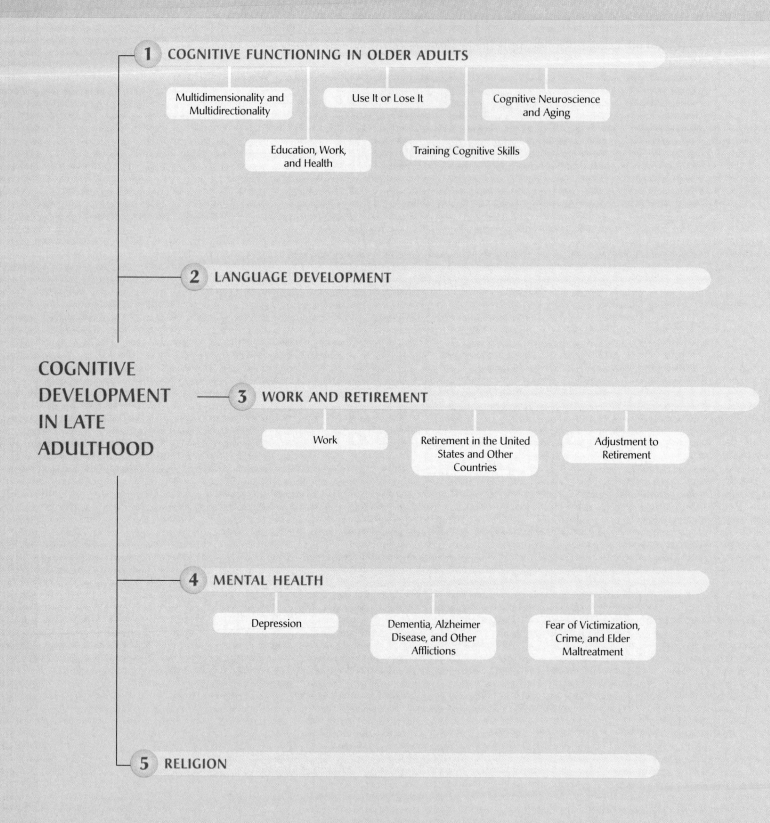

COGNITIVE DEVELOPMENT IN LATE ADULTHOOD

1 COGNITIVE FUNCTIONING IN OLDER ADULTS

- Multidimensionality and Multidirectionality
- Use It or Lose It
- Cognitive Neuroscience and Aging
- Education, Work, and Health
- Training Cognitive Skills

2 LANGUAGE DEVELOPMENT

3 WORK AND RETIREMENT

- Work
- Retirement in the United States and Other Countries
- Adjustment to Retirement

4 MENTAL HEALTH

- Depression
- Dementia, Alzheimer Disease, and Other Afflictions
- Fear of Victimization, Crime, and Elder Maltreatment

5 RELIGION

SUMMARY

1 Cognitive Functioning in Older Adults: *Describe the cognitive functioning of older adults*

Multidimensionality and Multidirectionality

Baltes emphasizes a distinction between cognitive mechanics (the neurophysiological architecture, including the brain) and cognitive pragmatics (the culture-based software of the mind). Cognitive mechanics are more likely to decline in older adults than are cognitive pragmatics. Researchers have found that sensory/motor and speed-of-processing dimensions decline in older adults. Some changes in attention take place in adulthood. In selective attention, older adults fare more poorly than younger adults in general, but when tasks are simple and sufficient practice is given, age differences are minimal. Likewise, for divided attention, on simple tasks, adult age differences are minimal, but on difficult tasks older adults do worse than younger adults. Older adults perform as well as middle-aged and younger adults on measures of sustained attention. Younger adults have better episodic memory than older adults. Regarding semantic memory, older adults have more difficulty retrieving semantic information, but they usually can eventually retrieve it. Researchers have found declines in working memory and perceptual speed in older adults. Older adults are more likely to show declines in explicit than in implicit memory. Prospective memory involves remembering what to do in the future, and the relation of prospective memory to aging is complex. An increasing number of studies are finding that people's beliefs about memory play an important role in their memory performance. Noncognitive factors such as health, education, and socioeconomic status are linked with memory in older adults. Wisdom is expert knowledge about the practical aspects of life that permits excellent judgment about important matters. Baltes and his colleagues have found that high levels of wisdom are rare, the time frame of late adolescence and early adolescence is the main window for wisdom to emerge, factors other than age are critical for wisdom to develop, and personality-related factors are better predictors of wisdom than cognitive factors such as intelligence.

Education, Work, and Health

Successive generations of Americans have been better educated. Education is positively correlated with scores on intelligence tests. Older adults may return to education for a number of reasons. Successive generations have had work experiences that include a stronger emphasis on cognitively oriented labor. The increased emphasis on information processing in jobs likely enhances an individual's intellectual abilities. Poor health is related to decreased performance on intelligence tests in older adults. Exercise is linked to higher cognitive functioning in older adults.

Use It or Lose It

Researchers are finding that older adults who engage in cognitive activities, especially challenging ones, have higher cognitive functioning that those who don't use their cognitive skills.

Training Cognitive Skills

There are two main conclusions that can be derived from research on training cognitive skills in older adults: (1) Training can improve the cognitive skills of many older adults, and (2) there is some loss in plasticity in late adulthood.

Cognitive Neuroscience and Aging

There has been considerable increased interest in the cognitive neuroscience of aging that focuses on links between aging, the brain, and cognitive functioning. This field especially relies on fMRI and PET scans to assess brain functioning while individuals are engaging in cognitive tasks. One of the most consistent findings in this field is a decline in the functioning of specific regions in the prefrontal cortex in older adults and links between this decline and poorer performance on complex reasoning, working memory, and episodic memory tasks.

2 Language Development: *Characterize changes in language in older adults*

For many individuals, knowledge of words and word meanings continues unchanged or may even improve late adulthood. However, some decline in language skills may occur as a consequence of declines in hearing or memory, speed of processing information, or as a result of disease.

3 Work and Retirement: *Discuss aging and adaptations to work and retirement*

Work

Today, the percentage of men over 65 who continue to work full-time is less than at the beginning of the twentieth century. An important change in older adults' work patterns is the increase in part-time work. Some individuals continue a life of strong work productivity throughout late adulthood.

Retirement in the United States and Other Countries

A retirement option for older workers is a late-twentieth-century phenomenon in the United States. The United States has extended the mandatory retirement age upward, and efforts have been made to reduce age discrimination in work-related circumstances. Although the United States has moved toward increasing the age for retirement, many European countries are encouraging early retirement.

Adjustment to Retirement

Individuals who are healthy, have adequate income, are active, are better educated, have an extended social network

643

of friends and family, and are satisfied with their lives before they retire adjust best to retirement.

 Mental Health: *Describe mental health problems in older adults*

Depression

Depression has been called the "common cold" of mental disorders. However, a majority of older adults with depressive symptoms never receive mental health treatment.

Dementia, Alzheimer Disease, and Other Afflictions

Dementia is a global term for any neurological disorder in which the primary symptoms involve a deterioration of mental functioning. Alzheimer disease is by far the most common dementia. This progressive, irreversible disorder is characterized by gradual deterioration of memory, reasoning, language, and eventually physical functioning. Special efforts are being made to discover the causes of Alzheimer disease and effective treatments for it. The increase in amyloid plaques and neurofibrillary tangles in Alzheimer patients may hold important keys to improving our understanding of the disease. Alzheimer disease involves a predictable, progressive decline, characterized by a deficiency in acetylcholine that affects memory. Also, in Alzheimer disease, the brain shrinks and deteriorates as plaques and tangles form. An important concern is caring for Alzheimer patients and the burdens this places on caregivers. In addition to Alzheimer disease, other types of dementia are multi-infarct dementia and Parkinson disease.

Fear of Victimization, Crime, and Elder Maltreatment

Some of the physical decline and limitations that characterize development in late adulthood contribute to a sense of vulnerability and fear among older adults. Almost one-fourth of older adults say they have a basic fear of being the victim of a crime. Older women are more likely than older men to be victimized or abused.

 Religion: *Explain the role of religion in the lives of older adults*

Many older adults are spiritual leaders in their church and community. Religious interest increases in old age and is related to a sense of well-being in the elderly.

KEY TERMS

cognitive mechanics 619
cognitive pragmatics 619
selective attention 620
divided attention 620
sustained attention 620

episodic memory 621
semantic memory 621
explicit memory 622
implicit memory 622

source memory 622
prospective memory 623
wisdom 623
major depression 633

dementia 634
Alzheimer disease 634
multi-infarct dementia 637
Parkinson disease 638

KEY PEOPLE

Paul Baltes 619
Lynn Hasher 622

K. Warner Schaie 626

Sherry Willis 626

Carolyn Nesselroade 626

E-LEARNING TOOLS

To help you master the material in this chapter, you'll find a number of valuable study tools on the LifeMap CD-ROM that accompanies this book and on the Online Learning Center for *Life-Span Development,* eleventh edition, at **www.mhhe.com/santrockld11.**

Video Clips

In the margins of this book there are icons directing you to the LifeMap CD-ROM that accompanies the book. There you'll find a video for chapter 19 called "Retirement." Today's adults are among the first generation able to conceive of retirement as an *option.* This segment considers the psychological factors, rather than the purely economic motives, involved in the decision to retire or continue working.

Self-Assessment

Connect to **www.mhhe.com/santrockld11** to reflect on aging and the workplace by completing the self-assessment, *My Perception of Older Workers.*

Taking It to the Net

Connect to **www.mhhe.com/santrockld11** to research the answers to these questions.

1. Jasper's 66-year-old father thinks he was passed over for a promotion because of his age. How can Jasper investigate whether his father has a legal claim against his company based on age discrimination. What rights do older workers have in their jobs?

2. Angela is interested in finding out more about how the causes, the nature, and the treatment of depression change over the life span. Her Aunt Sadie has become very depressed as she has gotten older, and Angela worries that her aunt might harm herself. What can Angela find out about the extent of depression in the elderly population and why depression often goes undiagnosed, as well as the causes and the best treatment for depression?

3. Juan's grandfather has just been diagnosed with Alzheimer disease. What do Juan and his family members need to know about caring for his grandfather's physical needs? What legal and financial issues may need to be considered by Juan's family to help them better deal with this situation?

Health and Well-Being, Parenting, and Education Exercises

Build your decision-making skills by trying your hand at the health and well-being, parenting, and education exercises. Connect to **www.mhhe.com/santrockld11** to research the answers and complete the exercises.

Chapter 20

SOCIOEMOTIONAL DEVELOPMENT IN LATE ADULTHOOD

I am the family face; Flesh perishes, I live on, Projecting trait and trace Through time to times anon, And leaping from place to place Over oblivion.

—THOMAS HARDY
English Novelist and Poet, 19th Century

CHAPTER OUTLINE		LEARNING GOALS
THEORIES OF SOCIOEMOTIONAL DEVELOPMENT	**1**	**Discuss five theories of socioemotional development and aging**
Erikson's Theory		
Disengagement Theory		
Activity Theory		
Socioemotional Selectivity Theory		
Selective Optimization with Compensation		
Theory		
PERSONALITY, THE SELF, AND SOCIETY	**2**	**Describe links between personality and morality, and identify changes in the self and society in late adulthood**
Personality		
The Self		
Older Adults in Society		
FAMILIES AND SOCIAL RELATIONSHIPS	**3**	**Characterize the families and social relationships of aging adults**
Lifestyle Diversity		
Older Adult Parents and Their Adult Children		
Great-Grandparenting		
Friendship		
Social Support and Social Integration		
Altruism and Volunteerism		
ETHNICITY, GENDER, AND CULTURE	**4**	**Summarize how ethnicity, gender, and culture are linked with aging**
Ethnicity		
Gender		
Culture		
SUCCESSFUL AGING	**5**	**Explain how to age successfully**

Bob Cousy, as a Boston Celtics star when he was a young adult (*left*) and as an older adult (*right*). What are some changes he has made in his life as an older adult?

Bob Cousy was a star player on Boston Celtics teams that won numerous National Basketball Association championships. In recognition of his athletic accomplishments, Cousy was honored by ESPN as one of the top 100 athletes of the twentieth century. After he retired from basketball, he became a college basketball coach and then into his seventies was a broadcaster of Boston Celtics basketball games. Now in his eighties, Cousy has retired from broadcasting but continues to play golf and tennis on a regular basis. He has a number of positive social relationships, including a marriage of more than 50 years, children and grandchildren, and many friends.

As is the case with many famous people, their awards usually reveal little about their personal lives and contributions. Two situations exemplify his humanitarian efforts to help others (McClellan, 2004). When Cousy played for the Boston Celtics, his African American teammate, Chuck Cooper, was refused a room on a road trip because of his race. Cousy expressed anger to his coach about the situation and then accompanied an appreciative Cooper on a train back to Boston. In a second situation, "Today the Bob Cousy Humanitarian Fund honors individuals who have given their lives to using the game of basketball as a medium to help others" (p. 4). The Humanitarian Fund reflects Cousy's motivation to care for others, be appreciative and giving something back, and make the world less self-centered.

PREVIEW

Bob Cousy's life as an older adult reflects some of the themes of socioemotional development in older adults that we will discuss in this chapter. These include the important role that being active plays in life satisfaction, adapting to changing skills, and the positive role of close relationships with friends and family in an emotionally fulfilling life.

1 THEORIES OF SOCIOEMOTIONAL DEVELOPMENT

| Erikson's Theory | Activity Theory | Selective Optimization with Compensation Theory |

| Disengagement Theory | Socioemotional Selectivity Theory |

We will explore five main theories of socioemotional development that focus on late adulthood: Erikson's theory, disengagement theory, activity theory, socioemotional selectivity theory, and selective optimization with compensation theory.

Erikson's Theory

We initially described Erik Erikson's (1968) eight stages of the human life span in chapter 2, and as we explored different periods of development in this book we examined the stages in more detail. Here we will discuss his final stage.

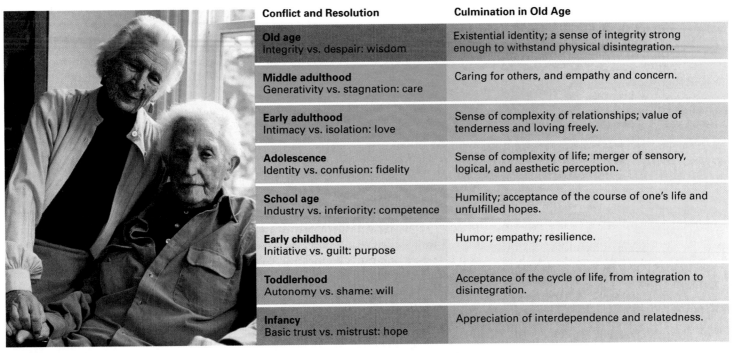

Conflict and Resolution	Culmination in Old Age
Old age Integrity vs. despair: wisdom	Existential identity; a sense of integrity strong enough to withstand physical disintegration.
Middle adulthood Generativity vs. stagnation: care	Caring for others, and empathy and concern.
Early adulthood Intimacy vs. isolation: love	Sense of complexity of relationships; value of tenderness and loving freely.
Adolescence Identity vs. confusion: fidelity	Sense of complexity of life; merger of sensory, logical, and aesthetic perception.
School age Industry vs. inferiority: competence	Humility; acceptance of the course of one's life and unfulfilled hopes.
Early childhood Initiative vs. guilt: purpose	Humor; empathy; resilience.
Toddlerhood Autonomy vs. shame: will	Acceptance of the cycle of life, from integration to disintegration.
Infancy Basic trust vs. mistrust: hope	Appreciation of interdependence and relatedness.

FIGURE 20.1 Erikson's View of How Positive Resolution of the Eight Stages of the Human Life Span Can Culminate in Wisdom and Integrity in Old Age. In Erikson's view, each stage of life is associated with a particular psychosocial conflict and a particular resolution. In this chart Erikson describes how the issue from each of the earlier stages can mature into the many facets of integrity and wisdom in old age. At left, Erikson is shown with his wife Joan, an artist.

Integrity versus despair is Erikson's eighth and final stage of development, which individuals experience during late adulthood. This stage involves reflecting on the past and either piecing together a positive review or concluding that one's life has not been well spent. Through many different routes, the older adult may have developed a positive outlook in each of the preceding periods. If so, retrospective glances and reminiscences will reveal a picture of a life well spent, and the older adult will be satisfied (integrity). But if the older adult resolved one or more of the earlier stages in a negative way (being socially isolated in early adulthood or stagnated in middle adulthood, for example), retrospective glances about the total worth of his or her life might be negative (despair). Figure 20.1 portrays how positive resolutions of Erikson's eight stages can culminate in wisdom and integrity for older adults.

Robert Peck's Reworking of Erikson's Final Stage Robert Peck (1968) reworked Erikson's final stage of development, integrity versus despair, by describing three developmental tasks, or issues, that men and women face when they become old:

- **Differentiation versus role preoccupation** involves redefining one's worth in terms of something other than work roles. Peck believes older adults need to pursue a set of valued activities so that time previously spent in an occupation and with children can be filled.
- **Body transcendence versus body preoccupation** involves coping with declining physical well-being. As older adults age, they may experience a chronic illness and considerable deterioration in their physical capabilities. For men and women whose identity has revolved around their physical well-being, the decrease in health and deterioration of physical capabilities may present a severe threat to their identity and feelings of life satisfaction.

integrity versus despair Erikson's eighth and final stage of development, which individuals experience in late adulthood. This involves reflecting on the past and either piecing together a positive review or concluding that one's life has not been well spent.

differentiation versus role preoccupation One of the three developmental tasks of aging described by Peck, in which older adults must redefine their worth in terms of something other than work roles.

body transcendence versus body preoccupation A developmental task of aging described by Peck, in which older adults must cope with declining physical well-being.

What characterizes a life review in late adulthood?

However, while most older adults experience illnesses, many enjoy life through human relationships that allow them to go beyond a preoccupation with their aging body.

- **Ego transcendence versus ego preoccupation** involves recognizing that while death is inevitable and likely not very far away, it is adaptive to be at ease with oneself by realizing one's contributions to the future through rearing of children or through vocations or ideas.

Life Review Life review is prominent in Erikson's final stage of integrity versus despair. Life review involves looking back at one's life experiences, evaluating them, interpreting them, and often reinterpreting them. Distinguished aging researcher Robert Butler (1975, 1996) believes the life review is set in motion by looking forward to death. Sometimes the life review proceeds quietly, at other times it is intense, requiring considerable work to achieve some sense of personality integration. The life review may be observed initially in stray and insignificant thoughts about oneself and one's life history. These thoughts may continue to emerge in brief intermittent spurts or become essentially continuous. One 76-year-old man commented, "My life is in the back of my mind. It can't be any other way. Thoughts of the past play on me. Sometimes I play with them, encouraging and savoring them; at other times I dismiss them."

Life reviews can include sociocultural dimensions, such as culture, ethnicity, and gender (Covan, 2005). Life reviews also can include interpersonal, relationship dimensions, including sharing and intimacy with family members or a friend (Cappeliez & O'Rourke, 2006). And life reviews can include personal dimensions, which might involve the creation and discovery of meaning and coherence. These personal dimensions might unfold in such a way that the pieces do or don't make sense to the older adult. In the final analysis, each person's life review is to some degree unique.

As the past marches in review, the older adult surveys it, observes it, and reflects on it (Cully, LaVoie, & Gfeller, 2001; Elford & others, 2005). Reconsideration of previous experiences and their meaning occurs, often with revision or expanded understanding taking place. This reorganization of the past may provide a more valid picture for the individual, providing new and significant meaning to one's life (Bohlmeijer & others, 2005; Stinson & Kirk, 2006). It may also help prepare the individual for death, in the process reducing fear (Cappeliez, O'Rourke, & Chaudhury, 2005).

One recent study of reminiscence in German and Dutch adults from 40 to 85 years of age focused on what individuals regretted the most in their lives (Timmer, Westerhof, & Dittmann-Kohli, 2005). Regrets involved four major themes: (1) mistakes and bad decisions, (2) hard times, (3) social relationships, and (4) missed educational opportunities.

Some clinicians use *reminiscence therapy* with their older clients. Reminiscence therapy involves discussing past activities and experiences with another individual or group. The therapy may include the use of photographs, familiar items, and video/audio recordings. Some research indicates that reminiscence therapy improves the mood of older adults (Ando, Tsuda, & Moorey, 2006; Woods & others, 2005).

Disengagement Theory

Disengagement theory states that to cope effectively, older adults should gradually withdraw from society. This theory was proposed almost half a century ago (Cumming & Henry, 1961). In this view, older adults develop increasing self-preoccupation, decrease their emotional ties with others, and show less interest in society's affairs. By following these strategies of disengagement, it was believed, older

ego transcendence versus ego preoccupation A developmental task of aging described by Peck, in which older adults must come to feel at ease with themselves by recognizing that although death is inevitable and probably not too far away, they have contributed to the future through raising their children or through their vocations and ideas.

disengagement theory The theory that to cope effectively, older adults should gradually withdraw from society.

adults would enjoy enhanced life satisfaction. Some researchers have observed that society, in turn, may contribute to this phenomenon by becoming disengaged from older adults (Antonucci, 2004).

The theory generated a storm of protest and met with a quick death. We mention it because of its historical relevance. Although not formally proposed until 1961, it summarized the prevailing beliefs about older adults in the first half of the twentieth century.

Activity Theory

Activity theory states that the more active and involved older adults are, the more likely they are to be satisfied with their lives. Thus, activity theory is the exact opposite of disengagement theory. Researchers have found strong support for activity theory, beginning in the 1960s and continuing into the twenty-first century (Haber & Rhodes, 2004; Neugarten, Havighurst, & Tobin, 1968; Riebe & others, 2005; Warr, Butcher, & Robertson, 2004). These researchers have found that when older adults are active, energetic, and productive, they age more successfully and are happier than if they disengage from society.

One recent large-scale longitudinal study of older adults in Manitoba, Canada, examined the relation between everyday activities and indicators of successful aging, namely, well-being, functioning, and mortality, over a six-year period (Menec, 2003). Participants were asked to fill out a 21-item activities checklist to indicate their participation in each of the activities within the past week. The activities were grouped into three categories: social activities (visiting family or relatives, for example), productive activities (volunteer work, doing light housework/gardening, for example), and solitary activities (collecting hobbies, for example). Well-being was assessed by asking participants how happy they were on a five-point scale ranging from 1 = happy and interested in life to 5 = so unhappy that life is not worthwhile. Function was evaluated in terms of whether cognitive impairment or physical difficulties were present. Mortality (whether participants were dead or alive) was determined by examining data from the Office of Vital Statistics. The results indicated that greater overall activity (but especially social and productive activity) was related to happiness, better functioning, and a lower mortality rate.

Activity theory suggests that many individuals will achieve greater life satisfaction if they continue their middle-adulthood roles into late adulthood. If these roles are stripped from them (as in early retirement), it is important for them to find substitute roles that keep them active and involved.

Should adults stay active or become more disengaged as they become older? Explain.

www.mhhe.com/santrockld11

Activities Resources for Older Adults

Socioemotional Selectivity Theory

Socioemotional selectivity theory states that older adults become more selective about their social networks. Because they place a high value on emotional satisfaction, older adults spend more time with familiar individuals with whom they have had rewarding relationships. Developed by Laura Carstensen (1995, 1998, 2006; Carstensen, Mikels, & Mather, 2006; Carstensen & others, 2003), this theory argues that older adults deliberately withdraw from social contact with individuals peripheral to their lives while they maintain or increase contact with close friends and family members with whom they have had enjoyable relationships. This selective narrowing of social interaction maximizes positive emotional experiences and minimizes emotional risks as individuals become older.

Socioemotional selectivity theory challenges the stereotype that the majority of older adults are in emotional despair because of their social isolation (Carstensen,

activity theory The theory that the more active and involved older adults are, the more likely they are to be satisfied with their lives.

socioemotional selectivity theory The theory that older adults become more selective about their social networks. Because they place a high value on emotional satisfaction, older adults often spend more time with familiar individuals with whom they have had rewarding relationships.

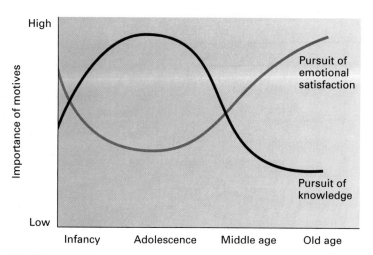

FIGURE 20.2 **Idealized Model of Socioemotional Selectivity Through the Life Span.** In Carstensen's theory of socioemotional selectivity, the motivation to reach knowledge-related and emotion-related goals changes across the life span.

2006; Carstensen & Löckenhoff, 2004; Carstensen, Mikels, & Mather, 2006). Rather, older adults consciously choose to decrease the total number of their social contacts in favor of spending increasing time in emotionally rewarding moments with friends and family. That is, they systematically hone their social networks so that available social partners satisfy their emotional needs.

Is there research evidence to support life-span differences in the composition of social networks? Longitudinal studies reveal far smaller social networks for older adults than for younger adults (Lee & Markides, 1990; Palmore, 1981). In one study of individuals 69 to 104 years of age, the oldest participants had fewer peripheral social contacts than the relatively younger participants but about the same number of close emotional relationships (Lang & Carstensen, 1994).

Socioemotional selectivity theory also focuses on the types of goals that individuals are motivated to achieve (Carstensen, 2006; Carstensen, Mikels, & Mather, 2006; Charles & Carstensen, 2004; Kennedy, Mather, & Carstensen, 2004). It states that two important classes of goals are (1) knowledge-related and (2) emotional. This theory emphasizes that the trajectory of motivation for knowledge-related goals starts relatively high in the early years of life, peaking in adolescence and early adulthood, and then declining in middle and late adulthood (see figure 20.2). The emotion trajectory is high during infancy and early childhood, declines from middle childhood through early adulthood, and increases in middle and late adulthood.

One of the main reasons given for these changing trajectories in knowledge-related and emotion-related goals involves the perception of time (Carstensen, 2006; Carstensen, Mikels, & Mather, 2006; Charles & Carstensen, 2004). When time is perceived as open-ended, as it is when individuals are younger, people are more strongly motivated to pursue information, even at the cost of emotional satisfaction. But as older adults perceive that they have less time left in their lives, they are motivated to spend more time pursuing emotional satisfaction.

Researchers have found that across diverse samples (Norwegians, Catholic nuns, African Americans, Chinese Americans, and European Americans) older adults report better control of their emotions and fewer negative emotions than younger adults (Lawton & others, 1992; Mroczek, 2001). Compared with younger adults, the feelings of older adults mellow. Emotional life is on a more even keel with fewer highs and lows. It may be that although older adults have less extreme joy, they have more contentment, especially when they are connected in positive ways with friends and family. To read further about how emotion changes across the life span, see the Research in Life-Span Development interlude.

RESEARCH IN LIFE-SPAN DEVELOPMENT

Changes in Emotion Across Adulthood

One study examined how emotion changes across the adulthood years in 2,727 persons from 25 to 74 years of age in the United States (Mroczek & Kolarz, 1998). Participants completed a survey that assessed the frequency of their positive and negative emotions over a 30-day time frame. Two six-item scales were created, one for positive emotion, the other for negative emotion. Participants rated each of the following items from 1 = none of the time to 5 = all of the time:

Positive Affect	*Negative Affect*
1. Cheerful	1. So sad nothing could cheer you up
2. In good spirits	2. Nervous
3. Extremely happy	3. Restless or fidgety
4. Calm or peaceful	4. Hopeless
5. Satisfied	5. That everything was an effort
6. Full of life	6. Worthless

Thus, scores could range from 6 to 30 for positive affect and for negative affect.

The results were that older adults reported experiencing more positive emotion and less negative emotion than younger adults and the increase in positive emotion with age in adults increased at an accelerating rate (see figure 20.3). In sum, researchers have found that the emotional life of older adults is more positive than once believed (Carstensen, 1998; Mroczek, 2001).

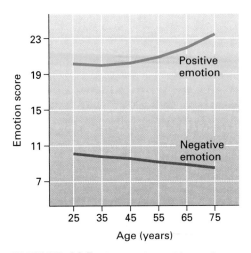

FIGURE 20.3 Changes in Positive and Negative Emotion Across the Adult Years. Positive and negative scores had a possible range of 6 to 30 with higher scores reflecting positive emotion and lower scores negative emotion. Positive emotion increased in the middle adulthood and late adulthood years while negative emotion declined.

Selective Optimization with Compensation Theory

Selective optimization with compensation theory states that successful aging is linked with three main factors: selection, optimization, and compensation (SOC). The theory describes how people can produce new resources and allocate them effectively to the tasks they want to master (Freund, 2006; Riediger, Li, & Lindenberger, 2006). *Selection* is based on the concept that older adults have a reduced capacity and loss of functioning, which require a reduction in performance in most life domains. *Optimization* suggests that it is possible to maintain performance in some areas through continued practice and the use of new technologies. *Compensation* becomes relevant when life tasks require a level of capacity beyond the current level of the older adult's performance potential. Older adults especially need to compensate in circumstances with high mental or physical demands, such as when thinking about and memorizing new material very fast, reacting quickly when driving a car, or running fast. When older adults develop an illness, the need for compensation is obvious.

Selective optimization with compensation theory was proposed by Paul Baltes and his colleagues (Baltes, 2003; Baltes & Baltes, 1990; Baltes, Lindenberger, & Staudinger, 2006; Baltes & Smith, 2003; Freund & Baltes, 2002; Marsiske & others, 1995; Riediger, Li, & Lindenberger, 2006). They describe the life of the late Arthur Rubinstein to illustrate their theory. When he was interviewed at 80 years of age, Rubinstein said that three factors were responsible for his ability to maintain his status as an admired concert pianist into old age. First, he mastered the weakness of old age by reducing the scope of his performances and playing fewer pieces (which reflects selection). Second, he spent more time at practice than earlier in his life (which reflects optimization). Third, he used special strategies, such as slowing down before fast segments, thus creating the image of faster playing (which reflects compensation).

The process of selective optimization with compensation is likely to be effective whenever people pursue successful outcomes. What makes SOC attractive to aging researchers is that it makes explicit how individuals can manage and adapt to losses. By using SOC, they can continue to live satisfying lives, although in a more restrictive manner. Loss is a common dimension of old age, although there are wide variations in the nature of the losses involved. Because of this individual variation, the specific form of selection, optimization, and compensation will likely vary depending on the person's life history, pattern of interests, values, health, skills, and resources. To read about some strategies for effectively engaging in selective optimization with compensation, see the Applications in Life-Span Development interlude.

selective optimization with compensation theory The theory that successful aging is related to three main factors: selection, optimization, and compensation.

APPLICATIONS IN LIFE-SPAN DEVELOPMENT

Strategies for Effectively Engaging in Selective Optimization with Compensation

What are some good strategies that aging adults can engage in to attain selective optimization with compensation? According to Paul Baltes and his colleagues (Baltes, Lindenberger, & Staudinger, 2006; Freund & Baltes, 2002), these strategies are likely to be effective:

Selection Strategies

- *Focus on the most important goal at a particular time.*
- *Think about what you want in life and commit yourself to one or two major goals.*
- *To reach a particular goal, you may need to abandon other goals.*

Optimization Strategies

- *Keep working on what you have planned until you are successful.*
- *Persevere and keep trying until you reach your goal.*
- *When you want to achieve something, you may need to be patient until the right moment arrives.*

Compensation

- *When things don't go the way they used to, search for other ways to achieve what you want.*
- *If things don't go well for you, be willing to let others help you.*
- *When things don't go as well as in the past, keep trying other ways until you can achieve results that are similar to what you accomplished earlier in your life.*

In Baltes' view (2000, 2003; Baltes, Lindenberger, & Staudinger, 2006; Baltes & Smith, 2003; Krampe & Baltes, 2002), the selection of domains and life priorities is an important aspect of development. Life goals and priorities likely vary across the life course for most people. For many individuals, it is not just the sheer attainment of goals, but rather the attainment of *meaningful* goals, that makes life satisfying. In one study, younger adults were more likely to assess their well-being in terms of accomplishments and careers, whereas older adults were more likely to link well-being with good health and the ability to accept change. And as you read earlier in our discussion of socioemotional selectivity theory, emotion-related goals become increasingly important for older adults (Carstensen, 1998, 2006).

In one cross-sectional study, the personal life investments of 25- to 105-year-olds were assessed (Staudinger, 1996) (see figure 20.4). From 25 to 34 years of age, participants said that they personally invested more time in work, friends, family, and independence, in that order. From 35 to 54 and 55 to 65 years of age, family became more important than friends to them in terms of their personal investment. Little changed in the rank ordering of persons 70 to 84 years old, but for participants 85 to 105 years old, health became the most important personal investment. Thinking about life showed up for the first time on the most important list for those who were 85 to 105 years old.

One point to note about the study just described is the demarcation of late adulthood into the subcategories of 70 to 84 and 85 to 105 years of age. This fits with our comments on several occasions that researchers increasingly do not study late adulthood as a homogeneous category, an important point in Paul Baltes' view of aging.

FIGURE 20.4 Degree of Personal Life Investment at Different Points in Life. Shown here are the top four domains of personal life investment at different points in life. The highest degree of investment is listed at the top (for example, work was the highest personal investment from 25 to 34 years of age, family from 35 to 84, and health from 85 to 105).

Recall from chapter 1 that Baltes (2003) believes optimization is more difficult for the oldest-old (85 years and older) than the young-old (65 to 84 years of age). He argues that the oldest-old often experience losses in cognitive potential and ability to learn; an increase in chronic stress; the presence of dementia; high levels of frailty; and dying with decreased dignity. However, Baltes trumpets the following good news about aging: The young-old are experiencing an increase in life expectancy; substantial potential for better physical and mental fitness, including gains in these areas for successive cohorts; cognitive and emotional reserves in an aging mind; successful aging; high levels of emotional and personal well-being; and effective strategies for mastering the gains and losses of late life.

Review and Reflect • LEARNING GOAL 1

1 Discuss five theories of socioemotional development and aging

Review
- What is Erikson's theory of late adulthood?
- What is disengagement theory?
- What is activity theory?
- What is socioemotional selectivity theory and how does research support it?
- What is selective optimization with compensation theory?

Reflect
- Which of the five theories best describes the lives of older adults you know? Explain.

2 | PERSONALITY, THE SELF, AND SOCIETY

| Personality | The Self | Older Adults in Society |

Is personality linked to mortality in older adults? Do self-perceptions and self-control change in late adulthood? How are older adults perceived and treated by society?

Personality

Might certain personality traits be related to how long older adults live? Researchers have found that some personality traits are associated with the mortality of older adults (Mroczek, Spiro, & Griffin, 2006).

We described the big five factors of personality in chapter 17, "Socioemotional Development in Middle Adulthood." Two of the big five factors were linked to older adults' mortality in a recent study, with low conscientiousness and high neuroticism predicting earlier death (Wilson & others, 2004).

Affect and outlook on life are also linked to mortality in older adults (Mroczek, Spiro, & Griffin, 2006). Older adults characterized by negative affect don't live as long as those who display more positive affect, and optimistic older adults who have a positive outlook on life live longer than their counterparts who are more pessimistic and have a negative outlook on life (Levy & others, 2002; Maruta & others, 2000).

The Self

Our exploration of the self focuses on changes in self-esteem and self-acceptance. In chapter 13, we described how self-esteem drops in adolescence, especially for girls. How does self-esteem change in the adult years?

Self-Esteem   In the cross-sectional study of self-esteem described in chapter 13, a very large, diverse sample of 326,641 individuals from 9 to 90 were assessed (Robins & others, 2002). About two-thirds of the participants were from the United States. The individuals were asked to respond to the item "I have high self-esteem" on the following five-point scale:

| 1 | 2 | 3 | 4 | 5 |
| Strongly Disagree | | | | Strongly Agree |

Self-esteem increased in the twenties, leveled off in the thirties and forties, rose considerably in the fifties and sixties, and then dropped significantly in the seventies and eighties (see figure 20.5). Through most of the adult years, the self-esteem of males was higher than the self-esteem of females. However, in the seventies and eighties, the self-esteem of males and females converged.

Why might self-esteem decline in older adults? Explanations include deteriorating physical health and negative societal attitudes toward older adults, although these factors were not examined in the large-scale study just described. Further research is needed to verify these developmental changes in self-esteem.

Is self-esteem more stable at some points in the life span than at others? A recent meta-analysis revealed that self-esteem was the least stable in early childhood (Trzesniewski, Donnellan, & Robins, 2003). One reason for this may be that young children don't completely understand the questions they are asked about their self-esteem but rather provide responses based on their current mood. The

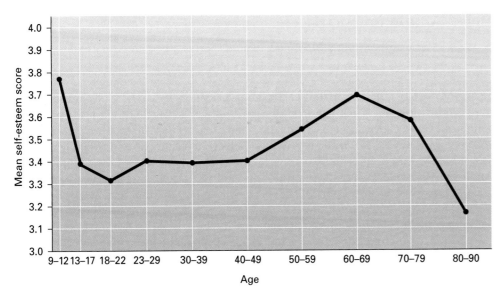

FIGURE 20.5 Self-Esteem Across the Life Span. One cross-sectional study found that self-esteem was high in childhood, dropped in adolescence, increased through early and middle adulthood, then dropped in the seventies and eighties (Robins & others, 2002). More than 300,000 individuals were asked the extent to which they have high self-esteem on a 5-point scale, with 5 being "Strongly Agree" and 1 being "Strongly Disagree."

stability of self-esteem increased in late adolescence and early adulthood. By late adolescence, individuals are experiencing less dramatic physical changes (compared to pubertal change, for example) and are able to better engage in self-control that likely contributed to the increase in stability of self-esteem. The stability of self-esteem decreased in late adulthood, a time during which dramatic life changes and shifting social circumstances (such as death of a loved one and deteriorating health) may occur.

Self-Acceptance   Another aspect of the self that changes across the adult years is self-acceptance. In one study, the self-acceptance of individuals at different points in adult development depended on whether they were describing their past, present, future, or ideal selves (Ryff, 1991). As shown in figure 20.6, young and middle-aged adults showed greater acceptance of their ideal and future selves than their present and past selves. However, in older adults there was little difference in acceptance of various selves because of decreased acceptance of ideal and future selves and increased acceptance of past selves.

Self-Control   Although older adults are aware of age-related losses, most still effectively maintain a sense of self-control. The negative effects of age-typical problems, such as a decline in physical and cognitive skills and an increase in illness, may be buffered by a flexible, accommodating control style. Researchers have found that *accommodating control strategies* (changing one's goals to fit a given circumstance) increase in importance and *assimilative control strategies* (changing a situation to meet one's goals) decrease in importance beginning in middle adulthood (Brandstädter & Renner, 1990).

However, it is important to consider not just general self-control but how people self-regulate their behavior in specific areas of their lives. One study examined individuals from 13 to 90 years of age. For the oldest group (60 to 90 years of age), self-control was lowest in the physical domain; for the youngest group (13 to 18 years of age), it was lowest in the social domain (Bradley & Webb, 1976). Other researchers have found a decline in perceived self-control in cognitive functioning in older adults (Bertrand & Lachman, 2003; Lachman, 1991; Lachman & others, 1982).

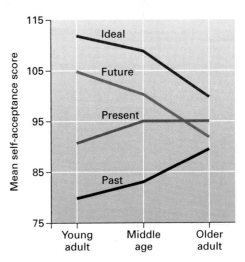

FIGURE 20.6 Changes in Self-Acceptance Across the Adult Years. Acceptance of ideal and future selves decreases with age, acceptance of past selves increases with age, and acceptance of present selves increases slightly in middle age and then levels off.

Older Adults in Society

Does society negatively stereotype older adults? What are some social policy issues in an aging society?

Stereotyping Older Adults   Social participation by older adults is often discouraged by **ageism,** which is prejudice against others because of their age, especially prejudice against older adults (Hepworth, 2004; Hess, 2006; Hinrichsen, 2006; Rupp, Vodanovich, & Crede, 2005). They are often perceived as incapable of thinking clearly, learning new things, enjoying sex, contributing to the community, or holding responsible jobs. Many older adults face painful discrimination and might be too polite and timid to attack it (Cunningham, 2004; Williams, Kemper, & Hummert, 2004). Because of their age, older adults might not be hired for new jobs or might be eased out of old ones; they might be shunned socially; and they might be edged out of their family life.

The personal consequences of negative stereotyping about aging can be serious. A physician (60 years old himself) recently told an 80-year-old: "Well, of course, you are tired. You just need to slow down. Don't try to do so much. After all you are very old." Many older adults accept this type of advice even though it is rooted in age stereotyping rather than medical records.

Ageism is widespread (Lovell, 2006; Robinson & Umphery, 2006). One recent study found that men were more likely to negatively stereotype older adults than were women (Rupp, Vodanovich, & Crede, 2005). Research indicates that the most frequent form is disrespect for older adults, followed by assumptions about ailments or frailty caused by age (Palmore, 2001, 2004). However, the increased number of adults living to an older age has led to active efforts to improve society's image of older adults, obtain better living conditions for older adults, and gain political clout.

Policy Issues in an Aging Society   The aging society and older persons' status in this society raise policy issues about the well-being of older adults. These include the status of the economy and the viability of the Social Security system, the provision of health care, supports for families who care for older adults, and generational inequity, each of which we consider in turn (Neugarten, 1988).

An important issue involving the economy and aging is the concern that our economy cannot bear the burden of so many older persons, who by reason of their age alone are usually consumers rather than producers. However, not all persons 65 and over are non-workers and not all persons 18 to 64 are workers. And considerably more individuals in the 55-to-64 age group are in the workforce—three out of five men—than a decade ago. Thus, it is incorrect to simply describe older adults as consumers and younger adults as producers.

An aging society also brings with it various problems involving health care (Ferraro, 2006; Havrda & others, 2005; Moen & Spencer, 2006; Moon, 2006). Escalating health-care costs are currently causing considerable concern. One factor that contributes to the surge in health costs is the increasing number of older adults (Rice & Fineman, 2004). Older adults have more illnesses than younger adults, despite the fact that many older adults report their health as good. Older adults see doctors more often, are hospitalized more often, and have longer hospital stays. Approximately one-third of the total health bill of the United States is for the care of adults 65 and over, who comprise only 12 percent of the population. The health-care needs of older adults are reflected in Medicare, the program that provides health-care insurance to adults over 65 under the Social Security system (Bass, 2005; Chisholm & Roberts, 2006). Of interest is the fact that the United States is the only industrialized nation that provides health insurance specifically for older adults rather than to the population at large, and the only industrialized nation currently without a national health-care system. Older adults themselves still pay about one-third of their total health-care costs. Thus, older adults as well as younger adults are adversely affected by rising medical costs (Tjia & Schwartz, 2006).

The Gray Panthers are actively involved in pressuring Congress on everything from health insurance to housing costs. Along with the American Association for Retired Persons, they have developed a formidable gray lobbying effort in state and national politics. *What are some of the policy issues in an aging society?*

ageism   Prejudice against other people because of their age, especially prejudice against older adults.

A special concern is that while many of the health problems of older adults are chronic rather than acute, the medical system is still based on a "cure" rather than a "care" model (Stone, 2006). Chronic illness is long-term, often lifelong, and requires long-term, if not life-term, management (Flesner, 2004). Chronic illness often follows a pattern of an acute period that may require hospitalization, followed by a longer period of remission, and then repetitions of this pattern. The patient's home, rather than the hospital, often becomes the center of managing the patient's chronic illness. In a home-based system, a new type of cooperative relationship between doctors, nurses, patients, family members, and other service providers needs to be developed (May & others, 2004). Health-care personnel need to be trained and be available to provide home services, sharing authority with the patient and perhaps yielding it to them over the long term.

Eldercare is the physical and emotional caretaking of older members of the family, whether that care is day-to-day physical assistance or responsibility for arranging and overseeing such care. An important issue involving eldercare is how it can best be provided (Monahan & Hopkins, 2002; Tuch, Parrish, & Romer, 2003; Zahn, 2005). With so many women in the labor market, who will replace them as caregivers? An added problem is that many caregivers are in their sixties, and many of them are ill themselves. They may find it especially stressful to be responsible for the care of relatives who are in their eighties or nineties.

In one study, two distinct systems of eldercare were found: individualistic and collectivistic (Pyke & Bengtson, 1996). Individualists approached parental caregiving reluctantly and considered it a burden. They often reported that they did not have adequate time for it and they relied on formal supports. In contrast, in collectivistic families, parental caregiving was assumed by family members, who emphasized family ties.

Some gerontologists advocate that the government should provide financial support to families to help with home services or substitute for the loss of income if a worker reduces outside employment to care for an aging relative (England & others, 1991). Some large corporations are helping workers with parent-caring by providing flexible work schedules and creating more part-time or at-home jobs. Government supports have been slow to develop. One reason for their slow development is that some individuals believe such government interventions will weaken the family's responsibility and thus have a negative effect on the well-being of older, as well as younger, adults.

Yet another policy issue involving aging is **generational inequity** (discussed initially in chapter 1): The view that our aging society is being unfair to its younger members because older adults pile up advantages by receiving an inequitably large allocation of resources. Some authors have argued that generational inequity produces intergenerational conflict and divisiveness in the society at large (Longman, 1987). The generational equity issue raises questions about whether the young should be required to pay for the old. One claim is that today's baby boomers, now in their forties and fifties, will receive lower Social Security payments than are presently being paid out, or none at all, when they reach retirement age if the economy takes a downturn.

Income   Also of special concern are older adults who are poor (Borg, Hallberg, & Blomqvist, 2006; Holden & Hatcher, 2006). One recent analysis found that lower health-related quality of life in U.S. older adults was linked with income of $15,000 or less (Centers for Disease Control and Prevention, 2003).

Recent census data suggest that although the overall number of older people living in poverty has declined since the 1960s, the percentage of older persons living in poverty has consistently remained in the 10 to 12 percent range since the early 1980s (U.S. Bureau of the Census, 2004). More than 25 percent of older women who live alone live in poverty. Also, the number of older single women just above the poverty line remains substantial. Poverty rates among ethnic minorities

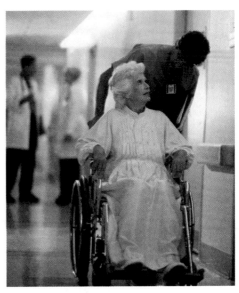

What are some concerns about health care for older adults?

eldercare Physical and emotional caretaking for older members of the family, whether by giving day-to-day physical assistance or by being responsible for overseeing such care.

generational inequity The view that our aging society is being unfair to its younger members because older adults pile up advantages by receiving inequitably large allocations of resources.

are two to three times higher than the rate for Whites. Combining sex and ethnicity, 60 percent of older African American women and 50 percent of older Latino women who live alone live in poverty. Also, the oldest-old are the age subgroup of older adults most likely to be living in poverty.

Many older adults are understandably concerned about their income (Holden & Hatcher, 2006; Morris, 2006). The average income of retired Americans is only about half of what they earned when they were fully employed. Although retired individuals need less income for job-related and social activities, adults 65 and over spend a greater proportion of their income for food, utilities, and health care. They spend a smaller proportion for transportation, clothing, pension and life insurance, and entertainment than do adults under the age of 65. Social Security is the largest contributor to the income of older Americans (38 percent), followed by assets, earnings, and pensions. There is a special concern about poverty in older women and the role of Social Security in providing a broad economic safety net for them (Rupp, Strand, & Davies, 2003).

Social Aging Resources
Social Psychology of Aging
Ageism Resources

Living Arrangements   One stereotype of older adults is that they are often residents in institutions—hospitals, mental hospitals, nursing homes, and so on. However, nearly 95 percent of older adults live in the community. Almost two-thirds of older adults live with family members—spouse, a child, a sibling, for example—while almost one-third live alone. The older people become, the greater are their odds for living alone. Half of older women 75 years and older live alone. The majority of older adults living alone are widowed, with three times as many of these individuals being women than men (U.S. Bureau of the Census, 2004). Older adults who live alone often report being more lonely than their counterparts who live with someone (Routasalo & others, 2006). However, as with younger adults, living alone as an older adult does not mean being lonely (Kasper, 1988). Older adults who can sustain themselves while living alone often have good health and few disabilities, and they may have regular social exchanges with relatives, friends, and neighbors.

For many years researchers who studied the living arrangements of older adults focused on special situations such as nursing homes, public housing, mobile-home parks, welfare hotels, or retirement communities. However, less than 10 percent of older adults live in these types of housing arrangements. Nonetheless, the quality of housing for older adults is far from perfect. The vast majority of older adults prefer to live independently—either alone or with a spouse—rather than with a child, with a relative, or in an institution. However, too many older adults have inadequate housing. One study examined the relation between older adults' physical living environment and their self-rated health (Krause, 1996). Older adults who had the most dilapidated housing gave themselves worse health ratings than their counterparts who had better housing.

Only 5 percent of adults 65 years of age and older live in institutions, but the older adults become, the more likely they are to live in an institution. For example, 23 percent of adults 85 years and over live in institutions. The majority of the older adults in institutions are widows, many of whom cannot physically navigate their environment, are mentally impaired, or are incontinent (cannot control their excretory functions). Because the population is aging and because wives' life expectancies are increasing more rapidly than husbands', even greater numbers of widows are likely to be in institutions in the future.

Our coverage of older adults' housing arrangements so far has focused on the United States. One recent study examined living arrangements of older adults in 43 developing countries (Bongaarts & Zimmer, 2002). Older adult females were more likely to live alone than older adult males. Co-residence of older adults with their adult children was most prevalent in Asia and least prevalent in Africa.

Technology   The Internet plays an increasingly important role in access to information and communication in adults as well as youth (Cutler, 2006; Scialfa &

Fernie, 2006). How well are older adults keeping up with changes in technology? Older adults are less likely to have a computer in their home and less likely to use the Internet than younger adults, but older adults are the fastest-growing segment of Internet users (Brinthall-Peterson, 2003; Czaja & others, 2006). A 2003 survey indicated that 32 percent of 65 and older U.S. adults (about 11 million) and 61 percent of 50- to 64-year-olds are online (Harris Interactive, 2003). Older adults log more time on the Internet (an average of 8.3 hours per week), visit more Web sites, and spend more money on the Internet than their younger adult counterparts. They are especially interested in learning to use e-mail and going online for health information (Melenhorst, Rogers, & Bouwhuis, 2006). Increasing numbers of older adults use e-mail to communicate with relatives. As with children and younger adults, cautions about the accuracy of information—in areas such as health care—on the Internet need to always be kept in mind (Cutler, 2006; Sauri, 2005; Scialfa & Fernie, 2006).

Are the close relationships of older adults different from those of younger adults? What are the lifestyles of older adults like? What characterizes the relationships of older adult parents and their adult children? Is the role of great-grandparents different from the role of grandparents? What do friendships and social networks contribute to the lives of older adults? How might older adults' altruism and volunteerism contribute to positive outcomes?

Are older adults keeping up with changes in technology?

Review and Reflect ● LEARNING GOAL 2

(2) Describe links between personality and mortality, and identify changes in the self and society in late adulthood

Review
- How are personality traits related to mortality in older adults?
- How do self-esteem and self-acceptance change in late adulthood?
- How are older adults perceived and treated by society?

Reflect
- What do you envision your life will be like as an older adult?

---

3 FAMILIES AND SOCIAL RELATIONSHIPS

| Lifestyle Diversity | Great-Grandparenting | Social Support and Integration |

| Older Adult Parents and Their Adult Children | Friendship | Altruism and Volunteerism |

Lifestyle Diversity

The lifestyles of older adults are changing. Formerly, the later years of life were likely to consist of marriage for men and widowhood for women. With demographic shifts toward marital dissolution characterized by divorce, one-third of adults can now expect to marry, divorce, and remarry during their lifetime. Let's now explore some of the diverse lifestyles of older adults, beginning with those who are married or partnered.

What are some adaptations that many married older adults need to make?

Grow old with me! The best is yet to be, The last of life, For which the first was made.

—ROBERT BROWNING
English Poet, 19th Century

Married Older Adults In 2000, older adult men were more likely to be married than older adult women—74 percent of men, 43 percent of women (U.S. Bureau of the Census, 2002). Almost half of all older adult women were widows (45 percent). There were more than four times as many widows as widowers.

The time from retirement until death is sometimes referred to as the "final stage in the marriage process." Retirement alters a couple's lifestyle, requiring adaptation (Dickson, Christian, & Remmo, 2004; Pruchno & Rosenbaum, 2003). The greatest changes occur in the traditional family, in which the husband works and the wife is a homemaker. The husband may not know what to do with his time, and the wife may feel uneasy having him around the house all of the time. In traditional families, both partners may need to move toward more expressive roles. The husband must adjust from being the provider outside of the home to being a helper around the house; the wife must change from being the only homemaker to being a partner who shares and delegates household duties. Marital happiness as an older adult is also affected by each partner's ability to deal with personal conflicts, including aging, illness, and eventual death (Field, 1996).

Individuals who are married or partnered in late adulthood are usually happier and live longer than those who are single (Lee, 1978). One recent study found that older adults were more satisfied with their marriages than were young and middle-aged adults (Bookwala & Jacobs, 2004). Indeed, the majority of older adults evaluate their marriages as happy or very happy (Huyck, 1995). Marital satisfaction is often greater for women than for men, possibly because women place more emphasis on attaining satisfaction through marriage than men do. However, as more women develop careers, this sex difference may not continue. Also, a recent longitudinal study of adults 75 years of age and older revealed that individuals who were married were less likely to die across a span of seven years (Rasulo, Christensen, & Tomassini, 2005).

Divorced and Remarried Older Adults Divorced and separated older adults represented only 8 percent of older adults in 2000 (U.S. Bureau of the Census, 2002). However, their numbers (2.6 million) have increased considerably since 1990 (1.5 million). Many of these individuals were divorced or separated before they entered late adulthood.

There are social, financial, and physical consequences of divorce for older adults (Jenkins, 2003). Divorce can weaken kinship ties when it occurs in later life, especially in the case of older men (Cooney, 1994). Divorced older women are less likely to have adequate financial resources than married older women, and as earlier in adulthood, divorce is linked to more health problems in older adults (Lillard & Waite, 1995).

Rising divorce rates, increased longevity, and better health have led to an increase in remarriage by older adults (Coleman, Ganong, & Fine, 2000). What happens when an older adult wants to remarry or does remarry? Researchers have found that some older adults perceive negative social pressure about their decision to remarry (McKain, 1972). These negative sanctions range from raised eyebrows to rejection by adult children. However, the majority of adult children support the decision of their older adult parents to remarry. Researchers have found that remarried parents and stepparents provide less support to adult stepchildren than parents in first marriages (White, 1994).

Cohabiting Older Adults An increasing number of older adults cohabit (Brown, Lee, & Bulanda, 2006). In 1960, hardly any older adults cohabited (Chevan, 1996). Today, approximately 3 percent of older adults cohabit (U.S. Bureau of the Census, 2004). It is expected that the number of cohabiting older adults will increase even further when baby boomers begin to turn 65 in 2010 and bring their historically more nontraditional values about love, sex, and relationships to late adulthood. In many cases, the cohabiting is more for companionship than for love. In other cases, for example, when one partner faces the potential for expensive care, a couple may decide to maintain their assets separately and thus not marry. One recent study found that older adults who cohabited had a more a more positive, stable relationship than younger adults who cohabited, although cohabiting older adults were less likely to have plans to marry their partner (King & Scott, 2005).

Does cohabiting affect an individual's health? One recent study of more than 8,000 51- to 61-year-old adults revealed that the health of couples who cohabited did not differ from the health of married couples (Waite, 2005). However, another recent study of individuals 50 years of age and older found that those who cohabited were more depressed than their married counterparts (Brown, Bulanda, & Lee, 2005).

Romance and Sex in Older Adults' Relationships Few of us imagine older couples taking an interest in sex or romantic relationships. We might think of them as being interested in a game of bridge or a conversation on the porch, but not much else. In fact, a number of older adults date. The increased health and longevity of older adults have resulted in a much larger pool of active older adults. And the increased divorce rate has added more older adults to the adult dating pool.

Regarding their sexuality, older adults may express their sexuality differently than younger adults, especially when engaging in sexual intercourse becomes difficult. Older adults especially enjoy touching and caressing as part of their sexual relationship. When older adults are healthy, they still may engage in sexual activities. And with the increased use of drugs to treat erectile dysfunction, older adults can be expected to increase their sexual activity (Seftel, 2005). However, companionship often becomes more important than sexual activity in older adults. Older couples often emphasize intimacy over sexual prowess. One recent study of individuals 60 years and older revealed that attitudes had a stronger influence on sexual desire than biomedical factors (DeLamater & Sill, 2005).

What are some ways that older adults retain their sexuality?

Older Adult Parents and Their Adult Children

Approximately 80 percent of older adults have living children, many of whom are middle-aged. About 10 percent of older adults have children who are 65 years or older. Adult children are an important part of the aging parent's social network. Researchers have found that older adults with children have more contacts with relatives than those without children (Johnson & Troll, 1992).

Increasingly, diversity characterizes older adult parents and their adult children. Divorce, cohabitation, and nonmarital childbearing are more common in the history of older adults today than in the past (Allen, Blieszner, & Roberto, 2000). Also, one study found that only 10 of 45 older adults had adult children who were characterized as conventional in terms of marriage and parenting (Allen & others, 1999).

Gender plays an important role in relationships involving older adult parents and their children. Adult daughters rather than adult sons are more likely to be involved in the lives of aging parents. For example, adult daughters are three times more likely than are adult sons to give parents assistance with daily living activities (Dwyer & Coward, 1991).

An extremely valuable task that adult children can perform is to coordinate and monitor services for an aging parent who becomes disabled. This might involve locating a nursing home and monitoring its quality, procuring medical services, arranging public service assistance, and handling finances. In some cases, adult children provide direct assistance with daily living, including such activities as eating, bathing, and dressing. Even less severely impaired older adults may need help with shopping, housework, transportation, home maintenance, and bill paying.

Researchers have found that ambivalence characterized by both positive and negative perceptions is often present in relationships between adult children and their aging parents. These perceptions include love, reciprocal help, and shared values on

*B*eing embedded in a family is a positive aspect of life for many older adults.

—LILLIAN TROLL
*Contemporary Developmental Psychologist,
University of California at San Francisco*

www.mhhe.com/santrockld11

Older Adults and Their Families

At the beginning of the twentieth century, the three-generation family was common, but now the four-generation family is common as well. Thus, an increasing number of grandparents are also great-grandparents. The four-generation family shown here is the Jordans—author John Santrock's mother-in-law, daughter, granddaughter, and wife.

the positive side and isolation, family conflicts and problems, abuse, neglect, and caregiver stress on the negative side (Fowler, 1999). One recent study of 1,599 adult children's relationships with their older adult parents found that ambivalence was likely to be present when relationships involved in-laws, those in poor health, and adult children with poor parental relationships in early life (Wilson, Shuey, & Elder, 2003).

Great-Grandparenting

Because of increased longevity more grandparents today than in the past are also great-grandparents. At the turn of the twentieth century, the three-generation family was common, but now the four-generation family is common. One contribution of great-grandparents is to transmit family history by telling their children, grandchildren, and great-grandchildren where the family came from, what their members achieved, what they endured, and how their lives changed over the years (Harris, 2002).

There has been little research on great-grandparenting. One study examined the relationship between young adults and their grandparents and great-grandparents (Roberto & Skoglund, 1996). The young adults interacted with and participated in more activities with their grandparents than great-grandparents. They also perceived their grandparents to have a more defined role and as more influential in their lives than great-grandparents.

Lillian Troll (1994, 2000) has found that older adults who are embedded in family relationships have much less distress than those who are family deprived. Next, we will consider these other aspects of social relationships in late adulthood: friendship, social support, and social integration.

Friendship

Aging expert Laura Carstensen (1998) concluded that people choose close friends over new friends as they grow older. And as long as they have several close people in their network, they seem content, says Carstensen.

In one recent study of 128 married older adults, women were more depressed than men if they did not have a best friend, and women who did have a friend reported lower levels of depression (Antonucci, Lansford, & Akiyama, 2001). Similarly, women who did not have a best friend were less satisfied with life than women who did have a best friend.

In one study of young-old and old-old adult friendships, there was more continuity than change in amount of contact with friends (Field, 1999). There were, however, more changes in older adult male than older adult female friendships. Older men declined in number of new friends, in their desire for close friendships, and in involvement beyond family activities, whereas older women did not change in these areas.

Two recent studies documented the importance of friendship in older adults:

What are some characteristics of older adults' friendships?

- A study of almost 1,700 U.S. adults 60 years and older revealed that friendships were more important than family relationships in predicting mental health (Fiori, Antonucci, & Cortina, 2006). Even when the researchers controlled for health, age, income, and other factors, older adults whose social contacts were mainly restricted to their family members were more likely to have depressive symptoms. Friends likely provide emotional intimacy and companionship, as well as integration into the community.

- A recent longitudinal study of adults 75 years of age and older revealed that individuals with close ties with friends were less likely to die across a seven-year age span (Rasulo, Christensen, & Tomassini, 2005). The findings were stronger for women than men.

Social Support and Social Integration

In the *social convoy* model of social relations, individuals go through life embedded in a personal network of individuals from whom they give and receive social support (Antonucci & Akiyama, 2002; Antonucci, Lansford, & Akiyama, 2001; Antonucci, Vandewater, & Lansford, 2000). Social support can help individuals of all ages cope more effectively.

Social support can improve the physical and mental health of older adults (Bisschop & others, 2004; Erber, 2005; Fiori & others, 2006). Social support is linked with a reduction in symptoms of disease and with the ability to meet one's own health-care needs (Cohen, Teresi, & Holmes, 1985). Social support also decreases the probability that an older adult will be institutionalized (Antonucci, 1990). Social support is associated with a lower incidence of depression in older adults (Joiner, 2000).

The social support of older adults may depend on the gender of the older adult (Lyyra & Heikkinen, 2006). One recent study showed that among married older adults, men primarily received emotional support from their spouses, whereas women were more likely to draw heavily on friends, relatives, and children for emotional support (Gurung, Taylor, & Seeman, 2003).

Social integration plays an important role in the lives of many older adults (Erber, 2005; Holtzman & others, 2004; Moren-Cross & Lin, 2006). Remember from our earlier discussion of socioemotional selectivity theory that many older adults choose to have fewer peripheral social contacts and more emotionally positive contacts with friends and family. Thus, a decrease in the overall social activity of many older adults may reflect their greater interest in spending more time in the small circle of friends and families where they are less likely to have negative emotional experiences. However, being lonely and socially isolated is a significant health risk factor in older adults (Moren-Cross & Lin, 2006). In one study, being part of a social network was related to longevity, especially for men (House, Landis, & Umberson, 1988). In a longitudinal study, both women and men with more organizational memberships lived longer than their counterparts with low participation in organizations (Tucker & others, 1999). And in another longitudinal study, poor social connections, infrequent participation in social activities, and social disengagement predicted cognitive decline in older adults (Zunzunegui & others, 2003). A recent study of African Americans 65 years and older found that a larger number of social networks and a higher level of social engagement were linked to less cognitive decline (Barnes & others, 2004a).

What role does social support play in the health of older adults?

Altruism and Volunteerism

A common perception is that older adults need to be given help rather than give help themselves. However, researchers recently have found that when older adults engage in altruistic behavior and volunteering they benefit from these activities. One recent study followed 423 older adult couples for five years (Brown & others, 2003). At the beginning of the study, the couples were asked about the extent to which they had given or received emotional or practical help in the past year. Five years later, those who said they had helped others were half as likely to have died. One possible reason for this finding is that helping others may reduce the output of stress hormones, which improves cardiovascular health and strengthens the immune system.

Researchers also have found that volunteering as an older adult is associated with a number of positive outcomes (George, 2006). An early study of individuals 65 years and older found that volunteer workers compared with nonvolunteers were more satisfied with their lives and were less depressed and anxious (Hunter & Linn, 1980). A study of 2,000 older adults in Japan revealed that those who gave more assistance to others had better physical health than their elderly counterparts who

Edna Wharf, who is retired, volunteers her time as a reading tutor at Claxton Elementary School in Ashville, North Carolina. *What are some of the benefits of volunteering for older adults?*

gave less assistance (Krause & others, 1999). And in a recent study, being a volunteer as an older adult was associated with more positive affect and less negative affect (Greenfield & Marks, 2004). Among the reasons for the positive outcomes of volunteering are its provision of constructive activities and productive roles, social integration, and enhanced meaningfulness.

Review and Reflect • LEARNING GOAL 3

3 Characterize the Families and Social Relationships of Aging Adults

Review

- How would you profile the diversity of adult lifestyles?
- What characterizes the relationships of older adult parents and their adult children?
- Is the role of great-grandparents different than for grandparents?
- What is the friendship of older adults like?
- What roles do social support and social integration play in late adulthood?
- How are altruism and volunteerism linked to positive outcomes in older adults?

Reflect

- If you were going to create a research study on close relationships in older adults, what topic would you want to study? Describe a study that you think would be interesting to conduct. Is it a correlational study or an experimental study? What type of measure (observation, interview, survey, for example) would you use?

---

4 ETHNICITY, GENDER, AND CULTURE

Ethnicity	Gender	Culture

How is ethnicity linked to aging? Do gender roles change in late adulthood? What are the social aspects of aging in different cultures?

Ethnicity

Of special concern are ethnic minority older adults, especially African Americans and Latinos, who are overrepresented in poverty statistics (Angel & Angel, 2006; Angel & others, 2004; Erber, 2005; Hinrichsen, 2006). Consider Harry, a 72-year-old African American who lives in a run-down hotel in Los Angeles. He suffers from arthritis and uses a walker. He has not been able to work for years, and government payments are barely enough to meet his needs.

Comparative information about African Americans, Latinos, and Whites indicates a possible double jeopardy for elderly ethnic minority individuals. They face problems related to *both* ageism and racism (Barnes & others, 2004b; Hinrichsen, 2006; Robert & Ruel, 2006). One recent study of more than 4,000 older adults found that African Americans perceived more discrimination than non-Latino Whites (Barnes & others, 2004b). Both the wealth and the health of ethnic minority older adults decrease more rapidly than for elderly Whites (Angel & Angel, 2006; Edmonds, 1993). Older ethnic minority individuals are more likely to become ill but less likely to receive treatment (Hinrichsen, 2006). They also are more likely to have a history of less education, unemployment, worse housing conditions, and shorter life expectancies than their older White counterparts (Himes, Hogan, & Eggebeen, 1996). And many ethnic minority workers never enjoy the Social Security and Medicare benefits to which their earnings contribute, because they die before reaching the age of eligibility for benefits.

Despite the stress and discrimination older ethnic minority individuals face, many of these older adults have developed coping mechanisms that allow them to survive in the dominant White world (Markides & Rudkin, 1996). Extension of family networks helps older minority-group individuals cope with the bare essentials of living and gives them a sense of being loved (Antonucci, Vandewater, & Lansford, 1998). Churches in African American and Latino communities provide avenues for meaningful social participation, feelings of power, and a sense of internal satisfaction (Hill & others, 2006). And residential concentrations of ethnic minority groups give their older members a sense of belonging. Thus, it always is important to consider individual variations in the lives of aging minorities (Whitfield & Baker-Thomas, 1999). To read about one individual who is providing help for aging minorities, see the Careers in Life-Span Development profile.

Gender

Do our gender roles change when we become older adults? Some developmentalists believe there is decreasing femininity in women and decreasing masculinity in men when they reach the late adulthood years (Gutmann, 1975). The evidence suggests that older men do become more feminine—nurturant, sensitive, and so on—but it appears that older women do not necessarily become more masculine—assertive, dominant, and so on (Turner, 1982). Keep in mind that cohort effects are especially important to consider in areas such as gender roles. As sociohistorical changes take place and are assessed more frequently in life-span investigations, what were once perceived to be age effects may turn out to be cohort effects (Jacobs, 1994).

One study found that time spent in committed activities by older adults had shifted in opposite ways for women and men (Verbrugge, Gruber-Baldini, & Fozard, 1996). Between 1958 and 1992, older men decreased their time in paid work and spent more time doing housework, home repairs, yard work, shopping, and child care. By contrast, older women engaged in more paid work and decreased their time in housework.

A possible double jeopardy also faces many women—the burden of *both* ageism and sexism (Lopata, 1994). The poverty rate for older adult females is almost double that of older adult males. According to Congresswoman Mary Rose Oakar, the number one priority for middle-aged and older women should be economic security. She predicts that 25 percent of all women working today can expect to be poor in old age. Yet only recently has scientific and political interest in the aging woman developed. For many years, the aging woman was virtually invisible in aging research and in protests involving rights for older adults (Markson, 1995). An

CAREERS in LIFE-SPAN DEVELOPMENT

Norma Thomas
Social Work Professor and Administrator

Dr. Norma Thomas has worked for more than three decades in the field of aging. She obtained her undergraduate degree in social work from Pennsylvania State University and her doctoral degree in social work from the University of Pennsylvania. Norma's activities are varied. Earlier in her career, as a social work practitioner, she provided services to older adults of color in an effort to improve their lives. She currently is a professor and academic administrator at Widener University in Chester, Pennsylvania, a fellow of the Institute of Aging at the University of Pennsylvania, and the chief executive officer and cofounder of the Center on Ethnic and Minority Aging (CEMA). CEMA was formed to provide research, consultation, training, and services to benefit aging individuals of color, their families, and their communities. Norma has created numerous community service events that benefit older adults of color, especially African Americans and Latinos. She has also been a consultant to various national, regional, and state agencies in her effort to improve the lives of aging adults of color.

Norma Thomas.

important research and political agenda for the twenty-first century is increased interest in the aging and the rights of older adult women.

Not only is it important to be concerned about older women's double jeopardy of ageism and sexism, but special attention also needs to be devoted to female ethnic minority older adults (Locher & others, 2005). They face what could be described as triple jeopardy—ageism, sexism, and racism (Burton, 1996; Markides, 1995). More information about being female, ethnic, and old appears in the Diversity in Life-Span Development interlude.

DIVERSITY IN LIFE-SPAN DEVELOPMENT

Being Female, Ethnic, and Old

A special concern is the stress faced by older African American women, many of whom view religion as a source of strength to help them cope. What are some other characteristics of being female, ethnic, and old?

Part of the unfortunate history of ethnic minority groups in the United States has been the negative stereotypes against members of their groups (Fernandez & Goldstein, 2004). Many also have been hampered by their immigrant origins in that they are not fluent or literate in English, may not be aware of the values and norms involved in American social interaction, and may have lifestyles that differ from those of mainstream America (Organista, 1994). Often included in these cultural differences is the role of women in the family and in society. Many, but not all, immigrant ethnic groups traditionally have relegated the woman's role to family maintenance. Many important decisions may be made by a woman's husband or parents, and she is often not expected to seek an independent career or enter the workforce except in the case of dire financial need.

Some ethnic minority groups may define an older woman's role as unimportant, especially if she is unable to contribute financially. However, in some ethnic minority groups, an older woman's social status improves. For example, older African American women can express their own needs and can be given status and power in the community. Despite their positive status in the African American family and the African American culture, African American women over the age of 70 are the poorest population group in the United States. Three of five older African American women live alone; most of them are widowed. The low incomes of older African American women translate into less than adequate access to health care. Substantially lower incomes for African American older women are related to the kinds of jobs they hold, which either are not covered by Social Security or, in the case of domestic service, are not reported even when reporting is legally required.

A portrayal of older African American women in cities reveals some of their survival strategies. They highly value the family as a system of mutual support and aid, adhere to the American work ethic, and view religion as a source of strength (Perry & Johnson, 1994). The use of religion as a way of coping with stress has a long history in the African American culture, with roots in the slave experience. The African American church came to fulfill needs and functions once met by religion-based tribal and community organizations that African Americans brought from Africa. In one study, the older African American women valued church organizations more than their male counterparts did, especially valuing the church's group activities (Taylor, 1982).

In sum, older African American women have faced considerable stress in their lives (Edmonds, 1993; Locher & others, 2005). In the face of this stress, they have shown remarkable adaptiveness, resilience, responsibility, and coping skills.

Culture

What factors are associated with whether older adults are accorded a position of high status in a culture? Seven factors are most likely to predict high status for older adults in a culture (Sangree, 1989):

- Older persons have valuable knowledge.
- Older persons control key family/community resources.
- Older persons are permitted to engage in useful and valued functions as long as possible.
- There is role continuity throughout the life span.
- Age-related role changes involve greater responsibility, authority, and advisory capacity.
- The extended family is a common family arrangement in the culture, and the older person is integrated into the extended family.
- In general, respect for older adults is greater in collectivistic cultures (such as China and Japan) than in individualistic cultures (such as the United States). However, some researchers are finding that this collectivistic/individualistic difference in respect for older adults is not as strong as it used to be and that in some cases older adults in individualistic cultures receive considerable respect (Antonucci, Vandewater, & Lansford, 2000).

Cultures vary in the prestige they give to older adults. In the Navajo culture, older adults are especially treated with respect because of their wisdom and extensive life experiences. *What are some other factors that are linked with respect for older adults in a culture?*

Review and Reflect ● LEARNING GOAL 4

4 **Summarize how ethnicity, gender, and culture are linked with aging**

Review
- How does ethnicity modify the experience of aging?
- Do gender roles change in late adulthood? Explain.
- How is aging experienced in different cultures?

Reflect
- What can America do to make being an older adult a more positive experience?

5 SUCCESSFUL AGING

For too long, the positive dimensions of late adulthood were ignored (Carstensen, Mikels, & Mather, 2006; Hendricks & Hatch, 2006; Klein, Council, & McGuire, 2005). Throughout this book, we have called attention to the positive aspects of aging. There are many robust, healthy older adults (Motta & others, 2005). With a proper diet, an active lifestyle, mental stimulation and flexibility, positive coping skills, good social relationships and support, and the absence of disease, many abilities can be maintained or in some cases even improved as we get older (Aldwin, Spiro, & Park, 2006; George, 2006). Even when individuals develop a disease, improvements in medicine mean that increasing numbers of older adults can still lead active, constructive lives (Topp, Fahlman, & Boardley, 2004).

Being active is especially important to successful aging (Kramer, Fabiani, & Colcombe, 2006; McReynolds & Rossen, 2004). Older adults who get out and go

www.mhhe.com/santrockld11

Old Age Across Cultures and Time
Culture and Aging

John Glenn's space mission is emblematic of our rethinking of older adults in terms of successful aging.

to meetings, participate in church activities, go on trips, and exercise regularly are more satisfied with their lives than their counterparts who disengage from society (Menec, 2003). Older adults who are emotionally selective, optimize their choices, and compensate effectively for losses increase their chances of aging successfully (Baltes, Freund, & Lee, 2005; Baltes, Lindenberger, & Staudinger, 2006; Riediger, Li, & Lindenberger, 2006).

Successful aging also involves perceived control over the environment (Mroczek, Spiro, & Griffin, 2006). In chapter 18, we described how perceived control over the environment had a positive effect on nursing home residents' health and longevity. In recent years, the term *self-efficacy* has often been used to describe perceived control over the environment and the ability to produce positive outcomes (Bandura, 2000; DeVellis & DeVellis, 2001). Researchers have found that many older adults are quite effective in maintaining a sense of control and have a positive view of themselves (Brandstädter, Wentura, & Greve, 1993; George, 2006). For example, one recent study of centenarians found that many were very happy and that self-efficacy and an optimistic attitude were linked to their happiness (Jopp & Rott, 2006). Examining the positive aspects of aging is an important trend in life-span development and is likely to benefit future generations of older adults.

Review and Reflect ● LEARNING GOAL 5

5) Explain how to age successfully

Review
- What factors are linked with aging successfully?

Reflect
- How might aging successfully in late adulthood be related to what people have done earlier in their lives?

REACH YOUR LEARNING GOALS

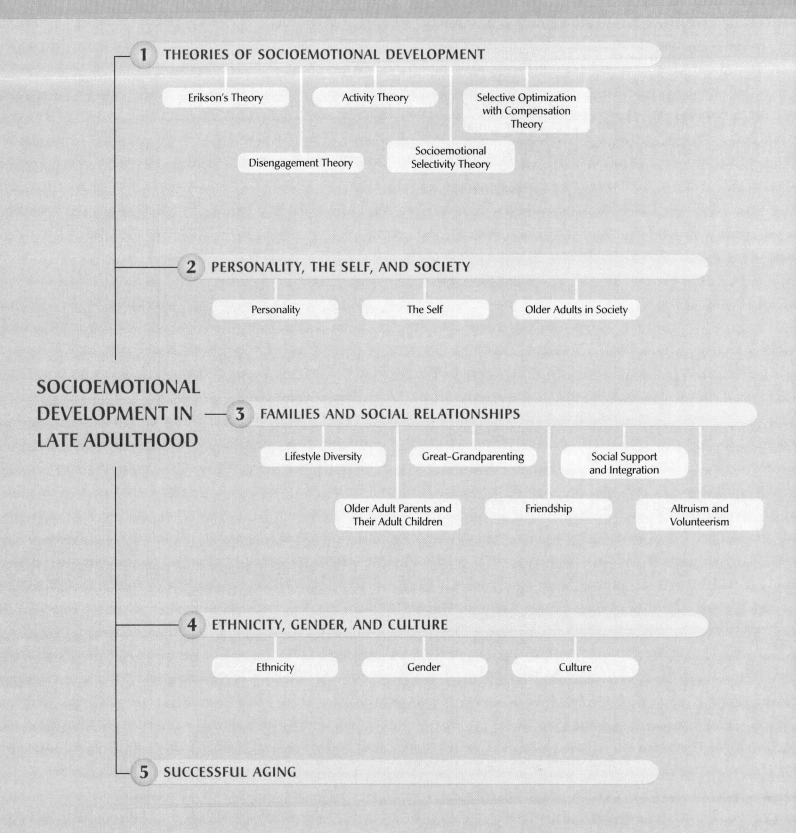

SOCIOEMOTIONAL DEVELOPMENT IN LATE ADULTHOOD

1 THEORIES OF SOCIOEMOTIONAL DEVELOPMENT

Erikson's Theory

Activity Theory

Selective Optimization with Compensation Theory

Disengagement Theory

Socioemotional Selectivity Theory

2 PERSONALITY, THE SELF, AND SOCIETY

Personality

The Self

Older Adults in Society

3 FAMILIES AND SOCIAL RELATIONSHIPS

Lifestyle Diversity

Great-Grandparenting

Social Support and Integration

Older Adult Parents and Their Adult Children

Friendship

Altruism and Volunteerism

4 ETHNICITY, GENDER, AND CULTURE

Ethnicity

Gender

Culture

5 SUCCESSFUL AGING

SUMMARY

1. Theories of Socioemotional Development: *Discuss Five Theories of Socioemotional Development and Aging*

Erikson's Theory
Erikson's eighth and final stage of development, which individuals experience in late adulthood, involves reflecting on the past and either integrating it positively or concluding that one's life has not been well spent. Peck described three developmental tasks that older adults face: (1) differentiation versus role preoccupation, (2) body transcendence versus preoccupation, and (3) ego transcendence versus ego preoccupation. Life review is an important theme in Erikson's stage of integrity versus despair.

Disengagement Theory
Disengagement theory is no longer a viable view. It stated that to be satisfied with their lives older adults need to withdraw from society.

Activity Theory
Activity theory states that the more active and involved older adults are, the more likely they are to be satisfied with their lives. This theory has been strongly supported.

Socioemotional Selectivity Theory
Socioemotional selectivity theory states that older adults become more selective about their social networks. Because they place a high value on emotional satisfaction, they are motivated to spend more time with familiar individuals with whom they have had rewarding relationships. Knowledge-related and emotion-related goals change across the life span, with emotion-related goals being more important when individuals get older.

Selective Optimization with Compensation Theory
Selective optimization with compensation theory states that successful aging is linked with three main factors: (1) selection, (2) optimization, and (3) compensation. These are especially likely to be relevant when loss occurs.

2. Personality, the Self, and Society: *Describe Links between Personality and Mortality, and Identify Changes in the Self and Society in Late Adulthood*

Personality
Low conscientiousness, high neuroticism, negative affect, pessimism, and a negative outlook on life are related to earlier death in late adulthood.

The Self
In one large-scale study, self-esteem increased through most of adulthood but declined in the seventies and eighties. Further research is needed to verify these developmental changes in self-esteem. The stability of self-esteem declines in older adults. Changes in types of self-acceptance occur through the adult years as acceptance of ideal and future selves decreases with age and acceptance of past selves increases. Most older adults effectively maintain a sense of self-control although self-regulation may vary by domain. For example, older adults often show less self-regulation in the physical domain than younger adults.

Older Adults in Society
Ageism is prejudice against others because of their age. Too many negative stereotypes of older adults continue to exist. Social policy issues in an aging society include the status of the economy and the viability of the Social Security system, the provision of health care, eldercare, and generational inequity. Of special concern are older adults who are in poverty. Poverty rates are especially high among older women who live alone and ethnic minority older adults. Most older adults live in the community, not in institutions. Almost two-thirds of older adults live with family members. Older adults are less likely to have a computer in their home and less likely to use the Internet than younger adults, but they are the fastest-growing age segment of Internet users.

3. Families and Social Relationships: *Characterize the Families and Social Relationships of Aging Adults*

Lifestyle Diversity
Older adult men are more likely to be married than older adult women. Almost half of older adult women are widowed. Retirement alters a couple's lifestyle and requires adaptation. Married older adults are often happier than single older adults. There are social, financial, and physical consequences of divorce for older adults. More divorced older adults, increased longevity, and better health have led to an increase in remarriage by older adults. Some older adults perceive negative pressure about their decision to remarry, although the majority of adult children support the decision of their older adult parents to remarry. An increasing number of older adults cohabit. Older adults especially enjoy touching and caressing as part of their sexual relationship.

Older Adult Parents and Their Adult Children
Approximately 80 percent of older adults have living children, many of whom are middle-aged. Increasingly, diversity characterizes older parents and their adult children. Adult daughters are more likely than adult sons to be involved in the lives of aging parents. An important task that adult children can perform is to coordinate and monitor services for an aging parent who becomes disabled. Ambivalence can characterize the relationships of adult children with their aging parents.

Great-Grandparenting

Because of increased longevity more grandparents today are also great-grandparents. One contribution of great-grandparents is family history. One research study found that young adults have a more involved relationship with grandparents than great-grandparents.

Friendship

There is more continuity than change in friendship for older adults, although there is more change for males than for females.

Social Support and Integration

Social support is linked with improved physical and mental health in older adults. Older adults who participate in more organizations live longer than their counterparts who have low participation rates. Older adults often have fewer peripheral social ties but a strong motivation to spend time in relationships with close friends and family members that are rewarding.

Altruism and Volunteerism

Altruism is linked to having a longer life. Volunteering is associated with higher life satisfaction, less depression and anxiety, better physical health, and more positive affect and less negative affect.

 4   Ethnicity, Gender, and Culture: *Summarize How Ethnicity, Gender, and Culture Are Linked with Aging*

Ethnicity

Aging minorities face special burdens, having to cope with the double burden of ageism and racism. Nonetheless, there is considerable variation in aging minorities.

Gender

There is stronger evidence that men become more feminine (nurturant, sensitive) as older adults than there is that women become more masculine (assertive). Older women face a double jeopardy of ageism and sexism.

Culture

Historically, respect for older adults in China and Japan was high, but today their status is more variable. Factors that predict high status for the elderly across cultures range from their valuable knowledge to integration into the extended family.

5   Successful Aging: *Explain How to Age Successfully*

Increasingly, the positive aspects of older adults are being studied. Factors that are linked with successful aging include an active lifestyle, positive coping skills, good social relationships and support, and the absence of disease.

KEY TERMS

integrity versus despair 649	ego transcendence versus ego preoccupation 650	socioemotional selectivity theory 651	ageism 658
differentiation versus role preoccupation 649	disengagement theory 650	selective optimization with compensation theory 653	eldercare 659
body transcendence versus body preoccupation 649	activity theory 651		generational inequity 659

KEY PEOPLE

Erik Erikson 648	Robert Butler 650	Paul Baltes 653
Robert Peck 649	Laura Carstensen 651	

E-LEARNING TOOLS

To help you master the material in this chapter, you'll find a number of valuable study tools on the LifeMap CD-ROM that accompanies this book and on the Online Learning Center for *Life-Span Development*, eleventh edition, at **www.mhhe.com/santrockld11**.

Video Clips

In the margins of this book there are icons directing you to the LifeMap CD-ROM that accompanies the book. In chapter 20 you'll find a video called "Being in Love in Late Adulthood." This segment inquires into the sexual and emotional needs of older adults in various relationships. An older couple describe how the nature of their affection for each other has changed over the years.

Self-Assessment

Connect to **www.mhhe.com/santrockld11** to reflect on your life satisfaction by completing the self-assessment, *How Satisfied Am I with My Life?*

Taking It to the Net

1. How much Social Security income can you expect to receive when you are normal retirement age? First, ascertain what will be your normal retirement age—it depends on the year in which you are born—and see how much you will receive. How much will you receive if you retire early? How much will you receive if you work past your normal retirement age?

2. Ted is the activities director at an adult retirement community. A friend who is a social worker suggested that Ted might want to develop a program in which the residents engage in reminiscence and life review. What benefits could the residents gain from such an activity?

3. Jessica, 33, a single mother of three, has been diagnosed with breast cancer. Just as a precaution, Jessica has made arrangements for her parents to raise the children if she dies. What types of services and financial assistance would be available to Jessica's parents if they need to take on the responsibility for their grandchildren?

Health and Well-Being, Parenting, and Education Exercises

Build your decision-making skills by trying your hand at the health and well-being, parenting, and education exercises. Connect to **www.mhhe.com/santrockld11** to research the answers and complete the exercises.

Chapter 21

DEATH AND GRIEVING

Sustained and soothed by an unfaltering trust, approach thy grave, Like one who wraps the Drapery of his couch About him, and lies down to pleasant dreams.

—WILLIAM CULLEN BRYANT
American Poet, 19th Century

LEARNING GOALS

1 Evaluate issues in determining death and decisions regarding death

2 Describe the roles of sociohistorical and cultural contexts in understanding death

3 Discuss death and attitudes about it at different points in development

4 Explain the psychological aspects involved in facing one's own death and the contexts in which people die

5 Identify ways to cope with the death of another person

Images of Life-Span Development
Paige Farley-Hackel and Ruth McCourt

Paige Farley-Hackel and her best friend Ruth McCourt teamed up to take McCourt's 4-year-old daughter, Juliana, to Disneyland. They were originally booked on the same flight from Boston to Los Angeles, but McCourt decided to use her frequent flyer miles and go on a different airplane. Both their flights exploded 17 minutes apart after terrorists hijacked them, then rammed them into the twin towers of the World Trade Center in New York City on 9/11/2001.

Forty-six year old Farley-Hackel was a writer, motivational speaker, and spiritual counselor who lived in Newton, Massachusetts. She was looking forward to the airing of the first few episodes of her new radio program, "Spiritually Speaking," and wanted to eventually be on "The Oprah Winfrey Show," said her husband, Allan Hackel. Following 9/11, Oprah included a memorial tribute to Farley-Hackel, McCourt, and Juliana.

Forty-five year old Ruth McCourt was a homemaker from New London, Connecticut, who met Farley-Hackel at a day spa she used to own in Boston. McCourt gave up the business when she became married but the friendship between the two women lasted. They often traveled together and shared their passion for reading, cooking, and learning.

PREVIEW

In this final chapter of the book, we will explore many aspects of death and dying. Among the questions that we will ask are: How can death be defined? How is death viewed in other cultures? What are some links between development and death? How do people face their own death? How do people cope with the death of someone they love?

1 DEFINING DEATH AND LIFE/DEATH ISSUES

Issues in Determining Death	Decisions Regarding Life, Death, and Health Care

Is there one point in the process of dying that is *the* point at which death takes place, or is death a more gradual process? What are some decisions individuals can make about life, death, and health care?

Issues in Determining Death

Twenty-five years ago, determining if someone was dead was simpler than it is today. The end of certain biological functions, such as breathing and blood pressure, and the rigidity of the body (rigor mortis) were considered to be clear signs of death. In the past several decades, defining death has become more complex (Corr, Nabe, & Corr, 2003; Joffe & Anton, 2006; Okuyz & others, 2004; Skrabal & others, 2005). Consider the circumstance of Philadelphia Flyers hockey star Pelle Lindbergh, who slammed his Porsche into a cement wall on November 10, 1985. The newspaper headline the next day read, "Flyers' Goalie Is Declared Brain Dead." In spite of the claim that he was "brain dead," the story reported that Lindbergh was listed in "critical condition" in the intensive care unit of a hospital.

Brain death is a neurological definition of death, which states that a person is brain dead when all electrical activity of the brain has ceased for a specified period of time. A flat EEG (electroencephalogram) recording for a specified period of time is one criterion of brain death. The higher portions of the brain often die sooner than the lower portions. Because the brain's lower portions monitor heartbeat and respiration, individuals whose higher brain areas have died may continue breathing and have a heartbeat. The definition of brain death currently followed by most physicians includes the death of both the higher cortical functions and the lower brain stem functions (Bernat, 2005).

Some medical experts argue that the criteria for death should include only higher cortical functioning. If the cortical death definition were adopted, then physicians could claim a person is dead who has no cortical functioning even though the lower brain stem is functioning. Supporters of the cortical death policy argue that the functions we associate with being human, such as intelligence and personality, are located in the higher cortical part of the brain. They believe that when these functions are lost, the "human being" is no longer alive.

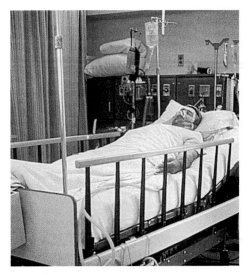

Advances in medical technology have complicated the definition of death. *What is the nature of the controversy about the criteria that should be used for determining when death occurs?*

Decisions Regarding Life, Death, and Health Care

In cases of catastrophic illness or accidents, patients might not be able to respond adequately to participate in decisions about their medical care. To prepare for this situation, some individuals make choices earlier.

Natural Death Act and Advanced Directive For many patients in a coma, it has not been clear what their wishes regarding termination of treatment might be if they still were conscious (Aiken, 2000). Recognizing that terminally ill patients might prefer to die rather than linger in a painful or vegetative state, the organization "Choice in Dying" created the living will. This document is designed to be filled in while the individual can still think clearly; it expresses the person's desires regarding extraordinary medical procedures that might be used to sustain life when the medical situation becomes hopeless.

Physicians' concerns over malpractice suits and the efforts of people who support the living will concept have produced natural death legislation in many states. For example, California's Natural Death Act permits individuals who have been diagnosed by two physicians as terminally ill to sign an *advanced directive,* which states that life-sustaining procedures shall not be used to prolong their lives when death is imminent (Giger, Davidhizar, & Fordham, 2006). An advanced directive must be signed while the individual still is able to think clearly (Wareham, McCallin, & Diesfeld, 2005). Laws in all 50 states now accept advanced directives as reflecting an individual's wishes.

Euthanasia Euthanasia ("easy death") is the act of painlessly ending the lives of individuals who are suffering from an incurable disease or severe disability. Sometimes euthanasia is called "mercy killing." Distinctions are made between two types of euthanasia: passive and active.

- **Passive euthanasia** occurs when a person is allowed to die by withholding available treatment, such as withdrawing a life-sustaining device. For example, this might involve turning off a respirator or a heart-lung machine.
- **Active euthanasia** occurs when death is deliberately induced, as when a lethal dose of a drug is injected.

Technological advances in life-support devices raise the issue of quality of life. Nowhere was this more apparent in the highly publicized case of Terri Schiavo, who suffered severe brain damage related to cardiac arrest and a lack of oxygen to the brain. She went into a coma and spent 15 years in a vegetative state. Across the 15 years, whether passive euthanasia should be implemented or whether she should be kept in the vegetative state with the hope that her condition might change for the better was debated between family members and eventually at a number of

brain death A neurological definition of death. A person is brain dead when all electrical activity of the brain has ceased for a specified period of time. A flat EEG recording is one criterion of brain death.

euthanasia The act of painlessly ending the lives of persons who are suffering from incurable diseases or severe disabilities; sometimes called "mercy killing."

passive euthanasia The withholding of available treatments, such as life-sustaining devices, allowing the person to die.

active euthanasia Death induced deliberately, as by injecting a lethal dose of a drug.

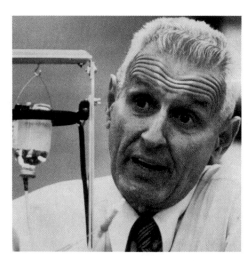

Dr. Jack Kevorkian assisted a number of people in Michigan to end their lives through active euthanasia. *Where do you stand on the use of active euthanasia?*

www.mhhe.com/santrockld11

Choice in Dying
Assisted Suicide
Exploring Euthanasia

levels in the judicial system. At one point toward the end of her life in early spring, 2005, a court ordered her feeding tube be removed. However, subsequent appeals led to its reinsertion twice. The feeding tube was removed a third and final time on March 18, 2005, and she died 13 days later.

Should individuals, like Terri Schiavo, be kept alive in a vegetative state? The trend is toward acceptance of passive euthanasia in the case of terminally ill patients (Branthwaite, 2006). The inflammatory argument that once equated this practice with suicide rarely is heard today. However, experts do not yet entirely agree on the precise boundaries or the exact mechanisms by which treatment decisions should be implemented (Phillips & others, 2005; Massetti & others, 2005). Can a comatose patient's life-support systems be disconnected when the patient has left no written instructions to that effect? Does the family of a comatose patient have the right to overrule the attending physician's decision to continue life-support systems? These questions have no simple or universally agreed-upon answers (Kelly & McLoughlin, 2002; Jeffrey, 2006). In one study of Canadian health-care workers, there was considerable variability in their decisions about whether to withdraw life support from critically ill patients (Cook & others, 1995).

The most widely publicized cases of active euthanasia involve "assisted suicide" (Hicks, 2006; Wolf, 2005). Jack Kevorkian, a Michigan physician, has assisted a number of terminally ill patients to end their lives (Roscoe & others, 2002). After a series of trials, Kevorkian was convicted of second-degree murder and given a long prison sentence.

Active euthanasia is a crime in most countries and in all states in the United States except one—Oregon (Hedberg, Hopkins, & Kohn, 2003). In 1994, the state of Oregon passed the Death with Dignity Act, which allows active euthanasia. Through 2001, 91 individuals were known to have died by active euthanasia in Oregon. Active euthanasia is legal in the Netherlands and Uruguay (Sheldon, 2005). In January 2006, the U.S. Supreme Court upheld Oregon's active euthanasia law.

A survey of more than 900 physicians assessed their attitudes about active euthanasia (Walker, Gruman, & Blank, 1999). Most opposed active euthanasia, said that adequate pain control often eliminates the need for it, and commented that the primary role of the physician is to preserve life. They also reported that the potential for abuse in active euthanasia is substantial, and many believe that it is morally wrong.

Needed: Better Care for Dying Individuals Death in America is often lonely, prolonged, and painful (Institute of Medicine, 1997). Dying individuals often get too little or too much care. Scientific advances sometimes have made dying harder by delaying the inevitable (Kaufman, 2005; Muth, 2000). Also, even though painkillers are available, too many people experience severe pain during the last days and months of life (Fine & Peterson, 2002; Lo & Rubenfeld, 2005). Many health-care professionals have not been trained to provide adequate end-of-life care or to understand its importance. In 1997, a panel of experts recommended that regulations be changed to make it easier for physicians to prescribe painkillers for dying patients who need them (Institute of Medicine, 1997).

End-of-life care should include respect for the goals, preferences, and choices of the patient and his or her family (Boyle, Miller, & Forbes-Thompson, 2005; Nidetz & others, 2005). Many patients who are nearing death want companionship.

Care providers are increasingly interested in helping individuals experience a "good death" (International Work Group on Death, Dying, and Bereavement & others, 2006; Wortman & Boerner, 2007). One view is that a good death involves physical comfort, support from loved ones, acceptance, and appropriate medical care (Carr, 2003).

There are few fail-safe measures for avoiding pain at the end of life. Still, you can follow these suggestions (Cowley & Hager, 1995):

- Make a living will, and be sure there is someone who will draw your doctor's attention to it.

- Give someone the power of attorney and make sure this person knows your wishes regarding medical care.
- Give your doctors specific instructions—from "Do not resuscitate" to "Do everything possible"—for specific circumstances.
- If you want to die at home, talk it over with your family and doctor.
- Check to see whether your insurance plan covers home care and hospice care.

**Hospice Net
Hospice Foundation of America
Better Care for the Dying**

Hospice is a program committed to making the end of life as free from pain, anxiety, and depression as possible. Whereas a hospital's goals are to cure illness and prolong life, hospice care emphasizes **palliative care,** which involves reducing pain and suffering and helping individuals die with dignity (King & Quill, 2006; Shah & others, 2006). Health-care professionals work together to treat the dying person's symptoms, make the individual as comfortable as possible, show interest in the person and the person's family, and help them cope with death (Chochinov & others, 2006; Hays & others, 2006).

The hospice movement began toward the end of the 1960s in London, when a new kind of medical institution, St. Christopher's Hospice, opened. Little effort is made to prolong life at St. Christopher's—there are no heart-lung machines and there is no intensive care unit, for example. A primary goal is to bring pain under control and to help dying patients face death in a psychologically healthy way. The hospice also makes every effort to include the dying individual's family; it is believed that this strategy benefits not only the dying individual but family members as well, probably diminishing their guilt after the death (Reb, 2003; Johnson & others, 2005).

The hospice movement has grown rapidly in the United States (Casarett & others, 2005; Ferris & Librach, 2005; Lund, 2006). More than 1,500 community groups are involved nationally in establishing hospice programs. Hospices are more likely to serve people with terminal cancer than those with other life-threatening conditions (Kastenbaum, 2004). Hospice advocates underscore that it is possible to control pain for almost any dying individual and that it is possible to create an environment for the patient that is superior to that found in most hospitals (Hayslip, 1996).

Today more hospice programs are home-based, a blend of institutional and home care designed to humanize the end-of-life experience for the dying person. Whether the hospice program is carried out in the dying person's home, through a blend of home and institutional care, or in an institution often depends on medical needs and the availability of caregivers, including family and friends (Dougherty & Long, 2006; Terry & others, 2006). To read about the work of a home hospice nurse, see the Careers in Life-Span Development profile.

Researchers have found that family members provide more positive evaluations of a loved one's quality of life and better psychological adjustment themselves following the loved one's death when in-home hospice services are used than when the loved one is cared for in the final weeks of life in nursing homes, hospitals, or at home with home health nursing services (Teno & others, 2004).

CAREERS in LIFE-SPAN DEVELOPMENT

Kathy McLaughlin
Home Hospice Nurse

Kathy McLaughlin is a home hospice nurse in Alexandria, Virginia. She provides care for individuals with terminal cancer, Alzheimer disease, and other diseases. There currently is a shortage of home hospice nurses in the United States.

Kathy says that she has seen too many people dying in pain, away from home, hooked up to needless machines. In her work as a home hospice nurse, she comments, "I know I'm making a difference. I just feel privileged to get the chance to meet this person who is not going to be around much longer. I want to enjoy the moment with this person. And I want them to enjoy the moment. They have great stories. They are better than novels" (McLaughlin, 2003, p. 1).

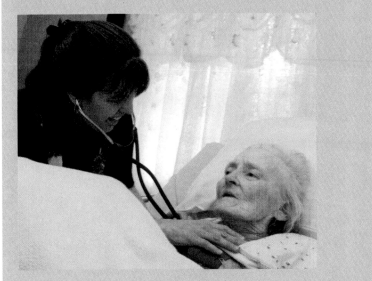

Kathy McLaughlin checks the vital signs of Kathryn Francis, 86, who is in an advanced stage of Alzheimer disease.

hospice A program committed to making the end of life as free from pain, anxiety, and depression as possible. The goals of hospice contrast with those of a hospital, which are to cure disease and prolong life.

palliative care Emphasized in hospice care, involves reducing pain and suffering and helping individuals die with dignity.

One study also revealed that hospice care reduced the increased mortality linked with bereavement by loved ones (Christakis & Iwashyna, 2003).

Review and Reflect • LEARNING GOAL 1

1 **Evaluate issues in determining death and decisions regarding death**

Review
- What are some issues regarding the determination of death?
- What are some decisions to be made regarding life, death, and health care?

Reflect
- Do you think assisted suicide should be legal? Explain your answer.

---

2   DEATH AND CULTURAL CONTEXTS

Changing Historical Circumstances	Death in Different Cultures

When, where, and how people die have changed historically in the United States. Also, attitudes toward death vary across cultures.

Changing Historical Circumstances

We have already described one of the historical changes involving death—the increasing complexity of determining when someone is truly dead. Another historical change involves the age group in which death most often strikes. Two hundred years ago, almost one of every two children died before the age of 10, and one parent died before children grew up. Today, death occurs most often among older adults (Lamb, 2003). Life expectancy has increased from 47 years for a person born in 1900 to 78 years for someone born today (U.S. Bureau of the Census, 2006). In 1900, most people died at home, cared for by their family. As our population has aged and become more mobile, more older adults die apart from their families. In the United States today, more than 80 percent of all deaths occur in institutions or hospitals. The care of a dying older person has shifted away from the family and minimized our exposure to death and its painful surroundings.

Death in Different Cultures

Cultural variations characterize the experience of death and attitudes about death (Talib, 2005; Warren, 2005; Yasien-Esmael & Rubin, 2005). To live a full life and die with glory was the prevailing goal of the ancient Greeks. Individuals are more conscious of death in times of war, famine, and plague. Whereas Americans are conditioned from early in life to live as though they were immortal, in much of the world this fiction cannot be maintained. Death crowds the streets of Calcutta in daily overdisplay, as it does the scrubby villages of Africa's Sahel. Children live with the ultimate toll of malnutrition and disease, mothers lose as many babies as survive into adulthood, and it is rare that a family remains intact for many years. Even in peasant areas where life is better, and health and maturity may be reasonable expectations, the presence of dying people in the house, the large attendance at funerals, and the daily contact with aging adults prepare the young for death and provide them with guidelines on how to die. By contrast, in the United States it is not uncommon to reach adulthood without having seen someone die.

Most societies throughout history have had philosophical or religious beliefs about death, and most societies have a ritual that deals with death (Lobar, Youngblut, & Brooten, 2006) (see figure 21.1). Death may be seen as a punishment for one's sins, an act of atonement, or a judgment of a just God. For some, death means loneliness; for others, death is a quest for happiness. For still others, death represents redemption, a relief from the trials and tribulations of the earthly world. Some embrace death and welcome it; others abhor and fear it. For those who welcome it, death may be seen as the fitting end to a fulfilled life. From this perspective, how we depart from earth is influenced by how we have lived.

In most societies, death is not viewed as the end of existence—though the biological body has died, the spiritual body is believed to live on (Emmons, 2003; Morgan, 2003). This religious perspective is favored by most Americans as well (Gowan, 2003). Cultural variations in attitudes toward death include belief in reincarnation, which is an important aspect of the Hindu and Buddhist religions (Dillon, 2003; Truitner & Truitner, 1993). In the Gond culture of India, death is believed to be caused by magic and demons. The members of the Gond culture react angrily to death. In the Tanala culture of Madagascar, death is believed to be caused by natural forces. The members of the Tanala culture show a much more peaceful reaction to death than their counterparts in the Gond culture.

In many ways, we in the United States are death avoiders and death deniers (Norouzieh, 2005; Taylor, 2003). This denial can take many forms:

- The tendency of the funeral industry to gloss over death and fashion lifelike qualities in the dead
- The adoption of euphemistic language for death—for example, *exiting, passing on, never say die,* and *good for life,* which implies forever
- The persistent search for a fountain of youth
- The rejection and isolation of the aged, who may remind us of death
- The adoption of the concept of a pleasant and rewarding afterlife, suggesting that we are immortal
- The medical community's emphasis on prolonging biological life rather than on diminishing human suffering

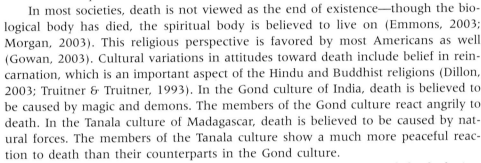
FIGURE 21.1 A Ritual Associated with Death. Family memorial day at the national cemetery in Seoul, South Korea.

www.mhhe.com/santrockld11

Dying and Medicine in America

Review and Reflect ● LEARNING GOAL 2

2 **Describe the roles of sociohistorical and cultural contexts in understanding death**

Review
- What are some changing sociohistorical circumstances regarding death?
- What are some variations in death across cultures?

Reflect
- Why is the United States such a death-denying culture? How could this be changed?

3 A DEVELOPMENTAL PERSPECTIVE ON DEATH

Causes of Death

Attitudes Toward Death at Different Points in the Life Span

Do the causes of death vary across the human life span? Do we have different expectations about death as we develop through the life span? What are our attitudes toward death at different points in our development?

Causes of Death

Death can occur at any point in the human life span. Death can occur during prenatal development through miscarriages or stillborn births. Death can also occur during the birth process or in the first few days after birth, which usually happens because of a birth defect or because infants have not developed adequately to sustain life outside the uterus. In chapter 5, we described *sudden infant death syndrome (SIDS)*, in which infants stop breathing, usually during the night, and die without apparent cause (Hunt & Hauck, 2006). SIDS currently is the leading cause of infant death in the United States, with the risk highest at 4 to 6 weeks of age (American Academy of Pediatrics Task Force on Infant Sleep Position and SIDS, 2000).

In childhood, death occurs most often because of accidents or illness. Accidental death in childhood can be the consequence of such things as an automobile accident, drowning, poisoning, fire, or a fall from a high place. Major illnesses that cause death in children are heart disease, cancer, and birth defects.

Compared with childhood, death in adolescence is more likely to occur because of motor vehicle accidents, suicide, and homicide. Many motor vehicle accidents that cause death in adolescence are alcohol-related. We will examine suicide in greater depth shortly.

Older adults are more likely to die from chronic diseases, such as heart disease and cancer, whereas younger adults are more likely to die from accidents. Older adults' diseases often incapacitate before they kill, which produces a course of dying that slowly leads to death. Of course, many young and middle-aged adults die of diseases, such as heart disease and cancer.

Attitudes Toward Death at Different Points in the Life Span

The ages of children and adults influence the way they experience and think about death. A mature, adult-like conception of death includes an understanding that death is final and irreversible, that death represents the end of life, and that all living things die. Most researchers have found that as children grow, they develop a more mature approach to death (Hayslip & Hansson, 2003).

Childhood Most researchers believe that infants do not have even a rudimentary concept of death. However, as infants develop an attachment to a caregiver, they can experience loss or separation and an accompanying anxiety. But young children do not perceive time the way adults do. Even brief separations may be experienced as total losses. For most infants, the reappearance of the caregiver provides a continuity of existence and a reduction of anxiety. We know very little about the infant's actual experiences with bereavement, although the loss of a parent, especially if the caregiver is not replaced, can negatively affect the infant's health.

Even children 3 to 5 years of age have little or no idea of what death means. They may confuse death with sleep or ask in a puzzled way, "Why doesn't it move?"

Preschool-aged children rarely get upset by the sight of a dead animal or by being told that a person has died. They believe that the dead can be brought back to life spontaneously by magic or by giving them food or medical treatment. Young children often believe that only people who want to die, or who are bad or careless, actually die. They also may blame themselves for the death of someone they know well, illogically reasoning that the event may have happened because they disobeyed the person who died.

Sometime in the middle and late childhood years more realistic perceptions of death develop. In one early investigation of children's perception of death, children 3 to 5 years of age denied that death exists, children 6 to 9 years of age believed that death exists but only happens to some people, and children 9 years of age and older recognized death's finality and universality (Nagy, 1948). In a review of research on children's conception of death, it was concluded that children probably do not view death as universal and irreversible until about 9 years of age (Cuddy-Casey & Orvaschel, 1997). Most children under 7 do not see death as likely. Those who do, perceive it as reversible.

An expert on death and dying, Robert Kastenbaum (2000) takes a different view on developmental dimensions of death and dying. He contends that even very young children are acutely aware of and concerned about *separation* and *loss,* just as attachment theorist John Bowlby (1980) does. Kastenbaum also says that many children work hard at trying to understand death. Thus, instead of viewing young children as having illogical perceptions of death, Kastenbaum thinks a more accurate stance is to view them as having concerns about death and striving to understand it.

The following clarification of children's experience with the death of others was provided by Bert Hayslip and Robert Hansson (2003). They concluded that "experiences with the deaths of grandparents, friends, heros (sports figures, rock stars), and parents are particularly powerful influences on children's awareness of death, as are culturally relevant experiences such as the Columbine High School shootings in 1999, . . . the terrorist attack on the World Trade Center in 2001, and the deaths of such public figures as Kurt Cobain, Dale Earnhardt, Sr., Selena, Princess Diana, (and) John F. Kennedy" (Hayslip & Hansson, 2003, p. 440). The death of a parent is especially difficult for children (Sood & others, 2006). When a child's parent dies, the child's school performance and peer relationships often worsen. For some children, as well as adults, a parent's death can be devastating and result in a hypersensitivity about death, including a fear of losing others close to the individual. In some cases, loss of a sibling can result in similar negative outcomes (Sood & others, 2006). However, a number of factors, such as the quality of the relationship and type of the death (whether due to an accident, long-standing illness, suicide, or murder, for example), can influence the individual's development following the death of a person close to the individual.

Most psychologists consider that honesty is the best strategy in discussing death with children. Treating the concept as unmentionable is thought to be an inappropriate strategy, yet most of us have grown up in a society in which death is rarely discussed. In one study, the attitudes of 30,000 young adults toward death were evaluated (Shneidman, 1973). More than 30 percent said they could not recall any discussion of death during their childhood. An equal number said that, although death was discussed, the discussion took place in an uncomfortable atmosphere. Almost one of every two respondents said that the death of a grandparent was their first personal encounter with death.

In addition to honesty, what other strategies can be adopted in discussing death with children? The best response to the child's query about death might depend on the child's maturity level (Aiken, 2000). For example, the preschool child requires a less elaborate explanation than an older child. Death can be explained to preschool children in simple physical and biological terms. Actually, what young children need more than elaborate explanations of death is reassurance that they are loved and will not be abandoned. Regardless of children's age, adults should be sensitive and sympathetic, encouraging them to express their own feelings and ideas.

What are children's and adolescents' attitudes about death?

www.mhhe.com/santrockld11

Grieving Children
Association for Death Education
and Counseling

It is not unusual for terminally ill children to distance themselves from their parents as they approach the final phase of their illness. The distancing may be due to the depression that many dying patients experience, or it may be a child's way of protecting parents from the overwhelming grief they will experience at the death. Most dying children know they have a terminal illness. Their developmental level, social support, and coping skills influence how well they cope with knowing they will die.

Adolescence
In adolescence, the prospect of death, like the prospect of aging, is regarded as a notion so remote that it does not have much relevance. The subject of death may be avoided, glossed over, kidded about, neutralized, and controlled by a cool, spectator-like orientation. This perspective is typical of the adolescent's self-conscious thought; however, some adolescents do show a concern for death, both in trying to fathom its meaning and in confronting the prospect of their own demise (Baxter, Stuart, & Stewart, 1998).

Deaths of friends, siblings, parents, or grandparents bring death to the forefront of adolescents' lives. Deaths of peers who commit suicide "may be especially difficult for adolescents who feel . . . guilty for having failed to prevent the suicide or feel that they should have died, or . . . feel they are being rejected by their friends who hold them responsible for the death" (Hayslip & Hansson, 2003, p. 441).

Adolescents develop more abstract conceptions of death than children do. For example, adolescents describe death in terms of darkness, light, transition, or nothingness (Wenestam & Wass, 1987). They also develop religious and philosophical views about the nature of death and whether there is life after death.

You will also recall (from chapter 12) the concepts of adolescent egocentrism and personal fable—adolescents' preoccupation with themselves and their belief that they are invincible and unique. Thus, it is not unusual for adolescents to think that they are somehow immune to death and that death is something that happens to other people but not to them.

Adulthood
There is no evidence that a special orientation toward death develops in early adulthood. An increase in consciousness about death accompanies individuals' awareness that they are aging, which usually intensifies in middle adulthood. In our discussion of middle adulthood, we indicated that midlife is a time when adults begin to think more about how much time is left in their lives. Researchers have found that middle-aged adults actually fear death more than do young adults or older adults (Kalish & Reynolds, 1976). Older adults, though, think about death more and talk about it more in conversation with others than do middle-aged and young adults. They also have more direct experience with death as their friends and relatives become ill and die (Hayslip & Hansson, 2003). Older adults are forced to examine the meanings of life and death more frequently than are younger adults.

Younger adults who are dying often feel cheated more than do older adults who are dying (Kalish, 1987). Younger adults are more likely to feel they have not had the opportunity to do what they want to with their lives. Younger adults perceive they are losing what they might achieve; older adults perceive they are losing what they have.

In old age, one's own death may take on an appropriateness it lacked in earlier years. Some of the increased thinking and conversing about death, and an increased sense of integrity developed through a positive life review, may help older adults accept death. Older adults are less likely to have unfinished business than are younger adults. They usually do not have children who need to be guided to maturity, their spouses are more likely to be dead, and they are less likely to have work-related projects that require completion. Lacking such anticipations, death may be less emotionally painful to them. Even among older adults, however, attitudes toward death vary. One 82-year-old woman declared that she had

How might older adults' attitudes about death differ from those of younger adults?

lived her life and was ready to see it come to an end. Another 82-year-old woman declared that death would be a regrettable interruption of her participation in activities and relationships.

*W*e keep on thinking and rethinking death after we have passed through childhood's hour.

—ROBERT KASTENBAUM
*Contemporary Gerontologist,
Arizona State University*

Review and Reflect ● LEARNING GOAL 3

3 Discuss death and attitudes about it at different points in development

Review
- What are some developmental changes in the cause of death?
- What are some attitudes about death at different points in development?

Reflect
- What is your current attitude about death? Has it changed since you were an adolescent? If so, how?

---

4 FACING ONE'S OWN DEATH

Kübler-Ross' Stages of Dying	Perceived Control and Denial	The Contexts in Which People Die

Knowledge of death's inevitability permits us to establish priorities and structure our time accordingly. As we age, these priorities and structurings change in recognition of diminishing future time. Values concerning the most important uses of time also change. For example, when asked how they would spend six remaining months of life, younger adults described such activities as traveling and accomplishing things they previously had not done; older adults described more inner-focused activities— contemplation and meditation, for example (Kalish & Reynolds, 1976).

Most dying individuals want an opportunity to make some decisions regarding their own life and death (Kastenbaum, 2004). Some individuals want to complete unfinished business; they want time to resolve problems and conflicts and to put their affairs in order. Might there be a sequence of stages we go through as we face death?

Kübler-Ross' Stages of Dying

Elisabeth Kübler-Ross (1969) divided the behavior and thinking of dying persons into five stages: denial and isolation, anger, bargaining, depression, and acceptance.

Denial and isolation is Kübler-Ross' first stage of dying, in which the person denies that death is really going to take place. The person may say, "No, it can't be me. It's not possible." This is a common reaction to terminal illness. However, denial is usually only a temporary defense. It is eventually replaced with increased awareness when the person is confronted with such matters as financial considerations, unfinished business, and worry about surviving family members.

Anger is Kübler-Ross' second stage of dying, in which the dying person recognizes that denial can no longer be maintained. Denial often gives way to anger, resentment, rage, and envy. The dying person's question is, "Why me?" At this point, the person becomes increasingly difficult to care for as anger may become displaced and projected onto physicians, nurses, family members, and even God.

www.mhhe.com/santrockld11

Kübler-Ross on Dying

---

denial and isolation Kübler-Ross' first stage of dying, in which the dying person denies that she or he is really going to die.

anger Kübler-Ross' second stage of dying, in which the dying person's denial gives way to anger, resentment, rage, and envy.

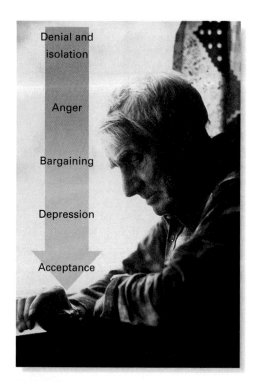

FIGURE 21.2 Kübler-Ross' Stages of Dying. According to Elisabeth Kübler-Ross, we go through five stages of dying: denial and isolation, anger, bargaining, depression, and acceptance. *Does everyone go through these stages, or go through them in the same order? Explain.*

bargaining Kübler-Ross' third stage of dying, in which the dying person develops the hope that death can somehow be postponed.

depression Kübler-Ross' fourth stage of dying, in which the dying person comes to accept the certainty of her or his death. A period of depression or preparatory grief may appear.

acceptance Kübler-Ross' fifth stage of dying, in which the dying person develops a sense of peace, an acceptance of her or his fate, and, in many cases, a desire to be left alone.

The realization of loss is great, and those who symbolize life, energy, and competent functioning are especially salient targets of the dying person's resentment and jealousy.

Bargaining is Kübler-Ross' third stage of dying, in which the person develops the hope that death can somehow be postponed or delayed. Some persons enter into a bargaining or negotiation—often with God—as they try to delay their death. Psychologically, the person is saying, "Yes, me, but . . ." In exchange for a few more days, weeks, or months of life, the person promises to lead a reformed life dedicated to God or to the service of others.

Depression is Kübler-Ross' fourth stage of dying, in which the dying person comes to accept the certainty of death. At this point, a period of depression or preparatory grief may appear. The dying person may become silent, refuse visitors, and spend much of the time crying or grieving. This behavior is normal and is an effort to disconnect the self from love objects. Attempts to cheer up the dying person at this stage should be discouraged, says Kübler-Ross, because the dying person has a need to contemplate impending death.

Acceptance is Kübler-Ross' fifth stage of dying, in which the person develops a sense of peace, an acceptance of one's fate, and in many cases, a desire to be left alone. In this stage, feelings and physical pain may be virtually absent. Kübler-Ross describes this fifth stage as the end of the dying struggle, the final resting stage before death. A summary of Kübler-Ross' dying stages is presented in figure 21.2.

What is the current evaluation of Kübler-Ross' approach? According to Robert Kastenbaum (2004), there are some problems with Kübler-Ross' approach:

- The existence of the five-stage sequence has not been demonstrated by either Kübler-Ross or independent research.
- The stage interpretation neglected the patients' situations, including relationship support, specific effects of illness, family obligations, and institutional climate in which they were interviewed.

However, Kübler-Ross' pioneering efforts were important in calling attention to those who are attempting to cope with life-threatening illnesses. She did much to encourage attention to the quality of life for dying persons and their families.

Because of the criticisms of Kübler-Ross' stages, some psychologists prefer to describe them not as stages but as potential reactions to dying. At any one moment, a number of emotions may wax and wane. Hope, disbelief, bewilderment, anger, and acceptance may come and go as individuals try to make sense of what is happening to them.

In facing their own death, some individuals struggle until the end, desperately trying to hang on to their lives. Acceptance of death never comes for them. Some psychologists believe that the harder individuals fight to avoid the inevitable death they face and the more they deny it, the more difficulty they will have in dying peacefully and in a dignified way; other psychologists argue that not confronting death until the end may be adaptive for some individuals (Lifton, 1977).

The extent to which people have found meaning and purpose in their lives is linked with how they approach death. A recent study of 160 individuals with less than three months to live revealed that those who had found purpose and meaning in their lives felt the least despair in the final weeks, while dying individuals who saw no reason for living were the most distressed and wanted to hasten death (McClain, Rosenfeld, & Breitbart, 2003). In this and other studies, spirituality helped to buffer dying individuals from severe depression (Smith, McCullough, & Poll, 2003).

Perceived Control and Denial

Perceived control may work as an adaptive strategy for some older adults who face death. When individuals are led to believe they can influence and control events—such as prolonging their lives—they may become more alert and cheerful. Remember from chapter 18 that giving nursing home residents options for control improved their attitudes and increased their longevity (Rodin & Langer, 1977).

Denial also may be a fruitful way for some individuals to approach death. It can be adaptive or maladaptive. Denial can be used to avoid the destructive impact of shock by delaying the necessity of dealing with one's death. Denial can insulate the individual from having to cope with intense feelings of anger and hurt; however, if denial keeps us from having a life-saving operation, it clearly is maladaptive. Denial is neither good nor bad; its adaptive qualities need to be evaluated on an individual basis.

The Contexts in Which People Die

For dying individuals, the context in which they die is important. More than 50 percent of Americans die in hospitals, and nearly 20 percent die in nursing homes. Some people spend their final days in isolation and fear (Clay, 1997). An increasing number of people choose to die in the humane atmosphere of a hospice.

Hospitals offer several important advantages to the dying individual; for example, professional staff members are readily available, and the medical technology present may prolong life. But a hospital may not be the best place for many people to die. Most individuals say they would rather die at home (Kalish & Reynolds, 1976). Many feel, however, that they will be a burden at home, that there is limited space there, and that dying at home may alter relationships. Individuals who are facing death also worry about the competency and availability of emergency medical treatment if they remain at home.

> *M*an is the only animal that finds his own existence a problem he has to solve and from which he cannot escape. In the same sense man is the only animal who knows he must die.
>
> —ERICH FROMM
> *American Psychotherapist, 20th Century*

Review and Reflect • LEARNING GOAL 4

4 **Explain the psychological aspects involved in facing one's own death and the contexts in which people die**

Review
- What are Kübler-Ross' five stages of dying? What conclusions can be reached about them?
- What roles do perceived control and denial play in facing one's own death?
- What are the contexts in which people die?

Reflect
- How do you think you will psychologically handle facing your own death?

5 COPING WITH THE DEATH OF SOMEONE ELSE

Communicating with a Dying Person	Making Sense of the World	Forms of Mourning

Grieving	Losing a Life Partner

Loss can come in many forms in our lives—divorce, a pet's death, loss of a job—but no loss is greater than that which comes through the death of someone we love and care for—a parent, sibling, spouse, relative, or friend. In the ratings of life's stresses that require the most adjustment, death of a spouse is given the highest

www.mhhe.com/santrockld11

Exploring Death and Dying
Death and Dying Resources

number. How should we communicate with a dying individual? How do we cope with the death of someone we love?

Communicating with a Dying Person

Most psychologists believe that it is best for dying individuals to know that they are dying and that significant others know they are dying so they can interact and communicate with each other on the basis of this mutual knowledge (Banja, 2005). What are some of the advantages of this open awareness for the dying individual? First, dying individuals can close their lives in accord with their own ideas about proper dying. Second, they may be able to complete some plans and projects, can make arrangements for survivors, and can participate in decisions about a funeral and burial. Third, dying individuals have the opportunity to reminisce, to converse with others who have been important in their life, and to end life conscious of what life has been like. And fourth, dying individuals have more understanding of what is happening within their bodies and what the medical staff is doing to them (Kalish, 1981).

In addition to keeping communication open, what are some suggestions for conversing with a dying individual? Some experts believe that conversation should not focus on mental pathology or preparation for death but should focus on strengths of the individual and preparation for the remainder of life. Since external accomplishments are not possible, communication should be directed more at internal growth. Keep in mind also that important support for a dying individual may come not only from mental health professionals, but also from nurses, physicians, a spouse, or intimate friends (DeSpelder & Strickland, 2005). In the Applications in Life-Span Development interlude, you can read further about effective communication strategies with a dying person.

APPLICATIONS IN LIFE-SPAN DEVELOPMENT

Communicating with a Dying Person

Effective strategies for communicating with a dying person include these:

1. Establish your presence, be at the same eye level; don't be afraid to touch the dying person—dying individuals are often starved for human touch.
2. Eliminate distraction—for example, ask if it is okay to turn off the TV. Realize that excessive small talk can be a distraction.
3. Dying individuals who are very frail often have little energy. If the dying person you are visiting is very frail, you may not want to visit for very long.
4. Don't insist that the dying person feel acceptance about death if the dying person wants to deny the reality of the situation; on the other hand, don't insist on denial if the dying individual indicates acceptance.
5. Allow the dying person to express guilt or anger; encourage the expression of feelings.
6. Don't be afraid to ask the person what the expected outcome for the illness is. Discuss alternatives, unfinished business.
7. Sometimes dying individuals don't have access to other people. Ask the dying person if there is anyone he or she would like to see that you can contact.
8. Encourage the dying individual to reminisce, especially if you have memories in common.
9. Talk with the individual when she or he wishes to talk. If this is impossible, make an appointment and keep it.
10. Express your regard for the dying individual. Don't be afraid to express love, and don't be afraid to say good-bye.

What are some good strategies for communicating with a dying person?

Grieving

Our exploration of grief focuses on dimensions of grieving, the dual process model of coping with bereavement, and cultural diversity in healthy grieving.

Dimensions of Grieving **Grief** is the emotional numbness, disbelief, separation anxiety, despair, sadness, and loneliness that accompany the loss of someone we love. Grief is not a simple emotional state but rather a complex, evolving process with multiple dimensions (Bonanno & others, 2005; Langner & Maercker, 2005; Levin, 2004; Neimeyer, 2005, 2006; Shear & others, 2005; Smith, 2005). In this view, pining for the lost person is one important dimension. Pining or yearning reflects an intermittent, recurrent wish or need to recover the lost person. Another important dimension of grief is separation anxiety, which not only includes pining and preoccupation with thoughts of the deceased person but also focuses on places and things associated with the deceased, as well as crying or sighing. Grief may also involve despair and sadness, which include a sense of hopelessness and defeat, depressive symptoms, apathy, loss of meaning for activities that used to involve the person who is gone, and growing desolation (Ringdal & others, 2001).

These feelings occur repeatedly shortly after a loss (Moules & others, 2004). As time passes, pining and protest over the loss tend to diminish, although episodes of depression and apathy may remain or increase. The sense of separation anxiety and loss may continue to the end of one's life, but most of us emerge from grief's tears, turning our attention once again to productive tasks and regaining a more positive view of life (Carrington & Bogetz, 2004; Powers & Wampold, 1994).

The grieving process is more like a roller-coaster ride than an orderly progression of stages with clear-cut time frames (Lund, 1996). The ups and downs of grief often involve rapidly changing emotions, meeting the challenges of learning new skills, detecting personal weaknesses and limitations, creating new patterns of behavior, and forming new friendships and relationships (Bruce, 2002; Feldon, 2003; Mitchell & Catron, 2002). For most individuals, grief becomes more manageable over time, with fewer abrupt highs and lows (Bonanno, 2004). But many grieving spouses report that even though time has brought some healing, they have never gotten over their loss. They have just learned to live with it.

Cognitive factors are involved in the severity of grief after a loved one has died. One recent study focused on 329 adults who had suffered the loss of a first-degree relative (Boelen, van den Bout, & van den Hout, 2003). The more negative beliefs and self-blame the adults had, the more severe were their symptoms of traumatic grief, depression, and anxiety.

Long-term grief is sometimes masked and can predispose individuals to become depressed and even suicidal (Davis, 2001; Feldon, 2003; Kastenbaum, 2004). Good family communication can help reduce the incidence of depression and suicidal thoughts. For example, in one study, family members who communicated poorly with each other had more negative grief reactions six months later than those who communicated effectively with each other just after the loss of a family member (Schoka & Hayslip, 1999).

An estimated 80 to 90 percent of survivors experience normal or uncomplicated grief reactions that include sadness and even disbelief or considerable anguish. By six months after their loss, they accept it as a reality, are more optimistic about the future, and function competently in their everyday lives. However, six months after their loss, approximately 10 to 20 percent of survivors have difficulty moving on with their life, feel numb or detached, believe their life is empty without the deceased, and feel that the future has no meaning. Increasingly, the term **complicated grief** is being used to describe this type of grief that involves enduring despair and is still unresolved over an extended period of time. Complicated grief usually has negative consequences for physical and mental health (Ng, 2005; Shear & others, 2005; Wortman & Boerner, 2007; Zuckoff & others, 2006). A person

It is sweet to mingle tears with tears; griefs, where they wound in solitude, wound more deeply.

—SENECA
Roman Poet, 1st Century

grief The emotional numbness, disbelief, separation anxiety, despair, sadness, and loneliness that accompany the loss of someone we love.

complicated grief Grief that involves enduring despair and is still unresolved over an extended period of time.

who loses someone he or she was emotionally dependent on is often at greatest risk for developing complicated grief (Prigerson, 2004, 2005). A recent study found that therapy focused on motivational interviewing, emotion coping, and communication skills was effective in reducing complicated grief (Zuckoff & others, 2006).

Dual-Process Model of Coping with Bereavement The **dual-process model** of coping with bereavement consists of two main dimensions: (1) loss-oriented stressors and (2) restoration-oriented stressors (Stroebe, Schut, & Stroebe, 2005, p. 50). Loss-oriented stressors focus on the deceased individual and can include grief work, as well as positive (such as "relief at the end of suffering") and negative reappraisal ("yearning and rumination") of the meaning of the loss. Restoration-oriented stressors involve the secondary stressors that emerge as indirect outcomes of bereavement. They can include a changing identity (such as from "wife" to "widow") and mastering skills (such as dealing with finances). Restoration rebuilds "shattered assumptions about the world and one's own place in it."

In the dual-process model, effective coping with bereavement often involves an oscillation between coping with loss and coping with restoration. Earlier models often emphasized a sequence of coping with loss through such strategies as grief work as an initial phase, followed by restoration efforts. However, in the dual process model, coping with loss and engaging in restoration can be carried out concurrently. Oscillation might occur in the short term during a particular day as well as across weeks, months, and even years. Although loss and restoration coping can occur concurrently, over time there often is an initial emphasis on coping with loss followed by greater emphasis on restoration over time.

Coping and Type of Death The impact of death on surviving individuals is strongly influenced by the circumstances under which the death occurs (Carr, Nesse, & Wortman, 2005; Hebert, Dang, & Schulz, 2006; Wortman & Boerner, 2007). Deaths that are sudden, untimely, violent, or traumatic are likely to have more intense and prolonged effects on surviving individuals and make the coping process more difficult for them (Murphy & others, 2003). Such deaths often are accompanied by post-traumatic stress disorder (PTSD) symptoms, such as intrusive thoughts, flashbacks, nightmares, sleep disturbance, problems in concentrating, and others.

Cultural Diversity in Healthy Grieving Some approaches to grieving emphasize the importance of breaking bonds with the deceased and returning to autonomous lifestyles. People who persist in holding on to the deceased are believed to be in need of therapy. Recent analyses, however, have cast doubt on whether this recommendation is always the best therapeutic advice (Reisman, 2001; Stroebe & others, 1992).

Analyses of non-Western cultures suggest that beliefs about continuing bonds with the deceased vary extensively. Maintenance of ties with the deceased is accepted and sustained in the religious rituals of Japan. In the Hopi of Arizona, the deceased are forgotten as quickly as possible and life is carried on as usual. Their funeral ritual concludes with a break-off between mortals and spirits. The diversity of grieving is nowhere more clear than in two Muslim societies—one in Egypt, the other in Bali. In Egypt, the bereaved are encouraged to dwell at length on their grief, surrounded by others who relate similarly tragic accounts and express their own sorrow. By contrast, in Bali, the bereaved are encouraged to laugh and be joyful.

In a longitudinal study of bereavement in the Netherlands, many people tended to maintain contact with the deceased, despite the contemporary emphasis on breaking such bonds (Stroebe & Stroebe, 1991). Many of the widowed persons were not planning a major break with their pasts, but rather were integrating the loss experience into their lifestyles and trying to carry on much as before the death of a loved one. Well over half "consulted" the deceased when having to make a decision. One

dual-process model A model of coping with bereavement that emphasizes oscillation between two dimensions: (1) loss-oriented stressors and (2) restoration-oriented stressors.

widow said that she gained considerable comfort from knowing that her decision was exactly what her deceased husband would have wanted her to do.

Similar findings have been reported among American widows and among the parents of sons who died in two Israeli wars, 13 and 4 years earlier (Rubin & Malkinson, 2001; Schuchter & Zisook, 1993). Even many years after the death of their son, the Israeli parents showed a strong involvement with him. They idealized the lost son in ways that were not present in the descriptions by a control group of parents of sons who had recently left home.

In summary, people grieve in a variety of ways (Matzo & others, 2003). The diverse grieving patterns are culturally embedded practices (Haas, 2003). Thus, there is no one right, ideal way to grieve. There are many different ways to feel about a deceased person and no set series of stages that the bereaved must pass through to become well adjusted. The stoic widower may need to cry out over his loss at times. The weeping widow may need to put her husband's wishes aside as she becomes the financial manager of her estate. What is needed is an understanding that healthy coping with the death of a loved one involves growth, flexibility, and appropriateness within a cultural context.

Making Sense of the World

One beneficial aspect of grieving is that it stimulates many individuals to try to make sense of their world (Kalish, 1981, 1987). A common occurrence is to go over again and again all of the events that led up to the death. In the days and weeks after the death, the closest family members share experiences with each other, sometimes reminiscing over family experiences. In one recent study, women who became widowed in midlife were challenged by the crisis of their husband's death to examine meaningful directions for their lives (Danforth & Glass, 2001). Another recent study found that mourners who expressed positive themes of hope for a positive future showed better adjustment than those who focused on negative themes of pain and suffering (Gamino & Sewell, 2004).

Each individual may offer a piece of death's puzzle. "When I saw him last Saturday, he looked as though he were rallying," says one family member. "Do you think it might have had something to do with his sister's illness?" remarks another. "I doubt it, but I heard from an aide that he fell going to the bathroom that morning," comments yet another. "That explains the bruise on his elbow," says the first individual. "No wonder he told me that he was angry because he could not seem to do anything right," chimes in a fourth family member. So it goes in the attempt to understand why someone who was rallying on Saturday was dead on Wednesday.

When a death is caused by an accident or a disaster, the effort to make sense of it is pursued more vigorously. As added pieces of news come trickling in, they are integrated into the puzzle. The bereaved want to put the death into a perspective that they can understand—divine intervention, a curse from a neighboring tribe, a logical sequence of cause and effect, or whatever it may be. A recent study of more than 1,000 college students found that making sense was an important factor in their grieving of a violent loss by accident, homicide, or suicide (Currier, Holland, & Neimeyer, 2006).

Mary Assanful (*front right* with other former restaurant workers) worked at Windows on the World restaurant located in the World Trade Center and lost her job when terrorist attacks came. She says that she still is not herself and regularly has nightmares. A Ghana native, Mary is still unemployed. She has joined several other workers who are now planning to return by opening a restaurant near Ground Zero. They hope the new restaurant will honor their co-workers who died and provide a focus and meaning for their still-unsettled lives. Mary says that since they have been working on this new project, her mind has calmed somewhat.

Losing a Life Partner

Those left behind after the death of an intimate partner often suffer profound grief and often endure financial loss, loneliness, increased physical illness, and psychological

Grief and Bereavement
WidowNet

disorders, including depression (Bonanno, Wortman, & Nesse, 2004; Carr, Wortman, & Neese, 2005; Li & others, 2005; Neimeyer, 2005, 2006; Savikko & others, 2005). How surviving spouses cope varies considerably (Bennett, Smith, & Hughes, 2005; Bisconti, Bergeman, & Boker, 2004; Ong, Bergeman, & Bisconti, 2004; Wortman & Boerner, 2007). In a recent study that included data from 3 years predeath to 18 months postdeath, nearly half of surviving spouses experienced low levels of distress consistently over the $4\frac{1}{2}$ years (Bonanno, Wortman, & Nesse, 2004). In another recent study, widowed individuals were more likely to increase their religious and spiritual beliefs following the death of a spouse and this increase was linked with a lower level of grief (Brown & others, 2004).

Widows outnumber widowers by the ratio of 5 to 1, because women live longer than men, because women tend to marry men older than themselves, and because a widowed man is more likely to remarry. Widowed women are probably the poorest group in America. One study found that most widows in the United States and Germany experienced a decline in living standards in the year following their husband's death, and many fell into poverty when they became widows (Hungerford, 2001). Also, a recent study of Mexican Americans revealed that widows were more likely than widowers to report financial strain, welfare dependency, and use of Medicaid than widowers (Angel, Douglas, & Angel, 2003). In this study, widows received more emotional support than widowers. Another recent study of African American widows found that storytelling was at the heart of widows' description of their bereavement experience (Rodgers, 2004). Six themes were identified in their stories: awareness of death, caregiving, getting through, moving on, changing feelings, and financial security.

Many widows are lonely. The poorer and less educated they are, the lonelier they tend to be. The bereaved are also at increased risk for many health problems, including death (Manor & Eisenbach, 2003; Neimeyer, 2006; Williams, 2004). The following Research in Life-Span Development interlude examines the relation of widowhood to health.

RESEARCH IN LIFE-SPAN DEVELOPMENT

The Women's Health Initiative Study of Widowhood and Health

One recent three-year longitudinal study of more than 130,000 women 50 to 79 years of age in the United States as part of the Women's Health Initiative examined the relation of widowhood to physical and mental health, health behaviors, and health outcomes (Wilcox & others, 2003). Women were categorized as (1) remaining married, (2) transitioning from married to widowed, (3) remaining widowed, and (4) transitioning from widowed to married. Widows were further subdivided into the recently widowed (widowed for less than one year) and longer-term widowed (widowed for more than one year).

The measures used to assess the older women's health were:

- *Physical health.* Blood pressure was assessed after five minutes of quiet rest using the average of two readings with 30 seconds between the readings. Hypertension was defined as more than 140/90. Body mass index (BMI) was calculated and used to determine whether a woman was obese. A health survey assessed physical function and health status.
- *Mental Health.* Depressive symptoms were assessed by a six-item depression scale, with participants rating the frequency of their depressed thoughts during the past week. The participant's self-report of antidepressant medicine use was also obtained. Information about social functioning and mental health was based on participants' responses on the Social Functioning Scale (Ware, Kosinski, & Dewey, 2000).

- *Health Behaviors.* Dietary behaviors were assessed with a modified version of the National Cancer Institute—Health Habits and History Questionnaire (Patterson & others, 1999). Participants also were asked if they smoked tobacco, and if so, how much. To assess physical activity, participants were asked how often they walked outside the home each week and the extent to which they engaged in strenuous or moderate exercise. To assess health-care use, they were asked whether they had visited their doctor in the past year.
- *Health Outcomes.* Cardiovascular disease and cancer occurrences were assessed annually and any overnight hospitalizations were noted.

At the beginning of the three-year study, married women reported better physical and mental health, and better health in general, than widowed women. Women who remained married over the 3-year period of the study showed stability in mental health, recent widows experienced marked impairments in mental health, and longer-term widows showed stability or slight improvements in mental health. Both groups of widows (recent and longer-term) reported more unintentional weight loss across the three years. The findings underscore the resilience of older women and their capacity to reestablish connections but point to the need for services that strengthen social support for those who have difficulty during the transition from marriage to widowhood.

Optimal adjustment after a death depends on several factors (Leming & Dickinson, 2002). Women do better than men largely because, in our society, women are responsible for the emotional life of a couple, whereas men usually manage the finances and material goods (Fry, 2001). Thus, women have better networks of friends, closer relationships with relatives, and more experience in taking care of themselves psychologically (Antonucci & others, 2001). Older widows do better than younger widows, perhaps because the death of a partner is more expected for older women. For their part, widowers usually have more money than widows do, and they are much more likely to remarry.

For either widows or widowers, social support helps them adjust to the death of a spouse (Boerner & Wortman, 1998; Wortman & Boerner, 2007). The Widow-to-Widow program, begun in the 1960s, provides support for newly widowed women. Volunteer widows reach out to other widows, introducing them to others who may have similar problems, leading group discussions, and organizing social activities. The program has been adopted by the American Association of Retired Persons and disseminated throughout the United States as the Widowed Person's Service. The model has since been adopted by numerous community organizations to provide support for those going through a difficult transition.

One recent study found that psychological and religious factors—such as personal meaning, optimism, the importance of religion, and access to religious support—were related to the psychological well-being of older adults following the loss of a spouse (Fry, 2001). Other studies have indicated that religiosity and coping skills are related to well-being following the loss of a spouse in late adulthood (Fry, 1999).

Forms of Mourning

One decision facing the bereaved is what to do with the body. Approximately 80 percent of corpses are disposed of by burial, the remaining 20 percent by cremation (Aiken, 2000; Cremation Association of America, 2000). Cremation is more popular in the Pacific region of the United States, less popular in the South. Cremation also is more popular in Canada than in the United States and most popular of all in Japan and many other Asian countries.

The funeral is an important aspect of mourning in many cultures. In one recent study, bereaved individuals who were personally religious derived more psychological

A widow leading a funeral procession in the United States.

A crowd gathered at a cremation ceremony in Bali, Indonesia, balancing decorative containers on their heads.

Buddhist Funeral Rites

benefits from a funeral, participated more actively in the rituals, and adjusted more positively to the loss (Hayslip, Edmondson, & Guarnaccia, 1999).

The funeral industry has been the source of controversy in recent years. Funeral directors and their supporters argue that the funeral provides a form of closure to the relationship with the deceased, especially when there is an open casket. Their critics claim that funeral directors are just trying to make money and that embalming is grotesque. One way to avoid being exploited during bereavement is to purchase funeral arrangements in advance. However, in one survey, only 24 percent of individuals 60 and over had made any funeral arrangements (Kalish & Reynolds, 1976).

In some cultures, a ceremonial meal is held after death; in others, a black armband is worn for one year following a death. Cultures vary in how they practice mourning (Adamolekun, 2001; Shepard, 2002). To learn about two cultures with extensive mourning systems, see the Diversity in Life-Span Development interlude.

DIVERSITY IN LIFE-SPAN DEVELOPMENT

The Amish, Traditional Judaism, and Mourning

The family and the community have important roles in mourning in some cultures. Two of those cultures are the Amish and traditional Judaism (Worthington, 1989).

The Amish are a conservative group with approximately 80,000 members in the United States, Ontario, and several small settlements in South and Central America. The Amish live in a family-oriented society in which family and community support are essential for survival. Today, they live at the same unhurried pace as that of their ancestors, using horses instead of cars and facing death with the same steadfast faith as their forebears. At the time of death, close neighbors assume the responsibility of notifying others of the death. The Amish community handles virtually all aspects of the funeral.

The funeral service is held in a barn in warmer months and in a house during colder months. Calm acceptance of death, influenced by a deep religious faith, is an integral part of the Amish culture. Following the funeral, a high level of support is given to the bereaved family for at least a year. Visits to the family, special scrapbooks and handmade items for the family, new work projects started for the widow, and quilting days that combine fellowship and productivity are among the supports given to the bereaved family.

The family and community also have specific and important roles in mourning in traditional Judaism. The program of mourning is divided into graduated time periods, each with its appropriate practices. The observance of these practices is required of the spouse and the immediate blood relatives of the deceased. The first period is *aninut,* the period between death and burial. The next two periods make up *avelut,* or mourning proper. The first of these is *shivah,* a period of seven days, which commences with the burial. It is followed by *sheloshim,* the 30-day period following the burial, including shivah. At the end of sheloshim, the mourning process is considered over for all but one's parents. For parents, mourning continues for 11 months, although observances are minimal.

The seven-day period of the shivah is especially important in traditional Judaism. The mourners, sitting together as a group through an extended period, have an opportunity to project their feelings to the group as a whole. Visits from others during shivah may help the mourner deal with feelings of guilt. After shivah, the mourner is encouraged to resume normal social interaction. In fact, it is customary for the mourners to walk together a short distance as a symbol of their return to society. In its entirety, the elaborate mourning system of traditional Judaism is designed to promote personal growth and to reintegrate the individual into the community.

An Amish funeral procession in Pennsylvania. The funeral service is held in a barn in the warmer months and in a house during the colder months. Following the funeral, a high level of support is given to the bereaved family for at least a year.

Review and Reflect ● LEARNING GOAL 5

5 **Identify ways to cope with the death of another person**

Review
- What are some strategies for communicating with a dying person?
- What is the nature of grieving?
- How is making sense of the world a beneficial outcome of grieving?
- What are some characteristics and outcomes of losing a life partner?
- What are some forms of mourning? What is the nature of the funeral?

Reflect
- Is there a best or worst way to grieve? Explain.

We have arrived at the end of this book. I hope this book and course have been a window to the life span of the human species and a window to your own personal journey in life.

Our study of the human life span has been long and complex. You have read about many physical, cognitive, and socioemotional changes that take place from conception through death. This is a good time to reflect on what you have learned. Which theories, studies, and ideas were especially interesting to you? What did you learn about your own development?

I wish you all the best in the remaining years of your journey though the human life span.

John W. Santrock

REACH YOUR LEARNING GOALS

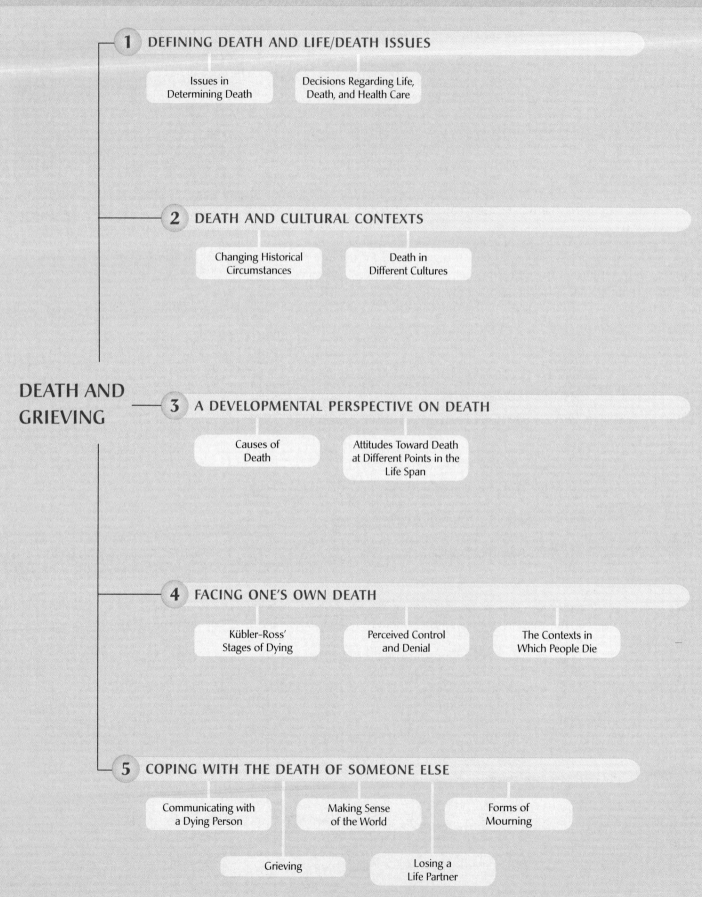

DEATH AND GRIEVING

1 DEFINING DEATH AND LIFE/DEATH ISSUES

Issues in Determining Death

Decisions Regarding Life, Death, and Health Care

2 DEATH AND CULTURAL CONTEXTS

Changing Historical Circumstances

Death in Different Cultures

3 A DEVELOPMENTAL PERSPECTIVE ON DEATH

Causes of Death

Attitudes Toward Death at Different Points in the Life Span

4 FACING ONE'S OWN DEATH

Kübler-Ross' Stages of Dying

Perceived Control and Denial

The Contexts in Which People Die

5 COPING WITH THE DEATH OF SOMEONE ELSE

Communicating with a Dying Person

Making Sense of the World

Forms of Mourning

Grieving

Losing a Life Partner

SUMMARY

1 Defining Death and Life/Death Issues: *Evaluate issues in determining death and decisions regarding death*

Issues in Determining Death

Twenty-five years ago, determining if someone was dead was simpler than it is today. Brain death is a neurological definition of death, which states that a person is brain dead when all electrical activity of the brain has ceased for a specified period of time. Medical experts debate whether this should mean the higher and lower brain functions or just the higher cortical functions. Currently, most states have a statute endorsing the cessation of brain function (both higher and lower) as a standard for determining death.

Decisions Regarding Life, Death, and Health Care

Decisions regarding life, death, and health care can involve whether to have a living will, euthanasia, and hospice care. Living wills and advanced directives are increasingly used. Euthanasia is the act of painlessly ending the life of a person who is suffering from an incurable disease or disability. Distinctions are made between active and passive euthanasia. Hospice care emphasizes reducing pain and suffering rather than prolonging life.

2 Death and Cultural Contexts: *Describe the roles of sociohistorical and cultural contexts in understanding death*

Changing Historical Circumstances

When, where, and why people die have changed historically. Today, death occurs most often among older adults. More than 80 percent of all deaths in the United States now occur in a hospital or other institution; our exposure to death in the family has been minimized. Most societies throughout history have had philosophical or religious beliefs about death, and most societies have rituals that deal with death.

Death in Different Cultures

Most cultures do not view death as the end of existence—spiritual life is thought to continue. The United States has been described as a death-denying and death-avoiding culture.

3 A Developmental Perspective on Death: *Discuss death and attitudes about it at different points in development*

Causes of Death

Although death is more likely to occur in late adulthood, death can come at any point in development. In children and younger adults, death is more likely to occur because of accidents; in older adults, death is more likely to occur because of chronic diseases.

Attitudes Toward Death at Different Points in the Life Span

Infants do not have a concept of death. Preschool children also have little concept of death. Preschool children sometimes blame themselves for a person's death. In the elementary school years, children develop a more realistic orientation toward death. Most psychologists believe honesty is the best strategy for helping children cope with death. Death may be glossed over in adolescence. Adolescents have more abstract, philosophical views of death than children do. There is no evidence that a special orientation toward death emerges in early adulthood. Middle adulthood is a time when adults show a heightened consciousness about death and death anxiety. The deaths of some persons, especially children and younger adults, are often perceived to be more tragic than those of others, such as very old adults, who have had an opportunity to live a long life. Older adults often show less death anxiety than middle-aged adults, but older adults experience and converse about death more. Attitudes about death may vary considerably among adults of any age.

4 Facing One's Own Death: *Explain the psychological aspects involved in facing one's own death and the contexts in which people die*

Kübler-Ross' Stages of Dying

Kübler-Ross proposed five stages: denial and isolation, anger, bargaining, depression, and acceptance. Not all individuals go through the same sequence.

Perceived Control and Denial

Perceived control and denial may work together as an adaptive orientation for the dying individual. Denial can be adaptive or maladaptive, depending on the circumstance.

The Contexts in Which People Die

Most deaths in the United States occur in hospitals; this has advantages and disadvantages. Most individuals say they would rather die at home, but they worry that they will be a burden and they worry about the lack of medical care.

5 Coping with the Death of Someone Else: *Identify ways to cope with the death of another person*

Communicating with a Dying Person

Most psychologists recommend an open communication system with the dying. Communication should not dwell on pathology or preparation for death but should emphasize the dying person's strengths.

Grieving

Grief is the emotional numbness, disbelief, separation, anxiety, despair, sadness, and loneliness that accompany the loss of someone we love. Grief is multidimensional and in some cases may last for years. Complicated grief involves enduring despair and is still unresolved after an extended period of time. In the dual-process model of coping with bereavement, oscillation occurs between two dimensions: (1) loss-oriented stressors and (2) restoration-oriented stressors. Grief and coping vary with the type of death. There are cultural variations in grieving.

Making Sense of the World

The grieving process may stimulate individuals to strive to make sense out of their world; each individual may contribute a piece to death's puzzle.

Losing a Life Partner

Usually the most difficult loss is the death of a spouse. The bereaved are at risk for many health problems, although there are variations in the distress experienced by a surviving spouse. Social support benefits widows and widowers.

Forms of Mourning

Forms of mourning vary across cultures. Approximately 80 percent of corpses are disposed of by burial, 20 percent by cremation. An important aspect of mourning in many cultures is the funeral. In recent years, the funeral industry has been the focus of controversy. In some cultures, a ceremonial meal is held after death.

KEY TERMS

brain death 679	hospice 681	bargaining 688	complicated grief 691
euthanasia 679	palliative care 681	depression 688	dual-process model 692
passive euthanasia 679	denial and isolation 687	acceptance 688	
active euthanasia 679	anger 687	grief 691	

KEY PEOPLE

Robert Kastenbaum 685   Bert Hayslip and Robert Hansson 685   Elisabeth Kübler-Ross 687

E-LEARNING TOOLS

To help you master the material in this chapter, you'll find a number of valuable study tools on the LifeMap CD-ROM that accompanies this book and on the Online Learning Center for *Life-Span Development*, eleventh edition, at **www.mhhe.com/santrockld11**.

Video Clips

In the margins of this book there are icons directing you to the LifeMap CD-ROM that accompanies the book. In chapter 21 you'll find a video segment called "On Dying at Age 72." Our attitude toward death changes as we get older. This segment features an interview with an elderly man who has begun to think differently about death.

Self-Assessment

Connect to **www.mhhe.com/santrockld11** to reflect on your feelings about the end of life by completing the self-assessments, *How Much Anxiety Do I Have About Death?* and *The Living Will*.

Taking It to the Net

Connect to **www.mhhe.com/santrockld11** to research the answers to these questions.

1. Herman's mother has Parkinson's disease. He wants her to make some difficult end-of-life decisions while she still can. He and his mother discuss the options of a durable power of attorney for health care, a living will, and/or a DNR (Do Not Resuscitate) order. What are the purposes of these documents, and what is the family's involvement in these decisions?

2. Letitia, a recent widow, is interested in starting a program for widowed women in her community. To start the process and request funding, she is exploring her options regarding foundation grants. As part of this process, she needs to investigate the available data on the nature and the extent of widowhood in the United States today, including the age, sex, and socioeconomic status of widowed people. What type of information is available to her?

Health and Well-Being, Parenting, and Education Exercises

Build your decision-making skills by trying your hand at the health and well-being, parenting, and education exercises. Connect to **www.mhhe.com/santrockld11** to research the answers and complete the exercises.

A

AB error Occurs when infants make the mistake of selecting the familiar hiding place (A) rather than the new hiding place (B) as they progress into substage 4 in Piaget's sensorimotor stage. 183

acceptance Kübler-Ross' fifth stage of dying, in which the dying person develops a sense of peace, an acceptance of her or his fate, and, in many cases, a desire to be left alone. 688

accommodation Piagetian concept of adjusting schemes to fit new information and experiences. 178

acquired immune deficiency syndrome (AIDS) A sexually transmitted disease caused by the HIV virus, which destroys the body's immune system. 475

active euthanasia Death induced deliberately, as by injecting a lethal dose of a drug. 679

active (niche-picking) genotype-environment correlations Correlations that exist when children seek out environments they find compatible and stimulating. 92

activity theory The theory that the more active and involved older adults are, the more likely they are to be satisfied with their lives. 651

addiction A pattern of behavior characterized by an overwhelming involvement with using a drug and securing its supply. 471

adolescent egocentrism The heightened self-consciousness of adolescents. 409

adoption study A study in which investigators seek to discover whether, in behavior and psychological characteristics, adopted children are more like their adoptive parents, who provided a home environment, or more like their biological parents, who contributed their heredity. Another form of the adoption study is to compare adoptive and biological siblings. 91

aerobic exercise Sustained exercise (such as jogging, swimming, or cycling) that stimulates heart and lung activity. 467

affectionate love In this type of love, also called companionate love, an individual desires to have the other person near and has a deep, caring affection for the other person. 502

affordances Opportunities for interaction offered by objects that fit within our capabilities to perform functional activities. 160

ageism Prejudice against other people because of their age, especially prejudice against older adults. 658

Alzheimer disease A progressive, irreversible brain disorder characterized by a gradual deterioration of memory, reasoning, language, and eventually physical function. 634

amnion The life-support system that is a bag or envelope that contains a clear fluid in which the developing embryo floats. 104

androgyny The presence of positive masculine and feminine characteristics in the same individual. 366

anger Kübler-Ross' second stage of dying, in which the dying person's denial gives way to anger, resentment, rage, and envy. 687

anger cry A cry similar to the basic cry, with more excess air forced through the vocal cords. 211

animism The belief that inanimate objects have "lifelike" qualities and are capable of action. 248

anorexia nervosa An eating disorder that involves the relentless pursuit of thinness through starvation. 406

Apgar Scale A widely used method to assess the health of newborns at one and five minutes after birth. The Apgar Scale evaluates infants' heart rate, respiratory effort, muscle tone, body color, and reflex irritability. 123

aphasia A loss or impairment of language ability caused by brain damage. 196

arthritis Inflammation of the joints that is accompanied by pain, stiffness, and movement problems; especially common in older adults. 604

assimilation Piagetian concept of the incorporation of new information into existing schemes. 178

assimilation The absorption of ethnic minority groups into the dominant group, which often involves the loss of some or virtually all of the behavior and values of the ethnic minority group. 442

associative play Play that involves social interaction with little or no organization. 304

attachment A close emotional bond between an infant and a caregiver. 219

attachment-related anxiety Involves the extent to which individuals feel secure or insecure about whether a partner will be available, responsive, and attentive. 497

attachment-related avoidance Involves the degree to which individuals feel secure or insecure in relying on others, opening up to them, and being intimate with them. 497

attention The focusing of mental resources. 185

attention deficit hyperactivity disorder (ADHD) A disability in which children consistently show one or more of the following characteristics: (1) inattention, (2) hyperactivity, and (3) impulsivity. 320

authoritarian parenting A restrictive punitive style in which parents exhort the child to follow their directions and to respect work and effort. The authoritarian parent places firm limits and controls on the child and allows little verbal exchange. Authoritarian parenting is associated with children's social incompetence. 288

authoritative parenting A parenting style in which parents encourage their children to be independent but still place limits and controls on their actions. Extensive verbal give-and-take is allowed, and parents are warm and nurturant toward the child. Authoritative parenting is associated with children's social competence. 288

autonomous morality The second stage of moral development in Piaget's theory, displayed by older children (about 10 years of age and older). The child becomes aware that rules and laws are created by people and that, in judging an action, one should consider the actor's intentions as well as the consequences. 280

average children Children who receive an average number of both positive and negative nominations from peers. 371

B

bargaining Kübler-Ross' third stage of dying, in which the dying person develops the hope that death can somehow be postponed. 688

basal metabolism rate (BMR) The minimum amount of energy a person uses in a resting state. 243

basic cry A rhythmic pattern usually consisting of a cry, a briefer silence, a shorter inspiratory whistle that is higher pitched than the main cry, and then a brief rest before the next cry. 211

basic-skills-and-phonics approach The idea that reading instruction should teach both phonics and the basic rules for translating written symbols into sounds. 343

Bayley Scales of Infant Development Scales developed by Nancy Bayley that are widely used in the assessment of infant development. The current version has three components: a mental scale, a motor scale, and an infant behavior profile. 189

becoming parents and a family with children The third stage in the family life cycle. Adults who enter this stage move up a generation and become caregivers to the younger generation. 513

behavior genetics The field that seeks to discover the influence of heredity and environment on individual differences in human traits and development. 90

big five factors of personality Openness to experience, conscientiousness, extraversion, agreeableness, and neuroticism (emotional stability). 568

biological age A person's age in terms of biological health. 20

biological processes Changes in an individual's physical nature. 16

blastocyst The inner layer of cells that develops during the germinal period. These cells later develop into the embryo. 103

body transcendence versus body preoccupation A developmental task of aging described by Peck, in which older adults must cope with declining physical well-being. 649

bonding The formation of a close connection, especially a physical bond between parents and their newborn in the period shortly after birth. 130

brain death A neurological definition of death. A person is brain dead when all electrical activity of the brain has ceased for a specified period of time. A flat EEG recording is one criterion of brain death. 679

brainstorming A technique in which individuals are encouraged to come up with creative ideas in a group, play off each other's ideas, and say practically whatever comes to mind. 328

Brazelton Neonatal Behavioral Assessment Scale (NBAS) A test given 24 to 36 hours after birth to assess newborns' neurological development, reflexes, and reactions to people. 124

breech position The baby's position in the uterus that causes the buttocks to be the first part to emerge from the vagina. 123

Broca's area An area in the brain's left frontal lobe involved in speech production. 196

bulimia nervosa An eating disorder in which the individual consistently follows a binge-and-purge pattern. 406

C

care perspective The moral perspective of Carol Gilligan, which views people in terms of their connectedness with others and emphasizes interpersonal communication, relationships with others, and concern for others. 362

case study An in-depth look at a single individual. 55

cataracts Involve a thickening of the lens of the eye that causes vision to become cloudy, opaque, and distorted. 600

cellular clock theory Leonard Hayflick's theory that the maximum number of times that human cells can divide is about 75 to 80. As we age, our cells have less capability to divide. 593

centration The focusing of attention on one characteristic to the exclusion of all others. 249

cephalocaudal pattern The sequence in which the earliest growth always occurs at the top—the head—with physical growth in size, weight, and feature differentiation gradually working from top to bottom. 139

child-centered kindergarten Education that involves the whole child by considering both the child's physical, cognitive, and social development and the child's needs, interests, and learning styles. 263

child-directed speech Language spoken in a higher pitch than normal with simple words and sentences. 198

chromosomes Threadlike structures that come in 23 pairs, one member of each pair coming from each parent. Chromosomes contain the genetic substance DNA. 77

chronic disorders Disorders that are characterized by slow onset and long duration. They are rare in early adulthood, they increase during middle adulthood, and they become common in late adulthood. 530

chronological age The number of years that have elapsed since birth. 20

climacteric The midlife transition in which fertility declines. 538

clique A small group that ranges from 2 to about 12 individuals, averaging about 5 to 6 individuals, and can form because adolescents engage in similar activities. 435

cognitive developmental theory of gender The theory that children's gender typing occurs after they have developed a concept of gender. Once they consistently conceive of themselves as male or female, children often organize their world on the basis of gender. 285

cognitive mechanics The "hardware" of the mind, reflecting the neurophysiological architecture of the brain as developed through evolution. Cognitive mechanics involve the speed and accuracy of the processes involving sensory input, attention, visual and motor memory, discrimination, comparison, and categorization. 619

cognitive pragmatics The culture-based "software programs" of the mind. Cognitive pragmatics include reading and writing skills, language comprehension, educational qualifications, professional skills, and also the type of knowledge about the self and life skills that help us to master or cope with life. 619

cognitive processes Changes in an individual's thought, intelligence, and language. 16

cohort effects Effects due to a person's time of birth, era, or generation but not to actual age. 59

commitment Marcia's term for the part of identity development in which adolescents show a personal investment in what they are going to do. 425

complicated grief Grief that involves enduring despair and is still unresolved over an extended period of time. 691

connectedness Connectedness consists of two dimensions: mutuality (sensitivity to and respect for others' views) and permeability (openness to others' views). 427

consensual validation An explanation of why individuals are attracted to people who are similar to them. Our own attitudes and behavior are supported and validated when someone else's attitudes and behavior are similar to our own. 499

conservation In Piaget's theory, awareness that altering an object's or a substance's appearance does not change its quantitative properties. 249

constructive play Play that combines sensorimotor and repetitive activity with symbolic representation of ideas. Constructive play occurs when children engage in self-regulated creation or construction of a product or a problem solution. 305

constructivist approach A learner-centered approach that emphasizes the importance of individuals actively constructing their knowledge and understanding with guidance from the teacher. 372

contemporary life-events approach Emphasizes that how a life event influences the individual's development depends not only on the life event, but also on mediating factors, the individual's adaptation to the life event, the life-stage context, and the sociohistorical context. 362

context The setting in which development occurs, which is influenced by historical, economic, social, and cultural factors. 8

continuity–discontinuity issue Focuses on the extent to which development involves gradual, cumulative change (continuity) or distinct stages (discontinuity). 23

controversial children Children who are frequently nominated both as someone's best friend and as being disliked. 371

conventional reasoning The second, or intermediate, level in Kohlberg's theory of moral development. At this level, individuals abide by certain standards but they are the standards of others such as parents or the laws of society. 358

convergent thinking Thinking that produces one correct answer and is characteristic of the kind of thinking tested by standardized intelligence tests. 328

cooperative play Play that involves social interaction in a group with a sense of group identity and organized activity. 304

coordination of secondary circular reactions Piaget's fourth sensorimotor substage, which develops between 8 and 12 months of age. Actions become more outwardly directed, and infants coordinate schemes and act with intentionality. 180

correlation coefficient A number based on statistical analysis that is used to describe the degree of association between two variables. 56

correlational research The goal is to describe the strength of the relationship between two or more events or characteristics. 56

creative thinking The ability to think in novel and unusual ways and to come up with unique solutions to problems. 328

crisis Marcia's term for a period of identity development during which the adolescent is choosing among meaningful alternatives. 425

critical thinking Thinking reflectively and productively, as well as evaluating the evidence. 328

cross-cultural studies Comparison of one culture with one or more other cultures. These provide information about the degree to which development is similar, or universal, across cultures, and the degree to which it is culture-specific. 11

cross-sectional approach A research strategy in which individuals of different ages are compared at one time. 58

crowd A larger group structure than a clique, a crowd is usually formed based on reputation, and members may or may not spend much time together. 435

crystallized intelligence Accumulated information and verbal skills, which increase with age, according to Horn. 541

cultural-familial retardation Retardation that is characterized by no evidence of organic brain damage, but the individual's IQ is between 50 and 70. 341

culture The behavior patterns, beliefs, and all other products of a group that are passed on from generation to generation. 11

culture-fair tests Tests of intelligence that are designed to be free of cultural bias. 339

D

date or acquaintance rape Coercive sexual activity directed at someone with whom the perpetrator is at least casually acquainted. 477

dating scripts The cognitive models that individuals use to guide and evaluate dating interactions. 437

deferred imitation Imitation that occurs after a delay of hours or days. 186

dementia A global term for any neurological disorder in which the primary symptoms involve a deterioration of mental functioning. 634

denial and isolation Kübler-Ross' first stage of dying, in which the dying person denies that she or he is really going to die. 687

depression Kübler-Ross' fourth stage of dying, in which the dying person comes to accept the certainty of her or his death. A period of depression or preparatory grief may appear. 688

descriptive research Has the purpose of observing and recording behavior. 56

development The pattern of change that begins at conception and continues through the life span. Most development involves growth, although it also includes decline brought on by aging and dying. 5

developmental quotient (DQ) An overall score that combines subscores in motor, language, adaptive, and personal-social domains in the Gesell assessment of infants. 189

developmentally appropriate practice Education that focuses on the typical developmental patterns of children (age-appropriateness) and the uniqueness of each child (individual-appropriateness). 265

differentiation versus role preoccupation One of the three developmental tasks of aging described by Peck, in which older adults must redefine their worth in terms of something other than work roles. 649

difficult child A child who tends to react negatively and cry frequently, who engages in irregular daily routines, and who is slow to accept new experiences. 214

direct instruction approach A structured, teacher-centered approach that is characterized by teacher direction and control, mastery of academic skills, high expectations for students' progress, maximum time spent on learning tasks, and efforts to keep negative affect to a minimum. 372

disease model of addiction The view that addictions are biologically based, lifelong diseases that involve a loss of control over behavior and require medical and/or spiritual treatment for recovery. 471

disengagement theory The theory that to cope effectively, older adults should gradually withdraw from society. 650

dishabituation Recovery of a habituated response after a change in stimulation. 161

divergent thinking Thinking that produces many answers to the same question and is characteristic of creativity. 328

divided attention Concentrating on more than one activity at the same time. 620

DNA A complex molecule that contains genetic information. 77

doula A caregiver who provides continuous physical, emotional, and educational support for the mother before, during, and after childbirth. 120

Down syndrome A chromosomally transmitted form of mental retardation, caused by the presence of an extra copy of chromosome 21. 81

dual-process model A model of coping with bereavement that emphasizes oscillation between two dimensions: (1) loss-oriented stressors and (2) restoration-oriented stressors. 692

dynamic systems theory The perspective on motor development that seeks to explain how motor behaviors are assembled for perceiving and acting. 151

dyslexia A category of learning disabilities involving a severe impairment in the ability to read and spell. 320

E

easy child A child who is generally in a positive mood, who quickly establishes regular routines in infancy, and who adapts easily to new experiences. 214

eclectic theoretical orientation An orientation that does not follow any one theoretical approach, but rather selects from each theory whatever is considered the best in it. 51

ecological theory Bronfenbrenner's environmental systems theory that focuses on five environmental systems: microsystem, mesosystem, exosystem, macrosystem, and chronosystem. 48

ecological view The view that perception functions to bring organisms in contact with the environment and to increase adaptation. 159

ego transcendence versus ego preoccupation A developmental task of aging described by Peck, in which older adults must come to feel at ease with themselves by recognizing that although death is inevitable and probably not too far away, they have contributed to the future through raising their children or through their vocations and ideas. 650

egocentrism The inability to distinguish between one's own perspective and someone else's (salient feature of the first substage of preoperational thought). 247

elaboration An important strategy that involves engaging in more extensive processing of information. 327

eldercare Physical and emotional caretaking for older members of the family, whether by giving day-to-day physical assistance or by being responsible for overseeing such care. 659

embryonic period The period of prenatal development that occurs two to eight weeks after conception. During the embryonic period, the rate of cell differentiation intensifies, support systems for the cells form, and organs appear. 103

emerging adulthood The transition from adolescence to adulthood (approximately 18 to 25 years of age) that involves experimentation and exploration. 459

emotion Feeling, or affect, that occurs when a person is in a state or interaction that is important to them. Emotion is characterized by behavior that reflects (expresses) the pleasantness or unpleasantness of the state a person is in or the transactions being experienced. 209

emotional intelligence A form of social intelligence that involves the ability to monitor one's own and others' feelings and emotions, to discriminate among them, and to use this information to guide one's thinking and action. 356

empty nest syndrome A decrease in marital satisfaction after children leave home, because parents derive considerable satisfaction from their children. 573

epigenetic view Emphasizes that development is the result of an ongoing, bidirectional interchange between heredity and environment. 93

episodic memory The retention of information about the where and when of life's happenings. 621

equilibration A mechanism that Piaget proposed to explain how children shift from one stage of thought to the next. 178

Erikson's theory Includes eight stages of human development. Each stage consists of a unique developmental task that confronts individuals with a crisis that must be resolved. 41

ethnic gloss Using an ethnic label such as African American or Latino in a superficial way that portrays an ethnic group as being more homogeneous than it really is. 64

ethnic identity An enduring, basic aspect of the self that includes a sense of membership in an ethnic group and the attitudes and feelings related to that membership. 427

ethnicity A characteristic based on cultural heritage, nationality characteristic, race, religion, and language. 11

ethology Stresses that behavior is strongly influenced by biology, is tied to evolution, and is characterized by critical or sensitive periods. 47

euthanasia The act of painlessly ending the lives of persons who are suffering from incurable diseases or severe disabilities; sometimes called "mercy killing." 679

evocative genotype-environment correlations Correlations that exist when the child's genotype elicits certain types of physical and social environments. 92

evolutionary psychology Emphasizes the importance of adaptation, reproduction, and "survival of the fittest" in shaping behavior. 74

experiment A carefully regulated procedure in which one or more of the factors believed to influence the behavior being studied are manipulated while all other factors are held constant. 56

explicit memory Memory of facts and experiences that individuals consciously know and can state. 186, 622

F

family at midlife The fifth stage in the family life cycle, a time of launching children, linking generations, and adapting to midlife developmental changes. 514

family in later life The sixth and final stage in the family life cycle, involving retirement and, in many families, grand-parenting. 514

family with adolescents The fourth stage of the family life cycle, in which adolescent children push for autonomy and seek to develop their own identities. 514

fertilization A stage in reproduction whereby an egg and a sperm fuse to create a single cell, called a zygote. 78

fetal alcohol syndrome (FAS) A cluster of abnormalities that appears in the offspring of mothers who drink alcohol heavily during pregnancy. 108

fetal period The prenatal period of development that begins two months after conception and lasts for seven months, on the average. 105

fine motor skills Motor skills that involve more finely tuned movements, such as finger dexterity. 157

first habits and primary circular reactions Piaget's second sensorimotor substage, which develops between 1 and 4 months of age. In this substage, the infant coordinates sensation

and two types of schemes: habits and primary circular reactions. 179

fluid intelligence The ability to reason abstractly, which steadily declines from middle adulthood on, according to Horn. 541

fragile X syndrome A genetic disorder involving an abnormality in the X chromosome, which becomes constricted and, often, breaks. 81

free-radical theory A microbiological theory of aging that states that people age because inside their cells normal metabolism produces unstable oxygen molecules known as free radicals. These molecules ricochet around inside cells, damaging DNA and other cellular structures. 594

friendship A form of close relationship that involves enjoyment, acceptance, trust, respect, mutual assistance, confiding, understanding, and spontaneity. 500

fuzzy trace theory States that memory is best understood by considering two types of memory representations: (1) verbatim memory trace and (2) gist. In this theory, older children's better memory is attributed to the fuzzy traces created by extracting the gist of information. 327

G

games Activities engaged in for pleasure that include rules and often competition with one or more individuals. 305

gender The psychological and sociocultural dimensions of being female or male. 11

gender identity The sense of being male or female, which most children acquire by the time they are 3 years old. 282

gender role A set of expectations that prescribes how females or males should think, act, and feel. 282

gender schema theory The theory that an individual's attention and behavior are guided by an internal motivation to conform to gender-based sociocultural standards and stereotypes. 285

gender stereotypes Broad categories that reflect our impressions and beliefs about females and males. 363

generational inequity The view that our aging society is being unfair to its younger members because older adults pile up advantages by receiving inequitably large allocations of resources. 659

genes Units of hereditary information composed of DNA. Genes direct cells to reproduce themselves and manufacture the proteins that maintain life. 77

genotype A person's genetic heritage; the actual genetic material. 79

germinal period The period of prenatal development that takes place in the first two weeks after conception. It includes the creation of the zygote, continued cell division, and the attachment of the zygote to the uterine wall. 103

gifted Having above-average intelligence (an IQ of 130 or higher) and/or superior talent for something. 341

glaucoma Damage to the optic nerve because of the pressure created by a buildup of fluid in the eye. 600

gonads The sex glands—the testes in males and the ovaries in females. 391

goodness of fit Refers to the match between a child's temperament and the environmental demands with which the child must cope. 215

grasping reflex A neonatal reflex that occurs when something touches the infant's palms. The infant responds by grasping tightly. 153

grief The emotional numbness, disbelief, separation anxiety, despair, sadness, and loneliness that accompany the loss of someone we love. 691

gross motor skills Motor skills that involve large-muscle activities, such as walking. 154

H

habituation Decreased responsiveness to a stimulus after repeated presentation of the stimulus. 161

hardiness A personality style characterized by a sense of commitment (rather than alienation), control (rather than powerlessness), and a perception of problems as challenges (rather than threats). 537

heritability The fraction of variance in a population that is attributed to genetics and is computed using correlational techniques. 335

heteronomous morality (Kohlberg's theory) Kohlberg's first stage in preconventional reasoning in which moral thinking is tied to punishment. 358

heteronomous morality The first stage of moral development in Piaget's theory, occurring from approximately 4 to 7 years of age. Justice and rules are conceived of as unchangeable properties of the world, removed from the control of people. 280

hormonal stress theory The theory that aging in the body's hormonal system can lower resilience to stress and increase the likelihood of disease. 594

hormones Powerful chemical substances secreted by the endocrine glands and carried through the body by the bloodstream. 391

hospice A program committed to making the end of life as free from pain, anxiety, and depression as possible. The goals of hospice

contrast with those of a hospital, which are to cure disease and prolong life. 681

hypothalamus A structure in the higher portion of the brain that monitors eating, drinking, and sex. 391

hypotheses Specific assumptions and predictions that can be tested to determine their accuracy. 39

hypothetical-deductive reasoning Piaget's formal operational concept that adolescents have the cognitive ability to develop hypotheses, or best guesses, about ways to solve problems, such as an algebraic equation. 408

I

identity achievement Marcia's term for adolescents who have undergone a crisis and have made a commitment. 426

identity diffusion Marcia's term for adolescents who have not yet experienced a crisis (explored meaningful alternatives) or made any commitments. 425

identity foreclosure Marcia's term for adolescents who have made a commitment but have not experienced a crisis. 426

identity moratorium Marcia's term for adolescents who are in the midst of a crisis, but their commitments are either absent or vaguely defined. 426

identity versus identity confusion Erikson's fifth developmental stage, which occurs during adolescence. At this time, individuals are faced with deciding on who they are, what they are all about, and where they are going in life. 424

imaginary audience Involves adolescents' belief that others are as interested in them as they themselves are; attention-getting behavior motivated by a desire to be noticed, visible, and "on stage." 409

immanent justice The concept that, if a rule is broken, punishment will be meted out immediately. 291

implicit memory Memory without conscious recollection; involves skills and routine procedures that are automatically performed. 186

inclusion Educating a child with special education needs full-time in the regular classroom. 322

individual differences The stable, consistent ways in which people are different from each other. 331

individualism, instrumental purpose, and exchange The second Kohlberg stage of moral development. At this stage, individuals pursue their own interests but also let others do the same. 358

individuality Individuality consists of two dimensions: self-assertion (the ability to have

and communicate a point of view) and separateness (the use of communication patterns to express how one is different from others). 427

individualized education plan (IEP) A written statement that spells out a program tailored to a child with a disability. The plan should be (1) related to the child's learning capacity, (2) specially constructed to meet the child's individual needs and not merely a copy of what is offered to other children, and (3) designed to provide educational benefits. 322

indulgent parenting A style of parenting in which parents are highly involved with their children but place few demands or controls on them. Indulgent parenting is associated with children's social incompetence, especially a lack of self-control. 288

infinite generativity The ability to produce an endless number of meaningful sentences using a finite set of words and rules. 190

information-processing theory Emphasizes that individuals manipulate information, monitor it, and strategize about it. Central to this theory are the processes of memory and thinking. 44

innate goodness The idea presented by the French philosopher Jean-Jacques Rousseau that children are inherently good. 6

insecure avoidant babies Babies that show insecurity by avoiding the caregiver. 200

insecure disorganized babies Babies that show insecurity by being disorganized and disoriented. 200

insecure resistant babies Babies that often cling to the caregiver, then resist her by fighting against the closeness, perhaps by kicking or pushing away. 200

integrity versus despair Erikson's eighth and final stage of development, which individuals experience in late adulthood. This involves reflecting on the past and either piecing together a positive review or concluding that one's life has not been well spent. 649

intelligence Problem-solving skills and the ability to learn from and adapt to the experiences of everyday life. 331

intelligence quotient (IQ) A person's mental age divided by chronological age, multiplied by 100. 331

intermodal perception The ability to relate and integrate information from two or more sensory modalities, such as vision and hearing. 167

internalization of schemes Piaget's sixth and final sensorimotor substage, which develops between 18 and 24 months of age. In this substage, the infant develops the ability to use primitive symbols. 180

intimacy in friendships Self-disclosure and the sharing of private thoughts. 375

intuitive thought substage Piaget's second substage of preoperational thought, in which children begin to use primitive reasoning and want to know the answers to all sorts of questions (between 4 and 7 years of age). 248

J

justice perspective A moral perspective that focuses on the rights of the individual; individuals independently make moral decisions. 362

juvenile delinquent An adolescent who breaks the law or engages in behavior that is considered illegal. 443

K

kangaroo care A way of holding a preterm infant so that there is skin-to-skin contact. 126

Klinefelter syndrome A chromosomal disorder in which males have an extra X chromosome, making them XXY instead of XY. 81

kwashiorkor A condition caused by a deficiency in protein in which the child's abdomen and feet become swollen with water; usually appears between 1 to 3 years of age. 149

L

laboratory A controlled setting in which many of the complex factors of the "real world" are removed. 53

language acquisition device (LAD) Chomsky's term that describes a biological endowment that enables the child to detect the features and rules of language, including phonology, syntax, and semantics. 196

language A form of communication, whether spoken, written, or signed, that is based on a system of symbols. 190

lateralization Specialization of function in one hemisphere of the cerebral cortex or the other. 141

launching The process in which youth move into adulthood and exit their family of origin. 513

learning disability Includes three components: (1) a minimum IQ level; (2) a significant difficulty in a school-related area (especially reading and/or mathematics); and (3) exclusion of only severe emotional disorders, second-language background, sensory disabilities, and/or specific neurological deficits. 319

least restrictive environment (LRE) The concept that a child with a disability must be educated in a setting that is as similar as possible to the one in which children who do not have a disability are educated. 322

leaving home and becoming a single adult The first stage in the family life cycle. It involves launching. 573

leisure The pleasant times after work when individuals are free to pursue activities and interests of their own choosing. 547

life expectancy The number of years that will probably be lived by the average person born in a particular year. 589

life span The upper boundary of life, the maximum number of years an individual can live. The maximum life span of human beings is about 120 to 125 years of age. 588

life-history record A record of information about a lifetime chronology of events and activities that often involve a combination of data records on education, work, family, and residence. 55

life-process model of addiction The view that addiction is not a disease but rather a habitual response and a source of gratification and security that can be understood only in the context of social relationships and experiences. 471

life-span perspective The perspective that development is lifelong, multidimensional, multidirectional, plastic, multidisciplinary, and contextual; involves growth, maintenance, and regulation; and is constructed through biological, sociocultural, and individual factors working together. 7

longitudinal approach A research strategy in which the same individuals are studied over a period of time, usually several years or more. 58

long-term memory A relatively permanent type of memory that holds huge amounts of information for a long period of time. 326

low birth weight infants An infant that weighs less than $5\frac{1}{2}$ pounds at birth. 125

M

macular degeneration A disease that involves deterioration of the macula of the retina, which corresponds to the focal center of the visual field. 600

major depression A mood disorder in which the individual is deeply unhappy, demoralized, self-derogatory, and bored. The person does not feel well, loses stamina easily, has poor appetite, and is listless and unmotivated. Major depression is so widespread that it has been called the "common cold" of mental disorders. 633

marasmus A wasting away of body tissues in the infant's first year, caused by severe protein-calorie deficiency. 149

matching hypothesis States that although we prefer a more attractive person in the abstract, in the real world we end up choosing someone who is close to our own level. 499

meaning-making coping Involves drawing on beliefs, values, and goals to change the meaning of a stressful situation, especially in times of chronic stress as when a loved one dies. 549

meiosis A specialized form of cell division that occurs to form eggs and sperm (or gametes). 78

memory A central feature of cognitive development, pertaining to all situations in which an individual retains information over time. 186

menarche A girl's first menstruation. 391

menopause The complete cessation of a woman's menstruation, which usually occurs in the late forties or early fifties. 538

mental age (MA) Binet's measure of an individual's level of mental development, compared with that of others. 331

mental retardation A condition of limited mental ability in which an individual has a low IQ, usually below 70 on a traditional test of intelligence, and has difficulty adapting to everyday life. 340

metacognition Cognition about cognition, or knowing about knowing. 330

metalinguistic awareness Refers to knowledge about language, such as knowing what a preposition is or the ability to discuss the sounds of a language. 343

middle adulthood The developmental period beginning at approximately 40 years of age and extending to about 60 to 65 years of age. 530

mitochondrial theory The theory that aging is caused by the decay of mitochondria, tiny cellular bodies that supply energy for function, growth, and repair. 594

mitosis Cellular reproduction in which the cell's nucleus duplicates itself with two new cells being formed, each containing the same DNA as the parent cell, arranged in the same 23 pairs of chromosomes. 78

Montessori approach An educational philosophy in which children are given considerable freedom and spontaneity in choosing activities and are allowed to move from one activity to another as they desire. 264

moral development Development that involves thoughts, feelings, and actions regarding rules and conventions about what people should do in their interactions with other people. 279

Moro reflex A neonatal startle response that occurs in reaction to a sudden, intense noise or movement. When startled, the newborn arches its back, throws its head back, and flings out its arms and legs. Then the newborn rapidly closes its arms and legs to the center of the body. 153

morphology Units of meaning involved in word formation. 191

multi-infarct dementia Sporadic and progressive loss of intellectual functioning caused by repeated temporary obstruction of blood flow in cerebral arteries. 637

mutual interpersonal expectations, relationships, and interpersonal conformity Kohlberg's third stage of moral development. At this stage, individuals value trust, caring, and loyalty to others as a basis of moral judgments. 358

myelination The process by which the nerve cells are covered and insulated with a layer of fat cells, which increases the speed at which information travels through the nervous system. 240

N

natural childbirth Developed in 1914 by Dick-Read, this method attempts to reduce the mother's pain by decreasing her fear through education about childbirth and relaxation techniques during delivery. 121

naturalistic observation Observing behavior in real-world settings. 53

nature-nurture issue Refers to the debate about whether development is primarily influenced by nature or nurture. Nature refers to an organism's biological inheritance, nurture to its environmental experiences. The "nature proponents" claim biological inheritance is the most important influence on development; the "nurture proponents" claim that environmental experiences are the most important. 21

neglected children Children who are infrequently nominated as a best friend but are not disliked by their peers. 371

neglectful parenting A style of parenting in which the parent is very uninvolved in the child's life; it is associated with children's social incompetence, especially a lack of self-control. 288

Neonatal Intensive Care Unit Neurobehavioral Scale (NNNS) An "offspring" of the NBAS, the NNNS provides a more comprehensive analysis of the newborn's behavior, neurological and stress responses, and regulatory capacities. 124

neo-Piagetians Developmentalists who have elaborated on Piaget's theory, giving more emphasis to information processing, strategies, and precise cognitive steps. 325

neuron Nerve cell that handles information processing at the cellular level. 142

new couple Forming the new couple is the second stage in the family life cycle. Two

individuals from separate families of origin unite to form a new family system. 513

non-normative life events Unusual occurrences that have a major impact on an individual's life. 9

nonshared environmental experiences The child's own unique experiences, both within the family and outside the family, that are not shared by another sibling. Thus, experiences occurring within the family can be part of the "nonshared environment." 92

normal distribution A symmetrical distribution with most scores falling in the middle of the possible range of scores and a few scores appearing toward the extremes of the range. 331

normative age-graded influences These are influences that are similar for individuals in a particular age group. 9

normative history-graded influences Influences that are common to people of a particular generation because of historical circumstances. 9

O

object permanence The Piagetian term for understanding that objects and events continue to exist, even when they cannot directly be seen, heard, or touched. 181

onlooker play Play in which the child watches other children play. 303

operations In Piaget's theory, internalized sets of actions that enable children to do mentally what they formerly did physically. 247

organic retardation Mental retardation that involves some physical damage and is caused by a genetic disorder or brain damage. 340

organization Piaget's concept of grouping isolated behaviors into a higher-order, more smoothly functioning cognitive system. 178

organogenesis Organ formation that takes place during the first two months of prenatal development. 104

original sin The view that children were basically bad and born into the world as evil beings. 6

osteoporosis A chronic condition that involves an extensive loss of bone tissue and is the main reason many older adults walk with a marked stoop. Women are especially vulnerable to osteoporosis. 604

P

pain cry A sudden appearance of loud crying without preliminary moaning, followed by breath holding. 211

palliative care Emphasized in hospice care, involves reducing pain and suffering and helping individuals die with dignity. 681

parallel play Play in which the child plays separately from others, but with toys like those the others are using or in a manner that mimics their play. 304

Parkinson disease A chronic, progressive disease characterized by muscle tremors, slowing of movement, and partial facial paralysis. 638

passive euthanasia The withholding of available treatments, such as life-sustaining devices, allowing the person to die. 679

passive genotype-environment correlations Correlations that exist when the natural parents, who are genetically related to the child, provide a rearing environment for the child. 91

perception The interpretation of what is sensed. 159

personal fable The part of adolescent egocentrism that involves an adolescent's sense of uniqueness and invincibility. 409

personality type theory John Holland's view that it is important for individuals to select a career that matches up well with their personality type. 482

phenotype The way an individual's genotype is expressed in observed and measurable characteristics. 79

phenylketonuria (PKU) A genetic disorder in which an individual cannot properly metabolize an amino acid. PKU is now easily detected but, if left untreated, results in mental retardation and hyperactivity. 82

phonology The sound system of the language, including the sounds that are used and how they may be combined. 191

Piaget's theory States that children actively construct their understanding of the world and go through four stages of cognitive development. 43

pituitary gland An important endocrine gland that controls growth and regulates other glands. 391

placenta A life-support system that consists of a disk-shaped group of tissues in which small blood vessels from the mother and offspring intertwine. 104

pluralism The coexistence of distinct ethnic and cultural groups in the same society. Individuals with a pluralistic stance usually advocate that cultural differences be maintained and appreciated. 442

popular children Children who are frequently nominated as a best friend and are rarely disliked by their peers. 371

postconventional reasoning The highest level in Kohlberg's theory of moral development. At this level, the individual recognizes alternative moral courses, explores the options, and then decides on a personal moral code. 359

postformal thought A form of thought that is qualitatively different from Piaget's formal operational thought. It involves understanding that the correct answer to a problem can require reflective thinking, that the correct answer can vary from one situation to another, and that the search for truth is often an ongoing, neverending process. It also involves the belief that solutions to problems need to be realistic and that emotion and subjective factors can influence thinking. 479

postpartum depression Characteristic of women who have such strong feelings or sadness, anxiety, or despair that for at least a two-week period they have trouble coping with daily tasks in the postpartum period. 130

postpartum period The period after childbirth when the mother adjusts, both physically and psychologically, to the process of childbirth. This period lasts for about six weeks or until her body has completed its adjustment and returned to a near prepregnant state. 128

practice play Play that involves repetition of behavior when new skills are being learned or when physical or mental mastery and coordination of skills are required for games or sports. 304

pragmatics The appropriate use of language in different contexts. 192

preconventional reasoning The lowest level in Kohlberg's theory of moral development. The individual's moral reasoning is controlled primarily by external rewards and punishment. 358

preoperational stage Piaget's second stage, lasting from 2 to 7 years of age, during which children begin to represent the world with words, images, and drawings and symbolic thought goes beyond simple connections of sensory information and physical action; stable concepts are formed, mental reasoning emerges, egocentrism is present, and magical beliefs are constructed. 247

prepared childbirth Developed by French obstetrician Ferdinand Lamaze, this childbirth strategy is similar to natural childbirth but includes a special breathing technique to control pushing in the final stages of labor and a more detailed anatomy and physiology course. 121

pretense/symbolic play Play in which the child transforms the physical environment into a symbol. 304

preterm infants Those born three weeks or more before the pregnancy has reached its full term. 125

Project Head Start A government-funded program that is designed to provide children from low-income families the opportunity to acquire the skills and experiences important for school success. 265

prospective memory Involves remembering to do something in the future. 623

proximodistal pattern The sequence in which growth starts at the center of the body and moves toward the extremities. 140

psychoanalytic theories Describe development as primarily unconscious and heavily colored by emotion. Behavior is merely a surface characteristic, and the symbolic workings of the mind have to be analyzed to understand behavior. Early experiences with parents are emphasized. 40

psychoanalytic theory of gender A theory deriving from Freud's view that the preschool child develops a sexual attraction to the opposite-sex parent, by approximately 5 or 6 years of age renounces this attraction because of anxious feelings, and subsequently identifies with the same-sex parent, unconsciously adopting the same-sex parent's characteristics. 283

psychological age An individual's adaptive capacities compared with those of other individuals of the same chronological age. 20

psychosocial moratorium Erikson's term for the gap between childhood security and adult autonomy that adolescents experience as part of their identity exploration. 425

puberty A period of rapid physical and sexual maturation that occurs mainly during early adolescence. 390

R

rape Forcible sexual intercourse with a person who does not consent to it. 476

rapport talk The language of conversation; a way to establish connections and negotiate relationships; preferred by women. 519

reciprocal socialization Socialization that is bidirectional; children socialize parents, just as parents socialize children. 224

reflexes Built-in reactions to stimuli that govern the newborn's movements, which are automatic and beyond the newborn's control. 153

reflexive smile A smile that does not occur in response to external stimuli. It happens during the month after birth, usually during sleep. 211

rejected children Children who are infrequently nominated as a best friend and are actively disliked by their peers. 371

report talk Language designed to give information, including public speaking; preferred by men. 519

restrained eaters Individuals who chronically restrict their food intake to control their weight. Restrained eaters are often on diets, are very conscious of what they eat, and tend to feel guilty after splurging on sweets. 466

rite of passage A ceremony or ritual that marks an individual's transition from one

status to another. Most rites of passage focus on the transition to adult status. 441

romantic love Also called passionate love, or eros, romantic love has strong sexual and infatuation components and often predominates in the early period of a love relationship. 502

rooting reflex A newborn's built-in reaction that occurs when the infant's cheek is stroked or the side of the mouth is touched. In response, the infant turns his or her head toward the side that was touched, in an apparent effort to find something to suck. 153

S

schemes In Piaget's theory, actions or mental representations that organize knowledge. 171

secondary circular reactions Piaget's third sensorimotor substage, which develops between 4 and 8 months of age. In this substage, the infant becomes more object-oriented, moving beyond preoccupation with the self. 180

securely attached babies Babies that use the caregiver as a secure base from which to explore the environment. 220

selective attention Focusing on a specific aspect of experience that is relevant while ignoring others that are irrelevant. 620

selective optimization with compensation theory The theory that successful aging is related to three main factors: selection, optimization, and compensation. 653

self-concept Domain-specific evaluations of the self. 354

self-efficacy The belief that one can master a situation and produce favorable outcomes. 355

self-esteem The global evaluative dimension of the self. Self-esteem is also referred to as self-worth or self-image. 354

self-understanding The child's cognitive representation of self, the substance and content of the child's self-conceptions. 277

semantic memory A person's knowledge about the world—including a person's fields of expertise, general academic knowledge of the sort learned in school, and "everyday knowledge." 621

semantics The meaning of words and sentences. 191

sensation The product of the interaction between information and the sensory receptors—the eyes, ears, tongue, nostrils, and skin. 159

sensorimotor play Behavior engaged in by infants to derive pleasure from exercising their existing sensorimotor schemas. 304

sensorimotor stage The first of Piaget's stages, which lasts from birth to about 2 years of age; infants construct an understanding of the world by coordinating sensory experiences with motoric actions. 178

separation protest An infant's distressed reaction when the caregiver leaves. 212

sequential approach A combined cross-sectional, longitudinal design. 59

seriation The concrete operation that involves ordering stimuli along a quantitative dimension (such as length). 324

service learning A form of education that promotes social responsibility and service to the community. 415

sexually transmitted infections (STIs) Infections that are contracted primarily through sexual contact, which is not limited to sexual intercourse. Oral-genital and anal-genital contact also can transmit STIs. 397, 479

shape constancy The recognition that an object's shape remains the same even though its orientation to us changes. 164

shared environmental experiences Siblings' common environmental experiences, such as their parents' personalities and intellectual orientation, the family's socioeconomic status, and the neighborhood in which they live. 92

short-term memory The memory component in which individuals retain information for up to 30 seconds, assuming there is no rehearsal of the information. 256

sickle-cell anemia A genetic disorder that affects the red blood cells and occurs most often in people of African descent. 82

simple reflexes Piaget's first sensorimotor substage, which corresponds to the first month after birth. In this substage, sensation and action are coordinated primarily through reflexive behaviors. 179

size constancy The recognition that an object remains the same even though the retinal image of the object changes. 164

slow-to-warm-up child A child who has a low activity level, is somewhat negative, and displays a low intensity of mood. 214

small for date infants Also called small for gestational age infants, these infants' birth weights are below normal when the length of pregnancy is considered. Small for date infants may be preterm or full term. 125

social age Social roles and expectations related to a person's age. 20

social clock The timetable according to which individuals are expected to accomplish life's tasks, such as getting married, having children, or establishing themselves in a career. 564

social cognitive theory The view of psychologists who emphasize behavior, environment, and cognition as the key factors in development. 46

social cognitive theory of gender A theory that emphasizes that children's gender development occurs through the observation and imitation of gender behavior and through the rewards and punishments children experience for gender-appropriate and gender-inappropriate behavior. 284

social constructivist approach An approach that emphasizes the social contexts of learning and that knowledge is mutually built and constructed. Vygotsky's theory reflects this approach. 250

social contract or utility and individual rights The fifth Kohlberg stage. At this stage, individuals reason that values, rights, and principles undergird or transcend the law. 359

social conventional reasoning Thoughts about social consensus and convention, in contrast to moral reasoning, which stresses ethical issues. 362

social play Play that involves social interactions with peers. 304

social policy A national government's course of action designed to promote the welfare of its citizens. 13

social referencing "Reading" emotional cues in others to help determine how to act in a particular situation. 212

social role theory A theory that gender differences result from the contrasting roles of men and women. 283

social smile A smile in response to an external stimulus, which, early in development, typically is a face. 211

social systems morality The fourth stage in Kohlberg's theory of moral development. Moral judgments are based on understanding the social order, law, justice, and duty. 359

socioeconomic status (SES) Refers to the grouping of people with similar occupational, educational, and economic characteristics. 11

socioemotional processes Changes in an individual's relationships with other people, emotions, and personality. 16

socioemotional selectivity theory The theory that older adults become more selective about their social networks. Because they place a high value on emotional satisfaction, older adults often spend more time with familiar individuals with whom they have had rewarding relationships. 651

solitary play Play in which the child plays alone and independently of others. 303

source memory The ability to remember where one learned something. 622

stability-change issue Involves the degree to which we become older renditions of our early experience (stability) or whether we develop into someone different from who we were at an earlier point in development (change). 21

standardized test A test with uniform procedures for administration and scoring. Many standardized tests allow a person's performance to be compared with the performance of other individuals. 54

stereotype threat The anxiety that one's behavior might confirm a negative stereotype about one's group. 338

Strange Situation An observational measure of infant attachment that requires the infant to move through a series of introductions, separations, and reunions with the caregiver and an adult stranger in a prescribed order. 220

stranger anxiety An infant's fear and wariness of strangers; it tends to appear in the second half of the first year of life. 211

strategies Deliberate mental activities to improve the processing of information. 258

sucking reflex A newborn's built-in reaction to automatically suck an object placed in its mouth. The sucking reflex enables the infant to get nourishment before he or she has associated a nipple with food. 153

sudden infant death syndrome (SIDS) A condition that occurs when an infant stops breathing, usually during the night, and suddenly dies without an apparent cause. 146

sustained attention The state of readiness to detect and respond to small changes occurring at random times in the environment. 620

symbolic function substage Piaget's first substage of preoperational thought, in which the child gains the ability to mentally represent an object that is not present (between 2 and 4 years of age). 247

syntax The ways words are combined to form acceptable phrases and sentences. 191

T

tabula rasa The idea, proposed by John Locke, that children are like a "blank tablet." 6

telegraphic speech The use of short and precise words without grammatical markers such as articles, auxiliary verbs, and other connectives. 195

temperament An individual's behavioral style and characteristic way of emotionally responding. 213

teratogen Any agent that can potentially cause a birth defect or negatively alter cognitive and behavioral outcomes. 105

tertiary circular reactions, novelty, and curiosity Piaget's fifth sensorimotor substage, which develops between 12 and 18 months of age. In this substage, infants become intrigued by the many properties of objects and by the many things that they can make happen to objects. 180

theory An interrelated, coherent set of ideas that helps to explain and make predictions. 39

theory of mind Refers to the awareness of one's own mental processes and the mental processes of others. 258

top-dog phenomenon The circumstance of moving from the top position in elementary school to the lowest position in middle or junior high school. 412

transitivity The ability to logically combine relations to understand certain conclusions. 324

triarchic theory of intelligence Sternberg's theory that intelligence consists of analytical intelligence, creative intelligence, and practical intelligence. 333

trophoblast The outer layer of cells that develops in the germinal period. These cells provide nutrition and support for the embryo. 103

Turner syndrome A chromosome disorder in females in which either an X chromosome is missing, making the person XO instead of XX, or the second X chromosome is partially deleted. 81

twin study A study in which the behavioral similarity of identical twins is compared with the behavioral similarity of fraternal twins. 91

Type A behavior pattern A cluster of characteristics—being excessively competitive, hard-driven, impatient, and hostile—thought to be related to the incidence of heart disease. 537

Type B behavior pattern Being primarily calm and easygoing. 537

U

umbilical cord A life-support system containing two arteries and one vein that connects the baby to the placenta. 104

universal ethical principles The sixth and highest stage in Kohlberg's theory of moral development. Individuals develop a moral standard based on universal human rights. 359

unoccupied play Play in which the child is not engaging in play as it is commonly understood and might stand in one spot, or perform random movements that do not seem to have a goal. 303

V

visual preference method A method used to determine whether infants can distinguish one stimulus from another by measuring the length of time they attend to different stimuli. 161

Vygotsky's theory A sociocultural cognitive theory that emphasizes how culture and social interaction guide cognitive development. 44

W

Wernicke's area An area of the brain's left hemisphere that is involved in language comprehension. 196

whole-language approach An approach to reading instruction based on the idea that instruction should parallel children's natural language learning. Reading materials should be whole and meaningful. 343

wisdom Expert knowledge about the practical aspects of life that permits excellent judgment about important matters. 623

working memory Closely related to short-term memory but places more emphasis on mental work. Working memory is like a "workbench" where individuals can manipulate and assemble information when making decisions, solving problems, and comprehending written and spoken language. 544

X

XYY syndrome A chromosomal disorder in which males have an extra Y chromosome. 82

Z

zone of proximal development (ZPD) Vygotsky's term for tasks too difficult for children to master alone but that can be mastered with assistance. 251

zygote A single cell formed through fertilization. 78

AARP (2004). *The divorce experience: A study of divorce at midlife and beyond.* Washington, DC: AARP.

Abbassi, V. (1998). Growth and normal puberty. *Pediatrics (Suppl.), 102 (2)* 507–511.

Abbott, A. (2003). Restless nights, listless days. *Nature, 425,* 896–898.

Abbott, R. D., White, I. R., Ross, G. W., Masaki, K. H., Curb, J. D., & Petrovitch, H. (2004). Walking and dementia in physically capable elderly men. *Journal of the American Medical Association, 292,* 1447–1453.

ABC News. (2005, December 12). Larry Page and Sergey Brin. Available at http://abcnews.go.com?Entertainment/12/8/05

Abel, E. L. (2006). Fetal alcohol syndrome: A cautionary note. *Current Pharmacy Design, 12,* 1521–1529.

Abeles, R., Fozard, J., Kausler, D., & Storandt, M. (2006). Evaluating progress in the study of the psychology of aging. In J. E. Birren & K. W. Schaie (Eds.), *Handbook of the psychology of aging* (6th ed.). San Diego: Academic Press.

Aboud, F., & Skerry, S. (1983). Self and ethnic concepts in relation to ethnic constancy. *Canadian Journal of Behavioral Science, 15,* 3–34.

Abu-Amero, S., Monk, D., Apostoloidou, S., Stanier, P., & Moore, G. (2006). Imprinted genes and their role in human fetal growth. *Cytogentic and Genome Research, 113,* 262–270.

Accornero, V. H., Anthony, J. C., Morrow, C. E., Xue, L., & Bandstra, E. S. (2006). Prenatal cocaine exposure: An examination of childhood externalizing and internalizing behavior problems at age 7 years. *Epidemiology, Psychiatry, and Society, 15,* 20–29.

Acebo, C., & Carskadon, M. A. (2002). Influence of irregular sleep patterns on waking behavior. In M. A. Carskadon (Ed.), *Adolescent sleep patterns.* New York: Cambridge University Press.

Ackerman, P. L., & Lohman, D. F. (2006). Individual differences in cognitive function. In P. A. Alexander & P. H. Winne (Eds.), *Handbook of educational psychology* (2nd ed.). Mahwah, NJ: Erlbaum.

Adamolekun, K. (2001). Survivors' motives for extravagant funerals among the Yorubas of western Nigeria. *Death Studies, 25,* 609–619.

Adams, G. R., Gulotta, T. P., & Montemayor, R. (Eds.). (1992). *Adolescent identity formation.* Newbury Park, CA: Sage.

Adams, G., & Snyder, K. (2006). Child care subsides and low-income parents. In N. Cabrera, R. Hutchens, H. E. Peters, & L. Peters (Eds.), *From welfare to childcare.* Mahwah, NJ: Erlbaum.

Adams-Curtis, L. E., & Forbes, G. B. (2004). College women's experiences of sexual coercion: A review of cultural, perpetrator, victim, and situational variables. *Trama, Violence, and Abuse, 5,* 91–122.

Adamson, H. D. (2004). *Language minority students in American schools.* Mahwah, NJ: Erlbaum.

Addis, A., Magrini, N., & Mastroiacovo, P. (2001). Drug use during pregnancy, *Lancet, 357,* 800.

Adgent, M. A. (2006). Environmental tobacco smoke and sudden infant death syndrome: A review. *Birth Defects Research, 77,* 69–85.

Adler, T. (1991, January). Seeing double? Controversial twins study is widely reported, debated. *APA Monitor, 22,* 1, 8.

Adolph, K. E. (1997). Learning in the development of infant locomotion. *Monographs of the Society for Research in Child Development, 62* (3, Serial No. 251).

Adolph, K. E. (2002). Learning to keep balance. In R. Kail (Ed.), *Advances in child development and behavior.* San Diego: Academic Press.

Adolph, K. E., & Avolio, A. M. (2000). Walking infants adapt locomotion to changing body dimensions. *Journal of Experimental Psychology: Human Perception and Performance, 26,* 1148–1166.

Adolph, K. E., & Berger, S. E. (2005). Physical and motor development. In M. H. Bornstein & M. E. Lamb (Eds.), *Developmental psychology* (5th ed.). Mahwah, NJ: Erlbaum.

Adolph, K. E., & Berger, S. E. (2006). Motor development. In W. Damon & R. Lerner (Eds), *Handbook of child psychology* (6th ed.). New York: Wiley.

Adolph, K. E., & Joh, A. S. (2007). Motor development: How infants get into the act. In A. Slater & M. Lewis (eds.), *Infant Development* (2nd ed.). New York: Oxford University Press.

Aggarwal, N. T., Wilson, R. S., Beck, T. L., Bienias, J. L., Berry-Kravis, E., & Bennett, D. A. (2005). The apolipoprotein E epsilon 4 allele and incident Alzheimer's disease in persons with mild cognitive impairment. *Neurocase, 11,* 3–7.

Agras, W. S., & others. (2004). Report of the National Institutes of Health workshop on overcoming barriers to treatment research in anorexia nervosa. *International Journal of Eating Disorders, 35,* 509–521.

Aguiar, A., & Baillargeon, R. (2002). Developments in young infants' reasoning about occluded objects. *Cognitive Psychology, 45,* 263–336.

Aguirre, D., Nieto, K., Lazos, M., Pena, Y. R., Palma, I., Kofman-Alfaro, S., & Queipo, G. (2006). Extragonal germ cell tumors are often associated with Klinefelter syndrome. *Human Pathology, 37,* 447–484.

Ahluwalia, I. B., Tessaro, I., Grumer-Strawn, L. M., MacGowan, C., & Benton-Davis, S. (2000). Georgia's breastfeeding promotion program for low-income women. *Pediatrics, 105,* E-85–E-87.

Ahmed, N. U., Smith, G. L., Flores, A. M., Pamies, R. J., Mason, H. R., Woods, K. F., & Stain, S. C. (2005). Racial/ethnic disparity and predictors of leisure-time activity among U.S. men. *Ethnicity and Disease, 15,* 40–52.

Ahrons, C. (2004). *We're still family.* New York: HarperCollins.

Aiken, L. (2000). *Dying, death, and bereavement* (4th ed.). Mahwah, NJ: Erlbaum.

Aiken, L. R., & Groth-Marnat, G. (2006). *Psychological testing and assessment* (12th ed.). Boston: Allyn & Bacon.

Ainsworth, M. D. S. (1979). Infant-mother attachment. *American Psychologist, 34,* 932–937.

Aitken, M. E., Graham, C. J., Killingsworth, J. B., Mullins, S. H., Parnell, D. N., & Dick, R. M. (2004). All-terrain injury in children: Strategies for prevention. *Injury Prevention, 10,* 180–185.

Akaike, A. (2006). Preclinical evidence of neuroprotection by cholinesterase inhibitors. *Alzheimer Disease and Associated Disorder, 20,* Suppl 1, S8–S11.

Akerlund, M. (2006). Targeting the oxytocin receptor to relax the myometrium. *Expert Opinion on Therapeutic Targets, 10,* 423–427.

Akiyama, H., & Antonucci, T. C. (1999, November). *Mother-daughter dynamics over the life course.* Paper presented at the meeting of the Gerontological Association of America, San Francisco.

Alan Guttmacher Institute. (1998). *Teen sex and pregnancy.* New York: Alan Guttmacher Institute.

Albers, L. L., Selder, K. D., Bedrick, E. J., Teaf, D., & Peralta, P. (2005). Midwifery care measures in the second stage of labor and reduction of genital tract trauma at birth: A randomized trial. *Journal of Midwifery and Women's Health, 50,* 365–372.

Aldwin, C. M., & Levenson, M. R. (2001). Stress, coping, and health at midlife: A developmental perspective. In M. E. Lachman (Ed.), *Handbook of midlife development.* New York: John Wiley.

Aldwin, C. M., Spiro, A., Levenson, M. R., & Cupertino, A. P. (2001). Longitudinal findings from the Normative Aging Study: III. Personality, individual health trajectories, and mortality. *Psychology and Aging, 16,* 450–465.

Aldwin, C. M., Spiro, A., & Park, C. L. (2006). Health, behavior, and optimal aging. In J. E. Birren & K. W. Schaie (Eds.), *Handbook of the psychology of aging* (6th ed.). San Diego: Academic Press.

Alegre, M. & Welsch, D. (2003). *Maxine Hong Kingston after the fire.* www.powers.com./authors.

Alexander, P. A. (2006). *Psychology in learning and instruction.* Upper Saddle River NJ: Prentice Hall.

Alexander, R. T., & Radisch, D. (2005). Sudden infant death syndrome risk factors with regards to sleep position, sleep surface, and co-sleeping. *Journal of Forensic Science, 50,* 147–151.

Alexopoulos, P., Grimmer, T., Perneczky, R., Domes, G., & Kurz, A. (2006). Do all patients with mild cognitive impairment progress to dementia? *Journal of the American Geriatric Society, 54,* 1008–1010.

Aliyu, M. H., Salihu, H. M., Blankson, M. L., Alexander, G. R., & Keith, L. (2004). Risks in triplet pregnancy: Advanced maternal age, premature rupture of membranes, and risk of mortality. *Journal of Reproductive Medicine, 49,* 721–726.

Allan, R., & Scheidt, S. (Eds.). (1996). *Heart and mind.* Washington, DC: American Psychological Association.

Allen, J. P., Hauser, S. T., & Borman-Spurrell, E. (1996). Attachment security and related sequelae of severe adolescent psychopathology: An eleven-year follow-up study. *Journal of Consulting and Clinical Psychology, 64,* 254–263.

Allen, J. P., Kuperminc, G. P., Moore, C. (2005, April). *Stability and predictors of change in attachment security across adolescence.* paper presented at the Meeting of the Society for Research on Child Development, Atlanta.

Allen, J. P., Marsh, P. A., McFarland, F. C., McElhaney, K. B., Land, D. J., Jodl, K. M., et al. (2002). Attachment and autonomy as predictors of the development of social skills and deviance during mid-adolescence. *Journal of Consulting & Clinical Psychology, 70,* 56–66.

Allen, J. P., McElhaney, K. B., Land, D. J., Kuperminic, G. P., Moore, C. W., O-Beirne-Kelly, H., & Kilmer, S. L. (2003). A secure base in adolescence: Markers of attachment security in the mother-adolescent relationship. *Child Development, 74,* 292–307.

Allen, J. P., Moore, C., Kuperminc, G., & Bell, K. (1998). Attachment and adolescent psychosocial functioning. *Child Development, 69,* 1406–1419.

Allen, J. P., Philliber, S., Herring, S., & Kuperminic, G. P. (1997). Preventing teen pregnancy and academic failure: Experimental evaluation of a developmentally-based approach. *Child Development, 68,* 729–742.

Allen, K. R., Blieszner, R., & Roberto, K. A. (2000). Families in middle and later years: A review and critique of research in the 1990s. *Journal of Marriage and the Family, 62,* 911–926.

Allen, K. R., Blieszner, R., Roberto, K. A., Farnsworth, E., & Wilcox, K. L. (1999). Older adults and their children: Family patterns of structural diversity. *Family Relations, 48,* 151–157.

Allen, M., Brown, P., & Finlay, B. (1992). *Helping children by strengthening families.* Washington, DC: Children's Defense Fund.

Allen, V. M., Wilson, R. D., & Cheung, A. (2006). Pregnancy outcomes after assisted reproductive technology. *Journal of Obstetrics and Gynecology Canada, 28,* 220–225.

Alm, B., Lagercrantz, H., & Wennergren, G. (2006). Stop SIDS—sleeping solitary supine, sucking smoother, stopping smoking substitutes. *Acta Paediatrica, 95,* 260–262.

Almeida, D., & Horn, M. (2004). Is daily life more stressful during middle adulthood? In G. Brim, C. D. Ryff, & R. Kessler (Eds.), *How healthy we are: A national study of well-being in midlife.* Chicago: University of Chicago Press.

Al-Suleiman, S. A., Al-Janna, F. E., Rhaman, J., & Rhaman, M. S. (2006). Obstetric complications and perinatal outcomes in triplet pregnancies. *Journal of Obstetrics and Gynecology, 26,* 200–204.

Alvik, A., Haldorsen, T., Groholt, B., & Lindemann, R. (2006). Alcohol consumption before and during pregnancy comparing concurrent and retrospective reports. *Alcohol: Clinical and Experimental Research, 30,* 510–515.

Amabile, T. M. (1993). Commentary. In D. Goleman, P. Kaufman, & M. Ray. *The Creative Spirit.* New York: Plume.

Amabile, T. M., & Hennessey, B. A. (1992). The motivation for creativity in children. In A. K. Boggiano & T. S. Pittman (Eds.), *Achievement and motivation.* New York: Cambridge.

Amato, P. (2004). To have not: Marriage and divorce in the United States. In M. Coleman & L. Ganong (Eds.), *Handbook of contemporary families.* Thousand Oaks, CA: Sage.

Amato, P. (2005). Historical trends in divorce and dissolution. In M. A. Fine & J. H. Harvey (Eds.), *Handbook of divorce and relationship dissolution.* Mahwah, NJ: Erlbaum.

Amato, P. R. (2000). The consequences of divorce for adults and children. *Journal of Marriage and the Family, 62,* 1269–1287.

Amato, P. R., & Booth, A. (1996). A prospective study of divorce and parent-child relationships. *Journal of Marriage and the Family, 58,* 356–365.

Amato, P. R., & Cheadle, J. (2005). The long reach of divorce: Divorce and child well-being across three generations. *Journal of Marriage and the Family, 67,* 191–206.

Amato, P., & Irving, S. (2006). Historical trends in divorce and dissolution. In M. A. Fine & J. H. Harvey (Eds.), *Handbook of divorce and relationship dissolution.* Mahwah, NJ: Erlbaum.

Ambrosio, J. (2004). No child left behind. *Phi Delta Kappan, 85,* 709–711.

American Academy of Pediatrics (AAP) Work Group on Breastfeeding. (1997). Breastfeeding and the use of human milk. *Pediatrics, 100,* 1035–1039.

American Academy of Pediatrics Task Force on Infant Positioning and SIDS. (2000). Changing concepts of sudden infant death syndrome. *Pediatrics, 105,* 650–656.

American Association of Retired Persons (2002). *Tracking Study of the Baby Boomers in Midlife.* Washington, DC: AARP

American Psychological Association (2003). *Psychology: Scientific problem solvers.* Washington, DC: Author.

American Public Health Association. (2006). *Understanding the health culture of recent immigrants to the United States.* Available on the Internet at www.apha.org/ppp/red/Intro.htm

Amin, A., Monabati, A., Tadayon, A., Attaran, S. Y., & Kumar, P. V. (2006). Testicular fine needle aspiration cytology in male infertility. *Acta Cytologica, 50,* 147–150.

Amsterdam, B. K. (1968). *Mirror behavior in children under two years of age.* Unpublished doctoral dissertation. University of North Carolina, Chapel Hill.

Anastasi, A., & Urbina, S. (1996). *Psychological testing* (7th ed.). Upper Saddle River, NJ: Prentice Hall.

Anderson, C. A., & Bushman, B. J. (2001). Effects of violent video games on aggressive behavior, aggressive cognition, aggressive affect, physiological arousal, and prosocial behavior: A meta-analytic review of the scientific literature. *Psychological Science, 12,* 353–359.

Anderson, D. R., Huston, A. C., Schmitt, K., Linebarger, D. L., & Wright, J. C. (2001). Early childhood viewing and adolescent behavior: The recontact study. *Monographs of the Society for Research in Child Development, 66* (1, Serial No. 264).

Anderson, D. R., Lorch, E. P., Field, D. E., Collins, P. A., & Nathan, J. G. (1985, April). *Television viewing at home: Age trends in visual attention and time with TV.* Paper presented at the biennial meeting of the Society for Research in Child Development, Toronto.

Anderson, E., Greene, S. M., Hetherington, E. M., & Clingempeel, W. G. (1999). The dynamics of parental remarriage. In E. M. Hetherington (Ed.), *Coping with divorce, single parenting, and remarriage.* Mahwah, NJ: Erlbaum.

Anderson, J. E., Ebrahim, S., Floyd, L., & Atrash, H. (2006, in press). Prevalence of risk factors for adverse pregnancy outcomes during pregnancy and the preconception period—United States, 2002–2004. *Maternal and Child Health Journal.*

Anderson, J. E., Santelli, J. S., & Morrow, B. (2006). Trends in adolescent contraceptive use, unprotected and poorly protected sex, 1991–2003. *Journal of Adolescent Health, 38,* 734–739.

Anderson, J. L., Waller, D. K., Canfield, M. A., Shaw, G. M., Watkins, M. L., & Werler, M. M. (2005). Maternal obesity, gestational diabetes, and central nervous system birth defects. *Epidemiology, 16,* 87–92.

Anderson, J., Moffatt, L., & Shapiro, J. (2006). Reconceptualizing language education in early childhood: Socio-cultural perspectives. In B. Spodek & O. N. Saracho (Eds.), *Handbook of research on the education of young children* (2nd ed.). Mahwah, NJ: Erlbaum.

Anderson, L. M., Shinn, C., Fullilove, M. T., Scrimshaw, S. C., Fielding, J. E., Normand, J., & Carande-Kulis, V. G. (2003). The effectiveness of early childhood development programs: A systematic review. *American Journal of Preventive Medicine, 24* (3 Supplement), 32–46.

Anderson, P. A., (2006). Sex differences that make a difference: Social evolution and reproduction. In K. Dindia & D. J. Canary (Eds.), *Sex differences and similarities in communication.* Mahwah, NJ: Erlbaum.

Anderson, S. L., Terry, D. F., Wilcox, M. A., Babineau, T., Malek, K., & Perls, T. T. (2005). Cancer in the oldest old. *Mechanisms of Aging and Development, 126,* 263–267.

Anderton, B. H. (2002). Aging of the brain. *Mechanisms of Aging and Development, 123,* 811–817.

Ando, M., Tsuda, A., & Moorey, S. (2006). Preliminary study of reminiscence therapy on depression and self-esteem in cancer patients. *Psychological Reports, 98,* 339–346.

Andrade, S. E., Gurwitz, J. H., Davis, R. L., Chan, K. A., Finkelstein, J. A., Fortman, K., McPhillips, H., Raebel, M. A., Roblin, D., Smith, D. H. Yood, M. U., Morse, A. N., & Platt, R. (2004). Prescription drug use in pregnancy. *American Journal of Obstetrics and Gynecology, 191,* 398–407.

Andrulis, D. P. (2005). Moving beyond the status quo in reducing racial and ethnic disparities in children's health. *Public Health Reports, 120,* 370–377.

Angel, J. L., Douglas, N., & Angel, R. J. (2003). Gender, widowhood, and long-term care in the older Mexican population. *Journal of Women and Aging, 15,* 89–105.

Angel, R. J., & Angel, J. L. (2006). Diversity and aging in the United States. In R. H. Binstock & L. K. George (Eds.), *Handbook of aging and the social sciences* (6th ed.). San Diego: Academic Press.

Angel, R. J., Frisco, M., Angel, J. L., & Chiriboga, D. A. (2004). Financial strain and health among elderly Mexican-origin individuals. *Journal of Health and Social Behavior, 44,* 536–551.

Annesi, J. J. (2005). Correlations of depression and total moods disturbance with physical activity and self-concept in preadolescents enrolled in an afterschool exercise program. *Psychological Reports, 96,* 891–898.

Ano, G. G., & Vasconcelles, E. B. (2005). Religious coping and psychological adjustment to stress: A meta-analysis. *Journal of Clinical Psychology, 61,* 461–480.

Anstey, K. J., & Smith, G. A. (1999). Interrelationships among biological markers of aging, health, activity, acculturation, and cognitive performance in late adulthood. *Psychology and Aging, 14,* 605–618.

Antai-Otong, D. (2003). Suicide: Life span considerations. *Nursing Clinics of North America, 38,* 137–150.

Antelmi, I., de Paula, R. S., Shinzato, A. R., Peres, C. A., Mansur, A. J., & Grupi, C. J. (2004). Influence of age, gender, body mass index, and functional capacity heart rate variability in a cohort of subjects without heart disease. *American Journal of Cardiology, 93,* 381–385.

Anthony Greenwald & Associates. (2000). *Current views toward retirement: A poll.* New York: Author.

Anton, R. F., & others. (2006). Combined pharmacotherapies and behavioral interventions for alcohol dependence. *Journal of the American Medical Association, 295,* 2003–2017.

Antonacci, P. A. P., & O'Callaghan, C. M. (2006). *A handbook for literacy instructional and assessment strategies, K-8.* Boston: Allyn & Bacon.

Antonucci, T. C. & Akiyama, H. (2002). Aging and close relationships over the life span. *International Society for the Study of Behavioural Development Newsletter* (1, Serial No. 41), 2–5.

Antonucci, T. C. (1989). Understanding adult social relationships. In K. Kreppner & R. M. Lerner (Eds.), *Family systems and life-span development*. Hillsdale, NJ: Erlbaum.

Antonucci, T. C. (1990). Social supports and relationships. In R. H. Binstock & L. K. George (Eds.), *Handbook of aging and the social sciences*. San Diego: Academic Press.

Antonucci, T. C. (2004). Unpublished review of Santrock *Life-Span development (10th Ed.)*. New York: McGraw-Hill.

Antonucci, T. C., Lansford, J. E., & Akiyama, H. (2001). The impact of positive and negative aspects of marital relationships and friendships on the well-being of older adults. In J. P. Reinhardt (Ed.), *Negative and positive support*. Mahwah, NJ: Erlbaum.

Antonucci, T. C., Lansford, J. E., & Schaberg, L., Smith, J., Baltes, M., Akiyama, H., Takahashi, K., & Fuhrer, R. (2001). Widowhood and illness: A comparison of social network characteristics in France, Germany, Japan, and the United States. *Psychology and Aging, 16*, 655–665.

Antonucci, T. C., Vandewater, E. A., & Lansford, J. E. (1998). Extended family relationships. In H. S. Friedman (Ed.), *Encyclopedia of mental health* (Vol. 2). San Diego: Academic Press.

Antonucci, T. C., Vandewater, E. A., & Lansford, J. E. (2000). Adulthood and aging: Social processes and development. In A. Kazdin (Ed.), *Encyclopedia of psychology*. Washington, DC, & New York: American Psychological Association and Oxford University Press.

Apostolova, L. G., Dutton, R. A., Dinov, I. D., Hayashi, K. M., Toga, A. W., Cummings, J. L., & Thompson, P. M. (2006). Conversion of mild cognitive impairment to Alzheimer disease predicted by hippocampal atrophy maps. *Archives of Neurology, 63*, 693–699.

Aquilino, W. S. (2005). Impact of family structure on parental attitudes toward the economic support of adult children over the transition to adulthood. *Journal of Family Issues, 26*, 143–167.

Araceli, G., Castro, J., Cesena, J., & Toro, J. (2005). Anorexia nervosa in male adolescents: Body image, eating attitudes, and psychological traits. *Journal of Adolescent Health, 36*, 221–226.

Arbuckle, T. Y., Maag, U., Pushkar, D., & Chalkelsen, J. S. (1998). Individual differences in trajectory of intellectual development over 45 years of adulthood. *Psychology and Aging, 13*, 663–675.

Archer, S. L. (1989). The status of identity: Reflections on the need for intervention. *Journal of Adolescence, 12*, 345–359.

Archer, S. L., & Waterman, A. S. (1994). Adolescent identity development: Contextual perspective. In C. B. Fisher & R. M. Lerner (Eds.), *Applied developmental psychology*. New York: McGraw-Hill.

Archibald, A. B., Graber, J. A., & Brooks-Gunn, J. (1999). Associations among parent-adolescent relationships, pubertal growth, dieting, and body image in young adolescent girls: A short-term longitudinal study. *Journal of Research on Adolescence, 9*, 395–415.

Archibald, A. B., Graber, J. A., & Brooks-Gunn, J. (2003). Pubertal processes and physical growth in adolescence. In G. R. Adams & M. Berzonsky (Eds.), *Handbook on adolescence*. Malden, MA: Blackwell.

Archibald, S. L., Fennema-Notetine, C., Gamst, A., Riley, E. P., Mattson, S. N., & Jernigan, T. L. (2001). Brain dysmorphology* in individuals with severe prenatal alcohol exposure. *Developmental Medicine and Child Neurology, 43*, 148–154.

Arehart, D. M., & Smith, P. H. (1990). Identity in adolescence: Influences on dysfunction and psychosocial task issues. *Journal of Youth and Adolescence, 19*, 63–72.

Arenas, A., Bosworth, K., Kwadayi, H. P., & Compare, A. (2006). Civic service through schools: an international perspective. *Journal of Comparative Education, 36*, 23–40.

Arendt, R., Angelopoulos, J., Salvator, A., & Singer, L. (1999). Motor development of cocaine-exposed children at age two years. *Pediatrics, 103*, 86–92.

Areosa, S., A., Sheriff, F., & McShane, R. (2005). Memantine for dementia. *Cochrane Database systems Review, 18*, CD003154.

Ariagno, R. L., Van Liempt, S., & Mirmiran, M. (2006, in press). Fewer spontaneous arousals during prone sleep in preterm infants at 1 and 3 months corrected age. *Journal of Perinatology*.

Arias, I. (2004). The legacy of child maltreatment: Long-term health consequences for women. *Journal of Women's Health, 13*, 468–473.

Arif, A. A., & Rohrer, J. F. (2006). The relationship between obesity, hyperglycemia symptoms, and health-related quality of life among Hispanic and non-Hispanic white children and adolescents. *BMC Family Practice, 7*, 3.

Arima, A. N. (2003). Gender stereotypes in Japanese television advertisements. *Sex Roles, 49*, 81–90.

Armour, K. L., & Callister, L. C. (2005). Prevention of triplets and higher order multiples: Trends in reproductive medicine. *Journal of Perinatal and Neonatal Nursing, 19*, 103–111.

Arnett, J. J. (1995, March). *Are college students adults?* Paper presented at the meeting of the Society for Research in Child Development, Indianapolis.

Arnett, J. J. (2000). Emerging adulthood. *American Psychologist, 55*, 469–480.

Arnett, J. J. (2004). *Emerging adulthood*. New York: Oxford U. Press.

Arnett, J. J. (2006). Emerging adulthood: Understanding the new way of coming of age. In J. J. Arnett, J. L. Tanner (Eds.), *Emerging adults in America*. Washington, DC: American Psychological Association.

Arnett, J. J., & Tanner, J. (Eds.) (2006), *Advances in emerging adulthood*. Washington, DC: American Psychological Association.

Aron, A., Fisher, H., Mashek, D. J., Strong, G., Li, H., & Brown, L. L. (2005). Reward, motivation, and emotion are associated with early-stage intense romantic love. *Journal of Neurophysiology, 94*, 327–337.

Aronson, E. (1986, August). *Teaching students things they think they already know about: The case of prejudice and desegregation*. Paper presented at the meeting of the American Psychological Association, Washington, DC.

Aronson, J. M. (2002). Stereotype threat: Contending and coping with Unnerving Expectations. *Improving academic achievement*. San Diego: Academic Press.

Aronson, J. M., Fried, C. B., & Good, C. (2002). Reducing the effects of stereotype threat on African American college students by shaping theories of intelligence. *Journal of Experimental Social Psychology, 38*, 113–125.

Aronson, J. M., Lustina, M. J., Good, C., Keough, K., Steele, C. M., & Brown, J. (1999). When white men can't do math: Necessary and sufficient factors in stereotype threat. *Journal of Experimental Social Psychology, 35*, 29–46.

Arpanantikul, M. (2004). Midlife experiences of Thai women. *Journal of Advanced Nursing, 47*, 49–56.

Arria, A. M., & others. (2006). Methamphetamine and other substance use during pregnancy: Preliminary estimates from the Infant Development, Environment, and Lifestyle (IDEAL) Study. *Maternal and Child Health Journal, 5*, 1–10.

Arshad, S. H. (2005). Primary prevention of asthma and allergy. *Journal of Allergy and Clinical Immunology, 116*, 3–14.

Arvanitakis, Z., Wilson, R. S., Aggarwad, N. T., & Bennett, D. A. (2006). Diabetes and function in different cognitive systems in older adults without dementia. *Diabetes Care, 29*, 560–565.

Aschkenasy, M. T., & Rothenhaus, T. C. (2006). Trauma and falls in the elderly. *Emergency Clinics of North America, 24*, 413–432.

Ashdown-Lambert, J. R. (2005). A review of low birth weight: Predictors, precursors, and morbidity outcomes. *Journal of Research in Society and Health, 125*, 76–83.

Asher, J., & Garcia, R. (1969). The optimal age to learn a foreign language. *Modern Language Journal, 53*, 334–341.

Ashkenazi, A., & Silberstein, S. D. (2006). Hormone-related headache: Pathophysiology and treatment. *CNS Drugs, 20*, 125–141.

Ashy, M. A. (2004). Saudi Arabia. In K. Malley-Morrison (Ed.), *International perspectives on family violence and abuse*. Mahwah, NJ: Erlbaum.

Aslin, R. N., Jusczyk, P. W., & Pisoni, D. B. (1998). Speech and auditory processing during infancy: Constraints on and precursors to language. In W. Damon (Ed.), *Handbook of child psychology, 5th Ed, Vol. 2*. New York: Wiley.

Atchley, R. C., & Barusch, A. (2004). *Social forces and aging* (10th ed). Belmont, CA: Wadsworth.

Ateah, C. A. (2005). Maternal use of physical punishment in response to child misbehavior: Implications for child abuse prevention. *Child Abuse and Neglect, 29*, 169–185.

Atiyeh, G. N., & El-Mohandes, A. (2005) Preventive healthcare of infants in a region of Lebanon: Parental beliefs, attitudes, and behaviors. *Maternal and Child Health Journal 9*, 83–90.

Atkinson, A. P., & Wheeler, M. (2004). The grain of domains: The evolutionary-psychological case against domain-general cognition. *Mind and Language, 19*, 147–176.

Atkinson, R. (1988). *The teenage world: Adolescent self-image in ten countries*. New York: Plenum Press.

Atkinson, R. M., Ryan, S. C., & Turner, J. A. (2001). Variation among aging alcoholic patients in treatment. *American Journal of Geriatric Psychiatry, 9*, 275–282.

Attie, I., Brooks-Gunn, J. (1989). Development of eating problems in adolescent girls: A longitudinal study. *Developmental Psychology, 25*, 70–79.

Auchus, R. J., & Rainey, W. E. (2004). Adrenarche— physiology, biochemistry, and human disease. *Clinical Endocrinology. 60*, 288–296.

Aud, M. A., Bostick, J. E., Marek, K. D., & McDaniel, R. W. (2006). Introducing baccalaureate student nurses to gerontological nursing. *Journal of Professional Nursing, 22*, 73–78.

Avgil, M., & Ornoy, A. (2006). Herpes simplex virus and Epstein-Barr virus infections in pregnancy: Consequences of neonatal or intrauterine infection. *Reproductive Toxicology, 21*, 436–445.

Avis, N. E. (1999). Women's health at midlife. In S. L. Willis & J. D. Reid (Eds.), *Life in the middle: Psychological and social development in middle age*. San Diego: Academic Press.

Avis, N. E., Zhao, X., Johannes, C. B., Ory, M., Brockwell, S., & Greendale, G. A. (2005). Correlates of sexual function among multi-ethnic middle-aged women: Results from the Study of Women's Health Across the Nation (SWAN). *Menopause, 12*, 385–398.

Aviv, A., Shay, J., Christensen, K., & Wright, W. (2005). The longevity gap: Are telomeres the explanation? *Science of Aging, Knowledge, and Environment, 8*, 16.

Avolio, B. J., & Sosik, J. J. (1999). A life-span framework for assessing the impact of work on white-collar workers. In S. L. Willis & J. D. Reid (Eds.), *Life in the middle: Psychological and social development in middle age*. San Diego: Academic Press.

Awan, T. M., Sattar, A., & Khattak, E. G. (2005). Frequency of growth hormone deficiency in short statured children. *Journal of the College Physicians and Surgeons Pakistan, 15,* 295–298.

Ayres, A., & Johnson, T. R. (2005). Management of multiple pregnancy: Prenatal care—part I. *Obstetrical and Gynecological Survey, 60,* 527–537.

Azar, S. T. (2002). Parenting and child maltreatment. In M. H. Bornstein (Ed.), *Handbook of parenting* (2nd ed., Vol. 4). Mahwah, NJ: Erlbaum.

Azar, S. T. (2003). Adult development and parenting. In J. Demick & C. Andreoletti (Eds.), *Handbook of adult development.* New York: Kluwer.

Babalola, O. E., Murdoch, I. E., Cousens, S., Abiose, A., & Jones, B. (2003). Blindness: How to assess numbers and causes. *British Journal of Ophthalmology, 87,* 282–284.

Babor, T. F., & Del Boca, F. K. (Eds.) (2003). *Treatment matching in alcoholism.* Cambridge: Cambridge University Press.

Bacak, S. J., Baptiste-Roberts, K., Amon, E., Ireland, B., & Leet, T. (2005). Risk factors for neonatal mortality among extremely-low-birthweight infants. *American Journal of Obstetrics and Gynecology, 192,* 862–867.

Bacchini, D., Magliulo, F. (2003). Self-image and perceived self-efficacy during adolescence. *Journal of Youth and Adolescence, 32,* 337–350.

Bachman, J. G., Johnston, L. D., O'Malley, P., & Schulenberg, J. (1996). Transitions in drug use during late adolescence and young adulthood. In J. A. Graber, J. Brooks-Gunn, & A. C. Petersen (Eds.), *Transitions through adolescence.* Mahwah, NJ: Erlbaum.

Bachman, J. G., O'Malley, P. M., Schulenberg, J., Johnston, L. D., Bryant, A. L., & Merline, A. C. (2002). *The decline of substance abuse in young adulthood.* Mahwah, NJ: Erlbaum.

Backman, L., Small, B. J., & Wahlin, A. (2001). Aging and memory: Cognitive and behavioral processes. In J. E. Birren & K. W. Schaie (Eds.), *Handbook of the psychology of aging* (5th ed.). San Diego: Academic Press.

Baddeley, A. (2000). Short-term and working memory. In E. Tulving & F. I. M. Craik (Eds.), *The Oxford handbook of memory.* New York: Oxford University Press.

Bagwell, C. L. (2004). Friendships, peer networks, and antisocial behavior. In J. B. Kupersmidt & K. A. Dodge (Eds.), *Children's peer relations.* Washington, DC: American Psychological Association.

Bahl, R., Frost, C., Kirkwood, B. R., Edmond, K., Martines, J., Bhandari, N., & Arthur, P. (2005). Infant feeding patterns and risk of death and hospitalization in the first half of infancy: Multicentre cohort study. *Bulletin of the World Health Organization, 83,* 418–426.

Bahrick, H. P. (1984). Semantic memory content in permastore: Fifty years of memory for Spanish learned in school. *Journal of Experimental Psychology: General, 113,* 1–35.

Bailey, B. N., Delaney-Black, V., Covington, C. Y., Ager, J., Janisse, J., Hannigan, J. H., & Sokol, R. J. (2004). Prenatal exposure to binge drinking and cognitive and behavioral outcomes at age 7 years. *American Journal of Obstetrics and Gynecology, 191,* 1037–1043.

Bailey, L. B., & Berry, R. J. (2005). Folic acid supplementation and the occurrence of congenital heart defects, orofacial clefts, multiple births, and miscarriage. *American Journal of Clinical Nutrition, 81,* 1213S–1217S.

Bailit, J. L., Love, T. E., & Dawson, N. V. (2006). Quality of obstetric care and risk-adjusted primary cesarean delivery rates. *American Journal of Obstetrics and Gynecology, 194,* 402–407.

Baillargeon, R. (1995). The object concept revisited: New directions in the investigation of infants' physical knowledge, In C. E. Granrud (Ed.), *Visual perception and cognition in infancy.* Hillsdale, NJ: Erlbaum.

Baillargeon, R. (2004). The acquisition of physical knowledge in infancy: A summary in eight lessons. In U. Goswami (Ed.), *Blackwell handbook of childhood cognitive development.* Malden, MA: Blackwell.

Baillargeon, R., & Devos, J. (1991). Object permanence in young children: Further evidence. *Child Development, 62* (1991), 1227–1246.

Baird, A. A., Gruber, S. A., Cohen, B. M., Renshaw, R. J., & Yurgelun-Todd, D. A. (1999). MRI of the amygdala in children and adolescents. *American Academy of Child and Adolescent Psychiatry, 38,* 195–199.

Bakeman, R, & Brown, J. V. (1980). Early interaction: Consequences for social and mental development at three years. *Child Development, 51,* 437–447.

Baker, S.R. (2006). Towards an idiopathic understanding of the role of social problem solving in daily event, mood, and health experiences: A prospective daily diary approach. *British Journal of Health Psychology, 11,* 513–531.

Baldwin, J. D., & Baldwin, J. I. (1998). Sexual behavior. In H. S. Friedman (Ed.), *Encyclopedia of mental health* (Vol. 3). San Diego: Academic Press.

Baldwin, S., & Hoffman, J. F. (2002). The dynamics of self-esteem: A growth curve analysis. *Journal of Youth and Adolescence, 31,* 101–113.

Ball, K., & others. (2003). Effects of cognitive training interventions with older adults. *Journal of the American Medical Association, 288,* 2271–2281.

Ballem, K. D., & Plunkett, K. (2005). Phonological specificity in children at 1; 2. *Journal of Child Language, 32,* 159–173.

Balota, D. A., Dolan, P. O., & Ducheck, J. M. (2000). Memory changes in healthy older adults. In E. Tulving & F. I. M. Craik (Eds.), *The Oxford handbook of memory.* New York: Oxford University Press.

Baltes, P. B. (1987). Theoretical propositions of life-span developmental psychology: On the dynamics between growth and decline. *Developmental Psychology, 23,* 611–626.

Baltes, P. B. (2000). Life-span developmental theory. In A. Kazdin (Ed.), *Encyclopedia of psychology* Washington, DC, & New York: American Psychological Association and Oxford University Press.

Baltes, P. B. (2003). On the incomplete architecture of human ontogeny: Selection, optimization, and compensation as foundation for developmental theory. In U. M. Staudinger & U. Lindenberger (Eds.), *Understanding human development.* Boston: Kluwer.

Baltes, P. B., & Baltes, M. M. (1990). Psychological perspectives on successful aging: The model of selective optimization with compensation. In P. B. Baltes & M. M. Baltes (Eds.), *Successful aging: Perspectives from the behavioral sciences.* New York: Cambridge University Press.

Baltes, P. B., & Kunzmann, U. (2003). Wisdom. *The Psychologist, 16,* 131–132.

Baltes, P. B., & Lindenberger, U. (1997). Emergence of a powerful connection between sensory and cognitive functions across the adult life span: A new window to the study of cognitive aging? *Psychology and Aging, 12,* 12–21.

Baltes, P. B., & Smith, J. (1990). The psychology of wisdom and its ontogenesis. In R. J. Sternberg (Ed.), *Wisdom.* New York: Cambridge University Press.

Baltes, P. B., & Smith, J. (2003). New frontiers in the future of aging: From successful aging of the young old to the dilemmas of the fourth age. *Gerontology, 49,* 123–135.

Baltes, P. B., Freund, A. M., & Li, S.-C. (2005). The psychological science of human aging. In M. Johnson, V. L. Bengtson, P. G. Coleman & T. Kirkwood (Eds.), *The Cambridge handbook of age and aging.* Cambridge: Cambridge University Press.

Baltes, P. B., Glück, J., & Kunzmann, U. (2002). Wisdom: Its structure and function in regulating successful life span development. In C. R. Snyder & S. J. Lopez (Eds.), *Handbook of positive psychology.* New York: Oxford University Press.

Baltes, P. B., Lindenberger, U., & Staudinger, U. (2006). Life-span theory in developmental psychology. In W. Damon & R. Lerner (Eds.), *Handbook of child psychology* (6th ed.). New York: Wiley.

Baltes, P. B., Reuter-Lorenz, P., & Rösler. F. (Eds.) (2006). *Lifespan development and the brain.* New York: Cambridge University Press.

Banci, A., & Singh, V. (2004), Dopamine dysregulation syndrome in Parkinson's disease patients: From reward to penalty. *Annals of Neurology, 59,* no. 5, 852–858.

Bandura, A. (1986). *Social foundations of thought and action: A social cognitive theory.* Englewood Cliffs, NJ: Prentice Hall.

Bandura, A. (1997). *Self-efficacy: The exercise of control.* New York: W. H. Freeman.

Bandura, A. (1998, August). *Swimming against the mainstream: Accentuating the positive aspects of humanity.* Paper presented at the meeting of the American Psychological Association, San Francisco.

Bandura, A. (1999). Moral disengagement in the perpetuation of inhumanities. *Personality and Social Psychology Review, 3,* 193–209.

Bandura, A. (2001). Social cognitive theory. *Annual Review of Psychology* (Vol. 52). Palo Alto, CA: Annual Reviews.

Bandura, A. (2002). Selective moral disengagement in the exercise of moral agency. *Journal of Moral Education, 31,* 101–119.

Bandura, A. (2004, May). *Toward a psychology of human agency.* Paper presented at the meeting of the American Psychological Society, Chicago.

Bandura, A. (2006). Going global with social cognitive theory: From prospect to paydirt. In S. I. Donaldson, D. E. Berger, & K. Pezdek (Eds.), *The rise of applied psychology: New frontiers and rewarding careers.* Mahwah, NJ: Erlbaum.

Banister, N. A., Jastrow, S. T., Hodges, V., Loop, R., & Gillham, M. B. (2004). Diabetes self-management training program in a community clinic improves patient outcomes at modest cost. *Journal of the American Diet Association, 104,* 807–810.

Banja, J. (2005). Talking to the dying. *Case Manager, 16,* 37–39.

Bank, L., Burraston, B., & Snyder, J. (2004). Sibling conflict and ineffective parenting as predictors of adolescent boys' antisocial behavior and peer difficulties: Additive and interactive effects. *Journal of Research on Adolescence, 14,* 99–125.

Banks, E. C. (1993, March). *Moral education curriculum in a multicultural context: The Malaysian primary curriculum.* Paper presented at the biennial meeting of the Society for Research in Child Development, New Orleans.

Banks, J. A. (2003). *Teaching strategies for ethnic studies* (7th ed.). Boston: Allyn & Bacon.

Banks, J. A. (2006). *Cultural diversity and education* (5th ed.). Boston: Allyn & Bacon.

Banks, M. S. (2005). The benefits and costs of combining information between and within the senses. In J. J. Reiser, J. J. Lockman, & C. A. Nelson (Eds.), *The role of action in learning and development.* Mahwah, NJ: Erlbaum.

Banks, M. S., & Salapatek, P. (1983). Infant visual perception. In P. H. Mussen (Ed.), *Handbook of child psychology* (4th ed., Vol. 2). New York: Wiley.

Bannon, L. (2005). *Gender: Psychological perspectives* (4th ed.). Boston: Allyn & Bacon.

Barbaresi, W. J., Katusic, S. K., Colligan, R. C., Weaver, A. L., Leibson, C. L., & Jacobsen, S. J. (2006). Long-term stimulant medication treatment of attention-deficit/hyperactivity disorder: Results from a population-based study. *Journal of Developmental and Behavioral Pediatrics, 27,* 1–10.

Barber, B. L. (2006). To have loved and lost... Adolescent romantic relationships and rejection. In A. C. Crouter & A. Booth (Eds.), *Romance and sex in adolescence and emerging adulthood.* Mahwah, NJ: Erlbaum.

Barefoot, J. C., Mortensen, E. L., Helms, J., Avlund, K., & Schroll, M. (2001). A longitudinal study of gender differences in depressive symptoms from age 50 to 80. *Psychology and Aging, 16,* 342–345.

Barker, R., & Wright, H. F. (1951). *One boy's day.* New York: Harper & Row.

Barling, J., Kelloway, E. K., & Frone, M. R. (Eds.) (2004). *Handbook of work and stress.* Thousand Oaks, CA: Sage.

Barnes, L. L., Mendes de Leon, C. F., Wilson, R. S., Bienias, J. L., & Evans, D. A. (2004a). Social resources and cognitive decline in a population of older African Americans and Whites. *Neurology, 63,* 2322–2326.

Barnes, L. L., Mendes de Leon, C. F., Wilson, R. S., Bienias, J. L., Bennett, D. A., & Evans, D. A. (2004b). Racial differences in perceived discrimination in a community population of older Blacks and Whites. *Journal of Aging and Health, 16,* 315–317.

Barnet, B., Arroyo, C., Devoe, M., Duggan, A. K. (2004). Reduced school dropout rates among adolescent mothers receiving school-based prenatal care. *Archives of Pediatric and Adolescent Medicine, 158,* 262–268.

Barnett, R. C. (2001). Work-family balance. In J. Worell (Ed.), *Encyclopedia of women and gender.* San Diego: Academic Press.

Barnett, R. C., Gareis, K. C., James, J. B., & Steele, J. (2001, August). *Planning ahead: College seniors' concerns about work-family conflict.* Paper presented at the meeting of the American Psychological Association, San Francisco.

Baron, N. S. (1992). *Growing up with language.* Reading, MA: Addison-Wesley.

Barone, D., Hardman, D., & Taylor, J. (2006). *Reading first in the classroom.* Boston: Allyn & Bacon.

Bar-Oz, B., Levicheck, Z., Moretti, M. E., Mah, C., Andreou, S., & Koren, G. (2004). Pregnancy outcome following rubella vaccination: A prospective study. *American Journal of Medical Genetics, 130A,* 52–54.

Barr, H. M., & Streissguth, A. P. (2001). Identifying maternal self-reported alcohol use associated with fetal alcohol disorders. *Alcoholism: Clinical and Experimental Research, 25,* 283–287.

Barrett, A. E., & Turner, R. J. (2005). Family structure and mental health: The mediating effects of socioeconomic status, family process, and social stress. *Journal of Health and Social Behavior, 46,* 156–169.

Barrett, D. E., Radke-Yarrow, M., & Klein, R. E. (1982). Chronic malnutrition and child behavior: Effects of calorie supplementation on social and emotional functioning at school age. *Developmental Psychology, 18,* 541–556.

Barton, W. H. (2004). Bridging juvenile justice and positive youth development. In S. F. & M. A. Hamilton (Eds.), *The youth development handbook.* Thousand Oaks, CA: Sage.

Barton, W. H. (2005). Juvenile justice policies and programs. In J. M. Jenson & M. W. Fraser (Eds.), *Social policy for children and families.* Thousand Oaks, CA: Sage.

Baskett, L. M., & Johnson, S. M. (1982). The young child's interaction with parents versus siblings. *Child Development, 53,* 643–650.

Bass, S. A. (2005). Medicare reform—a wolf in sheep's clothing. *Journal of Aging and Social Policy, 17,* 1–17.

Bassett, S. S., Yousem, D. M., Cristinzio, C., Kusevic, I., Yassa, M. A., Caffo, B. S., & Zeger, S. L. (2006). Familial risk for Alzheimer's disease alters fMRI activation patterns. *Brain, 129,* 1229–1239.

Bateman, B. T., & Simpson, L. L. (2006). Higher rate of stillbirth at the extremes of reproductive age: A large nationwide sample of deliveries in the United States. *American Journal of Obstetrics and Gynecology, 194,* 840–845.

Bates, A. S., Fitzgerald, J. F., Dittus, R. S., & Wollinsky, F. D. (1994). Risk factors for underimmunization in poor urban infants. *Journal of the American Medical Association, 272,* 1105–1109.

Bates, E. (1990). Language about me and you: Pronomial reference and the emerging concept of self. In D. Cicchetti & M. Beeghly (Eds.), *The self in transition: Infancy to childhood* (pp. 165–182). Chicago: University of Chicago Press.

Baud, P. (2005). Personality traits as intermediary phenotypes in suicidal behavior: Genetic issues. *American Journal of Medical Genetics, 133C,* 34–42.

Bauer, P. J. (2004). Early memory development. In *handbook of childhood cognitive developments.* Malden, MA: Blackwell. U. Goswami (Ed.).

Bauer, P. J. (2005). Developments in declarative memory. *Psychological Science, 16,* 41–47.

Bauer, P. J. (2006). Event memory. In W. Damon & R. Lerner (Eds.), *Handbook of child psychology* (6th ed.). New York: Wiley.

Bauer, P. J., Wenner, J. A., Dropik, P. L., & Wewerka, S. S. (2000). Parameters of remembering and forgetting in the transition from infancy to early childhood. *Monographs of the Society for Research in Child Development, 65* (4, Serial No. 263).

Bauer, P. J., Wiebe, S. A., Carver, L. J., Waters, J. M., & Nelson, C. A. (2003). Developments in long-term explicit memory late in the first year of life: Behavioral and electrophysiological indices. *Psychological Science, 14,* 629–635.

Bauman, K. E., Ennett, S. T., Foshee, V. A., Pemberton, M., King, T. S., & Koch, G. G. (2002). Influence of a family program on adolescent smoking and drinking prevalence. *Prevention Science, 3,* 35–42.

Baumeister, R. F., Campbell, J. D., Krueger, J. I., & Vohs, K. D. (2003). Does high self-esteem cause better performance, interpersonal success, happiness, or healthier lifestyles? *Psychological Science in the Public Interest, 4* (No. 1), 1–44.

Baumeister, R. F., & Vohs, K. D. (2002). The pursuit of meaningfulness in life. In C. R. Snyder & S. J. Lopez (Eds.), *Handbook of positive psychology.* New York: Oxford University Press.

Baumrind, D. (1971). Current patterns of parental authority. *Development Psychology Monographs, 4* (1, Pt. 2).

Baumrind, D. (1999, November). Unpublished review of J. W. Santrock's *Child Development* (9th ed.). New York: McGraw-Hill.

Baumrind, D., Larzelere, R. E., & Cowan, P. A. (2002). Ordinary physical punishment: Is it harmful? Comment on Gershoff. *Psychological Bulletin, 128,* 590–595.

Bauserman, R. (2002). Child adjustment in joint-custody versus sole-custody arrangements: A meta-analytic review. *Journal of Family Psychology, 16,* 91–102.

Baxter, G. W., Stuart, W. J., & Stewart, W. J. (1998). *Death and the adolescent.* Toronto: University of Toronto Press.

Bayley, N. (1943). Mental growth during the first three years. In R. G. Barker, J. S. Kounin, & H. F. Wright (Eds.), *Child behavior and development.* New York: McGraw-Hill.

Bayley, N. (1969). *Manual for the Bayley Scales of Infant Development.* New York: Psychological Corporation.

Bayley, N. (1970). Development of mental abilities. In P. H. Mussen (Ed.), *Manual of child psychology* (3rd ed., Vol. 1). New York: Wiley.

Beachy, J. M. (2003). Premature infant massage in the NICU. *Neonatal Network, 22,* 39–45.

Beal, C. R. (1994). *Boys and girls: The development of gender roles.* Boston: McGraw-Hill.

Bearman, P. S., & Moody, J. (2004). Suicide and friendships among American adolescents. *American Journal of Public Health, 94,* 89–95.

Bechtold, A. G., Bushnell, E. W., & Salapatek, P. (1979, April.) *Infants' visual localization of visual and auditory targets.* Paper presented at the meeting of the Society for Research in Child Development, San Francisco.

Beck, C. T. (2002). Theoretical perspectives of postpartum depression and their treatment implications. *American Journal of Maternal/Child Nursing, 27,* 282–287.

Beck, C. T. (2006). Postpartum depression: It isn't just the blues. *American Journal of Nursing, 106,* 40–50.

Beck, M. (1992, December 7). Middle Age. *Newsweek,* pp. 50–56.

Becker-Blease, K. A., Deater-Deckard, K., Eley, T., Freyd, J. J., Stevenson, J., & Plomin, R. (2004). A genetic analysis of individual differences in dissociative behaviors in childhood and adolescence. *Journal of Child Psychology and Psychiatry, 45,* 522–532.

Bednar, R. L., Wells, M. G., & Peterson, S. R. (1995). *Self-esteem* (2nd ed.). Washington, DC: American Psychological Association.

Beeghly, M., Martin, B., Rose-Jacobs, R., Cahral, H., Heeren, T., Augustyn, M., Bellinger, D., & Frank, D. A. (2006). Prenatal cocaine exposure and children's language functioning at 6 and 9.5 years: moderating effects of child age, birthweight, and gender. *Journal of Pediatric Psychology, 31,* 98–115.

Beeri, M. S., & others. (2006). Coronary disease is associated with Alzheimer disease neuropathology in APOE4 carriers. *Neurology, 66,* 1399–1404.

Belk, C., & Borden, V. (2007). *Biology* (2nd ed.). Upper Saddle River, NJ: Prenctice Hall.

Bell, M. A., & Fox, N. A. (1992). The relations between frontal brain electrical activity and cognitive development during infancy. *Child Development, 63,* 1142–1163.

Bell, S. M., & Ainsworth, M. D. S. (1972). Infant crying and maternal responsiveness. *Child Development, 43,* 1171–1190.

Bellastella, A., Esposito, D., Conte, M., Ruocco, G., Bellastella, G., Sinisi, A. A., & Pasquali, D. (2005). Sexuality in the aging male. *Journal of Endocrinology Investigations, 28* Suppl 2, S55–S60.

Belle, D. (1999). *The after school lives of children.* Mahwah, NJ: Erlbaum.

Bellevia, G., & Frone, M. R. (2004). Work-family conflict. In J. Baring, E. K. Kelloway, & M. R. Frone (Eds.), *Handbook of work stress.* Thousand Oaks, CA: Sage.

Bellinger, D. C. (2005). Teratogen update: Lead and pregnancy. *Birth Defects Research, 73,* 409–420.

Bellinger, D. C., Leviton, A., Waternaux, C., Needleman, H., & Rabinowitz, M. (1987). Longitudinal analysis of prenatal and postnatal lead exposure and early cognitive development. *New England Journal of Medicine, 316,* 1037–1043.

Belloc, N. B., & Breslow, L. (1972). Relationships of physical health status and health practices. *Preventive Medicine, 1,* 409–421.

Belsky, J. (1981). Early human experience: A family perspective. *Developmental Psychology, 17,* 3–23.

Belsky, J., & Eggebeen, D. (1991). Early and extensive maternal employment/child care and 4–6-year-olds socioemotional development: Children of the National Longitudinal Survey of Youth. *Journal of Marriage and the Family, 53,* 1083–1099.

Belsky, J., Jaffe, S., Hsieh, K., & Silva, P. (2001). Child-rearing antecedents of intergenerational relations in young adulthood: A prospective study. *Developmental Psychology, 37,* 801–813.

Belsky, J., & Pasco Fearon, R. (2002a). Early attachment security, subsequent maternal sensitivity, and later child development: Does continuity in development depend upon continuity of caregiving? *Attachment & Human Development, 4,* 361–387.

Belsky, J., & Pasco Fearon, R. (2002b). Infant-mother attachment security, contextual risk, and early development: A moderational analysis. *Development and Psychopathology, 14,* 293–310.

Belson, W. (1978). *Television violence and the adolescent boy.* London: Saxon House.

Bendersky, M., & Sullivan, M. W. (2002). Basic methods in infant research. In A. Slater & M. Lewis (Eds.), *Infant development.* New York: Oxford University Press.

Benenson, J. F., & Health, A. (2006). Boys withdraw more in one-on-one situations, whereas girls withdraw more in groups. *Developmental Psychology, 42,* 272–282.

Benenson, J. F., Apostoleris, N. H., & Parnass, J. (1997). Age and sex differences in dyadic and group interaction. *Developmental Psychology, 33,* 538–543.

Benfey, P. (2005). *Essentials of genomics.* Upper Saddle River, NJ: Prentice Hall.

Bengtson, V. L. (1985). Diversity and symbolism in grandparental roles. In V. L. Bengtson & J. Robertson (Eds.), Grandparenthood. *Newbury Park, CA: Sage.*

Bengtson, V. L. (2001). Beyond the nuclear family: The increasing importance of multigenerational bonds. *Journal of Marriage and the Family, 63,* 1–16.

Benjet, C., & Kazdin, A. E. (2003). Spanking children: The controversies, findings, and new directions. *Clinical Psychology Review, 23,* 197–224.

Benn, P. A., Fang, M., & Egan, J. F. (2005). Trends in the use of second trimester maternal serum screening from 1991 to 2003. *Genetics in Medicine, 7,* 328–331.

Bennett, C. I. (2007). *Comprehensive multicultural education* (6th ed.). Boston: Allyn & Bacon.

Bennett, K. M. (2004). Why did he die? The attributions of cause of death among women widowed in later life. *Journal of Health Psychology, 9,* 345–353.

Bennett, K. M., Smith, P. T., & Hughes, G. M. (2005). Coping, depressive feelings, and gender differences in late life widowhood. *Aging and Mental Health, 9,* 348–353.

Bennett, S. E., & Assefi, N. P. (2005). School-based teenage pregnancy prevention programs: A systematic review of randomized controlled trials. *Journal of Adolescent Health, 36,* 72–81.

Bennett, W. I., & Gurin, J. (1982). *The dieter's dilemma: Eating less and weighing more.* New York: Basic Books.

Benson, P. L., Scales, P. C., Hamilton, S. F., & Sesma, A. (2006). Positive youth development. In W. Damon & R. Lerner (Eds.), *Handbook of child psychology* (6th ed.). New York: Wiley.

Bensore, E. (2003, February). Intelligence across cultures. *Monitor on Psychology, 34,* No. 2, 56–58.

Benz, E. J. (2004). Genotypes and phenotypes—another lesson from the hemoglobinpathies. *New England Journal of Medicine, 351,* 1532–1538.

Berado, F. M. (2003) Widowhood and its social implication. In C.D. Bryant (Ed.), *Handbook of death and dying.* Thousand Oaks, CA: Sage.

Berardi, A., Parasuraman, R., & Haxby, J. V. (2001). Overall vigilance and sustained attention decrements in healthy aging. *Experimental Aging Research, 27,* 19–39.

Berenbaum, S. A., & Bailey, J. M. (2003). Effects on gender identity of prenatal androgens and genital appearance: Evidence from girls with congenital adrenal hyperplasia. *Journal of Endocrinology and Metabolism, 88,* 1102–1106.

Berenson, G. S. (2005). Obesity—A critical issue in preventive cardiology: The Bogalusa Heart Study. *Preventive Cardiology, 8,* 234–241.

Berenson, G. S., Srinivasan, S. R., & the Bogalusa Heart Study Group (2005). Cardiovascular risk factors in youth with implications for aging: The Bogalusa Heart Study. *Neurobiology of Aging, 26,* 303–307.

Bergen, D. (1988). Stages of play development. In D. Bergen (Ed.), *Play as a medium for learning and development.* Portsmouth, NH: Heinemann.

Berk , L. E. (1994). Why children talk to themselves. *Scientific American, 271* (5), 78–83.

Berk, L. E., & Spuhl, S. T. (1995). Maternal interaction, private speech, and task performance in preschool children. *Early Childhood Research Quarterly, 10,* 145–169.

Berko Gleason, J. (2004). Unpublished review of J. W. Santrock's *Life-span development* 9th ed. (New York: McGraw-Hill).

Berko Gleason, J. (2005). *The development of language* (6th ed.). Boston: Allyn & Bacon.

Berko, J. (1958). The child's learning of English morphology. *Word, 14,* 15–177.

Berkowitz, C. D. (2004). Cosleeping: Benefits, risks, and cautions. *Advances in Pediatrics, 51,* 329–349.

Berkowitz, R. L., Roberts, J., & Minkoff, H. (2006). Challenging the strategy of maternal age-based prenatal genetic counseling. *Journal of the American Medical Association, 295,* 1446–1448.

Berlin, L., & Cassidy, J. (2000). Understanding parenting: Contributions of attachment theory and research. In J. D. Osofsky & H. E. Fitzgerald (Eds.), *WAIMH handbook of infant mental health* (Vol. 3). New York: Wiley.

Berlyne, D. E. (1960). *Conflict, arousal, and curiosity.* New York: McGraw-Hill.

Bern, S. L. (1977). On the utility of alternative procedures for assessing psychological androgyny. *Journal of Consulting and Clinical Psychology, 45,* 196–205.

Bernat, J. L. (2005). The concept and practice of brain death. *Progress in Brain Research, 150,* 369–379.

Berndt, T. J. (2002). Friendship quality and social development. *Current Directions in Psychological Science, 11,* 7–10.

Berndt, T. J., & Perry, T. B. (1990). Distinctive features and effects of early adolescent friendships. In R. Montemayor (Ed.), *Advances in adolescent research.* Greenwich, CT: JAI Press.

Berninger, V. W. (2006). Learning disabilities. In W. Damon & R. Lerner (Eds.), *Handbook of child psychology* (6th ed.). New York: Wiley.

Berninger, V. W., & Abbott, R. (2005, April). *Paths leading to reading comprehension in at-risk and normally developing second-grade readers.* Paper presented at the meeting of the Society for Research in Child Development, Atlanta.

Bernstein, J. (2004). The low-wage labor market: Trends and policy implications. In A. C. Crouter & A. Booth (Eds.), *Work-family challenges for low-income families and their children.* Mahwah, NJ: Erlbaum.

Berry, J. W. (2006). Acculturation. In M. H. Bornstein & L. R. Cote (Eds.), *Acculturation and parent-child relationships.* Mahwah, NJ: Erlbaum.

Berry, J. W., Phinney, J. S., Sam, D. L., & Vedder, P. (Eds.) (2006). *Immigrant youth in cultural transition.* Mahwah, NJ: Erlbaum.

Berscheid, E. (1988). Some comments on love's anatomy: Or, whatever happened to old-fashioned lust? In R. J. Sternberg (Ed.), *Anatomy of love.* New Haven, CT: Yale University Press.

Berscheid, E. (2000). Attraction. In A. Kazdin (Ed.), *Encyclopedia of psychology.* Washington, DC, & New York: American Psychological Association and Oxford University Press.

Berscheid, E., & Fei, J. (1977). Sexual jealousy and romantic love. In G. Clinton & G. Smith (Eds.), *Sexual jealousy.* Englewood Cliffs, NJ: Prentice-Hall.

Berscheid, E., & Reis, H. T. (1998). Attraction and close relationships. In D. T. Gilbert, S. T. Fiske, & G. Lindzey (Eds.), *Handbook of social psychology* (4th ed., Vol. 2). New York: McGraw-Hill.

Berscheid, E., Snyder, M., & Omoto, A. M. (1989). Issues in studying close relationships: Conceptualizing and measuring closeness. In C. Hendrick (Ed.), *Close relationships.* Newbury Park, CA: Sage.

Bertenthal, B. (2005). Theories, methods, and models: Discussion of the chapters by Newcombe, Thelen, & Whitmeyer. In J. J. Reiser, J. J. Lockman, & C. A. Nelson (Eds.), *The role of action in learning and development.* Mahwah, NJ: Erlbaum.

Bertrais, S., Beyeme-Ondoua, J. P., Czernichow, S., Galan, P., Hercberg, S., & Oppert, J. M. (2005). Sedentary behaviors, physical activity, and metabolic syndrome in middle-aged French subjects. *Obesity Research, 13,* 936–944.

Bertrand, R. M., & Lachman, M. E. (2003). Personality development in adulthood and old age. In I. B. Weiner (Ed.), *Handbook of psychology, Vol. VI.* New York: Wiley.

Best, D. (2001). Cross-cultural gender roles. In J. Worell (Ed.), *Encyclopedia of women and gender.* San Diego: Academic Press.

Best, J. W., & Kahn, J. V. (2006). *Research in education* (10th ed.). Boston: Allyn Bacon.

Betts, L. R., Taylor, C. P., Sekuler, A. B., & Bennett, P. J. (2005). Aging reduces center-surround antagonism in visual motion processing. *Neuron, 45,* 361–366.

Betz, N. E. (2006). Women's career development. In J. Worell & C. D. Goodheart (Eds.), *Handbook of girls' and women's psychological health.* New York: Oxford University Press.

Beutel, M. E., Weidner, W., & Brahler, E. (2006). Epidemiology of sexual dysfunction in the male population. *Andrologia, 38,* 115–121.

Beyene, Y. (1986). Cultural significance and physiological manifestations of menopause: A biocultural analysis. *Culture, Medicine and Psychiatry, 10,* 47–71.

Bhutta, Z. A., Darmstadt, G. L., Hasan, B. S., & Haws, R. A. (2005). Community-based interventions for improving perinatal and neonatal health outcomes in developing countries: A review of the evidence. *Pediatrics, 115,* 519–616.

Bialystok, E. (1993). Metalinguistic awareness: The development of children's representations in language. In C. Pratt & A. Garton (Eds.), *System of representation in children.* London: Wiley.

Bialystok, E. (1997). Effects of bilingualism and biliteracy on children's emerging concepts of print. *Developmental Psychology, 33,* 429–440.

Bialystok, E. (1999). Cognitive complexity and attentional control in the bilingual mind. *Child Development, 70,* 537–804.

Bialystok, E. (2001). *Bilingualism in development: Language, literacy, and cognition.* New York: Cambridge University Press.

Bianca, S., Ingegnosi, C., Tetto, C., Cataliotti, A., & Ettore, G. (2005). Prenatally detected trisomy 20 mosaicism and genetic counseling. *Prenatal Diagnosis, 25,* 725–726.

Bianchetti, A., Ranieri, P., Margiotta, A., & Trabucchi, M. (2006). Pharmacological treatment of Alzheimer's disease. *Aging: Clinical and Experimental Research, 18,* 158–162.

Bianchi, S. M., & Spani, D. (1986). *American women in transition.* New York: Russell Sage Foundation.

Bierman, E. J., Comijs, H. C., Jonker, C., & Beekman, A. T. (2005). Effects of anxiety versus depression on cognition in later life. *American Journal of Geriatric Psychiatry, 13,* 686–693.

Bierman, K. L. (2004). *Peer rejection.* New York: Guilford.

Bigler, R. S., Averhart, C. J., & Liben, L. S. (2003). Race and the workforce: Occupational status, aspirations, and stereotyping among African American children. *Developmental Psychology, 19,* 572–580.

Bijur, P. E., Wallston, K. A., Smith, C. A., Lifrak, S., & Friedman, S. B. (1993, August). *Gender differences in turning to religion for coping.* Paper presented at the meeting of the American Psychological Association, Toronto.

Bildt, D. (2005). Sexual harassment: Relation to other forms of discrimination and to health among women and men. *Work, 24,* 251–259.

Billman, J. (2003). *Observation and participation in early childhood settings: A practicum guide* (2ⁿᵈ ed.). Boston: Allyn & Bacon.

Billson, F. A., Fitzgerald, B. A., & Provis, J. M. (1985). Visual deprivation in infancy and childhood: Clinical aspects. *Australian and New Zealand Journal of Ophthalmology, 13,* 279–286.

Billy, J. O. G., Rodgers, J. L., & Udry, J. R. (1984). Adolescent sexual behavior and friendship choice. *Social Forces, 62,* 653–678.

BiMauro, S., Tanji, K., Bonilla, E, Palloti, F., & Schon, E. A. (2002). Mitochondrial abnormalities in muscle and other aging cells: Classification, causes, and effects. *Muscle and Nerve, 26,* 597–607.

Bindler, R. M., & Bruya, M. A. (2006). Evidence for identifying children at risk for being overweight, cardiovascular disease, and type 2 diabetes in primary care. *Journal of Pediatric Health Care, 20,* 82–87.

Bingham, C. R., & Crockett, L. J. (1996). Longitudinal adjustment patterns of boys and girls experiencing early, middle, and late sexual intercourse. *Developmental Psychology, 32,* 647–658.

Birch, E. E., Fawcett, S. L., Morale, S. E., Weakley, D. R., & Wheaton, D. H. (2005). Risk factors for accommodative estropia among hypermetropic children. *Investigations in Ophthalmology and Vision Science, 46,* 526–529.

Bird, G. W., & Schnurman-Crook, A. (2005). Professional identity and coping behaviors in dual-career couples. *Family Relations, 54,* 145–160.

Birks, J. (2006). Cholinesterase inhibitors for Alzheimer's disease. *Cochrane Database System Review, 1,* DC005593.

Birren, J. E. (2002). Unpublished review of J. W. Santrock's *Life-span development,* 9ᵗʰ ed. (New York: McGraw-Hill).

Birren, J. E. (Ed.). (1996). *Encyclopedia of gerontology.* San Diego: Academic Press.

Birren, J. E., & Schaie, K. W. (Eds.). (2001). *Handbook of the psychology of aging* (5ᵗʰ ed.). San Diego: Academic Press.

Birren, J. E., Woods, A. M., & Williams, M. V. (1980). Behavioral slowing with age: Causes, organization, & consequences. In L. W. Poon (Ed.), *Aging in the 1980s: Psychological issues.* Washington, DC: American Psychological Association.

Bisconti, T. L., Bergeman, C. S., & Boker, S. M. (2004). Emotional well-being in recently bereaved widows: A dynamical systems approach. *Journals of Gerontology: Psychological Sciences and Social Sciences, 59B,* 168–176.

Bishop, D. V., Laws, G., Adams, C., & Norbury, C. F. (2006). High heritability of speech and language impairments in 6-year-old twins demonstrated using parent and teacher report. *Behavior Genetics, 36,* 173–184.

Bisschop, M. I., Kriegsman, D. M., Beekman, A. T., & Deeg, D. J. (2004). Chronic diseases and depression. *Social Science Medicine, 59,* 721–733.

Bjarnason, T., Andersson, B., Choquet, M., Elekes, Z., Morgan, M., & Rapinett, G. (2003). Alcohol culture, family structure, and adolescent alcohol use: Multilevel modeling of frequency of heavy drinking among 15–16 year old students in 11 European countries. *Journal of Studies on Alcohol, 64,* 200–208.

Bjorklund, D. F. (2005). *Children's thinking* (4ᵗʰ ed.). Belmont, CA: Wadsworth.

Bjorklund, D. F., & Pellegrini, A. D. (2002). *The origins of human nature.* New York: Oxford University Press.

Black, M. M., & others. (2004). Special Supplemental Nutrition Program for Women, Infants, and Children participation and infants' growth and health: A multisite surveillance study. *Pediatrics, 114,* 169–176.

Black, R. A., & Hill, D. A. (2003). Over-the-counter medications in pregnancy. *American Family Physician, 67,* 2517–2524.

Blair, C., & Ramey, C. (1996). Early intervention with low birth weight infants: The path to second generation research. In M. J. Guralnick (Ed.), *The effectiveness of early intervention.* Baltimore: Paul H. Brookes.

Blair, J. M., Hanson, D. L., Jones, H., & Dworkin, M. S. (2004). Trends in pregnancy rates among women with human immunodeficiency virus. *Obstetrics and Gynecology, 103,* 663–668.

Blair, S. N. (1990, January). *Personal communication.* Aerobics Institute, Dallas.

Blair, S. N., Kohl, H. W., Paffenbarger, R. S., Clark, D. G., Cooper, K. H., & Gibbons, L. W. (1989). Physical fitness and all-cause mortality: A prospective study of healthy men and women. *Journal of the American Medical Association, 262,* 2395–2401.

Blasi, A. (2005). Moral character. A psychological approach. In D. K. Lapsley & F. C. Power (Eds.) *Character psychology and character education.* Notre Dame, IN: University of Notre Dame Press.

Blazer, D. (2002). *Depression in late life* (3ʳᵈ ed.). New York: Springer.

Blazer, D. G. (2003). Depression in late life: Review and commentary. *Journals of Gerontology A: Biological and Medical Sciences, 58,* M240–M265.

Blekesaune, M., & Solem, P. E. (2005). Working conditions and early retirement: A prospective study of retirement behavior. *Research on Aging, 27,* 3–30.

Bloch, M., Rotenberg, N., Koren, D., & Klein, E. (2005). Risk factors associated with the development of postpartum mood disorders. *Journal of Affective Disorders,* in press.

Block, J. (1993). Studying personality the long way. In D. Funder, R. D. Parke, C. Tomlinson-Keasey, & K. Widaman (Ed.), *Studying lives through time.* Washington, DC: American Psychological Association.

Block, J. H., & Block, J. (1980). The role of ego-control and ego-resiliency in the organization of behavior. In W. A. Collins (Ed.), *Minnesota symposium on child psychology* (Vol. 13). Minneapolis: University of Minnesota Press.

Bloom, B. (1985). *Developing talent in young people.* New York: Ballantine.

Bloom, B., & Dey, A. N. (2006). Summary health statistics for U.S. children: National Health Interview Survey, 2004. *Vital Health Statistics, 227,* 1–85.

Bloom, K. C., Bednarzyk, M. S., Devitt, D. L., Renault, R. A., Teaman, V., & Van Loock, D. M. (2004). Barriers to prenatal care for homeless pregnant women. *Journal of Obstetrics, Gynecologic, and Neonatal Nursing, 33,* 428–435.

Bloom, L. (1998). Language acquisition in developmental context. In W. Damon (Ed.), *Handbook of child psychology* (5ᵗʰ ed., Vol. 5). New York: Wiley.

Bloom, L., Lifter, K., & Broughton, J. (1985). The convergence of early cognition and language in the second year of life: Problems in conceptualization and measurement. In M. Barrett (Ed.), *Single word speech.* London: Wiley.

Bloor, C., & White, F. (1983). *Unpublished manuscript.* University of California at San Diego, LaJolla, CA.

Blum, J. W., Beaudoin, C. M., & Caton-Lemos, L. (2005). Physical activity patterns and maternal well-being in postpartum women. *Maternal and Child Health Journal, 8,* 163–169.

Blum, R., & Nelson-Mmari, K. (2004). Adolescent health from an international perspective. In R. Lerner & L. Steinberg (Eds.), *Handbook of adolescent psychology.* New York: Wiley.

Blumberg, J. (1993, June 2). Commentary in "Lowly vitamin supplements pack a big health punch." *USA Today* p. 3D.

Blumenfeld, P., Modell, J., Bartko, T., Secada, W., Fredricks, J., Friedel, J., & Paris, A. (2005). School engagement of inner city students during middle childhood. In C. R. Cooper, C. T. Garcia Coll, W. T. Bartko, H. M. Davis, & C. Chatman (Eds.). *Developmental pathways through middle childhood.* Mahwah, NJ: Erlbaum.

Blumenthal, J. A., Emery, C. F., Madden, D. J., George, L. K., Coleman, R. E., Riddle, M. W., McKee, D. C., Reasoner, J., & Williams, R. S. (1989). Cardiovascular and behavioral effects of aerobic exercise training in healthy older men and women. *Journal of Gerontology: Medical Sciences, 44,* M147–157.

Blumenthal, J., Jeffries, N. O., Castellanos, F. X., Liu, H., Zidjdenbos, A., Paus, T., Evans, A. C., Rapoport, J. L., & Giedd, J. N. (1999). Brain development during childhood and adolescence: A longitudinal MRI study. *Nature Neuroscience, 10,* 861–863.

Blumstein, H., & Gorevic, P. D. (2005). Rheumatologic illness: Treatment strategies for older adults. *Geriatrics, 60,* 28–35.

Blustein, D. L. (2006). *Psychology of working.* Mahwah, NJ: Erlbaum.

Bodkin, N. L., Ortmeyer, H. K., & Hansen, B. (2005). A comment on the comment: Relevance on nonhuman primate dietary restriction to aging in humans. *Journals of Gerontology A: Biological Sciences and Medical Sciences, 60,* 951–952.

Bodrova, E., & Leong, D. J. (2001). *Tools of the mind.* Geneva, Switzerland: International Bureau of Education, UNESCO. Available online at http://www.ibe.unesco.org/International/Publications/INNODATA Monograph/inno07.pdf

Bodrova, E., & Leong, D. J. (2007). *Tools of the mind* (2ⁿᵈ ed.). Geneva, Switzerland: International Bureau of Education, UNESCO.

Boelen, P. A., van den Bout, J., & van den Hout, M. A. (2003). The role of cognitive variables in psychological functioning after the death of a first degree relative. *Behavior Research and Therapy, 41,* 1123–1136.

Boerner, K., & Wortman, C. B. (1998). Grief and loss. In H. S. Freeman (Ed.), *Encyclopedia of mental health* (Vol. 2). San Diego: Academic Press.

Bogenschneider, K. (Ed.) (2006) *Family policy matters.* Mahwah, NJ: Erlbaum.

Bogenschneider, K., Olson, J. R., Mills, J., & Linney, K. D. (2006). How can we connect research and knowledge with state policymaking? In K. Bogenschneider (Ed.), *Family policy matters.* Mahwah, NJ: Erlbaum.

Bohlin, G., & Hagekull, B. (1993), Stranger wariness and sociability in the early years. *Infant Behavior and Development, 16,* 53–67.

Bohlmeijer, E., Valenkamp, M., Westerhof, G., Smit, F., Cuijpers, P. (2005). Creative reminiscence as an early intervention for depression: Results of a pilot project. *Aging and Mental Health, 9,* 302–304.

Bolen, J. C., Bland, S. D., & Sacks, J. J. (1999, April). *Injury prevention behaviors: Children's use of occupant restraints and bicycle helmets.* Paper presented at the meeting of the Society for Research in Child Development, Albuquerque.

Bolger, K. E., & Patterson, C. J. (2001). Developmental pathways from child maltreatment to peer rejection. *Child Development, 72,* 339–351.

Bonanno, G. A. (2004). Loss, trauma, and human resilience: Have we underestimated the human capacity to thrive after extremely aversive events? *American Psychologist, 59,* 20–28.

Bonanno, G. A., Papa, A., Lalande, K., Zhang, N., & Noll, J. G. (2005). Grief processing and deliberate grief avoidance: A prospective comparison of bereaved spouses and parents in the United States and the People's Republic of China. *Journal of Consulting and Clinical Psychology, 73,* 86–98.

Bonanno, G. A., Wortman, C. B., & Nesse, R. M. (2004). Prospective pattern s of resilience and maladjustment during widowhood. *Psychology and Aging, 19,* 260–271.

Bonari, L., Bennett, H., Elnarson, A., & Koren, G. (2004). Risk of untreated depression during pregnancy. *Journal of Family Health Care, 13,* 144–145.

Bonvillian, J. (2005). Unpublished review of Santrock, *Topical life-span development,* 3rd ed. New York: McGraw Hill.

Bookwala, J. (2005). The role of marital quality in physical health during the mature years. *Journal of Aging and Health, 17,* 85–104.

Bookwala, J., & Jacobs, J. (2004). Age, marital processes, and depressed affect. *The Gerontologist, 44,* 328–338.

Booth, A., & Johnson, D. (1988). Premarital cohabitation and marital success. *Journal of Family Issues, 9,* 255–272.

Booth, M. (2002). Arab adolescents facing the future: Enduring ideals and pressures to change. In B. B. Brown, R. W. Larson, & T. S. Saraswathi (Eds.), *The world's youth.* New York: Cambridge University Press.

Bopp, K. L., & Verhaeghen, P. (2005). Aging and verbal memory span: A meta-analysis. *Journals of Gerontology B: Psychological Sciences and Social Sciences, 60,* P223–P233.

Bor, W., McGee, T. R., & Fagan, A. A. (2004). Early risk factors for adolescent antisocial behavior: An Australian longitudinal study. *Australian and New Zealand Journal of Psychiatry, 38,* 365–372.

Borg, C., Hallberg, I. R., & Blomqvist, K. (2006). Life satisfaction among older people (65+) with reduced self-care capacity: The relationship to social, health, and financial aspects. *Journal of Clinical Nursing, 15,* 607–618.

Bornstein, M. H. (1975). Qualities of color vision in infancy. *Journal of Experimental Child Psychology, 19,* 401–409.

Bornstein, M. H. (2006). Parenting science and practice. In W. Damon & R. Lerner (Eds.), *Handbook of child psychology* (6th ed.). New York: Wiley.

Bornstein, M. H., Arterberry, M. E., & Mash, C. (2005). Perceptual development. In M. H. Bornstein & M. E. Lamb (Eds.), *Developmental psychology* (5th ed.). Mahwah, NJ: Erlbaum.

Bornstein, M. H., & Cote, L. R. (Eds.), (2006). *Acculturation and parent-child relationships.* Mahwah, NJ: Erlbaum.

Bornstein, M. H., & Sigman, M. D. (1986). Continuity in mental development from infancy. *Child Development, 57,* 251–274.

Borra, S. T., Kelly, L., Shirreffs, M. B., Neville, K., & Geiger, C. J. (2003). Developing health messages. *Journal of the American Dietetic Association, 103,* 721–728.

Boswell, W. R., Olson-Buchanan, J. B., & LePine, M. A. (2004). Relations between stress and work outcomes. *Journal of Vocational Behavior, 64,* 165–181.

Botwinick, J. (1978). *Aging and behavior* (2nd ed.). New York: Springer.

Bouchard, T. J. (1995, August). *Heritability of intelligence.* Paper presented at the meeting of the American Psychological Association, New York, NY.

Bouchard, T. J., Lykken, D. T., McGue, M., Segal, N. L., & Tellegen, A. (1990). Source of human psychological differences. The Minnesota Study of Twins Reared Apart. *Science, 250,* 223–228.

Bouchey, H. A., & Furman, W. (2003). Dating and romantic relationships in adolescence. In G. Adams & M. Berzonsky (Eds.), *Blackwell handbook of adolescence.* Malden, MA: Blackwell.

Boukydis, C. F. Z., Bigsby, R., & Lester, B. M. (2004). Clinical use of the Neonatal Intensive Care Unit Network Neurobehavioral Scale. *Pediatrics, 113* (Supplement), S679–S689.

Boustani, M., Zimmerman, S., Williams, C. S., Gruber-Baldini, A. L., Watson, L., Reed, P. S., & Sloane, P. D. (2005). Characteristics associated with behavioral symptoms related to dementia in long-term care residents. *Gerontologist, 45 (Suppl 1),* S56–S61.

Bower, B. (1985). The left hand of math and verbal talent. *Science News, 127,* 263.

Bower, T. G. R. (1966). Slant perception and shape constancy in infants. *Science, 151,* 832–834.

Bower, T. G. R. (2002). Space and objects. In A. Slater & M. Lewis (Eds.), *Introduction to infant development.* New York: Oxford University Press.

Bowlby, J. (1969). *Attachment and loss* (Vol. 1). London: Hogarth.

Bowlby, J. (1980). *Attachment and loss: Vol. 3. Loss, sadness, and depression.* New York: Basic Books.

Bowlby, J. (1989). *Secure and insecure attachment.* New York: Basic Books.

Bowles, T. (1999). Focusing on time orientation to explain adolescent self concept and academic achievement: Part II. Testing a model. *Journal of Applied Health Behaviour, 1,* 1–8.

Boyd-Franklin, N. (1989). *Black families in therapy. A multisystems approach.* New York: Guilford Press.

Boyer, K., & Diamond, A. (1992). Development of memory for temporal order in infants and young children. In A. Diamond (Ed.), *Development and neural bases of higher cognitive function.* New York: New York Academy of Sciences.

Boyle, D. K., Miller, P. A., & Forbes-Thompson, S. A. (2005). Communication and end-of-life care in the intensive care unit: Patient, family, and clinician outcomes. *Critical Care Nursing Quarterly, 28,* 302–316.

Boyle, M. A., & Long, S. (2007). *Personal nutrition* (6th ed.). Belmont, CA: Wadsworth.

Brabeck, M. M. (2000). Kohlberg, Lawrence. In A. Kazdin (Ed.), *Encyclopedia of psychology.* Washington, DC. & New York: American Psychological Association and Oxford University Press.

Brabyn, J. A., Schneck, M. E., Haegerstrom-Portnoy, G., & Lott, L. (2001). The Smith-Kettlewell Institute (SKI). Longitudinal Study of Vision Function and Its Impact Among the Elderly: An Overview. *Ophthalmology and Vision Science, 78,* 2464–2469.

Bracey, J. R., Bamaca, M. Y., & Umana-Taylor, A. J. (2004). Examining ethnic identity among biracial and monoracial adolescents. *Journal of Youth and Adolescence, 33,* 123–132.

Brach, J. S., Simonsick, E. M., Kritchevsky, S., Yaffe, K., Newman, A. B., & the Health, Aging and Body Composition Study Research Group. (2004). The association between physical function and lifestyle activity in the health, aging, and body composition study. *Journal of the American Geriatrics Society, 52,* 502–509.

Bracken, M. B., Eskenazi, B., Sachse, K., McSharry, J., Hellenbrand, K., & Lee-Summers, L. (1990). Association of cocaine use with sperm concentration, motility, and morphology. *Fertility and Sterility, 53,* 315–322.

Bradbury, F. D., Fincham, F. D., & Beach, S. R. H. (2000). Research on the nature and determinants of marital satisfaction: A decade in review. *Journal of Marriage and the Family, 62,* 964–980.

Bradley, R. E., & Webb, R. (1976). Age-related differences in locus of control orientation in three behavior domains. *Human Development, 19,* 49–55.

Bradley, R., & Corwyn, R. (2004). "Family process" investments that matter for child well-being. In A. Kalil & T. DeLeire (Eds.), *Family investments in children's potential.* Mahwah, NJ: Erlbaum.

Bradshaw, C. P., & Garbarino, J. (2004). Using and building family strengths to promote youth development. In In S. F. Hamilton & M. A. Hamilton (Eds.), *The youth development handbook.* Thousand Oaks, CA: Sage.

Brainerd, C. J., & Reyna, V. E. (1993). Domains of fuzzy-trace theory. In M. L. Howe & R. Pasnak (Eds.), *Emerging themes in cognitive development.* New York: Springer.

Brandenburg, H., Kolkman, J., Lie Fong, S., & Steegers, E. (2005). Long term post-natal follow-up after transabdominal chorion villus sampling compared to amniocentesis. *Prenatal Diagnosis, 25,* 261–263.

Brandenburg, H., Steegers, E. A., & Gittenberger-de Groot, A. C. (2005). Potential involvement of vascular endothelial growth factor in pathophysiology of Turner syndrome. *Medical Hypotheses, 65,* 300–304.

Brandtstädter, J., & Renner, G. (1990). Tenacious goal pursuit and flexible goal adjustment: Explication and age-related analysis of assimilative and accommodative strategies of coping. *Psychology and Aging, 5,* 58–67.

Brandtstädter, J., Wentura, D., & Greve, W. (1993). Adaptive resources of the aging self: Outlines of an emergent perspective. *Journal of Behavioral Development, 16,* 323–349.

Bransford, J. D., & Donovan, M. S. (2005). Scientific inquiry and How people learn. In M. S. Donovan & J. D. Bransford (Eds.), *How Students Learn.* Washington, DC: National Academies Press.

Braver, S., Goodman, M., & Shapiro, J. (2006). The consequences of divorce for parents. In M. A. Fine & J. H. Harvey (Eds.), *Handbook of divorce and relationship dissolution.* Mahwah, NJ: Erlbaum.

Brazelton, T. B. (1956). Sucking in infancy. *Pediatrics, 17,* 400–404.

Brazelton, T. B. (2004). Preface: The Neonatal Intensive Care Unit Network Neurobehavioral Scale. *Pediatrics, 113,* (Suppl) S632–S633.

Bredekamp, S., & Copple, C. (1997). Developmentally appropriate practice for 3- through 5-year-olds. In S. Bredekamp & C. Copple (Eds.), *Developmentally appropriate practice in early childhood programs.* Washington, DC: NAEYC.

Breheny, M., & Stephens, C. (2004). Barriers to effective contraception and strategies for overcoming them among adolescent mothers. *Public Health Nursing, 21,* 220–227.

Brehm, S. S. (2002). *Intimate relationships* (3rd ed.). New York: McGraw-Hill.

Breitner, J.C. (2006). Dementia—epidemiological considerations, nomenclature, and a tacit consensus definition. *Journal of Geriatric Psychiatry and Neurology, 19,* 129–136.

Bremner, G. (2004). Cognitive development: Knowledge of the physical world. In A. Fogel & G. Bremner (Eds.), *Blackwell handbook of infant development.* London: Blackwell.

Brener, N., Lowry, R., Barrios, L., Simon, T., & Eaton, D. (2005). Violence-related behaviors among high school students—United States, 1991–2003. *Journal of School Health, 75,* 81–85.

Brennan, K. A., Clark, C. L., & Shaver, P. R. (1998). Self-report measurement of adult romantic attachment: An integrative overview. In J. A. Simpson & W. S. Rholes (Eds.), *Attachment theory and close relationships.* New York: Guilford Press.

Brent, R. L. (2004). Environmental causes of human congenital malformations. *Pediatrics, 113,* (4 Suppl). 957–968.

Brent, R. L., & Fawcett, L. B. (2000, May), *Environmental causes of human birth defects: What have we learned about the mechanism, nature, and etiology of congenital malformations in the past 50 years?* Paper presented at the joint meetings of the Pediatric Academic Societies and the American Academy of Pediatrics, Boston.

Breslau, N., Paneth, N. S., & Lucia, V. C. (2004). The lingering academic deficits of low birth weight children. *Pediatrics, 114,* 1035–1040.

Bretherton, I., Fritz, J., Zahn-Waxler, C., & Ridgeway, D. (1986). Learning to talk about emotions: A functionalist perspective. *Child Development, 57,* 529–548.

Bretherton, I., Stolberg, U., & Kreye, M. (1981). Engaging strangers in proximal interaction: Infants' social initiative. *Developmental Psychology, 17,* 746–755.

Brewer, J. A. (2007). *Introduction to early childhood education* (6th ed.). Boston: Allyn & Bacon.

Breysse, P., Farr, N., Galke, W., Lanphear, B., Morely, R., & Bergofsky, L. (2004). The relationship between housing and health: Children at risk. *Environmental Health Perspectives, 112,* 1583–1588.

Brickel, C. O., Ciarrocchi, J. W., Sheers, N. J., Estadt, B. K., Powell, D. A., & Pargament, K. I. (1998). Perceived stress, religious coping styles, and depressive affect. *Journal of Psychology and Christianity, 17,* 33–42.

Briem, V., Radeborg, K., Salo, I., & Bengtsson, H. (2004). Developmental aspects of children's behavior and safety while cycling. *Journal of Pediatric Psychology. 29,* 369–377.

Briesacher, B. A., Limcangco, M. R., Simoni-Wastila, L., Doshi, J. A., Levens, S. R., Shea, D. G., & Stuart, B. (2005). The quality of antipsychotic drug prescribing in nursing homes. *Archives of Internal Medicine, 165,* 1280–1285.

Briggs, G. G., & Wan, S. R. (2006). Drug therapy during labor and delivery, part 1. *American Journal of Health-System Pharmacy, 63,* 1038–1047.

Briken, P., Habermann, N., Berner, W., & Hill, A. (2006). XYY chromosome abnormality in sexual homicide perpetrators. *American Journal of Medical Genetics B: Neuropsychiatry and Genetics, 141,* 198–200.

Bril, B. (1999). Dires sur l'enfant selon les cultures. Etat des lieux et perspectives. In B. Bril, P. R. Dasen, C. Sabatier, & B. Krewer (Eds.), *Propos sur l'enfant et l'adolescent. Quels enfants pour quelles cultures?* Paris: L'Harmattan.

Brim, G. (1992, December 7). Commentary, *Newsweek,* p. 52.

Brim, G., Ryff, C. D., & Kessler, R. (Ed.) (2004). *How healthy we are: A national study of well-being in midlife.* Chicago: University of Chicago Press.

Brim, O. (1999). *The MacArthur Foundation study of midlife development.* Vero Beach, FL: MacArthur Foundation.

Brintnall-Peterson, M. (2003). *Older adults are fastest growing Internet audience.* Available on the Internet at: www.uwex.edu/news/story.cfm/570

Briones, T. L. (2006). Environment, physical activity, and neurogenesis: Implications for the treatment of Alzheimer's disease. *Current Alzheimer's Research, 3,* 49–54.

Brissette, I., Scheier, M. F., & Carver, C. S. (2002). The role of optimism and social network development,

coping, and psychological adjustment during a life transition. *Journal of Personality and Social Psychology, 82,* 102–111.

Brittle, C., & Zint, M. (2003). Do newspapers lead with lead? A content analysis of how lead health risks to children are covered. *Journal of Environmental Health, 65,* 17–22, 30, 34.

Broadwater, K., Curtin, L., Martz, D. M., & Zrull, M. C. (2005, in press). College student drinking: Perception of the norm and behavioral intentions. *Addictive Behaviors.*

Brockmeyer, S., Treboux, D., & Crowell, J. A. (2005, April). *Parental divorce and adult children's attachment status and marital relationships.* Paper presented at the meeting of the Society for Research in Child Development. Atlanta.

Brody, N. (2000). Intelligence. In A. Kazdin (Ed.), *Encyclopedia of psychology.* Washington, DC, & New York: American Psychological Association and Oxford University Press.

Brody, N. (2006). Does education influence intelligence? In P. C. Kyllonen, R. D. Roberts, & L. Stankov (Eds.), *Extending intelligence.* Mahwah, NJ: Erlbaum.

Brodzinsky, D. M., Lang, R., & Smith, D. W. (1995). Parenting adopted children. In M. H. Bornstein (Ed.), *Handbook of parenting* (Vol. 3). Hillsdale, NJ: Erlbaum.

Brodzinsky, D. M., & Pinderhughes, E. (2002). Parenting and child development in adoptive families. In M. H. Bornstein (Ed.), *Handbook of parenting* (Vol. 1). Mahwah, NJ: Erlbaum.

Brodzinsky, D. M., Schechter, D. E., Braff, A. M., & Singer, L. M. (1984). Psychological and academic adjustment in adopted children. *Journal of Consulting and Clinical Psychology, 52,* 582–590.

Brom, B. (2005). *NutritionNow* (4th ed.). Belmont CA: Wadsworth.

Bronfenbrenner, U. (1986). Ecology of the family as a context for human development: Research perspectives. *Developmental Psychology, 22,* 723–742.

Bronfenbrenner, U. (1995, March). *The role research has played in Head Start.* Paper presented at the meeting of the Society for Research in Child Development, Indianapolis.

Bronfenbrenner, U. (2000). Ecological theory. In A. Kazdin (Ed.), *Encyclopedia of psychology.* Washington, DC, & New York: American Psychological Association and Oxford University Press.

Bronfenbrenner, U. (2004). *Making human beings human.* Thousand Oaks, CA: Sage.

Bronfenbrenner, U., & Morris, P. (1998). The ecology of developmental processes. In W. Damon (Ed.), *Handbook of child psychology* (5th ed., Vol. 1). New York: Wiley.

Bronfenbrenner, U., & Morris, P. A. (2006). The ecology of developmental processes. In W. Damon & R. Lerner (Eds.), *Handbook of child psychology* (6th ed.). New York: Wiley.

Bronstein, P. (2006). The family environment: Where gender role socialization begins. In J. Worell & C. D. Goodheart (Eds.), *Handbook of girls' and women's psychological health.* New York: Oxford University Press.

Brook, J. S., Brook, D. W., Gordon, A. S., Whiteman, M., & Cohen, P. (1990). The psychological etiology of adolescent drug use: A family interactional approach. *Genetic Psychology Monographs, 116,* no. 2.

Brooker, R. J. (2005). *Genetics* (2nd ed.), New York: McGraw-Hill.

Brooks, J. G., & Brooks, M. G. (2001). *The case for constructivist classrooms* (2nd ed.). Upper Saddle River, NJ: Erlbaum.

Brooks-Gunn, J., Currie, J., Emde, R. E., & Zigler, E. (2003). Do you believe in magic? What we

can expect from early childhood intervention programs. *SRCD Social Policy Report, 17 (1),* 3–15.

Brooks-Gunn, J., Graber, J. A., & Paikoff, R. L. (1994). Studying links between hormones and negative affect: Models and measures. *Journal of Research on Adolescence, 4,* 469–486.

Brooks-Gunn, J., Han, W. J., & Waldfogel, J. (2002). Maternal employment and child cognitive outcomes in the first three years of life: The NICHD Study of Early Child Care. *Child Development, 73,* 1052–1072.

Brooks-Gunn, J., & Paikoff, R. (1993). "Sex is a gamble, kissing is a game": Adolescent sexuality, contraception, and sexuality. In S. P. Millstein, A. C. Petersen, & E. O. Nightingale (Eds.), *Promoting the health behavior of adolescents.* New York: Oxford University Press.

Brooks-Gunn, J., & Warren, M. P. (1989). The psychological significance of secondary sexual characteristics in 9- to 11-year-old girls. *Child Development, 59,* 161–169.

Brosco, J. P., Mattingly, M., & Sanders, L. M. (2006). Impact of specific medical interventions on reducing the prevalence of mental retardation. *Archives of Pediatric and Adolescent Medicine, 160,* 302–309.

Brott, A. A. (2001). *The expectant father.* New York: Abbeville Press.

Brown, B. B. (1999). Measuring the peer environment of American adolescents. In S. L. Friedman & T. D. Wachs (Eds.), *Measuring environment across the life span.* Washington, DC: American Psychological Association.

Brown, B. B. (2003). Crowds, cliques, and friendships. In G. Adams & M. Berzonsky (Eds.), *Blackwell handbook of adolescence.* Malden, MA: Blackwell.

Brown, B. B. (2004). Adolescence relationships with peers. In R. Lerner & L. Steinberg (Eds.), *Handbook of adolescent psychology.* New York: Wiley.

Brown, B. B., & Larson, R. W. (2002). The kaleidoscope of adolescence: Experiences of the world's youth at the beginning of the 21st century. In B. B. Brown, R. W. Larson, & T. S. Saraswathi (Eds.), *The world's youth.* New York: Cambridge University Press.

Brown, B. B., & Lohr, M. J. (1987). Peer-group affiliation and adolescent self-esteem: An integration of ego-identity and symbolic-interaction theories. *Journal of Personality and Social Psychology, 52,* 47–55.

Brown, J. (2005). The compelling nature of romantic love: A psychosocial perspective. *Psychoanalysis, Culture, and Society, 10,* 23–43.

Brown, J. K. (1985). Introduction. In J. K. Brown & V. Kerns (Eds.), *In her prime: A new view of middle-aged women.* South Hadley, MA: Bergin & Garvey.

Brown, L. A., McKenzie, N. C., & Doan, J. B. (2005). Age-dependent differences in the attentional demands of obstacle negotiation. *Journal of Gerontology A: Biological Sciences and Medical Sciences, 60,* 924–927.

Brown, L. S. (1989). New voices, new visions: Toward a lesbian/gay paradigm for psychology. *Psychology of Women Quarterly, 13,* 445–458.

Brown, R. (1958). *Words and things.* Glencoe, IL: Free Press.

Brown, R. (1973). *A first language: The early stages.* Cambridge, MA: Harvard University Press.

Brown, S. L., Bulanda, J. R., & Lee, G. R. (2005). The significance of nonmarital cohabitation: Marital status and mental health benefits among middle-aged and older adults. *Journals of Gerontology B: Psychological Sciences and Social Sciences, 60,* S21–S29.

Brown, S. L., Lee, G. R., & Bulanda, R. (2006). Cohabitation among older adults: A national portrait. *Journals of Gerontology B: Psychological Sciences and Social Sciences, 61,* S71–S79.

Brown, S. L., Nesse, R. M., House, J. S., & Utz, R. L. (2004). Religion and emotional compensation: Results from a prospective study of widowhood. *Personality and Social Psychology Bulletin, 30,* 1165–1174.

Brown, S. L., Nesse, R. M., Vinokur, A. D., & Smith, D. M. (2003). Providing social support may be more beneficial than receiving it: Results from a prospective study of mortality. *Psychological Science, 14,* 320–327.

Brownell, K. (2000). Dieting. In A. Kazdin (Ed.), *Encyclopedia of psychology.* Washington, DC, & New York: American Psychological Association and Oxford University Press.

Brownell, K. D. (2002, June 18). Commentary. *USA Today,* p. 8D.

Brownell, P., & Heiser, D. (2006). Psycho-educational support groups for older women victims of family mistreatment: A pilot study. *Journal of Gerontological Social Work, 46,* 137–144.

Browning, C. A. (2000). Using music during childbirth. *Birth, 27,* 272–276.

Brownlee, S. (1998, June 15). Baby talk. *U.S. News & World Report,* 48–54.

Brownson, R. C., Boehmer, T. K., & Luke, D. A. (2005). Declining rates of physical activity in the United States: What are the contributors? *Annual Review of Public Health, 26,* 421–443.

Bruce, C. A. (2002). The grief process for patient, family, and physician. *Journal of the American Osteopathic Association, 102,* (9, Suppl. 3) S28–S32.

Bruce, J. M., Olen, K., & Jensen, S. J. (1999, April). *The role of emotion and regulation in social competence.* Paper presented at the meeting of the Society for Research in Child Development, Albuquerque.

Bruck, M., & Ceci, S. J. (1999). The suggestibility of children's memory. *Annual Review of Psychology, 50,* 419–439.

Bruck, M., & Melnyk, L. (2004). Individual differences in children's suggestibility: A review and a synthesis. *Applied Cognitive Psychology, 18,* 947–996.

Bruck, M., Ceci, S. J., & Hembrooke, H. (1998). Reliability and credibility of young children's reports: From research to policy and practice. *American Psychologist, 53(2),* 136–151.

Bruck, M., Ceci, S. J., & Principe, G. F. (2006). The child and the law. In W. Damon & R. Lerner (Eds.), *Handbook of child psychology* (6th ed.). New York: Wiley.

Brugman, G. M. (2006). Wisdom and aging. In J. E. Birren & K. W. Schaie (Eds.), *Handbook of psychology of aging* (6th Ed.). San Diego: Academic Press.

Bruner, J. S. (1983). *Child talk.* New York: W. W. Norton.

Bruner, J. S. (1996). *The culture of education.* Cambridge, MA: Harvard University Press.

Bryant, J. B. (2005). Language in social contexts: The development of communicative competence. In J. Berko Gleason, *The development of language* (6th ed.). Boston: Allyn & Bacon.

Bugental, D. B., & Grusec, J. E. (2006). Socialization processes. In W. Damon & R. Lerner (Eds.), *Handbook of child psychology* (6th ed.). New York: Wiley.

Buhrmester, D. (1998). Need fulfillment, interpersonal competence, and the developmental contexts of early adolescent friendship. In W. M. Bukowski & A. F. Newcomb (Eds.), *The company they keep: Friendship in childhood and adolescence.* New York: Cambridge University Press.

Buhrmester, D. (2001, April). *Romantic development: Does age at which romantic involvement start matter?* Paper presented at the meeting of the Society for Research in Child Development, Minneapolis.

Buhrmester, D. (2003). Unpublished review of Santrock, J. W., *Adolescence* (10th ed.) New York: ***M. Grow-Hill.

Buhrmester, D. (2005, April). *The antecedents of adolescents' competence in close relationships: A six-year study.* Paper presented at the meeting of the Society for Research in Child Development, Atlanta.

Buhs, E. S., & Ladd, G. W. (2001). Peer rejection as an antecedent of young children's school adjustment: An examination of mediating processes. *Developmental Psychology, 37,* 550–560.

Bukowski, W. M., & Adams, R. (2005). Peer relationships and psychopathology. *Journal of Clinical Child and Adolescent Psychology, 34,* 3–10.

Bulik, C. M., Sullivan, P. F., Tozzi, F., Furberg, H., Lichtenstein, P., & Pedersen, N. L. (2006). Prevalence, heritability, and prospective risk factors for anorexia nervosa. *Archives of General Psychiatry, 63,* 305–312.

Buller, D. J. (2005). Evolutionary psychology: The emperor's new paradigm. *Trends in Cognitive Science, 9,* 277–283.

Bullock, M., & Lutkenhaus, P. (1990). Who am I? Self-understanding in toddlers. *Merrill-Palmer Quarterly, 36,* 217–238.

Bullock, R., & Dengiz, A. (2005). Cognitive performance in patients with Alzheimer's disease receiving cholinesterase inhibitors for up to 5 years. *International Journal of Clinical Practice, 59,* 817–822.

Bulteau, A. L., Szweda, L. I., Friguet, B. (2006). Mitochondrial protein oxidation and degradation in response to oxidative stress and aging. *Experimental Gerontology, 41,* 653–657.

Bumpas, M. F., Crouter, A. C., & McHale, M. (2001). Parental autonomy granting during adolescence: Exploring gender differences in context. *Developmental Psychology, 37,* 163–173.

Bumpass L. L., & Aquilino, W. S. (Eds.) (1995). *A Social Map of Midlife: Family and Work over the Middle Life Course.* Vero Beach, FL: MacArthur Foundation Research Network: Successful Midlife Development.

Bumpass, L. L., & Lu, H. H. (2000). Trends in cohabitation and implications for children's family contexts in the United States. *Population Studies, 54,* 29–41.

Bumpass, L., & Aquilino, W. (1994). *A social map of midlife: Family and work over the middle life course.* Center for Demography & Ecology, University of Wisconsin, Madison, WI.

Burbank, P. M., Dowling-Castronova, A., Crowther, M. R., & Capezuti, E. A. (2006). Improving knowledge and attitudes toward older adults through innovative educational strategies. *Journal of Professional Nursing, 22,* 191–197.

Burchinal, M. (2006). Child care subsidies, quality, and preferences among low-income families. In N. Cabera, R. Hutchens & H. E. Peters (Eds.), *From welfare to childcare.* Mahwah, NJ: Erlbaum.

Bureau of Labor Statistics, U. S. (2005). *People.* Washington, DC: U.S. Department of Labor.

Burgess, E. O. (2004). Sexuality in midlife and later life couples. In J. H. Harvey & A. Wetzel (Eds.), *The handbook of sexuality in close relationships.* Mahwah, NJ: Erlbaum.

Burke, D. M., & Shafto, M. A. (2004). Aging and language production. *Current Directions in Psychological Science, 13,* 21–24.

Burke, H. M., Zautra, A. J., Davis, M. C., Schultz, A. S., & Reich, J. W. (2003). Arthritis and musculoskeletal conditions. In I. B. Weiner (Ed.), *Handbook of psychology,* Vol. IX. New York: Wiley.

Burke, S. N., & Barnes, C. A. (2006). Neural plasticity in the aging brain. *Nature Review: Neuroscience, 7,* 30–40.

Burkhauser, R. V., & Quinn, J. F. (1989). American patterns of work and retirement. In W. Schmall (Ed.), *Redefining the process of retirement.* Berlin: Springer.

Burnett, A. L. (2004). The impact of sildenafil on molecular science and sexual health. *European Urology, 46,* 9–14.

Burns, D. (1985). *Intimate connections.* New York: Morrow.

Burrows, E., Crockenberg, S., & Leerkes, E. (2005, April). *Developmental history of care and control, anger and depression: Correlates of maternal sensitivity in toddlerhood.* Poster presented at the Biennial Meetings of the Society for Research in Child Development, Atlanta.

Burt, S. A., McGue, M., Krueger, R. F., & Iacono, W. G. (2005). Sources of covariation among the child-externalizing disorders: Informant effects and the shared environment. *Psychological Medicine, 35,* 1133–1144.

Burton, L. M. (1996). The timing of child-bearing, family structure, and the role of responsibilities of aging Black women. In E. M. Hetherington & E. A. Blechman (Eds.), *Stress, coping, and resilience in children and families.* Hillsdale, NJ: Erlbaum.

Buss, D. M. (1995). Psychological sex differences: Origins through sexual selection. *American Psychologist, 50,* 164–168.

Buss, D. M. (2004). *Evolutionary psychology* (2nd ed.). Boston: Allyn & Bacon.

Buss, D. M., & Barnes, M. (1986). Preferences in human mate selection. *Journal of Personality and Social Psychology, 50,* 559–570.

Buss, D. M., & others. (1990). International preferences in selecting mates: A study of 37 cultures. *Journal of Cross-Cultural Psychology, 21,* 5–47.

Buss, D. M., & Schmitt, D. P. (1993). Sexual strategies theory: An evolutionary perspective on human mating. *Psychological Review, 100,* 204–232.

Busse, E. W., & Blazer, D. G. (1996). *The American Psychiatric Press textbook of geriatric psychiatry* (2nd ed.). Washington, DC: American Psychiatric Press.

Bussey, K., & Bandura, A. (1999). Social cognitive theory of gender development and differentiation. *Psychological Review, 106,* 676–713.

Butler, R. N. (1975). *Why survive? Being old in America.* New York: Harper & Row.

Butler, R. N. (1996). Global aging: Challenges and opportunities of the next century. *Ageing International, 21,* 12–32.

Butler, R. N., & Lewis, M. (2002). *The new love and sex after 60.* New York: Ballantine.

Buzwell, S., & Rosenthal, D. (1996). Constructing a sexual self: Adolescents' sexual self-perceptions and sexual risk-taking. *Journal of Research on Adolescence, 6,* 489–513.

Bybee, J. (Ed.). (1999). *Guilt and children.* San Diego: Academic Press.

Byrnes, J. P. (2003). Cognitive development during adolescence. In G. Adams & M. Berzonsky (Eds.), *Blackwell handbook of adolescence.* Malden, MA: Blackwell.

Byrnes, J. P. (2005). The development of regulated decision making. In J. E. Jacobs & P. A. Klaczynski (Eds.), *The development of judgment and decision making in children and adolescents.* Mahwah, NJ: Erlbaum.

Cabera, N., Hutchens, R., & Peters, H. E. (Eds.) (2006). *From welfare to childcare.* Mahwah, NJ: Erlbaum.

Cabeza, R. (2002). Hemispheric asymmetry reduction in older adults: The HAROLD model. *Psychology and Aging, 17,* 85–100.

Cabeza, R., Nyberg, L., & Park, D. (2005). Cognitive neuroscience of aging: Emergence of a new discipline. In Cabeza, R., Nyberg, L., & Park, D. (Eds.), *Cognitive Neuroscience of Aging: Linking Cognitive and Cerebral Aging.* New York: Oxford University Press.

Cabezon, C., Vigil, P., Rojas, I., Leiva, M. E., Riquelme, R., Aranda, W., & Garcia, C. (2005). Adolescent pregnancy prevention: An abstinence-centered randomized controlled intervention in a Chilean public high school. *Journal of Adolescent Health, 36,* 64–69.

Cacabelos, R. (2005). Pharmacogenomics and therapeutic prospects in Alzheimer's disease. *Expert Opinions in Pharmacotherapy, 6,* 1967–1987.

Cacioppo, J. T., & Hawkley, L. C. (2003). Social isolation and health, with an emphasis on underlying mechanisms. *Perspectives on Biology and Medicine, 46,* 3 Suppl., 539–552.

Cacioppo, J. T., Ernst, J. M., Burleson, M. H., McClintock, M. K., Malarkey, W. B., Hawkley, L. C., Kowalewski, R. B., Paulsen, A., Hobson, J. A., Hugdahl, K., Spiegel, D., Berntson, G. G. (2000). Lonely traits and concomitant physiological processes: The MacArthur Social Neuro-science Studies. *International Journal of Psychophysiology, 35,* 143–154.

Cairns, R. B., & Cairns, B. (2006). The making of developmental psychology. In W. Damon & R. Lerner (Eds.), *Handbook of child psychology* (6th. Ed.). New York: Wiley.

Calabrese, R. L., & Schumer, H. (1986). The effects of service activities on adolescent alienation. *Adolescence, 21,* 675–687.

Caley, L. M., Kramer, C., & Robinson, L. K. (2005). Fetal alcohol spectrum disorder. *Journal of School Nursing, 21,* 139–146.

Call, K. A., Riedel, A., Hein, K., McLoyd, V., Kupke, M., & Petersen, P. (2002). Adolescent health and well-being in the 21st century: A global perspective. *Journal of Research on Adolescence, 12,* 69–98.

Callan, J. E. (2001). Gender development: Psycho-analytic perspective. In J. Worrel (Ed.). *Encyclopedia of women and gender.* San Diego: Academic Press.

Callaway, L. K., Lust, K., & McIntyre, H. D. (2005). Pregnancy outcomes in women of very advanced maternal age. *Obstetric and Gynecology Survey, 60,* 562–563.

Calvaresi, E., & Bryan, J. (2001). B vitamins, cognition, and aging: A review. *Journal of Gerontology: Phychological Sciences, 56B,* 327–339.

Camaioni, L. (2004). The transition from communication to language. In A. Fogel & G. Bremner (Eds.), *Blackwell handbook of infant development.* Malden, MA: Blackwell.

Camenga, D. R., Klein, J. D., & Ray, J. (2006). The changing risk profile of the adolescent smoker: Implications for prevention programs and tobacco interventions. *Journal of Adolescent Health, 39,* 120.e1–120.e10.

Camilleri, B. (2005). Dynamic assessment and intervention: Improving children's narrative abilities. *International Journal of Language & Communication Disorders, 40,* 240–242.

Campbell, F. A. (2006). The malleability of the cognitive development of children of low-income African-American families: Intellectual test performance over twenty-one years. In P. C. Kyllonen, R. D. Roberts, & L. Stankov (Eds.), *Extending intelligence.* Mahwah, NJ: Erlbaum.

Campbell, F. A., Pungello, E. P., Miller-Johnson, S., Burchinal, M., & Ramey, C. T. (2001). The development of cognitive and academic abilities: Growth curves from an early childhood educational experiment. *Developmental Psychology, 37,* 231–243.

Campbell, L., Campbell, B., & Dickinson D. (2004). *Teaching and learning through multiple intelligences* (3rd ed.). Boston: Allyn & Bacon.

Campos, J. J. (2001, April). *Emotion in emotional development: Problems and prospects.* Paper presented at the meeting of the Society for Research in Child Development, Minneapolis.

Campos, J. J. (2005). Unpublished review of Santrock, J. W., *Life-span development* (11th ed.) New York: McGraw-Hill.

Campos, J. J., Langer, A., & Krowitz, A. (1970). Cardiac responses on the visual cliff in prelocomotor human infants. *Science, 170,* 196–197.

Canfield, J., & Hansen, M. V. (1995). *A second helping of chicken soup for the soul.* Deerfield Beach, FL: Health Communications.

Canfield, R. L., & Haith, M. M. (1991). Young infants' visual expectations for symmetric and asymmetric stimulus sequences. *Developmental Psychology, 27,* 198–208.

Canfield, R. L., Henderson, C. R., Cory-Slechta, D. A., Cox, C., Jusko, T. A., & Lanphear, B. P. (2003). Intellectual impairment in children with blood lead concentrations below 10 microg per deciliter. *New England Journal of Medicine, 348,* 1517–1526.

Canterino, J. C., Ananth, C. V., Smulian, J., Harrigan, J. T., & Vintzileos, A. M. (2004). Maternal age and risk of betal death in singleton gestation: United States, 1995–2000. *Obstetrics and Gynecology Survey, 59,* 649–650.

Cappeliez, P., & O'Rourke, N. (2006). Empirical validation of a model of reminiscence and health in later life. *Journals of Gerontology B: Psychological and Social Sciences, 61,* P237–P244.

Cappeliez, P., O'Rourke, N., & Chaudhury, H. (2005). Functions of reminiscence and mental health in later life. *Aging and Mental Health, 9,* 295–301.

Capri, M., & others. (2006). The genetics of human longevity. *Annals of the New York Academy of Sciences, 1067,* 252–263.

Carbone, D. J., & Seftel, A. D. (2002). Erectile dysfunctions: Diagnosis and treatment in older men. *Geriatrics, 57(9),* 18–24.

Carbonell, O. A., Alzte, G., Bustamante, M. R., & Quiceno, J. (2002). Maternal caregiving and infant security in two cultures. *Developmental Psychology, 38,* 67–78.

Carel, J. C. (2005). Growth hormone in Turner syndrome: Twenty years after, what can we tell our patients? *Journal of Clinical Endocrinology & Metabolism, 90,* 3793–3794.

Carey, S. (1978). The child as word learner. In M. Halle, J. Bresnan, & G. A. Miller (Eds.), *Linguistic theory and psychological reality* (pp. 264–293). Cambridge, MA: MIT Press.

Carlisle, J. F. (2004). Morphological processes that influence learning to read. In C. A. Stone, E. R. Silliman, B. J. Ehren, & K. Apel (Eds.), *Handbook of language and literacy.* New York: Guilford.

Carlo, G. (2006). Care-based and altruistically-based morality. In M. Killen & J. Smetana (Eds.), *Handbook of moral development.* Mahwah, NJ: Erlbaum.

Carlson, C., Cooper, C., & Hsu, J. (1990, March). *Predicting school achievement in early adolescence: The role of family process.* Paper presented at the meeting of the Society for Research in Adolescence, Atlanta.

Carlson, E. A., Sroufe, L. A., & Egeland, B. (2004). The construction of experience: A longitudinal study of representation and behavior. *Child Development, 75,* 66–83.

Carlson, K. S. (1995, March). *Attachment in sibling relationships during adolescence: Links to other familial and peer relationships.* Paper presented at the meeting of the Society for Research in Child Development, Indianapolis.

Carly, A. (2003). Anemia: When is it iron deficiency? *Pediatric Nursing, 29,* 127–133.

Carmichael, S. L., Shaw, G. M., & Nelson, V. (2002). Timing of prenatal care initation and risk of congenital malformations. *Teratology, 66,* 326–330.

Carnegie Corporation. (1996). *Report on education for children 3–10 years of age.* New York: The Carnegie Foundation.

Carnegie Council on Adolescent Development. (1995). *Great transitions.* New York: The Carnegie Corporation.

Carnethon, M. R., Gidding, S. S., Nehgme, R., Sidney, S., Jacobs, D. R., & Liu, K. (2003). Cardiorespiratory fitness in young adulthood and the development of cardiovascular disease risk factors. *Journal of the American Medical Association, 290,* 3092–3100.

Caron, S. (2006). *Sex matters for college students* (2nd ed.). Upper Saddle River, NJ: Prentice Hall.

Carpendale, J. I., & Chandler, M. J. (1996). On the distinction between false belief understanding and subscribing to an interpretive theory of mind. *Child Development, 67,* 1686–1706.

Carr, D. (2003). A "good death" for whom? Quality of spouse's death and psychological distress among older widowed persons. *Journal of Health & Social Behavior, 44,* 215–232.

Carr, D., Nesse, R., & Wortman, C. (Eds.). (2005). *Spousal bereavement in late life.* New York: Springer.

Carr, D., Wortman, C., & Nesse, R. (2005). Understanding late life widowhood: New directions in research, theory, and practice. In D. Carr, R. Nesse, & C. Wortman (Eds.), *Spousal bereavement in late life.* New York: Springer.

Carrington, N. A., & Bogetz, J. F. (2004). Normal grief and bereavement. *Journal of Palliative Medicine, 7,* 309–323.

Carroll, J. L. (2007). *Sexuality now* (2nd ed.). Belmont, CA: Wadsworth.

Carroll, J. S., & Doherty, W. J. (2003). Evaluating the effectiveness of premarital prevention programs: A meta-analytic review of outcome research. *Family Relations, 52,* 105–118.

Carskadon, M. A. (Ed.). (2002). *Adolescent sleep patterns.* New York: Cambridge University Press.

Carskadon, M. A. (2004). Sleep difficulties in young people. *Archives of Pediatric and Adolescent Medicine, 158,* 597–598.

Carskadon, M. A. (2005). Sleep and circadian rhythms in children and adolescents: Relevance for athletic performance of young people. *Clinical Sports Medicine, 26,* 319–328.

Carskadon, M. A. (2006, April). *Adolescent sleep: The perfect storm.* Paper presented at the meeting of the Society for Research on Adolescence, San Francisco.

Carskadon, M. A., Acebo, C., & Jenni, O. G. (2004). Regulation of adolescent sleep: implications for behavior. *Annals of the New York Academy of Sciences, 102,* 276–291.

Carson, C. C. (2003). Sildenafil: A 4-year update in the treatment of 20 million erectile dysfunction patients. *Current Urology Reports, 4,* 488–496.

Carstensen, L. L. (1995). Evidence for a life-span theory of socioemotional selectivity. *Current Directions in Psychological Science, 4,* 151–156.

Carstensen, L. L. (1998). A life-span approach to social motivation. In J. Heckhausen & C. Dweck (Eds.), *Motivation and self-regulation across the life span.* New York: Cambridge University Press.

Carstensen, L. L. (2006). The influence of a sense of time on human development. *Science, 312,* 1913–1915.

Carstensen, L. L., Charles, S. T., Isaacowitz, D., & Kennedy, Q. (2003). Life-span development and emotion. In R. J. Davidson, K. Scherer, & H. H. Goldsmith (Eds.), *Handbook of affective sciences.* New York: Oxford University Press.

Carstensen, L. L. & Löckenhoff, C. E. (2004). Aging, emotion, and evolution. The bigger picture. In P. Ekman, J. J. Campos, R. J. Davidson, & F. B. M. de Waal (Eds.), *Emotions inside out: 130 years after Darwin's The expression of the emotions in man and* *animals.* New York: Annals of the New York Academy of Sciences.

Carstensen, L. L., Mikels, J. A., & Mather, M. (2006). Aging and the intersection of cognition, motivation, and emotion. In J. E. Birren, & K. W. Schaie (Eds.), *Handbook of the psychology of aging* (6th ed.) San Diego: Academic Press.

Carter, B., & McGoldrick, M. (1989). Overview: The changing family life cycle—A framework for family therapy. In B. Carter & M. McGoldrick (Eds.), *The changing family life cycle* (2nd ed.). Boston: Allyn & Bacon.

Carter, P. A. (2004). Education and work as human rights for women. In R. D. Lakes & P. A. Carter (Eds.), *Globalizing education for work.* Mahwah, NJ: Erlbaum.

Carter-Saltzman, L. (1980). Biological and sociocultural effects on handedness: Comparison between biological and adoptive families. *Science, 209,* 1263–1265.

Carthenon, M. R., Gulati, M., & Greenland, P. (2005). Prevalence and cardiovascular disease correlates of low cardiorespiratory fitness in adolescents and adults. *Journal of the American Medical Association, 294,* 2981–2988.

Carver, K. Joyner, K., & Udry, J. R. (2003). National estimates of romantic relationships. In P. Florsheim (Ed.), *Adolescent romantic relations and sexual behavior.* Mahwah, NJ: Erlbaum.

Carver, L. J., & Bauer, P. J. (2001). The dawning of a past: The emergence of long-term explicit memory in infancy. *Journal of Experimental Psychology: General, 130*(4), 726–745.

Casarett, D., Crowley, R., Stevenson, C., Xie, S., & Teno, J. (2005). Making difficult decisions about hospice enrollment: What do patients and families want to know? *Journal of the American Geriatric Society, 53,* 249–254.

Case, R. (1987). Neo-Piagetian theory: Retrospect and prospect. *International Journal of Psychology, 22,* 773–791.

Case, R. (1999). Conceptual development in the child and the field: A personal view of the Piagetian legacy. In E. K. Skolnick, K. Nelson, S. A. Gelman, & P. H. Miller (Eds.), *Conceptual development.* Mahwah, NJ: Erlbaum.

Case, R., & Mueller, M. P. (2001). Differentiation, integration, and covariance mapping as fundamental processes in cognitive and neurological growth. In J. L. McClelland & R. S. Siegler (Eds.), *Mechanisms of cognitive development.* Mahwah, NJ: Erlbaum.

Case, R., Kurland, D. M., & Goldberg, J. (1982). Operational efficiency and the growth of short-term memory span. *Journal of Experimental Child Psychology, 33,* 386–404.

Casey, B. J., Durston, S., & Fossella, J. A. (2001). Evidence for a mechanistic model of cognitive control. *Clinical Neuroscience Research, 1,* 267–282.

Caspi, A., & Roberts, B. W. (2001). Personality development across the life course: The argument for change and continuity. *Psychological Inquiry, 12,* 49–66.

Caspi, A., & Shiner, R. L. (2006). Personality development. In W. Damon & R. Lerner (Eds.), *Handbook of child psychology* (6th, ed.). New York: Wiley.

Casson, I. F. (2006) Pregnancy in women with diabetes—after the CEMACH report, what now? *Diabetic Medicine, 23,* 481–484.

Castle, N. G. (2001). Innovation in nursing homes. *The Gerontologist, 41* (No. 2), 161–172.

Castle, N. G., & Engberg, J. (2005). Staff turnover and quality of care in nursing homes. *Medical Care, 43,* 616–626.

Cauffman, B. E. (1994, February). *The effects of puberty, dating, and sexual involvement on dieting and disordered eating in young adolescent girls.* Paper presented at the meeting of the Society for Research on Adolescence, San Diego.

Cavanaugh, J. (2000, January). Commentary. *American Psychologist, 31,* p. 25.

Cavanaugh, S. E. (2004). The sexual debut of girls in adolescence: The intersection of race, pubertal timing, and friendship group characteristics. *Journal of Research on Adolescence, 14,* 285–312.

Ceci, S. J. (2000). Bronfenbrenner, Urie. In A. Kazdin (Ed.), *Encyclopedia of psychology.* Washington, DC, & New York: American Psychological Association and Oxford University Press.

Ceci, S. J., & Gilstrap, L. L. (2000). Determinants of intelligence: Schooling and intelligence. In A. Kazdin (Ed.), *Encyclopedia of Psychology.* Washington, DC, & New York: American Psychological Association and Oxford University Press.

Ceci, S. J., Fitneva, S. A., & Gilstrap, L. L. (2003). Memory development and eye witness testimony. In A. Slater, & G. Bremner (Eds.), *An introduction to developmental psychology.* Malden, MA: Blackwell.

Center for Survey Research at the University of Connecticut. (2000). *Hours on the job.* Storrs: University of Connecticut, Center for Survey Research.

Centers for Disease Control and Prevention (2001). *Strategies for stopping smoking.* Atlanta, GA: Centers for Disease Control and Prevention.

Centers for Disease Control and Prevention (2002). *Adolescent pregnancy.* Atlanta & Centers for Disease Control and Prevention.

Centers for Disease Control and Prevention (2002). *Cohabitation,* Atlanta, GA: Centers for Disease Control and Prevention.

Centers for Disease Control and Prevention (2003). Physical activity levels among children aged 9–13—United States, 2002. *Morbidity and Mortality Weekly Report, 52,* 785–788.

Centers for Disease Control and Prevention (2003). Public health and aging: Health-related quality of life among low-income persons aged 45–64 years–United States. *Morbity and Mortality Weekly Reports, 21,* 1120–1124.

Centers for Disease Control and Prevention (2004, October 8). Smoking during pregnancy–United States, 1990–2002. *MMWR Morbidity and Mortality Report, 53,* 911–915.

Centers for Disease Control and Prevention (2005). *Obesity.* Atlanta: Centers for Disease Control and Prevention.

Centers for Disease Control and Prevention (2006). Racial and socioeconomic disparities in breasfeeding—United States, 2004. *MMWR Morbidity and Mortality Weekly Report, 55,* 335–339.

Centers for Disease Control and Prevention (2006). *Sexually transmitted diseases.* Atlanta: Centers for Disease Control and Prevention.

Chai, W., Du, Q., Shay, J. W., & Wright, W. E. (2006). Human telomeres have different overhang sizes at leading versus lagging strands. *Molecular Cell, 21,* 427–435.

Chambers, B., Cheung, A. C. K., & Slavin, R. F. (2006). Effective preschool programs for children at risk of school failure: A best-evidence synthesis. In B. Spodek & O. N. Saracho (Eds.), *Handbook of research on the education of young children.* Mahwah, NJ: Erlbaum.

Chang, F., Dell, G. S., & Bock, K. (2006). Becoming syntactic. *Psychological Review, 113,* 234–272.

Chang, L., Smith, L. M., LoPresti, C., Yonekura, M. L., Kuo, J., Walot, I., & Ernst, T. (2004). Smaller subcortical volumes and cognitive deficits in children with prenatal methamphetamine exposure. *Psychiatry Research, 132,* 95–106.

Chang, M. Y., Wang, S. Y., & Chen, C. H. (2002). Effects of massage on pain and anxiety during labor: A randomized controlled trial in Taiwan. *Journal of Advanced Nursing, 38,* 68–73.

Chang, S. C., & Chen, C. H. (2004). *Hu Li Za Zhi, 51,* 61–66. (Article in Chinese).

Chang, S. C., O'Brien, K. O., Nathanson, M. S.,

Mancini, J., & Witter, F. R. (2003). Characteristics and risk factors for adverse birth outcomes in pregnant black adolescents. *Journal of Obstetrics and Gynecology Canada, 25,* 751–759.

Chantry, C. J., Howard, C. R., & Aninger, P. (2006). Full breastfeeding duration and associated decrease in respiratory tract infection in U.S. children. *Pediatrics, 117,* 425–432.

Chao, R. (2001). Extending research on the consequences of parenting style for Chinese Americans and European Americans. *Child Development, 72,* 1832–1843.

Chao, R. K. (2005, April). *The importance of* Guan *in describing control of immigrant Chinese.* Paper presented at the meeting of the Society for Research in Child Development, Atlanta.

Chao, R., & Tseng, V. (2002). Parenting of Asians. In M. H. Bornstein (Series Ed.), *Handbook of parenting: Vol. 4. Social conditions and applied parenting* (2nd ed.). Mahwah, NJ: Erlbaum.

Chapman, D. J., Damio, G., Young, S., & Perez-Escamilla, R. (2004). Effectiveness of breastfeeding peer counseling in a low-income, predominantly Latina population: A randomized controlled trial. *Archives of Pediatric and Adolescent Medicine, 158,* 897–902.

Chapman, O. L. (2000). Learning science involves language, experience, and modeling. *Journal of Applied Developmental Psychology, 21,* 97–108.

Charles, S. T. & Carstensen, L. L. (2004). A life-span view of emotional functioning in adulthood and old age in P. Costa (Ed.), *Advances in cell aging and gerontology series.* New York: Elsevier.

Charlton, R. A., Morris, R. G., Nitkunan, A., & Markus, H. S. (2006). The cognitive profiles of CADASIL and sporadic small vessel disease. *Neurology, 66,* 1523–1526.

Charness, N., & Bosman, E. A. (1992). Human factors and aging. In F. I. M. Craik & T. A. Salthouse (Eds.), *The handbook of aging and cognition.* Hillsdale, NJ: Erlbaum.

Charness, N., Krampe, R. T., & Mayr, U. (1996). The role of practice and coaching in entrepreneurial skill domains: An international comparison of life-span chess skill acquisition. In K. A. Ericsson (Ed.), *The road to excellence: The acquisition of expert performance in the arts, sciences, sports, and games.* Mahwah, NJ: Erlbaum.

Chattin-McNichols, J. (1992). *The Montessori controversy.* Albany, NY: Delmar.

Chaudhuri, J. H., & Williams, P. H. (1999, April). *The contribution of infant temperament and parent emotional availability to toddler attachment.* Paper presented at the meeting of the Society for Research in Child Development, Albuquerque.

Chaytor, N., & Schmitter-Edgecombe, M. (2004). Working memory and aging: A cross-sectional and longitudinal analysis using a self-ordered pointing task. *Journal of the International Neuropsychological Society, 10,* 489–503.

Chee, M. W. I., Goh. J. O. S., Venkatraman, V., Tan. J. C., Gutchess, A., Sutton, B., Hebrank, A., Leshikar, E., & Park, D. (2006). Agerelated changes in object processing and contextual binding revealed using fMR adaptation. *Journal of Cognitive Neuroscience, 18,* 495–507.

Cheitlin, M. D. (2003). Sexual activity and cardiovascular disease. *American Journal of Cardiology, 92,* 3M–9M.

Chen, C., & Stevenson, H. W. (1989). Homework: A cross-cultural comparison. *Child Development, 60,* 551–561.

Chen, I. G., Durbin, D. R., Elliott, M. R., Kallan, M. J., & Winston, F. K. (2005). Trip characteristics of vehicle crashes involving child passengers. *Injury Prevention, 11,* 219–224.

Chen, P. S., Yang, Y. K., Lee, Y. S., Yeh, I. H., Chiu, N. T., & Chu, C. L. (2005). Correlation between different memory systems and striatal dopamine D2/D3 receptor density: A single photon emission computed tomography study. *Psychological Medicine, 35,* 197–204.

Chen, W., Srinivasan, S. R., Li, S., Xu, J., & Berenson, G. S. (2005). Metabolic syndrome variables at low levels in childhood are beneficially associated with adulthood cardiovascular risk: The Bogalusa Heart Study. *Diabetes Care, 28,* 126–131.

Chen, X., Hastings, P. D., Rubin, K. H., Chen, H., Cen, G., & Stewart, S. L. (1998). Childrearing attitudes and behavioral inhibition in Chinese and Canadian toddlers: A cross-cultural study. *Developmental Psychology, 34,* 677–686.

Chen, X., Striano, T., & Rakoczy, H. (2004). Auditory-oral matching behaviors in newborns. *Developmental Science, 7,* 42–47.

Chen, Z., & Siegler, R. S. (2000). Across the great divide: Bridging the gap between understanding of toddlers' and older children's thinking. *Monograph of the Society for Research in Child Development, 65* (No. 2).

Cherlin, A. J., & Furstenberg, F. F. (1994). Stepfamilies in the United States: A reconsideration. In J. Blake & J. Hagen (Eds.), *Annual review of sociology.* Palo Alto, CA: Annual Reviews.

Chernausek, S. D. (2004). Growth hormone treatment of short children born small for gestational age: A U.S. perspective. *Hormone Research, 62, Supplement 3,* S124–S127.

Chess, S., & Thomas, A. (1977). Temperamental individuality from childhood to adolescence. *Journal of Child Psychiatry, 16,* 218–226.

Chess, S., & Thomas, A. (1987). *Origins and evolution of behavior disorders.* Cambridge, MA: Harvard University Press.

Cheurprakobkit, S., & Bartsch, R. A. (2005). Security measures on school crime in Texas middle and high schools. *Educational Research, 47,* 235–250.

Chevan, A. (1996, August). As cheaply as one: Cohabitation in the older population. *Journal of Marriage and the Family, 58,* 656–667.

Chi, M. T. (1978). Knowledge structures and memory development. In R. S. Siegler (Ed.), *Children's thinking: What develops?* Hillsdale, NJ: Erlbaum.

Chiappetta, E. L., & Koballa, T. R. (2006). *Science instruction in the middle and secondary schools* (6th ed.). Upper Saddle River, NJ: Prentice Hall.

Child Trends. (2001). *Trends among Hispanic children, youth, and families.* Washington, DC: Author.

Child Trends. (2006). *Facts at a glance.* Washington, DC: Child Trends.

Chiriboga, D. (1997). Crisis, challenge, and stability in the middle years. In M. E. Lachman & J. B. James (Eds.), *Multiple paths of midlife development.* Chicago: University of Chicago Press.

Chiriboga, D. A. (1982). Adaptation to marital separation in later and earlier life. *Journal of Gerontology, 37,* 109–114.

Chiroro, P., Bohner, G., Viki, G. T., & Jarvis, C. I. (2004). Rape myth acceptance and rape proclivity: Expected dominance versus expected arousal as mediators in acquaintance rape situations. *Journal of Interpersonal Violence, 19,* 427–442.

Chisholm, J. S. (1989). Biology, culture and the development of temperament: A Navajo example. In J. K. Nugent, B. Lester, & T. B. Brazelton (Ed.), *The cultural context of infancy: Vol. 1. Biology, culture, and infant development* (pp. 341–364). Norwood, NJ: Ablex.

Chisholm, M. A., & Roberts, E. (2006). Medicare Part D coverage and its influence on transplant patients' out-of-pocket expenses. *American Journal of Transplantation, 6,* 1737–1742.

Chiuve, S. E., McCullough, M. L., Sacks, F. M., & Rimm, E. B. (2006). Healthy lifestyle factors in the primary prevention of coronary heart disease among men: Benefits among users and nonusers of lipid-lowering and antihypertensive medications. *Circulation, 114,* 160–167.

Chochivov, H. M., Krisjanson, L. J., Hack, T. F., Hassard, T., McClement, S., & Harlos, M. (2006). Dignity in the terminally ill. *Journal of Palliative Medicine, 9,* 662–672.

Choi, N. G. (2001). Relationship between life satisfaction and postretirement employment among older women. *International Journal of Aging and Human Development, 52,* 45–70.

Chomsky, N. (1957). *Syntactic structures.* The Hague: Mouton.

Chopra, M. (2003). Risk factors for under-nutrition of young children in a rural area of South Africa. *Public Health Nursing, 6,* 645–652.

Christakis, N. A., & Iwashyna, T. J. (2003). The health impact of health care on families: A matched cohort study of hospice use by decedents and mortality outcomes in surviving, widowed spouses. *Social Science and Medicine, 57,* 465–475.

Christensen, H., Korten, A., Jorm, A. F., Henderson, A. S., Scott, R., & MacKinnon, A. J. (1996). Activity levels and cognitive functioning in an elderly community sample. *Age and Aging, 25,* 72–80.

Christensen, L. (1996). *Diet-behavior relationships.* Washington, DC: American Psychological Association.

Christensen, L. B. (2007). *Experimental methodology* (10th ed.). Boston: Allyn & Bacon.

Christensen, S. L., & Thurlow, M. L. (2004). School dropouts: Prevention, considerations, interventions, and challenges. *Current Directions in Psychological Science, 13,* 36–39.

Christian, K., Bachman, H. J., & Morrison, F. J. (2001). Schooling and cognitive development. In. R. J. Sternberg & E. L. Grigorenko (Eds.), *Environmental effects on cognitive development.* Mahwah, NJ: Erlbaum.

Christian, P. Jiang, T., Khatry, S. K., LeClerq, S. C., Shrestha, S. R., & West, K. P. (2006). Antenatal supplementation with micronutrients and biochemical indicators of status and subclinical infection in rural Nepal. *American Journal of Clinical Nutrition, 83,* 788–794.

Christie, J. F., Vukellich, C., & Enz, B. J. (2007). *Teaching language and literacy.* Boston: Allyn & Bacon.

Chronis, A. M., Chacko, A., Fabiano, G. A., Wymbs, B. T., & Pelham, W. E. (2004). Enhancements to the behavioral parent training paradigm for families of children with ADHD: Review and future directions. *Clinical Child and Family Psychology Review, 7,* 1–27.

Chuang, M. E., Lamb, C. P., & Hwang, C. P. (2004). Internal reliability, temporal stability, and correlates of individual differences in paternal involvement: A 15-year longitudinal study in Sweden. In R. D. Day & M. E. Lamb (Eds.), *Conceptualizing and measuring father involvement.* Mahwah, NJ: Erlbaum.

Chun, K. M., & Akutsu, P. D. (2003). Acculturation among ethnic minority families. In K. M. Chun, P. B. Organista, & G. Marin (Eds.), *Acculturation.* Washington, DC: American Psychological Association.

Church, D. K., Siegel, M. A., & Fowler, C. D. (1988). *Growing old in America.* Wylie, TX: Information Aids.

Cicchetti, D. (2001). How a child builds a brain. In W. W. Hartup & R. A. Weinberg (Eds.), *Child psychology in retrospect and prospect.* Mahwah, NJ: Erlbaum.

Cicchetti, D., & Blender, J. A. (2004, December 14). A multiple-levels-of-analysis approach to the study of developmental processes in maltreated children. *Proceedings of the National Academy of Science USA, 101,* 17325–17326.

Cicchetti, D., & Toth, S. L. (2005). Child maltreatment. *Annual Review of Clinical Psychology, 1.* Palo Alto, CA: Annual Reviews.

Cicchetti, D., & Toth, S. L. (2006). Developmental psychopathology and preventive intervention. In W. Damon & R. Lerner (Eds.). *Handbook of child psychology* (6th ed.). New York: Wiley.

Cicchetti, D., Toth, S. L., & Rogusch, F. A. (2005) *A prevention program for child maltreatment.* Unpublished manuscript, University of Rochester, Rochester, NY.

Cicirelli, V. G. (1991). Sibling relationships in adulthood. *Marriage and Family Review, 16,* 291–310.

Cicirelli, V. G. (1994). Sibling relationships in cross-cultural perspective. *Journal of Marriage and Family, 56,* 7–20.

Cillessen, A. H. N., & Mayeux, L. (2004). Sociometric status and peer group behavior: Previous findings and current directions. In J. B. Kupersmidt & K. A. Dodge (Eds.), *Children's peer relations: From development to intervention.* Washington, DC: American Psychological Association.

Cisneros-Cohernour, E. J., Moreno, R. P., & Cisneros, A. A. (2000). Curriculum reform in Mexico: Kindergarten teachers' challenges and dilemmas. Proceedings of the Lilian Katz Symposium. In D. Rothenberg (Ed.), *Issues in early childhood education: Curriculum reform, teacher education, and dissemination of information.* Urbana-Champaign: University of Illinois.

Clark, E. V. (1993). *The lexicon in acquisition.* New York: Cambridge University Press.

Clark, R. D., & Hatfield, E. (1989). Gender differences in receptivity to sexual offers. *Journal of Psychology and Human Sexuality, 2,* 39–55.

Clarke, J., Preston, M., Raksin, J., & Bengtson, V. L. (1999). Types of conflicts and tensions between older adults and adult children. *Gerontologist, 39,* 261–270.

Clarke, R. (2006). Vitamin B 12, folic acid, and the prevention of dementia. *New England Journal of Medicine, 354,* 2817–2819.

Clarke-Stewart, K. A., Malloy, L. C., & Allhusen, V. D. (2004). Verbal ability, self-control, and close relationships with parents protect children against misleading statements. *Applied Cognitive Psychology, 18,* 1037–1058.

Clark-Plaskie, M. & Lachman, M. E. (1999). The sense of control in midlife. In S. L. Willis & J. D. Reid (Eds.), *Life in the middle.* Sam Diego: Academic Press.

Clarkson-Smith, L., & Hartley, A. A. (1989). Relationships between physical exercise and cognitive abilities in older adults. *Psychology and Aging, 4,* 183–189.

Clausen, J. A. (1993). *American lives.* New York: Free Press.

Clay, R. A. (1997, April). Helping dying patients let go of life in peace. *APA Monitor,* p. 42.

Cleary, P. D., Zaborksi, L. B., & Ayanian, J. Z. (2004). Sex differences in health over the course of midlife. In G. O. Brim, C. D. Ryff, & R. C. Kessler (Eds.), *How healthy are we?* Chicago: U. of Chicago Press.

Cleves, M. A., Hobbs, C. A., Collins, H. B., Andrews, N., Smith, L. N., & Robbins, J. N. (2004). Folic acid use by women receiving gynecologic care. *Obstetrics and Gynecology, 103,* 746–753.

Clifford, B. R., Gunter, B., & McAleer, J. L. (1995). *Television and children.* Hillsdale, NJ: Erlbaum.

Clifton, R. K., Morrongiello, B. A., Kulig, J. W., & Dowd, J. M. (1981). Developmental changes in auditory localization in infancy. In R. N. Aslin, J. R. Alberts, & M. R. Petersen (Eds.), *Development of perception* (Vol. 1). Orlando, FL: Academic Press.

Clifton, R. K., Muir, D. W., Ashmead, D. H., & Clarkson, M. G. (1993). Is visually guided reaching in early infancy a myth? *Child Development, 64,* 1099–1110.

Clinchy, B. M., Mansfield, A. F., & Schott, J. L. (1995, March). *Development of narrative and scientific modes of thought in middle childhood.* Paper presented at the meeting of the Society for Research in Child Development, Indianapolis.

Clingempeel, W. G., & Brand-Clingempeel, E. (2004). Pathogenic conflict: Families and children. In M. Coleman & L. Ganong (Eds.), *Handbook of contemporary families.* Thousand Oaks, CA: Sage.

Cnattingius, S., Bergstrom, R., Lipworth, L., & Kramer, M. S. (1998). Prepregnancy weight and the risk of adverse pregnancy outcomes. *New England Journal of Medicine, 338,* 147–152.

Cochran, S. D., & Mays, V. M. (1990). Sex, lies, and HIV. *New England Journal of Medicine, 322 (11),* 774–775.

Cohen, C. I., Teresi, J., & Holmes, D. (1985). Social networks, stress, adaptation, and health. *Research on Aging, 7,* 409–431.

Cohen, G. J. (2000). *American Academy of Pediatrics guide to your child's sleep: Birth through adolescence.* New York: Villard Books.

Cohen, G. L., & Sherman, D. K. (2005). Stereotype threat and the social and scientific contexts of the race achievement gap. *American Psychologist, 60,* 270–271.

Cohen, L. B. (1995). Violent video games: Aggression, arousal, and desensitization in young adolescent boys. Doctoral dissertation, University of Southern California, 1995). *Dissertation Abstracts International,* 57(2-B), 1463. University Microfilms No. 9616947.

Cohen, L. B., & Cashon, C. H. (2006). Infant cognition. In W. Damon & R. Lerner (Eds.), *Handbook of child psychology* (6th ed.). New York: Wiley.

Cohen, M. S. (2004). Fetal and childhood onset of adult cardiovascular diseases. *Pediatric Clinics of North America.* 51, 1697–1719.

Cohen, P., Kasen, S., Chen, H., Hartmark, C., & Gordon, K. (2003). Variations in patterns of developmental transitions in the emerging adulthood period. *Developmental Psychology, 39,* 657–669.

Cohn, A., & Canter, A. (2003). *Bullying: Facts for schools and parents.* Washington, DC: National Association of School Psychologists Center.

Cohn, E., & Harlow, K. (1993, October). Elders as victims: Randomized studies in two states. Paper presented at the meeting of the Geronotological Association of America, New Orleans.

Coie, J. (2004). The impact of negative social experiences on the development of antisocial behavior. In J. B. Kupersmidt & K. A. Dodge (Eds.), *Children's peer relations: From development to intervention.* Washington, DC: American Psychological Association.

Colby, A., Kohlberg, L., Gibbs, J., & Lieberman, M. (1983). A longitudinal study of moral judgment. *Monographs of the Society for Research in Child Development* (Serial No. 201).

Colcombe, S. J., Erickson, K. I., Raz, N., Webb, A. G., Cohen, N. J., McAuley, E., & Kramer, A. F. (2003). Aerobic fitness reduces brain tissue loss in aging humans. *Journals of Gerontology: Biological Sciences and Medical sciences, 58,* 176–180.

Colcombe, S. J., & Kramer, A. F. (2003). Fitness effects on the cognitive function of older adults: A meta-analytic study. *Psychological Science, 14,* 125–130.

Colcombe, S. J., Kramer, A. F., Rickson, K. I., Scalf, P., McAuley, E., Cohen, N. J., Webb, A., Jerome, G. J., Marquez, D. X., & Elavsky, S. (2004). Cardiovascular fitness, cortical plasticity, and aging. *Proceedings of the National Academy of Science, 101,* 3316–3321.

Cole, A. (2003). Retirement: Into extra time. *Health Services Journal, 113,* 26–28.

Cole, E. R., & Stewart, A. J. (1996). Black and white women's political activism: Personality development, political identity and social responsibility. *Journal of Personality and Social Psychology, 71,* 130–140.

Cole, M. (2005). Culture in development. In M. H. Bornstein & M. E. Lamb (Eds.), *Developmental science* (5th ed.). Mahwah, NJ: Erlbaum.

Cole, M. (2006). Culture and cognitive development in phylogenetic, historical, and ontogenetic perspective. In W. Damon & R. Lerner (Eds.), *Handbook of child psychology* (6th ed.). New York: Wiley.

Coleman, M., Ganong, L., & Fine, M. (2000). Reinvestigating remarriage: Another decade of progress. *Journal of Marriage and the Family, 62,* 1288–1307.

Coleman, M., Ganong, L., & Fine, M. (2004). Communication in stepfamilies. In A. L. Vangelisti (Ed.), *Handbook of family communication.* Mahwah, NJ: Erlbaum.

Coleman, P. D. (1986, August). *Regulation of dendritic extent: Human aging brain and Alzheimer's disease.* Paper presented at the meeting of the American Psychological Association, Washington, DC.

Coleman, V. H., Erickson, K., Schulkin, J., Zinberg, S., & Sachs, B. P. (2005). Vaginal birth after cesarean delivery: Practice patterns of obstetricians-gynecologists. *Journal of Reproductive Medicine, 50,* 261–266.

Coles, R. (1970). *Erik H. Erikson: The growth of his work.* Boston: Little, Brown.

Coley, R. (2001). *Differences in the gender gap: Comparisons across racial/ethnic groups in education and work.* Princeton: Educational Testing Service.

Coley, R. L. Li-Grining, & Chase-Lansdale, P. L. (2006). Low-income families' child care experiences. In N. Cabrera, R. Hutchens, H. E. Peters, & L. Peters (Eds.), *From welfare to childcare.* Mahwah, NJ: Erlbaum.

Coley, R. L., Morris, J. E., & Hernandez, D. (2004). Out-of-school care and problem behavior trajectories among low-income adolescents: Individual, family, and neighborhood characteristics and added risks. *Child Development, 75,* 948–965.

Coll, C. G., & Pachter, L. M. (2002). Ethnic and minority parenting. In M. H. Bornstein (Ed.), *Handbook of parenting* (2nd ed., Vol. 4). Mahwah, NJ: Erlbaum.

Collaku, A., Rankinen, T., Rice, T., Leon, A. S., Rao, D. C., Skinner, J. S., Wilmore, J. H., & Bouchard, C. (2004). A genome-wide linkage scan for dietary energy and nutrient intakes. *American Journal of Clinical Nutrition, 79,* 881–886.

Collins, M. (1996, Winter). The job outlook for 96 grades. *Journal of Career Planning,* pp. 51–54.

Collins, R. L. (2005). Sex on television and its impact on American youth: Background and results from the RAND television and adolescent sexuality study. *Child and Adolescent Psychiatry Clinics of North America, 14,* 371–385.

Collins, R. L., Elliott, M. N., Berry, S, H., Kanouse, D. E., Kunkel, D., Hunter, S. B., & Miu, A. (2004). Watching sex on television predicts adolescent initiation of sexual behavior. *Pediatrics, 114,* e280–e289.

Collins, W. A. & Laursen, B. (2004). Parent adolescent relationships and influences. In R. Lerner & L. Steinberg (Eds.), *Handbook of adolescent psychology.* New York: Wiley.

Collins, W. A. & Steinberg, L. (2006). Adolescent development in interpersonal context. In W. Damon & R. Lerner (Eds.), *Handbook of child psychology* (6th ed.). New York: Wiley.

Collins, W. A., Maccoby, E. E., Steinberg, L., Hetherington, E. M., & Bornstein, M. H. (2000). Contemporary research on parenting: The case for nature and nurture. *American Psychologist, 55,* 218–232.

Collins, W. A., Maccoby, E. E., Steinberg, L., Hetherington, E. M., & Bornstein, M. H. (2001).

Toward nature WITH nurture. *American Psychologist, 56,* 171–173.

Collins, W. A., Madsen, S. D., & Susman-Stillman, A. (2002). Parenting during middle childhood. In M. Bornstein (Ed.), *Handbook of parenting* (2nd ed.). Mahwah, NJ: Erlbaum.

Colman, R. A., & Widom, C. S. (2004). Childhood abuse and neglect and adult intimate relationships: A prospective study. *Child Abuse and Neglect, 28,* 1133–1151.

Combs, M. (2006). *Readers and writers in the primary grades* (3rd ed.). Upper Saddle River, NJ: Prentice Hall.

Comer, J. P. (1988). Educating poor minority children. *Scientific American, 259,* 42–48.

Comer, J. P. (2004). *Leave no child behind.* New Haven, CT: Yale University Press.

Comijs, H., Deeg, D., Dik, M., Twisk, J., & Jonker, C. (2002). *Memory complaints.* Unpublished manuscript, Department of Psychiatry, Vrije University, Amsterdam, The Netherlands.

Committee on Substance Abuse. (2000). Fetal alcohol syndrome and alcohol-related neurodevelopmental disorders. *Pediatrics, 106,* 258–261.

Commoner, B. (2002). Unraveling the DNA myth: The spurious foundation of genetic engineering. *Harper's Magazine, 304,* 39–47.

Commons, M. L., & Bresette, L. M. (2006). Illuminating major creative scientific innovators with postformal stages. In C. Hoare (Ed.), *Handbook of adult development and learning.* New York: Oxford University Press.

Commons, M. L., Sinnott, J. D., Richards, F. A., & Armon, C. (1989). *Adult development: Vol. 1. Comparisons and applications of developmental models.* New York: Praeger.

Compas, B. (2004). Processes of risk and resilience during adolescence: Linking contexts and individuals. In R. Lerner & L. Steinberg (Eds.), *Handbook of adolescent psychology.* New York: Wiley.

Compas, B. E., Connor-Smith, J. K., Saltzman, H., Thomsen, A. H., & Wadsworth, M. E. (2001). Coping with stress during childhood and adolescence: Problems, progress, and potential in theory and research. *Psychological Bulletin, 127,* 87–127.

Compas, B. E., & Grant, K. E. (1993, March). *Stress and adolescent depressive symptoms: Underlying mechanisms and processes.* Paper presented at the biennial meeting of the Society for Research in Child Development, New Orleans.

Comstock, G., & Scharrer, E. (2006). Media and popular culture. In W. Damon & R. Lerner (Eds.), *Handbook of child psychology* (6th ed.). New York: Wiley.

Conduct Problems Prevention Research Group. (2004). The Fast Track experiment: Translating the developmental model into a preventive design. In J. B. Kupersmidt & K. A. Dodge (Eds.), *Children's peer relations: From development to intervention.* Washington, DC: American Psychological Association.

Conger, R. D., & Chao, W. (1996). Adolescent depressed mood. In R. L. Simons (Ed.), *Understanding differences between divorced and intact families: Stress, interaction, and child outcome.* Thousand Oaks, CA: Sage.

Conger, R. D., & Ge, X. (1999). Conflict and cohesion in parent-adolescent relations: Changes in emotional expression. In M. J. Cox & J. Brooks-Gunn (Eds.), *Conflict and cohesion in families.* Mahwah, NJ: Erlbaum.

Conger, R., & Reuter, M. (1996). Siblings, parents, and peers: A longitudinal study of social influences in adolescent risk for alcohol use and abuse. In G. H. Brody (Ed.), *Sibling relationships: Their causes and consequences.* Norwood, NJ: Ablex.

Conner, K. R., Duberstein, P. R., Beckman, A., Heisel, M. J., Hirsch, J. K., Gamble, S., & Conwell, Y. (2006, in press). Planning of suicide attempts among depressed inpatients ages 50 and over. *Journal of Affective Disorders.*

Conner, M. E., & White, J. L. (Eds.) (2006). *Black fathers*. Mahwah, NJ: Erlbaum.

Consedine, N. S., Magai, C., & Conway, F. (2004). Predicting ethnic variation in adaptation to later life: Styles of socioemotional functioning and constrained heterotypy. *Journal of Cross Cultural Gerontology, 19,* 97–131.

Contemporary Research Press. (1993). *American working women: A statistical handbook.* Dallas: Author.

Conway, K. P., Swendsen, J. D., & Merikangas, K. R. (2003). Alcohol expectancies, alcohol consumption, and problem drinking: The moderating role of family history. *Addictive Behavior, 28,* 823–836.

Conway, K. S., & Kutinova, A. (2006). Maternal health: Does prenatal care make a difference? *Health Economics, 15,* 461–488.

Cook, D. J., Guyatt, G. H., Jaeschke, R., Reeve, J., Spanier, A., King, D., Molloy, D., William, A., & Streiner, D. (1995). Determinants in Canadian health care workers of the decision to withdraw life support from the critically ill. *Journal of the American Medical Association, 273,* 703–708.

Cook, J. A., & Hawkins, D. B. (2006). Hearing loss and hearing aid treatment options. *Mayo Clinic Proceedings, 81,* 234–237.

Cook, J. A., & others. (2005). Integration of psychiatric and vocational services: A multisite. randomized, controlled trial of supported employment. *American Journal of Psychiatry, 162,* 1948–1956.

Cook, M., & Birch, R. (1984). Infant perception of the shapes of tilted plane forms. *Infant Behavior and Development, 7,* 389–402.

Cooney, T. M. (1994). Young adults' relations with parents: The influence of recent parental divorce. *Journal of Marriage and the Family, 56,* 45–56.

Cooper, C. R., & Grotevant, H. D. (1989, April). *Individuality and connectedness in the family and adolescent's self and relational competence.* Paper presented at the meeting of the Society for Research in Child Development, Kansas City.

Cooper, C. R., Grotevant, H. D., Moore, M. S., & Condon, S. M. (1982, August). *Family support and conflict: Both foster adolescent identity and role taking.* Paper presented at the meeting of the American Psychological Association, Washington, DC.

Cooter, R. B. (Ed.) (2004). *Perspectives on rescuing urban literacy education.* Mahwah, NJ: Erlbaum.

Corbett, T. (2006). Foreward. In K. Bogenschneider (Ed.), *Family policy matters.* Mahwah, NJ: Erlbaum.

Cornish, K. (2004). The role of cognitive neuroscience in understanding atypical developmental pathways. *Journal of Cognitive Neuroscience, 16,* 4–5.

Corr, C. A., Nabe, C. M., & Corr, D. M. (2003). *Death and dying, life and living* (4th ed.). Belmont, CA: Wadsworth.

Corrigan, R. (1981). The effects of task and practice on search for invisibly displaced objects. *Developmental Review, 1,* 1–17.

Corsini, R. J. (1990). *The dictionary of psychology.* Philadelphia: Brunner/Mazel.

Cortesi, F., Giannotti, F., Sebastiani, T., & Vagnoni, C. (2004). Cosleeping and sleep behavior in Italian school-aged children. *Journal of Developmental and Behavioral Pediatrics, 25,* 28–33.

Cortina, L. M. (2004). Hispanic perspectives on sexual harassment and social support. *Personality and Social Psychology Bulletin, 30,* 574–584.

Cortina, L. M., & Wasti, S. A. (2005). Profiles in coping: Responses to sexual harassment across persons, organizations, and cultures. *Journal of Applied Psychology, 90,* 182–192.

Cosmides, L., Tooby, J., Cronin, H., & Curry, O. (Eds.). (2003). *What is evolutionary psychology? Explaining the new science of the mind.* New Haven, CT: Yale University Press.

Costa, P. T., & McCrae, R. R. (1995). Solid ground on the wetlands of personality: A reply to Black. *Psychological Bulletin, 117,* 216–220.

Costa, P. T., & McCrae, R. R. (1998). Personality assessment. In H. S. Friedman (Ed.), *Encyclopedia of mental health* (Vol. 3). San Diego: Academic Press.

Costa, P. T., & McCrae, R. R. (1999). Contemporary personality psychology: Implications for geriatric neuropsychiatry. In C. E. Coffey and J. L. Cummings (Eds.), *Textbook of geriatric neuropsychiatry* (2nd ed.), Washington, DC: American Psychiatric Press.

Costa, P. T., & McCrae, R. R. (2000). Contemporary personality psychology. In C. E. Coffey and J. L. Cummings (Eds.), *Textbook of geriatric neuropsychiatry.* Washington, DC: American Psychiatric Press.

Cote, J. E. (2006). Emerging adulthood as an instutionalized moratorium: Risks and benefits to identity formation. In J. J. Arnett and J. L. Tanner (Eds.), *Emerging adulthood in America.* Washington, DC: American Psychological Association.

Cotten, S. R. (1999). Marital status and mental health revisited: Examining the importance of risk factors and resources. *Family Relations, 48,* 225–233.

Council of Economic Advisors. (2000). *Teens and their parents in the 21st century: An examination of trends in teen behavior and the role of parent involvement.* Washington, DC: Author.

Courage, M. L., Edison, S. C., & Howe, M. L. (2004). Variability in the early development of visual self-recognition. *Infant Behavior and Development, 27,* 509–532.

Covan, E. K. (2005). Meaning of aging in women's lives. *Journal of Women and Aging, 17,* 3–22.

Cowan, C. P., & Cowan, P. A. (2000). *When partners become parents.* Mahwah, NJ: Erlbaum.

Cowley, G. (1998, April 6). Why children turn violent. *Newsweek,* pp. 24–25.

Cowley, G., & Hager, M. (1995, December, 4). Terminal care: Too painful, too prolonged. *Newsweek,* pp. 74–75.

Cox, B. J., Enns, M. W., & Clara, I. P. (2004). Psychological dimensions associated with suicidal ideation and attempts in the National Comorbidity Study. *Suicide and Life-Threatening Behavior, 34,* 209–219.

Cox, H., & Hammonds, A. (1998). Religiosity, aging, and life satisfaction. *Journal of Religion and Aging, 5,* 1–21.

Cox, J. (2006). Postnatal depression in fathers. *Lancet, 366,* 982.

Cox, J. L., Holden, J. M., & Sagovsky, R. (1987). Detection of postnatal depression: Development of the 10-items Edinburgh Postnatal Depression Scale. *British Journal of Psychiatry, 150,* 782–786.

Cox, M. J., Burchinal, M., Taylor, L. C., Frosch, B., Goldman, B., & Kanoy, K. (2004). The transition to parenting: Continuity and change in early parenting behavior and attitudes. In R. D., Conger, F. O. Lorenz, & K. A. S. Wickrama (Eds.), *Continuity and change in family relations.* Mahwah, NJ: Erlbaum.

Coyne-Beasley, T., Baccaglini, L., Johnson, R. M., Webster, B., & Wiebe, D. J. (2005). Do partners with children know about firearms in their home? Evidence of a gender gap and implications for practitioners. *Pediatrics, 115,* e662–e667.

Craik, F.I., & Bialystok, E. (2006). Cognition through the lifespan: Mechanisms of change. *Trends in cognitive science, 10,* 131–138.

Cremation Association of America. (2000). *Fact sheet.* Milwaukee, WI: Author.

Cress, S. W. (2004). Assessing standards in the "real" kindergarten classroom. *Early Childhood Education Journal, 32,* 95–99.

Crews, F. T., & others. (2005). Alcoholic neurobiology: Changes in dependency and recovery. *Alcoholism: Clinical and Experimental Research, 29,* 1504–1513.

Crews, J. E., & Campbell, V. A. (2004). Vision impairment and hearing loss among community-dwelling older Americans: Implications for health and functioning. *American Journal of Public Health, 94,* 823–829.

Crick, N. R. (2005, April). *Gender and psychopathology.* Paper presented at the meeting of the Society for Research in Child Development, Atlanta.

Crick, N. R., Ostrov, J. M., Appleyard, K., Jansen, E. A., & Casas, J. F. (2004). Relational aggression in early childhood. In M. Putallaz & K. L. Bierman (Eds.), *Aggression, antisocial behavior, and violence among girls.* New York: Guilford.

Crockenberg, S. B. (1986). Are temperamental differences in babies associated with predictable differences in caregiving? In J. V. Lerner & R. M. Lerner (Eds.), *Temperament and social interaction during infancy and childhood.* San Francisco: Jossey-Bass.

Crockett, L. J., Raffaelli, M., & Moilanen, K. (2003). Adolescent sexuality: Behavior and meaning. In G. Adams & M. Berzonsky (Eds.), *Blackwell handbook of adolescence.* Malden, MA: Blackwell.

Croog, S.H., Burleston, J.A., Sudilovsky, A., & Baume, R.M. (2006). Spouse caregivers of Alzheimer patients: Problem responses to caregiver burden. *Aging and Mental Health, 10,* 87–100.

Crosignani, P.G. (2006, in press). Hormones and cardiovascular health in women. *Human Reproduction Update.*

Crossfield, S., Kinman, G., & Jones, F. (2005). Crossover of occupational stress in dual-career couples: The role of work demands and supports, job commitment, and marital communication. *Community, Work, and Family, 8,* 211–232.

Crossman, A. M., Scullin, M. H., & Melnyk, L., (2004). Individual and developmental differences in suggestibility. *Applied Cognitive Psychology, 18,* 941–945.

Crouter, A. C., & Booth, A. (Eds.) (2004). *Work-family challenges for low-income families and their children.* Mahwah, NJ: Erlbaum.

Crouter, A. C., & McHale, S. (2005). The long arm of the job revisited: Parenting in dual-earner families. In T. Luster & L. Okagaki (Eds.), *Parenting.* Mahwah, NJ: Erlbaum.

Crowley, K., Callahan, M. A., Tenenbaum, H. R., & Allen, E. (2001). Parents explain more to boys than to girls during shared scientific thinking. *Psychological Science, 12,* 258–261.

Crowley, M., Lichter, D.T., & Qian, Z. (2006). Beyond gateway cities: Economic restructuring and poverty among Mexican immigrant families and children. *Family Relations, 55,* 345–360.

Csaba, A., Bush, M. C., & Saphier, C. (2006). How painful are amniocentesis and chorionic villus sampling? *Prenatal Diagnosis, 26,* 35–38.

Czaja, S. J. (2001). Technological change and the older worker. In J. E. Birren & K. W. Schaie (Eds.), *Handbook of the psychology of aging* (5th ed.). San Diego: Academic Press.

Csikszentmihalyi, M. (1995). *Creativity.* New York: HarperCollins.

Csikszentmihalyi, M. (1997). *Finding flow.* New York: Basic Books.

Csikszentmihalyi, M. (2000). Creativity: An overview. In A. Kazdin (Ed.), *Encyclopedia of psychology.* Washington DC, & New York: American Psychological Association and Oxford University Press.

Csikszentmihalyi, M., & Nakamura, J. (2006). Creativity though the life span from an evolutionary systems perspective. In C. Hoare (Ed.), *Handbook of adult development and learning.* New York: Oxford University Press.

Csikszentmihalyi, M., & Rathunde, K. (1998). The development of the person: An experiential perspective on the ontogenesis of psychological complexity. In W. Damon (Ed.), *Handbook of child psychology* (5th ed., Vol. 1). New York: Wiley.

Cuddy-Casey, M., & Orvaschel, H. (1997). Children's understanding of death in relation to child suicidality and homicidality. *Death Studies, 17,* 33–45.

Cuevas, K. D., Silver, D. R., Brooten, D., Youngblut, J. M., & Bobo, C. M. (2005). The cost of prematurity: Hospital charges at birth and frequency of rehospitalization and acute care visits over the first year of life: A comparison of gestational age and birth weight. *American Journal of Nursing, 105,* 56–64.

Cui, X., & Vaillant, G. E. (1996). Antecedents and consequents of negative life events in adulthood: A longitudinal study. *American Journal of Psychiatry, 153,* 123–126.

Cuijpers, P. (2001). Mortality and depressive symptoms in inhabitants of residential homes. *International Journal of Geriatric Psychiatry, 16,* 131–138.

Cullen, K. (2001). *Context and eating behavior in children.* Unpublished research, Children's Nutrition Research Center, Baylor School of Medicine, Houston.

Cully, J. A., LaVoie, D., & Gfeller, J. D. (2001). Reminiscence, personality, and psychological functioning in older adults. *The Gerontologist, 41 (No. 1),* 89–95.

Cumming, E., & Henry, W. (1961). *Growing old.* New York: Basic Books.

Cummings, E. M. (1987). Coping with background anger in early childhood. *Child Development, 58,* 976–984.

Cummings, E. M., Braungart-Rieker, J. M., & Du Rocher-Schudlich, T. (2003). Emotion and personality development. In I. B. Weiner (Ed,), *Handbook of psychology* (Vol. 6). New York: Wiley.

Cummings, M. (2006). *Human heredity* (7th ed.). Pacific Grove, CA: Brooks Cole.

Cunningham, M. (2004). Old is a three-letter word. *Geriatric Nursing, 25,* 277–280.

Cupertino, A. P., & Haan, M. N. (1999, November). *Religiosity and health among elderly Latinos.* Paper presented at the meeting of the Gerontological Society of America, San Francisco.

Curran, K., DuCette, J., Eisenstein, J., & Hyman, I. A. (2001, August). *Statistical analysis of the cross-cultural data: The third year.* Paper presented at the meeting of the American Psychological Association, San Francisco, CA.

Currier, J. M., Holland, J. M., & Neimeyer, R. A. (2006). Sense-making, grief, and the experience of violent loss: Toward a mediational model. *Death Studies, 30,* 403–428.

Cushner, K. H. (2006). *Human diversity in action* (3rd ed.). New York: McGraw-Hill.

Cutler, S. J. (2006). Technological change and aging. In R. H. Binstock & L. K. George (Eds.), *Handbook of aging and the social sciences* (6th ed.). San Diego: Academic Press.

Cutrona, C. E. (1982). Transition to college: Loneliness and the process of social adjustment. In L. A. Peplau & D. Perlman (Eds.), *Loneliness.* New York: Wiley.

Cyna, A. M., McAuliffe, G. L., & Andrew, M. I. (2004). Hypnosis for pain relief in labor and childbirth: A systematic review. *British Journal of Anesthesia, 93,* 505–511.

Czaja, S. J., Charness, N., Fisk, A. D., Hertzog, C., Nair, S. N., Rogers, W. A., & Sharit, J. (2006). Factors predicting the use of technology: Findings from the Center for Research and Education on Aging and Technology (CREATE). *Psychology and Aging, 21,* 333–352.

Czeizel, A. E., & Puho, E. (2005). Maternal use of nutritional supplements during the first month of pregnancy and decreased risk of Down's syndrome: Case-control study. *Nutrition, 21,* 698–704.

D'Augelli, A. (2000). Sexual orientation. In A. Kazdin (Ed.), *Encyclopedia of psychology.* Washington, DC, & New York: American Psychological Association and Oxford University Press.

D'Augelli, A. R. (1991). Gay men in college: Identity processes and adaptations. *Journal of College Student Development, 32,* 140–146.

Daaleman, T. P., Perera, S., & Studenski, S. A. (2004). Religion, spirituality, and health status in geriatric outpatients. *Annals of Family Medicine, 2,* 49–53.

Dahl, R. E. (2001). Affect regulation, brain development, and behavioral/emotional health in adolescence. *CNS Spectrums, 6,* 60–72.

Dahl, R. E. (2004). Adolescent brain development: A period of vulnerabilities and opportunities. *Annals of the New York Academy of Sciences, 1021,* 1–22.

Dahl, R. E. (2006). Sleeplessness and aggression in youth. *Journal of Adolescent Health, 38,* 641–642.

Dahl, R. E., & Lewin, D. S. (2002). Pathways to adolescent health sleep regulation and behavior. *Journal of Adolescent Health, 31* (6 Suppl.), 175–184.

Dale, P., & Goodman, J. (2004). Commonality and differences in vocabulary growth. In M. Tomasello & D. I. Slobin (Eds.), *Beyond nature-nurture.* Mahwah, NJ: Erlbaum.

Daley, S. E., & Hammen, C. (2002). Depressive symptoms and close relationships during the transition to adulthood: Perspectives from dysphoric women, their best friends, and their romantic partners. *Journal of Consulting and Clinical Psychology, 70,* 129–141.

Damon, W. (1988). *The moral child.* New York: Free Press.

Damon, W., & Hart, D. (1992). Self-understanding and its role in social and moral development. In M. H. Bornstein & M. E. Lamb (Eds.), *Developmental psychology: An advanced textbook* (3rd ed.). Hillsdale, NJ: Erlbaum.

Danforth, M. M., & Glass, J. C. (2001). Listen to my words, give meaning to my sorrow: A study in cognitive constructs in middle-aged bereaved widows. *Death Studies, 25,* 513–548.

Daniels, P., Noe, G. F., & Mayberry, R. (2006). Barriers to prenatal care among Black women of low socioeconomic status. *American Journal of Health Behavior, 30,* 188–198.

Daniels, S. R. (2005). What is the best method to identify cardiovascular risk related to obesity? *Journal of Pediatrics, 146,* A3.

Danielson, C. K., De Arellano, M. A., Kilpatrick, D. G., Saunders, B. E., & Resnick, H. S. (2005). Child maltreatment in depressed adolescents: Differences in symptomatology based on history of abuse. *Child Maltreatment, 10,* 37–48.

Danner D., Snowdon D., Friesen W. (2001). Positive emotions in early life and longevity: Findings from the Nun Study. *Journal of Personality and Social Psychology, 80* (5), 814–813.

Dansinger, M. L., Gleason, A., Griffith, J. L., Selker, H. P., & Schaefer, E. J. (2005). Comparisons of Atkins, Ornish, Weight Watchers, and Zone diets for weight loss and heart disease risk reduction. *Journal of the American Medical Association, 293,* 43–53.

Darling-Hammond, L., & Bransford, J. (Eds.) (2005). *Preparing teachers for a changing world.* San Francisco: Jossey-Bass.

Darwin, C. (1859). *On the origin of species.* London: John Murray.

Darwin, C. (1965). *The expression of the emotions in man and animals.* Chicago: University of Chicago Press. (Original work published 1872).

Das, S., & O'Keefe, J. H. (2006). Behavioral cardiology: Recognizing and addressing the profound impact of psychosocial stress on cardiovascular health. *Current Atherosclerosis Reports, 8,* 111–118.

Dasen, P. R. (1977). Are cognitive processes universal? A contribution to cross-cultural Piagetian psychology. In N. Warran (Ed.), *Studies in cross-cultural psychology* (Vol. 1). London: Academic Press.

Datar, A., & Sturm, R. (2004). Childhood overweight and parent- and teacher-reported behavior problems: Evidence from a prospective study of kindergartners. *Archives of Pediatric and Adolescent Medicine, 158,* 804–810.

Dattilio, F. M. (Ed.). (2001). Case studies in couple and family therapy. New York: Guilford.

Davenport, G. (2004). Rheumatology and musculoskeletal medicine. *British Journal of General Practice, 54,* 457–464.

Davidson, J. (2000). Giftedness. In A. Kazdin (Ed.), *Encyclopedia of psychology.* Washington, DC, & New York: American Psychological Association and Oxford University Press.

Davies, J., & Brember, I. (1999). Reading and mathematics attainments and self-esteem in years 2 and 6—an eight-year cross-sectional study. *Educational Studies, 25,* 145–157.

Davies, S. L., DiClemente, R. J., Wingood, G. M., Person, S. D., Dix, E. S., Harrington, K., Crobsy, R. A., & Oh, K. (2006). Predictors of inconsistent contraceptive use among adolescent girls: A prospective study. *Journal of Adolescent Health, 39,* 43–49.

Davila, J., & Steinberg, S. J. (2006). Depression and romantic dysfunction during adolescence. In T. E. Joiner, J. S. Brown, & J. Kistner (Eds.), *The interpersonal, cognitive, and social nature of depression.* Mahwah, NJ: Erlbaum.

Davis, B. E., Moon, R. Y., Sachs, M. C., & Ottolini, M. C. (1998). Effects of sleep position on infant motor development. *Pediatrics, 102,* 1135–1140.

Davis, D. K. (2005). Leading the midwifery renaissance. *RCM Midwives, 8,* 264–268.

Davis, E. P., Glynn, L. M., Dunkel-Schetter, C., Hobel, C., Chiez-Demet, A., & Sandman, C. A. (2006). Corticotropin-releasing hormone during pregnancy is associated with infant temperament. *Developmental Neuroscience, 27,* 299–305.

Davis, G. F. (2001). Loss and duration of grief. *Journal of the American Medical Association, 285,* 1152–1153.

Davis, K. E. (1985, February). Near and dear: Friendship and love compared. *Psychology Today,* pp. 22–29.

Davis, L., & Keyser, J. (1997). *Becoming the parent you want to be: A sourcebook of strategies for the first five years.* New York: Broadway

Davison, G. C., & Neale, J. M. (2007). *Abnormal psychology* (10th ed.). New York: Wiley.

Davison, K. K., & Birth, L. L. (2001). Weight status, parent reaction, and self-concept in five-year-old girls. *Pediatrics, 107,* 46–53.

Daws, D. (2000). *Through the night.* San Francisco: Free Association Books.

Day, N. L., Leech, S. L., Richardson, G. A., Cornelius, M. D., Robles, N., & Larkby, C. (2002). Prenatal alcohol exposure predicts continued deficits in offspring size at 14 years of age. *Alcohol: Clinical and Experimental Research, 26,* 1584–1591.

Day, R. H., & McKenzie, B. E. (1973). Perceptual shape constancy in early infancy. *Perception, 2,* 315–320.

Day-Stirk, F. (2005). The big push for normal birth. *RCM Midwives, 8,* 18–20.

De Bellis, M. D., Keshavan, M. S., Beers, S. R., Hall, J., Frustaci, K., Masalehdan, A., & Boring, N. J. (2001). Sex differences in brain maturation during childhood and adolescence. *Cerebral Cortex, 11,* 552–557.

De Graaf, C., Blom, W. A., Smeets, P. A., Stafleu, A., & Hendriks, H. F. (2004). Biomarkers of satiation and satiety. *American Journal of Clinical Nutrition, 79,* 946–961.

de Jong, J. (2004). Grammatical impairment. In L. Verhoeven & H. Van Balkom (Eds.), *The classification of language disorders.* Mahwah, NJ: Erlbaum.

de Jong-Gierveld, J. (1987). Developing and testing a model of loneliness. *Journal of Personality and Social Psychology, 53,* 119–128.

De la Fuente, M., Hernanz, A., & Vallejo, M. C. (2006). The immune system in the oxidative stress conditions of aging and hypertension: Favorable effects of antioxidants and physical exercise. *Antioxidants and Redox Signaling, 7,* 1356–1366.

de la Rochebrochard, E., & Thonneau, P. (2002). Paternal age and maternal age are risk factors for miscarriage: Results of a multicentre European study. *Human Reproduction, 17,* 1649–1656.

De Litvan, M. A., & Manzano, J. (2005). Inter-generational transmission of psychopathology. *International Journal of Psychoanalysis, 86,* 517–520.

de Vries, P. (2005). Lessons from home: Scaffolding vocal improvisation and song acquisition in a 2-year-old. *Early Childhood Education Journal, 32,* 307–312.

Deary, I. J., & Der, G. (2005). Reaction time explains IQ's association with death. *Psychological Science, 16,* 64–69.

Deater-Deckard, K. & Dodge, K. (1997). Externalizing behavior problems and discipline revisited: Non-linear effects and variation by culture, context and gender. *Psychological Inquiry, 8,* 161–175.

Deater-Deckard, K., Petrill, S. A., Thompson, L. A., & DeThorne, I. S. (2005). A cross-sectional behavioral genetic analysis of task persistence in the transition to middle childhood. *Developmental Science, 8,* F21–F26.

DeCasper, A. J., & Spence, M. J. (1986). Prenatal maternal speech influences newborn's perception of speech sounds. *Infant Behavior and Development, 9,* 133–150.

Decca, L., Daldoss, C., Fratelli, N., Lojacono, A., Slompo, M., Stegher, C., Valcamonico, A., & Frusca, T. (2004). Labor course and delivery in epidural amnesia: A case-control study. *Journal of Maternal-Fetal and Neonatal Medicine, 16,* 115–118.

Declercq, E., Menacker, F., & Macdorman, M. (2006). Maternal risk profiles and the primary cesarean rate in the United States, 1991–2002. *American Journal of Public Health, 96,* 867–872.

Deeg, D. J. M. (2005). The development of physical and mental health from late midlife to early old age. In S. L. Willis & M. Martin (Eds.) *Middle adulthood.* Thousand Oaks, CA: Sage.

DeLamater, J. D., & MacCorquodale, P. (1979). *Premarital sexuality.* Madison: University of Wisconsin Press.

DeLamater, J. D., & Sill, M. (2005). Sexual desire in later life. *Journal of Sex Research, 42,* 167–174.

Delemarre-van de Waal, H. A. (2005). Secular trend of timing puberty. *Endocrine Development, 8,* 1–14.

DeLoache, J. (2001). The symbol-mindedness of young children. In W. W. Hartup & R. A. Weinberg (Eds.), *Child psychology in retrospect and prospect.* Mahwah, NJ: Erlbaum.

DeLoache, J. S. (2004). Early development of the understanding and use of symbolic art: Facts. In U. Goswami (Ed.), *Blackwell handbook of childhood cognitive development.* Malden MA: Blackwell.

Delpisheh, A., Attia, E., Drammond, S., & Brabin, B. J. (2006). Adolescent smoking in pregnancy and birth outcomes. *European Journal of Public Health, 16,* 168–172.

DeMarie, D., Abshier, D. W., & Ferron, J. (2001, April). *Longitudinal study of predictors of memory improvement over the elementary school years: Capacity, strategies, and metamemory revisited.* Paper presented at the meeting of the Society for Research in Child Development, Minneapolis.

DeMaris, A., & Rao, K. (1992). Premarital cohabitation and subsequent marital stability in the United States: A reassessment. *Journal of Marriage and the Family, 54,* 178–190.

Demetriou, A. (2001, April). *Towards a comprehensive theory of intellectual development: Integrating psychometric and post-Piagetian theories.* Paper presented at the meeting of the Society for Research in Child Development, Minneapolis.

Demorest, R. A., & Landry, G. L. (2004). Training issues in elite young athletes. *Current Sports Medicine Reports, 3,* 167–172.

Dempster, F. N. (1981). Memory span: Sources of individual and developmental differences. *Psychological Bulletin, 80,* 63–100.

Dendinger, V. M., Adams, G. A., & Jacobson, J. D. (2005). Reasons for working and their relationship to retirement attitudes, job satisfaction, and occupational self-efficacy of bridge employees. *International Journal of Aging and Human Development, 61,* 21–35.

Denham, S. A. (1998). *Emotional development in young children.* New York: Guilford.

Denmark, F. L., Rabinowitz, V. C., & Sechzer, J. A. (2005). *Engendering psychology: Women and gender revisited* (2nd ed.). Boston: Allyn & Bacon.

Denmark, F. L., Russo, N. F., Frieze, I. H., & Eschuzur, J. (1988). Guidelines for avoiding sexism in psychological research: A report of the ad hoc committee on nonsexist research. *American Psychologist, 43,* 582–585.

Denney, N. W. (1986, August). *Practical problem solving.* Paper presented at the meeting of the American Psychological Association, Washington, DC.

Denney, N. W. (1990). Adult age differences in traditional and practical problem solving. *Advances in Psychology, 72,* 329–349.

Denny, C. B. (2001). Stimulant effects in attention deficit hyperactivity disorder. *Journal of Clinical Child Psychology, 30,* 98–109.

DePinho, B. M., & Morris, W. L. (2005). Singles in society and science. *Psychological Inquiry, 16,* 57–83.

DeRosier, M. E., & Marcus, S. R. (2005). Building friendships and combating bullying: Effectiveness of S. S. Grin at one-year follow-up. *Journal of Clinical Child and Adolescent Psychology, 34,* 140–150.

Desmarais, S., & Alksnis, C. (2004). Gender issues. In J. Barling, E. K. Kelloway, & M. R. Frone (Eds.), *Handbook of work and stress.* Thousand Oaks, CA: Sage.

DeSpelder, L. A., & Strikland, A. L. (2005). *The last dance: Encountering death and dying* (6th ed., rev. update). Mountain View, CA: Mayfield.

Deutsch, F. M. (1991). Women's lives: The story not told by theories of development. *Contemporary Psychology, 36,* 237–238.

Devanand, D. P., Pelton, G. H., Zamora, D., Liu, X., Tabert, M. H., Goodkind, M., Scarmeas, N., Braun, I., Stern, Y., & Mayeux, R. (2005). Predictive utility of apolipoprotein E genotype for Alzheimer disease in outpatients with mild cognitive impairment. *Archives of Neurology, 62,* 975–980.

DeVellis, B. M., & DeVellis, R. F. (2001). Self-efficacy and health. In A. Baum, T. A. Revenson, & J. E. Singer (Eds.), *Handbook of health psychology.* Mahwah, NJ: Erlbaum.

Dewey, K. G. (2003). Is breastfeeding protective against childhood obesity? *Journal of Human Lactation, 19,* 9–18.

Diamond, A. D. (1985). Development of the ability to use recall to guide action, as indicated by infants' performance on AB. *Child Development, 56,* 868–883.

Diamond, A. D. (2001). A model system for studying the role of dopamine in the prefrontal cortex during early development in humans: Early and continuously treated phenylketonuria. In C. Nelson & M. Luciana (Eds.), *Handbook of developmental cognitive neuroscience.* Cambridge, MA: MIT Press.

Diamond, L. M. (2003). Love matters: Romantic relationships among sexual-minority adolescents.

In P. Florsheim (Ed.), *Adolescent romantic relationships and sexual behavior.* Mahwah, NJ: Erlbaum.

Diamond, L. M., & Savin-Williams, R. C. (2003). The intimate relationships of sexual-minority youths. In G. Adams & M. Berzonsky (Eds.), *Blackwell handbook of adolescence.* Malden, MA: Blackwell.

Diao, G., & Lin, D. Y. (2006). Improving the power of association tests for quantitative traits in family studies. *Genetic Epidemiology, 30,* 301–313.

Diaz, C. F., Pelletier, C. M., & Provenzo, E. F. (2006). *Touch the future . . . teach!* Boston: Allyn & Bacon.

Diaz-Rico, L. T., & Weed, K. Z. (2006). *Cross-cultural language and academic development handbook* (3rd ed.). Boston: Allyn & Bacon.

Dick, D. M., & Bierut, L. J. (2006). The genetics of alcohol dependence. *Current Psychiatry Reports, 8,* 151–157.

Dickson, F. C., Christian, A., & Remmo, C. J. (2004). Exploration of marital and family issues of the later-life adult. In C. Segrin & J. Flora (Eds.), *Family Communication.* Mahwah, NJ: Erlbaum.

Diener, E. (2004) *Frequently Asked questions (FAQS) about subjective well-being (happiness and life-satisfaction).* Champaign, IL: University of Illinois, Department of Psychology.

Diener, E., Lucas, R. E., & Oishi, S. (2002). Subjective well-being: The science of happiness and satisfaction. In C. R. Snyder & S. J. Lopez (Eds.), *Handbook of positive psychology.* New York: Oxford University Press.

Diener, E., Lucas, R. E., & Oishi, S. (2002). Subjective well-being: The science of happiness and satisfaction. In C. R. Snyder & S. J. Lopez (Eds.), *Handbook of positive psychology.* New York: Oxford University Press.

Diener, E., & Seligman, M. E. P. (2002). Very happy people. *Psychological Science, 13,* 81–84.

Dietl, J. (2005). Maternal obesity and complications during pregnancy. *Journal of Perinatal Medicine, 33,* 100–105.

Dietz, W. H. (2004). Overweight in childhood and adolescence. *New England Journal of Medicine, 350,* 855–857.

Dietz, W. H., & Robinson, T. N. (2005). Clinical practice: Overweight children and adolescents. *New England Journal of Medicine, 352,* 2100–2109.

Dietz, W. H., & Robinson, T. N. (2005). Clinical practice: Overweight children and adolescents. *New England Journal of Medicine, 352,* 2100–2109.

DiGiorgio, L. F. (2005). Promoting breastfeeding to mothers in the Special Supplemental Nutrition Program for Women, Infants, and Children. *Journal of the American Diet Association, 105,* 716–717.

Dillon, J. (2003). Reincarnation: The technology of death. In C. D. Bryant (Ed.), *Handbook of death and dying.* Thousand Oaks, CA: Sage.

Dindia, K. (2005). Men are from North Dakota, women are from South Dakota. In K. Dindia & D. J. Canary (Eds.), *Sex differences and similarities in communication.* Mahwah, NJ: Erlbaum.

Dipoye, R., & Colella, A. (Eds.) (2005). *Discrimination at work.* Mahwah, NJ: Erlbaum.

Dirks, A. J., & Leeuwenburgh, C. (2006). Calorie restriction in humans: Potential pitfalls and health concerns. *Mechanisms of Aging and Development. 127,* 1–7.

Dishion, T. J., Nelson, S. E., & Yasui, M. (2005). Predicting early adolescent gang involvement from middle school adaptation. *Journal of Clinical Child and Adolescent Psychology, 34,* 62–73.

Dishman, R. K., & others. (2006). Neurobiology of exercise. *Obesity, 14,* 345–356.

Dittmann-Kohli, F. (2005). Middle age and identity in a cultural and life-span perspective. In S. L. Willis & M. Martin (Eds.), *Middle adulthood.* Thousand Oaks, CA: Sage.

Dittmann-Kohli, F. (2005). Middle age identity in cultural and life span perspective. In S. L. Willis & M. Martin (Eds.), *Middle adulthood*. Thousand Oaks, CA: Sage.

Dixit, N. K., Gerton, B. K., Dohn, P., Meyer-Lindenberg, A., & Berman. K. F. (2000, June). *Age-related changes in rCBF activation during an N-Back working memory paradigm occur prior to age 50.* Paper presented at the Human Brain Mapping meeting, San Antonio, TX.

Dixon, L., Browne, K., & Hamilton-Glachritsis, C. (2005). Risk factors of parents abused as children: A mediational analysis of the intergenerational continuity of child maltreatment (Part I). *Journal of Child Psychology and Psychiatry and Allied Disciplines, 46,* 47–57.

Dobrossy, M. D., & Dunnett, S. B. (2005). Optimizing plasticity: Environmental and training associated factors in transplant-mediated brain repair. *Review of Neuroscience, 16,* 1–21.

Dodd, V. L. (2005). Implications of kangaroo care for growth and development in preterm infants. *Journal of Obstetrical, Gynecological, and Neonatal Nursing, 34,* 218–222.

Dodge, K. A. (1983). Behavioral antecedents of peer social status. *Child Development, 54,* 1386–1399.

Dodge, K. A. (2000). Developmental psychology. In M. H. Ebert, P. T. Loosen, & B. Nurcombe (Eds.). *Current diagnosis and treatment in psychiatry.* East Norwalk, CT: Appleton & Lange.

Dodge, K. A. (2001). The science of youth violence prevention: Progressing from developmental psychopathology to efficacy to effectiveness in public policy. *American Journal of Preventive Medicine, 20,* 63–70.

Dodge, K. A., Coie, & J. D., Lynam, D. R. (2006). Aggression and antisocial behavior in youth. In W. Damon & R. Lerner (Eds.), *Handbook of child psychology* (6th ed.). New York: Wiley.

Doherty, T., Chopra, M., Nkonki, L., Jackson, D., & Greiner, T. (2006). Effects of the HIV epidemic on infant feeding in South Africa: "When they see me coming with the tins they laugh at me." *Bulletin of the World Health Organization, 84,* 90–96.

Doherty, W. J., & Beaton, J. M. (2004). Mothers and fathers parenting together. In A. L. Vangelisti (Ed.), *Handbook of family communication.* Mahwah, NJ: Erlbaum.

Dohrenwend, B. S., & Dohrenwend, B. P. (1978). Some issues in research on stressful life events. *Journal of Nervous and Mental Disease, 166,* 7–15.

Dohrenwend, B. S., & Shrout, P. E. (1985). "Hassles" in the conceptualization and measurement of life stress variables. *American Psychologist, 40,* 780–785.

Dolan, A. L., Koshy, E., Waker, M., & Goble, C. M. (2004). Access to bone densitometry increases general practitioners' prescribing for osteoporosis in steroid treated patients. *Annals of Rheumatoid Diseases, 63,* 183–186.

Donat, H., Ozean, A., Ozdirenc, M., Aksakoglu, G., & Aydinoglu, S. (2005). Age-related changes in pressure pain threshold, grip strength, and touch pressure in upper extremities of older adults. *Aging: Clinical and Experimental Research, 17,* 380–384.

Dondi, M., Simion, F., & Caltran, G. (1999). Can newborns discriminate between their own cry and the cry of another newborn infant? *Developmental Psychology, 35* (2), 418–426.

Donelson, F. E. (1998). *Women's experiences.* Mountain View, CA: Mayfield.

Donnellan, M. B., Trzniewski, K. H., & Robins, R. W. (2006). Personality and self-esteem development in adolescence. In D. K. Mroczek & T. D. Little (eds.), *Handbook of personality development.* Mahwah, NJ: Erlbaum.

Dorn, L. D., Williamson, D. E., & Ryan, N. D. (2002, April). *Maturational hormone differences in adolescents with depression and risk for depression.* Paper

presented at the meeting of the Society for Research on Adolescence, New Orleans.

Dorr, A., Rabin, B. E., & Irlen, S. (2002). Parents, children, and the media. In M. H. Bornstein (Ed.), *Handbook of parenting* (2nd ed., Vol. 5). Mahwah, NJ: Erlbaum.

Dow, B. J., & Wood, J. (Eds.) (2006). *The Sage handbook of gender and communication.* Thousand Oaks, CA: Sage.

Dowan, M. K. (2006). *Microbiology.* New York: McGraw-Hill.

Dowda, M., Ainsworth, B. E., Addy, C. L., Saunders, R., & Riner, W. (2001). Environmental influences, physical activity, and weight status in 8- to 16-year-olds. *Archives of Pediatric and Adolescent Medicine, 155,* 711–717.

Draghi-Lorenz, R., Reddy, V., & Costall, A. (2001). Rethinking the development of "nonbasic" emotions: A critical review of existing theories. *Development Review, 21,* 263–304.

Drake, A. J., & Walker, B. R. (2004). The intergenerational effects of fetal programming: Non-genomic mechanisms for the inheritance of low birth weight and cardiovascular risk. *Journal of Endocrinology, 180,* 1–16.

Drapeau, C., Hamel-Hebert, I., Robillard, R., Selmaoui, B., Filipini, D., & Carrier, J. (2006). Challenging sleep in aging: The effects of 220 mg of caffeine during the evening in young and middle-aged moderate caffeine consumers. *Journal of Sleep Research, 15,* 133–141.

Drew, C., & Hardman, M. L. (2000). *Mental retardation* (7th ed.). Columbus, OH: Merrill.

Drewes, A. A., Carey, L. J., & Schaefer, C. E. (Eds.), (2003) *School-based play therapy.* New York: Wiley.

Drewnowski, A., & Spector, S. E. (2004). Poverty and obesity: the role of energy density and energy costs. *American Journal of Clinical Nutrition, 79,* 6–16.

Driscoll, A., & Nagel, N. G. (2005). *Early childhood education, birth–8* (3rd ed.). Boston: Allyn & Bacon.

Driscoll, J. W. (2006). Postpartum depression: The state of the science. *Journal of Perinatal and Neonatal Nursing, 20,* 40–42.

Driver, J., Tabares, A., Shapiro, A., Nahm, E. Y., & Gottman, J. M. (2003). Interactional patterns in marital success and failure: Gottman laboratory studies. In F. Walsh (Ed.), *Normal family processes* (3rd ed.). New York: Guilford.

Droege, K. L. (2004). Turning accountability on its head. *Phi Delta Kappan, 85,* 610–612.

Dryfoos, J. G. (1990). *Adolescents at risk: Prevalence or prevention.* New York: Oxford University Press.

Dubay, L., Joyce, T., Kaestner, R., & Kenney, G. M. (2001). Changes in prenatal care timing and low birth weight by race and socioeconomic status: Implications for the Medicaid expansions for pregnant women. *Health Services Research, 36,* 373–398.

Duffy, T. M., & Kirkley, J. R. (Eds.) (2004). *Learner-centered theory and practice in distance education.* Mahwah, NJ: Erlbaum.

Duggan, A., Fuddy, L., Burrell, L., Higman, S. M., McFarlane, E., Windham, A., & Sia, C. (2004). Randomized trial of statewide home visiting program to prevent child abuse: Impact in reducing parental risk factors. *Child Abuse and Neglect, 28,* 623–643.

Duke, K., & Don, M. (2005). Acupuncture use for prebirth treatment. *Complementary Therapy in Clinical Practice, 11,* 121–126.

Dundek, L. H. (2006). Establishment of a Somali doula program at a large metropolitan hospital. *Journal of Perinatal and Neonatal Nursing, 20,* 128–137.

Dunkel-Schetter, C. (1998). Maternal stress and preterm delivery. *Prenatal and Neonatal Medicine, 3,* 39–42.

Dunkel-Schetter, C., Gurung, R. A. R., Lobel, M., & Wadhwa, P. D. (2001). Stress processes in

pregnancy and birth. In A. Baum, T. A. Revenson, & J. E. Singer (Eds.), *Handbook of health psychology.* Mahwah, NJ: Erlbaum.

Dunlosky, J., Kubat-Silman, A. K., & Hertzog, C. (2003). Training monitoring skills improves older adults' self-paced associative learning. *Psychology and Aging, 18,* 340–345.

Dunn, J. (1984). Sibling studies and the developmental impact of critical incidents. In P. B. Baltes & O. G. Brim (Eds.), *Life-span development and behavior* (Vol. 6). Orlando, FL: Academic Press.

Dunn, J., Davies, L. C., O'Connor, T. G., & Sturgess, W. (2001). Family lives and friendships: The perspectives of children in step-, single-parent, and nonstep families. *Journal of Family Psychology, 15,* 272–287.

Dunn, J., & Kendrick, C. (1982). *Siblings.* Cambridge, MA: Harvard University Press.

Dunn, K. S., & Horgas, A. L. (2004). Religious and nonreligious coping in older adults experiencing chronic pain. *Pain Management Nursing, 5,* 19–28.

Dunson, D. B., Baird, D. D., & Columbo, B. (2004). Increased fertility with age in men and women. *Obstetrics and Gynecology, 103,* 51–56.

Durodola, A., Kuti, O., Orji, E. O., & Ogunniyi, S. O. (2005). Rate of increase in oxytocin dose on the outcome of labor induction. *International Journal of Gynecology and Obstetrics,* in press.

Durrant, J. E. (2000). Trends in youth crime and well-being since the abolition of corporal punishment in Sweden. *Youth and Society, 3,* 437–455.

Dusek, J. B., & McIntyre, J. G. (2003). Self-concept and self-esteem development. In G. Adams & M. Berzonsky (Eds.), *Blackwell handbook of adolescence.* Malden, MA: Blackwell.

Dwyer, J. W., & Coward, R. T. (1991). A multivariate comparison of the involvement of adult sons versus daughters in the care of impaired parents. *Journal of Gerontology: Social Sciences, 46,* S259–S269.

Dychtwald, K., Erickson, T., & Morison, B. (2004). It's time to retire. *Harvard Business Review, 82,* 48–57, 126.

Eagly, A. H. (2000). Gender roles. In A. Kazdin (Ed.), *Encyclopedia of psychology.* Washington, DC, & New York: American Psychological Association and Oxford University Press.

Eagly, A. H. (2001). Social role theory of sex differences and similarities. In J. Worell (Ed.), *Encyclopedia of women and gender.* San Diego: Academic Press.

Eagly, A. H., & Crowley, M. (1986). Gender and helping: A meta-analytic review of the social psychological literature. *Psychological Bulletin, 108,* 233–256.

Eagly, A. H., & Diekman, A. B. (2003). The malleability of Sex differences in response to social roles. In L. G. Aspinwell & U. M. Staudinger (Eds.), *A psychology of human strengths.* Washington, DC: American Psychological Association.

Eagly, A. H., & Steffen, V. J. (1986). Gender and aggressive behavior: A meta-analytic review of the social psychological literature. *Psychological Bulletin, 100,* 309–330.

Eaton, D. K., & others. (2006). Youth risk behavior surveillance—United States, 2005. *MMWR Surveillance Summary, 55,* 1–108.

Ebersole, P., Hess, P., & Luggen, A. S. (2004). *Toward healthy aging* (6th ed.). St. Louis: Mosby.

Eby, J. W., Herrell, A., & Jordan, M. L. (2006). *Teaching K-12 schools: A reflective action approach* (4th ed.). Upper Saddle River, NJ: Prentice-Hall.

Eccles, J. (2003). Education: Junior and high school. In G. Adams & M. Berzonsky (Eds.), *Blackwell handbook of adolescence.* Malden, MA: Blackwell.

Eccles, J. S., & Goodman, J. (Eds.) (2002). *Community programs to promote youth development.* Washington, DC: National Academy Press.

Eccles, J. S., & Roeser, R. W. (2005). School and community influences on human development. In M. H. Bornstein & M. E. Lamb (Eds.), *Developmental psychology* (5th ed.). Mahwah, NJ: Erlbaum.

Echevarria, J. M., & Avellon, A. (2006). Hepatitis B virus: Genetic diversity. *Journal of Medical Virology, 78,* (Suppl. 1), S36–S42.

Eckel, R. H. (2005). The dietary approach to obesity. *Journal of the American Medical Association, 293,* 96–97.

Edelman, M. W. (1997, April). *Children, families and social policy.* Paper presented at the meeting of the Society for Research in Child Development, Washington, DC.

Edmonds, M. M. (1993). Physical health. In J. S. Jackson, L. M. Chatters, & R. J. Taylor (Eds.), *Aging in Black America.* Newbury Park, CA: Sage.

Educational Testing Service. (1992, February). *Cross-national comparison of 9–13 year olds' science and math achievement.* Princeton, NJ: Author.

Edwards, C. J. (2005). Immunological therapies for rheumatoid arthritis. *British Medical Bulletin, 73,* 71–82.

Edwards, C. P. (2002). Three approaches from Europe: Waldorf, Montessori, and Reggio Emilia. *Early Childhood Practice and Research, 4,* 36–40.

Edwards, J. D., Wadley, V. G., Vance, D. E., Wood, K., Roenker, D. L., & Ball, K. K. (2005). The impact of speed of processing training on cognitive and everyday performance. *Aging and Mental Health, 9,* 262–271.

Edwards, R., & Hamilton, M. A. (2004). You need to understand my gender role: An empirical test of Tannen's model of gender and communication. *Sex Roles, 50,* 491–504.

Edwards, S. L., & Sarwark, J. F. (2005). Infant and child motor development. *Clinical and Orthopedic Related Research, 434,* 33–39.

Egan, B.M. (2006). Sleep and hypertension: Burning the candle at both ends really is hazardous to your health. *Hypertension, 47,* 816–817.

Egeland, B., & Carlson, B. (2004). Attachment and psychopathology. In L. Atkinson & S. Goldberg (Eds.), *Attachment issues in psychopathology and intervention.* Mahwah, NJ: Erlbaum.

Egeland, B., Jacobvitz, D., & Sroufe, L. A. (1988). Breaking the cycle of abuse. *New Directions for Child Development, 11,* 77–92.

Eggen, P. D., & Kauchak, D. P. (2006). *Strategies and models for teachers: Teaching content and critical thinking* (5th ed.). Boston: Allyn & Bacon.

Egley, A. (2002). *National youth gang survey trends from 1996 to 2000.* Washington, DC: U.S. Department of Justice, Office of Justice Programs, Office of Juvenile Justice and Delinquency Prevention.

Eichmeyer, J. N., Northrup, H., Assel, M. A., Goka, T. J., Johnston, D. A., & Williams, A. T. (2005). An assessment of risk understanding in Hispanic genetic counseling patients. *Journal of Genetic Counseling, 14,* 319–328.

Eichorn, D. H., Clausen, J. A., Haan, N., Honzik, M. P., & Mussen, P. H. (Eds.). (1981). *Present and past in middle life.* New York: Academic Press.

Eidelman, A. I., & Feldman, R. (2004). Positive effect of human milk on neurobehavioral and cognitive development of premature infants. *Advances in Experimental Medicine and Biology, 554,* 359–364.

Eiferman, R. R. (1971). Social play in childhood. In R. Herron & B. Sutton-Smith (Eds.), *Child's play.* New York: Wiley.

Eilte, D. (2005). The moderating effects of peer substance abuse on the family structure-adolescent substance use association: Quantity versus quality of parenting. *Addictive Behaviors, 30,* 963–980.

Einstein, G. O., McDaniel, M. A., Manzi, M., Cochran, B., & Baker, M. (2000). Prospective memory and aging: Forgetting intentions over short delays. *Psychology and Aging, 15,* 671–683.

Einstein, G. O., M-Daniel, M. A. (2005). Prospective memory. *Current Directions in Psychological Science, 14,* 286–290.

Eisdorfer, C. (1996, December). Interview. *APA Monitor,* p. 35.

Eisenberg, A., Murkoff, H., & Hathaway, S. (2002). *What to expect when you're expecting* (3rd ed.). New York: Workman.

Eisenberg, N. (Ed.). (1982). *The development of prosocial behavior.* New York: Wiley.

Eisenberg, N. (2006). Empathy-related responding in children. In M. Killen & J. G. Smetana (Eds.), *Handbook of moral development.* Mahwah, NJ: Erlbaum.

Eisenberg, N., & Fabes, R. A. (1998). Prosocial development. In N. Eisenberg (Ed.), *Handbook of child psychology* (5th ed., Vol. 3). New York: Wiley.

Eisenberg, N., Fabes, R. A., Guthrie, I. K., & Reiser, M. (2002). The role of emotionality and regulation in children's social competence and adjustment. In L. Pulkkinen & A. Caspi (Eds.), *Paths to successful development.* New York: Cambridge University Press.

Eisenberg, N., Fabes, R. A., & Spinrad, T. L. (2006). Prosocial development. In W. Damon & R. Lerner (Eds.), *Handbook of child psychology* (6th ed.). New York: Wiley.

Eisenberg, N., Martin, C. L., & Fabes, R. A. (1996). Gender development and gender effects. In D. C. Berliner & R. C. Calfee (Eds.), *Handbook of educational psychology.* New York: Macmillan.

Eisenberg, N., & Morris, A. S. (2004). Moral cognitions and social responding in adolescence. In R. Lerner & L. Steinberg (Eds.), *Handbook of adolescent psychology.* New York: Wiley.

Eisenberg, N., Spinrad, T. L., & Sadovsky, A. (2006). Empathy-related responding in children. In M. Killen & J. G. Smetana (Eds.), *Handbook of moral development.* Mahwah, NJ: Erlbaum.

Eisenberg, N., Spinrad, T. L., & Smith, C. L. (2004). Emotion-related regulation: Its conceptualization, relations to social functioning, and socialization. In P. Philippot & R. S. Feldman (Eds.), *The regulation of emotion.* Mahwah, NJ: Erlbaum.

Eisinger, F., & Burke, W. (2003). Breast cancer and breastfeeding. *Lancet, 361,* 176–177.

Ekman, A., Hall, P., & Litton, J. E. (2005). Can we trust cancer information on the Internet? A comparison of cancer risk sites. *Cancer Causes and Control, 16,* 765–772.

Ekstrom, H. (2005). Trends in middle-aged women's reports of symptoms, use of hormone therapy and attitudes toward it. *Maturitas, 52,* 154–164.

Elder, G. H. (1998). The life course and human development. In W. Damon (Ed.), *Handbook of child development* (5th ed.). New York: Wiley.

Elder, G. H., & Shanahan, M. J. (2006). The life course and human development. In W. Damon & R. Lerner (Eds.), *Handbook of child psychology* (6th ed.). New York: Wiley.

Eley, T. C., Liang, H., Plomin, R., Sham, P., Sterne, A., Williamson, R., & Purcell, S. (2004). Parental family vulnerability, family environment, and their interactions as predictors of depressive symptoms in adolescents. *Journal of the American Academy of Child and Adolescent Psychiatry, 43,* 298–306.

Elford, H., Wilson, F., McKee, K. J., Chung, M. C., Bolton, G., & Goudie, F. (2005). Psychosocial benefits of solitary reminiscence writing: An exploratory study. *Aging and Mental Health, 9,* 305–314.

Elias, M. F., Elias, P. K., Sullivan, L. M., Wolf, P. A., & D'Agostino, R. B. (2005). Obesity, diabetes, and cognitive deficit: The Framington Heart Study. *Neurobiology of Aging, 26,* (Suppl 1), 11–16.

Elkind, D. (1970, April 5). Erik Erikson's eight ages of man. *New York Times Magazine.*

Elkind, D. (1976). *Child development and education: A Piagetian perspective.* New York: Oxford University Press.

Elkind, D. (1988, January). Educating the very young: A call for clear thinking. *NEA Today,* pp. 22–27.

Elliott, V. S. (2004). Methamphetamine use increasing. Available on the Internet at:www.amaassn.org/amednews/2004/07/26/hlsc0726.htm

Ellis, L., & Ames, M. A. (1987). Neurohormonal functioning and sexual orientation. *Psychological Bulletin, 101,* 233–258.

Elmes, D. G., Kantowitz, B. H., & Roediger, H. L. (2005). *Research methods in psychology* (8th ed.). Belmont, CA: Wadsworth.

Elovainio, M., Kivimaki, M., Vahtera, J., Ojanlatva, A., Korkeila, K., Suominen, S., Helenius, H., & Koskenvuo, M. (2003). Social support, early retirement, and a retirement preference: A study of 10,489 Finnish adults. *Journal of Occupational and Environmental Medicine, 45,* 433–439.

El-Toukhy, T., Khalaf, Y., & Braude, P. (2006). IVF results: Optimize not maximize. *American Journal of Obstetrics and Gynecology, 194,* 322–331.

Elwig, K. (2005). Fetal nutrition and adult disease, *Journal of Human Nutrition and Diet, 18,* 224–225.

Ely, R. (2005). Language and literacy in two school years. In J. Berko Gleason, *The development of language* (6th ed.). Boston: Allyn & Bacon.

Emde, R. N., Gaensbauer, T. G., & Harmon, R. J. (1976). Emotional expression in infancy: A biobehavioral study. Psychological Issues: *Monograph Series, 10* (37).

Emery, R. E. (1994). *Renegotiating family relationships.* New York: Guilford Press.

Emmers-Sommer, T. M., & Allen, M. (2005). *Safer sex in personal relationships: The role of sexual scripts in HIV infection and prevention.* Mahwah, NJ: Erlbaum.

Emmons, C. F. (2003). The spiritualist movement. In C. D. Bryant (Ed.), *Handbook of death and dying.* Thousand Oaks, CA: Sage.

Emsley, J. G., Mitchell, B. D., Kempermann, G., & Macklis, J. D. (2005). Adult neurogenesis and repair of the adult CNS with neural progenitors, precursors, and stem cells. *Progress in Neurobiology, 75,* 321–341.

Eng, P. M., Kawachi, I., Fitzmaurice, G., & Rimm, E. B. (2005). Effects of marital transitions on changes in dietary and other health behaviors in U.S. male health professionals. *Journal of Epidemiology and Community Health, 59,* 56–62.

Enger, E. (2007). *Concepts in biology* (12th ed.). New York: McGraw-Hill.

England, S. E., Linsk, N. L., Simon-Rusinowitz, L., & Keigher, S. M. (1991). Paying kin for care: Agency barriers to formalizing informal care. *Journal of Aging and Social Policy, 2,* 63–86.

Engler, A. J., Ludington-Hoe, S. M., Cusson, R. M., Adams, R., Bahnsen, M., Brumbaugh, E., Coates, P., Grief, J., McHargue, L., Ryan, D. L., Settle, M., & Williams, D. (2002). Kangaroo care: National survey of practice, knowledge, barriers, and perceptions. *American Journal of Maternal/Child Nursing. 27,* 146–153.

Engles, R. C., Vermulst, A. A., Dubas, J. S., Bot, S. M., & Gerris, J. (2005). Long-term effects of family functioning and child characteristics on problem drinking in young adulthood. *European Addiction Research, 11,* 32–37.

Enning, C. (2004). Waterbirth: Contemporary application for historic concepts. *Midwifery Today, 70,* 45.

Enright, R. D., Lapsley, D. K., Dricas, A. S., & Fehr, L. A. (1980). Parental influence on the development of adolescent autonomy and identity. *Journal of Youth and Adolescence, 9,* 529–546.

Enzinger, C., Fazekas, F., Matthews, P. M., Ropele, S., Schmidt, H., Smith, S., & Schmidt, R. (2005). Risk factors for progression of brain atrophy in aging:

Six-year follow-up of normal subjects. *Neurology, 64,* 1704–1711.

Epel, E. S., Lin, J., Wilhelm, F. H., Wolkowitz, O. M., Cawthon, R., Adler, N. E., Dolbier, C., Mendes, W. B., & Blackburn, E. H. (2006). Cell aging in relation to stress arousal and cardiovascular disease risk factors. *Psychoneuroimmunology, 31,* 277–287.

Erber, J. T. (2005). *Aging & older adulthood.* Belmont, CA: Wadsworth.

Ericsson, K. A., Krampe, R., & Tesch-Romer, C. (1993). The role of deliberate practice in the acquisition of expert performance. *Psychological Review, 100,* 363–406.

Erikson, E. H. (1950). *Childhood and society.* New York: W. W. Norton.

Erikson, E. H. (1962). *Young man Luther.* New York: W. W. Norton.

Erikson, E. H. (1968). *Identity: Youth and crisis.* New York: W. W. Norton.

Erikson, E. H. (1969). *Gandhi's truth.* New York: W. W. Norton.

Erixon-Lindroth, N., Farde, L., Wahlin, T. B., Sovago, J., Hallidin, C., & Backman, L. (2005). The role of the striatal dopamine transporter in cognitive aging. *Psychiatry Research, 138,* 1–12.

Ernst, C., Olson, A. K., Pinel, J. P., Lam, R. W., & Christie, B. R. (2006). Antidepressant effects of exercise: Evidence for an adult-neurogenesis hypothesis? *Journal of Psychiatry and Neuroscience, 31,* 84–92.

Escandon, S. (2006). Mexican American intergenerational caregiving model. *Western Journal of Nursing, 28,* 564–585.

Eskenazi, B., Stapleton, A. L., Kharrazi, M., & Chee, W. Y. (1999). Associations between maternal decafffeinated and caffeinated coffee consumption and fetal growth and gestational duration. *Epidemiology, 10,* 242–249.

Eslinger, P. J., Flaherty-Craig, C. V., & Benton, A. L. (2004). Developmental outcomes after early prefrontal cortex damage. *Brain and Cognition, 55,* 84–103.

Espelage, D. L., & Swearer, S. M. (Eds.). (2004). *Bullying in American schools.* Mahwah, NJ: Erlbaum.

Espy, K. A., McDiarmid, M. M., Cwik, M. F., Stalets, M. M., Hamby, A., & Senn, T. E. (2004). The contribution of executive functions to emergent mathematic skills in preschool children. *Developmental Neuropsychology, 26,* 465–486.

Etaugh, C. A., & Bridges, J. S. (2001). Midlife transitions. In J. Worell (Ed.), *Encyclopedia of women and gender.* San Diego: Academic Press.

Etaugh, C., & Bridges, J. S. (2004). *The psychology of Women* (2nd ed.), Boston: Allyn & Bacon.

Etaugh, C., & Bridges, J. S. (2006). *Women's lives: A topical approach.* Belmont, CA: Wadsworth.

Ettinger, D., Grady, D., Tosteson, N. A., Pressman, A., & Macer, J. L. (2003). Effect of the Women's Health Initiative on women's decisions to discontinue postmenopausal hormone therapy. *Obstetrics & Gynecology, 102,* 1225–1232.

Evans, E., Hawton, K., & Rodham, K. (2005). Suicidal phenomena and abuse in adolescents: A review of epidemiological studies. *Child Abuse and Neglect, 29,* 45–58.

Evans, G. W. (2004). The environment of childhood poverty. *American Psychologist, 59,* 77–92

Evans, G. W., English, G. W. (2002). The environment of poverty. *Child Development, 73,* 1238–1248

Evans, M. I., & Britt, D. W. (2005). Fetal reduction. *Seminars in Perinatology, 29,* 321–329.

Evans, M. I., Lluba, E., Landsberger, E. J., O'Brien, J. E., & Harrison, H. H. (2004). Impact of folic acid

fortification in the United States: markedly diminished high maternal serum alpha-fetoprotein values. *Obstetrics and Gynecology, 103,* 474–479.

Evans, M. I., & Wapner, R. J. (2005). Invasive prenatal diagnostic procedures: 2005. *Seminars in Perinatology, 29,* 215–218.

Evert, J., Lawler, E., Bogan, H., & Perls, T. (2003). Morbidity profiles of centenarians: Survivors, delayers, and escapers. *Journals of Gerontology A: Biological Sciences and Medical Sciences, 58,* 232–237.

Evertson, C. M., & Weinstein, C. S. (Eds.). (2006). *Handbook of classroom management.* Mahwah, NJ: Erlbaum.

Exploratorium (2004). *Young in mind.* Available on the Internet at: www.exploratorium.edu/exploring/ exploring_memory/ memory_2.html.

Eyres, P. S. (2005). Heading off harassment: Effective training is critical to limiting legal exposure of work-place harassment. *Occupational Health and Safety, 74,* 18, 20.

Fabes, R. A., Eisenberg, N., Jones, S., Smith, M., Gutherie, I., Poulin, R., Shepard, S., & Friedman, J. (1999). Regulation, emotionality, and preschoolers' socially competent peer interactions. *Child Development, 70,* 432–442.

Fabes, R. A., Hanish, L. D., & Martin, C. L. (2003). Children at play: The role of peers in understanding the effects of child care. *Child Development, 74,* 1039–1043.

Fabiani, M., Low, K. A., Wee, E., Sable, J. J., & Gratton, G. (2006). Reduced suppression or labile memory? Mechanisms of inefficient filtering of irrelevant information in older adults. *Journal of Cognitive Neuroscience, 18,* 637–650.

Fagan, J. F. (1992). Intelligence: A theoretical viewpoint. *Current Directions in Psychological Science, 1,* 82–86.

Fagot, B. I., Rodgers, C. S., & Leinbach, M. D. (2000). Theories of gender socialization. In T. Eckes & H. M. Trautner (Eds.), *The developmental social psychology of gender.* Mahwah, NJ: Erlbaum.

Fagot, B. L. (1995). Parenting boys and girls. In M. H. Bornstein (Ed.), *Handbook of parenting* (Vol. 1). Hillsdale, NJ: Erlbaum.

Fair Test. (2004). "No child left behind" after two years: A track record of failure. Retrieved at http://www.fairtest.org.

Falbo, T., & Poston, D. L. (1993). The academic, personality, and physical outcomes of only children in China. *Child Development, 64,* 18–35.

Falicov, C., & Karrer, B. (1980). Cultural variations in the family life cycle: The Mexican American family. In E. Carter & M. McGoldrick (Eds.), *The family life cycle: A framework for family therapy.* New York: Gardner Press.

Fallis, W. M., Hamelin, K., Symonds, J., & Wang, X. (2006). Maternal and newborn outcomes related to maternal warming during cesarean delivery. *Journal of Obstetric, Gynecologic, and Neonatal Nursing, 35,* 324–331.

Fang, G., Fang, F., Keller, M., & Edelstein, W. (2003). Social moral reasoning in Chinese children: A developmental study. *Psychology in the Schools, 40,* 125–138.

Fanos, J. H., Spangner, K. A., & Musci, T. J. (2006). Attitudes toward prenatal screening and testing for fragile X. *Genetics in Medicine, 8,* 129–133.

Fantz, R. L. (1963). Pattern vision in newborn infants. *Science, 140,* 296–297.

Faraone, S. V., Biederman, J., & Mick, E. (2006). The age-dependent decline of attention deficit hyperactivity disorder: A meta-analysis of follow-up studies. *Psychological Medicine, 36,* 159–165.

Faraone, S. V., & Doyle, A. E. (2001). The nature and heritability of attention deficit hyperactivity disorder. *Psychiatric Clinics of North America, 10,* 299–316.

Faravelli, C., Giugni, A., Salvatori, S., & Ricca, V. (2004). Psychopathology after rape. *American Journal of Psychiatry, 161,* 1483–1485.

Farrell, M. P., & Rosenberg, S. D. (1981). *Men at mid-life.* Boston: Auburn House.

Farrington, D. (2004). Conduct disorder, aggression, and delinquency. In R. Lerner & L. Steinberg (Eds.), *Handbook of adolescent psychology.* New York: Wiley.

Fasig, L. (2000). Toddlers' understanding of ownership: Implications for self-concept development. *Social Development, 9,* 370–382.

Federal Drug Administration. (2004, March 22). *FDA issues public health advisory on cautions for use of antidepressants in adults and children.* Washington, DC: U.S. Food and Drug Administration.

Federal Interagency Forum on Child and Family Statistics. (2002). *Key national indicators of well-being.* Washington, DC: U.S. Government Printing Office.

Federman, D. D. (2006). The biology of human sex differences. *New England Journal of Medicine, 354,* 1507–1514.

Feeney, J. A., Noller, P., & Callan, V. J. (1994). Attachment style, communication and satisfaction in the early years of marriage. In K. Bartholomew and D. Perlman (Eds.). *Advances in personal relationships Vol. 5: Attachment processes in adulthood.* London: Jessica Kingsley.

Feeney, S., Christensen, D., & Moravcik, E. (2006). *Who am I in the lives of children?* (7th ed.). Upper Saddle River, NJ: Prentice Hall.

Feenstra, J. S., Banyard, V. L., Rines, E. N., & Hopkins, K. R. (2001). First-year students' adaptation to college: The role of family variables and individual coping. *Journal of College Student Development, 42,* 106–113.

Fehr, B. (2000). The life cycle of friendships. In C. Hendrick & S. S. Hendrick (Eds.), *Close relationships.* Thousand Oaks, CA: Sage.

Fein, G. G. (1986). Pretend play. In D. Gorlitz & J. F. Wohlwill (Eds.), *Curiosity, imagination, and play.* Hillsdale, NJ: Erlbaum.

Feinberg, M., & Hetherington, E. M. (2001). Differential parenting as a within-family variable. *Journal of Family Psychology, 15,* 22–37.

Feiring, C. (1996). Concepts of romance in 15-year-old adolescents. *Journal of Research on Adolescence, 6,* 181–200.

Fekkes, M., Pijpers, F. I., & Verloove-Vanhorick, S. P. (2004). Bullying behavior and associations with psychosomatic complaints and depression in victims. *Journal of Pediatrics, 144,* 17–22.

Feldman, H. D. (2001, April). *Contemporary developmental theories and the concept of talent.* Paper presented at the meeting of the Society for Research in Child Development, Minneapolis.

Feldman, R., Greenbaum, C. W., & Yirmiya, N. (1999). Mother-infant affect synchrony as an antecedent of the emergence of self-control. *Developmental Psychology, 35,* 223–231.

Feldman, R., Weller, A., Sirota, L., & Eidelman, A. I. (2002). Skin-to-skin contact (kangaroo care) promotes self-regulation in premature infants: Sleep-wake cyclicity, arousal modulation, and sustained exploration. *Developmental Psychology, 38,* 194–207.

Feldman, R., Weller, A., Sirota, L., & Eidelman, A. I. (2003). Testing a family intervention hypothesis: The contribution of mother-infant skin-to-skin (kangaroo care) to family interaction, proximity, and touch. *Journal of Family Psychology, 17,* 94–107.

Feldman, S. S. (1999). Unpublished review of J. W. Santrock's *Adolescence,* 8th ed. New York: McGraw-Hill.

Feldman, S. S., & Elliott, G. R. (1990). Progress and promise of research on normal adolescent development. In S.S. Feldman & G. Elliott (Eds.), *At the threshold: The developing adolescent.* Cambridge, MA: Harvard University Press.

Feldman, S. S., Turner, R., & Aruajo, K. (1999). Interpersonal context as an influence on sexual timetables of youths: Gender and ethnic effects. *Journal of Research on Adolescence, 9,* 25–52.

Feldon, J. M. (2003). Grief as a transformative experience: Weaving through different lifeworlds after a loved one has committed suicide. *International Journal of Mental Health Nursing, 12,* 74–85.

Felkner, M., Suarez, L., Hendricks, K., & Larsen, R. (2003). Implementation and outcomes of recommended folic acid supplementation in Mexican-American women with prior neural tube defect-affected pregnancies. *Preventive Medicine, 40,* 867–871.

Ferber, S. G., & Makhoul, J. R. (2004). The effect of skin-to-skin (kangaroo care) shortly after birth on the neurobehavioral responses of the term newborn. *Pediatrics, 113,* 858–865.

Ferguson, D. M., Harwood, L. J., & Shannon, F. T. (1987). Breastfeeding and subsequent social adjustment in 6- to 8-year-old children. *Journal of Child Psychology and Psychiatry, 28,* 378–386.

Fernald, A. (2001). Two hundred years of research on the early development of language comprehension. In W. W. Hartup & R. A. Weinberg (Eds.), *Child psychology in retrospect and prospect.* Mahwah, NJ: Erlbaum.

Fernandes, O., Sabharwal, M., Smiley, T., Pastuszak, A., Koren, G., & Einarson, T. (1998). Moderate to heavy caffeine consumption during pregnancy and relationship to spontaneous abortion and abnormal fetal growth: A meta-analysis. *Reproductive Toxicology, 12,* 435–444.

Fernandez, A., & Goldstein, L. (2004). Primary care physicians who treat blacks and whites. *New England Journal of Medicine, 351,* 2126–2127.

Ferrando-Lucas, M. T. (2006). Attention deficit hyperactivity disorder: Its aetiological factors and endophenotypes. *Revista de Neurologia (Spanish), 42,* (Suppl), S9–S11.

Ferrara, C. M., Goldberg, A. P., Ortmeyer, H. K., & Ryan, A. S. (2006). Effects of aerobic and resistive exercise training on glucose disposal and skeletal muscle metabolism in older men. *Journals of Gerontology A: Biological Sciences and Medical Sciences, 61,* 480–487.

Ferrara, N. (2004). The aging heart and exercise training. *Archives of Gerontology and Geriatrics, 35,* (Suppl.), 145–156.

Ferraro, K. F. (2006). Health and aging. In R. H. Binstock & L. K. George (Eds.), *Handbook of aging and the social sciences* (6th ed.). San Diego: Academic Press.

Ferris, F. D., & Librach, S. L. (2005). Models, standards, guidelines. *Clinical Geriatric Medicine, 21,* 17–44.

Fiala, J. E., Egan, J. F., & Lashgari, M. (2006). The influence of body mass index on pregnancy outcomes. *Connecticut Medicine, 70,* 21–23.

Fiatarone, M. A., Marks, E. C., Meredith, C. N., Lipsitz, L. A., & Evans, W. J. (1990). High intensity strength training in nonagenarians: Effects on skeletal muscle. *Journal of the American Medical Association, 263,* 3029–3034.

Fidalgo, Z., & Pereira, F. (2005). Sociocultural differences and the adjustment of mothers' speech to their children's cognitive and language comprehension skills. *Learning & Instruction, 15,* 11–21.

Fied, T. M., Grizzle, N., Scafidi, F., & Schanberg, S. (1996). Massage and relaxation therapies' effects on depressed adolescent mothers. *Adolescence, 31,* 903–911.

Field, A. E., Cambargo, C. A., Taylor, C. B., Berkey, C. S., Roberts, S. B., & Colditz, G. A. (2001). Peer, parent, and media influences on the development of weight concerns and frequent dieting among preadolescent and adolescent girls and boys. *Pediatrics, 107,* 54–60.

Field, D. (1999). Review of relationships in old age by Hansson & Carpenter. *Contemporary Psychology, 41,* 44–45.

Field, D. (1999). A cross-cultural perspective on continuity and change in social relations in old age: Introduction to a special issue. *International Journal of Aging and Human Development, 48,* 257–262.

Field, T. M. (1992, September). Stroking babies helps growth, reduces stress. *Brown University Child and Adolescent Behavior Letter,* pp. 1, 6.

Field, T. M. (1998). Massage therapy effects. *American Psychologist, 53,* 1270–1281.

Field, T. M. (2001). Massage therapy facilitates weight gain in preterm infants. *Current Directions in Psychological Science, 10* 51–55

Field, T. M. (2002). Massage therapy. *Medical Clinics of North America, 86,* 163–171.

Field, T. M. (2003). Stimulation of preterm infants. *Pediatrics Review, 24,* 4–11.

Field, T. M., Henteleff, T., Hernandez-Reif, M., Martines, E., Mavunda, K., Kuhn, C., & Schanberg, S. (1998). Children with asthma have improved pulmonary functions after message therapy. *Journal of Pediatrics, 132,* 854–858.

Field, T. M., Hernandez-Reif, M., Feijo, L., & Freedman, J. (2006). Prenatal, perinatal, and neonatal stimulation. *Infant Behavior & Development, 29,* 24–31.

Field, T. M., Hernandez-Reif, M., & Freedman, J. (2004). Stimulation programs for preterm infants. *Social Policy Report, Society for Research in Child Development,* XVIII (No. 1), 1–19.

Field, T. M., Hernandez-Reif, M., Seligman, S., Krasnegor, J., & Sunshine, W. (1997). Juvenile rheumatoid arthritis: Benefits from massage therapy. *Journal of Pediatric Psychology, 22,* 607–617.

Field, T. M., Hernandez-Reif, M., Taylor, S., Quintino, O., & Burman, I. (1997). Labor pain is reduced by massage therapy. *Journal of Psychosomatic Obstetrics and Gynecology, 18,* 286–291.

Field, T. M., Lasko, D., Mundy, P., Henteleff, T., Kabat, S., Talpins, S., & Dowling, M. (1997). Brief report: Autistic children's attentiveness and responsivity improve after touch therapy. *Journal of Autism and Developmental Disorders, 27,* 333–338.

Field, T. M., Quintino, O., Hernandez-Reif, M., & Koslosky, G. (1998). Adolescents with attention deficit hyperactivity disorder benefit from massage therapy. *Adolescence, 33,* 103–108.

Field, T. M., Schanberg, S. M., Scafidi, F., Bauer, C. R., Vega-Lahr, N., Garcia, R., Nystrom, J., & Kuhn, C. M. (1986). Tactile/kinesthetic stimulation effects on preterm neonates. *Pediatrics, 77,* 654–658.

Fields, R. (2007). *Drugs in perspective* (6th ed.). New York: McGraw-Hill.

Filkins, K., & Koos, B. J. (2005). Ultrasound and fetal diagnosis. *Current Opinions in Obstetrics and Gynecology, 17,* 185–195.

Finch, C. E., & Seeman, T. E. (1999). Stress theories of aging. In V. L. Bengtson, & K. W. Schaie (Eds.) *Handbook of theories of aging.* New York: Springer.

Fine, M. A., & Harvey, J. H. (2006). Divorce and relationship dissolution in the United States. In M. A. Fine & J. H. Harvey (Eds.), *Handbook of divorce and relationship dissolution.* Mahwah, NJ: Erlbaum.

Fine, M. A., Ganong, L. H., & Demo, D. H. (2005). Divorce as a family stressor. In P. C. McKenry & S. J. Price (Eds.). *Families and change* (3rd ed.). Thousand Oaks, CA: Sage.

Fine, P. G., & Peterson, D. (2002). Caring about what dying patients care about caring. *Journal of Pain Symptom Management, 23,* 267–268.

Fingerman, K. L. (2000). Age and generational differences in mothers' and daughters' descriptions of enjoyable visits. *Journals of Gerontology B: Psychological and Social Sciences, 55,* P95–P106.

Fingerman, K. L. (2003, April). Commentary in "Researchers replace midlife myths with facts." *Monitor on Psychology, 34,* p. 40.

Fingerman, K. L. (2006). Social relations. In J. E. Birren & K. W. Schaie (Eds.), *Handbook of the psychology of aging* (6th ed.). San Diego: Academic Press.

Fingerman, K. L., & Lang, F. R. (2004). Coming together: A perspective on relationships across the life span. In F. R. Lang & K. L. Fingerman (Eds.), *Growing together.* New York: Cambridge University Press.

Finn, C. T., & Smoller, J. W. (2006). Genetic counseling in psychiatry. *Harvard Review of Psychiatry, 14,* 109–121.

Fiore, H., Travis, S., Whalen, A., Auinger, P., Ryan, S. (2006). Potentially protective factors associated with healthful body mass index in adolescents with obese and nonobese parents: A secondary data analysis of the Third National Health and Nutrition Examination Survey, 1988–1994, *Journal of The American Dietetic Association, 10,* 55–64.

Fiori, K. L., Antonucci, T. C., & Cortina, K. S. (2006). Social network typologies and mental health among older adults. *Journals of Gerontology B: Psychological Sciences and Social Sciences, 61,* P25–P32.

Fiori, K. L., McIlvane, J. M., Brown, E. E., & Antonucci, T. C. (2006). Social relations and depressive symptomatology: Self-efficacy as a moderator. *Aging and Mental Health, 10,* 227–239.

Firlik, R. (1996). Can we adapt the philosophies and practices of Reggio Emilia, Italy, for use in American schools? *Young Children, 51,* 217–220.

Fisch, S. M. (2004). *Children's learning from educational television.* Mahwah, NJ: Erlbaum.

Fischer, K. W., & Rose, S. P. (1995, Fall). Concurrent cycles in the dynamic development of brain and behavior. *SRCD Newsletter,* pp. 3–4, 15–16.

Fish, M. (2004). Attachment in infancy and preschool in low socioeconomic status rural Appalachian children: Stability and change and relations to preschool and kindergarten competence. *Developmental Psychopathology, 16,* 293–312.

Fisher, B. S., Cullen, F. T., Turner, M. G. (2000). *The sexual victimization of college women.* Washington, DC: National Institute of Justice.

Fisher, H. E. (2006). Broken hearts: The nature and risks of romantic rejection. In A. C. Crouter & A. Booth (Eds.), *Romance and sex in adolescence and emerging adulthood.* Mahwah, NJ: Erlbaum.

Fisher, S. E., & Marcus, G. F. (2006). The eloquent ape: Genes, brains, and the evolution of language. *Nature Reviews: Genetics, 7,* 9–20.

Fitzgerald, E. F., Hwang, S. A., Langguth, K., Cayo, M., Yang, B. Z., Bush, S., Worswick, P., & Lauzon, T. (2004). Fish consumption and other environmental exposures and their associations with serum PCB concentrations among Mohawk women at Akwesasne. *Environmental Research, 94,* 160–170.

Fitzgibbon, M. L., Stolley, M. R., Dyer, A. R., VanHorn, L., & Kaufer-Christoffel, K. (2002). A community-based obesity prevention program for minority children: Rationale and study design for Hip-Hop to Health Jr. *Preventive Medicine, 34,* 289–297.

Fitzgibbon, M. L., Stolley, M. R., Schiffer, L., Van Horn, L., Kaufer Christoffel, L., & Dyer, A. (2005). Two-year follow-up results for Hip-Hop to Health Jr: A randomized controlled trial for overweight prevention in preschool minority children. *Journal of Pediatrics, 146,* 618–625.

Fitzpatrick, L. A. (2004). Menopause and hotflashes: No easy answers to a complex problem. *Mayo Clinic Proceedings, 79,* 735–737.

Fivush, R. (1993). Developmental perspectives on autobiographical recall. In G. S. Goodman & B. Bottoms (Eds.), *Child victims and child witnesses: Understanding and improving testimony.* New York: Guilford.

Flanagan, C. (2004). Volunteerism. In R. Lerner & L. Steinberg (Eds.), *Handbook of adolescent psychology.* New York: Wiley.

Flannery, D. J., Hussey, D., Biebelhausen, L., & **Wester, K.** (2003). Crime, delinquency, and youth gangs. In G. Adams & M. Berzonsky (Eds.), *Blackwell handbook of adolescence*. Malden, MA: Blackwell.

Flavell, J. H. (1999). Cognitive development: Children's knowledge about the mind. *Annual Review of Psychology* (Vol. 50). Palo Alto, CA: Annual Reviews.

Flavell, J. H., (2004). Theory-of-mind development: Retrospect and prospect. *Merrill-Palmer Quarterly, 50,* 274–290.

Flavell, J. H., Friedrichs, A., & Hoyt, J. (1970). Developmental changes in memorization processes. *Cognitive Psychology, 1,* 324–340.

Flavell, J. H., Green, F. L., & Flavell, E. R. (1995). Young children's knowledge about thinking. *Monographs of the Society for Research in Child Development, 60* (1, Serial No. 243).

Flavell, J. H., Green, F. L., & Flavell, E. R. (1998). The mind has a mind of its own: Developing knowledge about mental uncontrollability. *Cognitive Development, 13,* 127–138.

Flavell, J. H., Green, F. L. & Flavell, E. R. (2000). Development of children's awareness of their own thoughts. *Journal of Cognition and Development, 1,* 97–112.

Flavell, J. H., Miller, P. H., & Miller, S. (2002). *Cognitive development* (4th ed.). Upper Saddle River, NJ: Prentice Hall.

Fleischman, D. A., Wilson, R. S., Gabrieli, J. D., Bienias, J. L., Bennett, D. A. (2004). A longitudinal study of implicit and explicit memory in older persons. *Psychology and Aging, 19,* 617–625.

Flesner, M. K. (2004). Care of the elderly as a global nursing issue. *Nursing Administration Quarterly, 28,* 67–72.

Fletcher, A. C., Steinberg, L., & Williams-Wheeler, M. (2004). Parental influences on adolescent problem behavior: Revisiting Stattin and Kerr. *Child Development, 75,* 781–796.

Fletcher, A. E., Breeze, E., & Shetty, P. S. (2003). Antioxidant vitamins and mortality in older persons. *American Journal of Nutrition, 78,* 999–1010.

Flick, L., White, D. K., Vemulapalli, C., Stulac, B. B., & Kemp, J. S. (2001). Sleep position and the use of soft bedding during bed sharing among African American infants at increased risk for sudden infant death syndrome. *Journal of Pediatrics, 138,* 338–343.

Flohr, J. W., Atkins, D. H., Bower, T. G. R., & Aldridge, M. A. (2001, April). *Infant music preferences.* Paper presented at the meeting of the Society for Research in Child Development, Minneapolis.

Flores, D. L., & Hendrick, V. C. (2002). Etiology and treatment of postpartum depression. *Current Psychiatry Reports, 4,* 461–466.

Flores, G., Abreu, M., & Tomany-Korman, S. C. (2005). Limited English proficiency, primary language at home, and disparities in children's health care: How language barriers are measured matters. *Public Health Reports, 120,* 418–420.

Florsheim, P., Moore, D., & Edgington, C. (2003). Romantic relationships among pregnant and parenting adolescents. In P. Florsheim (Ed.), *Adolescent romantic relations and sexual behavior.* Mahwah, NJ: Erlbaum.

Florsheim, P., Sumida, E., McCann, C., Winstanley, M., Fukui, R., Seefeldt, T., & Moore, D. (2003). The transition to parenthood among young African American and Latino couples: Relational predictors of risk for parental dysfunction. *Journal of Family Psychology, 17,* 65–79.

Flynn, J. R. (1999). Searching for justice: The discovery of IQ gains over time. *American Psychologist, 54,* 5–20.

Flynn, J. R. (2006). The history of the American mind in the 20th century: A scenario to explain gains over time and a case for the irrelevance of *g*. In P. C. Kyllonen, R. D. Roberts, & L. Stankov (Eds.), *Extending intelligence.* Mahwah, NJ: Erlbaum.

Fodor, I., G., & Franks, V. (1990). Women in midlife and beyond. The new prime of life? *Psychology of Women Quarterly, 14,* 445–449.

Fogoros, R. N. (2001). *Does stress really cause heart disease?* Retrieved October 10, 2001, from http://www.about.com

Foley, D., Ancoli-Israel, S., Britz, P., & Walsh, J. (2004). Sleep disturbances and chronic diseases in older adults: Results of the 2003 National Sleep Foundation Sleep in America survey. *Journal of Psychosomatic Research, 56,* 497–502.

Fontaine, K. R., & Haaz., S. (2006). Risk factors for lack of recent exercise in adults with self-reported, professionally diagnosed arthritis. *Journal of Clinical Rheumatology, 12,* 66–69.

Forbes-McKay, K. E., Ellis, A. W., Shanks, M. F., & Venneri, A. (2005). The age of acquisition of words produced in a semantic fluency task can reliably differentiate normal from pathological age related cognitive decline. *Neuropsychologia, 43,* 1625–1632.

Ford, D., & Tower, J. (2006). Genetic manipulation of life span in *Drosophilia Melanogaster.* In E. J. Masor & S. N. Austad (Eds.), *Handbook of the biology of aging.* San Diego: Academic Press.

Ford, N., Odallo, D., & Chorlton, R. (2003). Communication from a human rights perspective: Responding to the HIV/AIDS pandemic in eastern and southern Africa. *Journal of Health Communication, 8,* 599–602.

Fowler, G. (1999). *As we grow old: How adult children and their parents can face aging with candor and grace.* Valley Forge, PA: Judson Press.

Fox, B., & Hull, M. (2002). *Phonics for the teacher of reading* (8th ed.). Upper Saddle River, NJ: Merrill.

Fox, K. R. (2004). Childhood obesity and the role of physical activity. *Journal of Research in Social Health, 124,* 34–39.

Fox, M. K., Pac, S., Devaney, B., & Jankowski, L. (2004). Feeding infants and toddlers study: What foods are infants and toddlers eating? *American Dietetic Association Journal (Suppl.), 104,* S22–S30.

Fox, N. C., & Schott, J. M. (2004). Imaging cerebral atrophy: Normal aging to Alzheimer disease. *Lancet, 363,* 392–394.

Fox, P. G., Burns, K. R., Popovich, J. M., Belknap, R. A., & Frank-Stromberg, M. (2004). Southeast Asia refugee children: Self-esteem as a predictor of depression and scholastic achievement in the U.S. *International Journal of Nursing Research, 9,* 1063–1072.

Fozard, J. L. (1992, December 6). Commentary in "We can age successfully." *Parade Magazine,* pp. 14–15.

Fozard, J. L. (2000). Sensory and cognitive changes with age. In K. W. Schaie & M. Pietrucha (Eds.), *Mobility and transportation in the elderly.* New York: Springer.

Fozard, J. L., & Gordon-Salant, S. (2001). Changes in vision and hearing with aging. In J. E. Birren & K. W. Schaie (Eds.), *Handbook of the psychology of aging* (5th ed.). San Diego: Academic Press.

Fraga, C. G., Motchnik, P. A., Shigenaga, M. K., Helbock, H. J., Jacob, R. A., & Ames, B. N. (1991). Ascorbic acid protects against endogenous oxidative DNA damage in human sperm. *Proceedings of the National Academy of Sciences of the United States, 88,* 11003–11006.

Fraiberg, S. (1959). *The magic years.* New York: Scribner's.

Francis, J., Fraser, G., & Marcia, J. E. (1989). *Cognitive and experimental factors in moratorium-achievement (MAMA) cycles.* Unpublished manuscript, Department of Psychology, Simon Fraser University, Burnaby. British Columbia.

Francis, P. (2006). Targeting cell death in dementia. *Alzheimer Disease and Associated Disorders, 20* Suppl 1, S3–S7.

Franke, T. M. (2000, winter). The role of attachment as a protective factor in adolescent violent behavior. *Adolescent & Family Health, 1,* 29–39.

Frankl, V. (1984). *Man's search for meaning.* New York: Basic Books.

Franklin, S. S. (2006). Hypertension in older people: Part I. *Journal of Clinical Hypertension, 8,* 444–449.

Franz, C. E. (1996). The implications of preschool tempo and motoric activity level for personality decades later. Reported in A. Caspi, Personality development across-the life course, in W. Damon (Ed.), *Handbook of child psychology,* Vol. 3. New York: Wiley, p. 337.

Fraser, S. (Ed.). (1995). *The bell curve wars: Race, intelligence, and the future of America.* New York: Basic Books.

Frazier, P. A., & Cook, S. W. (1993). Correlates of distress following heterosexual relationship dissolution. *Journal of Social and Personal Relationships, 10,* 55–67.

Freda, M. C. (2004). Issues in patient educations. *Journal of Midwifery and Women's Health, 49,* 203–209.

Frede, E. C. (1995). The role of program quality in producing early childhood program benefits. *The Future of Children, No. 3,* 115–132.

Frederikse, M., Lu, A., Aylward, E., Barta, P., Sharma, T., & Pearlson, G. (2000). Sex differences in inferior lobule volume in schizophrenia. *American Journal of Psychiatry, 157,* 422–427.

Fredrickson, D. D. (1993). Breastfeeding research priorities, opportunities, and study criteria: What we learned from the smoking trial. *Journal of Human Lactation, 3,* 147–150.

Fredriksen, K., Rhodes, J., Reddy, R., & Way, N. (2004). Sleepless in Chicago: Tracking the effects of adolescent sleep loss during the middle school years. *Child Development, 75,* 84–95.

Freedman, D. S., Khan, L. K., Serdula, M. K., Dietz, W. H., Srinivasan, S. R., & Berensen, G. S. (2004). Inter-relationships among childhood BMI, childhood height, and adult obesity: The Bogalusa Heart Study. *International Journal of Obesity and Related Metabolic Disorders, 28,* 10–16.

Freedman, D. S., Khan, L. K., Serdula, M. K., Dietz, W. H., Srinivasan, S. R., & Berensen, G. S. (2005). The relation of childhood BMI to adult adiposity: The Bogalusa Heart Study. *Pediatrics, 115,* 22–27.

Freeman, S., & Herron, J. C. (2007). *Evolutionary analysis* (4th ed.). Upper Saddle River, NJ: Prentice-Hall.

French, S. E., Seidman, E., Allen, L., & Aber, J. L. (2006). The development of ethnic identity in adolescence. *Developmental Psychology, 42,* 1–10.

Frenn, M., Malin, S., Bansal, N., Delgado, M., Greer, Y., Havice, M., Ho, M., & Schweitzer, H. (2003). Addressing health disparities in middle school students' nutrition and exercise. *Journal of Community Health Nursing, 20,* 1–14.

Freud, A., & Dann, S. (1951). Instinctual anxiety during puberty. In A. Freud (Ed.), *The ego and its mechanisms of defense.* New York: International Universities Press.

Freud, S. (1917). *A general introduction to psychoanalysis.* New York: Washington Square Press.

Freund, A. M. (2006). Age-differential motivational consequences of optimization versus compensation focus in younger and older adults. *Psychology and Aging, 21,* 240–252.

Freund, A. M., & Baltes, P. B. (2002). Life-management strategies of selection, optimization, and compensation: Measurement by self-report and construct validity. *Journal of Personality and Social Psychology, 82,* 642–662.

Freund, A. M., & Riediger, M. (2003). Successful aging. In I. B. Weiner (Ed.), *Handbook of psychology,* Vol. VI. New York: Wiley.

Friedman, J. H., Trieschmann, M. E., Myers, R. H., & Fernandez, H. H. (2005). Monozygotic twins discordant for Huntington disease after 7 years. *Archives of Neurology, 62,* 995–997.

Friedman, M., & Rosenman, R. (1974). *Type A behavior and your heart.* New York: Knopf.

Friedman, N. J., & Zeiger, R. S. (2005). The role of breast-feeding in the development of allergies and asthma. *Journal of Allergy and Clinical Immunology, 115,* 1238–1248.

Friend, M. (2005). *Special education.* Boston: Allyn & Bacon.

Friend, M. (2006). *Special education* (IDEA 2004 Update ed.). Boston: Allyn & Bacon.

Frieske, D. A., & Park, D. C. (1999). Memory for news in young and old adults. *Psychology and Aging, 14,* 90–98.

Frisard, M., Ravussin, E. (2006). Energy metabolism and oxidative stress: Impact on the metabolic syndrome and the aging process. *Endocrine, 29,* 27–32.

Fry, P. S. (1999, November). *Significance of religiosity and spirituality to psychological well-being of older adults.* Paper presented at the meeting of the Gerontological Society of America, San Francisco.

Fry, P. S. (1999, November). *Widows' regrets of action and inaction in coping with spousal loss: A follow-up.* Paper presented at the meeting of the Gerontological Society of America, San Francisco.

Fry, P. S. (2001). The unique contribution of key existential factors to the prediction of psychological well-being of older adults following spousal loss. *The Gerontologist, 41,* 69–81.

Frye, D. (1999). Development of intention: The relation of executive function to theory of mind. In P. D. Zelazo, J. W. Astington, & D. R. Olson (Eds.), *Developing theories of intention: Social understanding and self-control.* Mahwah, NJ: Erlbaum.

Frye, D., Zelazo, P. D., Brooks, P. J., & Samuels, M. C. (1996). Inference and action in early causal reasoning. *Developmental Psychology, 32,* 120–131.

Fuente, M. L., Hernanz, A., & Vallejo, M. C. (2005). The immune system in the oxidative stress conditions of aging and hypertension: Favorable effects of antioxidants and physical exercise. *Antioxidants and Redox Signaling, 7,* 1356–1366.

Fujikado, T., Kuroa, T., Maeda, N., Ninomiya, S., Goto, H., Tano, Y., Oshika, T., Hiroshara, Y., & Mihashi, T. (2004). Light scattering and optical aberrations as objective parameters to predict visual deterioration in eyes with cataracts. *Journal of Cataract and Refractive Surgery, 30,* 1198–1208.

Fujita, S., & Volpi, E. (2006). Amino acids and muscle loss with aging. *Journal of Nutrition, 136 (Suppl 1),* 277S–280S.

Fukunaga, A., Uematsu, H., & Sugimoto, K. (2005). Influences of aging on taste perception and oral somatic sensation. *Journals of Gerontology A: Biological Sciences and Medical Sciences, 60,* 109–113.

Fuligni, A. J., Alvarez, J., Bachman, J., & Ruble, D. N. (2005). Family obligation and the motivation of young children from immigrant families. In C. R. Cooper, C. T. Garcia Coll, W. T. Bartko, H. M. Davis, & C. Chatman (Eds,), *Developmental pathways through middle childhood.* Mahwah, NJ: Erlbaum.

Fuligni, A. J., & Hardway, C. (2004). Preparing diverse adolescents for the transition to adulthood. *Future of Children, 14,* 99–119.

Fuligni, A. J., & Witkow, M. (2004). The postsecondary educational progress of youth from immigrant families. *Journal of Research on Adolescence, 14,* 159–183.

Fuligni, A. J., & Yoshikawa, H. (2004). Investments in children among immigrant families. In A. Kalil & T. DeLeire (Eds.), *Family*

Fulmer, T., Guadagno, L., & Bolton, M. M. (2004). Elder mistreatment in women. *Journal of Obstetrics, Gynecological, and Neonatal Nursing, 33,* 657–663.

Fung, H., & Carstensen, L. L. (2004) Motivational changes in response to blocked goals and foreshortened time: Testing alternatives to socioemotional selectivity theory. *Psychology and Aging, 19*(1), 68–78.

Furman, E. (2005). *Boomerang nation.* New York: Fireside.

Furman, W., Ho, M., & Low, S. (2005, April). *Adolescent dating experiences and adjustment.* Paper presented at the meeting of the Society for Research in Child Development, Atlanta.

Furman, W., & Shaffer, L. (2003). The role of romantic relationships in adolescent development. In P. Florsheim (Ed.), *Adolescent romantic relations and sexual behavior.* Mahwah, NJ: Erlbaum.

Furth, H. G., & Wachs, H. (1975). *Thinking goes to school.* New York: Oxford University Press.

Galambos, N. L. (2004). Gender and gender role development in adolescence. In R. Lerner & L. Steinberg (Eds.), *Handbook of adolescence.* New York: Wiley.

Galambos, N. L., & Maggs, J. L. (1989, April). *The afterschool ecology of young adolescents and self-reported behavior.* Paper presented at the biennial meeting of the Society for Research in Child Development, Kansas City.

Galinsky, E., & David, J. (1988). *The preschool years: Family strategies that work—from experts and parents.* New York: Times Books.

Gallahue, D. L., & Ozmun, J. C. (2006). Motor development in young children. In B. Spodak & O. N. Saracho (Eds.). *Handbook of research on the education of young children* (2nd ed.). Mahwah, NJ: Erlbaum.

Gallo, L. C., Troxel, W. M., Matthews, K. A., Kuller, L. W. (2003). Marital status and quality in middle-aged women: Associations with levels and trajectories of cardiovascular risk factors. *Health Psychology, 22,* 453–463.

Galloway, J. C., & Thelen, E. (2004). Feet first: Object exploration in young infants. *Infant Behavior & Development, 27,* 107–112.

Gallup, G. H. (1987). *The Gallup poll: Public opinion 1986.* Wilmington, DE: Scholarly Resources.

Galvin, J. E., Powlishta, K. K., Wilkins, K., McKeel, D. W., Xiong, C., Grant, E., Storandt, M., & Morris, J. C. (2005). Predictors of preclinical Alzheimer disease and dementia; A clinicopathologic study. *Archives of Neurology, 62,* 758–765.

Gamino, L. A., & Sewell, K. W. (2004). Meaning constructs as predictors of bereavement adjustment: A report from the Scott & White grief study. *Death Studies, 28,* 397–421.

Gandour, J., Wong, D., Dzemidzic, M., Lowe, M., Tong, Y., & Li, X. (2003). A cross-linguistic fMRI study of perception of intonation and emotion in Chinese. *Human Brain Mapping, 18,* 149–157.

Gannon, L. (1998). Menopause. In H. S. Friedman (Ed.), *Encyclopedia of mental health* (Vol. 2). San Diego: Academic Press.

Ganong, L., Coleman, M., & Hans, J. (2005). Divorce as prelude to stepfamily living and the consequences of re-divorce. In M. A. Fine & J. H. Harvey (Eds.), *Handbook of divorce and relationship dissolution.* Mahwah, NJ: Erlbaum.

Gao, Y., Elliott, M. E., & Waters, E. (1999, April). *Maternal attachment representations and support for three-year-olds' secure base behavior.* Paper presented at the meeting of the Society for Research in Child Development, Albuquerque.

Garbarino, J. (1999). *Lost boys: Why our sons turn violent and how we can save them.* New York: Free Press.

Garbarino, J. (2001). Violent children. *Archives of Pediatrics & Adolescent Medicine, 155,* 1–2.

Garbarino, J., Dubrow, N., Kostelny, K., & Pardo, C. (1992). *Children in danger.* San Francisco: Jossey-Bass.

Garcia Coll, C., & Pachter, L. M. (2002). Ethnic and minority parenting. In M. H. Bornstein (Ed.), *Handbook of parenting* (2nd ed., Vol. 4), Mahwah, NJ: Erlbaum.

Garcia-Alba, C. (2004). Anorexia and depression. *Spanish Journal of Psychology, 7,* 40–52.

Gard, J. W., Alexander, J. M., Bawdon, R. E., & Albrecht, J. T. (2002). Oxytocin preparation stability in several common intravenous solutions. *American Journal of Obstetrics and Gynecology, 186,* 496–498.

Gardner, H. (1983). *Frames of mind.* New York: Basic Books.

Gardner, H. (1993). *Multiple intelligences.* New York: Basic Books.

Gardner, H. (2002). The pursuit of excellence through education. In M. Ferrari (Ed.), *Learning from extraordinary minds.* Mahwah, NJ: Erlbaum.

Garity, J. (2006). Caring for a family member with Alzheimer's disease: Coping with caregiver burden post-nursing home placement. *Journal of Gerontological Nursing, 32,* 39–48.

Garofalo, R., Wolf, R. C., Wissow, L. S., Woods, E. R., & Goodman, E. (1999). Sexual orientation and risk of suicide attempts among a representative sample of youth. *Archives of Pediatrics and Adolescent Medicine, 153,* 487–493.

Garshasbi, A., & Faghih Zadeh, S. (2005). The effect of exercise on the intensity of low back pain in pregnant women. *International Journal of Gynecology and Obstetrics, 88,* 271–275.

Gartner, J., Larson, D. B., & Allen, G. D. (1991). Religious commitment and mental health: A review of the empirical literature. *Journal of Psychology and Theology, 19,* 6–25.

Gartner, L. M., Morton, J., Lawrence, R. A., Naylor, A. J., O'Hare, D., Schanler, R. J., Eidelman, A. I., & the American Academy of Pediatrics Section on Breastfeeding. (2005). Breastfeeding and the use of human milk. *Pediatrics, 115,* 496–506.

Gassio, R., Artuch, R., Vilaseca, M. A., Fuste, E., Boix, C., Sans, A., & Campistol, J. (2005). Cognitive functions in classical phenylketonuria and mild hyperphenylalaninemia: Experience in a pediatric population. *Developmental Medicine and Child Neurology, 47,* 443–448.

Gatz, M. (2006). Mental health and adjustment: In I. E. Birren, K. W. Schaie (eds.), *Handbook of the psychology of aging* (6th Ed.). San Diego: Academic Press.

Gatz, M., Reynolds, C. A., Franglioni, L., Johansson, B., Mortimer, J. A., Berg, S., Fiske, A., & Pedersen, N. L. (2006). Role of genes and environments for explaining Alzheimer disease. *Archives of General Psychiatry, 63,* 168–174.

Gatza, C., Hinkal, G., Moore, L., Dumble, M., & Donehower, L. A. (2006). p53 and mouse aging models. In E. J. Masoro & S. N. Austad (Eds.), *Handbook of the biology of aging* (6th ed.). San Diego: Academic Press.

Gazzaley, A., Cooney, J. W., Rissman, J., & D'Esposito, M. (2005). Top-down suppression deficit underlies working memory impairment in normal aging. *Nature Neuroscience, 8,* 1298–1300.

Ge, S., Goh, E. L., Sailor, K. A., Kitabatake, Y., Ming, G. L., & Song, H. (2006). GABA regulates synaptic integration of newly generated neurons in the adult brain. *Nature, 439,* 589–593.

Geissbuehler, V., Stein, S., & Eberhard, J. (2004). Waterbirths compared to landbirths: An observational study of nine years. *Journal of Perinatal Medicine, 32,* 308–314.

Gelhorn, H., Stallings, M., Young, S., Corley, R., Rhee, S. H., Christian, H., & Hewitt, J. (2006). Common and specific genetic influences on aggressive and nonaggressive conduct disorder domains. *Journal of the American Academy of Child and Adolescent Psychiatry, 45,* 570–577.

Gelles, R. J., & Cavanaugh, M. M. (2005). Violence, abuse, and neglect in families and intimate relationships. In P.C. McKenry & S. J. Price (Eds.), *Families and change* (3rd ed.). Thousand Oaks, CA: Sage.

Gelman, R. (1969). Conservation acquisition: A problem of learning to attend to relevant attributes. *Journal of Experimental Child Psychology, 7,* 67–87.

Gelman, S. A., & Kalish, C. W. (2006). Conceptual development. In W. Damon & R. Lerner (Eds.), *Handbook of child psychology* (6th ed.). New York: Wiley.

Gelman, S. A., & Opfer, J. E. (2004). Development of the animate-inanimate distinction. In U. Goswami (Ed.), *Blackwell handbook of childhood cognitive development.* Malden, MA: Blackwell.

Gennetian, L. A., Crosby, D. A., & Huston, A. C. (2006). Wefare and child care policy effects on very young children's child care experiences. In N. Cabrera, R. Hutchens, H. E. Peters, & L. Peters (Eds.), *From welfare to childcare.* Mahwah, NJ: Erlbaum.

Gentile, S. (2005). The role of estrogen therapy in postpartum psychiatric disorders: An update. *CNS Spectrum, 10,* 944–952.

Gentzler, A. L., & Kerns, K. A. (2004). Associations between insecure attachment and sexual experiences. *Personal Relationships, 11,* 249–266.

George, L. K. (2006). Perceived quality of life. In R. H. Binstock & L. K. George (Eds.), *Handbook of aging and the social sciences* (6th ed.). San Diego: Academic Press.

Gerard, J. M., Landry-Meyer, L., & Roe, J. G. (2006). Grandparents raising grandchildren: The role of social support in coping with caregiving challenges. *International Journal of Aging and Human Development, 62,* 359–383.

Geroff, A.J., & Olshaker, J.S. (2006). Elder abuse. *Emergency Medical Clinics of North America, 24,* 491–505.

Gerrotsen, M., Berg, I., Deelman, B., Visser-Keizer, A., & Jong, B. (2003). Speed of information processing after unilateral stroke. *Journal of Clinical and Experimental Neuropsychology, 25,* 1–13.

Gershoff, E. T. (2002). Corporal punishment by parents and associated child behaviors and experiences: A meta-analysis and theoretical review. *Psychological Bulletin, 128,* 539–579.

Gescheider, G. A. (1997). *Psychophysics: The fundamentals.* Mahwah, NJ: Erlbaum.

Gesell, A. L. (1928). *Infancy and human growth.* New York: Macmillan.

Gesell, A. L. (1934). *Infancy and human growth.* New York: Macmillan.

Gessert, C. E., Elliott, B. A., & Haller, I. V. (2003). Mortality patterns in middle and old age. *Journals of Gerontology A: Biological and Medical Sciences, 58,* B967.

Getahun, D., Demissie, K., Lu. S. E., & Rhoads, G. G. (2004). Sudden infant death syndrome among twin births: United States, 1995–1998. *Journal of Perinatology, 24,* 544–551.

Gewirtz, J. (1977). Maternal responding and the conditioning of infant crying: Directions of influence within the attachment-acquisition process. In B. C. Etzel, J. M. LeBlanc, & D. M. Bear (Eds.), *New developments in behavioral research.* Hillsdale, NJ: Erlbaum.

Ghetti, S., & Alexander, K. W. (2004). "If it happened, I would remember it": Strategic use of event memorability in the rejection of false autobiographical events. *Child Development, 75,* 542–561.

Ghosh, S., & Shah. D. (2004). Nutritional problems in urban slum children. *Indian Pediatrics, 41,* 682–696.

Giammattei, J., Blix, G., Marshak, H. H., Wollitzer, A. O., & Pettitt, D. J. (2003). Television watching and soft drink consumption: Associations with obesity in 11- to 13-year-old schoolchildren. *Archives of Pediatric and Adolescent Medicine, 157,* 882–886.

Giannarelli, F., Sonenstein, E., & Stagner, M. (2006). Child care arrangements and help for low-income families with young children: Evidence from the National Survey of America's Families. In N. Cabrera, R. Hutchens, & H. E. Peters (Eds.), *From welfare to childcare.* Mahwah, NJ: Erlbaum.

Gibbons, J. L. (2000). Gender development in cross-cultural perspective. In T. Eckes & H. M. Trautner (Eds.), *The developmental social psychology of gender.* Mahwah, NJ: Erlbaum.

Gibbons, J., & Ng, S. H. (2004). Acting bilingual and thinking bilingual. *Journal of Language & Social Psychology, 23,* 4–6.

Gibbs, J. C. (1993, March). *Inductive discipline's contribution to moral motivation.* Paper presented at the biennial meeting of the Society for Research in Child Development, New Orleans.

Gibbs, J. C. (2003). *Moral development & reality.* Thousand Oaks, CA: Sage.

Gibson, E. J. (1969). *Principles of perceptual learning and development.* New York: Appleton-Century-Crofts.

Gibson, E. J. (1989). Exploratory behavior in the development of perceiving, acting, and the acquiring of knowledge. *Annual Review of Psychology, 39.* Palo Alto, CA: Annual Reviews.

Gibson, E. J. (2001). *Perceiving the affordances.* Mahwah, NJ: Erlbaum.

Gibson, E. J., & Walk, R. D. (1960). The "visual cliff." *Scientific American, 202,* 64–71.

Gibson, E. J., Riccio, G., Schmuckler, M. A., Stoffregen, T. A., Rosenberg, D., & Taormina, J. (1987). Detection of the traversability of surfaces by crawling and walking infants. *Journal of Experimental Psychology: Human Perception and Performance, 13,* 533–544.

Gibson, J. H., Harries, M., Mitchell, A., Godfrey, R., Lunt, M., & Reeve, J. (2000). Determinants of bone density and prevalence of osteopenia among female runners in their second to seventh decades of age. *Bone, 26,* 591–598.

Gibson, J. J. (1966). *The senses considered as perceptual systems.* Boston: Houghton Mifflin.

Gibson, J. J. (1979). *The ecological approach to visual perception.* Boston: Houghton Mifflin.

Giedd, J., Jeffries, N., Blumenthal, J., Castellanos, F., Vaituzis, A., Fernandez, T., Hamburger, S., Liu, H., Nelson, J., Bedwell, J., Tran, L., Lenane, M., Nicolson, R., & Rapoport, J. (1999). Childhood-onset schizophrenia: Progressive brain changes during adolescence. *Biological Psychiatry, 46,* 892–898.

Giequel, C., & Le Boue, Y. (2006). Hormonal regulation of fetal growth. *Hormone Research, 65,* (Suppl. 3), 28–33.

Gifford-Smith, M. E., & Rabiner, D. L. (2004). Children's understanding and regulation of emotion in the context of their peer relations. In J. B. Kupersmidt & K. A. Dodge (Eds.), *Children's peer relations.* Washington, DC: American Psychological Association.

Giger, J. N., Davidhizar, R. E., & Fordham, P. (2006). Multi-cultural and multiethnic considerations and advanced directives: Developing cultural competency. *Journal of Cultural Diversity, 13,* 3–9.

Gilbert, P. E., Pirogovsky, E., Ferdon, S., & Murphy, C. (2006). The effects of normal aging on source memory for odors. *Journals of Gerontology B: Psychological Sciences and Social Sciences, 61,* P58–P60.

Gilhar, A., Ullman, Y., Karry, R., Shalaginov, R., Assy, B., Serafimovich, S., & Kalish, R. S. (2004). Aging of human epidermis. *Journals of Gerontology A: Biological and Medical Sciences, 59,* B411–B415.

Gilligan, C. (1982). *In a different voice.* Cambridge, MA: Harvard University Press.

Gilligan, C. (1992, May). *Joining the resistance: Girls' development in adolescence.* Paper presented at the symposium on development and vulnerability in close relationships, Montreal, Quebec.

Gilligan, C. (1996). The centrality of relationships in psychological development: A puzzle, some evidence, and a theory. In G. G. Noam & K. W. Fischer (Eds.), *Development and vulnerability in close relationships.* Hillsdale, NJ: Erlbaum.

Gilligan, C., Spencer, R., Weinberg, M. K., & Bertsch, T. (2003). On the listening guide: A voice-centered relational model. In P. M. Carnic & J. E. Rhodes (Eds.), *Qualitative research in psychology* Washington, DC: American Psychological Association.

Gilstrap, L. L., & Ceci, S. J. (2005). Reconceptualizing children's suggestibility: Bidirectional and temporal properties. *Child Development, 76,* 40–53.

Gingart, E., Helmes, E., & Speelman, C. P. (2005). Exploring attitudes toward older workers among Australian employers: An empirical study. *Journal of Aging and Social Policy, 17,* 85–103.

Girling, A. (2006). The benefits of using the Neonatal Behavioral Assessment Scale in health visiting practice. *Community Practice, 79,* 118–120.

Girls, Inc. (1991). *Truth, trusting, and technology: New research on preventing adolescent pregnancy.* Indianapolis: Author.

Girouard, H., & Iadecola, C. (2006). Neurovascular coupling in the normal brain and in hypertension, stroke, and Alzheimer disease. *Journal of Applied Physiology, 100,* 328–335.

Glantz, J. C. (2005). Elective induction vs. spontaneous labor associations and outcomes. *Journal of Reproductive Medicine, 50,* 235–240.

Glaser, R., & Kiecolt-Glaser, J. K. (2005). Stress-induced immune dysfunction: Implications for health. *Nature Review: Immunology, 5,* 243–251.

Glass, J. M., Park, D. C., Minear, M., & Crofford, L. J. (2005). Memory beliefs and function in fibromyalgia patients. *Journal of Psychosomatic Research, 58,* 263–269.

Glazier, R. H., Elgar, F. J., Goel, V., & Holzapfel, S. (2004). Stress, social support, and emotional distress in a community sample of pregnant women. *Journal of Psychosomatic Obstetrics and Gynecology, 25,* 247–255.

Glei, D. A. (1999). Measuring contraceptive use patterns among teenage and adult women. *Family Planning Perspectives, 31,* 73–80.

Gliori, G., Imm, P., Anderson, H. A., & Knobeloch, L. (2006). Fish consumption and advisory awareness among expectant women. *Wisconsin Medicine Journal, 105,* 41–44.

Godding, V., Bonnier, C., Fiasse, L., Michel, M., Longueville, E., Lebecque, P., Robert, A., & Galanti, L. (2004). Does in utero exposure to heavy maternal nicotine smoking induce nicotine withdrawal symptoms in neonates? *Pediatric Research, 55,* 645–651.

Goffin, S. G., & Wilson, C. S. (2001). *Curriculum models and early childhood education.* Upper Saddle River, NJ: Prentice Hall.

Golan, M., & Crow, S. (2004). Parents are key players in the prevention and treatment of weight-related problems. *Nutrition Review, 62,* 39–50.

Goldberg, M. (2005, January). Test mess 2: Are we doing any better a year later? *Phi Delta Kappan,* 389–395.

Golden, T., R., Morten, K., Johnson, F., Samper, E., & Melov, S. (2006). Mitochondria: A critical role in aging. In E. J. Masoro & S. N. Austad (Eds.), *Handbook* *of the biology of aging* (6th ed.). San Diego: Academic Press.

Goldman, N., Weinstein, M., Cornman, J., Singer, B., Seeman, T., Goldman, N., & Chang, M. C. (2004). Sex differentials in biological risk factors for chronic disease. *Journal of Women's Health, 13,* 393–403.

Goldsmith, H. H. (2002). Genetics of emotional development. In R. J. Davidson, K. R. Scherer, & H. H. Goldsmith (Eds.), *Handbook of affective sciences.* New York: Oxford University Press.

Goldstein, J. M., Seidman, L. J., Horton, N. J., Makris, N., Kennedy, D. N., Caviness, V. S., Faraone, S. V., & Tsuang, M. T. (2001). Normal sexual dimorphism of the adult human brain assessed by in vivo magnetic resonance imaging. *Cerebral Cortex, 11,* 490–497.

Goldstein, M. H., King, A. P., & West, M. J. (2003). Social interaction shapes babbling: Testing parallels between birdsong and speech. *Proceedings of the National Academy of Sciences, 100*(13), 8030–8035.

Goldstein, S. E, Davis-Kean, P. E., & Eccles, J. S. (2005). Parents, peers, and problem behavior: A longitudinal investigation of the impact of relationship perceptions and characteristics on the development of adolescent problem behavior. *Developmental Psychology, 41,* 401–413.

Goleman, D. (1995). *Emotional intelligence.* New York: Basic Books.

Golombok, S., MacCallum, F., & Goodman, E. (2001). The "test-tube" generation: Parent-child relationships and the psychological well-being of in vitro fertilization children at adolescence. *Child Development, 72,* 599–608.

Gonzales, N. A., Knight, G. P., Birman, D., & Sirolli, A. A. (2004). Acculturation and enculturation among Latino youths. In K. L. Maton, C. J. Schellenbach, & A. L. Solarz (Eds.), *Investing in children, families, and communities.* Washington, DC: American Psychological Association.

Gonzales, V., Yawkey, T. D., & Minaya-Rowe, L. (2006). *English-as-a-second-language (ESL) teaching and learning.* Boston: Allyn & Bacon.

Gonzalez-del Angel, A. A., Vidal, S., Saldan, Y., del Castillo, V., Angel, M., Macias, M., Luna, P., & Orozco, L. (2000). Molecular diagnosis of the fragile X and FRAXE syndromes in patients with mental retardation of unknown cause in Mexico. *Annals of Genetics, 43,* 29–34.

Goodman, G. S., Batterman-Faunce, J. M., & Kenney, R. (1992). Optimizing children's testimony: Research and social policy issues concerning allegations of child sexual abuse. In D. Cicchetti & S. Toth (Eds.), *Child abuse, child development and social policy.* Norwood, NJ: Ablex.

Goodman, J. H. (2004). Paternal postpartum depression, its relationship to maternal postpartum depression and implications for family health, *Journal of Advanced Nursing, 45,* 26–169.

Gooren, L. J. (2002). Psychological consequences. *Seminars in Reproductive Medicine, 20,* 285–296.

Goorhuis-Brouwer, S., Coster, H., Nakken, H., & Spelberg, H. L. (2004). Environmental factors in developmental language disorders. In L. Verhoeven & H. Van Balkom (Eds.), *The classification of language disorders.* Mahwah, NJ: Erlbaum.

Gordon-Salant, S., Yeni-Komshian, G.H., Fitzgibbons, P.J., & Barrett, J. (2006). Age-related differences in identification and discrimination of temporal cues in speech segments. *Journal of the Acoustical Society of America, 119,* 2455–2466.

Gostic, C. L. (2005). The crucial role of exercise and physical activity in weight management and functional improvement for seniors. *Clinical Geriatric Medicine, 21,* 747–756.

Gotesdam, K. G., & Agras, W. S. (1995). General population-based epidemiological survey of eating disorders in Norway. *International Journal of Eating Disorders, 18,* 119–126.

Gottfried, A. E., Gottfried, A. W., & Bathurst, K. (2002). Maternal and dual-earner employment status and parenting. In M. H. Bornstein (Ed.), *Handbook of parenting* (2nd ed., Vol. 2.) Mahwah, NJ: Erlbaum.

Gottlieb, G. (1998). Normally occurring environmental and behavioral influences on gene activity: From central dogma to probabilistic epigenesis. *Psychological Review, 105,* 792–802.

Gottlieb, G. (2003). *Developmental behavior genetics and the statistical concept of interaction.* Unpublished manuscript, Department of Psychology, University of North Carolina, Chapel Hill.

Gottlieb, G. (2004). Normally occurring environmental and behavioral influences on gene activity. In C. G. Coll, E. L. Bearer, & R. M. Lerner (Eds.), *Nature and nurture.* Mahwah, NJ: Erlbaum.

Gottlieb, G. (2005). Unpublished review of Santrock *Topical Life Span Development* (3rd ed.). New York: McGraw-Hill.

Gottlieb, G., Wahlsten, D., & Lickliter, R. (1998). The significance of biology for human development. In W. Damon & R. Lerner (Eds.), *Handbook of child psychology* (5th ed.). New York: Wiley.

Gottlieb, G., Wahlsten, D., & Lickliter, R. (2006). The significance of biology for human development: A developmental psychobiological systems view. In W. Damon & R. Lerner (Eds.), *Handbook of child psychology* (6th ed.). New York: Wiley.

Gottlieb, M. (2006). *Assessing English language learners.* Thousand Oaks, CA: Sage.

Gottman, J. M. (1994). *Why marriages succeed or fail.* New York: Simon & Schuster.

Gottman, J. M., Coan, J., Carrere, S., & Swanson, C. (1998). Predicting marital happiness and stability from newlywed interactions. *Journal of Marriage and the Family, 60,* 5–22.

Gottman, J. M., & DeClaire, J. (1997). *The heart of parenting: Raising an emotionally intelligent child.* New York: Simon & Schuster.

Gottman, J. M., & Levenson, R. W. (2000). The timing of divorce: Predicting when a couple will divorce over a 14-year period. *Journal of Marriage and the Family, 62,* 737–745.

Gottman, J. M., & Notarius, C. I. (2000). Decade review: Observing marital interaction. *Journal of Marriage and the Family, 62,* 927–947.

Gottman, J. M., & Parker, J. G. (Eds.). (1987). *Conversations of friends.* New York: Cambridge University Press.

Gottman, J. M., Ryan, K. D., Carrers, S., & Erley, A. M. (2002). Toward a scientifically based marital therapy. In H. A. Liddle & D. A. Santisteban (Eds.), *Family psychology.* Washington, DC: American Psychological Association.

Gottman, J. M., & Silver, N. (2000). *The seven principles for making marriages work.* New York: Crown.

Gould, E., Reeves, A. J., Graziano, M. S., & Gross, C. G. (1999). Neurogenesis in the neocortex of adult primates, *Science, 286* (1), 548–552.

Gould, M. S., Greenberg, T., Velting, D. M., & Shaffer, D. (2003). Youth suicide risk and preventive interventions: A review of the past 10 years. *Journal of the American Academy of Child and Adolescent Psychiatry, 42,* 386–405.

Gould, S. J. (1981). *The mismeasure of man.* New York: W. W. Norton.

Gouldner, H., & Strong, M. M. (1987). *Speaking of friendship.* New York: Greenwood Press.

Gouin-Decarie, T. (1996). Revisiting Piaget, or the vulnerability of Piaget's infancy theory in the nineties. In G. G. Noam & K. W. Fischer (Eds.), *Development and vulnerability in close relationships.* Hillsdale, NJ: Erlbaum.

Gove, W. R., Style, C. B., & Hughes, M. (1990). The effect of marriage on the well-being of adults: A theoretical analysis. *Journal of Health and Social Behavior, 24,* 122–131.

Gowan, D. E. (2003). Christian beliefs concerning death and life after death. In C. D. Bryant (Ed.), *Handbook of death and dying.* Thousand Oaks, CA: Sage.

Graber, J. (2004). Internalizing problems during adolescence. In R. Lerner & L. Steinberg (Eds.), *Handbook of adolescent psychology.* New York: Wiley.

Graber, J. A. (2003). *Early puberty and drug use.* Unpublished data, Department of Psychology, University of Florida, Gainesville, FL.

Graber, J. A., & Brooks-Gunn, J. (2001). Body image. In R. M. Lerner & J. V. Lerner (Eds.), *Adolescence in America.* Santa Barbara, CA: ABC-CLIO.

Graber, J. A., & Brooks-Gunn, J. (2002). Adolescent girls' sexual development. In G. M. Wingood & R. J. DiClemente (Eds.), *Handbook of sexual and reproductive health.* New York: Plenum.

Graber, J. A., Seeley, J. R., Brooks-Gunn, J., & Lewinsohn, P. M. (2004). Is pubertal timing associated with psychopathology in young adulthood? *Journal of the American Academy of Child and Adolescent Psychiatry, 43,* 718–726.

Grady, C. L., Springer, M. V., Hongwanishkul, D., McIntosh, A. R., & Winocur, G. (2006). Age-related changes in brain activity across the adult life span. *Journal of Cognitive Neuroscience, 18,* 227–241.

Grady, M. A., & Bloom, K. C. (2004). Pregnancy outcomes of adolescents enrolled in a Centering Pregnancy program. *Journal of Midwifery and Women's Health, 49,* 412–420.

Graham, J. E., Christian, L. M., & Kiecolt-Glaser, J. K. (2006, in press). Stress, age, and immune function: Toward a lifespan approach. *Journal of Behavioral Medicine.*

Graham, J. M., & Shaw, G. M. (2006). Gene-environment interactions in rare diseases that include common birth defects. *Birth Defects Research, 73,* 865–867.

Graham, J. E., Christian, L. M., & Kiecolt-Glaser, J. K. (2006). Stress, age, and immune function: toward a lifespan approach. *Journal of Behavioral Medicine, 29,* 389–400.

Graham, S. (1992). Most of the subjects were white and middle class. *American Psychologist, 47,* 629–637.

Graham, S. (2005, February 16). Commentary in *USA Today,* p. 2D.

Graham, S. (Ed.). (2006). Our children too: A history of the first 25 years of the Society for Research in Child Development. *Monographs of the Society for Research in Child Development, 71* (No. 1), 1–227.

Grambs, J. D. (1989). *Women over forty* (rev. ed.), New York: Springer.

Grant, J. (1993). *The state of the world's children.* New York: UNICEF and Oxford University Press.

Grant, J. P. (1996). *The state of the world's children.* New York: UNICEF and Oxford University Press.

Grant, J. P. (1997). *The state of the world's children.* New York: UNICEF and Oxford University Press.

Grantham-McGregor, S., Ani, C., & Fernald, L. (2001). The role of nutrition in cognitive development. In R. J. Sternberg & E. I. Grigorenko (Eds.), *Environmental effects on cognitive abilities.* Mahwah, NJ: Erlbaum.

Graves, M., Juel, C., & Graves, B. (2007). *Teaching reading in the 21st century* (4th ed.). Boston: Allyn & Bacon.

Gray, K. A., Day, N. L., Leech, S., & Richardson, G. A. (2005). Prenatal marijuana exposure: Effect on child depressive symptoms at ten years of age. *Neurotoxicology and Teratology, 27,* 439–448.

Gray, M. J., & Acierno, R. (2002). Symptom presentation of older adult crime victim description of a clinical sample. *Journal of Anxiety Disorders, 16,* 299–309.

Graziano, A. M., & Raulin, M. L. (2007). *Research methods* (6th ed.). Boston: Allyn & Bacon.

Greenberger, E., & Steinberg, L. (1986). *When teenagers work: The psychological social costs of adolescent employment.* New York: Basic Books.

Greene, V. L., Lovely, M. E., Miller, M. D., & Ondrich, J. I. (1995). Reducing nursing home use through community long-term care: An optimization analysis. *Journal of Gerontology: Social Sciences, 50B,* S259–S268.

Greenfield, L. A., & Marks, N. F. (2004). Formal volunteering as a protective factor for older adults' psychological well-being. *Journals of Gerontology B: Psychological Sciences and Social Sciences, 59,* S258–S264.

Greenfield, P. M. (1966). On culture and conservation. In J. S. Bruner, R. P. Oliver, & P. M. Greenfield (Eds.), *Studies in cognitive growth.* New York: Wiley.

Greenfield, P. M., Suzuki, L. K., & Rothstein-Fisch, C. (2006). Cultural pathways through human development. In W. Damon & R. Lerner (Eds.), *Handbook of child psychology* (6th ed.). New York: Wiley.

Greenfield, P. M., Trumbull, E., Keller, H., Rothstein-Fisch, C., Suzuki, L., & Quiroz, B. (2006). Cultural conceptions of learning and development. In P. A. Alexander & P. H. Winne (Eds.), *Handbook of educational psychology* (2nd ed.). Mahwah, NJ: Erlbaum.

Greenough, W. T. (1997, April 21). Commentary in article, "Politics of biology." *U.S. News & World Report,* p. 79.

Greenough, W. T. (1999, April). *Experience, brain development, and links to mental retardation.* Paper presented at the meeting of the Society for Research in Child Development, Albuquerque.

Greenough, W. T. (2001, April). *Nature and nurture in the brain development process.* Paper presented at the meeting of the Society for Research in Child Development, Minneapolis.

Greenough, W. T., Klintsova, A. Y., Irvan, S. A., Galvez, R., Bates, K. E., & Weiler, I. J. (2001). Synaptic regulation of protein synthesis and the fragile X protein. *Proceedings of the National Academy of Science, USA, 98,* 7101–7106.

Gregg, R. E. (2004). Restrictions on workplace romance and consensual relationship policies. *Journal of Medical Practice Management, 19,* 314–316.

Gregory, R. J. (2007). *Psychological testing* (5th ed.). Boston: Allyn & Bacon.

Grigorenko, E. (2000). Heritability and intelligence. In R. J. Sternberg (Ed.), *Handbook of intelligence.* New York: Cambridge University Press.

Grigorenko, E. L., Geissler, P., Prince, R., Okatcha, F. Nokes, C., Kenney, D. A., Bundy, D. A., & Sternberg, R. J. (2001). The organization of Luo Conceptions of intelligence: A study of implicit theories in a Kenyan village. *International Journal of Behavioral Development, 25,* 367–378.

Grigoriadis, S., & Kennedy, S. H. (2002). Role of estrogen in the treatment of depression. *American Journal of Therapy, 9,* 503–509.

Grolnick, W. S., Bridges, L. J., & Connell, J. P. (1996). Emotion regulation in two-year-olds: Strategies and emotional expression in four contexts. *Child Development, 67,* 928–941.

Grolnick, W. S., & Gurland, S. T. (2001). Mothering: Restrospect and prospect. In J. P. McHale & W. S. Grolnick (Eds.), *Retrospect and prospect in the psychological study of families.* Mahwah, NJ: Erlbaum.

Gronlund, N. W. (2006). *Assessment of student achievement* (8th ed.). Boston: Allyn & Bacon.

Gross, R. T. (1984). Patterns of maturation: Their effects on behavior and development. In M. D. Levine & P. Satz (Eds.), *Middle childhood: Development and dysfunction.* Baltimore: University Park Press.

Grossman, E., & Messerli, F. H. (2006). Long-term safety of antihypertensive therapy. *Progress in Cardiovascular Disease, 49,* 16–25.

Grossmann, K., Grossmann, K. E., Spangler, G., Suess, G., & Unzner, L. (1985). Maternal sensitivity and newborns' orientation responses as related to quality of attachment in northern Germany. In I. Bretherton & E. Waters (Eds.), Growing points of attachment theory and research. *Monographs of the Society for Research in Child Development, 50* (1–2, Serial No. 209).

Grosso, L. M., & Bracken, M. B. (2005). Caffeine metabolism, genetics, and perinatal outcomes: A review of exposure assessment during pregnancy. *Annals of Epidemiology, 15,* 460–466.

Grotevant, H. D. (2006, March). *Adjustment outcomes for adopted adolescents.* Paper presented at the meeting of the Society for Research on Adolescence, San Francisco.

Grotevant, H. D., & Cooper, C. R. (1985). Patterns of interaction in family relationships and the development of identity exploration in adolescence. *Child Development, 56,* 415–428.

Grotevant, H. D., & Cooper, C. R. (1998). Individuality and connectedness in adolescent development: Review and prospects for research on identity, relationships, and context. In E. Skoe & A. von der Lippe (Eds.), *Personality development in adolescence: A cross-national and life-span perspective.* London: Routledge.

Grotevant, H. D., van Dulmen, M. H. M., Dunbar, N., Nelson-Christinedaughter, J., Christensen, M., Fan, X., & Miller, B. C. (2006). Antisocial behavior of adoptees and nonadoptees: Prediction from early history and adolescent relationships. *Journal of Research on Adolescence, 16,* 105–131.

Groth, K. E., Gilmore, G. C., & Thomas, C. W. (2003). Impact of stimulus integrity on age differences in letter matching. *Experimental Aging Research, 29,* 155–172.

Grundy, S.M. (2006). Does a diagnosis of metabolic syndrome have value in clinical practice? *American Journal of Clinical Nutrition, 83,* 1248–1251.

Grusec, J. (2006). Development of moral behavior and conscience. In M. Killen & J. G. Smetana (Eds.), *Handbook of moral development.* Mahwah, NJ: Erlbaum.

Grusec, J., Davidov, M., & Lundell, L. (2002). Prosocial and helping behavior. In P. K. Smith & C. H. Hart (Eds.), *Blackwell handbook of childhood social development.* Malden, MA: Blackwell.

Guarente, L., & Picard, F. (2005). Calorie-restriction—the SIR2 connection. *Cell, 120,* 473–482.

Guastello, D. D., & Guastello, S. J. (2003). Androgyny, gender role behavior, and emotional intelligence among college students and their parents. *Sex Roles, 49,* 663–673.

Gudykunst, W. B. (2004). *Bridging differences* (4th ed.). Thousand Oaks, CA: Sage.

Guilford, J. P. (1967). *The structure of intellect.* New York: McGraw-Hill.

Gumora, G., & Arsenio, W. (2002). Emotionality, emotion regulation, and school performance in middle school children. *Journal of School Psychology, 40,* 395–413.

Gump, B., & Matthews, K. (2000 March). *Annual vacations, health, and death.* Paper presented at the meeting of American Psychosomatic Society, Savannah, GA.

Gunnar, M. R. (2000). Early adversity and the development of stress reactivity and regulation. In C. A. Nelson (Ed.), *The effects of early adversity on neurobehavioral development. The Minnesota Symposia on Child Psychology* (Vol. 31). Mahwah, NJ: Erlbaum.

Gunnar, M. R., & Davis, E. P. (2003), Stress and emotion in early childhood. In I. B. Weiner (Ed.), *Handbook of psychology* (Vol. 6). New York: Wiley.

Gunnar, M. R., Malone, S., & Fisch, R. O. (1987). The psychobiology of stress and coping in the human neonate: Studies of the adrenocortical activity in response to stress in the first week of life. In T. Field, P. McCabe, & N. Scheiderman (Eds.). *Stress and coping.* Hillsdale, NJ: Erlbaum.

Gunning, T. G. (2006). *Closing the literacy gap.* Boston: Allyn & Bacon.

Gur, R. C., Mozley, L. H., Mozley, P. D., Resnick, S. M., Karp, J. S., Alavi, A., Arnold, S. E., & Gur, R. E. (1995). Sex differences in regional cerebral glucose metabolism during a resting state. *Science, 267,* 528–531.

Gurung, R. A., Taylor, S. E., & Seeman, T. E. (2003). Accounting for changes in social support among older adults: Insights from the MacArthur Studies of Successful Aging. *Psychology and Aging, 18,* 487–496.

Gurwitch, R. H., Silovsky, J. F., Schultz, S., Kees, M., & Burlingame, S. (2001). *Reactions and guidelines for children following trauma/disaster.* Norman; Department of Pediatrics, University of Oklahoma Health Sciences Center.

Gustafsson, P. A., Duchen, K., Birberg, U., & Karlsson, T. (2004). Breastfeeding, very long polyunsaturated fatty acids (PUFA), and IQ at 6 1/2 years of age. *Acta Pediatrics, 93,* 1280–1287.

Gutchess, A. H., Welsch, R. C., Hedden, T., Bangert, A., Minear, M., Liu, L. L., & Park, D. C. (2005). Aging and the neural correlates of successful picture encoding: Frontal activations compensate for decreased medial-temporal activity. *Journal of Cognitive Neuroscience, 17,* 84–96.

Gutmann, D. L. (1975). Parenthood: A key to the comparative study of the life cycle. In N. Datan & L. Ginsberg (Eds.), *Life-span developmental psychology: Normative life crises.* New York: Academic Press.

Gutteling, B. M., de Weerth, C., & Buitellar, J. K. (2005). Maternal prenatal stress and 4–6 year old children's salivary cortisol concentrations pre- and post-vaccination. *Stress, 7,* 257–260.

Guymer, R. H., & Chong, E. W. (2006). Modifiable risk factors for age-related macular degeneration. *Medical Journal of Australia, 184,* 455–458.

Gyamfi, P., Brooks-Gunn, J., & Jackson, A. P. (2001). Associations between employment and financial and parental stress in low-income single Black mothers. In M. C. Lennon (Ed.), *Welfare, work, and well-being.* New York: Haworth Press.

Haager, D., & Klingner, J. K. (2005). *Differentiating instruction in inclusive classrooms.* Boston: Allyn & Bacon.

Haber, D., & Rhodes, D. (2004). Health contract with sedentary older adults. *Gerontologist, 44,* 827–835.

Hacker, K. A., Suglia, S. F., Fried, L. E., Rappaport, N., & Cabral, H. (2006). Developmental differences in risk factors for suicide attempts between ninth and eleventh graders. *Suicide and Life Threatening Behavior, 36,* 154–166.

Hadwin, J., & Perner, J. (1991). Pleased and surprised: Children's cognitive theory of emotion. *British Journal of Developmental Psychology, 9,* 215–234.

Hagestad, G. O. (1985). Continuity and connectedness. In V. L. Bengtson (Ed.), *Grandparenthood.* Beverly Hills, CA: Sage.

Hahn, C. S., & DiPietro, J. A. (2001). In vitro fertilization and the family: Quality of parenting, family functioning, and child psychosocial adjustment. *Developmental Psychology, 37,* 37–48.

Hahn, D. B., Payne, W. A., & Lucas, E. B. (2007). *Focus on health* (8th ed). New York: McGraw-Hill.

Hahn, W. K. (1987). Cerebral lateralization of function: From infancy through childhood. *Psychological Bulletin, 101,* 376–392.

Haith, M. M., & Benson, J. B. (1998). Infant cognition. In W. Damon (Ed.), *Handbook of child psychology* (5th ed., Vol. 2). New York: Wiley.

Haith, M. M., Hazen, C., & Goodman, G. S. (1988). Expectation and anticipation of dynamic visual events by 3.5 month old babies. *Child Development, 59,* 467–479.

Hakuta, K. (2000). Bilingualism. In A. Kazdin (ed.), *Encyclopedia of psychology.* Washington, DC, & New York: American Psychological Association and Oxford University Press.

Hakuta, K. (2001, April). *Key policy milestones and directions in the education of English language learners.* Paper prepared for the Rockefeller Foundation Symposium, Leveraging Change: An Emerging Framework for Educational Equity, Washington, DC.

Hakuta, K. (2005, April). *Bilingualism at the intersection of research and public policy.* Paper presented at the meeting of the Society for Research in Child Development, Atlanta.

Hakuta, K., Butler, Y. G., & Witt, D. (2000). *How long does it take English learners to attain proficiency?* Berkeley, CA: The University of California Linguistic Minority Research Institute Policy Report 2000–1.

Hales, D. (2006). *Personal health and wellness* (4th ed.). Belmont, CA: Wadsworth.

Hales, D. (2007). *An invitation to health* (12th ed.). Belmont, CA: Wadsworth.

Halford, G. S. (2004). Information processing models of cognitive development. In U. Goswami (Ed.), *Blackwell handbook of cognitive development.* Malden, MA: Blackwell.

Hall, G. S. (1994). *Adolescence* (Vols. 1 & 2). Englewood Cliffs, NJ: Prentice Hall.

Hall, J. (2005). Postnatal emotional wellbeing. *Practicing Midwife, 8,* 35–40.

Hallahan, D. P., & Kauffman, J. M. (2005). *Learning disabilities* (3rd ed.). Boston: Allyn & Bacon.

Hallahan, D. P., & Kauffman, J. M. (2006). *Exceptional learners* (10th ed.). Boston: Allyn & Bacon.

Hallfors, D. D., Waller, M. W., Ford, C. A., Halpern, C. T., Brodish, P. H., & Iritani, B. (2004). Adolescent depression and suicide risk: Association with sex and drug behavior. *American Journal of Preventive Medicine, 27,* 224–231.

Halonen, J., & Santrock, J. W. (1999). *Psychology: Contexts and Applications.* Boston: McGraw-Hill.

Halpern, D. (2001). Sex difference research: Cognitive abilities. In J. Worell (Ed.), *Handbook of women and gender.* San Diego: Academic Press.

Halpern, D. (2006). Assessing gender Gaps in learning and academic achievement. In P. A. Alexander & P. H. Wynne (Eds.), *Handbook of educational psychology* (2nd ed.). Mahwah, NJ: Erlbaum.

Hambleton, R. K. (2002). How can we make NAEP and state test score reporting scales and reports more understandable? In R. W. Lissitz & W. D. Schafer (Eds.), *Assessment in educational reform: Both means and ends.* Boston: Allyn & Bacon.

Hamburg, B., & Hamburg, D. (2004). *On the future of adolescent psychology.* In R. Lerner & L. Steinberg (Eds.), *Handbook of adolescent psychology.* New York: Wiley.

Hamburg, D. A. (1997). Meeting the essential requirements for healthy adolescent development in a transforming world. In R. Takanishi & D. Hamburg (Eds.), *Preparing adolescents for the 21st century.* New York: Cambridge University Press.

Hamilton, B. E., & Ventura, S. J. (2006). Fertility and abortion rates in the United States, 1960–2002. *International Journal of Andrology, 29,* 34–45.

Hamilton, S. F., & Hamilton, M. A. (2004). Contexts for mentoring: Adolescent-adult relationships in workplaces and communities. In R. Lerner & L. Steinberg (Eds.), *Handbook of adolescent psychology* (2nd ed.). New York: Wiley.

Hammen, C. (2003). Mood disorders. In I. B. Weiner (Ed.), *Handbook of psychology* (Vol. VIII). New York: Wiley.

Hamon, R. R., & Ingolds by, B. B. (Eds.) (2003). *Mate selection across cultures.* Thousand Oaks, CA: Sage.

Hampton, T. (2004). Panel reviews health effects data for assisted reproductive technologies. *Journal of the American Medical Association, 292,* 2961–2962.

Han, S. K., & Moen, P. (1998). *Clocking out: Multiplex time use in retirement.* Bronfenbrenner Life Course Center Working Paper Series #98–03m. Ithaca, NY: Cornell University.

Handelsman, D. J., & Liu, P. Y. (2006). Klinefelter's syndrome—a microcosm of male reproductive health. *Journal of Clinical Endocrinology and Metabolism, 91,* 1220–1222.

Hanevold, C., Walter, J., Daniels, S., Portman, R., & Sorol, J. (2004). The effects of obesity, gender, and ethnic group on left ventricular hypertrophy and geometry in hypertensive children: A collaborative study of the International Pediatric Hypertension Association. *Pediatrics, 113,* 328–333.

Hankin, B. L., Kassel, J. D., & Abela, J. R. (2005). Adult attachment dimensions and specificity of emotional distress symptoms: Prospective investigations of cognitive risk and interpersonal stress generation as mediating mechanisms. *Personality and Social Psychology Bulletin, 31,* 136–151.

Hankins, G. D., & Longo, M. (2006). The role of stillbirth prevention and late preterm (near-term) births. *Seminars in Perinatology, 30,* 20–23.

Hanley, J. (2006). The assessment and treatment of postnatal depression. *Nursing Times, 102,* 24–26.

Hannish, L. D., & Guerra, N. G. (2004). Aggressive victims, passive victims, and bullies: Developmental continuity or developmental change? *Merrill-Palmer Quarterly, 50,* 17–38.

Hansen, L. A. (2006). The neuropathology of aging, mild cognitive impairment, and Alzheimer disease. *Archives of Neurology, 63,* 647–648.

Hansen, M., Janssen, I., Schiff, A., Zee, P. C., & Dubocovich, M. L. (2005). The impact of school daily schedule on adolescent sleep. *Pediatrics, 115,* 1555–1561.

Harding, B., Risdon, R. A., & Krous, H. F. (2004). Shaken baby syndrome. *British Medical Journal, 328,* 719–720.

Hardman, M. L., Drew, C. J., & Egan, M. W. (2006). *Human exceptionality* (8th ed. Update). Boston: Allyn & Bacon.

Hardy, M. (2006). Older workers. In R. H. Binstock & L. K. George (Eds.), *Handbook of aging and the social sciences* (6th ed.). San Diego: Academic Press.

Hargreaves, D. A., & Tiagemann, M. (2004). Idealized body images and adolescent body image: "Comparing" boys and girls. *Body Image, 1,* 351–361.

Hargrove, K. (2005). What makes a "good" teacher "great"? *Gifted Child Today, 28,* 30–31.

Harkins, S. W., Price, D. D., & Martinelli, M. (1986). Effects of age on pain perception. *Journal of Gerontology, 41,* 58–63.

Harkness, S., & Super, C. M. (1995). Culture and parenting. In M. H. Bornstein (Ed.), *Handbook of parenting* (Vol. 3). Hillsdale, NJ: Erlbaum.

Harkness, S., & Super, C. M. (2002). Culture and parenting. In M. H. Bornstein (Ed.), *Handbook of parenting* (2nd ed., Vol. 2). Mahwah, NJ: Erlbaum.

Harlow, H. F. (1958). The nature of love. *American Psychologist, 13,* 673–685.

Harman, D. (2006). Alzheimer's disease pathogenesis: Role of aging. *Annals of the New York Academy of Science, 1067,* 454–460.

Harman, D. (2006). Free radical theory of aging: An update. *Annals of the New York Academy of Science, 1067,* 10–21.

Harman, S. M. (2006). Testosterone in older men after the Institute of Medicine Report: Where do we go from here? *Climacteric, 8,* 124–135.

Harmsen, P., Lappas, G., Rosengren, A., & Wilhelmsen, L. (2006). Long-term risk factors for stroke: Twenty-eight years of follow-up of 7457 middle-aged men in Goteborg, Sweden. *Stroke, 37,* 1663–1637.

Harold, R. D., Colarossi, L. G., & Mercier, L. R. (2007). *Smooth sailing or stormy waters: Family transitions through adolescence and their implications for practice and policy.* Mahwah, NJ: Erlbaum.

Harrell, J.S., Jessup, A., & Greene, N. (2006). Changing our future: Obesity and the metabolic syndrome in children and adolescents. *Journal of Cardiovascular Nursing, 21,* 322–330.

Harris, C. R. (2002). Sexual and romantic jealousy in heterosexual and homosexual adults. *Psychological Science, 13,* 7–12.

Harris, G. (2002). *Grandparenting: How to meet its responsibilities.* Los Angeles: The Americas Group.

Harris, G., Thomas, A., & Booth, D. A. (1990). Development of salt taste in infancy. *Developmental Psychology, 26,* 534–538.

Harris Interactive (2003, February 5). *Harris Poll # 8: Adults on the Internet.* Rochester, NY: Author.

Harris, J. B. (1998). *The nature assumption: Why children turn out the way they do: Parents matter less than you think and peers matter more.* New York: Free Press.

Harris, K. M., Gorden-Larsen, P., Chantala, K., & Udry, J. R. (2006). Longitudinal trends in race/ethnic disparities in leading health indicators from adolescence to young adulthood. *Archives of Pediatrics and Adolescent Medicine, 160,* 74–81.

Harris, L. (1975). *The myth and reality of aging in America.* Washington, DC: National Council on Aging.

Harris, L. (1997). *A national poll of children and exercise.* Washington, DC: Lou Harris & Associates.

Harris, P. L. (2006). Social cognition. In W. Damon & R. Lerner (Eds.), *Handbook of child psychology* (6th ed.). New York: Wiley.

Harris, S. M. (2004). The effect of health value and ethnicity on the relationship between hardiness and health behaviors. *Journal of Personality, 72,* 379–412.

Harrison-Hale, A. O., McLoyd, V. C., & Smedley, B. (2004). Racial and ethnic status: Risk and protective processes among African-American families. In K. L. Maton, C. J. Schellenbach, B. J. Leadbetter, & A. L. Solarz (Eds.). *Investing in children, families, and communities.* Washington, DC: American Psychological Association.

Hart, B., & Risley, T. R. (1995). *Meaningful difference in the everyday experience of young Americans.* Baltimore: Paul H. Brookes.

Hart, C. H., Yang, C., Charlesworth, R., & Burts, D. C. (2003, April). *Early childhood teachers' curriculum beliefs, classroom practices, and children's outcomes: What are the connections?* Paper presented at the biennial meeting of the Society for Research in Child Development, Tampa, FL.

Hart, D., & Karmel, M. P. (1996). Self-awareness and self-knowledge in humans, great apes, and monkeys. In A. Russon, K. Bard, & S. Parker (Eds.), *Reaching into thought.* New York: Cambridge University Press.

Hart, D., Atkins, R., & Donnelly, T. M. (2006). Community service and moral development. In M. Killen & J. Smetana (Eds.), *Handbook of moral development.* Mahwah, NJ: Erlbaum.

Hart, S. L., Boylan, L. M., Carroll, S. R., Musick, Y. A., Kuratko, C., Border, B. G., & Lampe, R. M. (2006). Brief report: Newborn behavior differs with decosahexaenoic acid levels in breast milk. *Journal of Pediatric Psychology, 31,* 221–226.

Hart, S., & Carrington, H. (2002). Jealousy in 6-month-old infants. *Infancy, 3,* 395–402.

Hart, S., Carrington, H., Tronick, E. Z., & Carroll, S. R. (2004). When infants lose exclusive maternal attention: Is it jealousy? *Infancy, 6,* 57–78.

Harter, S. (1990). Processes underlying adolescent self-concept formation. In R. Montemayor, G. R. Adams, &, R. P. Gulotta (Eds.), *From childhood to adolescence: A transitional period?* Newbury Park, CA: Sage.

Harter, S. (1999). *The construction of the self.* New York: Guilford.

Harter, S. (2002). Unpublished review of Santrock, *Child Development* (10th ed.). New York: McGraw-Hill.

Harter, S. (2006). The self. In W. Damon & R. Lerner (Eds.), *Handbook of child psychology* (6th ed.). New York: Wiley.

Harter, S., & Whitesell, N. (2001, April). *What we have learned from Columbine: The impact of self-esteem on suicidal and violent ideation among adolescents.* Paper presented at the meeting of the Society for Research in Child Development, Minneapolis.

Hartley, A. (2006). Changing role of the speed of processing construct in The cognitive psychology of human aging. In J. E. Birren & K. W. Schaie (Eds.), *Handbook of the psychology of aging* (6th, ed.). San Diego: Academic Press.

Hartmann, D. P., & Pelzel, K. E. (2005). Design, measurement, and analysis in developmental research. In M. H. Bornstein & M. E. Lamb (Eds.), *Developmental psychology* (5th ed.). Mahwah, NJ: Erlbaum.

Hartshorne, H., & May, M. S. (1928–1930). *Moral studies in the nature of character: Studies in the nature of character.* New York: Macmillan.

Hartup, W. W. (1983). The peer system. In P. H. Mussen (Ed.), *Handbook of child psychology* (4th ed., Vol. 4). New York: Wiley.

Hartup, W. W. (1996). The company they keep: Friendships and their development significance. *Child Development, 67,* 1–13.

Hartup, W. W. (1999, April). *Peer relations and the growth of the individual child.* Paper presented at the meeting of the Society for Research in Child Development, Albuquerque.

Hartup, W. W. (2000). Middle childhood: Socialization and social context. In A. Kazdin (Ed.), *Encyclopedia of psychology.* Washington, DC, & New York: American Psychological Association and Oxford University Press.

Hartup, W. W., & Abecassis, M. (2004). Friends and enemies. In P. K. Smith & C. H. Hart (Eds.), *Blackwell handbook of childhood social development.* Malden, MA: Blackwell.

Hartwell, L. (2008). *Genetics* (3rd ed.). New York: McGraw-Hill.

Hartwell, L., Hood, L., Goldberg, M. L., Silver, L. M., Veres, R. C., & Reynolds, A. (2004). *Genetics* (2nd ed.). New York: McGraw-Hill.

Harvald, B., Hauge, G., Kyvik, K. O., Christensen, K., Skythe, A., & Holm, V. V. (2004). The Danish twin registry: Past and present. *Twin Research, 7,* 318–335.

Harvey, J. A. (2004). Cocaine effects on the developing brain: Current status. *Neuroscience and Biobehavior Review, 27,* 751–764.

Harvey, J. H., & Weber, A. L. (2002). *The odyssey of the heart* (2nd ed.). Mahwah, NJ: Erlbaum.

Harwood, R. L., & Feng, X. (2006). Studying acculturation among Latinos in the United States. In M. H. Bornstein & L. R. Cote (Eds.), *Acculturation and parent-child relationships.* Mahwah, NJ: Erlbaum.

Harwood, R., Leyendecker, B., Carlson, V., Asencio, M., & Miller, A. (2002). Parenting among Latino families in the U.S. In M. H. Bornstein (Ed.), *Handbook of parenting* (2nd ed.). Mahwah, NJ: Erlbaum.

Hasher, L. (2003, February 28). Commentary in "The wisdom of the wizened." *Science, 299,* 1300–1302.

Hasher, L., Chung, C., May, C. P., & Foong, N. (2001). Age, time of testing, and proactive interference. *Canadian Journal of Experimental Psychology, 56,* 200–207.

Hass F. (2003). Bereavement care: Seeing the body. *Nursing Standards, 17,* 33–37.

Hauck, F. R., Omojokun, O. O., & Siadaty, M. S. (2005). Do pacifiers reduce the risk of sudden infant death syndrome? A meta-analysis. *Pediatrics, 116,* e717–e723.

Haugaard, J. J., & Hazan, C. (2004). Adoption as a natural experiment. *Developmental Psychopathology, 15,* 909–926.

Haugaard, J. J., & Hazan, C. (2004). Recognizing and treating uncommon behavioral and emotional disorders in children and adolescents who have been severely maltreated: Reactive attachment disorder. *Child Maltreatment, 9,* 154–160.

Hausman, B. L. (2005). Risky business: framing childbirth in hospital settings. *Journal of Medical Ethics, 26,* 23–38.

Havighurst, S. S., Harley, A., & Prior, M. (2004). Building preschool children's emotional competence. *Early Education and Development, 15,* 423–447.

Havrda, D. E., Omundsen, B. A., Bender, W., & Kirkpatrick, M. A. (2005). Impact of Medicare modernization act on low-income persons. *Annals of Internal Medicine, 143,* 600–608.

Hawkes, C. (2006). Olfaction in neurogenerative disorder. *Advances in Otorhinolaryngology, 63,* 133–151.

Hawkins, J. A., & Berndt, T. J. (1985, April). *Adjustment following the transition to junior high school.* Paper presented at the biennial meeting of the Society for Research in Child Development, Toronto.

Hawkins, N. M., & Dunn, F. G. (2006). The management of hypertension in ischemic heart disease. *Current Opinions in Cardiology, 21,* 273–278.

Hayden, K. M., & others (2006). Vascular risk factors for incident Alzheimer disease and vascular dementia: the Cache County Study. *Alzheimer Disease and Associated Disorders, 20,* 93–100.

Hayflick, L. (1977). The cellular basis for biological aging. In C. E. Finch & L. Hayflick (Eds.), *Handbook of the biology of aging.* New York: Van Nostrand.

Haykowsky, M., McGavock, J., Vonder Muhll, I., Koller, M., Mandic, S., Welsh, R., & Taylor, D. (2005). Effect of exercise training on peak aerobic power, left ventricular morphology, and muscle strength in older women. *Journals of Gerontology A: Biological Sciences and Medical Sciences, 60,* 307–311.

Haynes, W. G. (2005). Role of leptin in obesity-related hypertension. *Experimental Physiology, 90,* 683–688.

Hays, R. M., Valentine, J., Haynes, G., Geyer, J. R., Villareale, N., McKinstry, B., Varni, J. W., & Churchill, S. S. (2006). The Seattle pediatric palliative care project: Effects on family satisfaction and health-related quality of life. *Journal of Palliative Medicine, 9,* 716–228.

Hayslip, B. (1996). Hospice. In J. E. Birren (Ed.), *Encyclopedia of gerontology* (Vol. 1). San Diego: Academic Press.

Hayslip, B., Edmondson, R., & Guarnaccia, C. (1999, November). *Religiousness, perceptions of funerals, and bereavement adjustment in adulthood.* Paper presented at the meeting of the Gerontological Society of America, San Francisco.

Hayslip, B., & Hansson, R. (2003). Death awareness and adjustment across the life span. In C. D. Bryant (Ed.), *Handbook of death and dying.* Thousand Oaks, CA: Sage.

Hazan, C., & Shaver, P. R. (1987). Romantic love conceptualized as an attachment process. *Journal of Personality and Social Psychology, 52,* 522–524.

Health Management Resources. (2001). *Child health and fitness.* Boston: Author.

Heaman, M. I. (2005). Relationship between physical abuse during pregnancy and risk factors for preterm birth among women in Manitoba. *Journal of Obstetrical, Gynecologic and Neonatal Nursing, 34,* 721–731.

Heather, N. (2004). Addiction treatment: A strengths perspective. *Alcohol and Alcoholism, 39,* 70–71.

Hebert, R. S., Dang, Q., & Schulz, R. (2006). Preparedness for the death of a loved one and mental health in bereaved caregivers of patients with dementia: Findings from the REACH study. *Journal of Palliative Medicine, 9,* 683–693.

Hedberg, K., Hopkins, D., & Kohn, M. (2003). Five years of legal physician-assisted suicide in Oregon. *New England Journal of Medicine, 348,* 961–964.

Hedden, T., & Gabrieli, J. D. E. (2004). Insights into the aging mind: A view from cognitive neuroscience. *Nature Reviews: Neuroscience, 5,* 87–97.

Hedden, T., Lautenschlager, G., & Park, D. C. (2005). Contributions of processing ability and knowledge to verbal memory tasks across the adult lifespan. *Quarterly Journal of Experimental Psychology, 58A,* 169–190.

Heilman, A. W., Blair, T. R., & Rupley, W. H. (2002). *Principles and practices of teaching Reading* (10th ed.). Upper Saddle River, NJ: Merrill.

Heine, M. K., Ober, B. A., & Shenaut, G. K. (1999). Naturally occurring and experimentally induced tip-of-the-tongue experiences in three adult age groups. *Psychology and Aging, 14,* 445–457.

Heinicke, C. M. (2002). The transition to parenting. In M. H. Bornstein (Ed.), *Handbook of parenting* (2nd ed.). Mahwah, NJ: Erlbaum.

Helgeson, V. S. (2005). *Psychology of gender* (2nd ed.). Upper Saddle River, NJ: Prentice Hall.

Helms, J. E. (2005). Stereotype threat might explain the black-white test-score difference. *American Psychologist, 60,* 269–270.

Helmuth, L. (2003). The wisdom of the wizened. *Science, 299,* 1300–1302.

Helson, R. (1997, August). *Personality change: When is it adult development?* Paper presented at the meeting of the American Psychological Association, Chicago.

Helson, R., & Wink, P. (1992). Personality change in women from the early 40s to early 50s. *Psychology and Aging, 7,* 46–55.

Helson, R., Mitchell, V., & Moane, G. (1984). Personality change in women from college to midlife. *Journal of Personality and Social Psychology, 53,* 176–186.

Henderson, P., Martines, J., & de Zoysa, I. (2004). Mortality associated with reasons for not breastfeeding. *AIDS, 18,* 361–362.

Hendrick, C., & Hendrick, S. S. (2004). Sex and romantic love. In J. H. Harvey, A. Wenzel, & S. Sprecher (Eds.), *The handbook of sexuality in close relationships.* Mahwah, NJ: Erlbaum.

Hendrick, C., & Hendrick, S. S. (Eds.) (2000). *Close relationships.* Thousand Oaks, CA: Sage.

Hendrick, J., & Weissman, P. (2006). *The whole child* (8th ed.). Upper Saddle River, NJ: Prentice Hall.

Hendricks, J., & Hatch, L. R. (2006). Lifestyle and aging. In R. H. Binstock & L. K. George (Eds.), *Handbook of aging and the social sciences* (6th ed.). San Diego: Academic Press.

Hendry, J. (1995). *Understanding Japanese society.* London: Routledge.

Hendry, J. (1999). *Social anthropology.* New York: Macmillan.

Henninger, M. L. (2005). *Teaching young children* (3rd ed.). Boston: Allyn & Bacon.

Henriksen, T. B., Hjollund, N. H., Jensen, T. K., Bonde, J. P., Andersson, A. M., Kolstad, H., Ernst, E., Giwereman, A., Skakkebaek, N. E., & Olsen, J. (2004). Alcohol consumption at the time of conception and spontaneous abortion. *American Journal of Epidemiology, 160,* 661–667.

Henry, J. D., MacLeod, M. S., Philips, L. H., & Crawford, J. R. (2004). A meta-analytic review of prospective memory and aging. *Psychology and Aging, 19,* 27–39.

Henson, K. (2004). *Constructivist teaching strategies for diverse middle school classrooms.* Boston: Allyn & Bacon.

Hepper, P. G., Shahidullah, S., & White, R. (1990). Origins of fetal handedness. *Nature, 347,* 431.

Hepworth, M. (2004). Images of aging. In J. F. Nussbaum & J. Coupland (Eds.), *Handbook of communication and aging.* Mahwah, NJ: Erlbaum.

Herbst, M. A., Mercer, B. M., Beasley, D., Meyer, N., & Carr, T. (2003). Relationship of prenatal care and perinatal morbidity in low-birth-weight infants. *American Journal of Obstetrics and Gynecology, 189,* 930–933.

Herrera, V. M., Koss, M. P., Bailey, J., Yuan, N. P., & Lichter, E. L. (2006). An overview of policies that impact the psychological well-being of girls and women. In J. Worell & C. D. Goodheart (Eds.), *Handbook of girls' and women's psychological health.* New York: Oxford University Press.

Hertz, R.P., Unger, A.N., & Ferrario, C.M. (2006). Diabetes, hypertension, and dyslipidemia in Mexican Americans and non-Hispanic Whites. *American Journal of Preventive Medicine, 30,* 103–110.

Hertzog, C., & Dixon, R. A. (2005). Metacognition in middle life. In S. L. Willis & M. Martin (Eds.), *Middle adulthood.* Thousand Oaks, CA: Sage.

Hertzog, C., & Robinson, A. E. (2005). Metacognition and intelligence. In O. Wilhelm & R. W. Engle (Eds.), *Handbook of understanding and measuring intelligence.* Thousand Oaks, CA: Sage.

Heshmat, S., & Lo, K. C. (2006). Evaluation and treatment of ejaculatory duct obstruction in infertile men. *Canadian Journal of Urology, 13,* (Suppl. 1), 18–21.

Hess, T. (2006). Attitudes toward aging and their effects on behavior. In J. E. Birren & K. W. Schaie (Eds.), *Handbook of the psychology of aging* (6th ed.). San Diego: Academic Press.

Hess, T. M. (2005). Memory and aging in context. *Psychological Bulletin, 131,* 383–406.

Hess, T. M., Auman, C., Colcombe, S. J., & Rahhal, T. A. (2003). The impact of stereotype threat on age differences in memory performance. *Journals of Gerontology: Psychological and Social Sciences, 58B,* P3–P11.

Hess, T. M., Hinson, J. T., & Statham, J. A. (2004). Explicit and implicit stereotype activation effects on memory: Do age and awareness moderate the impact of priming? *Psychology and Aging, 19,* 495–505.

Hess, T. M., Osowski, N. L., & Leclerc, C. M. (2005). Age and experience influences on the complexity of social inferences. *Psychology and Aging, 20,* 447–459.

Hetherington, E. M. (1989). Coping with family transitions: Winners, losers, and survivors. *Child Development, 60,* 1–14.

Hetherington, E. M. (1993). An overview of the Virginia Longitudinal Study of Divorce and Remarriage with a focus on early adolescence. *Journal of Family Psychology, 7,* 39–56.

Hetherington, E. M. (1999). Social capital and the development of youth from non-divorced, divorced, and remarried families. In W. A. Collas & B. Laursen (Eds.), *Relationships as developmental contexts.* Mahwah, NJ: Erlbaum.

Hetherington, E. M. (2000). Divorce. In A. Kazdin (ed.), *Encyclopedia of Psychology.* Washington, DC, & New York: American Psychological Association and Oxford University Press.

Hetherington, E. M. (2005). Divorce and the Adjustment of Children. *Pediatrics in Review, 26,* 163–169.

Hetherington, E. M., Bridges, M., & Insabella, G. M. (1998). What matters? What does not? Five perspectives on the association between marital transitions and children's adjustment. *American Psychologist, 53,* 167–184.

Hetherington, E. M., & Kelly, J. (2002). *For better or for worse: Divorce reconsidered.* New York: Norton.

Hetherington, E. M., Reiss, D., & Plomin, R. (Eds.). (1994). *Separate social worlds of siblings: The impact of nonshared environment on development.* Hillsdale, NJ: Erlbaum.

Hetherington, E. M., & Stanley-Hagan, M. (2002). Parenting in divorced and remarried families. In M. H. Bornstein (Ed.), *Handbook of parenting* (2nd ed., Vol. 3). Mahwah, NJ: Erlbaum.

Heuwinkel, M. K. (1996). New ways of learning 5 new ways of teaching. *Childhood Education, 72,* 27–31.

Hewlett, S. A. (2002). *Creating a life: Professional women and the quest for children.* New York: Talk Miramax Books.

Hicks, M. H. (2006). Physician-assisted suicide: A review of the literature concerning practical and clinical implications for UK doctors. *BMC Family Practice, 22,* 39.

Higgins, M. M., & Barkley, M. C. (2004). Barriers to nutrition education for older adults, and nutrition and aging training opportunities for educators, healthcare providers, volunteers, and caregivers. *Journal of Nutrition for the Elderly, 23,* 99–121.

Hildebrand, V., Phenice, A., & Hines, R. P. (2000). *Knowing and serving diverse families.* Columbus, OH: Merrill.

Hill, C. R., & Stafford, R. P. (1980). Parental care of children: Time diary estimate of quantity, predictability, and variety. *Journal of Human Resources, 15,* 219–239.

Hill, J., Waldfogel, J., Brooks-Gunn, J., & Han, W. (2001, November). *Towards a better estimate of causal links in child policy: The case of maternal employment and child outcomes.* Paper presented at the Association for Public Policy Analysis and Management Fall Research Conference, Washington, DC.

Hill, J. L., Waldfogel, J., Brooks-Gunn, J., & Han, W. J. (2005). Maternal employment and child development: A fresh look at using newer methods. *Developmental Psychology, 41,* 833–850.

Hill, P. C., & Butter, E. M. (1995). The role of religion in promoting physical health. *Journal of Psychology and Christianity, 14,*.

Hill, P. C., & Pargament, K. I. (2003). Advances in conceptualization and measurement of religion and spirituality: Implications for physical and mental health research. *American Psychologist, 58,* 64–74.

Hill, S. E., & Nichols, S. (2006). Emergent literacy: symbols at work. In B. Spodek & O. N. Saracho (Eds.), *Handbook of research on the education of young children* (2nd ed.). Mahwah, NJ: Erlbaum.

Hill, T. D., & Angel, R. J. (2005). Neighborhood disorder, psychological distress, and heavy drinking. *Social Science and Medicine, 61,* 965–975.

Hill, T. D., Angel, J. L., Ellison, C. G., & Angel, R. J. (2005). Religious attendance and mortality: An 8-year follow-up of older Mexican Americans. *Journals of Gerontology B: Psychological Sciences and Social Sciences, 60,* S102–S109.

Hill, T. D., Burdette, A. M., Angel, J. L., & Angel, R. J. (2006). Religious attendance and cognitive functioning among older Mexican Americans. *Journals of Gerontology B: Psychological Sciences and Social Sciences, 61,* P3–P9.

Hillis, S. D., Anda, R. F., Dube, S. R., Felitti, V. J., Marchbanks, P. A., & Marks, J. S. (2004). The association between adverse childhood experiences and adolescent pregnancy, long-term psychological consequences, and fetal death. *Pediatrics, 113,* 320–327.

Himes, C. L., Hogan, D. P., & Eggebeen, D. J. (1996). Living arrangements of minority elders. *Journal of Gerontology. 51A,* S42–S48.

Hinrichsen, G. A. (2006). Why multicultural issues matter for practitioners working with older adults. *Psychology and Aging, 37,* 29–35.

Hintz, S. R., Kendrick, D. E., Vohr, B. R., Poole, W. K., Higgins, R. D., and the National Institute of Child Health and Human Development Neonatal Research Network. (2005). Changes in neurodevelopment outcomes at 18 and 22 months' corrected age among infants of less than 25 weeks' gestational age born in 1993–1999. *Pediatrics, 115,* 1645–1651.

Hiona, A., & Leeuwenburgh, C. (2005, in press). Life-long caloric restriction counteracts apoptotic effects of aging in the brain and bolsters the action of apoptosis inhibitors. *Neurobiology of Aging.*

Hipwell, A. E., Murray, L., Ducournau, P., & Stein, A. (2005). The effects of maternal depression and parental conflict on children's peer play. *Child Care, Health, and Development, 31,* 11–23.

Hirsch, B. J., & Rapkin, B. D. (1987). The transition to junior high school: A longitudinal study of self-esteem, psychological symptomatology, school life, and social support. *Child Development, 58,* 1235–1243.

Hitch, G. J., Towse, J. N., & Hutton, U. (2001). What limits children's working memory span? Theoretical accounts and applications for scholastic development. *Journal of Experimental Psychology: General, 130,* 184–198.

Hock, R. R., & Williams, S. (2006). *Human sexuality.* Upper Saddle River, NJ: Prentice Hall.

Hockenberry, M. (2005). *Wong's essentials of pediatric nursing* (7th ed.). St. Louis: Mosby.

Hodapp, R. M., & Dykens, E. M. (2006). Mental retardation. In W. Damon & R. Lerner (Eds.), *Handbook of child psychology* (6th ed.). New York: Wiley.

Hoern, B. (1995). Sweden. In H.-P. Blossfeld (Ed.), *The new role of women: Family formation in modern societies.* Boulder, CO: Westview Press.

Hofer, M. A. (2006). Psychobiological roots of early attachment. *Current Directions in Psychological Science, 15,* 84–88.

Hofer, S. M., & Sliwinski, M. J. (2006). Design and analysis of longitudinal studies on aging. In J. E. Birren & K. W. Schaie (Eds.), *Handbook of the psychology of aging* (6th ed.). San Diego: Academic Press.

Hoff, E. (2003). Language development in childhood. In I. B. Weiner (Ed.), *Handbook of psychology* (Vol. VI). New York: Wiley.

Hoff, E. (2006). How social contexts support and shape language development. *Developmental Review, 26,* 55–88.

Hoff, E., Laursen, B., & Tardif, T. (2002). Socioeconomic status and parenting. In M. H. Bornstein (Ed.), *Handbook of parenting* (2nd ed.), Mahwah, NJ: Erlbaum.

Hoffereth, S. L., & Casper, L. M. (Eds.). (2006). *Handbook of measurement issues in family research.* Mahwah, NJ: Erlbaum.

Hoffereth, S. L., & Reid, L. (2002). Early childbearing and children's achievement behavior over time. *Perspectives on sexual and reproductive health, 34,* 41–49.

Hoffman, L. W. (1989). Effects of maternal employment in the two parent family. *American Psychologist, 44,* 283–292.

Hoffman, L. W., & Youngblade, L. M. (1999). *Mothers at work: Effects on children's well-being.* New York: Cambridge.

Hoffman, M. L. (1970). Moral development. In P. H. Mussen (Ed.), *Manual of child psychology* (3rd ed., Vol. 2). New York: Wiley.

Hoffman, M. L. (2002). *Empathy and moral development.* New York: Cambridge University Press.

Hoffman, S. (2003). Sleep in the older adult. *Geriatric Nursing, 24,* 210–214.

Hoffmann, E. A. (2004). Selective sexual harassment: Differential treatment of similar groups of women. *Law and Human Behavior, 28,* 29–45.

Hofmanova, I. (2006). Pre-conception care and support for women with diabetes. *British Journal of Nursing, 15,* 90–94.

Holden, K., & Hatcher, C. (2006). Economic status of the aged. In R. H. Binstock & L. K. George (Eds.), *Handbook of aging and the social sciences* (6th ed.). San Diego: Academic Press.

Holding, S. (2002). Current state of screening for Down syndrome. *Annals of Clinical Biochemistry, 39,* 1–11.

Holland, J. L. (1987). Current status of Holland's theory of careers: Another perspective. *Career Development Quarterly, 36,* 24–30.

Hollich, G., Newman, R. S., & Jusczyk, P. W. (2005). Infants' use of synchronized visual information to separate streams of speech. *Child Development, 76,* 598–613.

Holmes, R. M., & Holmes, S. T. (2005). *Suicide in the U.S.* Thousand Oaks, CA: Sage.

Holmes, T. H., & Rahe, R. H. (1967). The social readjustment rating scale. *Journal of Psychosomatic Research, 11,* 213–218.

Holtzen, D. W. (2000). Handedness and professional tennis. *International Journal of Neuroscience, 105,* 101–119.

Holtzman, R. E., Rebok, G. W., Saczynski, J. S., Kouzis, A. C., Wilcox, D. K., & Eaton, W. W. (2004). Social network characteristics and cognition in middle-aged and older adults. *Journal of Gerontology B: Psychological Sciences and Social Sciences, 59,* P278–P284.

Holviala, J. H., Sallinen, J. M., Kraemer, W. J., Alen, M. J., & Hakkinen, K. K. (2006). Effects of strength training on muscle strength characteristics, functional capabilities, and balance in middle-aged and older women. *Journal of Strength and Conditioning Research, 20,* 336–344.

Hopkins, B. (1991). Facilitating early motor development: An intracultural study of West Indian mothers and their infants living in Britain. In J. K. Nugent, B. M. Lester, & T. B. Brazelton (eds.), *The cultural context of infancy, Vol. 2.* Norwood, NJ: Ablex.

Hopkins, B., & Westra, T. (1988). Maternal handling and motor development: An intracultural study. *Genetic Psychology Monographs, 14,* 377–420.

Hopkins, B., & Westra, T. (1990). Motor development, maternal expectations, and the role of handling. *Infant Behavior and Development, 13,* 117–122.

Hopkins, J. R. (2000). Erikson, Erik H. In A. Kazdin (Ed.), *Encyclopedia of psychology.* Washington, DC, & New York: American Psychological Association and Oxford University Press.

Horn, J. L., & Donaldson, G. (1980). Cognitive development II: Adulthood development of human abilities. In O. G. Brim & J. Kagan (Eds.), *Constancy and change in human development.* Cambridge, MA: Harvard University Press.

Horne, R. S., Franco, P., Adamson, T. M., Groswasser, J., & Kahn, A. (2002). Effects of body position on sleep and arousal characteristics in infants. *Early Human Development, 69,* 25–33.

Horne, R. S., Parslow, P. M., & Harding, R. (2004). Respiratory control and arousal in sleeping infants. *Pediatric Respiratory Review 5,* 190–198.

Hornor, G. (2005). Physical abuse: Recognition and reporting. *Journal of Pediatric Health Care, 19,* 4–11.

Horowitz, J. A., & Cousins, A. (2006). Postpartum depression treatment rates for at-risk women. *Nursing Research, 55* (Suppl. 2), S23–S27.

Horowitz, J. A., & Goodman, J. H. (2005). Identifying and treating postpartum depression. *Journal of Obstetrics, Gynecology, and Neonatal Nursing, 34,* 264–273.

Horton, D. M. (2001). The disappearing bell curve. *Journal of Secondary Gifted Education, 12,* 185–188.

Horton, R. (2006). The coming decade for global action on child health. *Lancet, 367,* 3–5.

Hosa, B., Pelham, W. E., Waschbusch, D. A., Kipp, H., & Owens, J. S. (2001). Academic task persistence of normal achieving ADHD and control boys. *Journal of Consulting and Clinical Psychology, 69,* 271–283.

Host, A., & Halken, S. (2005). Primary prevention of food allergy in infants who are at risk. *Current Opinions in Allergy and Clinical Immunology, 5,* 255–259.

Hough, C. J., & Ursano, R. J. (2006). A guide to the genetics of psychiatric disease. *Psychiatry, 69,* 1–20.

House, J. S. (1998). Commentary: Age, work, and well-being. In K. W. Schaie & C. Schooler (Eds.), *The impact of work on older adults.* New York: Springer.

House, J. S., Landis, K. R., & Umberson, D. (1988). Social relationships and health. *Science, 241,* 540–545.

Houston, P. D. (2005, February). NCLB: Dreams and nightmares. *Phi Delta Kappan 466–470.*

Houston-Price, C., Plunkett, K., & Harris, P. (2005). Word-learning wizardry at 1; 6. *Journal of Child Language, 32,* 175–189.

Howard, R. W. (2001). Searching the real world for signs of rising population intelligence. *Personality & Individual Differences, 30,* 1039–1058.

Howe, L. J. (2003). Management of age related macular degeneration: Still room for improvement. *British Journal of Ophthalmology, 87,* 375.

Howe, M. J. A., Davidson, J. W., Moore, D. G., & Sloboda, J. A. (1995). Are there early childhood signs of musical ability? *Psychology of Music, 23,* 162–176.

Howell, E. M., Pettit, K. L, & Kingsley, G. T. (2005). Trends in maternal and infant health in poor urban neighborhoods: Good news from the 1990s, but challenges remain. *Public Health Reports, 120,* 409–417.

Howell, K. K., Lynch, M. E., Platzman, K. A., Smith, G. H., & Coles, C. D. (2005, in press). Prenatal alcohol exposure and ability, academic achievement, and school functioning in adolescence: A longitudinal follow-up. *Journal of Pediatric Psychology.*

Howley, E. T. (2001). Type of activity: Resistance, aerobic and leisure versus occupational physical activity. *Medical Science and Sports Exercise, 33* (Suppl.), S364–S369.

Hoyer, W. J. & Roodin, P. A. (2003). *Adult development and aging* (5th ed.). New York: McGraw-Hill.

Hoyer, W. J., Stawski, R., Wasylyshyn, C., & Verhaeghen, P. (2004). Adult age and digit-symbol performance: A meta-analysis. *Psychology and Aging, 19,* 211–214.

Hoyer, W. J., & Verhaeghen, P. (2006). Memory aging. In J. E. Birren & K. W. Schaie (Eds.), *Handbook of the psychology of aging* (6th ed.). San Diego: Academic Press.

Hoyert, D. L., Mathews, T. J., Menacker, F., Strobino, D. M., & Guyer, B. (2006). Annual summary of vital statistics: 2004. *Pediatrics, 117,* 168–183.

Hsu, H-C. (2004). Antecedents and consequences of separation anxiety in first-time mothers: Infant, mother, and social-contextual characteristics. *Infant Behavior & Development, 27,* 113–133.

Hsu, L. K. (2004). Eating disorders: Practical interventions. *Journal of the American Medical Women's Association, 59,* 113–124.

Huang, C. M., Tung, W. S., Kuo, L. L., & Ying-Ju, C. (2004). Comparison of pain responses of premature infants to the heelstick between containment and swaddling. *Journal of Nursing Research, 12,* 31–40.

Huang, T., Owolabi, T., Summers, A. M., Meier, C., & Wyatt, P. R. (2005). The identification of risk of spontaneous fetal loss through second-trimester maternal serum screening. *American Journal of Obstetrics and Gynecology, 193,* 395–403.

Huebner, A. J., & Howell, L. W. (2003). Examining the relationship between adolescent sexual risk-taking and perceptions of monitoring, communication, and parenting styles. *Journal of Adolescent Health, 33,* 71–78.

Huebner, A. M., & Garrod, A. C. (1993). Moral reasoning among Tibetan monks: A study of Buddhist adolescents and young adults in Nepal. *Journal of Cross-Cultural Psychology, 24,* 167–185.

Huesmann, L. R. (1986). Psychological processes promoting the relation between exposure to media violence and aggressive behavior by the viewer. *Journal of Social Issues, 42,* 125–139.

Huesmann, L. R., Moise-Titus, Podolski, C., & Eron, L. D. (2003). Longitudinal relations between exposure to TV violence and their aggressive and violent behavior in young adulthood: 1977–1992. *Developmental Psychology, 39,* 201–221

Huffman, L. R., & Speer, P. W. (2000). Academic performance among at-risk children: The role of developmentally appropriate practices. *Early Childhood Research Quarterly, 15,* 167–184.

Huffman, S. B., Myers, J. E., Tingle, L. R., & Bond, L. A. (2005). Menopause symptoms and attitudes of African American women: Closing the knowledge gap and expanding opportunities for counseling. *Journal of Counseling & Development, 83,* 48–56.

Hughes, J. R. (2003). Motivating and helping smokers to stop smoking. *Journal of General Internal Medicine, 18,* 1053–1057.

Huizink, A. C., & Mulder, E. J. (2006). Maternal smoking, drinking, or cannibis use during pregnancy and neurobehavioral and cognitive functioning in human offspring. *Neuroscience and Biobehavioral Research, 30,* 24–41.

Hultsch, D. F., Hammer, M., & Small, B. J. (1993). Age differences in cognitive performance in later life: Relationships to self-reported health and activity life style. *Journal of Gerontology, 48,* P1–P11.

Hultsch, D. F., Hertzog, C., Small, B. J., & Dixon, R. A. (1999). Use it or lose it: Engaged lifestyle as a buffer of cognitive decline in aging? *Psychology and Aging, 14,* 245–263.

Hultsch, D. F., & Plemons, J. K. (1979). Life events and life-span development. In P. B. Baltes & O. G. Brim (Eds.). *Life-span development and behavior.* New York: Academic Press.

Hummer, R. A., Ellison, C. G., Rogers, R. G., Moulton, B. C., & Romero, R. R. (2004). Religious involvement and adult mortality in the United States: Review and perspective. *Southern Medical Journal, 97,* 1223–1230.

Humpheys, K. (2000). Alcoholics Anonymous. In A. Kazdin (Ed.), *Encyclopedia of psychology.* Washington, DC, & New York: American Psychological Association and Oxford University Press.

Humphreys, K. (2003). Alcoholics Anonymous and 12-step alcoholism treatment programs. *Recent Developments in Alcoholism, 16,* 149–164.

Hungerford, T. L. (2001). The economic consequences of widowhood on elderly women in the United States and Germany. *The Gerontologist, 41,* 103–110.

Hunsley, M., & Thoman, E. B. (2002). The sleep of co-sleeping infants when they are not co-sleeping: Evidence that co-sleeping is stressful. *Developmental Psychology, 40,* 14–22.

Hunt, C. E., & Hauck, F. R. (2006). Sudden infant death syndrome. *Canadian Medical Association Journal, 174,* 1861–1864.

Hunt, N. D., Hyun, D. H., Allard, J. S., Minor, R. K., Mattson, M. P., Ingram, D. K., & de Cabo, R. (2006). Bioenergetics of aging and calorie restriction. *Aging Research Review, 5,* 125–143.

Hunter, K. I., & Linn, M. W. (1980). Psychological differences between elderly volunteers and non-volunteers. *International Journal of Aging and Human Development, 12,* 205–213.

Hurd Clarke, L. (2006). Older women and sexuality: Experiences in marital relationships across the life course. *Canadian Journal of Aging, 25,* 129–140.

Hurt, H., Brodsky, N. L., Roth, H., Malmund, F., & Giannetta, J. M. (2005). School performance of children with gestational cocaine exposure. *Neurotoxicology and Teratology, 27,* 203–211.

Hurwitz, L. M., & others. (2006). Radiation dose to the fetus from body MDCT during early gestation. *American Journal of Roentgenology, 186,* 871–876.

Huston, A. C. (1983). Sex-typing. In P. H. Mussen (Ed.). *Handbook of child psychology* (4th ed., Vol. 4). New York: Wiley.

Huston, T. L., & Holmes, E. K. (2004). Becoming parents. In A. L. Vangelisti (Ed.), *Handbook of family communication.* Mahwah, NJ: Erlbaum.

Huttenlocher, J., Haight, W., Bruk, A., Seltzer, M., & Lyons, T. (1991). Early vocabulary growth: Relation to language input and gender. *Developmental Psychology, 27,* 236–248.

Huttenlocher, P. R., & Dabholkar, A. S. (1997). Regional differences in synaptogenesis in human cerebral cortex. *Journal of Comparative Neurology, 37* (2), 167–178.

Huyck, M. H. (1995). Marriage and close relationships of the marital kind. In R. Blieszner & V. H. Bedford (Eds.), *Handbook of aging and the family.* Westport, CT: Greenwood Press.

Huyck, M. H. (1999). Gender roles and gender identity in midlife. In S. L. Willis & J. D. Reid (Eds.), *Life in the middle.* San Diego: Academic Press.

Huyck, M. H., & Hoyer, W. J. (1982). Adult development and aging. Belmont, CA: Wadsworth.

Hvas, A. M., Nexos, E., & Nielsen, J. B. (2006). Vitamin B(12) and vitamin B(6) supplementation is needed among adults with phenylketonuria (PKU). *Journal of Inherited Metabolic Disorders, 29,* 47–53.

Hybels, C. F., & Blazer, D. G. (2004). Epidemiology of the late-life mental disorders. *Clinical Geriatric Medicine, 19,* 663–696.

Hyde, J. S. (2004). *Half the human experience* (5th ed.). Boston: Houghton Mifflin.

Hyde, J. S. (2005). The gender similarities hypothesis. *American Psychologist, 60,* 581–592.

Hyde, J. S. (2007). *Half the human experience* (7th ed.). Boston: Houghton Mifflin.

Hyde, J. S., & DeLamater, J. (2005). *Human sexuality* (8th ed., revised), New York: Guilford.

Hyde, J. S., & DeLamater, J. D. (2006). *Understanding human sexuality* (9th, ed.). New York: McGraw-Hill.

Hyde, J. S., & Mezulis, A. H. (2001). Gender difference research: Issues and critique. In J. Worell (Ed.), *Encyclopedia of women and gender.* San Diego: Academic Press.

Hyman, I., Kay, B., Tabori, A., Weber, M., Mahon, M., & Cohen, I. (2006). Bullying: Theory, research, and interventions. In C. M. Evertson & C. S. Weinstein (Eds.), *Handbook of classroom management:*

Research, practice, and contemporary issues. Mahwah, NJ: Erlbaum.

Hymel, S., McDougall, P., & Renshaw, P. (2004). Peer acceptance/rejection. In P. K. Smith & C. H. Hart (Eds.), *Blackwell handbook of childhood social development.* Malden, MA: Blackwell.

Hyson, M. C., Copple, C., & Jones, J. (2006). Early childhood development and education. In W. Damon & R. Lerner (Eds.), *Handbook of child psychology* (6th ed.). New York: Wiley.

Ianucci, L. (2000). *Birth defects* New York: Enslow.

Idler, E. L., Stanislav, V. K., & Hays, J. C. (2001). Patterns of religious practice and belief in the last year of life. *Journal of Gerontology: Social Sciences, 56B,* S326–S334.

Ievers-Landis, C. E., Hoff, A. L., Brez, C., Cancilliere, M. K., McConnell, J., & Kerr, D. (2005). Situational analysis of dietary challenges of the treatment regimen for children and adolescents with phenylketonuria and their primary caregivers. *Journal of Developmental and Behavioral Pediatrics, 26,* 186–193.

Ige, F., & Shelton, D. (2004). Reducing the risk of sudden infant death syndrome (SIDS) in African-American communities. *Journal of Pediatric Nursing, 19,* 290–292.

Iliyasu, Z., Kabir, M. Galadanci, H. S., Abubaker, I. S., & Aliyu, M. H. (2005. Awareness and attitude of antenatal clients toward HIV voluntary counseling and testing in Aminu Kano Teaching Hospital, Kano, Nigeria. *Nigerian Journal of Medicine, 14,* 27–32.

Ilola, L. M. (1990). Culture and health. In R. W. Brislin (Ed.), *Applied cross-cultural psychology.* Newbury Park, CA: Sage.

Ingelsson, E., Lind, L., Arnlov, J., & Sundstrom, J. (2006, in press). Sleep disturbances independently predict heart failure in overweight middle-aged men. *European Journal of Heart Failure.*

Inglehart, R. (1990). *Culture shift in advanced industrial society.* Princeton, NJ: Princeton University Press.

Inoff-Germain, G., Arnold, G. S., Nottelmann, E. D., Susman, E. J., Cutler, G. B., & Chrousos, G. P. (1988). Relations between hormone levels and observational measures of aggressive behavior of young adolescents in family interactions. *Developmental Psychology, 24,* 124–139.

Insel, P. M., & Roth, W. T. (2006). *Core concepts in health* (10th ed.). New York: McGraw-Hill.

Institute of Medicine. (1997, June). *Approaching death: Improving care at the end of life.* Washington, DC: National Academy Press.

International Human Genome Sequencing Consortium. (2004). Finishing the euchromatic sequence of the human genome. *Nature, 431,* 931–945.

International Montessori Council. (2006). Much of their success on Prime-Time Television. Available at www. Montessori.org/enews/ barbara_walters.html

Ireland, J. L., & Culpin, V. (2006). The relationship between sleeping problems and aggression, anger, and impulsivity in a population of juvenile and young offenders. *Journal of Adolescent Health, 38,* 649–655.

Irwin, S. A., Christmon, C. A., Grossman, A. W., Galvez, R., Kim, S. H., DeGrush, B. J., Weiler, I. J., & Greenough, W. T. (2005). Fragile X mental retardation protein levels increase following complex environment exposure in rat brain regions undergoing active synaptogenesis. *Neurobiology, Learning, and Memory, 83,* 180–187.

Isaacs, C. E. (2005). Human milk inactivates pathogens individually, additively, and synergistically. *Journal of Nutrition, 135,* 1286–1288.

Ishii-Kuntz, M. (2004). Asian American families. In M. Coleman & L. Ganong (Eds.), *Handbook of contemporary families.* Thousand Oaks, CA: Sage.

Issa, S. N., & Sharma, L. (2006). Epidemiology of osteoarthritis: An update. *Current Rheumatological Reports, 8,* 7–15.

Ito, A., Honma, Y., Inamori, E., Yada, Y., Momoi, M. Y., & Nakamura, Y. (2006). Developmental outcome of very low birth weight twins conceived by assisted reproduction techniques. *Journal of Perinatology, 26,* 130–136.

Itti, E., Gaw Gonzalo, I. T., Pawlikowska-Haddal, A., Boone, K. B., Mlikotic, A., Itti, L., Mishkin, F. S., & Swerdloff, R. S. (2006). The structural brain correlates of cognitive deficits in adults with Klinefelter's syndrome. *Journal of Clinical Endocrinology and Metabolism, 91,* 1423–1427.

Iverson, P., & Kuhl, P. K. (1996). Influences of phonetic identification and category goodness on American listeners' perception of /r/ and /l/. *Journal of the Acoustical Society of America, 99,* 1130–1140.

Iverson, P., Kuhl, P. K., Akahane-Yamada, R., Diesch, E., Tohkura, Y., Kettermann, A., & Siebert, C. (2003). A perceptual interference account of acquisition difficulties in non-native phonemes. *Cognition 87,* B47–57.

Jabbour, R. A., Hempel, A., Gates, J. R., Zhang, W., & Risse, G. L. (2005). Right hemisphere language mapping in patients with bilateral language. *Epilepsy & Behavior, 6,* 587–592.

Jackson, K. M., & Nazar, A. M. (2006). Breastfeeding, the immune response, and long–term health. *Journal of the American Osteopathic Association, 106,* 203–207.

Jackson, R. (2004). Evolutionary psychology. In W. E. Craighead & C. B. Nemeroff (Eds.). *The concise Corsini encyclopedia of psychology and behavioral science.* New York: Wiley.

Jackson, S. L. (2006). *Research methods and statistics: A critical thinking approach* (2nd ed.). Belmont, CA: Wadsworth.

Jacobs, J. E., & Klaczynski, P. A. (2002). The development of judgment and decision making during childhood and adolescence. *Current Directions in Psychological Science, 11,* 145–149.

Jacobs, J. E., & Potenza, M. (1990, March). *The use of decision-making strategies in late adolescence.* Paper presented at the meeting of the Society for Research in Adolescence, Atlanta.

Jacobs, J. E., & Tanner, J. L. (1999, August). *Stability and change in perceptions of parent-child relationships.* Paper presented at the meeting of the Gerontological Association of America, San Francisco.

Jacobs, N., Rijsdijk, F., Derom, C., Vlietinck, R., Delespaul, P., van Os, J., & Myin-Germeys, I. (2006). Genes making one feel blue in the flow of daily life: a momentary assessment study of gene-stress interaction. *Psychosomatic Medicine, 68,* 201–206.

Jacobs, R. H. (1994). His and her aging. Differences, difficulties, dilemmas, delights. *Journal of Geriatric Psychiatry, 27,* 113–128.

Jacobs-Lawson, J. M., Hershey, D. A., & Neukam, K. A. (2005). Gender differences in factors that influence time spent planning for retirement. *Journal of Women and Aging, 16,* 55–69.

Jacobson, J. L., & Jacobson, S. W. (2002). Association of prenatal exposure to an environmental contaminant with intellectual function in childhood. *Journal of Toxicology—Clinical Toxocology, 40,* 467–475.

Jacobson, J. L., Jacobson, S. W., Fein, G. G., Schwartz, P. M., & Dowler, J. (1984). Prenatal exposure to an environmental toxin: A test of the multiple-effects model. *Developmental Psychology, 20,* 523–532.

Jacobson, L. (2004). Pre-K standards said to slight social, emotional skills. *Education Week, 23* (No. 42), 13–14.

Jacoby, L. L., & Rhodes, M. G. (2006). False remembering in the aged. *Current Directions in Psychological Sciences, 15,* 49–53.

Jaffe, S. R. (2002). Pathways to adversity in young adulthood among early child childbearers. *Journal of Family Psychology, 16,* 38–49.

Jaffee, S., & Hyde, J. S. (2000). Gender differences in moral orientation: A metaanalysis. *Psychological Bulletin, 126,* 703–726.

Jalongo, M. R. (2007). *Early childhood language arts* (4ᵗʰ ed.). Boston: Allyn & Bacon.

James, D. C., & Dobson, B. (2005). Position of the American Dietetic Association: Promoting and supporting breastfeeding. *Journal of the American Dietetic Association, 105,* 810–818.

James, W. (1890/1950). *The principles of psychology.* New York: Dover.

James, W. H. (2005). Biological and psychosocial determinants of male and female human sexual orientation. *Journal of Biosocial Science, 37,* 555–567.

Jamner, M. S., Spruijt-Metz, D., Bassin, S., & Cooper, D. M. (2004). A controlled evaluation of a school-based intervention to promote physical activity among sedentary adolescent females: Project FAB. *Journal of Adolescent Health, 34,* 279–289.

Jang, K. L. (2005). *Genetics of psychopathology.* Mahwah, NJ: Erlbaum.

Jansen, I. (2006). Decision making in childbirth: The influence of traditional structures in a Ghanaian village. *International Nursing Review, 53,* 41–46.

Janssen, I., Craig, W. M., Boyce, W. F., & Pickett, W. (2004). Associations between overweight and obesity with bullying behaviors in school-aged children. *Pediatrics, 113,* 1187–1194.

Janssen, I., Katzmarzyk, P. T., Srinivasan, S. R., Chen, H., Malina, R. M., Bouchard, C., & Berenson, G. S. (2006). Utility of childhood BMI in the prediction of adulthood disease: Comparison of national and international references. *Obesity Research, 13,* 1106–1115.

Jenkins, C. L. (2003). Introduction: Widows and divorcees in later life. *Journal of Women and Aging, 15,* 1–6.

Jenkins, J. M., & Astington, J. W. (1996). Cognitive factors and family structure associated with theory of mind development in young children. *Development Psychology, 32,* 70–78.

Jensen, A. R. (1969). How much can we boost IQ and scholastic achievement? *Harvard Educational Review, 39,* 1–123.

Jenson, J. M., Anthony, E. K., & Howard, M. O. (2005). Policies and programs fro adolescent substance abuse. In J. M. Jenson & M. W. Fraser (Eds.), *Social policy for children and families.* Thousand Oaks, CA: Sage.

Jeste, D. V. (2005). Feeling fine at a hundred and three: Secrets of successful aging. *American Journal of Preventive Medicine, 28,* 323–324.

Ji, B. T., Shu, X. O., Linet, M. S., Zheng, W., Wacholde, S., Gao, Y. T., Ying, D. M., & Jin, F. (1997). Paternal cigarette smoking and the risk of childhood cancer among offspring of nonsmoking mothers. *Journal of the National Cancer Institute, 89,* 238–244.

Jiao, S., Ji, G., & Jing, Q. (1996). Cognitive development of Chinese urban only children and children with siblings. *Child Development, 67,* 387–395.

Jimenez, V., Herniquez, M., Llanos, P., & Riquelme, G. (2004). Isolation and purification of human placental plasma membranes from normal and pre-eclamptic pregnancies: A comparative study. *Placenta, 25,* 422–437.

Joffe, H., Sores, C. N., & Cohen, L. S. (2003). Assessment and treatment of hot flashes and menopausal mood disturbance. *Psychiatric Clinics of North America, 26,* 563–580.

Johnson, A. N. (2005). Kangaroo holding beyond the NICU. *Pediatric Nursing, 31,* 53–56.

Johnson, B. K. (1996). Older adults and sexuality. A multidimensional perspective. *Journal of Gerontological Nursing, 22,* 6–15.

Johnson, C. L., & Troll, L. E. (1992). Family functioning in late late life. *Journals of Gerontology, 47,* S66–S72.

Johnson, D. B., Gerstein, D. E., Evans, A. E., & Woodward-Lopez, G. (2006) Preventing obesity: A life cycle perspective. *Journal of the American Dietetic Association, 106,* 97–102.

Johnson, D. J., Jaeger, E., Randolph, S. M., Cauce, A., Ward, J., & National Institute of Child Health and Human Development Early Child Care Research Network (2003). Studying the effects of early child care experiences on the development of children of color in the United States. *Child Development, 74,* 1227–1244.

Johnson, F., & Wardle, J. (2005). Dietary restraint, body dissatisfaction, and psychological distress: A prospective analysis. *Journal of Abnormal Psychology, 114,* 119–125.

Johnson, G. B. (2006). *The living world* (4ᵗʰ ed.). New York: McGraw-Hill.

Johnson, J. S., & Newport, E. L. (1991). Critical period effects on universal properties of language: The status of subjacency in the acquisition of a second language. *Cognition, 39,* 215–258.

Johnson, K., & others (2006). Recommendations to improve preconception health and health care—United States. *MMWR Recommendations Report, 55,* 1–23.

Johnson, M. H. (2001). Functional brain development during infancy. In A. Fogel & G. Bremner (Eds.), *Blackwell handbook of infant development.* London: Blackwell.

Johnson, M. H. (2005). Developmental neuroscience, psychopathology, and genetics. In M. H. Bornstein & M. E. Lamb (Eds.), *Developmental science.* Mahwah NJ: Erlbaum.

Johnson, M. K., Beebe, T., Mortimer, J. T., & Snyder, M. (1998). Volunteerism in adolescence: A process perspective. *Journal of Research on Adolescence, 8,* 309–332.

Johnson, M. P., & Baker, S. R. (2004). Implications of coping repertoire as predictors of mens' stress, anxiety, and depression following pregnancy, childbirth, and miscarriage: A longitudinal study. *Journal of Psychosomatic Obstetrics and Gynecology, 25,* 87–94.

Johnson, S. C., & others. (2005, in press). Activation of brain regions vulnerable to Alzheimer's disease: The effect of mild cognitive impairment. *Neurobiology and Aging.*

Johnson, T. E. (2005). Genes, phenes, and dreams of immortality: The 2003 Kleemeier Award Lecture. *Journals of Gerontology A: Biological Science and Medical Sciences, 60,* 680–687.

Johnson, W., Bouchard, T. J., Krueger, R. F., McGue, M., & Gottesman, I. I. (2004). Just one g: Consistent results from three test batteries. *Intelligence, 32,* 95–107.

John-Steiner, V., & Mahn, H. (2003). Sociocultural contexts for teaching and learning. In I. B. Weiner (Ed.), *Handbook of psychology* (Vol. VII). New York: Wiley.

Johnston, C. S. (2005). Strategies for weight loss: From vitamin C to the glycemic response. *Journal of the American College of Nutrition, 24,* 158–165.

Johnston, L. D., O'Malley, P. M., & Bachman, J. G. (2004). *Monitoring the Future: 2003.* Ann Arbor, MI: Institute for Social Research, University of Michigan.

Johnston, L. D. O'Malley, P. M., Bachman, J. G., & Schulenberg, J. E. (2005). *Monitoring the Future national results on adolescent drug use: Overview of key findings, 2004* (NIH Publication No. 05-5726). Bethesda, MD: National Institute on Drug Abuse.

Johnston, L. D., O'Malley, P. M., Bachman, J. G., & Schulenberg, J. E. (2006). *Monitoring the Future national results on adolescent drug use: Overview of key findings, 2005.* Bethesda, MD: National Institute on Drug Abuse.

Joiner, T. E. (2000). Depression: Current developments and controversies. In S. H. Qualls & N. Abeles (Eds.), *Psychology and the aging revolution.* Washington, DC: American Psychological Association.

Jolly, C. A. (2005). Diet manipulation and prevention of aging, cancer, and autoimmune disease. *Current Opinions in Clinical Nutrition and Metabolic Care, 8,* 382–387.

Jones, A., Godfrey, K. M., Wood, P., Osmond, C., Goulden, P., & Phillips, D. I. (2006). Fetal growth and the adrenocortical response to psychological stress. *Journal of Clinical Endocrinology and Metabolism, 91,* 1868–1871.

Jones, B. F., Rasmussen, C. M., & Moffit, M. C. (1997). *Real-life problem solving.* Washington, DC: American Psychological Association.

Jones, M. C. (1965). Psychological correlates of somatic development. *Child Development, 36,* 899–911.

Jones, T. G., & Fuller, M. L. (2003). *Teaching Hispanic children.* Boston: Allyn & Bacon.

Jopp, D., & Rott, C. (2006). Adaptation in very old age: Exploring the role of resources and attitudes for centenarians' happiness. *Psychology and Aging, 21,* 266–280.

Jordan, S. (2005). Prescription drugs: Uses and effects. Antidepressants: Mental illness. *Nursing Standards, 19,* 72–74.

Jorgensen, M.E., Borch-Johnsen, K., & Bjerregaard, P. (2006). Lifestyle modifies obesity-associated risk of cardiovascular disease in a genetically homogeneous population. *American Journal of Clinical Nutrition, 84,* 29–36.

Jorm, A. F., Masaki, K. H., Petrovitch, H., Ross, G. W. & White, L. R. (2005). Cognitive deficits 3 to 6 years before dementia onset in a population sample: the Honolulu-Asia aging study. *Journal of the American Geriatric Society, 53,* 452–455.

Judge, B., & Billick, S. B. (2004). Suicidality in adolescence: Review and legal considerations. *Behavioral Science and the Law, 22,* 681.

Juffer, F., & van IJzendoorn, M. H. (2005). Behavior problems and mental health referrals of international adoptees: A meta-analysis. *Journal of the American Medical Association, 293,* 2501–2513.

Julien, D., Chartrand, E., Simard, M., Bouthillier, D., & Begin, J. (2003). Conflict, social support, and relationship quality: An observational study of heterosexual, gay male, and lesbian couples. *Journal of Family Psychology, 17,* 419–428.

Jung, C., (1933). *Modern man in search of a soul.* New York: Harcourt Brace.

Jusczyk, P. W. (2000). *The discovery of spoken language.* Cambridge, MA: MIT Press.

Jusczyk, P. W., & Hohne, E. A. (1997). Infants' memory for spoken words. *Science, 277,* 1984–1986.

Juurlink, D. N., Herrmann, N., Szalai, J. P., Kopp, A., & Redelmeier, D. A. (2004). Medical illness and the risk of suicide in the elderly. *Archives of Internal Medicine, 164,* 1179–1184.

Juvonen, J., Graham, S., & Schuster, M. A. (2003). Bullying among young adolescents. *Pediatrics, 112,* 1231–1237.

Kagan, J. (1987). Perspectives on infancy. In J. D. Osofsky (Ed.), *Handbook on infant development* (2ⁿᵈ ed.), New York: Wiley.

Kagan, J. (1992). Yesterday's promises, tomorrow's promises. *Developmental Psychology, 28,* 990–997.

Kagan, J. (2000). Temperament. In A. Kazdin (Ed.), *Encyclopedia of psychology.* Washington, DC, & New York:

American Psychological Association and Oxford University Press.

Kagan, J. (2002). Behavioral inhibition as a temperamental category. In R. J. Davidson, K. R. Scherer, & H. H. Goldsmith (Eds.), *Handbook of affective sciences.* New York: Oxford University Press.

Kagan, J. (2003). Biology, context, and developmental inquiry. *Annual Review of psychology* (Vol. 53). Palo Alto, CA: Annual Reviews.

Kagan, J., & Fox, N. (2006). Biology, culture, and temperamental biases. In W. Damon & R. Lerner (Eds.). *Handbook of child psychology* (6th ed.). New York: Wiley.

Kagan, J., & Herschkowitz, N. (2005). *A young mind in a growing brain.* Mahwah, NJ: Erlbaum.

Kagan, J., Kearsley, R. B., & Zelazo, P. R. (1978). *Infancy: Its place in human development.* Cambridge, MA: Harvard University Press.

Kagan, J., & Snidman, N. (1991). Infant predictors of inhibited and uninhibited behavioral profiles. *Psychological Science, 2,* 40–44.

Kagan, S. H. (2004). Faculty profile, University of Pennsylvania School of Nursing. Available on the Internet at: www.nursing. upenn.edu/faculty/ profile.asp?pid=33.

Kagan, S. L., & Scott-Little, C. (2004). Early learning standards. *Phi Delta Kappan, 82,* 388–395.

Kagitcibasi, C. (2006). An overview of acculturation and parent-child relationships. In M. H. Bornstein & L. R. Cote (Eds.), *Acculturation and parent-child relationships.* Mahwah, NJ: Erlbaum.

Kahn, A., Groswasser, J., Franco, P., Scaillet, S., Sawaguchi, T., Kelmanson, I., & Dan, B. (2004). Sudden infant deaths: Stress, arousal, and SIDS. *Pathophysiology, 10,* 241–252.

Kahn, J. A., Rosenthal, S. L., Succop, P. A., Ho, P. A., Ho, G. Y., & Burk, R. D. (2002). The interval between menarche and age of first sexual intercourse as a risk factor for subsequent HPV infection in adolescent and young adult women. *Journal of Pediatrics, 141,* 718–723.

Kaiser, B., & Rasminsky, J. S. (2003). *Challenging behavior in young children: Understanding, preventing, and responding effectively.* Boston: Pearson.

Kaizar, E. E., Greenhouse, J. B., Seltman, H., & Kelleher, K. (2006). Do antidepressants cause suicidality in children? A Bayesian meta-analysis. *Clinical Trials, 3,* 73–98.

Kalant, H. (2004). Adverse effects of cannabis on health: An update of the literature since 1996. *Progress in Neuropsychopharmacology and Biological Psychiatry, 28,* 849–863.

Kalichman, S. C., Simbayi, L. C., Jooste, S., Cherry, C., & Cain, D. (2005). Poverty related stressors and HIV AIDS transmission risks in two South African communities. *Journal of Urban Health, 82,* 237–249.

Kalick, S. M., & Hamilton, T. E. (1986). The matching hypothesis reexamined. *Journal of Personality and Social Psychology, 51,* 673–682.

Kalies, H., Heinrich, J., Borte, N., Schaf, B., von Berg, A., von Kries, R., Wichman, H. E., Bolte, G., & the LISA Study Group. (2005). The effect of breastfeeding on weight gain in infants: Results of a birth cohort study. *European Journal of Medical Research, 10,* 36–42.

Kalish, R. A. (1981). *Death, grief, and caring relationships.* Monterey, CA: Brooks/Cole.

Kalish, R. A. (1987). Death. In G. L. Maddox (Ed.), *Encyclopedia of aging.* New York: Springer.

Kalish, R. A., & Reynolds, D. K. (1976). *An overview of death and ethnicity.* Farmingdale, NY: Baywood.

Kalmuss, D. (2004). Nonvolitional sex and sexual health. *Archives of Sexual Behavior, 33,* 197–209.

Kamerman, S. B. (1989). Child care, women, work, and the family: An international overview of child-care service and related policies. In J. S. Lande, S. Scarr, & N. Gunzenhauser (Eds.), *Caring for children: Challenge to America.* Hillsdale, NJ: Erlbaum.

Kamerman, S. B. (2000a). Parental leave policies. *Social Policy Report of the Society for Research in Child Development, XIV* (No. 2), 1–15.

Kamerman, S. B. (2000b). From maternity to paternity child leave policies. *Journal of the Medical Women's Association, 55,* 98–99.

Kamii, C. (1985). *Young children reinvent arithmetic: Implications of Piaget's theory.* New York: Teachers College Press.

Kamii, C. (1989). *Young children continue to reinvent arithmetic.* New York: Teachers College Press.

Kanaka-Gantenbein, C. (2006). Hormone replacement therapy in Turner syndrome. *Pediatric Endocrinology Review, 3* (Suppl 1), 214–218.

Kanner, A. D., Coyne, J. C., Schaefer, C., & Lazarus, R. S. (1981). Comparison of two modes of stress measurement: Daily hassles and uplifts versus major life events. *Journal of Behavioral Medicine, 4,* 1–39.

Kanoy, K., Ulku-Steiner, B., Cox, M., & Burchinal, M. (2003). Marital relationship and individual psychological characteristics that predict physical punishment of children. *Journal of Family Psychology, 17,* 20–28.

Kaplan, R. (2006). Quality of life and aging. In J. E. Birren & K. W. Schaie (Eds.), *Handbook of the psychology of aging* (6th ed.). San Diego: Academic Press.

Kaplow, J. B., Curran, P. J., Dodge, K. A., & the Conduct Problems Prevention Research Group. (2002). Child, parent, and peer predictors of early-onset substance use: A multisite longitudinal study. *Journal of Abnormal Child Psychology, 30,* 199–216.

Kappor, A., Dunn, E., Kostaki, A., Andrews, M. H., & Matthews, S. G. (2006). Fetal programming of hypothalamo-pituitary-adrenal function: Prenatal stress and glutocorticoids. *Journal of Physiology, 572,* 31–44.

Karlin, B. E., & Norris, M. P. (2005, in press). Public mental health care utilization by older adults. *Administration and Policy in Mental Health.*

Karlsson, M. (2004). Has exercise an antifracture efficacy in women? *Scandinavian Journal of Medical Science and Sports, 14,* 2–15.

Karney, B. R., & Bradbury, T. N. (2005). Contextual influences on marriage. *Current Directions in Psychological Science, 14,* 171–175.

Karney, B. R., Garvan, C. W., & Thomas, M. S. (2003). *Family formation in Florida: 2003 baseline survey of attitudes, beliefs, and demographics relating to marriage and family formation.* Gainesville, FL: University of Florida.

Karnick, P. M. (2005). Feeling lonely: Theoretical perspectives. *Nursing Science Quarterly, 18,* 7–12.

Karniol, R., Grosz, E., & Schorr, I. (2003). Caring, gender-role orientation, and volunteering. *Sex Roles, 49,* 11–19.

Karoly, L. A., Kilburn, M. R., & Cannon, J. S. (2006). *Early childhood interventions: Proven results, future promise.* Santa Monica, CA: Rand.

Karp, H. (2002). *The happiest baby on the block.* New York: Bantam.

Karpansalo, M, Kauhanen, J., Lakka, T. A., Manninen, P., Kaplan, G. A., & Salonen, J. T. (2005). Depression and early retirement: Prospective population based study in middle aged men. *Journal of Epidemiology and Community Health, 59,* 70–74.

Kasper, J. D. (1988). *Aging alone: Profiles and projections.* Report of the Commonwealth Fund Commission: Elderly People Living Alone. Baltimore: Commonwealth Fund Commission.

Kastenbaum, R. J. (2000). *The psychology of death* (3rd ed.). New York: Springer.

Kastenbaum, R. J. (2004). *Death, society, and human experience* (8th ed.). Upper Saddle River, NJ: Prentice Hall.

Katakura, Y. (2006). Molecular basis for the cellular senescence program and its application to anticancer therapy. *Bioscience, Biotechnology, and Biochemistry, 70,* 1076–1081.

Kataoka-Yahiro, M., Ceria, C., & Caulfield, R. (2005). Grandparent caregiving role in ethnically diverse families. *Journal of Pediatric Nursing, 19,* 315–328.

Kato, T. (2005). The relationship between coping with stress due to romantic break-ups and mental health. *Japanese Journal of Social Psychology, 20,* 171–180.

Katz, L. (1999). Curriculum disputes in early childhood education. *ERIC Clearinghouse on Elementary and Early Childhood Education,* Document EDO-PS-99-13.

Katz, L. F. (1999, April). *Toward a family-based hypervigilance model of childhood aggression: The role of the mother's and the father's meta-emotion philosophy.* Paper presented at the meeting of the Society for Research in Child Development; Albuquerque.

Katz, L., & Chard, S. (1989). *Engaging the minds of young children: The project approach,* Norwood, NJ: Ablex.

Katz, P. A. (1987, August). *Children and social issues.* Paper presented at the meeting of the American Psychological Association, New York.

Katzmarzyk, P. T., Srinivasan, S. R. Chen, W., Malina, R. M., Bouchard, C., & Berensen, G. S. (2004). Body mass index, waist circumference, and clustering of cardiovascular disease risk factors in a biracial sample of children and adolescents. *Pediatrics, 114,* c198–e205.

Kauffman, J. M., & Hallahan, D. P. (2005). *Special education.* Boston: Allyn & Bacon.

Kauffman, J. M., McGee, K., & Brigham, M. (2004). Enabling or disabling? Observations on changes in special education. *Phi Delta Kappan, 85,* 613–620.

Kaufman, J., & Sternberg, R. J. (Eds.). (2006) *International handbook of creativity.* New York: Cambridge University Press.

Kaufman, S. R. (2005) *... And a time to die.* New York: Scribner.

Kavsek, M. (2004). Predicting IQ from infant visual habituation and dishabituation: A meta-analysis. *Journal of Applied Developmental Psychology, 25,* 369–393.

Kazdin, A. E., & Benjet, C. (2003). Spanking children: Evidence and issues. *Current Directions in Psychological Science, 12,* 99–103.

Keating, D. P. (1990). Adolescent thinking, In S. S. Feldman & G. R. Elliott (Eds.), *At the threshold: The developing adolescent.* Cambridge, MA: Harvard University Press.

Keating, D. P. (2004). Cognitive and brain development. In R. Lerner & L. Steinberg (Ed.), *Handbook of Adolescent Psychology,* New York: Wiley.

Keel, P. K., Mitchell, J. E., Miller, K. B., Davis, T. L., & Crowe, S. J. (1999). Long-term outcome of bulimia nervosa. *Archives of General Psychiatry, 56,* 63–69.

Keen, R. (2005). Unpublished review of Santrock *Topical life-span development,* 3rd ed. New York: McGraw-Hill.

Keller, A., Ford, L., & Meacham, J. (1978). Dimensions of self-concept in preschool children. *Developmental Psychology, 14,* 483–489

Keller, H. (2002). Culture and development: Developmental pathways to individualism and interrelatedness. In W. J. Lonner, D. L. Dinnel, S. A. Hayes, & D. N. Sattler (Eds.), *Online Readings in Psychology and Culture* (Unit 11, Chapter 1), retrieved April 29, 2006. from *http://www.wwu.edu/~culture,* Center for Cross-Cultural Research, Western Washington University, Bellingham, Washington.

Kelley, G. A., & Kelly, K. S. (2005, in press). Aerobic exercise and HDL(2)-C: A metaanalysis of randomized controlled trials. *Atherosclerosis.*

Kellman, P. J., & Arterberry, M. E. (2006). Infant visual perception. In W. Damon & R. Lerner (Eds.), *Handbook of child psychology* (6th ed). New York: Wiley.

Kellman, P. J., & Banks, M. S. (1998). Infant visual perception. In W. Damon (Ed.), *Handbook of child psychology* (5th ed., Vol. 2), New York: Wiley.

Kelly, B. D., & McLoughlin, D. M. (2002). Euthanasia, assisted suicide, and psychiatry: A Pandora's box. *British Journal of Psychiatry, 181,* 278–279.

Kelly, G. F. (2006). *Sexuality today* (8th, ed.). New York: McGraw-Hill.

Kelly, J. P., Borchert, J., & Teller, D. Y. (1997). The development of chromatic and achromatic sensitivity in infancy as tested with the sweep VEP. *Vision Research, 37,* 2057–2072.

Kelly, J. R. (1996). Leisure. In J. E. Birren (Ed.), *Encyclopedia of gerontology* (Vol. 2). San Diego: Academic Press.

Kemper, S., Greiner, L. H., Marquis, J. G., Prenovost, K., Mitzner, T. L. (2001). Language decline across the life span: Findings from the Nun Study, *Psychology and Aging, 16* (2), 227–239

Kempermann, G., Kuhn, G. G., & Gage, F. H. (1997). More hippocampal neurons in adult mice living in an enriched environment. *Nature, 386,* 493–495.

Kempermann, G., van Praag, H., & Gage, F. H. (2000). Activity-dependent regulation of neuronal plasticity and self repair. *Progress in Brain Research, 127,* 35–48.

Kempermann, G., Wiskott, L., & Gage, F. H. (2004). Functional significance of neurogenesis. *Current Opinions in Neurobiology, 14,* 186–191.

Kendall, G., & Peebles, D. (2005). Acute fetal hypoxia: The modulating effect of infection. *Early Human Development, 81,* 27–34.

Kennedy, E. T. (2006). Evidence for nutritional benefits in prolonging wellness. *American Journal of Clinical Nutrition, 83,* 410S–414S.

Kennedy, H. P., & Shanon, M. T. (2004). Keeping birth normal: Research findings on midwifery care during childbirth. *Journal of Obstetrical, Gynecologic, and Neonatal Nursing, 33,* 554–560.

Kennedy, Q., Mather, M., & Carstensen, L. L. (2004) The role of motivation in the age-related positive bias in autobiographical memory. *Psychological Science, 15*(3), 208–214.

Kennell, J. H. (2006). Randomized controlled trial of skin-to-skin contact from birth versus conventional incubator for physiological stabilization in 1200 g to 2199 g newborns. *Acta Paediatica (Sweden), 95,* 15–16.

Kennell, J. H., & McGrath, S. K. (1999). Commentary: Practical and humanistic lessons from the third world for perinatal caregivers everywhere. *Birth, 26,* 9–10.

Kephart, W. M. (1967). Some correlates of romantic love. *Journal of Marriage and the Family, 29,* 470–474.

Kerr, M. (2001). Culture as a context for temperament. In T. D. Wachs & G. A. Kohnstamm (Eds.), *Temperament in context.* Mahwah, NJ: Erlbaum.

Kerr, P. (2005). Midwifery reborn: Opportunities for a new generation. *RCM Midwives, 8,* 260–263.

Kessels, R. P., Bockhorst, S. T., & Postma, A. (2005). The contribution of implicit and explicit memory to the effects of errorless learning: A comparison between younger and older adults. *Journal of the International Neuropsychological Society, 11,* 144–151.

Kessen, W., Haith, M. M., & Salapatek, P. (1970). Human infancy. In P. H. Mussen (Ed.), *Manual of child psychology* (3rd ed., Vol. 1). New York: Wiley.

Ketcham, C. J., & Stelmack, G. E. (2001). Age-related declines in motor control. In J. E. Birren & K. W. Schaie (Eds.), *Handbook of the psychology of aging* (5th ed.). San Diego: Academic Press.

Ketterhagen, D., Vande Vusse, L, & Berner, M. A. (2002). *MCN American Journal of Maternal and Child Nursing, 27,* 335–340.

Keyes, C., & Ryff, C. (1999). Psychological well-being in midlife. In S. L. Willis & J. D. Reid (Eds.), *Life in the middle.* San Diego: Academic Press.

Keyman, A. (2003). Promoting sexual health to young people. *Journal of Research on Social Health, 123,* 6–7.

Kiarie, J. N., Richardson, B. A., Mbori-Ngacha, B., Nduati, R. W., & John-Stewart, T. M. (2004). Infant feeding practices of women in a perinatal HIV-1 prevention study in Nairobi, Kenya. *Journal of Acquired Immune Deficiency Syndrome, 35,* 75–81.

Kiecolt-Glaser, J. K., & Glaser, R. (1988). Behavioral influences on immune function. In T. Field, P. McCabe, & N. Schneiderman (Eds.), *Stress and coping across development.* Hillsdale, NJ: Erlbaum.

Kiecolt-Glaser, J. K., McGuire, L., Robles, T. F., & Glaser, R. (2002). Psychoneuroimmunology and psychosomatic medicine: Back to the future. *Psychosomatic Medicine, 64,* 15–28.

Kiecolt-Glaser, J. K., Preacher, K. J., MacCallum, R. C., Atkinson, C., Malarkey, W. B., & Glaser, R. (2003). Chronic stress and age-related increases in the proinflammatory cytokine IL-6. *Proceedings of the National Academy of Science USA, 100,* 9090–9095.

Kiecolt-Glaser, J. K., & Yehuda., R. (2005). Toward optimal health. *Journal of Women's Health, 14,* 294–298.

Kilbride, H. W., Thorstad, K., & Daily, D. K. (2004). Preschool outcome of less than 801-gram preterm infants compared with full-term siblings. *Pediatrics, 113,* 742–747.

Kilpatrick, D. G. (2004). What is violence against women? Defining and measuring the problem. *Journal of Interpersonal Violence, 19,* 1209–1234.

Kim, H. (2006). Older women's health and its impact on wealth. *Journal of Women's Aging, 18,* 75–81.

Kim, J., & Cicchetti, D. (2004). A longitudinal study of child maltreatment, mother-child relationship quality and maladjustment: The role of self-esteem and social competence. *Journal of Abnormal Child Psychology, 32,* 341–354.

Kim, J., & Cicchetti, D. (2006). Longitudinal trajectories of self-system processes and the depressive symptoms among maltreated and nonmaltreated children. *Child Development, 77,* 624–639.

Kim, J., & Sapienza, C. M. (2005). Implications of expiratory muscle strength training for rehabilitation of the elderly. *Journal of Rehabilitation Research and Development, 42,* 211–224.

Kim, J. E., & Moen, P. (2002). Retirement transitions, gender, and psychological well-being: A life-course, ecological model. *Journals of Gerontology B: Psychological Sciences and Social Sciences, 57,* P212–P222.

Kim, S., Hasher, L. (2005). The attraction effect in decision making: Superior performance by older adults. *Quarterly Journal of Experimental Psychology, 58A,* 120–133.

Kim, S. M., Han, J. H., & Park, H. S. (2006). Prevalence of low HDL-cholesterol levels and associated factors among Koreans. *Circulation Journal, 70,* 820–826.

Kimm, S. Y., Glynn, N. W., Kriska, A. M., Barton, B. A., Kronsberg, S. S., Daniels, S. R., Crawford, P. B., Sabry, Z. I., & Liu, K. (2002). Decline in physical activity in black girls and white girls during adolescence. *New England Journal of Medicine, 347,* 709–715.

Kimm, S. Y., & Obarzanek, E. (2002). Childhood obesity: A new pandemic of the new millennium. *Pediatrics, 110,* 1003–1007.

Kimura, D. (2000). *Sex and cognition.* Cambridge, MA: MIT Press.

King, B. M. (2005). *Human sexuality today* (5th ed.), Upper Saddle River, NJ: Prentice Hall.

King, D. A., & Quill, T. (2006). Working with families in palliative care: One size does not fit all. *Journal of Palliative Medicine, 9,* 704–715.

King, J. C. (2006, in press). Maternal obesity, metabolism, and pregnancy outcomes. *Annual Review of Nutrition.*

King, S., & Laplante, D. P. (2005). The effects of prenatal maternal stress on children's cognitive development: Project Ice Storm. *Stress, 8,* 35–45.

King, V., & Scott, M. E. (2005). A comparison of cohabiting relationships among older and younger adults. *Journal of Marriage and the Family, 67,* 271–285.

Kinney, J. (2006). *Loosening the grip: A handbook of alcohol information* (8th ed.). New York: McGraw-Hill.

Kiraly, M. A., & Kiraly, S. J. (2005). The effect of exercise on hippocampal integrity: Review of recent research. *International Journal of Psychiatry Medicine, 35,* 75–89.

Kirby, S. (2005). The positive effect of exercise as therapy for clinical depression. *Nursing Times, 101,* 28–29.

Kirkham, C., Harris, S., & Grzybowski, S. (2005). Evidence-based prenatal care II: Third-trimester care and prevention of infectious diseases. *American Family Physician, 71,* 1555–1560.

Kirungi, W. L., Musinguzi, J., Madraa, E., Mulumba, N., Callejja, T., Ghys, P., & Bessinger, R. (2006). Trends in antenatal HIV prevalence in urban Uganda associated with uptake of preventive sexual behavior. *Sexually Transmitted Infections, 82* (Suppl. 1), i36–i41.

Kisilevsky, B. S., Hains, S. M., Lee, K., Xie, X., Huang, H., Ye, H. H., Zhang, K., & Wang, Z. (2003). Effects of experience on fetal voice recognition. *Psychological Science, 14,* 220–224.

Kisilevsky, B. S., Hains, S. M., Jacquet, A. Y., Granier-Deferre, C., & Lecanuet, J. P. (2004). Maturation of fetal responses to music. *Developmental Science, 7,* 550–559.

Kistner, J. (2006). Children's peer acceptance, perceived acceptance, and risk of depression. In T. E. Joiner, J. S. Brown, & J. Kistner (Eds.), *The interpersonal, cognitive, and social nature of depression.* Mahwah, NJ: Erlbaum.

Kitchener, K. S., King, P. M., & DeLuca, S. (2006). The development of reflective judgment in adulthood. In C. Hoare (Ed.), *Handbook of adult development and learning.* New York: Oxford University Press.

Kivnick, H. Q., Sinclair, H. M. (1996). Grandparenthood. In J. E. Birren (Ed.), *Encyclopedia of gerontology* (Vol. 1). San Diego: Academic Press.

Klaczynski, P. A. (1997). Bias in adolescents' everyday reasoning and its relationship with intellectual ability, personal theories, and self-serving motivation. *Developmental Psychology, 33,* 273–283.

Klaczynski, P. A. (2005, in press). Metacognition and cognitive variability: A two-process model of decision making and its development. In J. Jacobs & P. Klaczynski (Eds.), *The development of decision making: cognitive, sociocultural, and legal perspectives.* Mahwah, NJ: Erlbaum.

Klaczynski, P. A., & Narasimham, G. (1998). Development of scientific reasoning biases: Cognitive versus ego-protective explanations. *Developmental Psychology, 34,* 175–187.

Klaus, M., & Kennell, H. H. (1976). *Maternal-infant bonding.* St. Louis: Moshv.

Klaus, M. H., Kennell, J. H., & Klaus, P. H. (1993). *Mothering the mother.* Reading, MA: Addison-Wesley.

Klein, D., Council, K., & McGuire, S. (2005). Education to promote positive attitudes about aging. *Educational Gerontology, 31,* 591–601.

Klesges, L. M., Johnson, K. C., Ward, K. D., & Barnard, M. (2001). Smoking cessation in pregnant women. *Obstetrics and Gynecological Clinics of North America, 28,* 269–282.

Kline, D. W., & Scialfa, C. T. (1996). Visual and auditory aging. In J. E. Birren & K. W. Schaie (Eds.), *Handbook of the psychology of aging* (4th ed.). San Diego: Academic Press.

Kline, G. H., Stanley, S. M., Markman, H. J., Olmos-Gallo, P. A., S. Peters, M., Whitton, S. W., & Prado, L. M. (2004). Timing is everything: Pre-engagement cohabitation and increased risk for poor marital outcomes. *Journal of Family Psychology, 18,* 311–318.

Kling, K. C., Hyde, J. S., Showers, C. J., & Buswell, B. N. (1999). Gender differences in self-esteem: A meta-analysis. *Psychological Bulletin, 125,* 470–500.

Klipstein, S., Regan, M., Ryley, D. A., Goldman, M. B., Alper, M. M., & Reindollar, R. H. (2005). One last chance for pregnancy: A review of 2,705 in vitro fertilization cycles initiated in women age 40 years and above. *Fertility and Sterility, 84,* 435–445.

Klonoff-Cohen, H. S., & Natarajan, L. (2004). The effect of advancing paternal age on pregnancy and live birth rates in couples undergoing in vitro fertilization or gamete intrafallopian transfer. *American Journal of Obstetrics and Gynecology, 191,* 507–514.

Klug, W. S., & Cummings, M. R. (2005). *Essentials of genetics* (5th ed.). Upper Saddle River, NJ: Prentice Hall.

Klug, W. S., Cummings, M. R., & Spencer, C. (2006). *Concepts of genetics* (8th ed.). Upper Saddle Rive, NJ: Prentice Hall.

Knackstedt, M. K., Hamelmann, E., & Arck, P. C. (2005). Mothers in stress: Consequences for the offspring. *American Journal of Reproductive Immunology, 54,* 63–69.

Knafo, A., Iervolino, A. C., & Plomin, R. (2005). Masculine girls and feminine boys: Genetic and environmental contributions to atypical gender development in early childhood. *Journal of Personality and Social Psychology, 88,* 400–412.

Knecht, S., Drager, B., Deppe, M., Bobe, L., Lohmann, H., Floel, A., Ringelstein, E. B., & Henningsen, H. (2000). Handedness and hemispheric language dominance in healthy humans. *Brains, 135,* 2512–2518.

Knight, B. G., Kaski, B., Shurgot, G. R., & Dave, J. (2006). Improving the mental health of older adults. In J. E. Birren & K. W. Schaie (Eds.), *Handbook of the psychology of aging* (6th ed.). San Diego: Academic Press.

Knight, B. G., Nordhus, I. H., & Satre, D. D. (2003). Psychotherapy with older adults. In I. B. Weiner (Ed.), *Handbook of psychology,* Vol. VIII. New York: Wiley.

Knight, B. G., Teri, L., Wohlford, P., & Santos, J. (Eds.). (1996). *Mental health services for older adults.* Washington, DC: American Psychological Association.

Knudtson, M. D., Klein, B. E., & Klein, R. (2006). Age-related eye disease, visual impairment, and survival: The Beaver Dam Eye Study. *Archives of Ophthalmology, 124,* 243–249.

Kobak, R. (1999). The emotional dynamics of disruptions in attachment relationships: Implications for theory, research, and clinical intervention. In J. Cassidy & P. Shaver (Eds.), *Handbook of attachment.* New York: Guilford.

Kobasa, S. C., Maddi, S. R., & Kahn, S. (1982). Hardiness and health: A prospective study. *Journal of Personality and Social Psychology, 42,* 168–177.

Kobasa, S. C., Maddi, S. R., Puccetti, M. C., & Zola, M. (1986). Relative effectiveness of hardiness, exercise, and social support as resources against illness. *Journal of Psychosomatic Research, 29,* 525–533.

Kobayashi, K., Tajima, M., Toishi, S., Fujimori, K., Suzuki, Y., & Udagama, H. (2005). Fetal growth restriction associated with measles virus infection during pregnancy. *Journal of Perinatal Medicine, 33,* 67–68.

Koenig, H. G. (Ed.). (1998). *Handbook of religion and mental health.* San Diego: Academic Press.

Koenig, H. G. (2001). Religion and medicine II: Religion, mental health, and related behaviors. *International Journal of Psychiatry, 31,* 97–109.

Koenig, H. G. (2004). Religion, spirituality, and medicine: Research findings and implications for clinical practice. *Southern Medical Journal, 97,* 1194–2000.

Koenig, H. G., & Blazer, D. G. (1996). Depression. In J. E. Birren (Ed.), *Encyclopedia of gerontology* (Vol. 1). San Diego: Academic Press.

Koenig, H. G., Cohen, H. J., Blazer, D. G., Pieper, C., Meador, K. G., Shelp, F., Goldi, V., & DiPasquale, R. (1992). Religious coping and depression in elderly hospitalized medically ill men. *American Journal of Psychiatry, 149,* 1693–1700.

Koenig, H. G., Larson, D. B. (1998). Religion and mental health. In H. S. Friedman (Ed.), *Encyclopedia of mental health* (Vol. 3). San Diego: Academic Press.

Koenig, H. G., Smiley, M., & Gonzales, J. A. T. (1988). *Religion, health, and aging.* New York: Greenwood Press.

Kohlberg, L. (1958). *The development on modes of moral thinking and choice in the years 10 to 16.* Unpublished doctoral dissertation, University of Chicago.

Kohlberg, L. (1966). A cognitive-developmental analysis of children's sex-role concepts and attitudes. In E. E. Maccoby (Ed.), *The development of sex differences.* Palo Alto, CA: Stanford University Press.

Kohlberg, L. (1969). Stage and sequence: The cognitive-developmental approach to socialization. In D. A. Goslin (Ed.), *Handbook of socialization theory and research.* Chicago: Rand McNally.

Kohlberg, L. (1986). A current statement of some theoretical issues. In S. Modgil & C. Modgil (Eds.), *Lawrence Kohlberg.* Philadelphia: Falmer.

Komitova, M., Mattsson, B., Johansson, B. B., & Eriksson, P. S. (2005). Enriched environment increases neural stem/progenitor cell proliferation and neurogenesis in the subventrical zone of stroke-lesioned adult rats. *Stroke, 36,* 1278–1282.

Kopp, C. B., & Neufeld, S. J. (2002). Emotional development in infancy. In R. Davidson & S. K. Scherer (Eds.), *Handbook of affective sciences.* New York: Oxford University Press.

Koppelman, K., & Goodhart, L. (2005). *Understanding human differences.* Boston: Allyn & Bacon.

Korantzopoulos, P., Kolettis, T. M., Galaris, D., & Goudevenos, J. A. (2006, in press). The role of oxidative stress in the pathogenesis and perpetuation of arterial fibrillation. *International Journal of Cardiology.*

Kornhaber, M., Fierros, E., & Veenema, S. (2004). *Multiple intelligences.* Boston: Allyn & Bacon.

Kotaska, A. J., Klein, M. C., & Liston, R. M. (2006). Epidural analgesia associated with low-dose oxytocin augmentation increases cesarean births: A critical look at the external validity of randomized trials. *American Journal of Obstetrics and Gynecology, 194,* 809–814.

Kotler, J. A., Wright, J. C., & Huston, A. C. (2001). Television use in families with children. In J. Bryant & J. A. Bryant (Eds.), *Television and the American Family.* Mahwah, NJ: Erlbaum.

Kotovsky, L., & Baillargeon, R. (1994). Calibration-based reasoning about collision events in 11-month-old infants. *Cognition, 51,* 107–129.

Kotre, J. (1984). *Outliving the self: Generativity and the interpretation of lives.* Baltimore: Johns Hopkins University Press.

Kottak, C. P. (2004). *Cultural anthropology* (10th ed.). New York: McGraw-Hill.

Kozol, J. (2005). *The shame of the nation.* New York: Crown.

Kozulin, A., Gindis, B., Ageyev, V. S., & Miller, S. M. (Eds.) (2003) *Vygotsky's educational theory in cultural context.* New York: Cambridge University Press.

Kraebel, K. S., Fable, J., & Gerhardstein, P. (2004). New methodology in infant operant kicking procedures. *Infant Behavior and Development, 127,* 1–18.

Kraehenbuhl, H., Preisig, M., Bula, C. J., & Waeber, G. (2004). Geriatric depression and vascular disease: What are the links? *Journal of Affective Disorders, 81,* 1–16.

Kramer, A. F., Colcombe, S. J., McAuley, E., Scalf, P. E., & Erickson, K. I. (2005). Fitness, aging, and neurocognitive function. *Neurobiology of Aging.*

Kramer, A. F., Erickson, K. I., & Colcombe, S. J. (2006, in press). Exercise, cognition, and the aging brain. *Journal of Applied Psychology.*

Kramer, A. F., Fabiani, M., & Colcombe, S. J. (2006). Contributions of cognitive neuroscience to the understanding of behavior and aging. In J. E. Birren & K. W. Schaie (Eds.), *Handbook of the psychology of aging* (6th ed.). San Diego: Academic Press.

Kramer, A. F., Hahn, S., Cohen, N. J., Banich, M. T., McAuley, E., Harrison, C., Chason, J., Vakil, E., Bardell, L., Boileau, R., & Colcombe, A. (1999, July). Aging, fitness, and neurocognitive function. *Nature, 400,* 418–419.

Kramer, A. F., Hahn, S., McAuley, E., Cohen, N. J., Banich, M. T., Harrison, C., Chason, J., Boileau, R. A., Bardell, L., Colcombe, A., & Vakil, E. (2002). Exercise, aging and cognition: Healthy body, healthy mind? In A. D. Fisk & W. Rogers (Eds.), *Human factors interventions for the health care of older adults.* Mahwah, NJ: Erlbaum.

Kramer, A. F., & Willis, S. L. (2002). Enhancing the cognitive vitality of older adults. *Current Directions in Psychological Research, 11,* 173–177.

Kramer, D. A., Kahlbaugh, P. E., & Goldston, R. B. (1992). A measure of paradigm beliefs about the social world. *Journal of Gerontology, 47,* 180–189.

Kramer, M. (2003). Commentary: Breastfeeding and child health, growth, and survival. *International Journal of Epidemiology, 32,* 96–98.

Kramer, P. (1993). *Listening to Prozac.* New York: Penguin Books.

Krampe, R. T., & Baltes, P. B. (2002). Intelligence as adaptive resource development and resource allocation: A new look through the lens of SOC and expertise. In R. J. Sternberg & E. L. Grigorenko (Eds.), *Perspectives on the psychology of abilities, competencies, and expertise.* New York: Cambridge University Press.

Krampe, R. T., & Baltes, P. B. (2003). Intelligence as adaptive resource development and resource allocation: A new look through the lens of SOC and expertise. In R. J. Stemberg & E. L. Grigorenko (Eds.), *Perspectives on the psychology of abilities, competencies, and expertise.* New York: Cambridge University Press.

Krause, N. (1996). Neighborhood deterioration and self-rated health in later life. *Psychology and Aging, 11,* 342–352.

Krause, N. (2003). Religious meaning and subjective well-being in late life. *Journal of Gerontology B: Psychological Sciences and Social Sciences, 58,* S160–S170.

Krause, N. (2004). Common facets of religion, unique facets of religion, and life satisfaction among older adults. *Journals of Gerontology B: Psychological Sciences and Social Sciences, 59,* S109–S117.

Krause, N. (2004). Religion, aging, and health: Exploring new frontiers in medical care. *Southern Medical Journal, 97,* 1215–1222.

Krause, N. (2006). Religion and health in late life. In J. E. Birren & K. W. Schaie (Eds.), *Handbook of the psychology of religion* (6th ed.). San Diego: Academic Press.

Krause, N. (2006). Social relationships in late life. In R. H. Binstock & L. K. George (Eds.), *Handbook of aging and the social sciences* (6th ed.). San Diego: Academic Press.

Krause, N. E. (2006). Religion and aging. In J. E. Birren & K. W. Schaie (Eds.), *Handbook of the psychology of aging*. San Diego: Academic Press.

Krause, N., Ingersoll-Dayton, B., Liang, J., & Sugisawa, H. (1999). Religion, social behavior, and health among the Japanese elderly. *Journal of Health and Social Behavior, 40*, 405–421.

Kreutzer, M., Leonard, C., & Flavell, J. H. (1975). An interview study of children's knowledge about memory. *Monographs of the Society for Research in Child Development. 40* (1, Serial No. 159).

Kriebs, J. M. (2006). Changing the paradigm: HIV in pregnancy. *Journal of Perinatal and Neonatal Nursing, 20*, 71–73.

Krimer, L. S., & Goldman-Rakic, P. S. (2001). Prefrontal microcircuits. *Journal of Neuroscience, 21*, 3788–3796.

Kristensen, J., Vestergaard, M., Wisborg, I. K., Kesmodel, U., & Secher, N. J. (2005). Pre-pregnancy weight and the risk of stillbirth and neonatal death. *British Journal of Obstetrics and Gynecology, 112*, 403–408.

Kroger, J. (2003). Identity development in adolescence. In G. Adams & M. Berzonsky (Eds.), *Blackwell handbook of adolescence*. Malden, MA: Blackwell.

Kroger, J. (2007). *Identity development: Adolescence through adulthood*. Thousand Oaks, CA: Sage.

Krogh, D. (2005). *Biology* (3rd ed.). Upper Saddle River, NJ: Prentice Hall.

Krogh, D. (2007). *Brief guide to biology*. Upper Saddle River, NJ: Prentice-Hall.

Krogh, K. L., & Slentz, S. I. (2001). *Teaching young children*. Mahwah, NJ: Erlbaum.

Ksir, C. J., Hart, C. L., & Ray, O. S. (2006). *Drugs, society, and human behavior* (11th, ed.). New York: McGraw-Hill.

Kübler-Ross, E. (1969). *On death and dying*. New York: Macmillan.

Kubrick, R. J., & McLaughlin, C. S. (2005). No Child Left Behind Act of 2001. In S. W. Lee (Ed.), *Encyclopedia of school psychology*. Thousand Oaks, CA: Sage.

Kuebli, J. (1994, March). Young children's understanding of everyday emotions. *Young Children*, pp. 36–48.

Kuehn, B. M. (2005). Better osteoporosis management a priority: Impact predicted to soar with aging population. *Journal of the American Medical Association, 293*, 2453–2458.

Kuhl, P. K. (1993). Infant speech perception: A window on psycholinguistic development. *International Journal of Psycholinguistics, 9*, 33–56.

Kuhl, P. K. (2000). A new view of language acquisition. *Proceedings of the National Academy of Science, 97* (22), 11850–11857

Kuhl, P. K., Stevens, E., Hayashi, A., Deguchi, T., Kiritani, S., & Iverson, P. (2006). Infants show a facilitation for native language phonetic perception between 6 and 12 months. *Developmental Science, 9*, F13–F21.

Kuhn, D. (1998). Afterword to Volume 2: Cognition, perception, and language. In W. Damon (Ed.), *Handbook of child psychology* (5th ed., Vol. 2). New York: Wiley.

Kuhn, D. (1999). A developmental model of critical thinking. *Educational Researcher, 28*, 16–25.

Kuhn, D. (2004). What is scientific thinking, and how does it develop? In U. Goswami (Ed.), *Blackwell handbook of childhood cognitive development*. Malden, MA: Blackwell.

Kuhn, D. (2005, in press). *Education for thinking*. Cambridge: Harvard University Press.

Kuhn, D., Amsel, E., & O'Laughlin, M. (1988). *The development of scientific thinking skills*. Orlando, FL: Academic Press.

Kuhn, D., & Franklin, S. (2006). The second decade: What develops (and how)? In W. Damon & R. Lerner (Eds.), *Handbook of child psychology* (6th ed.). New York: Wiley.

Kuhn, D., Schauble, L., & Garcia-Mila, M. (1992). Cross-domain development of scientific reasoning. *Cognition and Instruction, 9*, 285–327.

Kuiper, S., Maas, T., Schayck, C. P., Muris, J. W., Schonberger, H. J., Dompeling, E., Gijsbers, B., Weel, C., André Knottnerus, J., and the PREVASC group. (2005). The primary prevention of asthma in children study: Design of a multifaceted prevention program. *Pediatric Allergy and Immunology, 16*, 321–331.

Kukkonen-Harjula, K. T., Borg, P. T., Nenonen, A. M., & Fogelholm, M. G. (2005). Effects of a weight maintenance program with or without exercise on the metabolic syndrome: A randomized control trial in obese men. *Preventive Medicine, 41*, 784–790.

Kulczewski, P. (2005). Vygotsky and the three bears. *Teaching Children Mathematics, 11*, 246–248.

Kumar, R., Gautam, G., Gupta, N. P., Aron, M., Dada, R., Kucheria, K., Gupta, S. K., & Mitra, A. (2006). Role of testicular fine-needle aspiration cytology in infertile men with clinical obstructive azoospermia. *National Medical Journal of India, 19*, 18–20.

Kumari, A. S. (2001). Pregnancy outcome in women with morbid obesity. *International Journal of Gynecology and Obstetrics, 73*, 101–107.

Kupersmidt, J. B., & Cole, J. D. (1990). Preadolescent peer status, aggression, and school adjustment as predictors of externalizing problems in adolescence. *Child Development, 61*, 1350–1363.

Kupperman, M., Learman, L. A., Gates, E., Gregorich, S. E., Nease, R. F., Lewis, J., & Washington, A. E. (2006). Beyond race or ethnicity and socioeconomic status: Predictors of prenatal testing for Down syndrome. *Obstetrics and Gynecology, 107*, 1087–1097.

Kurdek, L. A. (1995). Developmental changes in relationship quality in gay and lesbian cohabiting couples. *Developmental Psychology, 31*, 86–94.

Kurdek, L. A. (1997). Adjustment to relationship dissolution in gay, lesbian, and heterosexual partners. *Personal Relationships, 4*, 145–161.

Kurdek, L. A. (2003). Differences between gay and lesbian cohabiting couples. *Journal of Social and Personal Relationships, 20*, 411–436.

Kurdek, L. A. (2004). Gay men and lesbian couples. In M. Coleman & L. Ganong (Eds.), *Handbook of contemporary families*. Thousand Oaks, CA: Sage.

Kurdek, L. A. (2006). Differences between partners from heterosexual, gay, and lesbian cohabiting couples. *Journal of Marriage and the Family, 68*, 509–528.

Kurjak, A., Carerra, J., Medic, M., Azumendi, G., Andonotopo, W., & Stanojevic, M. (2005). The antenatal development of fetal behavioral patterns assessed by four-dimensional sonography. *Journal of Maternal-Fetal and Neonatal Medicine, 17*, 401–416.

Kurrle, S. E. (2006). Improving acute care services for older people: A collaborative trial is needed. *Medical Journal of Australia, 184*, 427–428.

Kwak, H. K., Kim, M., Cho, B. H., & Ham, Y. M. (1999, April). *The relationship between children's temperament, maternal control strategies, and children's compliance*. Paper presented at the meeting of the Society for Research in Child Development, Albuquerque.

Kwan, M. L., Buffler, P. A., Abrams, B., & Kiley, V. A. (2004). Breastfeeding and the risk of childhood leukemia: A meta-analysis. *Public Health Reports, 119*, 521–535.

La Greca, A. M., & Harrison, H. M. (2005). Adolescent peer relations, friendships, and romantic relationships: Do they predict social anxiety and depression? *Journal of Clinical Child and Adolescent Psychology, 34*, 49–61.

Labouvie-Vief, G. (1986, August). *Modes of knowing and life-span cognition*. Paper presented at the meeting of the American Psychological Association, Washington, DC.

Labouvie-Vief, G. (2006). Emerging structures of adult thought. In J. J. Arnett & J. L. Tanner (Eds.), *Emerging adults in America*. Washington, DC: American Psychological Association.

Labouvie-Vief, G., & Diehl, M. (1999). Self and personality development. In J. C. Kavanaugh & S. K. Whitbourne (Eds.), *Gerontology: An interdisciplinary perspective*. New York: Oxford University Press.

Lachlan, R. F., & Feldman, M. W. (2003). Evolution of cultural communication systems. *Journal of Evolutionary Biology, 16*, 1084–1095.

Lachman, M. E. (1991). Perceived control over memory aging: Developmental and intervention perspective. *Journal of Social Issues, 47*(4), 159–175.

Lachman, M. E. (Ed.). (2001). *Handbook of midlife development*. New York: John Wiley.

Lachman, M. E. (2004). Development in midlife. *Annual Review of Psychology, Vol. 55*. Palo Alto, CA: Annual Reviews.

Lachman, M. E., Baltes, P. B., Nesselroade, J. R., & Willis, S. L. (1982). Examination of personality-ability relationships in the elderly: The role of the contextual (interface) assessment mode. *Journal of Research in Personality, 16*, 485–501.

Lachman, M. E., & Bertrand, R. M. (2001). Personality and the self in midlife. In M. E. Lachman (Ed.), *Handbook of midlife development*. New York: Wiley.

Lachman, M. E., & Firth, K. (2004). The adaptive value of feeling in control during midlife. In G. O. Brim, C. D. Ryff, & R. C., Kessler (Eds.), *How healthy we are:* A national study of well-being in midlife. Chicago: University of Chicago Press.

Lachman, M. E., Maier, H., & Budner, R. (2000). *A portrait of midlife*. Unpublished manuscript, Brandeis University, Waltham, MA.

Lachman, M. E., & Weaver, S. L. (1998). Sociodemographic variations in the sense of control by domain: Findings from the MacArthur Study of midlife. *Psychology and Aging, 13*, 553–562.

Ladd, G. W. (2006). *Peer relations and social competence of children and adolescents*. New Haven, CT: Yale University Press.

Ladd, G., Buhs, E., & Troop, W. (2004). School adjustment and social skills training. In P. K. Smith & C. H. Hart (Eds.), *Blackwell handbook of childhood social development*. Malden, MA: Blackwell.

Laditka, S. B., Laditka, J. N., Bennett, K., J. & Probst, J. C. (2005). Delivery complications associated with prenatal care access for Medicaid-insured mothers in rural and urban hospitals. *Journal of Rural Health, 21*, 158–166.

Lafrance, R., Brustoetsky, N., Sherburne, C., Delong, C., Delong, D., & Dubinsky, J. M. (2005). Age-related changes in regional in brain mitochondria from Fischer 344 rats. *Aging Cell, 4*, 139–145.

Laible, D. J., Carlo, G., & Raffaell, M. (2000). The differential relations of parent and peer attachment to adolescent adjustment. *Journal of Youth and Adolescence, 29*, 45–53.

Laird, R. D., Pettit, G. S., Dodge, K. A., & Bates, J. E. (2005). Peer relationship antecedents of delinquent behavior in late adolescence: Is there evidence of demographic group differences in developmental processes? *Development and Psychopathology, 17*, 127–144.

Lakes, R. D., & Carter, P. A. (2004). Globalization, vocational education, and gender equity: A review. In R. D. Lakes & P. A. Carter (Eds.), *Globalizing education for work.* Mahwah, NJ: Erlbaum.

Lamb, C. S., Jackson, L. A., Cassiday, P. B., & Priest, D. J. (1993). Body figure preferences of men and women: A comparison of two generations. *Sex Roles, 28,* 345–358.

Lamb, M. E. (1977). The development of mother-infant and father-infant attachments in the second year of life. *Developmental Psychology, 13,* 637–648.

Lamb, M. E. (1986). *The father's role: Applied perspectives.* New York: Wiley.

Lamb, M. E. (1994). Infant care practices and the application of knowledge. In C. B. Fisher & R. M. Lerner (Eds.), *Applied developmental psychology.* New York: McGraw-Hill.

Lamb, M. E. (2000). The history of research on father involvement: An overview. *Marriage and Family Review, 29,* 23–42.

Lamb, M. E. (2005). Attachments, social networks, and developmental contexts. *Human Development, 48,* 108–112.

Lamb, M. E., & Ahnert, M. E. (2006). Nonparental child care. In W. Damon & R. Lerner (Eds.), *Handbook of child psychology* (6th ed.). New York: Wiley.

Lamb, M. E., Bornstein, M. H., & Teti, D. M. (2002). *Development in infancy,* (4th ed.). Mahwah, NJ: Erlbaum.

Lamb, M. E., Frodi, A. M., Hwant, C. P., Frodi, M., & Steinberg, J. (1982). Mother and father-infant interaction involving play and holding in traditional and nontraditional Swedish families. *Developmental Psychology, 18,* 215–221.

Lamb, V. L. (2003). Historical and epidemiological trends in mortality in the United States. In C. D. Bryant (Ed.), *Handbook of death and dying.* Thousand Oaks, CA: Sage.

Lambert, S. (2005). Gay and lesbian families: What we know and where to go from here. *Family Journal, 13,* 43–51.

Lammers, W. J., & Badia, P. (2005). *Fundamentals of behavioral research.* Belmont, CA: Wadsworth.

Lan, T-Y. Deeg, D. J. H. Guralnik, J. M., Melzer, D. (2003). Responsiveness of the index of mobility limitation: Comparison with gait speed alone in the longitudinal aging study, Amsterdam.

Land, K. C., & Yang, Y. (2006). Morbidity, disability, and mortality. In R. H. Binstock & L. K. George (Eds.), *Handbook of aging and the social sciences* (6th ed.). San Diego: Academic Press.

Lane, H. (1976). *The wild boy of Aveyron.* Cambridge, MA: Harvard University Press.

Lane, M. A., Mattison, J. A., Roth, G. S., Brant, L. J., & Ingram, D. K. (2004). Effects of long-term diet restriction on aging and longevity in primates remain uncertain. *Journals of Gerontology A: Biological and Medical Sciences, 59,* B405–B407.

Lang, A. E., Mivasaki, J., Olanow, C. W., Stoessl, A. J., & Suchowersky, O. (2005). Progress in clinical neurosciences: A forum on the early management of Parkinson's disease. *Canadian Journal of Neurological Science, 32,* 277–286.

Lang, F. R., & Carstensen, L. L. (1994). Close emotional relationships in late life: Further support for proactive aging in the social domain. *Psychology and Aging, 9,* 315–324.

Langlois, J. A., Rutland-Brown, W., & Thomas, K. E. (2005). The incidence of traumatic brain injury among children in the United States: Differences by race. *Journal of Head and Trauma Rehabilitation, 20,* 229–238.

Langlois, J. H., & Liben, L. S. (2003). Child care research: An editorial perspective. *Child Development, 74,* 969–1226.

Langner, R., & Maercker, A. (2005). Complicated grief as a stress response disorder: Evaluating diagnostic criteria in a German sample. *Journal of Psychosomatic Research, 58,* 235–242.

Lantz, P. M., Low, L. K., Varkey, S., & Watson, R. L. (2005). Doulas as childbirth professionals: Results from a national survey. *Womens Health Issues, 15,* 109–116.

Lapierre, L. M., Spector, P. E., & Leck, J. D. (2005). Sexual versus nonsexual workplace aggression and victims' overall job satisfaction: A meta-analysis. *Journal of Occupational Health Psychology, 10,* 155–169.

Lapsley, D. K. (2006). Moral stage theory. In M. Killen & J. G. Smetana (Eds.), *Handbook of moral development.* Mahwah, NJ: Erlbaum.

Lapsley, D. K., & Narvaez D. (Eds.) (2004). *Moral development, self, and identity.* Mahwah, NJ: Erlbaum.

Lapsley, D. K., & Narvaez, D. (2006). Character education. In W. Damon & R. Lerner (Eds.), *Handbook of child psychology* (6th ed.). New York: Wiley.

Larson, F. B., Wang., L., Bowen, J. D., McCormick, W. C., Teri, L., Crane, P., & Kukull, W. (2006). Exercise is associated with reduced risk for incident dementia among persons 65 years of age and older. *Annals of Internal Medicine, 144,* 73–81.

Larson, R., & Richards, M. H. (1994). *Divergent realities.* New York: Basic Books.

Larson, R. W. (1999, September). Unpublished review of J. W. Santrock's *Adolescence,* 8th ed. New York: McGraw-Hill.

Larson, R. W. (2001). How U.S. children and adolescents spend their time: What it does (and doesn't) tell us about their development. *Current Directions in Psychological Science, 10,* 160–164.

Larson, R. W., Brown, B., & Mortimer, J. (2003). *Adolescents' preparation for the future: Perils and promises.* Malden, MA: Blackwell.

Larson, R., & Lampman-Petraitis, C. (1989). Daily emotional states as reported by children and adolescents. *Child Development, 60,* 1250–1260.

Larson, R. W., & Varma, S. (1999). How children and adolescents spend time across the world: Work, play, and developmental opportunities. *Psychological Bulletin, 125,* 701–736.

Larson, R. W., & Wilson, S. (2004). Adolescence across place and time: Globalization and the changing pathways to adulthood. In R. Lerner & L. Steinberg (eds.), *Handbook of adolescent psychology.* New York: Wiley.

Lasiuk, G. C., & Ferguson, L. M. (2005). From practice to midrange theory and back again: Beck's theory of postpartum depression. *Advanced Nursing Science, 28,* 127–136.

Lasker, J. N., Coyle, B., Li, K., & Ortynsky, M. (2005). Assessment of risk factors for low birth weight deliveries. *Health Care for Women International, 26,* 262–280.

Latham, N. K., Bennett, D. A., Stretton, C. M., & Anderson, C. S. (2004). Systematic review of resistance strength training in older adults. *Journals of Gerontology A: Biological Sciences and Medical Sciences, 59,* M48–M61.

Lauber, M. O., Marshall, M. I., & Meyers, J. (2005). Gangs. In S. W. Lee (Ed.), *Encyclopedia of school psychology.* Thousand Oaks, CA: Sage.

Laursen, B., & Collins, W. A. (2004). Parent-child communication during adolescence. In A. L. Vangelisti (Ed.), *Handbook of family communication.* Mahwah, NJ: Erlbaum.

Lautenschlager, N. T., & Almeida, O. P. (2006). Physical activity and cognition in old age. *Current Opinions in Psychiatry, 19,* 190–193.

Lawton, M. P., Kleban, M. H., Rajagopal, D., & Dean, J. (1992). The dimensions of affective experience in three age groups. *Psychology and Aging, 7,* 171–184.

Lazar, L., Darlington, R., & Collaborators. (1982). Lasting effects of early education: A report from the consortium for longitudinal studies. *Monographs of the Society for Research in Child Development, 47.*

Lazarus, R. S., & Folkman, S. (1984). *Stress, appraisal, and coping.* New York: Springer.

Leadbeater, B. J. R., & Way, N. (2001). *Growing up fast.* Mahwah, NJ: Erlbaum.

Leaper, C. (2002). Parenting girls and boys. In M. H. Bornstein (Ed.), *Handbook of parenting, Volume 1: Children and parenting* (2nd ed.). Mahwah, NJ: Lawrence Erlbaum.

Leaper, C., & Smith, T. E. (2004). A meta-analytic review of gender variations in children's language use: Talkativeness, affiliative speech, and assertive speech. *Developmental Psychology, 40,* 993–1027.

Leary, M. R. (2004). *Introduction to behavioral research methods* (4th ed.). Boston: Allyn & Bacon.

LeBrun, C. E., van der Schouw, Y. T., de Jong, F. H., Grobbee, D. E., & Lamberts, S. W. (2006). Fat mass rather than muscle strength is the major determinant of physical function and disability in postmenopausal women younger than 75 years of age. *Menopause, 13,* 474–481.

LeDoux, J. E. (1998). *The emotional brain: The mysterious underpinnings of emotional life.* New York: Simon & Schuster.

LeDoux, J. E. (2000). Emotion circuits in the brain. *Annual Review of Neuroscience, 23,* 155–184.

Lee, D. J., & Markides, K. S. (1990). Activity and mortality among aged persons over an eight-year period. *Journals of Gerontology: Social Sciences, 45,* S39–S42.

Lee, G. R. (1978). Marriage and morale in late life. *Journal of Marriage and the Family, 40,* 131–139.

Lee, H. Y., Lee, E. L., Pathy, P., & Chan, Y. H. (2005). Anorexia nervosa in Singapore: An eight-year retrospective study. *Singapore Medical Journal, 46,* 275–281.

Lee, I. M., & Skerret, P. J. (2001). Physical activity and all-cause mortality: What is the dose-response relation? *Medical Science and Sport Exercise, 33* (6 Suppl.), S459–S471.

Lee, I. M., Hsieh, C., & Paffenbarger, R. S. (1995). Exercise intensity and longevity in men. *Journal of the American Medical Association, 273,* 1179–1184.

Lee, I. M., Manson, J. E., Hennekens, C. H., & Paffenbarger, R. S. (1993). Bodyweight and mortality: A 27-year-follow-up. *Journal of the American Medical Association, 270,* 2823–2828.

Lee, J., & others. (2005). Maternal and infant characteristics associated with perinatal arterial stroke in the infant. *Obstetrical and Gynecological Survey, 60,* 430–431.

Lee, R. D., Ensminger, M. E., & LaVeist, T. A. (2005). The responsibility continuum: Never primary, coresident, and caregiver–heterogeneity in the African American grandmother experience. *International Journal of Aging and Human Development, 60,* 295–304.

Lee, S., Cho, E., Grodstein, F., Kawachi, I., Hu, F. B., & Colditz, G. A. (2005). Effects of marital transitions on changes in dietary and other health behaviors in U.S. women. *International Journal of Epidemiology, 34,* 69–78.

Lee, W. K. (2003). Women and retirement planning: Towards the "feminization of poverty" in an aging Hong Kong. *Journal of Women and Aging, 15,* 31–53.

Lefkowitz, E. S. (2005). "Things have gotten better": Developmental changes among emerging adults after the transition to university. *Journal of Adolescent Research, 20,* 40–63.

Lehman, H. C. (1960). The age decrement in outstanding scientific creativity. *American Psychologist, 15,* 128–134.

Lehr, C. A., Hanson, A., Sinclair, M. F., & Christensen, S. L. (2003). Moving beyond dropout prevention towards school completion. *School Psychology Review, 32,* 342–364.

Lehr, M. B., Rosenberg, K. D., & Lapidus, J. A. (2005). Bedsharing and maternal smoking in a population-based survey of new mothers. *Pediatrics, 116,* e530–e542.

Lehrer, R., & Schauble, L. (2006). Scientific thinking and science literacy: Supporting developmental change in learning contexts. In W. Damon & R. Lerner (Eds.), *Handbook of child psychology* (6th ed.). New York: Wiley.

Lehrer, R., Schauble, L., & Petrosino, A. (2001). Reconsidering the role of the experiment in science. In K. Crowley, C. Schunn, & T. Okada (Eds.), *Designing for science.* Mahwah, NJ: Erlbaum.

Leifer, A. D. (1973). *Television and the development of social behavior.* Paper presented at the meeting of the International Society for the Study of Behavioral Development, Ann Arbor, MI.

Leifer, M., Kilbane, T., Jacobsen, T., & Grossman, G. (2004). A three-generational study of transmission of risk for sexual abuse. *Journal of Clinical Child and Adolescent Psychology, 33,* 662–665.

Leming, M. R. (2003). The history of the hospice approach. In C. D. Bryant (Ed.), *Handbook of death and dying.* Thousand Oaks, CA: Sage.

Leming, M. R., & Dickinson, G. E. (2002). *Understanding death, dying and bereavement* (5th ed.). Belmont, CA: Wadsworth.

Lenders, C. M., McElrath, T. F., & Scholl, T. O. (2000). Nutrition in pregnancy. *Current Opinions in Pediatrics, 12,* 291–296.

Lenoir, C. P., Mallet, E., & Calenda, E. (2000). Siblings of sudden infant death syndrome and near miss in about 30 families: Is there a genetic link? *Medical Hypotheses, 54,* 408–411.

Lenton, A. P., & Blair, I. V. (2004). Gender roles. In W. E. Craighead & C. B. Nemeroff (Eds.), *The concise Corsini encyclopedia of psychology and behavioral science.* New York: Wiley.

Leonard, B. (2004). Women's conditions occurring in men: Breast cancer, osteoporosis, male menopause, and eating disorders. *Nursing Clinics of North America, 39,* 379–393.

Leonards, U., Ibanez, V., & Giannakopoulos, P. (2002). The role of stimulus type in age-related changes of visual working memory. *Experimental Brain Research, 146,* 172–183.

Lerner, H. G. (1989). *The dance of intimacy.* New York: Harper & Row.

Lerner, R. (2006). Developmental science, developmental systems, and contemporary theories of human development. In W. Damon & R. Lerner (Eds.), *Handbook of child psychology* (6th ed.). New York: Wiley.

Lesaux, N. K., & Siegel, L. S. (2003). The development of reading in children who speak English as a second language. *Development Psychology, 39,* 1005–1019.

Lesley, C. (2005). *Burning fence: A Western memoir of fatherhood.* New York: St. Martin's Press.

Lespessailles, E., & Prouteau, S. (2006). Is there a synergy between physical exercise and drug therapies for osteoporosis? *Clinical and Experimental Rheumatology, 24,* 191–195.

Lessow-Hurley, J. (2005). *The foundations of dual language instruction* (4th ed.). Boston: Allyn & Bacon.

Lester, B. (2000). Unpublished review of J. W. Santrock's *Life-span development.* 8th ed. (New York: McGraw-Hill).

Lester, B. M., Tronick, E. Z., & Brazelton, T. B. (2004). The Neonatal Intensive Care Unit Network Neurobehavioral Scale procedures. *Pediatrics, 113,* (Suppl) S641–S667.

Lester, B. M., Tronick, E. Z., LaGasse, L., Seifer, R., Bauer, C. R., Shankaran, S., Bada, H. S., Wright, L. L., Smeriglio, V. L., Lu, J., Finnegan, L. P., & Maza, P. L. (2002). The maternal lifestyle study: Effects of substance exposure during pregnancy on neurodevelopmental outcome in 1-month-old infants. *Pediatrics, 110,* 1182–1192.

Letterie, G. S. (2005). Three-dimensional ultrasound-guided embryo transfer—a preliminary study. *American Journal of Obstetrics and Gynecology, 192,* 1983–1987.

Leuenthal, T., & Brooks-Gunn, J. (2004). Diversity in developmental trajectories across Adolescence: Neighborhood influences. In R. Lerner & L. Steinberg (Eds.), *Handbook of adolescent psychology.* New York: Wiley.

Levant, R. F. (2002). Men and masculinity. In J. Worell (Ed.), *Encyclopedia of women and gender.* San Diego: Academic Press.

Levant, R. F., & Brooks, G. R. (1997). *Men and sex: New psychological perspectives.* New York: Wiley.

LeVay, S. (1991). A difference in the hypothalamic structure between heterosexual and homosexual men. *Science, 253,* 1034–1037.

Levelt, W. J. M. (1989). Speaking: From intention to articulation. Cambridge, MA: MIT Press.

Leventhal, A. (1994, February). *Peer conformity during adolescence: An integration of developmental, situational, and individual characteristics.* Paper presented at the meeting of the Society for Research on Adolescence, San Diego.

Levesque, J., Joanette, Y., Mensour, B., Beaudoin, G., Leroux, J. M., Bourgouin, P., & Beauregard, M. (2004). Neural basis of emotional self-regulation in childhood. *Neuroscience, 129,* 361–369.

Levin, B. G. (2004). Coping with traumatic loss. *International Journal of Emergency Mental Health, 6,* 25–31.

Levin, J. S., & Vanderpool, H. Y. (1989). Is religion therapeutically significant for hypertension? *Social Science and Medicine, 29,* 69–78.

Levin, J. S., Taylor, R. J., & Chatters, L. M. (1994). Race and gender differences in religiosity among older adults: Findings from four national surveys. *Journal of Gerontology, 49,* S137–S145.

Levin, M. P., & Smolak, L. (2006). *Prevention of eating problems and disorders.* Mahwah, NJ: Erlbaum.

LeVine, S. (1979). *Mothers and wives: Gusii women of East Africa.* Chicago: University of Chicago Press.

Levinson, D. J. (1978). *The seasons of a man's life.* New York: Knopf.

Levinson, D. J. (1996). *Seasons of a woman's life.* New York: Alfred Knopf.

Levy, B. R., Jennings, P., & Langer, E. J. (2001). Improving attention in old age. *Journal of Adult Development, 8,* 189–192.

Levy, B. R., Slade, M. D., Kunkel. S. R., & Kasl, S. V. (2002). Longevity increased by positive self-perceptions of aging. *Journal of Personality & Social Psychology, 83,* 261–270.

Lewin, B. (2006). *Essential genes.* Upper Saddle River, NJ: Prentice Hall.

Lewin-Fetter, V. (2005). Depression in elderly people. *Lancet, 366,* 544–545.

Lewis, A. C. (2005, January). States feeling the crunch of NCLB. *Phi Delta Kappan,* 339–340.

Lewis, C., & Carpendale, J. (2004). Social cognition. In P. K. Smith & C. H. Hart (Eds.), *Blackwell handbook of childhood social development.* Malden, MA: Blackwell.

Lewis, M. (1997). *Altering fate: Why the past does not predict the future.* New York: Guilford Press.

Lewis, M. (2001). Issues in the study of personality development. *Psychological Inquiry. 12,* 67–83.

Lewis, M. (2002). Early emotional development. In A. Slater & M. Lewis (Eds.), *Introduction to infant development.* New York: Oxford University Press.

Lewis, M. (2005). Selfhood. In B. Hopkins (Ed.), *The Cambridge Encyclopedia of Child Development* Cambridge: Cambridge University Press.

Lewis, M., & Brooks-Gunn, J. (1979). *Social cognition and the acquisition of the self.* New York: Plenum.

Lewis, M., Feiring, C., & Rosenthal, S. (2000). Attachment over time. *Child Development, 71,* 707–720.

Lewis, M., & Ramsay, D. S. (1999). Effect of maternal soothing and infant stress response. *Child Development, 70,* 11–20.

Lewis, M., Sullivan, M. W., Sanger, C., & Weiss, M. L. (2004). Variability in the early development of visual self-recognition. *Infant Behavior and Development, 27,* 509–532.

Lewis, R. (2005). *Human genetics* (6th ed.). New York: McGraw-Hill.

Lewis, R. (2007). *Human genetics* (7th ed.). New York. McGraw-Hill.

Li, D., Liao, C., Yi, C., & Pan, M. (2006). Amniocentesis for karyotyping prior to induction of abortion at second trimester. *Prenatal Diagnosis, 26,* 192.

Li, D. K., Willinger, M., Petitti, D. B., Odulil, R. K., Liu, L., & Hoffman, H. J. (2006). Use of a dummy (pacifier) during sleep and risk of sudden infant death syndrome (SIDS): Population-based case-control study. *British Medical Journal, 332,* 18–22.

Li, L., Liang, J, Toler, A., & Gu, S. (2005). Widowhood and depressive symptoms among older Chinese: Do gender and source of support make a difference? *Social Science Medicine, 60,* 637–647.

Li, S-C. (2006). Biocultural co-construction of life-Span development. In P. B. Baltes, P. Reuter-Lorenz, & F. Röster (Eds.), *Lifespan development and the brain.* New York: Cambridge University Press.

Li, S-C., Lindenberger, U., Hommel, B., Aschersleben, G., Prinz, W., & Baltes, P. B. (2004). Transformations in the couplings among intellectual abilities and constituent cognitive processes across the lifespan. *Psychological Science, 15,* 155–163.

Li, X., Li, S., Ulusovy, E., Chen, W., Srinivasan, S. R., & Berensen, G. S. (2004). Childhood adiposity as a predictor of cardiac mass in adulthood: The Bogalusa Heart Study. *Circulation, 110,* 3488–3492.

Liben, L. S. (1995). Psychology meets geography: Exploring the gender gap on the national geography bee. *Psychological Science Agenda, 8,* 6–9.

Lidral, A. C., & Murray, J. C. (2005). Genetic approaches to identify disease genes for birth defects with cleft lip/palate as a model. *Birth Defects Research, 70,* 893–901.

Lie, E., & Newcombe, N. (1999). Elementary school children's explicit and implicit memory for faces of preschool classmates. *Developmental Psychology, 35,* 102–112.

Lieberman, E., Davidson, K., Lee-Parritz, A., & Shearer, E. (2005). Changes in fetal position during labor and their association with epidural analgesia. *Obstetrics and Gynecology, 105,* 974–982.

Liederman, J., Kantrowitz, L., & Flannery, K. (2005). Male vulnerability to reading disability is not likely to be a myth: A call for new data. *Journal of Learning Disabilities, 38,* 109–129.

Lifshitz, F., Pugliese, M. T., Moses, N., & Weyman-Daum, M. (1987). Parental health beliefs as a cause of nonorganic failure to thrive. *Pediatrics, 80,* 175–182.

Lifton, R. J. (1977). The sense of immortality: On death and the continuity of life. In H. Feifel (Ed.), *New meanings of death.* New York: McGraw-Hill.

Lillard, L. A., & Waite, L. J. (1995). Til death do us part: Marital disruption and mortality. *American Journal of Sociology, 100,* 1131–1156.

Lim, S., & Cortina, L. M. (2005). Interpersonal mistreatment in the workplace: the interface and impact of general incivility and sexual harassment. *Journal of Applied Psychology, 90,* 483–496.

Limber, S. P. (1997). Preventing violence among school children. *Family Futures, 1,* 27–28.

Limber, S. P. (2004). Implementation of the Olweus Bullying Prevention Program in American schools: Lessons learned from the field. In D. L. Espelage & S. M. Swearer (Eds.), *Bullying in American schools.* Mahwah, NJ: Erlbaum.

Lin, J. W., Hwang, J. J., Dai, D. F., & Tseng, Y. Z. (2006). Using structural equation modeling to illustrate the relationship between metabolic risk factors and cardiovascular complications in Taiwan. *European Journal of Cardiovascular Prevention and Rehabilitation, 13,* 633–639.

Lin, M., Johnson, J. E., & Johnson, K. M. (2003). Dramatic play in Montessori kindergartens in Taiwan and Mainland China. Unpublished manuscript, Department of Curriculum and Instruction, Pennsylvania State University, University Park, PA.

Lindbohm, M. (1991). Effects of paternal occupational exposure in spontaneous abortions. *American Journal of Public Health, 121,* 1029–1033.

Lindenberger, U., & Baltes, P. B. (1994). Sensory functioning and intelligence in old age: A strong connection. *Psychology and Aging, 9,* 339–355.

Lindsay, A. C., Sussner, K. M., Kim, J., & Gortmaker, S. (2006) The role of parents in preventing childhood obesity. *Future of Children, 16* (No. 1), 169–186.

Linn, M. C., & Eylon, B. S. (2006). Science education: Integrating views of learning and instruction. In P. A. Alexander & P. H. Winne (Eds.), *Handbook of educational psychology* (2nd ed.). Mahwah, NJ: Erlbaum.

Linver, M. R., Fulini, A. J., Hernandez, M., & Brooks-Gunn, J. (2004). Poverty and child development. In P. Allen-Meares & M. Fraser (Eds.), *Intervention with children and adolescents.* Boston: Allyn & Bacon.

Lippa, R. A. (2005). *Gender, nature, and nurture* (2nd ed.). Mahwah, NJ: Erlbaum.

Lipsitz, J. (1983, October). *Making it the hard way: Adolescents in the 1980s.* Testimony presented at the Crisis Intervention Task Force, House Select Committee on Children, Youth, and Families, Washington, DC.

Litovsky, R. Y., & Ashmead, D. H. (1997). Development of binaural and spatial hearing in infants and children. In R. H. Gilkey & T. R. Anderson (Eds.), *Binaural and spatial hearing in real and virtual environments,* Mahwah, NJ: Erlbaum.

Litt, J., Taylor, H. G., Klein, N., & Hack, M. (2005). Learning disabilities in very low birth weight: Prevalence, neuropsychological correlates, and educational interventions. *Journal of Learning Disabilities, 38,* 130–141.

Liu, J., Raine, A., Venables, P. H., Dalais, C., & Mednick, S. A. (2003). Malnutrition at age 3 years and lower cognitive ability at age 11 years: Independence from psychosocial adversity. *Archives of Pediatric and Adolescent Medicine, 157,* 593–600.

Liu, J., Raine, A., Venables, P. H., & Mednick, S. A. (2004). Malnutrition at 3 years and externalizing behavior problems at age 8, 11, and 17 years. *American Journal of Psychiatry, 161,* 2005–2013.

Liu, Y. J., Xiao, P., Xiong, D. H., Recker, R. R., & Deng, H. W. (2005). Searching for obesity genes: Progress and prospects. *Drugs Today, 41,* 345–362.

Lively, W., & Bromley, D. (1973). *Person perception in childhood and adolescence.* New York: Wiley.

Livson, N., & Peskin, H. (1981). Psychological health at age 40. Prediction from adolescent personality. In

D. M. Eichorn, J. Clausen, N. Haan, M. Honzik, & P. Mussen (Eds.), *Present and past in middle life.* New York: Academic Press.

Lleo, A., Greenberg, S. M., & Growdon, J. H. (2006). Current pharmacotherapy for Alzheimer's disease. *Annual Review of Medicine, 57,* 513–533.

Lloyd, K., & Wise, K. (2004). Protecting children from exposure to environmental tobacco. *Nursing Times, 100,* 36–38.

Lo, B., & Rubenfeld, G. (2005). Palliative sedation in dying patients: "We turn to it when everything else hasn't worked." *Journal of the American Medical Association, 294,* 1810–1816.

Lobar, S. L., Youngblut, J. M., & Brooten, D. (2006). Cross-cultural beliefs, ceremonies, and rituals surrounding death of a loved one. *Pediatric Nursing, 32,* 44–50.

Locher, J. L., Ritchie, C. S., Roth, D. L., Baker, P. S., Bodner, E. V., & Allman, R. M. (2005). Social isolation, support, and capital and nutritional risk in an older sample: Ethnic and gender differences. *Social Science Medicine, 60,* 747–761.

Lock, A. (2004). Preverbal communication. In U. Goswami (Ed.), *Blackwell handbook of childhood cognitive development.* Malden, MA: Blackwell.

Lock, M. (1998). Menopause: Lessons from anthropology. *Psychosomatic Medicine, 60,* 410–419.

Locurto, C. (1990). The malleability of IQ as judged from adoption studies. *Intelligence, 14,* 275–292.

Loeb, S., Fuller, B., Kagan, S. L., & Carrol, B. (2004). Child care in poor communities: Early learning effects of type, quality, and stability. *Child Development, 75,* 47–65.

Loebel, M., & Yali, A. M. (1999, August). *Effect of positive expectancies on adjustment to pregnancy.* Paper presented at the meeting of the American Psychological Association, Boston.

Loeber, R., & Farrington, D. P. (Eds.). (2001). *Child delinquents: Development, intervention and service needs.* Thousand Oaks, CA: Sage.

Loeber, R., Farrington, D. P., Stouthamer-Loeber, M., Moffitt, T., & Caspi, A. (1998). The development of male offending: Key findings from the first decade of the Pittsburgh Youth Study. *Studies in Crime and Crime Prevention, 7,* 141–172.

Logsdon, M. C. (2004). Depression in adolescent girls: Screening and treatment strategies for primary care providers. *Journal of the American Women's Medical Association, 59,* 101–106.

London, K., Bruck, M., & Ceci, S. J. (2005). Disclosure of child sexual abuse: What does the research tell us about the ways that children tell? *Psychology, Public Policy, and Law, 11,* 194–226.

Long, T, & Long, L. (1983). *Latchkey children.* New York: Penguin.

Longman, P. (1987). *Born to pay: The new politics of aging in America.* Boston: Houghton Mifflin.

Loos, R. J., & Rankinen, T. (2005). Gene-diet interactions in body-weight changes. *Journal of the American Dietary Association, 105* (5, Pt. 2), 29–34.

Lopata, H. Z. (1994). *Circles and settings: Role changes of American women.* Albany State University of New York Press.

Lopez-Lluch, G., & others. (2006). Calorie restriction induces mitochondrial biogenesis and bioenergetic efficiency. *Proceedings of the National Academy of Science USA, 103,* 1768–1773.

Lorenz, F. O., Wickrama, K. A., Conger, R. D., & Elder, G. H. (2006). The short-term and decade-long effects of divorce on women's midlife health. *Journal of Health and Social Behavior, 47,* 117–125.

Lorenz, K. Z. (1965). *Evolution and the modification of behavior.* Chicago: University of Chicago Press.

Lott, B., & Maluso, D. (2001). Gender development: Social learning. In J. Worell (Ed.), *Encyclopedia of women and gender.* San Diego: Academic Press.

Loughlin, A. (2004). Depression and social support: effective treatments for homebound elderly adults. *Journal of Gerontological Nursing, 30,* 11–15.

Louria, D. B. (2005). Extraordinary longevity: Individual and societal issues. *Journal of the American Geriatric Society, 53* (9 Suppl), S317–S319.

Lovell, M. (2006). Caring for the elderly: Changing perceptions and attitudes. *Journal of Vascular Nursing, 24,* 22–26.

Low, A. (2004). Health inequities. *Health Services Journal, 114,* 26–27.

Lowe, M. R., & Kral, T. V. (2005). Stress-induced eating in restrained eaters may not be caused by stress or restraint. *Appetite.*

Lowe, M. R., & Timko, C. A. (2004). What a difference a diet makes: Towards an understanding of differences between retrained dieters and restrained nondieters. *Eating Behavior, 5,* 199–208.

Lowry, R., Galuska, D. A., Fulton, J. E., Burgeson, C. R., & Kann, L. (2005). Weight management goals and use of exercise for weight control among U.S. high school students, 1991–2001. *Journal of Adolescent Health, 36,* 320–326.

Lucas, R. E., Clark, A. E., Yannis, G., & Diener, E. (2004). Unemployment alters the setpoint for life satisfaction. *Psychological Science, 15,* 8–13.

Luders, E., Narr, K. L., Thompson, P. M., Rex, D. E., Jancke, L., Steinmetz, H., & Toga, A. W. (2004). Gender differences in cortical complexity. *Nature Neuroscience, 1,* 799–800.

Ludington-Hoe, S. M., Anderson, G. C., Swinth, J. Y., Thompson, C., & Hadeed, A. J. (2004). Randomized controlled trial of kangaroo care: Cardiorespiratory and thermal effects on healthy preterm infants. *Neonatal Network, 23,* 39–48.

Ludington-Hoe, S. M., & Golant, S. K. (1993). *Kangaroo care: The best you can do to help your preterm baby.* New York: Bantam Doubleday.

Ludington-Hoe, S. M., Lewis, T., Morgan, K., Cong, X., Anderson, L., & Reese, S. (2006). Breast and infant temperatures with twins during kangaroo care. *Journal of Obstetric, Gynecologic, and Neonatal Nursing, 35,* 223–231.

Lund, D. A. (1996). Bereavement and loss. In J. E. Birren (Ed.), *Encyclopedia of gerontology* (Vol. 1). San Diego: Academic Press.

Luo, S., & Klohnen, E. C. (2005). Assertive mating and marital quality in newlyweds: A couple-centered approach. *Journal of Personality and Social Psychology, 88,* 304–326.

Luria, A., & Herzog, E. (1985, April). *Gender segregation across and within settings.* Paper presented at the biennial meeting of the Society for Research in Child Development, Toronto.

Lyketsos, C. G., Toone, L., Tschanz, J., Corcoran, C., Norton, M., Zandi, P., Munger, R., Breitner, J. C., & Welsh-Bohmer, K. (2006). A population-based study of the association between coronary artery bypass graft surgery (CABG) and cognitive decline: The Cache County Study. *International Journal of Geriatric Psychiatry, 21,* 509–518.

Lyndaker, C., & Hulton, L. (2004). The influence of age on symptoms of perimenopause. *Journal of Obstetric, Gynecological, and Neonatal Nursing, 33,* 340–347.

Lynn, R. (1996). Racial and ethnic differences in intelligence in the U.S. on the Differential Ability Scale. *Personality and Individual Differences, 26,* 271–273.

Lyon, H. N., & Hirschhorn, J. N. (2005). Genetics of common forms of obesity: A brief overview. *American Journal of Clinical Nutrition, 82* (1 Suppl), 215S–217S.

Lyon, T. D., & Flavell, J. H. (1993). Young children's understanding of forgetting over time. *Child Development, 64,* 789–800.

Lyons, S. J., Henly, J. R., & Schuerman, J. R. (2005). Informal support in maltreating families: Its effects on parenting practices. *Children and Youth Services Review, 27,* 21–38.

Lyyra, T.-M., & Heikkinen, R.-L. (2006). Perceived social support and mortality in older people. *Journals of Gerontology B: Psychological Sciences and Social Sciences, 61,* S147–S152.

Maccoby, E. E. (1984). Middle childhood in the context of the family. In *Development during middle childhood.* Washington, DC: National Academy Press.

Maccoby, E. E. (1987, November). Interview with Elizabeth Hall: All in the family. *Psychology Today,* pp. 54–60.

Maccoby, E. E. (1992). The role of parents in the socialization of children: An historical overview. *Developmental Psychology, 28,* 1006–1018.

Maccoby, E. E. (1998). The two sexes: Growing up apart, coming together. Cambridge, MA: Harvard University Press.

Maccoby, E. E. (2002). Gender and group processes. *Current Directions in Psychological Science, 11,* 54–58.

Maccoby, E. E. (2003). Parenting effects. In J. G. Borkowski, S. L. Ramey, & M. Bristol-Power (Eds.), *Parenting and the child's world.* Mahwah, NJ: Erlbaum.

Maccoby, E. E., & Jacklin, C. N. (1974). *The psychology of sex differences.* Palo Alto, CA: Stanford University Press.

Maccoby, E. E., & Lewis, C. C. (2003). Less daycare or better daycare? *Child Development, 74,* 1069–1075.

Maccoby, E. E., & Martin, J. A. (1983). Socialization in the context of the family. In E. M. Hetherington (Ed.), *Handbook of child psychology: Vol. 4. Socialization, personality, and social development.* New York: Wiley.

Maccoby, E. E., & Mnookin, R. H. (1992). *Dividing the child: Social and legal dilemmas of custody.* Cambridge, MA: Harvard University Press.

MacFarlane, J. A. (1975). Olfaction in the development of social preferences in the human neonate. In *Parent-infant interaction.* Ciba Foundation Symposium No. 33. Amsterdam: Elsevier.

MacGeorge, E. L. (2003). Gender differences in attributions and emotions in helping contexts. *Sex Roles, 48,* 175–182.

MacGeorge, E. L. (2004). The myth of gender cultures: Similarities outweigh differences in men's and women's provisions of and responses to supportive communication. *Sex Roles, 50,* 143–175.

Maciokas, J. B., & Crognale, M. A. (2003). Cognitive and attentional changes with age: Evidence from attentional blink deficits. *Experimental Aging Research, 29,* 137–153.

Mackay, T. F. C., Roshina, N., Leips, J., & Pasyukova, E. G. (2006). Complex genetic architecture of *Drosophilia* longevity. In E. J. Mastor & S. N. Austad, (Eds.), *Handbook of the biology of aging.* San Diego: Academic Press.

Mackintosh, M. A., Gatz, M., Wetherell, J. L., & Pedersen, N. L. (2006). A twin study of lifetime generalized anxiety disorder (GAD) in older adults: Genetic and environmental influences shared by neuroticism and GAD. *Twin Research and Human Genetics, 9,* 30–37.

Macklem, G. L. (2003). *Bullying and teasing: Social power in children's groups.* New York: Kluwer Academic/Plenum.

Madan, A., Palaniappan, L., Urizar, G., Wang, Y., Fortmann, S. P., & Gould, J. B. (2006). Sociocultural factors that affect pregnancy outcomes in two dissimilar immigrant groups in the United States. *Journal of Pediatrics, 148,* 341–346.

Madden, D. J. (2001). Speed and timing of behavioral processes. In J. E. Birren & K. W. Schaie (Eds.), *Handbook of the psychology of aging* (5th ed.). San Diego: Academic Press.

Madden. D. J., Gottlob, L. R., Denny, L. L., Turkington, T. G., Provenzale, J. M., Hawk. T. C., et al. (1999). Aging and recognition memory: Changes in regional cerebral blood flow associated with components of reaction time distributions. *Journal of Cognitive Neuroscience, II,* 511–520.

Maddi, S. R., Harvey, R. H., Khoshaba, D. M., Lu, J. L., Persico, M., & Brow, M. (2006). The personality construct of hardiness, III: Relationships with repression, innovativeness, authoritarianism, and performance. *Journal of Personality, 74,* 575–597.

Maddux, J. (2002). The power of believing you can. In C. R. Snyder & S. J. Lopez (Eds.), *Handbook of positive psychology.* New York: Oxford University Press.

Mader, S. S. (2006). *Inquiry into life* (11th ed.). New York: McGraw-Hill.

Mader, S. S. (2007). *Biology* (9th ed.). New York: McGraw-Hill.

Magnuson, K. A., & Duncan, G. J. (2002). Poverty and parenting. In M. H. Bornstein (Ed.), *Handbook of parenting.* Mahwah, NJ: Erlbaum.

Magri, F., Cravello, L., Barili, L., Sarra, S., Cinchetti, W., Salmoiraghi, F., Micale, G., & Ferrari, E. (2006). Stress and dementia: The role of the hypothalamic-pituitary-adrenal axis. *Aging: Clinical and Experimental Research 18,* 167–170.

Maguire, S., Mann, M. K., Sibert, J., & Kemp, A. (2005). Are there patterns of bruising in childhood which are diagnostic or suggestive of abuse? A systematic review. *Archives of Diseases in Childhood, 90,* 182–186.

Mahler, M. (1979). *Separation-individuation* (Vol. 2). London: Jason Aronson.

Mahlstedt, D. L., & Welsh, L. A. (2005). Perceived causes of physical assault in heterosexual dating relationships. *Violence Against Women, 11,* 447–472.

Main, M. (2000). Attachment theory. In A. Kazdin (Ed.), *Encyclopedia of psychology.* Washington, DC, & New York: American Psychological Association and Oxford University Press.

Mainous, A. G., Majeed, A., Koopman, R. J., Baker, R., Everett, C. J., Tilley, B. C., & Diaz, V. A. (2006). Acculturation and diabetes among Hispanics: Evidence from the 1999–2002 National Health and Nutrition Examination Survey. *Public Health Reports, 121,* 60–66.

Maitland, T. E., Gomez-Marin, O., Weddle, D. O., & Fleming, L. E. (2006). Associations of nationality and race with nutritional status during perimenopause: Implications for public health practice. *Ethnicity and Disease, 16,* 201–216.

Majumdar, I., Paul, P., Talib, V. H., & Ranga, S. (2003). The effect of iron therapy on the growth of iron-replete and iron-deplete children. *Journal of Tropical Pediatrics, 49,* 84–88.

Mak, W. W. S., Chen, S. X., Wong, E. C., & Zane, N. W. S. (2005). A psychosocial model of stress-distress relationship among Chinese Americans. *Journal of Social and Clinical Psychology, 24,* 422–424.

Makrides, M., Neumann, M., Simmer, K., Pater, J., & Gibson, R. (1995). Are long-chain polyunsaturated fatty acids essential nutrients in infancy? *Lancet, 345,* 1463–1468.

Malat, J., Oh, H. J., & Hamilton, M. A. (2005). Poverty, experience, race, and child health. *Public Health Reports, 120,* 442–447.

Malley-Morrison, K. (Ed.). (2004). *International perspectives on family violence and abuse,* Mahwah, NJ: Erlbaum.

Mallis, D., Moisidis, K., Kirana, P.S., Papaharitou, S., Simos, G., & Hatzichristou, D. (2006). Moderate and severe erectile dysfunction equally affects life satisfaction. *Journal of Sexual Medicine, 3,* 442–449.

Malm, M., Martikainen, J., Klaukka, T., & Neuvonen, P. J. (2004). Prescription of hazardous drugs during pregnancy. *Drug Safety, 27,* 899–908.

Malmitis-Puchner, A., & Boutsikou, T. (2006). Adolescent pregnancy and perinatal outcome. *Pediatric Endocrinology Reviews, 3* (Suppl. 1), 170–171.

Mandler, J. M. (2000). Perceptual and conceptual processes in infancy. *Journal of Cognition and Development, 1,* 3–36.

Mandler, J. M. (2003). Conceptual categorization. In D. Rakison, & L. M. Oakes (Eds.), *Early category and concept development.* New York: Oxford University Press.

Mandler, J. M. (2004). *The foundations of mind.* New York: Oxford University Press.

Mandler, J. M. (2006). *Jean Mandler.* Available on the World Wide Web at: http://cogsci.ucsd.edu/-jean/.

Mandler, J. M., & McDonough, L. (1993). Concept formation in infancy. *Cognitive Development, 8,* 291–318.

Mandler, J. M., & McDonough, L. (1995). Long-term recall in infancy. *Journal of Experimental Child Psychology, 59,* 457–474.

Mannell, R. C. (2000). Older adults, leisure, and wellness. *Journal of Leisurability, 26,* 3–10.

Mannessier, L., Alie-Daram, S., Roubinet, F., & Brossard, Y. (2000). Prevention of fetal hemolytic disease: It is time to take action. *Transfusions in Clinical Biology, 7,* 527–532.

Manning, W. D., & Smock, P. J. (2002). First comes cohabitation and then comes marriage. *Journal of Family Issues, 23,* 1065–1087.

Manor, O., & Eisenbach, Z. (2003). Mortality after spousal loss: Are there sociodemographic differences? *Social Science and Medicine, 56,* 405–413.

Mansfield, A. (2005). Advancing midwifery practice. *Practicing Midwife, 8,* 4–5.

Mantler, J., Matejicek, A., Matheson, K., & Anisman, H. (2005). Coping with employment uncertainty: A comparison of employed and unemployed workers. *Journal of Occupational and Health Psychology, 10,* 200–209.

Manton, K. G., Corder, L., & Stallard, E. (1997, March 18). Chronic disability in elderly United States populations, 1982–1994. *Proceedings of the National Academy of Sciences, 94,* 2593–2598.

Manton, K. I. (1989). The stress-buffering role of spiritual support: Cross-sectional and prospective investigations. *Journal for the Scientific Study of Religion, 28,* 310–323.

Marcell, J. J. (2003). Sarcopenia: Causes, consequences, and preventions. *Journals of Gerontology A: Biological and Medical Sciences, 58,* M911–M916.

Marchman, V. (2003). Review of Santrock, J. W. *Child Development,* 10th Ed. (New York: McGraw-Hill).

Marchman, V., & Thal, D. (2005). Words and grammar. In M. Tomasello & D. I. Slobin (Eds.), *Beyond nature-nurture.* Mahwah, NJ: Erlbaum.

Marcia, J. E. (1980). Ego identity development. In J. Adelson (Ed), *Handbook of adolescent psychology.* New York: Wiley.

Marcia, J. E. (1987). The identity status approach to the study of ego identity development. In T. Honess & K. Yardley (Eds.), *Self and identity: Perspectives across the lifespan.* London: Routledge & Kegan Paul.

Marcia, J. E. (1994). The empirical study of ego identity. In H. A. Bosma, T. I. G. Grassfsma, H. D. Grotevant, & D. J. De Levita (Eds.), *Identity and development.* Newbury Park, CA: Sage.

Marcia, J. E. (1996). Unpublished review of J. W. Santrock's *Adolescence,* 7th ed. (Dubuque, IA: Brown & Benchmark).

Marcia, J. E. (2002). Identity and psychosocial development in adulthood. *Identity, 2,* 7–28.

Marcon, R. A. (2003). The physical side of development. *Young Children. 58* (No. 1), 80–87.

Marcovitch, H. (2004). Use of stimulants for attention deficit hyperactivity disorder: AGAINST. *British Medical Journal, 329,* 908–909.

Marcus, D. L., Mulrine, A., & Wong, K. (1999, September 13). How kids learn. *U.S. News & World Report,* pp. 44–50.

Marecek, J., Finn, S. E., & Cardell, M. (1988). Gender roles in the relationships of lesbians and gay men. In J. P. De Cecco (Ed.), *Gay relationships.* New York: Harrington Park Press.

Marek, K. D., Popejoy, L., Petroski, G., Mehr, D., Rantz, M., & Lin, W. C. (2005). Clinical outcomes of aging in place. *Nursing Research, 54,* 202–211.

Margolin, L. (1994). Child sexual abuse by uncles. *Child Abuse and Neglect, 18,* 215–224.

Mariani, E., Polidori, M. C., Cherubini, A., & Mecocci, P. (2005). Oxidative Stress in brain aging, neurodegenerative and vascular diseases: An overview. *Journal of Chromatography B.*

Marild, S., Hansson, S., Jodal, U., Oden, A., & Svedberg, K. (2004). Protective effect of breastfeeding against urinary tract infection. *Acta Pediatrics, 93,* 164–168.

Markides, K. S. (1995). Aging and ethnicity. *Gerontologist, 35,* 276–277.

Markides, K. S., & Rudkin, L. (1996). Race and ethnic diversity. In J. E. Birren (Ed.), *Encyclopedia of gerontology* (Vol. 2). San Diego: Academic Press.

Markson, E. W. (1995). Older women: The silent majority? *Gerontologist, 35,* 278–281.

Markus, H. R., Ryff, C. D., Curhan, K., & Palmersheim, K. (2004). In their own words: Well-being among high school and college-educated adults. In G. Brim, C. D. Ryff & R. Kessler (Eds.), *How healthy we are: A national study of well-being in midlife.* Chicago: University of Chicago Press.

Marsh-Prelesnik, J. (2006). Midwifery model of care—phase II: Midwife lessons. *Midwifery Today: International Midwife, 77,* 7–9.

Marsiglio, W. (2004). When stepfathers claim children: A conceptual analysis. *Journal of Marriage and the Family, 66,* 22–39.

Marsiske, M., Klumb, P. L., & Baltes, M. M. (1997). Everyday activity patterns and sensory functioning in old age. *Psychology and Aging, 12,* 444–457.

Marsiske, M., Lang, F. R., Baltes, M. M., & Baltes, P. B. (1995). Selective optimization with compensation: Life-span perspectives on successful human development. In R. A. Dixon & L. Backman (Eds.), *Compensating for psychological deficits and declines: Managing losses and promoting gains* (pp. 35–79). Hillsdale, NJ: Erlbaum.

Marsiske, M., & Margrett, J. A. (2006). Everyday problem solving and decision making. In J. E. Birren & K. W. Schaie (Eds.), *Handbook of the psychology of aging* (6th ed.). San Diego: Academic Press.

Martin, C. L., & Dinella L. (2001). Gender development: Gender schema theory. In J. Worell (Ed.), *Encyclopedia of women and gender.* San Diego: Academic Press.

Martin, C. L., & Fabes, R. A. (2001). The stability and consequences of young children's same-sex peer interactions. *Development Psychology, 37,* 431–446.

Martin, C. L., & Halverson, C. F. (1981). A schematic processing model of sex typing and stereotyping in children. *Child Development, 52,* 1119–1134.

Martin, C. L., & Ruble, D. (2004). Children's search for gender cues. *Current Directions in Psychological Science, 13,* 67–70.

Martin, E. D., & Sher, K. J. (1994). Family history of alcoholism, alcohol use disorders, and the five-factor model of personality. *Journal of Studies in Alcohol, 55,* 81–90.

Martin, J. A., Hamilton, B. E., Menacker, F., Sutton, P. D., & Matthews, T. J. (2005, November 15). Preliminary births for 2004: Infant and maternal health. *Health E-Stats.* Atlanta: National Center for Health Statistics.

Martin, J. A., Kochanek, K. D., Strobino, D. M., Guyer, B., & MacDorman, M. F. (2005). Annual summary of vital statistics—2003. *Pediatrics, 115,* 619–634.

Martin, M., & Willis, S. L. (2005). Midlife development: Past, present, and before directions. In S. L. Willis & M. Martin (Eds.), *Middle adulthood.* Thousand Oaks, CA: Sage.

Martin, M. T., Emery, R., & Peris, T. S. (2004). Children and parents in single-parent families. In M. Coleman & L. Ganong (Eds.), *Handbook of contemporary families.* Thousand Oaks, CA: Sage.

Martinez, E., & Halgunseth, L. (2004). Hispanics/Latinos. In M. Coleman & L. Ganong (Eds.), *Handbook of contemporary families.* Thousand Oaks, CA: Sage.

Martinez-Frias, M. L., Frias, J. P., Bermejo, F., Rodriguez-Pinilla, E., Prieto, L., & Frias, J. L. (2005). Pre-gestational maternal body mass index predicts an increased risk of congenital malformations in infants of mothers with gestational diabetes. *Diabetic Medicine, 22,* 775–781.

Marusic, A. (2005). History and geography of suicide: Could genetic risk factors account for the variation in suicide rates? *American Journal of Medical Genetics, 133C,* 43–47.

Maruta, T., Colligan, R. C., Malinchoc, M., & Offord, K. P. (2000). Optimists vs. pessimists: Survival rate among medical patients over a 30-year period, *Mayo Clinic Proceedings, 75,* 140–143.

Mason, P., & Narad, C. (2005). International adoption: A health and developmental perspective. *Seminars in Speech and Language, 26,* 1–9.

Masoro, E. J. (2006). Are age-associated diseases an integral part of aging? In E. J. Masoro & S. N. Austad (Eds.), *Handbook of the biology of aging* (6th ed.). San Diego: Academic Press.

Massetti, M., & Tasle, M., Le Page, O., Deredec, R., Babatasi, G., Burklas, D., Thuadet, S., Charbonneau, P., Hamon, M., Grollier, G., Gerard, J. L., & Khayat, A. (2005). Back from irreversibility: Extracorporeal life support for prolonged cardiac arrest. *Annals of Thoracic Surgery, 79,* 178–183.

Massey, Z., Rising, S. S., & Ickovics, J. (2006). CenteringPregnancy group prenatal care: Promoting relationship-centered care. *Journal of Obstetric, Gynecologic, and Neonatal Nursing, 35,* 286–294.

Masten, A. S. (2004). Regulatory processes, risk and resilience in adolescent development. *Annals of the New York Academy of Sciences, 1021,* 310–319.

Masten, A. S. (2005). Peer relationships and psychopathology in developmental perspective: Reflections on progress and promise. *Journal of Clinical Child and Adolescent Psychology, 34,* 87–92.

Mastropieri, M. A., & Scruggs, T. E. (2007). *Inclusive classroom* (3rd ed.). Upper Saddle River, NJ: Prentice-Hall.

Masur, E. F., Flynn, V., & Eichorst, D. L. (2005). Maternal responsive and directive behaviors and utterances as predictors of children's lexical development. *Journal of Child Language, 32,* 63–91.

Matheny, A. P., & Phillips, K. (2001). Temperament and context: Correlates of home environment with temperament continuity and change. In T. D. Wachs & G. A. Kohnstamm (Eds.), *Temperament in context.* Mahwah, NJ: Erlbaum.

Mathews, T. J., Menacker, F., & MacDorman, M. F. (2003). Infant mortality statistics from the 2001 period linked birth/infant death data set. *National Vital Statistics Reports, 52,* 1–28.

Mathole, T., Lindmark, G., Majoko, F., & Ahlberg, B. M. (2004). A qualitative study of women's perspectives of antenatal care in rural areas of Zimbabwe. *Midwifery, 20,* 122–132.

Matijasevich, A., Barros, F. C., Santos, I. S., & Yemini, A. (2006). Maternal caffeine consumption and fetal death: A case-control study in Uruguay. *Pediatric and Perinatal Epidemiology, 20,* 100–109.

Matlin, M. W. (2004). *The psychology of women* (5th ed.). Belmont, CA: Wadsworth.

Matsumoto, D. (2004). *Culture and psychology* (3rd ed.). Belmont, CA: Wadsworth.

Matthews, D. B., & others. (2005). Complex genetics of interactions of alcohol and CNS function and behavior. *Alcoholism: Clinical and Experimental Research, 29,* 1706–1719.

Matthias, R. F., Lubben, J. E., Atchison, K. A., & Schweitzer, S. O. (1997). Sexual activity and satisfaction among very old adults: Results from a community-dwelling Medicare population survey. *Gerontologist, 37,* 6–14.

Matzo, M. L., Sherman, D. W., Lo, K., Egan, K. A., Grant, M., & Rhome, A. (2003). Strategies for teaching loss, grief, and bereavement. *Nursing Education, 28,* 71–76.

Mauck, K. F., & Clarke, B. L. (2006). Diagnosis, screening, prevention, and treatment of osteoporosis. *Mayo Clinic Proceedings, 81,* 662–672.

Maurer, D., & Salapatek, P. (1976). Developmental changes in the scanning of faces by young infants. *Child Development, 47,* 523–527.

Mauro, V. P., Wood, I. C., Krushel, L., Crossin, K. L., & Edelman, G. M. (1994). Cell adhesion alters gene transcription in chicken embryo brain cells and mouse embryonal carcinoma cells. *Proceedings of the National Academy of Sciences USA, 91,* 2868–2872.

Maxwell, C. J., Hicks, M. S., Hogan, D. B., Basran, J., & Ebby, E. M. (2005). Supplemental use of antioxidant vitamins and subsequent risk of cognitive decline and dementia. *Dementia and Geriatric Cognitive Disorders, 20,* 45–51.

May, C. P., Hasher, L., & Foong, N. (2005). Implicit memory, age, and time of day: Paradoxical priming effects. *Psychological Science, 16,* 96–100.

May, F. B. (2006). *Teaching reading creatively: Reading and writing as communication* (7th ed.). Upper Saddle River, NJ: Prentice Hall.

May, V., Onarcan, M., Oleschowski, C., & Mayron, Z. (2004). International perspectives on the role of home care and hospice in aging and long-term care. *Caring, 23,* 14–17.

Mayes, L. (2003). Unpublished review of J. W. Santrock's *Tropical life-span development,* 2nd ed. (New York: McGraw Hill).

Mayeux, R. (2005). Mapping the new frontier: Complex genetic disorders. *Journal of Clinical Investigations, 115,* 1404–1407.

Mayhew, P. M., Thomas, C. D., Clement, J. G., Loveridge, N., Beck, T. J., Bonfield, W., Burgoyne, C. J., & Reeve, J. (2005). Relations between age, femoral neck cortical stability, and hip fracture risk. *Lancet, 366,* 129–135.

Maynard, J. (2005). Permanency mediation: A path to open adoption for children in out-of-home care. *Child Welfare, 84,* 507–526.

Mbonye, A. K., Neema, S., & Magnussen, P. (2006). Treatment-seeking practices for malaria in pregnancy among rural women in Mukono district, Uganda. *Journal of Biosocial Science, 38,* 221–237.

McAdams, D. P. (2001). Generativity in midlife. In M. E. Lachman (Ed.), *Handbook of midlife development.* New York: Wiley.

McAdoo, H. P. (2002). African-American parenting. In M. H. Bornstein (Ed.), *Handbook of parenting* (2nd ed., Vol. 4), Mahwah, NJ: Erlbaum.

McBurney, D. H., & White, T. L. (2007). *Research methods* (7th ed.). Belmont, CA: Wadsworth.

McCarter, R. J. M. (2006). Differential aging among skeletal muscles. In E. J. Masoro & S. N. Austad (Eds.), *Handbook of the biology of aging* (6th ed.). San Diego: Academic Press.

McCartney, K. (2003, July 16). Interview with Kathleen McCartney in A. Bucuvalas, "Child care and behavior." *HGSE News,* pp. 1–4. Cambridge, MA: Harvard Graduate School of Education.

McCarty, M. E., & Ashmead, D. H. (1999). Visual control of reaching and grasping in infants. *Developmental Psychology, 35,* 620–631.

McClain, C. S., Rosenfeld, B., & Breitbart, W. S. (2003, March). *The influence of spirituality on end-of-life despair in cancer patients close to death.* Paper presented at the meeting of American Psychosomatic Society, Phoenix.

McClellan, M. D. (2004, February 9). Captain Fantastic: The interview. *Celtic Nation,* pp. 1–9.

McConkie-Rosell, A., Finucane, B., Cronister, A., Abrams, L., Bennett, R. L., & Pettersen, B. J. (2005). Genetic counseling for fragile x syndrome: Updated recommendations of the national society of genetic counselors. *Journal of Genetic Counseling, 14,* 249–270.

McCool, W. F., & Simeone, S. A. (2002). Birth in the United States: An overview of trends past and present. *Nursing Clinics of North America, 37,* 735–746.

McCormick, C. B. (2003). Metacognition and learning. In I. B. Weiner (Ed.), *Handbook of psychology,* Vol. VII. New York: Wiley.

McCoy, S. J., Beal, J. M., & Watson, G. H. (2003). Endocrine factors and postpartum depression: A selected review. *Journal of Reproductive Medicine, 48,* 402–408.

McCrady, B. S., Zucker, R. A., Molina, B. S., Ammon, L., Ames, G. M., & Longabaugh, R. (2006). Social environmental influences on the development of alcohol problems. *Alcoholism: Clinical and Experimental Research, 30,* 688–699.

McCrae, R. R. (2001). Traits through time. *Psychological Inquiry, 12,* 85–87.

McCrae, R. R., & Costa, P. T. (1990). *Personality in adulthood.* New York: Guilford.

McCrae, R. R., & Costa, P. T. (2003). *Personality in adulthood* (2nd ed.). New York: Guilford.

McCrae, R. R., & Costa, P. T. (2006). Cross-cultural perspectives on adult personality trait development. In D. K. Mroczek & T. D. Little (Eds.), *Handbook of personality development.* Mahwah, NJ: Erlbaum.

McCrae, R. R., Costa, P. T., Lima, M. P., Simoes, A., Ostendorf, F., et al. (1999). Age differences in personality across the adult lifespan: Parallels in five cultures. *Developmental Psychology, 35,* 466–477.

McCray, T. M. (2004). An issue of culture: The effects of daily activities on prenatal care utilization patterns in rural South Africa. *Social Science Medicine, 59,* 1843–1855.

McCullough, J. L, & Kelly, K. M. (2006). Prevention and treatment of skin aging. *Annals of the New York Academy of Science, 1067,* 323–331.

McCullough, M. E. (1995). Prayer and health: Conceptual issues, research review, and research agenda. *Journal of Psychology and Theology, 23,* 15–29.

McCullough, M. E., Enders, C. K., Brion, S. L., & Jain, A. R. (2005). The varieties of religious development in adulthood: A longitudinal investigation of religion and rational choice. *Journal of Personality and Social Psychology, 89,* 78–89.

McCullough, M. E., Hoyt, W. T., Larson, D. B., Koening, H. G., & Thoresen, C. (2000). Religious involvement and mortality: A meta-analytic review. *Health psychology, 19,* 211–222.

McCullough, M. E., & Laurenceau, J. P. (2005). Religiousness and the trajectory of self-rated health across adulthood. *Personality and Social Psychology Bulletin, 31,* 560–573.

McDaniel, M. A., Einstein, G. O., Stout, A. C., & Morgan, Z. (2003). Aging and maintaining intentions over delays: Do it or lose it. *Psychology and Aging, 18,* 823–835.

McDaniels, G., Issac, M., Brooks, H., & Hatch, A. (2005). Confronting K-3 challenges in an era of accountability. *Young Children, 60* (no. 2), 20–26.

McDermott, N.M., & others (2006). Obesity, weight change, and functional decline in peripheral arterial disease. *Journal of Vascular Surgery, 43,* 1198–1204.

McDonald, S., Murphy, K., Beyene, J., & Ohlsson, A. (2005). Perinatal outcomes of in vitro fertilization twins: A systematic review and meta-analyses. *American Journal of Obstetrics and Gynecology, 193,* 141–152.

McDougall, G. J. (2004). Memory's self-efficacy and memory performance among black and white elders. *Nursing Research, 53,* 323–331.

McDougall, G. J., Strauss, M. E., Holston, E. C., & Martin, M. (1999, November). *Memory self-efficacy and memory-anxiety as predictors of memory performance in at-risk elderly.* Paper presented at the meeting of the Gerontological Society of America, San Francisco.

McFarlane, J., Malecha, A., Gist, J., Watson, K., Batten, E., Hall, I., & Smith, S. (2005). Intimate partner sexual assault against women and associated victim substance use, suicidality, and risk factors for femicide. *Issues in Mental Health Nursing, 26,* 953–967.

McGarvey, C., McDonnell, M., Hamilton, K., O'Regan, M., & Matthews, T. (2006). An 8 year study of risk factors for SIDS: Bed-sharing versus non-bed-sharing. *Archives of Disease in Childhood, 91,* 318–323.

McGuire, L., Kiecolt-Glaser, J. K., & Glaser, R. (2002). Depressive symptoms and lymphocyte proliferation in older adults. *Journal of Abnormal Psychology, 111,* 192–197.

McHale, J. P., Johnson, D., & Sinclair, R. (1999). Family dynamics, preschoolers' family representations, and preschool peer relationships. *Early Education and Development, 10,* 373–401.

McHale, J. P., Khazan, I., Erera, P., Rotman, T., DeCourcey, W., & McConnell, M. (2002). Coparenting in diverse family systems. In M. H. Bornstein (Ed.), *Handbook of parenting* (2nd ed., Vol. 3). Mahwah, NJ: Erlbaum.

McHale, J. P., Kuersten-Hogan, R., & Rao, N. (2004). Growing points for coparenting theory and research. *Journal of Adult Development, 11,* 221–234.

McHale, S. M., Crouter, A. C., & Whiteman, S. D. (2003). The family contexts of gender development in childhood and adolescence. *Social Development, 12,* 125–152.

McHugh, K., Kiely, E. M., & Spitz, L. (2006, in press). Imaging of conjoined twins. *Pediatric Radiology.*

McIntyre, J. (2005). Preventing mother-to-child transmission of HIV: Successes and challenges. *British Journal of Obstetrics and Gynecology, 112,* 1196–1203.

McKain, W. C. (1972). A new look at older marriages. *The Family Coordinator, 21,* 61–69.

McKee, J. K., Poirier, F. E., & McGraw, W. S. (2005). *Understanding human evolution* (5th ed.), Upper Saddle River, NJ: Prentice Hall.

McKellar, J., Stewart, E., & Humphreys, K. (2003). Alcoholics Anonymous involvement and positive alcohol-related outcomes. *Journal of Consulting and Clinical Psychology, 71,* 302–308.

McKenna, J. J., Mosko, S. S., & Richard, C. A. (1997). Bedsharing promotes breastfeeding. *Pediatrics, 100,* 214–219.

McKnight, A. J., & McKnight A. S. (1993). The effect of cellular phone use upon driver attention. *Accident Analysis and Prevention, 25,* 259–265.

McLaughlin, K. (2003, December 30). Commentary in K. Painter, "Nurse dispenses dignity for dying." *USA Today,* Section D, pp. 1–2.

McLean, I. A., Balding, V., & White, C. (2005). Further aspects of male-on-male rape and sexual assault in greater Manchester. *Medical Science and Law, 45,* 225–232.

McLearn, K. T. (2004). Narrowing the income gaps in preventive care for young children: Families in healthy steps. *Journal of Urban Health, 81,* 556–567.

McLeod, J. D. (1996). Life events. In J. E. Birren (Ed.,) *Encyclopedia of gerontology* (Vol. 1). San Diego: Academic Press.

McLoyd, V. C. (2005). Pathways to academic achievement among children from immigrant families: A commentary. In C. R. Cooper, C. T. Garcia Coll, W. T. Bartko, H. M. Davis, & C. Chatman (Eds.), *Developmental pathways through middle childhood.* Mahwah, NJ: Erlbaum.

McLoyd, V. C., Aikens, N. L., & Burton, L. M. (2006). Childhood poverty, policy, and practice. In W. Damon & R. Lerner (Eds.), *Handbook of child psychology* (6th ed.). New York: Wiley.

McMillan, J. H., & Schumacher, S. (2006). *Research in education: Evidence based inquiry* (6th ed.). Boston: Allyn & Bacon.

McNamara, F., & Sullivan, C. E. (2000). Obstructive sleep apnea in infants. *Journal of Pediatrics, 136,* 318–323.

McReynolds, J. L., & Rossen, E. K. (2004). Importance of physical activity, nutrition, and social support for optimal aging. *Clinical Nurse Specialist, 18,* 200–206.

McTigue, K. M., Garrett, J. M., & Popkin, B. M. (2002). The natural history of the development of obesity in a cohort of young U.S. adults between 1981 and 1998. *Annals of Internal Medicine, 136,* 857–864.

McVeigh, C. (2005). Perimenopause: More than hot flashes and night sweats for some Australian women. *Journal of Obstetric, Gynecological, and Neonatal Nursing, 34,* 21–37.

McVeigh, C. A., Baafi, M., & Williamson, M. (2002). Functional status after fatherhood: An Australian study. *Journal of Obstetrics, Gynecology, and Neonatal Nursing, 31,* 165–171.

McWhorter, K. T. (2006). *Vocabulary simplified* (2nd ed.). Upper Saddle River, NJ: Prentice Hall.

MedLine Plus. (2006). *Medical encyclopedia.* Available on the Internet at: www.nim.nih.gov/medlineplus/ency/

Mehra, S., & Agrawal, D. (2004). Adolescent health determinants for pregnancy and child health outcomes among the urban poor. *Indian Pediatrics, 41,* 137–145.

Mehta, A., Hindmarsch, P. C., Stanhope, R. G., Turton, J. P., Cole, T. J., Preece, M. A., & Dattani, M. T. (2005). The role of growth hormone in determing birth size and early postnatal growth, using congenital growth hormone deficiency (GHD) as a model. *Clinical Endocrinology, 63,* 223–231.

Meier, S., Brauer, A. U., Heimrich, B., Nitsch, R., & Savaskan, N. E. (2004). Myelination in the hippocampus during development and following lesion. *Cellular and Molecular Life Sciences, 61,* 1082–1094.

Meis, P. J., & Peaceman, A. M. (2003). Prevention of recurrent preterm delivery by 17-alpha-hydroxyprogesterone caproate. *New England Journal of Medicine, 348,* 2379–2385.

Melenhorst, A.-S., Rogers, W. A., & Bouwhuis, D. G. (2006). Older adults' motivated choice for technological innovation: Evidence from benefit-driven selectivity. *Psychology and Aging, 21,* 190–195.

Melgar-Quinonez, H. R., & Kaiser, L. L. (2004). Relationship of child-feeding practices to overweight in low-income Mexican-American preschool-aged children. *Journal of the American Dietetic Association, 104,* 1110–1119.

Meltzoff, A. N. (1988). Infant imitation and memory: Nine-month-old infants in immediate and deferred tests. *Child Development, 59,* 217–225.

Meltzoff, A. N. (2002). Elements of a developmental theory of imitation. In A. N. Meltzoff, & W. Prinz (Eds.), *The imitative mind: Development, evolution, and brain bases.* Cambridge: Cambridge University Press.

Meltzoff, A. N. (2004). Imitation as a mechanism of social cognition: Origins of empathy, theory of mind, and the representation of action. In U. Goswami (Ed.), *Blackwell handbook of childhood cognitive development.* Malden, MA: Blackwell.

Meltzoff, A. N. (2005). Imitation. In B. Hopkins (Ed.), *Cambridge encyclopedia of child development.* Cambridge: Cambridge University Press.

Meltzoff, A. N., & Moore, M. K. (1999). A new foundation for cognitive development in infancy: The birth of the representational infant. In E. K. Skolnick, K. Nelson, S. A. Gelman, & P. H. Miller (Eds.), *Conceptual development.* Mahwah, NJ: Erlbaum.

Menec, V. H. (2003). The relation between everyday activities and successful aging: A 6-year longitudinal study. *Journals of Gerontology B: Psychological Sciences and Social Sciences, 58,* 574–582.

Menec, V. H., MacWilliam, L., & Aoki, F. Y. (2002). Hospitalizations and death due to respiratory illnesses during influenza seasons: A comparison of community residents, senior housing residents, and nursing home residents. *Journal of Gerontology: Biological and Medical Science A, 57,* M629–M635.

Menn, L., & Stoel-Gammon, C. (2005). Phonological development: Learning Sounds and Sound Patterns. In J. Berko Gleason (Ed.), *The development of language* (6th ed.). Boston: Allyn & Bacon.

Menshikova, E. V., Ritov, B. V., Fairfull, L., Ferrell, R. E., Kelley, D. E., & Goodpaster, B. H. (2006). Effects of exercise on mitochondrial content and function in aging human skeletal muscle. *Journals of Gerontology A: Biological Sciences and Medical Sciences, 61,* 534–540.

Menyuk, P., Liebergott, J., & Schultz, M. (1995). *Early language development in full-term and premature infants.* Hillsdale, NJ: Erlbaum.

Merchant, R. H., & Lala, M. M. (2005). Prevention of mother-to-child transmission of HIV—an overview. *Indian Journal of Medical Research, 121,* 489–501.

Meredith, N. V. (1978). Research between 1960 and 1970 on the standing height of young children in different parts of the world. In H. W. Reece & L. P. Lipsitt (Eds.), *Advances in child development and behavior* (Vol. 12). New York: Academic Press.

Merlob, P., Sapir, O., Sulkes, J., & Fisch, B. (2005). The prevalence of major congenital malformations during two periods of time, 1986–1994 and 1995–2002 in newborns conceived by assisted reproduction technology. *European Journal of Medical Genetics, 48,* 5–11.

Merrick, J., Morad, M., Halperin, I., & Kandel, I. (2005). Physical fitness and adolescence. *International Journal of Adolescent Medicine, 17,* 89–91.

Merrill, S. S., & Verbrugge, L. M. (1999). Health and disease in midlife. In S. L. Willis & J. D. Reid (Eds.), *Life in the middle: Psychological and social development in middle age.* San Diego: Academic Press.

Metts, S. (2004). First sexual involvement in romantic relationships. In J. H. Harvey, A. Wenzel, & S. Sprecher (Eds.), *The handbook of sexuality in close relationships.* Mahwah, NJ: Erlbaum.

Metz, E. C., & Youniss, J. (2005). Longitudinal gains in civic development through school-based required service. *Political Psychology, 26,* 413–437.

Meyer, I. H. (2003). Prejudice, social stress, and mental health in gay, lesbian, and bisexual populations: Conceptual issues and research evidence. *Psychological Bulletin, 129,* 674–697.

Michael, R. T., Gagnon, J. H., Laumann, E. O., & Kolata, G. (1994). *Sex in America.* Boston: Little, Brown.

Michel, G. L. (1981). Right-handedness: A consequence of infant supine head-orientation preference? *Science, 212,* 685–687.

Milan, S., Ickovics, J. R., Kershaw, T., Leis, J., Meade, C., & Ethier, K. (2004). Prevalence, course, and predictors of emotional distress in pregnant and parenting adolescents. *Journal of Consulting and Clinical Psychology, 72,* 328–340.

Miller Johnson, S., Coie, J., & Malone, P. S. (2003). *Do aggression and peer rejection in childhood predict early adult outcomes?* Paper presented at the meeting of the Society for Research in Child Development, Tampa.

Miller, B. C., Benson, B., & Galbraith, K. A. (2001). Family relationships and adolescent pregnancy risk: A research synthesis. *Developmental Review, 21,* 1–38.

Miller, B. C., Fan, X., Christensen, M., Grotevant, H. D., & von Dulmen, M. (2000). Comparisons of adopted and nonadopted adolescents in a large, nationally representative sample. *Child Development, 71,* 1458–1473.

Miller, E. R., Pastor-Barriuso, R., Dalal, D., Riemersma, R. A., Appel, L. J., & Gullar, E. (2005, in press). Meta-analysis: High-dosage vitamin E supplementation may increase allcause mortality. *Annals of Internal Medicine.*

Miller, J. B. (1986). *Toward a new psychology of women* (2nd ed.). Boston: Beacon Press.

Miller, J. G. (2006). Insights into moral development from cultural psychology. In M. Killen & J. G. Smetana (Eds.), *Handbook of moral development.* Mahwah, NJ: Erlbaum.

Miller, L. C. (2005). International adoption, behavior, and mental health. *Journal of the American Medical Association, 293,* 2533–2535.

Miller, L., Chan, W., Comfort, K., & Tirella, L. (2005). Health of children adopted from Guatemala: Comparison of orphanage and foster care. *Pediatrics, 115,* e710–e717.

Miller, P. H., & Seier, W. I. (1994). Strategy utilization deficiencies in children: When, where, and why. In H. W. Reese (Ed.), *Advances in child development and behavior* (Vol. 24). New York: Academic Press.

Miller-Day, M. A. (2004). *Communication among grandmothers, mothers, and adult daughters.* Mahwah, NJ: Erlbaum.

Miller-Jones, D. (1989). Culture and testing. *American Psychologist, 44,* 360–366.

Miller-Loncar, C., Lester, B. M., Seifer, R., Lagasse, L. L., Bauer, C. R., Shankaran, S., Bada, H. S., Wright, L. L., Smeriglio, V. L., Bigsby, R., & Liu, J. (2005). Predictors of motor development in children prenatally exposed to cocaine. *Neurotoxicology and Teratology, 27,* 213–220.

Milsom, A., & Gallo, L. L. (2006). Bullying in middle schools: Prevention and intervention. *Middle School Journal, 37,* 12–19.

Mimura, M., & Yano, M. (2006). Memory impairment and awareness of memory deficits in early-stage Alzheimer's disease. *Review of Neuroscience, 17,* 253–266.

Minczykowski, A., Gryczynska, M., Ziemnicka, K., Sowinksi, J., & Wysocki, H. (2005). The influence of growth hormone therapy on ultrasound myocardial tissue characterization in patients with childhood onset GH deficiency. *International Journal of Cardiology, 101,* 257–263.

Minino, A. M., Heron, M. P., & Smith, B. L. (2006, June 28). Deaths: Preliminary data for 2004. *National Vital Statistics Report, 54,* 1–49.

Minkler, M., & Fuller-Thompson, E. (2005). African American grandparents raising grandchildren: A national study using the Census 2000 American Community Survey. *Journals of Gerontology B: Psychological Sciences and Social Sciences, 60,* S82–S92.

Minnes, S., Robin, N. H., Alt, A., Kirchner, H. L., Satayathum, S., Salbert, B. A., Ellison, L., & Singer, L. T. (2005). Dysmorphic and anthropometric outcomes in 6-year-old prenatally exposed children. *Neurotoxicology and Teratology, 28,* 28–38.

Minns, R. A., & Busuttil, A. (2004). Patterns of presentation of the shaken baby syndrome: Four types of inflicted brain injury predominate. *British Medical Journal, 328,* 766.

Minuchin, P. (2001). Looking toward the horizon: Present and future in the study of family systems. In J. P. McHale & W. S. Grolnick (Eds.), *Retrospect and prospect in the psychological study of families.* Mahwah, NJ: Erlbaum.

Minuchin, P. O., & Shapiro, E. K. (1983). The school as a context for social development. In P. H. Mussen (Ed.), *Handbook of child psychology* (4th ed., Vol. 4). New York: Wiley.

Mir, P., Matsunaga, K., Gilio, F., Quinn, N. P., Siebner, H. R., & Rothwell, J. C. (2005). Dopaminergic drugs restore facilitatory premotor-motor interactions in Parkinson disease. *Neurology, 64,* 1906–1912.

Miranda, M. L. (2004). The implications of developmentally appropriate practices for the kindergarten general music classroom. *Journal of Research in Music Education, 52,* 43–53.

Mirescu, C., & Gould, E. (2006). Stress and adult neurogenesis. *Hippocampus, 16,* 233–238.

Missonier, P., Gold, G., Leonards, U., Costa-Fazio, L., Michel, J. P., Ibanez, V., & Giannakopoulos, P. (2004). Aging and working memory: Early deficits in EEG activation of posterior cortical areas. *Journal of Neural Transmission, 111,* 1141–1154.

Mitchell, E. A., Blair, P. S., & L'Hoir, M. P. (2006). Should pacifiers be recommended to prevent sudden infant death syndrome? *Pediatrics, 117,* 1811–1812.

Mitchell, E. A., Stewart, A. W., Crampton, P., & Salmond, C. (2000). Deprivation and sudden infant death syndrome. *Social Science and Medicine, 51,* 147–150.

Mitchell, K. J., Raye, C. L., Johnson, M. K., & Greene, E. J. (2006). An fMRI investigation of short-term source memory in young and older adults. *Neuroimage, 30,* 627–633.

Mitchell, K. S., & Mazzeo, S. E. (2004). Binge and psychological distress in ethnically diverse undergraduate men and women. *Eating Behavior, 5,* 157–169.

Mitchell, M., & Catron, G. (2002). Teaching grief and bereavement: Involving support groups in educating student midwives. *The Practicing Midwife, 5,* 26–27.

Mitchell, M. L. & Jolley, J. M. (2007). *Research design explained* (6th ed.). Belmont, CA: Wadsworth.

Mitchell, R. W. (1993). Mental models of mirror-self-recognition: Two theories. *New Ideas in Psychology, 11,* 295–325.

Mitchell, V., & Helson, R. (1990). Women's prime of life. Is it the 50s? *Psychology of Women Quarterly, 14,* 451–470.

Miyake, K, Chen, S., & Campos, J. (1985). Infants' temperament, mothers' mode of interaction and attachment in Japan: An interim report. In I. Bretherton & F. Waters (Eds.), *Growing points of attachment theory and research, Monographs of the Society for Research in Child Development, 50* (1–2, Serial No. 109), 276–297.

Moberg, D. O. (2005). Research in spirituality, religion, and aging. *Journal of Gerontological Social Work, 45,* 11–40.

Modell, J., & Elder, G. H. (2002). Child development in history: So what's new? In W. W. Hartup & R. A. Weinberg (Eds.), *Child psychology in retrospect and prospect.* Mahwah, NJ: Erlbaum.

Moen, P. (1998). Recasting careers: Changing reference groups, risks, and realities. *Generations, 22,* 40–45.

Moen, P., Spencer, D. C. (2006). Converging divergences in age, gender, health, and well-being: Strategic selection in the third age. In R. H. Binstock & L. K. George (Eds.), *Handbook of Aging and the Social Sciences* (6th ed.). San Diego: Academic Press.

Moen, P., & Wethington, E. (1999). Midlife development in a life course context. In S. L. Willis & J. D. Reid (Eds.), *Life in the middle: Psychological and social development in middle age.* San Diego: Academic Press.

Moise, K. J. (2005). Fetal RhD typing with free DNA I maternal plasma. *American Journal of Obstetrics and Gynecology, 192,* 663–665.

Mok, K. H., Lee, V. W., & So, K. F. (2004). Retinal nerve fiber loss in high- and normal-tension glaucoma by optical coherence tomography. *Optometry and Vision Science, 81,* 369–372.

Molina, I. A., Dulmus, C. N., Sower, K. M. (2005). Secondary prevention for youth violence: A review of selected school-based programs. *Brief Treatment & Crisis Intervention, 5,* 1–3.

Monastirli, A., & others. (2005). Short stature, type E brachydactyly, gynecomastia, and cryptorchidism in a patient with 47, XYY/45, X/46, XY mosaicism. *American Journal of Medical Science, 329,* 208–210

Monsour, M. (2006). Communication and gender among adult friends. In B. J. Dow & J. Wood (Eds.), *The Sage handbook of gender and communication.* Thousand Oaks, CA: Sage.

Montemayor, R. (1982). The relationship between parent-adolescent conflict and the amount of time adolescents spend with parents, peers, and alone. *Child Development, 53,* 1512–1519.

Moon, M. (2006). Organization and financing of health care. In R. H. Binstock & L. K. George (Eds.), *Handbook of aging and the social sciences* (6th ed.). San Diego: Academic Press.

Moon, R. Y., Oden, R. P., & Grady, K. C. (2004). Back to sleep: An educational intervention with women, infants, and children program clients. *Pediatrics, 113,* 542–547.

Mooney, C. G. (2006). *Theories of childhood.* Upper Saddle River, NJ: Prentice Hall.

Mooradian, A.D., & Korenman, S.G. (2006). Management of the cardinal features of andropause. *American Journal of Therapy, 13,* 145–160.

Moore, D. (2001). *The dependent gene.* New York: W. H. Freeman.

Moore, V. M., & Davies, M. J. (2005). Diet during pregnancy, neonatal outcomes, and later health. *Reproduction, Fertility, and Development, 17,* 341–348.

Moos, M. K. (2006). Prenatal care: Limitations and opportunities. *Journal of Obstetric, Gynecologic, and Neonatal Nursing, 35,* 278–285.

Moos, R. H. (1986). Work as a human context. In M. S. Pallack & R. Perloff (Eds.), *Psychology and work: Productivity, change, and employment.* Washington, DC: American Psychological Association.

Moos, R. H., & Moos, B. S. (2005). Sixteen-year changes and stable remission among treated and untreated individuals with alcohol use disorders. *Drug and Alcohol Dependence.*

Moran, S., & Gardner, H. (2006). Extraordinary achievements. In W. Damon & R. Lerner (Eds.).

Handbook of child psychology (6th ed.). New York: Wiley.

Moreira, P. I., Zhu, X., Nunomura, A., Smith, M. A., & Perry, G. (2006). Therapeutic options in Alzheimer's disease. *Expert Reviews in Neurotherapy, 6,* 897–910.

Morelli, G. A., Rogoff, B., Oppenheim, D., & Goldsmith, D. (1992). Cultural variation in infants' sleeping arrangements: Questions of independence. *Developmental Psychology, 28,* 604–613.

Moren-Cross, J. L., & Lin, N. (2006). Social networks and health. In R. H. Binstock & L. K. George (Eds.), *Handbook of aging and the social sciences* (6th ed.). San Diego: Academic Press.

Moreno, A., Posada, G. E., & Goldyn, D. T. (2006). Presence and quality of touch influence coregulation in mother-infant dyads. *Infancy, 9,* 1–20.

Moretti, R., Torre, P., Antonello, R. M., & Cazzato, G. (2006). Behavioral alterations and vascular dementia. *Neurologist, 12,* 43–47.

Morgan, J. D. (2003). Spirituality. In C. D. Bryant (Ed.), *Handbook of death and dying.* Thousand Oaks, CA: Sage.

Morgentaler, A., Barada, J., Niederberger, C., Donatucci, C., Garcia, C. S., Natanegara, F., Ahuja, S., & Wong, D. G. (2006). Efficacy and safety of tadalafil across ethnic groups and various risk factors in men with erectile dysfunction: Use of a novel noninferiority study design. *Journal of Sexual Medicine, 3,* 492–503.

Morley J. E. (2003). Anorexia and weight loss in older persons. *Journals of Gerontology A: Biological and Medical Sciences, 58,* M131–M137.

Morris, K. (2006). Issues and answers: Women and retirement. *Ohio Nurses Review, 81,* 11–12.

Morris, S. N., & Johnson, N. R. (2005). Exercise during pregnancy: A critical appraisal of the literature. *Journal of Reproductive Medicine, 50,* 181–188.

Morrison, G. (2006). *Teaching in America* (4th ed.). Boston: Allyn & Bacon.

Morrison, G. S. (2006). *Fundamentals of early childhood education* (4th ed.). Upper Saddle River, NJ: Prentice Hall.

Morrongiello, B. A., Fenwick, K. D., & Chance, G. (1990). Sound localization acuity in very young infants: An observer-based testing procedure. *Developmental Psychology, 26,* 75–84.

Morrow, C. E., Bandstra, E. S., Anthony, J. C., Ofir, A. Y., Xue, L., & Reyes, M. B. (2003). Influence of prenatal cocaine exposure on early language development: Longitudinal findings from four months to three years of age. *Journal of Developmental and Behavioral Pediatrics, 24,* 39–50.

Morrow, L. (1988, August 8). Through the eyes of children. *Time,* pp. 32–33.

Mortimer, J. T., & Larson, R. W. (2002). Macrostructural trends and the reshaping of adolescence. In J. T. Mortimer & R. W. Larson (Eds.), *The changing adolescent experience.* New York: Cambridge University Press.

Moscicki, E. K., & Caine, E. D. (2004). Opportunities of life: Preventing suicide in elderly patients. *Archives of Internal Medicine, 164,* 1171–1172.

Mosconi, L., Tsui, W. H., De Santi, S., Li, J., Rusinek, H., Convit, A., Li, Y., Bopanna, M., & de Leon, M. J. (2005). Reduced hippocampal metabolism in MCI and AD: Automated FDG-PET analysis. *Neurology, 64,* 1860–1867.

Moss, T. J. (2006). Respiratory consequences of preterm birth. *Clinical and Experimental Pharmacology and Physiology, 33,* 280–284.

Motta, M., Bennati, E., Ferlito, L., Malaguarnera, M., & Mottal, L. (2005). Successful aging in

centenarians: Myths and realty. *Archives of Gerontology and Geriatrics, 40,* 241–251.

Moules, N. J., Simonson, K., Prins, M., Angus, P., & Bell, J. M. (2004). Making room for grief. *Nursing Inquiry, 11,* 99–107.

Mounts, N. S. (2002). Parental management of adolescent peer relationships in context: The role of parenting style. *Journal of Family Psychology, 16,* 58–69.

Moya, J., Bearer, C. F., & Etzel, R. A. (2004). Children's behavior and physiology and how it affects exposure to environmental contaminants. *Pediatrics, 113* (Suppl. 4), 996–1006.

Mozingo, J. N., Davis, M. W., Droppleman, P. G., & Merideth, A. (2000). "It wasn't working": Women's experiences with short-term breast feeding. *American Maternal Journal of Nursing, 25,* 120–126.

Mroczek, D. K. (2001). Age and emotion in adulthood. *Current Directions in Psychological Science, 10,* 87–90.

Mroczek, D. K., Almeida, D. M., Spiro, A., & Pafford, C. (2006). Intraindividual stability and change in personality. In D. K. Mroczek & T. D. Little (Eds.), *Handbook of personality development.* Mahwah, NJ: Erlbaum.

Mroczek, D. K., & Kolarz, C. M. (1998). The effect of age on positive and negative affect: A developmental perspective on happiness. *Journal of Personality and Social Psychology, 75,* 1333–1349.

Mroczek, D. K., Spiro, A., & Griffin, P. W. (2006). Personality and aging. In J. E. Birren & K. W. Schaie (Eds.), *Handbook of the psychology of aging* (6th ed.). San Diego: Academic Press.

Mufti, P., Setna, F., & Nazir, K. (2006). Early neonatal mortality: Effects of interventions on survival of low birth babies weighing 1000–2000g. *The Journal of the Pakistan Medical Association, 56,* 174–176.

Mullick, S., Beksinska, M., & Msomi, S. (2005). Treatment for syphilis in antenatal care. *Sexually Transmitted Infections, 81,* 220–222.

Mullis, I. V. S. (1999, April). *Using TIMSS to gain new perspectives about different school organizations and policies.* Paper presented at the meeting of the American Educational Research Association, Montreal.

Mumme, D. L., Fernald, A., & Herrera, C. (1996). Infants' responses to facial & emotional signals in a social referencing paradigm. *Child Development, 67,* 3219–3237.

Munakata, Y. (2006). Information processing approaches to development. In W. Damon & R. Lerner (Eds.), *Handbook of child psychology* (6th ed.). New York: Wiley.

Murnane, R. J., & Levy, F. (1996). *Teaching the new basic skills.* New York: Free Press.

Murphy, D. J., Fowlie, P. W., & McGuire, W. (2004), Obstetric issues and preterm birth. *British Medical Journal, 329,* 783–786.

Murphy, J. G., McDevitt-Murphy, M. E., & Barnett, N. P. (2005). Drink and be merry? Gender, life satisfaction, and alcohol consumption among college students. *Psychology of Addictive Behaviors, 19,* 184–191.

Murphy, M. C. (1996). Stressors on the college campus: A comparison of 1985 and 1993. *Journal of College Student Development, 37,* 20–28.

Murphy, S. A., Johnson, L. C., Chung, I., Beaton, R. D. (2003). The prevalence of PTSD following the violent death of a child and predictors of change 5 years later. *Journal of Traumatic Stress, 16,* 17–25.

Murray, C. S., Woodcock, A., Smillie, F. I., Cain, G., Kissen, P., & Castovie, A. (2004). Tobacco smoke exposure, wheeze, and atopy. *Pediatric Pulmonology, 37,* 492–498.

Murray, J. P. (2006). The violent face of television: Research and discussion. In N. Pecora, J. P. Murray, & E. A. Wartella (Eds.), *Children and television*. Mahwah, NJ: Erlbaum.

Muskesh, B. N., Le, A., Dimitrov, P. N., Ahmed, S., Taylor, H. R., & McCarty, C. A. (2006). Development of cataract and associated risk factors: The Visual Impairment Project. *Archives of Ophthalmology, 124*, 79–85.

Mussen, P. H., Honzik, M., & Eichorn, D. (1982). Early adult antecedents of life satisfaction at age 70. *Journal of Gerontology, 37*, 316–322.

Mustanski, B. S., Chivers, M. L., & Bailey, J. M. (2003). A critical review of recent biological research on human sexual orientation. *Annual Review of Sex Research, 13*, 89–140.

Muth, A. S. (Ed.). (2000). *Death and dying sourcebook: Basic consumer health information for the layperson about end-of-life care and related ethical issues*. Detroit: Omnigraphics.

Myers, A., & Hansen, C. (2006). *Experimental psychology* (6th ed.). Belmont, CA: Wadsworth.

Myers, B. J., Dawson, K. S., Britt, G. C., Lodder, D. E., Meloy, L. D., Saunders, M. K., Meadows, S. L., & Elswick, R. K. (2003). Prenatal cocaine exposure and infant performance on the Brazelton Neonatal Behavioral Assessment Scale. *Substance Use and Misuse, 38*, 2065–2096.

Myers, D. G. (2000). *The American paradox*. New Haven, CT: Yale University Press.

Myers, D. L. (1999). *Excluding violent youths from juvenile court: The effectiveness of legislative waiver*. Doctoral dissertation, University of Maryland, College Park, MD.

Myers, M. G., & MacPherson, L. (2004). Smoking cessation efforts among substance abusing adolescents. *Drug and Alcohol Dependency, 73*, 209–213.

Myerson, J., Rank, M. R., Raines, F. Q., & Schnitzler, M. A. (1998). Race and general cognitive ability: The myth of diminishing returns in education. *Psychological Science, 9*, 139–142.

Nader, K. (2001). Treatment methods for childhood trauma. In J. P. Wilson, M. J. Friedman, & J. Lindy (Eds.), *Treating psychological trauma and PTSD*. New York: Guilford Press.

Naess, H., Nyland, H. I., Thomassen, L., Aarseth, J., & Myher, K. M. (2004). Etiology of and risk factors for cerebral infarction in young adults in western Norway: A population-based case-control study. *European Journal of Neurology, 11*, 25–30.

NAEYC. (2002). *Early learning standards: Creating the conditions for success*. Washington, DC: National Association for the Education of Young Children.

NAEYC. (2005). *Critical facts about young children and early childhood in the United States*. Washington, DC: Author.

Naglieri, J. (2000). Stanford-Binet Intelligence Scale. In A. Kazdin (Ed.), *Encyclopedia of psychology*. Washington, DC, & New York: American Psychological Association and Oxford University Press.

Nagy, M. (1948). The child's theories concerning death. *Journal of Genetic Psychology, 73*, 3–27.

Nagy, Z., Westerberg, H., & Klingberg, T. (2004). Maturation of white matter is associated with the development of cognitive functions during childhood. *Journal of Cognitive Neuroscience, 16*, 1227–1233.

Nair, K. S. (2005). Aging muscle. *American Journal of Clinical Nutrition, 81*, 953–963.

Nakai, K., & others. (2004). The Tohoku Study of Child Development: A cohort study of effects of perinatal exposure to methylmercury and environmentally persistent organic pollutants on neurobehavioral development in Japanese children. *Tohoku Journal of Experimental Medicine, 202*, 227–237.

Nakamura, J., & Csikszentmihalyi, M. (2002). The concept of flow. In C. R. Snyder & S. J. Lopez (Eds.), *Handbook of positive psychology*. New York: Oxford University Press.

Nakano, H., & Blumstein, S. E. (2004). Deficits in thematic processes in Broca's and Wernicke's aphasia. *Brain and Language, 88*, 96–107.

Nansel, T. R., Overpeck, M., Pilla, R., Ruan, W., Simons-Morton, B., & Scheidt, P. (2001). Bullying behaviors among U.S. youth. *Journal of the American Medical Association, 285*, 2094–2100.

Nardi, P. M. (2006). *Doing survey research* (2nd ed.). Boston: Allyn & Bacon.

Narkiewicz, K., Phillips, B. S., Kato, M., Hering, D., Bieniaszewski, L., & Somers, V. K. (2005). Gender-selective interaction between aging, blood pressure, and sympathetic nerve activity. *Hypertension, 45*, 522–525.

Nash, J. M. (1997, February 3). Fertile minds. *Time*, pp. 50–54.

Nash, S. G., McQueen, A., & Bray, J. H. (2005). Pathways to adolescent alcohol use: Family environment, peer influence, and parental expectations. *Journal of Adolescent Health, 37*, 19–28.

National Assessment of Educational Progress. (2000). *The nation's report card*. Washington, DC: National Center for Education Statistics.

National Assessment of Educational Progress. (2005). *The nation's report card*. Washington, DC: National Center for Education Statistics.

National Center for Addiction and Substance Abuse. (2001). *2000 teen survey*. New York: National Center for Addiction and Substance Abuse, Columbia University.

National Center for Children Exposed to Violence. (2001). *Statistics*. New Haven, CT: Author.

National Center for Children in Poverty. (2004). *Low-income children in the United States*. New York: National Center for Children in Poverty, Columbia University.

National Center for Education Statistics. (2002). *Work during college*. Washington, DC: U.S. Office of Education.

National Center for Education Statistics. (2003). *Digest of Education Statistics, Table 52*. Washington, DC: Author.

National Center for Education Statistics. (2005). *Dropout rates in the United States: 2003*. Washington, DC: U.S. Department of Education.

National Center for Health Statistics. (1999). Current estimates from the National Health Interview Survey, 1996. *Vital and Health Statistics, Series 10* (No. 200). Atlanta: Centers for Disease Control and Prevention.

National Center for Health Statistics. (2000). *Health United States, 2000, with adolescent health chartbook*. Bethesda, MD: U.S. Department of Health and Human Services.

National Center for Health Statistics. (2002). *Health United States, 2002*. Hyattsville, MD: U.S. Department of Health and Human Services.

National Center for Health Statistics. (2004) *Health United States*. Atlanta: Centers for Disease Control and Prevention.

National Center for Health Statistics. (2005). *Prevalence of overweight among children and adolescents*. Atlanta: Centers for Disease Control and Prevention.

National Center for Health Statistics. (2006). *Health United States*. Atlanta: Centers for Disease Control and preventation.

National Clearinghouse on Child Abuse and Neglect. (2002). *What is child maltreatment?* Washington, DC: Administration for Children and Families.

National Clearinghouse on Child Abuse and Neglect. (2004). *What is child abuse and neglect?* Washington, DC: U.S. Department of Health and Human Services.

National Commission on the High School Year. (2001). *Youth at the crossroads: Facing high school and beyond*. Washington, DC: The Education Trust.

National Council on Aging. (2000, March). *Myths and realities survey results*. Washington, DC: Author.

National Institutes of Health. (2004). *Women's Health Initiative Hormone Therapy Study*. Bethesda, MD: National Institutes of Health.

National Research Council. (1999). *How people learn*. Washington, DC: National Academy Press.

National Vital Statistics Reports. (2003). *Death rates for suicide, Table 46*. Atlanta: Centers for Disease Control and Prevention.

National Vital Statistics Reports. (2005, March 7). *Deaths: Leading causes for 2002*. Atlanta: Centers for Disease Control and Prevention.

Natsopoulos, D., Kiosseoglou, G., Xeromeritou, A., & Alevriadou, A. (1998). Do the hands talk on the mind's behalf? Differences in language between left- and right-handed children. *Brain and Language, 64*, 182–214.

Nauck, B., & Suckow, J. (2006). Intergenerational relations in cross-cultural comparison: How social networks frame intergenerational relations between mothers and grandmothers in Japan, Korea, China, Indonesia, Israel, Germany, and Turkey. *Journal of Family Issues, 27*, 1159–1185.

Nazarian, J. (2004). Cardiopulmonary rehabilitation after treatment for lung cancer. *Current Treatment Options in Oncology, 5*, 75–82.

Needham, A., Barrett, T., & Peterman, K. (2002). A pick-me-up for infants' exploratory skills: Early simulated experiences reaching for objects using `sticky mittens' enhances young infants' object exploration skills. *Infant Behavior and Development, 25*, 279–295.

Negalia, J. P., Friedman, D. L., Yasui, Y., Mertens, A., Hammond, S., Stoval, S., & Donaldson, M. (2001). Second malignant neoplasms in five-year survivors of childhood cancer. *Journal of the National Cancer Institute, 93*, 618–629.

Neimeyer, R. A. (2005). Widowhood, grief, and the quest for meaning: A narrative perspective on resilience. In C. B. Wortman (Ed.), *Late life widowhood in the United States*. New York: Springer.

Neimeyer, R. A. (2006). *Lessons of loss* (2nd ed.). New York: Routledge.

Neisser, U. (2004). Memory development: New questions and old. *Developmental Review, 24*, 154–158.

Neisser, U., Boodoo, G., Bouchard, T. J., Boykin, A. W., Brody, N., Ceci, S. J., Halpern, D. F., Loehlin, J. C., Perloff, R. J., Sternberg, R., & Urbina, S. (1996). Intelligence: Knowns and unknowns. *American Psychologist, 51*, 77–101.

Nelson, C. A. (2003). Neural development and lifelong plasticity. In R. M. Lerner, F. Jacobs, & D. Wertlieb (Eds.), *Handbook of applied developmental science* (Vol. 1). Thousand Oaks, CA: Sage.

Nelson, C. A. (2005). Neurobehavioral development in the context of biocultural co-constructivism. In P. B. Baltes & P. Reuter-Lorenz (Eds.), *Brain, mind, and culture*. New York: Oxford University Press.

Nelson, C. A., Thomas, K. M., & de Haan, M. (2006). Neural bases of cognitive development. In W. Damon, R. Lerner, D. Kuhn, & R. Siegler (Eds.), *Handbook of child psychology* (6th ed., Vol. 2). New York: Wiley.

Nelson, F. A., Yu, L. M., Williams, S., & the International Child Care Practices Study Group Members. (2005). International Child Care Practices

Study: Breastfeeding and pacifier use. *Journal of Human Lactation, 21,* 289–295.

Nelson, K. (1999). Levels and modes of representation: Issues for the theory of conceptual change and development. In E. K. Skolnick, K. Nelson, S. A. Gelman, & P. H. Miller (Eds.), *Conceptual development.* Mahwah, NJ: Erlbaum.

Nelson, L. J., Badger, S., & Wu, B. (2004). The influence of culture in emerging adulthood: Perspectives of Chinese college students. *International Journal of Behavioral Development, 28,* 26–36.

Nelson, L. J., & Barry, C. M. (2005). Distinguishing features of emerging adulthood: The role of self-classification as an adult. *Journal of Adolescent Research, 20,* 242–262.

Nelson, M. E., Fiatarone, M. A., Moranti, C. M., Trice, I., Greenberg, R. A., & Evans, W. J. (1994). Effects of high-intensity strength training on multiple risk factors for osteoporotic fractures: A randomized controlled trial. *Journal of the American Medical Association, 272,* 1909–1914.

Neno, R., & Neno, N. (2006). Promoting a healthy diet for older people in the community. *Nursing Standards, 20,* 59–65.

Nester, E. W., Anderson, D. G., Roberts, C. E., & Nester, M. T. (2007). *Microbiology* (5th ed.). New York: McGraw-Hill.

Neugarten, B. L. (1964). *Personality in middle and late life.* New York: Atherton.

Neugarten, B. L. (1986). The aging society. In A. Pifer & L. Bronte (Eds.), *Our aging society: Paradox and promise.* New York: W. W. Norton.

Neugarten, B. L. (1988, August). *Policy issues for an aging society.* Paper presented at the meeting of the American Psychological Association, Atlanta.

Neugarten, B. L., & Weinstein, K. K. (1964). The changing American grandparent. *Journal of Marriage and the Family, 26,* 199–204.

Neugarten, B. L., Havighurst, R. J., & Tobin, S. S. (1968). Personality and patterns of aging. In B. L. Neugarten (Ed.), *Middle age and aging.* Chicago: University of Chicago Press.

Neuman, S. B., & Roskos, K. (2005). Whatever happened to developmentally appropriate practice in early literacy? *Young Children, 60* (no. 4), 22–27.

Neville, H., & Bavelier, D. (2002). Human brain plasticity: Evidence from sensory deprivation and altered language experience. *Progress in Brain Research, 138,* 177–188.

New, R. (2005). The Reggio Emilia approach: Provocations and partnerships with U.S. early childhood educators. In J. I. Roopnarine & J. E. Johnson (Eds.), *Approaches to early childhood education* (4th ed.). Columbus, OH: Merrill/Prentice Hall.

Newcomb, M. D., & Bentler, P. M. (1980). Assessment of personality and demographic aspects of cohabitation and marital success. *Journal of Personality Development, 4,* 11–24.

Newcomb, M. D., & Bentler, P. M. (1988). Substance use and abuse among children and teenagers. *American Psychologist, 44,* 242–248.

Newcombe, N. S., Drummey, A. B., Fox, N. A., Lile, E., & Ottinger-Alberts, W. (2000). Remembering early childhood: How much, how, and why (or why not)? *Current Directions in Psychological Science, 9,* 55–58.

Newell, K. M., Vaillancourt, D. E., & Sosnoff, J. J. (2006). Aging, complexity, and motor performance. In J. E. Birren & K. W. Schaie (Eds.), *Handbook of the psychology of aging* (6th ed.). San Diego: Academic Press.

Newell, K., Scully, D. M., McDonald, P. V., & Baillargeon, R. (1989). Task constraints and infant grip configurations. *Developmental Psychobiology, 22,* 817–832.

Newman, A. B., and others. (2003). Effects of subclinical cardiovascular disease. *Archives of Internal Medicine, 163,* 2315–2322.

Newman, A. B., & others (2006). Association of long-distance corridor walk performance with mortality, cardiovascular disease, mobility limitation, and disability. *Journal of the American Medical Association, 295,* 2018–2026.

Newson, R. S., & Kemps, E. B. (2005). General lifestyle activities as a predictor of current cognition and cognitive change in older adults: A cross-sectional and longitudinal examination. *Journals of Gerontology B: Psychological Sciences and Social Sciences, 60,* P113–P120.

Newton, A. W., & Vandeven, A. M. (2005). Update on child maltreatment with a special focus on shaken baby syndrome. *Current Opinions in Pediatrics, 17,* 246–251.

Newton, A. W., & Vandeven, A. M. (2006). Unexplained infant death: A review of sudden infant death syndrome, sudden unexplained infant death, and child maltreatment facilities in shaken baby syndrome. *Current Opinions in Pediatrics, 18,* 196–200.

Ng, B. Y. (2005). Grief revisited. *Annals of the Academy of Medicine Singapore, 34,* 352–355.

NHANES. (2001, March). *National Health and Nutrition Examination Surveys.* Washington, DC: U.S. Department of Health and Human Services.

NICHD Early Child Care Research Network (2000). Factors associated with fathers' caregiving activities and sensitivity with young children. *Developmental Psychology, 14,* 200–219.

NICHD Early Child Care Research Network (2001). Nonmaternal care and family factors in early development: An overview of the NICHD Early Child Care Research Network study of Early Child Care. *Journal of Applied Developmental Psychology, 22,* 457–492.

NICHD Early Child Care Research Network (2002). Structure of Process and Outcome: Direct and indirect effects of child care quality on young children's development. *Psychological Science, 13,* 199–206.

NICHD Early Child Care Research Network (2003). Does amount of time spent in child care predict socioemotional adjustment during the transition to kindergarten? *Child Development, 74,* 976–1005.

NICHD Early Child Care Research Network (2004). Are child developmental outcomes related to before—and after—School care arrangement? *Child Development, 75,* 280–295.

NICHD Early Child Care Research Network (2004). Type of child care research network and children's development at 54 months. *Early Childhood Research Quarterly, 19,* 203–230.

NICHD Early Child Care Research Network (2005). *Child care and development.* New York: Guilford.

NICHD Early Child Care Research Network (2005). Duration and developmental timing of poverty and children's cognitive and social development from birth through third grade. *Child Development, 76,* 795–810.

NICHD Early Child Care Research Network (2005). Predicting individual differences in attention, memory, and planning in first graders from experiences at home, child care, and school. *Developmental Psychology, 41,* 99–114.

NICHD Early Child Care Research Network (2006). Infant-mother attachment classification: Risk and protection in relation to changing maternal caregiving quality. *Developmental Psychology, 42,* 38–58.

Nicholls, S. J., Rye, K. A., & Barter, P. J. (2005). High-density lipoproteins as therapeutic targets. *Current Opinions in Lipidology, 16,* 345–349.

Nichols, S., & Good, T. L. (2004). *America's teenagers—myths and realities.* Mahwah, NJ: Erlbaum.

Nicklas, T. A., Demory-Luce, D., Yang, S. J., Baranowski, T., Zakeri, I., & Berensen, G. (2004b). Children's food consumption patterns have changed over two decades (1973–1994): The Bogalusa Heart Study. *Journal of the American Dietetic Association, 104,* 1127–1140.

Nicklas, T. A., Morales, M., Linares, A., Yang, S. J., Baranowski, T., De Moor, C., & Berensen, G. (2004a). Children's meal patterns have changed over a 21-year-period: The Bogalusa Heart Study. *Journal of the American Dietetic Association, 104,* 753–761.

Nicklas, T. A., Webber, L. S., Jonson, C. S. Srinivasan, S. R., & Berensen, G. S. (1995). Foundations for health promotion with youth: A review of observations from the Bogalusa Heart Study. *Journal of Health Education, 26,* 518–526.

Nicklas, T. A., Yang, S. J., Baranowski, T., Zakeri, I., & Berensen, G. (2003). Eating patterns and obesity in children. The Bogalusa Heart Study. *American Journal of Preventive Medicine, 25,* 9–16.

Nicolaides, K. H. (2005). First-trimester screening for chromosomal abnormalities. *Seminars in Perinatology, 29,* 190–194.

Nidetz, A., Fishman, E., Jacobs, M., Daniels, C., & Tamang, S. (2005). Palliative care management services in a Medicare social HMO. *Journal of Pain and Symptom Management, 29,* 109–111.

Nielsen, S. J., Siega-Riz, A. M., & Popkin, B. M. (2002). Trends in energy intake between 1977 and 1986: Similar shifts seen across age groups. *Obesity Research, 10,* 370–378.

Nieves, J. W. (2005). Osteoporosis: The role of micronutrients. *American Journal of Clinical Nutrition, 81,* 1232S–1239S.

Nisbett, R. (2003). *The geography of thought.* New York: Free Press.

Nock, S. (1995). A comparison of marriages and cohabitating relationships. *Journal of Family Issues, 16,* 53–76.

Nohr, E. A., Bech, B. H., Davies, M. J., Fryenberg, M., Henriksen, T. B., & Olsen, J. (2005). Prepregnancy obesity and fetal death: A study with the Danish National Birth Cohort. *Obstetrics and Gynecology, 106,* 250–259.

Noice, H., Noice, T., & Staines, G. (2004). A short-term intervention to enhance cognitive and affective functioning in older adults. *Journal of Aging Health, 16,* 562–585.

Nolan, K., Schell, L. M., Stark, A. D., & Gomez, M. I. (2002). Longitudinal study of energy and nutrient intakes for infants from low-income, urban families. *Public Health Nutrition, 5,* 405–412.

Noland, J. S., Singer, L. T., Short, E. J., Minnes, S., Arendt, R. E., Kirchner, H. L., & Bearer, C. (2005). Prenatal drug exposure and selective attention in preschoolers. *Neurotoxicology and Teratology, 27,* 429–438.

Nolen-Hoeksema, S. (1990). *Sex differences in depression.* Stanford, CA: Stanford University Press.

Nolen-Hoeksema, S. (2007). *Abnormal psychology* (4th, ed.). New York: McGraw-Hill.

Nolen-Hoeksema, S., & Ahrens, C. (2002). Age differences and similarities in correlates of depressive symptoms. *Psychology and Aging, 17,* 116–124.

Nordahl, C. W., Ranganath, C., Yonelinas, A. P., Decarli, C., Fletcher, E., & Jagust. W. J. (2006). White matter changes compromise prefrontal cortex function in healthy elderly individuals. *Journal of Cognitive Neuroscience, 18,* 418–429.

Nordberg, A. (2006). Mechanisms behind neuroprotective actions of cholinesterase inhibitors in Alzheimer disease. *Alzheimer Disease and Associated Disorders, 20* (Suppl 1), S12–S18.

Nordlund, A., Rolstad, S., Hellstrom, P., Sjogren, M., Hansen, S., & Wallin, A. (2005). The Goteberg MCI study: Mild cognitive impairment is a heterogeneous condition. *Journal of Neurology, Neurosurgery, and Psychiatry, 76,* 1485–1490.

Norgard, B., Puho, E., Czeizel, A. E., Skriver, M. V., & Sorensen, H. T. (2005). Aspirin use during early pregnancy and the risk of congenital abnormalities. *American Journal of Obstetrics & Gynecology, 192,* 922–923.

Noriko, S. (2005). Identity development of pre- and post-empty nest women. *Japanese Journal of Developmental Psychology, 15,* 52–64.

Norman, J. F., Crabtree, C. E., Herrmann, M., Thompson, S. R., Shular, C. F., & Clayton, A. M. (2006). Aging and the perception of 3-D shape from dynamic patterns of binocular disparity. *Perception and Psychophysics, 68,* 94–101.

Norouzieh, K. (2005). Case management of the dying child. *Case Manager, 16,* 54–57.

Nottelmann, E. D., Susman, E. J., Blue, J. H., Inoff-Germain, G., Dorn, L. D., Loriaux, D. L., Cutler, G. B., & Chrousos, G. P. (1987). Gonadal and adrenal hormone correlates of adjustment in early adolescence. In R. M. Lerner & T. T. Foch (Eds.), *Biological-psychological interactions in early adolescence.* Hillsdale, NJ: Erlbaum.

Nour, K., Laforest, S., Gauvin, L., & Ginac, M. (2006). Behavior change following a self-management intervention for housebound older adults with arthritis: An experimental study. *International Journal of Nutrition and Physical Activity, 30,* 12.

Nowak, C. A. (1977). Does youthfulness equal attractiveness? In L. E. Troll, J. Israel, & K. Israel (Eds.), *Looking ahead: A woman's guide to the problems and joys of growing older.* Englewood Cliffs, NJ: Prentice Hall.

Nsamenang, A. B. (2002). Adolescence in sub-Saharan Africa: An image constructed from Africa's triple heritage. In B. B. Brown, R. W. Larson, & T. S. Saraswathi (Eds.), *The world's youth.* New York: Cambridge University Press.

Nugent, K., & Brazelton, T. B. (2000). Preventive infant mental health: Uses of the Brazelton scale. In J. D. Osofsky & H. E. Fitzgerald (Eds.), *WAIMH Handbook of infant mental health* (Vol. 2). New York: Wiley.

Nunomura, A., Castellani, R. J., Zhu, X., Moreira, P. I., Perry, G., & Smith, M. A. (2006). Involvement of oxidative stress in Alzheimer disease. *Journal of Neuropathology and Experimental Neurology, 65,* 631–641.

O'Connell, E. (2005). Mood, energy, cognition, and physical complaints: A mind/body approach to symptom management during the climacteric. *Journal of Obstetric, Gynecological, and Neonatal Nursing, 34,* 274–279.

O'Connor, T. G., Ben-Shlomo, Y., Heron, J., Golding, J., Adams, D., & Glover, V. (2005). Prenatal anxiety predicts individual differences in cortisol in pre-adolescent children. *Biological Psychiatry, 58,* 211–217.

O'Dowd, A. (2004). Why are midwife numbers in crisis? *Nursing Times, 100,* 12–13.

O'Hanlon, L, Kemper, S., & Wilcox, K. A. (2005). Aging, encoding, and word retrieval: Distinguishing phonological and memory processes. *Experimental Aging Research, 31,* 149–171.

O'Leary, C. (2004). Fetal alcohol syndrome. *Journal of Pediatric Child Health, 40,* 2–7.

O' Rand, A. M. (2006). Stratification and the life course. In R. H. Binstock & L. K. George (Eds.), *Handbook of aging and the social sciences* (6th ed.). San Diego: Academic Press.

Oakes, L. M., Kannass, K. N., & Shaddy, D. J. (2002). Developmental changes in endogenous control of attention: The role of target familiarity on infants' distraction latency. *Child Development, 73,* 1644–1655.

Obler, L. K. (2005). Development in the older years. In Berko Gleason (Ed.), *The development of language* (6th ed.). Boston: Allyn & Bacon.

Occupational Outlook Handbook. (2006–2007). Washington, DC: U.S. Department of Labor, Bureau of Labor Statistics.

Oehninger, S. (2001). Strategies for the infertile man. *Seminars in Reproductive Medicine, 19,* 231–238.

Offer, D., Ostrov, E., Howard, K. I., & Atkinson, R. (1988). *The teenage world: Adolescents' self, image in ten countries.* New York: Plenum.

Offer, D., Ostrov. E., & Howard, K. I. (1989). *The offer self-image questionnaire for adolescents: A manual.* Chicago: Michael Reese-Hospital.

Ogbu, J. U. (1989, April). *Academic socialization of Black children: An inoculation against future failure?* Paper presented at the meeting of the Society for Research in Child Development, Kansas City.

Ogbu, J., & Stern, P. (2001). Caste status and intellectual development. In R. J. Sternberg & E. L., Grigorenko (Eds.), *Environmental effects on cognitive abilities.* Mahwah, NJ: Erlbaum.

Ogden, C. L., Troiano, R. P., Briefel, R. R., Kuczmarski, R. J., Flegal, K. M., & Johnson, C. L. (1997). Prevalence of overweight in preschool children in the United States, 1971 through 1994. *Pediatrics, 99,* El.

Ohgi, S., Akiyama, T., & Fukuda, M. (2005). Neurobehavioral profile of low-birthweight infants with cystic periventricular leukomalacia. *Developmental Medicine and Child Neurology, 47,* 221–228.

Ohgi, S., Akiyama, T., Arisawa, K., & Shigemori, K. (2004). Randomized controlled trial of swaddling versus massage in the management of excess crying in infants with cerebral injuries. *Archives of Disease in Childhood, 89,* 212–216.

Ohgi, S., Fukuda, M., Moriuchi, H., Kusumoto, T., Akiyama, T., Nugent, J. K., Brazelton, T. B., Arisawa, K., Takahashi, T., & Saitoh, H. (2002). Comparison of kangaroo care and standard care: Behavioral organization, development, and temperament in healthy, low birth weight infants through 1 year. *Journal of Perinatology, 22,* 374–379.

Okagaki, L. (2000). Determinants of intelligence: Socialization of intelligence. In A. Kazdin (Ed.), *Encyclopedia of psychology.* Washington, DC, & New York: American Psychological Association and Oxford University Press.

Okah, F. A., Cal, J., & Hoff, G. L. (2005). Term-gestation low birth weight and health-compromising behaviors during pregnancy. *Obstetrics and Gynecology, 105,* 543–550.

Okazaki, K., Iwasaki, K., Prasad, A., Palmer, M. D., Martini, E. R., Fu, Q., Arbab-Zadeh, A., Zhang, R., & Levine, B. D. (2005). Dose-response relationship of endurance training for autonomic circulatory control in healthy seniors. *Journal of Applied Physiology, 99,* 1041–1049.

Okuyaz, C., Gucuyener, K., Karabacak, N. I., Aydin, K., Serdaroglu, A., & Cingi, E. (2004). Tc-99m-HMPAO SPECT in the diagnosis of brain death in children. *Pediatric International, 46,* 711–714.

Olpin, M., & Hesson, M. (2007). *Stress management for life.* Belmont, CA: Wadsworth.

Olshansky, S. J., Carnes, B. A., Hershow, R., Passaro, D., Laydn, J., Brody, J., Hayflick, L., Butler, R. N., Allison, D. B., & Ludwig, D. S. (2005). Misdirection on the road to Shangri-La. *Science of aging knowledge environment, 28,* 15.

Olsho, L. W., Harkins, S. W., & Lenhardt, M. L. (1985). Aging and the auditory system. In J. E. Birren & K. W. Schaie (Eds.), *Handbook of the psychology of aging* (2nd ed.). New York: Van Nostrand Reinhold.

Olson, A. K., Eadie, B. D., Ernst, C., & Christie, B. R. (2006). Environmental enrichment and voluntary exercise massively increase neurogenesis in the adult hippocampus via dissociable pathways. *Hippocampus, 16,* 250–260.

Olson, L. M., Tang, S. F., & Newacheck, P. W. (2005). Children in the United States with discontinuous health insurance coverage. *New England Journal of Medicine, 353,* 418–419.

Ong, A. D., Bergeman, C. S., & Bisconti, T. L. (2004). The role of daily positive emotions during conjugal bereavement. *Journals of Gerontology B: Psychological Sciences and Social Sciences, 59,* P168–P176.

Ono, Y. (2004). Suicide prevention program for the elderly. *Keio Journal of Medicine, 53,* 1–6.

Onwuegbuzi, A. J., & Daley, C. E. (2001). Racial differences in IQ revisited: A synthesis of nearly a century of research. *Journal of Black Psychology, 27,* 209–220.

Organista, K. C. (1994). Overdue overview of elderly Latino mental health. *Contemporary Psychology, 39,* 61–62.

Ornstein, A. C., Lasley, T., & Mindes, G. (2005). *Secondary and middle school methods.* Boston: Allyn & Bacon.

Ornstein, P., Gordon, B. N., & Larus, D. (1992). Children's memory for a personally experienced event: Implications for testimony. *Applied Cognition and Psychology, 6,* 49–60.

Osipow, S. (2000). Work. In A. Kazdin (Ed.), *Encyclopedia of psychology.* Washington, DC, & New York: American Psychological Association and Oxford University Press.

Osterlind, S. J. (2006). *Modern measurement theory.* Upper Saddle River, NJ: Prentice Hall.

Ostrov, J. M., & Keating, C. F. (2004). Gender differences in preschool aggression during free play and structured interactions: An observational study. *Social Development, 13,* 255–277.

Oswald, R. F., & Clausell, E. (2005). Same-sex relationships and their dissolution. In M. A. Fine & J. H. Harvey (Eds.) *Handbook of divorce and relationship dissolution.* Mahwah, NJ: Erlbaum.

Otiniano, M. E., Du, X. L., Maldonado, M. R., Ray, L., & Markides, K. (2005). Effect of metabolic syndrome on heart attack and mortality in Mexican-American elderly persons: Findings of 7-year follow-up from the Hispanic established population for the epidemiological study of the elderly. *Journals of Gerontology: Biological Sciences and Medical Sciences, 60,* 466A–470A.

Ouellette, S. C., & DiPlacido, J. (2001). Personality's role in the protection and enhancement of health. In A. Baum, T. A. Revenson, & J. E. Singer (Eds.), *Handbook of health psychology.* Mahwah, NJ: Erlbaum.

Ovando, C. J., Combs, M. C., & Collier, V. P. (2006). *Bilingual and ESL classrooms* (4th ed.). New York: McGraw-Hill.

Overton, W. F. (2006). Development psychology: Philosophy, concepts, methodology. In W. Damon & R. Lerner (Eds.), *Handbook of child psychology* (6th ed.). New York: Wiley.

Owen, C. G., Martin, R. M., Whincup, P. H., Smith, G. D., & Cook, D. G. (2005). Effect of infant feeding on the risk of obesity across the life course: A quantitative review of published evidence. *Pediatrics, 115,* 1367–1377.

Owen, C. J. (2005). The empty nest transition: The relationship between attachment style and women's use of this period as a time for growth and change. *Dissertation Abstracts International, Section B: The Sciences and Engineering, 65,* p. 3747.

Oxford, M. L., Gilchrist, L. D., Gillmore, M. R., & Lohr, M. J. (2006). Predicting variation in the life course of adolescent mothers as they enter adulthood. *Journal of Adolescent Health, 39,* 20–26.

Oztop, E., Bradley, N. S., & Arbib, M. A. (2004). Infant grasp learning: A computational model. *Experimental Brain Research, 158,* 480–503.

Padilla, A. M. (2006). Second language learning: Learning issues in research and teaching. In P. A. Alexander & P. H. Winne (Eds.), *Handbook of educational psychology* (2nd ed.). Mahwah, NJ: Erlbaum.

Padma-Nathan, H. (2006, in press). Sildenafil citrate (Viagra) treatment for erectile dysfunction: An updated profile of response and effectiveness. *International Journal of Impotence Research.*

Paffenbarger, O., Hyde, R. T., Wing, A. L., & Hsieh, C. (1986). Physical activity, all cause mortality, and longevity of college alumni. *New England Journal of Medicine, 324,* 605–612.

Paikoff, R. L., Buchanan, C. M., & Brooks-Gunn, J. (1991). Hormone-behavior links at puberty, methodological links in the study of. In R. M. Lerner, A. C. Petersen, & J. Brooks-Gunn (Eds.), *Encyclopedia of adolescence.* New York: Garland.

Pakpreo, P., Ryan, S., Auinger, P., Aten, M. (2004, March). *The association between parental lifestyle behaviors and adolescent knowledge, attitudes, intentions, and nutritional and physical activity behaviors.* Paper presented at the meeting of the Society for Adolescent Medicine, St. Louis.

Pal, P. K., & Netravathi, M. (2005). Management of neurogenerative disorders: Parkinson's disease and Alzheimer's disease. *Journal of the Indian Medical Association, 103,* 168–170, 172, 174–176.

Palmer, S. E. (2004). Custody and access issues with children whose parents are separated or divorced. *Canadian Journal of Community Mental Health, 4* (Suppl.), 25–38.

Palmore, E. B. (1981). *Social patterns in normal aging: Findings from the Duke Longitudinal Study.* Durham, NC: Duke University Press.

Palmore, E. B. (2001). The ageism survey: First findings. *The Gerontologist, 41,* 572–575.

Palmore, E. B. (2004). Research note: Ageism in Canada and the United States. *Journal of Cross Cultural Gerontology, 19,* 41–46.

Paloutzian, R. (2000). *Invitation to the psychology of religion* (3rd ed.). Boston: Allyn & Bacon.

Paloutzian, R. F., & Park, C. L. (Eds.) (2005). *Handbook of the psychology of religion and spirituality.* New York: Guilford.

Pan, B. A. (2005). Semantic development. In J. Berko Gleason, *The development of language* (6th ed.). Boston: Allyn & Bacon.

Pan, B. A., Rowe, M. L., Singer, J. D., & Snow, C. E. (2005). Maternal correlates of growth in toddler vocabulary production in low-income families. *Child Development, 76,* 763–782.

Pang, V. O. (2005). *Multicultural education.* (3rd ed.). New York: McGraw-Hill.

Papalia, D. E., Sterns, H. L., Feldman, R. D., & Camp, C. J. (2002). *Adult development and aging* (2nd ed.). New York: McGraw-Hill.

Papp, C., & Papp, Z. (2003). Chorionic villus sampling and amniocentesis: What are the risks in current practice? *Current Opinions in Obstetrics and Gynecology, 15,* 159–165.

Parazzini, F., Chatenoud, L., Surace, M., Tozzi, L., Salerio, B., Bettoni, G., & Benzi, G. (2003). Moderate alcohol drinking and risk of preterm birth. *European Journal of Clinical Nutrition, 57,* 1345–1349.

Paredes, I., Hidalgo, L., Chedraui, P., Palma, J., & Eugenio, J. (2005). Factors associated with inadequate prenatal care in Ecuadorian women. *International Journal of Gynecology and Obstetrics, 88,* 168–172.

Paris, S. G., & Paris, A. H. (2006). Assessment of early reading. In W. Damon & R. Lerner (Eds.),

Handbook of child psychology (6th ed.). New York: Wiley.

Parise, G., Brose, A. N., & Tarnopolsky, M. A. (2005). Resistance exercise training decreases oxidative damage to DNA and increases cytochrome oxidase activity in older adults. *Experimental Gerontology, 40,* 173–180.

Parish-Stephens, M. A., & Marson, D. (2006). Everyday problem solving. In J. E. Birren & K. W. Schaie (Eds.), *Handbook of the psychology of aging* (6th ed.). San Diego: Academic Press.

Park, C. L. (2005). Religion as a meaning-making system. Psychology of Religion Newsletter, 30 (No. 2), 1–9.

Park, C. L., & Folkman, S. (1997). Meaning in the context of stress and coping. *Review of General Psychology, 1* (2), 115–144.

Park, D. (2001). Commentary in Restak, R. *The secret life of the brain.* Washington, DC: Joseph Henry Press.

Park, D. C., & Gutchess, A. H. (2005). Long-term memory and aging: A cognitive neuroscience perspective. In R. Cabeza, L. Nyberg, & D. Parke, (Eds.), *Cognitive neuroscience of aging: Linking cognitive and cerebral aging.* New York: Oxford University Press.

Park, D. C., & Gutchess, A. H. (2006). The cognitive neurosciences of aging and culture. *Current Directions in Psychological Science, 15,* 105–108.

Parke, R. D. (2000). Father involvement: A developmental psychology perspective. *Marriage and Family Review, 29,* 43–58.

Parke, R. D. (2002). Fathering. In M. H. Bornstein (Ed.), *Handbook of parenting* (2nd ed.). Mahwah, NJ: Erlbaum.

Parke, R. D. (2004). Development in the family. *Annual Review of Psychology* (Vol. 55). Palo Alto, CA: Annual Reviews.

Parke, R. D., & Buriel, R. (2006). Socialization in the family: Ethnic and ecological perspectives. In W. Damon & R. Lerner (Eds.), *Handbook of child psychology* (6th ed.). New York: Wiley.

Parke, R. D., & Clarke-Stewart, K. A. (2003). Developmental psychology. In I. B. Weiner (Ed.), *Handbook of psychology* (Vol. 1). New York: Wiley.

Parker, A., & Fischhoff, B. (2002, April). *Individual differences in decision-making competence.* Paper presented at the meeting of the Society for Research on Adolescence, New Orleans.

Parker, J. G., & Asher, S. R. (1987). Peer relations and later personal adjustment: Are low accepted children at risk? *Psychological Bulletin, 102,* 357–389.

Parker, P. S. (2004). *Race, gender, and leadership.* Mahwah, NJ: Erlbaum.

Parkes, K.R. (2006). Physical activity and self-rated health: Interactive effects of activity in work and leisure domains. *British Journal of Health Psychology, 11,* 533–550.

Parlee, M. B. (1979, April). The friendship bond: PT's survey report on friendship in America. *Psychology Today,* pp. 43–54, 113.

Parmar, R. C., Muranjan, M. N., & Swami, S. (2002). Trisomy 21 with XYY. *Indian Journal of Pediatrics, 11,* 979–981.

Parnes, H. S., & Sommers, D. G. (1994). Shunning retirement: Work experiences of men in their seventies and early eighties. *Journal of Gerontology, 49,* S117–S124.

Parra-Cardona, J. R., Bulock, L. A., Imig, D. R., Villarruel, F. A., & Gold, S. J. (2006). "Trabajanco duro todos los dias": Learning from the life experiences of Mexican-origin migrant families. *Family Relations, 55,* 361–375.

Parsons, P. A. (2003). From the stress theory of aging to energetic and evolutionary explanations for longevity. *Biogerontology, 4,* 63–73.

Parten, M. (1932). Social play among preschool children. *Journal of Abnormal Social Psychology, 27,* 243–269.

Partnership for a Drug-Free America. (2005). *Partnership Attitude Tracking Study.* New York: Author.

Pascal-Bonaro, D., & Kroeger, M. (2004). Continuous female companionship during childbirth: A crucial resource in times of stress or calm. *Journal of Midwifery and Women's Health, 49* (No. 4, Supplement 1), 19–27.

Pasch, L. A. (2001). Confronting fertility problems. In A. Baum, T. A. Revenson, & J. E. Singer (Eds.), *Handbook of health psychology.* Mahwah, NJ: Erlbaum.

Pasley, K., & Moorefield, B. S. (2004). Stepfamilies. In M. Coleman & L. Ganong (Eds.), *Handbook of contemporary families.* Thousand Oaks, CA: Sage.

Pasquino, A. M., Pucarelli, I., Segni, M., Tarani, L., Calcaterra, V., & Larizza, D. (2005). Adult height in sixty girls with Turner syndrome treated with growth hormone matched with an untreated group. *Journal of Endocrinological Investigation, 28,* 350–356.

Passuth, P. M., Maines, D. R., & Neugarten, B. L. (1984). *Age norms and age constraints twenty years later.* Paper presented at the annual meeting of the Midwest Sociological Society, Chicago.

Pastor, A. D., & Evans, S. M. (2003). Alcohol outcome expectancies for alcohol use problems in women with and without a family history of alcoholism. *Drug and Alcohol Dependency, 70,* 201–214.

Patterson, B., Ryan, J., & Dickey, J. H. (2004). The toxicology of mercury. *New England Journal of Medicine, 350,* 945–947.

Patterson, C. J. (2002). Lesbian and gay parenthood. In M. H. Bornstein (Ed.), *Handbook of parenting* (2nd ed., Vol. 3). Mahwah, NJ: Erlbaum.

Patterson, C. J. (2004). What differences does a civil union make? Changing public policies and the experiences of same-sex couples: Comment on Solomon, Rothblum, and Balsam (2004). *Journal of Family Psychology, 18,* 287–289.

Patterson, G. R., De Baryshe, B. D., & Ramsey, E. (1989). A developmental perspective on antisocial behavior: *American Psychologist, 44,* 329–355.

Paul, P. (2003, September/October). The PermaParent trap. *Psychology Today, 36* (5), 40–53.

Pavlov, I. P. (1927). In G. V. Anrep (Trans.), *Conditioned reflexes.* London: Oxford University Press.

Pawelec, G., Koch, S., Franceschi, C., & Wikby, A. (2006). Human immunosenescence: does it have an infectious component? *Annals of the New York Academy of Science, 1067,* 56–65.

Payer, L. (1991). The menopause in various cultures. In H. Burger & M. Boulet (Eds.), *A portrait of the menopause.* Park Ridge, NJ: Parthenon.

Peck, R. C. (1968). Psychological developments in the second half of life. In B. L. Neugarten (Ed.), *Middle age and aging.* Chicago: University of Chicago Press.

Pecora, N., Murray, J. P., & Wartella, E. A. (Eds.). (2006). *Children and television.* Mahwah, NJ: Erlbaum.

Pederson, D. R., & Moran, G. (1996). Expressions of the attachment relationship outside of the Strange Situation. *Child Development, 67,* 915–927.

Pelayo, R., Owens, J., Mindell, J., & Sheldon, S. (2006). Bed sharing with unimpaired parents is not an important risk for sudden infant death syndrome: Letter to the editor, *Pediatrics, 117,* 993–994.

Pelkonen, M., & Marttunen, M. (2003). Child and adolescent suicide: Epidemiology, risk factors, and approaches to prevention. *Pediatric Drug, 5,* 243–265.

Pellizzer, C., Adler, S., Corvi, R., Hartung, T., & Bremer, S. (2004). Monitoring of teratogenic effects in vitro by analyzing a selected gene expression pattern. *Toxicology in Vitro, 18,* 325–335.

Peluso, M. A., & Andrade, L. H. (2005). Physical activity and mental health: The association between exercise and mood. *Clinics, 60,* 61–70.

Peplau, L. A. (2002). *Current research on gender and sexuality.* Paper presented at the meeting of the American Psychological Association, Chicago.

Peplau, L. A. (2003). Human sexuality: How do men and women differ? *Current Directions in Psychological Science, 12,* 37–40.

Peplau, L. A., & Beals, K. P. (2002). Lesbians, gays, and bisexuals in relationships. In J. Worell (Ed.), *Encyclopedia of women and gender.* San Diego: Academic Press.

Peplau, L. A., & Beals, K. P. (2004). Family lives of lesbians and gay men. In A. L. Vangelisti (Ed.), *Handbook of family communication.* Mahwah, NJ: Erlbaum.

Peplau, L. A., Fingerhut, A., & Beals, K. P. (2004). Sexuality in the relationships of lesbians and gay men. In J. H. Harvey & K. Wenzel (Eds.), *The handbook of sexuality in close relationships.* Mahwah, NJ: Erlbaum.

Perez-Febles, A. M. (1992). *Acculturation and interactional styles of Latina mothers and their infants.* Unpublished honors thesis, Brown University, Providence, RI.

Perez-Perdomo, R., Perez-Cardona, C., Disdier-Flores, O., & Cintron, Y. (2003). Prevalence and correlates of asthma in the Puerto Rican population: Behavioral risk factor surveillance system, 2000. *Journal of Asthma, 40,* 465–474.

Perlman, D., & Peplau, L. A. (1998). Loneliness. In H. S. Friedman (Ed.), *Encyclopedia of mental health* (Vol. 2). San Diego: Academic Press.

Perlman, G., & Shaffer, S. M. (2004). *Mom, can I move back in with you?* New York: Jeremy Tarcher.

Perls, T. (2005). *The New England Centenarian Study.* Boston: Boston University School of Medicine.

Perls, T. T. (2006). The different paths to 100. *American Journal of Clinical Nutrition, 83,* 484S–487S.

Perner, J., Stummer, S., Sprung, M., & Doherty, M. (2002). Theory of mind finds its Piagetian perspective: Why alternative naming comes with understanding belief. *Cognitive Development, 17,* 1451–1472.

Perrig-Chiello, P., & Perren, S. (2005). The impact of past transitions on well-being in middle age. In S. L. Willis & M. Martin (Eds.), *Middle adulthood.* Thousand Oaks, CA: Sage.

Perry, C. M., & Johnson, C. L. (1994). Families and support networks among African American oldest-old. *International Journal of Aging on Human Development, 38,* 41–50.

Perry, W. G. (1970). *Forms of intellectual and ethical development in the college years.* New York: Holt, Rinehart & Winston.

Perry, W. G. (1999). *Forms of ethical and intellectual development in the college years: A scheme.* San Francisco: Jossey-Bass.

Persson, J., Nyberg, L., Lind, J., Larsson, A., Nilsson, L. G., Ingvar, M., & Bucker, R. L. (2005). Structure-function correlates of cognitive decline in aging. *Cerebral Cortex.*

Pesce, C., Guidetti, L., Baldari, C., Tessiotore, A., & Capranica, L. (2005). Effects of aging on visual attentional focusing. *Gerontology, 51,* 266–276.

Peskin, H. (1967). Pubertal onset and ego functioning. *Journal of Abnormal Psychology, 72,* 1–15.

Peters, J. M., & Stout, D. L. (2006). *Concepts and inquiries for teaching elementary school science* (5th ed.). Upper Saddle River, NJ: Prentice Hall.

Peters, R. (2006). Aging and the brain. *Postgraduate Medical Journal, 82,* 84–88.

Petersen, A. C. (1979, January). Can puberty come any faster? *Psychology Today,* pp. 45–56.

Petersen, A. C. (1993). Creating adolescents: The role of context and process in developmental trajectories. *Journal of Research on Adolescence, 3,* 1–18.

Petersen, A. M., & Pedersen, B. K. (2005). The anti-inflammatory effect of exercise. *Journal of Applied Physiology, 98,* 1154–1162.

Peterson, B. E. (2002). Longitudinal analysis of midlife generativity, intergenerational roles, and caregiving. *Psychology and Aging, 17,* 161–168.

Peterson, B. E., & Stewart, A. J. (1996). Antecedents and contexts of generativity motivation at midlife. *Psychology and Aging, 11,* 21–33.

Peterson, C. C. (1996). The ticking of the social clock: Adults' beliefs about the timing of transition events. *International Journal of Aging and Human Development, 42,* 189–203.

Peterson, C. C. (1999). Grandfathers' and grandmothers' satisfaction with the grandparenting role: Seeking new answers to old questions. *International Journal of Aging and Human Development, 49,* 61–78.

Peterson, K. S. (1997, September 3). In high school, dating is a world into itself. *USA Today,* pp. 1–2D.

Petrella, J. R., Krishnan, S., Slavin, M. J., Tran, T. T., Murty, L., & Doraiswamy, P. M. (2006). Mild cognitive impairment: Evaluation with 4-T functional MR imaging. *Radiology, 240,* 177–186.

Petrini, J. (2004). *Preterm birth: A public health priority.* White Plains, NY: National March of Dimes.

Petrovitch, H., & others (2000). Midlife blood pressure and neurotic placques, neurofibrillary tangles, and brain weight at death: The HAAS Honolulu-Asia aging study. *Neurobiology of Aging, 21,* 57–62.

Pettito, L. A., Kovelman, I., & Harasymowycz, U. (2003, April). *Bilingual language development: Does learning the new damage the old?* Paper presented at the meeting of the Society for Research in Child Development, Tampa.

Pfeifer, M., Goldsmith, H. H., Davidson, R. J., & Rickman, M. (2002). Continuity and change in inhibited and uninhibited children. *Child Development, 73,* 1474–1485.

Philippakis, A., Hemenway, D., Alexe, D. M., Dessypris, N., Spyridopoulos, T., & Petridou, E. (2004). A quantification of preventable unintentional childhood injury mortality in the United States. *Injury Prevention, 10,* 79–82.

Phillips, D. (2006). Child care as risk or protection in the context of welfare reform. In N. Cabrera, R. Hutchens, & H. E. Peters (Eds.), *From welfare to childcare.* Mahwah, NJ: Erlbaum.

Phillips, J. M., Brennan, M., Schwartz, C. E., & Cohen, L. M. (2005). The long-term impact of dialysis discontinuation on families. *Journal of Palliative Medicine, 8,* 79–85.

Phillips, S. (2003). Adolescent health. In I. B. Weiner (Ed.), *Handbook of psychology* (Vol. IX). New York: Wiley.

Phinney, J. S. (1996). When we talk about American ethnic groups, what do we mean? *American Psychologist, 51,* 918–927.

Phinney, J. S. (2003). Ethnic identity and acculturation. In K. M. Chun, P. S. Organista, & G. Marin (Eds.), *Acculturation.* Washington, DC: American Psychological Association.

Phinney, J. S. (2006, April). *Acculturation and adaptation of immigrant adolescents in thirteen countries.* Paper presented at the meeting of the Society for Research on Adolescence, San Francisco.

Phinney, J. S., & Alipuria, L. L. (1990). Ethnic identity in college students from four ethnic groups. *Journal of Adolescence, 13,* 171–183.

Phinney, J. S., Berry, J. W., Vedder, P., & Liebkind, K. (2006). The acculturation experience: Attitudes, identities, and behaviors of immigrant youth. In J. W. Berry, J. S. Phinney, D. L. Sam, & P. Vedder (Eds.), *Immigrant youth in cultural transition.* Mahwah, NJ: Erlbaum.

Piaget, J. (1932). *The moral judgment of the child.* New York: Harcourt Brace Jovanovich.

Piaget, J. (1952). Jean Piaget. In C. A. Murchison (Ed.), *A history of psychology in autobiography* (Vol. 4). Worcester, MA: Clark University Press.

Piaget, J. (1952). *The origins of intelligence in children.* (M. Cook, Trans.). New York: International Universities Press.

Piaget, J. (1954). *The construction of reality in the child.* New York: Basic Books.

Piaget, J. (1962). *Play, dreams, and imitation.* New York, W.W. Norton.

Piaget, J., & Inhelder, B. (1969). *The child's conception of space,* (F. J. Langdon & J. L. Lunger, Trans.). New York: W. W. Norton.

Pianta, R. C. (2005). Prevention. In H. W. Lee (Ed.), *Encyclopedia of school psychology.* Thousand Oaks, CA: Sage.

Pierce, K. M., Hamm, J. V., & Vandell, D. L. (1997, April). *Experiences in after-school programs and children's adjustment at school and at home.* Paper presented at the meeting of the Society for Research in Child Development, Washington, DC.

Pinette, M. G., Wax, J., Blackstone, J., Cartin, A., & McCrann, D. (2004). Timing of early amniocentesis as a function of membrane fusion. *Journal of Clinical Ultrasound, 32,* 8–11.

Pinheiro, R. T., Magalhaes, P. V., Horta, B. L., Pinheiro, K. A., da Silva, R. A., & Pinto, R. H. (2006). Is paternal postpartum depression associated with maternal postpartum depression? Population-based study in Brazil. *Acta Psychiatrica Scandinavia, 113,* 230–232.

Pinker, S. (1994). *The language instinct.* New York: HarperCollins.

Pinquart, M., & Sorensen, S. (2006). Gender differences in caregiver stressors, social resources, and health: An updated meta-analysis. *Journals of Gerontology B: Psychological Sciences and Social Sciences, 61,* P33–P45.

Piper, M. D. W., Mair, W., & Partridge, L. (2005). Counting the calories: The role of specific nutrients in extension of life span by food restriction. *Journals of Gerontology A: Biological Sciences and Medical Sciences, 60,* 549–555.

Pipp, S. L., Fischer, K. W., & Jennings, S. L. (1987). The acquisition of self and mother knowledge in infancy. *Developmental Psychology, 23,* 86–96.

Pitkanen, T., Lyyra, A. L., & Pulkkinen, L. (2005). Age of onset of drinking and the use of alcohol in adulthood: A follow-up study from age 8–42 for females and males. *Addiction, 100,* 652–661.

Pitt-Catsouphes, Kossek, E. E., & Sweet, S. (Eds.) (2006). *The work and family handbook.* Mahwah, NJ: Erlbaum.

Pittman, K., & Diversi, M. (2003). Social policy for the 21st century. In R. Larson, B. Brown, & J. Mortimer (Eds.), *Adolescents' preparation for the future. Perils and promise.* Malden, MA: Blackwell.

Piwoz, E. G., & Ross, J. S. (2005). Use of population-specific infant mortality rates to inform policy decisions regarding HIV and infant feeding. *Journal of Nutrition, 135,* 1113–1119.

Pizzamiglio, A. P., Saygin, S. L., Small, S., & Wilson, S. (2005). Language and the brain. In M. Tomasello & D. A. Slobin (Eds.), *Beyond nature-nurture.* Mahwah, NJ: Erlbaum.

Pleck, J. H. (1995). The gender-role strain paradigm. In R. F. Levant & W. S. Pollack (Eds.), *A new psychology of men.* New York: Basic Books.

Plomin, R. (1993, March). *Human behavioral genetics and development: An overview and update.* Paper presented at the biennial meeting of the Society for Research in Child Development, New Orleans.

Plomin, R. (1999). Genetics and general cognitive ability. *Nature, 402* (Suppl.), C25–C29.

Plomin, R. (2004). Genetics and developmental psychology. *Merrill-Palmer Quarterly, 50,* 341–352.

Plomin, R., DeFries, J. C., Craig, I. W., & McGuffin, P. (Eds.). (2003). *Behavioral genetics in the postgenomic era.* Washington, DC: APA Books.

Plomin, R., Reiss, D., Hetherington, E. M., & Howe, G. W. (1994). Nature and nurture: Contributions to measures of the family environment. *Developmental Psychology, 30,* 32–43.

Polivy, J., Herman, C. P., Mills, J., & Brock, H. (2003). Eating disorders in adolescence. In G. Adams & M. Berzonsky (Eds.), *Blackwell handbook of adolescence.* Malden, MA: Blackwell.

Pollack, W. (1999). *Real boys.* New York: Owl Books.

Pollitt, E. P., Gorman, K. S., Engle, P. L., Martorell, R., & Rivera, J. (1993). Early supplementary feeding and cognition. *Monographs of the Society for Research in Child Development, 58* (7, Serial No. 235).

Pollock, B. G. (2005). The pharmacokinetic imperative in late-life depression. *Journal of Clinical Psychopharmacology, 25* (4 Suppl 1), S19–S23.

Pontecorvo, C. (2004). Thinking with others: The social dimension of learning in families and schools. In A. Perret-Clermont, L. B. Resnick, C. Pontecorvo, T. Zittoun, & Burge, B. (Eds.) *Joining society.* New York: Cambridge University Press.

Ponterotto, J. G., Casas, J. M., Suzuki, L. A., & Alexander, C. M. (Eds.) (2001). *Handbook of multicultural counseling.* Thousand Oaks, CA: Sage.

Poole, D. A., & Lindsay, D. S. (1995). Interviewing preschoolers: Effects of nonsuggestive techniques, parental coaching and leading questions on reports of nonexperienced events. *Journal of Experimental Child Psychology, 60,* 129–154.

Poole, D. A., & Lindsay, D. S. (1996). *Effects of parents' suggestions, interviewing techniques, and age on young children's event reports paper.* Presented at the NATO Advanced Study Institute, Porte de Bourgenay, France.

Popenoe, D., & Whitehead, B. D. (2005). *The state of our unions: 2005.* Piscataway, NJ: The National Marriage Project, Rutgers University.

Popovic, V., & Duntas, L. H. (2005). Leptin TRH and ghrelin: Influence on energy homeostasis at rest and during exercise. *Hormone and Metabolism Research, 37,* 533–537.

Porath, A. J., & Fried, P. A. (2005). Effects of prenatal cigarette and marijuana exposure on drug use among offspring. *Neurotoxicology and Teratology, 27,* 267–277.

Porges, S. W., Doussard-Roosevelt, J. A., & Maiti, A. K. (1994). Vagal tone and the physiological regulation of emotion. In N. A. Fox (Ed.), *Emotion regulation: Behavioral and biological considerations. Monographs of the Society for Research in Child Development, 59* (Serial No. 240), 167–196.

Posner, J. K., & Vandell, D. L. (1994). Low-income children's after-school care: Are there benefits of after-school programs? *Child Development, 65,* 440–456.

Potvin, L., Champagne, F., & Laberge-Nadeau, C. (1988). Mandatory driver training and road safety: The Quebec experience. *American Journal of Public Health, 78,* 1206–1212.

Poudevigne, M. S., & O'Connor, P. J. (2005). Physical activity and mood during pregnancy. *Medical Science and Sports Exercise, 37,* 1374–1380.

Poudevigne, M. S., & O'Connor, P. J. (2006). A review of physical activity patterns in pregnant women and their relationship to psychological health. *Sports Medicine, 36,* 19–38.

Powell, D. R. (2005). Searching for what works in parenting interventions. In T. Luster & L. Okagaki (Eds.), *Parenting* (2nd ed.). Mahwah, NJ: Erlbaum.

Powell, D. R. (2006). Families and early childhood interventions. In W. Damon & R. Lerner (Eds.), *Handbook of child psychology* (6th ed.). New York: Wiley.

Powell, G. N. (2004). *Managing a diverse workforce* (2nd ed.). Thousand Oaks, CA: Sage.

Powers, L. E., & Wampold, B. E. (1994). Cognitive-behavioral factors in adjustment to adult bereavement. *Death Studies, 18,* 1–24.

Pratt, H. D., Patel, D. R., & Greydanus, D. E. (2003). Behavioral aspects of children's sports. *Pediatric Clinics of North America, 50,* 879–899.

Pratt, M. W., Danse, H. A., Arnold, M. L., Norris, J. E., & Filyer, R. (2001). Adult generativity and the socialization of adolescents. *Journal of Personality, 69,* 89–120.

Pressley M. (2000). What should comprehension instruction be the instruction of? In M. Kamil (Ed.), *Handbook of reading research.* Mahwah, NJ: Erlbaum.

Pressley, M., Allington, R., Wharton-McDonald, R., Block, C. C., & Morrow, L. M. (2001). *Learning to read: Lessons from exemplary first grades.* New York: Guilford.

Pressley, M., Cariligia-Bull, T., Deane, S., & Schneider, W. (1987). Short-term memory, verbal competence, and age as predictors of imagery instructional effectiveness. *Journal of Experimental Child Psychology, 43,* 194–211.

Pressley, M., Dolezal, S. E., Raphael, L. M., Welsh, L. M., Bogner, K., & Roehrig, A. D. (2003). *Motivating primary-grades teachers.* New York: Guilford.

Pressley, M., & Harris, K. R. (2006). Cognitive strategies instruction. In P. A. Alexander & P. H. Winne (Eds.), *Handbook of educational psychology* (2nd ed.). Mahwah, NJ: Erlbaum.

Pressley, M., & Hilden, K. (2006). Cognitive strategies. In W. Damon & R. Lerner (Eds.), *Handbook of child psychology* (6th ed.). New York: Wiley.

Pressley, M., Raphael, L. Gallagher, D., & DiBella, J. (2004). Providence-St. Mel School: How a school that works for African-American students works. *Journal of Educational Psychology, 96,* 216–235.

Pressman, S. D., Cohen, S., Miller, G. E., Barkin, A., Rabin, B. S., & Treanor, J. J. (2005). Loneliness, social network size, and immune response to influenza vaccination in college freshmen. *Health Psychology, 24,* 297–306.

Preston, A. M., Rodriguez, C., Rivera, C. E., & Sahai, H. (2003). Influence of environmental tobacco smoke on vitamin C status in children. *American Journal of Clinical Nutrition, 77,* 167–172.

Preville, M., Hebert, R., Boyer, R., Bravo, G., & Seguin, M. (2005). Physical health and mental disorders in elderly suicide: A case-control study. *Aging and Mental Health, 9,* 576–584.

Price, C. A., & Joo, E. (2005). Exploring the relationship between marital status and women's retirement satisfaction. *International Journal of Aging and Human Development, 61,* 37–55.

Prickaerts, J., Koopmans, G., Blokland, A., & Scheepens, A. (2004). Learning and adult neurogenesis: Survival with or without proliferation? *Neurobiology of Learning and Memory, 81,* 1–11.

Prigerson, H. G. (2004). Complicated grief: When the path to adjustment leads to a dead end. *Bereavement Care, 23,* 38–40.

Prigerson, H. G. (2005, July 12). *Research to validate diagnostic criteria for complicated grief.* Paper presented at the 7th International Conference on Grief and Bereavement in Contemporary Society, Kings College, London.

Pringle, P. J., Geary, M. P., Rodeck, C. H., Kingdom, J. C., Kayamba-Kays, S., & Hind-Marsh, P. C. (2005). The influence of cigarette smoking on antenatal growth, birth size, and the insulin-like growth factor axis. *Journal of Clinical Endocrinology and Metabolism, 90,* 2556–2562.

Pritchard, F. F., & Whitehead, F. F. (2004). *Serve and learn.* Mahwah, NJ: Erlbaum.

Probst, T. M. (2004). Economic stressors. In J. Baring, E. K. Kelloway, & M. R. Frone (Eds.), *Handbook of work stress.* Thousand Oaks, CA: Sage.

Promislow, D. E. L., Fedorka, K. K., & Burger, J. M. S. (2006). Evolutionary biology of aging: Future directions. In E. J. Masoro & S. N. Austad (Eds.), *Handbook of the biology of aging* (6th ed.). San Diego: Academic Press.

Province, M. A., Hadley, E. C., Hornbrook, M. C., Lipitz, L. A., Miller, J. P., Mulrow, C. D., Ory, M. G., Sattin, R. W., Tinetti, M. E., & Wolf, S. L. (1995). The effects of exercise on falls in elderly patients. *Journal of the American Medical Association, 273,* 1341–1347.

Pruchno, R., & Rosenbaum, J. (2003). Social relationships in adulthood and old age. In I. B. Weiner (Ed.), *Handbook of psychology* (Vol. VI). New York: Wiley.

Pryor, J. H., Hurtado, S., Saenz, V. B., Lindholm, J. A., Korn, W. S., & Mahoney, K. M. (2005). *The American freshman: National norms for fall 2005.* Los Angeles: Higher Education Research Institute, UCLA.

Pujol, J., Lopez-Sala, A., Sebastian-Galles, N., Deus, J., Cardoner, N., Soriano-Mas, C., Moreno, A., & Sans, A. (2004). Delayed myelination in children with developmental delay detected by volumetric MRI. *Neuroimage, 22,* 897–903.

Punzalan, C., Paxton, K.C., Guentzel, H., Bluthenthal, R.N., Staunton, A.D., Mejia, G., Morales, L., & Miranda, J. (2006). Seeking community input to improve implementation of a lifestyle modification program. *Ethnicity and Disease, 16* (Suppl 1), S79–S88.

Putnam Investments (2006). *Survey of the working retired.* Franklin, MA: Putnam Investments.

Putnam, S. P., Sanson, A. V., & Rothbart, M. K. (2002). Child temperament and parenting. In M. H. Bornstein (Ed.), *Handbook of parenting* (2nd ed.). Mahwah, NJ: Erlbaum.

Putneg, N. M., & Bengtson, V. L. (2001). Families, intergenerational relationships, and kinkeeping in midlife. In M. E. Lachman (Ed.), *Handbook of midlife development.* New York: Wiley.

Pyke, K. D., & Bengtson, V. L. (1996). Caring more or less: Individualistic and collectivist systems of family eldercare. *Journal of Marriage and the Family, 58,* 379–392.

Quadrel, M. J., Fischoff, B., & Davis, W. (1993). Adolescent (in) vulnerability. *American Psychologist, 48,* 102–116.

Quilliam, S. (2004). Hormone replacement therapy (HRT). *Journal of Family Planning and Health Care, 30,* 59–61.

Quinsey, V. L. (2003). The etiology of anomalous sexual preferences in men. *Annals of the New York Academy of Science, 989,* 105–117.

Rafaelli, M., & Crockett, L. J. (2003). Sexual risk taking in adolescence: The role of self-regulation and attraction to risk. *Developmental Psychology, 39,* 1036–1046.

Raffaelli, M., & Ontai, L. L. (2001). "She's sixteen years old and there's boys calling over to the house": An exploratory study of sexual socialization in Latino families. *Culture, Health, and Sexuality, 3,* 295–310.

Raffaelli, M., & Ontai, L. L. (2004). Gender socialization in Latino/a families: Results from two retrospective studies. *Sex Roles, 50,* 287–299.

Rahal, T. A., May, C. P., & Hasher, L. (2002). Truth and character: Sources that older adults can remembers. *Psychological Science, 13,* 101–105.

Rajah, M. N., & D'Esposito, M. (2005). Region-specific changes in prefrontal function with age: A review of PET and fMRI studies on working memory and episodic memory. *Brain, 128,* 1964–1983.

Rajeshwari, R., Yang, S. J., Niclas, T. A., & Berensen, G. S. (2005). Secular trends in children's sweetened-beverage consumption (1973 to 1994): The Bogalusa Heart Study. *Journal of the American Dietetic Association, 105,* 208–214.

Rajfer, J., Aliotta, P.J., Steidie, C.P., Fitch, W.P., Zhao, Y., & Yu, A. (2006, in press). Tadalafil dosed once a day in men with erectile dysfunction: A randomized, double-bind, placebo-controlled study in the U.S. *International Journal of Impotence Research.*

Ramacciotti, C. E., Coli, E., Paoli, R., Gabriellini, G., Schulte, F., Castrogiovanni, S., Dell'Osso, L., & Garfinkel, R. E. (2005). The relationship between binge eating disorder and non-purging bulimia nervosa. *Eating and Weight Disorders, 10,* 8–12.

Ramey, C. T., & Campbell, F. A. (1984). Preventive education for high-risk children: Cognitive consequences of the Carolina Abecedarian Project. *American Journal of Mental Deficiency, 88,* 515–523.

Ramey, C. T., & Ramey, S. L. (1998). Early prevention and early experience. *American Psychologist, 53,* 109–120.

Ramey, C. T., Ramey, S. L., & Lanzi, R. G. (2001). Intelligence and experience. In R. J. Sternberg & E. I. Grigorenko (Eds.), *Environment effects on cognitive development.* Mahwah, NJ: Erlbaum.

Ramey, C. T., Ramey, S. L., & Lanzi, R. G. (2006). Children's health and education. In W. Damon & R. Lerner (Eds.), *Handbook of child psychology* (6th ed.). New York; Wiley.

Ramey, S. L. (2005). Human developmental science serving children and families: Contributions of the NICHD study of early child care. In NICHD Early Child Care Network (Eds.), *Child care and development.* New York: Guilford.

Rampage, C., Eovaldi, M., Ma, C., & Weigel-Foy, C. (2003). Adoptive families. In F. Walsh (Ed.), *Normal family processes: Growing diversity and complexity* (3rd ed.). New York: Guilford Press.

Ramphal, C. (1962). *A study of three current problems in education.* Unpublished doctoral dissertation, University of Natal, India.

Ramsey, P. S., Nuthalapaty, E. S., Lu, G., Ramin, S., & Ramin, K. D. (2004). A survey of maternal-fetal medicine providers. *American Journal of Obstetrics and Gynecology, 191,* 1497–1502.

Randall, O. S., Kwagyan, J., Huang, Z., Xu, S., Ketete, M., & Magbool, A. R. (2005). Effect of diet and exercise on pulse pressure and cardiac function in morbid obesity: Analysis of 24-hour ambulatory blood pressure. *Journal of Clinical Hypertension, 7,* 445–463.

Randolph, S., & Kochanoff, A. (2004). Child care research at the dawn of a new millennium. In J. G. Bremner & A. Fogel (Eds.), *Blackwell handbook of infant development.* Malden, MA: Blackwell.

Rantz, M. J., Hicks, L., Petroski, G. F., Madsen, R. W., Mehr, D. R., Conn, V., Zwygart-Staffacher, & Mass, M. (2004). Stability and sensitivity of nursing home quality indicators. *Journals of Gerontology A: Biological and Medical Sciences, 59,* M79–M82.

Rao, G. D., & Tan, S. L. (2005). In vitro maturation of oocytes. *Seminars in Reproductive Medicine, 23,* 242–247.

Rapaport, S. (1994, November 28). Interview. *U.S. News & World Report,* p. 94.

Rasulo, D., Christensen, K., & Tomasini, C. (2005). The influence of social relations on mortality in later life: A study on elderly Danish twins. *Gerontologist, 45,* 601–608.

Ratey, J. (2006, March 27). Commentary in L. Szabo, "ADHD treatment is getting a workout." *USA Today,* 6D.

Rathbun, R. C., Lockhart, S. M., & Stephens, J. R. (2006). Current HIV treatment guidelines—A review. *Current Pharmacology Design, 12,* 1045–1063.

Rathunde, K., & Csikszentmihalyi M. (2006). The developing person: An experiential perspective. In W. Damon & R. Lerner (Eds.), *Handboook of child psychology* (6th ed.). New York: Wiley.

Raudenbush, S. (2001). Longitudinal data analysis. *Annual Review of Psychology* (Vol. 52). Palo Alto, CA: Annual Reviews.

Ravid, D., Levie, R., & Ben-Zvi, G. A. (2004). Morphological disorders. In L. Verhoeven & H. Van Balkom (Eds.), *The classification of language disorders.* Mahwah, NJ: Erlbaum.

Raymo, J. M., & Sweeney, M. M. (2006). Work-family conflict and retirement preferences. *Journals of Gerontology B: Psychological Sciences and Social Sciences, 61,* S161–S169.

Raymo, J. M., Liang, J., Sugisawa, H., Kobayashi, E., & Sugihara, Y. (2004). Work at older ages in Japan: Variation by gender and employment status. *Journals of Gerontology B: Psychological Social Sciences, 59,* S154–S163

Reaven, G. M. (2006). The metabolic syndrome: Is this diagnosis necessary? *The American Journal of Clinical Nutrition, 83,* 1237–1247.

Reb, A. M. (2003). Palliative and end-of-life care: Policy analysis. *Oncology Nursing Forum, 30,* 35–50.

Rebollo, M. A., & Montiel, S. (2006) Attention and the executive functions. *Revista de Neurologia (Spanish), 42* (Suppl.), S3–S7.

Redinbaugh, E. M., MacCallum, J., & Kiecolt-Glaser, J. K. (1995). Recurrent syndromal depression in caregivers. *Psychology and Aging, 10,* 358–368.

Reed, S. K. (2007). *Cognitive psychology* (7th ed.). Belmont, CA: Wadsworth.

Reese, C. M., & Cherry, K. E. (2004). Practical memory concerns in adulthood. *International Journal of Aging and Human Development, 59,* 235–253.

Reeves, G., & Schweitzer, J. (2004). Pharmacological management of attention deficit hyperactivity disorder. *Expert Opinions in Pharmacotherapy, 5,* 1313–1320.

Regalado, M., Sareen, H., Inkelas, M., Wissow, L. S., & Halfon, N. (2004). Parents' discipline of young children: Results from the National Survey of Early Childhood Health. *Pediatrics, 113,* 1952–1958.

Regev, R. H., Lusky, A., Dolfin, T., Litmanovitz, I., Arnon, S., Reichman, B., & the Israel Neonatal Network. (2003). Excess mortality and morbidity among small-for-gestational-age premature infants: A population-based study. *Journal of Pediatrics, 143,* 186–191.

Reid, J. D., & Willis, S. L. (1999). Middle age: New thoughts, new directions. In S. L. Willis & J. D. Reid (Eds.), *Life in the middle.* San Diego: Academic Press.

Reid, P. T., & Zalk, S. R. (2001). Academic environments: Gender and ethnicity in U.S. higher education. In J. Worell (Ed.), *Encyclopedia of women and gender.* San Diego: Academic Press.

Reinders, H., & Youniss, J. (2006). School-based required community service and civic development in adolescence. *Applied Developmental Science, 10,* 2–12.

Reiner, W. G., & Gearhart, J. P. (2004). Discordant sexual identity in some genetic males with cloacal exstrophy assigned to female sex at birth. *New England Journal of Medicine, 350,* 333–341.

Reis, O., & Youniss, O. (2004). Patterns of identity change and development in relationships with mothers and friends. *Journal of Adolescent Research, 19,* 32–44.

Reisberg, B. (2006). Diagnostic criteria in dementia: A comparison of current criteria, research challenges, and implications for DSM-V. *Journal of Geriatric Psychiatry and Neurology, 19,* 137–146.

Reisman, A. S. (2001). Death of a spouse: Basic assumptions and continuation of bonds. *Death Studies, 25,* 445–460.

Reitzes, D. C., & Mutran, E. J. (2004). Grandparenthood: Factors influencing frequency of grandparent-grandchildren contact and grandparent role satisfaction. *Journals of Gerontology B: Psychological and Social Sciences, 59,* S9–S16.

Religion in America. (1993). Princeton, NJ: Princeton Religious Research Center.

Renninger, K. A., & Sigel, I. E. (2006). Applying research to practice. In W. Damon & R. Lerner (Eds.), *Handbook of child psychology* (6th ed.). New York: Wiley.

Rest, J. R., Narvaez, D., Bebeau, M. J., & Thoma, S. J. (1999). *Postconventional moral thinking.* Mahwah, NJ: Erlbaum.

Resta, R. G. (2005). Changing demographics of advanced maternal age (AMA) and the impact on the predicted incidence of Down syndrome in the United States: Implications for prenatal screening and genetic counseling. *American Journal of Medical Genetics A, 133,* 31–36.

Reuter-Lorenz. P. A., Jonides, J., Smith. E. S., Hartley, A., Miller, A., Marshuetz, C., et al. (2000). Age differences in the frontal lateralization of verbal and spatial working memory revealed by PET. *Journal of Cognitive Neuroscience, 12,* 174–187.

Revelle, S. P. (2004). High standards + high stakes = high achievement in Massachusetts. *Phi Delta Kappan, 85,* 591–597.

Reyna, V. F. (2004). How people make decisions that involve risk: A dual-process approach. *Current Directions in Psychological Science, 13,* 60–66.

Reyna, V. F., & Brainerd, C. J. (1995). Fuzzy-trace theory: An interim analysis. *Learning and Individual Differences, 7,* 1–75.

Reynolds, A. J. (1999, April). *Pathways to long-term effects in the Chicago Child-Parent Center Program.* Paper presented at the meeting of the Society for Research in Child Development, Albuquerque.

Rhodes, G. M. (2005). *Estimated HIV prevalence in the United States at the end of 2003.* Paper presented at the National HIV Prevention Conference, Atlanta.

Rice, D. P., & Fineman, N. (2004). Economic implications of increased longevity in the United States. *Annual Review of Public Health, 25,* 457–473.

Richardson, C. R., Faulkner, G., McDevitt, J., Skrinar, G. S., Hutchinson, D. S., Piette, J. D. (2005). Integrating physical activity into mental health services for persons with serious mental illness. *Psychiatric Services, 56,* 324–331.

Richardson, G. A., Ryan, C., Willford, J., Day, N. L., & Goldschmidt, L. (2002). Prenatal alcohol and marijuana exposure: Effects on neuropsychological outcomes at 10 years. *Neurotoxicology and Teratology, 24,* 309–320.

Richter, L. (2003). Poverty, underdevelopment, and infant mental health. *Journal of Pediatric and Child Health, 39,* 243–248.

Rickards, T., & deCock, C. (2003). Understanding organizational creativity: Toward a paradigmatic approach. In M. A. Runco (Ed.), *Creativity research handbook.* Cresskill, NJ: Hampton Press.

Rickert, V. I., Wiemann, C. M., & Vaughan, R. D. (2005). Disclosure of date/acquaintance rape: Who reports and when. *Journal of Pediatric and Adolescent Gynecology, 18,* 17–24.

Riddell, M. C., & Iscoe, K. E. (2006). Physical activity, sport, and pediatric diabetes. *Pediatric Diabetes, 7,* 60–70.

Ridgeway, D., Waters, E., & Kuczaj, S. A. (1985). Acquisition of emotion-descriptive language: Receptive and productive vocabulary norms for ages 18 months to 6 years. *Developmental Psychology, 21,* 901–908.

Riebe, D., Garber, C. E., Rossi, J. S., Greaney, M. L., Nigg, C. R., Lees, F. D., Burbank, P. M., & Clark, P. G. (2005). Physical activity, physical function, and stages of change in older adults. *American Journal of Health Behavior, 29,* 70–80.

Riediger, M., Li, S.-C., & Lindenberger, U. (2006). Selection, optimization, and compensation as developmental mechanisms of adaptive resource allocation: Review and preview. In J. E. Birren & K. W. Schaie (Eds.), *Handbook of the psychology of aging* (6th ed.). San Diego: Academic Press.

Riekmann, T. R., Wadsworth, M. E., & Deyhle, D. (2004). Cultural identity, explanatory style, and depression in Navajo adolescents. *Cultural Diversity & Ethnic Minority Psychology, 10,* 365–382.

Rifas-Shiman, S. L., Rich-Edwards, J. W., Willett, W. C., Kleinman, K. P., Oken, E., & Gillman, M. W. (2006). Changes in dietary intake from the first to the second trimester of pregnancy. *Pediatric and Perinatal Epidemiology, 20,* 35–42.

Rigby, K. (2002). *New perspectives on bullying.* London: Jessica Kingsley Publishers.

Riggs, N. R., Elfenbaum, P., & Pentz, M. A. (2006). Parent program component analysis in a drug abuse prevention trial. *Journal of Adolescent Health, 39,* 66–72.

Righetti-Veltema, M., Conne-Perreard, E., Bousquest, A., & Manzano, J. (2002). Postpartum depression and mother-infant relationship at 3 months old. *Journal of Affective Disorders, 70,* 291–306.

Riley, E. H., Fuentes-Afflick, E., Jackson, R. A., Escobar, G. J., Brawarsky, P., Schreiber, M., & Haas, J. S. (2005). Correlates of prescription drug use during pregnancy. *Journal of Women's Health, 14,* 401–409.

Riley, K. P., Snowdon, D. A., Derosiers, M. F., & Markesbery, W. R. (2005). Early life linguistic ability, late life cognitive function, and neuropathology: Findings from the Nun Study. *Neurobiology of Aging, 26,* 341–347.

Riley, K. P., Snowdon, D. A., & Markesbery, W. R. (2002). Alzheimer's neurofibrillary pathology and the spectrum of cognitive function: Findings from the Nun Study. *Annals of Neurology, 5,* 567–577.

Riley, L. D., & Bowen, C. (2005). The sandwich generation: Challenges and coping strategies of multigenerational families. *Family Journal, 13,* 52–58.

Rimberg, H. M., & Lewis, R. J. (1994). Older adolescents and AIDS: Correlates of self-reported safer sex practices. *Journal of Research on Adolescence, 4,* 453–464.

Rimm, E. B., Stampfer, M. J., Ascherio, A., Giovannucci, E., Colditz, G. A., & Willett, W. C. (1993). Vitamin E consumption and the risk of coronary heart disease in men. *New England Journal of Medicine, 328,* 1450–1456.

Rincon, M., Muzumdar, R., & Barzilai, N. (2006). Aging, body fat, and carbohydrate metabolism. In E. J. Masoro & S. N. Austad (Eds.), *Handbook of the biology of aging* (6th ed.). San Diego: Academic Press.

Ringdal, G. I., Jordhoy, M. S., Ringdal, K., & Kaasa, S. (2001). The first year of grief and bereavement in close family members to individuals who have died of cancer. *Palliative Medicine, 15,* 91–105.

Ringman, J. M., & Cummings, J. L. (2006). Current and emerging pharmacological treatment options for dementia. *Behavioral Neurology, 17,* 5–16.

Rivera, C., & Collum, E. (Eds.). (2006) *State assessment policy and practice for English language learners.* Mahwah, NJ: Erlbaum.

Rizzo, M. S. (1999, May 8). Genetic counseling combines science with a human touch. *Kansas City Star,* p. 3.

Robert, S. A., & Ruel, E. (2006). Racial segregation and health disparities between black and white older adults. *Journals of Gerontology B: Psychological Sciences and Social Sciences, 61,* S203–S211.

Roberto, K. A., Allen, K. R., Blieszner, R. (2001). Grandfathers' perceptions and expectations of relationships with their adult grandchildren. *Journal of Family Issues, 22,* 407–426.

Roberto, K. A., & Skoglund, R. R. (1996). Interactions with grandparents and great-grandparents: A comparison of activities, influences, and relationships. *International Journal of Aging and Human Development, 43,* 107–117.

Roberts, B. L., Dunkle, R., & Haug, M. (1994). Physical, psychological, and social resources as moderators of stress to mental health of the very old. *Journal of Gerontology, 49,* S35–S43.

Roberts, B. W. (2006). Personality development and organizational dynamics across the life span. In B. M. Staw (Ed.), *Research on organizational behavior.* London: Elsevier Science/JAI Press.

Roberts, B. W., & Helson, R. (1997). Changes in culture, changes in personality: The influence of individualism in a longitudinal study of women. *Journal of Personality and Social Psychology, 72,* 641–651.

Roberts, B. W., Walton, K. E., & Bogg, T. (2005). Conscientiousness and health across the life course. *Review of General Psychology, 9,* 156–168.

Roberts, B. W., Walton, K. E., & Viechtbauer, W. (2006). Patterns of mean-level change in personality traits across the life course: A meta-analysis of longitudinal studies. *Psychological Bulletin, 132,* 1–25.

Roberts, D. F., Hennikson, L., & Foehr, V. G. (2004). Adolescents and the media. In R. Lerner & L. Steinberg (Eds.). *Handbook of adolescent psychology.* New York: Wiley.

Roberts, D. F., Henriksen, L., & Foehr, V. G. (2004). Adolescents and the media. In R. Lerner & L. Steinberg (Eds.), *Handbook of adolescent psychology.* New York: Wiley.

Roberts, S. B., & Rosenberg, I. (2006). Nutrition and aging: Changes in the regulation of energy metabolism with aging. *Physiology Review, 86,* 651–667.

Roberts, W. B. (2005). *Bullying from both sides.* Thousand Oaks, CA: Sage.

Robins, R. W., Trzesniewski, K. H., Tracey, J. L., Potter, J., & Gosling, S. D. (2002). Age differences in self-esteem from age 9 to 90. *Psychology and Aging, 17,* 423–434

Robinson, J. H., & Clay, D. L. (2005). Potential school violence: Relationship between teacher anxiety and warning-sign identification. *Psychology in the Schools, 42,* 623–635.

Robinson, K. M., Buckwalter, K. C., & Reed, D. (2005). Predictors of use of services among dementia caregivers. *Western Journal of Nursing, 27,* 126–140.

Robinson, T., & Umphery, D. (2006). First- and third-person perceptions of images of older people in advertising: An intergenerational evaluation. *International Journal of Aging and Human Development, 62,* 159–173.

Roche, H. M., Phillips, C., & Gibney, M. J. (2005). The metabolic syndrome: The crossroads of diet and genetics. *Proceedings in Nutrition Science, 64,* 371–377.

Rode, S. S., Chang, P., Fisch, R. O., & Sroufe, L. A. (1981). Attachment patterns of infants separated at birth. *Developmental Psychology, 17,* 188–191.

Rodin, J. (1983). Behavioral medicine: Beneficial effects of self-control training in aging. *International Review of Applied Psychology, 32,* 153–181.

Rodin, J., & Langer, E. J. (1977). Long-term effects of a control-relevant intervention with the institutionalized aged. *Journal of Personality and Social Psychology, 35,* 397–402.

Rodrigo, J., Fernandez, A. P., Serrano, J., Peinado, M. A., & Martinez, A. (2005). The role of free radicals in cerebral hypoxia and ischemia. *Free Radical Biology & Medicine, 39,* 26–50.

Rodriguez-Cano, T., Beato-Fernandez, L. & Llario, A. B. (2006). Body dissatisfaction as a predictor of self-reported suicide attempts in adolescents: A Spanish community perspective. *Journal of Adolescent Health, 38,* 684–688.

Rodrigues, A. E., Hall, J. H., & Fincham, F. D. (2006). What predicts divorce and relationship dissolution. In M. A. Fine & J. H. Harvey (Eds.). *Handbook of divorce and relationship dissolution.* Mahwah, NJ: Erlbaum.

Roefs, A., Herman, C. P., Macleod, C. M., Smulders, F. T., & Jansen, A. (2005). At first sight: How do restrained eaters evaluate high-fat palatable foods? *Appetite, 44,* 103–114.

Roese, N. J., & Summerville, A. (2005). What we regret most ... and why. *Personality and Social Psychology Bulletin, 31,* 1273–1285.

Rogers, L. S. (2004). Meaning of bereavement among older African American widows. *Geriatric Nursing, 25,* 10–16.

Rogerson, P. A., & Kim, D. (2005). Population distribution and redistribution of the baby-boom cohort in the United States: Recent trends and implications. *Proceedings of the National Academy of Science, USA.*

Rohner, R. P., & Rohner, E. C. (1981). Parental acceptance-rejection and parental control: Cross-cultural codes. *Ethnology, 20,* 245–260.

Rohrer, J. F., Pierce, J. R., & Blackburn, C. (2005). Lifestyle and mental health. *Preventive Medicine, 40,* 483–443.

Roman, G. C., Sachdev, P., Royall, D. R., Bullock, R. A., Orgogozo, J. M., Lopez-Pousa, S., Arizaga, R., & Wallin, A. (2004). Vascular cognitive disorder: A new diagnostic category updating vascular cognitive impairment and vascular dementia. *Journal of Neurological Science, 226,* 81–87.

Ronnlund, M., Nyberg, L., Backman, L., & Nilsson, L. G. (2005). Stability, growth, and decline in adult life span development of declarative memory: Cross-sectional and longitudinal data from a population-based study. *Psychology and Aging, 20,* 3–18.

Roopnarine, J. L., Fouts, H. J., Lamb, M. E., & Lewis-Elligan, T. Y. (2005). Mothers' and fathers' behaviors toward their 3- to 4-month-old infants in lower, middle, and upper socioeconomic status African American families. *Developmental Psychology, 41,* 723–732.

Roopnarine, J. L., & Metindogan, A. (2006). Early childhood education research in cross-national perspective. In B. Spodek & O. N. Saracho (Eds.), *Handbook of research on the education of young children.* Mahwah, NJ: Erlbaum.

Roper Starch Worldwide. (2000). *Attitudes toward retirement: A poll.* New York: Author.

Rosa, E. F., Silva, A. C., Ihara, S. S., Mora, O. A., Aboulafia, J., & Nouailhetas, V. L. (2005). Habitual exercise program protects murine intestinal, skeletal, and cardiac muscles against aging. *Journal of Applied Physiology, 99,* 1569–1575.

Roscoe, L. A., Malphurs, J. E., Dragovic, L. J., & Cohen, D. (2002). A comparison of characteristics of Kevorkian euthanasia cases and physician-assisted suicides in Oregon. *The Gerontologist, 41,* 439–446.

Rose, L. C., & Gallup, A. M. (2000). The 32nd annual Phi Delta Kappa/Gallup Poll of the public's attitudes toward the public schools. *Phi Delta Kappan, 82* (No. 10), 41–58.

Rose, M. R., & Mueller, L. D. (2006). *Evolution and ecology of the organism.* Upper Saddle River, NJ: Prentice Hall.

Rose, S. A. (1990). Cross-modal transfer in human infants: What is being transferred? *Annals of the New York Academy of Sciences, 608,* 38–47.

Rose, S. A., Feldman, J. F., & Wallace, I. F. (1992). Infant information processing in relation to six-year cognitive outcomes. *Child Development, 63,* 1126–1141.

Rose, S., & Frieze, I. R. (1993). Young singles' contemporary dating scripts. *Sex Roles, 28,* 499–509.

Rosen, G. D. (Ed.). (2006). *The dyslexic brain.* Mahwah, NJ: Erlbaum.

Rosenberg, T. J., Garbers, S., Lipkind, H., & Chiasson, M. A. (2005). Maternal obesity and diabetes as risk factors for adverse pregnancy outcomes: Differences among 4 racial/ethnic groups. *American Journal of Public Health, 95,* 1545–1551.

Rosenblith, J. F. (1992). *In the beginning* (2nd ed.). Newbury Park, CA: Sage.

Rosenblum, G. D., & Lewis, M. (2003). Emotional development in adolescent care. In G. Adams & M. Berzonsky (Eds.), *Blackwell handbook of adolescence.* Malden MA: Blackwell.

Rosenfeld, A., & Stark, E. (1987, May). The prime of our lives. *Psychology Today,* pp. 62–72.

Rosenstein, D., & Oster, H. (1988). Differential facial responses to four basic tastes in newborns. *Child Development, 59,* 1555–1568.

Rosenthal, C. J., Martin-Matthews, A., & Matthews, S. H. (1996). Caught in the middle? Occupancy in multiple roles and help to parents in a national probability sample of Canadian adults. *Journals of Gerontology B: Psychological Sciences and Social Sciences, 51,* S274–S283.

Rosenzweig, M. R. (1969). Effects of heredity and environment on brain chemistry, brain anatomy, and learning ability in the rat. In M. Monosevitz, G. Lindzey, & D. D. Thiessen (Eds.), *Behavioral genetics.* New York: Appleton-Century-Crofts.

Rosilio, M., Carel, J. C., Ecosse, E., & Chaussainon, J. L. (2005). Adult height of prepubertal short children born small for gestational age treated with GH. *European Journal of Endocrinology, 152,* 835–843.

Rosnow, R. L., & Rosenthal, R. L. (2005). *Beginning behavioral research* (5th ed.). Upper Saddle River, NJ: Prentice Hall.

Ross, C., Kirby, G. (2006). Welfare-to-work transitions for parents of infants. In N. Cabrera, R. Hutchens, H. E. Peters, & L. Peters (Eds.), *From welfare to childcare.* Mahwah, NJ: Erlbaum.

Ross, M.E.T., & Aday, L.A. (2006). Stress and coping in African American grandparents who are raising their children. *Journal of Family Issues, 27,* 912–932.

Rossi, A. S. (1989). A life-course approach to gender, aging, and intergenerational relations. In K. W. Schaie & C. Schooler (Eds.), *Social structure and aging.* Hillsdale, NJ: Erlbaum.

Rossi, A. S. (2004). The menopausal transition and aging processes. In G. Brim, C. D. Ryff, & R. Kessler (Eds.), *How healthy we are: A national study of well-being in midlife.* Chicago: University of Chicago Press.

Rossi, S., Miniussi, C., Pasqualetti, P., Babiloni, C., Rossini, P. M., & Cappa, S. F. (2005). Age-related functional changes of prefrontal cortex in long-term memory: A repetitive transcranial magnetic stimulation study. *Journal of Neuroscience, 24,* 7939–7944.

Roth, G. S., Lane, M. A., Ingram, D. K., Mattison, J. A., Elahi, D., Tobin, J. D., Muller, D., & Metter, E. J. (2002). Biomarks of caloric restriction may predict longevity in humans. *Science, 297,* 811.

Roth, J. L., Brooks-Gunn, J., Murray, L., & Foster, W. (1998). Promoting healthy adolescents: Synthesis of youth development program evaluations. *Journal of Research on Adolescence, 8,* 423–459.

Rothbart, M. K. (2004). Temperament and the pursuit of an integrated developmental psychology. *Merrill-Palmer Quarterly, 50,* 492–505.

Rothbart, M. K., & Bates, J. E. (1998). Temperament. In W. Damon (Ed.), *Handbook of child psychology* (5th ed., Vol. 3). New York: Wiley.

Rothbart, M. K., & Bates, J. E. (2006). Temperament. In W. Damon & R. Lerner (Eds.), *Handbook of child psychology* (6th ed.). New York: Wiley.

Rothbart, M. K., & Putnam, S. P. (2002). Temperament and socialization. In L. Pulkkinen & A. Caspi (Eds.), *Paths to successful development.* New York: Cambridge University Press.

Rothbaum, F., Poll, M., Azuma, H., Miyake, K., & Weisz, J. (2000). The development of close relationships in Japan and the United States: Paths of symbiotic harmony and generative tension. *Child Development, 71,* 1121–1142.

Routasalo, P. E., Savikko, N., Tilvis, R. S., Strandberg, T. E., & Pitkala, K. H. (2006). Social contacts and their relationship to loneliness among aged people—a population-based study. *Gerontology, 52,* 181–187.

Rovee-Collier, C. (1987). Learning and memory in children. In J. D. Osofsky (Ed.), *Handbook of infant development* (2nd ed.). New York: Wiley.

Rovee-Collier, C. (2002). Infant learning and memory. In U. Goswami (Ed.), *Blackwell handbook of childhood cognitive development.* Malden, MA: Blackwell.

Rovee-Collier, C., & Barr, R. (2004). Infant learning and memory. In G. Bremner & A. Fogel (Eds.), *Blackwell handbook of infant development.* Malden, MA: Blackwell.

Rowe, R., Maughn, B., Worthman, C. M., Costello, E. J., & Angold, A. (2004). Testosterone, antisocial behavior, and social dominance in boys: Pubertal development and biosocial interaction. *Biological Psychiatry, 55,* 546–552.

Rowe, S. M., & Wertsch, J. V. (2004). Vygotsky's model of cognitive development. In U. Goswami (Ed.), *Blackwell handbook of childhood cognitive development.* Malden, MA: Blackwell.

Rubenstein, D. (2004). Language games and natural resources. *Journal of the Theory of Social Behavior, 34,* 55–71.

Rubin, D. (2006). *Gaining word power* (7th ed.). Upper Saddle River, NJ: Prentice Hall.

Rubin, D. H., Krasilnikoff, P. A., Leventhal, J. M., Weile, B., & Berget, A. (1986, August 23). Effect of passive smoking on birthweight. *The Lancet,* 415–417.

Rubin, K. (2000). Middle childhood: Social and emotional development. In A. Kazdin (Ed.), *Encyclopedia of psychology.* Washington, DC, & New York: American Psychological Association and Oxford University Press.

Rubin, K. H., Bukowski, W., & Parker, J. G. (1998). Peer interactions, relationships, and groups. In N. Eisenberg (Ed.), *Handbook of child psychology* (5th ed., Vol. 3). New York: Wiley.

Rubin, K. H., Bukowski, W., & Parker, J. G. (2006). Peer interactions, relationships, and groups. In W. Damon & R. Levner (Eds.), *Handbook of child psychology* (6th ed.). New York: Wiley.

Rubin, S., & Malkinson, R. (2001) *Parental response to child loss across the life-cycle: Clinical and research perspectives.* In M. Stroebe, R. Hansson, W. Stroebe & H. Schut (Eds), *Handbook of bereavement research: consequences, coping and care.* Washington, DC: American Psychological Association.

Rubin, Z. (1970). Measurement of romantic love. *Journal of Personality and Social Psychology, 16,* 265–273.

Rubin, Z., & Mitchell, C. (1976). Couples research as couples counseling. *American Psychologist, 31,* 17–25.

Ruble, D. (1983). The development of social comparison processes and their role in achievement-related self-socialization. In E. Higgins, D. Ruble, & W. Hartup (Eds.), *Social cognitive development: A social-cultural perspective.* New York: Cambridge University Press.

Ruble, D. N., Martin, C. L., & Berenbaum, S. (2006). Gender development. In W. Damon & R. Lerner (Eds.), *Handbook of child psychology* (6th ed.). New York: Wiley.

Ruddell, R. B. (2006). *Teaching children to read and write* (4th ed.). Boston: Allyn & Bacon.

Rudolph, K. L., Chang, S., Lee, H., Gottlieb, G. J., Greider, C., & DePinho, R. A. (1999). Longevity, stress response, and cancer in aging telomerase-deficient mice. *Cell, 96,* 701–712.

Rueda, R., & Yaden, D. B. (2006). The literacy education of linguistically and culturally diverse young children: An overview of outcomes, assessment, and large-scale interventions. In B. Spodek & O. N. Saracho (Eds.), *Handbook of research on the education of young children.* Mahwah, NJ: Erlbaum.

Rueter, M. A., & Kwon, H. K. (2005). Developmental trends in adolescent suicide ideation. *Journal of Research on Adolescence, 15,* 205–222.

Ruff, H. A., & Capozzoli, M. C. (2003). Development of attention and distractibility in the first 4 years of life. *Developmental Psychology, 39,* 877–890.

Ruff, H. A., & Rothbart, M. K. (1996). *Attention in early development.* New York: Oxford University Press.

Rumberger, R. W. (1995). Dropping out of middle school: A multilevel analysis of students and schools. *American Education Research Journal, 3,* 583–625.

Runco, M. A. (2004). Creativity. *Annual Review of Psychology* (Vol. 55). Palo Alto, CA: Annual Reviews.

Runco, M. A. (Ed.). (2006). *Creativity research handbook.* Creskill, NJ: Hampton Press.

Rupp, D. E., Vodanovich, S. J., & Crede, M. (2005). The multidimensional nature of ageism: Construct validity and group differences. *Journal of Social Psychology, 145,* 335–362.

Rupp, K., Strand, A., & Davies, P. S. (2003). Poverty among elderly women: Assessing the SSI options to strengthen Social Security reform. *Journals of Gerontology B: Psychological and Social Sciences, 58,* S359–S368.

Rupp, R., Rosenthal, S. L., & Stanberry, L. R. (2005). Pediatrics and herpes simple virus vaccines. *Seminars in Pediatric Infectious Diseases, 16,* 31–37.

Rusak, B., Robertson, H. A., Wisden, W., & Hunt, S. P. (1990). Light pulses that shift rhythms induce gene expression in the suprachiasmatic nucleus. *Science, 248,* 1237–1240.

Rusbult, C. E., Olsen, N., Davis, J. L., & Hannon, P. A. (2001). Commitment and relationship maintenance mechanisms. In J. H. Harvey & A. Wenzel (Eds.), *Close romantic relationships.* Mahwah, NJ: Erlbaum.

Russek, L. G., & Schwartz, G. E. (1997). Feelings of parental caring predict health status in midlife: A 35-year follow-up of the Harvard Mastery Study of Stress. *Journal of Behavioral Medicine, 30,* 1–13.

Russell, D. W. (1996). UCLA Loneliness Scale (Version 3): Reliability, validity and factor structure. *Journal of Personality Assessment, 66,* 20–43.

Russell, S. T., & Joyner, K. (2001). Adolescent sexual orientation and suicide risk: Evidence from a national study. *American Journal of Public Health, 91,* 1276–1281.

Ruxton, C. (2004). Obesity in children. *Nursing Standards, 18,* 47–52.

Ryan, A. S. (1997). The resurgence of breastfeeding in the United States. *Pediatrics, 99,* E12.

Ryan, R. M., Fauth, R. C., & Brooks-Gunn, J. (2006). Childhood poverty: Implications for school readiness and early childhood education. In B. Spodek & O. N. Saracho (Eds.), *Handbook of research on the education of young children.* Mahwah, NJ: Erlbaum.

Ryan, S. D., Pearlmutter, S., & Groza, V. (2004). Coming out of the closet: Opening agencies to gay and lesbian adoptive parents. *Social Work, 49*, 85–95.

Ryff, C. D. (1984). Personality development from the inside: The subjective experience of change in adulthood and aging. In P. B. Baltes & O. G. Brim (Eds.), *Life-span development and behavior.* New York: Academic Press.

Ryff, C. D. (1991). Possible selves in adulthood and old age: A tale of shifting horizons. *Psychology and Aging, 6*, 286–295.

Ryff, C. D., & Singer, B. (2000). Interpersonal flourishing: A positive health agenda for the new millennium. *Personality and Social Psychology Review, 4*, 30–44.

Ryff, C. D., Singer, B., Wing, E. H., & Love, G. D. (2001). Elective affinities and uninvited agonies: Mapping emotion with significant others onto health. In C. D. Ryff & B. Singer (Eds.), *Emotion, social relationships, and health.* New York: Oxford University Press.

Rypma, B., Berger, J. S., & D'Esposito, M. (2002). The influence of working memory demand and subject performance on prefrontal cognitive activity. *Journal of Cognitive Neuroscience, 14*, 721–731.

Saarni, C. (1999). *The development of emotional competence.* New York: Guilford.

Saarni, C. (2002). Unpublished review of J. W. Santrock's *Life-span development*, 10th ed. (New York: McGraw-Hill).

Saarni, C. (2006). Emotion regulation and personality development in childhood. In D. K. Mroczek & T. D. Little (Eds.), *Handbook of personality development.* Mahwah, NJ: Erlbaum.

Saarni, C., Campos, J., Camras, L. A., & Witherington, D. (2006). Emotional development. In W. Damon & R. Lerner (Eds.), *Handbook of child psychology* (6th ed.). New York: Wiley.

Sabol, W. J., Coulton, C. J., & Korbin, J. E. (2004). Building community capacity for violence prevention. *Journal of Interpersonal Violence, 19*, 322–340.

Sachs-Ericsson, N., Blazer, D., Plant, A. E., & Arnow, B. (2005). Childhood sexual and physical abuse and the 1-year prevalence of medical problems in the National Comorbidity Study. *Health Psychology, 24*, 32–40.

Sackett, P. R., Hardison, C. M., & Cullen, M. J. (2004). On interpreting stereotype threat as accounting for African-American White differences in cognitive tests. *American Psychologist, 59*, 7–13.

Saczynski, J., & Willis, S. L. (2001). *Cognitive training and maintenance of intervention effects in the elderly.* Unpublished manuscript. University Park, PA: Pennsylvania State University.

Sadaf Farooqi, I. (2005). Genetic and hereditary aspects of childhood obesity. *Best Practice & Research: Clinical Endocrinology and Metabolism, 19*, 359–374.

Safar, M. E., & Smulyan, H. (2004). Hypertension in women. *American Journal of Hypertension, 17*, 82–87.

Saffran, J. R., Werker, J. F., & Werner, L. A. (2006). The infant's auditory world: Hearing, speech, and the beginnings of language. In W. Damon & R. Lerner (Eds.), *Handbook of child psychology* (6th ed.). New York: Wiley.

Sagan, C. (1977). *The dragons of Eden.* New York: Random House.

Sagi, A., Koren-Karie, N., Gini, M., Ziv, Y., & Joels, T. (2002). Shedding further light on the effects of various types and quality of early child care on infant-mother attachment relationship: The Haifa study of early child care. *Child Development, 73*, 1166–1186.

Sahu, G., Mohanty, S., & Dash, J. K. (2005). Vulnerable victims in sexual assault. *Medical Science and Law, 45*, 256–260.

Sakai, K. L., Tatsuno, Y., Suzuki, K., Kimura, H., & Ichida, Y. (2005). Sign and speech: A modal commonality in left hemisphere dominance for comprehension of sentences. *Brain, 128*, 1407–1417.

Sakraida, T. J. (2005). Divorce transition differences of midlife women. *Issues in Mental Health Nursing, 26*, 225–249.

Salmon, J., Campbell, K. J., & Crawford, D. A. (2006). Television viewing habits associated with obesity risk factors: A survey of Melbourne children. *Medical Journal of Australia, 184*, 64–67.

Salovey, P., & Mayer, J. D. (1990). Emotional intelligence. *Imagination, Cognition, and Personality, 9*, 185–211.

Salthouse, T. A. (1991). *Theoretical perspectives on cognitive aging.* Mahwah, NJ: Erlbaum.

Salthouse, T. A. (1994). The nature of influence of speed on adult age differences in cognition. *Developmental Psychology, 30*, 240–259.

Salthouse, T. A. (1996). General and specific speed mediation of adult age differences in memory. *Journal of Gerontology, 51A*, P30–P42.

Salthouse, T. A. (2000). Adulthood and aging: Cognitive processes and development. In A. Kazdin (ed.), *Encyclopedia of psychology.* Washington, DC, & New York: American Psychological Association and Oxford University Press.

Salthouse, T. A. (2005). From description to explanation in cognitive aging. In R. J. Sternberg & J. E. Pretz (Eds.), *Cognition and intelligence.* New York: Cambridge University Press.

Salthouse, T. A., & Baltes, P. B. (2006). Theoretical development in the psychology of aging. In J. E. Birren & K. W. Schaie (Eds.), *Handbook of the psychology of aging.* San Diego: Academic Press.

Salthouse, T. A., & Miles, J. D. (2002). Aging and time-sharing aspects of executive control. *Memory and Cognition, 30*, 572–582.

Salthouse, T. A., & Skovronek, E. (1992). Within-context assessment of working memory. *Journal of Gerontology, 47*, P110–P117.

Salvia, S. N. (2004). Health behaviors and physical activity: Are they related? *Journal of Adolescent Health, 34*, 128.

Sambrook, P., & Cooper, C. (2006). Osteoporosis. *Lancet, 367*, 2010–2018.

Samii, A., Nutt, J. G., & Ransom, B. R. (2004). Parkinson's disease. *Lancet, 363*, 1783–1793.

Samour, P. Q., Helm, K. K., & Lang, C. E. (Eds.). (2000). *Handbook of pediatric nutrition* (2nd ed.). Aspen, CO: Aspen.

Sanchez-Johnsen, L. A., Fitzgibbon, M. L., Martinovich, Z., Stolley, M. R., Dyer, A. R. & Van Horn, L. (2004). Ethnic differences in correlates of obesity between Latin-American and black women. *Obesity Research, 12*, 652–660.

Sandiford, R. (2006). Keeping it natural. *Nursing Times, 102*, 22–23.

Sands, R. G., & Goldberg-Glen, R. S. (2000). Factors associated with stress among grandparents raising their grandchildren. *Family Relations, 49*, 97–105.

Sandstrom, M. J., & Zakriski, A. L. (2004). Understanding the experience of peer rejection. In J. B. Kupersmidt & K. A. Dodge (Eds.), *Children's peer relations: From development to intervention.* Washington, DC: American Psychological Association.

Sangree, W. H. (1989). Age and power: Life-course trajectories and age structuring of power relations in East and West Africa. In D. I. Kertzer & K. W. Schaie (Eds.), *Age structuring in comparative perspective.* Hillsdale, NJ: Erlbaum.

Sanson, A., & Rothbart, M. K. (1995). Child temperament and parenting. In M. H. Bornstein (Ed.), *Handbook of parenting* (Vol. 4). Hillsdale, NJ: Erlbaum.

Santiago-Delefosse, M. J., & Delefosse, J. M. O. (2002). Three positions on child thought and language. *Theory and Psychology, 12*, 723–747.

Santrock, J. W. (2006). *Educational psychology* (2nd ed. Update). New York: McGraw-Hill.

Santrock, J. W. (2007). *Adolescence* (11th ed.). New York: McGraw-Hill.

Santrock, J. W., & Halonen, J. (2006). *Your Guide to College Success* (4th ed.). New York: Wadsworth.

Santrock, J. W., Sitterle, K. A., & Warshak, R. A. (1988). Parent-child relationships in stepfather families. In P. Bronstein & C. P. Cowan (Eds.), *Fatherhood today: Men's changing roles in the family.* New York: Wiley.

Santrock, J. W., & Warshak, R. A. (1979). Father custody and social development in boys and girls. *Journal of Social Issues, 35*, 112–125.

Sanz, A., Caro, P., Ibanez, J., Gomez, J., Gredilla, R., & Barja, G. (2005). Dietary restriction at old age lowers mitochondrial oxygen radical production and leak at complex I and oxidative DNA damage in rat brain. *Science of Aging, Knowledge, Environment, 20*, e14.

Sarigiani, P. A., & Petersen, A. C. (2000). Adolescence: Puberty and biological maturation. In A. Kazdin (Ed.), *Encyclopedia of psychology.* Washington, DC, & New York. American Psychological Association and Oxford University Press.

Sarkisian, N., Gerena, M., & Gerstel, N. (2006). Extended family ties among Mexicans, Puerto Ricans, and Whites: Superintegration or disintegration? *Family Relations, 55*, 331–334.

Sarrel, P., & Masters, W. (1982). Sexual molestation of men by women. *Archives of Human Sexuality, 11*, 117–131.

Sarsam, S. E., Elliott, J. P., & Lam, G. K. (2005). Management of wound complications from cesarean delivery. *Obstetrical and Gynecological Survey, 60*, 462–473.

Sato, R. L., Li, G. G., & Shaha, S. (2006, in press). Antepartum seafood consumption and mercury levels in newborn cord blood. *American Journal of Obstetrics and Gynecology.*

Saudino, K. J. (2005). Behavioral genetics and child temperament. *Journal of Developmental and Behavioral Pediatrics, 26*, 214–223.

Sauri, M. (2005). Influences on drug marketing. *Maryland Medicine, 6*, 24–25.

Savell, V. H., Hughes, S. M., Bower, C., & Parham, D. M. (2004). Lymphocytic infiltration in pediatric thyroid carcinomas. *Pediatric and Developmental Pathology, 7*, 487–492.

Savikko, N., Routasalo, P., Tilvis, R. S., Strandberg, T. E., & Pitkala, K. H. (2005). Predictors and subjective causes of loneliness in an aged population. *Archives of Gerontology and Geriatrics, 41*, 223–233.

Savin-Williams, R. C. (2001). *Mom, dad, I'm gay.* Washington, DC: American Psychological Association.

Savin-Williams, R. C. (2005). *The new gay teenager.* Cambridge, MA: Harvard University Press.

Savin-Williams, R. C., & Diamond, L. (2004). Sex. In R. Lerner & L. Steinberg (Eds.), *Handbook of adolescent psychology.* New York: Wiley.

Sayer, L. C. (2006). Economic aspects of divorce and relationship dissolution. In M. A. Fine & J. H. Harvey (Eds.), *Handbook of divorce and relationship dissolution.* Mahwah, NJ: Erlbaum.

Scafidi, F., & Field, T. M. (1996). Massage therapy improves behavior in neonates born to HIV-positive mothers. *Journal of Pediatric Psychology, 21*, 889–897.

Scaramella, L. V., & Conger, R. D. (2004). Continuity versus discontinuity in parent and adolescent negative affect. In R. D. Conger, F. O.

Lorenz, & K. A. S., Wickrama (Eds.), *Continuity and change in family relations.* Mahwah, NJ: Erlbaum

Scarr, S. (1993). Biological and cultural diversity: The legacy of Darwin for development. *Child Development, 64,* 1333–1353.

Scarr, S. (2000). Day care. In A. Kazdin (Ed.), *Encyclopedia of Psychology.* Washington, DC, & New York: American Psychological Association and Oxford University press.

Scarr, S. A., & Weinberg, R. A. (1983). The Minnesota adoption studies: Genetic differences and malleability. *Child Development, 54,* 182–259.

Schaalma, H. P., Abraham, C., Gillmore, M. R., & Kok, G. (2004). Sex education as health promotion: What does it take? *Archives of Sexual Behavior, 33,* 259–269.

Schaap, L. A., Pluijm, S. M., Deeg, D. J., & Visser, M. (2006). Inflammatory markers and loss of muscle mass (sarcopenia) and strength. *American Journal of Medicine, 119*(6), e9–e17.

Schachter, S. C., & Ransil, B. J. (1996). Handedness distributions in nine professional groups. *Perceptual and Motor Skills, 82,* 51–63.

Schaffer, D. V., & Gage, F. H. (2004). Neurogenesis and neuroadaptation. *Neuromolecular Medicine, 5,* 1–9.

Schaffer, H. R. (1996). *Social development.* Cambridge, MA: Blackwell.

Schaie, K. W. (1993). The Seattle longitudinal studies of adult intelligence. *Current Directions in Psychological Science, 2,* 171–175.

Schaie, K. W. (1994). The life course of adult intellectual abilities. *American Psychologist, 49,* 304–313.

Schaie, K. W. (1996). *Intellectual development in adulthood: The Seattle Longitudinal Study.* New York: Cambridge University Press.

Schaie, K. W. (2000). Unpublished review of J. W. Santrock's *Life-span development,* 8th ed. (New York: McGraw: Hill).

Schaie, K. W. (2005). *Developmental influences on adult intelligence: The Seattle Longitudinal Study.* New York: Oxford University Press.

Schaie, K. W. (2006). Intelligence. In R. Schultz (Ed.), *Encyclopedia of aging* (4th Ed.). New York: Springer.

Schaie, K. W. (2007). Generational differences: The age-cohort period model. In J. E. Birren (Ed.), *Encyclopedia of gerontology* (2nd ed.). Oxford: Elsevier.

Schaie, K. W., & Elder, G. (2006). Historical influences on aging. In J. E. Birren & K. W. Schaie (Eds.), *Handbook of the psychology of aging* (6th, ed.). San Diego: Academic Press.

Schaie, K. W., & Willis, S. L. (2000). A stage theory model of adult development revisited. In R. Rubinstein, M. Moss, & M. Kleban (Eds.), *The many dimensions of aging: Essays in honor of M. Powell Lawton.* New York: Springer.

Schaie, K. W., & Willis, S. L. (2002). *Adult development and aging* (5th ed.). Upper Saddle River, NJ: Prentice Hall.

Schaie, K. W., & Zanjani, F. A. K. (2006). Intellectual development across adulthood. In C. Hoare (Ed.), *Handbook of adult development and learning.* New York: Oxford University Press.

Schapira, A. H. (2005). Present and future drug treatment for Parkinson's disease. *Journal of Neurology, Neurosurgery, and Psychiatry, 76,* 1472–1478.

Schattschneider, C., Fletcher, J. M., Francis, D. J., Carlson, C. D., & Foorman, B. R. (2004). Kindergarten prediction of reading skills: A longitudinal comparative analysis. *Journal of Educational Psychology, 96,* 265–282.

Schauble, L. (1990). Belief revision in children: The role of prior knowledge and strategies for generating evidence. *Journal of Experimental Child Psychology, 49,* 31–57.

Scheer, S. D. (1996, March). *Adolescent to adult transitions: Social status and cognitive factors.* Paper presented at the meeting of the Society for Research on Adolescence, Boston.

Schegel, A. (2000). The global spread of adolescent culture. In L. J. Crockett & R. K. Silbereisen (Eds.), *Negotiating adolescence in time of social change.* New York: Cambridge University Press.

Scheidt, R. J., & Windley, P. G. (2006). Environmental gerontology. In J. E. Birren & K. W. Schaie (Eds.), *Handbook of the psychology of aging* (6th ed.). San Diego: Academic Press.

Scheinfeld, N., & Bangalore, S. (2006). Facial edema induced by isotretinoin use: A case and a review of the side effects of isotretinoin. *Journal of Drugs and Dermatology, 5,* 467–468.

Schellenbach, C., Leadbeater, B., & Moore, K. A. (2004). Enhancing the developmental outcomes of adolescent parents and their children. In K. I. Maton, C. J. Schellenbach, B. J. Leadbeater, & A. L. Solarz (Eds.), *Investing in children, youth, families, and communities.* Thousand Oaks, CA: Sage.

Schieber, F. (2006). Vision and aging. In J. E. Birren & K. W. Schaie (Eds.), *Handbook of the psychology of aging* (6th ed.). San Diego: Academic Press.

Schieman, S., Van Gundy, K. S., Taylor, J. (2002). The relationship between age and depressive symptoms: A test of competing explanatory and suppression influences. *Journal of Aging Health, 14,* 260–285.

Schindler, A.E. (2006). Climacteric symptoms and hormones. *Gynecological Endocrinology, 22,* 151–154.

Schmidt, M. E., & Anderson, D. R. (2006). The impact of television on cognition and educational achievement. In N. Pecora, J. P. Murray, & E. A. Wartella (Eds.), *Children and television.* Mahwah, NJ: Erlbaum.

Schmidt, U. (2003). Aetiology of eating disorders in the 21st century: New answers to old questions. *European Child and Adolescent Psychiatry, 12* (Suppl. 1), I130–I137.

Schmier, J. K., Jones, M. L., & Halpern, M. T. (2006). The burden of age-related macular degeneration. *Pharmacoeconomics, 24,* 319–334.

Schmitt, D. P., & Pilcher, J. J. (2004). Evaluating evidence of psychological adaptation: How do we know one when we see one? *Psychological Science, 15,* 643–649.

Schnake, E. M., Peterson, N. M., & Corden, T. E. (2005). Promoting water safety: The physician's role. *Wisconsin Journal of Medicine, 104,* 45–49.

Schneider, D., Freeman, N. C., & McGarvey, P. (2005). Asthma and respiratory dysfunction among urban, primarily Hispanic children. *Archives of Environmental Health, 59,* 4–13.

Schneider, W., & Pressley, M. (1997). *Memory development from 2 to 20* (2nd ed.). Mahwah, NJ: Erlbaum.

Schneiderman, N., Antoni, M. H., Saab, P. G., & Ironson, G. (2001). Health psychology: Psychological and biobehavioral aspects of chronic disease management. *Annual Review of Psychology* (Vol. 52). Palo Alto, CA: Annual Reviews.

Schnorr, T. M., & others. (1991). Video-display terminals and the risk of spontaneous abortion. *New England Journal of Medicine, 324,* 727–733.

Schoen, R., & Standish, N. (2001). The entrenchment of marriage: Results from marital status life tables for the United States, 1995." *Population and Development Review, 27,* 553–563.

Schoka, E., & Hayslip, B. (1999, November). *Grief and the family system: The roles of communication, affect, and cohesion.* Paper presented at the meeting of the Gerontological Society of America, San Francisco.

Schooler, C. (2001). The intellectual effects of the demands of the work environment. In R. J. Sternberg & E. L. Grigorenko (Eds.), *Environmental effects on cognitive abilities.* Mahwah, NJ: Erlbaum.

Schooler, C., Mulatu, M. S., & Oates, G. (2004). Occupational self-direction, intellectual functioning, and self-directed orientation in older workers: Findings and implications for individuals and societies. *Social Psychology Quarterly, 67,* 16–32.

Schooler, C., Mulatu, S., & Oates, G. (1999). The continuing effects of substantively complex work on the intellectual functioning of older workers. *Psychology and Aging, 14,* 483–506.

Schrag, S. G., & Dixon, R. L. (1985). Occupational exposure associated with male reproductive dysfunction. *Annual Review of Pharmacology and Toxicology, 25,* 467–592.

Schroots, J. J. F. (1996). Time: Concepts and perceptions. In J. E. Birren (Ed.), *Encyclopedia of gerontology* (Vol. 2). San Diego: Academic Press.

Schuchter, S., & Zisook, S. (1993). The course of normal grief. In M. Stroebe, W. Stroebe, & R. O. Hanson (Eds.), *Handbook of bereavement.* New York: Cambridge University Press.

Schulenberg, J. E., Bryant, A. L., & O'Malley, P. M. (2004). Taking hold of some kind of life: How developmental tasks relate to trajectories of well-being during the transition to adulthood. *Development and Psychopathology, 16,* 1119–1140.

Schulenberg, J., O'Malley, P. M., Bachman, J. G., & Johnson, L. D. (2000). "Spread your wings and fly": The course of health and well-being during the transition to young adulthood. In L. Crockett & R. Silbereisen (Eds.), *Negotiating adolescence in times of social change.* New York: Cambridge University Press.

Schulenberg, J. E., & Zarrett, N. R. (2006). Mental health during emerging adulthood: Continuities and discontinuities in course, content, and meaning. In J. J. Arnett & J. Tanner (Eds.), *Advances in emerging adulthood.* Washington, DC: American Psychological Association.

Schultz, J. H., & Borowski, A. (2006). Economic security in retirement: Reshaping the public-private pension mix. In R. H. Binstock & L. K. George (Eds.), *Handbook of aging and the social sciences* (6th ed.). San Diego: Academic Press.

Schultz, R., & Curnow, C. (1988). Peak performance and age among super athletes: Track and field, swimming, baseball, tennis, and golf. *Journal of Gerontology, 43,* P113–P120.

Schunk, D. H. (1991). Self-efficacy and academic motivation. *Educational Psychologist, 25,* 71–86.

Schunk, D. H. (2001). Social cognitive theory and self-regulated learning. In B. J. Zimmerman & D. H. Schunk (Eds.), *Self-regulated learning and achievement* (2nd ed.). Mahwah, NJ: Erlbaum.

Schunk, D. H. (2004). *Learning theories: An educational perspective* (4th ed.). Upper Saddle River, NJ: Prentice Hall.

Schunk, D. H., & Zimmerman, B. J. (2003). Self-regulation and learning. In I. B. Weiner (Ed.), *Handbook of psychology* (Vol. 7). New York: Wiley.

Schunk, D. H., & Zimmerman, B. J. (2006). Competence and control beliefs. In P. A. Alexander & P. H. Wynne (Eds.), *Handbook of educational psychology* (2nd ed.). Mahwah, NJ: Erlbaum.

Schwartz, D. L., Lin, X., Brophy, J., & Bransford, J. D. (1999). Toward the development of flexibly adaptive instructional designs. In C. M. Reigelut (Ed.), *Instructional design theories and models* (Vol. II). Mahwah, NJ: Erlbaum.

Schwarzer, R., & Schultz, U. (2003). Stressful life events. In I. B. Weiner (Ed.), *Handbook of psychology,* Vol. IX. New York: Wiley.

Schweinhart, L. J., Montie, J., Xiang, Z., Barnett, W. S., Belfield, C. R., & Nores, M. (2005). *Lifetime*

Effects: The High/Scope Perry Preschool Study Through Age 40. Ypsilanti, MI: High/Scope Press.

Schwerha, D. J., & McMullin, D. L. (2002). Prioritizing ergonomic research in aging for the 21st century American workforce. *Experimental Aging Research, 28,* 99–110.

Schwimmer, J. B., Burwinkle, T. M., & Varni, J. W. (2003). Health-related quality of life of severely obese children and adolescents. *Journal of the American Medical Association, 289,* 1813–1819.

Scialfa, C. T., & Fernie, G. R. (2006). Adaptive technology. In J. E. Birren & K. W. Schaie (Eds.), *Handbook of the psychology of aging* (6th ed.). San Diego: Academic Press.

Scott, C. M., & Popovich, D. J. (2001). Undiagnosed alcoholism and prescription drug misuse among the elderly. *Caring, 20,* 20–23.

Scott, J. A., Binns, C. W., Oddy, W. H., & Graham, K. I. (2006). Predictors of breastfeeding duration: Evidence from a cohort study. *Pediatrics, 1117,* e646–e655.

Scott-Jones, D. (1995, March). *Incorporating ethnicity and socioeconomic status in research with children.* Paper presented at the meeting of the Society for Research in Child Development, Indianapolis.

Scourfield, J., Van den Bree, M., Martin, N., & McGuffin, P. (2004). Conduct problems in children and adolescents: A twin study. *Archives of General Psychiatry, 61,* 489–496.

Search Institute. (1995). *Barriers to participation in youth programs.* Unpublished manuscript, the Search Institute, Minneapolis.

Sears, R. R., & Feldman, S. S. (Eds.). (1973). *The seven ages of man.* Los Altos, CA: Kaufmann.

Seeman, T. E., & Chen, X. (2002). Risk and protective factors for physical functioning in older adults with and without chronic conditions: MacArthur Studies of Successful Aging. *Journal of Gerontology: Social Sciences, 57B,* S135–S144.

Seeman, T. E., Charpentier, P. A., Berkman, L. F., Tinetti, M. E., Guralnik, J. M., Albert, M., Blazer, D., & Rowe, J. W. (1994). Predicting changes in physical performance in a high-functioning elderly cohort: MacArthur Studies of Successful Aging. *Journal of Gerontology, 49,* M97–M108.

Seftel, A. D. (2005). From aspiration to achievement: Assessment and noninvasive treatment of erectile dysfunction in aging men. *Journal of the American Geriatric Society, 53,* 119–130.

Segerberg, O. (1982). *Living to be 100: 1200 who did and how they did it.* New York: Scribner's.

Seguin, R., & Nelson, M. E. (2003). The benefits of strength training for older adults. *American Journal of Preventive Medicine, 25* (Suppl. 2), 141–149.

Seidell, J. C. (2005). Epidemiology of obesity. *Seminars in Vascular Medicine, 5,* 3–14.

Seidenfeld, M. E., Sosin, E., & Rickert, V. I. (2004). Nutrition and eating disorders in adolescents. *Mt. Sinai Journal of Medicine, 71,* 155–161.

Seifert, K. L. (2006). Cognitive development and the education of young children. In B. Spodek & O. N. Saracho (Eds.), *Handbook of research on the education of young children.* Mahwah, NJ: Erlbaum.

Selim, A. J., Fincke, G., Berlowitz, D. R., Miller, D. R., Qian, S. X., Lee, A., Cong, Z., Rogers, W., Selim, B. J., Ren, X. S., Spiro, A., Kazis, L. E. (2005). Comprehensive health status assessment of centenarians: Results from the 1999 Large Health Survey of Veteran Enrollees. *Journals of Gerontology: Biological Sciences and Medical Sciences, 60,* 515–519.

Selman, R. L., & Dray, A. J. (2006). Risk and prevention. In W. Damon & R. Lerner (Eds.), *Handbook of child psychology* (6th ed.). New York: Wiley.

Seltzer, J. (2004). Cohabitation and family change. In M. Coleman & L. Ganong (Eds.), *Handbook of contemporary families.* Thousand Oaks. CA: Sage.

Seroczynski, A. D., Jacquez, F. M., & Cole, D. (2003). Depression and suicide during adolescence. In G. Adams & M. Berzonsky (Eds.), *Blackwell handbook of adolescence.* Malden, MA: Blackwell.

Serpell, R. (1974). Aspects of intelligence in a developing country. *African Social Research, 17,* 576–596.

Serpell, R. (2000). Culture and intelligence. In A. Kazdin (Ed.), *Encyclopedia of psychology.* Washington, DC, & New York: American Psychological Association and Oxford University Press.

Setterson, R. A. (2006). Aging and the life course. In R. H. Binstock & L. K. George (Eds.), *Handbook of aging and the social sciences* (6th ed.) San Diego: Academic Press.

Shah, S., Blanchard, M., Tookman, A., Jones, L., Blizard, R., & King, M. (2006). Estimating needs in life-threatening illness: A feasibility study to assess the views of patients and doctors. *Palliative Medicine, 20,* 205–210.

Shakhatreh, F. M., & Mas'ad, D. (2006). Menopausal symptoms and health problems of women aged 50–65 years of age in southern Jordan. *Climacteric, 9,* 305–311.

Shan, Z. Y., Liu, J. Z., Shagal, V., Wang, B., & Yue, G. H. (2006). Selective atrophy of the left hemisphere and frontal lobe of the brain in old men. *Journals of Gerontology A: Biological Sciences and Medical Sciences, 60,* 165–174.

Shankar, A. V., Sastry, J., Erande, A., Joshi, A., Suryawanshi, N., Phadke, M. A., & Bollinger, R. C. (2005). Making the choice: The translation of global HIV and infant feeding policy to local practice among mothers in Pune, India. *Journal of Nutrition, 135,* 960–965.

Shanley, D.P., & Kirkwood, T.B. (2006, in press). Caloric restriction does not enhance longevity in all species and is unlikely to do so in humans. *Biogerontology.*

Shao, B., Oda, M. N., Vaisa, T., Oram, J. F., & Heinecke, J. W. (2006). Pathways for oxidation of high-density lipoprotein in human cardiovascular disease. *Current Opinions in Molecular Therapeutics, 8,* 198–205.

Sharma, A. R., McGue, M. K., & Benson, P. L. (1996). The emotional and behavioral adjustment of adopted adolescents: Part I: Age at adoption. *Children and Youth Services Review, 18,* 101–114.

Sharma, A. R., McGue, M. K., & Benson, P. L. (1998). The psychological adjustment of United States adopted adolescents and their nonadopted siblings. *Child Development, 69,* 791–802.

Sharma, S., & Kaur, G. (2005). Neuroprotective potential of dietary restriction against kainate-induced excitotoxicity in adult male Wistar rats. *Brain Research Bulletin, 67,* 482–491.

Sharma, V. (2002). Pharmacotherapy of postpartum depression. *Expert Opinions on Pharmacotherapy, 3,* 1421–1431.

Sharp, L., Cardy, A. H., Cotton, S. C., & Little, J. (2004). CYP17 gene polymorphisms: Prevalence and associations with hormone levels and related factors, a HuGE review. *American Journal of Epidemiology, 160,* 729–740.

Sharpless, N. E., & DePinho, R. A. (2004). Telomeres, stem cells, senescence, and cancer. *Journal of Clinical Investigation, 113,* 160–168.

Shatz, M., & Gelman, R. (1973). The development of communication skills: Modifications in the speech of young children as a function of the listener. *Monographs of the Society for Research in Child Development, 38* (Serial No. 152).

Shave, P. (1986, August). *Being lonely, falling in love: Perspectives from attachment theory.* Paper presented at the meeting of the American Psychological Association, Washington, DC.

Shavers, V. L., & Shavers, B. S. (2006). Racism and health inequity among Americans. *Journal of the National Medical Association, 98,* 386–396.

Shaw, D., Gilliom, M., Ingoldsby, E. M., & Nagin, D. S. (2003). Trajectories leading to school-age conduct problems. *Developmental Psychology, 39,* 189–200.

Shaw, G. M. (2001). Adverse human reproductive outcomes and electromagnetic fields. *Bioelectromagnetics, 5* (Supplement), s5–s18.

Shay, J. W., & Wright, W. E. (1999). Telomeres and telomerase in the regulation of cellular aging. In V. A. Bohr, B. F. Clark, & T. Stevenser (Eds.), *Molecular biology of aging.* Copenhagen, Denmark: Munksgaard.

Shay, J. W., & Wright, W. E. (2000). The use of telomerized cells for tissue engineering. *Nature Biotechnology, 18,* 22–23.

Shay, J. W., & Wright, W. E. (2004). Telomeres are double-strand DNA breaks hidden from DNA damage responses. *Molecular Cells, 14,* 420–421.

Shay, J. W., & Wright, W. E. (2005). Mechanism-based combination telomerase inhibition therapy. *Cancer Cell, 7,* 1–2.

Shay, J. W., & Wright, W. E. (2006, in press). Telomerase therapeutics for cancer: Challenges and new directions. *Nature Reviews: Drug Discovery.*

Shaya, F. T., Gu, A., & Saunders, E. (2006). Addressing cardiovascular disparities through community interventions. *Ethnicity and Disease, 16,* 138–144.

Shea, A., Walsh, C., MacMillan, H., & Steiner, M. (2005). Child maltreatment and HPA axis dysregulation: Relationship to major depressive disorder and post traumatic stress disorder in females. *Psychoneuroendocrinology, 30,* 162–178.

Sheahan, S. L., & Free, T. A. (2005). Counseling parents to quit smoking. *Pediatric Nursing, 31,* 98–102, 105–109.

Shear, K., Frank, E., Houck, P. R., & Reynolds, C. F. (2005). Treatment of complicated grief: A randomized controlled trial. *Journal of the American Medical Association, 293,* 2601–2608.

Sheets, R. H. (2005). *Diversity pedagogy.* Boston: Allyn & Bacon.

Sheldon, T. (2005). Dutch euthanasia law should apply to patients "suffering through living," report says. *British Medical Journal, 330,* 61.

Shepard, G. H. (2002). Three days for weeping: Dreams, emotions, and death in Peruvian Amazon. *Medical Anthropology Quarterly, 16,* 200–209.

Sherker, S., Ozanne-Smith, J., Rechnitzer, G., & Grzebieta, R. (2005). Out on a limb: Risk factors for arm fracture in playground equipment falls. *Injury Prevention, 11,* 120–124.

Sherwood, A., Light, K. C., & Blumenthal, J. A. (1989). Effects of aerobic exercise training on hemodynamic responses during psychosocial stress in normotensive and borderline hypertensive Type A men: A preliminary report. *Psychosomatic Medicine, 51,* 123–136.

Shi, L., & Stevens, G. D. (2005). Disparities in access to care and satisfaction among U.S. children: The roles of race/ethnicity and poverty status. *Public Health Reports, 120,* 431–441.

Shields, S. A. (1991). Gender in the psychology of emotion. In K. T. Strongman (Ed.), *International Review of Studies of Emotion* (Vol. 1). New York: Wiley.

Shiner, R. L. (2006). Temperament and personality in childhood. In D. K. Mroczek & T. D. Little (Eds.),

Handbook of personality development, Mahwah, NJ: Erlbaum.

Shiraev, E., & Levy, D. (2007). *Cross-cultural psychology: Critical thinking and critical applications* (3rd ed.). Belmont, CA: Wadsworth.

Shiri, R., Koskimaki, J., Hakama, M., Hakkinen, J., Tammela, T. L., Huhtala, H., & Auvinen, A. (2003). Effect of chronic diseases on incidence of erectile dysfunction. *Urology, 62,* 1097–1102.

Shneidman, E. S. (1973). *Deaths of man.* New York: Quadrangle/New York Times.

Shore, L. M., & Goldberg, C. B. (2005). Age discrimination in the work place. In R. L. Dipobye & A. Colella (Eds.), *Discrimination at work.* Mahwah, NJ: Erlbaum.

Shulman, S., & Ben-Artzi, E. (2003). Age-related differences in the transition from adolescence to adulthood and links with family relationships. *Journal of Adult Development, 10,* 217–226.

Shweder, R., Goodnow, J., Hatano, G., LeVine, R. A., Markus, H., & Miller, P. (2006). The cultural psychology of development. In W. Damon & R. Lerner (Eds.), *Handbook of child psychology* (6th ed.). New York: Wiley.

Shweder, R., Goodnow, J., Hatano, G., Levine, R., Markus, H., & Miller, P. (2006). The cultural psychology of development. In W. Damon & R. Lerner (Eds.), *Handbook of child psychology* (6th ed.). New York: Wiley.

Siega-Riz, A. M., Kranz, S., Blanchette, D., Haines, P. S., Guilkey, D. K., & Popkin, B. M. (2004). The effect of participation in the WIC program on preschoolers' diets. *Journal of Pediatrics, 144,* 229–234.

Siegel, L. S. (2003). Learning disabilities. In I. B. Weiner (Ed.), *Handbook of psychology* (Vol. VI). New York: Wiley.

Siegler, I. C., & Costa, P. T. (1999, August). *Personality change and continuity in midlife: UNC Alumni Heart Study.* Paper presented at the meeting of the American Psychological Association, Boston.

Siegler, I. C., Bosworth, H. B., & Poon, L. W. (2003). Disease, health, and aging. In I. B. Weiner (Eds.), *Handbook of psychology* (Vol. VI). New York: Wiley.

Siegler, R. S. (1998). *Children's thinking* (3rd ed.). Upper Saddle River, NJ: Prentice Hall.

Siegler, R. S. (2003). Relations between short-term and long-term cognitive development. *Psychological Science Agenda, 16,* 8–10.

Siegler, R. S. (2006). Microgenetic analysis of learning. In W. Damon & R. Lerner (Eds.), *Handbook of child psychology* (6th ed.). New York: Wiley.

Siegler, R. S., & Alibali, M. W. (2005). *Children's thinking* (4th ed.). Upper Saddle River, NJ: Prentice Hall.

Sigal, J., & others. (2005). Cross-cultural reactions to academic sexual harassment: Effects of individualist and collectivist culture and gender of participants. *Sex Roles, 52,* 201–215.

Sigler, R. S. (2006). Microgenetic analysis of learning. In W. Damon & R. Lerner (Eds.). *Handbook of child psychology* (6th ed.). New York: Wiley.

Sigman, M., Cohen, S. E., & Beckwith, L. (2000). Why does infant attention predict adolescent intelligence? In D. Muir & A. Slater (Eds.), *Infant development: Essential readings.* Malden, MA: Blackwell.

Signore, R. J. (2004). Bradley method offers option for natural childbirth. *American Family Physician, 70,* 650.

Silberman, M. (2006). *Teaching actively.* Boston: Allyn & Bacon.

Silva, C. (2005, October 31). When teen dynamo talks, city listens. *Boston Globe,* pp. 81–84.

Silva, C., & Martins, M. (2003). Relations between children's invented spelling and children's phonological awareness. *Educational Psychology, 23,* 3–16.

Silverstein, M., Conroy, S. J., Wang, H., Giarrusso, R., & Bengtson, V. L. (2002). Reciprocity in parent-child relation over the adult life course. *Journals of Gerontology: Psychological Sciences and Social Sciences, 57B,* S3–S13.

Silverstein, M., Gans, D., & Yang, F.M. (2006). Intergenerational support to aging parents. *Journal of Family Issues, 27,* 1068–1084.

Sim, T. N., & Ong, L. P. (2005). Parent punishment and child aggression in a Singapore Chinese preschool sample. *Journal of Marriage and the Family, 67,* 85–99.

Simmons, R. G., & Blyth, D. A. (1987). *Moving into adolescence.* Hawthorne, NY: Aldine.

Simons, J. S., Dodson, C. S., Bell, D., & Schacter, D. L. (2004). Specific- and partial-source memory: Effects on aging. *Psychology and Aging, 19,* 689–694.

Simons-Morton, B. G. (2002). Prospective analysis of peer and parent influences on smoking initiation among early adolescents. *Prevention Science, 3,* 275–283.

Simons-Morton, B., Haynie, D. L., Crump, A. D., Eitel, P., & Saylor, K. E. (2001). Peer and parent influences on smoking and drinking among early adolescents. *Health Education and Behavior, 28,* 95–107.

Simonton, D. K. (1996). Creativity. In J. E. Birren (Ed.), *Encyclopedia of aging.* San Diego: Academic Press.

Simkin, P., & Bolding, A. (2004). Update on nonpharmacological approaches to relieve labor pain and prevent suffering. *Journal of Midwifery and Women's Health, 49,* 489–504.

Simpson, C. F., Punjabi, N. M., Wolfenden, L., Shardell, M., Shade, D. M., & Fried, L. P. (2005). Relationship between lung function and physical performance in disabled older women. *Journals of Gerontology: Biological Sciences and Medical Sciences, 60,* A350–A354.

Simpson, J. A., Rholes, W. S., & Nelligan, J. S. (1992). Support-seeking and support-giving within couple members in an anxiety-provoking situation: The role of attachment styles. *Journal of Personality and Social Psychology, 62,* 434–446.

Sinclair, D. A., & Howitz, K. T. (2006). Dietary restrictions, hormesis, and small molecule mimetics. In E. J. Masoro & S. N. Austad (Eds.), *Handbook of the biology of aging* (6th ed.). San Diego: Academic Press.

Sinclair, J. M., Harriss, L., Baldwin, D. S., & King, E. A. (2005). Suicide in depressive disorders: A retrospective case-control study of 127 suicides. *Journal of Affective Studies, 87,* 107–113.

Singer, L. T., Arendt, R., Fagan, J., Minnes, S., Salvator, A., Bolek, T., & Becker, M. (1999). Neonatal visual information processing in cocaine-exposed and non-exposed infants. *Infant Behavior and Development, 22,* 1–15.

Singer, T., Lindenberger, U., & Baltes, P. B. (2003). Plasticity of memory for new learning in very old age: Six-year longitudinal findings in the Berlin Aging Study (BASE). *Psychology and Aging, 18,* 318–331.

Singer, T., Verhaeghen, P., Ghisletta, P., Lindenberger, U., & Baltes, P. B. (2003). The fate of cognition in very old age: Six-year longitudinal findings in the Berlin Aging Study (BASE). *Psychology and Aging, 18,* 318–331.

Singh, A. S., Chin, A., Paw, M. J., Bosscher, R. J., & van Mechelen, W. (2006). Cross-sectional relationship between physical fitness components and functional performance in older persons living in long-term care facilities. *BMC Geriatrics, 6,* 4.

Singh, K. K. (2006). Mitochondria damage checkpoint, aging, and cancer. *Annals of the New York Academy of Science, 1067,* 182–190.

Singh, M. A. F. (2002). Exercise comes of age: Rationale and recommendations for a geriatric exercise prescription. *Journal of Gerontology: Medical Sciences, 57A,* M262–M282.

Singh, M. A. F. (2004). Exercise and aging. *Clinical Geriatric Medicine, 20,* 201–221.

Singh, N. A., Clements, K. M., & Fiataroen, M. A. (1997). A randomized controlled trial of progressive resistance training in depressed elders. *Journal of Gerontology, 52A,* M27–M35.

Singh, S., Darroch, J. E., Vlasoff, M., & Nadeau, J. (2004). *Adding it up: The benefits of investing in sexual and reproductive health care.* New York: The Alan Guttmacher Institute.

Singh, S., Wulf, D., Samara, R., & Cuca, Y. P. (2000). Gender differences in the timing of first intercourse: Data from 14 countries. *International Family Planning Perspectives, 26,* 21–28, 43.

Sizer, F., & Whitney, E. (2006). *Nutrition* (10th ed.). Belmont, CA: Wadsworth.

Skinner, B. F. (1938). *The behavior of organisms: An experimental analysis.* New York: Appleton-Century-Crofts.

Skinner, B. F. (1957). *Verbal behavior.* New York: Appleton-Century-Crofts.

Skoog, I., Blennow, K., & Marcusson, J. (1996). Dementia. In J. E. Birren (Ed.), *Encyclopedia of gerontology* (Vol. 1). San Diego: Academic Press.

Skrabal, C. A., Thompson, L. O., Potapov, E. V., Southard, R. E., Joyce, D. L., Youker, K. A., Noon, G. P., & Loebe, M. (2005). Organ-specific regulation of pro-inflammatory molecules in heart, lung, and kidney following brain death. *Journal of Surgical Research, 123,* 118–125.

Skrha, J., Kunesova, M., Hilgertova, J., Weiserova, H., Krizova, J., Kotrlikova, E. (2005). Short-term very low calorie diet reduces oxidative stress in obese type 2 diabetic patients. *Physiological Research, 54,* 33–39.

Slade, E. P., & Wissow, L. S. (2004). Spanking in early childhood and later behavior problems: A prospective study. *Pediatrics, 113,* 1321–1330.

Slama, R., Bouyer, J., Windham, G., Fenster, L., Werwatz, A., & Swan, S. H. (2005). Influence of paternal age on the risk of spontaneous abortion. *American Journal of Epidemiology, 161,* 816–823.

Slater, A. (2004). Visual perception. In A. Fogel & G. Bremner (Eds.), *Blackwell handbook of infant development.* London: Blackwell.

Slater, A., Field, T., & Hernandez-Reif, M. (2002). The development of the senses. In A. Slater & M. Lewis (Eds.), *Introduction to infant development.* New York: Oxford University Press.

Slater, A., Morison, V., & Somers, M. (1988). Orientation discrimination and cortical function in the human newborn. *Perception, 17,* 597–602.

Sleet, D. A., & Mercy, J. A. (2003). Promotion of safety, security, and well-being. In M. H. Bornstein, L. Davidson, C. L. M., Keyes, & K. A. Moore (Eds.), *Well-being.* Mahwah, NJ: Erlbaum.

Sleight, P. (2003). Current opinions in the management of coronary heart disease. *American Journal of Cardiology, 92,* 4N–8N.

Slijper, F. M., Drop, S. L., Molenaar, J. C., & de Muinck Keizer-Schrama, S. M. (1998). Long-term psychological evaluation of intersex children. *Archives of Sexual Behavior, 27,* 125–144.

Sljivic, S., & others. (2006). Possible interactions of genetic and immuno-neuroendocrine regulatory mechanisms in pathogenesis of congenital anomalies. *Medical Hypotheses, 67,* 57–64.

Slobin, D. (1972, July). Children and language: They learn the same way around the world. *Psychology Today,* 71–76.

Slomkowski, C., Rende, R., Novak, S., Lloyd-Richardson, E., & Niaura, R. (2005). Sibling effects on smoking in adolescence: Evidence for social influence from a genetically informative design. *Addition, 100,* 430–438.

Slomkowski, C., Rende, R., Conger, K. J., Simons, R. L., & Conger, R. D. (2001). Sisters, brothers, and delinquency: Social influence during early and middle adolescence. *Child Development, 72,* 271–283.

Small, S. A. (1990). *Preventive programs that support families with adolescents.* Washington, DC: Carnegie Council on Adolescent Development.

Smetana, J. (2006). Social domain theory. In M. Killen & J. G. Smetana (Eds.), *Handbook of moral development.* Mahwah, NJ: Erlbaum.

Smetana, J., Campione-Barr, N., & Metzger, A. (2006). Adolescent development in interpersonal and societal contexts. *Annual Review of Psychology,* Vol. 57. Palo Alto, CA: Annual Reviews.

Smetana, J., & Turiel, E. (2003). Moral development during adolescence. In G. Adams & M. Berzonsky (Eds.), *The Blackwell handbook of adolescence.* Malden, MA: Blackwell.

Smith, A. D. (1996). Memory. In J. E. Birren (Ed.), *Encyclopedia of gerontology* (Vol. 2). San Diego: Academic Press.

Smith, B. (2007). *The psychology of sex and gender.* Boston: Allyn & Bacon.

Smith, C. A., & Crowther, C. A. (2004). Acupuncture for the induction of labor. *Cochrane Database of Systematic Review, 1,* CD0029262.

Smith, D. (2005). *Working with gifted and talented pupils in the secondary school.* Thousand Oaks, CA: Sage.

Smith, D. D. (2007). *Introduction to special education* (6th ed.). Boston: Allyn & Bacon.

Smith, K. (2002). *Who's minding the kids? Child care arrangements: Spring 1977.* Current Population Reports, P70–86. Washington, DC: U.S. Census Bureau.

Smith, L. A., Oyeku, S. O., Homer, C., & Zuckerman, B. (2006). Sickle cell disease: A question of equity and quality. *Pediatrics, 117,* 1763–1770.

Smith, L. B. (1999). Do infants possess innate knowledge structures? The con side. *Developmental Science, 2,* 133–144.

Smith, L. M., Chang, L., Yonekura, M. L., Gilbride, K., Kuo, J., Poland, R. E., Walot, I., & Ernst, T. (2001). Brain proton magnetic resonance spectroscopy and imaging in children exposed to cocaine in utero. *Pediatrics, 107,* 227.

Smith, S. H. (2005). Anticipatory grief and psychological adjustment to grieving in middle-aged children. *American Journal of Palliative Care, 22,* 283–286.

Smith, T. B., McCullough, M. E., & Poll, J. (2003). Religiousness and depression: Evidence for a main effect and the moderating influence of stressful life events. *Psychological Bulletin, 129,* 614–636.

Smits, A. K., Paladine, H. L., Judkins, D. Z., & Huber, T. (2006). Clinical inquiries. What are the risks to the fetus associated with diagnostic radiation exposure during pregnancy? *Journal of Family Practice, 55,* 441–442, 444.

Smock, P. J., Manning, W. D., & Porter, M. (2005). "Everything's there except the money": How money shapes decisions to marry among cohabitors. *Journal of Marriage and the Family, 67,* 680–696.

Smoreda, Z., & Licoppe, C. (2000). Gender-specific use of the domestic telephone. *Social Psychology Quarterly, 63,* 238–252.

Smulian, J. C., Ananth, C. V., Vintzileos, A. M., Scorza, W. E., & Knuppel, R. A. (2002). Parental age difference and adverse perinatal outcomes in the United States. *Pediatric and Perinatal Epidemiology, 16,* 320–327.

Snarey, J. (1987, June). A question of morality. *Psychology Today,* pp. 6–8.

Snell, J. L., & Hirschstein, M. (2005) Bullying and victimization. In S. W. Lee (Ed.), *Encyclopedia of school psychology.* Thousand Oaks, CA: Sage.

Snow, C. E., & Yang, J. Y. (2006). Becoming bilingual, biliterate, and bicultural. In W. Damon & R. Lerner (Eds.), *Handbook of child psychology* (6th ed.). New York: Wiley.

Snowdon, D. A. (1995). *An epidemiological study of aging in a select population and its relationship to Alzheimer's disease.* Unpublished manuscript, Sanders. Brown Center on Aging. Lexington, KY.

Snowdon, D. A. (1997). Aging and Alzheimer's disease: Lessons from the Nun Study. *Geronologist, 37,* 150–156.

Snowdon, D. (2002). *Aging with grace: What the Nun Study teaches us about leading longer, healthier, and more meaningful lives.* New York: Bantam.

Snowdon, D. A. (2003). Healthy aging and dementia: Findings from the Nun Study. *Annals of Internal Medicine, 139,* 450–454.

Snowdon, D. A., Tully, C. L., Smith, C. D., Riley, K. P., & Markesbery, W. R. (2000). Serum folate and the severity of atrophy of the neocortex in Alzheimer's disease: Findings from the Nun Study. *American Journal of Clinical Nutrition, 71,* 993–998.

Snowdon, L. R., & Cheung, F. K. (1990). Use of inpatient mental health services by members of ethnic minority groups. *American Psychologist, 45,* 347–355.

Snowling, M. J. (2004). Reading development and dyslexia. In U. Goswami (Ed.), *Blackwell handbook of childhood cognitive development.* Malden, MA: Blackwell.

Snyder, H. N., & Sickmund, M. (1999, October). *Juvenile offenders and victims: 1999 national report.* Washington, DC: National Center for Juvenile Justice.

Sobieszczyk, M. E., Talley, A. K., Wilkin, T., & Hammer, S. M. (2005), Advances in anti-retroviral therapy. *Topics in HIV Medicine, 13,* 24–44.

Soenens, B., Elliot, A. J., Goossens, L., Vansteenkiste, M., Luyten, P., & Duriez, B. (2005). The intergenerational transmission of perfectionism: Parents' psychological control as an intervening variable. *Journal of Family Psychology, 19,* 358–366.

Soergel, P., Pruggmayer, M., Schwerdtfeger, R., Mulhaus, K., & Scharf, A. (2006). Screening for trisomy 21 with maternal age, fetal nuchal translucency, and maternal serum biochemistry at 11–14 weeks: A regional experience from Germany. *Fetal Diagnosis and Therapy, 21,* 264–268.

Sollod, R. N. (2000). Religious and spiritual practices. In A. Kazdin (Ed.), *Encyclopedia of psychology.* Washington, DC, & New York: American Psychological Association and Oxford University Press.

Solomon, D., Battistich, V., Watson, M., Schaps, E., & Lewis, C. (2000). A six-district study of educational change: Direct and mediated effects of the Child Development Project. *Social Psychology of Education, 4,* 3–51.

Solot, D., & Miller, M. (2002). *Unmarried to each other.* New York: Marlowe.

Soltero, S. W. (2004). *Dual language: teaching and learning in two languages.* Boston: Allyn & Bacon.

Sommer, B. (2001). Menopause. In J. Worell (Ed.), *Encyclopedia of women and gender.* San Diego: Academic Press.

Sood, A. B., Razdan, A., Weller, E. B., & Weller, R. A. (2006). Children's reactions to parental and sibling death. *Current Psychiatry Reports, 8,* 115–120.

Sophian, C. (1985). Perseveration and infants' search: A comparison of two- and three-location tasks. *Developmental Psychology, 21,* 187–194.

Sorof, J. M., Lai, D., Turner, J., Poffenberger, T., & Portman, R. J. (2004). Overweight, ethnicity, and the prevalence of hypertension in school-aged children. *Pediatrics. 113,* 475–482.

Sorokin, P. (2002). New agents and future directions in biotherapy. *Clinical Journal of Oncological Nursing, 6,* 19–24

Souder, E. (2005). Neuropathology in Alzheimer's disease: Target of psychopharmacotherapy. *Journal of the American Academy of Nurse Practitioners, 17* (Suppl), S3–S5.

Sowell, E., & Jernigan, T. (1998). Further MRI evidence of late brain maturation: Limbic volume increases and changing asymmetries during childhood and adolescence. *Developmental Neuropsychology, 14,* 599–617.

Spafford, C. S., & Grosser, G. S. (2005). *Dyslexia and reading difficulties* (2nd ed.). Boston: Allyn & Bacon.

Spandel, V. (2001). *Creating young writers.* Boston: Allyn & Bacon.

Spandorfer, S. D., Davis, O. K., Barmat, L. I., Chung, P. H., & Rosenwaks, Z. (2004). Relationship between maternal age and aneuploidy in in vitro fertilization pregnancy loss. *Obstetrics and Gynecology Survey, 59,* 773–774.

Sparks, D. L., Hunsaker, J. C., Scheff, S. W., Kryscio, R. J., Henson, H., & Markesbery, W. R. (1990). Cortical senile plaques in coronary artery disease, aging, and Alzheimer's disease. *Neurobiology of Aging, 11,* 601–607.

Spear, L. P. (2000). Neurobehavioral changes in adolescence. *Current Directions in Psychological Science, 4,* 111–114.

Spear, L. P. (2004). Adolescent brain development and animal models. *Annals of the New York Academy of Sciences, 1021,* 23–26.

Spearman, C. E. (1927). *The abilities of man.* New York: Macmillan.

Spelke, E. S. (1979). Perceiving bimodally specified events in infancy. *Developmental Psychology, 5,* 626–636.

Spelke, E. S. (1991). Physical knowledge in infancy: Reflections on Piaget's theory. In S. Carey & R. Gelman (Eds.), *The epigenesis of mind: Essays on biology and cognition.* Hillsdale, NJ: Erlbaum.

Spelke, E. S. (2000). Core knowledge. *American Psychologist, 55,* 1233–1243.

Spelke, E. S., Breinlinger, K., Macomber, J., & Jacobson, K. (1992). Origins of knowledge. *Psychological Review, 99,* 605–632.

Spelke, E. S., & Hespos, S. J. (2001). Continuity, competence, and the object concept. In E. Dupoux (Ed.), *Language, brain, and behavior.* Cambridge, MA: Bradford/MIT Press.

Spelke, E. S., & Newport, E. L. (1998). Nativism, empiricism, and the development of knowledge. In W. Damon (Ed.), *Handbook of child psychology* (5th ed., Vol. 2). New York: Wiley.

Spelke, E. S., & Owsley, C. J. (1979). Intermodal exploration and knowledge in infancy. *Infant Behavior and Development, 2,* 13–28.

Spence, A. P. (1989). *Biology of human aging.* Englewood Cliffs, NJ: Prentice Hall.

Spence, J. T., & Buckner, C. E. (2000). Instrumental and expressive traits, trait stereotypes, and sexist attitudes: What do they signify? *Psychology of Women Quarterly, 24,* 44–62.

Spence, J. T., & Helmreich, R. (1978). *Masculinity and feminity: Their psychological dimensions.* Austin: University of Texas Press.

Spence, M. J., & DeCasper, A. J. (1987). Prenatal experience with low-frequency maternal voice sounds influences neonatal perception of maternal voice samples. *Infant Behavior and Development, 10,* 133–142.

Spencer, J. P., Vereijken, B., Diedrich, F. J., & Thelen, E. (2000). Posture and the emergence of manual skills. *Developmental Science, 3,* 216–233.

Spencer, M. B. (2006). Phenomenology and ecological systems theory. In W. Damon & R. Lerner (Eds.), *Handbook of child psychology* (6th ed.). New York: Wiley.

Spencer, S. (2005). Giving birth on the beach: hypnosis and psychology. *Practicing Midwife, 8,* 27–29.

Speranza, M., Corcos, M., Loas, G., Stéphan, P., Guilbaud, O., Perez-Diaz, F., Vénisse, J. L., Bizouard, P., Halfon, O., Flament, M., & Jeammet, P. (2005). Depressive personality dimensions and alexithymia in eating disorders. *Psychiatry Research, 135,* 153–163.

Spielberger, C. D., & Grier, K. (1983). Unpublished manuscript, University of South Florida, Tampa.

Spinelli, M. G. (2005). Neuroendocrine effects on mood. *Reviews in Endocrine and Metabolic Disorders, 6,* 109–115.

Spiro, A. (2001). Health in midlife: Toward a lifespan view. In M. E. Lachman (Ed.), *Handbook of midlife development.* New York: John Wiley.

Spitzer, A. R. (2005). Current controversies in the pathophysiology and prevention of sudden infant death syndrome. *Current Opinion in Pediatrics, 17,* 181–185.

Sprei, J. E., & Courtois, C. A. (1988). The treatment of women's sexual dysfunctions arising from sexual assault. In R. A. Brown & J. R. Fields (Eds.), *Treatment of sexual problems in individual and group therapy.* Great Neck, NY: PMA.

Spring, J. (2006). *American education* (12th ed.). New York: McGraw-Hill.

Spring, J. (2007). *Deculturalization and the struggle for equality* (5th ed.). New York: McGraw-Hill.

Springer, M. V., McIntosh, A. R., Winocur, G., & Grady, C. L. (2005). The relation between brain activity during memory tasks and years of education in young and older adults. *Neuropsychology, 19,* 181–192.

Springer, S. P., & Deutsch, G. (1985). *Left brain, right brain.* New York: W. H. Freeman.

Sprinthall, R. C. (2007). *Basic statistical analysis* (8th ed.). Boston: Allyn & Bacon.

Sroufe, L. A. (2000, Spring). The inside scoop on child development: Interview, *Cutting through the hype.* Minneapolis: College of Education and Human Development, University of Minnesota.

Sroufe, L. A., Egeland, B., & Carlson, E. A. (1999). One social world: The integrated development of parent-child and peer relationships. In W. A. Collins & B. Laursen (Eds.), *Minnesota symposium on child psychology* (Vol. 31). Mahwah, NJ: Erlbaum.

Sroufe, L. A., Egeland, B., Carlson, E., & Collins, W. A. (2005). The place of early attachment in developmental context. In K. E. Grossman, K. Krossman, & E. Waters (Eds.), *The power of longitudinal attachment research: From infancy and childhood to adulthood.* New York: Guilford Press.

Sroufe, L. A., Waters, E., & Matas, L. (1974). Contextual determinants of infant affectional response. In M. Lewis & L. Rosenblum (Eds.), *Origins of fear.* New York: Wiley.

Stahl, S. (2002, January), *Effective reading instruction in the first grade.* Paper presented at the Michigan Reading Recovery conference, Dearborn, MI.

Stanford University Medical Center (2006). *Diabetes and other endocrine and metabolic disorders.* Palo Alto, CA: Stanford University Medical Center.

Stanley, S. M., Amato, P. R., Johnson, C. A., & Markman, H. J. (2006). Premarital education, marital quality, and marital stability: Findings from a large, household survey. *Journal of Family Psychology, 20,* 117–126.

Stanner, S. (2006). New thinking about diet and cardiovascular disease. *Journal of Family Health Care, 16,* 71–74.

Stanwood, G. D., & Levitt, P. (2004). Drug exposure early in life: Functional repercussions of changing neuropharmacology during sensitive periods of brain development. *Current Opinions in Pharmacology, 4,* 65–71.

Starr, C. (2006). *Biology* (6th ed.). Pacific Grove, CA: Brooks Cole.

Stattin, H. & Magnusson, D. (1990). *Pubertal maturation in female development: Paths through life* (Vol. 2). Hillsdale, NJ: Erlbaum.

Statz, D. L. (2006). State of the science: Use of human milk and breast-feeding for vulnerable infants. *Journal of Perinatal and Neonatal Nursing, 20,* 51–55.

Staub, T. R., Bulgakova, M., Leurgans, S., Bennett, D. A., Fleischman, D., Turner, D. A., & DeToledo-Morrell, L. (2005). MRI predictors of risk of incident Alzheimer disease: A longitudinal study. *Neurology, 64,* 1520–1524.

Staudinger, U. M. (1996). Psychologische Produktivität und Selbstenfaltung im Alter. In M. M. Baltes & L. Montada (Eds.), *Produktives Leben im Alter.* Frankfurt: Campus.

Staudinger, U. M., & Bluck, S. (2001). A view on midlife development from lifespan theory. In M. E. Lachman (Ed.), *Handbook of midlife development.* New York: John Wiley.

Stebbins, R. A. (2005). Choice and experiential definitions of leisure. *Leisure Sciences, 27,* 349–352.

Steele, C. M., & Aronson, J. (1995). Stereotype threat and the intellectual test performance of African-Americans. *Journal of Personality and Social Psychology, 69,* 797–811.

Steele, C. M., & Aronson, J. A. (2004). Stereotype threat does not live by Steele and Aronson (1995) alone. *American Psychologist, 59,* 47–48.

Steele, J., Waters, E., Crowell, J., & Treboux, D. (1998, June). *Self-report measures of attachment: Secure bonds to other attachment measures and attachment theory.* Paper presented at the meeting of the International Society for the Study of Personal Relationships, Saratoga Springs, NY.

Steeman, E., de Casterlé, B. D., Godderis, J., & Grypdonck, M. (2006). Living with early stage dementia: A review of qualitative studies. *Journal of Advanced Nursing, 54,* 722–738.

Steffens, D. C., & others, (2006). Perspectives on depression, mild cognitive impairment, and cognitive decline. *Archives of General Psychiatry, 63,* 130–138.

Stegelin, D. A. (2003). Application of Reggio Emilia approach to early childhood science curriculum. *Early Childhood Education Journal, 30,* 163–169.

Steinberg, L. (2004). Risk taking in adolescence: What changes, and why? *Annals of the New York Academy of Sciences, 1021,* 23–26.

Steinberg, L. (2005). Cognitive and affective development in adolescence. *Trends in Cognitive Science, 9,* 69–74.

Steinberg, L. (2006, April). *A new approach to the study of adolescent cognitive development.* Paper presented at the meeting of the Society for Research on Adolescent Development, San Francisco.

Steinberg, L., Blatt-Eisengart, I., & Cauffman, E. (2006). Patterns of competence and adjustment among adolescents from authoritative, authoritarian, indulgent, and neglectful homes: A replication in a sample of serious juvenile offenders. *Journal of Research on Adolescence, 16,* 47–58.

Steinberg, L., & Cauffman, E. (2001). Adolescents as adults in court. *Social Policy Report, SRC D. XV* (No. 4), 1–13.

Steinberg, L. D. (1986). Latchkey children and susceptibility to peer pressure: An ecological analysis. *Developmental Psychology, 22,* 433–439.

Steinberg, L. D., & Levine, A. (1997). *You and your adolescent* (2nd ed.). New York: Harper Perennial.

Steinberg, L. D., & Silk, J. S. (2002). Parenting adolescents. In M. Bornstein (Ed.), *Handbook of parenting* (2nd ed., Vol. 1). Mahwah, NJ: Erlbaum.

Steiner, J. E. (1979). Human facial expressions in response to taste and smell stimulation. In H. Reese & L Lipsitt (Eds.), *Advances in child development* (Vol. 13). New York: Academic Press.

Stek, M. L., Gussekloo, J., Beekman, A. T. F., van Tilburg, W., & Westendorp, R. G. J. (2004). Prevalence, correlates, and recognition of depression in the oldest old: the Leiden 85-plus study. *Journal of Affective Disorders, 78,* 193–200.

Stenkley, N. C., Vik, O., & Laukli, E. (2004). The aging ear. *Acta Otolaryngology, 124,* 69–76.

Stephenson, J. (2004). FDA warns on mercury in tuna. *Journal of the American Medical Association, 291,* 171.

Steptoe, A., & Ayers, S. (2005). Stress, health, and illness. In S. Sutton, A. Baum, & M. Johnston (Eds.), *The SAGE handbook of health psychology.* Thousand Oaks, CA: Sage.

Stern, D. N., Beebe, B., Jaffe, J., & Bennett, S. L. (1977). The infant's stimulus world during social interaction: A study of caregiver behaviors with particular reference to repetition and timing. In H. R. Schaffer (Ed.), *Studies in mother-infant interaction.* London: Academic Press.

Stern, J. S. (1993, June 2). Commentary in "Lowly vitamin supplements pack a big health punch." *USA Today,* p. 3D.

Sternberg, R. J. (1986). *Intelligence applied.* San Diego: Harcourt Brace Jovanovich.

Sternberg, R. J. (1988). *The triangle of love.* New York: Basic Books.

Sternberg, R. J. (2002). Intelligence: The triarchic theory of intelligence. In J. W. Gutherie (Ed.), *Encyclopedia of education* (2nd ed.). New York: Macmillan.

Sternberg, R. J. (2003). Contemporary theories of intelligence. In I. B. Weiner (Ed.), *Handbook of Psychology* (Vol. VIII). New York: Wiley.

Sternberg, R. J. (2004). Individual differences in cognitive development. In U. Goswami (Ed.), *Blackwell handbook of childhood cognitive development.* Malden, MA: Blackwell.

Sternberg, R. J. (2006). *Cognitive psychology* (4th ed.). Belmont, CA: Wadsworth.

Sternberg, R. J., Grigorenko, E. L., & Kidd, K. K. (2005). Intelligence, race, and genetics. *American Psychologist, 60,* 46–59.

Sternberg, R. J., Grigorenko, E. L., & Kidd, K. K. (2006). Racing toward the finish line. *American Psychologist, 61,* 178–179.

Sternberg, R. J., Grigorenko, E. L., & Singer, J. L. (Eds.). (2004). *Creativity: From potential to realization.* Washington, DC: American Psychological Association.

Sternberg, R. J., Nokes, K., Geissler, P. W., Prince, R., Okatcha, F., Bundy, D. A., & Grigorenko, E. L. (2001). The relationship between academic and practical intelligence: A case study in Kenya. *Intelligence, 29,* 401–418.

Sterns, H. & Huyck, M. H. (2001) The role of work in midlife. In M. Lachman (Ed.), *Handbook of Midlife Development.* New York: Wiley.

Stetsenko, A. (2002). Adolescents in Russia: Surviving the turmoil and creating a brighter future. In B. B. Brown, R. W. Larson, & T. S. Saraswathi (Eds.), *The world's youth.* New York: Cambridge University Press.

Steur, F. B., Applefield, J. M., & Smith, R. (1971). Televised aggression and interpersonal aggression of preschool children. *Journal of Experimental Child Psychology, 11,* 442–447.

Stevens, J., & Killeen, M. (2006). A randomized controlled trial testing the impact of exercise on cognitive symptoms and disability of residents with dementia. *Contemporary Nurse, 21,* 32–40.

Stevenson, D. G. (2006). Nursing home consumer complaints and quality of care: A national view. *Medical Care Research Review, 63,* 347–368.

Stevenson, H. W. (1995). Mathematics achievement of American students: First in the world by 2000? In C. A. Nelson (Ed.), *Basic and applied perspectives in learning, cognition, and development.* Minneapolis: University of Minnesota Press.

Stevenson, H. W. (2000). Middle childhood: Education and schooling. In A. Kazdin (Ed.), *Encyclopedia of psychology.* Washington, DC, & New York: American Psychological Association and Oxford University Press.

Stevenson, H. W., Lee, S., Chen, C., Stigler, J. W., Hsu, C., & Kitamura, S. (1990). Contexts of achievement. *Monograph of the Society for Research in Child Development, 55* (Serial No. 221).

Stevenson, H. W., Lee, S., & Stigler, J. W. (1986). Mathematics achievement of Chinese, Japanese, and American children. *Science, 231,* 693–699.

Stevenson, H. W., & Mofer, B. K. (1999). Education policy in the United States and abroad: What we can learn from each other. In G. J. Cizek (Ed.), *Handbook of educational policy.* San Diego: Academic Press.

Stevenson, H. W., & Newman, R. S. (1986). Long-term prediction of achievement and attitudes in mathematics and reading. *Child Development, 57,* 646–659.

Stevenson, H. W., & Zusho, A. (2002). Adolescence in China and Japan: Adapting to a changing environment. In B. B. Brown, R. W. Larson, & T. S. Saraswathi (Eds.), *The world's youth.* New York: Cambridge University Press.

Stewart, A. J., Ostrove, J. M., & Helson, R. (2001). Middle aging in women: Patterns of personality change from the 30s to the 50s. *Journal of Adult Development, 8,* 23–37.

Stice, E., Presnell, K., & Spangler, D. (2002). Risk factors for binge eating onset in adolescent girls: A 2-year prospective investigation. *Health Psychology, 21,* 131–138.

Stiffer, E., Sacu, S., Weghaupt, H., Konig, F., Richter-Muksch, S., Thaler, A., Velikay-Parel, M., & Radner, W. (2004). Reading performance depending on the type of cataract and its predictability on the visual outcome. *Journal of Cataract and Refractive Surgery, 30,* 1259–1267.

Stine, E. A. L., Soederberg, L. M., & Morrow, D. G. (1996). Language and discourse processing through adulthood. In F. Blanchard-Fields & T. M. Hess (Eds.), *Perspectives on cognitive change in adulthood and aging.* New York: McGraw-Hill.

Stine-Morrow, E.A., Miller, L.M., & Hertzog, C. (2006). Aging and self-regulated language processing. *Psychological Bulletin, 132,* 582–606.

Stinson, C. K., & Kirk, E. (2006). Structured reminiscence: An intervention to decrease depression and increase self-transcendence in older women. *Journal of Clinical Nursing, 15,* 208–218.

Stipek, D. J. (2002). *Motivation to learn* (4th ed.). Boston: Allyn & Bacon.

Stipek, D. J. (2004). Head Start: Can't we have our cake and eat it too? *Education Week, 23* (No. 34), 52–53.

Stipek, D. J. (2005, February 16). Commentary in *USA Today,* p. 1D.

Stipek, D., Recchia, S., & McClintic, S. (1992). Self-evaluation in young children. *Monographs of the Society for Research in Child Development, 57* (1, Serial No. 226).

Stocchi, F. (2005). Optimizing levodopa therapy for the management of Parkinson's disease. *Journal of Neurology, 252* (Suppl 4), Siv43–Siv48.

Stocchi, F. (2006). The levodopa wearing-off phenomenon in Parkinson's disease: Pharmacokinetic considerations. *Expert Opinions in Pharmacotherapy, 7,* 1399–1407.

Stocker, C., & Dunn, J. (1990). Sibling relationships in adolescence: Links with friendships and peer relationships. *British Journal of Developmental Psychology, 8,* 227–244.

Stokstad, E. (2003). Nutrition: The vitamin D deficit. *Science, 302,* 1886–1888.

Stolley, M. R., Fitzgibbon, M. L., Dyer, A., Van Horn, L., Kaufer Christoffel, K., & Schiffer, L.

(2003). Hip-Hop to Health Jr., an obesity prevention program for minority preschool children: Baseline characteristics of the participants. *Preventive Medicine, 36,* 320–329.

Stone, R. I. (2006). Emerging issues in long-term care. In R. H. Binstock & L. K. George (Eds.), *Handbook of aging and the social sciences* (6th ed.). San Diego: Academic Press.

Stouthamer-Loeber, M., Loeber, R., Wei, E., Farrington, D. P., & Wikstrom, P. M. (2002). Risk and promotive affects in the explanation of serious delinquency in boys. *Journal of Consulting and Clinical Psychology, 70,* 111–123.

Strain, L. A., Grabusie, C. C., Searle, M. S., & Dunn, N. J. (2002). Continuing and ceasing leisure activities in later life: A longitudinal study. *The Gerontologist, 42,* 217–223.

Strasser, A., Skalicky, M., & Viidik, A. (2006). Impact of moderate physical exercise—in comparison with dietary restrictions—on age-associated decline in cell-mediated immunity of Sprague-Dawley rats. *Aging: Clinical and Experimental Research, 18,* 179–186.

Strauss, M. A., Sugarman, D. B., & Giles-Sims, J. (1997). Spanking by parents and subsequent anti-social behavior in children. *Archives of Pediatrics and Adolescent Medicine, 151,* 761–767.

Strauss, R. S. (2001). Environmental tobacco smoke and serum vitamin C levels in children. *Pediatrics, 107,* 540–542.

Streissguth, A. P., Martin, D. C., Sandman, B. M., Kirchner, G. L., & Darby, B. L. (1984). Intrauterine alcohol and nicotine exposure: Attention and reaction time in four-year-old children. *Developmental Psychology, 20,* 533–543.

Streri, A. (1987) Tactile discrimination of shape and intermodal transfer in two- to three-month-old infants. *British Journal of Developmental Psychology, 5,* 213–220.

Striegel-Moore, R. H., Franko, D. L., Thompson, D., Barton, B., Schreiber, G. B., & Daniels, S. R. (2004). Changes in weight and body image over time in women with eating disorders. *International Journal of Eating Disorders, 36,* 315–327.

Striegel-Moore, R. H., Silberstein, L. R., & Rodin, J. (1993). The social self in bulimia nervosa: Public self-consciousness, social anxiety, and perceived fraudulence. *Journal of Abnormal Psychology, 102,* 297–303 (p. 406).

Stringer, M., Ratcliffe, S. J., Evans, E. C., & Brown, L. P. (2005). The cost of prenatal care attendance and pregnancy outcomes in low-income working women. *Journal of Obstetrical, Gynecologic, and Neonatal Nursing, 34,* 551–560.

Stroebe, M., Gergen, M. H., Gergen, K. J., & Stroebe, W. (1992). Broken hearts or broken bonds: Love and death in historical perspective. *American Psychologist, 47,* 1205–1212.

Stroebe, M., Schut, H., & Stroebe, W. (2005). Attachment in coping with bereavement: A theoretical integration. *Review of General Psychology, 9,* 48–66.

Stroebe, M., & Stroebe, W. (1991). Does "grief work" work? *Journal of Consulting and Clinical Psychology, 59,* 57–65.

Strong, B., Sayad, B. W., DeValut, C., & Yarber, W. L. (2005). *Human sexuality* (5th ed.). New York: McGraw-Hill.

Studenski, S., Carlson, M. C., Fillet, H., Greenough, W. T., Kramer, A., & Rebok, G. W. (2006). From bedside to bench: Does mental and physical activity promote cognitive vitality in late life? *Science of Aging, Knowledge, and Environment, 10,* e21.

Substance Abuse and Mental Health Services Administration. (2003). *Aging and substance abuse.* Washington, DC: U.S. Department of Health and Human Services.

Sue, S. (1990, August). *Ethnicity and culture in psychological research and practice.* Paper presented at the meeting of the American Psychological Association, Boston.

Sugita, Y. (2004). Experience in early infancy is indispensable for color perception. *Current Biology, 14,* 1267–1271.

Sullivan, H. S. (1953). *The interpersonal theory of psychiatry.* New York: W. W. Norton.

Sullivan, K., & Sullivan, A. (1980). Adolescent-parent separation. *Developmental Psychology, 16,* 93–99.

Suls, J., & Swain, A. (1998). Type A-Type B personalities. In H. S. Friedman (Ed.), *Encyclopedia of mental health* (Vol. 3). San Diego: Academic Press.

Sumer, N., & Cozzarelli, C. (2004). The impact of adult attachment on partner and self-attributions and relationship quality. *Personal Relationships, 11,* 355–371.

Sung, H. E., Richter, L., Vaughn, R., Johnson, P. B., & Thom, B. (2005). Nonmedical use of prescription opiods among teenagers in the United States: Trends and correlates. *Journal of Adolescent Health, 37,* 44–51.

Suomi, S. J., Harlow, H. F., & Domek, C. J. (1970). Effect of repetitive infant-infant separations of young monkeys. *Journal of Abnormal Psychology, 76,* 161–172.

Susanne, G. O., Sissel, S., Ulla, W., Charlotta, G., & Sonja, O. L. (2006). Pregnant women's responses to information about an increased risk of carrying a baby with Down syndrome. *Birth, 33,* 64–73.

Susman, E. J. (2006, April). *Puberty revisited: Models, mechanisms, and the future.* Paper presented at the meeting of the Society for Research on Adolescence, San Francisco.

Susman, E. J., & Rogol, A. (2004). Puberty and psychological development. In R. Lerner & L. Steinberg, (Eds.), *Handbook of adolescence.* New York: Wiley.

Susman, E. J., Dorn, L. D., & Schiefelbein, V. L. (2003). Puberty, sexuality, and health. In R. M. Lerner, M. A. Easterbrooks, & J. Mistry (Eds.), *Comprehensive handbook of psychology: Developmental psychology* (Vol. 6). New York: Wiley.

Sutterly, J. A., & Frost, J. (2006). Creating play environments for early childhood: Indoors and out. In B. Spodek & O. N. Saracho (Eds.), *Handbook of research on the education of young children* (2nd ed.). Mahwah, NJ: Erlbaum.

Sutton-Smith, B. (2000). Play. In A. Kazdin (Ed.), *Encyclopedia of psychology.* Washington, DC, & New York: American Psychology Association and Oxford University Press.

Suzman, R. (1997, March 18). Commentary, *USA Today,* p. 1A.

Suzman, R. M., Harris, T., Hadley, E. C., Kovar, M. G., & Weindruch, R. (1992). The roubust oldest old: Optimistic perspectives for increasing healthy life expectancy. In R. M. Suzman, D. P. Willis, & K. G. Manton (Eds.), *The oldest old.* New York: Oxford University Press.

Suzuki, T. A., Qiang, Y., Sakuragawa, S., Tamura, H., & Oajima, K. (2006). Age-related changes of reaction time and p300 for lowcontrast color stimuli: Effects of yellowing of the aging human lens. *Journal of Physiological Anthropology, 25,* 179–187.

Swaab, D. F., Chun, W. C., Kruijver, F. P., Hofman, M. A., & Ishunina, T. A. (2002). Sexual differentiation of the human hypothalamus. *Advances in Experimental Medicine and Biology, 511,* 75–100.

Swain, S. O. (1992). Men's friendships with women. In P. Nardi (Ed.), *Gender in intimate relationships.* Belmont. CA: Wadsworth.

Swanson, J. M., & others. (2001). Clinical relevance of the primary findings of MTA: Success rates based on severity of ADHD and ODD symptoms at the end of treatment. *Journal of the American Academy of Child and Adolescent Psychiatry, 40,* 168–179.

Swarztrauber, K., Koudelka, C., & Brodsky, M. A. (2006). Initial pharmacotherapy in a population of veterans with Parkinson disease. *Neurology, 66,* 1425–1426.

Swaab, D. F., Chang, W. C., Kruijver, F. P., Hofman, M. A., & Ishunina, T. A. (2001). Structural and functional sex differences in the human hypothalamus. *Hormones and Behavior, 40,* 93–98.

Swick, D., Senkfor, A.J., & Van Petten, C. (2006, in press). Source memory retrieval is affected by aging and prefrontal lesions: Behavioral and ERP evidence. *Brain Research.*

Sykes, C. J. (1995). *Dumbing down our kids: Why America's children feel good about themselves but can't read, write, or add.* New York: St. Martin's Press.

Symonds, E. M., & Symonds, I. M. (2004). *Essential obstetrics and gynecology* (4th ed.). New York: Elsevier.

Taaffe, D.R. (2006). Sarcopenia—exercise as a treatment strategy. *Australian Family Physician, 35,* 130–134.

Tager-Flusberg, H. (2005). Morphology and syntax in the preschool years. In J. Berko Gleason, *The development of language* (6th ed.). Boston: Allyn & Bacon.

Takai, Y., Sato, M., Tan, R., & Hirai, T. (2005). Development of stereoacuity: Longitudinal design using a computer-based random-dot stereo test. *Japanese Journal of Ophthalmology, 49,* 1–5.

Talib, N. (2005). Dilemmas surrounding passive euthanasia—a Malaysian perspective. *Medicine Law Review, 24,* 605–613.

Tamura, T., & Picciano, M. F. (2006). Folate and human reproduction. *American Journal of Human Reproduction, 83,* 993–1016.

Tang, C. H., Wu, M. P., Liu, J. T., Liu, H. C., & Hsu, C. C. (2006). Delayed parenthood and the risk of cesarean delivery—is paternal age an independent risk factor? *Birth, 33,* 18–26.

Tang, M. P., Chon, H. C., Tsao, K. I., & Hsich, W. S. (2004). Outcome of very low birth weight infants with sonographic enlarged occipital horn. *Pediatric Neurology, 30,* 42–45.

Tannen, D. (1990). *You just don't understand: Women and men in conversation.* New York: Ballantine.

Tanner, J. L. (2006). Recentering during emerging adulthood: A critical turning point in life span development. In J. J. Avnett, & J. L. Tanner (Eds.), *Emerging adults in America.* Washington, DC: American Psychological Association.

Tantillo, M., Kesick, C. M., Hynd, G. W., & Dishman, R. K. (2002). The effects of exercise on children with attention-deficit hyperactivity disorder. *Medical Science and Sports Exercise, 34,* 203–212.

Tappan, M. B. (1998). Sociocultural psychology and caring psychology: Exploring Vygotsky's "hidden curriculum." *Educational Psychologist, 33,* 23–33.

Tappia, P. S., & Gabriel, C. A. (2006). Role of nutrition in the development of the fetal cardiovascular system. *Expert Review of Cardiovascular Therapy, 4,* 211–215.

Tariot, P. N. (2006). Contemporary issues in the treatment of Alzheimer's disease: Tangible benefits of current therapies. *Journal of Clinical Psychiatry, 67,* Supp 3, S15–S22.

Tarpenning, K. M., Hawkins, S. A., Marcell, T. J., & Wiswell, R. A. (2006). Endurance exercise and leg strength in older women. *Journal of Aging and Physical Activity, 14,* 3–11.

Tashiro, T., & Frazier, P. (2003). "I'll never be in a relationship like that again": Personal growth following romantic relationship breakups. *Personal Relationships, 10,* 113–128.

Tashiro, T., Frazier, P., & Berman, M. (2005). Stress-related growth following divorce and relationship dissolution. In M. A. Fine & J. H. Harvey (Eds.) *Handbook of divorce and relationship dissolution.* Mahwah, NJ: Erlbaum.

Tasker, F. L., & Golombok, S. (1997). *Growing up in a lesbian family: Effects on child development.* New York: Guilford.

Tassell-Baska, J., & Stambaugh, T. (2006). *Comprehensive curriculum for gifted learners* (3rd ed.). Boston: Allyn & Bacon.

Taylor, C. (2006). How a flexible approach can make retirement easier. *Nursing Times, 102,* 38–39.

Taylor, C. S., Smith, P. R., Taylor, V. A., von Eye, A., Lerner, R. M., Balsano, A. B., Anderson, P. M., Banik, R., & Almerigi, J. B. (2005). Individual and ecological assets and thriving among African American adolescent male gang and community-based organization members: A report from wave 3 of the "Overcoming the Odds" study. *Journal of Early Adolescence, 25,* 72–93.

Taylor, F. M. A., Ko, R., & Pan, M. (1999). Prenatal and reproductive health care. In E. J. Kramer, S. L. Ivey, & Y.-W. Ying (Eds.), *Immigrant women's health.* San Francisco: Jossey-Bass.

Taylor, S. E. (2003). *Health psychology* (5th ed.). New York: McGraw-Hill.

Taylor, S. P. (1982). Mental health and successful coping among Black women. In R. C. Manuel (Ed.), *Minority aging.* Westport, CT: Greenwood Press.

Teague, M. L., Mackenzie, S. L. C., & Rosenthal, D. M. (2007). *Your health today.* New York: McGraw-Hill.

Temple, C. A., Makinster, J. G., Buchmann, L. G., Logue, J., Mrvova, G., & Gearan, M. (2005). *Intervening for literacy.* Boston: Allyn & Bacon.

Tenenbaum, H. R., Callahan, M., A., Alba-Speyer, C., & Sandoval, L. (2002). Parent-child science conversations in Mexican descent families: Educational background, activity, and past experience as moderators. *Hispanic Journal of Behavioral Sciences, 24,* 225–248.

Teno, J. M., Clarridge, B. R., Casey, V., Welch, L. C., Wetie, T., Shield, R., & Mor, V. (2004). Family perspectives on end-of-life are at the last place of care. *Journal of the American Medical Association, 291,* 88–93.

Terman, D. L., Larner, M. B., Stevenson, C. S., & Behrman, R. E. (1996). Special education for students with disabilities: Analysis and recommendations. *The Future of Children, 6* (1), 4–24.

Terman, L. (1925). *Genetic studies of genius. Vol. 1: Mental and physical traits of a thousand gifted children.* Stanford, CA: Stanford University Press.

Terry, D. F., Wilcox, M. A., McCormick, M. A., & Perls, T. T. (2004). Cardiovascular disease delay in centenarian offspring. *Journals of Gerontology A: Biological and Medical Sciences, 59,* M385–M389.

Terry, W. S. (2006). *Learning and memory* (3rd ed.). Boston: Allyn & Bacon.

Teti, D. M. (2001). Retrospect and prospect in the study of sibling relationships. In J. P. McHale & W. S. Grolnick (Eds.), *Retrospect and prospect in the psychological study of families.* Mahwah, NJ: Erlbaum.

Teti, D. M., Sakin, J., Kucera, E., Caballeros, M., & Corns, K. M. (1993, March). *Transitions to siblinghood and security of firstborn attachment: Psychosocial and psychiatric correlates of changes over time.* Paper presented at the biennial meeting of the Society for Research in Child Development, New Orleans.

Thaithumyanon, P., Limpongsanurak, S., Praisuwanna, P., & Punnahitanon, S. (2006). perinatal effects of amphetamine and heroin use during pregnancy on the mother and infant. *Journal of the Medical Association of Thailand, 88,* 1506–1513.

Thapar, A., Fowler, T., Rice, F., Scourfield, J., Van Den Bree, M., Thomas, S., Harold, G., & Hay, D. (2003). Maternal smoking during pregnancy and attention deficit hyperactivity disorder symptoms in offspring. *American Journal of Psychiatry, 160,* 1985–1989.

Tharp, R. G. (1994). Intergroup differences among Native Americans in socialization and child cognition: An erthogenetic analysis. In P. M. Greenfield & R. Cocking (Eds.), *Cross-cultural roots of minority child development.* Mahwah, NJ: Erlbaum.

Tharp, R. G., & Gallimore, R. (1988). *Rousing minds to life: Teaching, learning, and schooling in social context.* New York: Cambridge University Press.

The Conduct Problems Prevention Research Group. (2002). Evaluation of the first 3 years of the Fast Track prevention trial with children at high risk for adolescent conduct problems. *Journal of Abnormal Child Psychology, 30,* 19–35.

Thelen, E. (1995). Motor development: A new synthesis. *American Psychologist, 50,* 79–95.

Thelen, E. (2000). Perception and motor development. In A. Kazdin (Ed.), *Encyclopedia of psychology.* Washington, DC & New York: American Psychological Association and Oxford University Press.

Thelen, E. (2001). Dynamic mechanisms of change in early perceptual-motor development. In J. L. McClelland & R. S. Siegler (Eds.), *Mechanisms of cognitive development.* Mahwah, NJ: Erlbaum.

Thelen, E., Corbetta, D., Kamm, K., Spencer, J. P., Schneider, K., & Zernicke, R. F. (1993). The transition to reaching: Mapping intention and intrinsic dynamics. *Child Development, 64,* 1058–1098.

Thelen, E., & Smith, L. B. (1998). Dynamic systems theory. In W. Damon (Ed.), *Handbook of child psychology* (5th ed., Vol. 1.). New York: Wiley.

Thelen, E., & Smith, L. B. (2006). Dynamic development of action and thought. In W. Damon & R. Lerner (Eds.), *Handbook of child psychology* (6th ed.). New York: Wiley.

Thelen, E., & Whitmeyer, V. (2005). Using dynamic systems theory to conceptualize the interface of perception, action, and cognition. In J. J. Reiser, J. J. Lockman, & C. A. Nelson (Eds.), *The role of action in learning and development.* Mahwah, NJ: Erlbaum.

Thiessen, E. D., Hill, E. A., & Saffan, J. R. (2005). Infant-directed speech facilitates word segmentation. *Infancy, 7,* 53–71.

Thobois, S. (2006). Proposed dose equivalence for rapid switch between dopamine receptor agonists in Parkinson's disease: A review of the literature. *Clinical Therapy, 28,* 1–12.

Tholin, S., Rasmussen, F., Tynelius, P., & Karlsson, J. (2005). Genetic and environmental influences on eating behavior: The Swedish Young Male Twins Study. *American Journal of Clinical Nutrition, 81,* 564–569.

Thomas, A., & Chess, S. (1991). Temperament in adolescence and its functional significance. In R. M. Lerner, A. C. Petersen, & J. Brooks-Gunn (Eds.), *Encylopedia of adolescence* (Vol. 2). New York: Garland.

Thomas, D. R. (2003). The relationship between functional status and inflammatory disease in older adults. *Journal of Gerontology A: Biological and Medical Science, 58,* M995–M998.

Thomas, K. (1998, November 4). Teen cyberdating is a new wrinkle for parents, too. *USA Today,* P. 9D.

Thomas, R. M. (2005). *Comparing Theories of Child development* (6th ed.). Belmont CA: Wadsworth.

Thompson, B., Thompson, A., Thompson, J., Fredickson, C., & Bishop, S. (2003). Heavy smokers: A quantitative analysis of attitudes and beliefs concerning cessation and continued smoking. *Nicotine and Tobacco Research, 5,* 923–933.

Thompson, J. (2005). Breastfeeding: Benefits and implications. Part One. *Community Practice, 78,* 183–184.

Thompson, P. M., Giedd, J. N., Woods, R. P., MacDonald, D., Evans, A. C., & Toga, A. W. (2000). Growth patterns in the developing brain detected by using continuum mechanical tensor maps. *Nature, 404*, 190–193.

Thompson, R., & Murachver, T. (2001). Predicting gender from electronic discourse. *British Journal of Social Psychology, 40*, 193–208.

Thompson, R. A. (1994). Emotion regulation: A theme in search of a definition. *Monographs of the Society for Research in Child Development, 59* (Serial No. 240), 2–3.

Thompson, R. A. (2006). The development of the person. In W. Damon & R. Lerner (Eds.), *Handbook of child psychology* (6th ed.). New York: Wiley.

Thompson, R. A., Easterbrooks, M. A., & Walker, L. (2003). Social and emotional development in infancy. In I. B. Weiner (Ed.), *Handbook of psychology* (Vol. 6). New York: Wiley.

Thompson, R. A., & Goodvin, R. (2005). The individual child: Temperament, emotion, self and personality. In M. J. Bornstein & M. E. Lamb (Eds.) *Developmental psychology* (5th ed.). Mahwah, NJ: Erlbaum.

Thompson, R. A., & Lagattuta, K. H. (2005). Feeling and understanding: Early emotional development. In K. McCartney & D. Phillips (Eds.), *The Blackwell handbook of early childhood development*. Malden, MA: Blackwell.

Thompson, R. A., & Nelson, C. A. (2001). Developmental science and the media. *American Psychologist, 56*, 5–15.

Thoni, A., & Moroder, L. (2004). Waterbirth: A safe and natural delivery method. Experience after 1355 waterbirths in Italy. *Midwifery Today, 70*, 44–48.

Thoppil, J., Riuteel, T. I., & Nalesnik, S. W. (2005). Early intervention for perinatal depression. *American Journal of Obstetrics and Gynecology, 192*, 1446–1448.

Thoresen, C. E., & Harris, A. H. S. (2002). Spirituality and health: What's the evidence and what's needed? *Annals of Behavioral Medicine, 24*, 3–13.

Thorne, C., & Newell, M. L. (2005). Treatment options for the prevention of mother-to-child transmission of HIV. *Current Opinion in Investigational Drugs, 6*, 804–811.

Thornton, P. L., Kieffer, E. C., Salbarian-Pena, Y., Odoms-Young, A., Willis, S. K., Kim, H., & Salinas, M. A. (2006). Weight, diet, and physical activity-related health beliefs and practices among pregnant and postpartum Latino women: The role of social support. *Maternal and Child Health Journal, 10*, 95–104.

Thornton, A., & Camburn, D. (1989). Religious participation and sexual behavior and attitudes. *Journal of Marriage and the Family, 49*, 117–128.

Thornton, R., & Light, L. L. (2006). Aging and language. In J. E. Birren & K. W. Schaie (Eds.), *Handbook of the psychology of aging* (6th Ed.). San Diego: Academic Press.

Thornton, W. J., & Dumke, H. A. (2005). Age differences in everyday problem-solving and decision-making effectiveness: A meta-analytic review. *Psychology and Aging, 20*, 85–99.

Thrasher, J. F., Campbell, M. K., & Oates, V. (2004). Behavior-specific social support for healthy behaviors among African American church members: Applying optimal matching theory. *Health Education and Behavior, 31*, 193–205.

Thung, S. F., & Grobman, W. A. (2005). The cost-effectiveness of routine antenatal screening for maternal herpes simplex virus-1 and -2 antibodies. *American Journal of Obstetrics and Gynecology, 192*, 483–488.

Thurstone, L. L. (1938). *Primary mental abilities*. Chicago: University of Chicago Press.

Tierney, M. C., Yao, C., Kiss, A., & McDowell, I. (2005). Neuropsychological tests accurately predict incident Alzheimer disease after 5 and 10 years. *Neurology, 64*, 1853–1859.

Timko, C., Finney, J. W., & Moos, R. H. (2005). The 8-year course of alcohol abuse: Gender differences in social context and coping. *Alcoholism: Clinical and Experimental Research, 29*, 612–621.

Timmer, E., Westerhof, G. J., & Dittmann-Kohli, F. (2005). "When looking back on my past life I regret ...": Retrospective regret in the second half of life. *Death Studies, 29*, 625–644.

Tinsley, B. J. (2003). *How Children learn to be healthy*. New York: Cambridge University Press.

Tjia, J., & Schwartz, J. S. (2006). Will the Medicare prescription drug benefit eliminate cost barriers for older adults with diabetes mellitus? *Journal of the American Geriatric Society, 54*, 606–612.

Tobin, A. J., & Dusheck, J. (2005). *Asking about life* (3rd ed.). Pacific Grove, CA: Brooks Cole.

Tobin, J. J., Wu, D. Y. H., & Davidson, D. H. (1989). *Preschool in three cultures*. New Haven, CT: Yale University Press.

Toga, A. W., Thompson, P. M., & Sowell, E. R. (2006). Mapping brain maturation. *Trends in Neuroscience, 29*, 148–159.

Tolan, P. H. (2001). Emerging themes and challenges in understanding youth violence. *Journal of Clinical Child Psychology, 30*, 233–239.

Tomasello, M. (2002). The emergence of grammar in early child language. In T. Givon & B. Malle (Eds.), *The Evolution of Language out of Prelanguage*. Amsterdam: John Benjamins.

Tomasello, M. (2003). *Constructing a language: A usage-based theory of language acquisition*. Cambridge, MA: Harvard University Press.

Tomasello, M. (2006). Acquiring linguistic constructions. In W. Damon & R. Lerner (Eds.), *Handbook of child psychology* (6th ed.). New York: Wiley.

Tomasello, M. & Slobin, D. I. (Eds.). (2005). *Beyond nature & nurture*. Mahwah, NJ: Erlbaum.

Tompkins, G. E. (2006). *Literacy for the 21st century* (4th ed.). Upper Saddle River, NJ: Prentice Hall.

Tong, E. K., England, L., & Glantz, S. A. (2005). Changing conclusions on secondhand smoke in a sudden infant death syndrome review funded by the tobacco industry. *Pediatrics, 115*, e356–e366.

Topp, R., Fahlman, M., & Boardley, D. (2004). Healthy aging: Health promotion and disease prevention. *Nursing Clinics of North America, 39*, 411–422.

Tough, S. C., Newburn-Cook, C., Johnston, D. W., Svenson, L. W., Rose, S., & Belik, J. (2002). Delayed childbearing and its impact on population rate changes in lower birth weight, multiple birth, and preterm delivery. *Pediatrics, 109*, 399–403.

Tovnetta, P., Hirsch, E. F., Howard, R., McConnell, T., & Ross, E. (2004). Skeletal injury patterns in older females. *Clinical Orthopedics, 422*, 556–561.

Tozer, S. E., Senese, G., & Violas, P. C. (2005). *School and society* (5th ed.). New York: McGraw-Hill.

Trappe, R., Laccone, F., Cobilanschi, J., Meins, M., Huppke, P., Hanefeld, F., & Engel, W. (2001). MECP2 mutations in sporadic cases of Rett syndrome are almost exclusively of paternal origin. *American Journal of Human Genetics, 68*, 1093–1101.

Trasler, J. (2000). Paternal exposures: Altered sex ratios. *Teratology, 62*, 6–7.

Trasler, J. M., & Doerksen, T. (2000, May). *Teratogen update: Paternal exposure-reproductive risks*. Paper presented at the joint meeting of the Pediatric Academic Societies and American Academy of Pediatrics, Boston.

Traustadottir, T., Bosch, P. R., & Matt, K. S. (2005). The HPA axis response to stress in women: Effects of aging and fitness. *Psychoneuroendocrinology, 30*, 392–402.

Treffers, P. E., Eskes, M., Kleiverda, G., & Van Alten, D. (1990). Home births and minimal medical interventions. *Journal of the American Medical Association, 246*, 2207–2208.

Trehub, S. E., Schneider, B. A., Thorpe, L. A., & Judge, P. (1991). Observational measures of auditory sensitivity in early infancy. *Developmental Psychology, 27*, 40–49.

Tremblay, M. S., Perez, C. E., Ardern, C. I., Bryan, S. N., & Katzmarzyk, P. T. (2005). Obesity, overweight, and ethnicity. *Health Reports, 16*, 23–34.

Tremblay, T., Monetta, L., & Joanette, Y. (2004). Phonological processing of words in right- and left-handers. *Brain and Cognition, 55*, 427–432.

Trimble, J. E. (1988, August). *The enculturation of contemporary psychology*. Paper presented at the meeting of the American Psychological Association, New Orleans.

Tritten, J. (2004). Embracing midwives everywhere. *Practicing Midwife, 7*, 4–5.

Trivedi, A. N., & Ayanian, J. Z. (2006). Perceived discrimination and use of preventive health services. *Journal of General Internal Medicine, 21*, 553–558.

Troll, L. E. (1994). Family-embedded versus family-deprived oldest-old: A study of contrasts. *International Journal of Aging and Human Development, 38*, 51–64.

Troll, L. E. (2000). Transmission and transmutation. In J. E. Birren & J. J. F. Schroots (Eds.), *A history of geropsychology in autobiography*. Washington, DC: American Psychological Association.

Trommsdorff, G. (2002). An eco-cultural and interpersonal relations approach to development of the lifespan. In W. J. Lonner, D. L. Dinnel, S. A. Hayes, & D. N. Sattler (Eds.), *Online Readings in Psychology and Culture* (Unit 12, Chapter 1), retrieved April 29, 2006. from *http://www.wwu.edu/~culture*, Center for Cross-Cultural Research, Western Washington University, Bellingham, Washington.

Truitner, K., & Truitner, N. (1993). Death and dying in Buddhism. In D. P. Irish & K. F. Lundquist (Eds.), *Ethnic variations in dying, death, and grief: Diversity in universality*. Washington, DC: Taylor & Francis.

Trzesniewski, K. H., Donnellan, M. B., & Robins, R. W. (2003). Stability of self-esteem across the life span. *Journal of Personality and Social Psychology, 84*, 205–220.

Tsigos, C., & Chrousos, G. P. (2002). Hypothalamic-pituitary-adrenal axis, neuroendocrine factors, and stress. *Journal of Psychosomatic Research, 53*, 865–871.

Tsujimoto, S., Yamamoto, T., Kawaguchi, H., Koizumi, H., & Sawaguchi, T. (2004). Prefrontal cortex activation associated with working memory in adults and preschool children: An event-related optical topography study. *Cerebral Cortex, 14*, 703–712.

Tubman, J. G., & Windle, M. (1995). Continuity of difficult temperament in adolescence: Relations with depression, life events, family support, and substance abuse. *Journal of Youth and Adolescence, 24*, 133–152.

Tuch, H., Parrish, P., & Romer, A. L. (2003). Integrating palliative care into nursing homes. *Journal of Palliative Medicine, 6*, 297–309.

Tucha, O., Prell, S., Meclinger, L., Bormann-Kischkel, C., Kubber, S., Linder, M., Walitza, S., & Lange, K. W. (2006). Effects of methylphenidate on multiple components of attention in children with attention deficit hyperactivity disorder. *Psychopharmacology 185*, 315–326.

Tucker, J. S., Ellickson, P. L., & Klein, M. S. (2003). Predictors of the transition to regular smoking during adolescence and young adulthood. *Journal of Adolescent Health, 32*, 314–324.

Tucker, J. S., Schwartz, J. E., Clark, K. M., & Friedman, H. S. (1999). Age-related changes in the associations of social network ties with mortality risk. *Psychology and Aging, 14*, 564–571.

Tudge, J. (2004). Practice and discourse as the intersection of individual and social in human development. In A. N. Perret-Clermont, L. Resnick, C. Pontecorvo, & B. Burge (Eds.), *Joining society: Social interactions and learning in adolescence and youth.* New York: Cambridge University Press.

Tulving, E. (2000). Concepts of memory. In E. Tulving & F. I. M. Craik (Eds.), *The Oxford handbook of memory.* New York: Oxford University Press.

Turgeon, J. L., McDonnell, D. P., Martin, K. A., & Wise, P. M. (2004). Hormone therapy: Physiological complexity belies therapeutic simplicity. *Science, 304,* 1269–1273.

Turiel, E. (1998). The development of morality. In N. Eisenberg (Ed.), *Handbook of child psychology* (5th ed., Vol. 3). New York: Wiley.

Turiel, E. (2003). *The culture of morality.* New York: Cambridge University Press.

Turiel, E. (2006). The development of morality. In W. Damon & R. Lerner (Eds.), *Handbook of child psychology* (6th ed.), New York: Wiley.

Turk, D. C., Rudy, T. E., & Salovey, P. (1984). Health protection: Attitudes and behaviors of LPN's teachers and college students. *Health Psychology, 3,* 189–210.

Turnbull, A., Turnbull, H. R., & Tompkins, J. R. (2007). *Exceptional lives* (5th ed.). Upper Saddle River, NJ: Prentice-Hall.

Turner, B. F. (1982). Sex-related differences in aging. In B. B. Wolman (Ed.), *Handbook of developmental psychology.* Englewood Cliffs, NJ: Prentice Hall.

Turner, C. H., & Robling, A. G. (2005). Mechanisms by which exercise improves bone strength. *Journal of Bone and Mineral Metabolism, 23* (Suppl.), S16–S22.

Turner, J. M. (2006). X-inactivation: Close encounters of the X kind. *Current Biology, 16,* R259–R261.

Turvey, C. L., Carney, C., Arndt, S., & Wallace, R. B. (1999, November). *Conjugal loss and syndromal depression in a sample of elders ages 70 years and older.* Paper presented at the meeting of the Gerontological Society of America, San Francisco.

U.S. Bureau of the Census (2001). *Census data: 2000.* Washington, DC: U.S. Bureau of the Census.

U.S. Bureau of the Census (2002). *Statistical abstracts of the United States.* Washington, DC: U.S. Government Printing Office.

U.S. Bureau of the Census (2003). *Population statistics.* Washington, DC: U.S. Food and Drug Administration.

U.S. Bureau of the Census (2004). *Statistical abstracts of the United States.* Washington, DC: U.S. Government Printing Office.

U.S. Bureau of the Census (2005). *People.* Washington, DC: U.S. Bureau of the Census.

U.S. Bureau of the Census (2006). *Statistical abstract of the United States, Table 96.* Washington, DC: U.S. Bureau of the Census.

U.S. Department of Education (1996). *Number and disabilities of children and youth served under IDEA.* Washington, DC: Office of Special Education Programs, Data Analysis System.

U.S. Department of Education (2003, December 23). *The NCES fast facts: What are the trends in the educational level of the United States Population?* Washington, DC: V. S. Office of Education.

U.S. Department of Energy (2001). *The human genome project.* Washington, DC: U.S. Department of Energy.

U.S. Food and Drug Administration (2004, March 19). *An important message for pregnant women and women of childbearing age who may become pregnant about the risk of mercury in fish.* Washington, DC: U.S. Bureau of the Census.

U.S. Department of Health and Human Services (2003). *Child abuse and neglect statistics.* Washington, DC: U.S. Department of Health and Human Services.

U.S. Surgeon General's Report (1990). *The health benefits of smoking cessation.* Bethesda, MD: U.S. Department of Health and Human Services.

Ubell, C. (1992, December 6). We can age successfully. *Parade,* pp. 14–15.

Uchino, B. N., Berg, C. A., Smith, T. W., Pearce, G., & Skinner, M. (2006). Age-related differences in ambulatory blood pressure during daily stress: Evidence for greater blood pressure reactivity with age. *Psychology and Aging, 21,* 231–239.

Uchino, B. N., Holt-Lunstad, J., Bloor, L. E., & Campo, R. A. (2005). Aging and cardiovascular reactivity to stress: Longitudinal evidence for changes in stress reactivity. *Psychology and Aging, 20,* 134–143.

Umana-Taylor, A. J. (2004). Ethnic identity and self-esteem: Examining the role of social contexts. *Journal of Adolescence, 27,* 139–146.

UNAIDS (2006). *2006 report on the global AIDS epidemic.* Geneva, UNICEF.

Underwood, M. K. (2003). *Social aggression among girls.* New York: Guilford.

Underwood, M. K. (2004). Sticks and stones and social exclusion: Aggression among boys and girls. In P. K. Smith & C. H. Hart (Eds.), *Blackwell handbook of childhood social development.* Malden, MA: Blackwell.

Unger, B., Kemp, J. S., Wilkins, D., Psara, R., Ledbetter, T., Graham, M., Case, M., & Thach, B. T. (2003). Racial disparity and modifiable risk factors among infants dying suddenly and unexpectedly. *Pediatrics, 111,* E127–E131.

UNICEF (2003). *The state of the world's children 2003.* Geneva: UNICEF.

UNICEF (2004). *The state of the world's children 2004.* Geneva: UNICEF.

UNICEF (2006). *The state of the world's children 2006.* Geneva: UNICEF.

United Nations (2002). *Improving the quality of life of girls.* New York: United Nations.

Urbano, M. T., & Tait, D. M. (2004). Can the irradiated uterus sustain a pregnancy? *Clinical Oncology, 16,* 24–28.

Vacca, J. A. L., Vacca, R. T., Gove, M. K., Burkey, L. C., Lenhart, L. A., & McKeon, C. A. (2006). *Reading and learning to read* (6th ed.). Boston: Allyn & Bacon.

Vaillant, G. (2005). Conversation with George Vaillant. *Addiction, 100,* 274–280.

Vaillant, G. E. (1977). *Adaptation to life.* Boston: Little, Brown.

Vaillant, G. E. (1992). Is there a natural history of addiction? In C. P. O'Brien & J. H. Jaffe (Eds.), *Addictive states.* Cambridge, MA: Harvard University Press.

Vaillant, G. E. (2002). *Aging well.* Boston: Little, Brown.

Valencia, R. R., & Suzuki, L. A. (2001). *Intelligence testing and minority students.* Thousand Oaks, CA: Sage.

Valeri, S. M. (2003). Social factors: Isolation and loneliness versus social activity. In A. Spirito & J. C. Overholser (Eds.), *Evaluating and treating adolescent suicide attempters.* San Diego: Academic Press.

Valuck, R. J., Lily, A. M., Sills, M. R., Giese, A. A., & Allen, R. A. (2004). Antidepressant treatment and risk of suicide attempt by adolescents with major depressive disorder: A propensity-adjusted retrospective cohort study. *CNS Drugs Review, 18,* 1119–1132.

Van Buren, E., & Graham, S. (2003). *Redefining ethnic identity: Its relationship to positive and negative school adjustment outcomes for minority youth.* Paper presented at the meeting of the Society for Research in Child Development, Tampa.

van den Boom, D. C. (1989). Neonatal irritability and the development of attachment. In G. A. Kohnstamm, J. E. Bates, & M. K. Rothbart (Eds.), *Temperament in childhood.* New York: Wiley.

Van Egeren, L. A., & Hawkins, D. P. (2004). Coming to terms with coparenting: Implications of definition and measurement. *Journal of Adult Development, 11,* 165–178.

Van Evra, J. (2004). *Television and child development.* Mahwah, NJ: Erlbaum.

van Gool, C. H., Kempen, G. I., Bosma, H., van Boxtel, M. P., Jolles, J., & van Eijk, J. T. (2006, in press). Associations between lifestyle and depressed mood: Longitudinal results from the Maastricht Aging Study. *American Journal of Public Health.*

van Hooren, S. A., Valentijn, S. A., Bosma, H., Ponds, R. W., van Boxtel, M. P., & Jolles, J. (2005). Relation between health status and cognitive functioning: A 6-year follow-up of the Maastricht Aging Study. *Journals of Gerontology B: Psychological Sciences and Social Sciences, 60,* 57–60.

van IJzendoorn, M. H., & Kroonenberg, P. M. (1988). Cross-cultural patterns of attachment: A meta-analysis of the Strange Situation. *Child Development, 59,* 147–156.

van IJzendoorn, M. H., Juffer, F., & Poelhuis, C. W. (2005). Adoption and cognitive development: A meta-analytic comparison of adopted and nonadopted children's IQ and school performance. *Psychological Bulletin, 131,* 301–316.

Van Mierlo, J., & Van den Buick, J. (2004). Benchmarking the cultivation approach to video game effects. *Journal of Adolescence, 27,* 97–111.

van Praag, H., Shubert, T., Zhao, C., & Gage, F. H. (2005). Exercise enhances learning and hippocampal neurogenesis in aged mice. *Journal of Neuroscience, 25,* 8680–8685.

van Solinge, H., & Henkens, K. (2005). Couples' adjustment to retirement: A multiactor panel study. *Journals of Gerontology B: Psychological Sciences and Social Sciences, 60,* S11–S20.

VanBeveren, T. T. (2005, January). *Personal conversation.* Richardson, TX: Department of Psychology, U. of Texas at Dallas.

Vandell, D. L. (2004). Early child care: The known and unknown. *Merrill-Palmer Quarterly, 50,* 387–414.

Vandell, D. L., & Wilson, K. S. (1988). Infants' interactions with mother, sibling, and peer: Contrasts and relations between interaction systems. *Child Development, 48,* 176–186.

Vandewater, E. A., Ostrove, J. M., & Stewart, A. J. (1997). Predicting women's well-being in mid-life: The importance of personality development and social role involvements. *Journal of Personality and Social Development, 72,* 1147–1160.

VandeWeerd, C., & Paveza, G. (1999, November). *Physical violence in old age: A look at the burden of women.* Paper presented at the meeting of the Gerontological Society of America, San Francisco.

Varkey, P., Chutka, D.S., & Lesnick, T.G. (2006). The aging game: Improving medical students' attitudes toward caring for the elderly. *Journal of of the American Medical Directors Association, 7,* 224–229.

Vastag, B. (2004). Does video game violence sow aggression? *Journal of the American Medical Association, 291,* 1822–1824.

Vaughn, S. S., Bos, C. S., & Schumm, J. S. (2007). *Teaching students who are exceptional, diverse, and at risk in the general education classroom* (4th ed.). Boston: Allyn & Bacon.

Vaupel, J.W., & Loichinger, E. (2006). Redistributing work in aging Europe. *Science, 312,* 1911–1913.

Venners, S. A., Wang, X., Chen, C., Wang, L., Chen, D., Guang, W., Huang, A., Ryan, L., O'Connor, J., Lasley, B., Overstreet, J., Wilcox, A., & Xu, X. (2005). Paternal smoking and pregnancy loss: A prospective study using a biomarker of pregnancy. *American Journal of Epidemiology, 159,* 993–1001.

Verbrugge, L. M., Gruber-Baldini, A. L., & Fozard, J. L. (1996). Age differences and age changes in activities: Baltimore Longitudinal Study of Aging. *Journal of Gerontology: Social Sciences, 51B,* S30–S41.

Verhaeghen, P., Marcoen, A., & Goossens, L. (1995). Facts and fiction about memory aging: A quantitative integration of research findings. *Journal of Gerontology, 48,* P157–P171.

Verma, S., & Saraswathi, T. S. (2002). Adolescence in India: Street urchins or Silicon Valley millionaires? In B. B. Brown, R. W. Larson, & T. S. Saraswathi (Eds.), *The world's youth.* New York: Cambridge University Press.

Verster, J. C., van Duin, D., Volkerts, E. R., Schreueder, A. H., & Verbaten, M. N. (2002). Alcohol hangover effects on memory functioning and vigilance performance after an evening of binge drinking. *Neuropsychopharmacology, 28,* 740–746.

Vicario, A., Martinez, C. D., Baretto, D., Diaz Casale, A., & Nicolosi, L. (2005). Hypertension and cognitive decline: Impact of executive function. *Journal of Clinical Hypertension, 7,* 598–604.

Vidaeff, A. C., & Mastrobattista, J. M. (2003). In utero cocaine exposure: A thorny mix of science and mythology. *American Journal of Perinatology, 20,* 165–172.

Vidal, F. (2000). Piaget's theory. In A. Kazdin (Ed.), *Encyclopedia of psychology.* Washington, DC, & New York: American Psychological Association and Oxford University Press.

Vijg, J., & Suh, Y. (2005). Genetics of longevity and aging. *Annual Review of Medicine, 56,* 193–212.

Villareal, T.T., Banks, M., Sinacore, D.R., Siener, C., & Klein, S. (2006). Effect of weight loss and exercise on frailty in obese older adults. *Archives of Internal Medicine, 166,* 860–866.

Vina, J., Borras, C., Gambini, J., Sastre, J., & Pallardo, F. V. (2005). Why females live longer than males: Control of longevity by hormones. *Science of Aging Knowledge Environment, 23,* e17.

Vintzileos, A. M., Guzman, E. R., Smulian, J. C., Scorza, W. E., & Knuppel, R. A. (2002). Second-trimester genetic sonography in patients with advanced maternal age and normal triple screen. *Obstetrics and Gynecology, 99,* 993–995.

Virnig, B., Huang, Z., Lurie, N., Musgrave, D., McBean, A. M., & Dowd, B. (2004). Does Medicare managed care provide equal treatment for mental illness across race? *Archives of General Psychiatry, 61,* 201–205.

Virts, E. L., Phillips, J. A., & Thoman, M. L. (2006). A novel approach to thymic rejuvenation in the aged. *Rejuvenation Research, 9,* 134–142.

Visher, E., & Visher, J. (1989). Parenting coalitions after remarriage: Dynamics and therapeutic guidelines. *Family Relations, 38,* 65–70.

Vitiello, M. V., Larsen, L. H., & Moe, K. E. (2004). Age-related sleep change: Gender and estrogen effects on the subjective-objective sleep quality relationships of healthy, noncomplaining older men and women. *Journal of Psychosomatic Research, 56,* 503–510.

Voelker, R. (2004). Stress, sleep loss, and substance abuse create potent recipe for college depression. *Journal of American Medical Association, 291,* 2177–2179.

Voeller, K. K. (2004). Attention-deficit hyperactivity disorder. *Journal of Child Neurology, 19,* 798–814.

Vogler, G. P. (2006). Behavior genetics and aging. In J. E. Birren & K. W. Schaie (Eds.), *Handbook of the psychology of aging* (6th ed.). San Diego: Academic Press.

Vogler, M. A. (2006). Update: Preventing mother-to-child transmission of HIV. *Current HIV/AIDS Reports, 3,* 59–65.

Volling, B. L. (2002). Sibling relationships. In M. H. Bornstein, L. Davidson, C. L. M. Keyes, & K. A. Moore (Eds.), *Well-being.* Mahwah, NJ: Erlbaum.

Volterra, M. C., Caselli, O., Capirci, E., & Pizzuto, E. (2004). Gesture and the emergence and development of language. In M. Tomasello & D. I. Slobin (Eds.), *Beyond nature-nurture.* Mahwah, NJ: Erlbaum.

Votruba-Drzal, E., Coley, R. L., & Chase-Lansdale, P. L. (2004). Child care and low-income children's development: Direct and moderated effects. *Child Development, 75,* 296–312.

Voydanoff, P. (1990). Economic distress and family relations: A review of the eighties. *Journal of Marriage and the Family, 52,* 1099–1115.

Vurpillot, E. (1968). The development of scanning strategies and their relation to visual differentiation. *Journal of Experimental Child Psychology, 6,* 632–650.

Vygotsky, L. S. (1962). *Thought and language.* Cambridge, MA: MIT Press.

Wachs, T. D. (1994). Fit, context and the transition between temperament and personality. In C. Halverson, G. Kohnstamm, & R. Martin (Eds.), *The developing structure of personality from infancy to adulthood.* Hillsdale, NJ: Erlbaum.

Wachs, T. D. (1995). Relation of mild-to-moderate malnutrition to human development: Correlational studies. *Journal of Nutrition Supplement, 125,* 2245s–2254s.

Wachs, T. D. (2000). *Necessary but not sufficient.* Washington, DC: American Psychological Association.

Wadhwa, P. D. (2005). Psychoneuroendocrine processes in human pregnancy influence fetal development and health. *Psychoneuroendocrinology, 30,* 724–743.

Wadsworth, S. J., Olson, R. K., Pennington, B. F., & DeFries, J. C. (2004). Differential genetic etiology of reading disability as a function of IQ. *Journal of Learning Disabilities, 33,* 192–199.

Wagstaff, A., Bustreo, F., Bryce, J., Claeson, M., and the WHO-World Bank Child Health and Poverty Working Group. (2004). Child health: Reaching the poor. *American Journal of Public Health, 94,* 726–736.

Wainryb, C. (2006). Moral development in culture: Diversity, tolerance, and justice. In M. Killen & J. G. Smetana (Eds.), *Handbook of moral development.* Mahwah, NJ: Erlbaum.

Waite, L. (2005, June). *The case for marriage.* Paper presented at the 9th annual Smart Marriages conference, Dallas.

Walden, T. (1991). Infant social referencing. In J. Garber & K. Dodge (Eds.), *The development of emotional regulation and dysregulation.* New York: Cambridge University Press.

Waldman, I. D., & Gizer, I. R. (2006 in press). The genetics of attention deficit hyperactivity disorder. *Clinical Psychology Review.*

Walker, A. (2006). Aging and politics: An international perspective. In R. H. Binstock & L. K. George (Eds.), *Handbook of aging and the social sciences* (6th ed.). San Diego: Academic Press.

Walker, C., Gruman, C., & Blank, K. (1999, November). *Physician-assisted suicide: Looking beyond the numbers.* Paper presented at the meeting of the Gerontological Society of America, San Francisco.

Walker, E. F. (2002). Adolescent neurodevelopment and psychopathology. *Current Directions in Psychological Science, 11,* 24–28.

Walker, H. (1998, May 31). Youth violence: Society's problem. *Eugene Register Guard,* p. 1C.

Walker, L. (1982). The sequentiality of Kohlberg's stages of moral development. *Child Development, 53,* 1130–1136.

Walker, L. (2001). Battering in adult relationships. In J. Worell (Ed.). *Encyclopedia of women and gender.* San Diego: Academic Press.

Walker, L. J. (2002). In W. Damon (Ed.), *Bringing in a new era of character education.* Stanford, CA: Hoover Press.

Walker, L. J. (2004). Progress and prospects in the psychology of moral development. *Merrill-Palmer Quarterly, 50,* 546–557.

Walker, L. J. (2006). Gender and morality. In M. Killen & J. G. Smetana (Eds.), *Handbook of moral development.* Mahwah, NJ: Erlbaum.

Walker, S. O., Petrill, S. A., & Plomin, R. (2005). A genetically sensitive investigation of the effects of the school environment and socioeconomic status on academic achievement in seven-year-olds. *Educational Psychology, 25,* 55–63.

Walker-Sterling, A. (2005). African Americans and obesity: Implications for clinical nurse specialist practice. *Clinical Nurse Specialist, 19,* 193–198.

Wallace Foundation. (2004). *Out-of-school learning: All work and no play.* New York City: Author.

Wallace-Bell, M. (2003). The effects of passive smoking on adult and child health. *Professional Nurse, 19,* 217–219.

Wallerstein, J. S., & Johnson-Reitz, L. (2004). Communication in divorced and single parent families. In A. L. Vaneglisti (Ed.), *Handbook of family communication.* Mahwah, NJ: Erlbaum.

Wallerstein, J. S., & Lewis, J. M. (2005). The reality of divorce: Reply to Gordon. *Psychoanalytic Psychology, 22,* 452–454.

Walsh, L. A. (2000, Spring). The inside scoop on child development: Interview. *Cutting through the hype.* Minneapolis: College of Education and Human Development, University of Minnesota.

Walsh, L. V. (2006). Beliefs and rituals in traditional birth attendant practice in Guatemala. *Journal of Transcultural Nursing, 17,* 148–154.

Walshaw, C. A., & Owens, J. M. (2006). Low breastfeeding rates and milk insufficiency. *British Journal of General Practice, 56,* 379.

Walters, E., & Kendler, K. S. (1994). Anorexia nervosa and anorexia-like symptoms in a population based twin sample. *American Journal of Psychiatry, 152,* 62–71.

Waltman, P. A., Brewer, J. M., Rogers, B. P., & May, W. L. (2004). Building evidence for practice: A pilot study of newborn bulb suctioning at birth. *Journal of Midwifery and Women's Health, 49,* 32–38.

Wandel, M., & Roos, G. (2005). Work, food, and physical, activity: A qualitative study of coping strategies among men in three occupations. *Appetite, 44,* 93–102.

Wang, J., Eslinger, P. J., Smith, M. B., & Yang, Q. X. (2005). Functional magnetic resonance imaging study of human olfaction and normal aging. *Journals of Gerontology A: Biological Sciences and Medical Sciences, 60,* 510–514.

Wang, S. M., DeZinno, P., Fermo, L., William, K., Caldwell-Andrews, A. A., Bravemen, F., & Kain, Z. N. (2005). Complementary and alternative medicine for low-back pain in pregnancy: A cross-sectional survey. *Journal of Alternative and Complementary Medicine, 11,* 459–464.

Warburton, D. E., Nicol, C. W., & Bredin, S. S. (2006). Health benefits of physical activity: the evidence. *Canadian Medical Association Journal, 174,* 801–809.

Ward, L. M. (2003). Understanding the role of entertainment media in the sexual socialization of American youth: A review of empirical research. *Developmental Review, 23,* 347–388.

Ward, L. M., & Caruthers, A. (2001). Media influences. In J. Worell (Ed.), *Encyclopedia of women and gender.* San Diego: Academic Press.

Ward, L. M., & Friedman, K. (2006). Using TV as a guide: Associations between television viewing and adolescents' sexual attitudes and behavior. *Journal of Research on Adolescence, 16,* 133–156.

Ward, L. M., Hansbrough, E., & Walker, E. (2005). Contributions of music video exposure to Black adolescents' gender and sexual schemas. *Journal of Adolescent Research, 20,* 143–166.

Ward, R. A., & Spitze, G. D. (2004). Marital implications of parent-adult child coresidence: A longitudinal view. *Journals of Gerontology B: Psychological and Social Sciences, 59*, S2–S8.

Ward, W. F., Qi, W., Van Remmen, H., Zackert, W. E., Roberts, L. J., & Richardson, A. (2005). Effects of age and caloric restriction on lipid peroxidation: Measurement of oxidative stress by F-isoprostane levels. *Journals of Gerontology A: Biological Sciences and Medical Sciences, 60*, 847–851.

Wardlaw, G. M. (2006). *Contemporary nutrition* (6th ed.). New York: McGraw-Hill.

Wardlaw, G. M., & Hampl, J. (2007). *Perspectives in nutrition* (7th ed.). New York: McGraw-Hill.

Wardlaw, G. M., & Smith, A. M. (2007). *Contemporary nutrition* (6th ed. Updated). New York: McGraw-Hill.

Ware, J. E., Kosinski, M., & Dewey, J. E. (2000). *How to score Version 2 of the SF-36 Health Survey.* Boston: QualityMetric.

Wareham, P., McCallin, A., & Diesfeld, K. (2005). Advance directives: The New Zealand context. *Nursing Ethics, 12*, 349–359.

Wark, G. R., & Krebs, D. L. (2006, in press). The construction of moral dilemmas in everyday life. *Journal of Moral Education.*

Warr, P. (1994). Age and employment. In M. Dunnette, L. Hough, & H. Triandis (Eds.), *Handbook of industrial and organizational psychology* (Vol. 4). Palo Alto, CA: Consulting Psychologists Press.

Warr, P. (2004). Work, well-being, and mental health. In J. Baring, E. K. Kelloway, & M. R. Frone (Eds.), *Handbook of work stress.* Thousand Oaks, CA: Sage.

Warr, P., Butcher, V., & Roberts, I. (2004). Activity and psychological well-being in old people. *Aging and Mental Health, 8*, 172–183.

Warren, B. J. (2005). The cultural expression of death and dying. *Case Manager, 16*, 44–47.

Warren, M. P., & Valente, J. S. (2004). Menopause and patient management. *Clinical Obstetrics and Gynecology, 47*, 450–470.

Warrick, P. (1992, March 1). The fantastic voyage of Tanner Roberts. *Los Angeles Times*, pp. E1, 12, 13.

Warshak, R. A. (2004, January). Personal communication, Department of Psychology, University of Texas at Dallas, Richardson.

Watemberg, N., Silver, S., Harel, S., & Lerman-Sagie, T. (2002). Significance of microencephaly among children with developmental disabilities. *Journal of Child Neurology, 17*, 117–122.

Waterman, A. S. (1985). Identity in the context of adolescent psychology. In A. S. Waterman (Ed.), *Identity in adolescence: Processes and contents.* San Francisco: Jossey-Bass.

Waterman, A. S. (1989). Curricula interventions for identity change: Substantive and ethical considerations. *Journal of Adolescence, 12*, 389–400.

Waterman, A. S. (1992). Identity as an aspect of optimal psychological functioning. In G. R. Adams, T. P. Gullotta, & R. Montemayor (Eds.), *Adolescent identity formation.* Newbury Park, CA: Sage.

Waters, E., Corcoran, D., & Anafara, M. (2005). Attachment, other relationships, and the theory that all good things go together. *Human Development, 48*, 85–88.

Waters, G., & Caplan, D. (2005). The relation between age, processing speed, working memory capacity, and language comprehension. *Memory, 13*, 403–413.

Wathen, C.N. (2006). Health information seeking in context: How women make decisions regarding hormone replacement therapy. *Journal of Health Communication, 11*, 477–493.

Watson, D. L., & Tharp, R. G. (2007). *Self-directed behavior* (9th ed.). Belmont, CA: Wadsworth.

Watson, J. A., Randolph, S. M., & Lyons, J. L. (2005). African-American grandmothers as health educators in the family. *International Journal of Aging and Human Development, 60*, 343–356.

Watson, J. B. (1928). *Psychological care of infant and child.* New York: W. W. Norton.

Watson, J. B., & Rayner, R. (1920). Conditioned emotional reactions. *Journal of Experimental Psychology, 3*, 1–14.

Watson, M., Kash, K. M., Homewood, J., Ebbs, S., Murday, V., & Eeles, R. (2005). Does genetic counseling have any impact on management of breast cancer risk? *Genetic Testing, 9*, 167–174.

Watson, R., & DeMeo, P. (1987). Premarital cohabitation vs. traditional courtship and subsequent marital adjustment: A replication and follow-up. *Family Relations, 36*, 193–197.

Wattendorf, D. J., & Muenke, M. (2005). Fetal alcohol spectrum disorders. *American Family Physician, 72*, 279–282, 285.

Watts, C., & Zimmerman, C. (2002). Violence against women: Global scope and magnitude. *Lancet, 359*, 1232–1237.

Waxman, S. R. (2004). Early word-learning and conceptual development. In U. Goswami (Ed.), *Blackwell handbook of infant development.* Malden, MA: Blackwell.

Waxman, S. R., & Lidz, J. L. (2006). Early word learning. In W. Damon & R. Lerner (Eds.), *Handbook of child psychology* (6th ed.). New York: Wiley.

Waylen, A., & Wolke, D. (2004). Sex `n' rock `n' roll: The meaning and consequences of pubertal timing. *European Journal of Endocrinology, 151* (Supplement), U151–U159.

Weber, E. (2005). *MI strategies in the classroom and beyond.* Boston: Allyn & Bacon.

Wechsler, H., & Nelson, T. F. (2006). Relationship between level of consumption and harms in assessing drink cut-points for alcohol research: Commentary on: "Many college freshmen drink at levels far beyond the binge threshold" by White et al. *Alcoholism: Clinical and Experimental Research, 30*, 922–927.

Wechsler, H., Davenport, A., Sowdall, G., Moetykens, B., & Castillo, S. (1994). Health and behavioral consequences of binge drinking in college. *Journal of the American Medical Association, 272*, 1672–1677.

Wechsler, H., Lee, J. E., Kuo, M., Seibring, M., Nelson, T. F., & Lee, H. (2002). Trends in college binge drinking during a period of increased prevention efforts: Findings from 4 Harvard School of Public Health college alcohol study surveys: 1993–2001. *Journal of American College Health, 50*, 203–217.

Weerdesteyn, V., Rijken, H., Geurts, A. C., Smits-Engelsman, B. C., Mulder, T., & Duysens, J. (2006). A five-week exercise program can reduce falls and improve obstacle avoidance in the elderly. *Gerontology, 52*, 131–142.

Wegman, M. E. (1987). Annual summary of vital statistics—1986. *Pediatrics, 80*, 817–827.

Wehren, L. E., Hawkes, W. G., Hebel, J. R., Orwig, D. L., & Magaziner, J. (2005). Bone mineral density, soft tissue body composition, strength, and functioning after hip fracture. *Journals of Gerontology: Biological Sciences and Medical Sciences, 60*, A80–A84.

Wehrens, X. H., Offermans, J. P., Snijders, M., & Peeters, L. L. (2004). Fetal cardiovascular response to large placental chorioangiomas. *Journal of Perinatal Medicine, 32*, 107–112.

Wei, M., Vogel, D. L., Ku, T-Y., & Zakalik, R. A. (2005). Adult attachment, affect regulation, negative mood, and interpersonal problems: The mediating roles of emotional reactivity and emotional cutoff. *Journal of Counseling Psychology, 52*, 14–24.

Weijers, H. G., Wiesbeck, G. A., Wodarz, N., Keller, H., Michel, T., & Boning, J. (2003). Gender and personality in alcoholism. *Archives of Women's Mental Health, 6*, 245–252.

Weikert, D. P. (1993). [Long-term positive effects in the Perry Preschool Head Start Program.] Unpublished data, High Scope Foundation, Ypsilanti, MI.

Weincke, J. K., Thurston, S. W., Kelsey, K. T., Varkonyi, A., Wain, J. C., Mark, E. J., & Christiani, D. C. (1999). Early age at smoking initiation and tobacco carcinogen DNA damage in the lung. *Journal of the National Cancer Institute, 91*, 614–619.

Weinraub, M., Horvath, D. L., & Gringlas, M. B. (2002). Single parenthood. In M. H. Bornstein (Ed.), *Handbook of parenting* (2nd ed., Vol. 3). Mahwah, NJ: Erlbaum.

Weinstein, N. D. (1984). Reducing unrealistic optimism about illness susceptibility. *Health Psychology, 3*, 341–457.

Weinstock, M. (2005). The potential influence of maternal stress hormones on development and mental health of the offspring. *Brain, Behavior, and Immunology, 19*, 296–308.

Weisz, A. N., & Black, B. M. (2002). Gender and moral reasoning: African American youth respond to dating dilemmas. *Journal of Human Behavior in the Social Environment, 5*, 35–52.

Welch-Carre, E. (2005). The neurodevelopmental consequences of prenatal alcohol exposure. *Advances in Neonatal Care, 5*, 217–219.

Wellman, H. M. (2004). Understanding the psychological world: Developing a theory of mind. In U. Goswami (Ed.), *Blackwell handbook of childhood cognitive development.* Malden, MA: Blackwell.

Wellman, H. M., Cross, D., & Watson, J. (2001). Meta-analysis of theory-of-mind development: The truth about false belief. *Child Development, 72*, 655–684.

Wellman, H. M., & Woolley, J. D. (1990). From simple desires to ordinary beliefs: The early development of everyday psychology. *Cognition, 35*, 245–275.

Welti, C. (2002). Adolescents in Latin America: Facing the future with skepticism. In B. B. Brown, R. W. Larson, & T. S. Saraswathi (Eds.), *The world's youth.* New York: Cambridge University Press.

Wen, S. W., & Walker, M. (2005). An exploration of health effects of folic acid in pregnancy beyond reducing neural tube defects. *Journal of Obstetrics and Gynecology Canada, 27*, 13–19.

Wenestam, C. G., & Wass, H. (1987). Swedish and U. S. children's thinking about death: A qualitative study and cross-cultural comparison. *Death Studies, 11*, 99–121.

Weng, N. P. (2006). Aging of the human immune system: How much can the adaptive immune system adapt? *Immunity, 24*, 495–499.

Wenger, N. S., & others. (2003). The quality of medical care provided to vulnerable community-dwelling older patients. *Annals of Internal Medicine, 139*, 740–747.

Wenk, G. L. (2006). Neuropathologic changes in Alzheimer's disease: Potential targets for treatment. *Journal of Clinical Psychiatry, 67* (Suppl 3), S3–S7.

Wentworth, R. A. L. (1999). *Montessori for the millennium.* Mahwah, NJ: Erlbaum.

Wentzel, K. R., & Asher, S. R. (1995). The academic lives of neglected, rejected, popular, and controversial children. *Child Development, 66*, 754–763.

Wentzel, K. R., Barry, C. M., & Caldwell, K. A. (2004). Friendships in middle school: Influences on motivation and school adjustment. *Journal of Educational Psychology, 96*, 195–203.

Wenze, G. T., & Wenze, N. (2004). Helping left-handed children adapt to school experiences. *Childhood Education, 81*, 25–31.

Werts, M. G., Culatta, R. A., & Tompkins, J. R. (2007). *Fundamentals of special education* (3rd ed.). Upper Saddle River, NJ: Prentice-Hall.

West, J. R., & Blake, C. A. (2005). Fetal alcohol syndrome: An assessment of the field. *Experimental Biology and Medicine, 230*, 354–356.

Wethington, E., Kessler, R. C., & Pixley, J. E. (2004). Turning points in adulthood. In O. G. Brim, C. D. Ryff, & R. C. Kessler (Eds.), *How healthy are we?* Chicago: University of Chicago Press.

Wexler, R., & Auckerman, G. (2006). Nonpharmacologic strategies for managing hypertension. *American Family Physician, 73*, 1953–1956.

Weyandt, L. L. (2006). *An ADHD primer*. Mahwah, NJ: Erlbaum.

Whiffen, V. (2001). Depression. In J. Worell (Ed.), *Encyclopedia of women and gender*. San Diego: Academic Press.

Whincup, P.H., Papacosta, O., Lennon, L., & Haines, A. (2006). Carboxyhemoglobin levels and their determinants in older British men. *BMC Public Health, 18*, 189.

Whitbourne, S. K. (2000). Adult development and aging: Biological processes and physical development. In A. Kazdin (Ed.), *Encyclopedia of psychology*. Washington, DC, & New York: American Psychological Association and Oxford University Press.

Whitbourne, S. K. (2001). The physical aging process in midlife: Interactions with psychological and sociocultural factors. In M. E. Lachman (Ed.), *Handbook of midlife development*. New York: John Wiley.

Whitbourne, S. K. (2006). Sexual behavior and aging. In J. E. Birren & K. W. Schaie (Eds.), *Handbook of the psychology of aging* (6th ed.), Thousand Oaks, CA: Sage.

Whitbourne, S. K., & Connolly, L. A. (1999). The developing self in midlife. In S. L. Willis & J. D. Reid (Eds.), *Life in the middle*. San Diego: Academic Press.

White, A. M., Kraus, C. L., & Swartzwelder, H. (2006). Many college freshmen drink at levels far beyond the binge thresholds. *Alcoholism: Clinical and Experimental Research, 30*, 1006–1010.

White, C. B., & Catania, J. (1981). Psychoeducational intervention for sexuality with the aged, family members of the aged, and people who work with the aged. *International Journal of Aging and Human Development*.

White, C. W., & Coleman, M. (2000). *Early childhood education*. Columbus, OH: Merrill.

White, J. W. (2001). Aggression and gender. In J. Worell (Ed.), *Encyclopedia of gender and women*. San Diego: Academic Press.

White, J. W., & Frabutt, J. M. (2006). Violence against girls and women. In J. Worell & C. D. Goodheart (Eds.), *Handbook of girls' and women's psychological health*. New York: Oxford University Press.

White, L. (1994). Stepfamilies over the life course: Social support. In A. Booth and J. Dunne (Eds.), *Stepfamilies: Who benefits and who does not*. Hillsdale, NJ: Erlbaum.

White, L. (2001). Sibling relationships over the life course. *Journal of Marriage and the Family, 63*, 555–568.

Whitehead, B. D., & Popenoe, D. (2003). *The State of our Unions: 2003*. New Brunswick, NJ: Rutgers University.

Whitehead, D., Keast, J., Montgomery, V., & Hayman, S. (2004). A preventive health education program for osteoporosis. *Journal of Advanced Nursing, 47*, 15–24.

Whitescarver, K. (2006, April). *Montessori rising: Montessori education in the United States, 1955-present*. Paper presented at the meeting of the American Education Research Association, San Francisco.

Whitfield, K. (2006). Health disparities and minority aging. In J. E. Birren & K. W. Schaie (Eds.), *Handbook of the psychology of aging* (6th ed.). Thousand Oaks, CA: Sage.

Whitfield, K. E., & Baker-Thomas, T. (1999). Individual differences in aging minorities. *International Journal of Aging and Human Development, 48*, 73–79.

Whiting, B. B., & Edwards, C. P. (1988). *Children of different worlds*. Cambridge, MA: Harvard University Press.

Whiting, J. (1981). Environmental constraint on infant care practices. In R. H. Munroe & B. Whiting (Eds.), *Handbook of cross-cultural human development*. New York: Garland STPM Press.

Whitman, T. L., Borkowski, J. G., Keogh, D. A., & Weed, K. (2001). *Interwoven lives*. Mahwah, NJ: Erlbaum.

Wickelgren, I. (1999). Nurture helps to mold able minds. *Science, 283*, 1832–1834.

Wiese, A. M., & Garcia, E. E. (2006). Educational policy in the United States regarding bilinguals in early childhood education. In B. Spodek & O. N. Saracho (Eds.), *Handbook of research on the education of young children*. Mahwah, NJ: Erlbaum.

Wieser, M., & Haber, P. (2006, in press). The effects of systematic resistance training in the elderly. *International Journal of Sports Medicine*.

Wiesner, M., & Ittel, A. (2002). Relations of pubertal timing and depressing symptoms to substance use in early adolescence. *Journal of Early Adolescence, 22*, 5–23.

Wigfield, A., Eccles, J. S., Schiefele, U., Roeser, R., & Davis-Kean, P. (2006). Development of achievement motivation. In W. Damon & R. Lerner (Eds.), *Handbook of child psychology* (6th ed.). New York: Wiley.

Wilbur, J., Miller, A. M., McDevitt, J., Wang, E., & Miller, J. (2005). Menopausal status, moderate-intensity walking, and symptoms in midlife women. *Research and Theory in Nursing Practice, 19*, 163–180.

Wilcox, S., Evenson, K. R., Aragaki, A., Wassertheil-Smoller, S., Mouton, C. P., & Loevinger, B. L. (2003). The effects of widowhood on physical and mental health, health behaviors, and health outcomes: The women's health initiative. *Health Psychology, 22*, 513–522.

Wiley, D., & Bortz, W. M. (1996). Sexuality and aging—usual and successful. *Journal of Gerontology, 51A*, M142–M146.

Wilkinson-Lee, A. M., Russell, S. T., Lee, F. C. H., & the Latina/o Teen Pregnancy Prevention Workgroup (2006). Practitioners' perspectives on cultural sensitivity in Latina/o pregnancy prevention. *Family Relations, 55*, 376–389.

Willcox, B. J., Willcox, M. D., & Suzuki, M. (2002). *The Okinawa Program*. New York: Crown.

Williams, A., & Nussbaum, J. F. (2001). *Intergenerational communication across the life span*. Mahwah, NJ: Erlbaum.

Williams, J. E., & Best, D. L. (1989). *Sex and psyche: Self-concept viewed cross-culturally*. Newbury Park, CA: Sage.

Williams, K. (2004). The transition to widowhood and the social regulation of health: Consequences for health and health risk behavior. *Journals of Gerontology B: Psychological Sciences and Social Sciences, 59*, S343–S349.

Williams, K., Kemper, S., & Hummert, M. L. (2004). Enhancing communication with older adults: Overcoming elderspeak. *Journal of Gerontologial Nursing, 30*, 17–25.

Williams, M. H. (2005). *Nutrition for health, fitness, & sport* (7th ed.). New York: McGraw-Hill.

Williams, N. L., & Risking, J. H. (2004). Adult romantic attachment and cognitive vulnerabilities to anxiety and depression: Examining the interpersonal base of vulnerability models. *Journal of Cognitive Psychotherapy, 18*, 7–24.

Williams, R. B. (1995). Coronary prone behaviors, hostility, and cardiovascular health. In K. Orth-Gomer & N. Schneiderman (Eds.), *Behavioral medicine approaches to cardiovascular disease prevention*. Mahwah, NJ: Erlbaum.

Williams, R. B. (2001). Hostility (and other psychosocial risk factors): Effects on health and the potential for successful behavioral approaches to prevention and treatment. In A. Baum, T. A. Revenson, & J. E. Singer (Eds.). *Handbook of health psychology*. Mahwah, NJ: Erlbaum.

Willis, S. L., Martin, M. (2005). Preface. In S. C. Willis & M. Martin (Eds), *Middle adulthood*. Thousand Oaks, CA: Sage.

Willis, S. L., & Nesselroade, C. S. (1990). Long-term effects of fluid ability training in old age. *Developmental Psychology, 26*, 905–910.

Willis, S. L., & Reid, S. L. (Eds.) (1999). *Life in the middle: Psychological and social development in middle age*. San Diego: Academic Press.

Willis, S. L., & Schaie, K. W. (1986). Training the elderly on the ability factors of spatial orientation and inductive reasoning. *Psychology and Aging, 1*, 239–247.

Willis, S. L., & Schaie, K. W. (1994). Assessing everyday competence in the elderly. In C. Fisher & R. Lerner (Eds.), *Applied developmental psychology*. Hillsdale, NJ: Erlbaum.

Willis, S. L., & Schaie, K. W. (1999). Intellectual functioning in midlife. In S. L. Willis & J. D. Reid (Eds.), *Life in the middle: Psychological and social development in middle age*. San Diego: Academic Press.

Willis, S. L., & Schaie, K. W. (2005). Cognitive trajectories in midlife and cognitive functioning in old age. In S. L. Willis & M. Martin (Eds.), *Middle adulthood*. Thousand Oaks, CA: Sage.

Willis, W. O., Eder, C. H., Lindsay, S. P., Chavez, G., & Shelton, S. T. (2004). Lower rates of low birth weight and preterm births in the California Black Infant Health Program. *Journal of the National Medical Association, 96*, 315–324.

Wills, T. A., Resko, J. A., Ainette, M. G., & Mendoza, D. (2004). Role of parental support and peer support in adolescent substance use: A test of mediated effects. *Psychology of Addictive Behaviors, 18*, 122–134.

Wilmoth, J. M., & Chen, P. C. (2003). Immigrant status, living arrangements, and depressive symptoms among middle-aged and older adults. *Journals of Gerontology B: Psychological and Social Sciences, 58*, S305–S313.

Wilson, A. E., Shuey, K. M., & Elder, G. H. (2003). Ambivalence in relationships of adult children to aging parents and in-laws. *Journal of Marriage and the Family, 65*, 1055–1072.

Wilson, B. (2001, April). *The role of television in children's emotional development and socialization*. Paper presented at the meeting of the Society for Research in Child Development, Minneapolis.

Wilson, R. S., Mendes de Leon, C. F., Barnes, L. L., Schneider, J. A., Bienias, J., Evans, D. A., & Bennett, D. A. (2002). Participation in cognitively stimulating activities and risk of incident Alzheimer disease. *Journal of the American Medical Association, 287*, 742–748.

Wilson, R. S., Mendes de Leon, C. F., Bienias, J. L., Evans, D. A., & Bennett, D. A. (2004). Personality and mortality in old age. *Journal of Gerontology: Psychological Sciences, 59B*, 110–116.

Windle, W. F. (1940). *Physiology of the fetus*. Philadelphia: W. B. Saunders.

Wineberg, H. (1994). Marital reconciliation in the United States: Which couples are successful? *Journal of Marriage and the Family, 56*, 80–88.

Wink, P., & Dillon, M. (2002). Spiritual development across the adult life course: Findings from a longitudinal study. *Journal of Adult Development, 9*, 79–94.

Winner, E. (1986, August.). Where pelicans kiss seals. *Psychology Today*, pp. 24–35.

Winner, E. (1996). *Gifted children: Myths and realities.* New York: Basic Books.

Winner, E. (2000). The origins and ends of giftedness. *American Psychologist, 55,* 159–169.

Winner, E. (2006). Development in the arts. In W. Damon & R. Lerner (Eds.), *Handbook of child psychology* (6th ed.). New York: Wiley.

Winsler, A., Carlton, M. P., & Barry, M. J. (2000). Age-related changes in preschool children's systematic use of private speech in a natural setting. *Journal of Child Language, 27,* 665–687.

Winsler, A., Diaz, R. M., & Montero, I. (1997). The role of private speech in the transition from collaborative to independent task performance in young children. *Early Childhood Research Quarterly, 12,* 59–79.

Winstead, B., & Griffin, J. L. (2001). Friendship styles. In J. Worell (Ed.), *Encyclopedia of women and gender.* San Diego: Academic Press.

Wintre, M. G., & Vallance, D. D. (1994). A developmental sequence in the comprehension of emotions: Intensity, multiple emotions, and valence. *Developmental Psychology, 30,* 509–514.

Wise, P. M. (2006). Aging of the female reproductive system. In E. J. Masoro & S. N. Austad (Eds.), *Handbook of the biology of aging* (6th ed.). San Diego: Academic Press.

Wiseman, C. V., Sunday, S. R., & Becker, A. E. (2005). Impact of the media on adolescent boy image. *Child and Adolescent Psychiatric Clinics of North America, 14,* 453–471.

Witkin, H. A., Mednick, S. A., Schulsinger, R., Bakkestrom, E., Christiansen, K. O., Goodenough, D. R., Hirchhorn, K., Lundsteen, C., Owen, D. R., Philip, J., Rubein, D. B., & Stocking, M. (1976). Criminality in XYY and XXY men. *Science, 193,* 547–555.

Wocadlo, C., & Rieger, I. (2006). Educational and therapeutic resource dependency at early school age in children who were born very preterm. *Early Human Development, 82,* 29–37.

Wolf, G. (2006). Calorie restriction increases life span: A molecular mechanism. *Nutrition Review, 64,* 89–92.

Wolf, S. M. (2005). Physician-assisted suicide. *Clinical Geriatrics Medicine, 21,* 179–192.

Wolff, J. L., & Kasper, J. D. (2006). Caregivers of frail elders: Updating a national profile. *Gerontologist, 46,* 344–356.

Wolinsky, F. D., Miller, D. K., Andersen, E. M., Malmstrom, T. K., & Miller, J. P. (2004). Health-related quality of life in middle-aged African Americans. *Journals of Gerontology B: Psychological and Social Sciences, 59,* S118–S123.

Wong, A. H., Gottesman, I. I., & Petronis, A. (2005). Phenotypic differences in genetically identical organisms: The epigenetic perspective. *Human Molecular Genetics, 15* (1), 11–18.

Wong, A. M., Lin, Y. C., Chou, S. W., Tang, F. T., & Wong, P. Y. (2001). Coordination exercise and postural stability in elderly people: Effect of Tai Chi Chuan. *Archives of Physical Medicine & Rehabilitation, 82,* 608–612.

Wong, C. H., Wong, S. F., Pang, W. S., Azizah, M. Y. Dass, M. J. Habitual walking and its correlation to better physical function: Implications for prevention of physical disability in older persons,

Wong, D. L. (2006). *Maternal child nursing and virtual clinical excursions 3.0 Package* (3rd ed.). St. Louis, MO: Mosby.

Woo, K. S., Chook, P., Yu, C. W., Suung, R. Y., Qiao, M., Leung, S. S., Law, C. W., Metreweli, C., & Celermajer, D. S. (2004). Effects of diet and exercise on obesity-related vascular dysfunction in children. *Circulation, 109,* 1981–1986.

Wood, A. G., Harvey, A. S., Wellard, R. M., Abbott, D. F., Anderson, V., Kean, M., Saling, M. M., &

Jackson, G. D. (2004). Language cortex activation in normal children. *Neurology, 63,* 1035–1044.

Wood, J. M. (2002). Age and visual impairment decrease driving performance as measured on a closed-road circuit. *Human Factors, 44,* 482–494.

Wood, J. T. (2001). *Gendered lives.* Belmont, CA: Wadsworth.

Wood, M. D., Read, J. P., Mitchell, R. E., & Brand, N. H. (2004). Do parents still matter? Parent and peer influences on alcohol involvement among recent high school graduates. *Psychology of Addictive Behaviors, 18,* 19–30.

Wood, M. J., & Atkins, M. (2006). Immersion in another culture: One strategy for increasing cultural competency. *Journal of Cultural Diversity, 13,* 50–54.

Woods, B., Spector, A., Jones, C., Orrell, M., & Davies, S. (2005). Reminiscence therapy for dementia. *Cochrane Database System Review, 18,* CD001120.

Woodward, A. L., & Markman, E. M. (1998). Early word learning. In D. Kuhn & R. S. Siegler (Eds.), *Handbook of child psychology* (5th ed., Vol. 2), New York: Wiley.

Woodward, J., & Kelly, S. M. (2004). A pilot study for a randomized controlled trial of waterbirth versus landbirth. *British Journal of Obstetrics and Gynecology, 111,* 537–545.

Woodward, N. J., & Wallston, B. S. (1987). Age and health-care beliefs: Self-efficacy as a mediator of low desire for control. *Psychology and Aging, 2,* 3–8.

Worell, J. (2006). Pathways to healthy development: Sources of strength and empowerment. In J. Worell & C. D. Goodheart (Eds.), *Handbook of girls' and women's psychological health.* New York: Oxford University Press.

Worell, J., & Goodheart, C. D. (Eds.) (2006). *Handbook of girls' and women's psychological health: Gender and well-being across the life span.* New York: Oxford University Press.

Worku, B., & Kassie, A. (2005). Kangaroo mother care: A randomized controlled trial on effectiveness of early kangaroo care for low birthweight infants in Addis Ababa, Ethiopia. *Journal of Tropical Pediatrics, 51,* 93–97.

World Health Organization. (2000, February 2). *Adolescent health behavior in 28 countries.* Geneva: Author.

World Health Organization. (2002). *The world health report 2002.* Geneva: World Health Organization.

Worobey, J., & Belsky, J. (1982). Employing the Brazelton scale to influence mothering: An experimental comparison of three strategies. *Developmental Psychology, 18,* 736–743.

Worthington, E. L. (1989). Religious faith across the life span: Implications for counseling and research. *Counseling Psychologist, 17,* 555–612.

Wortman, C. B., & Boerner, K. (2007). Reactions to death of a loved one: Beyond the myths of coping with loss. In H. S. Friedman & R. C. Silver (Eds.), *Foundations of health psychology.* New York: Oxford University Press.

Wright, M. R. (1989). Body image satisfaction in adolescent girls and boys. *Journal of Youth and Adolescence, 18,* 71–84.

Wright, P.J. (2006, in press). Comparison of phosphodiesterase type 5 (PDE5) inhibitors. *International Journal of Clinical Practice.*

Wu, P., Robinson, C. C., Yang, C., Hart, C. H., Olsen, S. F., & Porter, C. L. (2006, in press). Similarities and differences in mothers' parenting of preschoolers in China and the United States. *International Journal of Behavioural Development.*

Xiong, G., & Doraiswamy, P. M. (2005). Combination drug therapy for Alzheimer's disease: What is evidence-based, and what is not? *Geriatrics, 60,* 22–26.

Xu, X., Hudspeth, C.D., & Bartkowski, J. P. (2006). The role of cohabitation in remarriage. *Journal of Marriage and the Family, 68,* 261–274.

Xu, Y., Cook, T. J., & Knipp, G. T. (2006). Methods for investigating placental fatty acid transport. *Methods of Molecular Medicine, 122,* 265–284.

Yaffe, K., Barnes, D., Nevitt, M., Lui, L., & Covinsky, K. (2001). A prospective study of physical activity and cognitive decline in elderly women. *Archives of Internal Medicine, 161,* 1703–1708.

Yand, N. (2005). Effects of individualism-collectivism on perceptions and outcomes of work-family interfaces: A Sino-U.S. comparison. In S. A. Y. Poelmans (Ed.), *Work and family.* Mahwah, NJ: Erlbaum.

Yang, C. K., Kim, J. K., Patel, S. R., & Lee, J. H. (2005). Age-related changes in sleep/wake patterns among Korean teenagers. *Pediatrics, 115* (Suppl 1), S250–S256.

Yang, J. H., Chung, J. H., Shin, J. S., Choi, J. S., Ryu, H. M., & Kim, M. Y. (2005). Prenatal diagnosis of trisomy 18: Report of 30 cases. *Prenatal Diagnosis, 25,* 119–122.

Yang, J., McCrae, R. R., & Costa, P. T. (1998). Adult age differences in personality traits in the United States and the People's Republic of China. *Journals of Gerontology: Psychological Sciences, 53B,* P375–P383.

Yang, S. N., Liu, C. A., Chung, M. Y., Huang, H. C., Yeh, G. C., Wong, C. S., Lin, W. W., Yang, C. H., & Tao, P. L. (2006). Alterations of postsynaptic density proteins in the hippocampus of rat offspring from the morphine-addicted mother: Beneficial effects of dextromethorphan. *Hippocampus, 16,* 521–530.

Yang, S., & Sternberg, R. J. (1997). Taiwanese Chinese people's conceptions of intelligence. *Intelligence, 25,* 21–36.

Yang, Y., May, Y., Ni, L., Zhao, S., Li, L., Zhang, J., Fan, M., Liang, C., Cao, J., & Xu, L. (2003). Lead exposure through gestation-only caused long-term memory deficits in young adult offspring. *Experimental Neurology, 184,* 489–495.

Yasien-Esmael, H., & Rubin, S. S. (2005). The meaning structures of Muslim bereavements in Israel: Religious traditions, mourning practices, and human experience. *Death Studies, 29,* 495–518.

Yasui, M., Dorham, C. L., & Dishion, T. J. (2004). Ethnic identity and psychological adjustment: A validity analysis for European American and African American adolescents. *Journal of Adolescent Research, 19,* 807–825.

Yates, M. (1995, March). *Political socialization as a function of volunteerism.* Paper presented at the meeting of the Society for Research in Child Development, Indianapolis.

Yates, W. R. (2004). The link between religion and health: Psychoneuroimmunology and the faith factor. *American Journal of Psychiatry, 161,* 586.

Yeats, D. E., Folts, W. E., & Knapp, J. (1999). Older workers' adaptation to a changing workplace: Employment issues for the 21st century. *Educational Gerontology, 25,* 331–347.

Young, D. (2001). The nature and management of pain: What is the evidence? *Birth, 28,* 149–151.

Young, K. T. (1990). American conceptions of infant development from 1955 to 1984: What the experts are telling parents. *Child Development, 61,* 17–28.

Young, S. K., & Shahinfar, A. (1995, March). *The contributions of maternal sensitivity and child temperament to attachment status at 14 months.* Paper presented at the meeting of the Society for Research in Child Development, Indianapolis.

Yu, B. P. (2006, in press). Why caloric restriction would work for human longevity. *Biogerontology.*

Yu, V. Y. (2000). Developmental outcome of extremely preterm infants. *American Journal of Perinatology, 17,* 57–61.

Yu, Z. Y., Wang, W., Fritschy, J. M., Witte, O. W., & Redecker, C. (2006, in press). Changes in neocortical and hippocampal GABA(A) receptor subunit distribution during brain maturation and aging. *Brain Research.*

Zaffanello, M., Maffeis, C., & Zamboni, G. (2005). Multiple positive results during a neonatal screening program. *Journal of Perinatal Medicine, 33,* 246–251.

Zarit, S. H., & Knight, B. G. (Eds.). (1996). *A guide to psychotherapy and aging.* Washington, DC: American Psychological Association.

Zarof, C. M., Knutelska, M., & Frumkes, T. E. (2003). Variation in stereoacuity: Normative description, fixation disparity, and the roles of aging and gender. *Investigative Ophthalmology and Vision Science, 44,* 891–900.

Zaslow, M. (2004). Child-care for low-income families: Problems and promises. In A. C. Crouter & A. Booth (Eds.), *Work-family challenges for low-income parents and their children.* Mahwah, NJ: Erlbaum.

Zdravkovic, T., Genbacev, O., McMaster, M. T., & Fisher, S. J. (2005). The adverse effects of maternal smoking on the human placenta: A review. *Placenta, 26* (Suppl. A), S81–S86.

Zelazo, P. D., & Muller, U. (2004). Executive function in typical and atypical development. In U. Goswami (Ed.), *Blackwell handbook of cognitive development.* Malden, MA: Blackwell.

Zelazo, P. D., Muller, U., Frye, D., & Marcovitch, S. (2003). The development of executive function in early childhood. *Monographs of the Society for Research in Child Development, 68* (3, Serial No. 274).

Zentall, S. S. (2006). *ADHD and education.* Upper Saddle River, NJ: Prentice Hall.

Zeskind, P. S., Klein, L., & Marshall, T. R. (1992). Adults' perceptions of experimental modifications of durations and expiratory sounds in infant crying. *Developmental Psychology, 28,* 1153–1162.

Zhan, H. J. (2005). Aging, health care, and elder care: perpetuation of gender inequalities in China. *Health Care for Women International, 26,* 693–712.

Zhang, F., Chen, Y., Heiman, M., & Dimarchi, R. (2005). Leptin: Structure, function, and biology. *Vitamins and Hormones, 71,* 345–372.

Zhu, C.W., Scarmeas, N., Torgan, R., Albert, M., Brandt, J., Blacker, D., Sano, M., & Stern, Y. (2006). Clinical features associated with costs in early AD: Baseline data from the Predictors Study. *Neurology, 66,* 1021–1028.

Zhuang, Z. P., Kung, M. P., & Kung, H. F. (2006). Synthesis of biphenyltrienes as probes for beta-amyloid plaques. *Journal of Medical Chemistry, 49,* 2841–2844.

Zigler, E. F., & Styfco, S. J. (1994). Head Start: Criticisms in a constructive context. *American Psychologist, 49,* 127–132.

Zimmerman, B. J., & Schunk, D. H. (2004). Self-regulating intellectual processes and outcomes: A social cognitive perspective. In D. Y. Dai & R. J. Sternberg (Eds.), *Motivation, emotion, and cognition.* Mahwah, NJ: Erlbaum.

Zimmerman, R. S., Khoury, E., Vega, W. A., Gil, A. G., & Warheit, G. J. (1995). Teacher and student perceptions of behavior problems among a sample of African American, Hispanic, and non-Hispanic White students. *American Journal of Community Psychology, 23,* 181–197.

Zimmerman, S., Sloane, P. D., Williams, C. S., Reed, P. S., Preisser, J. S., Eckert, J. K., Boustani, M., & Dobbs, D. (2005). Dementia care and quality of life in assisted living and nursing homes. *Gerontologist, 45* (Suppl 1), S133–S146.

Zinn, M. B., & Wells, B. (2000). Diversity within Latino families: New lessons for family social science. In D. M. Demo, K. R. Allen, & M. A. Fine (Eds.), *Handbook of family diversity.* New York: Oxford University Press.

Zitanova, I., Korytar, P., Sobotova, H., Horakova, L., Sustrova, M., Pueschel, S., & Durackova, Z. (2006). Markers of oxidative stress in children with Down syndrome. *Clinical Chemistry and Laboratory Medicine, 44,* 306–310.

Zucker, A. N., Ostrove, J. M., & Stewart, A. J. (2002). College educated women's personality development in adulthood: Perceptions and age differences. *Psychology and Aging, 17,* 236–244.

Zuckoff, A., Shear, K., Frank, E., Daley, D. C., Seligman, K., & Silowash, R. (2006). Treating complicated grief and substance use disorders: A pilot study. *Journal of Substance Abuse and Treatment, 30,* 205–211.

Zukow-Goldring, P. (2002). Sibling caregiving. In M. H. Bornstein (Ed.), *Handbook of parenting* (2nd ed., Vol. 3). Mahwah, NJ: Erlbaum.

Zunzunegui, M., Alvarado, B. E., Del Ser, T., & Otero, A. (2003). Social networks, social integration, and social engagement determine cognitive decline in community-dwelling Spanish older adults. *Journals of Gerontology B: Psychological Sciences and Social Sciences, 58,* S93–S100.

Zverev, Y. P. (2006). Cultural and environmental pressure against left-hand preference in urban and semi-urban Malawi. *Brain and Cognition, 60,* 295–303.

CREDITS

Text and Line Art Credits

Chapter 1

Figure 1.3: From "Percentage of Children 7 to 18 Years of Age Around the World Who Have Never Been to School of Any Kind," 2004, *The State of the World's Children*, Geneva, Switzerland: UNICEF, Fig. 5, p. 27. **Figure 1.9**: From Ronald Inglehart, *Culture Shift in Advanced Industrial Society*. © 1990 Princeton University Press. Reprinted by permission of Princeton University Press.

Chapter 2

Figure 2.5: From "Bronfenbrenner's Ecological Theory of Development," C. B. Kopp & J. B. Krakow, 1982, *Child Development in the Social Context*, p. 648. Addison-Wesley Longman, Inc. Reprinted by permission of Pearson Education, Inc. **Figure 2.9**: From Santrock, *Children* 9/e, Figure 2.12. Copyright © 2007 The McGraw-Hill Companies. Reproduced by permission of The McGraw-Hill Companies.

Chapter 3

Figure 3.1: From Santrock, *A Topical Approach to Life-Span Development*, 2/e. Copyright © 2005 The McGraw-Hill Companies. Reproduced with permission of The McGraw-Hill Companies. **Figure 3.2**: Baltes, P. B., Staudinger, U. M., & Lindenberger, U., 1999, "Lifespan Psychology," Annual Review of Psychology, 50, p. 474, Fig. 1. With permission, from the Annual Review of Psychology, Volume 50 © 1999 by Annual Reviews, www.annualreview.org **Figure 3.3**: From Santrock, *Psychology*, 7/e. Copyright © 2003 The McGraw-Hill Companies. Reproduced by permission of The McGraw-Hill Companies. **Figure 3.6**: From Santrock, *Children*, 9/e, Figure 3.5. Copyright © 2007 The McGraw-Hill Companies. Reproduced by permission of The McGraw-Hill Companies. **pp. 87–88**: Text from D. Brodzinsky and E. Pinderhughes, "Parenting and Child Development in Adoptive Families" in M. Bornstein (Ed.) *Handbook of Parenting*, 2e, Vol. 1, pp. 280–282. Mahwah, NJ: Lawrence Erlbaum Associates, Inc. Reprinted by permission. **p. 89**: Text from D. Brodzinsky and E. Pinderhughes, "Parenting and Child Development in Adoptive Families" in M. Bornstein (Ed.) *Handbook of Parenting*, 2e, Vol. 1, pp. 288–292. Mahwah, NJ: Lawrence Erlbaum Associates, Inc. Reprinted by permission. **TA 3.10**: From Santrock, *Children*, 9/e, Figure 3.10. Copyright © 2007 The McGraw-Hill Companies. Reproduced by permission of The McGraw-Hill Companies.

Chapter 4

Figure 4.3: From Santrock, *Children*, 9/e, Figure 4.3. Copyright © 2007 The McGraw-Hill Companies. Reproduced by permission of The McGraw-Hill Companies. **Figure 4.4**: Adapted from K. L. Moore and T. V. N. Persaud from *Before We Are Born*, page 130. © 1993 with permission from Elsevier. **Figure 4.6**: From Santrock, *Children*, 9/e, Figure 4.6. Copyright © 2007 The McGraw-Hill Companies. Reproduced by permission of The McGraw-Hill Companies. **Figure 4.7**: From Virginia A. Apgar, 1975, "A Proposal for a New Method of Evaluation of a Newborn Infant," in *Anesthesia and Analgesia*, Vol. 32, pp. 260–267. Reprinted by

permission of Lippincott Williams & Wilkins. **Figure 4.8**: From Santrock, *Child Development*, 10/e, Figure 4.9. Copyright © 2004 The McGraw-Hill Companies. Reproduced by permission of The McGraw-Hill Companies. **Figure 4.9**: From Santrock, *Child Development*, 10/e, Figure 4.11. Copyright © 2004 The McGraw-Hill Companies. Reproduced by permission of The McGraw-Hill Companies. **p. 119**: From P. Warrick, "The Fantastic Voyage of Tanner Roberts," *Los Angeles Times*, March 1, 1992, pp. E1, E12, E13. Copyright © 1991, Los Angeles Times. Reprinted with permission.

Chapter 5

Figure 5.1: From Santrock, *Children*, 9/e, Figure 6.1. Copyright © 2007 The McGraw-Hill Companies. Reproduced by permission of The McGraw-Hill Companies. **Figure 5.5**: From Santrock, *Child Development*, 10/e, Figure 5.2. Copyright © 2004 The McGraw-Hill Companies. Reproduced by permission of The McGraw-Hill Companies. **Figure 5.7**: From Santrock, *A Topical Approach to Life-Span Development*. Copyright © 2002 The McGraw-Hill Companies. Reproduced by permission of The McGraw-Hill Companies. **Figure 5.10**: From Santrock, *Child Development*, 11/e, Figure 5.13. Copyright © 2007 The McGraw-Hill Companies. Reproduced by permission of The McGraw-Hill Companies. **Figure 5.11**: From Santrock, *Child Development*, 10/e, Figure 5.11. Copyright © 2004 The McGraw-Hill Companies. Reproduced by permission of The McGraw-Hill Companies. **Figure 5.12**: From Santrock, *Children*, 5/e. Copyright © 1997 The McGraw-Hill Companies. Reproduced by permission of The McGraw-Hill Companies. **Figure 5.14**: Reprinted from *Journal of Pediatrics*, Vol. 71, W. K. Frankenburg and J. B. Dobbs, "The Denver Development Screening Test," pp. 181–191. Copyright © 1967, with permission from Elsevier. **Figure 5.16 (illustration)**: Adapted from "The Origin of Form Perception" by R. L. Frantz. Copyright © 1961 by Scientific American, Inc. **Figure 5.17**: From A. Slater, V. Morison, & M. Somers, 1988, "Orientation Discrimination and Cortical Functions in the Human Newborn," *Perception*, Vol. 17, pp. 597–602, Fig. 1 and Table 1. Reprinted by permission of Pion. London. **Figure 5.19**: From Santrock, *Child Development*, 10/e, Figure 5.18. Copyright © 2004 The McGraw-Hill Companies. Reproduced by permission of The McGraw-Hill Companies.

Chapter 6

Figure 6.3: From R. Baillargeon & J. DeVoe, "Using the Violation of Expectations Method to Study Object Permanence in Infants," 1991, "Object Permanence in Young Children: Further Evidence," *Child Development*, 62, pp. 1227–1246. Reprinted by permission of Blackwell Publishing. **Figure 6.6**: From "The Rule Systems of Language," from S. L. Haight, *Language Overview*. Used by permission. **Figure 6.8**: From Santrock, *Children*, 9/e. Copyright © 2007 The McGraw-Hill Companies. Reproduced by permission of The McGraw-Hill Companies. **Figure 6.9**: From Santrock, *Children*, 9/e, Figure 7.11. Copyright © 2007 The McGraw-Hill Companies. Reproduced by permission of The McGraw-Hill Companies. **Figure 6.10**: From

Santrock, *Child Development*, 10/e, Figure 10.2. Copyright © 2004 The McGraw-Hill Companies. Reproduced by permission of The McGraw-Hill Companies. **Figure 6.12**: From Hart & Risley, (1995), *Meaningful Differences in the Everyday Experiences of Young American Children*, Baltimore: Paul H. Brookes Publishing Co. Reprinted by permission of Paul H. Brookes Publishing Co. **p. 176**: From J. Piaget, *The Origins of Intelligence*, pp. 27, 159, 225, 273, 339. Reprinted with permission by International Universities Press, Inc. and Taylor & Francis Books.

Chapter 7

Figure 7.4: From Santrock, *Life-Span Development*, 4/e. Copyright © 1999 The McGraw-Hill Companies. Reproduced by permission of The McGraw-Hill Companies. **Figure 7.6**: From van Ijzendoorn & Kroonenberg, 1988, "Cross Cultural Patterns of Attachment," *Child Development*, 59, 147–156. Adapted by permission of Blackwell Publishing. **Figure 7.7**: From Jay Belsky, "Early Human Experiences: A Family Perspective," in *Developmental Psychology*, Vol. 17, pp. 2–23. Copyright © 1981 by the American Psychological Association. Reprinted by permission.

Chapter 8

Figure 8.1: From Santrock, *Children*, 9/e, Figure 9.3. Copyright © 2007 The McGraw-Hill Companies. Reproduced by permission of The McGraw-Hill Companies. **Figure 8.2**: From G. J. Schirmer (ed.) *Performance Objectives for Preschool Children*, Adapt Press: Sioux Falls, SD, 1974. **Figure 8.3**: From G. J. Schirmer (ed.) *Performance Objectives for Preschool Children*, Adapt Press: Sioux Falls, SD, 1974. **Figure 8.5**: From Sleet & Mercy, 2003, "Promotion of Safety, Security, and Well-Being," in M. H. Bornstein, et al. (eds.), *Well Being*, Mahwah, NJ: Lawrence Erlbaum Associates, Inc., Table 7.2. Reprinted by permission. **Figure 8.6**: From Santrock, *Psychology*, 7/e. Copyright © 2003 The McGraw-Hill Companies. Reproduced by permission of The McGraw-Hill Companies. **Figure 8.7**: "The Symbolic Drawings of Young Children," reprinted courtesy of D. Wolf and J. Nove. Reprinted by permission of Dennie Palmer Wolf, Annenberg Institute, Brown University. **p. 251**: From E. C. Frede, 1995, "The Role of Program Quality in Producing Early Childhood Program Benefits," in *The Future of Children*, a publication of the David and Lucile Packard Foundation. Used with permission. **Figure 8.11**: From Bodrova, E. & Leong, D. J. (2001, 2007). Tools of the mind. Geneva, Switzerland: International Bureau of Education, UNESCO. http://ibe.unesco.org/InternationalPublications/INNODATAMonograph/inno07.pdf. Reprinted with permission from the authors. **p. 257** From Bruck, M. and Ceci, S. J. (1999). The suggestibility of children's memory. *Annual Review of Psychology*, 50, pp. 429-430. Reprinted with permission of M. Bruck. **Figure 8.13**: From Santrock, *Children*, 7/e. Copyright © 2003 The McGraw-Hill Companies. Reproduced by permission of The McGraw-Hill Companies. **Figure 8.17**: From Jean Berko, 1958, "The Child's Learning of English Morphology," in *Word*, Vol. 14, p. 154. Reprinted courtesy of Jean Berko Gleason. **p. 262** From Jean Berko Gleason, *The Development of Language*, 3rd ed., figure 10.11. p. 336. Published by Allyn & Bacon,

Boston, MA. Copyright ©1993 by Pearson Education. Reprinted by permission of the publisher. **Figure 8.18**: Adapted and excerpted, by permission, from S. Bredekamp and C. Copple, "Developmentally Appropriate Practice for 3- through 5-Year-olds," in *Developmentally Appropriate Practice in Early Childhood Programs,* Rev. ed., eds. S. Bredekamp and C. Copple (Washington, DC: NAEYC, 1997), 123–38. Reprinted with permission from the National Association for the Education of Young Children.

Chapter 9

Figure 9.1: From Santrock, *Children,* 7/e. Copyright © 2003 The McGraw-Hill Companies. Reproduced by permission of The McGraw-Hill Companies. **Figure 9.3**: From Santrock, *Child Development,* 10/e, Figure 13.3. Copyright © 2004 The McGraw-Hill Companies. Reproduced by permission of The McGraw-Hill Companies. **Figure 9.6**: From K. Curran, J. DeCette, J. Eisenstein, & I. Hyman, August 2001, "Statistical Analysis of the Cross-Cultural Data: The Third Year," Paper presented at the meeting of the American Psychological Association, San Francisco, CA. Reprinted by permission. **p. 276:** From *Burning Fence* by Craig Lesley, Copyright © 2005 by author and reprinted by permission of St. Martin's Press, LLC.

Chapter 10

Figure 10.2: From Santrock, *Children,* 9/e, Figure 12.5. Copyright © 2007 The McGraw-Hill Companies. Reproduced by permission of The McGraw-Hill Companies. **Figure 10.5**: From "The Role of Expertise in Memory," from M. T. H. Chi, "Knowledge Structures and Memory Development," in R. S. Siegler (ed.), *Children's Thinking: What Develops?* Mahwah, NJ: Lawrence Erlbaum Associates, Inc. Reprinted by permission. **Figure 10.9**: From "The Rise in IQ Scores from 1932 to 1997," from "The Increase in IQ Scores from 1932 to 1997," from "The Increase in IQ Scores from 1932 to 1997," by Ulric Neisser. Reprinted by permission.

Chapter 11

Figure 11.2: From Colby, et al., "A Longitudinal Study of Moral Judgment," *Monographs of the Society for Research in Child Development,* Serial No. 201. Reprinted with permission by Blackwell Publishing. **Figure 11.4**: From Nansel, et al., 2001, "Bullying Behaviors Among U.S. Youth," *Journal of the American Medical Association,* Vol. 285, pp. 2094-2100. **Figure 11.5**: Reprinted with permission from Stevenson, Lee & Stigler, 1986, Figure 6, "Mathematics Achievement of Chinese, Japanese and American Children," *Science,* Vol. 231, pp. 693-699. Copyright 1986 AAAS.

Chapter 12

p. 388: From "Through the Eyes of Children" by L. Morrow, *Time,* Aug. 8, 1988, pp. 32-33. © Time Inc. Reprinted by permission. **Figure 12.1**: From J. M. Tanner, et al., "Standards from Birth to Maturity for Height, Weight, Height Velocity and Weight Velocity: British Children, 1965" in *Archives of Diseases in Childhood* 41, 1966. With permission from BMJ Publishing Group. **Figure 12.2**: From Santrock, *Adolescence,* 10/e, Figure 3.1. Copyright © 2005 The McGraw-Hill Companies. Reproduced by permission of The McGraw-Hill Companies. **Figure 12.3**: From A. F. Roache, "Secular Trends in Stature, Weight and Maturation," *Monographs of the Society for Research in Child Development,* n. 179. © Blackwell Publishing. Used with permission. **Figure 12.4**: From R. G. Simmons, D. A. Blyth, and K. L. McKinney, "The Social and Psychological Effects of Puberty on White Females. In J. Brooks-Gunn & A. C. Petersen (eds.), *Girls at Puberty: Biological and Psychological Perspectives,* pp. 229–272, 1983. With kind permission of Springer Science and Business Media. **Figure 12.6**: From Santrock, *Child Development,* 10/e, Figure 6.14. Copyright © 2004 The McGraw-Hill Companies. Reproduced by permission of The McGraw-Hill Companies. **Figure 12.7**: From

Santrock, *Children,* 9/e, Figure 15.12. Copyright © 2007 The McGraw-Hill Companies. Reproduced by permission of The McGraw-Hill Companies. **Figure 12.8**: From "Trends in Drug Use by U.S. Eighth-, Tenth- and Twelfth-Grade Students," by J. D. Johnston, P. M. O'Malley, and J. G. Bachman, 2001, *The Monitoring of the Future: National Results on Adolescent Drug Use,* Washington, DC: National Institute on Drug Abuse. **Figure 12.9**: From "Young Adolescents' Reports of Alcohol Use in the Family Matters Program," from K. E. Bauman, S. T. Ennett, et al., 2002, "Influence of a Family Program on Adolescent Smoking and Drinking Prevalence," *Prevention Science* 3, 2002, pp. 35–42. With kind permission of Springer Science and Business Media. **pp. 404–405:** From "Young Adolescents' Reports of Cigarette Smoking in the Family Matters Program," from K. E. Bauman, S. T. Ennett, et al., 2002, "Influence of a Family Program on Adolescent Smoking and Drinking Prevalence," *Prevention Science,* 3, 2002 pp. 35–42. With kind permission of Springer Science and Business Media.

Chapter 13

Figure 13.2: From *Divergent Realities* by Reed Larson. Copyright © 1994 by Reed Larson and Maryse Richards. Reprinted by permission of Basic Books, a member of Perseus Books, L.L.C. **Figure 13.5**: "Age of Onset of Romantic Activity" from *Romantic Development: Does Age at Which Romantic Involvement Starts Matter?* by Duane Buhrmester, April 2001, paper presented at the meeting of the Society for Research in Child Development, Minneapolis, MN. Used with permission.

Chapter 14

Figure 14.1: "Self-Perceptions of Adult Status," from J. Arnett, "Emerging Adulthood" in *American Psychologist,* Vol. 55, pp. 469–480, Fig. 2. Copyright © 2000 by the American Psychological Association. Reprinted by permission. **Figure 14.2**: From Diener and Seligman, "Very Happy People," 2002, *Psychological Science,*Vol. 13, pp. 81–84. Reprinted by permission of Blackwell Publishing. **Figure 14.5**: From Pate, et al., *Journal of the American Medical Association,* 273, 404. Copyright © 1995 American Medical Association. Reprinted by permission. **Figure 14.7**: From *Sex in America* by John Gagnon. Copyright © 1994 by CSG Enterprises, Inc., Edward O. Laumann, Robert T. Michael, and Gina Kolata. By permission of Little, Brown and Co., Inc. and Brockman, Inc. **Figure 14.8**: From Santrock, *Children,* 9/e, Figure 15.8. Copyright © 2007 The McGraw-Hill Companies. Reproduced by permission of The McGraw-Hill Companies. **Figure 14.9**: From "Completed Rape and Attempted Rape of College Women According to Victim-Offender Relationship," from Fisher, Cullen & Turner, 2000, *The Sexual Victimization of College Women,* Exhibit 8, p. 19. Reprinted by permission of the National Institute of Justice. **Figure 14.10**: Reproduced by special permission of the publisher, Psychological Assessment Resources, Inc., 16204 N. Florida Avenue, Lutz, FL 33549 from *Making Vocational Choices,* third edition. Copyright 1973, 1985, 1992, 1997 by PAR, Inc. All rights reserved. **Figure 14.12**: From "Changes in the Percentage of U.S. Traditional and Dual-Career Couples," from "Word-Family Balance," by R. Barnett, in *Encyclopedia of Women and Gender: Sex Similarities and Differences and the Impact of Society on Gender,* 2 Volume Set, by Judith Worell (Ed.). Reprinted with permission from Elsevier.

Chapter 15

p. 494: Pages 44–45 from *The Dance of Intimacy* by Harriet Goldhor Lerner. Copyright © 1989 by Harriet Goldhor Lerner. Reprinted by permission of HarperCollins Publishers. **Figure 15.1**: From "Temperament in Childhood, Personality in Adulthood, and Intervening Contexts," from Wachs, T. D. "Fit, Context, and the Transition Between Temperament and Personality," in C. Halverson, G. Kohnstamm, & R. Martin (Eds.) *The Developing Structure of Personality from Infancy to Adulthood.* Mahwah, NJ: Lawrence Erlbaum

Associates, Inc. Reprinted by permission. **Figure 15.3**: From "Examples of Positive Changes in the Aftermath of a Romantic Breakup," by T. Tashiro & P. Frazier, 2003, "I'll Never Be in a Relationship Like That Again: Personal Growth Following Romantic Relationship Breakups," *Personal Relationships,*10, after Table 1, p. 120. Reprinted with permission from Blackwell Publishing. **Figure 15.5**: "Percentage of Married Persons Age 18 and Older with 'Very Happy' Marriages" from D. Popenoe & B. Whitehead, *The State of Our Minds: The Social Health of Marriage in America,* 2005 Fig. 4, p. 18. The National Marriage Project, Rutgers University, Piscataway, NJ. Used by permission. **Figure 15.6**: From B. R. Karney and T. N. Bradbury, "Contextual Influences on Marriage," 2005, *Current Directions I Psychological Science,* 14, pp. 171–175, Figure 2. Reprinted with permission from Blackwell Publishing. **Figure 15.10**: From Holland, *Making Vocational Choices: A Theory of Vocational Personalities and Work Environments,* 2e, © 1984. Published by Allyn and Bacon, Boston, MA. Copyright © 1985 by Pearson Education. Reprinted by permission of the publisher. **pp. 517-518:** E. Mavis Hetherington and John Kelly. From *For Better or for Worse: Divorce Reconsidered* by E. Mavis Hetherington & John Kelly. Copyright © 2002 by E. Mavis Hetherington and John Kelly. Used by permission of W. W. Norton & Company, Inc.

Chapter 16

p. 528 From Jim Croce, "Time in a Bottle." Copyright © 1972, 1985 Denjac Music Co. Reprinted with permission. **Figure 16.1**: Adapted from *Newsweek,* "Health for Life," Special Section, Fall/Winter 2001. Copyright © Newsweek, Inc. All rights reserved. Reprinted by permission. **Figure 16.2**: Adapted from *Newsweek,* "Health for Life," Special Section, Fall/Winter 2001. Copyright © Newsweek, Inc. All rights reserved. Reprinted by permission. **Figure 16.5**: From *Sex in America* by John Gagnon. Copyright © 1994 by CSG Enterprises, Inc., Edward O. Laumann, Robert T. Michael, and Gina Kolata. By permission of Little, Brown and Co., Inc.

Chapter 17

Figure 17.1: From "Changes in Generativity and Identity Certainty from the 30s through the 50s," from Stewart, Osgrove, & Helson, 2002, "Middle Aging in Women: Patterns of Personality Change from the 30s to the 50s," Fig. 3, *Journal of Adult Development,* Vol. 8, pp. 23–37. With kind permission of Springer Science and Business Media. **Figure 17.2**: From "Items Used to Assess Generativity and Identify Certainty," from Steward, Osgrove, & Helson, 2002, "Middle Aging in Women: Patterns of Personality Change from the 30s to the 50s," Table II, *Journal of Adult Development,* Vol. 8, pp. 23–37. With kind permission of Springer Science and Business Media. **Figure 17.7**: From "Individuals' Conceptions of the Right Age for Major Life Events and Achievements: Late 1950s and Late 1970s," from D. F. Hultsch and J. K. Plemons, "Life Events and Life Span Development," in *Life Span Development and Behavior,* Vol. 2, by P. B. Baltes and O. G. Brun (eds.). Reprinted with permission from Elsevier. **Figure 17.8**: From Santrock, *Psychology,* 7/e, Figure 12.11. Copyright © 2003 The McGraw-Hill Companies. Reproduced by permission of The McGraw-Hill Companies.

Chapter 18

Figure 18.1: From *The Psychology of Death, Dying and Bereavement,* by Richard Schultz. Copyright © 1978 The McGraw-Hill Companies. Reproduced by permission of The McGraw-Hill Companies. **Figure 18.2**: From *The Okinawa Diet Plan* by Bradley J. Willcox, M.D., D. Craig Willcox, Ph.D., and Makoto Suzuki, M.D. with Leah Feldon, copyright © 2004 by Bradley J. Willcox and D. Craig Willcox. Used by permission of Clarkson Potter/Publishers, a division of Random House, Inc. **Figure 18.6**: Adapted from *Newsweek,* "Health for Life," Special Section, Fall/Winter 2001. Copyright ©

Figure 18.8: Adapted from J. A. Brabyn et al. The Smith-Kettlewell Institute (SKI) Longitudinal Study of Vision Function and Its Impact on the Elderly: An Overview. *Optometry and Vision Science* 78 , pp. 2464–2469. Used with permission by Dr. John Brabyn. **Figure 18.11:** From "Age and the Consumption of Five or More Drinks on at Least One Day in the United States," from National Center for Health Statistics, 2002.

Chapter 19

Figure 19.1: From S.-C. Li, et al., 2004, *Psychological Science,* 15, p. 158. Reprinted by permission of Blackwell Publishing. **Figure 19.6:** From J. Kielcot-Glaser, et al., 2003, "Comparison of IL-6 Levels in Alzheimer's Caregivers and a Control Group of Non-Caregivers," from "Chronic Stress and Age-Related Increases in the Proinflammatory Cytokine IL-g," *Proceedings of the National Academy of Science USA,* 100, after Figure 1. Copyright © 2003 National Academy of Sciences, U.S.A. used with permission.

Chapter 20

Figure 20.2: From L. Carstensen, et al., "The Social Context of Emotion," in the *Annual Review of Geriatrics and Gerontology,* by Schaie/Lawton, 1997, Vol. 17, p. 331. Copyright © 1997 by Springer Publishing Company. Adapted by permission of Springer Publishing Company, New York. **Figure 20.3:** From "Changes in Positive and Negative Emotion Across the Adult Years," from D. Mroczek and C. M. Kolarz, "The Effect of Age in Positive and Negative Affect," in *Journal of Personality and Social Psychology,* Vol. 75, pp. 1333–1349. Copyright © 1998 by the American Psychological Association. Reprinted by permission. **Figure 20.5:** From "Self-Esteem Across the Life Span," from Robins, et al., "Age Differences in Self-Esteem from 9 to 90," in *Psychology and Aging,* Vol. 17, pp. 423–434. Copyright © 2002 by the American Psychological Association. Reprinted by permission.

Photo Credits

Chapter 1

Opener: © Bob Torrz/Stone/Getty Images; p. 4 (top): © Seana O'Sullivan/CORBIS/Sygma; p. 4 (bottom): © AP/Wide World Photos; p. 6: © Archives of the History of American Psychology/Louise Bates Ames Gift; p. 8: Courtesy of Paul Baltes, Margaret Baltes Foundation; p. 9 (top): © Adam Tanner/Reuters/Corbis; p. 9 (bottom): © Paul Bartan/CORBIS; p. 10 (top): Courtesy of Luis Vargas; p. 10 (bottom): © National Association for the Education of Young Children, Robert Maust/Photo Agora; p. 11: © Nancy Agostini; p. 13 (top): © James Pozarik; p. 13 (bottom): Courtesy of Marian Wright Edelman, The Children's Defense Fund, photograph by Rick Reinhard; p. 14: © Nathan Benn/CORBIS; p. 15: © Dennis Brack Ltd./Black Star/Stock Photo; 1.7 (prenatal): Courtesy of Landrum Shettles, MD; 1.7 (infancy): John Santrock; 1.7 (early childhood): © Joe Sohm/The Image Works; 1.7 (middle/late childhood): © CORBIS website; 1.7 (adolescence): © James L. Shaffer; 1.7 (early adulthood): © Vol. 155/CORBIS; 1.7 (middle adulthood): © CORBIS website; 1.7 (late adulthood): © CORBIS website; p. 20 (top): © Jay Syverson/CORBIS; p. 20 (bottom): © Owaki-Kulla/CORBIS; p. 22: © Joel Gordon 1995

Chapter 2

Opener: © Michael Krasowitz/FPG/Getty Images; p. 40 and p. 42: © Bettmann/CORBIS; p. 43: © Yves de Braine/Black Star/Stock Photo; p. 44: A.R. Lauria/Dr. Michael Cole, Laboratory of Human Cognition, University of California, San Diego; p. 46 and p. 47: © Bettmann/CORBIS; p. 48: Photo by Nina Leen/Timepix/Getty Images; p. 49: Courtesy of Urie Bronfenbrenner; p. 50: © Julian Hirshowitz/CORBIS; p. 54 (Freud): © Bettmann Archive; p. 51 (Pavlov):

© Bettmann Archive; p. 51 (Piaget): © Yves de Braine/Black Star/Stock Photo; p. 51 (Vygotsky): A. R. Lauria/Dr. Michael Cole, Laboratory of Human Cognition, University of California, San Diego; p. 51 (Skinner): © Harvard University News Office; p. 51 (Erikson): © UPI/Bettmann Newsphotos; p. 51 (Bandura): © Bettmann/CORBIS; p. 51 (Bronenbrenner): Courtesy of Urie Bronfenbrenner; p. 53: © Richard T. Nowitz/Photo Researchers; p. 55 (top): © Bettmann/CORBIS; p. 55 (bottom): © S. Fraser/Photo Researchers; 2.13a: © Photo Researchers; 2.13b&c: © AP/Wide World Photos; 2.13d: © Bettmann/CORBIS; 2.13e: © Sukie Hill Photography; 2.13f: © Lawrence Migdale/Photo Researchers; p. 61: © McGraw-Hill Companies, John Thoeming photographer; p. 64: Courtesy of Pam Trotman Reid; p. 65 (left): © AFP/Getty Images; p. 65 (right): © Stuart McClymont/Stone/Getty Images

Chapter 3

Opener: © Hua China Tourism Press, Shao/The Image Bank/Getty Images; p. 72: © Enrico Ferorelli Enterprises; p. 73: © Frans Lemmens/CORBIS; p. 76: © David Wilke; p. 78: © Rick Rickman/Matrix; 3.4: © Sundstrom/Liaison Agency/Gamma; 3.5a&b: © Custom Medical Stock Photo; p. 81: © Joel Gordon 1989; p. 82: © Andrew Eccles/Janet Botaish Group; p. 84: Courtesy of Holly Ishmael; p. 85: © Jacques Pavlousky/Sygma/CORBIS; p. 87: © Randy Santos/SuperStock; p. 91: © Myrleen Ferguson Cate/Photo Edit

Chapter 4

Opener: Photo Lennart Nilsson/Albert Bonniers Forlag AB, *A Child Is Born,* Dell Publishing Company; p. 102: © John Santrock; 4.3 (All): Photo Lennart Nilsson/Albert Bonniers Forlag AB., *A Child Is Born,* Dell Publishing Company; 4.5: Courtesy of Ann Streissguth; p. 110: © John Chiasson; p. 112: © Betty Press/Woodfin Camp & Associates; p. 113: © Alon Reininger/Contract Press Images; p. 114: © R.I.A./Liaison Agency/Gamma; p. 115: © David Young-Wolff/PhotoEdit; p. 116: © Sharon Schindler Rising, Centering Pregnancy Program; p. 118: © Vivian Moos/CORBIS; p. 120: © Marjorie Shostak/Anthro-Photo; p. 121: © Roger Tully/Stone/Getty; p. 122: Courtesy of Linda Pugh; p. 123: © SIU/Peter Arnold, Inc.; 4.7: © Stephen Marks, Inc./The Image Bank/Getty Images; p. 125: © Charles Gupton/Stock Boston; p. 126: Courtesy of Dr. Susan M. Ludington; p. 127: Courtesy of Dr. Tiffany Field; p. 130: © Ariel Skelley/CORBIS

Chapter 5

Opener: © Joe McNally; p. 138 (top): © Wendy Stone/CORBIS; p. 138 (bottom): © Dave Bartruff/CORBIS; 5.2: © 1999 Kenneth Jarecke/Contact Press Images; 5.4: © A. Glauberman/Photo Researchers; 5.8a&b: Courtesy of Dr. Harry T. Chugani, Children's Hospital of Michigan; 5.9a: © David Grugin Productions, Inc. Reprinted by permission; 5.9b: Image courtesy of Dana Boatman, Ph.D., Department of Neurology, Johns Hopkins University, reprinted with permission from *The Secret Life of the Brain,* Joseph Henry Press; p. 146: © SuperStock; p. 148 (top): © Bruce McAllister/Image Works; p. 148 (bottom) © Bob Daemmrich/The Image Works; p. 148: Courtesy of T. Berry Brazelton; p. 150: Hawaiian Family Support Healthy Start Program; p. 151: Courtesy of Esther Thelen; p. 153 (top): © Elizabeth Crews/The Image Works; p. 153 (bottom): © Petit Format/Photo Researchers; p. 154: © Fabio Cardos/zefa/Corbis; 5.13 (left & right): Courtesy Dr. Karen Adolph, New York University; p. 157 (top): © Michael Greenlar/The Image Works; p. 157 (bottom): © Frank Baily Studios; 5.15: Courtesy Amy Needham, Duke University; 5.16: © David Linton; 5.18 (all): Courtesy of Dr. Charles Nelson; 5.20: © Enrico Ferorelli Enterprises; 5.21a: © Michael Siluk; 5.21b: © Dr. Melanie Spence, University of Texas; 5.22: © Jean Guichard/Sygma/CORBIS; 5.23 a-c: From D. Rosenstein and H. Oster, "Differential Facial Responses to Four Basic Tastes in

Newborns," *Child Development,* Vol. 59, 1988, © Society for Research in Child Development, Inc.

Chapter 6

Opener: © Spencer Grant/Photo Edit; p. 180: © PunchStock; 6.2 (left & right): © Doug Goodman/Photo Researchers; 6.4: Courtesy of Dr. Carolyn Rovee-Collier; 6.5: © Enrico Ferorelli Enterprises; p. 188: Courtesy of John Santrock; 6.7 (top & bottom): © 2003 University of Washington, Institute for Learning and Brain Sciences (I-LABS); p. 195: © ABPL Image Library/Animals Animals/Earth Scenes; 6.11: © Michael Goldstein, Cornell University; p. 199: © John Carter/Photo Researchers

Chapter 7

Opener: © Jamie Marcial/SuperStock; p. 208: © Rick Gomez/CORBIS; 7.1 (all): © Michael Lewis, Institute for the Study of Child Development, Robert Wood Johnson Medical School; 7.2: © Sybil L. Hart, Texas Tech University; p. 211: © Andy Cox/Stone/Getty Images; p. 215 (top): © Michael Tcherevkoff/The Image Bank/Getty Images; p. 215 (bottom): © Judith Oddie/Photo Edit; p. 218: © Vol. 63 PhotoDisc/Getty Images; 7.5: © Martin Rogers/Stock Boston; p. 220: © David Young-Wolff/Photo Edit; p. 222: © Penny Tweedie/Stone/Getty Images; 7.7: © BrandXPictures/Getty Images; p. 225: © John Henley/CORBIS; p. 226: © Owen Franken/CORBIS; p. 228: Courtesy of Rashmi Nakhre, The Hattie Daniels Day Care Center; p. 229: © Lawrence Migdale/Stone/Getty Images

Chapter 8

Opener: © Ariel Skelley/The Stock Market/CORBIS; p. 238: From 'Open Window' © 1994 Municipality of Reggio Emilia Infant-Toddler Centers and Preschools Published by Reggio Children; p. 239: © Bob Daemmrich/The Image Works; p. 241: © Joel Gordon 1993; p. 242: © Eyewire Vol. EP078 /Getty Images; p. 246: © AP/Wide World Photos; 8.8: © Paul Fusco/Magnum Photos; 8.10: © Elizabeth Crews/The Image Works; p. 252: Courtesy of Barbara Rogoff; 8.11a&b: Images courtesy of E. Bodrova and D. J. Leong, from *Tools of the Mind,* 2007; 8.12 (left): A. R. Lauria/Dr. Michael Cole, Laboratory of Human Cognition, University of California, San Diego; 8.12 (right): © Bettmann/CORBIS; p. 257: © 1999 James Kamp; p. 259: © John Flavell; p. 262: © Roseanne Olson/Stone/Getty Images; p. 264: © AP/Wide World Photos; p. 267: Courtesy of Yolanda Garcia; p. 268: © Ronnie Kaufman/The Stock Market/CORBIS

Chapter 9

Opener: © Ariel Skelley/CORBIS; p. 278: © Michael Lewis, Institute for the Study of Child Development, Robert Wood Johnson Medical School; p. 279: © LWA-Dann Tardif/zefa/CORBIS; p. 280: © Yves de Braine/Black Star/Stock Photo; p. 281: © Randy Faris/CORBIS; p. 284: © Digital Stock; 9.5: © Ariel Skelley/CORBIS; p. 290: © Jose Luis Pelaez/CORBIS; p. 291: © PunchStock; p. 292: Courtesy of Darla Botkin; p. 293: © David M. Wells/CORBIS; p. 293: © Prevent Child Abuse America; p. 295: © Ariel Skelley/CORBIS; p. 297: © PunchStock; p. 298: © Shelly Gazin/The Image Works; p. 300: © Spencer Grant/Photo Edit; p. 299: © Karen Kasmauski/Woodfin Camp; p. 302: © Ariel Skelley/CORBIS; p. 303: © Richard Hutchings/Photo Edit; p. 305: © Bryan Peterson; p. 306: © Franco Vogt/CORBIS

Chapter 10

Opener: © Michael Pole/CORBIS; p. 316 (top): © Aerial Skelley/CORBIS; p. 316 (bottom): © Gabe Palmer/CORBIS; p. 317: Courtesy of Sharon Mcleod; p. 318: © L. Perez/zefa/CORBIS; p. 321: © David Young-Wolff/Photo Edit; p. 322: © Will McIntyre/Photo Researchers; p. 325: © Bernheim/Woodfin Camp; p. 326: © Gabe Palmer/CORBIS; p. 329: © Francisco Cruz/SuperStock; p. 330: © Sherry Brown; p. 334: © Joe McNally; p. 339: © Will & Deni McIntyre/CORBIS;

SUBJECT INDEX

A

Abecedarian Intervention program, 337–338
AB error, 183
Abstract, research article, 61
Abstract thinking, 44, 407–408
Acceptance, of dying person, 688
Accidents
　adolescents, 401
　children, 244, 316
　infants, 155
　late adulthood, 604–605
Accommodation
　Piaget's theory, 178
　visual, 532
Acculturation
　in Mexican American families, 579–580
　and parenting, 300–301
Accutane, teratogenic effects, 107
Acetylcholine, and Alzheimer disease, 596
Achievement
　and attention, 256
　cross-cultural view, 380
　and poverty, 14
　and self-efficacy, 355
　and self-esteem, 354
　and self-regulation, 429
　social cognitive view, 47
　and socioeconomic status, 377–378
　and TV viewing, 58–59, 307
Active (niche-picking) genotype-
　environment correlations, 92
Active euthanasia, 679–680
Activity theory of aging, 651
Acupuncture, during childbirth, 122
Adaptation, defined, 177
Adaptive behavior
　evolutionary theory, 73–74
　Piaget's theory, 43
Adderall, 321
Addiction
　defined, 471
　drug treatment, 472
　theories of, 471–472
Adolescence
　adopted children, 89
　attachment, 430–431
　autonomy, 430–431
　brain development, 394
　cognitive development, 44, 407–409
　critical thinking, 410–411
　cross-cultural view, 388–389, 400,
　　438–441
　dating, 436–438
　death, causes of, 401, 684
　death, understanding of, 686
　decision-making, 410
　depression/suicide, 401, 446–449
　eating disorders, 405–406
　education and learning, 411–415
　egocentrism, 409
　emotions in, 394, 428–429
　ethnic minorities, 441–443
　exercise/physical activity, 400
　friendships, 434–435
　health status, 400
　identity development, 424–428
　juvenile delinquency, 443–446

memory, 327
obesity, 400
parent-teen relationship, 431–433
peer relations, 435
perspective-taking, 441–442
physical development. *See* Puberty
pregnancy. *See* Teen pregnancy
problems, prevention strategies, 402,
　404–405, 413, 446, 449–450
risk-taking, 401–402
rites of passage, 441
self-esteem, 6, 422–423
self-regulation, 394
sexuality, 394–397
sexually transmitted disease (STD), 397
sleep, 400–401
substance use/abuse, 402–405
time span of, 18
transition to adulthood, 458–462
Adopted children, 87–89
　IQ scores, 88
　parenting challenges, 89
　research related to, 88–89
　screening flexibility, 87–88
Adoption studies
　intelligence, 335
　purpose of, 91
　temperament, 215
Adult children. *See* Caregiving;
　Intergenerational relationships
Adult development. *See* Early adulthood;
　Late adulthood; Middle adulthood
Adult education, 624
Adultery, 473
Advance directives, 679
Aerobic exercise, 467, 606, 625, 627
Affectionate love, 502, 503
Affordances, 160
African Americans
　ageism/racism/sexism problem, 666–668
　educational inequality, 378–379
　exercise, lack of, 400
　health conditions of, 536, 604
　homicide, death by, 401
　identity development, 427–428
　intelligence test issue, 338–339
　life expectancy, 589, 604
　obesity and women, 243, 465–466
　older women, stress of, 660
　parenting style, 289
　poverty, 660
　preterm/low-birthweight infants, 125
　religious participation, 640
　sickle-cell anemia, 82–83
　and sudden infant death syndrome
　　(SIDS), 146
Afterbirth, 119
Age
　conceptualizations of, 20
　cross-sectional studies, 58
　functional age, 593
　and happiness, 19
　parental, and prenatal abnormalities, 81,
　　113–114
Age-grades, normative age-graded
　influences, 9
Ageism
　defined, 658
　and ethnic minority women, 668

older adult stereotyping, 610, 630,
　639, 658
Aggression
　bullying, 373–374
　Freud's view, 40–41
　gender differences, 365, 367
　laboratory observation of, 53
　and nutritional deficiencies, 244
　and rejected children, 371–372
　relational aggression, 365
　and TV viewing, 305–306
Aging of population, 15, 529
Aging theories
　activity theory, 651
　cellular clock theory, 593–594
　disengagement theory, 650–651
　free-radical theory, 594
　hormonal stress theory, 594–595
　mitochondrial theory, 594
　socioemotional selectivity theory,
　　651–652
AIDS
　breast-feeding and transmission, 111, 148
　cross-cultural view, 474–475
　death of children, 246
　newborn AIDS, 111
　prevention of, 475–476
　statistics on, 474
Alcoholics Anonymous (AA), 471
Alcoholism
　defined, 470
　and elderly, 605
　treatment of, 470–471
Alcohol use
　adolescents, 403
　binge drinking, 403, 469, 605
　cross-cultural view, 468–469
　elderly, 605
　gender differences, 469
　pregnancy guidelines, 109
　and prenatal abnormalities, 108–109
　young adults, 403, 468–469
Altruism, older adults, 665–666
Alzheimer disease, 634–637
　brain changes in, 634–635
　caregiver problems, 636–637
　drug treatment, 635–636
　early and late-onset, 634
　early detection, 635
　exercise as preventive, 635
　language, intact, 628–629
　and neurotransmitters, 596
　risk factors, 634–635
American Psychological Association (APA),
　on research ethics, 62–63
Amnesia, childhood amnesia, 186–187
Amniocentesis, 85
Amnion, 104
Amniotic fluid, 104
Amygdala, 215, 394
Amyloid plaques, 634
Anal stage, 40
Androgens
　functions of, 282, 364
　and puberty, 364
　See also Testosterone
Androgyny
　defined, 366
　traits related to, 366

Anemia, iron-deficiency, 243
Anesthesia, childbirth, 120–121
Anger
　and cardiovascular disease, 537
　of dying person, 687–688
Anger cry, 211
Animism, preoperational stage, 248
Anorexia nervosa, 405–406
Anoxia, 123
Antibiotics, teratogenic, 107
Antidepressants
　older adults, 633
　for postpartum depression, 130
　for smoking cessation, 471
　and suicidal thoughts, 448
Antioxidants, and aging, 608
Antisocial behavior, juvenile delinquency,
　443–446
Anxiety
　attachment-related, 497
　Freud's view, 40–41
　maternal and pregnancy, 113
　stranger anxiety, 211–212
Apgar scale, 123–124
Aphasia, 196
Apolipoprotein E, 634
Aricept, 635
Arthritis, 535
Asian Americans
　achievement, 442
　dating relationships, 437
　diversity of group, 536
　identity development, 427–428
　parenting style, 289
　in workplace, 485–486
Asians, pregnancy, view of, 118
Aspirin, teratogenic effects, 107
Assimilation
　of ethnic minorities, 442
　Piaget's theory, 178
Assisted suicide, 680
Associative play, 304
Athletes, peak performance, age of, 463–464
Atkins diet, 466
Attachment
　as adaptive behavior, 73
　and adolescent behavior, 430–431
　adolescent-parent, 430–431
　adopted children/parents, 89
　Bowlby's theory, 219
　and caregiver styles, 222–223
　cross-cultural view, 221–222
　defined, 219
　Erikson's theory, 219
　ethological theory, 47–48, 219
　Freud's theory, 219
　Harlow monkey experiment, 219
　infant cry, parental response, 213
　insecure avoidant infants, 220–221, 223
　insecure disorganized infants, 221, 223
　insecure resistant infants, 220
　and later adult relationships, 496–497
　and life-span development, 221–222
　measurement of, 220–221, 497
　mother-infant bonding, 130–131
　related anxiety, 497
　related avoidance, 497
　secure attachment, 220–222
　stages in development of, 220

SI·1